AREA HANDBOOK
for the
SOVIET UNION

Co-Authors

Eugene K. Keefe

Arsene A. Boucher

Sarah J. Elpern

William Giloane

James M. Moore

Terence L. Ogden

Stephen Peters

John P. Prevas

Nancy E. Walstrom

Eston T. White

Research and writing were completed on
March 13, 1970

Published 1971

DA Pam 550-95

Library of Congress Catalog Card Number: 71-609246

For sale by the Superintendent of Documents, U.S. Government Printing Office
Washington, D.C. 20402—Price $5.25

FOREWORD

This volume is one of a series of handbooks prepared by Foreign Area Studies (FAS) of The American University, designed to be useful to military and other personnel who need a convenient compilation of basic facts about the social, economic, political, and military institutions and practices of various countries. The emphasis is on objective description of the nation's present society and the kinds of possible or probable changes that might be expected in the future. The handbook seeks to present as full and as balanced an integrated exposition as limitations on space and research time permit. It was compiled from information available in openly published material. An extensive bibliography is provided to permit recourse to other published sources for more detailed information. There has been no attempt to express any specific point of view or to make policy recommendations. The contents of the handbook represent the work of the authors and FAS and do not represent the official view of the United States government.

An effort has been made to make the handbook as comprehensive as possible. It can be expected, however, that the material, interpretations, and conclusions are subject to modification in the light of new information and developments. Such corrections, additions, and suggestions for factual, interpretive, or other change as readers may have will be welcomed for use in future revisions. Comments may be addressed to:

The Director
Foreign Area Studies
The American University
5010 Wisconsin Avenue, N.W.
Washington, D.C. 20016

PREFACE

On November 7, 1967, the Soviet Union celebrated the fiftieth anniversary of the revolution that brought it into existence. From its inception, this relatively new state has proclaimed its allegiance to an official ideology—a particular style of socialism known as Marxism-Leninism—that it claims will eventually, and inevitably, spread to all countries of the world. The processes of continuity and change that transformed the former Russian Empire into the Soviet Union and fostered the development of that nation into a military and industrial power have prompted this study of its political, economic, and social life. This handbook by Foreign Area Studies of The American University has the objective of presenting an overview of the various aspects of Soviet society as they have developed under Communist Party leadership.

The *Area Handbook for the Soviet Union* is designed to explain the Soviet system. The effort in writing the handbook has been toward objectivity; it does not bring forth unique ideas or new analyses, nor is it exhaustive in any area. Because of a penchant for secrecy on the part of its leaders, the Soviet state has been described as an enigma; nevertheless, a major world power cannot exist in a vacuum. Investigations and analyses by scholars, correspondents, diplomats, and others have been possible and from these, voluminous materials have been published. The amount of published material itself presents a staggering problem for analysts, and the fact that so much material is written from preconceived ideas compounds the problem.

In writing this handbook, the authors have consciously attempted to set aside their own preconceptions in order to better present a picture of the Soviet Union as it was at the beginning of the 1970's. In essence, this handbook is an attempt to explore and expose the pertinent aspects of the system that will lead to a better understanding of internal and international Soviet affairs.

Sources used were mostly secondary, although Soviet sources, particularly newspapers, periodicals, and documents were extensively analyzed. In the selection of source materials and in the writing of the handbook, there were constant dangers of omission or of overstatement that could have caused imbalances in presentation. Aware of these inherent dangers, the authors have attempted to set down, often in the absence of much needed authentic Soviet evidence, a balanced overview of the Soviet Union in 1970.

This handbook is an introduction to a very complex society and is intended primarily for the layman who desires to familiarize himself with Soviet economic, political, and social life. The advanced student of Soviet affairs and the so-called Kremlinologist will find little here that has not been exposed in much greater detail by specialists in a variety of disciplines. It is hoped that this volume will provide in convenient form a basis of general knowledge for the average reader who desires such or a solid foundation for one who intends to increase his knowledge of the country through specialized study.

Grateful acknowledgment is made to Thomas D. Roberts, who served initially as Team Chairman; to David M. Evans, who wrote Chapter 18, Science and Technology; to Fran N. Gjupanovich, who wrote Chapter 22, The Legal System; and to Rodney E. Steele, who wrote Chapter 36, Fiscal and Monetary System.

Transliteration generally follows the rules of the *Romanization Guide* of the United States Board on Geographic Names; however, names of places and persons that have acquired a familiar spelling in the West are given in that familar spelling, for example, Moscow and Georgia, Trotsky and Podgorny. Acronyms such as USSR, RSFSR, and CPSU, which also have become familiar, are used frequently and are fully explained in the Glossary. Russian acronyms are used where necessary and are explained in the text and in the Glossary. Territorial designations—*kray*, *oblast*, *rayon*—are used and explained rather than using imprecise English equivalent terms.

COUNTRY SUMMARY

1. COUNTRY: Union of Soviet Socialist Republics (short title: the Soviet Union). From ninth century until 1922, known as Russia. Composed of fifteen union republics.

2. GOVERNMENT: Constitution of 1936 provides for a federal union of constituent republics and popular elections. Bicameral legislature meets briefly twice a year. In practice, Communist Party is above the government and controls elections. Party leaders occupy positions of authority in both Party and government, providing an interlocking of authority at all levels. Ultimate power rests in the Political Bureau (Politburo) and Secretariat of the Party's Central Committee.

3. SIZE AND LOCATION: Area, 8.65 million square miles, the largest country in the world. Extends 6,000 miles from the Baltic Sea in the west to the Bering Strait in the east and almost 3,000 miles from the Pamirs in the south to the Arctic Ocean in the north. Bordered on the north by the Arctic Ocean; on the east by the Pacific Ocean; on the south by North Korea, Communist China, Mongolia, Iran, Afghanistan, Turkey, and the Black Sea; and on the west by Rumania, Hungary, Czechoslovakia, Poland, the Baltic Sea, Finland, and Norway.

4. TOPOGRAPHY: A vast plain broken by low mountains and hills extends from the western borders about half-way across the country to the Yenisey River in the east and to the high mountains in the southern and eastern parts of Soviet Central Asia. The area extending eastward from the Yenisey River to the Pacific Ocean consists of hilly plateaus and mountains intersected by many rivers, most of which flow in a northerly direction. The southern rim of mountains extending westward from the upper Yenisey to the Black Sea includes all or part of the Pamirs and the Sayan, Altai, Tien Shan, and Caucasus ranges.

5. CLIMATE: Predominantly cold and continental with long winters and hot, dry, and windy summers. The precipitation pattern shows a broad zone, varying from sixteen to forty inches annually, that extends from the western borders to just beyond the Ural Mountains; precipitation decreases to the north, east, and south of this zone. The lowest annual precipitation, less than four inches, occurs in the desert regions of Soviet Central Asia. Permafrost covers about 40 percent of the total land area and, with lack of

precipitation and extreme temperatures, the amount of arable land is severely restricted.

6. POPULATION: About 241.1 million, estimated in January 1970. Growth rate slower during the 1960's than during the previous decade. About 87 males per 100 females. About 55 percent of total population living in cities. The Russian ethnic group comprises about half the total, with the remainder divided among more than 100 different ethnic groups.

7. LABOR FORCE: Approximately 129.4 million in 1970, about 54 percent of the total population. About two-thirds of labor force engaged in nonagricultural branches of the economy. Persons employed in the socialist sector of the economy comprised about 90 percent of the labor force, with the remaining 10 percent employed on small private agricultural plots in the free farm markets, or in individual handicraft operations. Women constituted about half the total labor force, predominating in such fields as communications, trade, health, education, agriculture, and social insurance.

8. LANGUAGES: Russian, the official national language, is used throughout the country in government and commerce, although official use of local languages is not prohibited. In census of 1959, 80 percent of population listed Russian, Ukrainian, or Belorussian as mother tongue. Uzbek with 6 million speakers, Tatar with 4.9 million, and Kazakh with 3.6 million led a long list of other languages, including thirteen that had more than 1 million native speakers and several that had 1,000 or fewer.

9. RELIGION: Atheism is official policy of the state, but about 40 percent of population considered to be religious believers. Most believers are members of the Russian Orthodox Church, but Muslims, Buddhists, Jews, Roman Catholics and several Protestant denominations also represented. Practice of religion is strictly regulated by state.

10. ECONOMY: Under complete government control. Increasingly industrialized, with emphasis on production of capital goods, yet agriculture still employs roughly one-third of the labor force and contributes from one-fifth to one-fourth of gross national product. Industrial raw materials abundant but unfavorably located; adverse climatic conditions limit cultivated agricultural area to 10 percent of country's land area. Industrial and agricultural activity heavily concentrated west of the Ural Mountains. Preponderant emphasis on heavy industry growth, with consequent lag in development of agriculture and light industry, responsible for continuing and widespread shortages of consumer goods.

11. IMPORTS AND EXPORTS: Foreign trade of relatively minor but growing importance. Two-thirds of total trade with other Communist countries, primarily those of Eastern Europe; about one-fifth with industrially developed West; and one-tenth with develop-

ing countries. Major exports consist of machinery and raw and processed materials. Machinery exported only to Communist and developing countries, because not competitive in West. Major imports consist of machinery and goods. Western industrial states are main source of technologically advanced equipment and grain. Because of legal restrictions imposed by the United States on trade with Communist countries, trade with the United States is insignificant.

12. FINANCE: The Ministry of Finance and the state banking system, as integral parts of the planned economy, carry out economic and financial programs. The basic monetary unit is the ruble, which is not freely convertible on the world currency market and is defined by the government to be worth .987412 grams of gold or the equivalent of US$1.11.

13. JUSTICE: The so-called regular courts form a single system found at all levels of government and administered by the Supreme Court of the USSR. Irregular or comrades' courts found on farms, in factories, or in housing developments deal with social crimes of a less serious nature. Soviet law consists of a system of rules established by the government under the direction and guidance of the Communist Party. Both regular and irregular courts hand down decisions by judges with no juries involved.

14. INTERNATIONAL ORGANIZATIONS: Member of the United Nations and some of its specialized agencies. Also belongs to the Warsaw Pact Organization, the Council for Economic Mutual Assistance (CEMA), the International Red Cross, and the Red Crescent. Through bilateral agreements, provides extensive aid to some developing nations, with particular emphasis on aid to Arab states.

15. HEALTH: Rapid advancements in medical science and a widespread system of health services resulted in a life expectancy of sixty-six years for men and seventy-four years for women by 1970, and a generally good state of health for the general population. Malaria, once widespread, has been virtually eliminated. Cancer and cardiovascular diseases are the major causes of death.

16. EDUCATION: Emphasis on education to develop loyalty to communism and produce the skills and capabilities required for a modernized industrial society virtually eliminated illiteracy, produced a large pool of professional and technically skilled personnel, and substantially raised the education level of the population. The education system is tightly controlled by central Party and state authorities.

17. COMMUNICATIONS: Strictly controlled and censored by the state. Facilities, all operated under government direction, include 8 million telephones, 70,000 telegraph and postal stations, 1,000 radio stations, and 900 television stations. The 8,000 newspapers and nearly 5,000 periodicals are subject to political control. *Pravda*

is the daily journal of the Central Committee of the Communist Party; *Izvestia* is the government's official newspaper. *TASS* and *Novosti* are the official news agencies.

18. AIRLINES AND AIRFIELDS: Nearly all air transport accomplished by Aeroflot, the government airline under control of the Ministry of Civil Aviation. Freight-carrying capability of the system has developed more slowly than passenger service, which increased more than twentyfold between 1955 and 1967.

19. RAILROADS: Carry 85 percent of total freight and by far the greatest number of passengers. Total track length is over 80,000 miles. About 95 percent of the system is diesel or electric powered. Track gauge is five feet. Although several new lines have been constructed east of the Ural Mountains since 1945, the major portion of the system is in European USSR. Moscow is the hub of the nation's important rail lines.

20. WATERWAYS: Approximately 90,000 miles are navigable but are closed for varying periods because of ice. Country has several of the world's largest river systems, but nearly all run generally north-south, while the greatest need for transportation is east-west. Ports on the White and Baltic seas in the north are linked through the system of inland waterways with ports on the Black and Caspian seas in the south.

21. HIGHWAYS: Paved roads account for approximately 10 percent of the country's more than 900,000 miles total. Most improved roads are in the European USSR. Major national road nets are lacking. Spring thaws and autumn rains make most dirt roads impassable in large areas of the country.

22. PORTS: The most important of the more than twenty-five major ports are: Murmansk on the Barents Sea; Arkhangelsk on the White Sea; Vladivostok on the Sea of Japan; Baku on the Caspian Sea; Odessa on the Black Sea; Riga on the Baltic Sea; and Leningrad on the Gulf of Finland. Most of the major ports are closed to shipping for varying periods each year because of ice. Even Odessa usually experiences a few days annually when shipping becomes impossible.

23. ARMED FORCES: Personnel strength of about 3.2 million men in five military services. The army, which maintains about 140 divisions in varying degrees of combat readiness, has well over half the total personnel. The navy has modernized rapidly, building a surface fleet to complement its traditional submarine strength. Antiaircraft and antimissile defense, using artillery, missiles, and aircraft, constitutes a separate service. The Long Range Air Force, also a separate service, has declined in importance. The fifth service is the Strategic Rocket Force, which has received considerable emphasis and has become increasingly powerful.

24. SECURITY: The security function is controlled and adminis-

tered by the Committee for State Security and the Ministry of Internal Affairs, both of which have subordinate agencies at every level of government. The Ministry of Internal Affairs controls most of the prisons and labor colonies and directs the local police. The Committee for State Security, a much more powerful agency, is responsible for safeguarding the country against any possible threat with the exception of an outright military invasion, to which the armed forces would respond. To accomplish its tasks, the committee has agents throughout the Party and government structures, in the military forces, in economic enterprises, and in all Soviet agencies operating abroad.

UNION OF SOVIET SOCIALIST REPUBLICS

TABLE OF CONTENTS

		Page
FOREWORD		iii
PREFACE		v
COUNTRY SUMMARY		vii

SECTION I. GENERAL SURVEY

Chapter 1. Nature of the Soviet System 1

2. Physical Environment 11
Natural Features—Boundaries and Political Sub-divisions—Regional Analysis

3. Historical Setting 37
Pre-Muscovite Period—Muscovy—Imperial Russia (1721–1917)—Reform and Repression—Revolution—Bolshevik Control—Stalin and Stalinism—Stalin's Heirs—Krushchev in Power

4. The Social System 73
Marxist-Leninist Social Theories—Historical Background—Social Stratification—Other Social Divisions —Social Dynamics

5. The Political System 87
Ideological Basic of the Political System—Development of the System—Soviet Achievements Measured Against Goals

6. The Economic System 101
Nature of the Economy—Economic Structure—Economic Performance

7. The State Security System 119
Historical Background—Position in the Government —The Border Troops—State Security Organization and Operations Since World War II

8. The Internal Security System 139
Historical Background—Position in the Government —Organization and Training—Developments in the Post-Stalin Period

SECTION II. SOCIAL

Chaper 9. Ethnic Groups 157
European Area—The Caucasian Area—Central Asia

— Paleo-Siberia — Population Movements — Official
Policies

10. Languages and Social Communication 181
Indo-European Languages—Uralic-Altaic Languages
—Caucasian Languages—Paleo-Asiatic Languages—
Other Languages—Official Policies and Practices—
Uses of Language

11. Family 199
Historical Background—Ideological and Legal Back-
ground—Forms of the Family and the Household—
Family Life Cycles—Family and Society

12. Living Conditions 221
Health and Sanitation—Patterns of Living and lei-
sure—Consumption Patterns—Food and Clothing—
Housing—Welfare Activities

13. Religion 239
State Atheism—Christianity—Islam—Buddhism—
Judaism

14. Social Values 261
Value Traditions—Individuals—Personal Relations
—Individual and Society—Patterns of Change

15. The Educational System 275
Historical Background—The Communist Educational
System—Education and Society

16. Artistic Expression 305
Architecture — Painting — Literature — Music —
Ballet — Theater — Cinema — Non-Russian Artistic
Expression in the Soviet Union

17. Intellectual Expression 331
Soviet Ideology—Marxism and the Russian Intel-
lectual Tradition—The Communist Party and Soviet
Scholarship—Marxist-Leninism and Intellectual Expression — Soviet Historiography — Philosophy and
Higher Education—Contemporary Intellectual Groupings—The Party and Contemporary Intellectual Life

18. Science and Technology 347
Early Development—Post-Stalin Years—Scientific
Endeavor—Technological Progress—The Scientist and
the State

SECTION III. POLITICAL

Chapter 19. Formal Structure of the Union Government 377
Constitutional Development—The Constitution of
1918—The Constitution of 1924—The Constitution of
1936—Amendment Process—Fundamental Rights and
Duties of Citizens—The Supreme Soviet—Commissions—Deputies—The Presidium of the Supreme
Soviet—The Council of Ministers—Ministries—The
Electoral System—Electoral Procedures—Civil Service—Arms and the Flag

Page

20. Component Political Subdivisions 399
    The Union Republics—Administrative Subdivisions
    —Autonomous or National Area Subdivisions

21. Political Dynamics 419
    The Communist Party of the Soviet Union—Political
    Socialization and Recruitment—Political Developments

22. The Legal System 441
    Before the Revolution—Under Communist Rule

23. The Police (Militia) and Correctional Systems 471
    Crimes, Criminals, and Punishment—The Militia—
    Local Volunteer Forces—Sentences Not Involving
    Deprivation of Freedom—Penal Institutions

24. Foreign Relations 487
    Determinants and Mechanisms—The United States
    — Communist China — Vietnam — Eastern Europe —
    Western Europe—The Arab States—Turkey, Iran, and
    Afghanistan—Other Asian and African Countries—
    Latin America—International Organizations

25. Public Information 515
    Government and Freedom of the Press—The Nature
    and Functions of the Mass Media—The Press—Radio
    —Television—Films

26. Agitation and Propaganda 541
    The Department of Propaganda and Agitation—
    Domestic Agitation—Domestic Propaganda—External
    Propaganda and Agitation

27. Political Attitudes and Reactions 555
    Determinants of Values and Attitudes—People's
    Attitude Toward the Government—Political Attitudes
    of the National Minorities—National Symbols and
    Holidays

28. The Armed Forces 569
    Historical Background—Position in the Government
    —The Military Establishment—Foreign Military Re-
    lations—The Military Establishment and the National
    Economy

SECTION IV. ECONOMIC

Chapter 29. Economic Planning and Control 603
    Nature of Planning—Planning Mechanism—Plan-
    ning Process—Methodology of Planning—Economic
    Control

30. Industry 623
    Industrial Resources—Structure of Industry—Labor
    and Productivity—Technology and Innovation—Prices
    —Production—Construction

31. Agriculture 653
    Background — Policy and Administration — Farm
    Organization—Land Use—Production

		Page
32.	The Labor Force	671
	Population Structure—Population Dynamics—Population Policy—Size and Composition of the Labor Force —Labor Requirements and Supply—Sources of Skilled Manpower—Labor Turnover—Labor Placement—Productivity	
33.	Labor Relations and Organization	687
	The Worker and Trade Unions in Soviet Society— Governmental Agencies and Regulation of Labor— Working Conditions—Trade Union Organization and Functions—Participation in International Labor Activities	
34.	Domestic Trade	705
	Distribution of Producer Goods—Wholesale Trade —Retail Trade—Transportation and Communications	
35.	Foreign Economic Relations	721
	Foreign Trade — The Customs System — Foreign Loans and Investments—Balance of Payments—Foreign Economic Assistance—Membership in International Organizations	
36.	Fiscal and Monetary System	745
	The Budget—The Banking and Currency System	
BIBLIOGRAPHY	....	763
GLOSSARY	....	807
INDEX	....	811

LIST OF ILLUSTRATIONS

Figure		Page
1	Main Political Subdivision of the Soviet Union	xviii
2	Relief and Drainage of the Soviet Union	15
3	Climatic Regions of the Soviet Union	17
4	Natural Vegetation Zones of the Soviet Union	19
5	Language Distribution in the Soviet Union	183
6	Soviet Union General Organization of Government	378
7	Soviet Union Council of Ministers, July 1969	392
8	Administrative and National Structure of the Soviet Union	400
9	Population Pyramid, January 1, 1970, Soviet Union	673

LIST OF TABLES

Table		Page
1	Soviet Union Industrial Production Plans, 1966–70 and 1970	116
2	Police System of the Soviet Union	142
3	Union Republics of the Soviet Union	403
4	Kraya of the Soviet Union	407
5	Autonomous Soviet Socialist Republics of the USSR	412
6	Autonomous Oblasti of the Soviet Union	415

SECTION I. GENERAL SURVEY

CHAPTER 1

NATURE OF THE SOVIET SYSTEM

The Union of Soviet Socialist Republics, more commonly referred to as the Soviet Union, is the world's largest country, covering the eastern half of Europe and the northern third of Asia. It also ranks third in population, which was estimated at over 241 million in January 1970. A highly industrialized nation that emerged from World War II as one of the world's leading powers, the Soviet Union is a multinational state descended from the former Russian Empire. The empire of the tsars, known for the severity of its absolutism and authoritarianism, fell to a popular revolution in early 1917. The Provisional Government that assumed control promised a constituent assembly, amnestied all political prisoners and exiles, and tried to bring order out of the chaos of war and revolution. The weak Provisional Government failed and fell to a coup d'etat staged in November 1917 by the Bolshevik wing of the Russian Social Democratic Workers Party, which eventually became the Communist Party of the Soviet Union (CPSU). The brief respite from absolutism and authoritarianism ended as the Bolsheviks reinstituted secret police and censorship and suppressed all opposition.

The nature of the Soviet system is indissolubly linked with the nature of the CPSU, which not only rules the country through the established government but also dictates standards for every facet of Soviet life: political, economic, social, and military. The CPSU, as the only political party, has monopolized power since the early 1920's and, developing without competition from other political groupings, has become a system in itself rather than a party in the conventionally accepted sense of the term. Credit for the theoretical basis and the implementation of the theory that led to the founding and development of the Party belongs to Vladimir Ilyich Lenin, who has been practically deified by his successors and is continually cited as the fount of all wisdom.

Lenin, born Vladimir Ilyich Ulyanov in 1870, was practically a legend by the time of his death in January 1924. Characterized by a fellow revolutionary and political adversary as the "uncrowned king" of the Party, even his most severe critics admitted that without him the Bolshevik movement most probably would have failed.

Directing his Bolshevik revolutionaries from exile between 1903 and 1905 and again from 1906 until April 1917, Lenin had the iron will and leadership abilities needed to keep the movement alive. After the popular revolution that forced the abdication of the tsar, Lenin returned to Russia to lead the virulent opposition to the Provisional Government, which brought about the downfall of that government within eight months. Lenin then led his revolutionary government through the difficult years of civil warfare and foreign intervention. Assuming dictatorial power over both Party and government, he tolerated no opposition and established a regime that rivaled and surpassed tsarism in its authoritarianism.

The Party, because of its monopolization of control over Soviet society, is the most important element contributing to the nature of the system. In more than fifty years in power, the CPSU had adjusted to industrialization and modernization of the country without relinquishing any of its authority. Membership in the Party was larger in 1970 than ever before in its history but, in comparison to population, it still constituted only a small percentage. Joseph Stalin, Lenin's successor, once commented that actual influence within the Party is confined to a minute percentage of the membership—an elite within the elite. Stalin's assessment would be as valid in 1970 as it was during the 1930's. Of the more than 13 million members in 1970, perhaps only one-half to three-quarters of a million wield any real influence in important political affairs, and the pyramid of power narrows rapidly toward the apex.

The 195 voting members and 165 nonvoting, candidate members of the Party's Central Committee would be considered very important persons in any ranking order, but even some of this elite assembly are members only because they occupy prestige positions in the arts and sciences or in the military hierarchy. The actual power of the Central Committee has reportedly increased in the post-Stalin era, and there is definite evidence to support this thesis. Ultimate power rests, however, with the policymaking Politburo and the operational Secretariat, which have eleven and ten members, respectively. These are the true molders of the Soviet system, and in 1970 three individuals occupied positions in both of these supreme bodies. Leonid Brezhnev, the general secretary, and two of his fellow secretaries, Andrei Kirilenko and Mikhail Suslov, were concurrently members of the Politburo.

Classical Marxism divided society into two major and several minor classes. The two major classes were the bourgeoisie and the proletariat, that is, the owners of the important means of production and the workers who had nothing to sell but their labor. The minor classes included the intelligentsia, usually those involved in mental work; small businessmen, often called petty bourgeoisie; landlords; peasants; and a group referred to by Marx and his collaborator,

2

Friedrich Engels, as the *lumpenproletariat*, the dregs of society. According to Marxist-Leninist theory, the ultimate stage of history will be communism and, when that stage has been achieved, there will be no class divisions among people.

The Soviet Union, referred to as a Communist state by most Westerners, is called socialist by its own leaders and people. *Socialism*, in their terminology, is a transitional stage between capitalism and communism, during which all citizens are required to contribute to the building of communism. With regard to class divisions, in the present stage, that of socialism, Soviet authorities assert that only two classes exist: workers and peasants. They also recognize a separate stratum of society known as the intelligentsia, which they claim originated from and overlaps both classes. The old bourgeoisie, petty bourgeoisie, landlords, and the *lumpenproletariat* disappeared during the establishment of a socialist society, according to Soviet ideologues, and the remaining classes will fuse into a single proletarian society when communism has been established.

The role of ideology in the nature of the system is ambiguous, and ideological tenets are often altered or rationalized to meet practical requirements. This was as true in 1917 as it was in 1970. Lenin had stated that all workers should be employees of the state and, accomplishing their share of work equally, they would be paid equally. Stalin, a few years later, stated that egalitarianism was nonsense and that workers should be paid according to their skill levels and production. The ideology is unequivocal in its definition of the coming classless society, yet the rise of the Soviet Union as a modern technological state has seen the concurrent rise of new classes, such as managers and technicians, who compete for prestige with the already existing classes of Party elite and bureaucrats. The aspirations of the people of the new classes are much the same as those of people in similar classes in the so-called bourgeois societies.

From a primarily peasant, agricultural background, the Soviet Union has been transformed into an urban, industrialized nation, and programs of mass education have practically eliminated illiteracy. Soviet Communists, from the beginning of their era, have proclaimed the coming of the "new Soviet man," in essence, a basic change in human nature that would eventually bring about the classless society. The Communist leadership has discovered that mass education and indoctrination have not brought about the selflessness that Karl Marx predicted for those living under a socialist system. Instead, Soviet man in 1970 shared the basic instincts and desires of mankind everywhere. The desire for better food, clothing, and shelter—a higher standard of living in general—is a basic attitude as are the desires for personal and family security and the desires to see one's children achieve higher education and a better life than that of the preceding generations.

3

At the Twenty-third Party Congress in 1966, the Communist leaders, in speech after speech, ignored ideology and concentrated on means of making the country more powerful in the international arena and raising the standard of living at home. Party rules call for a congress to be held every four years but, as of March 1970, the twenty-fourth Party congress had not been scheduled. If a congress is held in 1970 or 1971, the actions and expressed attitudes of the leaders since 1966 indicate that emphasis would again be placed on international power and an attempt to satisfy rising material expectations of the Soviet people.

The nature of the Soviet system, however, cannot be described in terms of Communist Party affairs alone, despite the fact that nothing within the system is exempt from control by the Party. The government and the people also contribute to, and are part of, the system. The government, according to Marxist-Leninist dogma, is destined to wither away when the world has reached the stage of communism but, in its first half century of existence, it has become a vast bureaucracy showing no signs of eventual disappearance. The people, from a great variety of ethnic backgrounds, also vary widely in degrees of education and modernization as well as in aspirations.

The government is the instrument through which the Party administers the huge country. In addition to providing the structure for the usual governmental functions and controls, the government also provides one of the bases through which the Party maintains contact with the masses. In structure the government is a pyramid of soviets, over 40,000 in all, with regular elections held every two years for lower level soviets and every four years for republic and national level bodies. Only one candidate for each office appears on a ballot, but that is part of the nature of the system, and most Soviet citizens have grown up knowing no other system and accepting the one they have.

In 1966 there was public discussion concerning the value of having more than one name on a ballot, an idea proposed by a high-ranking Party and government official. The idea received little or no support from the hierarchy and, as far as could be ascertained, the people did not demonstrate any great support for the proposal. The idea never got out of the discussion stage, but a few years earlier such discussions would have been considered heretical.

The most significant development in the political sphere during the 1960's was the advent of collegial rule after the ouster of Nikita Khrushchev, who had eventually acquired Party and government control after Stalin's death. Since its inception, the Soviet state has proclaimed collective leadership as one of its foremost achievements, but the dictatorship of Stalin and the near-dictatorship of Khrushchev belied this contention. After the downfall of Khrushchev in 1964, most Western observers predicted that a new dictator would emerge because, in their view, the system itself inherently demanded control by a single leader with dictatorial power. At the beginning of 1970, however, the collective leadership that succeeded Khrushchev was still operating as a collective. Party leadership and government leadership, combined in the person of Stalin, and again by Khrushchev in his time, continued in early 1970 to be divided between the general secretary of the CPSU, Leonid Brezhnev, and the chairman of the Council of Ministers, Aleksei Kosygin.

Another important development of the 1960's has been the appearance of open dissent, albeit on a small scale and primarily confined to intellectual circles. Actually, an atmosphere for dissent was created by the curbing of arbitrary police powers after the death of Stalin, but it was not until after Khrushchev's denunciation of the former dictator that writers began openly to condemn the excesses of the past. Soviet periodicals began publishing material about life in Stalin's camps; subjects that had only been whispered about previously began to appear in print and seemed to electrify the Soviet people. At the same time, many individuals who had been purged by Stalin were rehabilitated, even though often posthumously; and groups of people castigated as collaborators during the war were pardoned, some being allowed to return to their original homelands.

A period of liberalization appeared to be at hand, but by the mid-1960's criticism of past leadership appeared to be too close to criticism of current leadership and of the system itself. The regime reacted with arrests and trials of writers who were condemned for "anti-Soviet attitudes." Public demonstrations in Moscow and some other cities in support of imprisoned authors were a new phenomena for the regime, which quickly stamped out the public manifestations of dissent. Many intellectuals and writers were silenced either by agreeing to conform to prescribed standards or by imprisonment.

Covert dissent proved to be more difficult to deal with, and an underground press was active during the 1960's and into 1970. Since 1968 a typed manuscript newspaper has appeared regularly on the last day of every other month. Titled *Khronika Tekushchikh Sobyty* (The Chronicle of Current Events), the manuscript is distributed clandestinely and is reportedly retyped by many recipients in order to achieve wider distribution. In contrast to underground literary publications that publish stories and poetry, this newspaper deals only with newsworthy items and purports to be a newspaper rather than a disseminator of opinions. Because the government has not eliminated it and because of the regularity of its publication, *Khronika Tekushchikh Sobyty*, in effect, has become an opposition newspaper—the only one to exist since Lenin silenced all opposition newspapers in 1917.

The Soviet Union in 1970 was the world's second ranking industrial nation, a nuclear power, and a nation proud of its accomplishments in space. The huge airliners of Aeroflot, the state airline, had become familiar sights in most of the world's capitals, and at home Aeroflot linked together some of the most remote towns of the country. The Soviet Union, however, had not entered the automobile age along with the rest of the world's industrialized nations. Its automotive industry had for years concentrated on the production of trucks, tractors, farm machines, and military vehicles rather than passenger cars but, through an arrangement with the Fiat Company of Italy to build and equip a huge plant, the Soviets predict greatly increased production of automobiles in the early 1970's. It seems unlikely that the expressed aspirations of many citizens to own private automobiles can soon be fulfilled, yet the aspirations are real and the regime is taking some steps to meet them.

The nature of the economic system derives from state ownership and operation of the entire industrial sector and part of the agricultural sector of the economy. The collective sector of agriculture is also tightly controlled and directed by the state. In addition to state control, the entire economy has been centrally planned since Stalin's First Five-Year Plan began in 1928. Despite modifications and greatly heralded reforms, the basic nature of the system has not changed; it remains a system of centrally planned socialism.

At the beginning of 1970 the economy appeared to be in trouble. Contradictory reports by officials and editorials in *Pravda* clouded the issues, but statements by Brezhnev left no doubt that economic performance in the late 1960's had not pleased the leadership. Economic growth rates, which had been spectacular during earlier periods of rapid industrialization, have slowed to a degree evidently unacceptable to the leadership. Some Soviet economists practically admit that the economic problems arise from outmoded ideological doctrines. These are the reformers who have urged decentralization, more power to managers, more incentives to workers, more profitability, and other non-Marxist innovations. Some of their ideas have been incorporated into the system, but an opposing school of Soviet economists, as well as many Party politicians, have opposed the reforms with enough strength to make them ineffective. The opposition has been based primarily on ideology.

The direction and operation of the economy are key functions of the CPSU and, throughout the Soviet era, Party men without training in economics, technology, or management have had inordinate influence on economic operations. The struggle is between the Party man and the technocrat, and it does not appear likely that the Party will diminish or eliminate its role in the running of the system. Therefore, in 1970, the economy seemed likely to continue along the same path it had followed during the 1966—70 plan, with inadequate growth rates and unfulfilled promises of higher living standards for the people. The technocrats would probably continue to recommend cures that would be ideologically unacceptable to the Party. The economic system did not appear to be in danger of collapse, but neither could it become dynamic in such an impasse.

An official census, the first since 1959, was conducted in January 1970, but it is expected that several months will be spent in analysis and compilation of statistics before results are published. The 1959 census showed about 55 percent of the total population to be ethnic Russians, but estimates in 1969 placed the ratio at about fifty-fifty. The 1959 census also showed about 10 percent of the non-Russian peoples claimed Russian as their native language, and this number is expected to show increase in the new census. Soviet officials at the time of the 1970 census-taking predicted that the number of ethnic Russians will probably be under 50 percent of the total population for the first time in history. Despite any percentage decrease, however, the Russians remain by far the most numerous ethnic group, and Russian dominance in the politics, economics, and culture of the entire country is unquestioned. How to handle the problems of ethnicity that have plagued all Soviet rulers continues to be of critical importance as the Brezhnev-Kosygin regime enters the decade of the 1970's.

Basically, the ethnic problem involves the methods to be used in maintaining centralized control over a vast multinational state while granting some measures of autonomy to the ethnic minorities. Some Soviet scholars subscribe to assimilation as an on-going process that will eventually erode national differences. Others predict that nationalism will flourish, but without intergroup rancor or animosity, because of the peoples' allegiance to socialism and the building of communism.

Similar ambivalence is to be found in the positions of Western observers. Some stress the anti-Russian sentiments prevalent among many non-Russian groups, but others counter such arguments by pointing out that anti-Russian and pro-Soviet views are not necessarily incompatible. Another telling argument against separatist ideas is the fact that regional economies have been securely linked and the planned economy militates against separatism. Cultural autonomy with economic and political homogeneity seem to be the probable future course of Soviet nationalism.

Religious affiliations often go hand in hand with ethnic differentiations. The Russian Orthodox Church claims adherents among the Russians, Ukrainians, and Belorussians as well as among many smaller ethnic groups. Lutheranism is strongest in Estonia and Latvia, and Roman Catholicism is found in Lithuania and the former Polish territories of the Soviet Union. Islam, which is second only to Russian Orthodoxy in numbers of believers, encompasses many ethnic groups, primarily in the republics of Soviet Asia but also in some regions north of the Caucasus Mountains. There are other religions associated with ethnic groups, such as Buddhism, found among the Buryats, Kalmyks, and Soviet Koreans. Soviet Jews are considered to be an ethnic group as well as a religious group.

Religion, in the view of staunch ideologists, should have disappeared or been stamped out during the more than fifty years of Communist rule. The practice of religion, however, has defied all assaults and doggedly persists. Official tolerance has become part of the system, and people representing many denominations do attend religious services. Marxism-Leninism itself has become a pseudo-religion, and Soviet people line up for blocks to view the embalmed remains of Lenin just as people line up to visit a famous cathedral or to listen to a famous evangelist in other societies.

In international affairs the Soviet Union operates on two planes, one being its relations with the almost ninety Communist parties of the world and the second being its regular nation-to-nation diplomatic relations. In its dealings with other parties, the CPSU has lost its hegemony over the world movement, primarily since the appearance of the open rift with China, but actually the first split in what then appeared to be an international Communist monolith came in 1948 with Stalin's expulsion of Yugoslavia from the Cominform (Communist Information Bureau—see Glossary). The feud between Stalin and Josip Broz Tito, the Yugoslav Communist leader, was considered by many observers to be a minor crack in an otherwise monolithic structure, but the sustained Sino-Soviet dispute actually divided the international Communist movement into hostile camps. The ideological struggle between Communist China and the Soviet Union had always encompassed questions of national interest as well as ideology, but, in 1969, national interests became of foremost importance as the two nations engaged in combat along their mutual borders. The basic Marxist tenet of solidarity among socialist states was shown to be meaningless, if it had not already been revealed as a myth by the Soviet invasions of Hungary in 1956 and Czechoslovakia in 1968.

On the fiftieth anniversary of the Bolshevik Revolution, Albania and China refused to participate in the Moscow celebrations, while the leaders of Cuba, North Korea, and North Vietnam chose to send representatives rather than attend in person. During the anniversary celebrations, with most of the world's notable Communists present and some notably absent, Brezhnev reportedly tried and failed to get a consensus for the condemnation of China as an ideological deviant. Other such attempts have been made by Brezhnev at international Communist meetings, with the same result. Moscow has become one of the centers of international communism instead of the only center.

In the usual international affairs, as opposed to inter-Communist affairs, the Kremlin leadership appears to be more cautious than Khrushchev and less belligerent than Stalin. They have continued to support North Vietnam with money and military hardware. They have also continued financial support of Cuba despite Fidel Castro's intermittent insults and anti-Soviet statements. Through support of the Arab States, the Soviets have become a Mediterranean power—an unfulfilled dream of many former tsars. But Soviet ships, naval and merchant, are plying all the seas, not just the Mediterranean; in 1970 the Soviet Union was a trading nation, bidding for markets wherever they could be found regardless of the ideological proclivities of the prospective trading partners. In addition to trade, the Soviet Union has also become a grantor of aid, and, since 1954, several billion rubles (1 ruble equals US$1.10) in the form of long-term loans have been granted to various underdeveloped nations.

In its military posture the Soviet Union stands out as a first rank power among the nations of the world. It maintains an armed force of about 3.2 million men with modern equipment for conventional army, navy, and air forces as well as for its missile forces. The armed forces are generally assessed by Western observers to be well equipped, trained, and motivated. The bulk of the forces consists of conscripts who apparently have good morale and accept military service as a normal fact of life. A conscript's term of service is characterized by rigid discipline and intensive programs of military training and political indoctrination. The officer corps and the nucleus of noncommissioned officer corps are composed of professionals who display their professionalism, dedication, and loyalty. Political controls in the armed forces no longer subject a commander to the humiliation of having orders countermanded by a political commissar. With about 85 percent of the forces made up of Party or Komsomol (Young Communist League—see Glossary) members, loyalty is not questioned to the extent that it was at various times in the past. Political officers exist in all units but are deputies to commanding officers rather than political overseers.

CHAPTER 2

PHYSICAL ENVIRONMENT

The Union of Soviet Socialist Republics, the world's largest state in area (8.65 million square miles) and the third most populous in the world (240 million inhabitants in 1969), occupies a dominant position in eastern Europe and northern Asia and covers much of central Asia. It extends over 6,000 miles from the Baltic Sea in the west to the Bering Strait in the east and somewhat more than 3,000 miles from the Pamir Mountains in the south to the Arctic Ocean north of the Arctic Circle. This multinational state, comprising between one-sixth and one-seventh of the landmass of our planet, includes within its borders more than 40 percent of the area of Europe and Asia and over 100 ethnic groups.

The country is outlined in the north by the seas of the Arctic Ocean. To the west there is the Baltic Sea and, as a part of Europe, the Soviet Union has land frontiers with Norway, Finland, Poland, Czechoslovakia, Hungary, and Rumania. To the south in Europe there is the Black Sea. Southern boundaries in Asia are with Turkey, Iran, Afghanistan, Communist China, the Mongolian People's Republic, and Korea (see fig. 1).

The seas of the Arctic Ocean along the Soviet Union's northern coast include the White Sea, east of Finland, and the Barents Sea, which stretches to the islands of Franz Josef Land in the extreme north. Farther east lie sizable islands, including Novaya Zemlya and Vaygach, beyond which is the Kara Sea reaching the western coast of the Severnaya island group, just north of the Taymyr Peninsula. Beyond are the Laptev Sea and several chains of islands, and farther east are the East Siberian Sea and Wrangel Island. From north to south the Chukchi Sea, Bering Strait, and the Bering Sea separate Siberia from Alaska.

A major feature of the country's Pacific coastline is the Kamchatka Peninsula with its offshore Karaginsky and Commander islands. To the southwest is the Sea of Okhotsk, separated from the Pacific Ocean proper by the Kuril island chain which runs north to south from Kamchatka to Japan. The large Soviet island of Sakhalin forms the northern limit to the Sea of Japan and lies east of the Soviet mainland.

In Europe the country's coastline south of Finland stretches along the Gulf of Finland and the Baltic Sea, which border the Leningrad region, Estonia (with its two offshore islands of Hiiumaa and Saaremaa), Latvia, Lithuania, and the Kaliningrad (formerly Koenigsberg) region. The Black Sea limits the country on the south along the coasts of the Ukraine, including the Crimea, and the western Caucasus. To the east the Black Sea joins the Sea of Azov, which in turn delimits the eastern Crimea, southern Ukraine and northwestern Caucasus. The Soviet Union has a coastline of a total of over 30,000 miles.

In relief, the country consists of a huge plain that extends from the western borders eastward on a broad front up to the moderately elevated Ural Mountains, separating Russia proper from Siberia, and continues across central Siberia. Farther on the land becomes a succession of plateaus and mountains that reach the sea along the country's eastern extremity. Mountain ranges, mostly of great elevation, extend along practically all of the southern border.

The country is rich in rivers and waterways, and its geographers claim that it possesses the greatest hydroelectric power potential in the world. Inland waters include the Caspian Sea, the largest inland body of water in the world, whose shores are shared in the south with Iran; the Aral Sea, just to the east in central Asia; Lake Baikal, in eastern Siberia; Lake Ladoga and Lake Onega, east of Leningrad; and Lake Balkhash, in eastern Kazakhstan.

Worldwide surveys of known resources indicate that the country has about half of the world's reserves of coal and peat, over one-third of the iron ore, and a large percentage of the manganese and potassium. Its proved reserves of copper, lead, zinc, nickel, bauxite, tungsten, mercury, and sulfur are estimated to be greater than in any other country, and it has extensive oil and gas fields (see ch. 30, Industry). The forests comprise about one-fourth of the total forested area of the world and vary widely by species, but their economic potential is limited by relative inaccessibility in some areas.

By far the greater part of the country lies north of the 50th parallel, and some 10 percent is within the Arctic Circle. The essentially landlocked nature of the Soviet Union and its remoteness from warm water result in a continental climate for the greater part of the landmass.

Because of this fact and the northern location, winters are long and very cold, and warm summers are short. The region of permafrost, where the subsoil is permanently frozen and only the higher layers thaw during the summer, covers about 40 percent of the total land area. There are a few relatively small areas of subtropical climate along the Black Sea and the southern border in central Asia.

The amount of agriculturally productive land is limited by shortage of rainfall. The overall result is a generally disadvantageous climatic situation that has led to a pattern of settlement severely restricted by the usefulness of the soil and the rigors of the climate.

A great triangle of Soviet population can be drawn from Leningrad in the northwest eastward to Novosibirsk in western Siberia and from this apex westward to Rostov-on-the-Don, leaving an open-ended western funnel coinciding with the western frontiers of the Soviet state. Here reside the great majority of the inhabitants. North and east of the region stretch vast coniferous forests and in the extreme north the tundra, which barely supports life. Broadleaf forests still abound within the great triangle. For many centuries they have provided for the Eastern Slav the base of life—plentiful logs for *izbi* (log cabins), firewood for fuel and warmth, wood for utensils and tools—assured the retention of subsurface moisture, the enrichment of the soil by humus, and the maintenance of wildlife.

The greatest cities are Moscow, capital of the Soviet Union and of the Russian Soviet Federated Socialist Republic, situated in central Russia, with over 6.5 million inhabitants; Leningrad, formerly Saint Petersburg, with nearly 4 million people, on the Gulf of Finland; Kiev, mother of Russian cities and capital of the Ukraine, with about 1.5 million; and Tashkent, capital of Uzbekistan in central Asia, with a population of about 1.3 million. Other urban places with populations exceeding 1 million include Baku, on the Caspian Sea; Kharkov, in the eastern Ukraine; Gorky, northeast of Moscow on the Volga; Novosibirsk, in western Siberia, the largest industrial city east of the Urals; Kuybyshev, on the Volga; and Sverdlovsk, leading industrial city of the Urals. All of these cities except Tashkent and Baku are situated within the great triangle of population described above.

NATURAL FEATURES

The great plain that comprises so much of the Soviet Union reaches from the western frontiers in Europe to the center of Asia. In the west it is broken by higher ground along the Barents Sea and the border with Finland, extending southward nearly to the Black Sea through the center of European Russia. In the southwest the hilly region of the Ukraine extends eastward to uplands along the Volga River and southward to the mountains of the Caucasus. Farther east, the great plain is interrupted by the chain of the Ural Mountains, which traditionally have been considered a dividing line between Europe and Asia (see fig. 2).

South of the Ural Mountains and extending eastward around the Caspian Sea, lowlands extend into Asia as far as the foothills of the high ranges of the Pamirs and the Tien Shan, Altai, and Sayan mountains that rise abruptly along the Soviet Union's southern border. Lowlands continue to the north beyond Lake Balkhash and the moderately elevated uplands of Kazakhstan and slope as a wide plain across West Siberia to the shores of the Arctic Ocean. Farther east, beyond the Yenisey River, the land rises to form a hilly plateau region across central Siberia that merges into a complex of mountains and drainage basins extending to the country's eastern seaboard.

Europe's greatest river, the Volga, from a source in the Valdai Hills southeast of Leningrad, flows southeastward past Moscow and then directly southward in the extreme east of Europe into the Caspian Sea. The Volga River, together with its tributaries, is of more importance for transportation purposes than all the other rivers of the country combined. The greatest rivers in point of flow and length, however, are east of the Ural Mountains. These include the Irtysh-Ob, Yenisey, Angara, and the Lena. They all flow northward into the seas of the Arctic Ocean, and their value for transportation purposes is further limited by the fact that in the main their direction crosses, rather than coincides with, the great traffic routes across central Asia.

The country's northern seacoasts are never completely ice free except for the northeast coastal region of the Kola Peninsula with the port of Murmansk, which remains ice free because of the effects of the Gulf Stream. The remainder of the northern coastline is noteworthy only for its insignificant ports and a need for icebreakers and spotter planes to assist shipping even in the summer when the ice breaks up for a few months. The Pacific seaboard, by contrast, has weather modified by the maritime influence of the Pacific Ocean. Its port city of Vladivostok overlooks Peter the Great Bay which, although icebound in winter, is free of ice in the warm weather months.

The Baltic ports in the far west of the country are closed by ice for several months each winter. The Baltic Sea itself may be viewed as an inland lake rather than an open sea. To reach an open sea, Soviet shipping must go on to the North Sea beyond Denmark and Norway.

To the south the Black Sea, like the Baltic, resembles a lake. In this case it opens into an even greater one, the Mediterranean Sea. Despite its Black Sea location, Odessa, the leading southern Soviet port, is frozen in for about six weeks each winter.

The climate of most of the country is continental, under the predominant influence of dry polar airmasses and not greatly affected by tropical or maritime conditions. Because of the northern location, summers are short, and winters are long and severe. The normally prevailing flow of dry arctic air over the greater part of the country, distance from open, warm oceans, and the screening effect of high mountains on the east and south—all combine to result in a general pattern of precipitation that is not abundant (see fig. 3).

14

Except for a small belt influenced by maritime air masses from the Pacific Ocean, the precipitation pattern shows a broad maximum zone that stretches east-west across the country. From this zone, the rain and snow decreases toward the north and toward the south. Within the maximum zone, there is a decrease from west to east. Particularly along the south of the maximum zone, precipitation in many areas is unreliable, and there may be years of severe drought. The lowest precipitation occurs in the southern lowland areas of west and central Asia where the annual average may be less than four inches per year and the evaporation rate is very high. Some parts of northeastern Siberia, inland from the seacoast, are almost as dry. Most favored by rainfall are the shores along the eastern part of the Black Sea where annual rainfall may exceed forty inches.

Four major zones of natural vegetation cross the country from its western borders almost to the Pacific seaboard. There are some local modifications, and the higher mountains introduce variations resulting from differences in elevation. The general nature of the country's soils is closely related to the patterns of natural vegetation and has a similar zonal arrangement in east-west belts. There are gradations in each belt largely caused by variations in moisture and in insolation or the pattern of sunshine received (see fig. 4).

A treeless zone of tundra extends southward from the Arctic seaboard to an irregular line roughly approximating the Arctic Circle except in the White Sea-Kola Peninsula area of the far northwest. In its southern part there are scattered, stunted bushes, but elsewhere the vegetation consists of low shrubs, mosses, and lichens. This is a region of permafrost where the subsoil is permanently frozen and the upper layers, even when thawed during the short summer season, are boggy because of poor drainage.

South of the tundra is the taiga—a great coniferous forest, with an area of some 3 million square miles—which is the largest in the world. In the northern reaches, trees grow slowly and to no great height. Farther south, where the climate is more favorable, there are excellent stands of pine, spruce, and larch. These become interspersed with birch, oak, maple, and other deciduous hardwoods along the southern edge, and the forest becomes mixed, particularly in European Russia, where the original cover either has been much modified by man or cleared for farming. Gray or brown acid soils predominate throughout this vegetation zone. These are generally low in humus and of only moderate fertility, although their agricultural productivity improves toward the south.

A belt of grassland, consisting mainly of steppe with natural cover of short, bunched grasses, lies south of the zone of forest. This belt is widest in European Russia and extends through the Ukraine in a narrowing triangle across western Siberia. The steppe lands usually have an exceptionally rich black soil, high in organic content and mineral nutrients. These soils provide the best agricultural land in the country, but because they develop only where the rainfall is very moderate, they can be farmed only at the risk of occasional failure from drought (see ch. 31, Agriculture).

A wide belt of arid steppe and desert extends from the mountains along the country's southern border westward from central Asia to the northern slopes of the Caucasus. The arid steppe is broadest in western Siberia and Kazakhstan and is characterized by lack of trees, scanty grasses, and poor chestnut-brown soils low in humus content. Generally south of the arid steppe, the land becomes a true desert made up of sandy areas, rock and gravel, and salt flats. Some parts of the desert have soils of enough mineral content to be very fertile, and with irrigation they offer important agricultural advantages.

BOUNDARIES AND POLITICAL SUBDIVISIONS

International Boundaries

The Soviet Union has common territorial frontiers with twelve countries. In the far northwest extending inland from the Barents Sea, the boundary with Norway runs generally southwest for about 120 miles to the Finnish tripoint at Krokfjell, a few miles west of the Pasvikely River. For most of its length the boundary follows natural water features. It has been marked by boundary pillars throughout. The boundary was established by the 1826 Treaty of Petersburg and, although subsequent agreements have made minor rectifications and adjustments, the alignment has remained essentially unchanged.

From the Norwegian tripoint, the boundary between the Soviet Union and Finland extends in a generally southerly direction for about eight hundred miles to the Gulf of Finland at a point about one hundred miles west of Leningrad. The boundary has been delimited for the most part by straight lines, and geographic features are rarely utilized except as turning points. Stream lines are virtually ignored, and drainage divides and ridge lines are not followed at all. As a consequence, the border is very complex. It has been demarcated, however, by boundary pillars throughout its entire length. The modern basis for the boundary rests on agreements negotiated at the end of World War I, the Winter War of 1939—40 between Finland and the Soviet Union, and World War II, which resulted in various territorial transfers and changes in the alignment. In 1969 there were no known disputes concerning the border.

The line indicating the frontier with Poland was established as a result of World War II military action and agreements made at the

Yalta and Potsdam conferences. From a point on the shore of the Gulf of Danzig, some 30 miles southwest of Kaliningrad, the boundary runs east and then generally south for a distance of about 650 miles to the Czechoslovakian tripoint, about 80 miles southwest of L'vov. Except for a stretch of about 100 miles where the boundary follows the course of the Bug River, natural features are disregarded.

The boundary with Czechoslovakia extends roughly south for about sixty miles from Poland on the north to the Hungarian tripoint, a short distance southwest of the important railway junction of Chop. It results from cession by Czechoslovakia of trans-Carpathian Ruthenia to the Soviet Union, formalized by the Moscow Agreement of June 29, 1945. So far as is known, there is no dispute over delimitation of the boundary. Southeast of the Czechoslovakian frontier the Soviet Union borders on Hungary for a distance of about 75 miles. The boundary, which makes little use of natural features, has been fully demarcated. The basic boundary delimitation was established by agreements originating at the Paris Peace Conference in 1919 when the line formed part of the boundary between newly established Czechoslovakia and Hungary. World War II treaties and agreements have confirmed the boundary, and there are no known disputes concerning it.

From the Hungarian tripoint, the Soviet Union borders on Rumania along a generally easterly to southeasterly line for a distance of about 850 miles. The boundary ends at the Black Sea at one of the northern exits of the Danube River after crossing the Transylvanian Basin, the Carpathian Mountains, the Moldavian-Bessarabian Plateau, and the plains and delta of the lower Danube Valley. The boundary derives from Rumania's cession of territory to the Soviet Union in 1940, recognized by the Treaty of Peace with Rumania, signed in Paris in 1947. There are no disputes over the precise alignment of the boundary, but indirectly Rumania has hinted reservations concerning the 1940 cession of territory.

East of the Black Sea, the Soviet Union's border with Turkey extends for about 350 miles to the Iranian tripoint. The boundary begins on the coast of the Black Sea about 15 miles southwest of Batumi and follows an irregular course conforming to streamlines, drainage divides, and old administrative boundaries. The boundary was delimited in the 1921 Treaties of Moscow and Kars and has remained unchanged since that time. It was demarcated in 1925—26 by a mixed commission.

Beginning at the Turkish tripoint in the center of the main channel of the Aras River about 40 miles southeast of Yerevan, the Soviet Union shares over 1,000 miles of land frontier with Iran, of which some 450 miles lie west of the Caspian Sea. The boundary follows the Aras River through mountainous country until it approaches the lowlands west of the Caspian Sea and then utilizes a number of streamlines and drainage divides until it reaches the sea, about 150 miles south of Baku. East of the Caspian Sea the frontier follows an irregular course generally eastward along stream and ridge lines to the Afghan tripoint in the main channel of the Hari Rud (river), about 100 miles northwest of Herat in Afghanistan.

West of the Caspian Sea the boundary was defined early in the nineteenth century by the Treaties of Gulistan and Turkmanchai. To the east delimitation was provided a half century later by the Tehran Conventions of 1881 and 1893. Neither Iran nor the Soviet Union has strong territorial claims in the border area, and after minor rectifications culminating in a demarcation protocol signed in 1957, the boundary has been stabilized. Limits of national sovereignty in the Caspian Sea have not been determined. Since the Soviet Union and Iran are the only countries that border on those waters, they appear to have a condominium status, and there is a question whether the normal rules of territorial waters apply.

The border with Afghanistan follows a very irregular, but eastward trending trace for about 1,300 miles. In the west it crosses a thinly populated, hilly region for about 400 miles between the Iranian border and the Amu Darya (Oxus River). It then follows the main channel of the Amu Darya and two of its tributaries upstream through high mountains to Lake Victoria, from which it continues along ridge lines of the Pamirs to the Chinese tripoint high in the mountain cluster north of Kashmir. Several bilateral agreements involving Great Britain, Afghanistan, and Russia established the greater part of the border with Afghanistan. The first direct Afghan-Russian agreement on their common boundary was concluded in 1921 and was followed by another bilateral agreement in 1946 that completed the delimitation. Demarcation was carried out by a mixed commission, and there appear to be no disputes over the alignment.

Over 4,000 miles long, the boundary with Communist China, stretching from the Pamirs in central Asia to within a few miles of the Sea of Japan, is divided into two nearly equal sectors by the Mongolian People's Republic. On the west the Sinkiang-Turkestan section generally follows main drainage divides for about half its length and then crosses valleys and streamlines to the western tripoint with the Mongolian People's Republic in the Altai range. On the east, by far the greater part of the boundary is defined by the Argun, Amur, and Ussuri rivers.

Although most of the boundary has been delimited by a series of Sino-Russian treaties concluded during the Tsarist and Manchu period, a number of territorial problems exist along the frontier. In the extreme west, no treaty delimits the border in the area of the Pamirs. East of the Mongolian People's Republic, there are disputes not only over the exact course of parts of the river line boundaries but also over the validity and interpretation of some of the treaties and protocols upon which the general alignment has been based (see ch. 24, Foreign Relations).

Between the eastern and western sectors of the border with Communist China, the Soviet Union's boundary with the Mongolian People's Republic extends for about 1,700 miles in an irregular arc south of Lake Baikal, with only limited utilization of natural features. The boundary is the one essentially agreed upon in the Treaty of Kyakta, concluded in 1727 between the Russian and Chinese empires, with the exception of about 700 miles along the southern border of the Tuvinskaya ASSR (formerly Tannu Tuva). This territory was absorbed by the Soviet Union in 1944, and its border was agreed to by the Mongolian People's Republic.

Extending a distance of about ten miles from the Communist China tripoint to the Sea of Japan, the boundary with Korea follows the lower course of the Tumen River. There has been no treaty delimiting this border, but there are no known disputes concerning its alignment, which appears to follow the main navigation channel of the river.

Main Political Subdivisions

The Soviet Union is federal in form and made up of fifteen separate union republics (see fig. 1). This territorial organization reflects the multinational character of the population and efforts on the part of the Communist government to incorporate national identities and languages into the country's administrative structure. At the time the structure was worked out in 1922, with establishment of the Union of Soviet Socialist Republics, a union republic was formed for most of the major peoples or nationality groups. For this reason and because the country was formed by a process of imperial expansion, the boundaries of the main subdivisions are based less on topography than on ethnic and political considerations (see ch. 3, Historical Setting).

By far the largest of the union republics is the Russian Soviet Federated Socialist Republic (RSFSR), which contains over half the total population of the Soviet Union, stretches from Europe across the northern half of western Siberia, and continues to the Pacific Ocean seaboard. West of the RSFSR and bordering on the Baltic Sea are the three relatively small republics of Estonia, Latvia, and Lithuania, each with its own language and national traditions. Inland from the Baltic seaboard and extending along the Soviet Union's western borders are the Belorussian (White Russian) and Ukrainian union republics, both of which have Slavic languages closely akin to Russian. To the south is the Rumanian-speaking

25

Bessarabia, known as the Moldavian Soviet Socialist Republic (SSR).

East of the Black Sea, along the country's southern frontier, the Transcaucasia area, with an age-old history of population movements and political changes, has the Georgian, Armenian, and Azerbaijan union republics. The people of the last-named territory speak a Turkic language. Four other major subdivisions whose inhabitants mostly use forms of Turkic are in Central Asia, south of the RSFSR. These include the Kazakh republic, which is next in size to the RSFSR but is comparatively underpopulated, and the Turkmen, Uzbek, and Kirgiz republics. The Tadzhik Soviet Socialist Republic, bordering on Afghanistan and Communist China in the south, has a largely Iranian-speaking population.

There are several kinds of subordinate administrative subdivisions within the union republics. Nominally endowed with varying degrees of autonomy, they have been established either to grant recognition to a predominant nationality or to facilitate economic planning and development. The names and boundaries of these units have often been changed (see ch. 20, Component Political Subdivisions).

REGIONAL ANALYSIS

Baltic-Belorussia Region

This region is made up of a broad glacial plain that stretches from the shores of the Baltic Sea southward along the Soviet Union's western borders across the lowlands of the Pripet Marshes to the higher elevations of the Ukraine. Its area includes Estonia, Latvia, Lithuania, and the Belorussian union republic and the area on the Baltic Sea around Kaliningrad, once Prussian Koenigsberg. The main urban places include the Baltic port cities of Tallin, Riga, and Kaliningrad. Inland are Vilnius and Minsk, administrative capitals of Lithuanian and the Belorussian union republic, respectively and Brest-Litovsk, an important railway junction for traffic between the Soviet Union and the rest of Europe.

Most of the region is below 500 feet in elevation, and a good deal of the land, especially in the south, is either boggy or interspersed with small lakes and swamps. From a low divide that crosses the center of the region, the Western Dvina and Bug rivers and their tributaries drain northwestward to the Baltic Sea. South of the divide, drainage into the Pripet and Dnepr rivers flows to the Black sea. A canal between the Pripet and Bug rivers provides barge service across the border with Poland.

The climate of this region is more tempered by marine influences than those parts of the Soviet Union in Europe that lie farther inland. Temperature extremes are not so great as elsewhere, but polar airmasses bring cold periods during the winter. An annual precipitation of from twenty to twenty-five inches, of which a considerable part is snow, is adequate for general agriculture, and drought is rare. Natural vegetation consists of mixed deciduous and coniferous forest with a number of valuable species, including spruce, fir, hemlock, oak, and maple, which are exploited for wood products and timber. The forest cover in this long-settled land has been much modified by man, and where the soil is suitable, has been extensively cleared for agriculture except in the north.

The south of the region is noted for the poverty of its acid, boggy soil, even though efforts have been made to reclaim the marshy areas. Toward the north, the land is better, but the soil tends to be acid and deficient in organic nutrients. Root crops, such as beets and potatoes, are widely grown, and the chief grains are rye, oats, and barley. Stockbreeding and dairying are important in the costal areas, and there is some fishing, both along the coast and in inland waters. There are few usable mineral resources of any great value. Peat is taken from boggy areas and is an important local source of fuel. Minor deposits of phosphate rock and limestone are found inland along the coast, and there are oil-bearing shales in the north.

Industries are almost wholly concerned with food processing, metal working, and marine repairs in the port cities; the manufacture of wood products, including pulp and paper; leather production; and other light industrial operations, largely for local consumption. The region is well served by railways. The main line between Leningrad and Warsaw passes through Vilnius. The main line between Moscow and Warsaw passes through Minsk. Highway facilities, especially in the south where the swampy terrain is a serious obstacle, are not well developed, but one of the country's principal superhighways gives Minsk a direct connection with Moscow on the east and Warsaw on the west.

Ukraine-Moldavia Region

A land of broad plains and low, rolling hills, with a few wide river valleys, this region extends for roughly 800 miles across the southern part of Russia in Europe as far as the hilly area north of the Sea of Azov on the western side of the Don river. Politically, the area includes the Ukrainian and the Moldavian union republics, of which the former is by far the larger and more populous. From the edge of the Carpathian Mountains on the west, the land descends to the east. Most of the region is below 1,500 feet in elevation and of nearly featureless relief. Major drainage is to the south and east. The Dnepr River flows to the Black Sea though the center of the region, roughly paralleled on the west by the Dniester and Prut rivers and on the east by the Donets River and other tributaries of the Don River.

The climate is transitional between the continental extremes of central Russia to the northeast and the more temperate regions of Europe on the west. Except along the south coast of the Crimean Peninsula, where the weather is much moderated by maritime influences, there are marked seasonal contrasts. Summers are warm, and temperature averages for July range from about 60°F. in the north to over 70°F. in the south. During the winter months, intrusions of masses of Arctic air bring very cold temperatures that often fall well below 0°F. in most of the region. Average January temperatures range from about 18°F. in the north to 37°F. along the southern Crimean coast. Generally speaking, April and September are the months of last and first frosts, respectively.

Precipitation during normal years is barely adequate for nonirrigated farming. Decreasing from north to south, the average ranges from about twenty-five inches to about twelve inches in the driest zone along the Black Sea. Variations in rainfall below the average resulting in crop failures have been of common occurrence. The summer rains usually come in the form of heavy downpours associated with thunderstorms. Snow provides heavy cover for the ground in the north, but toward the south the ground is frequently bare during winter months.

Mediocre bog or forest soils, acid and deficient in plant nutrients, found in the north in association with mixed deciduous forest and forest-steppe give way to the fertile black earth known as chernozem in the southern half of the region. This soil is rich in minerals and is provided with abundant humus. Its chemical and mechanical composition produces an easily worked, moisture-conserving soil. Although soil of this general type is found in other areas farther east, the Ukraine has the greatest part, and it constitutes a valuable agricultural resource.

This is one of the main agricultural regions of the country. In addition to wheat, rye, and corn, of which it is an important producer, the region furnishes much of the country's beet sugar supply together with root crops, oil seeds, vegetables, and dairy products. Well over half of this region's land area is tillable, a condition that is exceptional, for only 20 percent of the country as a whole is estimated to be agriculturally useful.

The region has great mineral wealth advantageously situated, including coal, iron, manganese, nickel, and natural gas. The Donets Basin in the east has major coal deposits and is a center for heavy industry. The Krivoi Rog and Kerch regions, also in the east, account for perhaps 25 percent of the Soviet Union's immense iron ore resources. Light industries in the region include textile, food processing, metal goods, and wood products plants. The Dnepr

28

River provides power from six hydroelectric plants (see ch. 30, Industry).

The largest cities are Kiev and Kharkov, each with over a million inhabitants. Rich in historical importance, Kiev is the capital of the Ukrainian Soviet Socialist Republic and a major transportation center. Kharkov is a manufacturing and rail center. In the late 1960's other cities with populations exceeding a half million were Donetsk, center for heavy industry; Odessa, the country's principal Black Sea port; Dnepropetrovsk; and L'vov. Railway transportation is well developed throughout the region, and there are international connections with Czechoslovakia, Hungary, and Rumania. The Dnepr River and its tributaries form an extensive system of inland waterways, but these are closed by ice for several months each year. The highway system is relatively underdeveloped as is the case elsewhere in the country.

Transcaucasia

This area is made up of the Transcaucasian union republics of Georgia, Armenia, and Azerbaijan, situated between the Black and Caspian seas and bordering on Turkey and Iran in the south. The region includes most of the high range of the Caucasus Mountain system, some of the summits of which reach 15,000 feet or more. In Georgia, the Black Sea and the shelter of the mountains assure a moderate, almost subtropical, climate and exceptionally high precipitation for the union. Armenia to the south is very mountainous, and the land under cultivation is arid and requires irrigation. Farther to the east in Azerbaijan, a similar situation exists except for the southern triangle, which is subtropical. In Georgia forests abound, alternating with mountain meadow and steppe soils.

Very sizable deposits of manganese are mined in Georgia. Mountain streams provide abundant hydroelectric power resources for the entire area. Baku and its environs in the east of the region in Azerbaijan union republic provide a considerable, albeit declining, output of petroleum for the country. The city of Baku itself, situated on the Caspian Sea, with a population of over a million, is the major industrial center. The other main cities are Tbilisi, capital of Georgia, with nearly a million inhabitants, and Yerevan, capital of Armenia, with over a half million.

The Russian Soviet Federated Socialist Republic in Europe

Extending eastward from the Baltic-Belorussian-Ukrainian regions and including the land north of Transcaucasia, the Russian Soviet Federated Socialist Republic (RSFSR) in Europe is largely a plain, interrupted by a few ranges of hills and wide river valleys that terminate at the Ural Mountain chain, generally considered as marking the dividing line between Europe and Asia. In the far north a narrow belt of tundra extends inland from the Arctic shoreline. Most of the northern half of the region, however, has natural vegetation, consisting of coniferous forest interspersed with peat bogs and marshes. South of this main belt are deciduous mixed forests that become steppes with trees farther south, the steppe recurring in the region of the northern Caucasus. East of the mouth of the Volga River and northeast of the Caspian Sea begins the Great Central Asian area of semideserts and deserts. The Ural Mountains, which divide Europe and Asia, are covered by mountain forests as is the Caucasus barrier in the south, which has a belt of warm temperate, broadleaf forest.

The region has in general a continental climate. The mitigating effects of the sea and warm ocean currents are felt only in the extreme northwest. Elsewhere, Arctic airmasses sweep unchecked until they reach the tall peaks along the southern border. The northern half of the region annually averages only about 30 days with a mean temperature of 68°F. or above. Only the northeast Caucasus and the southern half of the Crimea have over 90 days with a mean temperature of 68°F. or above. An imaginary line traced just to the east of the Baltic republics, Belorussia, and slightly north of the Ukraine and the entire Caucasus divides Russia into two zones. The northern zone averages over 120 days with a mean temperature of 32°F. or below; the southern zone averages fewer than 120 such days per year. Throughout most of this great region, precipitation is not abundant but excepting in occasional bad years is adequate for most types of agriculture.

The soil pattern ranges from tundra on the maritime edge of the Kola Peninsula and along the Arctic coast from the Kanin Peninsula through the Pechora Basin in the Ural range. South of the tundra are poor, acid soils with a thin peaty layer of acid humus originating from the coniferous vegetation. Farther south gray forest soils alternate with fertile black earth that reaches south to the northwestern Caucasus, to the east of which chestnut soils enclose the northern shores of the Caspian Sea. The gray forest soils combine the characteristics of the leached acid soils of the north with those found in black grassland soils that have a deep rich humus layer produced by grassy vegetation. The chestnut soils mark a transition between grassland and desert.

The region is very rich in mineral deposits. The Ural Mountains have considerable reserves of iron ore, bauxite, magnesium, gold, platinum, zinc, copper, chromium, beryllium, and vanadium. To the west near Kursk are additional sources of iron ore. Just south of the Arctic Circle uranium is mined. The Kola Peninsula has large iron deposits as has the Ladoga-Onega lake region, which also contains copper.

The principal petroleum-bearing areas are in fields east of Saratov, on the Volga River extending over a wide area into the Ural Mountains and beyond. Other sources include Grozny and fields in the Kuban area northwest of the Caucasus Mountains near the mouth of the Volga River. Extensive coal deposits exist in the Pechora Basin just west of the Ural Mountains near the Arctic Circle, and in central Russia the Moscow lignite basin extends in an arc from south of Moscow to Lake Onega, northeast of Leningrad. Where there is coal there is industry, and major industrial areas are located in the Urals, with manufacturing being included in the great urban centers of Moscow and Leningrad and the great industrial cities on the Volga, such as Gorky and Kuybyshev.

The greatest rivers of the region are the Volga, the Dnepr, and the Don. The Volga River, largest in Europe and over 2,000 miles long, has its source in the Valdai Hills north of Moscow and flows winding north and east but mainly southward to the Caspian Sea near Astrakhan. The main cities on its banks are Gorky, east of Moscow, Kuybyshev, and Volgograd to the southeast. With its tributary the Kama, the Volga River carries over half the river traffic of the entire Soviet Union. The Dnepr River also rises in the Valdai Hills and eventually crosses Belorussia and the Ukraine to flow into the Black Sea. The Don River rises in the central Russian hills and flows southeast and southwest into the Sea of Azov.

The central government has expanded waterways and linked rivers and seas in the country by an intricate system of canals. In 1933 a canal linking the White and Baltic seas was opened. The Volga River itself has been linked with waterways to the north that reach the Gulf of Finland and the Baltic Sea and with the Don River in the south via the Volga-Don (V. I. Lenin) Canal, completed in 1952, to reach the Sea of Azov and the Black Sea. It is possible to ship freight from the White Sea or the Baltic Sea in the north to the Black Sea or the Caspian Sea in the south by means of waterways alone.

The region's railway network, which is extensive and dense, is centered on Moscow, industrial hub of the entire region. The generally flat country facilitates the construction and maintenance of railways, which have as elsewhere in the Soviet Union provided the chief means of transportation of passengers and freight.

The population is concentrated south of 60° latitude, and the major urban centers coincide with major industrial and manufacturing zones. The capital of the entire Soviet Union and its largest city is Moscow, capital of the RSFSR and center of the Moscow administrative area. Situated on the Moskva River, which flows into the Oka River and is linked to the Volga River by the Moscow-Volga Canal, completed in 1937, it is in effect a port city with access north to the Arctic Ocean, west to the Baltic Sea, south to the Black Sea as well as the Caspian Sea. It is the greatest industrial and manufacturing center of the country and its leading cultural city.

Leningrad (formerly Saint Petersburg and Petrograd) is the second largest city of the union and the RSFSR. Situated on the Gulf of Finland and founded by Peter the Great, it has highly developed industries with emphasis on metalworking, electrotechnical, chemical, lumbering, light industries, and food processing. It is also a leading cultural center.

The Russian Soviet Federated Socialist Republic in Asia

This broad region stretching eastward from the Ural Mountains north of the Kazakh union republic, Communist China, and the Mongolian People's Republic consists of Siberia proper, which reaches over 2,000 miles from the Ural Mountains to the Lena River, and the Far East, extending thence to the Pacific seaboard. It covers over half the total area of the Soviet Union and is potentially the richest area.

In relief, the region consists of the west and the north Siberian Lowlands interrupted by the Irtysh, Ob', and Yenisey rivers. The last-named marks the beginning of the Central Siberian Plateau. This plateau is, in turn, interrupted by a large triangular plain, the Central Yakutsk Lowlands, formed by the bend of the Lena River. Beyond the Lena River, the high and confused Verkhoyansk, Cherski, and Kolyma mountain systems range northeast toward the Bering Strait. Along its southern borders the region is delimited by the Altai and Sayan mountains, the Mongolian desert, and the Amur and Ussuri rivers.

Except along the Pacific seaboard where maritime influences come into play, the climate is in the main strictly continental with very cold and lengthy winters, hot but fleeting summers, as well as marginal precipitation. All of the region except a southern belt north of Kazakhstan and an enclave along the southern maritime coast has more days of frost than of thaw during each year. Similarly, all of this area except a relatively narrow belt of land north of Kazakhstan and another along the Amur and Ussuri rivers in the Far East has less than thirty warm days (temperatures above 68° F.) per year.

Precipitation is fairly well distributed the year round, the annual total averaging around twenty inches in the west and in the area south of Lake Baikal and on the Kamchatka Peninsula and the southern maritime territories. Elsewhere the totals decrease from west to east and from north to south to totals of ten to twelve inches. Large areas have insufficient precipitation and suffer from a form of permanent drought.

32

The general soil pattern leaves much to be desired. Tundra soils occur along the Arctic seaboard and inland for varying distances. Farther south the soils are quite acid, leached, and deficient in nutrients, with frequent peat bogs in the west and along the Lena River where salt flats are also found. In the southern half of the region, coinciding with the great triangle of Soviet population, stretches a belt of gray forest soils through north-central Asia. Farther east these fairly fertile soils become a combination of mountain forest and mountain tundra soils under the deepening influence of continental climatic conditions. But even here oases of gray forest soil and some black earths continue to occur. Nearer the Pacific and along its coast are found leached, acid soils and peat bogs with occasional strips of gray forest soils. Permafrost extends south from the Arctic seaboard in the north, the center, and the east exclusive of the southern maritime region.

Mosses, lichens and stunted shrubs grow in the belt of tundra soils in the north. All through the center and east stretch great forests of larch interspersed with tundra vegetation. In the southern maritime region and on the island of Sakhalin are mountain forests, south of which grow deciduous mixed forests. In western Siberia there are pine, fir, and birch forests and steppe with trees along the border with Kazakhstan in Central Asia. In the region west and south of Lake Baikal, there is a combined pattern of mountain forest, steppe with trees, tundra vegetation, and open steppe. Along the more populated belt that extends eastward across the southern part of the region, food crops, such as wheat, rye, barley, root crops, oil seeds, and vegetables, are raised. Flax is grown between the Ural Mountains and Lake Baikal, and there is a considerable livestock population.

The natural resources of this great region have not been fully explored, and some known resources of great value cannot be exploited economically until techniques to overcome obstacles of distances and climatic conditions are developed. Of all the coal reserves of the Soviet Union, 90 percent are estimated to be in the eastern part of the region. About 80 percent of the hydroelectric power potential of the country lies in the region's rivers. Over three-fourths of the country's forested areas are situated in Siberia, and they account for at least one-fourth of this resource in the world. The region has at least one-third of the country's iron ore resources as well as most of its gold, a great part of its diamonds, and large reserves of nonferrous and rare metals.

Compared with most of the Soviet Union in Europe, the RSFSR in Asia is sparsely inhabited, largely because of the severity of the climate. The population is concentrated in the south, with the main urban areas extending along the line of the Trans-Siberian Railway and its branches from the Ural Mountains to the Pacific seaboard.

Just east of the Ural Mountains, a cluster of industrial cities includes Sverdlovsk, with nearly a million inhabitants; Chelyabinsk; and Magnitogorsk. Farther east on the upper reaches of the Ob' River, Novosibirsk, with a population of over a million, is the great Siberian center of industry and manufacturing and the most rapidly growing city in the Soviet Union in 1968. To the southeast extends the Kuznets Basin, rich in coal and iron ore. Irkutsk, near the southern end of Lake Baikal, is another industrial center of growing importance. Khabarovsk, where the Amur and Ussuri rivers join, is the commercial and political center of the Soviet Far East, and Vladivostok, the terminus of the Trans-Siberian Railway, is the area's main seaport.

Central Asia Region

South of the RSFSR in Asia and extending eastward some fifteen hundred miles to the mountainous border of Communist China, this region reaches farther south than any other part of the Soviet Union. It includes as major political units the Kazakh, Turkmen, Uzbek, Tadzhik, and Kirgiz union republics. From the high mountains that rise along the southern and southeastern part of this region, the ground descends to much lower elevations with drainage to the north. Beyond the foothills, the land consists largely of flat to moderately hilly plateau country, crossed by a few major river valleys, and of lowland plains along the Caspian and Aral seas.

The climate is marked by seasonal extremes of temperature, with a range between the means for January and July of over 50°F. In the Tashkent area the average temperature for July is about 86°F., whereas the January average is about at the freezing-point. In the far north of the region, summers are not so warm and winters are much colder. Minimum temperatures during January may reach - 40°F., and the monthly averages may be around 5°F. The average temperature for July, which is the warmest month, is about 80°F.

Despite their distance from the sea, the high mountains in the south, from the Pamirs to the Altai range, have from twenty to eighty inches of precipitation per year in the form of both rain and snow. Runoff feeds the watercourses that drain the mountain slopes and forms a number of major streams, including the Amu Darya, the Syr Darya and the Ili rivers. These provide water for irrigation in the lower oasis valleys that are scattered along the southern part of the region. Northward from the mountains, precipitation decreases rapidly to averages of from four to twelve inches in the middle belt of the region to sixteen inches in the north where dryfarming, although sometimes precarious, is practicable.

Below the glaciers and snowfields of the higher mountains, the natural vegetation consists of mountain meadows interspersed in favorable exposures with forests of elm, aspen, and birch with very few coniferous species. Beyond the foothills there are wide expanses of desert country with salt flats, areas of rock or sand, and little vegetation except poor ephemeral grasses and stunted shrubs. Toward the north, with more rainfall the land becomes grassy steppe or steppe with deciduous trees. With the aid of irrigation, agriculture has long been highly developed in the south, and a great variety of crops, including cotton, rice, sugar beets, and fruits, and vegetables, are raised. In the north where the soils of the steppe are very fertile, extensive areas have been opened up to the mechanized farming of wheat and other grains.

The region is very rich in minerals. The area of Karaganda in the northeast is a major producer of high grade coal, much of which supplies the steel mills in the Ural industrial complex. Only a few hundred miles south of Karaganda, near Lake Balkhash, iron and copper ores are mined. There is lead, zinc, mercury, antimony, and some gold in the south in the general area of Tashkent. The Emba oilfields at the northern end of the Caspian Sea deliver the crude product by pipeline to the Ural industrial area, and there are other producing fields of less importance along the eastern side of the Caspian Sea, extending south to the Turkmen Field near the Iranian border.

The region is fairly well served by railway transportation, both in the form of feeder trunklines that extend roughly south from the main east-west axis of the Trans-Siberian Railway system, and by local branch lines. There is also a Trans-Caspian system that swings eastward along the southern border from Krasnovodsk on the Caspian Sea via Ashkhabad, Tashkent, and Alma Ata to the Trans-Siberian line at Novosibirsk, the principal city in West Siberia. As in large parts of the Soviet Union, the highway system was rudimentary in 1969 but under active development, especially in the grain farming region of the north.

Compared with the Soviet Union in Europe, Soviet Central Asia is sparsely populated, and large desert areas have fewer than three inhabitants per square mile. Settlement is heaviest in the oasis valleys of the south, some of which, like the 180-mile-long Fergana Valley, support populations with densities exceeding three hundred persons per square mile largely by irrigated agriculture. Tashkent, capital of the Uzbek union republic, is the region's leading city and industrial center and has a population of about 1 million. Other main urban areas, all with at least several hundred thousand inhabitants, are the coal cities of Karaganda, Alma Ata, and Frunze, political capitals in the far southeast, and Dushanbe (once Stalinabad) near the Afghan border and capital of the Tadzhik union republic.

CHAPTER 3
HISTORICAL SETTING

The Russian Communist regime attempted to project its coup d'etat of November 1917 as a revolution that heralded the dawn of a new and better epoch. The leaders, however, recognized much in the Russian past that should not, and could not, be expunged. Lenin understood that a blending of old and new would be necessary during the creation and development of the new Soviet state, and the Communists did not ignore the past and date history from November 7, 1917.

During the first decade of Bolshevik rule, non-Marxist historians continued to write and teach alongside their Marxist colleagues; only those who became politically active were silenced. Difficulties in getting works published arose as much from economic reasons as from ideological.

Toward the end of the 1920's, a period coinciding with Stalin's full consolidation of power, historiography came under rigid control of the regime, and historical scholarship became a tool of the new power elite. At about the same time that "Socialist Realism"— that is, depiction of mankind's struggle for social justice—became a mandatory doctrine for artists and writers, historians were compelled to write history in a manner that would justify and glorify the Communist regime. Soviet historiography had not been barren or confined solely to propaganda since the early 1930's, however, and Soviet citizens were not ignorant of Russian history. Much valuable work was accomplished, and many valuable contributions to the world's store of knowledge on Russia's past were made, but Soviet writers of history were guilty of sins of omission, particularly in dealing with their own era (see ch. 17, Intellectual Expression).

The great problem lies in making historical writing conform to Marxist dogma as well as to a current party line. The Marxist school of history demands that economic bases be found to explain just about all historical phenomena. Thus, the Soviet historian's account of the wars of Peter the Great or of Napoleon's invasion has been different from that of the prerevolutionary historian, who may have approached the same subject matter from a social, political, or patriotic point of view. In addition to being tied to a rigid dogma, the Soviet historian has also had to meet the demands of Communist propaganda, with the result that accounts of Leon Trotsky's leading role in the revolution, for example, cannot be found in Soviet history books. Similarly, a host of other leading Bolsheviks of the revolutionary period later disappeared from history's pages because of real or alleged counterrevolutionary activities. The historian's task has been further complicated by the subsequent rehabilitation of some of these.

Despite the machinations of politicians and the manipulation of historiography to fit political needs, the Soviet citizen in 1969 was a product of his country's entire history, not just the fifty-odd years since the revolution. The Communist period is the latest chapter in a long history.

PRE-MUSCOVITE PERIOD

Slavic tribes, the earliest ancestors of the Russians, inhabited various river valleys in what is now the European part of the Soviet Union from a very early time. Just how early and where they came from are subjects of great controversy among historians, but Slavs were present in the area for many centuries before the appearance of the first Russian state. The historical heritage of the Soviet Union is the sum of the lasting influences exerted on the people and on their institutions during the centuries of development from primitive times to the present.

The early Slavic clans and tribes, which were relatively peaceful, agriculturally oriented, and spread out over large areas, were easy prey for mounted nomads from Asia or for the warlike Germanic tribes from the north. The vast open steppes and the north-south river routes provided natural avenues for invasion by seemingly endless waves of peoples who swept back and forth across the country for centuries. These invasions were not merely fleeting moments in history; more often they were mass migrations, spearheaded by powerful warrior groups, which left indelible imprints on the people and the land. The Scythians held sway for five-hundred years; the Sarmatians, for four hundred; and the Goths, Huns, Khazars, and Avars, among others, all ruled for varying periods of time.

Meanwhile, the Slavs paid taxes and tribute to their conquerors, fought when possible, retreated when necessary, assimilated many of the invaders, multiplied in numbers, and continued their cultivation of the land, their hunting, fishing, and beekeeping. Pushed by invaders or simply seeking more peaceful lands, the Slavs themselves moved in all directions, and their migrations during the early Christian Era resulted in three general groupings. The West Slavs include the Poles, Czechs, Slovaks, and Lusatians; the South Slavs became the Serbs, Croats, Macedonians, Slovenes, Montenegrins, and Bulgars. The East Slavs are the Russians, Ukrainians, and Belorussians.

By the middle of the eighth century A.D., the land of the East Slavs consisted of several city-states, each of which dominated its surrounding territory. Extensive trade in foodstuffs and furs had been carried on for centuries, usually through foreign overlords, but now a class of Slavic merchants had developed and had built prosperous trading centers. The most pressing problem of the merchants was the vulnerability of their profitable commerce. They needed protection against Viking marauders and Asian nomads, as well as against their own subject peoples, who often rebelled against exploitation by the wealthy merchants. In the ninth century A.D. the protection of trade was provided by a group of Vikings known as Varangians, and a new epoch in Russian history began.

Whether the Varangians were invited by the Slav merchants to "come rule and reign over us," as related in the ancient chronicles, or whether they forcefully appropriated a profitable commercial structure is still a subject of controversy but, in either case, by about the year A.D. 862 the Varangians had assumed control. Their semilegendary leader was a Dane called Rurik, a trader-pirate-adventurer who founded a dynasty that would rule for more than seven hundred years. With the advent of Rurik it is proper to use the term "Rus." Once again historians differ as to whether the Varangians brought the term or adopted it from an indigenous Slavic tribe but, from the time of Rurik on, the most numerous and most powerful branch of the East Slavs would be known as Rus or Russian. Although the new rulers were Scandinavian in origin, they did not lead a great migration. They took over a Slavic civilization and culture and called themselves Rus, and within two or three generations they had been absorbed, completely Slavicized.

Rurik himself settled in the northern trading town of Novgorod, but Oleg, his successor, moved south and established himself as prince of Kiev. The subsequent flowering of Kievan commerce and culture marks the beginning of the first truly Russian state. At the height of its power, Kievan Russia encompassed a vast territory that included several large, prosperous trading centers. From the beginning, Kievan Russia was expansionist in nature, a trait passed on to future Russian states. The lifeblood of Kiev was trade, and the princes fought continually to expand that trade and encompass more potential routes and territories.

The flourishing commercial enterprises of the Kievan Russians, however, were paralleled by other aspects of their society. Most important in the rich Kievan legacy was the Orthodox religion, which the princes had adopted from the Byzantine Empire and had urged on their subjects in place of primitive pagan beliefs. Orthodox Christianity became a dominant theme in Russian life, and the considerable influence of the Church affected development of the character of the people, whether of the nobility or of the peasantry.

Religion as a dominant theme in Russian life remained until the Bolshevik revolution proclaimed official atheism but, even after more than fifty years of militant antireligion, Orthodoxy continued to be a force in the lives of many Russians (see ch. 13, Religion).

In addition to the large ecclesiastical establishment and the commercial structure, Russia also inherited from Kiev a system of agriculture, a money economy, a military tradition, and a stratification of society. The beginnings of Russian art, architecture, and literature are also traced to the Kievan period.

Weakened by internal strife and constant warfare, Kievan Russia was in an advanced stage of decline when the last great mass movement of Asians swept over the land, eventually occupying much of Eurasia. The Golden Horde, led by the successors of Ghengis Khan, held Russia in bondage for over two hundred years, and Mongol influences are integral to subsequent development. The Horde destroyed the city of Kiev in 1240; khan replaced prince as ruler of practically all of what had been Kievan Rus. Thus, the first East Slavic state disappeared and Russia was again subject to an Asian invader.

The Mongols were ruthless in their treatment of Russia and the Russians. They destroyed cities, slaughtered or enslaved citizens, and forced princes to swear allegiance to the khan and to collect taxes for his treasury. They did not, however, systematically eradicate Russian culture and customs. The Mongol aim was to maintain control and exploit the wealth of the country even though at first their terrible campaigns laid waste most of the cities. After the initial waves of destruction, the Mongols adopted the role of absentee landlord, humiliating the Russian princes and intimidating the country with their military might, which had so far proved to be nearly invincible.

Victory over the Horde in the battle of Kulikovo in 1380 was an event to be commemorated ever after. Led by a prince of Moscow, a Russian army defeated a Mongol force in a battle fought over nonpayment of tribute. The battle was actually inconclusive, and tribute payments continued, but the victory was very important to the developing state of Muscovy. A century later Ivan the Great of Moscow refused to pay tribute, and the khan did not force the issue. The stranglehold of the Mongols was broken.

Two and a half centuries of a harsh, brutal occupation designed for utmost exploitation inhibited the development of all aspects of Russian life. Russia was effectively cut off from contact with the west during the Mongol period. Its cities with their crafts, industries, and trade declined, and the country became predominantly agricultural. The Orthodox Church, although suffering great losses of churches and monasteries, emerged stronger than before because religion had gained a wider base among the people. Arts and literature suffered as the civilizing influences that had taken root in Kiev withered under the occupation. Most important during this period was the emergence of Muscovy as a new Russian state, establishing itself as the true successor to Kiev, the foundation of modern Russia.

MUSCOVY

The town of Moscow was first mentioned by the ancient chroniclers in 1147, at which time its only claim to fame was its location on a river route. Moscow was ranked low among Russian principalities, but after the decline of Kiev ambitious princes took steps to raise Moscow to first rank. All of the Russian princes had served at the sufferance of the khan during the period of domination. The prince of Kiev had been known as grand prince, but later that title was given to more important cities such as Novgorod and Tver.

In 1325 Ivan I of Moscow convinced the khan that he should be named grand prince, with the result that the prestige of Moscow soared. Ivan I was known to his people as "Moneybags," apparently with good reason. As grand prince, his duty was to collect taxes from all lesser princes to be given as tribute to the Mongol overlords. Enough of this wealth stayed in Moscow to enable Ivan to purchase various poorer princedoms as well as towns and villages surrounding Muscovy. Ivan also convinced the Metropolitan of the Russian Orthodox Church to transfer the metropolitanate to Moscow, a move that did much to enhance the prestige of Moscow and its prince. Ivan I succeeded so well in the enlargement and aggrandizement of Muscovy that his immediate successor assumed the new title of Grand Prince of All the Russians.

As the power of the Miscovite princes increased, that of the lesser princes proportionately decreased, and a trend toward centralization was definitely in evidence. The importance of towns and cities was reduced under the Mongols, whereas agricultural landlords tended to increase their control over the land and, with it, over the peasantry. In embryonic form, the institution of serfdom was slowly taking hold. When Ivan III (the Great) came to power in 1462, Muscovy was almost as large as Kiev had been in its heyday. It was difficult to administer such a large territory and there were enemies on the borders, but during his forty-three-year reign Ivan III solidified central control, created a bureaucracy, ended the Mongol domination, and regained large territories in the west which had been absorbed by the Polish-Lithuanian Empire. Ivan also broke the power of such Russian strongholds as Novgorod, Tver, and Ryazan, incorporating them into Muscovy.

Ivan III referred to himself as Sovereign of All Russia and in international relations, called himself tsar. Early chronicles tell of a prince of Kiev who had led his cavalry into battle, roasted his own food over an open fire, and slept on the ground with his saddle for a pillow. The dynasty of Rurik had come a long way from that early warrior-prince. The court of Ivan III had become regal and ritualistic, with Ivan declaring, "we hold our appointment from God." Thus, divine right was introduced, and autocracy was firmly established with the Russian Orthodox Church as its handmaiden.

Sixteenth-century Russian history is dominated by Ivan IV (the Terrible), whose reign lasted from 1533 to 1584. Since Ivan was a child of three when he succeeded to the throne, Russia was ruled by a regency council for several years. At age seventeen, however, Ivan was crowned tsar in a glittering ceremony designed to impress every Russian with the fact that the grand prince of Moscow was indeed Tsar of All the Russias with all the power inferred by that lofty title. Ivan, despite his youthfulness, ruled with an iron fist. For the next thirty-seven years he was the complete autocrat, running the country as if it were a private estate, changing its size and shape as well as its internal complexion.

During the years before his coronation, Ivan the Terrible learned to hate the nobles, known as boyars, who wielded extensive power at the Muscovy court. Scheming and conniving for influence, various noble families offended the young tsar and, in so doing, sealed their fate by leading Ivan to the conviciton that he would have to destroy the influence of the hereditary boyars and eliminate all differences between boyars and the service gentry created by his grandfather, Ivan the Great. Under Ivan IV, it became impossible to be a landlord without paying homage and rendering service to the tsar.

In the years immediately following his coronation, Ivan was advised by a small council, chosen by himself from among the middle classes rather than from the nobility whom he despised. Various enlightened reforms were initiated during this period which contrast sharply with the mad excesses of the latter part of Ivan's reign. A new legal code was enacted, new Church regulations were enforced, and a new system of local government was adopted which gave some citizens a voice in selecting local officials. Ivan also called the first Zemsky Sobor (Assembly of the Land), which contained representatives of the merchant class in addition to hereditary nobles and service gentry. Ivan called the assembly to advise him, but the inclusion of merchants and service gentry was simply another step to lessen the prestige of the boyars who had traditionally formed the tsar's advisory council.

On the international scene, Ivan established close commercial relations with England but was unsuccessful in his attempt to form a military alliance with that country against his Baltic enemies. For the most part, Ivan's other international relations consisted of warfare with Russia's neighboring states. The remnants of the Golden Horde still maintained independent khanates in Siberia, Kazan, Astrakhan, and Crimea. During Ivan's reign the first three of these Tatar khanates were conquered and incorporated into Muscovy, extending the eastern and southeastern boundaries far beyond Ivan's inheritance. The Crimean Tatars, eventually under Turkish suzerainty, held out for another two centuries. On his western borders, Ivan was less successful and lost the Baltic outlet at Narva, which had been secured by his predecessors. Western Europe was becoming alarmed by the burgeoning Muscovite giant; consequently the Scandinavian countries allied themselves with the German Baltic knights to reinforce Poland-Lithuania against incursions by the forces of Ivan the Terrible.

In the midst of his foreign wars, Ivan instituted a reign of terror designed to eliminate all opposition and resistance to his policies. A six-thousand-man political police, Russia's first and answering only to the tsar, ravaged the country, terrorizing boyar and peasant alike. Tracking down traitors became the chief task of Ivan's police, and the designation "traitor" was applied loosely and arbitrarily as the regime used any measure to establish tsarist absolutism. As with later purges, the terrorism of Ivan ultimately turned inward as his purgers destroyed one another. Russian cities, such as Novgorod, which the tsar suspected of mass disloyalty, were completely devastated. When the terror finally subsided, the state, although weakened and almost ruined, was completely under the control of its central authority.

Shortly before his death, Ivan the Terrible struck and killed his son and heir, an event that had far-reaching effects on the development of Russia. Ivan's remaining son, the simple-minded Fyodor I, died without an heir, ending the Rurik line and setting the stage for a dynastic struggle.

The Time of Troubles brought such great strife and upheaval throughout the land that it is remarkable that Muscovy managed to survive as a political entity. The struggle for the crown between 1605 and 1613 became a confusing succession of pretenders, charlatans, and foreign princes, all trying to ascend Muscovy's throne. Poland and Sweden, seeing opportunity for territorial gain and settlement of long-standing disputes, intervened in force. Cossack freebooters arose in the steppes, swept north, enlisting thousands of peasants into their armies, and sometimes threatened Moscow itself. At one time, a cossack band installed its own tsar in a town near Moscow and, in effect, Muscovy had two tsars with rival courts, rival armies, and rival tax collectors.

In 1610, with Polish armies occupying Moscow, both tsars were deposed and a council of boyars took control. At this point, feelings of nationalism stirred in the Russian people and, rallied by the

Patriarch of Moscow, they came to the defense of Holy Russia. Freebooters and foreign armies were finally driven out, and in 1613 the interregnum ended with the election by a Zemsky Sobor of Tsar Michael Romanov, the first of a new dynasty that would rule Russia for 304 years.

The first three Romanov tsars, whose reigns covered most of the seventeenth century, were all weak rulers. Although the Time of Troubles, historically speaking, ended in 1613, the foreign wars, peasant uprisings, and boyar intrigues continued to plague Russian tsars. With the help of strong personal advisers, the Zemsky Sobor, and various boyar councils, the first three Romanovs did manage to bring about a measure of internal order. The cossacks were won over by treaty, resulting in the annexation of the Ukraine. The Poles and Swedes were bought off in the west, postponing what seemed to be an inevitable military confrontation. A new law code was promulgated which bound every Russian to service to the crown, legalizing the hated institution of serfdom. In religious affairs, a blunt, undiplomatic patriarch forced corrections in liturgy and ritual, which alienated great numbers of Russians and caused a schism in Russian Orthodoxy that has never been healed. The religious dissension made it easy for the next ruler, a strong tsar, to usurp church prerogatives and downgrade clerical authority among the people.

IMPERIAL RUSSIA (1721-1917)

Near the end of the seventeenth century, a powerful Romanov came to the throne—Peter I (the Great). During his reign he transformed Russia from a backward principality into a powerful empire. Peter's furious energy drove him to interest himself in almost every aspect of Russian life. Impatient with the old, lethargic, inward-looking ways of his homeland, Peter determined to modernize it, using western Europe as his model. He changed the administrative structure of the government to make it more efficient as well as more responsive to the tsar. He modernized the army and built a navy—necessary reforms for a monarch who was at war for forty of the forty-two years of his reign. He changed the structure of society, establishing a table of ranks for military and civil service in which ability rather than heredity determined position. He abolished the office of patriarch in the Orthodox Church, putting a layman in Russia's top religious office and making the Church an extension of the autocracy.

Peter considered beards to be a symbol of backwardness and personally sheared some of his boyars; others quickly decided that a clean-shaven face was best in court circles. Nothing was too small or insignificant to escape the tsar's personal attention if it contributed to ending Russia's backwardness. Among other achievements, he changed the ancient Russian calendar, introduced Arabic numerals, revised the Cyrillic alphabet, published the first newspaper, established compulsory schools for children of the gentry, and founded an Academy of Sciences.

Peter, however, was not a systematic reformer nor a great theoretician. He was a man of action who brooked no opposition and little procrastination. Although his reforms were sometimes ill-conceived and poorly executed, some of his achievements had lasting effects on the development of the empire over the next two hundred years. Peter did nothing for the Russian serf except to make him more of a slave than he had ever been before; later, peasant uprisings became epidemic throughout the countryside.

Russia was at war with Sweden from 1700 until 1721, fought Turkey during many of the same years, and also was forced to use regular troops to put down serf insurrections. Peter suffered some humiliating defeats at the hands of the Swedes, but setbacks engendered greater efforts and, after studying the tactics of the enemy and adapting them to his own forces, the tsar personally led an army that destroyed Swedish land power, and his navy was equally victorious at sea. Sweden was eliminated as the preeminent power in northern Europe, and Peter obtained his long-sought outlet to the sea and his "window on Europe," as he termed the new capital of St. Petersburg. Upon his return from the Swedish war, Peter accepted the title of emperor from the Senate (one of his administrative creations), and Russia emerged as a full-blown power on the European scene.

With all of his reforms, Peter carefully avoided any innovation that might limit the authority of the tsar. In his view, Russia could only progress under the direction of an absolute monarch. Therefore, importation of European political thought did not accompany importation of goods, services, and techniques. Peter the Great also used terror in eliminating opposition, and his reign was marred by excesses reminiscent of the time of Ivan the Terrible. Like Ivan, Peter participated in tortures and executions, including the torture of his own son, who subsequently died from his injuries.

A series of weak rulers followed Peter, resulting in rule by court favorites and cliques from the time of Peter's death to the rise of Catherine the Great in 1762. This was not, however, a retrogressive period for Russia. Peter had established his country as a European power, and certain processes went forward despite the quality of rule. In external affairs, Russian armies warred successfully against the Turks and, at the same time, brought Frederick the Great of Prussia to the brink of disaster. Internally, the position of the peasantry became worse than ever, leaving little to distinguish serfdom from slavery. At the coronation of Peter's daughter, Elizabeth, serfs were omitted from the classes swearing allegiance to the new monarch, and in a revised law code they were listed simply under the heading of property. As the official status of the serfs degenerated into slavery, the gentry class accumulated greater wealth, prestige, and privileges. During the short reign of Peter III in 1762, the gentry managed to push through repeal of the law that bound them to state service. Thus, the gentry became a free class with few restraints on their power and control over the serfs.

Peter the Great had created elite Guards regiments for the protection of the tsar and of the capital. These regiments became the tsar's personal army, often performing secret police functions under Peter's supervision. In the power vacuum brought about by the death of the strong tsar, the St. Petersburg regiments became politically potent, twice determining the succession to the throne.

Catherine, princess of the small German state of Anhalt-Zerbst, married the grandson of Peter the Great, was converted to Orthodoxy, and took up residence in the court of St. Petersburg in 1744. Catherine was intelligent, determined, and supremely self-confident. Her position as a German princess in a Russian court that often despised and distrusted all Germans, was tenuous, but the force of her personality, her will power, and her dexterity in court intrigue served her well in the long years of waiting for her husband to become tsar. In 1762 Catherine (later to be called the Great), backed by the Guards, deposed her husband, bypassed her son, and had herself proclaimed empress of Russia. As empress, she quickly established herself as the absolute autocrat and became the most powerful monarch since Peter the Great.

After consolidating her power, Catherine fostered administrative reforms but, despite her celebrated correspondence with Voltaire and other philosophers of the Enlightenment, she believed that Russia could only succeed under an absolute monarch, and she intended to be that monarch. Much of Catherine's liberal philosophy fell victim to Russian reality, and the shock of the French Revolution finally converted her to conservatism. Revolution was anathema to Catherine. She vowed never to recognize the new United States of America, for example, and at her death in 1796 recognition had not been granted. (Official diplomatic relations between the United States and Russia were inaugurated in 1809.) With all her fear of revolutions and uprisings, Catherine would not confront serfdom, the root cause of Russia's internal problems. On the contrary, she compounded the problem by placing hundreds of thousands of peasants in bondage during her reign. Following the examples of earlier rulers, Catherine made lavish gifts of state lands to her favorites. Each gift included the peasants living on the land, thus swelling ranks of bonded serfs year after year.

Part of the reality of Russia during Catherine's time was the growing gap between gentry and peasantry. Peter the Great had wrenched his country out of its backwardness and had transformed it into a more or less modern European power, but had left the semifeudal structure of serfdom that could only impede progress. During Catherine's reign, the growing animosity between the relatively few landowners and the millions of serfs exploded into Russia's most famous serf rebellion. Led by Yemelyan Pugachev, a Don cossack, the insurrection spread rapidly, encompassing a huge territory and recruiting thousands of adherents to the cause. The Pugachev revolt (1773-75) was similar to many that had preceded it and many more that followed, but for sheer size and audacity it was a landmark in Russian history. Doomed to failure by poor organization and poor leadership, the revolt nevertheless frightened the privileged gentry class for decades to come. Instead of reform, Pugachev's escapade fostered further repression. Catherine attempted reforms but, because she sought always to maintain central authority, the reforms merely served to solidify the semislave status of the serfs and the feudal lord status of the landowner.

In foreign affairs Catherine followed the centuries-old expansionist policies of her predecessors. Vast new lands were acquired, and Russia's position as a participant in European power politics was reinforced. At the expense of Turkey, Russia finally reached the Black Sea coast and occupied the Crimean Peninsula. The empress also participated with the Prussian and Austrian rulers in three partitions of Poland that gave Russia most of the Ukraine and Belorussia along with several million new citizens. At the end of Catherine's reign, the Russians, though overwhelmingly poor and illiterate, possessed one of the most glittering courts in Europe, a huge standing army, and a smothering bureaucracy. Russia was acknowledged as one of Europe's foremost powers. Catherine was succeeded by her son Paul I, who for thirty-four years had waited for the throne which he had always considered to be rightfully his. Five years of Paul's madness brought about a palace revolt, Paul's murder, and the placing of his son Alexander I on the Romanov throne.

REFORM AND REPRESSION

Alexander I became tsar in 1801 in the midst of a revolutionary age. The new Russian ruler appeared at first to be a liberal reformer, and the early years of his reign seemed to forecast a relaxation of the all-pervasive power of the autocracy. He reorganized the central administrative organs to reduce bureaucratic confusion. He instituted educational reforms, financed the building of universities and schools, and decreed that education would be open to all classes rather than just to upper class children. He made obvious his own distaste for serfdom, but did not take official steps to abolish it. The high promise of Alexander's early years was eventually worn down by the size of Russia's problems and, in the middle of his reign, the tsar despaired of finding solutions to those problems. He complained that he needed thousands of officials to administer the huge country, but could not find fifty who were trustworthy.

Externally, Alexander's reign was essentially a continuation of the expansionist policies of his ancestors. Worried about Napoleon's designs on the continent, Alexander abrogated an inherited alliance with France, then sent his troops to engage French forces in Prussia. The Russian army suffered two severe military defeats, but distance saved the homeland and Napoleon was generous in his treatment of the tsar at their famed meeting in Tilsit. Russia was once again aligned with France. The new Franco-Russian alliance was barren, however, because of the incompatibility of national interests, and in 1812 Napoleon led the Grand Army in its ill-fated invasion of Russia. Two years later Alexander rode triumphantly into Paris. With the tsar playing a leading role as peacemaker at the Congress of Vienna in 1815, Russia gained in prestige and Alexander emerged as one of Europe's leading monarchs.

Internally, Russia remained an absolute monarchy even though Alexander granted constitutions to the Kingdom of Poland, of which he was king, and to the Grand Duchy of Finland, of which he was grand duke. He had one of his closest advisers draw up a constitutional plan for Russia, but nothing was ever done with it. Alexander discontinued the practice of crown grants in land and peasants, and the serfs of the Baltic provinces were emancipated, but the vast majority of Russian serfs were unaffected by the wave of liberalism that rolled over Europe in the wake of the French Revolution and the Napoleonic wars.

Official opposition prevented the infiltration of revolutionary ideas, but many of the officers who had followed Alexander across Europe returned with liberal ideas and imprecise notions of doing something to relieve the oppression of the masses in their homeland. Alexander's sudden death in 1825 while on a trip in the south brought confusion concerning the succession and a seemingly opportune time for a revolutionary movement. An abortive revolution known as the Decembrist uprising followed. The Decembrist leaders, with no agreed goals or plans of action, tried to incite various army garrisons to revolt and to demand a constitution, but no revolutionary preparation had been accomplished among the soldiery or among the people, with the result that the revolt was quickly suppressed and the leaders were either hanged or exiled to Siberia.

Although the Decembrist movement ended in disaster and was little more than a caricature of a revolution, it became a symbol for revolutionaries, radicals, liberals, and patriots for the remainder of the turbulent nineteenth century. It was also a symbol for Nicholas I, brother and successor to Alexander, who devoted his thirty-year reign to the suppression of liberal ideas. Nicholas I became the defender of the status quo, and his reign was notable for autocratic oppression even to the point of sending Russian troops abroad to quell revolution in neighboring states. The days of Russian influence in European affairs were numbered, however, as the government of Nicholas I blundered into the Crimean War against a coalition of powers. The bravery of the individual Russian soldier and sailor could not hold back the modern weapons and tactics of the French and British forces, and in a humiliating defeat Russia was exposed as a giant without power. Nicholas I died in 1855 and was succeeded by his son Alexander II before the Crimean debacle was finally concluded.

The new tsar, as conservative as his father but more practical, realized that the harsh measures of the past had to be tempered and, more important, that serfdom was an anachronism which Russia could no longer afford. From an economic viewpoint, serf labor was expensive and inefficient. Writers decried the system for what it did to human values and human dignity. Alexander II, more and more concerned over the fifteen hundred peasant uprisings of the first sixty years of the century, freed the serfs by imperial proclamation in March 1861.

The evils of a system that had virtually enslaved millions of Russians for centuries lived on after the abolishment of the system. Former serfs found themselves in a new type of bondage as they borrowed money to buy land which they had to have for simple existence. Landowners felt that they should be paid for the loss of serf labor. The emperor proclaimed emancipation, but could not proclaim peace and prosperity for the emancipated.

Alexander II initiated a series of reforms but, attempting to retain complete autocracy, he often tried to emasculate the measures that his government introduced. Reforms once initiated, however, proved difficult to restrain, and Alexander II is often referred to in histories as "Tsar-Liberator" and "Great Reformer." The reforms carried through in local government, the judicial system, the military forces, in education, and in the fiscal system placed Russia on the threshold of a new era while the rigidity of the autocracy kept the door open to the past.

On the international scene, Alexander could do little to regain prestige and influence in Europe so soon after the Crimean defeat. On the Asian mainland, however, the tsar could and did continue the tradition of expansion that had been going on since Muscovy first added to its original six hundred square miles. Alexander's armies conquered the remaining khanates and secured the trans-Caspian region. At the expense of troubled China, Russia acquired vast territories around the Amur and Ussuri rivers, leading to years of claims, counterclaims, and continual boundary disputes. The Caucasus mountain region also came under effective control after years of conflict with the various nationalistic Caucasian tribes (see ch. 9, Ethnic Groups).

Despite the aggrandizement of empire through new conquests, the freeing of millions of subjects, and the host of reforms, Russia remained a troubled country. A spirit of revolution, growing out of abject poverty and fed by the writings of the radical intelligentsia, was prevalent throughout the cities and towns. Overthrow of the tsarist system was the aim of the most radical groups, whereas moderates thought that constitutionalism could cure Russia's ills. Anarchistic and nihilistic underground groups sprung up.

A secret society called Land and Freedom had as its goal a mass peasant uprising, but thought it necessary to educate the peasantry toward this goal before success could be possible. In this movement hundreds of revolutionaries were arrested by the tsar's police, and many others were beaten or turned over to the police by the suspicious peasants. With the countryside proving to be unreceptive to, and suspicious of, city-bred revolutionaries, the latter turned their propagandizing efforts toward the more fertile areas of the universities and factories. Extremists turned to acts of terrorism, making several attempts on the life of Alexander II, who was finally killed by a terrorists' bomb in 1881.

The reactionary attitude introduced by Alexander III after the murder of his father became the hallmark of the remaining years of Russian tsardom. The few political and individual rights that were gained so slowly over the centuries slipped away as many reforms were annulled or ignored. People were subjected to arbitrary arrest, trial, and sentencing with little or no recourse to legal proceedings as the regimes of Alexander III and Nicholas II sought to perpetuate absolute monarchy. Russia, in effect, was a police state.

In areas other than political, the Russian Empire under its last two tsars was not stagnating. Industrialization, arriving late in Russia as compared with western Europe, once started, grew at an amazing rate. In the wake of Russia's industrial revolution came all the adverse effects that had earlier beset other industrialized nations. Poor peasants flocked to new industrial centers, depressing the labor market and creating instant slums. Women and children were exploited in factories and mines alongside their husbands and fathers. The unsafe, unhealthy working and living conditions were as bad or worse than those in the industrialized West.

Russia also had the problem of a shortage of indigenous capital and was flooded by foreign investment with the concurrent lack of concern for local conditions. Because of the poverty of local consumers, Russian producers were forced to seek export markets, but their products could not compete with those of the more industrially developed countries. New markets were found in the east, while the government, prodded by its enlightened and able finance minister, Serge Witte, aided industrialization by establishing banks and building railroads. The famous Trans-Siberian Railway, completed in 1904, provided a necessary link between European Russia and the Pacific coast (see ch. 2, Physical Environment).

In the face of industrialization and the complexities of modernization, Alexander III and his son Nicholas II both persevered in their attempts to run the empire in the style of Peter the Great or Ivan the Terrible—as a personal estate. Alexander was strong-willed and reactionary in the mold of Nicholas I and so many other predecessors who had reacted to liberal trends with severe repression. Nicholas II had inherited his father's reactionary attitudes but not his strong will. Nicholas' weakness of character and his tendency toward vacillation eventually contributed to the downfall of imperial Russia.

REVOLUTION

At the turn of the century the economy, still overwhelmingly agricultural, was staggered by a depression that further impoverished the populace, increased dissatisfaction with the government, and gave impetus to the growing forces of revolution. Nicholas, surrounded by incompetent advisers (he had a propensity for dismissing good ones), allowed Russia to stumble into what proved to be a disastrous war with Japan. A series of defeats revealed the ineptitude of the tsar as a leader and demonstrated the gross inefficiency of the bureaucracy in administering the affairs of the nation.

The spark needed to ignite revolution came when an order to fire on a workers' demonstration was given to the St. Petersburg militia. The demonstration had been peaceful. The workers of the capital with their wives and children had marched to the Winter Palace to petition the tsar to intervene on their behalf against the intolerable conditions brought about by depression and war. The demonstrators, carrying religious icons and pictures of the tsar, sang hymns as they marched to the palace. The militia opened fire at close range, and the resulting massacre, known in Russian history as Bloody Sunday, was the first act of violence of the Revolution of 1905.

For the remainder of the year Russia was torn by strikes and civil strife, and at times the tsardom itself seemed to be in danger of collapse. By granting concessions of certain civil liberties and, more important, a legislature (Duma), Nicholas managed to survive. The importance of the Revolution of 1905 lay in the fact that the masses of Russian people had risen against extreme oppression. This was not a revolt instigated by the Marxist Bolsheviks or Mensheviks, the Socialist Revolutionaries, or any other radical group. This was the voice of the long-suffering Russian people making themselves heard by means of a popular revolution—a fact seemingly missed or ignored by Nicholas, who returned to his autocratic ways.

By the end of 1905 revolutionary fervor was waning, and opposition to the monarchy was divided between the Bolshevik-led groups that wanted complete overthrow and those less radical factions that were willing to settle for the minimal constitutionalism promised by the tsar. Elections were held in December, and the first Duma convened in St. Petersburg in May 1906. Nicholas, expecting a subservient Duma because of the restrictive election laws, was horrified by the liberal demands of the new legislative body and forthwith dissolved the first Duma by imperial decree. New elections were held, but a second Duma was heavily socialist in membership and, after meeting for only three months, met the same fate as its predecessor.

After considerable manipulation of the electoral laws, a third Duma met with the tsar's grudging approval and served its full five-year term. The fourth and final Duma sat through the war years until it was abolished by the Bolsheviks, ending Russia's brief experiment with parliamentarianism. Despite the extreme limitations placed on the Duma, it was a rudimentary legislature. Nicholas thought of his powers as God-given and viewed any constitutional limitation as sinful and heretical. He was guided by the idea that the throne of the Romanovs should be passed on to his son as he had received it from his father: absolute and autocratic.

In the face of inevitable change presaged by the Revolution of 1905, the intransigent tsar gave ground slowly and only when there was no alternative. During the Duma period of limited constitutionalism, a strong man emerged as prime minister. Peter Stolypin, a monarchist who dedicated himself to preservation of the autocracy, was also a practical man who realized that certain reforms were necessary for the survival of the regime. Stolypin's first move was a program of pacification by which he planned to eliminate the nuclei of revolution. The new prime minister established military courts to deal with revolutionaries, and soon references to the "Stolypin necktie" became common as more and more enemies of the regime were summarily tried and hanged.

As pacification progressed, Stolypin introduced land reforms, which began the transformation of the Russian countryside from the centuries-old communal system to a capitalistic farming structure. During the reform period hundreds of thousands of peasants were allowed to break their ties with the village communes and acquire land in their own names. The reformers hoped to create a new class of independent farmers who, as landowners, would be conservative in their politics and loyal to the tsar. The reforms were rather slow moving, however, and Stolypin, a hard-driving person impatient with inefficiency and corruption, was making enemies on all sides. In 1911 he was assassinated by a revolutionary. A class of small landholders had been established, but the reforms had not progressed to the desired extent and, without the forcefulness of Stolypin, the reform movement languished. Meantime, along with Europe's other nations, Russia blundered along the path toward World War I.

When Russia entered the war in August 1914, the tsar was able to mobilize millions of men but, despite the progress of the previous decade, the industrial base was not equal to the task of supplying and moving a modern war machine. Russian troops fought valiantly, inflicting serious defeats on Austrian and Turkish armies and forcing the Germans to engage in a two-front war at a time when France and England were in dire need of help; however, Russian losses in killed, wounded, and prisoners were huge and, with the breakdown of supply and transport, there were times when as many as 25 percent of the frontline troops were without weapons. Soldiers were instructed to retrieve rifles of fallen comrades on the battlefield.

As the fierce fighting and massive losses failed to halt the German advance, morale at the front deteriorated dangerously, and at home similar discontent grew as every village watched rapidly mounting casualty lists. Political unrest, fostered by active revolutionary propaganda, became endemic and was increased when Nicholas assumed personal command of the forces. Petrograd, which had formerly been known as St. Petersburg, was left in the hands of Empress Alexandra, the German-born wife of the tsar, whose autocratic views had never endeared her to the Russian people and who was now widely accused of being a German agent. Alexandra's chief adviser and confidant was the ignorant peasant-monk Rasputin, whose escapades offended the Orthodox sensibilities of most Russians, whether nobles or peasants. Rasputin's hold over Alexandra, and through her over Nicholas, gave him such enormous power that he actually held the reins of government, dismissing and appointing officials at a dizzying rate.

Once again in the midst of a disastrous war, the Russian monarchy was shaken and, despite the murder of Rasputin in December 1916, the whole structure of tsardom crashed in the revolution of March 1917. As in 1905, it was the people of Russia, almost leaderless, revolting against conditions that had become intolerable. Spurred on by revolutionary propaganda but reacting to conditions rather than to exhortations, the masses stirred as the housewives of Petrograd took to the streets demanding bread. The women were soon joined by workers. Troops ordered to suppress the disturbances joined the demonstrators. Four days later Nicholas II was forced to abdicate, ending the three-century rule of the Romanovs. The Russian monarchy, which traced its beginnings to Rurik in the year 862, passed into history.

In the first days of the revolution, there was chaos in Petrograd. A Provisional Government was formed by the Duma, but concurrently a Soviet (Council) of Workers' and Soldiers' Deputies, which had emerged briefly in 1905, reappeared and established itself as a rival governing body. Although this soviet nominally gave allegiance to the Provisional Government, in effect Russia now had two governments, both of which were issuing laws and executive orders, often countermanding one another.

The most prominent revolutionaries of the time were not present in Petrograd to take advantage of the unexpected revolution in March 1917. Lenin, living in Switzerland, had despaired of seeing a Russian revolution in his lifetime and was taken by surprise by the March events. Unable to exploit the situation from abroad, Lenin quickly began planning his return to Russia. Trotsky, working in New York and not yet committed to Lenin's Bolshevism, returned to Petrograd to join the soviet which, at first, consisted mostly of non-Bolshevik deputies. Stalin, in Siberian exile, took advantage of the amnesty granted to political prisoners by the Provisional Government and hurried to Petrograd to renew his Bolshevik activities.

With the fall of the tsar, administration collapsed throughout the country as provincial governors and other appointed officials followed their leader into disrepute. Even the Zemtsvos (organs of rural self-government), which had been revived during the reforms of Alexander II, fell into disuse with the collapse of the central government. Quick action to restore a viable regime at the top was essential if Russia was to survive as a nation, but so many disparate elements following so many selfish interests made organization of a viable government almost impossible. Russia, already beyond the threshold of defeat in a terrible war, was torn by internal conflict at a time when unity was needed above all else.

Lenin, with his wife, his two chief lieutenants (Karl Radek and Gregory Zinoviev), and several other Russian socialists made arrangements with the German government for passage from Switzerland across Germany in a sealed train. The German High Command was hopeful that Lenin's disruptive influence would set the stage for Russia's withdrawal from the war. The Provisional Government, under pressure from Great Britain and France, had promised to uphold the commitments to the Allies. Defeatism and antiwar sentiment, however, were prevalent and, when Lenin arrived, propagandizing for immediate peace, he was welcomed at the railway station by a large, bipartisan throng. The main welcoming speech was made by the chairman of the Petrograd Soviet, a Menshevik, who expressed the hope that Lenin would set aside factional strife in favor of maintaining the revolution. Lenin quickly dashed these hopes by presenting his Bolshevik demands, which called for complete opposition to the Provisional Government.

By midsummer of 1917 as many as 350 councils similar to the Petrograd Soviet had been formed in cities and towns, and Lenin immediately saw the value of these councils as vehicles for his revolution. Loudly proclaiming that all power should be given to the soviets, Lenin set about infiltrating his people into the councils, most of which already contained Bolshevik minorities. Openly committed to complete opposition to the Provisional Government, Lenin became a thorn in the side of that interim ruling body and, as Bolshevik strength in the soviets increased, the ability of the Provisional Government to rule became more difficult and its position more tenuous.

The gravest error made by the Provisional Government was its decision to keep Russia in the war. The new leadership had misjudged the attitude of the people toward the war and, when Lenin arrived calling for immediate peace, he found receptive audiences. Lenin's ideas of land expropriation, socialist revolution, and Soviet power did not find consensus even among his own party hierarchy, but his insistence on immediate peace with Germany became a popular slogan.

Meanwhile, the Provisional Government had ordered a new offensive against the Germans. A breakdown of discipline led to widespread confusion in the armed forces and with the new order to attack, several units simply refused to fight, whereas others were rendered ineffective through mass desertion. Once again Petrograd was faced with military disaster. Internal bickering in the government, continued postponement of elections for the promised constituent assembly, and rising opposition from the soviets brought about a crisis that erupted in July with an abortive Bolshevik bid for power.

Alexander Kerensky, a Socialist Revolutionary, assumed the position of prime minister, and the Provisional Government survived the insurrection, but its days were numbered. Trotsky, who had recently proclaimed himself a Bolshevik, was imprisoned for his part in the July uprising. Lenin went into hiding to avoid arrest, but continued to direct the disruptive tactics of his party from nearby Finland. With all the pressure brought to bear from the Bolshevik Left, Kerensky was also threatened by a revolt from the Right. In order to combat the latter, many Bolsheviks were released from jail and asked to help protect the Provisional Government. In a very short time these erstwhile protectors became the enemy.

During the summer of confusion, the Bolsheviks achieved majorities in the Petrograd and Moscow soviets, providing the opportunity for Lenin to make his bid for complete power, which he did on November 7, 1917, in a near bloodless coup d'etat. The Bolsheviks imposed control on Petrograd through the soviet of that city. Very rapidly, through other soviets, they extended control over much of Russia. The Provisional Government was replaced by the Soviet government. Having seized power, the immediate objective of the new regime was to consolidate and secure it, but the country was on the verge of civil war.

BOLSHEVIK CONTROL

The new era in Russian history that began in November 1917 was not initiated by a mass movement of the people. The popular revolution of March had been unable to establish a nucleus of power to replace the system which it had overthrown. As a result, the revolution was taken away from the people and made the private preserve of a small but well organized party. The Bolsheviks soon became the only group in Russia displaying any unity of purpose and action, but Lenin's personal leadership was of paramount importance. Trotsky later said that the revolution could not have succeeded without Lenin. His will sustained the movement, his leadership ability commanded absolute devotion and loyalty among his close associates; and his oratorical skills brought roaring response from the crowds he harangued in Petrograd and in Moscow, which he again made the nation's capital.

Lenin was the prime mover of the Bolshevik success, but much credit also must be given to Trotsky. Trotsky's part in the November coup and the momentous events that followed cannot be found in Soviet history books. Nevertheless, his contributions were second only to those of Lenin and, together, these two revolutionaries stand out as giants among their contemporaries in the hierarchy of Bolshevism during its first six years.

The new government called itself the Soviet of People's Commissars as the top echelon of the Bolshevik party assumed the highest governmental posts. Lenin became chairman, with Trotsky as commissar of foreign affairs and Stalin as commissar of nationalities. The many years during which the new leaders had operated underground, from prison or from exile, colored the operation of the new government as secrecy and conspiratorial methods became fundamental. The use of terror also began early with the creation of a secret police structure within a month of the Bolshevik Revolution. Lenin had advocated a small, hard-core party and, in power, he continued to insist on the principle of selective membership despite opposition from those who feared such as elitist organization.

Conspiracy, terror, and the interlocking of party and government were basic because the Bolshevik regime, like so many of its tsarist predecessors, devoted much of its energies and resources to perpetuating itself in power. The Bolsheviks constituted only a small minority among Russia's political parties, but Lenin, advocating a one-party state, took steps toward that end. Within forty-eight hours of his seizure of power, he silenced the opposition press but to pacify horrified liberals he announced it as a temporary measure.

Lenin allowed elections for the Constituent Assembly, which had been talked about since the abdication of the tsar. In the election the Bolsheviks won only 24 percent of the vote. Immediately following the election, the Constitutional Democratic party was outlawed despite the fact that 2 million people had voted for that ticket. Eventually all other parties would meet the same fate, leaving only the Bolsheviks, who soon adopted the name Communist.

The Constituent Assembly, chosen in Russia's only free election, held one stormy meeting, during which the Bolsheviks, under the personal direction of Lenin, did everything in their power to disrupt parliamentary proceedings. Failing to deter the elected deputies with his obstructive tactics, Lenin called on the Red (Bolshevik) Guard to dissolve the assembly.

Lenin's most pressing problem as leader of the new government was the war and, toward the solution of that problem, he hastily arranged an armistice. Subsequent peace talks led to the Treaty of Brest-Litovsk in March 1918 which ended Russian participation in World War I. According to the terms of the treaty, Russia gave up one-quarter of its population, one-third of its industrial capacity, one-quarter of its railway system, and one-third of its arable land. The harsh terms of the treaty were regarded as shameful by many Russians and completely unacceptable by others, but Lenin recognized that his regime could not survive unless peace was obtained. The treaty served to increase opposition, but did not crystallize the dissident elements that had been fighting the Bolsheviks from the beginning.

After Brest-Litovsk, full-scale civil war raged throughout Russia and, with the signing of a separate peace, various former allies sent troops, ostensibly to prevent huge stocks of military supplies from falling into German hands. French, British, United States, and Japanese forces, among others, made up the forces of intervention, and their anti-Bolshevik sentiments became apparent immediately. Despite some fighting between interventionists and the Red Army, however, foreign troops never became a decisive factor in the civil war. Having foreign armies on Russian soil did, however, give the Communists a propaganda theme which they would reanimate periodically over the next fifty years.

Civil war began with a Don Cossack revolt in December 1917. For the next three years, warfare of varying intensity raged on many fronts across the length and breadth of Russia. Admiral Alexander Kolchak, veteran of the Russo-Japanese war and World War I, established a government at Omsk and commanded a large White (anti-Bolshevik) force. Kolchak's troops were joined by a Czech legion of approximately forty thousand men that had been stranded while trying to make its way to the western front. The Czechs soon controlled most of the major towns along the Trans-Siberian Railway.

General Anton Denikin, chief of staff under the Provisional Government, organized cossack troops in the Don region and, for a time, was very successful against the Red forces in southern Russia. Denikin later subordinated his troops to Baron Peter Wrangel, who then commanded all White forces in the south. From the Baltic region, a White army commanded by General Nikolai Yudenich attacked Petrograd, but was defeated on the outskirts of that city by superior Bolshevik forces.

In addition to the ring of White armies that had reduced Bolshevik-held territory to approximately the area of old Muscovy, the Reds also faced an array of foreign troops. Japanese and United States troops were in force in the Vladivostok area. British and French detachments occupied centers in southern Russian such as Baku, Batumi, and Odessa, while more United States, British, and French troops were present in Murmansk and Archangel in the far north. Ostensibly the Allies were in Russia to guard military supplies and to try to reopen an eastern front against the Germans, but their anti-Bolshevik sentiments were never hidden and at times they did fight against the Reds.

Bolshevik fortunes, which seemed at a low ebb throughout 1918, changed abruptly with the end of World War I in November of that year. As the war ended, the purpose of the continued presence of Allied troops in Russia became obscure. Shortly thereafter, their withdrawal began and the Red Army began its push toward victory (see ch. 28, The Armed Forces).

The Bolshevik Revolution owed its life to the organizational genius of Trotsky, who had become commissar of war. Using Draconian measures, Trotsky whipped the Red Army into shape and transformed it from a mass of raw conscripts into an effective fighting force. Men who demonstrated military talent, such as Frunze, Tukachevsky, Voroshilov, and Budyenny, were rapidly promoted to high rank and sent to the field to command Red armies. Trotsky himself traveled from front to front in an armored train, urging his armies on to greater achievement. Admiral Kolchak was eventually captured and executed; the Czech legion became inactive; and Wrangel was forced to retreat to Crimea, from where, with about one hundred thousand supporters, he was evacuated aboard Allied ships.

The reasons for the Red victory were many and complex, but chief among them was the unity of purpose on the part of the Reds as opposed to a great lack of cohesiveness among the Whites. Also, the Whites were never sure of their own aims, hence the peasants were never sure of the Whites. The peasants knew that the Bolsheviks would never countenance a return to the old landlord days, but they did not know what would happen if the Whites were victorious. The lack of a clear-cut policy toward the peasantry hurt the White cause immeasurably, and the feeble actions of the foreign interventionists did more harm than good.

The real tragedy, however, was not in the loss of property or production facilities but in the destruction of human life and human values. Troops on both sides pillaged and burned towns suspected of collaboration with the enemy. Both sides used systematic terror in maintaining order, in conscripting soldiers and, sometimes, in seemingly wanton orgies of vengeance. Added to the havoc created by the opposing forces were the depredations of roving bands of marauders as they plundered and terrorized the countryside, aligned sometimes with the Reds, sometimes with the Whites, but more often with neither side. The end of the civil war did not bring an end to the crimes of the outlaw bands or curtail the criminal activities of throngs of orphans, banded together for protection and for strength as they roamed the land in a terrible battle for survival. Estimates place the number of homeless children at between 7 and 9 million by the end of the civil war—a staggering problem for the Soviet government.

In the wake of the contesting armies came epidemics of cholera and typhus. Such plagues were not new in Russian history, but after years of internal strife and warfare the poorly housed, ill-fed people fell victims to disease in record numbers. Widespread drought in 1921 brought famine to the Russian land, and a catastrophe of major proportions was narrowly averted by the action of foreign as well as indigenous relief agencies. Americans returned to Russia in a peaceful intervention as Herbert Hoover led the American Relief Administration in its efforts to avert starvation for millions of Russians. In the spring of 1922, Hoover's organization was feeding 10 million Russians daily.

At this point, having decided that socialization could not progress under such conditions, Lenin prescribed a small dose of capitalism to cure the country's ills. The New Economic Policy (Novaya Ekonomicheskaya Politika—NEP) was a step backward for the Communists but, as always, Lenin proved that ideology could bend to practicality. During the NEP the Bolsheviks ceased the grain requisitions by which they had been taking all surplus grain and, according to Lenin's own admission, often had taken much more than just the surplus. Under NEP the peasant was able to trade produce on the open market. NEP also permitted small enterprises to be owned and operated by private entrepreneurs. The state retained control of banks, major factories, mines, and transportation—the "commanding heights" of the economy—but NEP saved the country from collapse and eventually restored the economy to prewar levels.

Meanwhile Russia had become the Union of Soviet Socialist Republics (USSR), containing the Russian, Ukranian, Belorussian, and Transcaucasian Soviet Socialist Republics. (In 1936, the Transcaucasian SSR was divided into the Georgian, Armenian, and Azerbaijanian SSR's.) The Communists had insured their monopoly over political affairs by outlawing all other political parties. The dual structure of Party and government was duplicated from the national level down to the lowest village, and Party supremacy in all matters went unquestioned. Key government posts were filled by top Party personnel, and ultimate power lay in the Party Political Bureau (Politburo), which was located in the Moscow Kremlin. Trotsky, in condemning Lenin's organizational schemes back in 1902, had argued that the system was tailor-made for an individual to take over completely, and his prophecy was borne out during the 1920's as Stalin gathered all power into his hands (see ch. 19, Formal Structure of the Union Government; ch. 21, Political Dynamics).

STALIN AND STALINISM

Joseph Vissarionovich Dzhugashvili (Stalin), a Georgian born in 1879, had been in the Party since its inception and had been a close collaborator of Lenin and a member of the original Politburo. In 1922 Stalin was appointed to the newly created position of general secretary, an office supposedly intended for coordination of Party affairs. Stalin quickly realized the potential of his new post, which had control of the vast Party patronage system, and he began to appoint Stalin men to positions throughout the Party-government structure. Lenin, who had been seriously wounded in an earlier assassination attempt, was still nominal leader, but a stroke in May 1922 had curtailed his activities, and successive strokes severely limited his participation until his death in January 1924. All during this time, Stalin was consolidating his own position and preparing for the inevitable power struggle that would come with Lenin's death. Trotsky, who closely adhered to the Leninist line of world revolution, seemed to be the leading heir, but Stalin, proclaiming "Socialism in One Country," managed to eliminate his chief rival along with several other old Bolsheviks who might possibly have contended with him for power.

In international affairs there was a dualism that paralleled the Party-state structure at home. Lenin had established the Comintern (Communist International) in 1919 to maintain liaison with Communist parties around the world—in effect, a headquarters for world revolution. Alongside the sometimes overt, sometimes covert activities of the Comintern ran the normal diplomatic relations of the Soviet Union. In the earliest days after the Treaty of Versailles, Russia was treated as a pariah among nations just like defeated Germany, and some of the Soviet Union's earliest international contacts were with Germany (see ch. 24, Foreign Relations).

During the 1920's diplomatic recognition from other major nations came slowly, usually following trade pacts, but it was not until 1933 that official relations between the United States and the Soviet Union were initiated. Most of the world's nations were concerned about the possibility of subversion because of Comintern activities within indigenous Communist parties. Despite Stalin's adherence to the building of socialism in his own country, he did not attempt to hide the fact that he merely considered this the first step on the road to world socialism.

Within four years after Lenin's death, Stalin was in complete control of the Party organization, the military forces, and the secret police. Although disdaining a position in the official governmental structure until 1941, Stalin was an absolute dictator by the end of 1927, by virtue of his post as secretary general of the Party (see ch. 19, Formal Structure of the Union Government). At this point he decided that the NEP, which Lenin himself had declared to be temporary, could be set aside and the Soviet Union could again be put on the path toward socialism. To Stalin this mean rapid industrialization and collectivization of agriculture, and in pursuit of these goals he decreed the first of the five-year plans, with extreme emphasis on heavy industry.

During the next dozen years the establishment of the so-called socialist state and the transformation of a backward agricultural nation into a ranking industrial and military power was given top priority. The cost in human lives and national wealth of this transformation equaled that of the catastrophic war years of 1914—1922, and the impact on the country was similar to that made by Peter the Great two centuries earlier.

Achievement of the goals of the first plan was proclaimed in 4½ years, and a second plan with greater goals but the same emphasis on heavy industry was embarked upon immediately. The third plan was interrupted by the Nazi invasion of 1941 but, as soon as the war ended, five-year planning was resumed (see ch. 29, Economic Planning and Control).

The forced industrialization of the 1930's was a key factor in preparing the country to withstand the onslaught of world war.

Stalin had stated in 1931 that the Soviet Union was fifty to one hundred years behind the advanced industrial nations and had predicted that the gap would have to be closed within ten years or the new Soviet state would be crushed. His words were prophetic and his time estimate accurate but, thanks in large measure to the transformation that he had engineered, the state was not crushed; however, the ruthlessness with which Stalin carried out his plans and the brutalization of the people angered and frightened observers around the world. While making his country into an industrial power, the dictator appeared to have also made it into one huge concentration camp.

Rapid industrialization brought millions of new workers to the industrial centers. The training, housing, and feeding of these workers provided staggering problems to the regime and resulted in the adoption of extreme measures, including the widespread use of slave labor. Feeding the new industrial proletariat put terrible burdens on the peasantry but, in addition, agricultural produce was badly needed for export in order to secure necessary capital. To encourage greater production and provide greater control, peasants were urged to join collectives. Resistance to collectivization was widespread, particularly among the relatively well-to-do peasants (*kulaki*), who rebelled against turning over their equipment and livestock to a collective. Resistance brought about forced collectivization, which resulted in a virtual civil war between the regime and the *kulaki*.

The centuries-old desire of the peasant to own the land he tilled had been fulfilled to some degree after the abolition of serfdom and the revolutions, but now, asked to give up their hard-won land, millions of peasants were willing to fight against this new type of bondage. Arrayed against the peasants were the Communist Party, the secret police, and sometimes the military; the outcome was never in doubt, but the havoc wreaked during this peasant revolt was incalculable. In their resistance the peasants resorted to the slaughter of livestock and draft animals to such a degree that it was thirty years before the livestock population regained the levels of 1929 (see ch. 31, Agriculture).

In internal politics and in international communism, the years of the first three five-year plans saw Stalin emerge as a supreme and unquestioned ruler. Stalin's great power rested on his absolute control of the Communist Party, and in the early 1930's he began taking drastic measures to ensure loyalty among the membership. From the beginning of the Bolshevik movement in 1903, Lenin had preached the necessity of limiting Party membership to the most active, the most enthusiastic, and the most revolutionary members of society. To this end, periodic expulsions, known as purges, of opportunists or of ideologically weak members had been carried out to keep the Party small and pure. Stalin gave a new meaning to the word *purge* as he executed rather than expelled many of those considered unworthy of Party membership.

During the purges of the 1930's, all potential opposition was eliminated in blood baths that overshadowed the excesses of Ivan the Terrible. The fury of industrialization and collectivization had been felt by the average citizen of the Soviet Union; the kulaks had been eliminated as a class, forced labor had become commonplace, and the differences between free workers and labor camp inmates were in many cases marginal. Now the fury was turned inward against the Communist Party itself.

Trotsky was tried in absentia and sentenced to death; the sentence was apparently carried out when Trotsky was murdered in Mexico in 1940. Many other old Bolsheviks were paraded into courts in person to "confess" to all kinds of crimes against the state for which they were usually executed. Most of the leaders of the revolutionary period disappeared during the convulsions of the 1930's.

Party stalwarts such as Gregory Zinoviev, who had been in Switzerland with Lenin, and Lev Kamenev, who had shared Siberian exile with Stalin were executed. Genrikh Yagoda, the chief of the security police who had been overseer of the purges and executioner, was himself purged and succeeded by Nikolai Yezhov. The latter administered the terrorism with such efficiency that the period from 1936 to 1938 is known in Russian as Yezhovshchina, a time of infamy and terror unequaled in Russian history. Yezhov was replaced in 1938 by Lavrenti Beria and disappeared. As the purge spread in ever-widening circles, the military hierarchy was attacked and Marshal Tukachevsky, civil war hero and leading military strategist, was accused of being a foreign agent, tried, and executed. Tukachevsky was the most famous, but purged with him were two others of the Soviet Union's five marshals, 13 of 15 army commanders, 57 of 85 corps commanders, and 110 of 195 division commanders.

As big names of the Party, the government, the military, and every other organ of Soviet officialdom fell victims to the purges, the terrorism reached out across the country. Bewildered citizens found themselves swept up in police nets and herded into labor camps. Estimates place the number of forced laborers at anywhere from 12 to 15 million; to maintain such figures, arrests had to proceed at a rapid rate, trials were abolished and sentencing became a police function. (see ch. 8, The Internal Security System).

In the midst of the purges the adoption of a new constitution was announced. For many years known as the Stalin Constitution but now called simply the Constitution of 1936, this document professed to be liberal, nominally providing all of the civil rights guaranteed under the most democratic of the world's constitutions. The paradox of a liberal constitution being promulgated by one of the world's most totalitarian dictators has been explained partly by Stalin's desire for closer ties with the western democracies because of the rapid rise of Hitler. Another reason was his increased self-assurance after the accelerated development of industry and the collectivization of agriculture. By the end of the decade Stalin had absolute control of the entire nation, complete loyalty from the Party, and a constitution that "proved" the democratic nature of his regime.

Secure at home, Stalin still faced the problem of facism on his doorstep in the form of a powerful, resurgent German aggressor. War between the rival dictatorships seemed inevitable, but the inevitable was postponed by the signing of the Soviet-German Nonaggression Pact of August 1939. Having defused any Soviet threat by the pact, Hitler invaded Poland; France and England lived up to their treaty obligations and, ten days after the Soviet-German agreement, World War II had started. Soviet troops occupied eastern Poland and, a few months later, invaded Finland. During the following summer Latvia, Lithuania, and Estonia were annexed and became republics of the Soviet Union.

In the east, tension between the Soviet Union and Japan had grown after the latter invaded China. Numerous border clashes led to at least two large-scale engagements but, since neither country was anxious for war, a nonaggression pact was negotiated and remained in force until abrogated by Stalin in the last few days of World War II.

Meantime, Nazi armies had achieved rapid successes in the west and in the Balkans. France had fallen, the Battle of Britain raged in the air, and Hitler decided that the time was ripe for his move to the east. Despite repeated British warnings that Hitler was preparing to attack, Stalin was apparently taken by surprise by the massive invasion of June 22, 1941. Churchill immediately offered British aid, and the United States began preparation of the Russian Lend-Lease program, which delivered US$11 billion in materiel to the Soviet Union during the next four years.

In May 1941 Stalin made himself premier, thus occupying the top position in government as well as in the Party. With the outbreak of war, he also made himself commissar of defense and later, as commander in chief of all Soviet forces, adopted the title of generalissimo. The Great Fatherland War, as it is known in the USSR, was once more a time for setting aside ideological goals in favor of practicality. Stalin appealed to feelings of patriotism and nationalism and played down the usual emphasis on the building of communism. He also eased pressure on the Orthodox Church and, in

1943, abolished the Comintern as a gesture of good faith to his western allies.

Hitler's forces aimed at Moscow, Leningrad (formerly known as Petrograd), and Kiev. Kiev fell to the enemy, but Leningrad withstood one of history's most terrible sieges while the Nazi blitzkrieg halted in the face of superior force on the threshold of Moscow. The first few months of the war were almost fatal for the Soviet Union, but the all-important centers of Moscow and Leningrad held fast, denying the quick victory sought by the Nazis. As the invaders faltered, the Russian winter set in, and soon the goals that Hitler had expected to gain in a matter of weeks became unattainable.

Soviet counteroffensives and winter weather managed to halt German attacks, but in the summer of 1942 the invaders again moved forward, particularly in the south where, because of the failures at Leningrad and Moscow, the Nazi strategists had decided to concentrate their main effort in an attempt to cut off the food, oil, and industrial output of the Ukraine and the Caucasus region. The battle for Stalingrad proved to be the turning point of the war. Field Marshal Paulus surrendered to the Soviet defenders in February 1943 with only 90,000 men remaining of his original force of 330,000. Two years of hard fighting remained, but after Stalingrad the Soviet forces went on the offensive and rarely gave it up as they cleared their own country and drove on to Berlin, which they entered by inter-Allied agreement in April 1945.

Stalin and Stalinism emerged from World War II stronger than ever. The cult of personality, born during the purges, was now a reality that would make the Soviet dictator one of the most feared leaders of all time. Combat, occupation, and a vengeful Nazi retreat had destroyed huge areas of the Soviet Union, had inflicted some 20 million deaths among civilians and soldiers alike, and had brought great suffering to the people as a whole. Stalin now demanded and received reparations and began the stripping of German and Japanese industry.

Having given so much to the war effort and having looked forward to a new life in the postwar world, the average Soviet citizen soon found that repression was again the order of the day, and forced-labor camps overflowed just as they had before the war. Instead of concentrating on the rebuilding of villages, towns, cities, roads, and bridges, the Soviet authorities returned to the concentration on heavy industry, forcing the people to tighten their belts again to endure the hardships of life with only the barest minimum of consumer essentials.

Xenophobia, which had surfaced periodically throughout Russian history, became especially pronounced after the war, and Soviet citizens who had contact with the West as displaced persons or as prisoners of war were treated as criminals. Hundreds of thousands of those returning to the Soviet Union were herded into camps for screening; many were sentenced for real or imagined offenses, and some were shot. Once again the entire country appeared to be one vast prison camp, and much of the good will engendered by the alliance against a common enemy began to melt away.

The postwar Soviet Union had more technological and administrative skills than during the earlier five-year plans, but the nation was again bearing the weight of Marxist dogma and the economy was again geared to a quota system of production emphasizing quantity over quality. Stalin himself seemed to be somewhat of an anachronism in the postwar world. Just as Nicholas II and other tsars had viewed Russia as a private estate, Stalin felt that his peculiar brand of brutal paternalism was sufficient to govern a nation that had emerged from the war as the world's second ranking military and industrial power. The extension of Soviet power into the colonial empire which Eastern Europe had become, increased apprehension in the West and made the Soviet Union seem to be a formidable foe rather than an ally. Stalin's pronouncement to his people in early 1946 that the danger of war would exist as long as capitalism existed did little to assuage the fears felt in Europe and America.

Within two years after the end of hostilities, there was no longer any common meeting ground for the former allies or any attempt at cooperation among them. The iron curtain, mentioned in a speech by Churchill in 1946, seemed to be real; as a matter of fact, there seemed to be two curtains, one separating Eastern and Western Europe and another separating Eastern Europe from the Soviet Union. The leaders in Moscow's Kremlin apparently did not look favorably on a free flow of peoples across eastern borders even though those borders were now between Communist states. To the war-weary people of Europe and most of the rest of the world, the very word "war" was anathema, even when preceded by the adjective "cold," but by 1946 cold war was a fact of life and nations began aligning themselves for this new type of war.

In 1948 Czechoslovakia was drawn into the Soviet orbit. Frightened by this further Communist movement into Europe, Great Britain, France, Belgium, the Netherlands, and Luxembourg signed a mutual assistance treaty against aggression. These nations, along with eleven others, also formed the Organization for European Economic Cooperation (OEEC), which was greatly aided by the American Marshall Plan. Faced with such initiatives, Stalin ordered the Berlin blockade, the first great test of Western will. Eleven months of airlifting supplies saved the blockaded city and made West Berlin a lasting symbol of resistance to Soviet cold war aggression.

In June 1950 the Soviet-trained, Soviet-equipped North Korean army invaded South Korea, providing the second major test of Western firmness in the face of Communist aggression. North Korea was a Soviet satellite at the time of the invasion, and China, whose armies soon joined the fray, was still under heavy Moscow influence. Resistance to the invasion was conducted by United Nations forces, with the United States playing the major role. After a year of fierce fighting, which raged up and down the Korean peninsula, the contending armies were occupying positions near the 38th Parallel, which had divided north and south before the invasion. Peace talks began, but were often stalemated while the fighting continued. No progress was made until Stalin died, then within a month the latest stalemate was broken, and within four months a truce was arranged.

In the first days of 1953 Stalin was seemingly preparing a new purge of the Party ranks, as evidenced by his announcement of a so-called "doctors' plot." Supposedly a group of Kremlin physicians were plotting the destruction of the Communist hierarchy. They were also accused of having murdered Andrei Zhdanov, a Party chieftain who had died mysteriously five years earlier. Beria, chief of the security police, was officially denounced for not having uncovered the plot, thus indicating that the secret police would be high on the purge list. All the elements for another great purge were present, but Stalin, producer, director, and leading man of the drama, died on March 5, 1953. The "doctors' plot" was forgotten as Stalin's political heirs gathered at his funeral and made plans for the inevitable power struggle.

STALIN'S HEIRS

Georgi Malenkov seemed to be in the best position to assume the role of dictator, as he had occupied the number two position in both Party and government under Stalin, but he soon relinquished his position as senior Party secretary to Nikita Khrushchev, a Party functionary little known outside official Soviet circles. Khrushchev assumed the title of first secretary, which was less ostentatious than the general secretary used by Stalin for thirty-one years. There was much jockeying for position among the leading dozen or so members of the Politburo (called Party Presidium from 1952 to 1966), each of whom could probably visualize himself in the shoes of the dead dictator.

If confusion reigned among the leaders about who should succeed Stalin, there seemed to be consensus about one who should not; that was Beria. As head of the secret police, Beria controlled a private army of half a million men armed with tanks, cannons, and aircraft. Against this formidable threat the other members closed ranks and quickly stripped Beria of all power. Sometime during the year he was either tried and executed or simply shot. At any rate, the last of a long line of dreaded police chiefs was dispatched, and no successor has ever been allowed to gain such power in that position.

The first public rift in the collegial rule of the Soviet Union after Beria's removal came unexpectedly in February 1955, when Malenkov accused himself of incompetence and resigned as premier. Malenkov had earlier promised an increase in consumer goods, which had been so long denied the people of Soviet Russia, but Khrushchev, from his position of power in the Party, had continually undermined the premier by initiating programs that demanded more concentration on heavy industry. Malenkov could not deliver on his promises and stepped aside in favor of Marshal Nikolai Bulganin, who became premier.

The world now witnessed the unprecedented spectacle of two top Kremlin leaders making state visits to a variety of nations. Bulganin and Khruschev visited India and England among several other nations, but most significant was their trip to Yugoslavia, which had been expelled from the Communist family of nations by Stalin. The visit to Marshal Tito caused consternation and confusion among Communist nations, including the Soviet Union itself where Tito had been vilified for years and where Titoism had become a high state crime, almost ranking in infamy with counterrevolution. The wooing of Tito would later be one of the points of difference with China and would be considered heresy in Albania.

At a Geneva summit conference in 1955, Premier Bulganin, closely shadowed by First Secretary Khrushchev, held cordial meetings with President Eisenhower, and a period of detente seemed to be at hand. The Khrushchev doctrine of peaceful coexistence appeared to be genuine despite its departure from the basic Marxist-Leninist tenet of inevitable warfare. Khrushchev stated that peaceful coexistence was actually a Leninist tenet of long-standing repute in the Soviet Union, but his speeches left no doubt that the advent of nuclear weapons gave new meaning to the doctrine. His own idea of peaceful coexistence ruled out war between his country and the United States, but did not alter the basic goal of world communization.

Meanwhile, the interplay of Kremlin politics, although usually veiled in deepest secrecy, was becoming apparent to observers as Khrushchev gained more and more power. In a momentous Party Congress in 1956, Khrushchev opened a Pandora's box for the Communist world by denouncing Stalin in a "secret" speech that soon reverberated around the globe. Communist parties everywhere were torn asunder by the denunciation of the dictator whose name had been synonymous with communism for over twenty-five years and whose body even now lay beside that of the great Lenin in the Red Square mausoleum. Khrushchev emerged from that Congress with a stronger hold on the Soviet Party, but the solidarity of the Communist bloc was irreversibly weakened.

Repercussions to the de-Stalinization speech soon came in Poland and Hungary. Polish workers rioted in Poznan, creating a crisis in which Polish defection was averted only by Soviet concessions. Polish First Secretary Gomulka, until recently imprisoned on Stalin's order, demanded and received Soviet concurrence in his plan to develop Polish communism along more nationalistic lines. In Hungary a similar situation took a different and tragic turn as that country staged a full-scale revolt against its own Communist regime. The revolt was quickly and brutally suppressed by Soviet troops.

Nationalism was at the root of the Polish and Hungarian troubles, and nationalistic feelings in the Soviet satellite empire continued to plague the Kremlin to the point that the term "satellite" became inapplicable in many instances. Albania dropped out of the Soviet orbit, Rumania continually, but warily, flaunted Soviet counsel; and Czechoslovakian nationalism brought a Soviet invasion of that country in August 1968.

Khrushchev survived the events of 1956, displaying his political acumen in the process. In the years since the death of Stalin, the aspiring dictator had displayed ability to estimate properly political situations and to exploit them to his own advantage. Basing his own power in his position as first secretary, Khrushchev proceeded to undercut the positions of his opponents in government. In a method of operation patterned after Stalin's rise to power, Khrushchev padded Party organs with his own supporters, then used this strength to eliminate the opposition which he had branded "the anti-Party group." First to fall were Malenkov, Molotov, and Kaganovich, Stalinists all, who were soon followed into obscurity by Premier Bulganin. Khrushchev promoted himself to premier, thus occupying top position in the government as well as in the Party, as Stalin had done before him. Soviet Russia had another dictator, powerful but not absolute, not another Stalin.

KHRUSHCHEV IN POWER

Khrushchev's tenure was short, but his imprint on the Soviet Union and on world communism was considerable. A grandson of serfs and son of poor peasants, he had come a long way from his humble beginnings when he assumed the role of autocrat of all Russia. *Apparatchik* is the term used for Khrushchev, since he was completely a man of the Party apparatus. The early years of abject poverty and the traditional brutalized and downtrodden life of the poor Russian peasantry had convinced the young Khrushchev that change was absolutely mandatory, and he soon became a revolutionary; by 1918 he had become a Bolshevik.

Khrushchev's subsequent rise to prominence as a Party functionary was on the coattails of Stalin. A scathing denunciation of Trotsky in the mid-1920's first brought the young rebel to Stalin's attention. Thirty years later his seven-hour denunciation of Stalin, his mentor, commanded worldwide attention.

In the intervening years Khrushchev had demonstrated unswerving allegiance to Stalin and had steadily climbed the Party ladder. His long years of apprenticeship might have made him a carbon copy of his harsh teacher, but once in power Khrushchev demonstrated his individuality and tried to divorce himself from the sins of the past. He altered the modus operandi of the Party by ending the extreme reliance on terror and, in so doing, he altered world communism.

Beria was dispatched in classical Communist style in 1953, but his was the last known execution of a high political figure. When Khrushchev eliminated the anti-Party group, the fallen comrades merely lost their power and were shunted off to regions distant from the Kremlin limelight. Molotov, for example, was made ambassador extraordinary and plenipotentiary to Mongolia, while Malenkov became director of a hydroelectric plant in eastern Kazakhstan. Had they been sent to another planet, they could not have been less influential in Soviet politics. Significantly, when his turn came, Khrushchev was retired, for reasons of age and health, and pensioned off to live quietly and inconspicuously in a Moscow suburb.

In addition to lessening the terror, Khrushchev's reforms led to a separation of the Soviet Party apparatus into industrial and agricultural components, much to the dismay of many ideologists, who saw the reorganization as a fractioning of Party strength. Khrushchev's reasoning was that greater efficiency could be had through the more intimate contact provided between the Party and the separate activities at all levels from national to local. In effect, this was a decentralization measure, as was his establishment of over a hundred regional economic councils intended to reduce the vast planning bureaucracy at the national level. Both reforms were repealed by Party stalwarts shortly after Khrushchev's downfall (see ch. 6, The Economic System).

On the international scene, Khrushchev pushed his peaceful coexistence theme with Western nations while striving to keep the thirteen other Communist nations under Soviet hegemony. The two goals were not always compatible. A cordial visit to President Eisenhower brought about the "spirit of Camp David," which seemed to herald a period of detente, and arrangements were made for a summit meeting of the Big Four in Paris. The Chinese Communist leadership let it be known that they considered such dalliance with the enemy to be highly un-Marxist.

On May 1, 1960, just before the scheduled Paris meeting, a United States reconnaissance plane was shot down over Sverdlovsk, deep in Soviet territory. The summit conference foundered as Khrushchev castigated President Eisenhower, canceled the latter's trip to Moscow, and demanded a public apology. The short-lived detente evaporated, and Khrushchev declared that he would wait for a new American president rather than have any further dealings with Eisenhower.

Later the same year the Soviet premier led a delegation to the United Nations General Assembly meeting, where he threatened withdrawal from that organization unless it were reorganized. He demanded that the secretary general be replaced by a three-man directorate. Khrushchev ranted and raved and finally pounded his shoe on the desk, but he did not force a vote on the issue and it was dropped.

By 1960 the long-smoldering Sino-Soviet feud was fully in the open. The Chinese considered that Khrushchev's de-Stalinization program had gone too far and, ideologically, had been a tactical error. The rivalry between the leaders of the two Communist giants had become intense and their polemics increasingly bitter. Despite the fact that Khrushchev visited Mao Tse-tung immediately after his tour of the United States, the Chinese distrusted the spirit of limited detente existing between East and West. As the Soviet leader reiterated the necessity for peaceful coexistence, Mao continually put forth the Marxist-Leninist tenet of inevitable war. Chinese Premier Chou En Lai, an invited guest at the 1961 Soviet Party Congress, walked out after much mutual verbal abuse.

Khrushchev's foreign policy next astounded the world when the presence of Soviet missiles in Cuba was disclosed. A United States naval "quarantine" (limited blockade) forced withdrawal of the missiles, but for a time the two powers appeared to be perilously close to war. The Chinese again vilified Khrushchev, declaring that he had sold out to the imperialists. A further attempt at reconciliation between the comrades took place in early 1963, but the Chinese continually charged Soviet departure from world revolutionary goals while the Russians argued that the world had changed since Lenin's day. The ideological rift seemed to be too wide, and the talks ended in failure. A few days later a nuclear test-ban treaty was signed in Moscow, which led to further Chinese castigation of the Soviet leadership, and the Communist schism appeared to be irreparable.

In April 1964, on the occasion of his seventieth birthday, Khrushchev received congratulations from world leaders and accepted the

Order of Lenin from Leonid Brezhnev, titular head of state and a Khrushchev protégé. Khrushchev appeared to be healthy, happy, and solidly in control, but in October the same colleagues who had lionized him in April accused him of high crimes against communism and deposed him. Brezhnev took over the reins of the Party, Aleksei Kosygin became premier, and Khrushchev retired into obscurity.

CHAPTER 4
THE SOCIAL SYSTEM

In 1970 the social order was similar to the kind found in modern industrial nations but modified by the official ideology. The Communist ideology proclaimed that only two classes—workers and peasants—existed in the country and that differences between the two were slight and rapidly disappearing. The obvious reality of everyday life, however, displayed many class distinctions, with a trend toward greater differentiation rather than toward a classless society. The criteria of class distinction were many and complex, but chief among them were Party affiliation, differences in income, ethnic background, education, and achievement. These differences divided the society into a hierarchical structure that was clearly discernible in life styles and attitudes.

Many of the component parts of the multinational Russian Empire, in 1917, were fairly recent acquisitions. Some of the older elements of the empire, and particularly those close to the culture of Russia—the nucleus of the empire—had become fairly well integrated into the whole. The Muslim peoples of central Asia and the Caucasus, however, were rather isolated until after the Bolshevik Revolution. The empire encompassed such a vast region that many parts of Siberia were virtually independent of state control. The Soviet state inherited these characteristics. The vast social changes set in motion by the Bolshevik Revolution altered the previous situation, both by increasing tendencies toward unification and also by increasing the sources of diversity.

The size, efficiency, and geographical reach of the Soviet bureaucracy in 1970 exceeded those of the tsarist state. Citizens of the Soviet Union were more aware of the central government than were their forebears in the Russian Empire. Universal suffrage had brought a feeling of participation, despite the fact that there was only one party and one candidate for office. A sense of being bound together in a union had also been imparted to the citizenry by the proliferation of Soviets. The most remote Arctic village had a soviet, and the villagers knew that their own soviet had ties, no matter how tenuous, with the central government in Moscow.

The leading role of the Russian ethnic group, its language, and its culture also tied together the components of the union. Russian is the most common second language for non-Russians; it is the language of the union government, and advanced studies in many fields were offered only in Russian (see ch. 10, Languages and Social Communication).

Despite the size and power of the union administration, the country's transportation and communication networks remained underdeveloped. Especially in bad weather and during spring thaws, large areas of the countryside become almost completely isolated for periods of time and, even during times of more favorable weather, the immense size of the country bars unification, particularly between urban and rural areas. Internal migration, especially that between countryside and city, which has been a concomitant of the industrialization process, has somewhat mitigated this effect of size.

MARXIST-LENINIST SOCIAL THEORIES

According to the first article of the Constitution, "The Union of Soviet Socialist Republics is a socialist state of workers and peasants." Ideologists continually reiterate that workers and peasants comprise the only two social classes that exist in the country; however, they distinguish a separate stratum of nonmanual workers, referred to as the intelligentsia. Official theories proclaim that the differences between workers, peasants, and intelligentsia are rather insignificant (compared to differences in capitalist societies) and are destined to disappear when the nation achieves the ultimate stage of communism. In the stage of socialism, during the construction of communism, relationships among workers, peasants, and intelligentsia are friendly, according to Soviet ideologists.

The existence of income differentials, obvious to every Soviet citizen, is considered in no way contradictory to the assertion that there are only two classes in the country, since classes are supposed to be based on ownership of the means of production. On the contrary, material rewards in the form of high salaries, bonuses, and special privileges are considered necessary in the transitional phase of socialism on the road to communism. Marx himself enunciated the principle, "from each according to his abilities, to each according to his work." The programs of both Lenin and Stalin perpetuated this principle and, as recently as 1959, Khrushchev declared that the inequality of material rewards made no difference in the social structure.

Material incentive to workers was a necessary item in the rapid industrialization of the Soviet Union because of the adverse conditions that have characterized most of its history. It has been predicted since 1961 that communism will be achieved in the twentieth century. When this is accomplished, it is generally supposed that state services will provide for all of the needs and many of the

74

luxuries of the citizens. Thus, it might be supposed that any differences in income that might survive from the period of socialism will be even less relevant, since everyone will be well provided for. If in the meantime these differentials seem to become even more pronounced, this is only to be expected in the dialectical process of social change.

HISTORICAL BACKGROUND

Although the rate of change, during the latter part of the tsarist era, may have seemed slow to would-be reformers, traditional society in the Russian Empire had undergone many changes since the beginning of the Muscovite state in the sixteenth century (see ch. 3, Historical Setting). In the nineteenth century increased changes occurred in the social system, one of the most important of which was the emancipation of the serfs in 1861. These changes, however, took place within a rather rigid framework, resulting in numerous incongruities and strains.

The basic system was feudal, although it differed in several aspects from the feudal system of western Europe. The people were grouped into estates, or classes, each with special legal rights and duties. The estates included the hereditary and personal nobility, the honored citizens, the merchants, and the peasants. The hereditary nobles were permitted to own serfs and were also generally large landowners. The personal nobles acquired their rank by service to the state, but could not pass it on to their children, who became honored citizens. Large-scale merchants retained their position only as long as they continued to pay certain fees to the state. The only taxable classes were the small merchants, artisans, and the peasants. All other classes were exempt from corporal punishment, the poll tax, and compulsory military service. Muslims, Jews, Orthodox clergy, and Cossacks were outside of the estate system.

The system centered on the tsar, who could raise individuals to high estate or lower them precipitately. The system had originated as a network of mutual services, from serf to tsar, and even in its last days, public service could be rewarded by appointment to the nobility. Both serfs and nobles could become merchants by paying the requisite fees, although they remained serfs or nobles. Most of the married clergy serving in rural areas were as poor as the serfs to whom they ministered.

Inheritance of wealth and position in the nobility did not depend on primogeniture (inheritance by the eldest son) as it did in the West, so that large landed estates could become fragmented and many nobles impoverished. The incipient industrialization of the tsarist era depended in large part on serf labor.

The tsar was the keystone of the whole system. The estates were unable to form any counterbalances to imperial power. Reforms in the second half of the nineteenth century weakened some of the legal supports of the estate system, but the tsar was never able to make substantial, far-reaching reforms. The government brought about its eventual fate by being too late with too little.

At the end of the tsar's reign, society was full of incongruities and imbalances, with only the potential beginnings of a new social system. The most articulate social group was the intelligentsia, composed of individuals drawn mostly from the nobility and merchant estates. Members of the intelligentsia, conscious of the many difficulties faced by their society, embraced a number of Western-inspired social movements, including Marxism.

When the Bolsheviks assumed power in 1917, their concern was to erase the old inequalities and to build a new social system. Western scholars have disagreed as to whether the new government intended a new egalitarianism—the classless society—or merely a new system of inequalities, based on different criteria. The Bolsheviks abolished the special titles and privileges of the nobility. They also turned upside down the old prestige ranking. Now, in descending order of importance were the ruling elite, the workers, the landless peasants, the intelligentsia, and the landowning peasants. At the bottom stood the clergy, the former nobility, merchants, formerly high ranking civil servants, and anyone possessing wealth. The higher groups had more access to food and housing, both scarce in the early years, while those at the bottom barely survived and were often called upon to do menial labor.

During the first wave of revolutionary fervor, many nobles lost their lives at the hands of peasants; and later, during the period of the First Five-Year Plan (1928—32) and enforced collectivization, more of them, together with clergy and many *kulaki* relatively well-to-do peasants, were liquidated. For many years afterward members of the former nobility, intelligentsia, merchant, and *kulak* classes and their families found it necessary to assume worker or peasant backgrounds in order to gain access to education and the amenities of living.

By the end of the First Five-Year Plan the old social order had been destroyed beyond all possibility of revival. The Soviet government was now able, and moreover found it necessary, to institute a system more compatible with the transition to a modern industrial state. The system of worker incentives was initiated, and the legal disabilities of the formerly privileged classes were abolished; all became equal before the law.

The egalitarian trends were compatible not only with both Marxist and Russian values but also with state control of the economy, rapid industrialization, and the trends in other industrial nations (see ch. 14, Social Values). Pay scales were standardized throughout the country, although a great differential existed between urban and rural income. Equality of opportunity and rapid social mobility were necessary in order to most efficiently use the nation's human resources. The austerity that characterized the early Soviet period had a great leveling effect.

SOCIAL STRATIFICATION

The social structure is basically that of a highly industrialized nation but shows strong effects of the unevenness of development among the various ethnic groups, some of which have only recently emerged from nomadism and, in early 1970, had not yet been integrated into the industrialized society. The structure is also affected by the large percentage of agricultural workers in an industrialized society and by the fact that agricultural earnings are traditionally lower than in the industrialized sector of the economy. Finally, under the Soviet system of state control and direction of the economy, there is no class of private entrepreneurs. With the exception of the small private trade permitted the collective farmers in their free markets, everyone is directly or indirectly employed by the state.

Nevertheless, there are individuals with high incomes, and the accumulation of large sums of money does occur. There is both a substantial middle class and a large working class and, although nonmanual work is valued above manual work, a number of skilled workers—the "worker aristocracy"—have incomes far greater than the lowest of the white-collar workers.

In the complex system of social stratification several criteria determine the position individuals attain in the class system; the bases of some of these criteria cannot be found in Marxist-Leninist ideology. Social classes in the Soviet Union, as elsewhere, are composed of individuals or families having common interests and goals, sharing equal prestige, considering each other acceptable for social interaction, and tending to marry within the class. Marx proclaimed that class standing depended on an individual's relation to the means of production, but in 1970 that definition was outdated in a country where class standing rested on many of the same criteria that applied in other industrial nations. The principal ranking criteria in 1970 appeared to be political power, education, occupation, income, life style, and personal associations.

In the early years of the Soviet period there was a leveling of incomes but, in 1931, Stalin made a famous speech in which he attacked egalitarianism, as it pertained to workers' incomes. Stalin maintained that both skilled workers and the intelligentsia should be given the benefits of higher wages in order to promote production and speed industrial advancement. Special rewards were to be given for innovative workers. Remuneration would be properly graduated for those involved in intellectual pursuits and for those having positions of high administrative responsibilities, such as factory managers, military officers, Party secretaries, and farm managers. Middle-level occupations were to be suitably rewarded and mostly included positions in the professions, such as doctor, scientist, engineer, foreman, and accountant. At the bottom of Stalin's scale of occupations stood schoolteachers, workers, and farmers, but even the lowest paid worker would be able to increase his income by overfulfillment of norms.

The most important division in occupation is between manual and nonmanual work. Despite the glorification of the image of the worker, manual work is not particularly sought after. Nonmanual work is considered cleaner and less tiring, and the prestige factor is important, since nonmanual positions are considered to be more dignified. Although pay scales overlap, nonmanual workers generally receive higher incomes than manual workers (see ch. 32, The Labor Force).

Within the category of manual labor, differentiation is made between skilled and unskilled positions. Factors in this assessment include not only pay and a required training period, but also the fact that unskilled work is generally dirty, tiring, and undignified. Unskilled jobs are often held by women, fewer of whom possess skills, possibly because of a residue of old Russian patriarchal attitudes toward women. Urban work is more highly valued than rural work. This is not merely because many of the amenities of urban living are often lacking in the countryside, because there are more unskilled jobs, or because such work is poorly paid, but it is primarily because the rural worker feels his condition to be one of despair; the work is hard and dirty, and there is little chance for advancement (see ch. 32, The Labor Force).

Two things are significant about the relationship of pay to occupation. First, the range of pay is vast, persons at the top making at least fifteen times as much as those at the bottom; the vast majority of wage earners fall toward the bottom end of the pay scale, although not at the bottom. Income taxes are low, but indirect taxes (such as on sales) are high; inheritance taxes as well as other benefits and bonuses favor the more affluent (see ch. 32, The Labor Force).

Second, pay is of significance for what it can do. The majority of people barely manage to subsist on a rather simple level; those in the higher income brackets can afford a cultured style of life and have easy access to higher education for their children. One thing money does not purchase for them is power; although wealth and power go together in the Soviet Union, those in power become wealthy instead of the reverse. Political power cannot be bought; this may be because of strongly held values, or it may be that in the Soviet era affluence is still acquired only by service.

Power and authority accompany increasingly higher positions in the Communist Party and in the government service. Those engaged in directing and managing economic affairs also acquire a great deal of power. Persons in such positions have high incomes, but few Soviet citizens would care to be in their places; the responsibility and precariousness of position are too great. Since the 1950's the trend has been for such positions to be filled by individuals possessing high levels of education and technical skills in addition to requisite political and social skills.

Education is of great importance in the formation of the Soviet system of social stratification. Not only does it play a major role in the determination of an individual's occupation, but it also permits one to follow the desirable cultured style of life (see ch. 14, Social Values).

Until 1958 only primary education was compulsory; after that year the educational requirement was extended to secondary education. Until recently tuition fees were charged to secondary students and, as of early 1970, other fees still had to be met. Various fees are also required of students in institutions of higher learning. Those students who do well receive stipends from the government, but those with lower grades must pay the greater part of their fees themselves (see ch. 15, The Educational System).

Programs of part-time education, from the primary level through the graduate level, are available for those who must work full time at their occupations. Such schools continue to be well attended, despite the difficulties of attending and keeping up with the required studies for those who emerge from their work tired and who live with little privacy in small apartments or rooms. The costs, even for secondary education, are a burden for those whose occupations fall at the lower end of the pay scale, even though these costs have decreased. Although good students at the university level may receive stipends, weak students from well-to-do families can receive university degrees while their poorer colleagues may have to drop out (see ch. 15, The Educational System).

The criterion of private association is based on the tendency of most people to associate with those with whom they have the most in common. The class system that has evolved during the Soviet era is very much present oriented or, often, future oriented. Social origin is no longer of great concern. What is important is an individual's present occupation, his present income, his present level of education, or what he is in the process of becoming. Such a class system is characteristic of modern industrial nations having a high rate of social mobility.

The individual's chances of engaging in a prestigious occupation increase with the level of education attained; those who have completed only the primary level can usually at best hope for a semi-skilled job, and those who have completed the secondary level either become skilled workers or join the ranks of the white-collar workers, depending upon the sort of secondary school attended. For entrance into the professions or the higher ranks of the bureaucracy, a higher level degree is required.

Although the Soviet government is attempting to achieve a high level of education throughout the entire population, at the same time it needs manual workers. For this and other reasons, access to higher education is limited. Although education is the chief means of upward social mobility, those who originate in the higher strata have greater access to this means than do those of lower origin. The intelligentsia has tended to become a self-perpetuating group.

Style of life seems rather an intangible criterion of social ranking. More important are such things as number of books read or periodicals subscribed to, taste in home furnishings and dress, and preferred entertainment and leisure activities. Education and income tend to determine the style of life. Also, government control over much of the cultural field and the absence of a strong popular culture are responsible for less differentiation in this area.

The Russian classics are popular for themselves, but much literature is unavailable. (see ch. 16, Artistic Expression; ch. 12, Living Conditions).

On the basis of occupation, Soviet citizens can be divided into six major groups, hierarchically arranged: the Party and government elite, the intelligentsia, the white-collar workers, the skilled workers, the ordinary workers, and the farm workers. Citizens seem to have little trouble placing themselves into one of these categories.

These strata do not correspond entirely with income variation. When income is considered, several groups emerge, arranged in several levels. At the top remain the Party and government elite, followed by the intelligentsia, that is, by those engaged in professional, intellectual, or artistic occupations. Next comes the working class aristocracy, that small group of workers who by their skill and diligence earn extra income that places them far above other workers. The next stratum includes the white-collar workers and the small number of well-placed farmers who have achieved a level of prosperity above their fellows. The next level consists of the average workers. At the bottom are the average farmers and the below-average workers.

The class system is based on occupation, but closely associated with it is the educational factor that makes possible the occupation and the income derived from it. These in turn tend to determine life style and private association. The criterion of power is associated directly with occupation and does not result in other factors of significance to the social structure. The classes are not separated, however, by distinct and rigid boundaries, and no special legal duties or privileges accrue to them. Furthermore, the possibility for and the amount of social mobility are still great.

Generally associated with a stable class system are well-defined class attitudes and identities; not only do individuals readily identify themselves as members of particular classes, but members of the various classes tend to hold in common ideas about social, political, and economic affairs. Such associations are only partly true in the Soviet Union. Individuals do identify themselves as members of particular classes, and they do hold definite attitudes about their own class and the other classes. But there are no great differences among the classes on political, social, and economic issues. This may be because the class system is of recent origin, or it may be because all of the classes owe their existence to the regime.

Intermarriage among the various social classes is entirely possible. Although no precise information is available, it seems likely that the limited opportunities for social interaction among the classes and the general tendencies for interaction to take place among those who are most similar tend to lower the rate of interclass marriage. For example, factory workers generally associate with other factory workers because of commonality of interests, and marriages often occur among coworkers. The same would apply, probably to an even greater degree, among collective farmers. The social classes are generally mixed in most urban housing, however, and all classes use the same public services and facilities, which would tend to promote interaction and the possibility of intermarriage.

Since the period of rapid social change preceding and following the Bolshevik Revolution, the class system has stabilized. The classes have tended to become crystallized and self-perpetuating. Children from the intelligentsia and white-collar strata have a better chance of receiving university educations so that they can emulate their parents. Workers' children have less opportunity, and farmers' children have the least. Sons of military officers often go to the Suvorov (military) and Nakhimov (naval) cadet schools where they prepare for military careers, and they often marry the daughters of officers (see ch. 28, The Armed Forces).

The other social classes also tend to marry within their grouping. Although class attitudes tend to be uniform, if the classes begin to perceive that they have different, even contradictory, interests in the system, class attitudes may vary, and bad feelings among the classes increase. There are some indications that this development may take place, but it is by no means certain from the available evidence.

OTHER SOCIAL DIVISIONS

Social divisions that either parallel or cut across lines of social distinction are those between city and country, or region; of ethnic group; of religion; and of sex. Membership or nonmembership in the Communist Party provides another cleavage.

Within a single collective farm, some families are more prosperous than others. The farms also differ greatly in degree of prosperity according to location, principal crops raised, and efficiency of management and operation. On a collective farm, members are paid by a system of work units in which the various kinds of work are equalized; the result is that workers in the simplest jobs must work longer to receive the same amount a skilled worker makes in a shorter period of time. Workers are not paid until other expenses of the farm are met. Each household is given a small plot of land on which it may raise whatever crops or animals are permitted by government regulations. A collective farm family may become prosperous if it has a favorable ratio of workers to dependents or many skilled workers to administrators or if it can manage to encompass more than one household and thus add another private plot with which private production could be increased. Families with many dependents or with only unskilled workers (often these are families headed by women) and those on less productive farms have a difficult time in providing for their needs (see ch. 31, Agriculture).

The administrative subdivisions of the Soviet Union, from the union republics down to the village soviets, especially when they correspond with separate ethnic groups, contain their own separate social hierarchies (see ch. 20, Component Political Subdivisions). These are based on the same criteria as the overall structure, of which they are a part.

The non-Slavic ethnic groups—particularly the Muslims, the Caucasians, and the tribal peoples—came from backgrounds very different from those of the peoples of the European part of the Russian Empire. Among these peoples the estate system had not been in operation. Kinship-based organizations, such as the clan, were the dominant features of social life. The Soviet government has made strenuous efforts to replace the native kinds of social organization with the one characteristic of the rest of the country. Except in remote regions, the clan organization no longer exists and, as everywhere in the Soviet Union, the occupational structure has been thoroughly transformed (see ch. 9, Ethnic Groups).

Because they share features of their lives with other peoples of the Soviet Union, members of the minority ethnic groups have become a part of the overall social structure. But very few non-Slavic peoples have become part of the union elite, although they can be found on all other levels of society (see ch. 9, Ethnic Groups).

Under the tsarist government, the Russian Orthodox Church was the official religion. Other religions were either not recognized, were merely tolerated, or were persecuted. Since the Bolshevik Revolution, atheism has been dominant, and religions have been persecuted or, at best, tolerated. Religious groups continue to maintain their own organizations in which individuals may advance. Membership in a religious group, however, totally precludes membership in the Party as well as advancement in the social class system. It is not known whether occupational or social class differences exist with respect to differences in religious affiliation (see ch. 13, Religion).

Since class membership is by family rather than by individual, it would seem that sex would be of little importance in the social structure. Because of the large number of women in the labor force, however, and the large number of families headed by women, sex does make a difference. Women outnumber men in some professions, particularly in medicine and agronomy, but women are still disproportionately represented in unskilled positions, and few women have made their way into the ranks of the bureaucratic elite (see ch. 11, Family; ch. 32, The Labor Force).

One of the biggest distinctions is between those who are members of the Communist Party and those who are not. The Party has its own quasi-military hierarchy, and class distinctions based on rank and power are traditional and noticeable. Income of members varies according to position and responsibilities, but it is an accepted fact that the ladder of success is more easily climbed by members of the Party. Social mobility and Party membership are interdependent despite individual social background.

SOCIAL DYNAMICS

The social system is far from rigid and is subject to change. Two kinds of social mobility exist. The vertical is up or down within a system of hierarchically arranged classes or other groupings, such as ethnic groups, and the horizontal is from one region to another or between social groups on the same level.

Education is the primary means of upward mobility, for it opens the way to positions in the bureaucracy, intelligentsia, and white-collar ranks. Education is especially important because of the state-controlled economy, which allows few options for private individuals with little formal education to succeed. It is also important in developing nations, as in the early Soviet era, in which individuals break away from the traditional occupational and class structure to found a new one by means of education and training. It also permits a higher, more cultured style of life, another of the determinants of social class.

Membership in the Communist Party generally assures upward social mobility. Migration from countryside to city or from more backward to more advanced regions, although technically an aspect of horizontal mobility, can result in increased opportunities for upward vertical mobility.

Precipitous declines in social standing have been less common and less drastic since the death of Stalin. Before then, thousands in bureaucratic, Party, or intelligentsia positions were removed for political reasons to find themselves, at best, performing menial labor for little pay. Positions within the elite group are still rather insecure. In addition to political reasons individuals may fall in social status following dismissal for reasons, of incompetence or corruption. Children of fortunate parents who choose not to acquire an education may find themselves on a lower social level when they leave home.

The biggest trend in horizontal mobility has been the movement from the countryside to the city. At the time of the Revolution, about 80 percent of the population was rural but, by early 1970, it was about 40 percent. Migrants have been motivated by the desire to escape rural life and to seek better jobs in the city. Such a movement was necessary for the expansion of industry, but it has had a detrimental effect on agriculture, particularly because of the heavy male migration to the cities. Soviet agricultural policies have not motivated the peasantry to remain on the farms. Increasing numbers of state farms on which peasants are wage earners similar to factory employees, plus official desires to create an agrarian proletariat, have caused increased migration to the cities. Many peasants openly demonstrate a desire to own the land that they till, an idea rooted in the tsarist past but completely at odds with Communist goals.

Although the peasants would prefer to be independent farmers rather than agricultural workers, they also want more of the comforts and cultural advantages of the city brought to the rural areas. Despite the fact that the bulk of the population movement has been toward the cities, the spread of values, standards, and tastes has been the opposite—from city to countryside. Urban standards have become dominant in Soviet cultural life.

Members of the non-European ethnic groups must generally acquire some, if not a great deal, of the Russian culture if they wish to advance. They must not only acquire an education but also transform themselves to a certain extent. Once transformed, they may do well (see ch. 9, Ethnic Groups).

There are indications that the political leaders seek to foster transforming peasants into an agricultural working class; both the state farms with their wage labor and the attempts at forming agro-towns have demonstrated this. What the peasants want are individual farms of their own, and the trend toward an agricultural working class may not become strong (see ch. 31, Agriculture).

The movement east, toward developing Siberia, is the other major aspect of horizontal mobility. For years the government has attempted to attract settlers to this region. In early 1970, despite the rigors of the climate and the pioneering quality of life, many had been attracted because of the new opportunities that existed there (see ch. 32, The Labor Force).

The only kind of horizontal mobility that exists between social groups is the assimilation of one from a non-Russian culture into the Russian culture, an adaptation that has been made by millions of non-Russians. Similarly, small non-Russian ethnic groups merge into other larger ones (see ch. 9, Ethnic Groups).

One of the principal and most successful means chosen to achieve industrial progress was that of material rewards for achievement. On the whole, these rewards have been to individuals, although work groups may be rewarded for outstanding achievement. The stress on individual rewards has resulted in individualism. In the race to succeed many do not consider the rights of others. Such attitudes are far from the selflessness of the ideal Communist. The family is seen as the focus of individualism; thus, despite the Soviet support for the family, there are nurseries, kindergartens, and boarding schools, which remove many responsibilities of child care from the family. Individualism is regularly denounced in the press but is, at the same time, supported by the principle and practice of, "From each according to his ability, to each according to his work."

CHAPTER 5

THE POLITICAL SYSTEM

In early 1970 the Communist Party of the Soviet Union (CPSU) exercised control over not only the political system but all other facets of society. Although power was concentrated in the Party, the state played a key role and exercised authority over a broad spectrum of activities and programs designed to achieve Party goals. Also, various social institutions, such as trade unions, had been given authority to carry out specified official functions. The pervasive, guiding, and directing role of the Party was assured by control of appointments to key positions and the monitorship of activities at all levels by some element of the Party organization (see ch. 19, Formal Structure of the Union Government; ch. 21, Political Dynamics).

The power to govern was based on the Party's avowed consecration to the laws of Marxism-Leninism, its link with history, and its authority to interpret this ideology. By invoking these relative abstract goals and imperatives, the Party leadership attempted to manipulate men and institutions as it chose. The mystique derived from the messianic mission of the Party stood as law and morality above all else and subordinated constitutional and legislative law to Party decisions and policies. The flexibility of the fundamental laws permitted the Party leadership to declare that which is useful to be "right" and "good."

Communist ideology placed much emphasis on the dictatorship of the proletariat, the so-called rule of society by the working people, but no legislative mechanism or institutions were provided to permit expression of the public will, except under guidance of the Party. Executive, legislative, and judicial powers all became prerogatives of the Party which, in effect, became the state.

The transformation of society from capitalism to communism has been held to be a fundamental goal. Soviet communism promises that it will create an ideal society in which the needs and desires of mankind will be fully satisfied. In the final stage of communism, according to theorists, there will be only one class—the workers; the state will have withered away, necessary social controls being provided by public organizations; and production and distribution will be on the basis of "from each according to his ability, to each according to his needs."

While these idealistic goals are continually emphasized to the people, in practice, the Party leadership has given highest priority to industrialization and modernization of the economy and to the building of military strength. A powerful industrial state has resulted and, with it, a strong state organization, a large bureaucracy, and privileged classes.

Along with the development of the state, groups of scientific, business, engineering, and cultural leaders have emerged, and the interests of these groups often transcend the narrowly political orientation of the Party leadership. There have been some relaxations in controls and greater freedom of expression in the post-Stalin era, but criticism and demands for change of policy are carefully maintained within boundaries established by the Party.

Work conditions and wages improved at an accelerated pace after the mid-1950's, but the standard of living of the masses of Soviet citizens lagged considerably behind that of other leading industrial nations (see ch. 12, Living Conditions). There was, in 1970, little momentum either to change the system of state capitalism that had emerged or to upset the system of social stratification of the highly developed bureaucracy.

Despite considerable indifference to the Party's propaganda effort, the leadership of the CPSU was generally accepted, and the masses looked to it to provide stability and direction for the realization of national objectives. The efforts over a period of more than four decades to create a monolithic society, fully responsive to Party desires, and the nontoleration of opposition both within and outside the Party have resulted in a pliant population generally attuned to Party leadership. There were diverse views on many Party programs and policies, but opposition that sought to provide alternatives outside the framework of Marxism-Leninism was, in early 1970, insignificant. Primary reliance was placed on voluntary cooperation but, when deemed necessary, the Party made use of its control over wages, welfare benefits, the courts, and the police to compel compliance with directives and support for its programs.

Party dynamics, which in the past relied heavily on the leadership of professional revolutionaries and on the maintenance of revolutionary zeal in the battle against world capitalism and internal class enemies, had become lethargic. Statements in the Soviet press and reports from foreign observers indicated that the Party's ideological appeal, which took shape during the period of Lenin's leadership and was oriented on effecting and securing the socialist revolution, did not correspond to the requirements of 1970. By the end of World War II, the Communist victory of 1917 was secure.

A new stage of development took form after the emergence of the Soviet Union as a leading world power. Policies and programs were concentrated primarily on national interests and Soviet objectives in the international power struggle. The split among the Communist nations, particularly the Sino-Soviet rift of the 1960's, made the appeal to the spirit of international communism even more difficult. The direction of Soviet development, beginning with the cold war in 1947, demanded new dynamics that were based on national interests and took into account commitment to the struggle for supremacy as a world power plus interests in a highly industrialized society.

The crucial test for the CPSU in 1970 was the revision of its proclaimed goals, its base of power, and its dynamics to meet the conditions and demands that confronted the Soviet Union as a highly industrialized and powerful nation. The CPSU was forced to consider these necessary revisions while guarding against the loss of its unique power position. In essence, the Party could not afford to set the stage for the development of pluralisms that could challenge or even replace its monopoly of power.

IDEOLOGICAL BASIS OF THE POLITICAL SYSTEM

Marxism-Leninism—the doctrinal basis for Soviet communism—is derived from the theories of Karl Marx and Friedrich Engels, the teachings of Lenin, and the experience of the CPSU. For Soviet theorists, it serves as a science to explain the laws of development of nature and society concerning class struggle and the construction of a Communist society. In early 1970, as in all periods of Communist rule, it permeated the Party's ideological effort to indoctrinate the masses and obtain their support for Party programs.

Dialectical materialism, from which historical determinism has been derived, was based on the thinking of the German philosopher Georg Hegel and developed by Marx and Engels. It maintains that any development has within itself the lifegiving quality of generating an opposite or antithesis; therefore, continuity of action is assured, and a safeguard against a fixed state of being is provided. Nothing is permanent, absolute, or sacred. The material nature of things is primary, and even thought and consciousness have the properties of matter. It is maintained that the materialistic dialectics encompass the whole of history—social development, economics, and politics—and provide a comprehensive, fully adequate and deterministic explanation for all developments and change (see ch. 17, Intellectual Expression).

The CPSU has applied historical materialism in explaining its role and the sequence of social developments. The Marx-Engel's analysis of societal formations provided for successive stages: primitive communal, slavery, feudalism, capitalism and finally socialism—the first stage of communism. The mainspring of history, according to Marxists-Leninists, is revolution, which develops from the class struggle between the owners of the means of production, the exploiters, and the nonowners. Under capitalism Marx maintained that a small capitalist class exploits the much larger working class. He concluded that capitalism could not be reformed because of its internal contradictions and that it must be destroyed by revolution of the proletariat against the capitalist owners, the bourgeoisie (see ch. 17, Intellectual Expression).

Marx saw the need for a political party of the proletariat to lead the ideological and political struggle, but he never gave particular emphasis to it in theory. The character and role of the CPSU are largely attributable to the work of Lenin. The Party as designed by him was an instrument for making revolution, a select and disciplined revolutionary elite, and a conspiratorial model of organization that concentrated control in the Party leadership. Lenin placed the Party in a vanguard role, as a professional manager, in a military bureaucratic system of organization and apart from the masses. He looked to the urban industrial workers as the most important element of society in the dictatorship of the proletariat.

Party ideology has continued to emphasize the leading role of the workers. A basic Party publication in the 1960's defined dictatorship of the proletariat as "power in the hands of the working people, led by the working class and having as its aim the building of socialism." The dictatorship of the proletariat, it is maintained, provides for a higher form of democracy because political power is used to benefit all working people rather than a privileged small element of society.

Marx, Engels, and contemporary Soviet leaders have held the position that the socialist transformation includes the eventual withering away of the state and the assumption of responsibility for required controls of society by public organizations. Lenin adopted the state machine that had been created in Russia and claimed that it became an institution in the hands of the proletariat to continue the struggle against the bourgeoisie. Stalin greatly expanded state power, however, admitting the contradiction. He justified his actions, claiming that the strengthening of the state would create the conditions for the eventual withering away of the state and that the requirement for a strong state would be a necessity as long as capitalism exists.

The allocations of functions and authority to the state have fluctuated during the various forms of leadership that have prevailed. Capabilities have been developed through education and training of leaders and the masses that provide great potential for public organizations to assume more responsibility for controls. Nevertheless, in early 1970 there were few evidences to indicate that state functions would be diminished, despite the trend toward increasing Party involvement in details of running the economy and organizing cultural and other activities.

Marxism-Leninism attempts to dignify the common working people. The masses are told that it is the people who are the driving force in the historical process and that it is the Party's indissoluble ties with the working class and with the broad masses that have enabled it to perform its vanguard role and score great victories. There is a constant effort to stimulate creativity and individual initiative to further Party efforts. The cult of the individual, which overemphasizes the importance of one person, is not accepted, because it undermines the development of initiative of the masses and destroys so-called socialist democracy. True leaders of the working class, it is maintained, have an important place and deserve the admiration and respect of the people.

The nature of human freedom under Soviet communism is based on the concept that man cannot act independently of the objective laws relating to nature, society, and thought, nor can he revoke or change them. The objective laws of Marxism-Leninism, it is argued, provide mankind with the oppontunity to form the kind of society that will make possible the enjoyment of a higher form of social freedom. The Party, purporting to follow these objective laws, assigns duties and obligation to all individuals and permits the exercise of rights that are consistent with Party policy. Individual freedom is measured in terms of cooperation and obedience to the Party will. Satisfaction for the individual is to be found in the fulfillment of the collective will. Unity and identity with the mass effort have been an obsession in all things undertaken in the name of the socialist transformation.

Despite the insistence on conformity, Party leaders have given considerable attention to the need for criticism. Marx saw criticism necessary in the analysis of the actual historical process. He considered it a material force when it sets men in motion by pointing out how they can attain their goals. Soviet leaders have encouraged both self criticism by individuals and criticism of programs as a dynamic for individual purity and efficiency, as well as to reflect inner party democracy. Care has been exercised, however, to ensure that the controlling Party leadership is not criticized. The practice has been for higher echelons of the Party and bureaucracy to criticize lower echelons and for the Party leadership to criticize deposed politicians as the political situation demands. The suggestion of alternatives to Party decisions is not condoned and is considered counterrevolutionary.

Marxist-Leninist views on international relations have developed in consonance with Soviet national interests and the nature of the struggle against capitalism. Marx envisioned relations between nations in the context of the revolution of the proletariat against capitalism, the strengthening of international working-class solidarity. Lenin, going a step beyond this, maintained that imperialism is a direct continuation of the fundamental properties of capitalism. He proposed to broaden the basis of socialist revolution by advocating actions to foment and support liberation movements against imperialism.

In 1920 Lenin declared that "as long as capitalism and socialism remain side by side we cannot live peacefully—the one or the other will be the victor in the end." At that time the Party had hopes that socialist revolutionary movements in other European countries would be successful and help secure communism in Russia. When support from outside did not materialize, the Party turned to the development of socialism in only its own country in the mid-1920's. Thereafter, national interests were given first priority. It became a matter of practical necessity that the Soviet state exist without war. During the period of Stalinist rule before World War II, this concept was rationalized as a temporary policy, as an expedient to gain time for preparation for the inevitable conflict with capitalism.

Further modifications were made after Stalin's death. During the period of Khrushchev's leadership, Party ideology dropped the premise that conflict with capitalism was inevitable and proposed that international disputes be resolved by peaceful means. Party leader Brezhnev, in a speech to the International Conference of Communists in 1969, reiterated these views, stating that "peaceful coexistence does not include the struggle of ideologies, and this must be given the most decisive emphasis."

Marxist-Leninists assert that ultimate peace depends on total victory of the socialist system over capitalism. Claiming that their goals are shared by the whole of so-called progressive mankind, they aspire to become rulers of the world and shapers of world culture.

DEVELOPMENT OF THE SYSTEM

The political system and methods of control in 1970 reflected the influences of the Leninist, Stalinist, and Khrushchev periods of leadership. The Party found itself confronted with the long-term utopian goals of Marxism-Leninism and, simultaneously, with immediate objectives and problems related to the continuance of Party rule and Soviet national objectives. The fundamental problems, dating from the first years of Communist rule, required great tactical and stragegic flexibility while adjusting goals and utilizing available instruments of power.

The Bolshevik Party, which emerged victorious in November 1917, was oriented primarily toward the utilization of the forces of discontent. Lacking the broad base of support from an exploited industrial working class such as Marx had envisioned, the Party of Lenin had to harness whatever resources were available and itself provide the momentum for establishing a Communist system of rule. From the beginning, in order to maintain control, it was necessary to insist on absolute obedience to a single will, that of the Party leaders, and for the leadership to insist on the self-perpetuation of Party rule.

The governing apparatus that Lenin established, with the Party as the guiding and directing force, incorporated the existing framework of administrative machinery and provided a hierarchical system of soviets, or people's councils. Other measures that helped shape the regime included the nationalization of banks and large syndicates; centralization of control over the economy, with provision for a plan in which there would be control of workers' organizations at the production level; acceptance of the already established organization of work at banks, the best factories, and other enterprises; state monopoly of foreign trade; and economic self-sufficiency to the degree possible.

Because of chaotic conditions after the Revolution, Lenin declared that a socialist system could not be established immediately. He proclaimed a period of "war communism" as an emergency measure to cope with civil warfare and foreign intervention. This period of war communism and civil warfare (from 1917 to 1921) brought great demands and, frequently, the resources and institutional machinery were inadequate. Much ad hoc improvisation was required, and many persons who were holdovers from the tsarist regime were, out of necessity, placed in responsible positions. Terror and coercion became a part of the totalitarianism that began to emerge. Included in the development of controls during this period were the monopoly of power by the Party, the concentration of control in the Party central organs, the purge of Party members to ensure purity, the emergence of a centralized bureaucracy, the establishment of the secret police as a political weapon, and the substitution of state control over all production and distribution for workers' control over industrial enterprises. The Party leadership further tightened its grip on the instruments of political power during the period of the New Economic Policy (Novaya Ekonomicheskaya Politika—NEP), despite the concessions to the peasants and private enterprises.

The industrialization and modernization of the economy at forced draft speed, with the concomitant collectivization of agriculture, were made the priority objectives of the late 1920's. This decision was based on the premise that heavy industry, the foundation of modern military power, was essential to guarantee the survival of the country and the socialist state. Catching up with and overtaking the more advanced industrial nations in terms of output became a political as well as an economic goal from this time on.

The masses of workers and peasants were called upon to make any sacrifice deemed necessary to fulfill Party plans. A steady barrage of propaganda directed at the whole population aimed to stimulate unity, patriotism, and revolutionary zeal and exalted the superiority of the Soviet system and the wisdom of the Party leadership. The secret police were utilized widely to enforce Party directives, and in some instances military units were called in during the period of collectivization. Millions were sent to corrective labor camps. The toll of deaths was large; the number remains a matter for conjecture (see ch. 8, The Internal Security System). Even persons who had committed no apparent offense were victimized in order to develop and maintain an atmosphere of anxiety and insecurity in the whole of society, thus hoping to ensure blind obedience to Party directives. The trials of Party notables and widespread purges in the 1930's eliminated any semblance of political opposition.

The system of soviets had never been given any real voice in government, despite Lenin's initial expressions that the laboring masses should take over the responsibilities of state administration. Under Stalin a state and bureaucracy developed as a strong arm of a personal dictatorship. Party membership was highly restrictive, never including more than 5 percent of the population in the Stalinist period. During periods of crisis, such as the 1929—31 period of forced collectivization, Stalin resorted to liberalized recruitment of persons from the working class to maximize his link with the masses.

The great losses of people and territory after the German invasion in June 1941 were, in part, the result of the inertness that derived from the rigid and pervasive system of controls under Stalin, as well as low morale. While the security of the Stalinist regime appeared to be hanging in the balance in the early phase of the war, the destructive and inhuman policies of the German invaders contributed significantly to the eventual success of the Party's redoubled appeals to patriotism. Studies of Soviet opposition to Stalin during World War II indicate that at least half a million ex-Soviet citizens were serving in the German army before the end of the war, and the total may well have been as high as a million.

The industrial base that had been built under great pressure in the 1930's was second only to the outstanding courage and tremendous human sacrifices of the people in bringing Soviet military successes in World War II. Adjustments were made in the system of political controls to meet the exigencies of war, but the absolutist and dictatorial system that had developed earlier remained in effect. During the postwar years of Stalinist rule, measures were again taken to tighten Party discipline and increase controls.

In his speech to the Twentieth Party Congress in 1956, Khrushchev characterized Stalinist rule as having been despotic, cruel, inhuman, and irrational, but these characteristics were attributable only in part to Stalin himself. Much of the basis for such traits was inherent in the Marxist-Leninist system. Lenin had set precedents and formulated precepts that facilitated the development of totalitarianism. He refused to tolerate minority views within the Party and rejected opposition from non-Party groups, utilized purge and terror to ensure Party control, and concentrated power in the leadership. The flexibility of interpretation of Marxist-Leninist doctrine also facilitated the development of despotic rule.

After Stalin's death in 1953, some controls were relaxed, and greater reliance was placed on voluntary cooperation. Masses of people were released from corrective labor camps, and terror was largely abandoned as an instrument of control.

The political system under Khrushchev's leadership was subjected to various innovations and reforms that generally attempted to broaden the Party's leadership and its involvement in the details of managing a modern industrialized society.

Less attention was given to ideology. Khrushchev rearranged the system of controls, shifting many functions from the state to the Party and broadening participation of the masses in administration to further his proclaimed objective of making the Party a party of the people. Regulations were changed to require greater turnover of membership of councils and committees of the Party and soviets; however, safeguards to permit continuity of the Party's central leadership were provided.

Various steps were taken to enlist greater support from the masses. These included criticism of the cult of the individual, or personality cult, as exemplified by Stalin and continued indictments of Stalin for his cruel and inhuman actions. The utopian program, to be realized by 1980, approved by the Twenty-second Party Congress, likewise aimed to further the concept of a party of the people. The extent of Khrushchev's avowed support for increasing the priority of consumer goods fluctuated with his political maneuverings for leadership. The Party's commitment to the means of production continued to prevail. Nevertheless, there were measures that brought modest improvements in human welfare.

The search for innovations included the widespread discussion concerning decentralization of control of the economic system and the introduction of profit criteria for industrial operations. Expressions of criticism on a scale previously considered dangerous and intolerable were permitted on various other aspects of the system.

Emphasis was placed on peaceful coexistence and economic competition in foreign relations. At the same time, Khrushchev implemented measures designed to enhance influence and prestige abroad. The challenge of Communist China in the early 1960's caused Khrushchev to attempt to exclude China from the Communist family of nations. This and many of his efforts to change the role of the Party were opposed by elements of the Party and bureaucracy and contributed to his removal.

The collective leadership, headed by Breznev and Kosygin, which followed Khrushchev, was generally more conservative. Measures were taken to enforce greater political and ideological conformity, and the highly optimistic program, outlined at the Twenty-second Party Congress, for a more abundant society was deemphasized. Generally, the 1965—70 period was one of caution and restraint, an acceptance of the status quo.

The limited economic reform introduced in 1965 brought a return to greater centralization of planning and management but did not produce the expected growth in output. The collective leadership showed little inclination to loosen Party controls and move off in new directions that might stimulate economic growth which, since the early 1960's, had not matched the levels of the previous decade (see ch. 30, Industry).

The institutional framework for governing the nation in early 1970 was little different from that which had prevailed during the preceding two decades. The CPSU, the guiding and directing force, monopolized power, and the major policy and decision making authority was concentrated in the Party leadership. The state, labor unions, and other institutions, all of whose leaderships were chosen by the Party, were accorded extensive authority to carry out assigned functions.

Primary reliance was placed on voluntary cooperation for attainment of objectives, but the Soviet system of controls, in comparison with those of non-Communist Western European nations, was highly compulsory. Failure to cooperate and avoidance of obligations could result in the reduction, or complete withholding, of social insurance or other benefits, exile, or other punishment (see ch. 22, The Legal System). A vast security police apparatus was available had the leadership desired to resort to force. Following the pattern that began after Stalin's death, the Party was inclined toward the use of incentives rather than widespread use of the police. There was little evidence of overt opposition. The system of controls was adequately maintaining criticism within manageable limits, but an undercurrent of social criticism by intellectuals sometimes attempted to breach the Party's monopoly of public communication.

Although the Party retained its leading position, interest groups, such as the state administration, the military, heavy industry, and the police were competing for a greater share of resources. There were persons in these groups whose professional interests transcended politics and whose training and experience commended them for leadership. The Party leadership was dominated by persons who were of the conventional dedicated kind of politician, but the indications were that the spectrum of talents would have to be broadened to provide required capabilities.

By early 1970 the Party leaders were predominately older persons. The average age of Politburo members was sixty-one, and the average age of the voting members of the Central Committee of the Party was over sixty. Although Kosygin's experience had been primarily in business and industry, most of the other top leaders were professional politicians, and there appeared to be little inclination to include elements in the leadership that could dilute its highly political and conservative character.

Despite a widespread lethargic attitude toward the Party's ideological efforts to maintain revolutionary zeal, the masses of people generally supported the Party's programs and looked to it for attainment of national objectives and improvement of their lot. The ordinary citizen took great pride in Soviet economic, scientific, and technical achievements and believed that, viewed as an entity, his society was moving forward. On the other hand, there was much lipservice to Party propaganda and a widespread feeling that the leaders had separated themselves from the masses. People generally appreciated the progress that had been made in living standards and the increases in privileges granted after the mid-1950's. Their expectations for greater personal freedom and material benefits were rising rapidly (see ch. 27, Political Attitudes and Reactions).

The political system was narrowly restricted in providing opportunities for increased freedom and contained no guarantees against encroachment on existing individual liberties and privileges. The soviets wielded no real political power and operated under Party guidance and direction. In order to strengthen its link with the masses, the Party encouraged participation in the work of the soviets, people's control committees, planning meetings, production conferences, and similar activities. Many of the slogans of the Khrushchev period promising a brighter future continued to be used, but some of the Khrushchev measures designed to increase participation in Party work were rescinded. The regulation adopted at the Twenty-second Party Congress requiring greater turnover of committee and council membership at all levels was dropped.

The system that Khrushchev established in 1962 to combine the Party and state control and inspection functions was changed in 1965. Under the new arrangement, Party work remained under Party control, and a People's Control Committee was established in the state administration in Moscow. In mid-1969 Kavanov, chairman of this committee, reported that 7 million volunteer inspectors and controllers were working at enterprise level and pointed out that the combination of state and public control was an outstanding democratic feature of a socialist society. In practice, the people's control committees supplement and assist the regular Party and state control organizations and provide an additional means to identify sources of inefficiency, waste, and deviations from the Party line.

SOVIET ACHIEVEMENTS MEASURED AGAINST GOALS

An evaluation of the Soviet political system in early 1970 revealed that considerable success had been achieved in the Party's priority effort to build a modern industrialized society. A comparison of promised and proclaimed achievements with actual conditions relating to distribution of political power, justice, equality, and an abundant life, on the other hand, showed that progress lagged in these areas and fell short of promised and proclaimed levels.

The rapid growth and development of the Soviet Union as an industrialized society indicated that the CPSU had worked out institutional forms and administrative processes that facilitated centralized control, long-range planning, and mobilization of the masses for implementation of Party directives. In many respects Soviet totalitarianism was a complete system, relating individuals to each other, to institutions, and to society as a whole. The country's position as one of the leading world powers was an indication that the system had successfully adapted itself to the building of a modern industrial society that is focused on growth of the means of production and military power.

The Party's success in putting an end to injustice and erasing differentiations in society fell short of the promises of Marxism-Leninism. While the system of soviets and Party organization was proclaimed as the most progressive kind of democracy, political power and the instruments of control were monopolized by the Party leadership. The public will could be exercised and expressed only within the boundaries established by the Party.

The stratifications of society resembled the pattern of differentiations that was commonly found in advanced industrialized nations. There was a great differential between the income and privileges of the elite as compared with the average worker. Living conditions improved during the 1953—70 period, but the standard of living lagged well behind that of other highly industrialized nations. There was little indication that the Party intended to share its monopoly of power or change the system of differentiations.

The promise to end the contradictions, irregularities, and waste that Marxists-Leninists had found and criticized in bourgeois society was not fulfilled. Massive irregularities were found in the economic system; frequently, industries produced those items that would bring the greatest credit for plan fulfillment rather than produce the goods that were most needed. The bureaucracy had the same impersonal character as in other highly industrialized societies, and the individual tended to lose his identity. The promise of a dynamic, constantly changing social order, offering new forms of social organization, was largely unfulfilled. There was little inclination to change the institution and processes that had largely taken form by the mid-1930's. The Party in early 1970 retained the Marxist-Leninist doctrine of revolution as a propaganda line, but maintenance of the status quo appeared to be its guiding principle.

CHAPTER 6

THE ECONOMIC SYSTEM

As the economy entered the final year of its five-year plan for 1966—70, it was certain that all but two of the published targets of that plan would not be met. The year 1970 was also the target year for the fulfillment of the confident forecast made by the leadership in the 1950's that the economy would overtake and surpass the economy of the United States in per capita production and consumption. Yet the gross national product (GNP) in 1970 was only about two-thirds as large as that of the United States according to official Soviet sources and not more than half as large according to Western economists using Western statistical concepts. On a per capita basis, the lag was still greater.

The failure to attain the planned goals reflected a prolonged economic slowdown, the reasons for which had been the subject of an extended debate in the Soviet Union and of intensive studies in Western countries. Western observers and several Soviet economists ascribed this slowdown to the inability of the traditional economic planning and management system to cope with problems of the increasingly complex, modern industrial economy. In their view, an improvement in economic performance could be achieved only through a revision of the existing centrally controlled system in the direction of a market economy. Western observers also attributed the economic difficulties to an insufficiency of resources for meeting the requirements of the leaders' competing goals for a military buildup, rapid economic growth, and a rising standard of living. They believed that a partial reallocation of resources from military and space programs to civilian production could result in a faster rate of growth. Neither a change in the economic system nor a significant reallocation of resources, however, was considered likely to occur in the near future, because the former would necessitate a surrender of economic control to a degree unacceptable to the Communist Party of the Soviet Union (CPSU) and the latter would jeopardize the goal of military supremacy.

NATURE OF THE ECONOMY

The Soviet economic system is a creation of the country's postrevolutionary leaders and reflects their authoritarian and autarchic tendencies. Although the prevailing economic theories and practices

101

are proclaimed to be grounded in the teachings of Karl Marx, Marx did not, in fact, provide any definite guidelines for the organization of a socialist economy. The basic features of the economy are an outgrowth of the pre-World War II political leaders' assessment of the economic development needs of the country in what they considered to be an unfriendly world environment and of their choice of methods for achieving the quickest possible results. These features include government ownership or control of all the means of production, a high degree of self-sufficiency, comprehensive planning and control by the government of all economic activities, and a scale of priorities in the allocation of resources that treats agriculture and the consumer as residual claimants. The discrimination in resource allocation has produced a two-tier economy, in which technologically advanced, highly productive enterprises in priority industries coexist with obsolete plants in less essential sectors and with a backward agricultural sector.

Beginning in the mid-1950's a number of measures were taken in the fields of labor and agriculture to reduce somewhat the rigidity and severity of the system without, however, significantly affecting its fundamental nature. These measures granted workers much greater freedom of movement and job selection and improved the lot of collective farmers by raising the government procurement prices for farm commodities. A continuing central problem for the economy has been the maintenance both of work incentives and efficiency at all levels of production and distribution in the absence of a profit motive and of an adequate supply of consumer goods on which workers' earnings could be spent. An economic reform instituted in 1965 in an effort to eliminate this problem has not proved effective.

The economy is organized on a sectoral and hierarchical basis. Overall control is vested in the Central Committee of the CPSU and the USSR Council of Ministers, some of whose members hold positions in both bodies. The Council of Ministers provides direction to a number of union ministries responsible for individual sectors of the economy and industry. Each ministry administers the sector under its jurisdiction through a series of main administrations responsible for groups of enterprises engaged in similar lines of activity. Individual enterprises at the bottom of the administrative pyramid are managed by government-appointed directors, who are responsible to the higher authorities. In a growing number of instances, associations of industrial enterprises form an additional administrative link, intermediate between the individual enterprise and the main administration. A parallel administrative organization, responsible to the USSR Council of Ministers, exists in each of the country's republics. As a rule, most important enterprises in any one sector are subject to union jurisdiction. Small local enterprises are controlled by lower levels of the CPSU and government structure. In addition to ministerial direction, collective and state farms are also subject to control of local CPSU committees.

The direction of the country's economic development has been determined by the relentless drive of Soviet leaders for national security and influence in world affairs through the attainment of military power second to none. The chosen means for achieving this end has been a high rate of economic growth, based on rapid industrialization with emphasis on heavy industry. At the same time, for ideological and internal political reasons, improvement in the living standard of the population has been repeatedly proclaimed as the major goal of economic development.

The primary economic functions of allocating available resources among competing claimants, specifying the nature of the production process and determining the composition and distribution of the national product, are performed by a central planning organization, with participation by enterprise management on the basis of directives issued by the Central Committee of the CPSU concerning major targets to be attained in the several sectors of the economy. Through a complex process of balancing resources with requirements, the planners translate these directives into broad national economic plans and detailed production plans having the force of law for each economic entity. As a rule, long-term goals have been embodied in five-year plans, whereas annual, quarterly, and monthly plans have served to guide current economic operations. A long-range plan centered on the year 1980 is also being developed (see ch. 29, Economic Planning and Control).

The scope of economic planning is all embracing, although major attention is given to the production of high-priority items and to industrial investment. The balancing process is a method of reconciling the resource requirements called for by the production and investment programs during a given period with anticipated supply availabilities and of distributing the final product among the various groups of consumers. It must ensure that each enterprise have at its disposal at the proper time the necessary materials, labor, and capital to carry out its assigned task. It must also ensure the availability of an adequate supply and assortment of foods and other consumer goods to the population throughout the country and equate the purchasing power of consumers with the value of the consumer goods output.

This planning of material balances is done primarily in physical terms, that is, in tons of coal and wheat and numbers of bulldozers, eggs, and man-hours. Corollary financial plans, developed through the application of fixed, government-established prices to the physical plans, serve mainly as a means of control over enterprise performance through the banking system.

The immense difficulty of planning the physical flow of productive resources and finished goods in an economy as large and complex as that of the Soviet Union inevitably entails serious planning errors, which produce various bottlenecks in production and distribution. Traditionally, shortages in high-priority sectors and industries have been alleviated by diverting resources from lower priority areas, primarily agriculture and the consumer industries. This method appears to have been applied somewhat less rigorously in the late 1960's, but widespread consumer goods shortages nevertheless continued in 1970.

The task of equating the disposable income and the effective demand of the population with the available supplies of goods and services has not always been amenable to satisfactory solution. Since the mid-1960's this fact has been evidenced by steeply rising savings deposits and by numerous shortages in the face of rising inventories of goods for which there has been no demand. The large savings deposits represent a deferred demand that exerts a strong pressure on the government for an increase in the supply of wanted consumer goods, the shortage of which has had a depressing effect on work incentives.

Another outgrowth of the difficulties presented by the time-consuming planning process is the impossibility of formulating, in the available period of time, several alternative plans that would allow the selection of the best plan from the point of view of the use of resources. Increased reliance on computers has been advocated by some economists and planners as a means of overcoming this problem, but others have expressed doubt that computers could compensate for the basic shortcomings of physical planning. The development of optimum production and investment plans has also been precluded by a reliance on administratively set prices for all commodities, which do not adequately reflect production costs and relative scarcities, and by a general disregard for true capital costs and rent.

To ensure compliance with production and resource utilization plans, a system of material rewards and punishments geared to the level of plan fulfillment has been in effect for enterprise management. Concurrently, an incentive payments system based on government-established output norms has been used to elicit a maximum productive effort from the workers.

In addition to the control exercised through the ministries and the banking system, close supervision over enterprise performance is also maintained by the CPSU through a specialized national control organization, party cells, trade unions, and individual workers. At the same time, great importance is attached to moral incentives, which include titles, honors, and favorable publicity for high achievement.

Management of the economy has been severely hampered by differences between the interests of the state and those of enterprise managers. Motivated by a drive for maximum economic growth, the government has consistently endeavored to set production goals high enough to force managers to exploit to the utmost all available resources. Managers, operating within a system that offers them large rewards for meeting or exceeding planned targets and penalizes them for falling short of the goals by even a very small margin, have naturally sought to protect themselves by creating reserves of equipment, materials, and labor through underestimating the productive potential of their plants and overstating their resource requirements. The need for such reserves has been accentuated by chronic supply difficulties induced by shortcomings in planning.

In an attempt to eliminate this management practice and to encourage greater efficiency, a much publicized economic reform was instituted in 1965. Gradually extended throughout most of the economy, this reform introduced charges for interest and rent as means of stimulating a more economical use of capital and natural resources and changed the standard for measuring enterprise performance from volume of output to profits in order to make managers more cost-conscious. It also reduced by a very small margin the number of performance targets dictated to the enterprise by superior authorities and allowed enterprises to use a portion of their profits for the benefit of the work force and for plant improvement.

At the time of its introduction, many Western observers believed this reform to constitute a major departure from traditional Marxist economics and a first step away from rigid central economic controls. By 1970, however, it became evident that the reform did not reflect any change in economic thinking on the part of the leadership or an intent to loosen central controls. Its purpose has been merely to provide additional incentives for more efficient performance. The mechanics of the reform, however, including price adjustments to compensate for added costs and to allow for a planned margin of profit, have largely negated its effectiveness. The reform has not significantly altered the functioning of the economy.

ECONOMIC STRUCTURE

Analysis of the economy is hampered by numerous statistical deficiencies, a fact repeatedly pointed out by Soviet economists concerned with economic structure. Data have never been published either on many of the essential industrial products and armaments or on the number, size and distribution of industrial establishments. Labor force statistics are not sufficiently detailed, and very little information has been published on earnings. Statistics on national income and the value of industrial and agricultural output are limited to percentage changes of these aggregates from year to year or to annual totals without adequate breakdowns into constituent parts. Definitions are often imprecise, and comparability over a period of time is destroyed by changes in pricing.

Western observers generally believe that physical output statistics are correctly reported by the Central Statistical Administration but that some of these statistics may in fact be exaggerated through improper reporting to the statistical authorities by enterprises intent on demonstrating their fulfillment of the plan. In agriculture several conditions are believed to exist that hamper the collection of accurate data and tend to overstate to an unknown degree both the absolute level and the rate of increase in the output of some farm products.

With regard to the validity of index number series for such items as national and real personal income, industrial production, and farm output, there is widespread skepticism among Western analysts, shared in part by some Soviet economists. Statistical results vary greatly depending upon the methods of calculation used. It is generally believed that official Soviet indexes reflect statistical practices that yield the most favorable data from the point of view of demonstrating superior economic performance.

There are significant differences between Soviet and Western statistical concepts and methods. For purposes of analysis and international comparisons, a number of Western economists have therefore undertaken to translate Soviet data into Western statistical terms. Because of the difficulties presented by a lack of essential information on the definitions and methods of calculation underlying these data, significantly differing results have been obtained with regard to magnitudes of economic aggregates, such as national income, and rates of growth. There is, nevertheless, general agreement that economic growth has not been so fast as that represented by official statistics.

The Soviet concept of GNP distinguishes between productive and unproductive activities and, in contrast to Western practice, excludes most services. Gross output in the Soviet Union also differs from the Western concept, in that it consists of the sum of the gross outputs of all productive enterprises rather than only of the sum of the values added by each enterprise in the productive process. These conceptual differences account very largely for the substantial disparity between Soviet GNP data that appear in official statistics and those published by Western scholars.

In Soviet terms the various economic sectors contributed the following percentage shares to the 1967 GNP of R502 billion (1 ruble equals US$1.10): industry, 63.9; construction, 10.0; agriculture,

16.1; transport and communications, 4.2; and trade, agricultural procurement, and material-technical supply, 5.8. This distribution was not significantly different from that in 1960. An increase of 1.7 percent in the share of industry was balanced by a similar decline in trade and construction.

A markedly different economic structure emerges in terms of Western concepts, as reflected by the percentage breakdown of the GNP by sectors of origin in 1964, the latest date for which this information is available, as follows: industry, 33.9; construction, 9.2; agriculture, 25.2; transport and communications, 9.7; commerce, 5.3; and services, 16.5. In Western terms the share of industry was only about half as large, and that of agriculture half again as large as their respective shares determined in accordance with Soviet statistical practice. The most notable feature of the economy's structure is the relatively high contribution of agriculture and low contribution of services to the national product.

About one-third of the labor force at the end of the 1960's was employed in agriculture. Nonagricultural employment was distributed among the various economic sectors roughly as follows: industry, 45 percent; construction, 8 percent; transport and communications, 12 percent; trade, 9 percent; and miscellaneous services, 26 percent. Chief among these services were health and education.

Although Marxist economics lays heavy stress on a balanced growth of the economy and assigns agriculture a major role in providing for the material well-being of the population, this sector has been sacrificed to the development of industry and primarily to the production of capital goods. According to official statistics, the gross output of industry rose almost 73-fold since 1913, including a 170-fold increase in capital goods and a 24-fold increase in consumer goods, while farm output rose by less than three times. Faulty though these statistics may be, they nevertheless provide striking evidence of the leadership's overwhelming preference for heavy industry at the expense of agriculture.

Natural conditions for agriculture are relatively unfavorable in terms of the availability of good arable land and of temperature and moisture conditions. The leadership's extreme emphasis on industrial development has deprived agriculture of urgently needed inputs, with disastrous results for production. Agriculture has also been strongly discriminated against through the official price structure and has thus been forced to bear the major burden of the cost of industrialization. Living conditions of collective farmers are among the poorest in the country (see ch. 31, Agriculture).

This decades-long neglect has been responsible for chronic shortages of foods and fibers and for an inadequate protein content in the average diet. It has also necessitated continuing, substantial imports of foods and massive imports of wheat in years of poor harvests. Although official concern has repeatedly been voiced about the low estate of agriculture and the need for radical improvement, these pronouncements have not been followed by an allocation of requisite resources. Western observers have, therefore, expressed doubt that the large volume of investment and the adjustment of prices needed to compensate for past neglect and to stimulate rapid growth would be soon forthcoming.

The full extent of the inefficiency of socialized agriculture in the 1960's—induced by the form of organization, capital starvation, and lack of price incentives—is made apparent by the magnitude of the output achieved on the small private plots of collective and state farm workers. Using little more than 3 percent of the total sown land, the private sector produced about two-thirds of the potato and egg output; two-fifths of the vegetable, meat, and milk production; and one-fifth of the wool output.

Industry has been the most rapidly growing sector of the economy. Strongly favored by the country's leadership and absorbing a major share of the available resources, it has attained second place in size among the industries of the world. Natural resources for industrial development are large, but most of these are unfavorably located with regard to terrain, climatic conditions, and established population centers. Exploitation of resources east of the Ural Mountains poses substantial technical difficulties and entails high labor and transportation costs that are, however, partly offset by the better quality of these resources. More readily accessible inferior mineral deposits in the western part of the country have been widely used, necessitating expensive processing.

For historic and climatic reasons, most industrial establishments are located in the European part of the country, although a substantial industrial development has taken place in the eastern regions, particularly since the beginning of World War II. The new industrial centers are mainly suppliers of raw materials and energy and provide only a small portion of the country's manufacturing output. Industrial enterprises tend to concentrate in large urban centers, both west and east of the Ural Mountains. A continuation of this trend is anticipated by planners concerned with industrial development to 1980, because of the attraction of the relatively superior amenities in the large cities. This factor poses a serious problem for the development of rich natural resources in remote areas of the north, Siberia, and the far eastern regions. Substantial wage differentials for workers in these areas have not provided a sufficient inducement to attract the required volume of labor.

Priority in the development of industry has been consistently accorded to electric power and the production of capital goods, particularly machinebuilding and metalworking. Relative emphasis on the development of particular industrial branches shifted from time to time in response to new goals or emerging disproportions. In the 1960's accelerated growth of the crude oil, natural gas, and chemical industries was stressed at the expense of the previously favored coal and steel industries. In the opinion of Soviet economists, heavy industry suffers from an excessive emphasis on investment in primary production, that is raw materials, fuels, and power, at the expense of processing industries.

As a consequence of the preference for capital goods, their share in the total industrial output rose from 39.5 percent in 1928 to 74.4 percent in 1966, according to official statistics, and remained at that level through 1969. A study published by the Academy of Sciences of the USSR, however, maintains that this figure is exaggerated by various statistical shortcomings and that the correct relationship between the outputs of producer and consumer goods cannot be determined on the basis of available data.

Development of the light and food industries has been hampered not only by the inadequacy of capital investments but also by their poor utilization. Existing capacities for food processing are insufficient to handle the available supplies of farm products, and their growth continues to lag behind the growth of state agricultural procurements. Light industry is limited primarily to the production of textiles, clothing, knitwear, leather goods, and footwear. It accounts for about one-third of the output of consumer goods. In the late 1960's some expansion and modernization of this industry were underway, based on imported equipment. Durable consumer goods, such as refrigerators, washing machines, television sets, bicycles, and household equipment, are produced predominantly by enterprises of heavy industry, in part from waste materials. The role of heavy industry in the consumer field is scheduled to rise, as the government strives to reduce consumer demand pressures by increasing the supply of industrial goods, in the absence of adequate supplies of foodstuffs and of agricultural raw materials for light industry.

The country's foreign trade is small by comparison with the trade of other major industrial states and absorbs less than 3 percent of the agricultural and industrial output. This is an outgrowth of an official policy of maximum self-sufficiency, which was pursued over several decades and began to be relaxed only in the mid-1950's. Subject to a state monopoly, foreign trade not only serves the purpose of acquiring essential goods in short supply domestically, including technologically advanced equipment and processes, but also is used as a means to bind more closely the Communist countries of Eastern Europe and to penetrate the former colonial, less developed areas of the world. In the latter context the Soviet Union has conducted a major economic and military foreign aid program, an important purpose of which has been to develop a group of client states along its borders (see ch. 35, Foreign Economic Relations). The impact of this program on the domestic economy cannot be adequately assessed, but foreign observers have no doubt that it constitutes a drain on the country's limited resources.

ECONOMIC PERFORMANCE

Economic progress from the end of World War II until the late 1950's was satisfactory from the point of view of the leadership intent on closing the gap between the Soviet economy and the economies of the most advanced Western industrial states. During that period the Soviet Union led all other countries in economic growth, with the possible exception of the Federal Republic of Germany (West Germany). After 1958, however, economic performance deteriorated and failed to recover by 1970. In Soviet statistical terms the growth of the national income declined from an average annual rate of 10.9 percent in the 1951—58 period to 7.1 percent from 1959 to 1969. The comparable decline for industrial production was from 12 to 8.6 percent and for farm output from 5.9 to 2.3 percent. In 1970 the planned rates of increase were only 6 percent for national income and 6.3 percent for industrial production, the lowest rate of peacetime industrial growth since 1928.

Since the early 1960's the CPSU and government leaders have repeatedly expressed grave concern over the slow progress of the economy, which they have attributed to a widespread waste of resources through inefficiencies caused by ineffective enterprise management and poor labor discipline. Corrective action, however, has been limited to the economic reform of 1965, which had not been entirely completed in 1970, and to a directive issued early in 1970 for the imposition of more severe penalties for infractions of labor discipline. The reform has not sufficed to reverse the unfavorable trend of economic progress, which has reflected a decline in the growth of employment and productivity, a lowering of the returns from capital investment, and a lag in the introduction and assimilation of technological innovation. Although a single-minded concentration on power-building aspects of economic development succeeded in raising the Soviet Union to a second-ranking world power, this achievement has been attained at the cost of creating an imbalance in the economic structure and of neglecting vital interests of the consumer.

By 1970 a progressive tightening of the labor supply produced labor shortages in the major industrial centers. Although nearly one-third of the total labor force was still engaged in agriculture, continued transfer of farmworkers to industry on the scale of earlier years was not considered feasible by Soviet planners without endangering agricultural output, because of the low productivity of farm labor and the inadequate rate of increase in farm mechanization. Neither was it considered possible to recruit significant numbers of additional workers from among members of households without gainful occupations, because nearly the entire able-bodied population of working age other than students was already employed. Further pressure on the labor supply for industry and the rest of the economy in future years was anticipated because of a declining rate of the natural population increase and a growing demand for labor in various social fields and in trade.

At the same time, larger increases in capital investment appeared to be precluded by continued heavy expenditures for military and space programs and by growing pressures for a long-delayed rise in the populations's standard of living, particularly in the areas of food and housing. A much stronger emphasis was therefore placed by the CPSU and government leadership on the need for greater productivity in all spheres of economic activity to maintain a satisfactory rate of economic growth. In the view of Western observers such an improvement in economic performance, which they believe to be contingent primarily on a reallocation of national priorities and a better management of technological progress, may be difficult to attain. They base their view on what they consider an evident reluctance on the part of the country's leaders to make a fundamental change in the existing economic pattern and on the demonstrated decline in the efficiency with which the economy used investment and other resources during the 1960's.

Economic growth in the Soviet Union has been sustained primarily by heavy inputs of labor and capital and, to a lesser degree, by a rise in productive efficiency. During the 1950's the demographic situation was favorable for a rapid increase in employment, and the civilian labor force was further augmented by partial postwar demobilization. After 1958 the growth of the labor force was adversely affected by the consequences of the low birth rates during the World War II and early postwar years. It became necessary to draw more heavily upon farm labor and the nonworking population of working age—housewives and students—and to release additional military manpower to supply the need for nonagricultural employment. The ratio of the gainfully employed to total population, which had already been considerably higher than the ratio in other major industrial states, was further increased. This high participation rate accounts for the unusually large share of women in total employment—50 percent or more— and, particularly, in agriculture, industry, construction, and transportation (see ch. 32, The Labor Force).

Despite these measures, the growth of the employed labor force

111

declined in the 1960's. The manpower shortage was accentuated by a reduction in the length of the workweek in industry from an average of 48 hours in 1957 to 41 hours in 1961. Although there were some small compensating gains in hourly productivity, these were not sufficient to offset the loss of man-hours worked. It has been suggested by a Western observer that the reduction in working hours at a time of a rising labor shortage may have been granted to workers as a substitute for additional consumer goods, the supply of which could not be increased under the then existing resource allocation priorities.

The decline in the growth of employment was accompanied by a sharp reduction in the rate of growth of labor productivity. In the 1960's, according to official statistics, the average annual rate on a man-year basis was about one-third lower in industry and 40 percent lower in construction compared with the previous decade. To some extent, this unfavorable development was probably brought about by the resort to marginal labor in terms of education and work experience. More important factors, however, were the progressive obsolescence and deterioration of a large portion of the existing capital stock of plants and equipment and a decline in the growth of new investment from an officially reported annual average of 13.5 percent in the 1950's to only 7.4 percent in the 1960's. In agriculture new investment failed to bring about a significant rise in productivity, partly because a portion of the investment merely replaced workers leaving the farms and also because work incentives for collective farmers were inadequate.

Over the years the Soviet Union has consistently devoted as much as one-third of its GNP to investment. Its ability to do so has been based on its power to control consumption and to siphon huge funds into the budget through a turnover (excise) tax (see Glossary) levied primarily on consumer goods. Since the introduction of the economic reform, a growing portion of the margin between the retail price and the cost of production has been collected by the state in the form of a tax on enterprise profits, but the turnover tax in 1969 still amounted to about 30 percent of the retail price (see ch. 36, Fiscal and Monetary System).

About 35 to 40 percent of the total investment has been channeled into industry. From 86 to 88 percent of the industrial investment has been regularly devoted to the branches producing capital goods, and the balance of only 12 to 14 percent—equivalent to less than 5 percent of total investment—to the branches manufacturing consumer goods. These shares have not varied significantly, despite periodic government promises of greater attention to consumer needs.

The share of agriculture in total investment rose slightly, from an average of 15 percent in the 1950's to between 17 and 18 percent after 1963. The amount invested in agriculture has been generally considered far below the needs for lifting this important sector out of its prolonged stagnation. Since agriculture is a major source of consumer goods and of raw materials for the consumer industries, its depressed condition has been an important contributing factor responsible for the unsatisfactory performance of these industries and for the relatively low consumption levels of the population.

Despite the serious, chronic shortage of housing, investment in housing construction declined from almost 22 percent of the total in the 1950's to only 16 to 17 percent from 1964 to 1967. In each of the four years 1961 to 1964, the absolute amount of investment was successively reduced below the level of the previous year. The housing shortage has hampered the movement of labor into major industrial centers, particularly in the developing eastern regions.

As in the case of employment, the decline in the rate of capital investment in the 1960's was paralleled by an unfavorable trend in the so-called capital output ratio, that is, the amount of new investment needed to produce an additional unit of output. According to Western estimates, the productivity of new capital investment declined by more than one-third after 1958.

Several reasons have been adduced for this phenomenon. A crash program for the development of new industries, such as oil, natural gas, and chemicals, and a rapid expansion of machine building entailed the suspension of many ongoing construction projects in traditional industries. At the same time, a lack of experience with the technologies of the new industries led to longer than usual delays in the completion of construction and the attainment of full-scale operation. This situation inevitable resulted in the immobilization of a substantial volume of capital.

Capital construction has traditionally been associated with a great waste of resources. Since capital could be obtained from the budget free of charge and since planners had no sound economic criteria for evaluating the relative merits of investment proposals, in the absence of a rational price system and given the prevalent Marxist disregard for economic rent, the volume of construction projects undertaken each year far surpassed the resources needed to complete them. The introduction of charges for interest and rent under the economic reform of 1965 has had no remedial effect, as evidenced by high-level CPSU criticism of conditions in the construction field in January 1970.

Individual construction projects outside the highest priority areas have dragged on for years, tying up large sums in unfinished buildings and in equipment awaiting installation. Construction difficulties have mounted with the growing complexity of modern industrial plants. One of numerous examples involves the construction of a papermill begun in 1964 and not yet completed in 1970, with two 228,000-ton annual capacity papermaking machines waiting at the site in their original crates. Completion of a large automobile plant being built with Italian aid is also far behind schedule. In an attempt to deal with the perennial construction problem, a number of administrative and operational changes were introduced in the building industry, effective January 1970. Simultaneously, the method of evaluating construction performance and the system of incentive payments in the construction industry were modified in line with the principles of the economic reform.

Another reason for the lowering of capital productivity has been the rising portion of the gross new investment used to compensate for the depreciation of existing facilities and the depletion of natural resources. This element has become increasingly important with the advancing age of the industrial plants and mines and a greater concern of the government with obsolescence. It has been further complicated by the fact that much of the equipment being produced is of poor quality and, therefore, short lived and that many obsolete kinds of machinery continue to be produced by enterprises that find it unprofitable to introduce technological improvements under the existing price system (see ch. 30, Industry). The poor quality of the equipment is reflected in an annual repair bill estimated by Soviet technicians at R10 billion. Soviet economists also estimated that from 40 to 60 percent of new investment in mining in the mid-1960's was needed to maintain production capacities at existing levels.

The productivity of capital has also been adversely affected by a general failure to translate scientific research findings into improved technological processes and by long delays in assimilating new technologies, including advanced developments imported from Western industrial nations in the form of machinery and complete industrial installations. Although Soviet scientific capabilities and achievements are of a high order, emphasis is being placed on research rather than development, and scientific research institutes are effectively separated from industrial design bureaus. The best talent and facilities are devoted to military and space research, so that industry must do with the second best. Major impediments to innovation are also inherent in the enterprise performance evaluation system, which penalizes management for the inevitable temporary production slowdown attendant upon the introduction of new technology and in the industrial price system under which technological and quality improvements entail a loss in profits (see ch. 18, Science and Technology; ch. 30, Industry).

Although the industrialization program had transformed the Soviet Union from a primarily agricultural country in the 1920's into an industrial power second only to the United States by 1970, the country's leaders found the rate of progress disappointing.

Some of the reasons for this disappointment become evident from a comparison of the industrial production targets projected for 1970 in the Five-Year Plan for 1966—70 with the annual economic plan targets for the same year announced in December 1969 (see table 1). Except for boots and shoes, the planned output of which surpasses the original goal, and for crude oil production, which is planned at the average of the projected five-year plan output range, all targets of the annual plan are below and, in some instances substantially below, the five-year plan goals. In 1970 the largest discrepancy appeared in the case of passenger cars, the scheduled output of which was less than half the original target. Production plans for other items for which comparable data are available were reduced by from 8 to 33 percent. Construction of housing through 1970 was expected to fall short of the five-year plan goal by 110 million square meters, or 17 percent, assuming that the 1970 construction target is attained. Similarly unsatisfactory performance has been the rule since 1959.

Official data on the output of major farm products during the 1966—69 period show agricultural performance to have been in line with the targets of the five-year plan, except for small shortfalls in the production of grain and potatoes. Nevertheless, a renewed decline in the numbers of livestock on the farms and concomitant shortages of livestock products in the country, particularly in the larger cities, were officially reported in 1969 and 1970. These food shortages were also noted by foreign correspondents of major Western newspapers.

The persistence of food shortages in the face of the agricultural plan fulfillment is a consequence of the stagnation of agricultural development since the forcible collectivization of the farms in the early 1920's. In 1956 the number of cattle on farms was the same as on the eve of the revolution forty years earlier, and the number of cows was 1 million less, whereas the population in the meantime had increased by 50 percent. The somewhat better situation in regard to hogs and sheep and the faster growth of the livestock population relative to the human population since 1956 have not sufficed to correct the imbalance appreciably.

In presenting his report on the annual economic plan for 1970 to the USSR Supreme Soviet, the chairman of the USSR State Planning Committee made it clear that, despite the production increases achieved since 1965 and planned for 1970, a variety of foods and consumer goods would remain in short supply.

Data on per capita consumption of foods in 1968, published in the official organ of the USSR State Planning Committee, show a substantial improvement in the average diet since 1960 through a reduced consumption of bread products and potatoes and an increase in the intake of protective foods. Yet, in relation to an

Table 1. *Soviet Union Industrial Production Plans, 1966–70 and 1970*

Product	Unit of measure	Five-year plan (1966–70)	Annual plan (1970)
Electric power	million kilowatt-hours	830–850	740
Crude oil	million metric tons	345–355	350
Natural gas	billion cubic meters	225–240	196
Coal	million metric tons	665–675	618
Steel	do	124–129	115
Rolled steel	do	95–99	80
Steel pipes	do	14–15	12
Fertilizers	do	62–65	58
Plastics	thousand metric tons	2,100–2,300	1,640
Synthetic fibers	do	780–830	696
Paper	do	5,000–5,300	4,130
Cement	million metric tons	100–105	94
Motor vehicles	thousand units	1,360–1,510	922
Trucks	do	600–650	522
Passenger cars	do	700–800	348
Tractors	do	600–625	456
Textiles	million square meters	9,500–9,800	8,900
Knitwear	million units	1,650–1,750	1,235
Boots and shoes	million pairs	610–630	675

Source: Adapted from *23d Congress of the Communist Party of the Soviet Union*, Moscow, n.d., p. 334; and *Pravda*, December 17, 1969, p. 2.

optimum diet for good health worked out by Soviet scientists, per capita consumption in 1968 was normal for sugar and excessive for bread products and potatoes by 24 and 36 percent, respectively. The intake levels of protective foods relative to the optimum standard ranged as follows: eggs, 49 percent; vegetables, 54 percent; meat, 59 percent; dairy products, 66 percent; fish, 79 percent; and vegetable oils, 89 percent.

The same study also reported textile consumption, excluding industrial uses, to have averaged 83 percent of the optimum norm. The available per capita housing space in 1969 was officially reported as 10.9 square meters. The availability of durable consumer goods per 100 families in 1970 was planned to be as follows: radios and wired sets, 71; television sets, 56; washing machines, 52; and refrigerators, 32. These figures are presumably based on past production and sales figures and would thus include equipment that is in need of repair and for which repairs are difficult or impossible to obtain.

CHAPTER 7

THE STATE SECURITY SYSTEM

The Committee for State Security (Komitet Gosudarstvennoy Bezopasnosti—KGB) had the responsibility on the eve of 1970 for the great majority of functions intended to guarantee the security of the state. These functions consisted mainly of border control and operation of the police apparatus that performed security activities outside the country as well as tasks inside the Soviet Union that were related to resident aliens or foreign nationals. Outside the Soviet Union some clandestine or intelligence collection work was done by the armed forces, the foreign service, the Communist Party of the Soviet Union (CPSU), and international Communist organizations. The work of these other organizations was, however, minor by comparison with that of the KGB. Not only did they operate on a smaller scale, but the KGB had personnel in all of them and may, in fact, have controlled their efforts or, in some cases, performed its own work from within their organizations.

In addition, KGB activities encompassed wide areas beyond those that could be regarded as within the province of security of the state externally, as opposed to internal security. It was, however, the organization at ministry level in the Soviet government that was charged with protection of the Soviet Union from external actions short of war that might weaken or endanger the country and with taking measures short of war that would enhance the position of the Soviet Union in relation to its enemies or potential enemies.

The various security functions have been arbitrarily shifted within the governmental structure during the period of Soviet history, and no single organ within the Soviet government has had responsibility for any sizable portion of the overall operation, such as KGB had in the 1960's, for more than a few years at a time. Changes in the allocation of responsibilities have reflected the ascendancy of individuals, efforts to keep the mission and organization of the police forces from being well understood by outsiders, or merely the results of periodic governmental reorganizations.

Even when the organizational structure has been established to provide separate state and internal security agencies, at various times one agency has assumed predominance over the other and has appropriated most or all of the major security responsibilities. A commissariat or ministry of state security did not exist until 1941.

Before that time its functions were accomplished within the internal security agencies and, until 1934, without recognition in the major organizational structure. Since 1941, on two different occasions the nominally coequal state security agency either has been abolished or the major portion of its activities taken over by the older internal security organization.

On the other hand, although on the eve of 1970 the KGB had preeminence over the existing internal security apparatus, it did not have the wide ranging responsibilities its predecessor, the Ministry of State Security, had enjoyed during the 1949—53 period. During that time the Ministry of Internal Affairs was relegated to being little more than an economic advisory agency with almost no control over, or association with, security work (see ch. 8, The Internal Security System).

The earliest Soviet security organ, established within a month of the Revolution, was dedicated to fighting counterrevolution, sabotage, and espionage. The national objectives of the new Bolshevik state, however, included the spread of communism and the "liberation" of the world's working classes, thus demanding more extensive efforts from the security police. In addition, the Soviet government did not hide its intention of undermining governments and economic systems in the non-Communist world. The efforts to control the world Communist movement also contributed to the extensive security activities abroad.

In the period after Stalin's death in 1953, security forces moderated their practices within the Soviet Union and, owing partially to the polycentrism of the Communist movement, the efforts abroad were carried on in relatively muted fashion. This resulted in conjecture that the work of the various security agencies had been curtailed. Information as to whether or not the costs of the programs and the numbers of people involved had been reduced was not available at the end of 1969, and statements concerning reduced activities abroad remained speculative.

HISTORICAL BACKGROUND

The Special Commission for the Fight Against Counterrevolution was established on December 4, 1917, less than four weeks after the Bolshevik Revolution. On December 20, 1917, it became the All-Russian Extraordinary Commission to Fight Counterrevolution, Sabotage, and Speculation, but this long title was usually shortened to the Extraordinary Commission (Chrezvychaynaya Kommisiya) or Cheka. Lenin had stated that the use of terror might be essential at certain times, under certain conditions, and the Cheka was his instrument of terror. This was the first in a series of security agencies that made terror a fact of life in the Soviet Union and kept it so until the death of Stalin in 1953.

The prerogatives of the security agencies and of individual agents were curtailed in 1953, but the apparatus was not destroyed; the Soviet system of government does not provide safeguards against abuses of power such as occurred between 1917 and 1953. Despite the absence of safeguards, however, observers of the post-Stalin scene generally reported that the attitudes of the Soviet people had changed noticeably when compared to those of the fear-ridden days of the Stalin era.

The Cheka was established by a decision of the Council of People's Commissars, but the council could not agree to the preparation of a formal decree, and no legislative authority existed for it until 1924, two years after it had been abolished. It had its forerunners in secret police institutions dating from Ivan the Terrible's sixteenth century private Oprichnina to the tsarist political secret police organization, the Okhrana, that operated between 1881 and the October Revolution in 1917. Construing that its mission against "counterrevolutionaries, spies, saboteurs, burglars, speculators, and other parasites" required measures that included "summary execution on the spot," the Cheka became the subject of increasing criticism both from abroad and within the Soviet Union and was abolished on February 6, 1922.

Lenin had originally believed that world revolution would occur almost spontaneously in the chaos that existed after World War I and, if properly stimulated, would spread in a chain reaction. Although nothing of the proportions he had anticipated developed, the external security efforts instituted then were carried on in the conviction that conditions would become ripe for revolution at another time. Continuing effort was necessary not only to speed up the process but to keep its control within the Moscow organization.

From the outset and continuing through 1969, state security activities have been directed toward Soviet citizens and emigres abroad, resident aliens and foreigners in the Soviet Union, penetration of foreign governments and national economies, or any activities that might further the cause of socialism and the national ambitions of the Soviet Union. Efforts before World War II emphasized agitation and subversion to an unprecedented degree and became systematic attempts to subvert and sabotage the societies and institutions of the countries whose hospitality Soviet diplomats and security personnel enjoyed. Embassy and consular staffs were expanded with agents whose military ranks and diplomatic status were purely honorary.

In an ostensible effort to make the police apparatus accountable to judicial machinery, the State Political Administration (Gosudarstvennoye Politicheskoye Upravleniye—GPU), which succeeded the Cheka, was placed under the People's Commissariat of Internal Affairs (Narodnyy Komisariat Vnutrennikh Del—NKVD). With the formation of the Union of Soviet Socialist Republics in 1923, the GPU was removed from subordination to the NKVD, became a separate people's commissariat, and was renamed the Unified State Political Administration (Ob'edinyonnoye Gosudarstvennoye Politicheskoye Upravleniye—OGPU). These changes had more apparent than real significance, since Felix Dzerzhinsky, who had founded and headed the Cheka, was also head of the NKVD, the GPU, and the OGPU. As such, until his death in 1926, he headed both the police apparatus and the ministry-level agency of the government that controlled it.

Irrespective of their subordination, from the October Revolution until 1953, during the Lenin and Stalin regimes, the internal and state security organizations were personal instruments of the dictator, and legal limitations were exercised or not exercised as he chose. Full development of both the police and internal and state security forces as well as of their operations and controls was reached during the OGPU's eleven years. It remained a separate commissariat until 1934, when it was absorbed within the NKVD.

State security remained under the People's Commissariat for Internal Affairs during the GPU, OGPU, and NKVD periods between 1922 and World War II, although it was recognized as a separate functional area and became a chief administration of the NKVD in 1934. During the period between the wars the security police grew tremendously in numerical strength and became a bureaucratic empire. Although there were occasional efforts to apply legal limitations to the exercise of its authority, it not only permeated the personal affairs of Soviet citizens, but its capabilities for collecting information and applying influence abroad steadily increased.

The People's Commissariat for State Security (Narodnyy Komisariat Gosudarstvennoy Bezopasnosti—NKGB) was created in 1941, and state security was for the first time divorced from the NKVD. With the German attack on the Soviet Union in June 1941, the old organization was temporarily reinstated, but the separation was again made in 1943. During World War II, in deference to its new allies, the Soviet Union abandoned its most provocative international activities, and most Communist agencies abroad became active in a campaign to elicit aid for the Soviet Union.

After the war the reservoir of good will that had been built up gave the Russians an opportunity to recommence their prewar activities. The wartime military alliance with the Allies had provided opportunities to infiltrate intelligence organizations, diplomatic services, foreign offices, and many industrial enterprises. The flow of refugees to the West was a source of embarrassment to the Soviet leadership but provided a vehicle useful for planting agents. Communist Party organizations had been allowed to flourish. Free travel, free speech and press, lenient regulations, and respect for the rights of an accused made the task easier in most of the countries of interest to the Soviet Union. A vast amount of sympathy for the people of the Soviet Union and sincere hopes that international cooperation would promote understanding and would result in mutual efforts to preserve the peace also worked to Soviet advantage.

Other factors worked to Soviet disadvantage. The Great Purge of 1936—39 had eliminated much of the senior leadership in the security organizations. During World War II, Communist organizations had been destroyed by the occupying German forces. This loss was still noticeable for several years after World War II. Postwar refugees supplied the West with valuable information on security techniques and, occasionally, on personalities in the system.

The term *Chekist* was coined to designate members of the first Soviet security police and, half a century later, remained in common usage despite the fact that the Cheka had been renamed in the early 1920's. In December 1967, during the fiftieth anniversary celebrations of the founding of the Cheka, various high security officials proudly referred to themselves as Chekists in speeches and articles. Party and government officials also praised the dedication of their Chekists.

Soviet conquests and repressive acts disenchanted all but the most staunch admirers of the Soviet system. Eastern Europe's recovery was slow, and the comparison between it and the reemerging Western countries was damaging to the Soviet image. Finally, Western security agencies had improved during the war and, when alerted to the fact that the Soviet Union did not want complete and open cooperation with its former allies, were better able to deal with new problems as they developed.

Shortly after World War II, in 1946, when the people's commissariats in the Soviet government were redesignated ministries, the People's Commissariat of Internal Security became the Ministry of Internal Affairs (Ministerstvo Vnutrennikh Del—MVD), and the People's Commissariat for State Security became the Ministry of State Security (Ministerstvo Gosudarstvennoy Bezopasnosti—MGB). (The NKVD and NKGB became the MVD and MGB.) Emphasis in the work of the state security agencies since the war has been on the collection of military intelligence; agitation against the North Atlantic Treaty Organization (NATO) and Western military installations in countries bordering on the Soviet Union; and activity in situations that could encourage internal dissatisfaction, minority problems, and social unrest in the non-Communist world.

Organizationally there were further name changes but, more importantly, there were widely fluctuating delineations of functions. Beginning about 1949, the MGB rapidly expanded its interests almost entirely at the expense of the MVD. In addition to state security, it took over all of MVD's internal, railway, and convoy troops; the local militia; control of the internal passport system; and even such basic administrative functions as the recording of births, deaths, and marriages (see ch. 8, The Internal Security System).

The MGB remained dominant until about 1953. In the power struggle that followed Stalin's death in early 1953, Lavrenti P. Beria used the MVD as the base from which he made his bid for power. As a result the MVD absorbed the MGB and for a short time again became the only agency exercising internal and state security functions. After Beria's execution, the state security organization re-emerged in March 1954 as the Committee for State Security (KGB) and rapidly regained its pre-1953 position relative to the MVD. The MVD was gradually reduced in status until, in 1960, it was decentralized to the point that the USSR MVD was abolished, and all of its functions were delegated to the union republic governments. From 1962 to 1968 the MVDs were renamed Ministries for the Preservation of Public Order.

POSITION IN THE GOVERNMENT

The KGB is a state committee, which is a ministry equivalent, under the Council of Ministers of the USSR. The chairman of the KGB is one of the core members of the Council of Ministers who form an elite and powerful group within that body. Since its establishment in 1954 the KGB was headed by Ivan A. Serov for four years, by Alexander N. Shelepin for three, Vladimir Y. Semichastny for six, and in 1969 by Yuri V. Andropov who took over in May of 1967. Serov rose to his position through work in the security apparatus. Those since 1958 have been Party functionaries; all four have been members of the Central Committee of the CPSU. Not since the death of Beria had the head of the security police concurrently occupied a seat on the Politburo. In 1967, however, Yuri Andropov was made chairman of the KGB and shortly thereafter was appointed a candidate member of the Politburo.

Whereas others who have headed the security agencies—Dzerzhinsky and Beria for examples—have been influential Party and government figures, the more recent leadership appeared not to have attained sufficient individual stature to have used the police apparatus as a personal vehicle from which it could challenge Party leadership. The governing board, or collegium, of the KGB consists

124

of a group of Communist Party members, some of whom have Chekist backgrounds and others who have only Party experience.

THE BORDER TROOPS

Border Controls

The perimeter of the Soviet Union is about 37,000 miles long. Much of it presents formidable natural barriers to penetration, particularly in the Arctic north and along the great mountain ranges of central Asia. The portion in Europe and much that separates the Soviet Union and Communist China, however, have few naturally separating features. The Border Troops, who are responsible for protecting the frontiers, date back to 1918, when they were known as the Border Chekas. The earliest known decree pertaining to them was enacted in 1922 and charges them to "assure the political security of the frontiers of the USSR." They have been subordinate since then to the GPU, OGPU, NKVD, MVD, MGB and, in 1957, came under the KGB.

Strictest controls are maintained on the borders with the European countries, Turkey, and on the Black Sea coast. Controls have been tightened adjacent to China with the deterioration of Sino-Soviet relations since about 1960. The elaborate barriers facing the West contrast markedly with the largely unmarked borders with Iran and Afghanistan. In the latter areas the inhabitants on both sides do not communicate or cooperate with the guards and cross the borders freely with grazing animals and on daily errands. Having decided years ago that the movements were harmless, the border forces ignore them.

The frontier zone is of unspecified depth, varying with the topography and sensitivity of relations with the neighboring nation. Admittance into this area is restricted and controlled by local militia (ordinary police). Within the zone Border Troops and local militia share authority. There are additional and stricter controls in the narrower frontier strip. Border troops have complete control within the strip, although there are militia in border towns, ports, and other cities near the seacoasts and borders.

The frontier strip is up to 1½ miles wide and, along the borders where crossings are prohibited, contains special barriers. Inside the border fence there is a strip that is kept freshly plowed or on which the snow is not disturbed so that footprints would be readily noticeable. Inside this there is another strip that may be patrolled by guards, sometimes with dogs. It may be kept floodlighted, equipped with warning signals, rows of barbed wire, traps, automatically firing weapons, or landmines. Observation posts may be visible or concealed.

125

Forces and Missions

The Border Troops are charged with repelling incursions into Soviet territory and protecting the population and property in frontier zones. They control entry and exit of people, currency, literature, and goods. Within the frontier zones they control the movement of the Soviet population, including resettlement of people from other areas of the Soviet Union. They maintain frontier markings and barriers. Along the land frontier, they are responsible for collecting information from a zone extending thirty miles from the border, on either side of it. In addition to illegal traffic, they are concerned with topographical information, border defenses or military installations of the neighboring country, assessment of existing or potentially dangerous conditions, and anything that might relate to border friction or possible incidents. This work involves establishing clandestine agents among the population on both sides of the border.

Along the coastlines in less populated areas, the border forces are responsible for a twelve-mile strip inland. The Soviet Union also claims twelve miles of coastal waters.

The majority of Border Troops are ground forces, referred to as the Land Border Troops. There are smaller Aviation Border Regiments and units of Maritime Border Troops. Little is known about the aviation and maritime units. Aircraft are presumably used in border patrol and possibly for photographic reconnaissance. The maritime forces perform coast guard functions—regulating shipping, assisting in coastal navigation, controlling fishing, preventing smuggling, and patrolling. Ships that do not comply with regulations or permit inspection within Soviet waters may be pursued on the high seas until they enter the coastal waters of another country.

Border units are prepared to execute a broad range of contingency plans, from action to be taken on such things as brush fires or customs violations, to major natural disasters, border incursions, or the outbreak of war. Troops can act individually against violators, can enforce quarantines in case of an epidemic disease, or can assemble large military formations to operate as army units in a major incident or during wartime. Border Troops performed a major role in the mass deportations of suspected ethnic groups during World War II.

In a wartime situation if the particular border area was in a quiet sector, border units would relieve the services from deployment of regular forces. In an active sector if Soviet forces advanced beyond the border, Border Troops would remain at the old demarcation line. If Soviet forces were forced to withdraw, the Border Troops would remain in the rear areas, maintaining order and controlling the movements of the population behind the lines.

In the normal peacetime situation the border units seek a considerable amount of cooperation from the local population. Local authorities are required to cooperate, and the civil population is urged to participate in people's squads, support brigades, and other Party and Komsomol (Young Communist League) groups that support the border forces. Some groups serve as active informer units and are valuable because they are more likely to notice unusual conditions or strange people than are the troops that are on duty in an unfamiliar area for relatively short periods. Other groups train to assist in the event of an emergency. Border unit commanders make an effort to foster good relations with the local population. They assist in harvests, local construction projects, transportation services, and in local emergency situations.

Personnel, Training, and Operations

Troops are taken from the group called annually for compulsory military service. Since the Border Troops are required to perform alone or in small groups and must use judgment in the review of passports, identification papers, and credentials, they are generally a more carefully selected and better educated group than the average recruit for the regular services. Men with skills required by the border units are furnished by the conscript selection teams. An attempt is made to keep troops from duty in their home areas and, to simplify the selection process, it has become practice to take the quotas from interior districts.

Early training is similar to that in the army. If a conscript has had premilitary training he gets two to four months of basic training with his unit. Special training is given in regulations, forms, passes, and the various documents pertaining to border transit. Extra emphasis is also placed on preparation for the problems that are likely to be encountered when men work in remote areas in small units that must be more than ordinarily self-sufficient. This training includes medical and veterinary instruction on the treatment of the most prevalent diseases, disease control, care of frostbite, quarantine, personal hygiene, radioactivity decontamination, as well as care and maintenance of equipment and mapreading. Special schools provide short courses in cooking, baking, tailoring, shoe repairing, vehicle operating, dog handling, and technical subjects.

A typical monthly program in a duty unit may include sixty-four hours of training. Political instruction accounts for nearly a third of the total. Border, tactical, and small arms training are given the next larger time blocks. Smaller periods are devoted to regulations, drill, health, mapreading, decontamination, animal care, and physical training.

Border service includes the most stringent of duty regimes, but these are at least partially compensated for in food, uniforms, and pay. The men receive the best food ration available to the military services. It is supplemented by a tobacco issue and occasional special distributions. Units in areas where the climate permits grow vegetables, melons, and fruit. Uniforms are good and are adapted for local weather conditions. Pay exceeds that in the regular services. There is a special effort to keep men in one unit for a complete tour of duty. It enables the man to acquire the maximum familiarity with the area and its people. It also permits his superiors to assess his character and reliability and serves to improve unit morale and discipline. Leave accrues at two days per month; but except in cases of serious family difficulties, illness of the soldier, or required assistance in a disaster situation, long absences are not permitted. If a man catches an important violator, or otherwise distinguishes himself, he may be allowed a special leave.

The daily schedule provides for three hours' training and allows time for housekeeping duties, attention to personal details, plus a certain amount of leisure. Units are frequently below authorized personnel strength, however, and when an emergency arises or a unit is cooperating in harvest or other community assistance, duty hours can reach sixteen per day. Training is canceled at this time. It is curtailed after thirteen hours so that the total duty time never exceeds sixteen hours except in an extreme emergency. The frontier is guarded twenty-four hours a day, every day of the year, so night, holiday, and bad weather duty go on regularly.

The military elements of the border forces man the guard posts and patrols and construct and maintain the barriers, lights, and physical characteristics of the frontier strip. They enforce border regulations and conduct checks, raids, and searches. They form and train civilian support groups that assist in overt activities in emergency situations. Security elements engage in clandestine work and recruit and train information collecting groups from both the civilian population and military personnel. Such groups operate on both sides of the border, gathering information on movements of people and goods, smuggling, or other illegal traffic. It is this element also that collects intelligence from the other side of the border.

Officers and Noncommissioned Officers

Noncommissioned officers are usually selected from those who appear most promising during basic training. They receive up to ten months of additional training and are then required to serve an additional year of mandatory duty.

Officers are ordinarily the products of the regular military cadet academies and officers' candidate schools. These officers have twenty-five-year service obligations. They may serve entirely within the Border Troops, or they may rotate into and out of these assignments at any point in their careers, most frequently after a course at one of the advanced military academies. The Frunze Military Academy, which is a command and staff college equivalent, offers a special one-year extension for Border Troops at the end of its three-year midcareer course. To be eligible for one of the longer midcareer courses from a border troop assignment, officers must have had five years as a unit commander or five years of security work.

The Higher Border Officers School is operated within the Border Troop organization, offering a variety of courses, most of which are tactical and are specialized in favor of the immediate requirements of the border forces. Officers may also be selected to attend any of the many special courses in the other military academies, in a range of subjects to include military law, ordnance, or tactical subjects such as tank warfare techniques.

Rank designations since World War II have been the same as in the Soviet Army. The state security titles, which ranged from sergeant of state security to commissar general of state security and which were the equivalent of army ranks between lieutenant and marshal of the Soviet Union, are no longer in use.

With proper career progression an officer is promoted from junior lieutenant to colonel in seventeen years. Failing promotion, he would ordinarily serve until he became overage in grade. In normal practice promotion has been considerably slower than the pace set as the norm, and usually those who fail to be promoted have remained on duty until the normal retirement age of fifty-five years. Aside from failing to measure up as an individual, the officer suffers from any evidence of poor performance in his unit. A violation of the frontier in his area, misconduct among any of his men, an unsatisfactory condition revealed in an inspection of his unit, or any other such occurrence would be sufficient reason to withhold promotion.

Awards and decorations are given for outstanding accomplishment or good and honorable routine service. Decorations include the Badge of the Honorable Chekist and Distinguished Service in Guarding the State Frontier. Ten years in border service is recognized by the Combat Services award; fifteen years by the Order of Lenin. Amenities include privileges to purchase scarce merchandise and luxury items, low rents, low cost resort holidays, and freedom from arrest except within their own organization.

STATE SECURITY ORGANIZATION AND OPERATIONS SINCE WORLD WAR II

The detailed organization of the KGB was not completely clear at the end of 1969. Since World War II nearly all of the major branches of the state security agencies either have changed titles, changed subordination within organizations or been shifted to different ministries. Administrative reorganizations have created new functional sections; others have been eliminated or grouped together into newly named sections. Available information about the changes made since World War II provides insight into the functions and operating techniques of the apparatus as it existed in 1969.

The Ministry of Internal Affairs

During the period immediately after Stalin's death, after the MGB had been absorbed into the MVD and before the newly created KGB had acquired the power and functions it was to assume during the next few years, the MVD's Moscow headquarters organization consisted of two major directorates, which were subdivided into about a dozen divisions each. The First Directorate included the Foreign, Operative, Secret, Information, Economic, Communications, Photographic, Coding, and Financial divisions, almost all of which dealt primarily with operations abroad.

The Foreign Division had the earliest antecedents, many of its functions having been carried on with little variation since Cheka days. It organized and directed the work of the other divisions which, in planning and programming, were subordinate to it. It controlled the assignment of personnel, directing the assignment of agents to the more important embassies, consulates, trade delegations, and other such posts. It was responsible for the organization of agent networks and for taking the necessary measures after exposures of individuals or activities.

The Secret Division provided identities for agents abroad. It collected passports, documents, identification cards, uniforms, badges and emblems, and anything that could be used or copied. It provided the agent with a total identity and the means to move as required.

The Information Division collected a quantity of general information from foreign news media. The division's goal was to glean all possible information on the attitude, opinions, and mood of the people as a group and of select individuals who might figure in news events or might be exploitable. The division had a reputation for concern with minutia such as gossip and rumors as well as social, cultural, political, and economic details.

The functions of the other divisions corresponded generally with their titles. In addition to supplying routine communications, the Communications Division could provide special transportation in unusual circumstances. The Economic Division cooperated closely

130

with the economic ministries in the Soviet government, joining their delegations abroad, as well as studying economic conditions in foreign countries.

The Second Directorate engaged in operational state security, and the major portion of its work was in the internal security category. Its Propaganda, Special, and Individual divisions, however, had important programs outside the Soviet Union. The Propaganda Division took over a major share of the work that had been done by the Agitation and Propaganda Bureau of the Comintern after that organization was abolished during World War II. In this capacity it maintained liaison with Communist parties abroad, especially where their activities had been forced underground. It furnished material and direction so that local parties would stay in proper alignment with the organization and policies of the Party in Moscow.

The Special Division organized guerrilla activities. Its predecessor organization had been effective against the Germans in World War II. It operated behind German lines and assisted the Balkan resistance groups during the war and the Greek insurgents afterward.

The Individual Division furnished Second Directorate personnel who accompanied musicians, artists, lecturers, scientists, sports groups, and other visiting or working groups abroad, and maintained a surveillance of emigres from the Soviet Union. Its operations internally consisted of the surveillance of foreigners, visiting or on assignments, in the Soviet Union.

The Allied Division worked in the East European countries, those of them that were at the time in satellite status. Mobile Groups for Special Operations were provided by the Second Directorate for surveillance of important defectors and liquidation, if considered necessary, of deserters. Leon Trotsky's murder in 1940 allegedly was performed by one of these groups.

The MVD division titles were selected by persons with a primarily internal security background, familiar with the practice, effective when applied with respect to the local population, of creating an aura of sinister mystique about the secret police apparatus. The KGB abandoned the old names and chose new ones less likely to make an impression of possibly hostile activities. Although administrative subordinations and titles were almost completely changed, security operations were not altered to any appreciable degree.

The Committee for State Security (KGB)

The KGB's major subdivisions were called administrations or directorates. In 1957 it was believed to have had ten main administrations, six of them related to its operation on the frontiers or outside the Soviet Union. The Main Administration of Border

Troops and the Political Administration of Border Troops controlled the forces and their operations on the frontiers of the Soviet Union.

The Foreign Administration was the oldest of the main administrations and had maintained a continuity from Cheka days. With the exception of the economics area, the Foreign Administration took over the bulk of the former MVD First Directorate functions, supervising the greater portion of intelligence activities abroad, controlling personnel, and setting objectives and targets. It also took over the Second Directorate Individual Division's relations with foreigners in the Soviet Union and Soviet citizens abroad.

The Economic Administration, as its name implies, was primarily concerned with collection of information on industry, trade, and other related interests. It also appeared capable of directing subversive and sabotage activities. The Administration for Counterintelligence was organized to collect information on a target country's police, national and local administrations, and its intelligence agencies.

Other KGB administrations had primary work within the Soviet Union but special functions to perform outside. The Administration of Special Sections operated with Soviet troops abroad. This administration was charged with ferreting out unreliable or politically suspect elements in the armed forces or in the environment of the forces that could be in contact with them. As such, it construed its duties as including a considerable effort directed against local populations adjacent to military installations. In the immediate post-World War II period, the predecessor of the Administration of Special Sections was the agency that screened and removed German scientists and industrialists to the Soviet Union. It was also active in combating Russian emigre organizations.

As the East European Communist countries evolved away from the satellite status of the post-war Stalin period, indigenous intelligence agencies have become more independent than during the early days in which they were little more than extensions of the Soviet organizations. The KGB, however, was believed to have close relationships in all of the East European capitals and to have access to all intelligence except that of purely local interest.

Special operational departments, superseding the MVD Mobile Groups for Special Operations, have handled especially important tasks and managed efforts that were undertaken against particular individuals—suspects, persons to be exploited, or persons requiring protection. These departments are also responsible for the security of sensitive projects and installations. The Central Index of Biographical Data in Moscow was probably maintained by one of the Special Operational Departments. This index not only contained card files on a large portion of the Soviet population but accumulated detailed information on foreigners. Files were maintained on prominent personalities, anyone considered sympathetic to the Soviet Union or to the Communist Party, as well as on persons considered vulnerable to exploitation. Auxiliary administrative branches of the KGB included communications, transportation, records, statistics, bookkeeping, printing, archives, cryptography, laboratory, personnel, financial and administrative management departments.

KGB effort in developing countries has been to gather information about the status and stability of the government and the economy and biographical data on influential personalities. Against potential enemies there were wider interests that included the military capability, all that could be learned of scientific and technical accomplishments, nuclear energy programs, transportation, public services, food supplies, civil defense and evacuation plans, and a wide variety of subjects related to industrial and economic conditions. In all countries there has been interest in governmental agencies and operations, the morale of the population, and the attitudes of the people toward communism.

There are local KGBs in each of the union republic governments, and smaller KGB branches at lower government levels—in the armed forces; in industrial, economic, trade, and scientific organizations; government administrative branches and CPSU organizations; and even in the labor camps, prisons, and forces of the internal security police and local militia. Their influence permeates the entire operation and control apparatus of the Soviet state. KGB subordination is always direct to Moscow, through its own organizational channels only. A functional section within a lower branch is subordinate to the chief of that branch and to the same functional sections of higher KGB units between it and Moscow, but the KGB of a union republic has no substantive subordination to the Council of Ministers of that republic. In the armed forces, for example, KGB personnel have communications channels to which the military commander has no access.

There is no reliable information as to the numbers of men in the KGB or of those involved in KGB's state security, as separate from its internal security, functions. The personnel in the regular military units of the Border Troops probably numbered about 150,000 in 1969. This figure represented about three-fifths of the uniformed military personnel in the security forces, the remainder of whom were in the internal security units. It did not include the probably larger numbers that are in convoy, railway, and guard troop organizations or the local militia. It also did not include clandestine, operational, and administrative personnel in KGB.

State Security Activities of Other Agencies

The Ministry of Foreign Affairs, the armed forces, and the Communist Party, as well as the KGB, are engaged in intelligence activities. The foreign ministry operates through its diplomatic contacts and specializes in political and economic information. The military works through its attaché system abroad, aiming primarily at evaluating military, scientific, and technical capabilities. It also performs photographic and electronic intelligence collection from aircraft, surface vessels, and reconnaissance satellites. The Communist Party apparatus engages in propaganda dissemination, attempting to attract new membership or support. The KGB, however, has permeated the foreign ministry, armed forces, and Party organizations and has maintained access to the material collected by the other agencies.

The relaxation of repression and calculated terror in police operations after Stalin's death created an impression of reduced efforts. Western observers suspected that there were reductions in personnel, but the routine activities of the security force continued, and probable reductions in the overall program were less than would be indicated from the decline in publicity.

Recruiting, Training, and Conditions of Service

KGB personnel recruited for foreign service are carefully selected and are trained in one or more of the so-called Checkist schools. Komsomol and Party members are preferred, and thorough surveillance of the candidates is continued during all training programs. Of the some 200 security police schools, about twenty to thirty train for work abroad. The basic curriculum is two to four years and features police work, political indoctrination, and physical conditioning. Sports feature the individually competitive contact types such as boxing, wrestling, and judo, and emphasize self-defense. Technical subjects include photography, chemistry, and laboratory techniques. Specialized training involves languages; interrogation and investigation techniques; and the tactics involved in agitation, crowd control, insurgency, and dissemination of propaganda.

Whereas it is practice to recruit individuals with no family attachments for security duties within the Soviet Union, it is advantageous to have agents for work abroad who have family ties, people remaining behind who would be held to account in case of defection. In any event, a good percentage of them are of select caliber and are well paid. While abroad, however, they receive only the living expenses and allowances required in the work, the bulk of their salaries being withheld in Moscow.

Recruiting abroad follows several different types of format. After World War II a large group of foreign agents was recruited. In the chaos of those times there were thousands of educated people, unemployed and barely existing in the rubble of European cities, who were seeking an ideology promising some escape from the recurring cycle of warfare that appeared to have become a pattern for Europe. The concept of supranationality was appealing, and the excitement of spying was, to some, an escape. This group provided the Russians with some information, and a few became excellent agents. When the less valuable of them were apprehended, they rarely had enough information to damage more serious Soviet efforts, and they absorbed the energies of local police forces. Their amateurish activities served to distract attention from better trained operatives who could remain separate and relatively secure in the background. On balance, however, they proved more problem than help; and after a period during which there were exposures, wranglings for power, and waverings of loyalties, more careful selection was ordered.

With few exceptions, after the early post-World War II period, foreigners were recruited by the KGB only when they could provide information from personal work or associations. They were usually recruited by the Communist Party organization in their own country or by the individual effort of a special agent. Target groups included newly naturalized citizens who did not yet identify themselves with their adopted country and who were having difficulties becoming accepted within it, individuals who had a sympathy with socialist ideology, or persons who had a dissatisfaction that could be exploited. Some who had access to desired information could be flattered, blackmailed, or would sell it for a price. Professional people were sought out in cultural societies or international associations when they could be persuaded that they were sharing scientific or professional opinion. Organizations or meetings on behalf of peace, minority groups, free trade, and many worthy causes were special targets.

Methods employed by the KGB varied widely, and its agents fell into a variety of categories determined largely by the capabilities demanded in different situations. Political agents specialized in government and administration, social conditions, morale of the people, and the country's tolerance toward communism. Many of these agents were provided with press credentials to facilitate their movement. They also assisted attachés and diplomatic personnel who had fewer opportunities to make contacts with working people and whose movements were restricted. Their interests included civil defense, defense installations, food supplies, public utilities, and other services.

A second group of agents consisted of those trained to collect technical and economic information. The technicians among them specialized in nuclear energy programs, military equipment and armament, and new industrial techniques. The economic specialists dealt with businessmen, industrialists, and government economic agencies, joining trade delegations and other such groups. They were sometimes involved with smuggling scarce or newly developed materials out of Western countries or with routing illegal shipments of goods to the Soviet Union via intermediary nations. The objective of the technical and economic agents was to determine the capacities of the target country's power, industry, and transportation systems, and the resiliency of the economy.

The third group consisted of those who dealt with individuals, to recruit or elicit assistance from local people. These agents also collected information on people of interest.

Developments in the 1960's

Developments in the late 1960's appeared aimed at ensuring that the security forces remain subordinate to the Party apparatus rather than to any single official in the agencies or to any one individual in the Party oligarchy. There may also have been an official intent to reestablish a balance between state and internal security agencies. In 1966 the Ministry for the Preservation of Public Order for the USSR was formed for the first time, signifying the return of an internal security agency to ministry status under the Council of Ministers of the USSR, rather than retaining its earlier complete decentralization in the union republic governments. In 1968 the Ministry for Preservation of Public Order designation was dropped, and the MVD was resurrected. Organizationally at least, the state and internal security agencies had again become equals. During the first year after these changes, it had still not become clear what the Soviet leadership considered a proper allocation of functions between the security agencies.

With the abandonment of terror as an instrument for controlling the population, all security forces' activities have shrunk into the background. The information that still seeps through, although less frequently, indicates that Soviet citizens who defect or are contemplating defection still fear the security police and have little doubt as to their continuing capabilities and resolve. Embassy and consular staffs are manned at levels as great as formerly, and there is no reason to believe that their functions have changed. Trade delegations, visiting groups, and Soviet officials abroad present much the same appearances that they did during Stalin's regime.

Visitors and foreign officials in the Soviet Union encounter the same limitations that have become familiar over the years. Phones are tapped, listening devices are found in hotel rooms, and surveillance is constant and obvious. Soviet citizens often shun personal contact with foreigners other than that which has been prearranged

136

and approved. Travel is restricted and strictly controlled. There is a residue of Stalinist methods of operation in the Soviet Union despite the fact that more tourists visited the Soviet Union during the 1960's and more Soviet citizens traveled abroad than ever before.

CHAPTER 8

THE INTERNAL SECURITY SYSTEM

In early 1970 the agencies at central government level responsible for internal security were the Ministry for Internal Affairs (Ministerstvo Vnutrennikh Del—MVD) and the Committee for State Security (Komitet Gosudarstvennoy Bezopasnosti—KGB). Both had ministerial status within the USSR Council of Ministers. Although they were government agencies, their personnel, historically, have been directly under the control of the dictator or collective leadership. The Politburo of the Central Committee of the Communist Party of the Soviet Union (CPSU) was considered to be the supreme authority over both the state and internal security agencies.

The MVD appeared to have had the major portion of the internal security mission and most of the routine functions related to a national police force. Since the KGB was the more powerful organization, it retained some specific internal security tasks, such as investigation of major crimes and, particularly, those considered to be in the category of "crimes against the state." In addition, KGB personnel were infiltrated throughout all Party and government institutions, including the MVD, to ensure political reliability (see ch. 7, The State Security System).

Between the October Revolution of 1917 and World War II, internal security was maintained by the same police agencies that had responsibility for state security. After World War II, however, separate internal and state security ministries were created. During most of the time since, the state security organizations have been much the more powerful agencies and have taken over all but the most routine internal security functions (see ch. 7, The State Security System).

A satisfactory state of national order and internal security has been regarded as the climate in which the Party and government leaders could operate most effectively to achieve a working socialist society and to perpetuate themselves in power. Soviet leaders have demanded more than an orderly society and have usually prevented any expression of opinion against the system. Police agencies have controlled the population with measures that have appeared to be overly severe by Western standards and at times have deliberately exercised control by terror.

There have always been safeguards in the legal system to protect the individual against police abuses or injustice in the courts, and sentences always could, constitutionally, be appealed for higher court review. Until the end of the Stalin period, however, the legal restraints were respected or ignored arbitrarily by the dictating elements. Police, at times, were authorized to investigate, arrest, try, and sentence suspects completely within the police organization.

Little overt dissidence, restiveness, or disrespect for law was discernible in the 1960's, and the incidence of crime was not high. There were outcries from artists, writers, and other intellectuals for more freedom, legality, and constitutionalism. At times, dissident writers were imprisoned or confined to mental institutions, but the bulk of the population appeared to be generally docile, and public manifestations of unrest were limited to juvenile delinquency and "hooliganism," that is, general rowdiness and drunkenness that could be considered only indirectly political in nature. Police forces have been effective enough to prevent any known organization of dissidents.

The militia corresponded to city and rural police forces in other countries. The militia organization was subordinated to the MVD but was generally locally oriented, locally responsible, and administered by local governments. In contrast, the political, secret, or internal police of the MVD and the KGB were responsible, through their own channels only, to the top-level authorities in Moscow. The militia were concerned with local crimes, whereas the MVD and the KGB were interested in the preservation of the social system, the Party, and the central government (see ch. 23, The Police [Militia] and Correctional Systems).

In an effort to improve the reputation of the police agencies, substantial reforms were undertaken after Stalin's death. Extrajudicial police powers were curbed. Economic agencies having only peripheral associations with security but which had previously been under the MVD were transferred to other government ministries. Labor colony regimes were made less severe, and colony populations were reduced. According to recent labor colony inmates, however, such as Anatoly Marchenko, it was also clear that the pendulum had not swung to the opposite side to the point that rehabilitation efforts involved soft treatment. Repressions against the masses of the population may still have been severe by world standards, but they too have been decreasing in scope and severity. The average Soviet citizen in early 1970 had less to fear from a sinister and unpredictable police system than had been the case since the 1920's and possibly in any period of modern Russian or Soviet history.

The formal relation of the Party to the security agencies as a whole could not be clearly determined in early 1970, but it was evident that it had changed radically since Stalin's death in 1953. In the earliest Soviet days Lenin had believed that every Communist should be a Chekist, but he would not authorize the Cheka to operate within the Party to purge its membership. Stalin, on the other hand, considered the remainder of the Party leadership a threat to his power. He used the security police to protect himself from any possible challenge from within the Party.

HISTORICAL BACKGROUND

The Cheka

When the Extraordinary Commission (Chrezvychaynaya Komis-siya—Cheka) was established on December 20, 1917, the Bolsheviks controlled only a small portion of what later became the Soviet Union and did not have complete control over the revolutionary movement. The Cheka's informal founding decree directed it to carry out preliminary investigations insofar as necessary and to hand over saboteurs and counterrevolutionaries for trial by revolutionary tribunals. Actually, it was directed to protect the new Bolshevik regime against counterrevolutionaries and political deviationists and to punish "spies, traitors, plotters, bandits, speculators, profiteers, counterfeiters, arsonists, hooligans, agitators, saboteurs, class enemies, and other parasites" (see table 2).

The Cheka rapidly became more independent in its operations. In February 1918 it performed its first execution without trial. It established its own courts in April and was then able to arrest, try, and sentence without restraint. By August of that year, after Lenin had been seriously wounded by a would-be assassin, the Cheka no longer confined its actions to legitimately suspected individuals. The nearly 400 provincial and district Chekas were directed to take hostages from the bourgeoisie and former army officers and to meet the least opposition with wholesale executions. This initiated the period known as the Red Terror.

Lenin's view of the operation of security police had been succinctly stated when he said, "We have never rejected terror on principle, nor can we do so. Terror is a form of military operation that may be usefully applied, or may even be essential in certain moments of the battle, under certain conditions." The excesses of the Cheka during the Red Terror had official sanction.

The Cheka also could send suspects to concentration camps for five years by administrative decision if investigation failed to provide enough evidence for trial. When trials were conducted, decisions could be reached without reference to the laws on which they were based, the accused were not necessarily present, and there was no defense or appeal.

The terror that the Cheka struck into the people caused many to calculate that it had executed hundreds of thousands. The actual

Table 2. *Police System of the Soviet Union*

Date	State security	Combined	Internal security
1917—22	. . . . . .	Cheka[1]	. . . . . .
1922—23	. . . . . .	GPU[2]	. . . . . .
1923—34	. . . . . .	OGPU[3]	. . . . . .
1934—41	. . . . . .	NKVD[4]	. . . . . .
1941	NKGB[5]	. . . . . .	NKVD
1941—43	. . . . . .	NKVD	. . . . . .
1943—46	NKGB	. . . . . .	NKVD
1946—53	MGB[6]	. . . . . .	MVD[7]
1953	. . . . . .	MVD	. . . . . .
1954—60	KGB[8]	. . . . . .	MVD
1960—66[9]	. . . . . .	KGB	. . . . . .
1966—68	KGB	. . . . . .	MOOP[10]
1968	KGB	. . . . . .	MVD

[1] Extraordinary Commission (Chrezvychaynaya Komissiya—Cheka).

[2] State Political Administration (Gosudarstvennoye Politicheskoye Upravleniye—GPU).

[3] Unified State Political Administration (Ob'edinyonnoye Gosudarstvennoye Politicheskoye Upravleniye (OGPU).

[4] People's Commissariat of Internal Affairs (Narodnyy Komisariat Vnutrennikh Del—NKVD).

[5] People's Commissariat for State Security (Narodnyy Komisariat Gosudarstvennoy Bezopasnosti—NKGB).

[6] Ministry of State Security (Ministerstvo Gosudarstvennoy Bezopasnosti—MGB).

[7] Ministry of Internal Affairs (Ministerstvo Vnutrennikh Del-VMD).

[8] Committee for State Security (Komitet Gosudarstvennoy Bezopasnosti—KGB).

[9] Continuity of internal security organization was maintained between 1960 and 1966 by the MVD, later renamed MOOP, at republic level. In 1966 a national MOOP was created in the USSR Council of Ministers.

[10] Ministry for the Preservation of Public Order (Ministerstvo Okhrany Obshchestvennogo Poryadka—MOOP).

figure was more likely to be around 50,000. The figures frequently quoted of 1 million or more deaths attributable to the Cheka included some or all civilian casualties, depending on the figure, among the dead from the civil warfare in the 1917—22 period.

The GPU and OGPU

Revulsion against the excesses of the Red Terror caused the Cheka to be abolished in name in February 1922, after an existence of just over four years. The State Political Administration (Gosudarstvennoye Politicheskoye Upravleniye—GPU) succeeded it for a year, which, in turn, was succeeded by the Unified State Political Administration (Ob'edinyonnoye Gosudarstvennoye Politicheskoye Upravleniye—OGPU) from 1923 to 1934.

The 1922—28 period was a time of consolidation with some respite from the horrors of world war, civil war, and terrorism. The OGPU's methods were restricted little by courts and legal procedures, but its efforts were directed mainly at criminals and active political deviationists and were not felt oppressively by the masses of ordinary citizens. Prisons were usually filled to their capacities of some 300,000, but the labor camp population in 1928 was probably as low as 30,000.

Lenin died in 1924. Under Stalin the police singled out the tsarist nobility, bourgeoisie, landowners, clergy, former White Army officers and White Guards, peasants who withheld produce, Mensheviks and others who opposed the government, and criminals. Arrests were numerous enough so that the population was constantly aware of the presence and influence of the security forces but, until the First Five-Year Plan went into operation in 1928, arrests did not approach the numbers that became commonplace from then until after 1950.

With the Five-Year Plan the OGPU became responsible for the confiscation and nationalization of the over 400,000 privately owned shops and small business enterprises that had been allowed to exist during the postrevolutionary period. Owners who resisted or did not move fast enough into the state industrial labor force were imprisoned, deported, or forced into the ranks of the labor camps.

In 1929 the OGPU also became the chief agency enforcing collectivization of agricultural lands. The approximately 1 million independent farmers, *kulaki*, opposed collectivization as a body and were uprooted en masse. The OGPU readopted Cheka practices of meting out long terms of imprisonment and death sentences on its own responsibility.

During the late 1920's and the early 1930's, a more general purge was directed toward the intelligentsia, managers, and engineers in the industrial sector. During the famine winter of 1932/33, the OGPU purged managers who had allegedly sabotaged the food supply. Those in positions of responsibility were vulnerable, because they could be held accountable for alleged shortcomings, for the failure of subordinates, or for failing to support superiors.

Political crimes had been expanded to include not only the commission of punishable acts, but also the failure to prevent them. Punishment was meted out to those accused of contemplating crimes or political deviation. When an offense had been committed and the guilty party was not apprehended, persons innocent of the crime but accused of having advance knowledge that it might be committed were arrested in lieu of the actual criminal.

The NKVD and the Great Terror

In 1934 the OGPU suffered the fate of the Cheka and the GPU. The security police forces then became directly administered by the

People's Commissariat of Internal Affairs (Narodnyy Komisariat Vnutrennikh Del—NKVD). In the legislation surrounding the transfer, it appeared that the NKVD would be subject to more legal restraint than its predecessors. Administrative deportations, exiles, and sentences to labor camps were again restricted, at this time to five years. The death sentence was not specifically mentioned but, since it was provided for within the authority of military tribunals and the military collegium of the Supreme Court, there was a strong implication that the NKVD would not exercise it. Furthermore, the Office of Procurator General of the USSR had been established in 1933 and had been charged with supervising the legality and regularity of security police actions. Whatever the intent of these restrictions, they became meaningless in the purge years that followed almost immediately (see ch. 22, The Legal System).

The NKVD gradually assumed a number of more administrative functions, such as maintaining population statistics and administering roads, automobile transport, survey and cartographic work, forest conservation, and weights and measures. This group of administrative tasks expanded the information and contacts available to the NKVD, increasing the scope of its control over the population.

Having destroyed the elements he considered dangerous in the industrial sector, among the intelligentsia, and in the rural population, Stalin now turned his attention to the Party, to political deviationists, and to possible challengers to his power. The repression culminated between 1936 and 1938 in the period known as the Great Purge or the Great Terror.

The purge was sparked initially by the assassination of Sergei Kirov in December 1934. Kirov was a Politburo member, head of the Leningrad Communist Party organization, and had been a Stalin henchman. There is conjecture as to whether Stalin, infuriated by Kirov's murder, started the purge thereafter or whether, having had the purge in mind, he instigated the incident, in which case Kirov could be termed the first of the purged.

The momentum of the purge built up slowly. Its first phase consisted of a purification of the Party rolls and did not involve arrests, imprisonment, or executions on a large scale. From screenings of Party rolls in 1935 and 1936, membership was reduced from 2.8 million to about 2 million. Those dropped were generally from opposition elements within the Old Bolshevik group—people who, because they had worked for the Revolution, held to the idea that they could voice opposition to Stalin and some of the policies of his regime.

The worst of the purge occurred between September 1936 and July 1938. This was the period when N. I. Yezhov, having replaced G. Yagoda, was head of the NKVD. This phase, known as the Yezhovshchina (The Yezhov Period) hit hard at the government, the armed forces, and the Party. A large majority of the Central Committee of the CPSU was eliminated, as were 90 percent of the officers in the senior grades of the military establishment. The purge of CPSU members was so thorough that less than 2 percent of the delegates to the Eighteenth Congress of the CPSU held in 1939 had attended the Seventeenth Congress five years earlier.

Having achieved his goals, Stalin disavowed the destruction of the Party and the country's leaders and turned the purge onto the purgers. Yezhov followed Yagoda to the executioner. Prisoners were joined in their cells by NKVD agents who had arrested and interrogated them earlier.

The purge had eliminated all of the active Bolshevik Old Guard, all others who appeared conceivably able to threaten Stalin and, finally, those of the purgers who knew the planning behind, and the extent of, the carnage. The population had been reduced to obedience, apathy, and silence. Nearly the entire Party leadership, including all but a small personal following of Stalin's, had been eliminated. Stalin had consolidated his power over the Party, the government, and the armed forces. In the last days, having turned on the purgers, Stalin posed as a champion of the people in doing away with those who "had tried to advance themselves by destroying honest Party members."

Labor camp populations continued to increase, even after the purge years of the late 1930's. Wholesale groups were removed from lands received from the partition of Poland in 1939 after the signing of the Soviet-German Nonaggression Pact. When the Soviet Union became involved in World War II, camp populations grew because of deportations of ethnic minorities from several suspect areas. Those removed from the Baltic States, plus the Volga Germans, Chechens, Balkars, Crimean Tatars, Kalmyks, Karachy, and German prisoners of war, swelled the population of prison camps. The Soviet population was screened in areas reoccupied after the Germans were driven back from the interior of the country. Efforts were made to identify those who had cooperated with the Germans or who had not actively resisted. Again mass deportations ensued. The last large group of deportees consisted of nearly 600,000 rural Baltic peoples who resisted collectivization of their farmlands in the 1948—49 period.

NKVD forces, known variously as Internal Troops or Troops of Special Purpose, were considered elite units during World War II. They were used as the forces of last resort in the critical hours of the 1941—42 defense of Moscow. Later in the war they functioned as "blocking troops," operating behind the front lines to prevent regular troops from retreating. They were also the military units involved in the deportations of the various allegedly unreliable ethnic groups.

The Postwar Stalin Period, 1946-53

In 1946 the NKVD was redesignated the MVD in the reorganization of the government, in which the former people's commissariats became ministries. Although the name change had nothing to do with it, the MVD went almost immediately into decline. By 1949 the state security agency that had been created during World War II and redesignated the Ministry of State Security (Ministerstvo Gosudarstvennoy Bezopasnosti—MGB) in 1946 had taken over all of the more important MVD functions (see ch. 7, The State Security System).

In January 1953 nine doctors, six of them Jewish, were arrested and accused of the murder of former Politburo member, A. A. Zhdanov, who had died mysteriously in 1948. The doctors were also accused of plotting further assassinations of top Communist leaders. The MGB was officially liberated for not having solved the Zhdanov murder years earlier and for being delinquent in protecting the country's leaders against "imperialist" plotters. To many observers, the so-called Doctors' Plot presaged another great purge, initially against Jewish elements of the population. The security police organizations would probably have been the brunt of a later phase of the purge, except that Stalin, the master purger, died in March 1953. Within a month *Pravda* announced that the Doctors' Plot had been a complete fabrication and that those involved had been released.

Control of the Population

The generally accepted mission of internal security forces is the protection of the country as a whole from lawless or nonconforming elements within the population. The major emphasis has been on the protection of the state and its institutions, occasionally from sizable numbers of its own people. In addition, much criminal activity that in most other countries would be considered a normal amount of antisocial behavior has been regarded as rebellion against Soviet authority or as unacceptable deviation from the principles of a socialist society.

As exercised by Lenin and Stalin, internal security had added elements calculated to strike fear into the populace in order to achieve obedience and conformity. As such, it became deliberate control by terror. Police powers were exercised arbitrarily, aimed at holding the people helpless in the face of overwhelming power. Security forces worked to achieve an atmosphere charged with a constant dread of unknown punishment.

Employment of terror had the effect of inducing isolation in many people. Afraid of expressing their thoughts, they kept dissident views to themselves, did not discuss questions about Party or government policies, and did not know whether or not their doubts were shared by others. Considered in relation to the size of the Soviet population and the length of the period of near-total police control, the excesses performed have not had a parallel in modern history.

Extrajudicial Police Tribunals

Preliminary investigation and trials have been provided for under Soviet law since early revolutionary days, but until Stalin's death the provisions usually were applied only in criminal cases. To steer a shorter course toward justice as they saw it, both Stalin and Lenin enabled their security police to sentence political suspects without the hindrances inherent in legal proceedings.

After the Cheka period the two most notorious police courts were the military tribunals and the Special Board. The military tribunals were originally set up to handle cases that involved security forces personnel only. With time their scope was expanded, enabling them to deal with civilian offenses, such as those arising from evasion of conscription, disclosure of state secrets, and noncompliance with martial law regulations. Political deviationists could be charged with crimes in the latter categories. During peacetime these tribunals were used in areas under martial law or where large-scale police activities, such as mass deportations, were underway. They were considerably restricted after Stalin died, but the decree curtailing them was not published for about four years (see ch. 22, The Legal System).

The Special Board was established in 1934. Trials in its courts consisted of a review of the evidence collected during investigation and interrogation of an accused. No defense was admitted, nor was the accused necessarily present during the trial. The basis of the sentence was the police recommendation to the court forwarded with the evidence. Special Board courts dealt with the larger portion of political offenders brought to trial during the purge of the late 1930's. The board was dissolved in September 1953, but its dissolution was not announced until 1956. Special assembly courts took over its functions until about 1965, when they also were abolished.

During the mid-1960's all political and about 65 percent of all criminal cases were investigated by the KGB or agents of the Ministry for the Preservation of Public Order (Ministerstvo Okhrany Obshchestvennogo Poryadka—MOOP). If legal processes were adhered to, however, trials, other than those for offenses committed by military or security service personnel, presumably were conducted in the regular civil court system.

Internal Passports and Labor Booklets

To control population mobility, a system of internal passports was introduced in 1932. This system effectively prevented any legal movement of the population that was not known and approved, and it greatly enhanced the power of the security agencies. Collective and state farmers did not receive passports and thus were barred from cities except on permitted visits when they were required to register with the militia and to carry certificates showing the purposes of the visits. The system also made it possible to exile any individual forcibly to another area, to prevent prisoners from returning to their homes after release, as well as to compile statistics on the population.

Labor booklets were issued to workers in state industries, a category that included almost everyone other than collective farmers. These booklets were retained by management and returned only when employment was terminated. A worker could not quit without his employer's permission. Work performance was recorded in the booklet, which was surrendered to any subsequent employer (see ch. 32, The Labor Force).

Internal passports and labor booklets served to hold population and labor mobility to a minimum, and it was not until 1956 that a worker could terminate employment of his own volition. Legislation in 1958 redirected emphasis to enforcement of the control systems, particularly to prevent any influx of "undesirables" into urban areas. The MVD was directed at that time to discover and expel from Moscow those who avoided socially useful work.

POSITION IN THE GOVERNMENT

The security police have at all times since 1917 been one of the basic elements of Communist power. They have consisted of forces organized into regular military units and of police agents who have operated individually or in small groups. The main mission of both categories of security forces has been to support Party objectives and to safeguard the regime.

Courts and government attorneys operate in relation to finite laws, although they have at times disregarded established rules and procedures. The armed forces are rigidly controlled. The security forces and political administration, on the other hand, have operated in a widely varying pattern, on the basis of instructions that could change in relation to daily events. The scope of their activities and the measures that they have employed have been determined as necessary to respond to the situation existing at any given moment.

Beginning with the Cheka, the security organization has been structurally within the governmental organization. It has had firmer ties to the Party and, although they have been separate and have had different functions, the Party and the police forces have been considered essential to each other. During the first thirty-five years of Soviet history, however, the security organizations were the tool of the dictator, responsible to him only.

The government may be considered to have had administrative control over the security establishment, but the Party and the dictator have directed it at the higher policymaking levels. Since Stalin, the role of the dictator has been assumed by the Politburo of the Central Committee of the CPSU. In this situation police force activities in relation to the Party have probably been limited to monitoring the rank and file of Party membership and its routine activities.

Although the predecessors of the MVD had a total monopoly over both state and internal security functions before World War II, state security agencies since that time have generally been more powerful than their internal security counterparts. The MVD, which had declined significantly by 1949, was revitalized briefly in 1953 by Lavrenti P. Beria, who had all security forces under his control and abolished the MGB altogether. A new state security agency, the KGB, was formed in March 1954, less than a year after Beria's execution. The MVD suffered a worse fate organizationally at the hands of the KGB than it had in relation to the MGB between 1949 and 1953. It lost ministerial status in the central government in 1960, and for six years, starting in 1962, lost its national identity altogether. The ministries for the preservation of public order that replaced it were for four more years also relegated to a decentralized republic status. In 1966, however, the Ministry for the Preservation of Public Order for the USSR was created, and in 1968 the organization reacquired the MVD name.

At its highest organizational level the MVD, as is the case with the KGB, is responsible to the Council of Ministers of the USSR and to the Supreme Soviet. Each union republic has a KGB and an MVD responsible, at least administratively, to the councils of ministers in the union republic governments as well as to their own organizations at higher government levels. The KGB, with more of its functions having strictly national concern, has little if any substantive subordination to local governments. Since the MVD has more locally oriented functions and since the internal security agencies had no ministries at USSR level from 1960 to 1966, it presumably has more substantive working relationships with the union republic governments than does the KGB.

MVD operations have been restricted by law to procedural controls relating it to the procuracy. These controls have antecedents in the decrees that established the GPU in 1922 and, except during purge periods and during deportations of mass groups of the population, these limitations have not been meaningless. Nonetheless, the security police have been essential to the survival of the dictatorship and have been maintained directly responsible to the dictator or the small dictating group. As such, the effective top-level control over the police system has been from within the Politburo of the Central Committee of the CPSU. The leaders have been able to relieve security forces from the restraints in constitutional safeguards whenever they have considered it necessary.

ORGANIZATION AND TRAINING

During the 1960's internal security functions have been accomplished within the MVD, the MOOP, and also the KGB. The KGB was by a considerable degree the most powerful agency and, during all of the early and mid-portion of the decade, had all of the important internal as well as state security functions.

Although a division of national security into state and internal categories has existed throughout Soviet history, actual delineation of responsibilities and functions has always been difficult to ascertain. With the establishment of the Ministry for the Preservation of Public Order within the USSR Council of Ministers in 1966, and its subsequent renaming as the Ministry of Internal Affairs in late 1968, there again existed two security agencies at the national level. Functional divisions were still clouded to the outside observer, but at the beginning of 1970 the KGB appeared to be the more powerful security organ.

The Committee for State Security (KGB)

The KGB has had directorates with internal security functions overlapping to some degree those of the MVD. These have included its Economic Administration, the State Construction Trust, the Secret Political Administration, the Road and Transport Administration, and the Main Administration of Prisons. Although not always the case, KGB's interests have not been the operation of the government enterprises so much as maintaining a surveillance over the people and the management, making sure of their political reliability. Production, however, sometimes has been used as a gauge of the reliability of the personnel.

The State Construction Trust makes use of the manpower in the Corrective Labor Colonies but has not had the vast quantities of prison labor that were available to security agencies during the Stalin years. The Economic Administration is concerned with "sabotage" and other offenses against state property, as well as production achievements. The Secret Political Administration maintains surveillance over all citizens and, before the death of Stalin, over the leadership of the Party, government, armed forces, and all major institutions. The KGB's Main Administration of Prisons has had its own special places of detention, presumably for interrogation and for maximum security criminal or important political prisoners. It has also maintained special operational departments for conducting investigations, checking political reliability, and for protecting leaders and some sensitive installations.

The Ministry of Internal Affairs (MVD)

Except for the three or four years before 1953 and the approximately ten years after about 1957, the MVD has had most of the internal security responsibilities. Its elements have ordinarily included the security responsibilities. Its elements have ordinarily included the security police, the Internal Troops, special units in the regular armed forces, the labor camps, a portion of the prisons, and certain courts.

Directorates within the MVD have included the main administrations of Internal Troops, Militia, Economy, Corrective Labor Colonies, Places of Detention, Local Air Defense, Fire Protection, Geodesy and Cartography, and State Archives. Guard Troops, Railway Troops, and Convoy Troops, sometimes held within the Internal Troops, at times have also been administered in separate main administrations.

The Internal Troops have been maintained directly subordinate to their main administration headquarters in Moscow but have had local administrative agencies in the union republics and possibly in some lower government echelons. Other administrations not only have had branches in the union republic and lower level governments but have performed most of their operations at those levels and have been subordinate in varying degrees to local authorities.

Official Soviet statements concerning the Internal Troops have consisted only of references to their existence. They were first identified as a separate force in 1923, when the Special Troops of the OGPU were created. Before that time there were Cheka Units of Special Purpose and GPU units that have been referred to as Guard Troops of the Internal Guard. Guard Troops, however, have been a separate force, and their continuity has dated back to 1920. The early Cheka and GPU units were probably small and attached within the regular Red Army establishment. As such they are believed to have been used during the Kronstadt mutiny and in the Antonov uprising, both of which occurred in 1921 (see Ch. 23, The Police [Militia] and Correctional Systems; ch. 28, The Armed Forces).

MVD Internal Troops have had a unique dual subordination. Their military organization has been centralized, with a chain of command extending downward from Moscow. Operationally, there has been an area and some functional subordination to local authorities. There has also been a district organization, but its areas have not conformed to those of military or border districts. Units have been stationed in or near most large towns.

Little is known about the changes in the military units of the security forces that have occurred since 1953. Internal Troops still exist, but the strengths and positive subordination of the various individual organizations could not be determined in late 1969. Official statements refer only to their existence. As of around 1957, the Internal Troops of the MVD were subdivided into Guard Troops, Railway Troops, Convoy Troops, and Troops of Special Purpose.

Routine guard duties at military installations, bridges, labor camps, and the like have been accomplished by the Guard Troops. Soviet railways have been of extraordinary importance, and the Railway Troops have been maintained as separate units. They guard railway stations, lines, and property. Convoy troops were formed to accompany and guard individuals under arrest or groups being involuntarily transported. The extent of their activities has decreased since the end of the mass deportations, resettlements, and purges that characterized the Stalin period. The Troops of Special Purpose were fully equipped units of up to division size.

During the late 1960's convoy, railway, and guard units were still in existence, and they were probably subordinated to the MVD. Organizations referred to as Units of Special Designation, Special Troops, Troops of Special Purpose, and other variations on these titles have always been maintained. They have been elite units and have had the more sensitive guard functions, such as safeguarding the most important installations, communications, and Kremlin security. They may operate in small groups but can assemble into sizable military formations. It is believed that the more elite of these units were under the KGB in 1969 but that the larger numbers of more ordinary security forces were MVD troops.

Troop strengths in internal security organizations have varied greatly. From a few small units scattered within the early Red Army, they expanded until, by 1930, there were about 750,000 men in the troops of the OGPU. For several years before and after World War II, they may have been considerably larger because during that period they expanded much as did the regular forces. The 1968 force strength was estimated at about 100,000 men. As has been the case with all forces subordinate to the central government's security agencies, men do not serve in areas near their native towns or villages.

Mobilization during peacetime would ordinarily consist of calling back men who had served tours in MVD units, had been discharged, and who were still under 50 years of age and carried in reserve status. In addition, rosters are maintained in regular army units of personnel having the political reliability required as members of the Internal Troops. These would be transferred if necessary. In time of war or threat of war, when the regular forces were also being augmented, the Internal Troops would be able to draw upon their own reserves and those allocated from newly drafted men only. In an extremely serious wartime situation, such as was the case during the defense of Moscow in 1941, the Internal Troops, because they are considered more reliable, might be augmented at the expense of regular army forces.

Internal Troops were recruited during the annual military conscription, as were regular military service personnel and the Border Troops of the KGB. Screening at induction attempted to ensure that only individuals with assured political reliability served with the Internal Troops and that those slated for convoy, railway, and guard troop units were men capable of operating individually or in small groups. Requirements for men with special skills were met, because the MVD forces needed extensive training facilities for policing functions, but being smaller than the regular army, could not maintain schools for all variety of communications, mechanical, and other required skills.

Before around 1960 educational backgrounds and percentages of membership in the Komsomol (Young Communist League) or the Party were higher in the security forces than in the regular services. As standards throughout the military establishment in 1969 were up considerably from those of a decade earlier, these conditions may no longer exist. The tour of duty had been a year longer than in the regular services, but 1968 legislation reduced the normal conscript tour to two years in both the regular and security forces.

Basic training featured individual combat techniques and small unit tactical exercises. These included counterinsurgency tactics against uprisings and group disorders, population and riot control, techniques for handling raids, individual and area searches, inspection of documents, investigation and arresting procedures, and methods for safeguarding large or sensitive installations. In subsequent training it was usual for the Troops of Special Purpose to engage in large-scale division-size maneuvers and for Convoy and Guard Troops to participate in battalion and regiment-size exercises. For all of the effort expended in basic training, special security service subjects, and military exercises, political indoctrination still accounted for 25 percent of training time.

Noncommissioned officers were usually selected at induction or during early basic training from among those who showed the competence and attitudes required. As is usually the case in the other forces, these men received up to a year of added training and were required to serve a year longer than the usual mandatory tour of duty.

Officers were ordinarily army career men who, as in the case of KGB officers, could rotate in and out of the Internal Troops or could serve within them for their entire careers. Advanced training opportunities, pay, special amenities, and service careers were similar to those in the KGB's Border Troops (see ch. 7, The State Security System).

Published reports have revealed that recruiting for agents or operatives was done individually. There have been security officers in all major universities, trade schools, and military units. Other recruiters have served in such capacities as welfare and social secretaries in central and local government offices, trade unions, factories, cooperatives, and state and collective farms. These people have been charged to seek out suitable candidates for policeman, prison warder, labor colony guard, and security agent.

According to these reports, after the recruiters recommended an individual, a preliminary check of his records was made. At this point it was helpful if he had family or relatives who had been in security police work. No immediate associate could have a record showing either political deviation or associations abroad, although a minor criminal record was not necessarily a bar to his selection. Orphans or individuals with no family ties were also favorably considered so long as their pasts could be completely accounted for.

If the initial check revealed no reason to eliminate an individual, he was then kept under careful observation for a period. If his personal habits, approach to work, and immediate associations also proved satisfactory, he was sent before a selection committee. Having favorably passed this hurdle, he could have been selected for any of about 200 Chekist schools, some of which have been established since the early 1920's. Most were specialized and had courses that ran upwards from a few days but were usually shorter than two years.

Comprehensive courses at a few schools ran from two to four years. General instruction in these included political indoctrination, military training, criminal law, investigative techniques, intelligence, and counterintelligence. A Moscow school for officials earmarked for promotion provided a midcareer advanced curriculum.

DEVELOPMENTS IN THE POST-STALIN PERIOD

From an internal security standpoint, the CPSU leadership evidently expected popular unrest when Stalin died. The Central Committee of the CPSU, the Council of Ministers, and the Presidium of the Supreme Soviet issued a joint statement requesting support, to ensure uninterrupted leadership and to prevent disarray and panic.

Beria gained control of the MVD and MGB within a month and consolidated both under the MVD, but he could not muster suffi-

154

cient support within the Party to extend his controls further. Two months later, having failed in his attempt to succeed Stalin as a one-man dictator, he was arrested. He may have been shot at the time of his arrest in June, but he was probably executed after a trial in December 1953.

The organizational subordination of the security agencies was changed completely after Beria's execution, and some twenty officials who had been closely associated with Beria were executed within the next few years. Although the police system was downgraded to some degree, condemnation for the excesses was directed at Beria and other individuals, who were said to have exploited police offices for personal advantage. The system itself received only moderate criticism and little, if any, challenge.

The KGB was formed in 1954 to replaced the MGB that Beria had abolished a year earlier. It steadily encroached upon MVD's preserves. In 1960 the MVD was so badly eroded that the ministry at the national level was dissolved, and all MVD activities were relagated to union republic and lower level governments. In 1962 the republics' MVDs were renamed ministries for the preservation of public order. For the next four years internal security appeared to be, at least in organizational status and prestige, at its lowest ebb.

A hint of a reversal in the fortunes of the deflated internal security agencies, however, occurred in 1966, when at the national level ministry for the preservation of public order of the USSR was established after four years of decentralization to the union republics. In 1968 the MVD reappeared, replacing the ministries for the preservation of public order at all government levels.

Since 1958 the leadership of the powerful KGB has been drawn primarily from Party officials. These were men who had Party, rather than police, experience but who appeared incapable of using the security organization as a means to personal power from which they could challenge the Party. There has probably been a planned program to keep the security agencies effectively subordinate to the Party, and it may have been considered further insurance to divide work between two ministries in a fashion that would prevent either from being able to exercise a power that could threaten the Party. Since 1954 the KGB has had close operating cooperation in certain of the Party's activities, but it is believed that the watchdog role at top levels has been reversed. No longer would the police force purge the ranking Party officials. The KGB might, at the request of the leadership, assist the Party in "purifying" its membership, but during the 1960's the Party leaders apparently were able to control the activities of the KGB units within the Party and to define their powers.

During the early 1960's, when much effort was directed toward eliminating the unsavory reputation the security forces had acquired from 1917 until the deaths of Stalin and Beria in 1953, the official Soviet press published straightforward comments on police activities, emphasizing efforts at reform. One police investigator stated that, although his business was to deal with persons who committed dangerous crimes against the state, there had not been a case of sabotage since the 1920's and that most of the still-active treason cases involved crimes from World War II. This official further stated that much of his recent activities had involved restoring the reputations of people defamed during the period up to 1953. He claimed that the courts were the exclusive instrument for handing down sentences and that the system was designed, and working, not only to punish all guilty persons but also to ensure that no innocent person was punished.

Operations of the security police have been modified in several significant ways. Extrajudicial powers have apparently been curbed, through the elimination of the military tribunal, Special Board, and Special Assembly courts. Security agencies have apparently been subordinated to a larger controlling group within the Party. A. N. Shelepin told the Twenty-second Party Congress in 1961 that the KGB, which he then headed, had been "cut down substantially." Economic and other agencies having only a peripheral association with internal security, but theretofore administered by the MVD, have been transferred to other government ministries. MVD responsibility for roads and highways has been transferred to a newly created Ministry of Transport and Highways. Enterprises that had used manpower from the labor colonies have also been transferred from MVD control to other ministries. Forced labor camps have been replaced by corrective labor colonies, and some degree of reform in the direction indicated by the change of name has been undertaken.

Since 1953 far fewer numbers have been sent to labor colonies, and their populations have declined drastically. The worst of the colonies have been closed because annual amnesties between 1953 and 1957 released those serving short sentences or imprisoned for minor crimes. Nearly all of those from the ethnic groups that were deported during World War II have been rehabilitated. Most were given some compensation. The Crimean Tatars, however, were not compensated, and the Baltic peoples have not been pardoned as a group, although most of the individuals have been amnestied.

SECTION II. SOCIAL

CHAPTER 9

ETHNIC GROUPS

There are over a hundred ethnic groups in the Soviet Union. The official 1959 census listed 109 nationalities or ethnic groups of varying size. Other lists have been even longer. Many groups are rather small and have been partly assimilated into neighboring and related groups. Others have been able to maintain a separate identity. All vary, however, in strength of self-identity.

In Russian the word *narody* (peoples) is used to mean ethnic groups or nationalities, or even, from an ethnocentric point of view, minorities. Some of these peoples have republics of their own, and many of them form distinct administrative units of some size (see ch. 20, Component Political Subdivisions).

Ethnic groups in the Soviet Union are formed on the basis of a common language and culture—or the recent historical presence of them—memories of a common history and, generally, a homeland. Despite the diversity of the population, physical differences are not the basis for ethnic differentiation. Two major elements have entered into the formation of the peoples, the Mongoloid and the Caucasoid. Caucasoids predominate in the western part of the country, in Europe, the Caucasus, and part of central Asia; they range from the northern, fairly blond with light colored eyes and hair, to the southern darker shades. The Mongoloids predominate in the eastern part of the country, including the Far North, Siberia, and part of central Asia. Population mixing has occurred primarily as a result of the Turkic and Mongolian invasions and is greatest in the central Asian and eastern Russian regions.

The ethnic diversity of the Soviet Union can be grouped into four major culture areas: Europe, central Asia, the Caucasus, and Paleo-Siberia, that is, areas of indigenous Siberian peoples. Although these areas are not internally homogeneous, they nevertheless can be distinguished on the basis of major languages and religions, culture, history, social structure, and ecology. Europe contains the most people and Europeans, especially the Russians, are politically and culturally dominant. The central Asians are next in importance, followed by the peoples of the Caucasus and, last, those of Paleo-Siberia.

157

Russian predominance is the result of expansions that began during the Kievan period of the ninth century A.D., and were largely completed by the mid-nineteenth century (see ch. 3, Historical Setting). It was not, however, until after the Bolshevik Revolution that the Russian influence was heavily felt in most areas. During the Soviet period the Russian language has been the language of government and a lingua franca among the nationalities, and the Russian culture has served as a model for developments in other areas.

Russians are to be found in large numbers throughout the country, often concentrated in the capital cities of the national areas where they serve as teachers, administrators, and technicians. They are also numerous in the developing areas of the northern part of central Asia and Siberia. During and after World War II members of several ethnic groups—including the Crimean Tatars and Volga Germans, as well as five groups from the Caucasus—were removed from their homelands for alleged cooperation with the Germans. Many inhabitants of the Baltic states found themselves in Siberian labor colonies. During the 1950's many of these peoples were permitted to return to their homelands.

Official policies toward ethnic groups are ambivalent. On the one hand, they recognize the variety in the country's peoples. In accordance with the slogan, "national in form, socialist in content," ethnic minorities are permitted to retain the part of their native cultures that is considered consonant with socialism, which is furthermore believed to be the ideal environment for the flourishing of national culture. In practice, not very much is considered consonant with socialism except the native language and some of the native folklore. Most of the ethnic groups, however, have managed to retain their distinctive features. Officially, every major ethnic group is supposed to be associated with a national territory, however small, and a national language, even if one had to be created. This policy, while permitting national self-expression, has also permitted the regime to divide the non-Russian peoples.

On the other hand, cultural variation within the Soviet Union is seen as a barrier to the creation of communism and national unity and even as an obsolescent stage of historical development. The blending of similar small groups is encouraged, as is their assimilation into the overall Russian culture. Russian language and culture are everywhere given a prominent place in the schools, and Russian words are added to native vocabularies. Blending (sblizheniye) and convergence (sliyaniye), two processes of culture change, are expected to result in a homogeneous or international Soviet culture, in which both the forms and content will be determined by socialism. According to Marxist theories, human beings can consciously direct their future and not just react passively to uncontrolled changes; from this arises the impetus to directed culture change.

Russians and other highly industrialized peoples may feel themselves superior to peoples who follow simpler modes of life and may be especially prone to do so in their role as culture bearers. At the same time, the non-Russians may resent the Russians in this same role and as conquerors. Among the non-Russians, those separated by thousands of miles of territory are without traditional attitudes toward each other, but within a culture area each group may have a particular reputation.

The role of Russian predominance in the social and cultural spheres has at times been officially recognized and at other times underplayed. Population shifts appear to be directing changes in the established patterns of ethnic group inter-relations within the Soviet Union. As the Russian population becomes proportionally smaller, the regime seems to give greater recognition to the other peoples within the limitations established by the Communist Party concerning expressions of nationalism.

EUROPEAN AREA

The European area stretches from the borders with Finland, Poland, Czechoslovakia, Hungary, Rumania on the west to the Ural Mountains in the east, and from the Arctic Ocean in the north to the Black Sea and the Caucasus Mountains and central Asian deserts on the south. This vast area encompasses millions of people and numerous ethnic groups but, despite its size and diversity, it is unified in its general character.

The area is largely a plain; there are forests, lakes, and bogs toward the north and dryer but more fertile earth toward the south (see ch. 2, Physical Environment). Traditional economy consisted largely of mixed farming—concentrating on cereals and potatoes—with pigs, cattle, and horses as the chief domestic animals. Forms of landholding and population distribution differed among the regions within the European area, but most persons were peasants cultivating fairly small holdings. Above the level of the family and kindred, locality was the basis for social organization.

Except for the Tatar presence, this region has been primarily oriented toward the West. Scandinavians founded Kievan Russia, and Peter the Great turned to Western Europe when he sought to reform the country. As a great power, Russia contended with other Western powers. The Slavic languages, spoken by a majority of Soviet Europeans, have most of their closest relatives to the West.

Soviet Europe, except for the Tatars, has historically been predominantly Christian, and of the Christians, largely Russian Orthodox (see ch. 13, Religion). In this respect it has been distinct from Catholic and Protestant Europe.

Slavic Subarea

Eastern Slavs have inhabited this area since prehistoric times. They formed a more or less homogeneous group for centuries, farming on the vast plains of their homeland. It was only comparatively recently that isolation and contacts with other peoples produced differentiation in language and social customs. The long Tatar rule isolated the Russians from the West and its developments, and the long period of Lithuanian and Polish rule turned the Belorussians and Ukrainians more toward the West. Many Ukrainians and Belorussians use Russian more than their native languages, or only Russian (see ch. 10, Languages and Social Communication).

Because of their westerly position and because of contacts with Poles and Lithuanians, some of the Ukrainians and Belorussians were Roman Catholics or Byzantine Catholics; that is, Orthodox who had become Uniates, recognizing the primacy of Rome (see ch. 13, Religion). This was a point of difference, often contention, with the Russians, who tended to identify with the Russian Orthodox Church. After World War II, Uniate Ukrainians officially became Orthodox, although the Uniate rite was reported to be observed illegally in some parts of the Ukraine.

Russians or Great Russians are the most numerous of the Slavs, as well as the largest ethnic group within the Soviet Union. The 1959 census found over 114 million of them. The Russians were the heart of the old Russian Empire and, under communism they have not only retained their essential character, but have institutionalized it in socialist development; for the non-Slavic peoples, socialization into the Soviet way of life has meant Russification.

Before the Bolshevik revolution most Russians lived in small villages strung out along country roads. Within the village, buildings were grouped according to function rather than by ownership, so that all the bathhouses were in one area and storehouses in another. Construction was of wood, either logs or planks. Land tenure was generally communal, held by the *mir*, a village commune with plots of farmland being redistributed periodically; later reforms increased the number of freeholding isolated peasants. Local government was exercised by the village council (*skhod*), which arrived at decisions by means of informal consensus. One council member (*starosta*) served as agent for the *skhod*. Every village had a priest, with a church and school supported by the community.

The village was a close, self-contained, and isolated community. Social control was maintained by means of gossip and public ridicule, as well as by the church. Within the family household, consisting of a man, his wife and children, and perhaps a grandmother, the husband was the undisputed head. Women could, however, own and control property themselves. Above the level of the family, close bilateral kin used to cooperate but did not form corporate groups.

Peasants were tied to the land, either on state lands or on lands owned by the aristocracy. Serfdom was abolished in 1861, but distinctions remained between the two groups of peasants, who generally maintained separate *mirs* and did not intermarry. The countryfolk supplemented their farming activities by migrant seasonal labor and various handicrafts. Despite their poverty, they had a rich folklore. Ceremonies and superstitions concerning courtship and marriage were elaborate.

There were over 37 million Ukrainians, or Little Russians, in 1959. Concentrated southwest of the Russians, they inhabit a more fertile and hospitable countryside. Ukrainian cities have become largely Russianized, so that it is the countryside that remains the Ukrainian homeland. Ukrainians have participated with the Russians in the development of the Soviet Union and have often been considered the same people as the Russians, by non-Slavs. Nevertheless, they have a tradition of separateness. In addition to the linguistic and religious differences, the Ukrainians generally lived on individual farms. The Soviet government has alternately encouraged and suppressed Ukrainian separatism according to expediency.

The 1959 census listed about 8 million Belorussians, or White Russians. They inhabit the land to the north of the Ukrainians and west of the Russians. Like the Ukrainians, they are sometimes Catholic and have been somewhat isolated geographically from the Russians. As in the Ukraine, the Belorussian language and culture have largely become limited to rural areas, but the cities have become Russian. Belorussian identity becomes largely a matter of sentiment.

Other Slavic peoples include the Poles (1,400,000), Czechs (25,000), Slovaks (15,000), Yugoslavs (5,000), and Bulgarians (324,000). These peoples have found themselves in the Soviet Union, either because of boundary adjustments in the west or because of population movements within the sphere of Communist countries. To judge by the low percentage of those still speaking their native languages, these Slavic minorities have become largely assimilated into the Russian majority.

The Baltic Subarea

Although the Baltic peoples have known only brief periods of independence from foreign rule, they nonetheless have a strong feeling of separate identity. Located along the Baltic Sea to the north of Belorussia, they are, proceeding from southwest to northeast, the Lithuanians, the Latvians, and the Estonians.

As might be expected from centuries of influence by Germans, Poles, Russians, and Scandinavians, the Baltic peoples are culturally mixed. Some are Lutheran, some are Roman Catholic, and some are Russian Orthodox. Russian or German settlement patterns had been imposed in some areas, but in general, the swampy terrain resulted in a distinctive pattern of isolated farmsteads. The rural farmhouse was similar to the Russian model, but many of the folk customs, including dress, were Scandinavian in origin.

In contrast to the Russians, the Baltic peoples generally did not favor communal farm labor. The Baltic peoples were not converted to Christianity until the late twelfth and thirteenth centuries, so that many pagan customs persisted, and the influence of the church was never as strong there. The customary diet leaned more heavily toward fish, milk products, and potatoes than the Russian, and the cooking style was generally Scandinavian.

In 1959 there were 2.4 million Lithuanians. They speak an Indo-European language that, together with Latvian, forms a distinct linguistic group. They have had close connections with the Poles and Belorussians, and they are predominantly Roman Catholic. The Latvians, numbering about 1.4 million, are closely related to the Lithuanians but have been more influenced by the Russians and Germans. Most of them are Lutheran. Ethnic Latvians are found mainly in the countryside, whereas the cities are more mixed, including both Russians and Germans. The Estonians, numbering about 1 million, speak a language related to Finnish rather than to the languages of Latvia and Lithuania. They have long been in contact with Finns and Scandinavians, and their culture is strongly Scandinavian. They are mostly Lutheran, but a few of them are Russian Orthodox. Like the Latvians, the Estonians generally are a rural people, concentrating on dairying and lumbering. Within Latvia, on the Baltic coast, are a few Livonians, who speak a language related to Estonian and who subsist as fishermen.

Uralian Peoples

Speaking a related group of languages, the Uralian peoples exist as islands on the margins and in the midst of Slavic peoples, where some lived before the advent of the Slavs. A number of them have specialized in hunting, fishing, and lumbering occupations.

The Mordvins, living close to Moscow, numbered about 1.3 million in 1959. Converted to the Russian Orthodox Church, they have retained a number of their old customs. Many of them speak Russian in addition to, or instead of, Mordvin.

The Komi and Permyaks are found in the north of the Russian area, just west of the Ural Mountains. There were about 400,000 of them in 1959 and, like the Mordvins, were largely assimilated into

162

the Russian majority. Because of their northerly homeland, their native economy includes reindeer herding, hunting, fishing, and lumbering, with some agriculture and industry toward the south.

The Mari, or Cheremis, are located along the Volga River almost directly east of Moscow. Numbering about 500,000 in 1959, they have managed to keep from being assimilated into the Russian sphere. Most of them were officially Russian Orthodox, with a few Muslims. During the nineteenth century a nativistic religion was developed, which played a large part in the maintenance of their separate identity. Their occupations are mainly lumbering and farming.

The Udmurts, or Votyaks, included over 600,000 in 1959. Situated to the south of the Komi, their culture has been heavily influenced by that of neighboring Turkic peoples. Most of them were traditionally pagan, although they had been formally converted to the Russian Orthodox Church.

There were about 170,000 Karelians in 1959 inhabiting the Karelian peninsula as well as the region southeast of Leningrad. Their way of life is much like that of the Finns—living on scattered farms. They are Russian Orthodox in religion. Increasing numbers of them have become assimilated into the Russian majority. There were a few thousand other Finnic peoples; about 93,000 ethnic Finns; 16,000 Vepsy; 1,800 Lapps (called Saami in Russian); and about 1,100 Ixhors, or Leningrad Finns. The Lapps and Izhors specialized in herding and lumbering, and the Finns and Vepsy are so scattered that they are undergoing a rapid process of assimilation.

Others

There is a sizable number of other groups, which cannot be fitted into any single category, although most of them are either Turkic or European in origin. Many of them became assimilated into the Russian majority by the 1960's.

The Chuvash, Bashkirs, and Tatars are all Turkic peoples. The Chuvash, however, are Russian Orthodox; and the Bashkirs and Tatars are Muslim with ties to their central Asian kinsmen. In 1959 there were about 1.5 million Chuvash, 1 million Bashkirs, and 5 million Tatars, not all of whom were within the European region of the Soviet Union. The Chuvash have been largely isolated from other Turkic peoples and have managed to preserve a sense of ethnic separateness. The Bashkirs, on the other hand, have become increasingly merged with the Tatars.

Tatars are to be found along the Volga, where they have an autonomous republic, and in the Crimea, along the Black Sea. At one time, they ruled the Russian people and, despite the centuries of contact with Christian Slavs, have managed to remain a separate people. The Crimean Tatars were deported during World War II for alleged collaboration with the Germans. Although they have been officially absolved of the charge against them, few have been allowed to return to their homeland. The rest—still concentrated around Tashkent in central Asia—have been increasingly vocal in their discontent.

Over 1.5 million Germans were identified in 1959. At one time they were concentrated in the Baltic States, as well as in the Ukraine, small areas in Siberia, and along the Volga, where they had an autonomous republic. After World War II, many of them were returned to Germany or were deported to the Tashkent region and to areas in Siberia. They are among the scattered peoples of the Soviet Union.

Around 2.3 million persons identified themselves as Jews in the 1959 census. Not all of these were European, for there are concentrations of Jews native to the Caucasus and central Asia. The official Jewish language is Yiddish, but only about one-fifth of the Soviet Jews speak it. They have an autonomous oblast in eastern Siberia, but few of them live there (see ch. 19, Formal Structure of the Union Government). Most of them have become assimilated into the Russian population, and many no longer follow Judaism. They are concentrated in the cities of Kiev, Leningrad, and Moscow.

Over 2 million Moldavians lived in Bessarabia, southeast of the Ukraine; it was acquired by the Soviet Union from Rumania in 1940 and is now known as the Moldavian Soviet Socialist Republic. An additional 106,000 persons identified themselves as Rumanians. These isolated mountain peasants speak a Romance language and are mostly Eastern Orthodox. Approximately 310,000 Greeks were counted in 1959; most of them were assimilated into the surrounding population of the southern Ukraine. There were also about 160,000 Hungarians, as well as a few thousand other Europeans, most of whom were assimilated into the Russian population.

THE CAUCASIAN AREA

The region of hills and high mountains between the Black Sea and the Caspian Sea is the smallest culture area in the Soviet Union but the most varied. Centuries of isolation in mountain valleys have produced a variety of languages and ethnic groups, most of them small, but independent and proud of their identity.

Throughout history the area's economic life was varied. Crops were widely diversified and included grapes and tea. The diet was similar to that of the Middle East, with an emphasis on mutton, rice, and many vegetables. A variety of livestock was raised, often in a transhumant or seminomadic manner. Many peoples of the Caucasus were famous for their handicrafts, including metalwork, felt cloaks, tapestries, and wooden and leather objects. In the mountains, houses were generally clustered together on the hillside, but in more open country scattered homesteads were the rule. Stone was often used in construction. By the nineteenth century, the old tribal organization had given way to feudal and village organization. Folklore and values upheld traditions of chivalry, honor, hospitality, and bravery.

Religious affiliations were similarly diverse, and during the 1960's the area had Muslims, both Sunni and Shia, and Jews. Most Christians were Byzantine Orthodox, but there were also Armenian Gregorian and Catholic, as well as a few Jacobites and Protestants (see ch. 13, Religion).

The Caucasian languages are unique to the area, with no known related languages elsewhere. There were also a number of representatives of other language families in the area, producing a linguistic mosaic. Many of these languages have had their own alphabets for many centuries, and the people are proud of their ancient literature and civilized traditions (see ch. 10, Languages and Social Communication).

Caucasian peoples have made an impression on the rest of the country out of proportion to their numbers. Joseph Stalin was a Georgian, although highly Russianized. The composer Aram Khachaturyan the former world chess champion Tigran Petrosian, and the politician Anastas Mikoyan are also from the Caucasus.

The Azerbaijani are the most numerous of the Caucasian peoples, encompassing about 3 million persons. Although they speak a Turkic language, they are Shia Muslims. An even larger group of Azerbaijani live across the border in Iran, but there are few ties between the two groups. Originally they were agricultural and herding people, both nomadic and sedentary, but since exploitation of the Baku oilfields in their region began, many of them have become industrial workers.

There are about 3 million Armenians in the Soviet Union and also large numbers of them elsewhere in the world, especially in the United States and the Middle East, where they fled after disturbances in Asia Minor in the early twentieth century. Although not independent, Soviet Armenia is the only Armenian state in existence and, as a cultural and national center, attracts the interest of Armenians throughout the world. Armenians are proud of their ancient Christian and literary traditions; their Gregorian Church is unique to them, and they have had a literary language since ancient times.

There are about 2.7 million Georgians. They speak one of the Caucasian languages, have been Christian since the fourth century, and have been in the Caucasus for centuries. Although they have a long history of contact with Europe and the Byzantine world, they have tenaciously held onto their identity and, even during the Soviet period, have resisted assimilation. They have a reputation as fierce and independent fighters. A few thousand Georgian-speaking Jews live around Tbilisi.

Next in number are the so-called Daghestan peoples, who inhabit an area to the north of the Azerbaijanis along the Caspian Sea. Altogether there are over 900,000 of them. Most of them, including the Avars, Laks, Dargins, Lezgians, Aguls, Rutuls, Tsakhur, and Tabasarans, speak Caucasian languages, but the Nogai and Kumyk are Turkic. Some groups, such as the Avars, Dargins, Laks, Tabasarans, and Kumuks, have their own literary languages, whereas others must use one of the languages of the larger groups and are in the process of becoming assimilated. The Daghestan peoples are all Sunni Muslims. The traditional economy is varied but tends toward stockraising and crafts. There were a number of even smaller groups within the Daghestan region, most of them only a few thousand in number, who are becoming assimilated.

The 1959 census enumerated 420,000 Chechens and 106,000 Ingush. These Sunni Muslims, speakers of Caucasian languages, were deported in 1943 to Kazakhstan for alleged collaboration with the Germans. In the late 1950's they were permitted to return to their homelands.

About 413,000 Ossets live in the central Caucasus. Speaking an Indo-European language closely related to that spoken in Afghanistan and the Pamirs, the Ossets are Eastern Orthodox or Sunni Muslim. Other Indo-European peoples in the Caucasus include the Talysh, Tats, and Kurds, as well as a few thousand ethnic Iranians. About one-half of the Tats are followers of Judaism. The Kurds extend into Turkey, Iran, Iraq, and Syria, and the Soviet government has encouraged their insurgency movements in some of those countries.

Because of alleged disloyalty, the Kalmyks, numbering 106,000, the Balkars (42,000), and the Karachay (81,000) were deported by the government in 1943 to areas in central Asia but have since been allowed to return. The Balkars and Karachay are Turkic, and the Kalmyks are Mongolian. All are Sunni, but the Kalmyks were distinctive in basing their subsistence on pastoral nomadism and fishing rather than on agriculture.

The Circassians are a large but divided group, some of whom are referred to as Kabardians and others as Adegey. Altogether there are about 314,000 Circassians; they are situated in the Caucasus Mountains to the north of Georgia. Speaking a language related to Georgian, most of them are Sunni Muslims. Many had fled to the Middle East in the midnineteenth century, when their homeland was conquered by the tsarist forces. Despite their maintenance of a separate identity in the Middle East, they have not served as a focal point for insurgent movements there.

There are several thousand ethnic Turks and Turkomans in the Caucasus. Most of these are Sunni, although a few in Georgia, called Gagauz, are Christians. The Assyrians, a small remnant of a once-large group that was widespread throughout Asia, speak Aramaic, which is a Semitic language; they are Jacobite Christians. Many Assyrians are also found in Iraq and Syria.

CENTRAL ASIA

Stretching east of the Caspian Sea to the borders with Mongolia and China lies a region about the size of the European area. Unlike Europe, however, this region contains large areas of desert and mountain and is much more sparsely inhabited. Most of the peoples within the area are speakers of Turkic languages and are mainly Islamic.

Central Asia has been subject to invasions and population movements for many centuries because of its location between the Far East and the Middle East and Europe, and it has served as a corridor for both traders and warriors. The earliest known inhabitants were the Soghdians, who were Iranian. After Cyrus the Great, the area became part of the Persian Empire, and Alexander the Great later conquered the area. To the east of the Iranians, in what is now Mongolia and China, lived Turkic peoples. During this early period, Buddhism was introduced. Later Nestorian Christian missionaries spread their Semitic alphabet into the area where it was adapted even for Mongolian languages; also, Manichaeanism arrived from Persia.

In the seventh and eight centuries of the Christian era, the Arab Muslims conquered central Asia and brought it into permanent contact with Middle Eastern civilization. Islam and the Arabic alphabet were established, as was classical scholarship. Shortly after this time, pagan Turks began to enter the area from the east; some remained nomadic, but others settled and became Muslims. The region eventually became almost entirely Turkic, although Iranian influence remained strong among sedentary peoples.

By the middle ages the central Asian life-pattern had become well established. Farmers made a prosperous living in oases and along the river banks. The oasis cities were great centers of science, literature, and religion, as well as being centers for the lucrative trade with the east. These cities formed nuclei for small and unstable states. In the dry areas away from the cities, pagan Turks moved about with their herds, trading with, and occasionally raiding, the sedentary peoples.

Central Asians, as participants in the advanced civilization of the

Islamic middle ages, made outstanding contributions to Western civilization. Ibn Sina, known as Avicenna, and Al Farabi wrote extensively on physiology, music, and philosophy; and al Khawarizmi, from Khiva, made important advances in algebra. Later, other central Asians built observatories for study of astronomy.

At the beginning of the thirteenth century, the Mongols invaded from the east. Unlike previous conquerors, who merely substituted their rule for that of their predecessors, the Mongols destroyed towns and farms, irrigation works, schools, mosques, libraries, and bazaars. Political stability was established, but at a great price. Eventually, prosperity and civilization began to return, but not until the twentieth century has marked progress been made.

By the sixteenth century, the trade routes across central Asia were being supplanted by sea routes to the Far East. The Russian Empire began to make inroads into the area and, by the midnineteenth century, much of central Asia had been incorporated into the empire. Since the Bolshevik revolution, more and more Russians have moved into the area, but the native peoples have resisted assimilation. The area has also served as a place of exile for disfavored nationalities, such as the Tatars and Germans, as well as the other peoples who have since returned home.

The Uzbeks are the most numerous of the central Asian peoples, encompassing over 6 million in 1959. These Sunni Muslim peoples are the sedentary descendants of one of the Turkic tribes that invaded the area after the seventh century. Their capital, Tashkent, was long a center for trade and learning and, as a result, their language was more influenced by Persian than were some of the other Turkic languages of the region. Tashkent has become the biggest industrial city in central Asia, and many Russians have moved there, creating a new city alongside the old. The exiled Tatars are located near there.

The Kazakhs are the next most numerous; there were about 3.6 million in 1959. The most northerly of the central Asian peoples, their area borders on the European area. It has been heavily settled by European farmers engaged in cultivating steppe lands that were formerly inhabited by pastoral nomads. Many of these nomadic Turks fled into Sinkiang (China) to join related peoples in an attempt to avoid collectivization and sedentarization, but many returned to escape the Communist Chinese regime. Kazakhstan has also been a focus for resettlement of exiled peoples.

The Tadzhiks, unlike most of the other peoples of central Asia, are Iranians, speaking a language similar to standard Persian. There are about 1.4 million Tadzhiks, inhabiting a small mountainous area bordering on Afganistan and regions within Iran and Afghanistan. Most of the Tadzhiks are Sunni Muslims, but a small group in remote mountain areas are Shiites. Some other small Iranian groups are found in the Pamirs.

Some 970,000 Kirgiz were counted in 1959. Both in language and way of life they closely resemble the Kazakh. Their mountainous land, however, necessitated a different variety of nomadism that involved movement between summer and winter pastures. Many Kirgiz are also located across the border in Sinkiang.

The 173,000 Karakalpaks are the next numerous, living south of the Aral Sea in an area that is devoted to cotton raising, but which was once given to mixed farming. Living among the Uzbek are numerous Uzbek-speaking Jews, particularly, in the ancient cities of Bukhara and Samarkand. Some 20,000 Dungans, (Chinese-speaking Muslims) and about 90,000 Uyghurs (a Turkic Muslim people from east of the Tien Shans) also live in this part of central Asia.

Over a million Turkmens live in a region bordering the Caspian Sea and the Iranian border and are also scattered in groups in the Caucasus and south into the Middle East. Living in an isolated region, many of them have retained their old nomadic ways or their traditional farming life. About 300,000 Koreans were brought from the Far East in the 1930's to introduce rice cultivation into central Asia. Since then, they have been concentrated in villages in the Syr Darya valley in southern Kazakhstan.

PALEO-SIBERIA

Before the Russian conquest and settlement, the vast region east of the Urals was inhabited by a variety of small groups. Some of these had affinities with Turkic and Mongolian peoples to the south, but others had a more isolated development. Their archaic way of life was well adapted to their rigorous climate and terrain. In the far north, most of the people subsisted by hunting, fishing, and gathering of wild plants. Farther south, reindeer herding and some agriculture were possible.

Most of the Paleo-Siberians lived in small communities, usually based on membership in patrilineal-descent groups. Within these exogamous clans, authority was generally patriarchal. Households were composed of nuclear families, but the entire community participated in joint economic activities, such as hunting and food gathering; the successful shared with the less fortunate.

The Paleo-Siberian peoples had no organized religion such as that found in more developed regions. They believed, however, in various nature spirits and often had cults of such large animals as the bear. One prominent feature was shamanism. The shaman was a person, male or female, who was believed to have special supernatural powers. Shamans held seances at which they communed with the spirits. After singing and drumming and falling into a trance, shamans upon returning to consciousness reported on what the spirits were supposed to have said. Shamans also claimed to be able to move objects without touching them. Individuals also made offerings to the spirits to avert harm or to ensure fertility of the animals they depended upon. Before the Bolshevik revolution, when Russians were actively colonizing Siberia, the Russian Orthodox Church sent missionaries to convert the natives (see ch. 13, Religion). Although most of the people were formally converted, they retained many of their old beliefs and practices, often in syncretist form.

The Paleo-Siberian peoples developed a complex material culture out of simple materials to deal with their harsh environment. Every part of any animal they killed was either eaten or used for clothing, housing, or hunting equipment. Nearly all edible wild plants were used as food. Fish and meat were preserved by drying, freezing, and smoking. Clothing was made out of furs and skins and decorated by dye or embroidery in geometric designs. Ingenious snares and other devices were used in hunting, as were skin boats and dugout canoes. Houses were made of bark and logs, or of skins or felt stretched over wood frames. Since many peoples migrated between winter and summer residences, they had different kinds of houses for the two seasons. Except for the reindeer herders, most people had only dogs as domesticated animals. The dogs carried burdens, pulled small sleds, herded animals, and aided in hunting.

Native folklore was distinctive. Songs with simple melodies and structure accompanied shamanist ceremonies and festive occasions. Epic narratives and myths were recited. Clothing and other utilitarian objects were decorated, and these decorations constituted the only forms of the visual arts.

The Paleo-Siberian peoples can be subdivided into two major groups, those of the south and those of the north. Altogether the Paleo-Siberian peoples do not number over 300,000 persons. Although Russian contacts with these peoples go as far back as the eleventh century, it was only after the 1860's and the freeing of the serfs that extensive contacts and colonization began. Contacts had also been long established with the Mongols and Chinese to the south. The native diet had been expanded to include tea, sugar, and a little flour; tobacco became popular, and the people began to use guns for hunting. As a result of European contacts, many of them turned to hunting fur-bearing animals for profit.

Southern Siberia

In the south are the Tuvins, numbering about 100,000. Although they are Turkic in origin, they have been heavily influenced by the

Mongols who ruled them. Formerly, they were mostly reindeer herders, with some reliance on hunting, fishing, and agriculture. Their country became a Russian protectorate in 1914 and was given independence after the Bolshevik revolution; but it was absorbed into the Soviet Union in 1944. Although shamanist in religion, many of the Tuvins had become Buddhists. About 57,000 Khakas live northwest of the Tuvins. Turkic in language, they encompass subgroups known as the Kachin, Sagay, Beltir, Kyzyl, and Koybal. They are mostly nomadic stockbreeders, although some are sedentary farmers. They have been nominally converted to Russian Orthodoxy.

Directly west of the Tuvins are the 45,000 Turkic Altay. At one time they were a powerful group in central Asia and their name, derived from the name of the mountains they inhabit, has been given to that large group of languages that includes the Turkic languages. Although they were converted by Russian Orthodox missionaries, they retained much of their old shamanistic religion. After 1904 a nativistic religious movement, based partly on Buddhism, sprang up in reaction to Russian domination of the area.

Some 300,000 Buryat Mongols inhabit the region east of Lake Baikal. Mongolian culture is similar to that of the Turkic peoples, although the Buryats are mostly Buddhists and sedentary farmers. Before the Russians entered their area, they were largely nomadic stockraisers, living in felt tents. During the twelfth and thirteenth centuries, they were part of Genghis Khan's empire.

Along the lower Amur River in southeastern Siberia and on Sakhalin Island in the Sea of Okhotsk lives a group of related peoples known collectively as Nanai or Goldi. Speaking Tungusic languages related to those spoken north of them, they have relatives in Manchuria. Altogether, there are over 12,000 Nanai, including the Ulchi, Udegeys, Oroks, Orochi, and the Negidals; they are mainly sedentary hunters and fishers. The Nanai have been under both Buddhist and Russian Orthodox influence.

Also in the same area are some 4,000 Nivkhy or Gilyak making a living mainly by fishing. There are also a few thousand Ainu on Sakhalin Island, but most of the Ainu are in Japan. About 15,000 Shors inhabit an area between the Khakas and Altai. These Turkic Muslim peoples formerly lived by hunting, but with the arrival of large numbers of Russians who came to exploit the extensive iron ore deposits in the area, they became largely assimilated. There are a few other Turkic peoples scattered about, including some Tatars and Tofalars. The Jewish Autonomous Oblast is located in southeastern Siberia, along the Amur River. There are few Jews in the oblast, however, and they are European, rather than Paleo-Siberian in culture.

Northern Siberia

Inhabiting a vast area of central Siberia is the largest northern Siberian ethnic group, the Yakuts. Speaking a Turkic language, the Yakuts, who numbered 237,000 in 1959, are one of the least isolated and most advanced of the Siberian peoples. Before the Russians arrived in large numbers during the eighteenth century, they subsisted as nomads herding cattle and horses or reindeer, and living in dome-shaped felt tents (yurts). Some subsisted by fishing, hunting, and gathering, and only in the south was agriculture found. The Russians introduced their Orthodox Church, but the old shamanist religion remained strong. Despite the Russian influence, the Yakuts have been able to resist assimilation. A few thousand Dolgans, speaking a related language, live along the Arctic Ocean.

In the far northwest along the Arctic Ocean are various Samoyedic-speaking groups, numbering in all about 27,600 in 1959. Subgroups are called the Nganasans, Ents, Selkups, and Nenets. Because of the rigorous climate of their Arctic land, fishing, hunting of sea animals, and some reindeer herding are the principal occupations. Other groups in the same general area include the Khanty and Mansi, together numbering about 26,000, and the Kets, of whom there are only about 1,000.

Scattered across a broad area of Siberia, from the Ob River to the Sea of Okhotsk, are the Evens, or Lamuts, and the Evenks, or Tungus. Despite the vast area in which they are found, there are only about 34,000 of these peoples, most of whom are reindeer herders.

East of the vast Yakut region, extending to the Pacific Ocean and down into the Kamchatka Peninsula, are a number of small groups, many of them partly assimilated into the Russian population of the area. The Chukchi, perhaps the best known, inhabit an area in the north, opposite Alaska. This group, about 12,000 in number, lives by fishing, hunting, and reindeer herding. Their way of life is similar to that of the Eskimos living among them and in the United States and Canada. The Koryaks, about 6,300 in number, and the Itelmens, about 1,000, speak related languages and have a similar way of life. The Eskimos and Aleuts, who also inhabit regions in Alaska and Canada, speak related languages and number about 1,500 altogether.

POPULATION MOVEMENTS

The great lands occupied by the Soviet Union have been the scene of population movements since prehistoric times. The homelands of both major linguistic groups within the country, the Indo-European and the Uralic-Altaic, are contained in or near the country's borders, but the present spreads reflect many changes.

Types and causes of population movements have been varied. Pressures from surrounding populations, conquests or dissolutions of other states, economic and other pressures on available resources, and desires to exploit new resources have provided reasons for wholesale population movements. Peoples have also moved to escape conquest or domination, to conquer others, or they have been moved to become exiles. Some population movements involved the wholesale transplantation of people and their culture into new areas; but others merely involved a domination on the top level, with perhaps a change in language or religion, but with the indigenous population remaining in place. Finally, some types of population movement involved the removal or destruction of native peoples without a subsequent replacement by the invaders.

The Slavs

The Russians and other Slavs originated in central and eastern Europe, where they had been since Neolithic times—about 10,000 B.C. They became separated about 1,000 B.C. from the Baltic peoples, who subsequently underwent a separate development. Somewhat later came pressures from the Celts and Germanic peoples and then an invasion by the Huns. After the breakup of the Hun state in the sixth century A.D., the Slavic peoples began to move west, south, and east. By this time the Slavs were divided into three groups, which became the basis for the later divisions into East, West, and South Slavs, but there were only minor cultural and regional dialectic differences among them.

By the ninth century A.D., the Slavs had arrived at their present-day distribution but were still largely undifferentiated. From the eighth to the eleventh century, the Slavs underwent increasing differentiation because of isolation, contacts with non-Slavic peoples, and internal economic and political divisions. During the tenth and eleventh centuries the East Slavs—ancestors of the Russians, Belorussians, and Ukrainians—were converted to Byzantine Orthodox Christianity, while the West and South Slavs became mainly Roman Catholic (see ch. 13, Religion). By the eleventh century, the East Slavs had divided into several small states headed by princes (see ch. 3, Historical Setting).

After the locus of power had shifted to Novgorod in the north and later to Moscow, and while the Poles and Lithuanians controlled much of the Ukraine and Belorussia, the Russians were already beginning to explore the region east of the Urals. Merchants from Novgorod were well aware of the economic potential of Siberia. Until well into the nineteenth century, Muscovite princes gradually extended Russian domination (see ch. 3, Historical Setting). It was not until after the freeing of the serfs in 1861 that large-scale settlement of Russians began in Siberia. Peasants, both Russian Orthodox and the dissident Old Believers, sought new opportunities. Entrepreneurs went in to trade guns and other Russian goods for furs, while missionaries tried to convert the native Siberians. The Russian government founded penal colonies and places of exile in remote areas of Siberia.

According to the 1959 census, Russians comprised 83 percent of the Russian Soviet Federated Socialist Republic and nearly 55 percent of the total population of the Soviet Union. In most of the other republics they constitute a large proportion of the population. In Kazakhstan they account for about 43 percent of the total—more than the Kazakhs—and in Kirgizia about 30 percent. Russians form a large minority in the Baltic republics of Latvia and Estonia and somewhat smaller minorities in the other Slavic republics; they are least numerous in Armenia. Within the union republics, the Russians often tend to concentrate in certain regions constituting a majority in some smaller level administrative units and are especially numerous in the capital cities.

The distribution of Russians outside their original area can be explained by administrative, cultural, and economic factors. The Russians are the dominant group within the Soviet Union; they predominate in higher level party and government positions, as well as in the lower levels, and in these positions are found chiefly in the administrative centers. Many Russians serve as teachers and directors of other cultural enterprises, as well as doctors, engineers, and other professional workers, and again are concentrated in capitals and other large cities. Industrial centers have been established to exploit the resources in remote Siberian regions, and the population of these cities is largely Russian, although the turnover is high.

The Kazakh region has been the scene of the virgin lands settlement program. Steppe lands, previously inhabited only by pastoral nomads, were settled by Russian farmers, and the lands were plowed and sowed in grain crops. The nomads had to settle or move elsewhere. Drought and dust storms, however, have reduced the appeal of the program, and the Russian population in the area may decrease.

The birth rate among the Russians is lower than that of non-Russians, particularly the central Asians and peoples of the Caucasus. It has been predicted that by 1970, when the next census is scheduled, the Russians will comprise less than 50 percent of the total population, although they will remain the largest ethnic group. Reports from Moscow in early 1969 indicated that the Russians were preparing for their prospective minority status. The multinational character of the Soviet state was being stressed, and the guiding role of the Russians deemphasized. Demographic realities seem to be guiding a return to early Bolshevik policies toward non-

Russian ethnic groups (see ch. 20, Component Political Subdivisions).

The Uralian-Altaians

The original home of the Turks, Mongols, and Tungus, as well as the Uralian peoples, lies in eastern Siberia. The characteristic Mongoloid facial structure is believed by many physical anthropologists to have originated in the intense dry and cold climate of Siberia, where it is well adapted. This structure subsequently spread to other areas where it was not at a selective disadvantage but may have disappeared because of the small numbers of its bearers.

By the time the first Slavs penetrated into what was to become Russia, the land was already inhabited by Uralian peoples, many of whom were either absorbed, pushed to the north, or allowed to remain as islands in the Slavic sea. The Samoyeds, Lapps, Mordvins, Komi, Permyaks, Mari, Udmurts, Vepsy, and Finns are modern representatives of these pre-Slavic peoples of Russia.

Subsequent population movements from the east into Russia were composed largely of Turkic peoples. The Huns arrived, coming through central Asia, in the fourth century A.D. They played an important role in the subsequent Slavic migrations. In the sixth century, a similar people, the Avars, appeared, to rule for over two centuries. A small remnant of them remains in the Caucasus. Both the Huns and the Avars were pagan nomadic herdsmen. The Khazars, who appeared in the next century were a similar people but were more sedentary and civilized. They have left no discernible remnants behind them, although they were a powerful force in their time.

Turkic peoples began to settle in central Asia during the first centuries of the Christian era, where they encountered Iranian peoples who had been there for at least two thousand years, and who had been in contact with their kinsmen in Iran and other neighboring countries. In the oasis regions, they were settled farmers who were for a time incorporated into the Persian and Greek Empires. To the north were the Scythians, who were horse nomads. Except for the Ossets and Mountain or Pamir Tadzhiks, they have left no linguistic survivors. Early Turkic settlers were either absorbed into the local Iranian populations or moved on to become a force in early Slavic and Byzantine history.

After the seventh century great numbers of Turks moved into central Asia where they encountered Islam; those who became sedentary became Muslim, but the nomadic Turks tended to remain pagan. So many Turks entered the region that it became known as Turkestan. Ethnic differentiations among these peoples are hard to establish, but they were composed of various tribal federations united under strong leaders. After the death of the leader the federation generally split, with the components later combining in another fashion under another leader. Some groups were more in contact with non-Turks than others, some being heavily influenced by the Iranians and others by the culturally similar Mongolians.

In the thirteenth century most of the Mongols as well as many Turks were united under Genghis Khan and swept westward into Russia across central Asia and the Caucasus. While the Khan still lived, unity prevailed but, after his death, the conquered territories were divided among three of his sons. They managed to extend his territory for a time. The Mongol territory was centered on Sarai on the lower Volga. The Mongols in Russian territory eventually became Turkicized. Those who remained in Russia proper eventually became known as Tatars, and their descendants—the Volga and Crimean Tatars, the Bashkirs, and the Chuvash—are the remnants of these peoples who once ruled Russia. In central Asia, the Mongol state split up into a number of small khanates based on the oasis cities of Samarkand, Tashkent, Khiva, and Bukhara, which were not conquered by the Russians until the nineteenth century. Their descendants are the Kazakhs, Uzbeks, Kirgiz, Karakalpaks, and Turkmens.

On the whole, the Turks and Mongols, being nomads, did not contribute a great deal to civilization in the areas they entered, except their languages. They did contribute indirectly to the isolation of Russia from general European developments and to the separate development of the Belorussian and Ukrainian peoples. They changed trade routes, set back development in central Asia, and altered the relations between peoples.

Others

Many of the peoples of Siberia speak Turkic languages or the related Tungusic languages. Inhabiting more northerly regions, they follow reindeer herding rather than mixed herding or subsist as hunters and fishers. Whether the Turkic peoples originated in the north, spread there from the south, or merely influenced the peoples in the north is not known for certain. The Paleo-Asiatic way of life is ancient, in many particulars not having changed a great deal since the Upper Paleolithic period. The primary reason for this conservatism is the rigorous climate. Even the Soviets bent on collectivization and reform of native cultures have not been able to make many changes and have had to give in to the climate.

The presence of the Caucasian languages, with a high degree of internal diversity and lack of known relatives outside the area, indicates that the Caucasian peoples have inhabited their area for many centuries. Some Soviet scholars have asserted that the Caucasians represent a survival of an ancient Mediterranean stratum of languages, but no proof exists for this hypothesis. Culturally and physically the Caucasians resemble their non-Caucasian neighbors (see ch. 10, Languages and Social Communication).

The period of intensive collectivization, which reached its peak during the 1930's, and the strong rule of Joseph Stalin resulted in the movement of sizable populations. Thousands of Kazakhs and Kirgiz moved across the border into Sinkiang (China) to join their ethnic kinsmen and escape the pressures for collectivization. During the 1960's many of these peoples have moved back across the border to escape the Communist Chinese regime. The Baltic peoples, the Estonians, Lithuanians, and Latvians, with their traditions of independent farms, also resisted collectivization. Many emigrated or were deported to detention centers elsewhere in the Soviet Union, to be replaced by Russians. During World War II some of them were charged with collaboration with the Germans, and consequently thousands more were deported.

The Volga Germans, the Crimean Tatars, and the Chechen-Ingush, Kalmyk, Karachay, and Balkars, all fell under suspicion during World War II for collaboration with the Germans. These populations were removed en masse from their homelands, and their autonomous regions were renamed or absorbed into other regions. Russians and Ukrainians replaced the deported peoples, who ceased to be officially recognized as ethnic groups, and whose rights as Soviet citizens were curtailed.

In the mid-1950's a partial reversal of policies occurred. The Caucasian groups were permitted to return home, and their administrative units were restored to them. They were all officially recognized in the 1959 census. The Germans were allowed to return home; they are again recognized officially as a people, although their autonomous republic was not restored.

The Crimean Tatars were absolved of their alleged crimes and were also supposed to be restored to their lands. Tatars were listed in the 1959 census, but it cannot be said whether the figures given include the Crimean Tatars since there are Tatar groups throughout the country. Crimean Tatars who were deported to a region near Tashkent, the capital of Uzbekistan, have claimed that they have not been allowed to return to their homeland and that their other rights have not been restored. Reluctant to disturb the settlement pattern of the Ukraine, into which the Crimean Tatar republic was absorbed, the government until 1969 had not acceded to the Crimean Tatar demands for permission to return. Some of their leaders had been jailed, and few have been allowed to resettle in the Crimea.

OFFICIAL POLICIES

The Bolsheviks took over a multinational state from the tsarist empire. Lenin's original impulse had been to proclaim self-determination for all the peoples contained therein, assuming that they would not take advantage of the proclamation because of economic ties to the Russians or because of local Communist movements. Instead, most of the non-Russian areas chose independence, and many were self-governing for several years. The Russians needed the resources of the non-Russian regions, and they also wished to extend their movement; and so, they reconquered the regions that had seceded. The reconquered regions were incorporated into an overall administrative and economic framework, and the process of directed culture change began.

Soviet policy toward ethnic minorities is governed by the slogan proposed by Stalin in 1930, "national in form, socialist in content," treating cultural form and content as separable entities. *Form* seems to refer mainly to local folklore; *content* refers to attitudes toward work, social organization, and techniques of production. Cultural items considered bourgeois or incompatible with socialism are to be transformed. Since such forms as abstract or geometric art forms and designs, non-Western modal scales or tense, rather than relaxed vocal-production in singing styles, and poems with tragic themes, may all be considered contrary to socialist realism—not to mention nonsocialist modes of production and distribution—no aspect of native culture can be considered invulnerable to directed culture change.

Functionalist theory in modern social science views the parts of a sociocultural system as interconnected, so that changes in one aspect result in changes elsewhere. Even Marxist theory is functionalist in this sense, regarding the economic sector as fundamental. In the evolution of world societies toward communism changes in the economic sector result in changes in other parts of society. Soviet theory, if not practice, would seem to be incompatible with classical Marxism.

Even without extensive directed culture change, the non-Russian cultures of the Soviet Union would be undergoing processes of change, by virtue of their contacts with the Russians and by their incorporation into the overall administrative and economic network. The process unquestionably has been more rapid under the Soviet regime.

At the same time, however, changes have not been as far reaching as was hoped. Active and passive resistance on the part of the peoples concerned, administrative inefficiency, changes and contradictions in policies, as well as the exigencies of geography in many areas have resulted in the retention of many native institutions. For

178

example, agriculture is not possible or is at best marginal and un-profitable in vast regions of Siberia and central Asia. Pastoral nomadism, as it evolved over many centuries, was found to be the most efficient economy in some areas. The Soviet need for Siberian furs has permitted the peoples of the Far North to retain most of their native way of life, although attempts have been made to sub-stitute the hunting of one animal on a cash basis for a subsistence-type economy involving more varied hunting, fishing, and gathering. Reindeer herding has been organized on a collective basis, but rein-deer brigades have often been based on indigenous clan organi-zations.

In practice as well as in explicit statements, the native culture comes to mean the native language, and even this is to undergo transformations. Words borrowed from languages such as Arabic and Persian, associated with cultures outside the Soviet Union, are to be replaced by words of native origin. Where, as was often the case, the native language contained no vocabulary for modern in-dustrial techniques and products, words had to be introduced; generally the introduction of Russian vocabulary seemed easiest (see ch. 10, Languages and Social Communication).

Officially, every major ethnic group is supposed to be associated with a national territory and a national literary language. Thus the Jews, regarded as an ethnic group rather than a religious group, were given a small and inhospitable territory in eastern Siberia with which they had no historical connection or interest. Their language is considered to be Yiddish even though most of them do not speak it. In central Asia, the Kirgiz and Kazakh differed little from each other except in subsistence and minor dialectic variations, but they were divided into two territories and given separate literary lan-guages. The old Turkic lingua franca, Chagatai, was replaced by separate literary languages—one for each group. The policy of let-ting each ethnic group have its own language and land has had the result, at least in part deliberate, of dividing and ruling. In the case of Turkic central Asia, the Soviet rulers wished to avert the threat of Pan-Turkic and Pan-Islamic movements developing, which would encompass Turkic peoples not only within the Soviet Union, but also those in Sinkiang (China) and the Middle East, mainly Turkey.

In Marxist theory, separate national and ethnic identities and cultures will merge into a new international Communist society. This merging is supposed to be the result of natural evolutionary processes, but the Soviet government attempts to hasten the process. Two subprocesses are distinguished: cultural convergence (*sblizheniye*) and cultural merging (*sliyaniye*). The first occurs when two similar or neighboring groups come closer together as a result of continuous contacts; the second, when smaller groups become assimilated into larger ones.

These natural processes have occurred at a more rapid rate under the Soviet regime, but at no time before the Bolshevik revolution can it be said that they were not going on. For example, small Mongol groups became assimilated into larger Turkic groups near them, or small Siberian groups might intermarry and become one. The Soviets attempted to assimilate various small Turkic groups in central Asia into the larger groupings of Kazakh, Kirgiz, Uzbek, and Turkmen. In other regions, assimilation into the Russian population was encouraged. A more vacillating policy was carried out in relation to the Ukrainians and Belorussians. At times separatism was fostered, and at other times ties with the Russians were encouraged.

Because of the predominant position of the Russians, both in numbers and in power, and because the Russians had the most highly industrialized society before the Bolshevik revolution, both Russians and non-Russians tend to identify Russian culture with Soviet culture and the process of building communism with Russianization. The Russians feel it is their duty to help the more backward peoples progress, that is, to become more like the Russians. Urban culture is also consciously extended into rural areas.

Theorists of the CPSU envision the future of Soviet society as international rather than Russian. National differences may still exist, in their view, but within a humanitarian and egalitarian system resembling nothing preceding it. The dedicated Communists within the Soviet Union believe that they are building communism but have not yet achieved it.

CHAPTER 10

LANGUAGES AND SOCIAL COMMUNICATION

Russian, a Slavic language, is the predominant and most important language in the Soviet Union, both from the viewpoint of the number of persons speaking it and from its position as the all-union language and lingua franca among the peoples (see fig. 5). Over 100 other languages, both of large and small groups, are also spoken but within more limited geographical regions and for more limited uses. Language is the chief criterion of ethnic group identity. Following the Leninist principles concerning the cultures of ethnic groups, linguistic autonomy is encouraged (see ch. 9, Ethnic Groups).

The Turkic languages are next in importance after the Slavic group. Although most numerous in Central Asia, they are also widespread in eastern and southern European Russia, the Caucasus, and Siberia. Languages of the related Uralic group are found as islands scattered within other language areas. Other languages, although they may be well developed, are confined to small groups. Many of the minor languages are disappearing as their speakers become assimilated into larger groups.

Official policies recognize the importance of Russian, which is the official language of the government and of the Communist Party of the Soviet Union (CPSU), but they also encourage the use of minority languages. Russian is also the lingua franca among the non-Russian nationalities and is taught in all their schools. Languages other than Russian, however, are used as the media of instruction in non-Russian areas. Languages are used both to divide peoples and to bind them to each other. Minority languages are used through propaganda, to promote the interests of the entire Soviet Union.

A considerable, but unknown, proportion of the adult non-Russian population is bilingual in Russian and some other language; fewer Russians are bilingual. In linguistically diverse regions such as the Caucasus, multilingualism is common. French, English, and German are the most commonly taught of the languages foreign to the Soviet Union.

The official communications media serve to uphold values, sanction behavior, and provide information. Informal channels of communication supplement the official media in these functions, but they are also important as supports for socially and politically deviant behavior. The postal, telephone, and telegraph systems are often technically unreliable—and private telephones not available to all—but they are still widely used. Telegrams are popular on the occasions of holidays (see ch. 25, Public Information).

INDO-EUROPEAN LANGUAGES

The Indo-European family of languages is predominant among the great variety of distinct languages spoken in the Soviet Union (see fig. 5). Speakers of Indo-European languages comprise 80 percent of the population and, by far, the great majority of these claim Russian as their native tongue. Russians, sometimes referred to as Great Russians to distinguish them from Ukranians and Belorussians, constituted more than 50 percent of the total population in 1969 (see ch. 9, Ethnic Groups).

Many scholars place the home of the ancestors of the Indo-European speakers somewhere either in the Caucasus region or in the southern Russian steppes. Linguistic differentiation began around 2000 B.C. as these people began to spread into Europe and India. Although it was once popular to identify the early Indo-Europeans with physical types found in modern Europe, particularly those of northern Europe, present-day speakers of Indo-European languages belong to no one physical type, and it is likely that their linguistic ancestors also did not.

Within the Soviet Union are found speakers of the Slavic, Iranian, Baltic, Italic, Germanic, Armenian, Indic, and Greek branches of the Indo-European family. Within these branches are groupings of languages and, on a lower level, the languages themselves and their dialects. Sometimes the Baltic and Slavic are grouped together because of their close affinities; Indic and Iranian form another such group.

Slavic Languages

All three groupings of the Slavic are present. The eastern is represented by Russian, Ukranian, and Belorussian; the western, by small numbers of Poles, Czechs, and Slovaks; and the southern, by Bulgarian and Old Church Slavonic, which is used by the Russian Orthodox Church (see ch. 13, Religion).

The entire eastern Slavic group—Russian, Belorussian, and Ukranian—is native to the Soviet Union and is largely confined there. Linguistic differentiation within the East Slavic branch goes back to the fourteenth century; however, before the Bolshevik Revolution the three languages often were regarded as forms or dialects of the same language, although each had its own separate literary tradition.

182

Russian itself has two major dialects, a northern and a southern. The speech of Moscow, a sort of median form, has become the standard. The northern dialect, which is more conservative, is the one that spread into Siberia. This dialect was being replaced by the standard one in the mid-twentieth century as the Soviet government carried out various economic and cultural development projects in Siberia. The two Russian dialects differ in phonology, morphology, and vocabulary. Spoken Russian also varies according to social class and social origins.

Literary Russian is based on the Moscow dialect; Russian writings from at least as far back as the eleventh century A.D. have been heavily influenced by Old Church Slavonic, a representative of the southern Slavic branch. One result has been pairs of words with roughly the same meaning, one from Russian and the other from Old Church Slavonic. Since the seventeenth century when Russians began to increase their contacts with the West, the Russian language has come under the influence, largely lexical, of various European languages. French, as the favored language of the aristocrats, was one of the most influential; German also was important. The Siberian Russian remained isolated from these later developments.

Word coinage has been an active process since the Bolshevik Revolution. One feature of interest is the creating of acronyms and shortened versions of long compounds. For example, *kolkhoz* (collective farm) is a shortened form of *kollektivnoye khozyaystvo*; *kul'tbaza* (a cultural outpost) is a shortened form of *kul'turnaya baza*; and *Donbas* (an industrial complex on the Don River), of *Donetsky Bassein*. The language also lends itself to play upon words, of which the Russians are fond. Diminutives abound, many of them with satirical or slightly pejorative connotations, but many with affectionate significations. They occur frequently as nicknames. For example, there is Sasha from Alexander, Misha from Mikhail, and Katya from Ekaterina.

Proverbs are popular among both rural and urban people. Like the rest of Russian folklore, they come from a general European background, and similar proverbs are found in English.

The Russian language, particularly its literary form, is complex and highly inflected. Many of the more complicated and obscure forms are learned by children only after they have attended school for a few years. Russian nouns have three grammatical genders, three declension paradigms, and six cases. There is no definite or indefinite article. Adjectives must agree with nouns in gender, number, and case. Verbs have two aspects, the perfective and imperfective; two conjugations; three tenses; and four moods: the imperative, indicative, subjunctive or conditional, and infinitive. There is no verb "to be" in the present tense. As a consequence of the high

185

degree of inflection, word order is less significant grammatically and is used for more subtle semantic nuances.

Russian is written in the Cyrillic alphabet, which was devised by Saints Cyril and Methodius, two Greek monks who were missionaries to the South Slavs (Bulgarians). They modified the Greek alphabet to suit the phonology of the South Slavic language, the precursor of Old Church Slavonic. As Orthodoxy spread into the land of the East Slavs, so did both the Cyrillic alphabet and the Old Church Slavonic.

The history of literary Ukranian parallels that of literary Belorussian. Because of its associations with nationalism, it was banned by the tsarist government. Ukranian writers published their works in L'vov, at that time part of the Austrian Empire; the language there came under the influence of Polish. Modern literary Ukrainian, written in a form of the ubiquitous Cyrillic alphabet, differs from the medieval literary Ukrainian.

Ukrainian has four major dialects, the northern, Carpathian, southeastern, and southwestern; of these, the southeastern, centered around Kiev, and the southwestern, centered around L'vov, are the most widely spoken. These formed the basis for the modern standard Ukrainian. White Ukrainian and Belorussian (although to a lesser extent) have become the languages used by countrypeople, Russian has become the language used in the cities. Spoken by over 30 million people, Ukrainian, unlike Belorussian, has been the focus of a strong nationalist movement.

Around 84 percent of the 8 million Belorussians listed in the census of 1959 reported that they considered Belorussian their native language. Belorussian tends to be the language of countrypeople, and the Belorussian Soviet Socialist Republic was, in 1968, still more than 65 percent agrarian. Although Belorussian has a literary form, Russian is generally used by people living in the cities and by educated people. Both languages are used in official communication.

Literary Belorussian began to evolve during the fourteenth century when the Belorussians were under the rule of Lithuania and, later, Poland and Lithuania; it was one of the official languages of the country. Polish replaced Belorussian as the official language and influenced it heavily. After the Russian Empire annexed the territory in the eighteenth century, the use of Belorussian was banned. Until the Bolshevik Revolution, Belorussian works were published in Poland, in the Latin alphabet. Modern literary Belorussian is written in a form of the Cyrillic alphabet that differs from Russian in a few letters.

There are two major dialects, the southwestern and the northeastern. The southwestern dialect served as the basis for the reconstruction of the literary language in the nineteenth century. Despite its use in the schools and in the government, the Belorussian language is declining in importance.

The western and southern Slavic branches are spoken only by small remnants of national groups whose centers lie outside the Soviet Union. Many of these people are coming to use Russian as their language. The West Slavic languages include Polish, Czech, and Slovak; representatives of South Slavic are Bulgarian, Serbo-Croatian, Slovene, and Macedonian.

Old Church Slavonic is a form of medieval South Slavic, the precursor of Bulgarian. It became the language of religion for the Eastern Slavs because of the missionary activities of Saints Cyril and Methodius and their successors; for a long time it was the only literary language as well.

Other Indo-European Languages

The Baltic languages, Lithuanian and Latvian (but not Estonian, which is Finnic), became separated from the Slavic languages around 1000 B.C. Speakers of these languages have inhabited the same territory since around that time, and the languages themselves, particularly Lithuanian, contain a number of archaic Indo-European features of interest to historical linguists.

Lithuanian and Latvian, although related, are not mutually intelligible. They both contain a number of borrowings from neighboring languages, Lithuanian more from Polish and Russian and Latvian chiefly from Livonian (a nearly extinct language related to Estonian) and Low German. Both use the Latin alphabet.

In the Middle Ages, although Lithuania was not only independent but also the center of a large state, Lithuanian was only a spoken language; Latin and the Belorussian form of East Slavic were the written languages. Two major dialects developed in Lithuania: Low Lithuanian, centering in East Prussia, and High Lithuanian, spoken in the rest of the country, including the region around the capital. Although written forms of the various dialects go back to the sixteenth century, modern literary Lithuanian, based on the High dialect, did not become important until the nineteenth century. It became the official language after independence in 1918 and is still the focus of national identity for the people.

Latvian has a history similar to that of Lithuanian. It, too, remained a peasant language until well into the nineteenth century, when it became associated with nationalist movements. Even in present-day Latvia, the native language is replaced in the cities by Russian and other languages. Latvian has three major dialects: eastern (or Upper), central, and western. The central, spoken around

Riga, the capital, is the standard and the basis for the literary language. Morphologically, it is somewhat less complex than Lithuanian.

Iranian languages are found in central Asia and the Caucasus. Of the two major branches of Iranian, Ossetic is the only representative of the eastern branch in the Soviet Union. It is spoken by the Ossets of the Caucasus region. It is closely related to the Pashto language of Afghanistan, and it has borrowed the complex consonantal system of its Caucasian neighbors. Like most of the languages of the Soviet Union, it is written in the Cyrillic alphabet.

The other Iranian languages belong to the western branch. One Iranian group includes Tadzhik and a number of closely related dialects spoken by small tribal groups in the Pamirs. The Kurds speak an Iranian language closely related to Persian, and some 8,000 Baluchi speakers have a language that is also spoken in Afghanistan. Speaking closely related languages are the Talysh and Tats, also of the Caucasus. There are also numerous ethnic Persians in central Asia and the Caucasus.

The western Iranian languages, like Armenian as well, share a lack of grammatical gender. All the Iranian languages have borrowed from Arabic, whose alphabet they formerly used, and also from Turkic. This is especially true of Tadzhik. After brief experiments with the Latin alphabet in the late 1930's, all the western Iranian languages were converted to the use of the Cyrillic.

The Romance branch of the Italic languages is represented by Moldavian, a dialect of Rumanian that is written in the Cyrillic alphabet. Rumanian is the most easterly of the languages descended from Latin. It has, however, a large admixture of words from Slavic languages. Over 2 million Soviet citizens speak Rumanian or Moldavian.

The western branch of the Germanic group is represented by German and Yiddish. German is spoken by a decreasing number of descendants of German settlers who arrived in Russia during the eighteenth century under the reign of Catherine the Great, herself a German. Yiddish is a variety of medieval German spoken by Jews descended from those who had lived in Germany but who had subsequently moved eastward into Poland and Russia. The language is written in the Hebrew alphabet and contains a large proportion of Hebrew words. In the Soviet Union it is considered to be the language of the Jewish people, although the Jewish communities in the Caucasus and central Asia speak local Iranian and Turkic languages. Some books and journals are published in Yiddish, and it is nominally the official language of the Jewish Autonomous Oblast. The number of Jews who actually claim Yiddish as their native language is not large; only one-fifth of them—about 500,000—reported it as such in the census of 1959.

Armenian forms a separate group of the Indo-European languages. Its written history goes back to the fifth century A.D., when the Armenians became Christians. The Armenian alphabet was devised by an early Armenian bishop and based on the Greek alphabet. The Classical Armenian language has changed little since that time; at present it is still used in the church. Two spoken dialects, eastern and western, developed out of Old (Classical) Armenian. Both have absorbed vocabulary items from Greek, Russian, Turkish, and French; their phonologies have been influenced by neighboring Caucasian languages, and their development generally isolated. The eastern is the one used by most of the Armenians in the Soviet Union, and the western by Armenians of Turkish origin scattered throughout the world. The two spoken dialects have been the basis for the two modern literary Armenian dialects. Despite attempts at reform of the Armenian alphabet begun in 1926, the old alphabet is still used. Although the Armenians are among the more cosmopolitan peoples of the Soviet Union, some 90 percent of them still speak their language, which is a concrete expression of their separate identity. The Armenian-language press flourishes in Soviet Armenia.

Other Indo-European languages spoken by relatively small numbers of people include Greek, spoken around the Black Sea, and Romany, an Indic language spoken by gypsies. These languages are fading into insignificance because of widespread use of Russian in daily affairs.

URALIC-ALTAIC LANGUAGES

The Uralic-Altaic languages are found from Northern and Eastern Europe all the way to the eastern shores of the Pacific Ocean. Peoples speaking these languages vary in physical form from Mongoloid to Caucasoid and in way of life from nomadic hunting to the most sophisticated of the urban milieus. There are the Hungarians, the Lapps, the Turks and Tatars, the Mongols, and simple Siberian hunters; even the Japanese and Koreans are included in the group by many linguists. In the Soviet Union Uralic-Altaic languages are spoken by almost 30 million people.

The Altaic language family has three parts—the Turkic, the Mongolic, and the Tungusic. This family is often grouped with the Uralic family, composed of the Finnic, Ugric, and Samoyedic languages, to form the Uralic-Altaic family on the basis of certain shared features, although not all linguists would concur in the larger grouping.

The Uralic Family

Of the three languages of the Uralic family—Finnic, Ugric, and Samoyedic—Finnic is the most numerous in the Soviet Union, although none are of major consequence. The Finnic-language group has three branches: the West Finnic, the East Finnic, and the Permian. Besides Finnish proper, spoken mostly in Finland, there are the closely related Estonian and Livonian, all belonging to West Finnic. Another West Finnic group includes Karelian, Veps, Izhor, and Lapp, of northwestern Russia. The East Finnic branch is represented by Mordvin and Mari, both spoken by people living along the Volga. The Permian branch comprises Udmurt, Komi, and Permyak, all spoken just west of the Urals.

The Ugric languages include Hungarian (of the Western branch), spoken by around 150,000 Soviet citizens; Ostyak, the language of the Khanty; and Vogul, the language of the Mansi. Both Ostyak and Vogul belong to the eastern branch. The Samoyedic languages are spoken by some small groups of the far north. The eastern Ugric languages and the Samoyedic languages are all found in northern Siberia and European Russia (see ch. 9, Ethnic Groups).

The total number of Uralic-language speakers in the Soviet Union amounts to barely 4 million. Of these, over one-half speak Finnic languages. Slightly less than one-half speak Ugric languages, and only approximately 25,000 speak the Samoyedic languages.

The Altaic Family

The Turkic languages are the most important of these; over 22 million Soviet peoples speak Turkic languages. Because of the mobility of these peoples, dialect boundaries are diffuse, most of the languages are more or less mutually intelligible, and the history of any one group is difficult to untangle. Furthermore, some groups have been under heavy influence from speakers of other languages, such as Mongolian, Persian, or Arabic. The Soviet government attempted, somewhat arbitrarily, to create separate languages out of the situation.

The Turkic languages are the next most numerous after the Slavic in the Soviet Union. They are found in Siberia, in southern Russia, in the Caucasus, and in central Asia. Across the borders they are also found in China, Mongolia, Afghanistan, Iran, and Turkey. Pan-Turkic sentiments have stirred these peoples since the nineteenth century and have posed problems for the government in Moscow since then. Around the time of the Bolshevik Revolution and the revolution in Ottoman Turkey, the Pan-Turkic movement was especially strong. Turkic peoples have always been able to move fairly freely across the remote mountainous borders, and many have done so in the twentieth century (see ch. 9, Ethnic Groups). The Soviet government has also been able to focus Turkic sentiment on the other side of the border to make difficulties for the Chinese government in the Chinese province of Sinkiang.

Because of the tangled history (in large part unwritten) of the Turkic peoples, the many foreign linguistic and cultural influences, and the lack of detailed research on many of them, there have been many varied classifications of the Turkic languages. The classification given here is based on phonological and morphological features, historical geography, and known history. Six major groups can be distinguished: the Yakut; the northeastern; the northwestern, or Kipchak; the southeastern, or Chagatai; the southwestern, or Oguz; and the Bulgar-Chuvash. Some linguists group the Yakut with the northeastern because both have undergone somewhat isolated development. Both the northeastern and the Bulgar-Chuvash contain archaic Turkic features.

The Yakut branch is represented by the Yakuts and Dolgans of central Siberia. The northeastern branch includes the speech of the Shors, Tuvins, the Khakas group, and the Altai, all inhabiting southern Siberia (see ch. 9, Ethnic Groups). These two branches together comprise some 500,000 people.

The northwestern, or Kipchak, branch comprises Kirgiz, Kazakh, and Karakalpak of central Asia; the Bashkir and Volga Tatar of southern Russia; Turkic peoples of the Caucasus; and the language of the Karaimy, or Karaites, a Turkic-speaking heterodox Jewish group inhabiting parts of the Crimea, Poland, and Lithuania. The southeastern, or Chagatai, branch includes primarily the sedentary Uzbek. The southwestern, or Oguz, branch includes the Azerbaijani, Turkmen, Gagauz, the Turkish of Turkey (called Osmanli, or Ottoman Turkish, and is also spoken by various small groups in central Asia and the Caucasus), and the Crimean Tatar. The Chuvash language is the only survivor of medieval Bulgar; the people of Bulgaria were Turkic before they became Slavic (see ch. 9, Ethnic Groups).

In the Soviet Union the Mongolic languages, represented by some 400,000 people, are found in the Caucasus and in Siberia. The Kalmyk Mongols of the Caucasus speak a language belonging to the western Mongolic branch, and the dialects of the Buryat Mongols belong to the eastern Mongolic branch.

The Tungusic languages are found scattered throughout Siberia. There are two branches—the northern and the southern. The northern branch includes the Evenk, the Even, and the Negidal. The southern branch includes the Ulchi, Udegey, Orochi, and Orok (see ch. 9, Ethnic Groups). About 25,000 people speak Tungusic languages.

Korean, which is the last member of the Altaic language family, and a dubious one at that, is found in central Asia and spoken by about 250,000 people. The government of the Soviet Union had brought them from Korea to introduce sericulture (see ch. 9, Ethnic Groups).

CAUCASIAN LANGUAGES

These are a group of languages found only in the Caucasus region. Attempts have occasionally been made to prove their relationship with other languages, many also still unclassified, but these attempts have never met with success.

The Caucasian languages are characterized by a complex and difficult phonology that has influenced the phonology of Indo-European languages in the same region. For example, Circassian has fifty-seven consonants but only seven vowels. Most of them have a complex noun system; nouns have many cases, and in one group of these languages nouns are associated into classes characterized by affix systems. Types of verb subjects are also classified, but the verb systems are otherwise not complex.

There are two major branches within the Caucasian languages, the northern and the southern. The relationship between the northeastern and northwestern groups of the northern branch has been established on the basis of structural and lexical similarities, but no particular relationship outside of geographical proximity has been demonstrated between these and the southern. Because of the mountainous terrain, there is a high degree of dialectical differentiation. Some languages and dialects are spoken only by the inhabitants of one or two villages.

Northwestern Caucasian languages include Chechen, Ingush, and other languages of Daghestan ethnic groups. There are other minor languages spoken whose speakers are not recognized as separate ethnic groups. The major languages have been given Cyrillic alphabets, while speakers of the minor languages must use one of the other languages for writing. About 1.5 million persons speak northeastern Caucasian languages, but the group is the most highly differentiated internally.

The northwestern Caucasian group includes Circassian, Abkhaz, and Ubykh. The Circassian is the most important of these, but many of its speakers have migrated to the Middle East (see ch. 9, Ethnic Groups). It uses a Cyrillic alphabet. There are about 500,000 speakers of northwestern Caucasian languages.

The southern group includes Georgian, Mingrelian, Svan, and Laz. Of these, Georgian, spoken by around 3 million people, is the most important; until the 1920's it was the only one to have a literature of its own. Georgian inscriptions from the fifth century A.D. have been found, and an extensive literature dates from the tenth century. The Georgian alphabet is based upon the Greek alphabet;

192

Cyrillic was never imposed. The other languages have since adopted the Cyrillic alphabet and have developed some literature.

PALEO-ASIATIC LANGUAGES

The Paleo-Asiatic group represents more of a geographic aggregate than a systematic linguistic grouping. Some languages have been proved to be related, but most of them remain independent. Nevertheless, there are certain similarities for the group as a whole, as well as to some of the North American Indian languages, Korean, Japanese, and to Samoyedic and Turkic languages. Some of these similarities may be the result more of borrowing than of common origin. Russian had also had a great influence, especially in vocabulary, on the Paleo-Asiatic languages.

The Chukchi, Koryak, and Itelmen languages are all related and are found in the far northeast of Siberia, from the Chukotka to the Kamchatka peninsulas. Eskimo and Aleut are related languages, more widespread in North America than in the Soviet Union. The Ainu speakers are found principally on Sakhalin Island; they are also found on, and are the original inhabitants of, the northernmost island of Japan. In northern Yakutia are found the speakers of Yukagir; they are not regarded as a separate ethnic group by the Soviet government because most of them have been assimilated into the Yakut ethnic group. Speakers of Gilyak are located on Sakhalin Island and along the lower Amur River. Ket is found the farthest to the west, in central Siberia.

At one time the Paleo-Asiatic languages were widespread and numerous in Siberia and northeastern Asia, but in the 1960's they occupied a marginal position. At the time of the 1959 census, there were only around 15,000 speakers of these languages. Since Europeans have been in contact with them, the number of their speakers has steadily declined because of death and assimilation into larger groups. Although the Soviet government has attempted to promote cultural development among speakers of these languages, including the donation of alphabets and establishment of native presses, it is likely that the trend toward assimilation will continue.

OTHER LANGUAGES

The Semitic languages are not spoken widely in the Soviet Union but are nonetheless of some importance. Hebrew is used only as a religious language by the Jews, but it has lent its alphabet and vocabulary to Yiddish. Arabic is the sacred language of Islam and, as such, has contributed greatly to the vocabularies of Muslim peoples in the Soviet Union. Until the latinizing reforms of the 1920's, its alphabet was the only one in use among most of the Muslim peoples of central Asia, the Caucasus, and southern Russia. A few native speakers of Arabic are found in central Asia. The Assyrians, a small, heterodox Christian people of the Caucasus, speak a modern version of Aramaic.

The Sino-Tibetan languages are represented only by Dungan, the variety of Chinese spoken by the Dungans, a Muslim people originally from Sinkiang who live in central Asia. Even they tend to use Chinese only in their homes. The Buddhist scriptures are in Pali, an ancient language of India.

OFFICIAL POLICIES AND PRACTICES

Official policies and practices concerning languages reflect both the dominant position of Russian and the desire to reach the national masses. Considering the ethnic composition of the country and the aims of the government, these policies are rational. They also represent a response to political exigencies. The 1961 Program of the CPSU indicates that linguistic and national policies have changed little since they were formulated in the 1930's by Stalin, who had been Lenin's expert on the nationality question (see ch. 9, Ethnic Groups).

In 1959 Russians constituted over one-half of the country's total population. In addition, various proportions of other ethnic groups used Russian as their primary language. Still many others used it as a second language, and as an avenue of social advancement for non-Russians. Few Russians are familiar with non-Russian languages. There can be no question that Russian is numerically the most important language.

Russian is also the language of the government in both internal and foreign affairs, the armed forces, and the CPSU. It forms a lingua franca among the nationalities and often is the only language in which advanced studies are taught. Recognizing these important functions of the language, in 1938 the teaching of Russian was made compulsory in all of the country's schools. Over 80 percent of books published are in Russian, and it is the primary language of broadcasting.

In non-Russian areas the native language is the primary language of instruction, and Russian is taught as a second language; this policy is not always actively pursued. In some areas, such as the Caucasus, additional languages may be taught because of their importance in the region. Departments of Russian have been established in the schools of the non-Russian republics, and in some regions special provisions had to be made to train instructors where the native teachers were not qualified to teach Russian. In the teaching profession, great interest exists in the field of teaching

Russian as a foreign language. Special linguistic methods, similar to those used elsewhere in the world for the teaching of foreign languages, have been developed (see ch. 15, The Educational System).

Because it is the lingua franca of the country, Russian is often spoken by persons with an imperfect knowledge of it. In development projects the workers often use a broken or nonstandard Russian. In the non-Russian parts of the country, the Russian used in the official communications media is not always correct. To combat this problem, the Soviet government has tried to promote the teaching of more correct Russian.

French, German, and English are the major languages foreign to the Soviet Union that are taught in schools. Chinese was popular before the rift between the Soviet Union and Communist China. Arabic is taught in central Asian schools. Foreign languages are accorded only a few hours of instruction per week in the schools (see ch. 15, The Educational System). Foreign literary works of importance are translated into Russian, which thus becomes the vehicle of world culture for the people of the Soviet Union.

As a means of promoting socialist development and national consciousness among the masses, the Soviet government has promoted the use of the native languages. Alphabets were created for unwritten languages, and the Cyrillic was generally imposed on written languages—except for Georgian, Armenian, Yiddish, and the languages of the Baltic nations. An intensive campaign was launched against illiteracy; the results have been very successful (see ch. 15, The Educational System). Presses for the publication of books, newspapers, magazines, and pamphlets have been established for the national languages; the works of Russian and foreign authors, as well as the works of Marx and Lenin, have been translated. Libraries and cultural centers have been established in even the most remote areas of the far north. Radio, regarded as an adjunct to the press, is also broadcast in the different national languages. Broadcasts are made on various political, economic, and cultural subjects (see ch. 25, Public Information).

In an attempt to quiet nationalist stirrings among the peoples of the country, the Soviet government created autonomous republics, autonomous *oblasti* (regions), and national *okruga* (areas) on the basis of ethnic groups. Most of these bear names derived from the dominant ethnic group. The language of that group is the official language (together with Russian, in every case). It is the language of administration, of court proceedings, and of instruction in the schools. It is found on public signs and in the official communications media. Interpreters are provided in courts for those who do not speak the local language, Russian also is found on public signs, and Russian schools are provided in most areas.

Language is the primary criterion of ethnicity and a symbol of national identity. At the time of the Bolshevik Revolution, group sentiment in many areas of central Asia, the Caucasus, and Siberia was focused more on religious or tribal affiliation than on ethnic or national group. Often the situation consisted of speakers of more or less mutually intelligible dialects; linguistic or ethnic unity was less meaningful than political, social, or religious unity. Wishing to make order out of chaos and wishing also to develop national sentiments that were neither religious nor sociopolitical, ethnic groups were somewhat arbitrarily formed. Related dialects were grouped, and ethnic standard languages were created. In central Asia those nomadic dialects regarded as purer were generally chosen as models. Small linguistic groups were attached to larger groups that spoke related languages or to which they had become partially assimilated (see ch. 9, Ethnic Groups).

Political requirements also dictated linguistic policies. One reason for focusing on ethnic groups was to weaken non-Soviet political groupings or to undermine religious and so-called bourgeois social sentiments. In addition, in order to more easily rule the divided groups, divisions were made within dialect groupings, such as between the closely related Kirgiz and Kazakh. Chagatai, the old Turkic lingua franca written in the Arabic script, was supplanted. Cyrillic was chosen not only to make literacy less esoteric, but also to cut peoples off from their past and from neighbors across the borders. At the same time, national self-expression was used as a point of propaganda aimed at these same border peoples (see ch. 9, Ethnic Groups).

Before the Bolshevik Revolution, many of the non-European languages were spoken by peoples who were without industrial and advanced scientific technologies and consequently lacked vocabularies dealing with these subjects. Moreover, many of them had borrowed terminology from Persian and Arabic, much of it concerning religious and philosophical concepts. The Soviet linguists have made some attempts to replace these words with words more suitable for Marxist-Leninist thought; these were either of Russian origin or built from preexisting roots. Most of the scientific and technological vocabulary has been borrowed directly from Russian.

Some non-Russian writers use Russian as the vehicle of their thoughts, claiming that their own languages cannot express them. Others deplore such tendencies as assimilative and believe that their writings should be primarily for their own people in their own languages.

USES OF LANGUAGE

Languages are not only means of communication but also modes of expression, means of social control, and symbols. Languages

196

exist on various levels of usage, in which the informal and less well known functions may be more important than the official and known.

Although the official means of mass communication, the radio and the press, serve to disseminate information and inculcate certain attitudes and behaviors, informal means are also important. These may have opposite aims and results from those of the official channels. Many people, particularly the better educated and those in more important positions, distrust what they receive on the radio and in the press. Some of them have access to other sources of information, and news may circulate by word of mouth. Such items both supplement and supplant the official news. Countrypeople and those with only primary or secondary educations rely more on the official media.

Informal channels—especially gossip—also may encourage attitudes and behavior contrary to those of the press and radio. Industrial managers may, for example, underestimate their productive capacities so that they can sell surplus on the black market. The official media consistently condemn such behavior, but it receives support from informal talk. Informal channels keep alive traditional modes of behavior proscribed under socialism. Grandmothers teach children about religion, polygyny is often condoned by central Asians, and private production is widespread on collective farms. Such practices are actively encouraged through informal communications among the individuals concerned.

Modern Soviet writers, especially those who are young and unestablished, often circulate privately printed (mimeographed) manuscripts that do not follow the "socialist realist" style officially favored. This practice is called *samizdat*. It gives the writers a chance to be evaluated by their colleagues on a professional, rather than political, basis. Some writers even hide manuscripts and smuggle them out to be published in foreign countries.

On the other hand, many of the informal channels support the official media. Most citizens have known no other system. Letters-to-the-editor sections of the newspapers provide channels for complaints about officials and practices contrary to what is expected by the citizens. Such complaints are directed toward individuals in charge rather than toward the system and do not touch on sensitive subjects, but they still serve to support official values. In the newspapers gossipy exposés of scandals, corruption, and the like, known as *feuilletons*, are popular items. Gossip also functions to support official goals and values, especially where an entire group is involved. For example, if a group within a factory is rewarded or sanctioned according to its output, the gossip reinforces the goal so that all may benefit.

Because of the dominant position of Russian, a knowledge of it is essential in social mobility. Increasing numbers of Soviet citizens are fluent in at least two languages. In some parts of the country, such as the Caucasus, where many languages are spoken within a relatively small area, children may study, in addition to their own language and Russian, another language of the region, and perhaps a non-Soviet foreign language such as English. This places a heavy burden on these children, and Soviet educators are aware of the problem.

Knowledge of non-Russian languages is not so essential for Russians. The study of the local languages is not required for Russians attending Russian schools in non-Russian areas. In some parts of the country, such as the Baltic states and the Caucasus, where national feeling is strong, however, Russians have had to use the local languages. The Russian reluctance to learn minority languages is resented by the non-Russians as being arrogant. National feelings may also result in a degree of apathy toward learning Russian. Some reports from Tadzhikistan indicate that relatively few Tadzhiks have availed themselves of the opportunity to study Russian.

Accessibility of channels of public communication—the postal service and the telephone and telegraph networks—varies within the regions of the country and between rural and urban areas. Private telephones are in short supply, although attempts have been made to catch up with the demand. Public telephones, however, are readily available, and the telephone bureau supplies services such as information. Long-distance calls must be paid in advance, and the telephone service is subject to breakdown and also to wiretapping. Nonetheless, telephones are in great demand and are widely used.

Both the postal and telegraph services are efficient. It has become customary for citizens to send telegrams to distant friends and relatives on holidays such as New Year's Day, Revolution Day, and May Day. It is possible to send telegrams in both the Cyrillic and the Latin alphabets. Because of the severity of the climate and the difficulties of travel in such a vast country, these three channels of communication are heavily used.

CHAPTER 11

FAMILY

The general theories of Marx and Engels concerning family life under communism appeared in *The Origin of the Family, Private Property and the State*, published by Engels after the death of his lifelong friend and collaborator. This work condemned bourgeois family life as merely another institution for the perpetuation of private property and capitalism. It did not condemn the family system per se, although it was widely misinterpreted to imply that the family system would be abolished under a classless society. This misinterpretation led to wide experimentation in the early days of the Soviet Union in familial relationships, marriage, and divorce. Engels had expressly argued that proletarian marriage would be inherently good as opposed to the evil institutions of the past.

When the experimentation and early revolutionary fervor had run their course, the exigencies of a developing economy and political system demanded stability of the society, as the state called upon its citizens for ever greater sacrifices in its drive toward industrialization. Stability was achieved, partly by enactment of more rigid codes for marriage, divorce, and family affairs in general. From the 1930's through the 1960's, the Party and state have proclaimed the importance of family life and have supported strong family ties.

Family life more than fifty years after the Bolshevik Revolution remains an important element of society. The family did not wither away, as some early revolutionaries had predicted, nor did the advocates of free love manage to abolish the institution of marriage. Most citizens retain traditional, even bourgeois, attitudes toward marital and familial relationships. The official moral code promulgated by the Party states the need for "mutual respect in the family and concern for the upbringing of children." Although the state strongly influences childrearing through the nurseries and kindergartens in which the children of working mothers spend much of their time, the family unit is still recognized as a stabilizing element.

Soviet families, in general, share many of the same problems of families in other industrialized, increasingly urbanized societies. The concerns of earning a living, aspiring to higher standards of living, getting children into the right schools, putting up with shortages in housing and transportation—all affect family life. Ideology seems to play only a minor role in family life, and the authorities appear to be more concerned about the declining birth rate than the creation of the "Socialist family" that has been written about since the Revolution.

Since so many of the early revolutionary ideals have not been realized, compromises have been made in the official ideology. Predictions are still made of the Communist future, and the family remains part of the picture. The picture, however, is far from clear. The family under communism is supposed to be pure and free from material considerations. Family relations will be voluntary, based on mutual affection and respect. Little has been said, however, of the functions the family will exercise in the future.

HISTORICAL BACKGROUND

Even before the Bolshevik Revolution, the Russian family had undergone a number of changes, gradually growing smaller in both scope of kin included and in size. In the non-Russian, and particularly non-Slavic, parts of the old Russian Empire, family forms and functions differed from those found in Russia; these too had been undergoing change, although less rapidly. The Revolution, however, initiated radical changes in the family life of the people.

Linguistic and archaeological evidence indicates that the early Slavs lived in extended families consisting of a man, his wife, unmarried children, married sons with their wives and children, and perhaps other relatives as well—that is, persons traced their descent through a single line from a common ancestor. Descent was patrilineal; family membership, names, and property descended through the male line. The families were grouped into clans, and these into tribes, all on a patrilineal basis. By around A.D. 600 the clan and tribal organization had ceased to function, although less formal relationships with patrilineal kin and close relatives by marriage continued.

As the East Slavs developed their civilization in the general area of the present European Soviet Union, their kinship organization underwent further changes. Affinal ties—those created by marriage—became more important, resulting in a bilateral kinship system. A patrilineal bias remained, and the people continued to reside in extended-family households.

By the nineteenth century economic and social conditions had continued to perpetuate the extended-family household among the Russians; among the Belorussians and Ukrainians, households tended to be smaller. Among all of the East Slavs, the households were linked by both patrilineal and affinal ties. Within the household the eldest male was the head; he also represented the family to the village and to the landlord or government.

In 1861 the serfs, who constituted well over half of the peasantry, were emancipated; peasants then constituted some 90 percent of the population. There followed a series of legal reforms affecting peasants and, beginning in 1906, the Stolypin land reforms brought further change (see ch. 31, Agriculture). The period from the emancipation of the serfs to the Bolshevik Revolution was characterized by a great deal of geographic and social mobility, famines, and deportations; whole villages became specialized economically; groups of men undertook seasonal labor outside the villages; and there arose a class of comparatively wealthy and independent peasants called kulaks.

All of these social changes had a profound effect upon the family. Both the range of kinship terminology and the scope of the family household became smaller. Households became more variable in size, and relationships through female kin became more important. Among urban workers, the family began to assume its modern form—a married couple, their children, and often an aged parent—that is, a nuclear or an expanded family.

Within the Caucasus region, the family assumed different forms. Since ancient times polygyny had been customary; a few men had two wives, fewer still had more, while most had only one. People lived in extended-family households, which were grouped into patrilineal clans. Marriages were generally arranged; in most areas a complex system of marriage restrictions was enforced. Among some Caucasian peoples, men were obliged to marry their deceased brothers' widows, a custom known as the levirate. Although most of the Caucasian peoples were either Christian or Muslim, neither Church law nor the Sharia was influential in the realm of marriage and the family; local customs prevailed.

After the Russians extended their rule into the Caucasus during the eighteenth and nineteenth centuries, they made some attempts to reform Caucasian customs. They attempted to suppress feuding and associated institutions, such as the clan organization, the complicated marriage restrictions, concubinage, arrangement of marriages, polygyny, the bridewealth, and the levirate. Under the Soviet regime, these attempts were intensified.

Family life in central Asia was similar to that in the Caucasus. In central Asia nearly all of the peoples were Muslims, and among the sedentary peoples, particularly the Iranians, the religious law, the Sharia, was more strictly followed; the nomads, however, relied more upon customary law.

Polygyny existed as a seldom realized ideal. The extended family was the rule. Males of the patrilineage constituted the core of the family; women born to the family left it upon marriage, and others came as brides, but some left because of divorce. The eldest man ruled the family, although the eldest woman, generally his wife, was in charge of household affairs. The fathers arranged marriages for their children, both boys and girls. The choice of mates was considered a family matter, involving economic and political ties between families, as well as the necessity to perpetuate the patrilineage.

Despite the Islamic law, women traditionally did not inherit from their families. They did, however, receive a dowry upon marriage and, in addition, there was the bridewealth, called *mahr* or *kalym*. According to Islamic law, the bridewealth was supposed to become the bride's personal property but, in practice, her family generally received most of it. Even among nomads the institution of the bridewealth did not make chattels of the women but rather represented an exchange of wealth between two families, serving to strengthen the ties between them; it also constituted a compensation to the woman's family for having raised her and served as a deterrent to divorce.

Among sedentary central Asians, no formal kinship organizations existed beyond the extended-family households. Among nomads, related families were grouped into camps, and these into exogamous clans; that is, men were expected to marry outside the clan. In earlier times there had been an inclusive tribal system, but this had broken down under the impact of Russian conquest.

In traditional central Asian society, the home was considered the proper sphere for women. Within the home the woman ran the household, subject to the ultimate authority of the eldest man. When women left the home, they were veiled; their husbands or kinsmen represented them publicly. It was not considered necessary that girls be educated and so, in a society in which few men received an education, still fewer women had the opportunity.

By the time ethnographers reached the peoples of Siberia and the Far North in the nineteenth century, family life had undergone a great amount of modification because of Russian settlements and the activities of traders. Polygyny existed as a possibility for a few well-to-do men, and extended families were common. Villages or nomadic camps were generally composed of related families. There was also a system of exogamous clans.

Throughout the old Russian Empire, families everywhere, whatever their form or size, had certain features in common. They served as the primary focus of life for most persons; people interacted mostly with kinsmen, for both work and recreation. The family was where children were not only raised to adulthood, but also where they learned their adult work; that is, a boy generally learned his father's trade, and a girl learned to keep house. Extrafamilial institutions for education or training were, on the whole, insignificant. The family was thus the source for the perpetuation of tradition.

Although there was always a chance for social mobility, in general an individual's place in society was determined by the status of his family. Not only were religion and ethnicity inherited, but also one's place on the social ladder.

Reflecting the importance of the family was its relation to religion. The major events in the life of the individual—birth, christening, circumcision, completion of religious education, attainment of adult status, marriage, and death—were marked by religious observances within a family context. Religious traditions were maintained and perpetuated by the family.

As one of the most important institutions of prerevolutionary Russia, the family was certain to attract the attention of the Bolsheviks; because it was so fundamental, any experiment with it resulted in highly visible results.

IDEOLOGICAL AND LEGAL BACKGROUND

As one of the two founders of Marxism, Friedrich Engels gave more attention to the family, publishing in 1884 *The Origin of the Family, Private Property and the State*. He based this work on the research of an American anthropologist, Lewis H. Morgan, who had proposed an evolutionary scheme of stages through which the family had passed. Morgan's theories are no longer considered valid in the West, but they remain an important component of Soviet social science.

According to Marxist theory, the form of the family and the nature of the relations within it are part of the social superstructure; that is, they are based on the system of property relations. Where these are characterized by material considerations and by exploitation, so also are family relations. Only under communism, then, can a pure form of the family exist.

Marx and Engels were not always clear in their writings in regard to the family. They were motivated not only to develop a scientific theory, but also to relieve mankind from suffering. The ambiguity of the ideas expressed by the founders of Marxism made possible a wide range of early Bolshevik theories on the family and also a great scope for experimentation with it.

Whatever their disagreements, however, Marxists have agreed with Morgan in placing monogamous marriage at the summit of human evolutionary progress. It has been the permanence of the union between man and woman and the functions of the family in childbearing that have been freest to vary theoretically.

The early Bolsheviks took a revolutionary approach to the family. They wished to eradicate all traces of bourgeois family relations, that is, those based upon material considerations. Lenin, moreover, regarded housework as a stultifying burden from which women should be freed so that they, too, could participate in the Revolution. The Bolsheviks also regarded the family as the source for reactionary beliefs and behavior.

In December 1917, one month after the Bolshevik Revolution, two decrees were promulgated. One of these substituted civil marriage for religious marriage, which had previously been the only form, and the other introduced divorce upon the application of one spouse, with no requirement for stating the grounds for the request. In the following year these decrees were replaced by a code on civil status. This contained the same provisions for marriage and divorce as the preliminary decrees but also instituted a new concept of the family. The code stated that birth was to be the basis of the family and that there was no difference between births in or out of wedlock; thus, common-law (and also religious marriages) were as valid as civil marriages. No provisions were made for parental responsibilities for, or authority over, their children.

In old Russia abortion, even for medical reasons, had been illegal. In 1920, after considering the ill effects of the numerous illegal abortions that had been performed in previous years, the Soviet government legalized abortions. Abortions were to be performed free, in government hospitals only. Private abortions remained illegal. The Health Commissariat, however, tried to discourage women from having abortions; it also made an effort to establish nurseries and kindergartens to provide for the children of working women.

In 1918, just a few months after the Bolsheviks assumed control, a decree abolishing inheritance was promulgated. This was one of the means whereby the material bases of the bourgeois family were to be undermined. The authorities seemingly did not realize that the inheritance of property often served as a form of social insurance for widows and orphans. By 1921, when the New Economic Policy (Novaya Ekonomicheskaya Politika—NEP) was initiated, the inheritance of property was reintroduced. There were restrictions on the type and amount of property and on the circle of heirs, but these restrictions were subsequently eroded away.

In 1926, during the period of the NEP, an even more revolutionary law, the Code on Domestic Relations, was enacted. Although it was said that new means of production and distribution of property had come into existence, permitting changes in the family, the opposite was actually the situation, for the NEP represented a necessary compromise with capitalism. Marriage registration became, in effect, the statement that a certain relationship existed; the divorce procedure merely established that a marriage had ended. In addition, homosexuality, adultery, and incest were no longer considered crimes.

In the Soviet Union the 1920's were years of social chaos and social experimentation. The relations between men and women were to be free and voluntary. Many considered that it was only a matter of time before the family would wither away, its functions being absorbed by the state. Parents had neither legal authority over children nor responsibility for their actions. The complete equality of men and women was stressed; some feminists considered that both sexes should have identical social roles as well. Many writers extolled the virtues of free love.

Reaction was inevitable. The rate of abortions continued to be high. Many persons took liberties with the divorce laws, either engaging in a series of short marriages or not even bothering to register their unions, and some men were polygynous. Although the new freedom of divorce had been intended to make women equal to men, a common result was that women and children suffered. As a result of the frivolous attitudes toward marriage and the family and because of the upheavals caused by World War I, the revolutions, and the civil war, large gangs of homeless and delinquent children roamed the countryside. The rate of population increase dropped. Although most families continued to carry on as best they could throughout this difficult period, family problems were nevertheless overwhelming.

By 1935 parents were made responsible for the actions of their children. In 1934 homosexual behavior was made a punishable offense, and in 1936 abortion was made illegal except for certain medical reasons. Soviet authorities began to proclaim that the family was an integral element of socialism and that free love was incompatible with socialist ethics and morality. Restrictions on divorce were initiated. Motherhood prizes and bonuses for child-bearing were introduced. Paradoxically, the 1936 Constitution of the USSR proclaimed that socialism had been attained; the legal trends of the mid-1930's, however, represented a step toward the bourgeois past.

One of the means by which the status of women was to be improved was through the provision of new opportunities for careers. In 1918 all levels of education were opened to women. The participation of women in all parts of the economy, including their employment in skilled, responsible, and professional occupations, was encouraged. Since women remained wives and mothers, it was necessary to assist them to enter the economy. Attempts were made to establish child-care facilities and to provide such services as public dining halls. Provisions were made for child support and alimony in case of divorce; even unwed mothers could sue the fathers of their children for support.

The number of child-care facilities and public services was never adequate to meet the demand. The housing shortage and lack of housekeeping appliances continued to burden working wives and mothers into the 1960's. Some mothers have been able to place their children in day nurseries; others have been fortunate to have an older female relative live with them and care for the household and the children. In some families the husband and wife were obliged to work on different shifts so that someone could be home to supervise the children (see ch. 12, Living Conditions).

Part of the reason for the meager support given to working mothers was that the state had to use most of its limited resources for the building of basic industry and armaments. The ambiguous attitude of Marxist theory toward the family was also involved, as was a lingering old-fashioned feeling on the part of many Party leaders. Many of them continued to uphold the rights of women while continuing to regard women ideally as being suited only for the roles of wife and mother. Such attitudes formed part of the basis for drastic changes made in family laws in the 1940's.

By the mid-1940's a drastic depopulation, particularly of males, had taken place because of World War II, the Great Purge, and the enforced collectivization that had begun with the First Five-Year Plan of 1928. The war had also resulted in a great deal of social dislocation and disruption of family life, including large numbers of temporary liaisons. Many unscrupulous unmarried mothers also filed paternity suits against men with whom they had no connection.

The 1944 legislation on marriage and the family had two major goals; to encourage as many births as possible in order to make up for the severe population losses suffered by the country; and to stabilize and strengthen the family. The means chosen to further these goals were somewhat contradictory. Unwed mothers were to be given allowances for child support or permitted to place their children in institutions. Insulting mother or child was made punishable by law, but on the child's birth certificate and other public documents the space for identification of the child's father was left blank. Paternity suits were completely abolished. In effect, the stigma of illegitimacy, which had been removed in 1918, was reinstituted.

Marriages continued to be performed by civil registry offices. Instructions were given that a dignified and festive ceremony should be made out of the registration procedure, which should be carried out in suitable surroundings. Only civil marriages were to be considered valid; the courts no longer upheld common-law marriages, although those who had such unions before 1944 were permitted to validate them by registration.

Divorce, although still considered to be a right of all Soviet citizens, was made nearly impossible. It involved the payment of large fees; the appearance of both plaintiff and defendant in two successive courts, one of which was to try to reconcile the couple; and the publication of the intent to file divorce in the local newspaper, a step that took both time and money. The determination of grounds for divorce was left to the discretion of the judge.

Parents continued to be held responsible for the actions of their minor children. Family bonuses and motherhood honors were continued. In 1945 the inheritance laws were revised, enlarging further the circle of eligible heirs; previously, in 1943, the heavy progressive tax on inheritance was abolished. In 1947 marriage to non-Soviet citizens was declared unlawful.

Collective farm members have been subject to different laws on inheritance. Although collective membership is individual, houses, garden plots, and farming equipment belong to households and are joint property. When one member, even the head, of a household dies, the survivors do not inherit, because the property already belongs to them. Personal property of collective farm members, however, is subject to the usual laws of inheritance. These have remained unchanged since the mid-1940's.

Official statements on the subject of marriage and the family extolled the virtues of motherhood and the importance of a stable family life. The family was no longer considered to be the source and perpetuator of reaction but, together with public institutions, the source of Communist morality and the molder of upright Soviet citizens. According to Anton Makarenko, a Soviet educator, the family is the primary cell of society, a small collective. In it and in the schools and youth organizations, children learned responsibility and self-descipline, consideration for others, and good behavior through the unobtrusive guidance of their elders and friendly criticism of their peers.

The family legislation of the mid-1940's had few good effects, although there was a rise in the rate of population increase after World War II. Nonetheless, many provisions became highly unpopular, particularly the humiliating blank space on the birth certificates of illegitimate children, the impossibility of proving paternity outside of marriage even when the father so desired, and the difficulties of divorce. Because divorce was so difficult, many couples merely separated, later to form irregular unions.

Many men took an irresponsible attitude toward sexual relationships, abandoning women whom they made pregnant. Unmarried fathers who wished to give their names and inheritance to their children were obligated to adopt them. The position of mothers and children became much as it had been before the Bolshevik Revolution and was contrary to the often-expressed Communist principles of the equality of all Soviet citizens.

It was not long before public debate and citizen complaints began on the marriage and family laws. In 1955 the ban on abortions was repealed. Consideration was again given to the health of women and the difficulty in prohibiting what so many women desired. Instead of increasing the birth rate, the prohibition resulted in a rise in hazardous, illegal abortions.

Despite the liberalization in family laws, the authorities still express the same support for a strong family that they have made since the 1930's. Documents of the Twenty-Second Congress of the Communist Party of the Soviet Union, held in 1961, proclaimed the importance of the family in Soviet life. Khrushchev, in a speech to the Congress, claimed that the family would not become obsolete during the transition to communism but would instead become stronger. While stressing the importance of parental example and guidance in the upbringing of children, he also stressed the role of schoolteachers and public institutions. Public and family education were not in opposition. He also suggested that boarding schools and preschool institutions be expanded, but the suggestion met with little public support, and the project never flourished.

The Third Program of the Communist Party of the Soviet Union (CPSU), announced at the same Congress, continued to stress women's rights and promised provisions to lighten the burdens of working women, including public canteens, increased public services, domestic appliances, lighter workloads, extended maternity leave, and development of various public educational and child-care facilities. Evidently, the Party has recognized that domestic work has been a barrier to the full participation of women in economic and political life.

While some authorities, including Khrushchev, took a conservative position, others, including jurists and pedagogical experts, favored reform. By the mid-1960's it seemed that reforms would be shelved. But in 1965, after Khrushchev left office, reforms were made in the divorce laws—expenses of divorce proceedings were decreased, the publication requirement was removed, and the court appearances were made simpler. Judges were also instructed to give more latitude in their judgments of divorce cases.

The 1965 divorce reforms, however, were only a stopgap, and the debate continued. The regime took great care to determine public opinion and to secure expert advice. The magazine *Literaturnaya Gazeta* (Literary Gazette) became the forum for professional articles and letters on the subject. Finally, in April 1968 the draft legislation was published in *Izvestia*, the government newspaper.

A central question in the discussion of reform was the correction of injustices and inefficacies. Three problems of chief concern were the contracting of marriages, divorce procedures, and the establishment of paternity. Many authorities feared that another change would only make matters worse and pointed out that one could not legislate morality.

In June of 1968 the Supreme Soviet of the USSR ratified the draft, which became effective in October of the same year. Items in the new legislation, called principles, gave only the major outlines that were to be followed by more detailed legislation in the individual republics.

The new principles reiterated that marriage was to be a voluntary union, that the family should raise the children in a spirit of responsibility and Communist morality, and that the interests of women and children must be guarded. In family relations women and men have equal property rights, and all citizens of the Soviet Union, regardless of origin, have equal rights in family relations. Only civil marriages are recognized. The minimum age for marriage is at legal majority, eighteen years, but the republics may lower it to sixteen years. Applicants must wait one month before registering their marriages. Polygamy is forbidden; other impediments to marriage include close relationship by legitimate or illegitimate consanguinity or adoption, and mental illness or retardation.

Spouses may retain their own surnames, choose one or the other for joint use, or combine the two. Both are free to choose their occupations and place of residence; both have authority within the family. Property acquired by either spouse during marriage becomes joint property; property acquired by inheritance or owned before marriage also becomes joint. In case of divorce they have equal rights to communal property. The spouses are required to support each other materially. In the case of divorce either may be liable for alimony, depending upon the circumstances.

Paternity of children is usually established by marriage. Where this does not exist, both parents may apply to establish paternity; or the court may decide upon the application of one parent on the bases of cohabitation, maintenance of a common household, and support of the child. Paternity suits can be filed only for children born after October 1, 1968; this was to remove the possibility of a wave of paternity suits. Unmarried mothers may record the father's surname and patronymic on the child's birth certificate; the notorious blank space has been abolished.

Parents have the duty to rear their children and support them materially. Parental rights cannot be exercised contrary to the interests of the children. If parents neglect their duties or abuse their children, their rights to them may be removed by the court; these rights may be restored upon evidence of reform. When a parent is deprived of his parental rights, the child is removed to a public institution or foster home or put under the care of a guardian. Adult children may be obligated to support needy parents. Support for minor children may devolve upon other relatives. The state now accepts a residual role in family welfare. In cases of divorce alimony payments are adjusted according to need and ability to pay (see ch. 12, Living Conditions).

Minor children may be adopted by married couples or single individuals. Adopted children have the same legal status as natural children, the same rights and obligations, including inheritance, and the same impediments to marriage with kin. In certain cases minor children may be put under the care of foster parents or guardians; in such cases they legally remain members of their original families.

Great changes were made in the divorce law. If both partners agree to a divorce and there are no minor children, the civil registry may grant a divorce after a three-month waiting period. It will also grant a divorce upon the application of one spouse if the other has been declared mentally incompetent, has disappeared without a trace, or has been sentenced to prison for more than three years. In all other cases application must be made to the local people's court, which seeks to protect the interests of mothers and minor children.

Marriage with foreign nationals is permitted Soviet citizens. A child born of such a marriage becomes a Soviet citizen if one of the parents resided in the Soviet Union at the time of birth; otherwise the parents determine the citizenship. Previous legislation has established that the nationality, or ethnic affiliation, which is registered on the passport of a Soviet citizen, derives from that of the parents; in the case of a mixed marriage, the child must make a choice upon attaining his majority.

FORMS OF THE FAMILY AND THE HOUSEHOLD

Since the Bolshevik Revolution, the country has experienced a trend toward smaller family size and nuclear family organization. This trend, taking place throughout the world under the impact of wars, urbanization, and industrialization, has been hastened in the Soviet Union by the ideology and practices of the Communist Party.

The Nuclear Family

The model form of the family in the Soviet Union, the nuclear family, consists of a man and his wife and their unmarried children. Among Russians and other Europeans this family type has been becoming more and more common. Since the Bolshevik Revolution environmental causes, such as housing shortages, increased urbanization and industrialization, hardship, war, famine, and information campaigns on the part of the authorities, have combined to make the nuclear family the typical form. This has also occurred, to a somewhat lesser degree, in the non-European parts of the country, where the extended-family type of organization was more common before the Revolution.

Relationship patterns within the family have also changed. The old Russian custom was patriarchal; by both law and tradition the father was the head of the household, and his wife and children had to obey him. The mother represented more of a loving and submissive, yet strong, figure. On the whole, family relations were close and affectionate.

The Russian family is still close and affectionate, but relationships have become more democratic. This trend again had its origins before the Revolution in the prevailing bilateral kinship organization and the custom of men's work cooperatives that left the villages to seek seasonal work. These customs resulted in an increased importance being given to women and, at times, they became the acting heads of families.

Since the Revolution the higher male death rate that was a result of war, collectivization, and political purges also resulted in an increased importance of women. In the countryside, since more males than females migrated to the cities, at least seasonally, women also had greater opportunities to assume authority. Communist ideology has placed great stress on the emancipation of women from the authority of men, and the Communists have implemented their programs with a great measure of success.

Partly out of necessity, because their wives have worked, and partly because of government campaigns, Soviet men have come to share the tasks of housekeeping and childrearing with their wives. This trend has not been without male resistance and, even in the 1960's, working wives have less time for sleep and leisure activities than their husbands. Many working wives complain that they get little assistance from their husbands in mundane household chores.

Changes have also occurred in the authority of parents over children. This was another area in which the Communists sought to destroy the old bourgeois family. One of the consequences of early legislation was a sharp decrease in parental authority and responsibility. At one point, children were encouraged to put the interests of the regime over that of their families. One boy was regarded by the authorities as a hero for having informed on his father. After his father was executed, however, a band of outraged peasants killed the boy.

The emancipation of children was carried to an extreme. Both as a consequence of legal provisions and of large-scale social disruption, juvenile delinquency became a serious problem. Since the mid-1930's parents have had authority over, and responsibility for, their children; no contrary trend appears to be evident.

Nonetheless, the authority of parents has been weakened. This has been partly a consequence of rapid social change in which children receive greater exposure to new ideas and thus find in their parents an image of tradition instead of final authority. Some parents have been aware of this but, instead of attempting to impose their ideas on them, have realized that their children will be living in a future to which they must be adjusted. The emphasis on peer group collectives—youth organizations and schools—has also weakened parental authority.

Among the Muslim peoples of central Asia and the Caucasus, the nuclear family has become common, although not so common as in the European parts of the country. Patriarchal traditions, however, have remained strong there, and the father has great authority over his family.

Affection and intimacy has continued to be strong within the family. Hardship, particularly political persecution, has often served to strengthen these feelings within the family. External pressures have resulted in a strengthening of the family as a refuge of peace and security.

Other Forms of the Family

A common variant of the nuclear family, with firm roots in tradition, is the expanded family. In this variant, some other relative resides with the nuclear family. Generally, it is an elderly female, usually the mother of one of the spouses. Although this pattern was typically rural, at the present time it is perhaps even more common in the cities. The grandmother thus finds a place to live in the crowded housing situation and something useful to do with herself; at the same time, the working mother has someone to help with the housekeeping and childrearing.

The economic bases for cooperation within the bilateral kinship group have been removed by collectivization and industrialization. Internal migration has resulted in the dispersal of groups of relatives over vast expanses of the country. Rural life more than urban life has favored the retention of informal ties with close kin.

Another common variant of the nuclear family is the partial family. Two forms of the partial family exist: a parent with minor children or an adult and an elderly parent. The first form, generally a mother with her children, has been caused by the death or desertion of the husband; or it may be only temporary, caused by remote employment. The other form generally consists of a single woman and her widowed mother. Partial families of the first type result in hardship for the women who must be both wage earner and mother and are a common source of juvenile delinquency. The other type, since it does not involve minor children, usually represents an amelioration of conditions, given the shortage of males in certain age groups and the crowded housing situation.

Joint and extended family households occur in isolated parts of the country outside of the European sector. The joint family household may consist of a group of brothers and their families living together or of a man with his wives and children. Polygyny may occur covertly among men who have the means and who seek traditional symbols of prestige; the second wives are taken according to religious law, and of course the marriages cannot be registered officially.

The clan organization has also been able to persist in some rural areas. Both in Siberia and in central Asia *kolkhoz* (collective farm) brigades and even *kolkhozy* (collective farms) have been organized around the prevailing clan organization. Other adjuncts of clan organization, such as exogamy (marrying outside of the group), the bridewealth, and the levirate, have also persisted, often in modified form. All of these customs are fast disappearing, however, under the impact of economic changes and pressures by the authorities.

FAMILY LIFE CYCLES

In the late 1960's young people everywhere in the Soviet Union had opportunity to meet one another. Schools, factories, union meetings, the Young Pioneers and the Komsomol (Young Communist League), as well as interest clubs and youth cafes, all provided places to meet. Formerly, the opportunities were limited to an individual's village or to villages where he had close relatives. In the Caucasus and central Asia, where parents arranged marriages, the young people considered themselves fortunate if they had even seen each other before the wedding.

The changes that have taken place in the relationship of the sexes in marriage have had concomitant changes in the reasons for marriage. Before Soviet social changes had taken effect, the usual peasant notion was that love was of little importance in the choice of a mate. Health, strength, and skills were the most important qualities for the peasant in search of a spouse. Among the aristocracy and in the Caucasus and central Asia, family social status was an important consideration. A family's financial status was often considered, particularly in the small middle class. Other marriage restrictions existed, stemming from religion or tradition; the church had a wide range of prohibited degrees, and most of the non-Europeans had exogamous clans.

Soviet law has reduced to a very narrow circle the number of prohibited kin. The rapid social mobility that has taken place under the Soviet regime has rendered the old status differences largely meaningless. Ethnicity remains a barrier to intermarriage; Muslims, and especially their women, rarely marry non-Muslims.

Marx, Engels, and Lenin favored marriage for love, and love, together with community of interests, has increasingly become the chief reason for marriage. Soviet citizens have come to expect more out of the personal relations within marriage. Trends toward smaller family size and scope, changes in values, and external pressures on families have all resulted in increased chances for greater personal satisfaction within marriage.

213

Numerous studies of the family by Soviet sociologists have shown that when a couple have not known each other long before marriage, the marriage is more likely to fail. These studies were of great interest to the framers of the new family law. They wished to deter these hasty marriages but at the same time realized that too great obstacles would result in cohabitation without marriage. A one-month waiting period and a continued stress on a solemn ceremony at registration were the result.

Although religious ceremonies of marriage have been discouraged by the regime and are no longer legally valid in themselves, they still take place among some segments of the population, usually in isolated rural areas. The religious ceremony, where it occurs, is often held to please older relatives and takes place up to a month after the civil registration. The young people often begin living together after the civil ceremony. If the religious ceremony is dispensed with, as is generally the case, after the civil ceremony at the registry office families like to hold a traditional-style reception and feast either at home or in a public hall. Traditionally, bride and groom returned to their new home—usually the groom's—after the ceremony. The institution of the honeymoon is virtually unknown.

Traditionally, childbirth was marked by religious or quasi-religious ceremonies; various folk customs, designed to protect mother and child or to associate the child with his appropriate sex role, also existed. As a part of the campaign against religion and traditional customs, the Soviet authorities have sought to replace these observances by ceremonies considered more appropriate to socialism. When the birth of a child is entered at the civil registry office, a ceremony is supposed to be made of the presentation of the birth certificate. Many people enjoy having celebrations at home; the old customs have lost their meaning for most, but at the same time the new ceremonies have not become customary.

The old coming-of-age ceremonies, such as the bar mitzvah, confirmation, and completion of Koranic studies, have had the expected fate. The secular substitution, graduation from secondary school, has become very popular. Families often spend great sums of money on clothes, beauty parlors, and parties for their children. In the Baltic states an attempt has been made to introduce a public coming-of-age ceremony for boys and girls who have attained the age of eighteen during the year. Dressed in their best clothes, the young people have a parade, then attend a public assembly, and conclude with feasting and dancing.

After they attain their majority, children hope to be able to leave home to make a life for themselves; throughout adolescence they have been becoming less and less dependent upon their families. Because of the housing shortage, however, many must remain at home until marriage or, sometimes, even afterwards. The state has provided some dormitories for single working people, but these are overcrowded and insufficient to meet the need.

Legally, a marriage ends by death or divorce. Widowhood is a problem that has been faced by numerous Soviet women, not only because of the difference in lifespans between men and women—in 1959 the average was seven years—but also because the hardships of the twentieth century have fallen more heavily upon men than upon women.

These same hardships have put a great strain on marriages. Conditions of crowded housing, close budgeting, long hours of difficult work, housekeeping chores under adverse conditions, lack of leisure time and facilities, and government political pressures have caused some families to grow closer together, but more of them have disintegrated under the strain. The dislocations of war and occupational migration have also had adverse effects, not only from the facts of physical separation alone, but from the tendency of lonely people to seek new companionship. Some men have used occupational migration as an escape from unhappy marital situations.

During the two decades after the Stalinist divorce laws were enacted, when divorce was virtually impossible, desertion and separation were the means many took. And even during that period, when the regime was trying to change attitudes toward divorce, people still attached no stigma to divorce; the divorce rate was low simply because it was so difficult to obtain a divorce.

During the early years of the Soviet period when divorce was easy to obtain, other factors as well contributed to the high divorce rates. The belief that marriage was an obsolescent institution and the bold talk about free love and the emancipation of women contributed to an insouciant attitude toward marriage. The difficult social conditions also resulted in more divorces. Since divorce had been all but impossible during the tsarist era, many unhappy couples finally had the chance to change their marital situations.

Since the divorce reforms of 1965, the divorce rate has again risen sharply. One factor has been the same one that operated after the end of the tsarist regime. Soviet demographers also attribute the growing economic independence of women and the diminishing functions of the family as causes. Attitudes toward divorce and divorced persons are lenient—another contributing factor.

FAMILY AND SOCIETY

Family Size

Continuing since the latter part of the nineteenth century, but accelerated during the Soviet period, has been a trend toward smaller family size. Environmental conditions have played a major role in this trend, but they have resulted in a change in values as

215

well. Despite the concern voiced by the Soviet regime, little has been done to effectively change the trend.

The environmental conditions affecting family size have in part been those peculiar to Soviet history. Elsewhere in the world the process of industrialization and accompanying urbanization also has resulted in a trend toward smaller families.

In 1959 the average size of the family, defined in the Soviet census as a group of people related by kinship or marriage and living under a common budget, was 3.7. The urban mean was 3.5 and the rural mean was 3.9. These figures include both partial and expanded families.

Figures on the declining birth rate and the trend toward smaller family size indicate that most Soviet couples regard one or two children as an ideal number. During the pre-Soviet era people either had no concept of ideal family size or desired to have as many children as possible. At that time conditions made such attitudes necessary. Many children not only were an economic asset on the farm but also, in the absence of social security, provided a form of old-age insurance as well. In the presence of high mortality rates, only a high birth rate could ensure the survival of sufficient children.

The authorities are still interested in the birth rate, which has fallen since the early 1960's, but they have retreated from the traditional Marxist position that, under socialism, regulation of the birth rate is unnecessary. Contraception has come to be preferable to abortion as a means of birth control. There have been some campaigns for the distribution of contraceptive devices and information. The authorities have apparently found it necessary to follow the trend toward smaller family size (see ch. 32, The Labor Force).

Public medical and welfare programs, pensions, and social security had made old age more secure by the late 1960's. The mortality rate has nearly reached the lowest point possible, given the composition of the population (see ch. 32, The Labor Force).

Inadequate housing and insufficient wages have made large families undesirable. Many working women now regard childbearing as a burden. In addition, both husbands and wives find that children detract from the time and energy they can devote to recreational and intellectual activities (see ch. 12, Living Conditions).

The improvement in the status of women has caused an inevitable change in the self-image of women. They no longer regard themselves as just housewives and mothers but as workers as well and no longer need to justify themselves by having many children, for they have other sources of personal satisfaction.

Even should improvements in the housing situation and the provision of services and child-care facilities, promised since the Bolshevik Revolution, be made, a large increase in the birth rate would probably not result because of the changes in values. Although the regime is not likely to abandon its campaign of glorifying motherhood, it is even less likely to retreat from the emancipation of women; the latter is entrenched in the Marxist system of values.

Socialization

Communism has resulted in the family's being supplemented in its role of socialization by various public institutions. The early Bolsheviks regarded the family not only as an institution fated to early extinction but also as a source of tradition and reaction. Such attitudes led to a deemphasization of the family, with adverse results. The family was reinstated as a necessary social institution but, given the continuing needs to perpetuate the Revolution, extrafamilial agents of socialization continued to be important. The family was, and is, regarded as compatible with socialism and as an adjunct to public agencies in producing man in a new image.

The schools not only provide education and occupational training, but also, together with youth organizations, give moral training and character building. Many preschool children spend the greater part of their day in nursery schools and, during the summer, in camps. Primary and secondary school children spend long hours in school and afterwards attend interest clubs and meetings of the Young Pioneers and the Komsomol. Summer camps and work projects also are available to them. In addition, there are boarding schools and institutions for orphans and illegitimate children (see ch. 15, The Educational System).

Soviet parents usually prefer to keep infants in the home for at least the first year, before leaving them in a nursery during working hours. The boarding schools and institutions have not been popular, even with unwed mothers. Although a great problem has existed in combining child supervision and work, parents have been reluctant to turn over all responsibilities to other persons. Parents want their children at home at least during the evenings and on weekends and want younger children within the family circle as much as possible.

Despite such parental attitudes, the role of the family in socialization has diminished. Most parents have recognized that times have changed and that resistance is futile.

The tone of Soviet socialization is highly moralistic. Following the lead of pedagogical experts, a great emphasis has been placed on raising responsible citizens in the new Soviet image. The moral principles of communism, enunciated in the Third Program of the CPSU in 1961, on the whole bear a striking resemblance to traditional moral principles known in the West. Exceptions are an emphasis on collectivism and on loyalty to the Communist cause. The program states that a citizen should be loyal and have a high sense of civic duty and responsibility. He should be honest, friendly, truthful, modest, and morally pure. Family relations were included in the moral code to the effect that they should be characterized by mutual respect and concern for the upbringing of children.

Childrearing methods, although not at all permissive, are kindly. Corporal punishment of children is regarded as not only unnecessary but unjustifiable. Parents prefer to train children by example and by appeal to their better judgment. Shaming is a final resort when children do not respond to milder methods. Although this method is one favored by the stress placed on collectivism, it was one of the traditional Russian methods of social control.

On the whole, the process of socialization has resulted in success, according to the goals chosen. Exceptions exist, but problem youths have generally had defective backgrounds. Either they come from broken or partial families or from relatively wealthy families in which money replaced parental responsibilities. The juvenile delinquents, although noteworthy in the Soviet press, remain in a minority.

Welfare and Security

Material welfare is another area in which the functions of the family have decreased. Except for a few religious and urban institutions, the family was the chief resource in the pre-Soviet era for the individual in need. The necessity for material security was one of the economic bases of the family that the Marxists had hoped to eradicate. Early Bolshevik pronouncements were consistent with this ideal. Implementation of ideals, however, proved to be difficult.

For many years, even into the 1960's, financial resources of the state were limited, a major proportion of funds going into basic industry and armaments. Early programs for pensions, workmen's compensation, and family allowances were severely limited. This was one of the reasons for the early reinstatement of inheritance. But even the earliest decrees recognized that the family, in conjunction with state programs, would continue to be responsible for the support of children, the aged, and the disabled. Although the achievement of socialism was announced in the 1936 Constitution, the family continued to be the chief institution responsible for individual security.

According to the 1968 family code, parents are responsible for the material support of minor children; they are also responsible for needy adult children. Spouses are responsible for each other's support. In certain cases, such as disablement or the existence of minor children, such obligations may continue for a period after a divorce. The obligations to support minor children and needy adults may devolve upon other kin, such as siblings, grandparents, and step-parents if a court so decides. The state, then, assumes responsibility for welfare only when the appropriate kin are missing or are unable to fulfill their responsibilities.

Family and Status

In the old Russian Empire there existed opportunities for social mobility, but these were limited; generally, individuals acquired their status from that of their families. Status included not only social class and economic standing, but also ethnic and religious affiliation, and occupation. The Communist revolutionaries hoped to eradicate such status differences, not to mention the family itself.

In part, they have been successful. Great opportunities for social mobility have been created, as educational and career possibilities have opened up throughout the country. Religious and ethnic differences, have, on the whole, been minimized. A father's trade and social standing are no longer restrictions on a child's economic opportunities.

Differences exist between the life styles of peasants and workers, and still greater differences exist between those of high-level intelligentsia and Party administrators and the proletariat. Children coming from the fortunate families have greater chances for advancement than do children from working-class families. Although such privilege is against the ideals of Soviet society, well-to-do parents do their best to perpetuate privileges for their children. The situation is recognized as a social problem, since it conflicts with basic values. The use of material rewards as incentive in occupations will doubtless continue, but attempts to increase the opportunities available to working-class children will also continue.

The Position of Women

The emancipation of women, from material dependency, exploitation by men, housekeeping, and childrearing, was one of the cornerstones of early family policy. This ideal was one more easily realized for, in part, it required smaller amounts of money and also because the state could not afford to waste the human resources of half the population—the women. Furthermore, women, since they had less exposure to the outside world, were more conservative than their husbands. In their role as rearers of children, they were in a position to pass on this conservatism to their children—a situation that the revolutionary Bolsheviks desired to end.

Outside of legal provisions, economic circumstances have been more influential in changing the position of women than have ideological campaigns. Among the Islamic peoples, who share a great tradition centering outside the Soviet Union, situations that seem to outsiders to indicate a low position of women actually have no such meaning. For example, the Russian ethnic group within the country regards the seclusion of women as exploitation and humiliation, but traditional Muslims who observe the custom feel that seclusion honors and protects women. The Russians consider the bridewealth to be a degrading symbol of chattel status, whereas the Muslims regard it as a symbol of the high regard for individual women as well as a source of security from want and repudiation by their husbands. In a number of the central Asian republis, the proportion of women who work is still very low, and girls still often drop out of secondary school to get married. Even in the most conservative regions, however, progress has been made toward the goal of equality of the sexes.

Numerous difficulties hindered the entrance of women into the working world but, nonetheless, by the late 1960's women were well represented in all sectors of the economy. Certain professions, such as medicine, have come to be regarded as feminine provinces, but discrepancies remain, and a great part of the women employed occupy unskilled positions. For example, in 1959 four-fifths of the women employed were in unskilled physical labor, generally in agriculture. At the same time, over half of the white-collar workers were women. Seventy-five percent of physicians are women, and women constitute one-third of the engineering profession.

Although women may find combining the home and a career a burden, neither they nor the men regard home and career as incompatible roles. Such a value change is a result of Soviet policy toward women and toward family relationships in general.

CHAPTER 12
LIVING CONDITIONS

Modernization had become the predominant influence in the cities and towns of the Soviet Union by early 1970, and tradition no longer played a central role in determining the urban manner of living. From the cities and towns of the European sector of the country, change was spreading to the relatively static society of the villages and the remote parts of the country. The growing rate of urbanization since the end of World War II had accelerated the changes in the lives of the people. Radio, motion pictures, television, newspapers, and improved transportation were all factors contributing to change.

Despite heavy migration to the cities, nearly half of the people still lived in villages and rural areas. The typical peasant was slow to accept change, and patterns of living in the village reflected his conservatism. Lacking many modern amenities and isolated by poor communications, the village way of life offered few of the material advantages enjoyed by the residents of the relatively modern and well-developed cities and towns.

Public health was a prime concern of ministries and departments at all governmental levels, from the central government in Moscow to the smallest of village governments. The greatest portion of clinical and hospital services was provided at the district, or country, level. There were about 600,000 physicians and 50,000 dentists; approximately 70 percent of physicians were women. Including nurses, midwives, technicians, and other medical practitioners, about 80 medical personnel were available for every 10,000 persons in the country.

Leisure activities encouraged by the state included civil and social work, self-improvement studies, hobbies, and sports. Study and training to improve individual productive capabilities were especially encouraged. Reading has remained the most popular and respected form of self-educational leisure activity, walking the most popular form of leisure exercise.

The Soviet diet consisted of approximately 50 percent starches. Meat and dairy products were scarce and expensive. Fruit and vegetables were plentiful in season, but storage facilities were inadequate to keep them available at all times. The developing textille industry was unable to meet consumer demands by 1970 and, although Western styles predominated, styling tended to be indifferent and colors drab.

Urban housing was short about thirty family-dwelling units per 1,000 population in 1970. New construction consisted mainly of standardized low-cost apartment blocks. Cooperative housing developments were encouraged; private construction was discouraged.

Welfare programs were comprehensive and included retirement pensions, disability benefits, family allowances, and welfare services for children. The entire population, including collective farmers, was eligible for pensions at retirement age, and more than 35 million persons were receiving disability or old age pensions in 1970.

HEALTH AND SANITATION

On the basis of Soviet data, the crude birth rate in 1969 was 18 live births per 1,000 population, and the infant mortality rate was 26 per 1,000 live births. Life expectancy at the age of one year was sixty-six years for men and seventy-four years for women (see ch. 32, The Labor Force).

Inadequate sanitation is the principal environmental factor affecting the level of health. Public sanitation is comparatively recent and is not well developed in the rural areas. In the villages sewage disposal and drainage are generally inadequate, and most dwellings have outdoor toilet facilities. Larger towns and cities have modern sewage disposal systems.

The water supply in rural areas tends to be unsafe, while that in the larger towns and cities is generally satisfactory. Water for domestic use in the villages usually comes from communal sources, including streams, springs, or wells, all of which are subject to pollution and are unlikely to be treated. Only the large cities have modern water supplies, and some of these remain deficient.

Infectious diseases have declined as major causes of death in the Soviet Union, primarily because of extensive health measures undertaken since the end of World War II. Cancer and various cardiovascular diseases were reported to be among the main causes of death in 1969. No deaths were officially attributed to smallpox, malaria, cholera, plague, or typhus—formerly the causes of considerable mortality. Tuberculosis did occur, but its incidence has decreased greatly since about 1950 as a result of effective campaigns aimed at its early detection and treatment. Other diseases endemic in the country included trachoma, respiratory ailments, and diphtheria. Malaria, once a widespread disease, averaging between 2 million and 3 million cases per year in the early part of the twentieth century, has been reduced to relative insignificance since World War II by drainage and extensive use of modern insecticides.

Organization and Administration of Soviet Health Services

Over 26,000 hospitals, 20,000 polyclinics, 30,000 ambulatory clinics, and 2,000 sanatoriums, rest homes, and homes for the aged, with a total rated capacity of close to 4 million beds, are organized, administered, and funded by the state. In addition, the government maintains rural health stations and disease control and treatment clinics throughout the nation. For cardiovascular diseases, a network of dispensaries provided periodic examinations for students and industrial workers. The government also maintained over 7,000 tuberculosis inpatient and outpatient treatment centers, over 2,000 cancer clinics and hospitals, over 6,000 venereal disease treatment centers, and close to 200 neuropsychiatric clinics. Treatment and drugs are provided free of charge, and surveys are kept on the incidence of all infectious diseases. The Red Cross and the Red Crescent, members of the International League of Red Cross Societies, maintained volunteer organizations, primarily to provide disaster relief.

The government also provides special care and protection for mothers and children through a system of clinical centers, under the Ministry of Public Health. The centers are maintained either in the form of separate gynecological clinics or as specialized departments of polyclinics or hospitals and provide assistance ranging from prenatal examinations and care to postnatal pediatric services for children up to sixteen years of age. In addition, the government maintains day nurseries for nearly 1.5 million children (see ch. 15, The Educational System).

By the late 1960's the emphasis on planning, coordination, and national control had resulted in a large bureaucratic structure. The USSR Ministry of Public Health has overall responsibility for the nation's health system; republic ministries of health and local agencies share that responsibility in varying degrees. These ministries, structurally subordinate to their respective councils of ministers, are required to carry out the directives from those councils as well as directives from the national ministry.

The USSR Ministry of Public Health, responsible for the general health of the country, is in charge of all medical and public health services. In fulfilling its functions, the USSR Ministry of Public Health has the power to propose health legislation and to promulgate directives for all subordinate health agencies. More specifically, it is charged with planning the nation's health service—determining the number of required physicians for each community, assisting local health agencies, planning medical research, ascertaining the needs for medical supplies as well as providing for their production and distribution, and maintaining international cooperation in medicine and public health. Authority vested in the various repub-

223

lics comprises overseeing the implementation of the decisions, regulations, and directives of the health ministries.

The USSR Ministry of Public Health implements the laws and decisions of the USSR Supreme Soviet and the USSR Council of Ministers concerning the protection of public health. The ministry is divided into several departments, each with a director and staff. The number of such departments has varied over the years according to advances in Soviet medicine and health care and in various governmental reorganizations. Directly under the ministry or its departments are national medical institutions, research organizations, and medically related business enterprises.

Republic ministries of public health maintain larger staffs with more departments, and their administrative structures are more complex than that of the national ministry. Both the size and the number of departments in a republic ministry depend on local conditions and the population of the republic, but the overall structure remains the same for all republic health ministries. The main concern of republic ministries of health is with operations rather than planning.

Directly below the republic ministries of public health are the health ministries for autonomous republics, provincial health departments, or regional health departments. Attached to these agencies are executives, secretaries, and accountants, as well as medical councils and administrative and operational sectors. Attached to the sectors are the medical and paramedical personnel who are responsible for the medical services in their specialties.

Beneath the regional health departments, but above the small municipal and rural departments, are those at the district levels, where the majority of medical services are performed. At this level there is a polyclinic, which comprises many specialized clinics and, in some cases, a hospital that provides major medical services. The polyclinic maintains all forms of health services of an outpatient nature; services are provided either in the polyclinic itself or in the patient's home, where the bulk of medical practice takes place. The staff of the polyclinic varies with the number of persons in the area it is intended to serve. Hospitals in the district are reserved for those cases that cannot be treated in the polyclinic or at home and, although hospital treatment may be recommended, the patient is generally advised to recuperate at home as much as possible.

Municipal and rural health departments in small cities, towns, and villages are the lowest administrative levels in the health system. These agencies are responsible for the local medical services in their areas and direct all phases of the health system, from financing programs and appointing and paying medical personnel to maintaining preventive measures against diseases. They are also required to cooperate with voluntary medical agencies, such as the Red Cross or the Red Crescent. Funds for the medical services directed by them come from the local Soviets and administrative bodies. They provide medical assistance of a minor nature to populations ranging from 2,000 to 4,000 persons. Small towns are sometimes cut off from the outside world by harsh weather conditions, and their residents are unable to obtain modern medical aid at times when they most need it.

Separate health facilities exist for the armed forces and for the personnel of specific governmental agencies, such as the Ministry of Transport and Highways, the Committee for State Security, and the Ministry of Internal Affairs. The service provided varies in proportion to the influence and authority of the patient. Members of the top elite have personal physicians in constant attendance, who prescribe work habits, diet, and physical exercises. Hospital care in the Kremlin Polyclinic is reportedly the best in the country. Those members of the elite who require rest are able to go to luxuriously appointed sanatoriums in the Crimea, along the Black Sea coast, or in the Caucasus Mountains. All provide pleasant, often luxurious, surroundings; excellent food; and prompt, immediate medical attention, far superior to the medical care available to the general public.

Medical services and facilities available to high government officials, Party members, and such members of the intelligentsia as famous writers and artists are less luxurious than for those of the elite but are much better than those available to the general population. One doctor is assigned to five or six persons. For persons entitled to the next lower level of care, the doctor-patient ratio is one doctor for about fifteen patients. Facilities for local Party and governmental officials generally comprise a separate wing in the local hospital.

Medical Personnel and Training

In the mid-1960's there were over 4 million persons engaged in medicine and its related fields, representing 1.7 percent of the nation's population and 5.6 percent of the total working force (see ch. 32, The Labor Force). There were nearly 600,000 physicians in the Soviet Union in 1967; about 400,000, or approximately 70 percent, of them were women. Including the nearly 2 million nurses, midwives, and technicians, there were nearly 80 medical personnel for every 10,000 persons in the country. Moscow and Leningrad had the highest ratios of physicians to population, with more than 60 physicians per 10,000 persons. This was more than three times the national ratio. The number of medical personnel was much smaller in rural and remote areas of the country, since many doctors, if possible, avoided practicing in villages that lacked modern medical equipment and facilities.

The professional training of physicians comprises a six-year program either at a medical institute or at a medical faculty attached to a university. Prior educational requirements consist of completion of the secondary level of general education. Over 150,000 students were enrolled in over 200 medical institutes in 1969. More than 25,000 students graduate each year.

Specialization in such areas as general medicine, pediatrics, public health (the three major specialities in Soviet medicine), gynecology, or gerontology is possible for the graduate of the six-year program. Three years of service in an area designated by the state are required as repayment for his educational expenses, after which he may usually practice in an area of his own choosing. Specialization usually requires years of work either in a hospital or clinic under the direction of an older physician. In order to keep up with new medical developments, Soviet doctors also have access to refresher courses at postgraduate institutes, which consist of two months' training every three years.

The training of paramedical personnel is also extensive. *Feldshers* —medical practitioners who assist physicians and who may perform medical functions, including minor surgery—receive four years of training in secondary medical schools, requiring seven to eight years of general education before admission. In 1969 over 250,000 students were enrolled in 560 such schools. Nurses train in a two-year program. Rural midwives receive four years of training—two years of basic education on the secondary school level and two years mainly of assisting in patient care.

PATTERNS OF LIVING AND LEISURE

Life for an average urban family has changed substantially since World War II in terms of both consumption patterns and traditional practices. Paternal authoritarianism, although still a widely accepted principle, has given way to wide freedom of action and thought among the various family members. Women maintain full-time jobs away from the home and dress according to the fashion of the day. Young people, away from home at school or at a summer camp, speak more freely in the presence of their elders. Through schools, newspapers, radios, and television, people have learned about the rest of the country but little about the rest of the world. (see ch. 25, Public Information).

Persons who live in the small scattered villages have scarcely been affected by modern influences. A few rough dwellings (usually built of stone and cement), a coffeehouse, a school, and the outlying fields and pastures constitute the surroundings in which most villagers pass their lives. Many villages lack electricity, running water, doctors, and teachers. In many places women still do much of the heavy work and are considered inferior to men.

Leisure-time activities that Soviet officials consider to be most desirable are those that are held to be contributors to the construction of society according to the principles of communism. Such activities include study to improve employment qualifications, self-improvement and self-education, civic and social work, hobbies, and sports.

Study or training to improve one's productive capability is encouraged, and much of it is done during working hours while the individual receives his full salary.

Self-improvement or self-education is encouraged through many other activities organized by the state. These include lectures, seminars, museum excursions, attendance at motion pictures and plays, group radio-listening, and instruction in approved political values (see ch. 15, The Educational System; ch. 21, Political Dynamics).

Reading is the most important form of leisure-time self-educational activity. It has been accorded much respect in Russian as well as Soviet society as a true indication of personal intellectuality. Books are both extremely inexpensive and available in great quantities.

Participation in social or civic work is encouraged. Such activities include attending meetings and lectures and working with juvenile delinquents, ideological delinquents, alcoholics, the handicapped, and so on. Hobbies are also important to the people. Those popular in the late 1960's included stamp collecting, working with electrical radios, dancing, and participation in amateur theatricals. Most rural villages and many urban neighborhoods have some form of dramatic club.

Sports and physical activity are important in Soviet society. Both sexes and all ages are urged to keep physically fit. Individual or informal sports activities do not exist; the state organizes all such activities and provides the necessary facilities.

Walking has always been a traditional and favorite form of leisure-time exercise. Overcrowded living conditions in urban apartments, the scarcity of balconies or yards, and the lack of automobiles have contributed to an overall lack of privacy for the individual. Strolling in the generally well-maintained streets and parks thus serves a dual purpose.

The theater and motion pictures are popular. Motion picture attendance is greater, because the cinemas are more readily available, lower priced, and their tickets more easily obtained. Foreign films, rarely seen outside the large cities of European Russia, are most popular with young people.

Foreign travel is severely restricted, but internal travel is relatively free. Private foreign travel is permitted only to the Communist nations of Eastern Europe; travel to Western European countries is rarely allowed except for artists, scientists, and government officials on approved visits. Although an internal passport is required, great numbers of citizens travel throughout the country, especially during the summer months. The shortage of hotel rooms inhibits such travel to some extent.

Young people spend much free time in restaurants and cafes, which provide a place to relax, drink alcoholic beverages, eat, and dance. Cafe relaxation is viewed by authorities with disdain as a contributor to alcoholism, juvenile delinquency, and un-Soviet sexual morality. The state has consequently attempted, without complete success, to draw youths from such activities by building youth centers. Measures were also taken in early 1970 that were aimed at reducing the consumption of alcohol.

Rural and urban areas of the country tend to observe different holidays. In rural areas, where religious beliefs are stronger, Christmas and Easter are celebrated in addition to the Muslim, Jewish, Buddhist, and the Soviet national holidays. Observance of religious holidays is tolerated, although not sanctioned, by local officials. In the cities only national holidays are celebrated. May Day, November 7 (anniversary of the Communist Revolution), and New Year's Day predominate. Where religious holidays are not celebrated, New Year's Day has become the occasion for exchanging gifts.

CONSUMPTION PATTERNS

Economic and industrial progress has increased the quantities of consumer goods, particularly since 1953. Improvements in transportation and the migration of people from rural areas to the cities have also served to make them available to a larger proportion of the population. Also, the transition from barter to a money system has resulted in an increase in the range of goods that can be purchased in rural areas. Most peasants now buy cotton textiles, factory-made shoes, household utensils, radios, and many other things. About two-thirds of the rural houses have radios. Villagers who have traditionally accepted poverty with equanimity now want the material comfort and prestige derived from the possession of consumer goods (see ch. 34, Domestic Trade).

Citizens with larger incomes, or those who belong to the political, military, and cultural elites, live much better than the general population. They obtain better foods; have a more nutritionally well-rounded diet; can obtain the best medical treatment available; can obtain more luxurious and larger living quarters, often with a *dacha* (summer cottage); can purchase high-priced luxury goods, such as jewelry, automobiles, and better clothing; and can usually send their children to the best schools.

Over one-half the average person's income is spent on food, and the remainder is expended mainly on transportation, personal care, and repair services. Food expenditures account for the largest part of money income, primarily because of the high prices of scarce meat and dairy products. Reflecting improvements in the standard of living, the number and availability of laundries, dry cleaners, and clothing and appliance repair shops have increased.

FOOD AND CLOTHING

The kinds of food eaten in the country vary from region to region. The average nationwide daily per capita caloric intake averaged roughly 3,100 calories in the late 1960's. The average diet, however, included a heavy concentration of cereals, potatoes, and starches, with a small proportion of dairy, meat, and vegetable products. Fruit is eaten in season, but the diet is relatively low in dairy and animal products. Meat, once scarce and extremely expensive owing to the failure of the meat industry to expand with increased public demand, has been more plentiful since 1964, but it is still expensive. Vegetables are still relatively scarce because of inadequate storage facilities. These things notwithstanding, by the mid-1960's the percentage of starches in the average person's daily diet had fallen from about 70 to slightly over 50.

There are regional variations in the traditional styles of clothing but, except in the more remote parts of the country, traditional costumes have virtually disappeared. People wear ordinary Western styles with few, if any, distinctive national characteristics. In rural areas clothing is often homemade, of durable quality, and utilitarian rather than decorative. One effect of modernization in the country is the villager's belief that city products are more desirable than those traditionally made in the home. As a result, the use of homemade clothing has declined in recent years, and people more ordinarily buy readymade garments in the specialized clothing or department stores (see ch. 34, Domestic Trade).

The availability of Western-style clothing has increased considerably since 1965. Western fashions have been reproduced but, in 1970, the textile industry had not caught up with the initial demand for them, and the first production styles and drab colors still predominated. No mass fashion industry had developed to provide inexpensive clothing because, for a considerable time after World War II, the nation's planners had concentrated on the development of heavy industries at the expense of the consumer industry (see ch. 6, The Economic System).

The quality of Soviet fabrics was poor, and prices for finished products were extremely high. Shoes in Moscow department stores cost about one-third the average worker's net monthly income in 1970; coats, nearly 100 percent. Western-styled clothing exhibited in shopwindows often was not available for sale inside the store, and people who did wear such clothing generally purchased it outside the country.

HOUSING

Housing has been one of the most serious problems facing the nation. Despite the huge demand for new housing that existed after World War II, the necessity to rebuild industry at the expense of other sectors of the economy forced the government to delay the construction of new housing until the late 1950's. At that time, construction quantity was emphasized at the expense of quality, and the result has been more housing but of extremely poor quality.

Soviet law guarantees every citizen living space. The amount of living space, however, is established on the republic level and varies from republic to republic. The Ukrainian republic has established about 160 square feet per person as the norm, while the Russian republic has established about 110 square feet per person. While this has officially been referred to as the minimum legally permissible, in practice it has served as the maximum. Housing construction required high priority programs merely to rebuild units destroyed during World War II and to keep pace with the expanding population and its migration to the cities. The proportion of the nation's population living in cities increased from about one-third to over one-half between 1939 and 1968. By about 1960, however, the average citizen had again attained the approximately 60 square feet of living space that was the national average in the mid-1920's. At the end of 1969, it was estimated that the housing shortage in the urban areas approximated 30 dwellings per 1,000 inhabitants.

For the average citizen, the consequences have been severe. Sanitation facilities have been overtaxed, personal and family privacy has been restricted, and family relationships have been strained. In 1965 an average of 2.3 persons inhabited one room in the nation's cities, even though the maximum number of persons per room had been set at 1.5. Lavatory and kitchen facilities were frequently shared by several families.

The government on both national and local levels has been unable to provide enough new housing units to accommodate the increased urban population. Since 1959, however, the government has given a high priority to new housing construction and has planned high annual goals which, for the most part, have not been realized. From 1956 to the end of 1966 investment outlays in housing as a percentage of total investment outlays, excluding collective farms investment, averaged slightly over 18 percent each year. In addition to complaints about the lack of housing facilities in the nation, most tenants of new housing units have complained about poor quality, shoddy workmanship, lack of prompt repairs, the inability

230

to bring problems to the attention of the authorities, administrative inefficiency, and the lack of utilities.

The lack of utilities has been the major consumer complaint. Electric lighting is found in the great majority of state housing in urban areas but is found less frequently in rural housing. Serious shortages of running water, sewers, and central heating services still existed. State housing, however, was usually better equipped. In 1965 less than 25 percent of all homes in the country were serviced with gas, and most of these were located in the urban areas.

State Housing

In 1969 state-owned housing accounted for the majority of all housing units in the nation. It was administered either by agencies of the local government or by large industrial enterprises for their workers which, however, had to conform to strict municipal regulations governing allocation.

Public housing is allocated on the basis of a waiting list. The waiting period is considerable owing to the great demand, and people have criticized the pressures applied by large enterprises to move favored employees higher on the list. Unofficially, local officials do consider the socially useful nature of an applicant's employment; and members of the military, political elite, and intelligentsia receive preferential treatment.

Once a person has obtained an apartment through this process, his tenure in it is relatively secure. He signs a lease for five years; it is renewable at his option, and he can force its renewal through the courts. He is free to break the lease and leave at any time, but he may be evicted only under certain narrowly defined conditions such as causing damage to the premises or being a continual nuisance. In all usual situations an eviction must be accompanied by the provision of other accommodations suitable to the tenant. Different rules apply to apartments maintained by industrial concerns. They can evict a tenant without providing new quarters if a tenant has ceased his employment voluntarily, committed a criminal offense, or has breached labor discipline.

Rents are low and average about 5 percent of the family's income. They depend on the size of the city, the condition of the apartment, and the tenant's income. On the other hand, authorities have used rent as a weapon against undesirables. Priests, for example, pay usually five times the average rent.

Cooperative Housing

Cooperative housing developed on a large scale after 1962. It offered an individual the opportunity to secure an apartment amenable to him but at his own expense, although the state provided generous legal and credit arrangements. In 1970 it was estimated that cooperative housing accounted for nearly 10 percent of all housing. A year earlier it had accounted for 15 percent of the total in Moscow.

The national government has favored the development of cooperative housing for several reasons. Cooperative housing is consonant with official Communist dogma, since it is a collective activity and avoids private ownership. The cooperative members are referred to as shareholders, or grantees, rather than as owners. In addition to helping alleviate the shortage, the cooperatives make possible a reduction in the state's contribution to housing.

The formation of a cooperative must meet certain state requirements. At least sixty persons must qualify as shareholders. They must elect an executive committee and be legally registered with the authorities. To join, each shareholder pays about 40 percent of the cost of his apartment. The remainder is financed over a ten- to fifteen-year period, at small interest rates, ranging between 0.5 and 1 percent per year. According to national law, the local municipality is required to supply the cooperative with a suitable plot of land, roads, water mains, powerlines, and sewers, as well as to bear the costs of constructing food and other service stores in the first floor of the building.

Cooperative housing generally costs more than state housing. A two-room apartment in 1969 cost from R3,500 (1 ruble equals US$1.10) to R4,500, after the down payment of R1,400 to R1,800, and the monthly payment ranged from R12 to R23. The one-room apartment cost from R3,000 to R3,500 with an initial payment of R1,200 to R1,400, and monthly payments ranged from R10 to R16.5. Larger apartments were priced proportionately higher.

Despite the many advantages of cooperative housing, drawbacks also existed. Local governments have failed to provide suitable land and the specified facilities. Often the land was located far from public transportation or from the factory where the cooperative members worked, and the shareholders were forced to pay for the services furnished.

Private Housing

The third alternative to the person desiring suitable living quarters is private housing. This form of housing constituted over one-third of all urban housing in the nation, but new construction declined in the 1960's, mainly as a result of the government's policy to discourage private homeownership. The government has prohibited the construction of private homes in the republic capitals, and it has become difficult to lease land and to obtain credit from state banks.

Consequently, most of the private dwellings in the country in 1969 were in rural areas.

In order to build a home, the individual must conform to state regulations. Land itself cannot be purchased; however permission to use it for local housebuilding purposes must be secured from local authorities. An agreement covering the details of construction must then be executed with the authorities. The state has limited credit to one-half the building costs, up to R700, the money repayable within seven years at 2 percent annual interest. Collective farmers are not able to receive long-term credit for home construction. The size of a privately built house is also regulated.

Other regulations have limited the ownership of private dwellings. A family can own only one house other than those considered summer cottages. If another is acquired through inheritance or any other way, one must be sold within a year (see ch. 22, The Legal System). If an owner charges a high rental for a house or uses the building in order to carry on an illegal business, the government may confiscate it without compensation. Constructing a house with unearned income, that is with illegally earned money, or with stolen building supplies will also result in its confiscation.

WELFARE ACTIVITIES

The state maintains a comprehensive welfare and social insurance system, providing retirement pensions, disability benefits, maternity benefits, family allowances, and welfare services for children. These programs are staffed by social insurance delegates and professional welfare workers. Unemployment insurance was discontinued in 1930 because the government declared that, since unemployment had been totally eliminated, such benefits were no longer required.

The state system of social insurance is operated by the trade unions. More than 4 million active trade union members participate in disbursing these funds. Trade union committees, elected by direct vote at all industrial enterprises, plan and manage the distribution of money, pay out grants for rest and rehabilitation, oversee labor protection and safety precautions, and make sure that establishments pay their social insurance dues on time.

Necessary funds to finance Soviet social insurance and welfare measures come largely from compulsory deductions from industrial and construction establishments, offices, and state farms, usually comprising a certain percentage over and above their regular payrolls. The remainder is in the form of special allocations from the national budget. The major portion of these funds is spent on old-age pensions and disability benefits.

In 1968, the last year for which statistics were available, over 35 million persons, including over 9 million collective farmers, were receiving old-age or invalid pensions. In 1965 over R10 billion, or more than 10 percent of the national budget, was spent on pensions. By 1966 this figure had grown to nearly R12 billion, which was 36 times greater than in 1940 and 1.6 times greater than in 1960.

In addition to the length of employment, time spent in vocational training, service in the armed forces, and study in higher or specialized secondary schools may contribute toward increased retirement benefits. The vast majority of pension applicants had more than the required years for seniority, and about one-third were entitled to an extra long-service bonus.

Retirement Pensions

Retirement pensions were first introduced in the nation in 1928 in the textile industry and somewhat later in mining, iron and steel, and rail and water transport. The pension was fixed at 50 percent of earnings and granted to men on reaching age sixty and women at fifty-five. Seniority requirements were twenty-five years for men and twenty for women. Coverage was gradually extended into other branches of the economy. In later programs the pensions were geared to wages; higher pensions were established to reward good work and long work records, and minimums were revised. In 1965 retirement pensions were introduced for collective farmers. This rounded out the nation's social insurance system, which then covered every section of the economy.

Retirement pensions in 1969 ranged from 50 to 100 percent of wages and were not taxed by the state. The lower the wage, the higher the percentage paid out in pensions—100 percent in the low-pay categories— thereby narrowing the gap between maximum and minimum pensions. The minimum pension was R30 a month, and the maximum R120. On the average, the retirement pension amounted to more than 70 percent of all wages.

Payments are based on average earnings over the last twelve months of work. But if this amounts to less than the person earned at a younger age, he may choose any five years out of the last ten. The amount of the pension is determined for every applicant, with due account given to his work record, living conditions, and family. Persons with families receive extra bonuses.

Pensions are also paid to families that have lost their breadwinner. This applies to children, brothers and sisters of the deceased younger than sixteen, aged parents, grandparents, grandchildren, able-bodied spouses if they look after children, or other dependents of the deceased. Orphans are eligible for pensions even if one parent works and earns a living and even if they are receiving scholarships.

The minimum retirement age varies for different categories of work. Textile workers engaged in heavy work with a job record of twenty or more years and some collective farmers with five or more children can receive their pensions at age fifty. Men who have worked not less than fifteen years in the Far North or not less than twenty years in other rigorous climate areas can retire at age fifty-five; women, at fifty. Ex-servicemen wounded in the war or in the line of duty or incapacitated by sickness contracted in the course of military service can retire at fifty.

Disability Insurance

Workers sustaining injuries or becoming ill in the course of employment receive compensation during the period of temporary disablement or, in cases of permanent disability, until the extent of invalidity is determined and a pension fixed. This compensation equals 100 percent of his earnings, regardless of seniority. An injured worker may be given an easier job. If it is a lower paid one, the difference in wages is made up from social insurance funds. Social insurance covers temporary change of jobs owing to tuberculosis or an occupational disease, absence from work when it is necessary to care for an ill member of the family, temporary layoff because of quarantine in the case of an infectious disease, and full or partial cost of resort or sanatorium accommodations.

Maternity leave and benefits are also allowed. Every year more than 2 million women workers receive the full amount of their earnings in the form of maternity grants while on maternity leave, which amounts to 112 days. They also receive an allowance to purchase items needed for the infant.

Sick benefits depend on the seniority of the worker. Compensation ranges from 50 percent of his earnings if he has worked less than three years to 100 percent for having worked for more than eight years. Those with work records of from five to eight years receive 80 percent of their usual earnings. Wage and salary earners under eighteen are entitled to receive 60 percent of their wages while sick.

Sick benefits are paid from the first day until the worker returns to his job or until a special medical commission finds that he cannot continue his work and is entitled to an invalid's pension. On the recommendation of the trade union, incapacity grants in cases of industrial accidents or occupational diseases amount to the worker's full earnings, irrespective of the period of employment. In 1965 nearly R2 billion, or approximately 20 percent of the total social insurance expenditure, was paid out in sick benefits. In addition, another R364 million was paid out in sanatorium-treatment grants and for the provision of dietetic food.

Family Allowances

The family allowance program introduced in 1944 is designed to maintain and strengthen the home environment, to prevent juvenile delinquency, and to help the family with a large number of children improve its standard of living. This program can provide lump-sum payments to a mother on the birth of her third child, monthly payments to a mother with four or more children, and monthly payments to an unmarried mother. Payments in each category increase in amount as the number of children increases.

Welfare Services for Children

Child welfare is the responsibility of several government ministries. Family allowances provide financial assistance within the social insurance system. The ministries of education are responsible for healthy children who require special attention. The ministries of social welfare at the republic level are responsible for children who are permanently disabled or severely retarded. The ministries of internal affairs are responsible for juvenile delinquents.

Various economic services are provided by educational, health, and trade union agencies. Tuition fees for nursery school and kindergarten are largely underwritten by the state for lower income families. No tuition is required for orphaned children. Summer camps are largely subsidized; the parents pay about one-third of the costs.

A variety of social services are available to children or are provided for their benefit. The ministries of social welfare, in addition to administering the family allowance program, find work for mothers; help parents to improve their living conditions; find employment for teenagers; maintain children in nurseries, kindergartens, and other schools; and intervene on behalf of neglected, abused, or unsupervised children.

Medical assistance in pediatric clinics is designed to follow a child's progress from birth to adulthood, to advise families on their social problems, and to treat mentally disturbed children. Mothers are helped by nurses and attorneys in the sociological bureaus, who assist in solving problems concerning living conditions, employment, and marital relations.

Social services provided by educational personnel are extensive. Educators are charged with a responsibility to work with parents on a constant basis to prevent or treat difficulties in the school environment. Teachers also cooperate closely with medical personnel and Party groups.

One of the functions of the courts is to prevent the dissolution of a marriage that might threaten the welfare of the children involved (see ch. 22, The Legal System). Courts entertain motions to deprive parents of the custody of their children when they are not fulfilling their parental obligations.

Other services for children consist of foster-family care, adoption, and institutional care. Foster-family care and adoption are discouraged by the state and rarely occur, except in instances where the adopting family is closely related to the child in question. Institutions maintained by the ministries of education care for dependent or defective children.

Welfare Personnel

Welfare services in the country are performed by a variety of persons. These include social insurance delegates and welfare workers, in addition to the physicians, nurses, and teachers who perform tasks in social welfare related to their primary obligations as medical and educational personnel.

Social insurance delegates are trade union members elected by their fellow employees, and their main duties consist of helping sick employees and workers. These delegates visit the sick at their homes or in the hospital and attend to many details for them: checking the medical services, food, and diets; looking into care at rest homes and sanatoriums; checking into family relations; explaining provisions of the social insurance laws; and assisting in applying for appropriate benefits.

Social insurance delegates also assist in finding employment for retired workers who wish to continue to pursue some kind of occupation, as well as work with unemployed pensioners to make sure that their living conditions are satisfactory. They are called upon to aid invalids; to advise alcoholics, juvenile delinquents, and couples having marital difficulties; and to assist in the recognition of mental disorders.

The delegates themselves receive very little training to help them in the performance of their duties. Some can take advantage of a special course in Leningrad, but most attend lectures, seminars, and conferences in lieu of specialized training.

Over 100,000 professional welfare workers, of whom over 70 percent are women, work under the jurisdiction of the republic ministries of social welfare. An unknown, but probably far larger, number of workers are assigned to local and district offices in the local governmental structure, where welfare work would ordinarily be an additional or part-time duty. Duties performed by these workers are varied, but the largest portion of the work consists of administering and deciding claims for the various social insurance plans.

237

CHAPTER 13

RELIGION

The existence of religion in the Soviet Union more than half a century after the Bolshevik Revolution is an anomaly and an embarrassment to the atheistic leadership of the Communist Party of the Soviet Union (CPSU). Despite official hostility, harassment, and massive antireligious programs, Christians, Muslims, Buddhists, and Jews continue to practice their faiths.

The history of government-church relations during the Soviet era has been erratic. Periods of violent antireligious activity have been followed by periods of compromise and apparent rapprochement, but the officially announced goal of eradicating all religion has never been altered (see ch. 1, Nature of the Soviet System).

Karl Marx's dictum about religion being the opiate of the people, had itself taken on the attributes of Holy Writ for devout Communists. Lenin was particularly vitriolic in his castigation of all things religious, and Stalin differed with this viewpoint only during World War II when he appealed for church support against fascism. Khrushchev personally demanded greater antireligious activity and, at the Twenty-second Party Congress in 1961, predicted the complete elimination of religion in the Soviet Union by 1980. Khrushchev's successors continue in the same tradition but have apparently ceased making predictions as to when religion will finally be eliminated; they have not, however, given up the ideological struggle against all religions.

Official statistics concerning numbers of believers are never published, but estimates place the number of adherents to Russian Orthodoxy at as many as 50 million. Islam constitutes the second largest religion with 30 million Muslims. Roman Catholics, Baptists, and Lutherans also number several millions, and there are approximately 3 million Jews living in the Soviet Union. About half a million Buddhists now reside in the Soviet Union. Roughly 40 percent of the population might be considered believers although, because of fear and harassment, many of them do not participate in religious services (see ch. 4, The Social System).

STATE ATHEISM

Doctrinal Communism as enunciated by Karl Marx views religion as the "opiate of the people." Marx meant that religion and every kind of religious organization were instruments of bourgeois reaction, serving as a defense of exploitation and for the duping of the working class. He believed that the struggle against religion could not be limited to abstract ideological preaching but also had to be directed against the social roots of religion itself. The party of the proletariat had to be the spiritual leader in the struggle against all kind of medievalism, which included religion.

The CPSU places special emphasis on the struggle against religion. Guided by the conviction that only deliberate and conscious planning of all the social and economic activities of the masses will cause religious prejudices to die out, the Party strives for the complete destruction not only of religious institutions, but also of the religious sentiments of the people through the widest possible scientific, educational, and antireligious propaganda. At the same time, the Party is aware of the necessity of not offending the religious sentiments of believers, since that would only strengthen religion. To achieve its program, the CPSU has at its disposal all state organizations and institutions, and its own members by which antireligious propaganda and instruction can be intimately related to the daily life of citizens.

The official policy on religion was enunciated by the government in a decree in early 1918 that separated the church from the state and totally abolished church ownership of property. Not only was all church property confiscated without compensation, but churches were denied the right to own any property in the future, including the objects used in their rites. Under the decree a church cannot be a corporation, have any legal status, or enter into any contract. If believers wish to have a place of worship, at least twenty must first sign a contract with the local soviet, which has the authority to permit such use of a church building. This permission, however, is discretionary and can be withdrawn at any time.

There is no charge for the use, but the congregation as a group is responsible for the upkeep and care of the building and its ornamentation, and the objects used in the services. If there is any loss, destruction, or deterioration even through normal use, the congregation is obliged to make restitution. The church is not permitted to hold public classes for religious instruction for children under eighteen years of age and can only instruct seminarians. Private religious instruction is limited to classes with no more than five students, but such classes cannot be held on a regular basis for the express purpose of imparting religious education.

The CPSU prohibits its members from belonging to any religious group and has established the antireligious program to be followed in the country. The League of the Militant Godless, formed directly under Party auspices, was given the primary responsibility for the nation's antireligious program in the 1920's and 1930's. Its membership campaign recruited over 4 million atheists in a year's time. The league commenced its attack on religion by harassing clergymen and believers who attended services and by closing many churches. Its tactics were harsh and created great hostility and resentment toward the league and the state on the part of the people. Accordingly, the Communist Party urged the league to proceed in more subtle ways and to avoid its earlier harshness in order not to antagonize the people.

Since World War II, physical attacks and personal intimidation have been restricted. Instead, the antireligious program has assumed a more psychological and scientific approach, usually by demonstrating to the people the successes of Soviet scientific achievements and thereby attempting to prove the incompatibility of religion and science. To disseminate scientific antireligious propaganda, the government has established several specialized bodies, such as the Znaniye (Knowledge Society), which sponsors atheistic lectures and is responsible for the publication of atheistic literature.

Another feature of the antireligious program is an individual form of countermissionary work with believers in an attempt to persuade them to deny their faith. Especially trained Party members try to convert believers to atheism usually by visiting people in their homes. Doctors and nurses are urged to stress at all times the harm that can be caused by religious beliefs and ceremonies, especially in maternity hospitals where they discourage baptism.

In order to match the emotional and aesthetic appeal of familiar religious rites, the government has established civil ceremonies and institutions, such as Wedding Palaces and Palaces of the Newly Born, in order to win believers from their faith. Initial failure of these measures to achieve their objective, however, has not deterred their continued use, and appeals were being made in the late 1960's to bring these secular ceremonies more in line with the emotional attachments of the people.

CHRISTIANITY

Christianity in the Soviet Union is represented by Russian and Georgian Orthodox, Armenian Gregorian, Roman Catholic, and various Protestant denominations, and comprises the major religious identification of the people. Of the Christian religions, Russian Orthodoxy is the largest, forming over 50 percent of the total religious membership in the country. Roman Catholicism has a relatively small membership, mainly in the former Polish and Lithuanian territories. Protestantism, represented by the Evangelical Christian, Baptist, Lutheran, and other minor sects, has won many new adherents since the revolution.

The Orthodox Church, or Eastern Orthodox Church, as it is sometimes called throughout the world, is a loose federation with no single prelate having absolute power. Within the Orthodox Church, there are fifteen self-governing churches with their own primates, usually called patriarchs, that are united with the rest of the church on matters of doctrine and tradition. There are also several other Orthodox churches that are not completely self-governing and are controlled by one of the partiarchs. The use of the vernacular is permitted in the liturgy. Orthodox Christians in the Soviet Union outnumber the adherents of any of the other Orthodox churches elsewhere. In recent years this has led the patriarch of Moscow, with the support of the Soviet state, to try to supplant the ecumenical patriarch of Constantinople as the ceremonial leader of Eastern Orthodoxy.

The Russian Orthodox Church

The Russian Orthodox Church dates from the conversion of the Slavs by missionaries from Byzantium, led by Saint Cyril and Saint Methodius, in the ninth century A.D. In the tenth century Christianity became the Russian state religion, and the chief official, the metropolitan, was established first at Kiev and later at Moscow. Until the downfall of the Eastern Roman Empire, the Russian metropolitanate was considered an integral part of the Byzantine Orthodox Church under the jurisdiction of the patriarch of Constantinople. When Byzantium fell to the Turks, Russian Orthodox believers assumed an independent attitude and a century later elected their own patriarch. The Russians considered themselves the sole defenders of the true faith.

The Russian Orthodox Church was favored by, and subordinated to, the Tsars. In 1721 Tsar Peter the Great by his Ecclesiastical Regulations deprived the church of its autonomy by abolishing the patriarchate. Peter placed the church under the administration of the Holy Synod, composed of clerics and laymen whom he had personally chosen. The tsar was represented in the Synod by the high procurator, and although this lay official had no vote, he nevertheless possessed enormous influence. No action could be taken by the Synod without the high procurator's approval.

Since the church was dominated by the tsar, it became a politically conservative element in Russian society during the next two centuries, and the hierarchy decried all liberal attempts to reorganize either the church or the imperial government. Some liberal priests and bishops were summarily removed from their posts and either exiled or imprisoned, and great attempts were made to check their influence.

Because of the tsar's domination, it became possible for Grigory Rasputin to gain a position of influence from which he was able to wield inordinate power over church and national affairs. Rasputin, an uneducated and unordained holy man, possessed of hypnotic powers, gained ascendancy over the tsarina through his successful ministrations to the hemophiliac heir to the throne. From March 1915 to December 1916, when Tsar Nicholas II was absent from Saint Petersburg in personal command of the Russian armies at the front, the government of the country was in the hands of the tsarina and Rasputin, who appointed and dismissed government ministers and church officials at will. His appointees were often self-seeking sycophants rather than qualified officials or clerics. In addition, Rasputin's own unsavory reputation discredited the church and weakened Russia's government (see ch. 3, Historical Setting).

The bizarre circumstances of Rasputin's murder brought further disarray and discredit to the church and the nation. Two noblemen, Prince Felix Yusupov and Grand Duke Dmitry Pavlovich, plus a prominent member of the legislature, were involved, and this did little to help the deteriorating position of the monarchy. Immediately after the March revolution, Rasputin's appointees were dismissed from the Synod and other high religious offices, but the damage done to the church's reputation was lasting and the weaknesses nurtured by Rasputin's venal appointees persisted, paving the way for the Bolshevik domination of church affairs after the November revolution.

After the revolution, the Russian Orthodox Church suffered great losses of both membership and installations and was forced to accommodate itself to the Soviet regime in order to preserve what remained. Soon after the revolution, the Communists nationalized all church property, including parish funds and investments. The government took over the civil registers that were traditionally the church's preserve. Some parish churches were closed and converted into schools. The Communist leaders seized all cloisters, ousted the monastics, and converted the buildings into hospitals and schools. While inventorying the contents of the seized cloisters, the Soviets uncovered alleged frauds concerning saints' relics, which they used to damage the prestige of the church in the propaganda campaign being waged at the time.

Relations between church and state became strained during the famine of 1921—22. When the government asked for contributions for the famine victims, the church responded by donating only a small portion of its wealth in precious metals. The government, not satisfied with the church's gifts, decided to expropriate church plate and vessels for relief. Disorders resulting in loss of life broke out in several cities when government officials tried to implement the expropriation decree. The government assumed that the patriarch and churchmen were acting in harmony against it and thus tried and executed a number of clergy.

Patriarch Tikhon died in 1925, and hostility between the church and state continued. The state sought compliance by not permitting the election of a new patriarch and by arresting all officials who sought to function in place of the patriarch. Finally in 1927 after several arrests and long negotiations, Metropolitan Sergius of Nizhniy Novgorod announced that he had reached agreement with the government and would be permitted to set up a central administration, although the government still refused to permit the election of a patriarch. Sergius called on believers to renounce hostility to the regime and ordered prayers for Soviet leaders.

With the advent of Stalin's forced industrialization and collectivization of agriculture in 1928, an all-out attack on religion was also begun. The church was considered a center of opposition against the Stalinist goals, but the people did not discard their beliefs despite ten years of the violent antireligious campaign on the part of the Communists. The government continued to diminish the ranks of the clergy through imprisonment and exile to labor camps, and churches were closed or converted to secular use.

The Young Communist League (Komsomol) became particularly virulent in its antireligious activities, and the national council of trade unions increased its atheistic program among the workers. The League of the Militant Godless, which had been formed during the 1920's, increased the intensity of its war against religion and, through intense recruitment drives, vastly increased its membership. The tactics and excesses, however, alienated many of the people.

As a result, governmental leaders decreed that the antireligious campaign must be careful of the feelings of the believers and avoid excesses. Finally in 1936 Stalin improved the status of the clergy and made them equal to other citizens by approving enactments permitting priests to vote, to hold elective office (none have ever been nominated), to educate their children, and to be under the same income-tax laws and regulations as doctors and lawyers (see ch. 22, The Legal System).

The intense period of purges of the late 1930's included terror and violence against church and clergy, but the German invasion in 1941 opened the way to at least partial reconciliation between church and state. In June Metropolitan Sergius issued a patriotic appeal to the Russian people to support the war effort, and a year later the state gave its approval for the holding of a patriarchal election. A council, consisting of nineteen bishops, elected Sergius and selected a Holy Synod. The state also permitted the church to proceed with its reorganization, to establish theological seminaries, and to publish an ecclesiastical periodical.

After the death of Sergius in 1944, the government approved the convocation of a new council to elect another patriarch and permitted representatives from other Orthodox churches to attend. During the remainder of the war, the new patriarch Alexius continued to support the government and to priase Stalin. With the end of hostilities, a new antireligious campaign called Scientific and Enlightening Propaganda was undertaken with the avowed purpose of overcoming the survivals of ignorance, superstition, and prejudice and of making strenuous efforts to instill Soviet youth with atheism. The Komsomol maintained that a youth could not be an effective, progressive citizen while clinging to outmoded superstitions.

Active persecution of the church during the early Communist period was not resumed in the immediate post-World War II years. Restrictions of various sorts were still in effect and were enforced, but the wartime detente between church and state continued in the early postwar years. The Communist leadership expected religion to disappear in the wake of scientific advancement and atheistic education.

By the time Khrushchev had achieved full power in the late 1950's, Communist ideologues were again calling for militant atheism, and the Khruschev era was marked by an intensification of antireligious campaigns. The Society for the Dissemination of Political and Scientific Knowledge, successor to the League of the Militant Godless, was ordered to increase its attack on religion. Legal codes were revised and strengthened to prohibit religious teaching and propaganda, and clerical authorities were stripped of the meager powers that they had attained during the war.

The Soviet Constitution of 1936 allows freedom of religious worship and freedom of antireligious propaganda (see ch. 19, Formal Structure of the Union Government). Religious propaganda is not permitted. In effect, the function of the clergy is limited exclusively to the conducting of services. The return to extreme antireligious activity under Khrushchev was capped by wholesale closing of churches and seminaries. Once again, clerics either were being imprisoned or confined to mental institutions without charges or trials or anything resembling due process of law (see ch. 22, The Legal System).

The post-Khrushchev leadership reaffirmed by its actions the goal of complete eradication of religion. Violence was modified, and emphasis was placed on the furtherance of atheism through education and propaganda. The Central Committee of the Communist Party sponsored the Institute of Scientific Atheism, the title of which defines its objectives; and every level of government has councils devoted to the affairs of religious cults, which in effect are control agencies and vehicles for the propagation of antireligion.

The Russian Orthodox Church is formally self governing. Its structure is basically similar to that of other Orthodox churches; its authority is vested in both the patriarch of Moscow and the periodically convened Church Assembly and the Holy Synod.

The country's seventy dioceses are large and few in number considering the size of the country. The Synod is comprised of bishops, priests, monks, and laymen, chosen by diocesan elections according to canonical law. The patriarch of Moscow, the president of the Synod, also plays a role in the selection of the membership. In administering the affairs of the church, the patriarch and Synod abide by the Regulations for Administering the Russian Orthodox Church, adopted by the Church Assembly in 1945. These regulations cover the administration of church affairs and define the rights and duties of the church hierarchy.

All bishops are selected by the patriarch in the same manner, conforming to the ancient belief that the higher clergy should be selected by the patriarch. Tenure is supposedly permanent, but historically bishops have frequently been moved from one diocese to another. If a bishop has been accused of a major crime, he is subject to removal action by the Synod and patriarch.

Some seventy bishops, each taking the title of his cathedral town, selected by the patriarch from the ranks of the unmarried monastics, wield control over their dioceses singly or with the aid of a council composed of from three to five persons. Many Russian Orthodox communicants believe that bishops and other ecclesiastical officials should be selected from the ranks of the married clergy. Russian Orthodox clergy may marry before or after ordination but, traditionally, married clerics are not promoted above the rank of priest. There is no prohibition in Orthodoxy against the selection of a bishop from the laity. Bishops have generally undergone extensive training at the seminary or have special abilities that make them outstanding.

Dioceses are divided into districts, headed by provosts appointed by the bishop. In addition to their religious duties, bishops have historically played important social and philanthropic roles in the life of the country depending on their individual talents, interests, and energy but have been greatly restricted by the state to purely religious duties. Bishops ordain priests and appoint them to, and remove them from, local parishes. A bishop must, however, submit important matters concerning his diocese, including those of a theological nature, to higher ecclesiastical officials for their approval. There have been differences between bishops over theology and church policy concerning the role of the church in relation to the Communist state but very little interference by one bishop in the affairs of another.

The village priest, representing organized religion in the villages, has been one of the most important figures, often of tremendous influence, in the villagers' lives. A typical product of the countryside, he generally comes from a poor family, is relatively uneducated, and is married and has children.

Formal religious education begins when a youth is about eighteen years old when his parents usually send him to a priest or bishop for individual training, since there are few seminaries. Training consists mainly of learning how to conduct religious services, and studying the Old Slavonic language sometimes used in the services, rather than training in theology. The three seminaries reported active in 1965 each had an enrollment of fewer than 100 students. Most of the teachers were clergymen. The majority of graduates enter the married clergy, and only a small percentage of extremely gifted individuals join the monastic clergy or become candidates for higher ecclesiastical office (see ch. 15, The Educational System).

Within their dioceses, the bishops appoint priests to parishes, and often the priest is a native of the parish to which assigned. Appointments are generally permanent, but a priest can be removed if the villagers object to his ministry. In addition to his duties as a priest, he may engage in other occupations in order to supplement his income. He is aided in the carrying out of the business affairs of the parish by a lay board elected by the parishioners. The members of this board assist the priest and are responsible for the finances of the parish and for the maintenance of the church and other religious buildings. Occasionally, depending on the circumstances, the priest can invoke the aid of the entire village to help in parish projects or can intervene with state authorities in behalf of the interests of his parishioners.

Monasticism has been important to the people and has enriched the religious, intellectual, and cultural activities of the country. Historically, monasticism was held in high regard by the people, because its simple asceticism seemed to denote the highest and purest forms of Christian teaching. Monks were respected for their learning and for their renunciation of the material world and its pleasures to lead a life devoted to prayer and contemplation.

The monastic community was especially important in preserving the heritage and traditions of the Orthodox Church, especially the forms of worship and the early writings of the founders of the church. The monks were generally better educated than the parish priest and made many important contributions to Christian thought and education. They were sought out by all the people not only for spiritual guidance, but also for advice and help in daily difficulties.

The most important monastery for the Russian Orthodox Church was Mount Athos in Greece, an autonomous community under the jurisdiction of the ecumenical Patriarch of Constantinople, but the number of Russians in residence has sharply declined. There were also a few convents for women, but with few nuns. Rarely was a nun seen by the majority of the people. These women for the most part lived within the confines of the convent and devoted themselves to a life of prayer and good works.

The doctrine of the Russian Orthodox Church involves an impressive body of knowledge fully intelligible only to a few extremely learned specialists. The basic beliefs are that Orthodoxy, including the synodical structure of the church, is the true and originally established Christian Church; that there are seven sacraments required for man's salvation; and that man is to be punished after death for the sins he committed. Christ is honored as the head of the church, and Mary is honored as his mother. Although the Orthodox believe in Mary's virgin birth, the Immaculate Conception is not defined. Orthodox Christians do not believe in indulgences, and they revere the relics of saints, pictures of holy objects, and the cross.

Baptism, the first sacrament administered to a newly born infant, symbolizes God's forgiveness of the original sin of Adam and Eve. It is followed by chrismation and the first communion, or the eucharistic ceremony, which marks a child's entrance into the community of the church. With maturity, confession and repentance must precede communion. Holy orders and marriage are sacraments that impart grace to the souls of the people, and extreme unction is the anointing of the person by a priest when an individual is close to death (see ch. 11, Family).

After death, Orthodox Christians believe that man's body returns to the earth from which it came, while his soul, remaining fully conscious and exercising all its faculties, is judged by God. The judgment immediately after death is called the particular judgment. A man's final judgment, however, will not occur until the time of the general judgment, when all men's souls are judged at the end of the world. During the interval between the particular and general judgments, men's souls have the foretaste of their eventual blessing or punishment.

The ritual of the Russian Orthodox Church has remained basically unchanged and is highly traditional. The Mass, or Eucharist, which is the center of Orthodox worship and its chief public act, is the principal religious service and symbolizes the unity between God and man. By participating in this ritual, man glorifies God and achieves divine grace, personal perfection, and self-fulfillment. The Divine Liturgy, basically the recital of the divine plan for man's salvation, reveals the trinitarian nature of the divine. It also re-creates step by step the sacrifice of the Son of God.

A church building's external architecture and interior design symbolically represent the union between the divine and the natural worlds. Most Russian Orthodox churches are built in the form of a Greek cross with a dome over the transept representing the heavenly world. The altar of the church is separated from the worshipers by an ornate screen with icons. The icons, pictures of holy objects and saints, are not subjects of prayer but are venerated as representations of the divine world. There are no pews in the church, and people stand throughout the service and are permitted to move about freely.

The splendor and pageantry of services as seen only in churches impressed poor villagers as a heavenly vision. The priest's ornate vestments similar to those worn by Emperor Constantine, are usually embroidered with precious gems and gold. The ornately wrought gold altar screens and ritualistic vessels and icons are distributed throughout the church, although the majority of these were seized by the state during the famine in 1921—22, and the churches retained only a bare minimum to conduct services. Services are accompanied by elaborate antiphonal chanting of the celebrant and server in a modal style representative of the Middle East, adding to the solemnity of the service. The pungent incense used contributes to the communicant's concentration on the meaning of the divine mysteries. Most of the service is conducted in the Old Slavonic language that is largely unintelligible to a speaker of modern Russian, but modern Russian has been introduced in some parts of the service since World War II.

Religion centers in the home, except for certain important ceremonies that must take place in the church. In each believer's house there is an icon occupying a place of honor. Below the icon, there is customarily a shrine before which the family makes the sign of the cross several times a day and to which everyone who enters the house pays homage. Traditionally, the faithful observe the severe fasts that are common to Orthodox Christianity. The average Russian Orthodox, especially the man, rarely attends church except at Easter or to attend a marriage or baptism within the family.

There are two categories of Orthodox believers: those who practice their faith regularly and openly and those who, because of the pressures of living in a Communist society, practice their faith privately. The persistence of belief and adherence through years of antireligious propaganda and activities and psychological pressures since the revolution suggest that the religious convictions of both groups are strong.

Practicing Orthodox believers demonstrate the strength of their faith by the public performance of their rites. During the traditional Easter services, the congregational parade around the church, with lit candles, continues to take place each year. During the 1969 Easter services in Moscow, youths who scoffed at the traditional procession were admonished by other onlookers to cease their taunts and to let the processioners alone. The believers' faith is also demonstrated when they apply for permission to use the facilities of a church building for religious exercises. The present law states that at least twenty individuals must sign such an application, thereby making their religious affiliations known to the local Soviets, exposing themselves to direct antireligious pressures and harassment on the part of the state-supported organizations dedicated to the eradication of religious beliefs.

Nonpracticing believers in the Orthodox faith, typically young family men who maintain hopes of governmental positions, of job advancement, of better education for their children, or of an improved standard of living, are reluctant to openly declare their religious beliefs. In recent years exposés of the membership of the CPSU have revealed many members who have retained religious beliefs, although secretly, and the Party has continuously called upon members to disavow such beliefs and to expose those who still adhere to religious idologies.

Orthodox in doctrine but not subject to the patriarch of Moscow or the Holy Synod, the Georgian Orthodox Church is an autonomous body headed by the patriarch of all Georgia whose seat is in Tbilisi, the capital of the Georgian Soviet Socialist Republic. There is also an Armenian Gregorian Church, with followers in Armenia, Georgia, Azerbaijan, and a number of cities in the Russian Soviet Federated Socialist Republic (RSFSR). The church is headed by a supreme patriarch whose residence is in the Echmiadzin Monastery near Yerevan, the capital of the Armenian Soviet Socialist Republic.

Catholicism

In the 1960's there were perhaps as many as 4 million Roman Catholics living in the Soviet Union, mostly in the Lithuanian Soviet Socialist Republic and other western areas of the country. In earlier times when the Russian empire contained large Polish populations, there were several million more Roman Catholics under Russian authority. Incompatibility has been the hallmark of relations between Roman Catholicism and Russian Orthodoxy for many centuries and, because Orthodoxy was a state religion, Roman Catholics fared poorly under the tsars. At the beinning of the seventeenth century when Roman Catholic Poles occupied Moscow, it was a patriotic call to defend Holy Russia and Orthodoxy that roused the Russian people to drive out the invaders (see ch. 3, Historical Setting).

During the period of intense Russification of the nineteenth-century tsars, Roman Catholics were suspect because of their allegiance to the Pope and were oppressed, as were other minority religions. Few ethnic Russians were Roman Catholics, but the shifting borders of empire often encompassed many millions of non-Russian peoples who embraced Roman Catholicism. From 1596 on, there were also large numbers of Uniates who retained Russian Orthodox ritual and liturgy while acknowledging the Roman Catholic Pope as their spiritual leader.

There was an easing of religious persecution in Russia during the

250

Revolution of 1905 with the tsar's Edict of Religious Toleration. Further liberalization came during the short-lived era of the provisional government between the revolutions of 1917, but the Bolsheviks soon enforced Marxist antireligiosity after they came to power in November 1917.

Bolshevik anti-Catholicism was particularly intense because Roman Catholics acknowledged outside control—the papacy—while the Bolsheviks officially fostered atheism. Catholics openly rejected decrees that nationalized church property and forbade the teaching of religion to children. The new Communist government reacted severely with arrests, exile, and execution of Catholic clergy. Soviet actions resulted in the imprisonment and deportation of most bishops and priests in addition to the closing of churches, monasteries, and seminaries. Most priests and monastics were forced to abandon their calling and to obtain productive employment in the economy.

The 1920's and 1930's were decades of continual oppression for Soviet Catholics and Uniates as well. The Great Purge brought destruction and desecration of churches and mass disappearances of clergy and laity.

During World War II there was some lessening of anti-Catholicism during Stalin's wartime period of religious tolerance, but most Soviet Catholics were in areas that had been quickly overrun by the Nazis and remained under German occupation until late in the war. After the war, the campaign against minority religions resumed despite the off-and-on detente between the Communist government and the Orthodox Church. For Roman Catholics the postwar period became a struggle for survival, but oppression was more subtle than the open violence of the pre-World War II era.

The Roman Catholic Church in the Soviet Union had so far survived all types of antireligious campaigns, but the Uniate Church was not so fortunate. A campaign was undertaken by the Soviet government through the secret police to force the Uniate clergy and laity to renounce their allegiance to the Pope of Rome. In some cases, force was not necessary, because various Uniate dioceses willingly returned to the Russian Orthodox fold as others had voluntarily done during the nineteenth and early twentieth centuries. For those who chose to retain their allegiance to Rome, force was used, and the viciousness of the campaign sometimes rivaled the purge period. At any rate, whether by force or voluntarily, between 1946 and 1950 the Uniate Church ceased to exist as a separate entity, and the entire Uniate body was co-opted into the Russian Orthodox Church. However, recent Soviet press reports indicate that an underground Uniate rite continues to be practiced.

In 1969 the Roman Catholic Church in the Soviet Union still existed, facing the same problems of all religions existing in an officially atheist nation. Constitutionally, religious freedom was guaranteed—actually Communist ideologues continually reiterated the basic Marxist tenet that religion must ultimately disappear under their form of government.

Despite this, in 1969 Catholic religious life persisted in the country, especially in the more remote areas. There still existed three archdioceses, six dioceses, and one Apostolic Exarchate. Latin rite churches existed in Moscow, Leningrad, Odessa, and Tbilisi, but for the most part, religious services and ceremonies are celebrated clandestinely. Services are often performed in the priest's living quarters, and it is not unusual for large crowds to gather once news of the services has spread. Priests continue to officiate at weddings, baptisms, and funerals, and the congregations grow yearly. Since priests are forbidden to receive money for their services, the parishioners at these underground services donate food, clothing, and other articles.

Protestantism

In the 1960's Evangelical Christians and Baptists constituted the most important Protestant element in the Soviet Union. Although official statistics were unavailable, some estimates placed the number of adherents at over 5 million. Protestantism entered Russia with the establishment of the Russian Baptist Union in 1884. Like the Catholics, Baptists represented an alien influence and were persecuted by the Orthodox tsarist government. In 1908 the Union of Evangelical Christians was founded, and although the new sect embraced principles similar to those of the Baptists, interpretations differed. Various attempts were made through the years to merge the two denominations, and in 1944 the Union of Evangelical Christians and Baptists was created.

Before and immediately after the Bolshevik Revolution, these sects were favored by the Communists. Before the Revolution, Baptists and Evangelical Christians represented a democratic influence in the nation, and after the Revolution, they represented a weapon that could be used to weaken the Russian Orthodox Church. Because of official tolerance by the government, the two sects rapidly attracted new members. In 1923, however, the government ended its official favor and moved to control their activities. Its first step was directed against the exemption from military service on religious grounds. In order to placate the authorities, both the Baptists and the Evangelical Christians openly supported military conscription for their members.

Central to the religious life of these two sects were evangelical prayer meetings and religious farming communes. During the 1930's, the Communists moved to check both practices by banning

Protestants from the newly created collective farms and by outlawing the prayer meetings in the farming centers. Protestant believers were scattered, clergymen were arrested and exiled, and the Great Purge of the late 1930's seriously damaged the structure of Protestantism in the Soviet Union.

The All-Union Council of Evangelical Christian Baptists established in the period of Soviet religious tolerance during the war maintains the structure and organization of the church and has tried to preserve cordial relations with the Soviet authorities. Public support of Soviet foreign policies, especially the ostensible campaign for peace, has been common with all religions. By 1950, there were approximately 4,000 congregations and by 1960 more than 5,000, with membership close to 5 million. Since 1957—58, the government, in its antireligious propaganda, has charged members of the sects with acting as spies for the United States and has sought to discredit Protestantism by the testimony of apostates and by demonstrations calculated to prove the essential incompatibility between science and religion.

The Lutheran Church is the next largest Protestant denomination in the country, with a total membership estimated at close to 1 million persons. The Lutheran Church originated in Germany and was located primarily in the Baltic States and in several major cities in European Russia. During the purges of the 1930's, the Lutheran Church lost most of its membership; there were no officiating pastors and no active congregations. The Lutheran Church again became active in the 1940's when the Baltic States were incorporated into Soviet territory. In the 1960's membership in the Latvian Lutheran Church was estimated to be about 500,000; and that of the Estonian Lutheran Church, about 350,000.

Protestant sects of lesser importance but numbering a few thousand adherents in each denomination include Seventh-Day Adventists, Mennonites, and Molokans. The latter sect is purely Russian, dating from the seventeenth century, and rejects all forms of ritual. All religious sects felt the increased pressure of official atheistic propaganda and activity during the 1960's.

ISLAM

Next to the Russian Orthodox Church, Islam claims the greatest number of followers in the Soviet Union. Estimates as to the number of Muslim believers vary, but it was reported to be decreasing and during the 1960's was roughly estimated to be about 18 million. Because of official disapproval, the number of mosques and institutions of religious learning has declined sharply since the Bolshevik revolution. According to the 1959 census, there were no more than 200 central mosques and 1,000 district mosques in

Soviet central Asia, as compared with the 12,000 in Turkestan alone before Soviet rule.

The government regulates the ecclesiastical affairs of Muslims in the country by laws drawn up in accordance with Article 124 of the Constitution (see ch. 19, Formal Structure of the Union Government). The Muslim organization is based on four regional boards operating under general supervision of the Council for the Affairs of Religion, a unit of the Council of Ministers of the Soviet Union. The boards are largely concerned with establishing mosques and with selecting and training religious leaders in their jurisdictions.

In the late 1960's the Board for Central Asia and Kazakhstan, located at Tashkent, handled Islamic affairs in the Turkmen, Uzbek, Tadzhik, Kirgiz, and Kazakh union republics. A second board located at Ufa, just west of the Ural Mountains, had jurisdiction over Muslims in European Russia, except the Caucasus, and in Siberia. Islamic affairs in Daghestan and the areas along the northern slopes of the Caucasus Mountains were under jurisdiction of a board at Buynaksk. A fourth board for Transcaucasia was situated at Baku.

Islam, which literally means submission to the will of God, was first preached by the Prophet Muhammad, born at Mecca in the Arabian Peninsula in A.D. 570. According to tradition, Muhammad received a call from God at about the age of forty. The calls continued, and Muhammad's preaching against prevailing pagan practices and beliefs earned the hostility of important personalities in Mecca who forced him to flee with his closest followers to Medina in 622. This flight, known as the hegira, is taken as the first year of the Muslim calendar. Muhammad became head of state in Medina, repelled the attacks of the Meccans, and ultimately brought the entire Arabian subcontinent under Islam. Mecca became the holy city of Islam. After Muhammad's death in 632, the countries of the Middle East quickly succumbed to Islamic conquerors.

From the Middle East, Islam spread all the way to the Turkic peoples of Central Asia and into India, Southeast Asia, and Indonesia. This initial contact was followed by the movement of Turkic tribes to the area south of the Caspian Sea where, under Persian and Arab influence, Islam became the religion. Turkic groups later moved into Anatolia and eventually conquered Byzantium in the name of their new religion. With the fall of Constantinople in 1453, Anatolian Islam no longer found organized opposition.

In urban areas the formal traditions of Arabic Islam were fostered by the administrators, schools, and religious officials. In rural areas formal tradition was modified by the local customs and traditions of the nomadic peoples. In many rural areas, the emphasis on emotion, intuition, and personal participation of the Sufi mystic orders appealed strongly to unlettered villagers, who found the intellectually oriented traditions of urban Islam remote and difficult to understand.

The oneness of God, as testified to by his Prophet, Muhammad, is the fundamental article of Islamic faith. This declaration of faith is stated in the Shahada "There is no god but God (Allah), and Muhammad is the messenger of God." Acceptance of the basic tenet also implies acceptance of other tenets: submission to the will of God, the existence of angels and other supernatural beings, the general resurrection and final judgment, and the acceptance of God as the ultimate source of all events. Every man is responsible for his own sins; man is neither perfect nor depraved.

Islam recognizes the Pentateuch, the Book of Psalms, the Gospels, and the Koran as books of scripture. Muslims view the Koran as containing the final revelations of God to man, climaxing the earlier revelations to Adam, Noah, Abraham, Moses, and Jesus. As the recipient of God's final revelations, Muhammad is the most important of all the prophets. He is, however, only a man and has no claim to divinity.

The Koran, a compilation of Muhammad's inspired statements, and the *hadith* (sayings), a record made by observers of his non-inspired acts and statements, and of those of his immediate followers, provide the basis for the *sunna* (tradition). The Sharia, the body of Islamic canon law that covers all behavior is based on the Koran, the *Sunna*, the *ijma* (consensus), and *qiyas* (reasoning by analogy). Theology, based on the *sunna* and on Greek and Roman philosophy, was also highly developed. The great majority of Muslims are Sunnites, and the remainder are Shiites.

Shiites believe that Muhammad's special relationship with the Divine Being descended in the family of Ali, his son-in-law, and that only these descendants (Imams) can legitimately lead the Islamic community. Their refusal to recognize the dynastic succession of caliphs (successors to Muhammad as head of the Islamic state) not in the line of Ali kept them in opposition to the Ottoman caliphs and others. They do not accept the Sunnite traditions but have a collection of their own, which they say is the *sunna*. They also differ somewhat in law, ceremony, religious duties, and beliefs from the Sunnites.

The Five Pillars of Islam recognized by all Muslims consist of the declaration of faith and four primary religious duties. The four duties necessary to assure salvation are prayer five times daily; fasting during the month of Ramadan; almsgiving; and, if possible, pilgrimage to Mecca. The daily prayers are announced from the minaret of the mosque at dawn, noon, midafternoon, sunset, and early evening. On Fridays devout Muslim men attend prayer services at the mosques. Women are not required to pray in the mosque and generally attend only on holy days.

Muslims recognize two major holidays, four lesser ones, and a month of fasting. Dates for these occasions follow a lunar calendar. Id al Fitr is the breaking of the month-long fast of Ramadan, which is held in thankfulness for the revelation of the Koran. Id al Adha falls 70 days later and celebrates the sacrifice of a ram made by Abraham, and also the sacrifices made by the pilgrims in Mecca at that time.

Lesser holidays include the first day of the Islamic year, the tenth day of the first month, which is a fast originating in Yom Kippur and is observed by Shiites as mourning for their martyrs. Muhammad's birthday is celebrated and also the day on which he had a vision of heaven and hell.

BUDDHISM

Buddhism in the Soviet Union is professed by the Buryats, and Kalmyks, Tuvins, Koreans, and a few small ethnic groups (see ch. 9, Ethnic Groups). As with all other major religious groups, Buddhism has suffered at the hands of Communist antireligious propaganda. In 1915 it was estimated that there were over 16,000 lamas (Buddhist monks) in the country. By 1960 this number had declined to about 300.

Buddhism, a religion adhered to by as many as 500 million people in the Asian mainland, originated in the teachings of Siddhartha Gautama, who lived in the sixth century B.C. in the northern Indian province of Maghada. Born the son of a wealthy nobleman, Gautama became dissatisfied with his princely life and renounced it to become a wandering ascetic. He spent six years in meditation searching for salvation and finally attained enlightenment while seated under a *bo*, or sacred fig tree. Thereafter he was known as Buddha, the Enlightened One.

After Buddha's death, the faith that he inspired was institutionalized for about 400 years in the monastic orders founded by his disciples, and his teachings were orally transmitted by them. Several centuries passed before this oral tradition appeared in manuscript.

Buddhism first spread throughout India and Ceylon and later was carried by monks to the rest of Asia. From Mongolia in the seventeenth century, it entered the Russian Empire, where it was adopted first by the Kalmyks and Buryats. Under the tsars, although not favored, Buddhism was not repressed and was permitted to grow.

After the Bolshevik Revolution the government considered the Mongol followers of Buddhism to be suitable agents to advance Soviet aims in the Far East. In 1926, the government permitted the country's Buddhists to hold a congress in Moscow, which praised Soviet nationalities policy. Buddhist-Communist collaboration was encouraged by a concocted theory called Neo-Buddhism, which compared the religion with the atheism of Marx and Lenin. Tolerance of Buddhism continued through the years of Lenin's New Economic Policy as lamas sought to preserve their faith by cooperating with the Communists.

Beginning in 1928, the government began a campaign against Buddhism. Buddhists were condemned by the League of the Militant Godless, which tried to prevent the observance of holy days, disrupted religious services, and closed the temples. The Great Purge took a heavy toll, but Buddhists refused to abandon their faith. Government attempts to suppress Buddhism continued until World War II when antireligious activity was abated in the interests of unifying the country against the German invaders. Since 1945, however, Buddhism, as well as the other religions in the country, has again been under attack. By cooperating with Soviet propaganda campaigns, lamas have attempted to protect their institutions, but the CPSU antireligious campaign has been severe.

Buddhism has absorbed many beliefs and practices from other religious systems. Some of these derive from the Indian background of Buddhism's development. Others were added after Buddhism reached beyond the Indian subcontinent. After reaching Russia, local conditions added or modified some practices, but the central core of faith was unchanged.

Central to the structure of Buddhist belief is the doctrine of *karma*, which holds that every act, word, and even thought has consequences, not resulting from the intervention of supernatural beings but from the operation of cosmic principle. Evil acts have evil consequences in that the doer may suffer misfortune in this world or suffer in future incarnations. Good acts yield good consequences—prosperity in this world, birth in heaven, or a high position in the world in some future life.

Each higher incarnation brings one closer to *nirvana*, the ultimate, unknowable state of contentment and fulfillment that can be achieved at the end of a final incarnation by recognizing the Four Noble Truths and following the Eightfold Path. Three fundamental teachings are that all is impermanent, sorrow is inherent in everything and the separate self has no reality. All existence is illusion, and no substantial reality underlies change. The principal source of sorrow is the desire to live and to experience material things. The human being is an elemental aggregate that dissolves at death, having no ego. All that continues is a bundle of attributes, merits, or demerits.

The Four Noble Truths are that all life is sorrow; sorrow is the result of desire; cessation of desire ends sorrow; and cessation of desire is attained by following the Eightfold Path. The Eightfold Path, known as the Middle Way, comprises right understanding, right purpose, right speech, right action, right livelihood, right effort, right attentiveness, and right concentration. There are a number of precepts enjoining abstention from certain acts, such as taking life and self-indulgence. A few of these are commonly accepted as the minimum requirements for acceptable social and ethical conduct. Lamas observe all the precepts as part of an extensive body of rules that govern their life.

According to the Mahayana system of beliefs followed in the Soviet Union, Buddha's greatest virtue lay in his selfless devotion to others and in his willingness to postpone his own entry into *nirvana* so that the secret of salvation could be shared with other human beings. The ideal Buddhist, therefore, is the saintly figure who has vowed not to enter *nirvana* until the whole human race has achieved salvation with him.

Soviet Buddhists solemnly observe six important holy days called *khurals*. Five are devoted to the memory of Buddha, whereas one commemorates the famous Buddhist reformer Tsongkhapa. The most solemn holy day, the Zagran-Sara Khural, or holiday of the White Moon, is devoted to Buddha and lasts fifteen days. According to the Buddhist calendar, this is the beginning of the New Year. During Zagran-Sara every believer is cleared of his sins and dedicates himself to a better life for the coming year.

JUDAISM

Jewish settlements in areas now controlled by the Soviet Union date from the early pre-Christian period. There were Jews living in the Caucasus region in ancient times, and the Hellenic colonies around the Black Sea contained Jewish minorities. The seventh century A.D. state of Khazaria in the lower Volga Region had Jewish settlements, and some historians claim that the ruling classes of that state embraced Judaism. Jewish colonies and trading centers in the southern steppes were scattered by the Tatar invasion, and most Jews migrated to western areas of the present-day Ukraine, Belorussia, and Poland, some settling also in the Moscow area.

After the defeat of the Tatars as the Muscovite principality developed into the Russian Empire, Jews were officially discriminated against on religious grounds. Under the tsars, Jews were accorded an inferior position, and many professions and all government positions were barred to them. With the partitioning of Poland in the late eighteenth century, great numbers of Polish Jews came under control of the tsardom, joining their Russian brethren in the miserable conditions decreed for all Jews.

Catherine the Great instituted the infamous "Pale of Settlement" that restricted Jewish residence to a certain few areas in the western part of the country and set the pattern for oppression that lasted as long as tsardom itself. Catherine's grandson, Alexander I, prohibited Jews from living in rural areas, thus forcing them into trade or handicrafts and preventing Jewish farming of the land. The final century of tsarism in Russia brought continual oppression to Russia's Jews, with restrictive laws and unofficial but controlled pogroms.

A highly restrictive quota system effectively limited the number of Jewish youth allowed into secondary and higher schools, while the general Russification policies of the nineteenth century against all minorities attempted to force Jews to abandon their faith. Little amelioration of the Jewish position resulted from the Revolution of 1905, but after the March 1917 revolution a brief respite occurred. Within a week after the overthrow of the tsar, the Provisional Government issued a decree abolishing all anti-Jewish legislation.

The liberalizing trend under the Provisional Government ended abruptly with the Bolshevik Revolution of November 1917. A severe anti-Jewish campaign destroyed untold numbers of synagogues and religious schools. Rabbis were arrested, and the teaching of the Hebrew language proscribed. Observance of the high holy days, although not officially forbidden, was greatly restricted, and ceremonies were often broken up by roving bands of Bolshevik activists.

Soviet economic policies of the period before Lenin's New Economic Policy, put thousands of Jewish merchants and shopkeepers out of business and, with the country torn by civil war, most Jews found themselves in dire poverty. Many tried to return to farming, an activity denied to them for over a century, but land was scarce and shifting battlefronts prevented a mass return to the land. Anti-Semitism also kept Jews landless and, in general, contributed to their miserable plight.

In 1928 the Soviet government announced that a Jewish "republic" would be established and, in 1934, the Jewish Autonomous Region was founded in far-eastern Siberia. The difficulties of migrating thousands of miles to a remote area with a harsh climate had little appeal to the masses of Russian Jews, and few responded to the Soviet offer of a Jewish "homeland". In the late 1960's Jews represented less than 9 percent of the incongruously named Jewish Autonomous Region.

The purge period of the 1930's wreaked havoc among Jewish believers as well as among many who had renounced their religion to join the Bolsheviks. Leon Trotsky, the most famous of the Bolshevik Jews, had been exiled and was later murdered in Mexico. But old Bolsheviks, such as Lev Kamenev and Grigory Zinoviev, both Jews who had reached the apex of Communist power in the early 1920's, were executed in 1936.

Soviet Jews supported the government during World War II, but their support brought no reward from Stalin. Anti-Judaism was resumed immediately after the war in contrast to relative tolerance of some other religious groups. Jewish religious life was all but halted by Stalin, at least in its public manifestations. Near the very end of his life Stalin was again preparing an openly anti-Semitic drive with his revelation of the so-called Jewish "doctors' plot" that was later described as groundless (see ch. 3, Historical Setting).

Throughout the late 1940's and in the 1960's, the official campaign against Jewry in the Soviet Union continued in more intensive fashion than against other religions. Typical Soviet anti-Semitic activities were the arrests and trials of Jews for Zionist activity, as agents of a foreign power, in line with the government's pro-Arab policy in the Middle East. By 1964 there were fewer than 100 Jewish communities regarded as such, and formal religious observances had been virtually suppressed. There was some diminution in the pressure after Khrushchev's removal, and the post-Khrushchev leadership, more sensitive to world public opinion and concerned to counter past charges of anti-Semitism, has appeared less hostile in its attitude toward Judaism. Anti-Semitism and other manifestations of nationalism were condemned by Premier Kosygin in 1965. The authorities permitted the chief rabbi of Moscow to visit Jewish communities in the United States and other western nations as evidence of Soviet tolerance of Judaism.

CHAPTER 14
SOCIAL VALUES

As a multinational society, the Soviet Union contains a number of indigenous value traditions. The state has its own system of values, which it has attempted to make universal. The situation existing in early 1970 was one of change. Not only were the official values being spread at the expense of indigenous traditions, but these were themselves changing because of increased technology and political necessity.

Foremost among the native traditions is the Russian value system, for it is shared by the people of the most numerous and most powerful ethnic group. Other non-Russian European value systems were similar in many respects to the Russian.

Second in importance to the Russian value tradition, but very different from it, is the Islamic. Like communism, it is derived in part from sources outside the country, but it has been shaped by native peoples. Other value traditions have been of more significance to their bearers than to the country as a whole.

The Communist values also originated outside the country. As they were adopted by Russian revolutionaries, a form of syncretism took place, and communism took on a strong Russian coloring. Soviet-style Marxism has been so heavily imbued with Russian values that it is often thought of as an indigenous system.

The government expends great effort to transmit and sanction the Communist system of values in its Russian form. At the same time, the indigenous value systems are by no means moribund, and various secondary syntheses are taking place as the peoples of the Soviet Union adapt themselves to changing conditions.

Officials have predicted that the planned census of 1970 will find that Russians, for the first time, constitute less than half of the total population. No change can be forecast for the Russian dominance in cultural, social, and political spheres, because Russians will still be, by far, the largest single ethnic group and Russian predominance is too deeply ingrained in the society to change in any short period of time. Because of increasing numerical strength of various minorities, however, non-Russian and non-Communist value systems will persist. Concurrently, the universalizing effects of the mass media will continue the process of Sovietization, which has been a hallmark of the Communist era.

Certain features of traditional culture and some of the social values that it shared with Marx's original formulations fitted tsarist Russia into the pattern of Marxism, even though Marx proclaimed his doctrines to be designed for highly industrialized nations. Marxism's professed universalism permitted it to fill the gap between the ideals and the reality of organized religion in Russia. Moreover, collectivism was a strong feature in the old Russia. Marxism has also been able to provide intellectual and spiritual satisfaction for some people. The majority of Soviet citizens continue to accept the official values, because they receive little exposure to, and less encouragement for, other systems.

VALUE TRADITIONS

Russian Tradition

The strongest of many value traditions in the multinational Soviet Union is also the newest. The Marxism introduced by the Bolshevik revolutionaries in 1917 became an official ideology. Properly called Marxism-Leninism because of the intensely Russian interpretation of Marxist doctrines by Lenin, the most important tenet of this official ideology concerns "the building of communism." Marx, Engels, and Lenin had all stated that changes in human nature would be necessary for mankind to live under communism, and they generally believed that the changes would occur during the period of building the Communist system. After the Revolution the creation of the "new Soviet Man" became the ideal, and he was pictured as a person who loved his group, his fellow workers, and his fellow man. He was also courageous and honest and had a comradely desire to be a "member of the team." This ideal man would also love work whatever his calling might be.

Membership or nonmembership in the Communist Party is not a criterion for determining numbers of people subscribing to Marxism-Leninism because, theoretically, all the people are builders of communism. Many Soviet citizens who have no Party connections and even some who condemn the Party for past excesses tend to participate in "the building of communism" in the hope of improving their lot in life.

The Russian value traditions predominate in a country that for centuries the Russians have dominated numerically, culturally, and politically. In building and maintaining the prerevolutionary empire, the Russians at times attempted to spread their own culture and values among subjugated peoples, but tsarist policies were ambivalent, alternating between periods of intolerance and indifference toward minority groups. Without any concerted, long-range efforts to destroy indigenous cultures and values, native traditions

262

among the country's diverse nationalities persisted until the Stalin era and, in some aspects, still persist.

Imperial Russia has been described as a land of "Autocracy, Orthodoxy, and Nationalism." The absolute monarchy lasted until the Revolution of 1905, Russian Orthodoxy was the official religion until the advent of the atheist Bolsheviks, and nationalism still exists despite ideological incompatibility with Marxist doctrine. Stalin's program of "socialism in one country" and the creation of a powerful state was un-Marxist but conducive to the spread of a Soviet nationalism that has not supplanted, but overshadows the many nationalistic interests of the minorities. Marxism-Leninism has to some extent supplanted the influence of the Russian Orthodox church, which, however, has proved to be extremely durable.

Russia had been primarily agricultural for many centuries and, until 1861, a majority of the peasants were held in bondage as serfs. Even as serfs, however, Russians and non-Russians alike had a great affinity for the land they tilled. This "love of the land" was strong enough to be a key factor in the Bolshevik propaganda and, in later action, as the peasants expropriated the landlords.

In addition to the great love of the land, a traditional value of the peasantry, particularly among the Russians, was a desire for collectivity. Even as serfs the Russian peasants usually formed a village commune known as the *mir*. The *mir* persisted until Stalin's collectivization drive of the 1930's.

Similarities were apparent between the old village organization and the Soviet *kolkhoz* (collective farm), but differences between the two were more pertinent in the 1930's. Chief among the differences was the temporary absence of communal spirit that disappeared in Stalin's brutal collectivization campaign. The spirit of collectivity, however, with deep roots among the Russians as well as many of the non-Russian peoples, did not die during the 1930's, and it became one of the values most emphatically preached by the Communist Party of the Soviet Union (CPSU). Loyalty to one's peer group—whether it be in the classrooms of first graders, in the shops of factory workers, or on the collective and state farms—is held as a principal virtue, officially and actually.

Other Traditions

Different value traditions existed among the non-Russian minorities, although many similarities can be perceived, particularly among other Slavs, and also among other essentially European peoples whose backgrounds included serfdom, Christianity, and, in some cases, the communal kind of rural organizations. The cultures and religions of the Armenians and Georgians antedated the Slavic institutions; the Ukrainians, Belorussians, and Baltic peoples had more experience with individual land tenure, and within all these nationalities traditions of national identity existed. Soviet hegemony has not successfully erased nationalism any more than tsarist autocracy had in the centuries preceding the Revolution. Pride in the Soviet Union as a powerful modern state is evident, however, among diverse ethnic groups whose forbears never entertained such attitudes toward the old Russian Empire.

Some inhabitants of the Soviet Far North and Siberia shared nomadic tribal traditions and, in many cases, these peoples have been assimilated into Soviet society although not necessarily Russianized. Intermingling and intermarriage between Slavs and tribal peoples have brought great changes to the latter. Modern education and a sedentary life have broken down ancient tribal traditions to the point where many ethnic groups can truly be termed *Soviets* despite the retention of linguistic identity and ancient folkways and customs.

The influence of Islam is of great importance. Muslims are second numerically only to the Slavic peoples and, as a group, they have resisted Russianization and Sovietization and retained much of their old cultures and their ancient traditions. Although the Islamic peoples belong to many different ethnic groups, they nevertheless exhibit an appearance of solidarity based on their religious beliefs.

Loyalty to the community of Islam is one of the strongest values among Muslims, even for those who do not actively practice the faith. Islamic teachings stress that all Muslims are brothers and that ethnic differences are insignificant compared to the strong bond of Islam. Associated with communal loyalty is adherence to traditional customs, particularly those centering around the family and the religion.

Ideologically, the Islamic communities are Muslim rather than Communist. Each of the Muslim political entities—republics, autonomous regions, and national areas—has its Communist Party, and Muslim membership has increased in the post-World War II period. Muslim peoples have also taken advantage of the greater educational opportunities and higher standards of living that have come with Soviet domination, but, in the main, they are still more Muslim than Soviet. Among educated Muslims who accept communism to some degree, there is a trend toward fusion between Muslim and Communist values. This is anathema to the Kremlin leadership, which recognizes only its own brand of communism as legitimate.

INDIVIDUALS

The ideal man is strong, capable of performing hard work and of enduring pain and fatigue. He also has strength of character and is able to withstand suffering and hardship. These characteristics also

264

are valued in women. In choosing a prospective bride, peasant men put physical strength among the prime requirements. Throughout Russian history, strength has been a necessity, for the people have had to work hard and endure much.

Sensitivity to the feelings of others is highly valued. Liveliness of personality and expressiveness of feelings are also valued and are typical. A person should be natural, unaffected, and unself-concious. It is not considered necessary to hide one's feelings for the sake of polite form. If, for example, one is bored or tired at a social gathering, there is no shame in admitting it and no necessity to hide it.

In dealing with others, people should be direct instead of devious. Intentions, feelings, and opinions are openly expressed. Spontaneity of action is characteristic.

But despite the emphasis placed on naturalness and expressiveness, politeness and consideration are nevertheless highly valued. One of the worst things that can be said of a person is that he is uncultured, by which can be meant many things. It can refer to a person who does not consistently observe the basic rules of personal hygiene, to one who pushes in crowds, to one who does not read very much, or to one who is inconsiderate and self-centered. Although there was a time after the Bolshevik Revolution when good manners were considered to be bourgeois survivals of no importance, the old standards quickly reasserted themselves. In a society characterized by rapid upward social mobility, the concern with cultured behavior is stronger than ever.

Russian expressiveness has given rise to a stereotype of Russian moodiness. Some Western writers have attempted to attribute this characteristic to the tight swaddling of infants, occasionally alternated by periods when the infant is unbound and free to move and to cry. The range of socially permissible self-expression is wider than that in the West.

Hard work is considered good but as a means rather than an end in itself. The old Russian peasants considered that their labor had given them right to the land, and Communist values give primacy to the goodness of labor and the right of workers to enjoy the fruits of their labor. Work gives meaning to existence, and the old leisured classes are remembered with disfavor.

For a time during the Stalin period, Western observers characterized Soviet society as puritanical. The stress placed on industrialization and modernization called for great personal sacrifice on the part of the masses and left little time for romance or romantic expression. Industrial themes become prominent, even in romantic literature, and emotions were channeled into building of communism rather than into normal human relationships. One observer attributed the apparent puritanism of Soviet people to shyness and modesty, and modesty certainly seems to be part of the makeup. Soviet women, however, are quite frank in their associations with men without appearing bold. In their society it is as equally acceptable for a girl to attempt to make the acquaintance of a boy who is attractive to her as vice versa. At any rate, attitudes toward such values appear to be quite natural and unaffected.

Women are expected to be feminine but not excessively so. Preference for ensemble costumes (blouse, skirt, and jacket) and a cultural distaste for thinness have given foreigners a deceptive conception of Russian feminity. The many years of privation necessary for industrial development have given this deceptive impression, but the slackening of the pace in the 1960's makes the original conceptions more obvious again. Although women wish to have children, they do not regard childbearing as a necessary proof of their femininity.

Most Soviet people characterize femininity by sweetness and understanding; motherly characteristics are valued. Although pre-revolutionary Russia was characterized by the patriarchal regime in family life, women were still considered strong and capable. There is little evidence of the idea that women are less capable, responsible, or intelligent than men and, under the Soviet regime, the egalitarian tendencies have been increased.

Men, too, are expected to be strong. They should be courageous; women have great scorn for men who are not. Although a clear-cut division of labor existed before the Revolution and there still exist ideas of what sorts of work better suit men or women, there is no particular shame for men to do women's work, or vice versa. There seems to be no particular anxiety over sex identity.

On the other hand, a widespread literary theme, particularly of the nineteenth century, "concerns strong women and weak men," and to a certain extent this reflects reality. One result of the twentiety-century Soviet history has been a differential death rate, with male deaths far in excess of female; women have had by necessity to take commanding roles in families that have lost husbands and fathers. At the same time, as is true in any society in which masculine identity had been bound to occupation, with rapid social change men have had to accept occupational egalitarianism, leaving few stable models with which to identify. The problems with male alcoholism and juvenile delinquency reflect to some extent the results of this difficulty.

An ideal life would be characterized by work, with enough material rewards to permit a comfortable life. Sociability is desired, and closeness to friends and family is important. The desire for culture—education and gentility—is strong.

Official values extoll the importance of building communism as one of the reasons for existence, one of the goals of life; many have internalized these goals and derive satisfaction from their work in furthering progress toward the Communist utopia. Most, however, are content with more modest goals: happy family life, satisfying work, sufficient material rewards, and cultural achievement. Dedicated Communists and religious believers both derive spiritual rewards, but there is a felt vacuum in this realm. The value systems are in a state of change; the direction is not yet clear.

PERSONAL RELATIONS

Other persons are generally conceived of as good and trustworthy. Thus they can be approached openly, the valued manner. Closeness and intimacy are valued in personal relationships, within the family, and between friends. Friendship is generally close and confined to relatively few persons; Soviets do not care to have diffuse, but shallow relationships.

The long period of political repression and purges had its effect on personal relations. Seeming friends might turn out to be police informers and, if a person was arrested, his friends and family might also be implicated. A great deal of suspicion and caution was the inevitable result. In general, however, people continued to maintain close friendships whenever they could. Since the mid-1950's, friendship has resumed a more normal course.

Although the people are conscious of status differences among individuals as well as differences in life style and education, they nevertheless value those who, without being condescending, act in an egalitarian manner. The underlying concept is a feeling that all belong to one family, or collective. A feeling of belonging gives the individual security and results also in the typically unselfconscious behavior. There is thus no need for pretense or excessive formality. The long period of peasant experience in collectives, first in the *mir* and later in the *kolkhoz*, and the feeling of *sobornost* (community spirit) generated by the Russian Orthodox church have also contributed to the sense of belonging.

On the whole, people are tolerant of personal differences except where they affect the group. If an individual does not care for another, the latter is generally ignored. Zeal, formerly for religion, but later for communism, has sometimes modified the pattern of tolerance, resulting in a tendency toward inflexibility.

During the tsarist period, relations between men and women were generally characterized as patriarchal, especially among the peasants, who constituted an overwhelming majority of the population. Among the aristocrats and the small class of intellectuals, more egalitarian relations prevailed. The Revolution brought with it an egalitarian ideal, stressing the emancipation of women (see ch. 11, Family). Necessity has brought this ideal close to realization. In a family that can afford to let the husband be the sole wage earner, there exists a tendency for the woman to assume a more traditional role as wife and mother; in most cases, however, patriarchy has disappeared and, although the husband may take a leading role, his wife plays a close second.

Children have generally been expected to respect their parents and other adults, especially the elderly. Often they would be raised by an old grandmother *(babushka)* and the old men controlled the *mir*. Law in tsarist times gave fathers nearly absolute control over their children. As in so many aspects of life, the period immediately following the Bolshevik Revolution represented a temporary, but drastic change. Children were expected to view their parents with suspicion as being potentially hostile to the regime; parental authority was minimized (see ch. 11, Family).

Subsequent developments stressed the necessity that children respect their parents. The work of A. S. Makarenko, a Soviet pedagogue, made a point of this. He also stressed the importance of parental responsibility toward children. Parents should teach their children by example and precept rather than by punishment, but, on the other hand, they should not spoil them. Indulgence of children tends to be a common adult response, however, although most parents conscientiously attempt to follow expert advice.

The rapid changes that have taken place in society during the last fifty years have produced great changes in the relations between children and adults. Parents are often viewed as old fashioned or as out of touch with current realities; even when they are regarded with respect, their opinions may not always count for much.

INDIVIDUAL AND SOCIETY

Strong group loyalty and identification result from the Russian sense of belonging. Peasants have always been loyal to their villages, often out of necessity. In an industrial context group loyalty and identification still prevail. The regime has used these characteristics to promote production by appealing to group sentiment and by promising group rewards or penalties.

Marxist thought emphasized the importance of the mass—the

workingmen's collectives. Such concepts readily found fertile soil for growth in postrevolutionary Russia. Individuals are supposed to act for the good of the collective. The raising and education of children are designed to encourage collective sensibilities. Official pronouncements have occasionally made individuals seem but cogs in some vast machine. On the whole, however, the tone of official exhortations and pedagogical works has had a tone familiar in Western morality. Individuals are urged not to be selfish, but to consider other people, and to work for the good of all people. The collective seems to be viewed, not as an undifferentiated mass, but as a group of persons.

Nevertheless, the peer group, or the collective, and the individual's relationship to it receive much attention. Social sanctions in factory and school groups are carried out by a process of group shaming, in which the deviant individual is pressed by all members to consider his faults and to do better. This singling out from the group is uncomfortable for the individual, who derives a sense of security from belonging to the group. Sanctions in the old village collective followed the same pattern. Russian Orthodoxy also emphasized the common sharing of religious experience as truly human and truly Christian.

Soviet behavior in public and typical friendship patterns are highly individualistic. Individuals seem generally unconscious of other persons in public places. They show no need to seem amiable and often appear rude or unconscious of others. Friends are chosen because they seem interesting and compatible. In the most crowded of housing conditions, individuals are still able to maintain a sense of privacy or individuality.

But the person who is too withdrawn and seems too much concerned with himself and his own feelings is considered antisocial. This conception, which receives endorsement from official values, also forms the basis for the government's policies toward the arts. Both romanticism and abstraction in the arts have been considered to be too individualistic, too concerned with private sensations to the detriment of society. Abstract and impressionistic visual painting and sculpture, lyric poetry and psychological novels, and nontonal music have been shunned for realistic art, tonal music, and literature stressing the collective. Part of these reactions have also resulted from lack of sophistication, for prerevolutionary Russia was in the forefront of the arts (see ch. 16, Artistic Expression).

Ideally, leaders, especially those in the highest positions, should be models for those below them and should personify the official virtues. Thus, they should be stronger and more humane, sympathetic, unselfish, unselfconscious, dedicated, and honest. Soviet citizens evince the most respect for leaders who are both strong and humane; in his day, Stalin was so conceived by official literature.

Soviet egalitarianism requires that the leaders be distant from the mass of the ruled. In old Russia the tsar was called the Little Father, although he was far removed from the world of the peasants. Lenin and, particularly, Stalin were also far from the people. Perhaps Khrushchev was seen as condescending too much. The image of the ruler is often that of the patriarchal father, just and wise, but ruling by himself. Soviet leaders following Khrushchev have moved increasingly away from the cult of personality, from image-making, but by early 1970 it was still too soon to determine whether this trend was to be a permanent change in authority patterns.

Russian history has been characterized by a gulf between the rulers and the ruled, between "they" and "us." Although Russians readily identified with their social groups and had a great love for their country, they had no particular identification with, or loyalty to, their government. For Soviet citizens the government is the government of their country, and they regard it as a necessary alternative to anarchy and chaos. But the distance between individuals and their government, compounded by a rigid bureaucracy and a shortage of materials for consumption and construction, has created a problem of graft and corruption.

One of the methods of beating the system has been through the use of *blat* (influence). *Blat* is often resorted to by minor industrial officials or small enterprise managers who, needing raw materials or parts, have been frustrated by red tape or shortages. *Blat* may involve small gifts of money or goods, or it may simply result from friendship. The ends are generally rather small, such as speeding an application, expediting a shipment, or overlooking some deficiency.

Blat seldom results in large-scale corruption or embezzlement but more nearly resembles petty graft. Soviet citizens find other ways to circumvent the rules of bureaucracy, either to make life a little easier, reduce the effect of production quotas, or to avoid responsibility. A bookkeeper may manipulate the books to avoid filling quotas or to make it possible to obtain otherwise scarce goods; a foreman may find loopholes in the rules that permit his workers to underfulfill production quotas that were placed too high. A factory may employ a person to travel about making unofficial arrangements for supplies with other factories. A factory may even manufacture supplies for itself or, occasionally, items for sale to consumers.

Official values deplore the practice of *blat*. It is often exposed in the newspapers, where such exposés are among the most popular items. Although it is supposed to be a form of dishonesty, those who engage in *blat* do not feel particularly guilty, because they feel that the government is so remote and that there is the necessity to humanize the large and rigidly centralized bureaucratic system.

Theft—although generally not from private individuals—was once a problem for the same reasons. With the increased availability of consumer goods, the problem has declined considerably.

Communist values stress man's ability to change himself and the world. Even control over the means of production, basic in Marxist theory, is capable of being changed—in fact, it must be, out of historical necessity. Communism is, in this sense, highly optimistic. Communist man is thought to be capable of any accomplishment. Old ways and inherited traditions cannot set limits and experience in the twentieth century—the Revolution that overthrew the seemingly permanent tsarist regime, the rapid industrialization and urbanization, and the near eradication of illiteracy in a backward country—all of these reinforce such assertions in the minds of many citizens. Yet, such optimism can result in the wishful thinking that has left a negative impression on Soviet biology, social science, and agronomy.

Darwinian-Mendelian concepts of genetics and evolution, generally held to be valid, attribute biological evolution to the interaction of natural selection and random mutation of genes. Environmental influence upon the process of evolution is indirect. Lamarckian evolutionary theory, on the other hand, holds that the environment acts directly on the process of evolution and that acquired characteristics can be transmitted genetically. Because of the Soviet stress on man's abilities to change the world and the pressing needs for agricultural development, Lamarckian theories were officially adopted and were considered valid for a long period. Agricultural failures, however, eventually resulted in an abandonment of Lamarckian theories (see ch. 18, Science and Technology).

The optimistic values of communism explain in part the continuing attack on religion. The Communists hold that religious teachings encourage fatalism, or the passive acquiescence of things as they exist. It is also considered that religion portrays man as sinful and weak, whereas in the Communist utopia man and society will be perfected on earth, by man himself. Therefore, the campaign against religion has been constant. Methods and tactics change, but the original antireligious statements of Marx and Lenin are regarded as infallible doctrine.

PATTERNS OF CHANGE

The Soviet value system contains sources of tension, of conflict, and change, augmented by outside sources. Since systems compete in the Soviet Union, one system having been imposed on people holding to another system, tension has been further increased. In addition to contradictory values, the discrepancy that exists between the real and the ideal, between promises and actions provides tension,

For example, within the Russian tradition, the desire for material betterment contradicts the disdain for material goods. The strong egalitarian tendency conflicts with dominant-submissive patterns of social relations. Antagonism toward outgroups opposes the widely held church teachings of love and brotherhood.

During the tsarist era, Russian values conflicted with those of Muslim peoples in southern Russia and the Caucasus, as well as with those of European peoples within the empire. But on the whole, the non-Russian peoples were left largely to their own devices.

The advent of the Communist movement made drastic changes. Members of the Communist Party have consistently attempted to impose their values on all other peoples. The Communist regime, moreover, contains within itself sources of tension, for there are often highly visible discrepancies between behavior and officially proclaimed values.

The mass collective aspect of communism has been one of the most important sources of value conflict. Although the old peasant life had its collective aspects in the *mir*, there were individualistic traditions as well. The peasant commune itself consisted of a small group of people who had known each other all their lives. Certain features—such as the joint responsibility for the labor force, for land tenure, and for taxes—had been imposed upon the village from without. Family heads attempted to favor their own families but, out of necessity, had to retain the potential for mutual aid with fellow villagers.

By the 1960's over half of the population was urban (see ch. 32, The Labor Force). Even where neighbors and fellow apartment dwellers know each other well, city life is generally more anonymous and impersonal than village life. Furthermore, the migration to the city has consisted of individuals rather than whole villages. Motivations for migration have generally been to seek individual social and economic betterment. Individualistic values have also been shown in the preference for single family apartments and houses, summer cottages rather than public camps, and in the tendency of middle class parents to use what influence and position they have to favor their own children's careers. Certain aspects of *blat*—especially the avoidance of responsibility—also reflect individualistic values.

These events have all taken place under the Communist regime and have moreover been in part a result of its actions. Soviet development has been largely industrial, the new labor force largely being drawn from the countryside. The overall prosperity and promise of future economic improvements have increased individualistic tendencies, and many incentives offered by the regime have been individual, such as automobiles and private housing, as well as high salaries and bonuses. Punishments, on the other hand, have more often been collective, such as the attempts to liquidate the class of *kulaki* (relatively well-to-do peasants) in the 1930's, or the mass deportations of the Crimean Tatars and several other peoples in the 1940's (see ch. 9, Ethnic Groups).

Although Communist universalism has something in common with religious movements and thus was enabled to draw upon the religious sensibilities of the people, its militant atheism nevertheless created many conflicts in the early years, particularly between parents and children. For many people, communism did not equal religion as a source of enduring spiritual values. Where parents and children differed, the parents were disturbed by their children's attitudes, while the children regarded their parents as old fashioned and had less respect for them. The conflict has lessened as more generations have been born, raised, educated, and indoctrinated under the atheistic system.

The values placed by communism on internationalism are contradictory to the old Russian tendencies of antagonism toward outgroups and to native ethnocentrism. These latter attitudes have reasserted themselved in a form of Russian chauvinism, including the patronizing attitudes toward the "younger brothers" (see ch. 9, Ethnic Groups). Attitudes toward outgroups have to a certain extent been transferred to non-Communist nations and, recently, to the Communist Chinese and other so-called deviationists.

A discrepancy often exists between the professed values of the regime and its actions. Such discrepancies do not necessarily result in negative attitudes toward the Communist movement as a whole; instead there may result a fundamentalist attitude that the government should adhere more fully to Marxist values.

Exploitation and injustice are supposed to be obsolescent in the socialist state. There was a time when mere suspicion or guilt by association was used as cause to arrest and punish thousands, and often there were no trials. Many classes of workers still work long hard hours for small pay. Most women must not only work but also keep up a household with inadequate equipment. Despite claims under socialism of the opportunity for personal freedom, its absence has often been the case. The official policy is that individual freedom is not to exist at the expense of the public good. Many of those who chafe at the restrictions feel that Marxist principles are not being applied fully enough.

Although considerable progress has been made in the more than fifty years since the Bolshevik Revolution, promises have nevertheless outstripped performance. The Soviet Union was proclaimed to have achieved socialism in the 1930's, but some areas of private enterprise still flourish. The CPSU announced in 1961 that the present generation of Soviet citizens would achieve the long-sought goal of communism but, at the end of the decade, promises again were vague, and the millennium was being talked about in more distant time references.

Values are transmitted in the socialization process, in families, and in the schools and other public institutions (see ch. 11, Family). Of these, the Komsomol (Young Communist League), Young Pioneers, and Little Octobrists organizations are of paramount importance. In these organizations official Communist values are transmitted, and appropriate behavior is encouraged. At the same time, since Young Pioneer and Octobrist membership is nearly universal among children, and Komsomol membership also is high, and since these are the only available youth organizations, a wide coverage of the population is assured.

Parents may hold to different values. When both parents work and nursery care is unavailable, the *babushka* who raises the children is even more removed from the values of the Young Pioneers and the Komsomol. Children may find themselves the focus of conflict in values. Nevertheless, as new generations of children grow up and become parents, the values of the Komsomol inevitably gain. But as long as the nation promotes strong family life, and there are no indications to the contrary, families will continue to be important agencies in the transmission of values.

Social control in the realm of values again has its similarities with practices elsewhere. For example, invidious gossip and ridicule single out the deviant; those who conform receive the reward of security and social approval. Where deviation takes the form of highly antisocial and criminal behavior, legal agencies take over. One practice, prevalent in all Communist countries and very common in the Soviet Union, is the singling out from the group of the deviant individual. He is then made not only to feel ashamed of his deviant behavior and to change it, but also to undergo a change of heart. In the old days the *mir* was the agent of such sanctions but, by the 1960's, factory unions, youth groups, and other collectives had taken over its role.

The Soviet Union also is prominent in the explicit use of the mass media to promote values. Public lectures, posters, newspaper items all convey the message to even the least sophisticated. Finally, those who are sincerely convinced of the truth of the message can derive personal satisfaction from working to implement the social values in the building of communism.

CHAPTER 15

THE EDUCATIONAL SYSTEM

Education in the Soviet Union since the Bolshevik Revolution has been all-encompassing in its effects on the people. The immediate postrevolutionary goal of education was to create a literate population, and claims to success in this area have been attested to by many impartial observers. As the new Soviet state developed, its educational system was called upon to produce the workers, technicians, and scientists necessary for a rapidly industrializing nation. Concurrently, the new regime desired to break with that part of the Russian past that was considered backward and bourgeois. Soviet education was heralded as the means of creating "the new Soviet man" with new loyalties and new concepts of life.

In pursuit of these goals, education in the country since 1917 has undergone a series of experiments, changes, and counterchanges. Different types of schools provided different types of education based on changing situations and changing needs. Overall central coordination, standardization, and planning have always been vested in the Communist Party operating through state administrative agencies. Educational policy seemed to vacillate between the belief that the pursuit of conventional knowledge was a good and necessary thing and the belief that Communists could afford to dispense with some theoretical knowledge in favor of practical vocational learning achieved by work tempered by the thoughts of Marx and Lenin. Soviet achievements in a wide range of disciplines attest to the fact that the nation's leaders adopted a compromise, pragmatic course in the development of the educational system, designed to implement efforts in the building of a socialist state.

The country's leaders, although not neglecting standard education, have stressed political and ideological indoctrination in the educational process. Ideology continues to permeate the content of subject matter, and the teaching schedule is supplemented by extracurricular activities in which all students must participate in order to increase their exposure to the tenets of communism. Teachers and students alike must adhere to the ideologically correct lines, and inspectors periodically visit classrooms to ensure nationwide conformity.

The Soviet educational system, with over 72 million students in 1969, consisted of preschool nurseries and kindergartens, primary schools, secondary schools, special schools, vocational and technical schools, institutes and universities, correspondence schools, adult and part-time schools, and nondegree schools. Most institutions of higher learning, with over 4 million students, have concentrated on the training of engineers, scientists, and technicians needed in the Soviet economy. With a total of more than 750 institutions of higher learning, only about 40 were universities. The remainder were institutes with highly specialized curricula for training professionals in fields ranging from agriculture to medicine to teaching. The number of pedagogical institutes has increased rapidly with the ever-increasing number of new schools.

Teaching is generally formalized with central government ministries responsible for the content of syllabi and textbooks. University students, however, are allowed to engage in individual research projects, but in most cases these must apply to current scientific or industrial needs.

Soviet leaders claim to have raised the literacy rate from 25 percent to about 100 percent since the establishment of the Communist regime. The seven-year general school was made compulsory in 1958, and official announcements have stated that the ten-year school will be compulsory by 1970. Preschool facilities had not been sufficiently developed to accommodate all children in the age group, but primary and secondary facilities enrolled between 93 percent and 95 percent of all school-age children.

Universities and institutes of higher learning are open to all who pass the highly competitive entrance examinations, but in 1969 only one in four graduates of secondary schools continued to a higher level. Choice of study was determined by the priorities established by the State Planning Committee and counterpart committees at lower governmental levels.

HISTORICAL BACKGROUND

Tsarist Education

Education developed in ancient Russia with the introduction of Christianity from Byzantium in the tenth century A.D. Although few schools existed before the sixteenth century, churches and monasteries accumulated libraries and became centers of learning, as in many other areas of medieval Europe. Early education was almost entirely religious in nature, and the language used was the Church-Slavonic rather than the vernacular of the people. Reading, writing, and arithmetic were incorporated into the curricula of the church schools, but for many centuries educational goals were concerned almost exclusively with the training of clergy rather than with popular education.

The period from Ivan the Great (1462—1500) to the Romanov succession (1613) was marked by a deep interest in culture and learning, although no extensive measures were taken to develop a system of education. Instead, the tsars went to great lengths to import from western nations professionals, such as physicians and engineers, at the same time stressing the values of secular education in the home, usually provided by imported private tutors.

During the reign of the first Romanov, Tsar Michael (1613—45), interest in cultural and intellectual pursuits grew. The government sent a group of students to English universities, and in 1631 the Russian Orthodox Church, in a continuing effort to counter the educational efforts of Roman Catholic Jesuits, opened the first Russian institution of higher learning.

In the latter part of the seventeenth century, additional educational institutions were established; however, they were either theological seminaries or religiously oriented secular schools that stressed religious teaching, philosophy, and theology. Most educational facilities were located in urban areas, and the great bulk of the population remained uneducated and illiterate.

The reign of Peter the Great (1682—1725) brought important changes in Russian education. Peter established the School of Mathematics and Navigation and the Engineering and Artillery School to train officers for his military forces. Patterned on western models, these schools improved Russian scientific and technological training. He also decreed the creation of mathematics schools in every province, and made attendance compulsory for gentry children from ten to fifteen years of age, but this reform failed to become a permanent feature of the country's educational system. Further educational reforms initiated by Peter the Great consisted of the establishment in Saint Petersburg (now Leningrad) of the Academy of Sciences, which contained a university and a secondary school.

The successors to Peter the Great continued his reformist educational policies. The University of Moscow, which brought liberal western educational philosophies and theories to Russia, was founded in 1755 (see ch. 16, Artistic Expression).

The reign of Catherine the Great during the latter half of the eighteenth century saw great strides in Russian education. Among the new educational institutions were the Smolny Institute in Moscow and the Yekaterinskiy Institute in Saint Petersburg, the first schools exclusively for women. A highlight of Catherine's reign was her great interest in the liberal educational policies of western Europe, especially of France. In 1782 she set up the Commission for the Establishment of Schools, which was given the responsibility for creating a public school system in the country. The schools that were established, however, were deficient in many aspects, and

Catherine became disenchanted with public education after several peasant uprisings and the French Revolution (see ch. 3, Historical Setting).

Alexander I (1801–25) made several educational changes early in his reign. Among these was the creation of a Ministry of Public Culture, Youth Education and Dissemination of Science, which was given control of most secular educational institutions in the country. This agency was charged with responsibility for creating a centralized educational system patterned after the system then current in France. Other changes were the establishment of the universities of Kharkov, Kazan, Odessa, and Saint Petersburg and the opening of the Pedagogical Institute (for training teachers), private schools, and a language institute. During the latter part of his reign, Alexander I strengthened the religious influence and training in schools.

Alexander's successor, Nicholas I, initiated a policy of educational repression. Largely because he considered the schools and their teaching primarily responsible for the growing democratic, anti-tsarist sentiments in the country, he prohibited peasants from attending secondary and higher schools, which were to be preserved for the middle and upper classes only. All universities were placed under state control, losing their autonomous status. University courses were carefully censored, and some were removed from the curriculum. The number of students in the universities was limited, and teachers were prohibited from traveling abroad.

To accommodate the growing demands for repeal of these repressive measures and to provide the proper atmosphere in which the country's growing intellectual ferment could flourish, Tsar Alexander II (1855–81) instituted the period of greatest reforms in Russian education. The limitations on the number of students who could attend universities were abolished, private schools were reopened; and secondary education for women was enlarged. Universities received their autonomy, more gymnasiums were established, and adult education for peasants was initiated. Throughout Alexander's reign, public interest in education was spurred by the growth of educational periodicals and other types of literature devoted to educational theories and problems.

The attempted assassination of Alexander in 1864 ended educational reform. From this time until his assassination universities were once again placed under state control; students and teachers were placed under strict police surveillance; all textbooks were censored, and teachers were forced to teach in an officially prescribed manner. Schools specializing in technical subjects were established for children of the lower classes, who were prohibited from attending universities. After the tsar's death, his successor, Alexander III, (1881–94), empowered the Ministry of Education to take charge of

278

university education, to appoint professors, and to repeal the rights of students. Since he heavily favored education for men, the educational opportunities for women were limited.

During the reign of the last tsar, Nicholas II (1894–1917) student riots and disturbances at the universities accompanied demands for greater educational freedom. Although some concessions were made, they were either not liberal enough or were made too late to quiet student agitation.

Some progress, however, was made in other aspects of education. Several new universities were established; women were granted the same educational privileges as men at all educational levels; greater educational opportunities were provided for lower class children; primary school attendance was made free and compulsory; and the number of students was increased considerably.

The continual fluctuation between periods of reform and repression was disruptive, and educational reform became one of the major goals of the revolutionaries. The literacy rate, which in 1917 was estimated to be as low as 25 percent, helped create the decisive social schism between the nobles, who formed a small percentage of the population, and the peasants, who constituted the majority. This schism reduced the effectiveness of the educational reforms of Nicholas II. Had they been implemented properly, many inequalities in the educational system might have been corrected. By 1917 the educational system was expanding, and it has been estimated that between 40 percent and 60 percent of all eligible children were attending some type of school.

Early Communist Reform and Reorganization

After the Communists seized power in 1917, education, viewed as the principal means of political indoctrination for the masses, underwent a series of experiments that left the educational system in confusion and disorganization (see ch. 26, Agitation and Propaganda). The Bolsheviks' aim was to simplify and intensify courses of study in order to foster both adult and child literacy. The training of technical manpower and the reorientation of the content of education to the principles and aims of the new socialist order were of paramount importance.

One of the first educational reforms was to replace the tsarist educational system with a new centralized administration, with the government having full and absolute control. Church control was abolished; all schools were placed under state control; and a new administrative structure was created. Structured in the form of a pyramid with the local councils at the bottom, Soviet education was directed from the top by the People's Commissariat of Education. By 1918 the educational system had been completely reorganized, universal compulsory education established, school fees abolished, and universities made semiautonomous.

The second major reform in education consisted of changes in curriculum. All courses considered unnecessary or bourgeois were replaced by subject matter consonant with the development of a socialist state. The study of the social sciences was revised to conform with the theories and principles of Marx and Lenin. The study of religion, Latin, and Greek was discontinued. All text materials were thoroughly examined, and new textbooks were written under the careful supervision of state officials to ensure proper ideological content.

The period from 1921 to 1930 was the time of greatest experimentation as educators strove to discover the system that would best achieve the aims of the revolution. It was during this decade that education became progressive: grades were abolished; pupils practically controlled their education; and discipline was minimal. Reaction against this system of progressive education intensified on the part of political leaders as well as the general public, which was angered at the excesses and ideological disdain of the students. Demands for reorganization and greater control became widespread.

After the experimentation and relative educational chaos of the 1920's, Communist Party authoritarianism began with Stalin's First Five-Year Plan (1928—33). The educational system established in the 1930's still existed in 1969 and reflected not only Communist centralism but also a return to some tsarist traditions in education. Progressive pedagogical methods were superseded by stern disciplinarian methods, and students were required to wear the school uniforms formerly worn by tsarist decree. National curricula were introduced and uniformity required for all schools. Students were taught discipline as well as obedience and loyalty to the group and the Soviet state. This abrupt change in the direction of Soviet education coincided with the rapid industrialization called for by the First Five-Year Plan. The level of productivity demanded in this plan made it imperative that schools be greatly improved and modernized to increase the supply of technically trained people necessary for the rapid development of the Soviet economy.

THE COMMUNIST EDUCATIONAL SYSTEM

Educational Policy

Communist educational policy evolved during the immediate postrevolutionary period, while the country, which had been devastated by war and revolution, was suffering the further ravages of a civil war. A critical shortage of teachers, facilities, and supplies, plus the uncertainty of the times, required that education and training concentrate only on the most essential concerns of the new regime. One of the ingredients considered essential was ideological orientation; therefore, the study of Marxism, Party history, and other political subjects were incorporated into the curricula. The goal of education became the creation of the "new Soviet man," and this particular aspect of Soviet education has not changed during the more than fifty years of the Communist era.

Specifically, Soviet education is based on two principles: schools must provide the literate and trained manpower needed to sustain the country as a modern socialist state, and all aspects of education must be under the direction of the Communist Party of the Soviet Union (CPSU). Implementation of these principles has taken many forms and has varied in intensity over the years. At times, emphasis has been placed on training qualified and competent manpower by encouraging the pursuit of learning in relative freedom and by making academic competence the basis for decisions in matters of admission, promotion, and selection of courses of study. Most of the time, however, emphasis has been on making education serve the socialist proletarian cause by giving ideological training precedence over subject matter and by emphasizing practical education through work, often at the expense of theoretical knowledge.

This so-called socialist education was designed to promote class consciousness and to encourage the continuing class struggle that would destroy old Russia and build the classless society. The reading materials and examples used in all courses up to those of university level include study of the political evils of the past. By contrasting these with its own achievements, the Communist government tries to develop dedication to its own aims and policies.

An integral part of socialist education is learning through labor. Its dual purpose is to eliminate the traditional distinction between scholarship and labor and to break down the traditional contempt of intellectuals for manual work and those who engage in it. All students were required to devote some time to physical work, which is considered as educational as book learning and essential to the formation of the "new Soviet man." Work-study schools became most prevalent in rural areas, where the need to employ all available manpower was an additional impetus for their creation.

Administration and Control of the School System

Formal governmental administration and control of education were outlined in the Constitution of 1936, and the network of centralized control of the 1960's has its basis in that document. The centralization is similar to that envisaged by educational reformers under the tsars but never fully realized until the Soviet era. The

Constitution provides for ministerial control of the educational system, but actual direction is provided by the Scientific and Educational Institutes Department of the Central Committee of the CPSU.

The USSR Ministry of Higher and Specialized Secondary Education and the USSR Ministry of Education are the two most prominent governmental organs directly involved in the educational system. The former is concerned with all higher education and various technical secondary schools. The latter coordinates all primary and regular secondary educational activities. These ministries operate through republic-level ministries that bear the same titles.

Other bodies concerned with education include the USSR Ministry of Culture and the All-Union Central Council of Trade Unions, both of which have counterpart agencies at lower governmental levels. As with other sectors of the Soviet structure, high-ranking officials in the educational system usually hold important Party positions in addition to their ministerial or academic posts.

Another national organization that exercises important influence on education is the USSR State Planning Committee (see ch. 19, Formal Structure of the Union Government). This body, which is part of the USSR Council of Ministers, influences the training and distribution of specialists in institutions of higher learning. The State Planning Committee is primarily concerned with the graduation of sufficient numbers of specialists necessary to meet the needs of the Soviet economy. In effect, it establishes the admission requirements for various specialties, or the student quota system, by directing the higher schools to admit only a precise number of students in each specialty.

This extensive planning, however, has not entirely eliminated the major manpower problems. Most planning has been based on immediate, rather than long-range, needs. Because of rapid industrialization and rapid technological progress, it has been difficult for planners to establish future priorities. For many years concentration has been on the training of engineers and other professional people, with inadequate attention given to the training of lower-level technical support personnel. According to Soviet educators, this aspect of training often has been too theoretical in nature, too time consuming, and too narrow in scope to satisfy the needs of a growing economy. Planners and educators alike have called for broader training of technicians to enable them to be employed in several related fields rather than in one field only.

At the republic level the ministries of education for each republic administer the primary and secondary educational institutions. The republic educational administration is further subdivided into province, district, and local school boards and committees. All republic bodies, however, are principally responsible for implementing the laws, regulations, and directives of the USSR Council of Ministers concerning curricula, methods of instruction, and texts. Republic bodies must also supervise the allocation of funds, the repair and construction of school buildings, the appointment and training of teachers, and the quality of instruction.

Overlapping the national and republic educational administration has been the extensive role played by the CPSU, which is not included within the official chain of control and administration. Laws and regulations on education originate in the CPSU Central Committee's Scientific and Educational Institutes Department and the Agitation and Propaganda Department (see ch. 26, Agitation and Propaganda). Party directives are given pro forma ratification by the USSR Council of Ministers and the USSR Supreme Soviet.

Not only does the CPSU initiate educational policy for the nation's schools, but it also executes it as well, thus ensuring the ideological conformity of all Soviet instruction. This executory role is fulfilled by school personnel and students who are at the same time Party members. Most administrators in the republic ministries of education, school directors, and teachers belong to the Party. In addition, the state publishing houses, responsible for the publication of textbooks for schools, are assisted by the Party to ensure the correct ideological line of the books. Members of the Komsomol (Young Communist League), which is controlled by the CPSU, constitute approximately 90 percent of the student population over fourteen years of age.

Aside from Party members who hold school positions, the Party also relies on the trade unions to control education, especially in the technical institutions. Trade unions actively participate in the choice and placement of teaching personnel, the determination of qualifications for new faculty members, and in the establishment of entrance requirements. In some instances, faculty appointments have been withheld because of an adverse report from the All-Union Central Council of Trade Unions.

The financing of the country's educational system is the responsibility of the USSR Council of Ministers. Generally, Soviet education has received generous appropriations from the state, which has provided all necessary support for school programs. Requests for funds are initiated with the individual educational institutions, through local governmental channels, and the requests are then authorized by the republic councils of ministers. Most higher educational institutions also receive additional funds from government ministries and local industry for contracted research, a source that reportedly accounts for almost half the annual budget of some institutions. In the 1966/67 school year the national government allocated 17.6 percent of its annual budget to education, which was approximately 9 percent to 10 percent of its gross national product (GNP), equivalent to R18,700 million (1 ruble equals US$1.10).

Preschool Education

Kindergartens and nursery schools are considered an important component of the school system. They serve educational aims by introducing the child at an early age to the ideas on which his thought processes should be based, and they serve economic needs by releasing women from child care and allowing them to engage in productive work. In most regions of the country, the development of preschool education is tied in with child welfare programs.

Nursery schools for children under three years of age are maintained primarily by collective farms and factories for the children of their female workers. Preschool children of nonemployees are not eligible to attend, and in 1969 only a small percentage of all preschool-age children attended nurseries. Since nurseries are concerned with the child's health, the staff consists of nurses and assistants, and a doctor is usually available.

Kindergartens have been established throughout the country for children between the ages of three and seven, but in 1969 there was still an insufficient number of such facilities. A system of priorities for admittance had to be established. First preference is given to children with two working parents, to those with one working parent and one dead parent, and to those of unmarried mothers. Children whose parents have a monthly income of less than R100, or who are from large families have next preference. In kindergarten the child is taught obedience and discipline; little attention is given to play or self-directed activities.

Primary Education

As of 1969 primary education in the Soviet Union consisted of four years of compulsory elementary schooling. The curriculum included Russian language or the native language, arithmetic, geography, history, and music. Ideological indoctrination is an important component of primary education, but political courses as such do not exist. Ideology is implanted through songs and slogans repeated daily, through examples used in language and history classes, and through participation in parades, demonstrations, and other extracurricular activities. Nearly all eligible children were enrolled in primary schools in the late 1960's.

In 1968 the traditional four-year course in primary education was reduced to three years, the fourth year being added to the secondary school, especially in the larger cities. This change, however,

284

encountered serious difficulties, and in late 1969 it was too early to determine whether the change would be incorporated into the entire educational system. The major criticisms were: the delay in issuing new textbooks to accommodate the change; the lack of preparation by teachers; the inadequacy of schools in rural areas for handling increased enrollments at the secondary level; and the shortage of boarding facilities in most secondary schools, caused by the additional students.

In primary schools, classes are usually forty-five minutes long and are separated by three breaks lasting ten minutes and one half-hour break. Teaching is by the rote method, consisting of constant repetition and drill, requiring memorization of the material. Discipline is considered the most important habit to be learned in the primary grades, and great effort, primarily of a psychological nature, is made to ensure that each student is conscious of order and obedience and loyalty to the school and to his class.

Students in primary grades learn the fundamentals of all the courses that they will study in more advanced form and greater detail in the secondary school (grades four to ten). Students are instructed in, and are expected to acquire basic familiarity with, the Russian language or their own native language and, in addition, a foreign language, arithmetic, natural sciences, geography, history, drawing, singing, handicrafts, and physical education. It is also expected that the children will learn and acquire those study habits deemed desirable by the authorities. If a child is found to be proficient in a particular area, such as drawing, music, ballet, or another field, arrangements will be made for training in a special school to develop that proficiency.

Secondary Education

Secondary schools build on the primary curriculum by adding courses in literature, history, mathematics, geography, physics, chemistry, biology, and foreign languages. It is also expected that graduates from secondary schools will have a good background of general knowledge and also will have acquired certain abilities. As of the 1966—67 period, according to Soviet sources, over 40 million students were enrolled in secondary schools representing 95 percent of all children in this age group.

The regular full-time secondary course lasted three or six years, depending on whether the student planned to continue into a program of higher education. Upon completion, diplomas were awarded only after final examinations and comprehensive state examinations were successfully passed.

Secondary education comprises regular secondary schools, technical or other specialized secondary schools, vocational training schools, and evening secondary schools offering a general education. The first-level secondary school was made compulsory in 1958, and by 1970 the upper three-year level is expected to be made compulsory throughout the country. Tuition fees have been abolished, but parents must pay for writing materials, textbooks, uniforms, and any boarding costs.

The regular secondary school offers some work training, either in industry or on farms, for fifty-four days a year. The technical or specialized secondary schools, which have certain admission requirements, provide regular training as well as specialized courses. These schools offer much theoretical training in addition to practical training. The vocational school, designed for students who want to go to work immediately after completing their secondary schooling, offers the student a one-, two-, or three-year part-time course directly related to his chosen field of employment. Vocational students receive apprentice wages. Evening or shift secondary schools provide a general education for full-time workers.

Class Lessons

Lectures in scheduled classes are the principal form of instruction. Classes are forty-five minutes long, with breaks of ten minutes after the first, third, and fourth lessons and a half-hour break after the second lesson. Grades five through seven have five hours of classes four days a week and six hours on two days. Grades eight through ten have five hours of classes three days a week and three days of six hours of classes.

In all Soviet secondary schools, classes largely follow formalized procedures. In each class the teacher reviews old material and introduces new material by elaboration, drill, and constant repetition. Each student is examined in class to determine if he has learned and understood the new material. Homework is explained and students are told how to complete it. Students are taught to listen, to learn, to accept without question what they read and are told, and to repeat what they have been assigned in a logical and correctly written form.

Discipline

The inculcation of discipline, which is considered the duty of both the state and the parents, is stressed in secondary schools. Discipline is used primarily to encourage conformity on the part of the children, and elaborate rules are published by the state for the benefit of parents in preparing their children for school. Children in Soviet schools are not subjected to corporal punishment, except in extreme cases. Verbal scolding also is rare and not approved by the state. The preferred method of punishment is to bring the errors and wrong actions of the child before an assembly of his classmates meeting at an afterschool session The ramifications of the child's error are brought out, and the correct behavior explained.

Curriculum

The curriculum followed by general secondary schools is formulated in detail by the Communist Party and the USSR Council of Ministers. Each course is provided with a detailed syllabus and outline, which indicates the exact material to be covered during the school year. No one is permitted to alter these instructions in any way. Courses covered in the secondary school comprise Russian and native language and literature, a foreign language, arithmetic and mathematics, natural science, geography, history, handicrafts and practical work, physical education and military training, physics, chemistry, astronomy, and the USSR Constitution.

Russian-language training in the secondary schools consists of spelling, grammar and punctuation, and reading some of the best literature. Students also study literary movements, and they must be able to critically analyze key works in these movements. The basic aim in teaching Russian is to give each student comprehension of the historical development of Russian literature and its significance in the society. Students must also grasp the meaning of theme, plot, characters, as well as language, and acquire an appreciation and respect for literature. Non-Russian students study their native language, and Russian is taught as a foreign language in addition to the foreign-language requirement.

Beginning in the first year of secondary education (grade five), each student is required to study one foreign language. He is expected to become fluent in the language; he must be able to read orally with correct pronunciation, understand the spoken foreign language, ask and answer questions, and translate written works in the foreign language with minimal use of a dictionary.

In secondary school students begin to study more complicated mathematics. Beginning with fractions, decimals, percentages, and proportions, they continue on to learn the use of slide rules and arithmometers and to study algebra, geometry, trigonometry, and calculus. Mathematics training is linked with the sciences, and students are given problems to complete that relate to the sciences.

Natural-science training is primarily designed so that students will develop the officially approved materialistic viewpoint of the world. Students learn about vegetation, animal and poultry breeding, botany, zoology, anatomy and physiology of man, hygiene and sex, principles of Darwinism, and general psychology. Aside from regular classrom instruction, students travel to collective and state farms and natural science museums; during summer vacations they are given projects in agriculture and animal husbandry.

The study of geography in the secondary schools acquaints students with physical geography, world geography, and geography of the Soviet Union. Each student must be able to identify geographic regions and nations and know the basics of economic geography, especially that of the Soviet Union, which concentrates on the country's economic development and its natural resources.

Secondary courses in history are calculated to familiarize students with the origin and development of social structures. Beginning with the ancient world, the courses continue in chronological order, culminating in modern world history, Russian history, and history of the Soviet Union. It is expected that students will know the major historical events and dates and the officially approved interpretation of these events. Specific topics taught in history courses include the development of human society, the inevitable victory of Communist society over the bourgeois-capitalist society, slavery and its disintegration, feudalism, and capitalism. Teachers are instructed to concentrate on the "struggles for liberation" that are presently occurring around the world.

Courses are also required in secondary schools in practical work or training. These courses are designed to familiarize students with basic production methods and the implements of building.

Physical and military training are also part of the secondary curriculum. Physical education is used to help students strengthen and develop through drills, gymnastics, and games, through which they acquire physical dexterity, habits of personal hygiene, and feelings of comradeship, courage, and discipline. Military training, which is not publicly mentioned, emphasizes drill practice, military tactics, regulations and courtesy, and instruction in weapons. Its inclusion in secondary school prepares male students for military service, shortens the period normally devoted to basic training, and creates an armed citizenry able to defend their country.

In grade six students begin a five-year course in physics, in which they study mechanics, hydrodynamics, heat, light, electricity, kinematics, dynamics and statics, molecular physics, optics, sound, and aerodynamics. Teaching is by demonstration, experimentation, laboratory work, lectures, and excursions.

Students study chemistry beginning in grade seven. The main concentration is on substances, elements, atomic-molecular structure, oxides, salts, the laws of weight preservation, oxygen, hydrogen, air, and water. Through demonstrations, experimentation, and class lecture, students are expected to be knowledgeable in the foundations of chemistry and to be able to apply chemical phenomena and laws to Soviet industry.

The course on the Constitution of the Soviet Union in grade ten teaches the country's governmental structure, the role of the Communist Party, and the constitutional rights of all Soviet citizens. Students are taught that the Soviet Union has attained the highest and purest form of democracy.

Grading and Examinations

In order to provide periodic assessments of each student's educational progress in secondary school, the state maintains a uniform system of both written and oral matriculation examinations, either in Russian or the student's native language; periodic quizzes; and quarterly subject examinations. The result of these examinations determine promotion into higher grades, possible entrance into an institution of higher learning, future position, and employment. During an oral examination, the student is tested and graded by a panel consisting of the teacher of the subject, a teacher of the same subject from a different school, the deputy director in charge of instruction, and the school director. The student is permitted twenty-five minutes to answer the questions. Homework assignments are another way of assessing the student's progress. It is estimated that approximately 10 percent of the students fail the examinations and must repeat them.

Supplemental Primary-Secondary Education

Aside from the general system of secondary education the state maintains an elaborate supplementary system, designed especially for those who are unable to, or who do not wish to, attend the regular schools. These supplemental schools comprise part-time schools, schools for illiterates and semi-illiterates, adult schools, correspondence schools, schools for working youth, evening and seasonal schools for rural youth, and schools for exceptional children.

Part-time education, defined by the government as education without interruption of production, is one of the major educational forms in the country and, in terms of numbers, it is the principal form. The vast majority of part-time students are full-time workers. Programs pursued are either general or technical and usually on a level equal to full-time study; part-time education consists of fewer hours per week and requires more years to complete than the regular day programs.

The years 1919 through 1929 mark the beginnings of Soviet part-time education. The Bolsheviks, realizing the critical need to raise the country's literacy rate in order to provide a sufficient supply of trained manpower, instituted massive state aid for part-time education and formed committees to do research in the field. In 1919 the

Soviets instituted the workers' school system to provide training for workers and peasants to prepare them for higher education. This system existed until 1939 and educated hundreds of thousands of students. Located in institutions of higher learning, the workers' schools gave students the opportunity to participate in accelerated day, evening and correspondence courses.

The government also established "radio universities" (standard courses broadcast daily) to provide training for workers and peasants, but this method was not accredited. In 1929 the government set up the workers' universities for students over eighteen years of age. Generally located in factories or on collective farms, these schools also provided correspondence courses.

By 1930 part-time education had grown considerably. Even though over 500,000 students were enrolled, state planners expanded part-time education even further, since the number of graduating trained specialists continued to fall below actual needs. A national network of correspondence institutes, primarily self-study, were opened, but later curriculum changes provided student-teacher consultation and criticism, regular classroom attendance, and some testing. The dropout rate for these schools, however, was high; it was estimated that 50 percent, sometimes more, failed to finish the courses.

Although part-time education is considered by the general public to have a lower status than regular day-time education, its growth and its importance in raising the educational level of the Soviet people cannot be underestimated. Since the 1940's the number of part-time schools increased more than five times. Enrollment in part-time courses tripled in the same period and comprised, by the school year 1966/67, over one-half of total school enrollments. In the area of graduate study, part-time education accounted for almost one-half the total graduate-school enrollment in the same school year.

Serious obstacles continued to hamper the government's efforts in the field of part-time education. The student dropout rate remained high, and graduating students were reported to be weak in the theories underlying their chosen specialties. The supply of textbooks, equipment, libraries, laboratories, and experienced teachers was inadequate, and students were unable to obtain necessary study aids and manuals.

On the other hand, part-time training continued to be favored by many Soviet students. It offered an opportunity for many students to fulfill educational objectives because costs were lower and no labor time was lost. Furthermore, full-time educational facilities were inadequate to meet the great demand for education.

Evening and seasonal schools, with regularly scheduled classes, are another form of part-time education. Designed for industrial and agricultural workers, these schools offer both the seven- and ten-year programs, although each takes an extra year. In the late 1960's an estimated 8 percent of the total number of all students were enrolled in this type of institution. The evening and seasonal school is established in places where industrial and agricultural workers live or work, such as factories, collective farms, and construction sites.

The study load for part-time students is heavy. Each student is required to attend five class periods each week. Subjects are prescribed by the government, and there are no elective courses. Each student must undergo consultations or tutoring if the instructor finds that such are necessary. In the non-Russian areas of the country, there is a heavy amount of study devoted to the Russian language. Because the students have regular full-time employment, the study load seems heavy, and in the 1960's the Soviet press was highly critical of the burdens placed on part-time students.

A part-time student's failure to abide by state-established regulations results in his dismissal with notice to his employer. Each student must attend classes regularly and fullfill all the requirements laid down by the school and teachers. Missing classes without appropriate excuses or careless studies may occasion his dismissal.

Special Education

A later development in the country's educational system has been the introduction of special-education schools for the physically handicapped, such as the mentally retarded, the blind or partially blind, and the deaf or hard of hearing and for the exceptionally bright, and the artistically gifted. Each school normally has 200 students, with about sixteen students per class. In the school year 1966/67, total enrollment in these special-education schools was estimated at about 1 million.

Special schools for the mentally retarded or educationally backward were established to enable such children to obtain a general or vocational education to the utmost of their abilities, to correct speech defects, to ensure good health, and to help them become self-reliant. In order to be admitted to such a school, each child must be thoroughly examined by a commission of doctors and found capable of learning. If it happens that the child, once admitted, is unable to master the course or if he shows no improvement after three years, he is either placed in a special home or returned to his parents. There is no tuition, but parents are expected to contribute to the student's room and board according to their means.

Schools for the blind or those with partial sight have also been established. An eye specialist gives each applicant a thorough examination, and an admissions commission composed of a doctor from a regular school, an inspector, the director and two teachers from the special school, and another eye specialist carefully review each application. The curriculum in these schools is eleven years and covers the material of the regular ten-year school. Each child is also provided with vocational training in the event that he does not plan to go on to higher education.

Children eligible to attend the special schools for the deaf include deaf-mutes, mentally retarded deaf-mutes, those whose deafness resulted from congenital causes but who can speak, those hard of hearing who have speech difficulties, and those children who became deaf or hard of hearing after birth. Such schools exist primarily in the large cities and serve the surrounding areas. Most classes are preparatory and last for eight years; few finish the ten-year school curriculum. Deaf children can go on to higher education without the usual entrance examinations, if they have shown a marked ability.

Children who are physically handicapped or who suffer from delicate health and illness are eligible to attend special sanatoriums, where they receive medical attention in addition to continuing their general studies. Although most of these schools are administered by the government, some are operated by factories or collective farms. Usually located on small farms near forest areas, they give children access to orchards, vegetable gardens, healthful climates, and nourishing food. The curriculum is shorter than the regular one: classes are shorter, and fresh air, correct diet, sleep and rest, artistic and creative self-expression, and nature studies are stressed. Children remain until they are rehabilitated or until they are seventeen or eighteen years old.

Schools for the exceptionally bright also exist. Such children are students in a regular school who have been observed by the teacher to have advanced ability. The student is then placed in a special study class under the jurisdiction of a university. Classes are small, and the students work directly under university professors and instructors, who provide them with the necessary tutoring. Children in these schools have access to all university facilities such as libraries and laboratories. When the child finishes his secondary education, he is autonomically eligible for admission to higher education.

Under the administration of the Ministry of Culture, the state also maintains a few schools of art, ballet, and music for the artistically gifted. Generally located in large cities, they are designed both to develop the natural ability and aptitude the child has shown and also to provide general education. Students receive the best possible professional advice and training, and Soviet citizens as well as authorities are proud of their special schools (see ch. 16, Artistic Expression).

Admission requires that the student demonstrate a remarkable ability or talent in a special aptitude examination. It takes the student eleven years to finish the ten-year study program, and much of his time is consumed with practice. If, after three years, his early promise has not continued, he will then be sent to another, lesser school to learn a related trade. On the other hand, those students who live up to their early promise can continue their training in this special school and after completing the secondary program, will be eligible for admission into an advanced institution.

To provide free care and education for war orphans of military personnel and to train future officers of the armed services, the state established military boarding schools during World War II. Several special cadet secondary schools exist in the Soviet Union. These are the Suvorov military schools and the Nakhimov naval schools, which usually enroll between 150 and 500 students. These offer the regular, general school curriculum, but it is supplemented by a heavy load of mathematics, military training, and physical education. School schedules are operated with strict military efficiency and discipline. Both military officers and civilians teach in these schools, and each teacher supervises the education and extracurricular and extrascholastic activities of a group of twenty-five boys, on each of whom he keeps a detailed dossier of skills, activities, and attitudes. Most Suvorov and Nakhimov graduates go on to higher military institutions (see ch. 28, The Armed Forces).

Vocational Training

The system of vocational training is distinct from the general and part-time educational systems in the country, and government leaders have stressed its importance. Vocational training was viewed principally as the solution to the short supply of skilled and unskilled manpower that had hampered the country's growth. The government maintains vocational training institutions for industry and agriculture.

Industrial Vocational Training

There were four types of industrial vocational training available to Soviet students in 1969: the elementary vocational school, the one- and two-year training program in specialized trades for secondary-school graduates, schools that offer a variety of vocational courses of from three months' to two years' duration, and on-the-job vocational training programs available in factories.

The first type of vocational training is the basic, or elementary, vocational school. Students under twenty-two years of age are eligible to enroll in one of the four elementary programs designed to produce semiskilled and skilled workers with a minimum of formal education. Located within factories, schools offer one- to one-and-half year courses in light industrial skills. Other schools train apprentices between the ages of sixteen and nineteen to be semiskilled workers for basic industries. Courses are generally from six to twelve months in duration. Two-year trade schools train young people between fourteen and seventeen years of age for a variety of jobs in water transportation, communications, and in the metallurgical, chemical, mining, and petroleum sectors of the economy. Special railroad schools train workers for jobs as mechanics, bookkeepers, traffic controllers, and many other railroad positions.

Vocational technical schools, the second form of vocational education, provide training in over 200 occupations in at least ten major industries. Any secondary school graduate between eighteen and twenty-five years of age is eligible for admission. There are no tuition fees, and most students receive governmental grants to cover living expenses. The usual period of instruction is generally one year, but a few programs require an additional year. The teaching staff is recruited from factory workers who have demonstrated marked abilities in their work and as instructors.

The third type of industrial vocational training is the school operated by employers to train new personnel in trades and services. No previous educational attainments are required to participate in these courses, which last from three months to two years.

The fourth form of industrial vocational training is on-the-job training, for new workers, for retraining older workers to keep them informed about modern production methods, and for providing advanced training for workers with special abilities. The training program for new employees, called the "individual-brigade," demonstrates a plant's production methods to new employees and lasts three to six months, promoting those who do well on the final examination. Advanced on-the-job training for exceptional workers consists of a two- to three-year training period, ending in the student's submission of an individual research project related to his specialty.

Agricultural Vocational Training

In 1969 the government supported a variety of institutions that provided vocational training in agriculture. Farmers and future farmers were able to study farm management, introductory farming, courses in agronomy, animal husbandry, farm machinery, and other technical subjects. Study programs usually last one, two, or three years, depending on the student's specialty. Students are expected to relate their classroom instruction with practical problems in their employment. They also are expected to work in an agriculture enterprise during school vacations. During the period of

294

study, students generally receive monthly living stipends, in addition to free tuition, textbooks, and laboratory material.

Teachers

Traditionally, teachers occupied an important position in Russian society and were held in high esteem. Under the egalitarian principles of the Communist government, which has stressed the importance of education for all people, this special position has continued and, in 1969, was even stronger. Teachers in public schools are government servants with the same rights and privileges as any other government servants, and salaries are based on the extent of education and experience. In the school year 1966/67 there were reported more than 2.5 million teachers and about 500,000 graduates from teaching schools.

Teacher Training

The state operates a three-level system of teacher training; the level for each prospective teacher depends on the grade he has chosen to teach. For training primary-grade teachers, two-year pedagogical schools are available for graduates of a secondary school. For teachers of grades five to seven, two-year pedagogical institutes have been established, but the student, after graduation, is expected to study at night to complete the regular four-year program. For teachers of grades eight to ten, four-year programs at special teacher-training institutes was the rule.

Teacher-training institutes are administered and controlled by the republic ministries of education, although the establishment of academic standards rests with the All-Union Ministry of Higher Education, specifically its Directorate of Pedagogical Institutions. Teachers spend a majority of their study time on their chosen specialty and, at the same time, carry a heavy load of Communist theory and practice-teaching (both during the regular school year and in the summers). Full-time teachers can increase their qualifications through part-time study with correspondence or evening schools. Teachers graduating from the university-level school at the top of their class may pursue graduate studies in the pedagogical sciences.

Appointment and Dismissal

For the first three years after graduation, the new teacher is sent to a school that has a vacancy in his field. After this obligatory period, he is given full choice as to where he wishes to teach, or he may chose not to teach. Teaching appointments are generally permanent, although they can be withdrawn on the basis of an adverse report by the Communist Party. Aside from his regular salary, the teacher receives remuneration for doing various extra tasks. The regular salary he receives is based on how long he has taught, his level of education, the grade and subject he is teaching, and the place in which he is teaching.

Higher Education

Higher education has been of particular concern to Soviet leaders. The inherent conflict, however, between the two cardinal aims of Communist educational policy—the need to produce well-educated and highly skilled manpower and the demand that politics take precedence over all else—has subjected higher education to continual changes in orientation that have had serious repercussions on the quality of education.

Since 1917 higher education has grown considerably in the numbers of students and institutions. In tsarist Russia there were only 13 universities with a total enrollment of 43,000. As higher education was preserved for the middle and upper classes, few peasants had access to it. In 1967 over 4 million students were enrolled at 3,980 technical colleges, and 767 universities and higher institutes. The country's 40 universities had an enrollment totaling more than 500,000. Two types of higher educational institutions exists: the regular university, which concentrated on the theories underlying the sciences and the humanities, and the specialized higher educational institution, concentrating on specific applied disciplines.

Moscow University, founded in 1755, is the largest higher educational institution and research center in the country; it has 13 faculties, 233 departments, 4 research institutes, 250 laboratories, 163 study rooms, 8 research training stations, 3 museums, 4 astronomical observatories, and a botanical garden. Over 32,000 students are taught by 3,700 professors and instructors, 400 of whom have doctorates and over 1,500 of whom hold master's degrees. Of the total number of students, more than half are enrolled in evening and correspondence divisions, and there are over 2,000 graduate students.

The importance of specialized, technical higher training is seen in the proportion of students enrolled in technical subjects and in the number of such institutions. In the school year 1960/61, 49 percent of all students were engaged in engineering specialties, and by school year 1967/68 the proportion had increased to over 50 percent. It has been estimated that between 85 percent and 90 percent of students are enrolled in scientific and specialized pursuits, and only 8 percent to 10 percent are enrolled in regular universities. Over 70 percent of Soviet higher educational institutes are devoted to industry, agriculture, and economics. In the mid-1960's women constituted 43 percent of all students enrolled in institutes of higher education.

A further breakdown of Soviet higher education shows that 48 institutions provide higher learning in the arts for almost 30,000 students. There are 22 music conservatories, 12 theatrical and stage designer schools, several art academies and art colleges, institutes of decorative and applied arts, industrial arts schools, literary institutes, and an institute of cinematography and a college of architecture.

The higher educational course usually lasts five years and leads to the "candidate" degree, considered to be between a master's degree and a doctorate. To receive the candidate degree, the student must take extensive examinations in his major field of study and must prepare a research paper of from 100 to 125 pages in length, approved by a special academic committee and the State Examination Committee. Approved diploma projects are often published in scientific and other journals.

Admission requirements are set by the state, including the State Planning Committee. The applicant must have completed the ten-year academic school and have received his diploma or certificate of merit. He must also have passed the highly competitive examinations and have completed the required two-year period of full-time employment, or be legally exempt from such requirement.

Tuition costs and living expenses for most students in higher institutions are primarily borne by either the state or by an industrial enterprise or collective farm. Students receive many additional benefits to help them obtain their education, such as no fees for lectures, laboratories and library; free textbooks, study aids, and literature of all types; and free sports facilities and equipment. Dormitories, hostels, and eating places, subsidized by the state, are maintained at low cost to the student. Students also receive free medical services and treatment and free passes to rest homes and to winter and summer resorts.

The government gives each qualified student a minimum stipend to cover higher training. Students who have received lower grades on the entrance examinations may have to pay most of their training costs without such aid. On the other hand, if one does well on periodical examinations, the state stipend is increased. Students are also urged to work during their vacations in factories or agricultural enterprises.

The required curriculum for institutions consists mostly of course work in a specialized area. Whether a student will ultimately pursue that particular study, however, depends on state needs as determined by the planners. Additional requirements are one foreign language and three courses in Communist indoctrination: history of the Communist Party of the Soviet Union, political economy, and historical materialism. The indoctrination courses form approximately 15 percent of the curriculum.

In recent years the major curriculum change has been the introduction of production practice and training as a supplement to the regular study load. This on-the-job training usually takes place in the last semesters of the student's program, and only a small percentage of time is devoted to course work. In 1969 this work-study program was in a state of flux and experimentation, since many problems had been noted and criticism of the program came from employers and students alike.

Teaching personnel in higher educational institutions consisted of professors, lecturers, and lecture assistants. The position of professor is filled by the appointing staffs of the various institutions, but with the approval of the state attestation boards. Lecturers hold the title of assistant professor in the institution, and the lecture assistant is the instructor. In the 1960's there were over 150,000 educators in the country, and 65 percent of them held advanced degrees. Each lecturer must have a license from the state to lecture, and lecture assistants must, in addition, demonstrate their capabilities before a student and professorial board. Lecture licenses are renewable each year, and there is no assurance of renewal, since all positions are filled on a competitive basis each year.

The undergraduate life of students is subject to close regimentation, which educators feel is necessary in order to achieve the planned results. Relations between students and teachers are informal and friendly, with a spirit of unity in seminars and respect on the students' part for their teachers. On the other hand, there has been frequent criticism that the first two years of undergraduate study are overlectured with too much note taking and too many progress examinations.

Postgraduate Training

Graduate training and study, either on a full-time basis or by correspondence, is another important facet of Soviet higher education. Two advanced degrees are awarded: the candidate of science and the doctor of science. The graduate study leading to the candidate degree comprises three years of work, training, and research, passing state examinations, and a dissertation of suitable merit, which is published. The study program is individualized. Graduate study is available at all higher institutions, government ministries, republic academies of science, and other specialized academies. Graduate programs must be related to some practical work and associated with scientific or industrial research projects, and each student's work is intended to support the overall research program of a higher school or scientific institution.

298

The doctor of science degree has been abolished as the culmination of a prescribed study program. In 1969 it was awarded only to a select number of individuals who were considered to be outstanding in a particular field or who had made original contributions in a specialized area. It can be awarded for past achievements or for a properly defended dissertation.

Professional Training

Medical training, technical training, and engineering-technical training require longer periods of study than the regular university program. A medical degree is awarded after completing six years of work (the last three being devoted to clinical internship) and the presentation of a dissertation. During his last two summers, the medical student works outside the university in practical medical work.

Technical training normally lasts for five years and ten months. The first two years are generally devoted to production training aside from the regular course work; the middle years, devoted exclusively to study; and the end of the studies, to full-time employment in industry.

For engineering students, the study program lasts five years and four months, in order to provide the student with the opportunity to devote more time to practical training seminars and course projects.

Foreign Students

In recent years, in line with the country's foreign policy, the opportunities for students from economically underdeveloped countries to study in the Soviet Union have increased greatly (see ch. 24, Foreign Relations). In 1969 there were over 20,000 students from 116 nations pursuing educational programs in the Soviet Union. Before a foreign student is officially admitted to a program of higher education, he must undergo training in the Russian language or completion of the secondary educational program. Foreign students can pursue courses in engineering, agriculture, medicine, physics, mathematics, natural science, history, philology, economics, and law. Friendship University in Moscow is the largest educational institution in the country devoted exclusively to foreign students. Over 3,700 students from 83 are enrolled; they are of both sexes, are under 25 years of age, and pursue four-year programs. The study of medicine, however, requires six years. Education for the foreign student is free of charge: from the Soviet government he receives living accommodations, a monthly grant to cover his living expenses, medical care, winter clothing, textbooks, and study aids.

Distribution of Schools

The number of children in rural areas of the country pursuing education was nearly less than half that of the total number of students enrolled in urban schools, despite the fact that rural children represented almost one-half the total number of children in the school-age group. Moreover there has been much criticism concerning the condition of rural education. Most critics point out that the recent school-expansion programs had tended to concentrate in urban areas, to the detriment of the rural schools, which lack science rooms, sufficient space, and enough teachers. According to press reports, the authorities plan to reorganize the school system to achieve parity between urban and rural schools and to send more personnel and staff into rural areas.

Textbooks

Textbooks are uniform throughout the country on all educational levels. This is consonant with avowed Soviet policy to maintain a uniform national educational system and to ensure the proper ideological content and the proper definition and exposition of Communist ideals to Soviet youth. Textbooks are approved by, and produced under the auspices of, the Communist Party and the Ministry of Education ensuring all-union uniformity. The State Publishing House for Teaching and Pedagogical Materials publishes all editions of books in the country for national distribution, it also prepares the approved translations of the textbooks into the various national languages.

Textbooks are constantly being revised, reflecting the constant change that occurs in the educational system. Although many currently used textbooks appear to be of poor quality, with cheap paper, they are not old, and the production standard and quality are rising. The revision of textbooks requires the services of a large number of experts in the particular subject, and a new book is tested in actual use in selected schools and changed before final release to incorporate the needs and suggestions of the teachers.

Each year the State Publishing House prepares a list of available textbooks. According to Soviet law, each school is required to select its books from this list and order them through the republic education ministries. The students purchase the textbooks at nominal cost and generally resell them at the end of the year.

Various criticisms have been made about the textbooks. The major criticism is that the study material has been limited to provide more space for political indoctrination. Other criticisms are directed against their publication. The publishing houses often print too many copies of one book, and the text becomes outdated before its supply is exhausted. Distribution remained poor, and not enough students acquire the books. Most Soviet textbooks, however, provide the most current information on any subject.

EDUCATION AND SOCIETY

Apart from the goal of mass literacy, official Soviet interest in educational content has always been that it develop loyalty to the government and to Communist ideals. The creation of the "new Soviet man" has been the ultimate goal; however, Soviet authorities have realistically developed programs of education that would fulfill the needs of a powerful, modern nation. Only rarely has dogma interfered with the pursuit of knowledge, as in the case of the biological sciences (see ch. 18, Science and Technology). Loyalty to the cause is an objective, but the operation of a huge, complex state in which everything is run by the state requires hard skills and advanced knowledge. The Soviet educational system is designed to fill all the needs of the country; indoctrination has a place in that system but does not supplant the system itself.

The government is making special efforts to promote national unity. Training in the Russian language is required in all schools, although the medium of instruction is the native language. Group sports and other group activities are included to promote physical health and the spirit of group cooperation.

The emphasis on patriotism is apparent in the curriculum itself and in the other school activities. The classes in Russian and Soviet history, for example, stress the roles of the country's heroes and sometimes the roles of the present leaders. In the civic courses, pupils learn about the nature of the government and their responsibilities to school, family, society, Party, and the government. In the course on morality, the student is taught Communist ethics. In the 1960's increased emphasis was placed on Russian, including tsarist, culture (see ch. 16, Artistic Expression).

Extracurricular Activities

Soviet education does not end in the classroom; it extends into a broad pattern of extracurricular activities designed for all students, for whom participation is an obligation. Extracurricular activities are heavily oriented toward ideological indoctrination but also encompass a wide range of nonpolitical affairs. The majority of these activities are run by the individual republic education ministries and financed by the state. Some, however, receive financial support from trade unions, although they are still under state control. In 1966 the post of organizer of extracurricular activities, equal to an assistant director, was created in the secondary schools.

From the fifth grade on, children are required to participate in

301

one or two so-called circles, each of which is devoted to one subject matter, is headed by a teacher, and meets once or twice a week after regular classes. Membership is according to each child's preference. The circle stresses learning and participation in such subjects as technology, natural sciences, physical culture and sports activities, history, and art. The work of these circles is publicly scrutinized by periodic inspections.

Secondary clubs, directed by the school director and an executive board composed of students and teachers, meet three or four times a week and hold various competitions open to the public in such fields as mathematics, astronomy, and sports. These clubs also organize excursions and field trips for members.

Children's Central Stations, under the jurisdiction of the Central Children's Technical Station in Moscow, founded in 1926, are established throughout the country. Technically oriented, they give students an opportunity to conduct various experiments in biology and agriculture. Membership is estimated at over 250,000.

Children's excursion-tourist stations provide an opportunity for students to travel about the country to study the natural resources and economic and cultural aspects of the various regions. Children's Railways permit members to learn all aspects of railroading including actual operation. Children's Sports Schools and Stadiums provide games and athletic contests for 10 million youths between the ages of ten and sixteen. More than 6,000 children's libraries provide books, reading rooms, and over 125 children's newspapers. All extracurricular activities, from primary school through university level, are closely interrelated with the three major youth organizations: the Little Octobrists, the Pioneers, and the Komsomol (Young Communist League) (see ch. 21, Political Dynamics).

Informal Education

In addition to maintaining institutions where working adults can pursue part-time educational programs for credit, the country has also established an elaborate system of informal, noncredit education throughout the nation. Primarily designed for those who do not wish to engage in formal education, it consists of clubs, palaces of culture, and people's universities, in addition to libraries and publishing houses.

Palaces of culture, usually closely associated with a factory or other enterprise, provide a broad range of social, artistic, technical, recreational, and hobby activities. The main purpose of these establishments is to continue the process of political indoctrination. They also stress the nation's achievements in science and technology through lectures, exhibits, and other means.

The people's universities were first opened in 1960. All workers are eligible to attend; the program consists of lectures held two or three times a month for one to three years, in such subjects as art, literature, cinema, theater, music, technology, agriculture, health and hygiene, education, and law. By 1967 over 6,500 peoples' universities had been established, with close to 1 million enrollees. The universities are operated chiefly by academic councils associated with the republic trade union councils and the All-Union Central Council of Trade Unions, which controls the universities. Teachers must be specialists in their field.

CHAPTER 16

ARTISTIC EXPRESSION

The people of the Soviet Union regard themselves as exceptionally endowed for the creative arts, especially dance, literature, music, and the theater. This is particularly true of the Russians, but applies also to several other Soviet nationalities that have long, rich, cultural traditions. The people are proud and appreciative of their world-famous writers, composers, musicians, and ballet and theatrical performers. They spend much of their leisure time reading, listening to recordings, or attending concerts and the legitimate or motion picture theater. The frequency of attendance and the increasing numbers of concert halls, theaters, and museums, as well as the numerous amateur dramatic clubs and literary discussion groups, attest to the demand for cultural activities. Students pay only nominal fees to attend concerts, plays, and ballet performances and are encouraged to spend time in such cultural pursuits.

The Soviet government publicizes with pride the great number of book titles that are published annually. Propaganda is plentiful on Soviet bookshelves, but good literature is also available in quantity and at reasonable prices. Increasingly during the 1960's, approved foreign authors have been published, but the greatest popularity is reserved for the Russian literary giants of the nineteenth century. The government does not permit the publication of pornography or of other material that would be considered in poor taste. Since publishing is a government monopoly, such material does not appear except in illegal private publications.

The Russian contribution to literature, music, and the arts is vast. In literature the names of Leo Tolstoy and Feodor Dostoevsky stand as hallmarks of creativity and vision. In music Tchaikovsky, Rimsky-Korsakov and, more recently, Stravinsky and Shostakovich have left an indelible mark. Ballet, with Pavlova and Ulanova in the past and Plisetskaya and other great ballerinas in the 1960's, has almost become a Muscovite preserve. The plays of Anton Chekhov and the "inner realism" direction of Konstantin Stanislavsky brought originality and inventiveness to the Russian stage. The name of Sergei Eisenstein will be prominent in any history of motion pictures because of his creativity and initiative in the early days of the art.

In the 1960's the Soviet Union stood at a crossroads in its pursuit of artistic achievement. One direction followed the traditions of greatness and creativity, while another stagnated in hack work produced for the furtherance of ideological goals. *Doctor Zhivago*, a Russian work published abroad in 1957 and acclaimed by critics around the world, was ignored at home until its author, Boris Pasternak, was awarded the Nobel Prize for Literature. With such acclaim the book could no longer be ignored but, because it was considered politically unsound, Pasternak was vilified and forced to refuse the Nobel award. He later "confessed" and apologized in a public letter to Premier Nikita Khrushchev. As of mid-1969 *Doctor Zhivago* had not been published within the Soviet Union.

During the 1960's there was increasing ferment in Soviet artistic circles as artists struggled against ideological controls that, they claimed, had stifled Soviet creativity. A literary floodgate was opened for a while with the publication of Aleksandr Solzhenitsyn's novel, *One Day in the Life of Ivan Denisovich*. This work was serialized in a popular Soviet literary magazine with the apparent approval of Nikita Khrushchev, who was then at the peak of his power in government and Party affairs in the Soviet Union.

Solzhenitsyn's novel described the horrors of Stalin's labor camps—a topic never before allowed in Soviet publications. Whether or not the permission to publish was motivated by Khrushchev's de-Stalinization campaign, the result was electrifying. The Soviet people were astounded to see such material in print, and Soviet authors rushed to emulate Solzhenitsyn with works on similar themes. Poets and writers took advantage of the apparent thaw in political attitudes to rush into print with poems, articles, and books of a similar nature.

The thaw was relatively short lived, since the Communist regime reprimanded several authors whose works had evidently gone beyond the bounds of Marxist-Leninist propriety. In a trial that brought worldwide attention in 1965, Yuli Daniel and Andrei Sinyavsky were charged with publishing anti-Soviet works abroad, and both were given severe sentences. The case of Daniel and Sinyavsky did not disappear with the imprisonment of the two authors. Dissent, albeit on a small scale, became commonplace in the Soviet Union. Other trials followed quickly as the Soviet government took steps against the dissidents who openly demonstrated and petitioned the government for release of the imprisoned authors. In July 1969 Anatoly Kuznetsov, Soviet author and Communist Party member, requested political asylum while on a visit to London. Kuznetsov claimed that he could no longer live and write under the restrictions imposed on authors in his homeland (see ch. 17, Intellectual Expression).

The Soviet leadership utilizes the arts for such political objectives as to control and indoctrinate its own people and to influence foreign populations in favor of the Communist ideal as exemplified by the Soviet Union. The Bolshevik revolutionaries spoke of their support of personal liberties and artistic freedom before their seizure of power. Once in control, however, they changed their position from one of freedom to express individual views and ideas to that of the expression of views and ideas conforming to official Marxist-Leninist teaching. To be approved, art must be useful to the attainment of the objectives of the Communist Party. All major cultural decisions are, of course, made only by the Party apparatus.

Nothing may be published in the Soviet Union unless it bears the stamp of approval of the official censoring organization known as Glavlit. Apart from censorship, the Party can bring its influence to bear on publishing houses, which are run either directly by government agencies or by quasi-governmental agencies, such as the Writers Union or the Academy of Sciences.

Approved authors, composers, screenwriters, playwrights, and performing artists include the richest members of the Soviet elite. The most successful of them receive royalties that permit them to live in great comfort. Among these have been Maxim Gorky, Vladimir Mayakovsky, Mikhail Sholokhov, and Aleksei Tolstoy. By contrast, writers and poets who have expressed themselves without regard for the political consequences have been severely treated by the Soviet authorities and often have difficulty making a living.

Undoubtedly some Soviet artists paint abstracts, some Soviet musicians abandon approved forms for wide experimentation, some authors write "stream of consciousness" novels, but such avant-garde art is not seen by the public—it must remain strictly private to avoid censure. Toward the end of the 1960's, there was no indication that the Communist regime was ready or willing to give up its control of artistic expression in the Soviet Union.

ARCHITECTURE

With the exception of a period of "Stalinist architecture," during which several ornate skyscrapers were constructed in Moscow, most Soviet building since the revolution has been utilitarian. Its emphasis has been upon function and rational planning with a style characterized by almost complete lack of decoration. Factories, workers' flats, and sanatoriums that were singled out for special favor were granted good plans and material. City planning for Moscow, the rebuilding of Stalingrad, and construction of new towns in Siberia and central Asia, according to Western architects, has been excellent, following the traditional European symmetrical method of laying out buildings and streets. But the chief drawbacks remain. They are the shoddiness and shabbiness of workmanship and materials combined with an established pattern of standardizing inferior housing models to fulfill quotas.

Early in 1968 Soviet Deputy Premier Vladimir Novikov complained about the current state of his country's mass production of architecture, describing it as "monotonous and unsatisfying." He warned against "skyscraper mania." Soviet architects have complained that for years they have been excluded from creative work on individual projects. Local authorities have objected to over-centralization and complained that they did not even have the right to select architectural designs suitable for their own climatic or geographical conditions.

Significant Russian architecture dates back to the early eleventh century. Kiev, the leading East Slav principality of the period, was christianized late in the tenth century and, along with Byzantine Christianity, adopted the Byzantine style in architecture. The style, mainly confined to ecclesiastical construction in Russia, was marked by the simple logical clarity of an interior space covered with at least one central dome shape. This imported imperial art was modified by the popular art of the early Russians that reflected their fondness for bright colors and a need to adapt to the rigors of the northern continental climate.

The Saint Sophia Cathedral of Kiev (1017—47) with its thirteen cupolas rivaled the Great Saint Sophia of Justinian in Constantinople. The Kiev structure was remarkable for the simplicity of its exterior and the magnificence of its interior decoration. The Saint Sophia Cathedral still stands with some of its interior recognizable as the original eleventh-century structure despite numerous additions and modifications through the ages. Since the Bolshevik Revolution, the cathedral has been used as a state museum.

During the same period, Novgorod, a principality in the northwest, maintained more versatile architectural traditions. Novgorodian builders combined European, Byzantine, native Russian, and early Scandinavian influences. Churches, although more numerous than those at Kiev, were of more modest proportions. The Novgorod Saint Sophia, in addition to being smaller, also shows much more Russian modification of the Byzantine form.

The northeastern principality of Vladimir-Suzdal was the third great center that cradled Russian architecture which, in addition to native Russian and Byzantine influences, became strongly tinged by Eastern styles, both originating in and coming by way of the Caucasus. The city was known for its magnificent churches, such as the Cathedral of the Dormition, and, despite borrowings from other cultures, the architecture of ancient Vladimir-Suzdal was unmistakably Russian.

The Mongol-Tatar occupation arrested the development of Russian architecture. Only Moscow, a principality dating back to the middle of the twelfth century, managed to thrive in the oppressive atmosphere of foreign domination. From the late fourteenth century, Moscow was the leading Russian duchy. Developing amid thick forests, Muscovite architecture depended more on wood and less on stone construction. The geometric clarity of the previous age, based on masonry, gave way to the traditional yet flexible possibilities of wood.

Muscovite architecture soon developed away from the religious motifs that had dominated Russian efforts in earlier centuries. It moved in the direction of the essentially simple and functional. The use of stone first appeared late in the fourteenth century. Finally, after the independence of Moscow in 1480, the wooden walls of the Kremlin, inner citadel of Muscovite sovereignty, were rebuilt with red brick and completed in 1516.

In the fifteenth and sixteenth centuries tsars Ivan III and Ivan IV depended on Italian Renaissance architects to plan many of the palaces, churches, and towers of the Kremlin. Italian contributions resulted in a melange of Russian color, Byzantine pomp, and Renaissance magnificence that made the Kremlin and Red Square memorable architectural sites.

Russian architecture of the eighteenth century began a new era with the founding of Saint Petersburg (Leningrad) by Peter the Great in 1703. The enormous personal energy of Peter, shown in his drive to transform Russia into a European power, was as evident in art and architecture as it was in every other aspect of Russian life (see ch. 3, Historical Setting). Peter imported architects from all over western Europe to plan and build his new capital and to make it a distinctively European city. French, Dutch, German, and Italian architects brought styles then prevalent in their own countries, but these styles were soon transformed to embody a native Russian taste and aesthetic sense.

The long reigns of Elizabeth I and Catherine the Great during the eighteenth century witnessed a continuation of the architectural surge begun by Peter the Great. Importation of many European architects continued, but Russian names such as Andrei Zakharov (Admiralty Building in Saint Petersburg) and Ivan Starov (Tauride Palace, Saint Petersburg) should be added because of their outstanding contributions.

The mixed Russian and western European style of architecture continued through the reigns of Alexander I (1799—1825) and Nicholas I (1825—55). Both spent money on a grand scale to continue the work begun by Peter the Great. In the process, Saint Petersburg grew into a city that was acclaimed by artists and architects as one of the most beautiful in the world.

Moscow architecture had not kept pace with that of the new capital city in quantity or grandness. Construction in Moscow, however, displayed more Russian originality, particularly in the homes of the nobility. A native picturesqueness grew up in Moscow that did not appear in the grand palaces of Saint Petersburg.

Architectural trends that had flowered in the final years of tsarism continued in the first years of Soviet rule and, in one form or another, until the early 1930's. Modernism, the attempt to create a completely new style free of historical borrowings and utilizing new technical possibilities, was in vogue from 1917 to 1932. Experimentalism, an offshoot of modernism, gave birth to bizarre constructions. Both were in keeping with the compulsive revolutionary need to completely renovate the face of the new Russia.

By the late twenties, a more moderate version of the international modern style prevailed. The Vesnin brothers (Leonid 1880—1933, Victor 1822—1950, and Alexander 1883—1959) were among the most gifted architects of the period. Victor Vesnin was responsible for the greatest architectural monument to modernism, the Dniepr hydropower station at Zaporozhye (1926—32). The great French architect Le Corbusier was imported for the building of the Commissariat of Light Industry (1932) in Moscow.

During the thirties, modernism gave way to neoclassicism, the only viable prerevolutionary architectural tradition. The trend was in keeping with the official return to patriotism and the reinstatement of Russian nationalism. The best representatives of neoclassicism were Karo Alabyan (1897—1959), an Armenian, and Boris Iofan (1891—   ). Iofan drew up the plans for the Palace of the Soviets (1937) in Moscow and the Soviet pavilions at the international expositions in Paris (1937) and New York (1939). Alabyan's finest effort was probably the star-shaped, porticoed Theater of the Red Army (1938—40) in Moscow.

The parallel trend toward nativist tendencies is best represented by Alexander Tamanyan (1878—1936), the prominent Armenian architect who synthesized contemporary and traditional forms, taking into account the building resources of the region and its climatic conditions. Tamanyan planned and built the Government House in Yerevan in Armenian style. National forms were also popular at the All-Union Agricultural Fair held in 1939—40 in Moscow, where critics praised the pavilions of the Ukrainians, Uzbeks, Georgians, and Armenians.

PAINTING

Of late, Soviet graphic art has reflected modernist trends. Promising Soviet artists, unrecognized at home, have received recognition in the West. Anatoli Zverev (1931—   ) exhibited his paintings in Paris in 1965 and was acclaimed for his success in shaking off all traces of socialist realist influence. At home, however, the Communist Party apparatus continues to regard modern art as a sign of bourgeois decadence, and Zverev's style is officially discouraged.

The conversion of the East Slavs to Orthodox Christianity led to imitation of Byzantine religious art. The painting of icons—religious images often made of gold, silver, and fine wood representing Christ, the Holy Family, or the saints—gradually assumed a specifically Russian character. Iconography became an art centered around Moscow, where in the fifteenth century it reached its highest level of achievement with the works of the Russian monk Andrei Rublev (1360—1420). His achievements can still be viewed in the Blagoveshchensk cathedral in the Kremlin and the Uspensky cathedral in Vladimir. Delicate impressionism with a distinctly personal technique, discrete highlights, and a spirit gentler and subtler than late Byzantine painting characterize this exceptional religious painter. Icon-painting as an art began to decline as a consequence of mass production, initiated in the seventeenth century.

The late sixteenth century in Russia, distinguished by the secular ambitions of Ivan IV, saw the beginnings of modern painting, which by the eighteenth century had fallen under the influence of European models with their penchant for stylized mythological scenes. During the nineteenth century, an inclusive Russian school of painting, "Peredvizhniki" (Society of Traveling Exhibitions), sought to produce a truly national art in its attempt to express the inner reality of Russia. Established in 1863, it endured into the twentieth century and included such renowned painters as Ilya Repin (1844—1930). Its romanticism tended toward the idealization of the people and resulted in innumerable standard paintings of the poor and the afflicted in rural and urban Russia.

In the last two decades of the nineteenth century, Russian art, led by Mikhail Vrubel (1865—1910) and Isaac Levitan (1868—1910), sought to free itself from its traditional mediocrity and struck toward regions as yet uncharted. *Mir Iskusstva* (The World of Art), a Western-oriented illustrated periodical, founded in 1898 by Sergei Diaghilev (1872—1929) and including Alexander Benois (1870—1960), exhibited a passionate interest in all aspects of art. Its members excelled in theatrical design and book illustrations. In painting the group was linked with Art Nouveau, a freer method of drawing that also influenced architectural development.

Around 1910 a young avant-garde group branched off from *Mir Iskusstva*, accusing its members of mere decorativeness and superficiality. They studied the French impressionists and early cubists. In 1911 one of their number, Vassili Kandinsky (1866—1944), painted his first abstract watercolor and helped establish a school of abstract painting. This was the first time that a worldwide artistic movement had found one of its sources in Russia. With Marc Chagall (1887—   ), Haim Soutine (1894—1943) and others, Saint Petersburg and Moscow were the most active workshops of modern art until the outbreak of the revolution. This era marked the second golden age of painting in Russia after that of the icon.

Russian art was initially religious in its essence and transcendental in its aspirations. Through the centuries, it has served many masters. Before Ivan the Terrible, it served the Orthodox faith; in the subsequent two centuries, the majesty of the Muscovite tsar; in the eighteenth and nineteenth centuries, imperial power; and in the latter part of the nineteenth century, a divinized conception of the people.

In the twenties Russian art was diminished by the exodus of many of its best painters. Kandinsky, Soutine, and Chagall were among those who emigrated after the revolution. Despite the appointment of the moderate Anatoli Lunacharsky as commissar of education with authority over arts and artists, Party leaders looked with growing disfavor at the Soviet version of modernism. By 1928 all private art groups and schools were abolished as the serious business of industrialization began, and art was programmed under a five-year plan.

By the thirties the doctrine of socialist realism as applied to art made itself felt. The Communist Party Central Committee decreed that the artist was to give a truthful and historically concrete representation of reality in its revolutionary development, keeping in mind the task of ideologically forming the new Soviet man. The ensuing general decline in taste was rapid. Gifted painters such as Kuzma Petrov-Vodkin (1878—1939) abandoned symbolism to paint images of heroic commissars in order to make a living. Mikhail Nesterov (1862—1942) left behind religious themes to become the portraitist of successful Soviet scientists.

The Soviet policy of irreconcilability to abstractionism, formalism, and other modern Western developments has been carried on with equal vehemence by Stalin, Khrushchev, and Brezhnev. As a consequence, impoverishment, provincialism, and a break with the recent past have marked Soviet art. So drab and dispiriting had Soviet art become that Khrushchev, speaking at the Twenty-second Communist Party Congress in 1961, urged that serious attention be given to aesthetic education and the forming of artistic tastes in all the Soviet people and called for a decisive struggle to be waged against tastelessness.

LITERATURE

The Communist Revolution of 1917 and its subsequent attempt to dominate the territories of the Russian Empire brought to an end the milieu that had nourished the flowering of great writers and poets of preceding decades. Even Maxim Gorky (1868—1936), staunch apologist of the revolution, fled Russia in the early twenties to live in Italy, where he stayed until 1928.

The renewal of literary activity was slow and gradual. Whereas most of the poets stayed (Alexander Blok, Vladimir Mayakovsky, Sergei Essenin, Anna Akhmatova, and Boris Pasternak), the greater part of the important prose writers became émigrés (Ivan Bunin, Alexander Kuprin, Dimitri Merezhkovsky, Aleksei Remizov, Aleksei Tolstoy, among others). Prerevolutionary groups that stayed sought to continue their earlier work, as was the case of the poet Valery Briussov (1873—1924). Young people who had been involved in the civil war felt the urge to express their personal experiences and hopes. Communist leaders, of whom many belonged to the old intelligentsia, were anxious to encourage literature that would express the ideology of the revolution. With the passing of time, the intervention of the Communist Party into literary life grew as literature became a tool for indoctrination and propaganda.

Literary movements such as acmeism, which sought clarity and vigor of expression in line with the doctrine of art for the sake of art, and symbolism, which suggested the invisible world and concerned itself with mystic revelations, found little room in the Soviet world. Almost to the exclusion of all else, the new leadership sought to organize and industrialize agrarian Russia along totalitarian guidelines. Nikolai Gumilev (1886—1921), the leader of the acmeists, was executed, and Alexander Blok, (1880—1921), greatest of the symbolist poets, died in 1921, both dismayed over the absence of personal freedom that followed the revolution.

Socialist realism became the accepted mode of literary expression as Stalin's power increased and authors lost their freedom of expression. Following critical realism, which revealed the numerous shortcomings of life under the tsars, socialist realism was concerned with the positive aspects of Communist achievement. It stressed loyalty to Party goals, idealism, and populism. The official founder of the method, Maxim Gorky, began life doing odd jobs along the Volga docks of his native Nizhni-Novgorod, since renamed Gorky. He acquired fame by describing the lives of hoboes and menial workers with a gusto and relish that sharply contrasted with the reigning Chekhovian pessimism of the late nineteenth and early twentieth centuries.

His celebrated play *The Lower Depths* (1902) revealed for the first time in Russian the sordid living conditions of the common people. As his attachment to Marxism grew, his creative talent declined; by 1914 he had already done his best work. *The Small Town of Okurov* (1910) and the autobiographical *Childhood* (1913) radiate prerevolutionary Russian country and village life, despite their condemnatory tone, and are considered his best efforts. Gorky never did write of life in Russia after the establishment of the Soviet Union. A Marxist to the end, he felt that man's sufferings were caused by faulty living conditions, which he described at length side by side with those revolutionary individuals that he felt would set things right. The model of socialist realism was set by *Mother* (1906), a proletarian and revolutionary novel that sanctified revolution.

Aleksei Tolstoy (1883—1945), an aristocrat by birth, became an émigré immediately after the revolution. He was one of those pre-revolutionary writers who soon decided that the New Russia would maintain Russian traditions. Tolstoy returned to Soviet Russia and brought out two major pieces of creative prose. They were *The Road to Calvary*, an epic trilogy of Russia in the throes of revolution, and *Peter I*, a vivid glorification of the founder of the modern Russian state who, like the Bolsheviks, did not hesitate to make revolutionary changes in Russian society and life.

Vladimir Mayakovsky (1893—1930), son of an impoverished nobleman, emerged as the Poet of the Revolution, although his best poetry, in the futurist vein, was probably written between 1914 and 1917. He did not hesitate to use the full force of his considerable talent to turn out in verse the most trivial sort of Soviet propaganda. A man of uncommon integrity, he wrote *The Bed Bug* (1928) and *The Bath House* (1930), plays deriding the vast bureaucracy into which the revolution had become mired. An opponent of mediocrity and pettiness, Mayakovsky, sensing himself isolated and doomed, committed suicide in 1930. Some years earlier in December 1925, dismayed by the changes brought about in rural life by the Soviet authorities, the peasant poet Sergei Essenin (1895—1925) had also killed himself.

An outstanding writer of the Soviet era has turned out to be Mikhail Sholokhov (1905—   ), a Don Cossack. His masterpiece, and the greatest epic novel since *War and Peace*, is *The Quiet Don* (1928—40), published in four installments. Greeted by Soviet critics with reactions ranging from disapproval to condemnation, it has weathered all storms to win its author the Nobel Prize in Literature for 1965. To prove his loyalty to the Party, Sholokhov also wrote *Virgin Soil Upturned*, a standard socialist realism novel glorifying collectivization. He became a spokesman for Soviet communism and was appointed to the Central Committee of the CPSU and elected to the Supreme Soviet.

The Soviet literary scene has known many a turn. In the twenties experimentalism was not yet openly discouraged. With the advent of industrialization and the five-year plans, stories abounded of the pleasures of collectivization on the farm and in the factory and in construction projects in remote regions. In the midthirties patriotism was reinstated as a primary value in Soviet life and became an approved literary theme.

During the war a certain freedom of expression was permitted in order to mobilize all Soviet people against the common enemy. It was the time of the war novels of Konstantin Simonov (1915—   ),

314

Victor Nekrassov (1915—   ), and Leonid Leonov (1899—   ). After World War II, the anticosmopolite campaign of Andrei Zhdanov, Stalin's agent for artistic control, engendered systematic Soviet self-praise and denigration of Western peoples and institutions. The personal lyrics of Anna Akhmatova (1889—1966) and the caustic satire of Mikhail Zoshchenko were proscribed.

Only with the death of Stalin and the emergence of Khrushchev did a thaw set in. It resulted in the suicide of the prominent writer Alexander Fadeyev (1901—56), who it was rumored had betrayed some of his fellow writers in the purges of the late thirties. De-Stalinization was not sufficient, however, to allow publication in the Soviet Union of *Doctor Zhivago* by Boris Pasternak (1890—1960).

Aleksandr Solzhenitsyn (1918—   ) is regarded by his admirers as the outstanding European writer of his time. An artillery captain by the end of the war, he was arrested and sentenced to jail for eight years because he had made a critical remark about Stalin in one of his letters. At the end of the term, he was given an additional three years in a camp. Thus, he spent eleven years from 1945 to 1956 as a convict. On his release he began to write seriously.

One Day in the Life of Ivan Denisovich, his first novel, deals with life in a concentration camp. It was completed in 1957 but did not appear in print until November 1962, when it was published in the literary magazine *Novy Mir* (New World) with the approval of Khrushchev. His other novels include *The First Circle*, first published in Russian in June 1968 in West Germany, and *The Cancer Ward*, first published in Russian in April 1968 in Switzerland.

The humanism, compassion, and sense of personal dignity that distinguished the great Russian literature of the nineteenth century live again in Solzhenitsyn's simply written, but deeply felt, stories of human life and tragedy. Sclzhenitsyn feels that good literature arises out of pain and claims that is why he pins his literary hopes on Eastern Europe, including Russia.

The new liberal generation includes the poets Evgeny Evtushenko (1933—   ), Andrei Voznesensky (1933—   ), and Bella Akhmadulina (1937—   ). The liberal literary journal *Novy Mir*, under the editorship of the outstanding poet Aleksandr Tvardovsky (1910—   ), has sought to encourage the publication of excellent material without regard to its political orientation. The other noteworthy literary periodical is *Yunost* (Youth), which had Evtushenko on its editorial board until July 1969. There has been considerable pressure on these two literary journals, which remain suspect to the Communist Party apparatus. The situation of literature and the arts has become tense and uncertain in the Soviet Union, especially since the Soviet occupation of Czechoslovakia in August 1968.

The practice of private printing *(samizdat)* and passing of copies of creative writing continues to flourish in the country, since interest in good literature continues unabated. Literature, a creative and synthetic art, has played and continues to play a crucial role in Russian and Soviet life. Concerned with human problems, it seeks to present and perhaps resolve the essential questions of life that face individuals and societies.

Written literature actually began in Russia as a consequence of the introduction of Christianity into the country in the tenth century. A rich store of songs, rhymes, and fairy tales already existed by then in the oral tradition. The Cyrillic alphabet was adapted from the Greek to provide the Orthodox Church with a medium for the teaching of its doctrine to the East Slavs. As a result, almost all books written between the tenth and eighteenth centuries dealt with religious subjects and sought to instruct. Oral folklore, pagan in origin, represented the other current of literary expression. The two combined to produce a basic Russian style distinguished by mysticism, spontaneity, and a strong attachment to the land. *The Lay of the Host of Igor,* a heroic epic of a military campaign and the first great monument of Russian literature, was probably composed by the late twelfth or early thirteenth century.

The Mongol occupation from about 1240 to 1480 tended to arrest literary development, and Russian literature proved unable to keep pace with the medieval literary flowering of Europe. After the throwing off of the Tatar yoke, translations, popular tales and songs, and chronicles were produced in greater quantities. Religious works in Church-Slavonic, a Slav dialect developed for ecclesiastical purposes, kept pace. In 1564 the first Russian printed book, *The Apostle,* came off the press in Moscow.

The ecclesiastical reforms of the late seventeenth century promulgated by the patriarch Nikon led to the Great Schism that split the Orthodox faithful into two groups: those who supported ecclesiastical reforms and those who refused to accept them. Out of it came an extraordinary work, *The Life of Arch-Presbyter Avvacum,* in which the Old Believer priest Avvacum (1620—82) fought for the old faith. He was burned at the stake as a schismatic in 1682, but his original and witty book remained as a milestone in the development of Russian literary expression. Its blend of idealism, realism, passion, and slyness stamps it as a valid creation of the Russian spirit.

The eighteenth century marked the reentry of Russia into the European world. Mikhail Lomonosov (1711—65) attained a reputation as an outstanding scholar in almost all fields of art and science. He helped found Moscow University in 1755, published a Russian grammar, and established the Russian language as a vehicle for literary expression. Moscow University is actually called Moscow M. V. Lomonosov State University, named in honor of Russia's great scholar.

With Alexander Pushkin (1799—1837), the modern Russian literary style was born. The style is a blend of dignified Church-Slavonic and expressive colloquial Russian set to order by the inimitable linguistic sense of Pushkin. The poet studied Russian from peasants and artisans as well as from country squires and created a series of fairytales, legends, and songs derived from the deepest sources of native folklore and tradition. His great achievement is in lyric poetry and includes his masterpiece, a novel in verse, *Eugene Onegin* (1823—31), whose hero is a well-read young nobleman who spends his days in futile occupations. He is the first of a long line of "superfluous men" in Russian literature. Caught up in court intrigues, Pushkin at age thirty-seven was killed in a duel.

After Pushkin's death, Mikhail Lermontov (1814—41) circulated his poem "A Poet's Death," which expressed the feelings of many educated Russians to whom the death of Pushkin was a national catastrophe. His attack on elements of the imperial court brought Lermontov to the attention of Tsar Nicholas I, who exiled the twenty-three-year-old poet to the Caucasus.

Lermontov's novel *A Hero of Our Times* (1837—40), written in clear prose, offers the superhuman figure of the hero Pechorin who, despite his talent and character, does not really know what to do with himself and merely plays with life. The novel, the first outstanding creative prose piece in Russian, set a standard of refinement and mood. Lermontov was also killed in a duel.

Nikolai Gogol (1809—52), son of a Ukrainian landowner, came to Saint Petersburg to become a government official. He brought with him an extraordinary gift for comic observation, which served him well in his prose. His masterpiece *Dead Souls* (1836—42) deals with the adventures of an impostor who goes about collecting the contracts of serfs who have died but still officially count until the next census. The characters in the novel are presented with an eye to their basic dishonesty.

Even more important in its literary consequences is Gogol's short story "The Overcoat" (1842). It is the tragicomic presentation of the sufferings and death of a poor and lonely government official. Its stress on humanity, compassion, and moral values prompted Dostoevsky to say that Russian literature emerged from Gogol's "Overcoat." Gogol's work marked the transition between romanticism and realism in Russian literature.

Ivan Goncharov (1812—91), son of a Simbirsk merchant, is famous for his masterpiece *Oblomov* (1859). The novel describes the life and times of an idle Russian nobleman tragically caught between the waning of the old slave economy and the rise of the new commercial age requiring more energy and adaptability than nobility and virtue.

Ivan Turgenev (1818—83), born into a landowning family ruled by a willful mother, spent most of his adult life in France. There he was a friend of the great writers of the day and helped introduce Russian literature to Western Europe and the United States. His novels extol the beauty of the Russian countryside and the strength and virtue of Russian women. His masterpiece *Fathers and Sons* (1862) presents a nihilist as the new type of Russian revolutionary who seeks to completely destroy the old order in order to establish a new society based on science and objectivity.

Feodor Dostoevsky (1821—81), son of an army doctor, joined a socialist circle in his youth. He was arrested and condemned to be executed but at the last moment received a reprieve and a sentence of exile to Siberia. A monarchist and a mystic profoundly concerned with the problems of suffering and evil, he wrote some of the most psychologically perceptive novels of the nineteenth century. *Crime and Punishment* (1866) dealt with the question of individual moral responsibility in a materialistic and opportunistic society. *The Brothers Karamazov* (1880) concerned itself with the basic problem of good and evil and condemned as morally sterile imported Western-type material progress.

Leo Tolstoy (1828—1910), a titled aristocrat with prominent forebears, wrote what many literary critics consider to be the greatest of all novels, *War and Peace* (1863—69). In *Anna Karenina* (1873—77) he recounted the story of a woman's tragic love with his usual psychological insight into the structure of modern society.

Mikhail Saltykov-Schedrin (1826—89) wrote satirical accounts of national follies, one of which was *The History of a Town.* His masterpiece *The Golovlyov Family* (1879) recounted with chilling precision the decline and disintegration of a landowning family beset by misfortune and unable to cope with changing times.

The 1880's was a period of political reaction and relative mediocrity in literature. Tolstoy wrote novelettes of social commentary, such as *The Kreutzer Sonata* and *Father Sergius.* Anton Chekhov (1860—1904) brought to the fore his short stories, blending wistful humor and strict observation. He developed his style to perfection to become Russia's greatest short-story writer with creations like "Ward No. 6." He depicted man as a victim of unseen forces and reflected the decline of confidence felt by the intelligentsia in the institutions of the Russian monarchy.

After 1905 and the first Russian revolution, a period of literary decadence overcame the country. A new movement known as symbolism gained ground among poets and some writers. An impressionism of manner and technique, its roots plunged deep into

Russian mysticism. Its greatest representative was Alexander Blok (1880—1921), the final flowering of Russian poetic culture going back to Pushkin. Blok, faced by the decline of the aristocracy and conscious of widespread inequities, traditionalist though he was, welcomed the Bolshevik Revolution.

MUSIC

Despite restrictions, Russian musical composition in the Soviet era has kept a high standard and maintained its place in the world. The antecedents of Soviet composition reside in prerevolutionary musical tradition. As a result of the revolution, Glazunov and Stravinsky did not return to their homeland, but Prokofiev did so in 1936.

Sergei Prokofiev (1891—1953), a student of Rimsky-Korsakov, had a very individualistic and colorful style, neoclassical in its clarity of form and structure. His music is characteristically witty and humorous. Prokofiev's compositions include operas—*Love for Three Oranges* (1919), film music for *Alexander Nevsky* (1938) and *Ivan the Terrible* (2 parts, 1944—46), in addition to vocal-orchestral pieces, concertos, and sonatas.

Dmitri Shostakovich (1906—   ) claims first place in popularity among Soviet composers. His style is said to generally reflect the Soviet point of view in music with its stress on clear motifs drawn from popular sources. His highly individualistic approach, however, has at times subjected him to severe criticism from the Party apparatus.

Shostakovich's work is characterized by directness and clarity, use of current subjects, and a gift for satirical treatment. Best known for his symphonies, he has delved into nearly all media. Among his best-known operas are the avant-garde *Nose* (1929), taken from Gogol; *The Age of Gold* (1930), a satire on the capitalist world; and *Lady MacBeth of the Mzensk District* (1934), a last foray into modernism. He also wrote a suite for jazz orchestra before abandoning his audacious technique in the late forties.

Aram Khachaturyan (1903—   ) has composed rousing music to pedestrian ballets *Gayane* (1942) with its "Sabre Dance," and *Spartak* (1952). He has orchestrated Lermontov's play *Masquerade* (1941) and scored a number of films, including *Othello* (1955). His piano and violin concertos are very popular.

The most celebrated Soviet opera was composed in 1927. *The Red Poppy*, renamed *The Red Flower* in 1957, dealt with the exploitation of the Far Eastern peoples by Western commercial interests. It was put together by Reinhold Gliere (1875—1956), who had delved into Russian folksongs with his third "Ilya Muromets" symphony in 1911. He also utilized the famous Repin painting of the Zaporog Cossacks drafting their insulting letter to the sultan for *The Zaporogs* in 1921. With his ballet *The Bronze Horseman* (1949), he returned to Pushkin for inspiration.

The Red Poppy typifies the didactic direction of Soviet musical composition. In 1946 Andrei Zhdanov, Stalin's agent for artistic control, advised simply conceived, clearly defined melodies, preferably of Russian folk origin, that were likely to please the widest possible audience. The story itself had to be current or popular, in some way abetting the Soviet cause, either by condemning Western practices or revealing the positive aspects of Communist achievement at home or abroad.

Especially during the last years of Stalin's rule, composers were admonished and even punished to keep them true to the Party line. Shostakovich himself had to resign from the faculty of the Moscow Conservatory for a time. To redeem himself, the composer had to admit his ideological failings publicly and write some approved music to show contrition.

The very composite nature of modern Russian music, drawn as it is from Italian, Austrian, German, French, Spanish, Near Eastern, and Oriental models, suffered from Soviet-enforced isolation. Its mosaic richness and variety traditionally drew sustenance from religious inspiration. The song of devotion and mystical celebration had permeated much of pre-Soviet music. It has since become unacceptable, and Soviet music, as a consequence, lost one of its major dimensions.

Soviet conservatories have, on the other hand, continued to produce outstanding musical performers. The violinists David Oistrakh (1908–   ) and Leonid Kogan (1924–   ) and the pianists Sviatoslav Richter (1914–   ) and Emile Gilels (1916–   ) are living proof of this, as is the cellist Mstislav Rostropovich (1927–   ). The Russian musical tradition has continued to thrive. There are indications that the full legacy of Russian prerevolutionary music is being reconsidered with pride and hope for the future by the current promising composers despite the maintenance of de facto state censorship. Modern trends are reflected in the works of the recently established composers. Boris Tishchenko (1939–   ) composed a *Cello Concerto* in 1963, which he wrote in the modern idiom. Rostropovich made a recording of it with the Leningrad symphony orchestra.

Despite official Party opposition to jazz and other modern styles and forms of musical composition originating in the West, the progressive-minded young Soviet public has kept abreast of their development.

Two sources of musical inspiration provided the main elements of Russian musical composition. The first dates back to the conversion of Kievan Russia to Orthodox Christianity when the Byzantine chant of the Eastern Church came to the East Slavs. The Byzantine

Greeks sought to convey the impression of splendor through the use of a very rich liturgy. They attempted to set to music the poetry of the Bible. Their chant was entirely vocal, unaccompanied by instruments, and followed only one melodic line (monophonic). To heighten the dramatic effect, antiphony was employed by the use of a choir divided into two groups that sang alternately. By the fourteenth century, the chant, known as the "znamenny," had become wholly Russian. Like its model it remained entirely vocal and unaccompanied by musical instruments.

The second great source of Russian musical composition arose in the folksongs of the East Slavs. Pagan in origin and basically European in character, rhythmic, and polyphonic, the music was played on a variety of stringed, wind, and percussion instruments. The music itself was maintained and transmitted by amateur musicians who would gather to sing and play at rural festivities.

By the seventeenth century, the postmedieval harmonized music of the West began to penetrate into Russia. Late in the century the patriarch Nikon officially did away with the "znamenny" chant. Russian liturgic music as a consequence lost its native vitality and began to slavishly imitate the music of western Europe, specifically Italy. This trend continued throughout the eighteenth and into the middle of the nineteenth century when a return to the sources of Russian liturgic music took place.

The first major Western impact on Russian music came from the Italian opera of the late eighteenth and early nineteenth centuries. Mikhail Glinka (1803—57), founder of modern Russian music, was a friend of Hector Berlioz and studied in Berlin. He blended folk themes of Russian song with the great traditions of European music, particularly those of Germany and Italy. His first great opera, *A Life for the Tsar* (1836), told the tale of a Russian peasant who sacrificed his life to lead astray Polish troops bent on killing the tsar. Glinka also made an opera of *Ruslan and Ludmilla* (1842), Pushkin's delightful fairytale of young love. Alexander Dargomijski (1813—69) also set fairytales to music: *Russalka* and *The Stone Guest.*

The "Five," a group of composers founded by M. Balakirev (1837—1910), included Caesar Cui (1835—1918), Modest Moussorgsky (1849—81), Alexander Borodin (1833—87), and Nikolai Rimsky—Korsakov (1844—1908). Its members, ardent nationalists, were particularly interested in folk music and composed meticulously. They willingly utilized Russian folk themes in conjunction with either an Oriental or Western flavor.

Borodin sought to combine both Oriental and Western motifs in his celebrated ballet *Prince Igor* and presented a Europeanized arrangement of Near Eastern motifs in his symphonic picture *In the Steppes of Central Asia.* Moussorgsky emerged as the greatest forerunner of modern music with his startling *Pictures at an Exhibition* (1874) and *Night on Bald Mountain*. His *Boris Godunov* (1868—72) recreates in operatic form Pushkin's tragic poem of 1830. Rimsky-Korsakov taught most of the coming composers at the Saint Petersburg Conservatoire. He himself stood out for his exceptional technical virtuosity. His compositions are marked by Orientalism and exoticism of harmony and subject. Among them the better known include *Sadko, Scheherezade, The Snow Maiden, Tsar Soltan,* and *Le Coq d'Or,* all drawn from popular fairytales and related sources. His *Great Russian Easter Overture* returns to the sources of Russian religious music, while *Capriccio Espagnol* reflects Spanish themes.

Peter Tchaikovsky (1840—93) was a professor at the Conservatoire. His perennial use of popular folk themes and characteristic romanticism have assured him a preeminent place in the hearts of Russian musiclovers. His memorable operas *Eugene Onegin* and *Queen of Spades* recreate Alexander Pushkin's greatest stories, whereas with *Romeo and Juliet* he returns once more to Italy.

Russian symphonic literature began in the last quarter of the nineteenth century, its expansion coinciding with the development of Russian nationalism. Among its outstanding representatives was Tchaikovsky who, with the aid of German harmony and orchestration, set moods that alternated melancholy with boisterous mirth. Rimsky-Korsakov, on the other hand, utilized brilliant and colorful orchestration to return to the sources of the national ethos. Moussorgsky moved away from the romantic toward the more modern idiom and, like Rimsky-Korsakov, broke away from nineteenth-century romanticism.

Sergei Rachmaninoff's (1873—1943) symphonies and piano concertos have an appeal akin to that of Tchaikovsky. His music has a nostalgic quality that has given it wide popularity. He is the last of the great pianist-composers of the romantic tradition.

Igor Stravinsky (1882—   ) has made a tremendous impact on musical composition since 1910, when his *Firebird* registered a signal success in Paris. It was then he left Russia. His prerevolutionary style was dynamic, fearlessly using a wide range of innovations: percussive use of the piano, highly dissonant harmony, polytonality, accentuation on unlikely parts of a measure, and a de-emphasis of melodic creation. Among his other early successes were *Petrouchka* and the celebrated *Rite of Spring*.

BALLET

The Soviet ballet, which performs both classical and modern works, is renowned throughout the world. Perhaps no other performing art is regarded by the Soviet authorities with greater favor. They see it as a badge of Russian-Soviet cultural superiority over other countries.

The particular Soviet influence, namely socialist realism, came to the fore shortly after the revolution. Action became more dramatic, and emphasis was placed on the "theatre of the proletariat" with special stress put on the creativity of the people and, since the midthirties, on patriotism. These unofficial directives proved more a hindrance than an aid to the creation of good ballet.

Among those who had to struggle with these "suggested directives" were Gliere, Khatchaturian, and Prokofiev, the leading composers of ballet under the Soviets. Boris Assafiev (1884—1949), among those who wrote chiefly for the ballet, is responsible for *The Flame of Paris* (1932) and *The Fountain of Bakhtchisarai* (1934).

Ballet schools under government patronage operate in Moscow and Leningrad and, since the forties, in the capitals of the other union republics of the Soviet Union. The gifted are given free study and, through a series of competitions, the opportunity to be singled out for further attention. Among the greatest achievements of the Soviet ballet have been the prima ballerinas produced since the late twenties. They include Galina Ulanova (1910—   ), Olga Lepechin-skaya (1916—   ), Natalia Dudinskaya (1912—   ), Maya Plisetskaya (1925—   ), and Raissa Struchkova (1925—   ).

The Soviet regime prides itself on the performances of the Bolshoi and Kirov ballet companies and in having the finest ballerinas in the world. It has spared no expense on the maintenance of its world standing in this field. The dependence on prerevolutionary choreography and composition however outweighs the innovations which apart from placing emphasis on acrobatic prowess have been few since the revolution. The Soviets do not encourage experimentation in ballet technique.

The French ballet companies performed in Russia as early as the seventeenth century. Permanent companies were formed in Saint Petersburg in 1736 and in Moscow in 1806. French choreographer Didelot (1767—1837) introduced ballet-pantomine to Russia early in the nineteenth century. As late as the end of the nineteenth century, a French choreographer, Marius Petipa (1827—1910), collaborated in the staging of the ballet compositions of Tchaikovsky at Saint Petersburg. Among the productions were *Swan Lake* (1876), *Sleeping Beauty* (1889), and *The Nutcracker Suite* (1892).

In 1905 the Italian Enrico Cechetti, who had taught at the Imperial School of Ballet, founded his own school in Saint Petersburg. It was attended by Tamara Karsavina, Anna Pavlova, and Vaslav Nijinsky and his sister Bronislava. These were the famous stars that were to give preeminence to the Russian ballet in the world of the dance by recreating the traditional splendor of the classical ballet.

At that time, Michael Fokine (1880—1942), dancer and choreographer, taught at the Mariinsky Theatre Ballet School. He sought to synthesize all the elements of ballet: music, gesture, dancing, decor. In 1908 he was a member of the Imperial Theatre Ballet Company which, under the direction of Sergei Diaghilev (1872—1929), went to Paris for the first season of Russian ballet. There they produced masterpiece on masterpiece until the outbreak of the war in 1914. Their productions included *Prince Igor* (1909), *Petrouchka* (1911), and *Le Coq d'Or* (1914).

Nijinsky (1890—1950), who in 1912 had independently created his first ballet, *L'Apres-midi d'un Faune*, had overshadowed Fokine by 1914. The Diaghilev company itself had broken away from the Mariinsky Theatre of Saint Petersburg by 1911. It was chiefly because of Diaghilev that there was a renaissance of ballet as an art form and a worldwide interest in it.

In Russia itself the ballet-master Gorsky (1871—1924) maintained choreographic traditions with productions such as *Don Quixote* and *Swan Lake*. Among his more original creations was *Clorinda, Queen of the Mountain Fairies*. He also evolved an ingenious system of dance notations.

THEATER

The People's Commissariat of Education established a department of theatrical affairs as early as January 1918. In 1919 all theaters, imperial and private, came under the control of the state. Maxim Gorky took a prominent role in setting up a revolutionary theater. In Petrograd he organized the Grand Theatre (formerly the Gorski). In Moscow the Bolshoi and the Maly and in Petrograd the Alexandriisky, renamed the Pushkin, and the Mariinsky, renamed the Kirov, became academic theaters under unified direction. Anatoli Lunacharsky (1875—1933), a literate Marxist critic and dramatist, became the Soviet equivalent of minister of culture in 1917 and did not step down until 1929. During his tenure a certain freedom of means of expression prevailed.

The dominant theme of theatrical writing was the heroism of a people devoting all their energies to the building of a new society. Among the first successes was *Mystery-Bouffe* (1918), a comedy depicting the collapse of capitalism and the marvels of communism, written by Vladimir Mayakovsky (1893—1930). The staging was by Vsevolod Meyerhold (1874—1942), like Mayakovsky a member of the LEF (Left Front) Movement, which sought to use all the means available, including post-symbolist currents (dada, futurism), to further scenic effects. Early enthusiasm and support led to the opening of new theaters. After 1923 the peak of the LEF movement receded as Marxist critics assailed it for its ideological inconsistencies.

By 1925 good plays depicting the civil war reached the stage. Among the best were *Armored Train 14—69* by Vsevolod Ivanov (1895—1963) and *First Cavalry Army* (1929) by Vsevolod Vishnevsky (1900—51). Some plays dealt with the difficulties of the transition from the old to the new for the old intelligentsia. *Fear* (1926) by Alexander Afinogenov (1904—41) considered this problem, as did an adaptation of the novel *The White Guard* by Mikhail Bulgakov (1891—1940).

By 1929 state control was reinstituted over drama, and socialist realism as a prescribed style for the Soviet theatre was set forth in 1932. Generally humorless and dull plays about industrialization ensued. As an example, *The Aristocrats* (1934) by Nikolai Pogodin (1900—62), "a serious comedy," presented the moral regeneration of criminals through forced labor. By 1937, at the height of the Great Purge, Meyerhold was demoted and exiled in a campaign condemning "Formalism, decadent Experimentalism, and Aestheticism."

World War II and the loosening of Party controls brought in their wake a series of poignant patriotic plays. *The Front* (1942) by Alexander Korneychuk (1905—)considered the essential problems faced by the military in the early campaigns. Konstantin Simonov (1915—), a prominent writer, traced the sympathetic portrait of *The Russian People* (1942) caught in the crucible of war. Leonid Leonov (1899—) concerned himself with the human equation in *Invasion* (1942) and *Lyomushka* (1943).

The postwar freeze edicted by Andrei Zhdanov assured the lowering of Soviet dramatic writing to the level of unalloyed propaganda. Nikolai Pogodin's *The Missouri Waltz*, a typical effort produced at the height of the cold war in 1950, attempted to discredit President Harry Truman. The safe subjects were Lenin and Soviet heroism in war and peacetime construction.

The Soviet theatre, well subsidized by the government, puts on magnificent productions of both mediocre new plays and revivals of past successes. In the way of original writing and staging, however, there has been little if anything of value since the late forties. In the main, the Soviet stage continues to provide a medium for the transmission of Communist cliches, slogans, and calumnies. Of all the performing arts, it has most suffered from the Soviet policy of utilizing the arts for its own specific political ends.

As far back as the eleventh century, clowns and jugglers were improvising small plays, usually farces, in the Russian countryside. The modern Russian theatre, however, has its origins in the seventeenth century, when European stage presentations were given before court circles. After 1750 Russian drama schools were established. In 1756 a permanent theatrical group was formed in Saint Petersburg; other companies followed in Yaroslavl and Nizhni-Novgorod.

In the nineteenth century the great centers of theatrical activity were at the Alexandriisky Theatre in Saint Petersburg and the Maly

Theatre in Moscow. The comedy of social criticism developed by Denis Fonvizin (1745—92) in his *The Minor* (1782) bloomed in the nineteenth century with Alexander Griboyedov's (1795—1829) *Tis Folly to be Wise* and Gogol's *The Inspector-General* (1836). All were ironic looks at the primitive outlines of an imported social structure and the uneasy relationship of the Russians to it. In a deeper sense the plays considered the problems posed by the modern world to a still feudal society.

Under the influence of liberal critic Vissarion Belinsky (1811—48), the idea of a realistic approach to playwriting and performing led to the balanced, yet biting social commentary of Alexander Ostrovsky (1823—86). In such plays as *The Thunderstorm* (1859), he brilliantly exposed the ills of Russian society: the tyranny of ignorance, the abuse of privilege, and the crass commercialism of the business communities.

The acting styles gradually changed from the overwrought romanticism of the great Russian tragedian Pavel Mochalov (1800—48) to the more restrained performances of Mikhail Schepkin (1788—1863) and Alexander Martynov (1816—60). With the advent of Konstantin Stanislavsky (1863—1938) and Nemirovich-Danchenko (1858—1943) and their Moscow Art Theatre, established in 1898, "inner realism" became a valuable new contribution to the art of acting. It consisted of the attempt on the part of the actor to wholly identify himself with the character he sought to portray by assuming his mental outlook, emotional reactions, and particular moods.

The subtle and touching plays of Anton Chekhov (1860—1904) staged by Stanislavsky at the turn of the century gave Russia a prominent place in the theatrical world. Between the end of the nineteenth century and the 1917 revolution, Russia emerged as a major innovating force in the dramatic arts.

CINEMA

Although the first Russian documentary films were made in 1896 and the first studio was established by 1908, tsarist Russian failed to produce a noteworthy film art. For the most part, French films were shown in Russian motion picture theaters before 1917. The few Russian films were largely adapted from literary classics, such as Turgenev's *Nest of Gentlefolk* and Pushkin's *Queen of Spades*. They were not, however, of a quality to attract the particular attention either of critics or the filmgoing public.

After the revolution the entire film industry passed under state control by an edict of August 1919. Lenin himself saw the great possibilities of the film art as a vehicle for revolutionary propaganda and as a medium for indoctrinating the masses. He stated that, of all the arts, the most important for the Communists was the cinema.

From the first, the permanent principles of Soviet film-making stressed documentary aspects directed toward a compact synthesis in film technique. Freedom to make films, however, was permitted only to those whose thinking was in line with the Marxist-Leninist outlook.

It was not until the midtwenties that there emerged distinguished Soviet film directors who drew the attention of film critics throughout the world. The first such talent, Sergei Eisenstein (1898—1948), was originally influenced by the work of the American director D. W. Griffith. Eisenstein embarked on his career in 1923 with *Strike*. In 1925, applying the cinéma vérité technique to the story of a mutiny aboard a tsarist cruiser in 1905, Eisenstein created what some critics consider to be the greatest masterpiece of the cinema, *The Battleship Potemkin*. With this production was conceived the idea of a film without a hero in which the masses themselves were the stars.

A prodigious technician and bold revolutionary, Eisenstein was distrustful of any form of artifice and resolutely rejected studio settings. He used montage, simultaneous appearance of two or more images on one screen and, in later films, the interrelation of sound and picture in a way that stressed the dynamics of the film. His greatest achievement in talking pictures was *Ivan the Terrible*, filmed both in black and white and in color in Soviet central Asia during World War II. Although the two-part film depicted the savagery and oppression of sixteenth-century Muscovy, many observers felt that it was an apology for Stalin. The ruthless determination of Ivan the Terrible in uniting his country was seen as a rationalization and justification of Stalin's brutal methods.

Vsevolod Pudovkin (1893—1953), a contemporary of Eisenstein, directed official Communist classics, such as Gorky's *Mother* (1926) and *The End of Saint Petersburg* (1927). After World War II he made standard chauvinistic films such as *Suvorov* and *Admiral Nakhimov*, Alexander Dovzhenko (1894—1956), the third great name of the era, directed in 1927 his first film masterpiece, *Zvenigora*, an epic of the Ukraine, which he followed with *Arsenal* (1929), a ringing antiwar film, and *Earth* (1930), an idyllic film of life on the land.

In the late thirties there was an upsurge of creativity with *The Childhood of Gorky* (1938) by Mark Donskoi (1901) and *Peter I* (1937—39) by Vladimir Petrov (1896—   ), films that drew the attention of Soviet filmgoers away from the vast purges that were sweeping across the country.

During World War II, some 150 cameramen recorded events on various fronts. After the Battle of Stalingrad there was an appreciable improvement in film technique. The best known war documentaries included *24 Hours of War in the USSR* (1942), *The*

Battle of the Urals (1943), and *The Fall of Berlin* (1945). The terrible poetry of war in all its heroism and sacrifice was most vividly brought home in *The Rainbow* (1944) by Mark Donskoi and *The Decisive Turning Point* (1945) by Friedrich Ermler.

After the war a chauvinistic reaction and a depreciation of the leading Western powers led to a series of mediocre films. Films sought to contrast Soviet "virtues" with Western, more particularly Anglo-American, "decadence." The death of Stalin in 1953 and the subsequent Khrushchev speech in 1956 denouncing Stalinism ensured a certain thaw in Soviet film circles that encouraged better films. *The Forty-First*, directed by Grigori Chukhrai in 1956, presented a White Guards officer in a very favorable light, in itself a break with Soviet tradition. *The Fate of Man* (1959) by Sergei Bondarchuk (1920—) recounted in moving detail the defeats, sorrows, and sufferings of a Soviet soldier in the war.

In the sixties both classics of literature and events and consequences of World War II vied as topics for films. In *Clear Skies* (1961) Grigori Chukhrai recounted the postwar sufferings of returning Soviet prisoners of war at the hands of Soviet authorities. *My Name Is Ivan* (1962) utilized technical innovations to tell the tragic story of an orphan caught in the war. Leo Tolstoy's *War and Peace* (1968) was adapted to the screen by Sergei Bondarchuk, and in 1969 Ivan Pyriev (1901—) wrote and directed an adaptation of Dostoevsky's *The Brothers Karamazov.*

NON-RUSSIAN ARTISTIC EXPRESSION IN THE SOVIET UNION

In 1917 Stalin, Lenin's commissar of nationalities, devised an ingenious compromise that allowed indigenous cultural expression among the various nationalities while maintaining unity of control by the Communist Party over the whole multinational Soviet structure. The languages of the various nationalities and their literature were allowed and even encouraged along specific Marxist and socialist realist lines.

At the same time, the policy of "divide and rule" became manifest under Soviet direction. It led the Turkic-speaking peoples of central Asia and the Caucasus to adopt a Cyrillic alphabet in the period after 1928 and divided the closely related Kazakh and Kirgiz peoples into separate cultural and political entities. Except for Armenia and Georgia, which as ancient cultures have their own well-developed languages and literature, and the Baltic peoples, who are still permitted to use Latin script, no significant national regional unit within the Soviet Union is allowed to use an alphabet that is not Cyrillic.

In architecture and painting there has been an attempt to combine features of popular local customs with the tenets of socialist realism, functional requirements of the project, and geographic considerations of place. Those aspects of literature that coincide with the socialist-Leninist outlook and that reveal antibourgeois, antireligious orientation are everywhere encouraged. Music that is considered too sad or exotic, such as that in Muslim central Asia, is discouraged and replaced by standard symphonic arrangement on the European pattern. With official encouragement ballet and theater in the European-Russian mold but with a Marxist flavor flourish in all the republics.

The Soviet nationality policy on culture evolved by Stalin has been expressed in the statement "national in form, socialist in content." In fact, since the early thirties, the Russian-Soviet forms have been in the ascendant, and any attempt on the part of the other republics to overemphasize their specific nationality has been condemned by Moscow as "bourgeois chauvinism." This epithet has not been applied to similar Russian efforts, for the Great Russians are regarded by the Soviet Party apparatus, itself dominated by Great Russians, as elder brothers in the constellation of peoples that comprise the Soviet Union.

Russian culture has been the product not only of the Russians but also of the many varied peoples who have inhabited the former empire and the Soviet Union. Individuals of non-Russian background have often expressed creativity using Russian artistic forms or Russian language in addition to those characteristic of their own particular cultures. Some cultures, such as Armenian and Georgian, are quite ancient with literary and artistic development antedating the Russian. Others, such as those of the Baltic area, are relatively recent; some remain quite primitive, as is the case with most Paleo-Siberian peoples. Other cultures belong in a grouping the center of which lies beyond the borders of the Soviet Union, as is true with many of the peoples inhabiting Soviet central Asia.

Specific mention should be made of the major Turkic ethnic groups which, apart from the East Slavic family, comprise the largest number of related peoples within the Soviet Union. These include the Uzbeks, Tatars, Kazakhs, Azers, Chuvash, Turkmens, Bashkirs, and the Kirgiz. Settled in central Asia and the eastern region of European Russia, these Turkic peoples constitute no less than 10 percent of the entire union population. Mostly Muslim by religious affiliation, they are also Middle Eastern Muslim (Iranic-Arabic-Turkish) in their cultural pursuits and achievements.

Their towns have usually been centered on the citadel overlooking a central fortress surrounded by the city proper, in turn encircled by suburbs. Their artwork has been nonrepresentational, consisting of geometric patterns and designs. The music, taking its source in Iran, has consisted of modal, melodic and, occasionally, rhythmic, skeletal formulas, upon which performers improvise on percussion, wind and, especially, string instruments. The literature is based on Arabic and Iranian religious books as well as classical Iranian poetry.

CHAPTER 17

INTELLECTUAL EXPRESSION

Marxism-Leninism has reshaped the intellectual atmosphere of the country. It has stressed allegiance and loyalty to the cause of profound social transformation and world revolution and has directed the thought and energies of the citizens by means of education and communications.

The major theme of the official ideology remained, on the eve of the 1970's, the construction of socialism, in anticipation of "the classless society," that is, communism. Efforts in the intellectual sphere were directed toward strengthening of the state at home and abroad. The Communist Party of the Soviet Union (CPSU) directed and controlled intellectual activities of a public nature. In the cause of industrialization the physical and natural sciences received the greatest support and encouragement from the government, but the prestige of the humanities had not appreciably waned. Poets and writers, no less than scientists, held honored places in society, which also rated scholars and teachers highly.

Nevertheless, weaknesses in the physical and natural sciences existed, resulting in part from restrictions maintained for many years especially in biology. Since the Communists were interested not only in changing society but also in changing man himself as the basic element of society, they embraced the nineteenth-century French biologist Lamarck's theories—that acquired characteristics during lifetime can be inherited—thereby rejecting the opposing views of Abbe Mendel, almost universally accepted in the West. A major figure in this development was the agronomist and the biologist, Trofim Denisovich Lysenko, whose research on heredity and its variability, based on a form of Lamarckism worked out by the Soviet scientist, Ivan V. Michurin, won him a position of ultimate authority in Soviet biology.

After the death of Stalin in 1953, Lysenko's theories were relegated to the background, and orthodox geneticists were given limited freedom in teaching and writing. In psychology, the Communists rejected all theories and methods except that of behaviorism, based, they said, on the work of the Russian Pavlov on conditioned reflexes. The effect was to make them diverge from most other work in psychology.

Through the 1960's Soviet successes in space exploration and atomic energy kept pace with advances in physics and mathematics. While applied research tended to lag, the president of the Academy of Sciences, Mstislav V. Keldysh, in mathematics, and nuclear expert Pyotr L. Kapitsa, in physics, continued to make outstanding contributions to basic research. An indication of the relaxation of strict controls on the freedom of scientists was the fact that Kapitsa, four time winner of the Order of Lenin and member of the Presidium of the Academy of Sciences, was permitted for the first time to visit the United States in late 1969. Pyotr Fedoseev emerged as the leading official spokesman of Marxism-Leninism in Communist publications.

Among the outstanding achievements of science has been work in physics. Among the Soviet recipients of the Nobel prize in physics have been Igor E. Tamm, Pavel Cherenkov, and Ilya Frank in 1958; Lev Landau in 1962; and Alexander M. Prokhorov and Nikolay G. Basov in 1964. Similiarly, in the field of chemistry Nikolay N. Semyonov received the award for 1956 (see ch. 18, Science and Technology).

In the late 1960's leading writers and scientists criticized government censorship and controls on intellectual expression. Aleksandr Solzhenitsyn, in a letter dated May 16, 1967, addressed himself to the Fourth All-Union Congress of Soviet Writers. He asked the congress to discuss the "no longer tolerable oppression to which our literature has been subjected from decade to decade and with which the Writers' Union can no longer reconcile itself." He proposed that the congress work energetically for the abolition of all censorship, both open and secret, of individual productions.

In the same vein, Andrei Sakharov, one of the most distinguished Soviet nuclear physicists, wrote a long essay entitled "Thoughts on Progress, Peaceful Coexistence, and Intellectual Freedom." It circulated in manuscript form in Moscow in 1968 and apparently reflected views widely held in intellectual circles. The essay called for greater political and intellectual freedom of expression in the Soviet Union and a rapprochement with the United States. Despite the tone of the essay and its known authorship, academician Sakharov, according to news reports, has continued to work prominently on nuclear research.

The educational establishment maintained by the state includes forty-seven major universities and several hundred institutes of higher learning. Compulsory universal education through the secondary level was to be initiated in 1970. Institutes of research in all fields of basic science are supported and encouraged by the CPSU and the government. Gifted students are assured of a free education through all levels, to which are added a living allowance and other benefits. In keeping with European tradition and Soviet aspirations, scholarship is encouraged in all fields except those that may weaken Marxism-Leninism as the official doctrine of the state (see ch. 15, The Educational System).

Party propaganda, which for years derided, ignored, or only grudgingly admitted the achievements of Russian royalty and religion, recognized since the mid-1960's the value of the monuments to present and future generations. It refers to the relics of the Russian past as the reflection of a gifted people whose artists and architects have the historic role of national heroes. Lenin's admonition that the beautiful must be preserved and taken as an example and followed even if it is old is being recalled.

Until 1963, only the intelligentsia deplored the state of disrepair of many irreplaceable monuments of the past. Restoration involved only a few specific sites and buildings. Since then volunteer societies for the preservation of historical monuments, numbering some 3 million members, have sprung up on private initiative across the length and breadth of the land. To keep pace, the government initially established scientific and restoration workshops in the four great historic cities of the East Slavs; Moscow, Leningrad, Kiev, and Novgorod.

By the summer of 1969 various Western news sources reported that the Soviet government was spending hundreds of millions of rubles in a massive effort to restore Orthodox churches, tsarist palaces, princely mansions, private residences, and even whole towns, as in the case of Suzdal. The extent of the rehabilitation of the past is exemplified by the Culture Ministry's project of compiling *A Summary of the Monuments of History and Culture of the Peoples of the USSR*, which will eventually comprise about eighty volumes.

SOVIET IDEOLOGY

The official philosophy is Marxism-Leninism. It is based on materialism, which holds that all nature, including man himself, consists of matter in a constant process of development. The laws of that development do not depend on man's will; they are intrinsic in nature itself and fully knowable.

The theory is that the development of human society takes place in accordance with objective laws. Marxism asserts that it has made history a genuine science capable of explaining the nature of every social system and the development of society from one system to another.

The theory is seen as a guide to action, developing as historical conditions alter and as new tasks arise in the struggle of the "progressive forces of mankind." It considers the international working class the vanguard and leader of "the great movement for emancipation of all the oppressed and exploited."

The foundation of the whole edifice is dialectical and historical materialism, which regards the world "as it actually is" in the light of the data provided by "progressive science" and social practice. Its philosophical materialism is presented as the logical outcome of scientific knowledge gained over the centuries. The immediate sources include French eighteenth-century materialism, the metaphysical materialism of Ludwig Feuerbach, the idealistic dialectic of Georg Hegel, English classical political economy, and utopian socialism.

Hegel held that any process of development has two inseparable aspects: the positive aspect of growth, the emergence of something new (thesis) and the negative aspect of rejection, the discarding of the old (antithesis). The conflict between these two elements leads to a synthesis, or combining of certain features of both elements to form a new concept. The synthesis becomes a new thesis, and the process continues endlessly.

Marx accepted Hegel's view that thought and the object of thought are one but rejected his theory regarding the immateriality of ultimate reality as well as the Christian concept of a spiritual world more real than the material world of sense experience. Instead he held that man is in direct contact with a world that has objective reality.

Marx turned to Ludwig Feuerbach for the reinforcement of his tendency toward materialism. Feuerbach asserted that man forms the conscious, thinking aspect of nature, of which he is an indelible part; man is to himself his own object of thought and God is, as a consequence, no more than an outward projection of man's inner nature. Marxism holds that the means of material production of a given society determine the character of that society, of its ideas and outlook, its political and legal institutions; and that substantial changes in the conditions of material production in society lead inevitably to a change in its structure.

The decisive role in history belongs to the main productive forces of society, namely the working masses, that is, the proletariat. Contradictions between productive forces and their relation to each other in society lead to the formation of antagonistic classes. The inevitable ensuing class struggle is the moving force of social development that leads to social change. In this matter feudalism gave way to capitalism, according to Marx.

Marx defined capitalism as a social structure based on private capitalist ownership of the means of production and on the exploitation of hired labor by capitalists. He noted that capitalism while increasing productive capacity enslaved the laboring masses no less than did feudalism and similarly used religion to confound the oppressed while using the fruits of their labor. Its inner socioeconomic contradictions were bound to bring about its replacement by a more equitable arrangement of society.

Marxism teaches that the next step, socialism, is to provide a society based on the overthrow of the bourgeois-capitalist class and the liquidation of all exploiting classes as well as the socialization of the means of production. Every citizen would give according to his ability and receive according to the value of his labor. In turn, socialism is to give way to communism.

A generalized definition of communism was formulated in the Program of the CPSU adopted by its Twenty-Second Congress, held in Moscow in October 1961. It states that communism is a classless social system with a single form of public ownership of the means of production and full social equality of all members of society; under it, the all-round development of people is to be accompanied by the growth of the productive forces through continuous progress in science and technology; all the springs of cooperative wealth are to flow more abundantly, and the principle "From each according to his ability, to each according to his needs" will be implemented.

MARXISM AND THE RUSSIAN INTELLECTUAL TRADITION

Similarities exist between the tenets of Soviet Marxism and Russian nineteenth-century thought. Messianism, the belief that a country or doctrine is destined to transform the entire world, is common to both. In the same sense both are extreme, in that they seek a final and ultimate resolution of the problems of life and society. Russian thought, religious in its orientation, looked about for a general solution that Soviet Marxism claimed to have found by scientific means.

The traditional Russian distaste for commercialism among the intelligentsia as well as the peasantry coincides with the Marxist socialist ethic that is diametrically opposed to capitalism. The *sobornost* (community spirit) that typified all Russian social thought is revealed in the essentially socialist economic orientation exemplified by the *obshchina* or *mir* (peasant commune). Both stand in opposition to the individualistic, free enterprise economic approach.

The antiaristocratic populism that permeated Russian intellectual circles from the 1860's on revealed an admiration and confidence in the peasantry such as Marx had in the working classes. The anarchism that characterized many Russian thinkers found its counterpart in Marxism, which condemns the state to eventually wither away.

The notion of a small ruling elite, the Party hierarchy, coincided in some degree with the Russian tradition of rule by a small privileged minority. Likewise, the idea of a revolutionary party predated the formation of the Social-Democratic Party, predecessor to the Communist Party of the Bolsheviks, led by Lenin. The roots of the political parties formed around the turn of the century were in the radical movements of the 1860's and 1870's.

In the late nineteenth century some of the leading thinkers of Russia flirted with Marxism. Among those so-called legal Marxists were Nicholas Berdiaev, Prince Eugene N. Trubetskoy, Semion L. Frank, and Sergei Bulgakov. By 1900, disappointed in the uncertain metaphysical foundations of Marxism, they veered toward religiousness and idealism.

Marx himself had a low opinion of Russia, whose pan-Slav aspirations, he felt, endangered the security of Europe. He regarded Germany as the most likely candidate for his brand of "scientific socialism."

There also are pronounced variants between the Russian intellectual tradition and Marxism. The deep attachment of the Russian intellectual for his native land and his faithfulness to native tradition stand in opposition to the rootless internationalism and obsession with radical change that characterize Marx. Russian mysticism and spirituality conflict with Marxist materialism and Germanic sense of organization. The Orthodox stress on gentleness of soul, submissiveness to fate, and accord with nature contrast markedly with Marx's aggressive approach and support for violent action.

THE COMMUNIST PARTY AND SOVIET SCHOLARSHIP

The key to the manipulation of Soviet scholarship lies in the decisionmaking power at the summit of the Communist Party supplemented by the system of Party bureaucracy, which includes specific agencies, such as the secret police and the state censorship board (see ch. 16, Artistic Expression).

In most fields of scholarship the Academy of Sciences, directly subordinate to the USSR Council of Ministers, is the agency for official supervision. With several branches located throughout the country and control over the activities of the fourteen union republic academies, the all-union academy constitutes a control network encompassing almost all scholarly endeavor.

Loyalty to the regime and to the Communist cause is a prime requisite for high scholarly rank, and loyalty is assured through various means. Many academicians are Party members, all are well paid and, in a society that places scholarship high on the ladder of achievement, prestige is an important incentive toward loyalty. Following the academicians in scholarly ranking are the corresponding members of the academy and research associates. In addition to their generous pay, scholars are often able to earn extra fees as

336

government consultants, lecturers, and editors. The privileges available to scholars naturally bring with them pressures to conform to the demands of Party and state.

The Party controls over scholarship include restrictions relating to topics of research. Since 1938 the secret police has held control over archival materials, foreign travel, and research. Research, before and after publication, is verified by the Party to see that it does not conflict with the basic postulates of Marxism-Leninism.

MARXISM-LENINISM AND INTELLECTUAL EXPRESSION

On seizing power Lenin, contrary to Marxist theory, reestablished a repressive state apparatus, including the armed forces, a secret police, and a bureaucracy which, based on the model of its tsarist predecessor, became excessive. The breakdown of the national economy brought about by foreign and civil war led to Lenin's decision in 1921 to take another step backward from Marxist theory by reestablishing a moderate form of free enterprise known as the New Economic Policy (Novaya Ekonomicheskaya Politika—NEP).

The NEP itself was a bitter blow to the pure revolutionaries who had hoped to establish a completely socialist economy at the close of hostilities. Alexander Blok, a great symbolist poet and avid supporter of revolution, died disillusioned with Bolshevism in 1921. In September 1922 a government decree banished from the Soviet Republic twenty-five known idealistic (antimaterialistic) thinkers and writers, including Nicholas Berdiaev, Semion Frank, Nicholas Lossky, and the novelist Aleksei Remizov.

The teachings of Marx and Engels that originated as a revolutionary doctrine took on the form of orthodoxy. Materialism in its most elementary form, harking back to the democratic radicalism of the 1860's, came close to becoming the accepted intellectual attitude. Not only religion but philosophy was denounced by responsible Party officials. Social phenomena and psychic processes came to be regarded as chemical functions subject to quantitative analysis, or the mechanistic theory.

The dialectical philosopher, Abram Deborin, intent on expanding the broad outlines of Marxian thought, refuted this elementary materialism as an inadequate conception of the universe. In April 1929 the adherents of the mechanistic theory were condemned and ejected from positions in educational institutions and the state publishing houses. In December 1930 the Deborinists, in turn, were condemned by Stalin and faded into obscurity.

The Central Committee of the CPSU determined in January 1931 that henceforth all theoretical work was to be based on the declarations of Stalin. Natural scientists had to support the general line of the Party, build the sciences on the methodology of dialectical materialism, and contribute to the socialist construction of the country. There were, however, no definite statements on the relation of Soviet philosophy to the natural sciences. The program established in 1931, identified as the "Bolshevization of Science," indicated that the Party leadership intended to submit both philosophers and scientists to the Party line rather than to abstract Marxist principles.

In the adaptations to political necessities Marxism, already revised by Lenin, was doomed to be transformed to fit the needs of the state. The accent was placed less on the material evolution of economic relations than on the political action of the Party. The emphasis became less on the class struggle and more on the organization of the state, less on the international solidarity of the proletarians than on the victory of "the revolution" in Russia. Communist theory as a consquence dissolved into empiricism, immediate practical needs being served exclusively. It was a philosophy tailored to a dictatorship. Despite its officially materialistic form, it became a kind of idealism based on a mystic faith both in the "New Russia" and in Stalin.

Lenin had been an internationalist who viewed Russia merely as a base from which he could spread the revolutionary conflagration that would envelop the world and lead to the victory of communism on the entire planet. The unexpected failure of external revolutions led to the situation of "socialism in one country." It meant the reinforcement of the external security of the state and, in the face of internal opposition, the development of a powerful secret police.

Stalin, a nationalist in his attitude, propelled the country into speedy industrialization and agricultural collectivization in order to strengthen the state, which he warned would otherwise be crushed by foreign foes. After 1934 patriotism became the principal moving force in the New Russia. In the name of the edification of a new and equitable society millions perished in the widespread collectivization campaign of the early 1930's and the extensive purges of the late 1930's. Old internationalist and previous elite elements were discarded and made way for new people who owed everything to Stalin and to the new hierarchy he had created.

The new people who had moved up to positions of responsibility in the 1930's came from the underprivileged classes. Educated in technical schools, they had little knowledge of the outside world or of prerevolutionary thought and culture. Their chief concern was to serve Stalinism, whose "general line" had triumphed after the elimination of all potential rivals.

The ideology, theoretically embracing all branches of knowledge, identified itself in fact with the progress of humanity. In the system the Soviet state emerged as the privileged protagonist; all that served it served humanity. Materialism, the essential idea of Marxism, was conserved. Conceptions, hypotheses, or methods generally accepted in the scientific world, such as Freudianism, Einstein's theory of relativity, and Planck's theory of quanta, were condemned as aberrations taking their source in idealism. Basic scientific research, crippled by prohibitions and completely subordinated to the material needs of the moment, proved unable to make concerted progress. No less an authority than the future president of the Soviet Academy of Sciences, academician Sergei Vavilov (1891—1951), admitted in 1935 to the great difficulty of adjusting Marxist philosophy and Soviet physics.

In the postwar period Andrei Zhdanov dominated philosophy and the natural sciences. A Politburo member, Zhdanov was assigned to the task of cleansing artistic and intellectual life of capitalist and bourgeois survivals. Cosmopolitanism, the undue admiration of Western intellectual achievements; and formalism, lack of concern for "socialist realism," were savagely attacked in the press and on the radio.

The Central Committee of the CPSU recalled that the mission of literature was to aid the state in the education of the people and that no apolitical writing or expression of thought devoid of Communist ideology could be tolerated. Zhdanov silenced the outstanding humorist, Mikhail Zoshchenko, because of his caustic satire. He also attacked the great lyric poetess, Anna Akhmatova, for the lack of Soviet ideology in her poetry.

The Writers' Union of Leningrad advised authors on subject matter. They were to reflect the greatness of victory, the pathos of the rebuilding programs and the constitution of socialism, and the heroic efforts of the Soviet peoples in view of the overfulfillment of the new Stalinist five-year plan. But none of these issues could be treated without a profound study of the doctrine of Marx and Lenin and without a clear understanding of the policy of the state and the Party. Zhdanov counseled writers to return to the tradition of the great nineteenth-century revolutionary democrats—Vissarion Belinsky, Nikolai Dobrolyubov, and Nikolai Chernyshevsky—and the scientifically formulated and elaborated thought of Lenin and Stalin as expressed in the latter's handbook *Questions of Leninism*.

In 1950 a large collection of essays dealing with *The History of Russian Philosophy* renewed the positions of elementary materialism dating back to the 1860's. Between 1930 and 1950, according to French historian of ideas Pierre Pascal, in his essay on the main currents of Russian thought, no creative thought was engendered even within the intimate circle of Soviet Marxists.

At the same time, the more extreme extensions of dialectical materialism were gradually eliminated. In 1952 the editors of

Philosophic Questions of Contemporary Physics acknowledged that many of the philosophic problems dealing with physics had not been resolved and published Vavilov's old statement to the effect that the role of philosophy vis-à-vis physics remained undecided. One of the basic shortcomings of the Marxist philosophers, it turned out, was their lack of knowledge of the latest advances in modern science.

After Stalin's death in 1953 a minor relaxation in intellectual controls took place. In 1954 the official ideologues of the CPSU writing in the periodical *Kommunist* protested against philosophic neutralism on the scientific front and, at the same time, opposed any dogmatism in the sciences. Although Soviet scientists indicate their official adherence to dialectical materialism, Western studies by Maxim Mikulak and Eric Ashby, among others, do not reveal any clear and direct relation between the dialectic and the approach to scientific research. In *Dialekticheskii Materializm* (Dialectical Materialism), published in Moscow in 1959, M. N. Rutkevich recognized that while dialectical laws are of a general nature, scientific laws are of a specific nature and that he for one could not correlate the two. The question of linking the general with the specific emerged as the essential problem. Vice President of the Academy of Sciences Pyotr Fedoseev admitted as much in June 1960.

SOVIET HISTORIOGRAPHY

The role of Marxism-Leninism as an operative philosophy interpreted by the Communist Party in Soviet intellectual life is exemplified by its relation to historical writing. After 1928 the relative freedom provided by the New Economic Policy ceased, and non-Marxist historians were not tolerated within official scholarly bodies of the state, such as the Academy of Sciences. Until 1934 the official historical school was exemplified by the Marxist internationalist, Mikhail Pokrovsky. Following directives issued by Stalin, Andrei Zhdanov, and Sergei Kirov in that year, a patriotic and even chauvinistic approach to the writing and teaching of Russian history was established and has continued to typify Soviet historical efforts.

The official 1948 manual *Soviet Methods of Teaching History* expressed the position that history is a powerful weapon of Communist education that must wholly serve the cause of the struggle for communism. This was to be accomplished by creating in the students and the readers "the conviction that capitalism is doomed and that everywhere, in all spheres of science and art, industry and agriculture, in the work of peace, and on the battlefields the Soviet people march in the forefront of other nations, and have created values which are unequaled anywhere in the world."

PHILOSOPHY AND HIGHER EDUCATION

Among the forty-seven educational institutions with university status, only six have departments of philosophy. These are the Kiev Shevchenko State University, the Leningrad Zhdanov State University, the Mordovian State University in Saransk, the Moscow Lomonosov State University, the Tbilisi State University, and the Urals Gorky State University in Sverdlovsk. The courses they offer invariably center on Marxism-Leninism and give only passing reference to other currents of thought. Courses include: the theory of scientific communism, dialectical materialism, historical materialism, Marxist ethics and aesthetics, atheism and religion, Marxist logic, Marxist psychology, the history of Marxist-Leninist philosophy, and the history of Soviet philosophy. The history of foreign philosophy was added in the 1960's. The limited interest of the CPSU in philosophy is indicated by the fact that within the Academy of Sciences, philosophy is combined with law in a single department. The only institute of philosophy in the country is located in Moscow.

CONTEMPORARY INTELLECTUAL GROUPINGS

The general social structure known as the intelligentsia is divided into two groups. The larger and more governmentally favored group is the *tekhnicheskaya intelligentsia* (the technical intelligentsia), made up of all the technical specialists; the lesser and more independently active group is the *tvorcheskaya intelligentsia* (creative intelligentsia), made up of writers and scientists, professors, and liberal arts students. The latter contains within itself a core of independent-thinking individuals, such as the writer Solzhenitsyn and the scientist Sakharov, who do not fear to criticize and suggest reforms in the regime. They retain the traditional characteristics of the pre-revolutionary intelligentsia in their outspoken opposition to those aspects of life that they find to be offensive or repressive to individual and social life.

The Soviet creative intellectual community has generally been divided into "liberals" and "conservatives." Liberals are considered as representing those intellectuals who are intent on the loosening of Party controls and the guaranteed establishment of civil rights assuring greater personal freedom. Conservatives stand for the maintenance of Stalinist orthodoxy and for the preservation of the status quo in the political life of the country. The liberal-to-conservative range is sometimes divided into more varied groupings, with unofficial affiliations based largely on attitudes toward art and culture as they are related to politics.

Each of these groupings present the ruling CPSU with its own

341

particular problems, but with few exceptions their patriotism and attachment to the socialist way of life are beyond doubt. The failure of the Party apparatus to distinguish between loyal opposition and political disloyalty has put a heavy strain on the life of the intelligentsia. Official ideology is viewed with growing skepticism by an ever increasing body of people. Side by side with the officially approved intelligentsia have arisen courageous men who have dared to speak their notion of the truth even when their statements offended the Party leadership. There are clear indications that such men are respected by large segments of the public.

The groupings of intellectuals include the "dogmatists" or Stalinists representing the Old Guard. They dominate the periodical *Oktyabr* (October), published by the Union of Soviet Writers, the Academy of Fine Arts, the Russian writers' organization, and the unions of composers and artists. Generally older intellectuals, they are fearful of losing their privileges in Soviet society. They have made themselves anathema to the preponderant majority of Soviet intellectuals by their superpatriotism and their espousal of "socialist realism" in art. Their support for official ideological and propaganda goals tends to hinder the Party in its effort to win the good will of the intellectual community at home and abroad.

The neo-Slavophiles represent intellectuals strongly influenced by the Orthodox Church and the rural *obshchina* (village commune) that characterized pre-Petrine Russia. Mainly from the younger generation, they are intensely patriotic and seek to keep the Soviet Union free of outside, chiefly Western, influences. They are useful to the regime insofar as they encourage patriotism, but their loyalties have nothing to do with Marxism-Leninism. Certain influential elements in the Komsomol (Young Communist League), including Sergei Pavlov and their literary journal *Molodaya Gvardia* (The Young Guard), have shown great sympathy for the movement. In 1965 the Komsomol organized Rodina (Land of Birth) clubs to study prerevolutionary Russian culture.

Among its adherents in the artistic world are the painter Ilia Glazunov and the writer Vladimir Soloukhin, both of whom have been published in the *Molodaya Gvardia*. The Smogisti, a term derived from the first letter of the words *slovo* (word), *mysl* (thought), *obraz* (form), and *glubina* (profundity), forms the extreme wing of the movement.

The traditionalists most closely resemble the prerevolutionary intelligentsia. Devoted to the restoration of a genuine Russian culture, they show little interest in Western political concepts. Less impervious to non-Russian influences than the neo-Slavophiles, they are considerably more dedicated to the elimination of Stalinism and its substitutes. The poet Aleksandr Tvardovsky, editor of the "liberal" *Novy Mir* (New World), published by the Union of Soviet

Writers, is one of its leading spokesmen. Aleksandr Solzhenitsyn, Vladimir Tendriakov, and Yuri Kazakov may be classified as traditionalists. Because his critique of the Soviet system is based on traditional Russian culture, history, and values, Andrei Sinyavsky might be considered a member of this group. In its unofficial affiliation this grouping includes those who are probably the most talented and influential of Soviet artists and writers and poses the most serious problem to the Party because of its demand for the right to free intellectual expression.

The liberal conservatives comprise men and women from all generations who believe that the CPSU and the intellectuals must work together toward a moderate change in society. In the Party Aleksei Rumyantsev has been the spokesman for this viewpoint. With supporters such as the former Stalinist writer Konstantin Simonov and appreciable weight in the Moscow and Leningrad writers' organizations as well as in the Ministry of Culture, this grouping has been influential in enlarging the variety of foreign literature available in Russian. Although attuned to the progressive faction of the Party, it has irritated the provincial Party and the police and military establishments, all of which oppose any signs of tolerance for Western cultural and political values.

The modern liberals are mainly composed of writers and artists in their thirties or early forties. Centered around the magazine *Yunost* (Youth) and the Contemporary Theater and Taganka Theater in Moscow and the Gorky Theater in Leningrad, they have been responsible for most of the refreshing and sophisticated writing in the country. Among their number are Bella Akhmadulina, Yuri Nagibin, Andrei Voznesensky, Vasili Aksionov, Victor Nekrasov, and Yevgeny Yevtushenko. The aim of these people is to relate the culture of a modernized, multinational Soviet Union with the cultures of the contemporary West. They have turned out to be excellent unofficial ambassadors for the country. Their openness to Western influences has, on the other hand, rendered them suspect to the Party.

THE PARTY AND CONTEMPORARY INTELLECTUAL LIFE

Since 1956 there has been a general loosening of Marxist philosophical controls. Soviet philosophers have more prominently attended international conferences. They have stated that there are only two binding dogmas of Marxism—the primacy of matter and the idea that the world is knowable. While the central principle of Communist morality remains devotion to communism and love of the Socialist Fatherland, more works of non-Soviet philosophers are being translated into Russian. Even the works of non-Marxist thinkers, such as those of Pierre Teilhard de Chardin, are being appraised in a more open manner. The works of tsarist, antirevolutionary authors such as Dostoevsky have been republished in popular editions. The one-volume 1963 edition of the *Philosophical Dictionary* reflected increasing Soviet interest in areas of contemporary thought that are also of concern to the West.

The fall of Khruschev in October 1964 brought about a period of uncertainty while the new leadership attempted to establish its own approach and style. Early in 1965 the Moscow and Leningrad sections of the Writers' Union in the course of stormy sessions managed to remove representatives of the "old guard." Mstislav Keldysh, the president of the Academy of Sciences since 1961, in a meeting of the academy condemned Lysenkoism and its deleterious effect on the development of the biological sciences. His report, supported by a CPSU decree for improving biology, assured the removal of Lysenko and his disciples from positions of responsibility in the biological and agricultural sciences (see ch. 18, Science and Technology).

Late in February 1965 *Pravda* acquired a new editor, Aleksei Rumyantsev who declared that genuine creation is only possible in an environment of search, experiment, and the free expression and collision of opinions; the presence of various schools and trends; and various styles and genres competing among themselves under the banner of socialist realism. In March, Leonid Ilichev, a hardliner on cultural matters, was removed from his post as ideological chief of the Central Committee Secretariat and replaced by the more moderate Pyotr Demichev.

The spring of 1965 marked a revival in creative and critical writing. Andrei Voznesensky, Yevgeny Yevtushenko, Vladimir Tendriakov, Vitali Siomin, and Vasili Aksionov contributed richly to the short-lived renaissance. Works by Franz Kafka, William Faulkner, and John Updike were translated and appeared in print.

By late July and August of 1965 the conservative critics began their attacks on the liberals Aksionov, Voznesensky, Tendriakov, and Yevtushenko. Komsomol (Young Communist League) chief Sergei Pavlov called for a revival of the atmosphere of the 1930's. At this juncture Rumyantsev writing in *Pravda*, in September criticized the people attacking liberal writers and journals.

In that month Rumyantsev was removed from his post as editor in chief of Pravda, and Andrei Sinyavski and Yuli Daniel were arrested. The two arrested writers came to represent the crucial issue of intellectual freedom in the country. Sinyavski was sentenced to seven years and Daniel to five years in a labor camp despite widespread protests from the intellectual community. This was the price they paid for publishing satirical and ironic tales of Soviet life in Western publications.

In March 1967 some twenty-five professors and students of

philosophy were arrested in Leningrad because their views were considered anti-Marxist. Since that time, the CPSU through its secret police and censorship board has maintained an oppressive intellectual atmosphere in the country. The defection of Soviet writer Anatoli Kuznetsov in the summer of 1969 only served to underscore this fact.

According to the revelations of Kuznetsov the basic features of Stalinism have merely been somewhat modified without really being changed. All Soviet intellectuals who are allowed to travel abroad are expected to submit on their return reports on the conduct of their colleagues and to explain their own. Writers and scientists are encouraged to collaborate with the Komitet Gosudarstvennoy Bezopasnosti (The Committee for State Security—KGB). Those who collaborate are given opportunities to be published and prosper. In another category are those who acknowledge their duty toward the KGB but refuse to collaborate directly; they are deprived of many privileges, such as facility in finding publishing outlets and travel abroad. In the final category belong those who refuse all collaboration with the KGB; in that case their works are not allowed to be published, and they are considered to be suspect and are subject to harassment.

CHAPTER 18

SCIENCE AND TECHNOLOGY

Science and technology have played a leading role in the development of the modern Soviet state and have become dominant forces in most areas of Soviet life. In the 1960's various scientific and technological achievements received worldwide acclaim, and scientists were honored with international plaudits and awards. On the basis of its scientific eminence and technological achievements, the Soviet Union occupied a prominent position in the world scientific community in early 1970.

Scientific achievement has been marked by outstanding success in many areas and by mediocrity or weakness, in others. Work in mathematics, physics, astronomy, the earth sciences, and medical research has been outstanding, but modern biology and many branches of chemistry have been weak. Rapid technological progress in the exploration of space and the development of nuclear energy have attracted world attention and won universal respect. Advanced technology can also be found in such industries as aviation, iron and steel, and machine tools but, in agriculture and almost every other science-based industry, technology in the 1960's was lagging. For a nation committed to automation and computerization, for example, computer technology was strikingly behind the times.

The weakness in much of Soviet technology results from the problem of innovation—translating ideas from scientific laboratories into production at industrial factories. Although the Soviet Union has always stressed the practical uses of science, it has devoted more resources and more attention to research than to development. The organization of science has separated scientific research institutes from industrial design bureaus, and there have been few incentives for innovation. Failure to apply the fruits of research to technological development led to complaints from world-famed Soviet physicist Pyotr Kapitsa, among others, of a technological gap between his country and the West. Political leaders listened to the scientists and promised action to rectify the situation, and neglected areas began to show improvement at the end of the 1960's.

The government and Party have given full support to science and technology since the early years of the Soviet state. Scientific achievements are extolled, and careers in science are eagerly sought.

The country devotes 3 percent of its gross national product (GNP) to scientific research and development and maintains a pool of technically trained manpower that numbers about 2¼ million persons. Close to 700,000 of these are university graduates and, of the latter, 40 percent are women. More than half of all university graduates received degrees in the sciences or in engineering.

Soviet scientists have been well rewarded for their work and enjoy a position of material comfort and prestige unequaled in any other profession, but they have also endured the restrictions of state direction and control and the absence of intellectual freedom. Most scientists find accommodation within the system, but a number have chosen to speak out in the post-Stalin era over political issues and in defense of intellectual freedom (see ch. 17, Intellectual Expression).

EARLY DEVELOPMENT

Science in Tsarist Russia

The founding of the Imperial Academy of Sciences in 1725 marked the beginning of significant scientific activity in tsarist Russia. Until the eighteenth century there had been little interest in science, and no scientific research centers had been established. The new academy, founded by Peter the Great and closely associated with his reforms in education, was designed to nurture the development of an indigenous science and to provide a nucleus of well-trained scientific personnel. It was initially staffed by scientists from Western Europe, principally Germany, and remained under foreign domination for many years. The first Russian academician was not elected until the 1740's, and native Russians did not win control of the academy until the latter part of the nineteenth century.

Western science provided the base for early scientific development in Russia and exerted a strong influence throughout the last two centuries of the empire. One of the most distinguished foreign scientists was the Swiss mathematician Leonhart Euler, whose work during the initial years of the academy helped to pave the way for future Russian achievement in mathematics. But Russia herself also contributed substantially to world science and produced a large number of outstanding scientists in all fields. One of the greatest figures in Russian science was Mikhail V. Lomonosov (1711-65), who entered the academy in 1742. This remarkable scientist and man of letters developed a number of original theories in such varied subjects as chemistry, physics, geography, astronomy, and metallurgy.

The academy's second charter in 1803 relieved it of all educational responsibilities. New universities were established at Saint Petersburg, Kazan, Dorpat, and Kharkov, and the academy was permitted to concentrate on scientific research. Physics, mathematics, and the natural sciences blossomed in the first half of the nineteenth century. To this period belong the mathematician Nikolay I. Lobachevskiy (1793—1856), famous for his work in absolute calculus and non-Euclidean geometry; V. J. Struve (1793—1864), astronomer and founder of the Pulkovo Observatory in 1839; and N. N. Zinin (1812—80), a distinguished chemist who discovered aniline dyes. In 1841 the Academy of Sciences absorbed the Russian Academy (a separate institution founded in 1783), which became the division for language and literature alongside a division for physico-mathematical sciences and one for history and philosophy. The academy retained this organizational structure until 1927.

Scientific activity continued to flourish in the late nineteenth century and early 1900's, and Russian scientists received worldwide recognition. But their progressive ideas and empirical methods often brought them into conflict with the tsarist government and the Orthodox Church. Many scientists had studied in Western Europe and returned with political doctrines that challenged the old order. Dmitry I. Mendeleyev (1843—1907), who first compiled the periodic table of the elements, was blackballed from membership in the academy in 1880. The biologist Ilya I. Mechnikov (1845—1916) was forced to leave Russian in 1888. Sofia V. Kovalevskaya (1850—91), a talented mathematician and the first woman member of the academy, received greater recognition in Sweden than in her own country.

Among the other outstanding scientists of the tsarist period was Ivan P. Pavlov (1849—1936), famous for his research on conditioned reflexes, who won the Nobel Prize for his work in physiology in 1904. Konstantin E. Tsiolkovskiy (1857—1935), a pioneer in modern rocketry, first published the theory of cosmic flight at the turn of the century. Despite the restrictions placed on science by the autocracy, tsarist Russia bequeathed a rich tradition of scientific achievement and individual distinction to the new Soviet state.

The Revolution and the 1920's

The Bolshevik Revolution of 1917 disrupted scientific progress and induced a number of prominent scientists to emigrate. The Communist Party of the Soviet Union (CPSU) soon realized, however, that it could achieve its goal of rapidly transforming the country into a great modern state only through a concentrated effort upon science and technology. Marx had stressed the importance of science, and the Bolsheviks promised to promote science as the principal means of building communism. Although the preoccupation with science can be explained in part by reference to Marxist idology, the primary concern of the early leadership was to establish a technological basis for the modernization of society and for industrial and military development.

The new government moved quickly to enlist the support of its scientists and to encourage scientific endeavor. In January 1918 the Commissariat of Education appealed to scientists to become actively involved in the building of the new sodialist state. Lenin spoke of the "wonders of technology" and attached great importance to technological progress. In April he outlined a much-celebrated "Plan for Scientific and Technical Work," which specified the role science was to play in industrial reorganization and economic development.

The Academy of Sciences, which had only one institute in 1917, began to expand. In 1918 alone such new research centers were established as the Optics Institute, the Hydrology Institute, the Institute of Industrial Chemistry, the Institute of Physico-Chemical Analysis, and the Karpov Chemical Institute. In the following years the Physico-Mathematical Institute, the Physiology Institute, and the Soil Institute were founded. In 1925 the Academy of Sciences was redesignated the Academy of Sciences of the USSR and placed under direct supervision of the Council of People's Commissars.

The living and working conditions of scientists gradually improved. Although the government passed a decree on "Improving the Conditions of Scientists" in 1919, scientists suffered from a serious lack of facilities, inadequate housing, and a shortage of food in the early years of Communist rule. But by the mid-1920's their lot had improved substantially, and many were allowed to travel abroad. Scientific investigations in a number of fields, notably biology, reached a high point. Several Western scientists were attracted to the Soviet Union by the original research being carried out. In these years ideological restrains were few, and scientists enjoyed considerable freedom in their work. In 1925 Gorky had no hesitation in eulogizing scientists as "heroes of free and ever inquiring thought!"

The Stalinist Years

Beginning in the late 1920's, science was increasingly pressed into serving the needs of the state and was subjected to increasing ideological control. Scientific activity was enlisted in direct support of the five-year plans, rapid industrialization, and the forced collectivization of agriculture. Work in chemistry, for example, was heavily emphasized as the country strove to develop a giant new chemical industry. Scientists were encouraged to engage in solving practical tasks, and those who did not devote themselves to the applied sciences were accused of being "formalists." The regime made many demands on its scientists and technical experts, but it depended heavily upon their skills in meeting the needs not only of economic development but also of national defense.

The Academy of Sciences, the center of all scientific activity, endured a number of organizational changes that brought it under increased Party control. The work of the academy was redirected toward "practical" problems in the applied sciences and away from the past preoccupation with theoretical research. In 1927 a new charter deprived the academy of the right to nominate its own members and required it to admit Party members regardless of scientific preeminence. The number of academicians was increased from forty-two to seventy-five, a move that facilitated the election of elements favorable to the regime. A Division of Physico-Mathematical Sciences and a Division of Social Sciences replaced the three previous divisions.

Further measures in 1928 strengthened Party influence over the work of the academy. Party members were first elected to membership in 1929, and by 1933 a high percentage of the staff was Communist. A graduate studies program was introduced in 1929, the first time the academy had engaged in educational activities since the eighteenth century. A new charter in 1930 further defined the academy's practical orientation. In 1934 the academy was transferred from Leningrad to Moscow, in a move to centralize its expanding activities and place it under direct government control. The following year yet another charter, which remained in force until 1957, tied the work of the academy even more closely to economic development and created a new Division of Technical Sciences. During World War II the academy worked closely with the Commissariat of Defense. Its institutes were dispersed, and a number of emergency commissions were established. The academy was recentralized after the war, and Party control was reenforced with the creation of a new Academic Secretariat headed by Party nominee Aleksandr V. Topchiev.

The Party also reexamined science in terms of Marxist idology. Theories that were compatible with the tenets of dialectical materialism were singled out and encouraged. Pavlov's theories on conditioning, for example, were well suited to the Marxist emphasis on changing man and his environment and therefore received special attention. Psychology and physiology developed under Pavlovian influences and Pavlov himself were glorified. Theories that challenged the dialectic were repressed, however, and leading developments in the West were often branded as "capitalist" or "bourgeois false sciences." These included, most notably, cybernetics, the theory of relativity, and quantum mechanics.

Biology suffered most severely under the impact of Marxist

idology. As a result of the great "genetics controversy," which reached its peak in 1948, and the rise to power of the notorious Trofim D. Lysenko, biology in the Soviet Union had become almost totally discredited as a science by the time of Stalin's death. In the 1920's, however, Soviet geneticists, led by Nikolay I. Vavilov, had achieved outstanding results and had won world recognition. Their works were based on Mendelian genetics, which stressed the role of the gene in heredity and had long been accepted in the West.

Beginning in 1929, the theories of Vavilov and his followers were increasingly challenged by Lysenko, an unorthodox agronomist who claimed that characteristics of living organisms could be altered by environment and that these acquired characteristics could then be inherited. Lysenko's belief in the importance of environment in heredity fit nicely into the Marxist framework, and his theories on plant breeding promised an answer to the problem of raising agricultural production. Parading under the slogan of "Michurinism" (I. V. Michurin had earlier advanced similar proposals), Lysenko won official recognition and received the support of Stalin himself.

A campaign of accusation, dismissal, and arrest was launched against Vavilov and his supporters. They were accused of "anti-Michurinism," derided as the "Knights of the Gene," and attacked for their "idealistic mistakes." Vavilov was ousted as director of both the Institute of Plant Breeding and the Institute of Genetics and as president of the Academy of Agricultural Sciences and replaced by Lysenko. Several contrived public disputes were organized, at which geneticists had to defend themselves or admit their errors. In 1940 Vavilov was arrested on trumped-up charges and sent to prison, where he died in 1943. By 1948 Lysenkoism had reached its peak, many prominent geneticists were forced to recant, and the Academy of Sciences of the USSR admitted its mistake in having ever given credence to "Western" genetics.

POST-STALIN YEARS

Stalin's death initiated a more relaxed era in science. Communication with Western science and scientists was gradually restored to what it had been before the Revolution. Periodicals began to be exchanged, and Western publications were increasingly translated and disseminated within the country. Soviet scientists began to reappear on the world scene, participating increasingly in international conferences. In 1956 Soviet scientist Nikolay N. Semyonov, won the Nobel Prize, the first such award in science the country had received since 1904. Programs of cultural exchange and scientific cooperation were undertaken with many countries in the West.

Ideological control over science was loosened. Many areas that had been suppressed were now given official sanction. The most striking example was cybernetics. Under Stalin this study of control systems in human beings and machines had been attacked as a "bourgeois science." Since it represented another universalist philosophy, cybernetics posed a challenge to Marxist idology and competed with dialectical materialism. But in the mid-1950's as the Soviet Union turned increasingly to automation and computer technology, the need for cybernetics became clear even to its former opponents and was openly supported. Ideologists succeeded in reconciling cybernetics with Marxism by considering the two on different levels—Marxism as the broad law of nature and society, and cybernetics as the more narrow science of control systems and communications. In early 1970 cybernetics enjoyed the most popularity and the most enthusiastic official support of any scientific study in the country.

In biology Lysenkoism had already come under attack before Stalin's death, and during the 1950's Lysenko's influence began to decline. For a while he staged a comeback and received the support of Khrushchev, who was interested in his experiments with plant breeding. In 1964, however, Lysenko was ousted as director of the Genetics Institute. Charged with incompetency the following year, he retired. Lysenko never endured the kind of treatment he caused to be inflicted on others, however, and remains a full member of the Academy of Sciences. A number of his followers still hold positions of responsibility and, on occasion, speak out in defense of his theories.

Despite the relaxation of control, ideologists still strive to relate science to Marxism. A critic wrote in 1969 that "the Marxist philosophers cannot ignore the connection of science with ideology," adding that this connection was "of extreme importance" in biology. A number of Western scientific theories are still under attack. The ideals of Malthus on population, for example, are accused of being a "reactionary sociological doctrine of the capitalist world." The Party supervises scientific activities through a Department of Science and Establishments of Higher Education under the CPSU Central Committee Secretariat, headed by Sergei P. Trapeznikov.

Beginning in 1959, efforts were made to improve the organization of science, particularly the coordination of research and development. The role of the Academy of Sciences in research activities came into question, and in 1961 a decree on "Improving the Coordination of Scientific Research" reduced the scope of the academy's work in applied research. Institutes of the academy that were related to industry were transferred to the appropriate ministries or state committees, and the size of the Technical Sciences Division was reduced. In 1963 the academy was relieved of its remaining responsibilities for applied research and development and placed in charge of all fundamental research. The academy has thus circumvented, from its original preoccupation with basic research to an emphasis on applied science in the Stalinist years, and back again to fundamental research in the 1960's. But even its efforts in basic research must have a practical orientation toward industrial development.

The USSR Academy of Sciences stands at the center of all scientific activity. It is one of the most prestigious bodies in the country and enjoys ministerial status. In early 1968 it had 203 full members, or academicians, and 381 corresponding members. The academy employed over 27,000 scientists in nearly 200 scientific institutions in 1966. It is divided into four sections: physico-technical and mathematical sciences, the earth sciences, chemico-technological and biological sciences, and the social sciences. All but one of the union republics have their own academies, which employed more than 29,000 scientists in about 350 establishments. There are also close to 500 special research academies, such as the Academy of Agricultural Sciences and the Academy of Medical Sciences, subordinated to various ministries and state committees. The USSR Academy of Sciences, the republican academies, and the specialized academies are known collectively as the Academy System.

In an effort to decentralize scientific research and at the same time to promote regional development, a "science city" was established in 1957 near Novosibirsk in Southwest Siberia. Considered to be "one of the most important measures taken in this century to organize science," the Novosibirsk center serves as the headquarters of the important Siberian Branch of the Academy and is the most developed research center in the nation. The experiment has proved so successful that similar centers are being developed elsewhere, notably at Irkutsk in central Siberia.

Efforts had been made as early as 1947 to establish a central coordinating body responsible for the translation of basic research findings into industrial development. But it was not until 1961 that a workable organization, the State Committee for Coordination of Scientific Research—renamed in 1965 the State Committee for Science and Technology—was created. The committee is responsible for the overall coordination of research and development, determines priorities, and works to introduce new technology with maximum economic effect and minimum expense.

The committee also supervises the activities of the almost 4,000 scientific institutes and laboratories of the various industrial ministries, known as the "branch" system, which employ well over 300,000 scientists. The chairman of the committee is Vladimir A. Kirillin, a deputy premier of the USSR Council of Ministers, a member of the CPSU Central Committee, and a leading thermodynamicist. One of his deputies is Dzerman Gvishiani, the son-in-law of Premier Kosygin. The committee has the rank of a ministry.

Scientific research, both pure and applied, is also conducted at the universities, principally in Moscow, Leningrad, Kiev, and Novosibirsk, and at over 700 institutes of higher education. Approximately 60,000 scientists are employed at all higher education establishments. The work of these establishments is concerned primarily with teaching, however, and plays a relatively minor role in overall research and development.

SCIENTIFIC ENDEAVOR

Mathematics, Physics, Astronomy

The Soviet Union has recognized the growing importance of mathematics in the modern world, and mathematical training receives a high priority. Emphasis on mathematics has enhanced work in the physical sciences and the development of technology in such areas as aerospace, nuclear energy, and computers and automation. Mathematical methods are also being applied increasingly to economics, biology, medicine, statistics, sociology, and other subjects. Continuing the rich tradition of mathematical excellence in tsarist Russia, Soviet mathematicians have proved themselves to be among the most outstanding in the world.

Mathematicians are prominent in most of the physical sciences and in science administration. They have also applied their skills with distinction in the advance of technology and in engineering and industry. Mstislav V. Keldysh, president of the Academy of Sciences and a member of the Party Central Committee, is an expert in mechanics and aerodynamics and has contributed much to the Soviet space program. Boris N. Petrov, an authority on automation, cybernetics, and computers, is also prominent in the space effort.

Mikhail A. Lavrentyev, a vice president of the Academy and chairman of its section physico-technical and mathematical sciences, as well as the organizer of the Novosibirsk research center and president of the Academy's Siberian branch, is a specialist in the peaceful uses of atomic energy. Nikolay N. Bogolyubov, director of the Joint Nuclear Research Institute at Dubna, has done outstanding work in physics as well. Mikhail D. Millionshchikov, a renowned and respected mechanical engineer, is another vice president of the Academy. Ivan G. Petrovskiy and Aleksandr D. Aleksandrov, both mathematicians, are the rectors of Moscow and Leningrad Universities, respectively.

All branches of pure mathematics are avidly pursued and, in the field of applied mathematics, important work is being done in fluid dynamics, aerodynamics, and the theory of elasticity. Cybernetics, information theory, game theory, and linear programming, which had been suppressed during the Stalinist years, have been revived in the 1960's and are among the most popular subjects of study.

Training in computer technology, systems analysis, and systems programming, as well as cybernetics, is receiving particular attention in an effort to provide the specialists required for the steadily increasing use of computers and the introduction of automation in industry and other fields. Andrey N. Kolmogorov, one of the greatest names in Soviet mathematics and a specialist in probability theory, was among the influential scientists who admitted the importance of cybernetics in the late 1950's and gave this heretofore controversial subject his support. He now encourages the study of systems analysis at Moscow University. Other mathematicians who made early contributions to cybernetics included I. P. Pavlov, N. M. Krylov, and Bogolyubov. Viktor M. Glushkov, director of the important Kiev Cybernetics Research Institute, is another leading authority on computer technology and systems analysis.

Soviet work in physics is outstanding. There have been exceptional achievements in all fields, and since Stalin's death six physicists have won the Nobel Prize: Pavel A. Cherenkov, Ilya M. Frank, and Igor E.Tamm, for their discovery and interpretation of the Cherenkov effect—radiation given off by particles traveling with velocity greater than light (1958); Lev D. Landau, for his theory on the superfluidity of liquid helium (1962); and Nikolay G. Basov and Aleksandr M. Prokhorov (together with Charles H. Townes of the University of California at Berkeley) for their theoretical predictions of the laser (1964).

In nuclear physics, the late Igor V. Kurchatov became famous for his direction of the intensive research program on the atomic bomb in the mid-1940s'. An early specialist in the atomic nucleus, Kurchatov discovered nuclear isomerism in 1935. Although he died in 1963, important work has been carried out in his name and directed by Anatoli P. Aleksandrov, at the Institute of Atomic Energy in Moscow. Boris P. Konstantinov, a vice president of the academy until his death in 1969, developed the technology of uranium-isotope separation in 1945, an important step in the production of fissionable material for nuclear weapons.

Two prominent physicists played a key role in research on the theory of the hydrogen bomb and thermonuclear power. In 1950 Nobel laureate Tamm and Andrey D. Sakharov, then only thirty-two and later to be dubbed the "father" of the Soviet hydrogen bomb, laid the basis for research in controlled thermonuclear reactions. Together with scientists from the Lebedev Physics Institute, they carried out the first calculations of thermal diffusion and conductivity across a magnetic field. Lev A. Artsimovich and Mikhail A.

Leontovich have also contributed to the study of controlled nuclear reactions with their work on obtaining high-temperature plasma.

Soviet work in particle physics is world famous. Vladimir I. Veksler and Aleksandr L. Mints did research in the late 1950's in the creation of a synchrophasotron of 10 billion electron-volts. Veksler had discovered the principle of the synchrocyclotron in 1944, independently of the American physicist Edwin McMillan. The largest particle accelerator in the world was constructed in 1968 at Serpukhov, near Moscow.

The development of new, and even more powerful, accelerators at the Novosibirsk Nuclear Physics Research Institute has raised the Soviet Union to a position of world leadership in elementary particle studies. The director of the institute, Gersh I. Budker, has invented a colliding beam accelerator with a destructive force far stronger than that of a cyclotron, a synchrotron, or a linear accelerator and a temperature of several tens of millions of degrees. Two such machines have been built at Novosibirsk, and two more are under construction.

Pyotr L. Kapitsa, a leading physicist well known in the West, has led work in low-temperature physics. Trained in England under Lord Rutherford in the interwar years and well established at Cambridge University in the early 1930's, Kapitsa was induced to remain in the Soviet Union while on vacation there in 1934. His entire laboratory was transferred to Moscow, and he was placed in charge of the new Institute of Physical Problems. Research in solid state physics was pioneered by the late A. F. Joffe, who led in the development of semiconductors and the theory of thermoelectric generators. Recently, Soloman I. Pekar of Kiev University has done significant work on electron behavior in crystals.

Impressive work in quantum radiophysics and radioelectronics dates back to the early 1940's, when Soviet physicists pointed out the possibility of light intensification by induced radiation. Prokhorov and his colleagues, G. A. Askaryan and G. O. Shipulo, who developed the first Soviet optical quantum generators, or lasers, are leading extensive research into laser application for various industrial and scientific uses. In radioelectronics Yevgeniy K. Zavoyskiy discovered in 1946 that certain materials absorb radio waves when placed in a magnetic field, and he has continued research in paramagnetic resonance. B. Vedenskiy, editor in chief of the *Great Soviet Encyclopedia* until his death in 1969, contributed greatly to the study of the distribution of ultra-short waves and the field of magnetism.

The country took pains to rebuild and modernize facilities for the study of astronomy, which had almost been destroyed in World War II. Astronomers have at their disposal a vast array of modern instruments and are active in both optical observation and radio-astron-

357

omy. They have made important contributions in observational and theoretical astronomy and have devoted particular attention to the study of stellar systems, galactic evolution, and interstellar space. Astronomical investigations of circumterrestrial space and of the sun and its energy are of increasing importance to plans for more extensive exploration of space. A number of radio-telescope installations have been built in recent years, both for astronomical studies and for tracking stations. Work is now nearing completion on the largest optical telescope in the world, situated over a mile high in the Caucasus, with a mirror 236 inches in diameter.

The Pulkovo Astronomical Observatory near Leningrad, the first great modern observatory of Imperial Russia, founded in 1839, is still the leading observatory in the country. Scientists there have compiled the famous *Pulkovo Star Catalogue* and have invented and developed a number of advanced telescopes. The observatory's work, directed by Aleksandr A. Mikhaylov, is concerned with research into conditions on the planets, of the solar system, interplanetary space and solar radiation, and with attempts to contact possible extraterrestrial civilizations. Pioneering work is also being done in "laboratory astrophysics," simulating conditions similar to those in a stellar atmosphere.

A great modern astrophysical observatory was built in the Crimea after the war. The largest telescope there is a 120-inch reflector, completed in 1960, which has been the largest in Europe. The work of the Crimean Astrophysical Observatory is concerned with stellar astronomy, solar physics, and solar-terrestrial relations. The observatory's director, Andrey B. Severny, is a specialist in the study of velocity and magnetic fields on the sun. A deep-space tracking system is also located in the Crimea.

Other important observatories include the Abastumani Astrophysical Observatory in Georgia, headed by Yevgeniy K. Kharadze, and the Byurakan Astrophysical Observatory on the slopes of Mount Agarat in Armenia, whose director is Viktor A. Ambartsumyan, an expert in stellar association. A number of important astronomical institutes are also located in Moscow and Leningrad.

The Earth Sciences

Earth sciences are a particularly important area of scientific activity and have a strong pratical orientation. The Soviet Union has been thoroughly mapped, and there is continuing emphases on the discovery and exploitation of the country's rich natural resources and mineral deposits. Geography, geology, geochemistry, and geophysics are used extensively in pursuing regional economic development goals in Siberia, central Asia, and the Soviet Far East and in expanding the power, gas, oil, and chemical industries. Scientists are preparing imaginative plans for changing the natural environment for purposes beneficial to man, such as altering the courses of rivers, influencing weather, and raising Arctic temperatures. Oceanographic research is carried out on a worldwide basis, and expeditionary research in the Arctic and Antarctic is particularly active.

Geography is a more comprehensive science than it is in the West and has a more practical application. Physical geography is emphasized most heavily. Other specializations include economic geography, geomorphology, soil science, botanical geography, hydrology, climatology, and cartography. The Academy of Sciences Institute of Geography, headed by Innokentiy P. Gerasimov, and the Geographical Society of the USSR, descended from the Russian Geographical Society, founded in 1845, are active in expeditionary and research activities.

Geologists have studied the structural regularity of the earth and have explored extensively from desert to tundra. They have bored through the earth's crust and have recently used electromagnetic probes in seeking information on the surface and lower layers. Two new methods of ore prospecting were employed in 1969: a gamma radiation device provided an exceptionally rapid and convenient method of ore analysis, and discovery of the link between subterranean helium pockets and ore-bearing faults led to new discoveries of gold. In recent years the science of aerology has been developed, and the use of aerological surveys has increased the coverage of heretofore inaccessible areas. Geochemical and geophysical methods, widely applied to studies of the earth, are of growing importance in space research. Pioneer analysis of the composition of the moon has been conducted by Aleksandr P. Vinogradov, a vice president of the academy and director of the Vernadskiy Institute of Geochemistry and Analytical Chemistry.

The country occupies a leading position in oceanographic research and exploration. Scientists attach great importance to the study and future utilization of the great natural and mineral wealth of the sea. They speak of opening up the "underwater virgin lands" and look to the establishment of an industrial fleet with floating factories and bases. In addition to continued interest in fish as a food source, scientists are studying distillation of salt water and the extraction from the sea of salt, minerals, and ores. In the future they see the oceans as an endless source of energy, supplying deuterium, the heavy hydrogen isotope employed in controlled thermonuclear reaction.

The Soviet Union maintains a sizable fleet of modern scientific research vessels that travel regularly throughout the world. The world's only nonmagnetic research ship has conducted studies of the magnetic and gravitational field of the earth since 1954. Meteorological studies are made from ships acting as floating weather

359

bureaus and stationed in distant seas. Marine scientists cooperate with their counterparts in other countries, and in 1969 a Soviet team headed by the noted marine geologist Aleksandr P. Lisitzin completed a three-month expedition with United States scientists. Early in 1970 the country planned to set out in the North Atlantic the largest array of research buoys ever to be moored in the ocean. The project, under Andrey S. Monin, director of the academy's Institute of Oceanology, is designed to measure ocean currents.

Scientists are continuing a long tradition of exploration in the Arctic, an area of major importance to the Soviet Union. The "North" expedition of 1969 was the largest in the history of polar exploration and carried out a broad program of study on ice flow and formation, climate, and solar radiation. The nineteenth in the "North Pole" series of drifting research stations, famed since their inception in the 1930's, set off in late 1969 for an extended stay in Arctic waters. Scientists are actively prospecting for oil and gas on the shelf of the Arctic Ocean. They believe the area is a continuation of the oil-bearing depression of Siberia and is rich in oil.

Systematic studies of the Antarctic, which began in 1955, are being pursued in accordance with the international treaty on Antarctica. An observatory and four research stations have been established there, including the first permanent weather rocket station, which transmits atmospheric information directly to meteorological stations in Moscow. A Soviet scientist has compiled the first map of the Antarctic's actual landmass, hidden beneath the ice. The fifteenth Soviet Antarctic expedition, for 1969—71, has embarked on a wide program of meteorological, geophysical, and oceanographic research. Soviet scientists also plan to survey the little-known coast of Oates Land in Antarctica and to erect a new research station there.

Chemistry, Biology, and Medical Research

Soviet work in chemistry has not been as strong, in general, as it has been in such fields as physics and mathematics. Major attention has been devoted, however, to chemical research since the late 1920's in order to develop a petrochemical industry and to meet the steadily increasing demand for such products as synthetic fibers and substances, artificial fertilizers, and medicinals. During the period between the two world wars, Soviet chemists won worldwide recognition for their outstanding work in several fields. But since World War II, chemistry has failed to keep pace with developments in Western countries, the apparent result of the isolation of chemists from the West and inadequate research facilities. Despite the emphasis on industrial application, translation of the results of chemical research into new processes and products has been slow.

360

Physical chemistry continues strong, under the leadership of Nikolai N. Semyonov, a vice president of the Academy of Sciences and director of the Institute of Chemical Physics. Since the 1920's Semyonov has directed valuable research in elementary chemical reactions and in the mechanism of chain reactions in explosions, for which he received the Nobel Prize in 1956. His work has had broad practical application in internal combustion engines and nuclear fission. In 1968 Boris V. Derjaguin of the Institute of Physical Chemistry discovered an anomalous form of water, called polywater, with a viscosity and density far greater than ordinary water. His finding is of considerable scientific importance, since it may lead to the discovery of anomalies in other substances as well. Research in electrochemistry, developed in the interwar period by Aleksandr N. Frumkin, director of the Institute of Electrochemistry, has been held in high regard for many years.

Progress in organic and inorganic chemistry has been weak in comparison. Work on the development of synthetic rubber, which had been pioneered by S. V. Lebedev in the late 1920's, continues, and recent efforts have been made to find industrial methods for the synthesis of isoprene. Aleksandr N. Nesmeyanov, former president of the academy and director of the Institute of Elemento-Organic Compounds, leads research in the compound of metals. Valentin A. Kargin, until his death in 1969, won worldwide recognition for his work in the chemistry of high molecular compounds and in the field of polymer structures. His research at the Topchiev Institute of Petrochemical Syntheses helped lay the foundation for production of plastics, rubber, and synthetic fibers. But the Soviet Union still lags in development of modern medicinals, dyes, herbicides, fertilizers, and a wide range of synthetic materials for industry and consumer goods. In inorganic chemistry, important to the metallurgic industry, and well developed in the 1930's, work is being revived after a long period of neglect.

The science of biology has been gradually revived since its decline under the influence of Lysenko during the Stalinist period. Although Lysenko has been removed from all positions of responsibility and discredited personally, many of his genetic theories on plant breeding and the effect of environmental conditions have not been discarded. Rather, these theories are now ascribed to the "outstanding Soviet plant-breeder" Michurin, who continues to be held in high official regard even as Lysenko is conveniently forgotten. Ideologists still argue that the dialectical method is significant in understanding the basis of heredity and the capacity for change in organisms.

The Soviet Union is attempting to stimulate as rapid a growth in the biological sciences as has occurred in such fields as physics. The emphasis in biological research on practical application in the improvement of human health and the raising of agricultural production remains strong. Biochemistry is being pursued in support of medical research, and the study of proteins, considered to be the "central problem of biology," is active. One of the best known biochemists, Aleksandr Y. Braunshteyn, is director of the Institute of Protein. Production of synthetic foods, such as synthetic aminoacids, fats, and various vitamins, is being emphasized. Biological research is being employed in efforts to improve soil texture, introduce high-yield crops, and to make greater use of fertilizers.

Genetics and molecular biology survived the worst years of Lysenko's domination, largely as a result of the protection they received from influential nuclear physicists, who were particularly interested in the effect of radiation on inheritance. After Lysenko's fall, research into these fields began again, as Western theories were cautiously introduced, new journals began to appear, and a number of new institutes sprang up.

A longtime opponent of Lysenko and a specialist on the role of nucleic acids and genetics, Vladimir A. Engelgardt became director of the newly formed Institute of Molecular Biology. The Institute of Genetics, of which Lysenko had been director, gradually declined. In its place a new Institute of General Genetics has been organized under Nikolay P. Dubinin. An able cytogeneticist who had been out of sight since 1948, Dubinin was among the first to strike back at Lysenko in 1955, blaming him for the Soviet failure to develop hybrid corn. In 1967 a distinguished Soviet geneticist, N. V. Timofeyev-Ressovskiy, was presented the Kimber Genetics Award by the United States National Academy of Sciences for his work in heredity—a ceremony symbolizing the restoration of Soviet genetics to worldwide recognition.

Medical research has been heavily emphasized, as the Soviet Union strives to build up a vast modern public health service centered around the polyclinic. The USSR academy of Medical Sciences controls most of the country's research activity, which is carried out in twenty-nine specialized institutes and four laboratories. The president of the academy is Vladimir D. Timakov, a specialist in microbiology. Although by Western standards medical facilities and practices seem backward and proposals and experiments are often unorthodox, medical research is well advanced in many areas. Increasing attention is being given to the computerization of disease diagnosis and treatment, and many doctors are taking courses in computer techniques and basic mathematical theory.

Outstanding work is being done on the theoretical and clinical aspects of organ and tissue transplantation, and in 1969 thirty-five institutes engaged in this effort were placed under a central transplant institute headed by Gleb Solovyov, a prominent specialist in

362

cardio-surgery and kidney transplantation. Progress in orthopedics and in the development of artificial limbs, given original impetus by the great number of wounded after the war, is excellent. The Moscow Surgery and Orthopedic Research Institute has made practical use of the bones and joints of cadavers in over 2,000 successful operations. Cardiology is strong, and Soviet surgeons were the first to operate on the heart. Heart transplants are still viewed cautiously, however, and of the 109 such operations in the world by the spring of 1969, only one has been performed in the Soviet Union.

Treatment of cancer is of major concern, and a giant oncological center is to be built in Moscow between 1971 and 1975, the biggest of its kind in the country. In 1969 Soviet scientists conducted bold experiments in efforts to delay death from acute leukemia. Although research and methods in blood transfusion are judged to be years behind those of the West, the Soviet transfusion service is impressive, and progress in such areas as developing organic substitutes for blood may be more advanced. Cadavers are used as a supply source for blood banks, a unique departure from Western practice. Research in the field of endocrinology has increased widely since around 1960. Large-scale research in the treatment of virus-caused diseases is conducted in part at the Ivanovskiy Virology Research Institute, named after the famous Russian scientist who discovered viruses in 1892.

Work in psychology is strong, and there has been rapid progress in neurophysiology. In 1960 a revival of more precise psychological research and new work on verbal behavior and perception led to a huge outpouring of new research. Pavlov's influence on conditioning remains, but research is now balanced by more objectivity and access to developments in the West. The emphasis is on complex psychological processes and intellectual operations that regulate skills, not simply with sequences of conditioned reflexes.

TECHNOLOGICAL PROGRESS

Soviet technology is well advanced in high-priority areas such as space and rocketry, nuclear energy, and defense research. But throughout industry as a whole and in virtually all civilian sectors of the economy, technological development is sluggish and lags far behind that of the industrialized West. Moreover, the gap appears to be widening, a subject of considerable concern to political leaders and responsible scientists. Overall spending on research and development is substantial, running at 3 percent of the GNP and amounting to R8.2 billion (1 ruble equals US$1.10) in 1967. But an unusually large share of the total, estimated to be possibly as high as 80 percent, was devoted to military and space work. Spending on space projects alone has been estimated at 1 percent of the GNP. There also appears to have been little benefit of new technology from defense- and space-related research and development for civilian industry.

Space

The strength of Soviet science and technology has been clearly evident in space. The launching of the first artificial earth satellite in 1957 drew worldwide attention to the high level of its technological development and marked the beginning of the space age. The first *sputnik* was soon followed by a series of spectacular space "firsts" in both manned and unmanned flights, which established an early Soviet lead in space exploration. During the 1960's Soviet interest in the further development of its space program remained high, and scientists looked forward to the utilization of space research in many areas of science, the economy, and public health.

The achievements in space have also demonstrated that the Soviet Union can mount coordinated and well-organized programs in high priority areas and translate the findings of scientific research quickly and effectively into technological development. The space program grew naturally out of the intensive postwar effort to develop and produce intercontinental ballistic missiles. This well-funded effort, directed by Dmitry F. Ustinov, then minister of armaments, brought together research laboratories and design bureaus and united scientists, engineers, and technicians in a common endeavor.

In the early years of the program the Soviets relied heavily on captured German rocket equipment and specialists in V-2 technology, but by 1949 Soviet scientists had largely taken over the work on rocket propulsion. The chief designer of the early Soviet rocket engines and spacecraft was the late Sergey P. Korolev, former head of the Central Design Bureau for Space and Intercontinental Rockets. Leonid I. Sedov, a specialist in mechanics and aerodynamics, has been deeply involved in the space program for many years and has been hailed abroad as the "father of the Russian sputniks."

It is believed that Ustinov has retained overall supervision of Soviet space and rocketry programs from his present positions in the Politburo (candidate member) and secretariat of the CPSU Central Committee. Government control over the space program in 1969 was probably exercised by Leonid V. Smirnov, a deputy premier and former chairman of the State Committee for Defense Technology, and by Sergey A. Zverev, the minister of defense industry. In the Academy of Sciences a Council for the Exploration and Utilization of Space is responsible for the purely scientific aspects of the space program. Keldysh himself, who has played a major role in space work and, as president of the academy, maintains personal supervision over all space research.

The Soviet Union vaulted into the leadership of the space age by using a 1957 model intercontinental ballistic missile, which had extremely powerful booster engines for that time and could place a relatively heavy spacecraft into orbit. For almost a decade Soviet rocket engines remained the most powerful in the world. *Sputnik I*, launched on October 4, 1957, weighed 184 pounds. The second *sputnik* launched a month later and carrying a dog, the first living creature in space, weighed 1,121 pounds. The first United States satellite, *Explorer I*, weighed 31 pounds in comparison.

The early advantage in booster power also enabled the Soviet Union to make rapid strides in manned flights. On April 12, 1961, Yuri Gagarin became the first man in space, orbiting the earth in *Vostok I*. In August of that year the Soviets launched the first group flight when *Vostok III* and *Vostok IV* came within 3.1 miles of each other. The first woman in space, Valentina Tereshkova, went into orbit on June 16, 1963, in *Vostok VI*. A large new spacecraft, the 12,000-pound *Voskhod I*, carried the first multiple space crew of three cosmonauts into space on October 12, 1964. In March 1965 Aleksey Leonov performed the first "space walk" from *Voskhod II*. But the country also suffered the first tragic death from a space flight when Vladimir Komarov perished on reentry of his *Soyuz I* on April 24, 1967.

Scientists worked to correct apparent design problems in the new Soyuz series, and no further manned flights were attempted until October 1968, when Georgi Beregovoi in *Soyuz III* rendezvoused with the unmanned *Soyuz II*. In January 1969 *Soyuz IV* and *Soyuz V* accomplished the first docking of two manned spacecraft and the first transfer of spacemen from one vehicle to another. Three dramatic launchings on three successive days in October 1969 placed seven men into orbit aboard *Soyuz VI*, *Soyuz VII*, and *Soyuz VIII*—the greatest number of men and spacecraft ever together in space on one mission. The cosmonauts carried out unique space welding experiments and conducted preliminary tests for the eventual construction of giant manned space stations in orbit around the earth.

Taking an early lead in unmanned flights to the moon, the Soviet *Luna I* missed the moon by about 4,000 miles but became the first artificial satellite of the sun. The second *Luna* scored the first hard landing on the moon on September 13, 1959. In October of that year *Luna III* photographed the hidden side of the moon for the first time. The first soft landing was made by *Luna IX* on February 3, 1966, and two months later *Luna X* entered the first lunar orbit. Further probes continued and in September 1968 *Zond V* became the first spacecraft to travel to the moon and return. *Zond V* was also the first Soviet spacecraft not to land over mainland Russia, splashing down in the Indian Ocean where it was recovered by a waiting ship. Despite its early advantage in booster power, the Soviet Union had failed to develop the powerful rockets and sophisticated technology required to send manned spacecraft to the moon in the 1960's. Following the successful United States landing of men on the moon in July 1969, Soviet scientists, Keldysh among them, disavowed any plans to send their own cosmonauts to the moon in the near future.

Interplanetary research probes have been sent to Mars and Venus. *Mars I*, launched in November 1, 1962, missed Mars but entered a solar orbit. Several later Mars probes have either failed at launch or missed their target. Flights to Venus have been more successful. *Venera III* made the first hard landing on the planet on March 1, 1966, following two earlier flybys. Subsequent Venera probes transmitted much valuable information about the planet's extremely high temperature and atmospheric pressure.

Space satellites have also been used for scientific and environmental research, weather observation, communications, navigation, and other purposes. Most of the scientific probes have been in the catchall Cosmos series, of which there have been more than 300 since they began in 1962. Extensive meteorological studies are conducted by satellites in the Meteor series. The Orbita communications system, using the *Molniya* satellite, provides television coverage across the entire Soviet Union, and plans call for satellite transmission of *Pravda* throughout the country. About 135 intelligence gathering reconnaissance satellites had been launched by the end of 1969, and Soviet testing of a space bomb delivery system has continued since late 1966.

Soviet leaders and scientists have proclaimed their intention to work for international cooperation in space and to use space for peaceful purposes. They have pointed to the launching of *Intercosmos I*, a product of space cooperation between the Soviet Union and Eastern Europe, on October 14, 1969, as the first step in achieving a joint space research program. The Soviet Union has also concluded an agreement with the United States on sharing the results of medical research in space and has agreed with France to place a French laser reflector on the moon in 1970.

Most space probes have been launched from a site near Tyuratam in central Kazakhstan, which the Soviets call the Baikonur cosmodrome. An earlier site at Kapustin Yar, near the Ural Mountains north of the Caspian Sea, has also been used. More recently a launching area near Plesetsk, south of Archangel, has been active, especially for scientific probes.

By the late 1960's the most powerful operational Soviet booster was the SL-12, capable of generating 3 to 4 million pounds of thrust. This rocket has been used in several lunar probes and in the fall of 1968 it launched the world's heaviest unmanned payload, *Proton IV*, which weighed 37,000 pounds. Also being developed are new rocket engines with increased booster power, possibly in the 10-million-pound-thrust category, which would be required to send manned flights beyond earth orbit and to conduct more distant probes of the planets. A gigantic untested rocket has been observed at a vast new launching complex at Baikonur, but it was reported to have exploded during a test launch in the summer of 1969. The Soviet Union is also probably beginning to use high energy fuels, such as liquid hydrogen; and, according to Petrov, nuclear-powered rockets in the Yantar series, powered by plasma motors, have already been launched.

Future Soviet plans for the exploration of space appear to be centered around the construction of manned orbital space stations, which Keldysh has predicted will be in use in the mid-1970's. A permanent staff on these stations will be maintained and exchanged regularly by space "shuttles." The orbital stations will be used for a variety of scientific research programs related to the study of the earth and its vicinity, as well as for the study of outer space. They will also serve as staging points for future manned flights to the moon and possibly to nearby planets.

Nuclear Energy

Soviet achievements in developing nuclear energy for both military and peaceful purposes are also the result of a well-coordinated, high priority effort originally designed to meet defense needs. In 1943 a special Scientific and Technical Council was organized to develop an atomic bomb. Overall direction of the program was assigned to an industrial administrator, Boris Vannikov, while research was headed by the eminent nuclear physicist Kurchatov. The Soviet scientists were aided by German nuclear specialists. An atomic bomb was quickly developed and first detonated in the fall of 1949. Progress in thermonuclear explosions was even more rapid, and the first Soviet hydrogen bomb was tested on August 12, 1953.

In 1953 the atomic energy program was placed under the Ministry of Medium Machine Building of the USSR Council of Ministers. The development of an advanced nuclear weapons technology has remained under this ministry, which in 1969 was headed by Y. P. Slaviskiy. In addition to a wide range of powerful nuclear weapons, the Soviet Union is building nuclear-powered submarines and deploying them abroad. Development of nuclear energy for peaceful uses has been supervised by a separate organization since 1956. Now called the State Committee for the Utilization of Atomic Energy, it is headed by A. M. Petrosyants.

Since the Atomic Test-Ban Treaty in 1963, the Soviet Union has continued to conduct nuclear testing underground, although it did not acknowledge doing so until the fall of 1969. The principal test areas have been in Novya Zemlya in the Arctic and the Semipalatinsk area of eastern Kazakhstan, but an explosion in the southern Ural Mountains was reported for the first time in September 1969. Scientists have minimized the danger from radioactive fallout and have explained that their testing program contains an elaborate built-in system of security checks to prevent harmful radiation.

The use of energy for peaceful purposes has been officially endorsed. Lavrentyev, as chairman of the Scientific Council on the Use of Explosions in the National Economy, recently stated that nuclear blasts hold an "important key to progress" and cited the use of such explosions to tap mineral deposits in Siberia, clear space for people to live, make artificial dams, prevent flooding, and aid in the exploration of Siberian oil and gas deposits.

In the fall of 1969 *Komsomolskaya Pravda* devoted an entire page to a rare description of a nuclear explosion designed to create a vast underground reservoir for oil and gas. Petrosyants has also stressed the importance of nuclear tests to satisfy industrial requirements.

Nuclear energy is being developed as an inexpensive source of power for the further economic development of the country. The world's first atomic power station was put into operation in 1954 at the Obninsk research center near Moscow. Built under the direction of Dmitriy Blokhintsev, an expert in theoretical physics at the Dubna Neclear Research Institute, it was capable of producing a modest 5,000 kilowatts of electrical power. Since then more powerful plants have been constructed, notably the I. V. Kurchatov plant at Beloyar and one at Novovoronezh, which is to have an eventual power capacity of 1.5-million kilowatts. By 1980 it is planned to commission dozens of reactors with a capacity of 1, 2, or more million kilowatts.

Unique portable nuclear reactors are being constructed for use in remote arctic and tundra regions, and new types of more efficient reactors are being developed. These include the Sever series of portable atomic power stations, capable of producing sufficient energy for a village of 3,000. A miniature power station the size of a pinhead, which can operate for decades, has also been developed, according to Soviet sources.

Soviet scientists have made important progress in harnessing the power of thermonuclear energy, a goal that could lead to unlimited and inexpensive electrical power. The control and application of thermonuclear energy are also likely to revolutionize production processes in the chemical and metallurgical industries. This work is directed at developing a reactor powered by atomic fusion instead of the fission, or splitting of atoms, used to produce energy in nuclear powerplants now in use. Fusion research efforts are being conducted at the Kurchatov Institute in Moscow.

Successful fusion experiments have been achieved by using a machine called the *Tokamak* 3, which is far superior to counterparts in the West in obtaining conditions required for fusion. A larger model, *Tokamak* 10, is now being planned that may serve as a prototype for eventual nuclear fusion powerplants. Early in 1969 a Soviet official predicted with confidence that his country would be able to control nuclear fusion within ten years. But Western experts, conceding the long headstart, believe that the Soviets will demonstrate controlled fusion within five or six years. Another specialist has termed the Soviet work in controlling nuclear fusing "the best yet achieved by any nation."

Despite the early interest in nuclear power, however, and despite the considerable advanced research in nuclear physics, technology has not kept pace with the level of research. The Soviet Union lags far behind the major industrialized nations in nuclear technology. Reasons for the lag in nuclear power development appear to have been the traditional reliance on hydroelectric power and a reluctance—sharply criticized by nuclear experts—on the part of Soviet planners to push for the production of nuclear power equipment.

Industry

The civilian industry most technologically advanced is aviation, which has benefited substantially from military research. Development work and the construction of prototypes are heavily emphasized and, unlike other industries, aviation designers and engineers reportedly outrank factory managers. The country has successfully developed the world's first supersonic transport, the TU-144, which was test-flown on December 31, 1968. Aviation scientists are already thinking of aircraft with speeds of 10,000 to 12,000 kilometers per hour and possibly, of "aerocosmic" craft for use in flying to orbital space stations.

Iron and steel as well as machine tooling are also advanced industries, largely as the result of the two-way flow between research institutes and factories. But technological development in the chemical industry, essential to the growth of other important industries such as metallurgy, plastics, textiles and consumer goods, as well as to agriculture, is notably weak. As a result, much chemical and synthetic fiber technology has been imported. Weakness in automobile design is also apparent and has forced the country to base its future production plans on Italian technology. In most other science-based industries, the application of modern technology is lagging.

The important field of automation and computerization is perhaps the most striking example of technological lag. The Soviet Union is eager to introduce automation into industrial facilities and is pressing the development of computerized production systems. Automatic production lines have been installed in the "Moskvich" automobile plant, and increased productivity as a result of computerization has been noted at a number of factories. Despite these efforts, however, computers have yet to be fully incorporated into the economy. Soviet computer technology is believed to be five to ten years behind that of the West, both quantitatively and qualitatively. Soviet machines work slower, have less memory capacity, and are less varied and adaptable to different tasks.

First generation computers, the M-20 and Ural 1, were not developed until 1959. Later models in the Ural series after 1961 appeared to be second generation machines, but the Ural 4 was infamously bad. Heavy computers in the Minsk and Besm series have been subsequently developed. The Besm-6 is the most advanced model now in general use, handling a million operations a second. Seventy percent of the medium and small computers have been developed at the Kiev Cybernetics Research Institute, a center for research into mass production of computers. These include the Mir series for scientific computations and the Dnepr for control of production processes. By 1975 the country hopes to have a nation-wide computer network linking 800 regional data-processing centers to handle commercial and scientific computation needs. The network will be equipped with a new series, the Rjad, to be produced at the Minsk plant.

Despite the large share of resources devoted to defense and space programs, the technological lag in industry does not appear to have been caused by funding problems alone; nor is it the result of an inadequate supply of professionally trained manpower, or any inherent weakness in either the research or development sectors themselves. Rather, the lag seems to result from a failure to innovate, that is, to translate the findings of basic research into the development of new products and manufacturing processes.

Despite the traditional Soviet emphasis on the practical application of science, more resources are devoted to research than to development. In general, the scientific establishment appears to prefer spending more time on research than development work. Scientists at the research institutes of the Academy of Sciences enjoy greater prestige and receive more financial rewards than do their colleagues in industry. Research institutes also lack the pilot plants and facilities necessary for experimentation with new production processes and the development of prototypes.

The organization of research and development presents a major obstacle to innovation. The basic research institutes of the academy are separated from corresponding design and development bureaus in industry. The same is true for research conducted by the universities and institutes of higher learning. Within industry itself there is little coordination between the ministries and the research institutes and factories subordinate to them. Overall, little attention has been paid to the assessment of future technological needs and to the direction of research and development work to meet them. Nor has there been an effort to eliminate a plethora of useless duplication. There has never been a well-coordinated, centrally directed research and development effort in the civilian economy that has been comparable to the crash programs in the space and defense industries.

Finally, there has been very little incentive for innovation in industrial development. Centralized planning appears to have discouraged innovation, and factory managers have been judged on their ability to meet and exceed production targets, not on their ability to develop and introduce new technology. New processes that have threatened to disturb the production pattern have been avoided. There has been no financial inducement to the factory manager, the industrial scientist, or the engineer to devote their energies to technological development, and therefore they have concentrated almost entirely on production.

Scientists and government officials have become increasingly aware of the serious problem in innovation and are attempting to speed up the introduction of new technology. They have admitted that it can take two or three times as long to put innovations into effect as it does in other industrialized nations. V. A. Trapeznikov, first deputy chairman of the State Committee for Science and Technology and a leading authority on automation, complained in July 1969 that although it should take five to eight years at most to put new technological breakthroughs into production, this process was taking as long as eight to twelve years. He put the blame on crippling delays at construction sites that tie up hard-pressed resources and urged a 50-percent cut in all construction projects.

Specific measures have been undertaken to improve the coordination of research and development and to establish a closer link between science and industry. These include the setting up of scientific production organizations, which combine research institutes and design bureaus with a production plant. Emphasis is being placed on the "science city" concept, such as in Novosibirsk, where a leading research center, a major university, and local industry all contribute to, and support the work of, one another. Increasing use is being made of giving industrial research and development contracts to establishments of higher learning in a move designed to bring the two areas more closely together.

Steps have also been taken to provide economic incentives to factories and other industrial research organizations to encourage innovation. Under a decree adopted in October 1968, the pay of scientists and inventors will be increased for effective innovations. Scientists also will have more influence over the direction of their work and will be relieved of assignments to experimental shops and laboratories. Scientific personnel in factories will qualify for the same pay scale as their heretofore privileged colleagues in research institutes. The decree also provides for eliminating those research and design offices that are shown to be consistently ineffective.

Just how effective these measures will be is uncertain. In the petrochemical industry a large project uniting several research institutes with branch offices has facilitated the orientation of research to practical problems and has improved the quality of project work. New "scientific production" organizations have been set up in the electrical engineering industry, and the Ministry of Power and Electrification has assessed the work of the research institutes subordinated to it and worked out an overall plan for research up to 1980. But a number of ministries, particularly the Ministry of Construction, have been slow in introducing the new measures, and innovation is still ineffective. A *Pravda* editorial in November 1959 warned that the contribution of every scientific organization to improved production would be assessed at intervals of at least three years and that those bodies which were found lacking would be reorganized or abolished.

THE SCIENTIST AND THE STATE

Scientists constitute an elite within Soviet society. For their important contribution to the rapid development of a modern, technologically advanced state, the government has rewarded them with material benefits and prestige superior to those of any other profession. In the opinion of one Western correspondent, Soviet scientists are "sure of their value and high station."

Salaries exceed those for other professionals and are well above average salaries in the economy as a whole. According to Soviet statistics for 1967, the average monthly wage for all scientific workers was R122. This compared to R112.7 in state and economic administration, R112 in industry, R96.4 in education and culture, and R93.3 in banking and finance. The averave monthly wage for the economy as a whole in 1967 was R103.4. Leading scientists reportedly earn much more. The director of a research institute receives a monthly salary of R500 to R600, and a department chief in an institute earns R250. Full members and corresponding members of the Academy of Sciences receive an extra allowance of R500 and R250 a month, respectively. Scientists are also able to earn substantial increments in addition to their usual salaries, particularly under the measures designed to provide greater financial incentives for innovation.

A sociological study of occupations, based on interviews with former Soviet citizens, reveals that scientists rank at the top of the list with respect to the popular regard and general desirability of professions. Scientists receive special privileges with respect to housing, rest and vacation facilities, foreign travel, and contacts with the West. The cosmonauts and scientists engaged in the space program live in a modern town created especially for them outside Moscow. In their work scientists enjoy considerable independence in research and relative freedom from official constraints. The Academy of Sciences enjoys a large measure of independence in its operations and, in the post-Stalin period, reportedly has several times refused to approve the membership of candidates proposed by the Party.

Although the repressive climate and ideological excesses of the Stalinist years have faded into the past, the totalitarian system and Marxist philosophy remain. Nor is science immune from the Party and state controls that more deeply affect such areas as philosophy, literature, music, and art. For many years scientists had remained politically docile. But as various aspects of life began to loosen up after the death of Stalin, scientists started to press increasingly for more freedom of expression, for the removal of censorship, and for fewer restrictions on experimentation and travel.

By the late 1960's many scientists, including a number of the country's most prominent names, had entered into virtual intellectual rebellion against Party tutelege and thought control. Dissident scientists have rejected the philosophy of dialectical materialism, have shunned Party and "voluntary" public tasks, and have openly criticized the government's repressive actions against other intellectuals, especially writers.

The growing disaffection of scientists had developed much more slowly and expressed itself less overtly than the revolt of some of the younger writers and social scientists. One of the earliest signs of awakening independence by scientists was the convening in 1958 of a national conference intended to demonstrate to ideologists the significance of subjects that had long been suppressed, such as biology, cybernetics, and the theory of relativity. In 1962 the noted physicist Kapitsa, already known for his liberal and outspoken opinions, published an article on defense of these same subjects.

A clear signal that all was not well among the scientific elite came in early 1966. In January and February several scientists protested against the trial and harsh punishment of the writers Andrei Sinyavsky and Yuli Daniel. In March a group of twenty-five distinguished public figures addressed a petition to the Twenty-third Party Congress protesting against the rumored rehabilitation of Stalin. Among those signing were such outstanding Soviet physicists as Kapitsa, Tamm, Sakharov, Artsimovich, and Leontovich. In 1967

Kapitsa, in publicly defending an artist whose works had aroused official displeasure, argued that "the clash of differing artistic manners, styles, and creative creeds is just as important for the development of art, as the struggle of opinions is for scientific progress."

An increasing number of petitions bearing the names of scientists began to circulate in 1968 in defense of writers who were either under attack or had been jailed. In January and February petitions supporting Alexander Ginzburg, Yuri Galanskov, and their colleagues appeared with the names of many prominent scientists and research workers, some of them from prestige institutes such as the Dubna Nuclear Research Institute. One such petition was signed by forty-six scientists from the Novosibirsk research center. In March ninety-nine mathematicians, including seven Lenin Prize winners and seven academicians, addressed a "Letter of 99" to the state authorities protesting the recent confinement of their colleague and philosopher Aleksandr Yesenin-Volpin in a mental hospital. In August many scientists organized spontaneous meetings at a number of research institutes to express their disapproval of the invasion of Czechoslovakia.

Scientists have also expressed their independence and resentment against Party control by refusing to participate in "voluntary" work projects and shunning the study of Marxism-Leninism. In June 1967 the Party press complained about the increasing reluctance of scientists at the Obninsk research center to undertake "public work." According to a survey at one institute there, only 14 percent of the scientists performed such tasks "with pleasure," while the remainder did so either "with great reluctance" or "as a duty."

The growing ideological disaffection of scientests has been revealed by public expressions of official concern. In July 1968 *Pravda* pointedly reminded young research workers that they were "under an obligation to make a profound study of Marxism-Leninism and to apply themselves persistently to the mastery of the dialectical-materialist methodology of enquiry." In September of that year the newspaper *Sovietskaya Rossiya* (Soviet Russia) charged that at Obninsk some people had "spread views alien to the Party" and that while "dubious people propagated incorrect views on the development of literature and art" no lectures had been presented on politics, political economy, or philosophy for a long time.

The most significant step in the scientists' struggle for intellectual freedom has been the critical essay "Progress, Coexistence, and Intellectual Freedom" writen by the eminent physicist Sakharov. It first appeared clandestinely in June 1968 and was smuggled out of the country and published a month later in the *New York Times*. In his 10,000-word essay Sakharov urged "peaceful coexistence and intellectual freedom" while the United States and the Soviet Union attempted to deal with the "great possibilities and dangers connected with the scientific-technical revolution."

Sakharov went further than any other influential scientist in advancing an explicit and detailed proposal for rapprochement and cooperation between the two world powers and in expressing his apprehension at the "mass myths that put entire peoples and continents under the power of cruel and treacherous demagogues." He devoted much of his discussion to the changes in his own society that he believed to be essential in consolidating the achievements of socialism. High among them was "intellectual freedom," which Sakharov considered "essential for human society" and "the key to a progressive restructuring of the system of government in the interests of mankind."

The publication of Sakharov's essay created a worldwide sensation, both because of the author's outspoken views on the Soviet system of government and because the draft had been discussed and edited by several scientists with similar feelings and had been given wide circulation among scientific personnel at major research institutions throughout the Soviet Union. The Sakharov essay represents an expression of honesty and a sense of personal responsibility among Soviet scientests of stature. It, and other tangible forms of protest or public expression of views, suggest that these scientists now have their own positive ideas about the kind of society, and world, they wish to help build. According to the writer Anatoli Kuznetsov, who became a self-exile in 1969, some of the "more intelligent and thinking people" in the Soviet Union are pinning their hopes for a more liberal and decent society on influential scientists and scholars like Sakharov.

In outspoken public statements and concern for intellectual freedom, scientists have shown themselves to be loyal to the system but concerned that ideology and political controls have failed to adjust to changing times and conditions. Their criticism, therefore, does not appear to have been aimed so much against the state as it has been at trying to influence and correct some of its policies. Kapitsa, for example, sharply criticized Soviet ideology early in 1969 for lagging behind the times and being virtually without influence in the outside world. But his remarks were those of a loyal critic of the system, designed to improve the effectiveness of ideological work by making it more responsive to present conditions.

Nevertheless, the ideological disaffection of its scientists represents one of the gravest problems facing the regime. Ironically, by giving priority to the creation of a scientific elite, the government has raised to a key position within the system a group fundamentally alienated from it. On the one hand, the regime must maintain an inquiring and inventive scientific intelligentsia capable of keeping the nation in the forefront of the world technological revolution, while on the other, it is determined to impose on its scientists a uniform, doctrinaire pattern of political and philosophical thought.

Officials have expressed concern over the rebellious scientists. In March 1968 Keldysh condemned the "isolated groups" of scholars who had written petitions in support of dissident intellectuals. The Academy of Sciences, he warned, was "disturbed and is taking measures to prevent similar occurrences" in the future. He charged that the dissident scientists "do not determine our science" and that "the development of science will go forward in any case." Kelkysh, it turned out, had special reason for concern, since his own sister and brother-in-law had both signed protests.

In an article in the Party's leading theoretical journal, *Kommunist*, at the end of 1968, the deputy head of the Central Committee Propaganda Department expressed appreciation for the achievements of scientists but warned that "the Party and people want to see in scientists not only creators and organizers of scientific and technical progress, but political workers, active fighters for the cause of communism." Continuing concern over the scientists' rejection of "philosophy" (dialectical materialism) was expressed in *Pravda* articles of October 1968 and January 1969, which recalled that Lenin's superior scientific insight was the result of his application of the Marxist dialectic.

The regime has also resorted to certain repressive measures. Mass dismissals and expulsion from the Party of hundreds of scientists have been reported. Among them have been world-famous physicists, such as Aleksandr Kronrod, and mathematicians, such as Igor Shafarevich and Yuri Manin. Perhaps in reaction to the favored status they had enjoyed, repression has been particularly severe at such research centers as Novosibirsk and Obninsk. Scientists of world stature, such as Sakharov, present a special problem for the regime, however, since their scientific reputation and value to the state render them largely invulnerable. Sakharov's belief in the ultimate convergence of the Soviet and Western systems has also been publicly endorsed by Kapitsa. But even Sakharov is known to have been reprimanded and disciplined, and he has reportedly been deprived of several consultant positions and barred from classified work.

SECTION III. POLITICAL

CHAPTER 19

FORMAL STRUCTURE OF THE UNION GOVERNMENT

The Soviet Constitution of 1936, as amended, defined the country's formal governmental structure in 1969. The constitution provides that the powers of the state be shared by a parliamentary body known as the Supreme Soviet; by its executive committee, known as the Presidium of the Supreme Soviet; and, by a government bureaucracy functioning under a Council of Ministers (see fig. 6). In fact, however, the formal structure of government constitutes an administrative framework within which the Communist Party of the Soviet Union (CPSU), which is not designated by the constitution as a ruling body, exercises complete control. The Communist leadership exercises this rigid control through the party structure itself, through the political police, and through the armed forces (see ch. 21, Political Dynamics).

The CPSU maintains a monopoly of power over the political system, and the organization of the government is designed to further that purpose. Although the constitution does refer to various administrative powers that the branches of the government are allowed to exercise, it makes no mention of the measures the Party enacts, either alone or in conjunction with the state organs, to determine the course which the government will follow. The real rulers of the Soviet Union are the members of the Central Committee of the Party, especially its Politburo. The government and the CPSU, in 1969, were interlocked through well-known personalities of the Party who were to be found in all the crucial posts (see ch. 21, Political Dynamics).

The Constitution of 1936 describes the Soviet Union as a federal state, but the country has most of the characteristics of a unitary state with a highly centralized government. The governmental structure is based on a pyramid of elected councils, known as soviets, which—since the Bolsheviks came to power—have served as the governing bodies at various levels beginning with the village. Below the national level there were fifteen union republics in 1969 that were further subdivided into autonomous republics and regions;

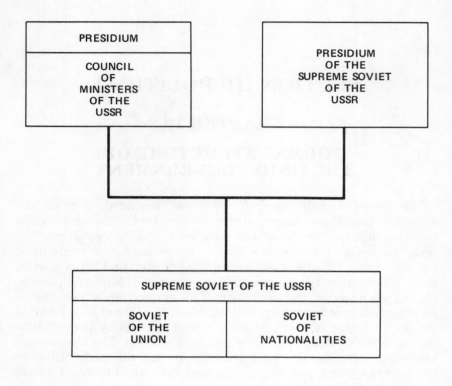

PRESIDIUM	PRESIDIUM OF THE SUPREME SOVIET OF THE USSR
COUNCIL OF MINISTERS OF THE USSR	

SUPREME SOVIET OF THE USSR	
SOVIET OF THE UNION	SOVIET OF NATIONALITIES

Note -- Presidium includes Chairman and Deputy Chairmen of the Council of Ministers.

Figure 6. Soviet Union General Organization of Government.

provinces; territories; and national areas on the basis of ethnic, historical or economic considerations. These subdivisions are formally assigned many powers of self-government, but in practice they function mainly to put into effect the decisions of the central government, channeled downward through a structure dominated by a political elite composed of professional government officials and CPSU leaders (see ch. 20, Component Political Subdivisions).

At the Twenty-first Party Congress in 1959, Nikita Khrushchev intimated that a revision of the constitution was necessary. At the Twenty-second Party Congress in 1961, he specifically mentioned the need for the drafting of a new document to replace the 1936 constitution under which the country had been operating. It was not until April 1962, however, that the Supreme Soviet unanimously approved a proposal for the formation of a commission to prepare the draft of a new constitution. Headed by Khrushchev, the commission consisted of ninety-six party and government dignitaries. With Khrushchev's removal in October 1964, the chairmanship of the commission was passed to Leonid Brezhnev, the new Party secretary. In 1969 the commission had not reported on its progress or presented a draft constitution. Thus the constitution adopted in 1936 continued to define the country's formal governmental structure.

CONSTITUTIONAL DEVELOPMENT

During the course of its history, the Soviet Union has had three constitutions, those of 1918, 1924, and 1936. However, the concept of constitutionalism—defined as an attempt to confine each branch of government to its prescribed role, to safeguard citizens against abuses of power by the officialdom, and to enforce the continuing responsibility of the governing authorities to the electorate—is alien to Soviet political thought. The constitutional documents have rarely been consulted by administrators as a guide to the organization and functioning of the government. The constitutions of the Soviet Union have never given an adequate picture of the actual political system; they have provided only an outline of the existing structures. More than in most other political systems, the real constitution remains largely unwritten.

From the point of view of the Soviet leaders, the constitutional documents of the Soviet Union serve several useful purposes. They make the formal governmental structure explicit, giving legitimacy and stability to the system of control. In addition, the constitutions have played an important role, both at home and abroad, as propaganda measures. Since the emphasis in Soviet constitutions has always been on the mass mobilization of the electorate and on its participation in the proceedings of the government, the regime has attempted to perpetuate an idea of monolithic popular support for itself. Finally, to meet ideological requirements, the Soviet constitutions have been carefully drafted to emphasize the economic security that the communist system claims to provide. The constitutions were designed to give the impression that ultimate power in the country resides in the hands of the workers.

THE CONSTITUTION OF 1918

On July 10, 1918 the Fifth All-Russian Congress of Soviets ratified the constitution which established the Russian Soviet Federated Socialist Republic (RSFSR). The structure of the state system as outlined in the constitution represented a formal codification of institutions that already existed and the first attempt of the new state to legitimize itself according to accepted Western standards. The Constitution of 1918 established formally many of the principles of political organization and control that have come to characterize the modern Soviet state.

In the debate preceding the drafting of the document, basic conflicts emerged between those revolutionaries who favored a strengthening of the central power of the new government and those who wished to safeguard the autonomy of the local soviets; between those who favored a concentration of legislative and executive powers in the supreme organs of the government and those who sought their separation and delimitation.

Under the guidance of Yakov Sverdlov and Joseph Stalin, the basic lines of policy that were drafted subordinated the local soviets to centralized authority, ensuring the concentration of legislative and executive power in the supreme governmental organs (which in turn were to be controlled by the Communist Party) and organizing the component subdivisions along nationality-territorial lines. The industrial working class was designated as the principal supporting pillar of the government. No specific mention of the Communist Party was made in the constitution.

In its final form the document consisted of two parts. The first part, the Declaration of the Rights of Toiling and Exploited Peoples, stated the policies and aims of the new regime and confirmed specific actions, which the government had taken prior to the ratification of the constitution. The Bill of Rights was cast in class terms in that the constitution provided for what it described as "real freedoms" of press, assembly, and association for the workers and peasants. Freedom of religious and antireligious propaganda was to be assured every citizen. The constitution further spelled out the duties as well as the rights of its citizens proclaiming that "he who does not work shall not eat."

The constitution established the principle that voting was to be indirect and based on unequal suffrage. Thus, the regime was able to deny the franchise to certain categories of persons that it considered hostile to the new order, such as priests and wealthy peasants. Urban voting strength was increased to five times that of rural voting power—one representative per 25,000 urban workers as opposed to one per 125,000 peasants. This indicated the general distrust of the rural voters held by the framers of the new constitution.

The second part of the constitution elaborated the general principles of the new governmental structure and spelled out the form it would assume. The constitution established the unicameral All-Russian Congress of Soviets as the supreme legislative body, and its executive arm was entrusted with discretionary powers between sessions of the congress. The executive committee or the All-Russian Central Executive Committee of the soviets consisted of approximately two hundred members elected by the congress. This committee in turn elected a Council of People's Commissars that was entrusted with the "general direction" of public and government affairs.

The provisions of the constitution were in accordance with Marxist theory in that they rejected the doctrine of the separation of powers as a subterfuge created by the capitalists. Legislative powers in the new state were not confined to the representative body, the congress of soviets, but were shared by the executive committee and the Council of People's Commissars. This reflected the view that the rapid rate of economic development necessary for the new state to survive, and the chaotic conditions of civil war in the country made it imperative that the council be able to issue rapid and urgent decrees without having to wait for parliamentary approval.

Below the level of the all-Russian central institutions the constitution provided for a hierarchical arrangement of local soviets that extended downward from the regional to the provincial, county, and village levels. Government under the constitution lacked stability both because of structural defects in the system and because of the disturbed conditions prevailing during the period of civil war. The pyramid of soviets resulted in a clash between centripetal and centrifugal tendencies. The basic principles of government organization outlined in the document, however, with few modifications, were carried over to form the basis for the subsequent constitutions of 1924 and 1936.

THE CONSTITUTION OF 1924

With the decision to form the Union of Soviet Socialist Republics made at the end of 1922, the government provided for the drafting of a new constitution. A commission was established for this purpose by the central executive committee and the document that this commission drafted became largely an embodiment of the views of Stalin and a few of his closest associates. This constitution like its predecessor in 1918 outlined the formal governmental structure of the new union, but concealed the dominating role of the CPSU behind an array of pseudo-representative institutions. Through the assumption of a constitutional disguise the Party was able to continue to conceal the reality of arbitrary power under a cloak of legitimacy.

The opening section of the constitution was an ideological manifesto that described the world as divided into rival camps of socialism and capitalism. The second section contained the treaty by which the partners to the union: the Russian, Ukrainian, Belorussian, and Transcaucasian republics declared their intention to unite in "one union state." The jurisdiction of the union republics was stated in residual form. The republics were authorized to exercise those powers that were not vested in the government of the Soviet Union. The stated authority of the central government was so broad, however, that the union republics had little in the way of initiative.

The constitution continued the formal role of the All-Russian Congress of Soviets as the supreme organ of authority in the country. The congress with over two thousand members was to meet once each year—after 1927, meetings became biennial. The unwieldly congress elected an executive committee that was supposed to act as a legislature between sessions of the complete body. This committee was made bicameral to give recognition to the varied ethnic groups but, with 750 members, the executive committee was also unwieldly, and actual legislative responsibilities rested in a 27-member presidium. Executive power was vested in a Council of People's Commissars appointed by the central executive committee.

Commissars appointed by the central executive committee were in every case the top leaders of the Communist Party, however, the Party was not mentioned in the constitution. Subsequently, the Council of People's Commissars arrogated to itself the power to annul decrees of the congress, the executive committee, the presidium, and all other state organs.

The constitution provided for a Supreme Court and a procurator, subordinated to the central executive committee. The jurisdiction of the Supreme Court included rendering opinions on questions of union legislation, examining decisions of the lower courts to discover infractions of union law, rendering decisions on the constitutionality of laws passed by the union republics, and settling disputes between them. The court had no power to pass on the constitutionality of union legislation nor could it declare any act of central government agencies to be in excess of legal authority. In the event the procurator disagreed with a decision of the Supreme Court, he had the right to protest before the Council of People's Commissars. The court was thus subordinated to the council, which retained supreme judicial as well as legislative and executive power (see ch. 22, The Legal System).

THE CONSTITUTION OF 1936

Although a new constitution had been discussed since June 1963, the constitution adopted by the congress of soviets in 1936 continued in 1969 to define the governmental structure of the country. This constitution has been amended a number of times during the course of its history, but the amendments have not significantly changed the document's character or the basic style of government.

Most of the changes have been minor, such as registering the admission of new union republics, making shifts in political subdivisions, and rearranging the administrative structure. The constitution, like its predecessors, does not fully describe the actual political system but only outlines the existing governmental structures.

On February 1, 1935, a plenum of the central committee of the CPSU proposed the drafting of a new constitution that would contain measures aimed at "further democratization of the electoral system" and would "make more precise" the social-economic bases of the constitution by bringing the document into conformity with the "present correlation of class forces in the Soviet Union." The congress of soviets unanimously approved the proposal, and its central executive committee designated a constitutional commission headed by Joseph Stalin, Nikolay Bukharin, and Karl Radek to draft the text of the new constitution. On June 12, 1936, the draft was published, and the people of the country were invited to engage in a nationwide discussion of its contents. Proposals for amendment were invited by the commission, but no changes of any consequence were made in the original draft.

The Constitution of 1936 was adopted during the period of Stalin's purges, which was a time of domestic uncertainty and potential weakness. Its adoption was politically important in that this act helped to establish a sense, or at least an impression, of unity under Stalin's leadership. Furthermore, the publication and adoption of the constitution was coordinated with the efforts of the Soviet foreign ministry to enlist the sympathy of the Western governments to inaugurate collective security against Nazi Germany. Ironically, both Bukharin and Radek, framers of the new constitution, became victims of the Great Purge within two years.

The 1936 constitution consists of thirteen chapters that not only establish the basic elements of the governmental structure but lay down the fundamental principles governing the country's social and economic structure. Chapter I states that the Soviet Union is a socialist state in which all power is vested in the workers and peasants. The economic base of the state is specified to be socialist ownership of the means of production, and the land, industries, means of transport, municipal enterprises, and city dwellings are proclaimed state property belonging to the whole people. A right to own personal property, including a dwelling, however, as well as the right of inheritance is stated. The principle that the country's economy will be guided and determined in accordance with a state economic plan is enunciated, and the chapter concludes with a statement establishing the duty of each citizen to work for the common benefit.

Chapter II establishes the overall structure of the state, but reference to the union as "federal" is not descriptive since all of the important operative statements and provisions fit the pattern of a centralized unitary state. Under Article 13, the Soviet Union is described as a state founded on the voluntary union of fifteen equal Soviet socialist republics (union republics). In theory no territory can acquire the status of a union republic unless it borders a foreign country because of the right to secession guaranteed each union republic by Article 17. Political theorists in the country consider this right to be very important, but there is a question whether the right could ever be freely exercised, and Stalin has been quoted as stating that secession would be a counter-revolutionary act.

Article 14 of the constitution lists twenty-four spheres in which the central government enjoys exclusive authority. Article 15 states that all other powers are to be exercised independently by the component union republics. The powers reserved to the central government are so broad and have been construed so liberally that little actually remains under independent authority of the lower political subdivisions (see ch. 20, Component Political Subdivisions).

Powers relating to foreign affairs reserved exclusively for the central government by Article 14 include: overall representation of the Soviet Union in international relations; the power to make or denounce treaties; and the establishment of procedures governing relations of the component union republics with foreign states. Questions of war and peace are under exclusive jurisdiction of the central government, together with matters concerning admission of new republics into the Soviet Union and the organization and direction of national defense. Jurisdiction over foreign trade is reserved to the central government, specifically on the basis of a state monopoly.

In domestic affairs, the central government has, under Article 14, a very broad range of exclusive powers over political and social affairs. These include control over observance of the constitution of the Soviet Union and ensuring conformity with it according to the constitutions of the component union republics, together with matters involving state security and fundamental aspects of the legal system. Under Article 14 the central government determines changes in the composition and boundaries of union republics, autonomous republics, and regions; it also legislates on citizenship and the rights of foreigners in the country and on acts of amnesty. Exclusive competence in social affairs includes labor legislation, definition of basic principles in public health and education, and legislation on marriage and the family.

In domestic economic matters, Article 14 gives the central government exclusive jurisdiction over economic planning for the country as a whole, together with budget control, which includes fixing taxes and allocating revenues to central government agencies and to component union republics and other local governments. Article 14 empowers the central government to administer the country's banking, industrial, agricultural, trading, construction, transportation and communications systems; the article also confers sole jurisdiction over money, credit and the state insurance organization. Powers to define the basic principles of land tenure and exploitation of natural resources are reserved to the central government, which is also given exclusive jurisdiction over organizing a uniform system of economic statistics.

Chapter III of the constitution outlines the organization of the government, providing for a bicameral legislature and an executive office. Chapter IV delineates a similar governmental structure for the union republics. Chapters V and VI set forth organizational structure for lower levels of government (see ch. 20, Component Political Subdivisions). Chapters VII and VIII provide for similar structures of government for the autonomous republics and the regions and territories of the country.

Chapter IX deals with the court system and the procurator's office. The constitution states that justice is administered by the Supreme Court of the Soviet Union and the Supreme Courts of the union republics as well as territorial, regional, and area courts created by the Supreme Soviet. All cases are to be tried with the participation of a people's assessor except in cases specially exempted by law. Supreme court justices are elected for a period of five years by the Supreme Soviet. People's assessors are elected by the Supreme Soviet for periods of two years.

A Procurator-General is provided for by Articles 113—117 of Chapter IX. He is appointed by the Supreme Soviet for a period of seven years and is given supreme supervisory power to ensure observance of the law both by governmental officials and the general public (see ch. 22, The Legal System).

AMENDMENT PROCESS

Amendments to the constitution have been frequent during its history, and the procedure is not complicated. Amendments are adopted by a majority of not less than two-thirds of the delegates voting in each chamber of the Supreme Soviet.

FUNDAMENTAL RIGHTS AND DUTIES OF CITIZENS

The Constitution of 1936 in Chapter X lists the rights of citizens and, in some cases, indicates how those rights are implemented and guaranteed. This inclusion is apparently an outgrowth of Marxist-Leninist thought. Because Soviet ideology contends that political liberties under bourgeois governments are meaningless, the framers of the constitution tried to demonstrate the meaningfulness of civil rights under socialism.

The constitution outlines five basic economic rights, guaranteed to each citizen by the socialist system: the right to paid employment; leisure; support in old age or in sickness; education; and, equality for women. Some of the enumerated rights are qualified by enunciation of duties. For example, the right to employment is limited in Article 130 by a stipulation that it is the duty of every citizen to maintain labor discipline and to respect the rules of socialist society (see ch. 33, Labor Relations and Organization).

The right to rest and leisure in the Soviet Union depends on the availability of the means to enjoy rest and leisure. Reductions in the length of the work week, improved housing facilities, social insurance benefits, and free medical care have contributed substance to this right.

Free education is provided by the state for primary and secondary schooling plus vocational training that will enable an individual to work either in the industrial or the agricultural sector of the economy. Students who gain admission to higher educational institutions usually receive extensive state aid (see ch. 15, The Educational System).

A constitutional prohibition against racial and national discrimination contained in Article 123 needs to be considered against the traditional tendency of the country's leaders to accord priority to the Russian nationality and to regard any display of local patriotism among the other nationalities as a threat to the unity of the state (see ch. 10, Ethnic Groups). Although official policy remains ostensibly opposed to racial or ethnic discrimination, such discrimination has persisted. Women are, however, accorded an equal status with men in most fields.

The constitutional guarantee of freedom of conscience and religious worship contained in Article 124 separates the church from the state and the school from the church. This clause also specifically provides for freedom of anti-religious propaganda (see ch. 13, Religion).

Article 125 guarantees the rights of freedom of speech, press, assembly, and demonstration. Enunciation of these rights is prefaced by the statement that they are guaranteed in "conformity with the interests of the working class and in order to strengthen the socialist system." This article further states that facilities essential to the exercise of these rights are placed "at the disposal of the working people and their organizations."

The constitution does not provide for any system of judicial review or review by the courts of law to determine whether or not governmental acts are in violation of the constitution. Therefore, there is no judicial recourse for a citizen who believes that his constitutional rights have been violated nor is there judicial means by which the validity of any law can be challenged (see ch. 22, The Legal System).

Articles 131 through 133 of the constitution establish the principle of universal military service and stipulate that it is the duty of every citizen to safeguard public property and to defend the country. Offenders against public socialist property are denounced as being enemies of the people; and desertion to the enemy, impairing the military power of the state, and espionage are listed as the most heinous of crimes, punishable with all the severity of the law.

THE SUPREME SOVIET

Article 30 of the constitution designates the Supreme Soviet of the Soviet Union as the highest organ of state power in the country. This parliamentary body is bicameral in structure, consisting of the Soviet of the Union and the Soviet of Nationalities. The Soviet of the Union is so constituted as to provide one deputy for each 300,000 of the population. The Soviet of Nationalities provides representation on a regional rather than on a population basis; it consists of thirty-two deputies from each union republic, eleven deputies from each autonomous republic, five deputies from each autonomous region, and one deputy from each national area (see ch. 20, Component Political Subdivisions).

The Soviets of Workers Deputies were first organized during the Revolution of 1905 as strike and insurrection committees. Lenin found in the soviets a potential means for ruling the state. During the March Revolution of 1917 soviets were again formed both in the factories and in the army. These revolutionary organizations sprang up throughout the country and elected delegates to a central congress, the precursor of the Supreme Soviet. The congress, which first met in June 1917, formed a power independent of the Provisional Government and exerted much influence in the capital city. The Bolsheviks were at first a minority in the soviets, and not until the autumn of 1917 were they able to gain majorities in the two most important, Petrograd and Moscow. Early in November 1917 the Bolsheviks overthrew the Provisional Government with the support of the Petrograd Soviet (see ch. 3, Historical Setting).

Thereafter, the soviets came to symbolize the people in their mass political activity. The soviets are nominally the democratic basis of government in the country. From the very beginning, however, complexity of government administration and the influence of the Party has reduced the soviets to little more than ratifying agencies and has enlarged the role of the executive committees. Because the

Supreme Soviet exercises little actual legislative power or initiative, it can be considered largely a symbol of the Revolution, a facade which the party uses as a basis for popular legitimacy.

The two chambers of the Supreme Soviet have equal rights of legislative initiative. The sessions of each chamber begin and end at the same time, and there are provisions for holding joint sessions. Deputies to both chambers serve for a term of four years, at the expiration of which the soviet is dissolved and new elections are held. The constitution stipulates that elections must be held within two months after dissolution, but in practice this rule is not closely followed. The Supreme Soviet may be dissolved before its expiration date if the chambers fail to resolve a disagreement between themselves; however, there has never been a known disagreement.

The public sessions of the Supreme Soviet rarely last for more than a few days. The stage of legislation that is crucial in the soviet system is the preparatory one. The major legislative measures originate within the secretariat of the Central Committee of the CPSU and in the Council of Ministers (see ch. 21, Political Dynamics). Legislative measures are often submitted to the soviet as joint resolutions of the Council of Ministers and the Central Committee of the CPSU and, thereupon, are formally enacted in statutory form by the Supreme Soviet.

COMMISSIONS

Each chamber of the Supreme Soviet establishes a number of committees or commissions to carry on the bulk of its legislative work. Before each session a committee of senior deputies meets to determine the agenda for the coming session. Meetings of the commissions are not public nor are commission proceedings reported in the press.

The commissions conduct preliminary examination of draft proposals that are to be submitted to the Supreme Soviet for confirmation. Aside from a Credentials Commission in each chamber, which is charged with the examination of deputies' credentials, there are commissions on foreign affairs, budget, legislation, industry, agriculture, health and social welfare, education, science, and culture.

The commissions, composed of from thirty to fifty members elected from among the deputies, usually sit more frequently and for longer periods than the Supreme Soviet. Between sessions of the Supreme Soviet, commission members are accountable to the chairman of the chamber that elected them, however, their activity is coordinated by the presidium. The sittings of the commissions are not open to the public, and they have the power to investigate government agencies. The commissions often form subcommittees that may include members who are not deputies, but who are experts in matters under investigation. The powers of the commissions are merely consultive, but sometimes they are able to influence the content of legislation. The budget and economic commissions of the Soviet of Nationalities are in a particularly good position to further the interests of the regions they represent. In the last resort the commissions, whose chairmen are invariably members of the Central Committee of the CPSU, can be made to conform through Party enforcement of discipline.

DEPUTIES

The composition of the Supreme Soviet reflects its character as a ratifying board for Party policy. Although the largest groups within the two chambers are composed of Party officials, the membership, in conformity with Marxist-Leninist theology, is designed to reflect a cross section of Soviet society. Thus, leading workers, collective farmers, teachers, scientists, engineers and others are included. Election to the Supreme Soviet is often a reward for exemplary service to the state. It is a body that assembles leading and representative figures, but is at most only a confirming body, since all important decisions are made by leaders of the CPSU.

The only qualification laid down in the constitution for a deputy to the Supreme Soviet is that he be a citizen over twenty-three years of age. When elected he continues to draw his salary from his regular employment, plus allowances for transportation and other emoluments related to sessions of the soviet. He is immune from criminal prosecution or arrest without the consent of the Supreme Soviet or its presidium.

Article 142 of the constitution stipulates that it is the duty of a deputy to report to his constituents on his work, and provides that he may be recalled at any time by decision of a majority of his electors in a manner to be established by law. There is a question whether the latter proviso has much importance since the elections are under tight CPSU controls. A deputy's main functions are to explain and popularize official policy and to represent his constituents. As intermediaries between the people and the state apparatus they generally play a useful role in listening to grievances and advancing the interests of their constituents.

THE PRESIDIUM OF THE SUPREME SOVIET

The Supreme Soviet meets semi-annually, each session lasting only a few days. Between active sessions, its legislative powers and certain powers of an executive nature are performed by the Presidium of the Supreme Soviet. Elected in a joint session of the two chambers of the Supreme Soviet, this organ consists of a president, fifteen vice presidents—one from each union republic—twenty members, and a secretary. The presidium functions as a collective body and, its president, often referred to as chairman, has no distinct powers of his own. Nevertheless, in practice the president of the presidium generally carries out the formal functions traditionally associated with a titular head of state, and is sometimes known outside the Soviet Union as the Soviet president.

The fifteen vice presidents of the presidium are selected because they are the presidents of the presidiums of the component union republics. The twenty ordinary members include some important CPSU leaders, who by virtue of this dual role in the government and the Party are the rulers of the country. The secretariat of the presidium provides coordination and continuity for the day to day activity of the presidium.

The presidium is assigned eighteen primary functions by Article 49 of the constitution. Among the most important of the legislative functions is the issuing of decrees that have the force of law. These are generally ratified by formal enactment of the Supreme Soviet at a later date, but the constitution has no specific provision requiring such action. Among other functions related to legislation, the constitution empowers the presidium to interpret the laws of the country, conduct nationwide referendums, and to annul decisions and orders of the Council of Ministers of the Soviet Union and of the councils of ministers of the union republics if they do not conform to law.

The presidium is also constitutionally responsible for the following: the convening and dissolution of the Supreme Soviet and ordering new elections; the appointment and removal of ministers when the Supreme Soviet is not in session; exercising the right of pardon; ratifying and denouncing treaties; instituting decorations, titles of honor, awards, military titles and diplomatic ranks; appointing and removing the high command of the armed forces; appointing and receiving diplomatic representatives; ordering mobilization and declaring martial law; and proclaiming a state of war if the Supreme Soviet is not in session. Under Article 48 of the constitution the presidium is accountable for all its activities to the Supreme Soviet, which may dissolve that body and elect a new one. The presidium does not have the right to veto any legislation passed by the Supreme Soviet (see ch. 5, The Political System; ch, 21, Political Dynamics).

THE COUNCIL OF MINISTERS

Described by the constitution as the highest executive and administrative organ of the state, the Council of Ministers of the

Soviet Union issues decisions and orders on the basis and in pursuance of laws in operation and verifies their execution. It is the central coordinator of operations within the government system, and controls the planning and administration of an economy in which the natural resources, and the processes of production are nationalized (see ch. 29, Economic Planning and Control). Constitutionally, the council is responsible and accountable to the Supreme Soviet and the Presidium of the Supreme Soviet. In practice, the more important members derive their very substantial powers from their standing in the CPSU by which they are selected for office and to which they are actually accountable.

The composition of the Council of Ministers is specified in the constitution. Its basic membership consists of the heads of the various ministries of the central government and the chairmen of the more important central government committees. The chairmen of the Councils of Ministers of the component union republics are ex officio members of the central government's Council of Ministers, and the entire organization is headed by a chairman, the equivalent of a prime minister, who is assisted by a varying number of vice chairmen (see fig. 7).

The number and titles of the ministries and committees represented on the Council of Ministers have been frequently changed, and with each change it becomes necessary to amend the constitution. The authority of the Council of Ministers, however, has always remained paramount and its decisions and orders are binding on all lower organs of government throughout the country. Under a strict construction, the constitution does not endow the council with powers of legislation. In practice, however, the council's decisions and orders frequently amount to new legislation and make changes in the law.

The chairman of the Council of Ministers (known as the Council of People's Commissars until 1946) had traditionally been the central figure in the government, but real power from the early 1920's had been in the hands of the general secretary of the party, Joseph Stalin. In 1941 Stalin made himself chairman, thus combining the top governmental and party posts for the first time since the death of Lenin. Nikita Khrushchev continued the practice until his removal from both posts in 1964. With the removal of Khrushchev, the Central Committee of the CPSU stressed "collective leadership" and, almost five years later, the two leading positions remained separate. Leonid Brezhnev, in 1969, retained the position of CPSU general secretary, and Aleksey Kosygin was the chairman of the Council of Ministers.

Because of the size of the Council of Ministers and the varied responsibilities of many of its members, its daily business is carried on by a much smaller inner group that operates as an ad hoc execu-

```
┌─────────────────────────────────────────────┐
│  Chairman                                     │
│  First Deputy Chairmen (2)                    │
│  Deputy Chairmen (9)                          │
└─────────────────────────────────────────────┘
```

Representation in its Council	Ministers in the Council
All-Union Industrial Ministries	21 Ministries
Union-Republic Industrial Ministries	18 Ministries
All-Union Nonindustrial Ministries (5)	Civil Aviation Foreign Trade Internal Affairs Merchant Marine Railways
Union-Republic Nonindustrial Ministries (12)	Agriculture — Geological Survey Culture — Higher and Secondary Education Defense — Public Health Education — Public Order Finance — Trade Foreign Affairs — Water Conservation
State Committees (Ministerial Status) (11)	Agricultural Procurement Construction Foreign Economic Relations Forestry Labor and Wages Material and Technical Supply People's Control Planning Science and Technology Security Vocational Training
Special Agencies (Ministerial Status) (3)	Administrative Board of State Bank All-Union Board for Supply of Farm Machinery, Fuel, and Fertilizers Central Statistical Administration
Chairmen of Union Republic Councils of Ministers (15)	Ex Officio Members (15)

Note: Membership in the Council of Ministers as shown in the constitution of the USSR.

Figure 7. *Soviet Union Council of Ministers, July 1969.*

tive body. This group normally consists of the chairman of the Council of Ministers and the deputy chairmen, who are often ministers without portfolio. It is in this group where the real policy-making of the Council of Ministers takes place.

MINISTRIES

The constitution specifically provides for two types of ministries to carry out governmental activities—the All-Union or central government ministries and the Union-Republic ministries. The All-Union ministries direct the branches of adminstration entrusted to them throughout the entire country either directly or through organs appointed by them. The union-republic ministries administer only those branches designated in a list confirmed by the Presidium of the Supreme Soviet.

Each ministry is organized along similar administrative guidelines. The minister and a number of deputies are in charge of several main divisions. Deputy ministers are usually technical specialists rather than politicians. Each minister is personally responsible to the Council of Ministers for the activities of his department and the actions of his subordinates.

THE ELECTORAL SYSTEM

The political life in the country is marked by frequent elections. The soviets of the central government and union republics are elected for terms of four years, and the lower soviets are elected for two-year terms. Elections for the central government and the union republic soviets do not coincide with each other or with local elections.

According to the Article 135 of the constitution, all citizens who have reached the age of eighteen, except those who are legally insane, are entitled to vote without distinction as to race, sex, social origin, or past activities. The article stipulates that each citizen has one vote and that all participate in elections on an equal footing. Voting for candidates is specified as being secret and direct, based on universal suffrage.

Elections in the Soviet Union do not result in a transfer of power from one organized political group to another. The Soviet view of government legitimacy does not rest on a system of popular electoral consent alone. It assigns the right of final approval to the Communist Party that is specified in Article 126 of the constitution as forming the vanguard of the working people and the leading core of all organizations of the working people (see ch. 21, Political Dynamics).

The country's elections serve primarily as public demonstrations of the legitimacy of the regime. Political leaders point to the response of the voters as a manifestation of the unity of the people and their approval of the government. Statistical triumphs of 99.95 percent turnout, and 99.47 percent favorable vote for the candidates of the Party are frequently heralded in the press as demonstrations of such unity and support.

Election campaigns provide valuable educational and propaganda opportunities for mass political indoctrination. The Communist Party members and the active Party supporters, for weeks before an election, engage in propaganda campaigns supporting official candidates and encouraging voters to go to the polls on election day. Intense pressure is brought to bear on the citizen to participate, and those who fail to vote are strongly criticized.

ELECTORAL PROCEDURES

To ensure CPSU control over all elections, the regime maintains a system of electoral commissions. These commissions are established for the purpose of ensuring that nominations of the candidates are made in accordance with Party directives, and that elections are conducted in accordance with the law. Nominations for public office must be approved by the commissions before they can be placed on the ballots. The commissions are the final judges in all cases of complaint or dispute since there is no appeal to or supervision of elections by the judiciary. Electoral commissions are present in every constituency and in every polling district. Polling stations are under the direct supervision of the district electoral commissions, and a commissioner is present to oversee the voting throughout the election day. The commissions normally consist of Party members and are solely responsible for tabulating the ballots and releasing election results.

The right to nominate a candidate for election to any of the soviets is, according to the constitution, reserved to mass organizations and the societies of the working people; namely, Communist Party organizations, trade unions, cooperatives, youth organizations, and cultural societies. Individuals do not have the right of nomination. Since CPSU members constitute the leading core of each organization that is eligible to nominate a candidate, the Party is assured that its candidate will be selected.

Because of the several million elective offices to be filled it is difficult for the Party to find enough members who can qualify as candidates and, thus in the lower elections, the CPSU sponsors some nonmember candidates. However, the proportion of candidates who are members of the CPSU rises as the importance of the legislative office increases. Party members may constitute fewer than one-fourth of the candidates for village soviets, but at the All-Union level the proportion often exceeds 75 percent.

During the course of an election campaign, candidates address the voters in their constituencies, however, they never voice disagreement with the policies or criticize the actions of the regime. Since the interests of the locality must defer to projects that are centrally determined, the role of the candidate as a spokesman for local interests is very limited. A candidate's first obligation is to follow Party directives.

The electoral lists contain one candidate's name for each office, and the voter is instructed to cross out the names of all candidates except the one for which he wishes to vote. Since only one name appears on the ballot, however, the only alternative to voting for the official candidate is for the voter to cross out the single name and thus indicate dissent. In each polling station provision is made for a private booth. Since a voter who supports the official candidate need only deposit his unmarked ballot into a receptacle, to retire into the voting booth would indicate to the electoral commissioners that his vote was one of dissent. Unless over half of the voters strike a candidate's name from the ballot he is elected. On occasion a candidate fails to win a majority in election to a local soviet, but this eventuality is unheard of in elections to the higher bodies.

CIVIL SERVICE

Because of state control of the economy, roughly two-thirds of the country's civilian labor force was listed in 1966 as being in government employment. All such individuals, whether high ministerial officials or workers in steel plants—excluding collective farm workers—are considered to be government employees (see ch. 32, The Labor Force). Soviet law and administrative rules, however, clearly distinguish between the general run of government workers and those individuals within the administrative organs of government who have duties involving public regulatory procedures or changes in the legal relations between individuals and institutions. The latter are considered office holders and correspond roughly to the groups that comprise the civil services in many other countries. Although this array of civil servants is very large, the central government has no formally constituted civil service with uniform recruitment standards, disciplinary rules, and promotion procedures.

Detailed information on conditions of service is scanty, but there is evidence indicating that officials in the higher levels enjoy a privileged position in the society (see ch. 4, The Social System). The civil service administrators work under conditions of the strictest discipline, and penalties for default and failure are severe. Soviet law contains many detailed and complicated provisions concerning the responsibilities of state officials and the sanctions that may be invoked for derelictions of various kinds. The criminal code defines special offenses that can be committed by office holders, such as abuses of official power, failure to perform prescribed duties, and embezzlement or fraud. Material damage caused by an official's neglect for example, may result in the responsible individual forfeiting up to three months' salary.

Disciplinary measures can be imposed upon state employees not only by the government and CPSU organs of control, but by those superiors in the office or institution to which the offender is assigned. Penalties range from reprimand, reduction in rank, or dismissal to criminal liability. There is in every case a right of appeal, but only to the next higher authority. The decision on an appeal is final, but there is a provision that a reprimand may be expunged from the record after a period of faultless service.

Good service to the government is well rewarded. The salaries and pensions for civil servants are higher than those available to the average Soviet citizen, and posts of responsibility entitle the occupants to many privileges not enjoyed by the average worker. Among these are priority access to scarce consumer goods, housing, recreational, and cultural facilities. Since the death of Stalin, there has been a trend toward curtailing the financial rewards of high office and a tightening of control over the proliferation of agencies and growth of higher staffs.

The government leaders, during the 1960's, paid increasing attention to the systematic training and recruitment of the various technicians and specialists needed to staff the expanding governmental system. To this end, a number of schools of university or quasi-university status have been established to meet the needs of particular ministries or governmental activities. Graduates of such schools find employment in the branch of production or service with which the particular ministry supervising the school is concerned.

Graduates of other higher educational establishments are recruited by the ministries for which the qualifications are appropriate and, in practice, considerable pressure is exerted on these graduates to accept the governmental posts offered (see ch. 15, The Educational System).

In general, recruiting is governed by legislative enactments that vary, depending on the governmental ministry or department. Among matters stressed in general enactments on recruiting for the civil service are prohibitions against discrimination on the grounds of ethnic origin, race, and sex. It is also specifically required that recruiting be done with due regard to the candidate's political, practical, and professional qualifications. Political qualification means loyalty to and understanding of the CPSU ideology. The practical and professional qualifications are determined by the employing agency in cooperation with the secretariat of the CPSU.

The general enactments on recruiting are contained not only in various legislative acts but in directives of the appropriate state committees on wages and labor of the councils of minister, which coordinate problems of employment and pay. Manning tables or lists, known as *nomenklatura*, are the bases for appointment to posts of higher responsibility in the central government. These tables not only establish the positions and titles, but specify the individuals in the governmental and CPSU hierarchies who must be consulted and formally approved before an appointment is considered valid.

Consultive groups known as collegiums are normally established in the ministries and other organs of the central government to provide a formal structure for planning and formulating policy. Such a group usually includes, in addition to the minister, the deputies and heads of main departments or other subordinate groups. Although appointed by the minister, the membership must be approved by the Council of Ministers as a whole. Technical experts or individuals with special knowledge of subjects on the agenda attend meetings on a case-by-case basis. These groups are wholly advisory and cannot bind the minister or chairman, who remains solely responsible for the decisions. The membership does not have the power to enforce a majority view upon the minister, but it can appeal his decisions to the Council of Ministers.

ARMS AND THE FLAG

The constitution specifies that the arms of the Soviet Union are a hammer and sickle against a globe, depicted in the rays of the sun and surrounded by ears of grain bearing the inscription "Workers of All Countries, Unite." At the top of the arms is a five-pointed star. The hammer and the sickle symbolize the implements of the working class and were adopted as the symbols of the new regime after the revolution. The ears of grain represent the prosperity promised by the new order and the rays of the sun the new world that the Communist order will bring forth. The motto is that used by Marx at the conclusion of his manifesto to rally what he termed the "enslaved classes" to revolution.

The state flag of the Soviet Union is of red cloth with the hammer and sickle depicted in gold in the upper corner near the staff; and above them is a five-pointed star bordered in gold. The ratio of width to length is one to two. The flag is flown at all official functions, and national holidays, and serves as the emblem of both the government and the Party.

CHAPTER 20

COMPONENT POLITICAL SUBDIVISIONS

The Soviet Union in early 1970 consisted of fourteen soviet socialist republics and one soviet federated socialist republic. Each republic, variously referred to as a union republic, a constituent republic, or a soviet socialist republic (Sovetskaya Sotsialisticheskaya Respublika—SSR—see Glossary), had its own constitution, supreme soviet, and supreme court, all patterned upon similar agencies at USSR level. All but the most minor foreign relations, foreign trade, defense policy, economic controls, and fiscal matters were delegated by the union republics to the central government.

Contained within, and subordinate to, some of the union republics were twenty so-called autonomous republics (Avtonomnaya Sovetskaya Sotsialisticheskaya Respublika—ASSR—see Glossary) and various levels of local governments of both administrative and national types from villages to regions. Sizes and boundaries of the administrative units were based upon economic and geographic considerations, whereas the national or autonomous units had been created to recognize various ethnic minorities.

Although the two general types of subdivisions, administrative and national, varied greatly in size and population, they did not constitute two separate governmental hierarchies. Not only were there fewer autonomous or national areas, all categories of which were generally less important than their administrative counterparts, but no autonomous or national area contained lower level autonomous areas. The SSR's were considered apart. They were national states, joined to form the USSR but, in time, have come to be considered its major administrative subdivisions.

The administrative local government units included *kraya* (territories), *oblasti* (provinces), *rayony* (districts), towns, settlements, and villages (see Glossary). *Kraya* and *oblasti* were regional subdivisions. *Rayony* were districts. The village level referred to the smallest point or area that merited a local soviet. It may have been a small town, a group of small villages or populated points, a workers' settlement, or an agricultural settlement (see fig. 8).

The *kraya* and *oblasti* were directly subordinate to the SSR's and, in turn, administered lower level governments within them. In early 1970 there were six *kraya* and just over 100 *oblasti*.

District-level governments included the rural *rayon* (equivalent to

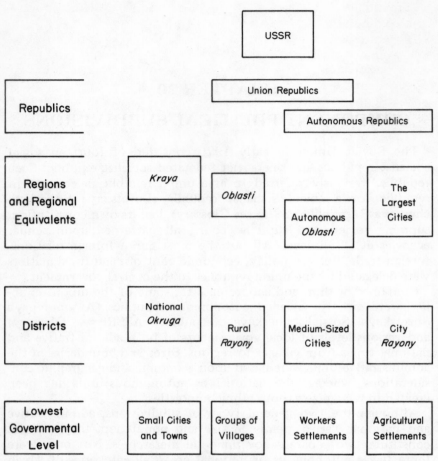

		USSR		

Republics		Union Republics		
			Autonomous Republics	

Regions and Regional Equivalents	*Kraya*	*Oblasti*	Autonomous *Oblasti*	The Largest Cities

Districts	National *Okruga*	Rural *Rayony*	Medium-Sized Cities	City *Rayony*

Lowest Governmental Level	Small Cities and Towns	Groups of Villages	Workers Settlements	Agricultural Settlements

Note: Vertical differentiation of the blocks indicates the relative importance of a unit within its administrative category. For example, the *kray, oblast,* and autonomous *oblast* regions are of descending importance. Since the size of cities varies widely, their governments are included at all levels of local administration.

Figure 8. Administrative and National Structure of the Soviet Union.

a county in the United States), medium-sized cities, and the boroughs of the large cities (known as city *rayony*). Rural *rayony* were the usual subdivisions of *kraya, oblasti,* the smaller SSR's, and of autonomous areas. In early 1970 there were probably a few more than 1,800 rural *rayony,* approximately the same number of cities governed at that level, and about 400 city *rayony.*

In the village category about 40,000 small towns, villages, or groups of villages had the lowest level of local government. An additional 3,000 to 3,500 populated areas were referred to as settlements. Workers settlements were ordinarily towns that had sprung up around an industrial enterprise; agricultural settlements were farm communities.

The national, or autonomous, units were created in an effort to solve some of the problems inherent in governing a land containing many nationalities, each wishing to preserve a certain amount of independence, national identity, culture, and language. Each category was granted a degree of autonomy that depended on the size and importance of the national group and the area in which it was predominant. They were represented, as were the SSR's, in the USSR Soviet of Nationalities, a representation that had no counterpart from the administrative subdivisions.

There were twenty autonomous republics, or ASSR's, in early 1970, administered in most respects the same as the union republics. Their autonomy consisted of a considerable degree of self-determination in the control of local governments beneath them and permitted the use of local languages in schools, courts, local trade, communications, and administration. National manners and customs were respected.

Autonomous *oblasti* were formed where there were smaller areas dominated by a national group, large enough to have individual significance but too small to be considered for republic status. Eight of them existed in early 1970.

The least important of the autonomous areas to be represented in the USSR Soviet of Nationalities were the national *okruga* (areas— see Glossary). Most of these consisted of sparsely inhabited spaces where there had as yet been no economic reason for colonization. There were ten national *okruga* in early 1970. They were administered at a level between the *oblast* and the *rayon* and were permitted, by virtue of their autonomous status, to retain local manners and customs.

Governments throughout the entire system were structurally similar. There was, however, a major demarcation separating the USSR and republic governments from those below, all of which were considered to be in the local government category. Basic to all were the soviets, but local soviets were sheared of the title *supreme*. Republic ministries and state committees were replaced in local governments by administrations or departments, and councils of ministers and presidiums by executive committees. Although the soviets and committees grew progressively smaller in the local governments, they were a means through which mass participation in state machinery was achieved. About 2 million deputies were elected to local soviets in 1969, and a roughly similar number of additional people were appointed to various groups supporting their executive committees.

Each element of a republican or local government was responsible at its own level to its soviet and presidium or executive committee.

It was also responsible to a parent agency in the government at the administrative level above. The Communist Party of the Soviet Union (CPSU) and local governments had generally parallel organizations. Party personnel were active in local government agencies, and it was usual practice for many of the key positions in both Party and government structures to be occupied by the same individual. The Party organization and the subordinations within the governmental system have served to hold actual power and controls tightly under the central government and the CPSU in Moscow (see ch. 5, the Political System; ch 21, Political Dynamics).

THE UNION REPUBLICS

The original USSR, proclaimed on January 31, 1924, was a "one-union state" consisting of four union republics: the Russian Soviet Federated Socialist Republic (Rossiyskaya Sovetskaya Federativnaya Sotsialisticheskaya Respublika—RSFSR—see Glossary), the Ukraine, Belorussia, and the Transcaucasus. The three republics in south-central USSR—Uzbek, Turkmen, and Tadzhik—were added to the union between then and 1930. In 1936 the Transcaucasus SSR was divided into three republics: Georgia, Azerbaijan, and Armenia. Kazakhstan and Kirgiz in south-central USSR became SSR's at about the same time. Kazakhstan had previously been an autonomous republic within the RSFSR (see table 3).

The Baltic states of Estonia, Latvia, and Lithuania were forcibly annexed to the Soviet Union and made soviet socialist republics in 1940. In the same year, Rumania was forced to cede Bessarabia and northern Bukovina to the Soviets, and that territory was combined with part of the existing Moldavian ASSR and given union republic status. Also in 1940, after the end of the Russo-Finnish War, the Karelo-Finnish SSR was formed, but in 1956 its union republic status was withdrawn, and it became an autonomous republic within the RSFSR. With the downgrading of the Karelo-Finnish republic in 1956, the number of union republics became fifteen and remained so in early 1970.

Stalin set rough guidelines as to the requirements for an area to become a union republic. He declared that an eligible area must be on the frontier of the USSR and must have a population in excess of 1 million and that the nationality for which it was to be named must constitute a majority among the local population. The fifteen union republics are constitutionally sovereign and independent states. Although each has the constitutional right "freely to secede," the USSR's national anthem speaks of "an unbreakable union of free republics." Each republic has a constitutional right to engage in independent relations with foreign powers and to organize

402

Table 3. *Union Republics of the Soviet Union*

Soviet Socialist Republic	Area (in square miles)	Population (in thousands)[1]	Density of population (per square mile)	Location
RSFSR[2]	6,593,000	127,911	19	Southwest European USSR
Ukraine	231,750	46,381	201	West-central European USSR
Belorussia	80,100	8,820	111	Transcaucasus
Georgia	26,900	4,659	173	Do.
Azerbaijan	33,425	4,917	147	Do.
Armenia	11,500	2,306	201	South-central USSR
Uzbek	173,500	11,266	71	Do.
Turkmen	188,200	2,029	11	Do.
Tadzhik	55,150	2,736	50	Do.
Kazakh	1,048,000	12,678	12	Do.
Kirgiz	76,500	2,836	37	Western USSR bordering Rumania
Moldavia	13,100	3,484	266	
Estonia	17,400	1,304	75	Western USSR on Baltic Sea
Latvia	24,600	2,298	93	Do.
Lithuania	25,140	3,064	122	Do.
Total	8,598,265[3]	236,689	27[4]	

[1] January 1, 1968.
[2] Russian Soviet Federated Socialist Republic.
[3] The total area of the USSR is usually given as approximately 8,650,000 square miles. This figure includes certain water areas that are not shown in the areas of the individual union republics.
[4] Average population density.

its own defense forces. None, however, has exercised more than token activity in either of these areas.

Other than the RSFSR, which contains the lion's share of European USSR and all of northern and eastern Siberia, five are located along the south-central USSR boundary east of the Caspian sea, adjacent to Iran, Afghanistan, Pakistan, and Communist China. Three are in the Transcaucasus, and the remaining six are along the western border of European USSR.

The union republics vary tremendously in size. The RSFSR contains over 76 percent of the area of the entire union and, combined with the second largest republic—Kazakhstan, 88 percent of the total land area is accounted for by just two of the union republics. In contrast, the Armenian SSR contains only 0.13 percent of the Soviet territory.

Variations in population are equally extreme. According to official Soviet statistics for January 1968 the RSFSR, with almost 128 million people, had about 55 percent of the population. The Ukrainian SSR, with over 46 million inhabitants, accounted for more than 19 percent of the total. Estonia, smallest in population among the SSR's, with 1.3 million people, had less than 1 percent of the total.

The constitutions and governments of the SSR's are patterned closely after that of the USSR. Each has, in addition to its constitution, a supreme soviet, presidium, council of ministers, and a supreme court. Although the SSR's are "free and independent," their constitutions must be approved by the USSR and cannot be in contradiction with its Constitution. All actions taken by any organ of the SSR government are subject to reversal by the Supreme Soviet, Presidium, or a ministry of the USSR. This could include an SSR action to secede.

The supreme soviets in the constituent republics are unicameral, representation being based on population rather than national groups. Below the USSR level, legislative bodies are unicameral; no republic or local government has a chamber that equates to the USSR Soviet of Nationalities. The RSFSR Supreme Soviet had 884 members in 1968; Estonia's had only 178. The others had numbers of deputies falling between these figures. The supreme soviets are required to meet twice a year, but the Soviet press indicates that some of them have failed to convene as frequently as is specified.

The central government has two types of ministries and state committees: all-union and union-republic. The republics usually have counterparts of the union-republic ministries, but the all-union agencies are not duplicated at lower levels. In 1968 there were about fifty union-republic ministries and state committees in the USSR Council of Ministers, most of which were duplicated in the governments of the constituent republics. The USSR Constitution states that union-republic ministries are subordinate both to the corresponding ministry at the federal level and to its own republic government.

In addition to the union-republic agencies, each republic also has a number of so-called republican ministries that have no counterparts at the federal level. The republican ministries are concerned exclusively with local affairs and are subordinate only to their own governments.

In 1968 a typical republic council of ministers had about forty-five members, including six to eight chairmen and vice chairmen, about twenty-five ministers, and about fifteen chairmen of state committees and other ministry-level establishments attached to the council. SSR presidiums had from three to five chairmen, deputy chairmen, and secretaries and from five to fifteen members. The RSFSR was an exception, having sixteen additional deputy chairmen, each representing an ASSR.

Each union republic sends thirty-two deputies to the Soviet of Nationalities of the USSR Supreme Soviet. Since the ASSR's are allocated a total of 220 deputies, the autonomous *oblasti* 40, and the national *okruga* a mere 10, the total of 480 deputies from the SSR's constitutes a preponderance of the membership of the chamber.

The revenues that the SSR's may use or may redistribute to the various governments under their jurisdiction are derived primarily from two sources: a percentage of the income from enterprises and a portion of the direct national taxes that are collected within their borders. In addition, they are allowed a small amount of local taxation. The percentage of total USSR revenues allocated to the SSR's has increased since the end of the Stalin period in 1953.

ADMINISTRATIVE SUBDIVISIONS

Kraya

Kraya were established originally to administer large, sparsely populated territories that had no individual national character or special economic significance. In administrative subordination they had status equal to, or greater than, the *oblast*, differing in that a typical *kray* was much larger and more thinly populated. Indicative of the possibly greater administrative importance of the *kray* in relation to the administrative *oblast*, five of the six *kraya* have autonomous *oblasti* within, and subordinate to, them. Although autonomous *oblasti* may also be subordinate directly to an SSR, none are subordinate to administrative oblasts. Only two of the six *kraya* that existed in early 1970, however, still conformed to the original size and population format. Two were no larger than the average *oblast*, and four had population densities that were equal to, or greater than, the average for the USSR (see table 4).

All six *kraya* are located within the RSFSR. Two of them, Khabarovsk and Maritime, are on the far east periphery of the USSR. The largest, Krasnoyarsk, is at the east-west center of the USSR and extends from within a few miles of Mongolia in the south into the islands of the Artic Ocean. Altay is in south-central Siberia and has a short common border with Mongolia. The two smallest, Krasnodar and Stavropol, are in the Caucasus.

Although they average more than twice the size and population of the typical ASSR, *kraya* are administrative subdivisions of the RSFSR and have no national autonomy. Therefore, they have no representation in the USSR Soviet of Nationalities, although autonomous *oblasti* and national areas within them do. They do not have supreme soviets or supreme courts, as do the SSR's and ASSR's. *Kray* soviets are considered local soviets and have executive committees in place of presidiums and councils of ministers and administrations or departments in place of ministries or state committees. *Kray* governments are directly subordinate to the RSFSR government and have direct administrative control over the autonomous *oblasti*, *rayony*, national areas, and towns of *rayon* status that are within them.

Oblasti

Oblasti are standard administrative subdivisions covering about half of the entire Soviet territory. Territorial breakdown, particularly below republic level, has been fluid throughout Soviet history, and *oblasti* have been created, abolished, combined, or subdivided on a routine basis to conform with growth of the population, changes in the economy, or governmental reorganization. *Oblast* size ranges from the 1,660 square miles of the Andizhan Oblast in the Uzbek SSR to the 554,000 square miles of the Tyumen Oblast in the RSFSR. The populations of the two *oblasti*, however, are not significantly different: about 1 million for Andizhan and slightly less than 1.4 million for Tyumen.

Although it was early practice to create new *oblasti* as previously undeveloped areas became economically significant, the tendency since 1953 has been to reduce their overall numbers. From about 145 at that time, they have been reduced to just over 100 by the late 1960's. These included about fifty in the RSFSR, twenty-five in the Ukraine, fifteen in Kazakhstan, ten in Uzbekistan, six in Belorussia, and one in Kirgizia. *Oblasti* had been eliminated from the ASSR's and the nine smaller SSR's, most of which corresponded roughly in size or population to the *oblasti*. Administrative *oblasti* are usually integral to an economic or geographic region

406

Table 4. Kraya of the Soviet Union

Kray	Area (in square miles)	Population (in thousands)[1]	Density of population (per square mile)	Location (all in RSFSR)[2]
Altay	101,000	2,723	27	South-central Siberia, northwest of Mongolia
Khabarovsk	318,500	1,336	4	Far East
Maritime (Primorskiy)	64,000	1,669	26	Do.
Krasnoyarsk	927,000	2,939	3	Central Siberia
Krasnodar	32,300	4,335	134	Caucasus
Stavropol	31,000	2,207	71	Do.
Total	1,473,800	15,209	10.3[3]	

[1] January 1, 1968.
[2] Russian Soviet Federated Socialist Republic.
[3] Average population density.

rather than, as in the case of the autonomous *oblasti*, to an ethnic group.

The population of an *oblast* is usually between 1 million and 2 million. It is less in some of the sparsely populated Siberian *oblasti* and considerably higher in areas of European USSR. The Moscow Oblast has more than 11 million people, and the Leningrad Oblast has about 5 million.

The union republics are empowered to create or redesignate *oblast* boundaries and, since there were in early 1970 no administrative *oblasti* in *kraya* or autonomous republics, all were subordinate to one of the six union republics. *Oblasti* are usually subdivided into rural *rayony* that, together with towns of *rayon* status, are directly subordinate to them. They may also contain nation *okruga*, which are administered and controlled on a level between the *oblast* and the *rayon*.

Oblasti may contain towns of *oblast* status that are responsible directly to the SSR. Moscow and Leningrad, for example, are within, and are the administrative centers of, otherwise typical oblasts, but each of their city governments is more important than that of its *oblast*. Of the nine cities in the USSR that were estimated to have populations exceeding 1 million in 1969, only Baku was not also the center of an *oblast* named for it. Baku is the capital of the Azerbaijan SSR, one of the republics that is not broken down into *oblasti* because of its small size.

Oblasti and *kraya* are considered regions and, therefore, are required to have soviets with a minimum of 100 deputies. They usually elect more than the minimum, and the average has been 150 to 200. In common with all the other local soviets, the primary executive and administrative functions are carried out by the executive committee and various departments. To comply with articles in the SSR constitutions, all committees have a chairman, vice chairman, and secretary. The numbers of members vary, usually between seven and fifteen. Departments and administrations are responsible to corresponding ministries and state committees at republic level, as well as to the *oblast* soviet and executive committee.

Rayony

The *rayon*, or district, is the subdivision of the smaller union republics, autonomous republics, *kraya*, *oblasti*, autonomous *oblasti*, and national *okruga*. In this form, when it constitutes an area having smaller towns, villages, settlements, or collective farms, it is usually referred to as a rural *rayon*. City *rayony* are the boroughs, of roughly 100,000 people each, of the larger cities. Medium-sized cities are administered at the same level as the rural and city *rayony*. Villages, agricultural settlements, workers' settlements, and small towns or cities are subordinate to the *rayony*, which in turn are responsible to the next higher government level.

There are some 4,000 *rayony* or *rayon*-equivalent districts distributed throughout all major territorial units and large cities. Like the *oblasti*, *rayon* boundaries are subject to change, and their numbers have varied widely. Khrushchev undertook to make the *rayon* conform to local economic conditions and reduced the overall numbers of rural *rayony* from nearly 3,500 to less than 1,300. Although Khrushchev's programs fell into disrepute after his ouster in 1964, the number of *rayony* has been brought back to hardly more than one-half of the pre-Khrushchev total. In early 1970 there were more than 1,800 rural *rayony*, nearly the same number of towns or cities of *rayon* status, and about 400 city boroughs.

Some regions have had less than ten rural *rayony*, others as many as sixty. There were fifty-seven in the Moscow Oblast in the mid-1960's. The *rayon* usually has about fifteen settlements or groups of villages subordinate to it. There have been as few as two, however, and occasionally there may be thirty or more.

Rayon governments are similar to, but scaled down from, those of the *oblasti*. In the early 1960's the typical *rayon* attempted to maintain the same administrative organization as its immediately superior government, although some agencies were grouped together and most were more modestly staffed. There apparently has been some effort to eliminate unnecessary departments in the *rayon* governments, but it cannot be determined whether or not any real reform has been achieved.

Rayon and other district-equivalent soviets must have at least seventy-five deputies. During the 1969 elections a total of about 500,000 deputies were elected to them, or an average of roughly 125 each. The soviets are scheduled to meet for a session at two-month intervals, and most of them convene as required. As in all local soviets, the executive committees are their administrative and executive agencies and perform all necessary governmental functions between sessions. In order to perform specialist work, a large number of departments and standing committees assist the executive committees. At the district level in 1969, some 350,000 deputies and about double that number of activists served on various commissions. The activists are people of the local communities who represent local agricultural, industrial, or trade activities; a majority of them apparently are not Party members. Their participation tends to bring local expertise into the government and to broaden the popular base.

Cities

Cities or towns, depending on their sizes, can be administered at any level beneath the republic. The smallest, sometimes referred to as urban-type settlements, are subordinate to *rayony*. The largest, even when they themselves are the administrative centers of *oblasti* that are named for them, have governments of *oblast* equivalence and are responsible directly to their SSR's. They have boroughs, or city *rayony*, within them.

City soviets must have a minimum of fifty deputies, but their numbers vary with the size of the city. The Moscow Soviet had over 800 in the late 1960's. Large as it was then, it was far smaller than during the mid-1950's when it had over 2,000 deputies. At that time its executive committee numbered seventy. It had its own ten-member presidium, and the presidium had a three-member bureau. When the soviet was reduced in size, its executive committee and presidium were also made smaller; the bureau disappeared altogether.

Administrative status changes with urban growth. Growing cities initially responsible to *rayony*, for example, may achieve *rayon* status and become subordinate to the next higher regional or republican government. From the numbers that are upgraded in individual administrative change announcements, it appears that they do so in routine, if not automatic, fashion.

As is the case in other local governments, the larger cities have departments and administrations corresponding to many of the republican ministries and state committees. The smaller ones have only those that are concerned with maintaining local public services and are maintained with far more modest staffs.

Villages and Settlements

The unit forming the bottom or the broad base of the governmental pyramid is the village or settlement soviet. The typical village, hamlet, or populated point is too small to justify a government of its own, and one soviet is usually elected by a group of them, numbering from two or three to as many as fifteen. Workers' settlements, agricultural settlements, or settlements of an urban type are usually larger, and most of them have their own individual soviets.

The village category of soviets has decreased in number from about 75,000 in 1953. Redistribution was necessary because state and collective farms, which had numbered about 250,000 in 1950, had been combined until, in 1967, there were only about 50,000. The larger farms frequently were subordinate to two or more village soviets, and one was subordinate to eight. Elections in 1969 indicated that there were about 40,000 village soviets and almost 3,500 settlement soviets.

Even more than at *rayon* level, attempts are made to get mass popular participation at the lowest level of government. Almost 1.5 million deputies were elected to village soviets in 1969. About two-thirds of them serve on various standing committees, and approximately another 1.5 million activists are appointed to the committees from the local population. In the smallest ones, however, all local administration may be accomplished by the executive committee alone. The committee could consist of only the three required persons—the chairman, vice chairman, and secretary of the soviet—who would then be the only persons involved in the daily village public service functions. Village soviets are ordinarily subordinate to *rayons.* Infrequently they may, however, be subordinate to *oblasts* or to large towns or cities.

AUTONOMOUS OR NATIONAL AREA SUBDIVISIONS

Autonomous Republics

The ASSR's were formed to grant a degree of political and cultural autonomy to large national minorities predominant in certain integral areas. Their constitutions refer to autonomy, as opposed to the sovereignty and independence that is referred to in the constitutions of the union republics. This autonomy entails, at the minimum, the right of the national group to retain its local language in schools, courts, news media, local business, and local administration. National manners and customs are respected. The ASSR's, constitutionally, are considered "national states within the constituent Soviet republics." As such, all of them are physically within, and subordinate to, a union republic. The autonomy they enjoy relative to the SSR is comparable to that enjoyed by the SSR's in relation to the USSR.

Sixteen of the twenty autonomous republics are in the RSFSR, two in Georgia, and one each in Azerbaijan and Uzbek. In the RSFSR five of the smaller ones are in a cluster east of Moscow, between the city and the Ural Mountains. Four other small ones are in the Caucasus between the Black and Caspian seas. The others are more widely spread. One is in south-central USSR, roughly surrounding the southern half of the Aral Sea. Two are in southern Siberia, bordering Mongolia. Two are in lesser populated areas in the northern portion of European RSFSR. The Yakut ASSR constitutes a large portion of east-central Siberia.

The areas of the autonomous republics represent wide extremes. The Yakut ASSR contains almost 1.2 million square miles. At the other extreme is the Adzhar ASSR, having only 1,160 square miles. The remaining eighteen fall between the two extremes, but none approaches the size of the huge Yakut area (see table 5).

Although the autonomous republics were created to recognize the predominance of a nationality within their areas, there are now

Table 5. Autonomous Soviet Socialist Republics of the USSR

Autonomous Soviet Socialist Republic[1]	Area (in square miles)	Population (in thousands)[2]	Density of population (per square mile)	Location
Bashkir	55,400	3,787	68	RSFSR,[3] European USSR, in a cluster between Moscow and the southern Ural Mountains
Chuvash	7,065	1,196	156	
Mari	8,950	657	73	
Mordovia	10,100	1,010	100	
Tatar	26,250	3,132	119	
Udmurt	16,300	1,386	85	
Chechen-Ingush	7,450	1,053	135	RSFSR,[3] Caucasus
Dagestan	14,600	1,392	95	
Kabardino-Balkarian	4,825	543	112	
Kalmyk	29,400	254	9	
North Ossetia	3,880	525	135	
Tuva	65,800	222	3	RSFSR,[3] south-central Siberia, northwest of Mongolia
Buryat	135,000	789	6	RSFSR,[3] south-central Siberia, east and south of Lake Baikal
Yakut	1,198,000	662	0.6	RSFSR,[3] northern and east-central Siberia
Karelia	66,540	701	11	RSFSR,[3] western USSR, bordering Finland
Komi	162,100	985	6	RSFSR,[3] northeast European USSR
Nakhichevan	2,100	194	92	Armenian SSR,[4] Transcaucasus[5]
Abkhaz	3,300	477	145	Georgian SSR,[4] Transcaucasus[5]
Adzhar	1,160	305	263	Do.
Kara-Kalpak	60,500	655	11	Uzbek SSR,[4] south-central USSR
Total	1,878,720	19,925	11[6]	

[1] ASSR.
[2] January 1, 1968
[3] Russian Soviet Federated Socialist Republic.
[4] Soviet Socialist Republic.
[5] Azerbaijan SSR, with which it has no physical contact.
[6] Average population density.

only a few in which the groups for which they were named remain in majority. In several, the national group was a majority when the republic was formed but is no longer. The indigenous Yakut population, for example, remained practically unchanged from 1926 to 1959, while the republic increased in population fourfold. The result was that the Yakuts numbered roughly one-fourth of the total after 1969. Similarly, the Komi people constituted 92.2 percent of their republic's population when it was formed in 1926. After important coal and oil resources were discovered, the population of the republic also quadrupled, and nearly all of the increase consisted of other nationalities.

In the Caucasian areas there are so many ethnic groups, and the groups are so scattered that it would be administratively inconceivable to create autonomous areas for all of them. Dagestan, the only ASSR deriving its name from an area rather than a people, contains at least thirty minority groups.

In other instances political motivations figured in the original boundary determinations. The existence of a Bashkir culture has been questionable for many years. About one-quarter of the ASSR population in 1959 claimed to be Bashkirs, but only one-half of these spoke the language. Many appear to claim or disclaim the nationality in differing situations. Many scholars believe that the state owed its existence originally to fears that sentiment for a large and potentially troublesome Muslim state encompassing Bashkir and areas to its south might develop if the area were not first fragmented along other lines.

The Karelian ASSR, adjacent to Finland, was a political pawn from its inception. The Karelians were a majority group within a definable area in 1923, but the ASSR borders were drawn up so that the majority of Karelians were outside them, and there has never been a Karelian majority within them. Even as it was formed, the Finnish population constituted about 1 percent of the total, but the Finnish language was made coequal to Russian and Karelian. This provided the necessary legality for publishing texts, news media, and the like that could be understood by Finland's population across the border.

The ASSR's have governments structured almost identically after those of the USSR and the SSR's, with comparable constitutions, supreme soviets, councils of ministers, presidiums, and supreme courts. There constitutions contain only local variations from those of their parent SSR's, and amendments must be approved by the higher echelon. Their supreme soviets are unicameral. A deputy represents people numbering from 20,000 in a populous ASSR to 4,000 in a more sparsely populated ASSR. The typical ASSR soviet in the mid-1960's had about 150 deputies. Each ASSR sends eleven deputies to the USSR Soviet of Nationalities.

The typical ASSR presidium has a chairman, two vice chairmen, a secretary, and a small number of additional members. A minimum of twelve ministries was provided for in all ASSR constitutions during the early 1960's. Other ministries are optional, their type and number depending upon the size, population, and economy of the ASSR, but most have somewhat fewer than do their parent SSR's. All are counterparts of, and are responsible to, corresponding SSR ministries.

Autonomous Oblasti

Autonomous *oblasti* usually contain minority groups in areas that are not important enough to constitute distinctive and integral economic regions. There were eight such regions in early 1970. As a group they are less important economically than are the autonomous republics or the more ordinary administrative *oblasti*. The autonomy granted their citizens amounts largely to recognition of their local culture. As in the autonomous republics, local manners, customs, and languages prevail in schools, courts, governmental administrations, and local news media. Since autonomous areas are never incorporated within other autonomous areas, the autonomous *oblasti* are subordinate either to the *kray* or to the union republic in which they are located. Each sends five deputies to the USSR Soviet of Nationalities.

Five of the eight are within the RSFSR, and the other three are in Georgia, Azerbaijan, and the Tadzhik SSR bordering on Afghanistan and Communist China. Of those in the RSFSR, two are in the Caucasus, two are in south-central Siberia, and one is in the Far East. Each of them is within a *kray* and is subordinate to it rather than to the republic. Those in the smaller SSR's, however, are directly responsible to the republic governments.

Populations in 1968 varied between about 95,000 and 465,000. The average of just over 200,000 was approximately one-fifth that of a typical administrative *oblast* or about one-fourth that of the typical autonomous republic. Generally located in the more remote areas, their population density averaged fifteen persons per square mile, as compared with about twenty-seven for the entire USSR (see table 6).

National Okruga

Like the ASSR's and autonomous *oblasti*, national *okruga* were formed to grant a degree of autonomy to various ethnic groups. They are large areas but are by far the most sparsely populated of any of the categories of territorial subdivision in the USSR. As such, they are maintained as parts of *kraya* or administrative *oblasti* and are subdivided into *rayony*. Local autonomy is limited; how-

Table 6. Autonomous Oblasti of the Soviet Union

Autonomous oblasti	Area (in square miles)	Population (in thousands)[1]	Density of population (per square mile)	Location
Karachay-Cherkess .	5,500	335	61	RSFSR,[2] Caucasus
Adygey	1,740	371	214	Do.
Khakass	23,700	466	20	RSFSR,[2] South-central Siberia
Gorno-Altay	35,750	168	5	Do.
Jewish	13,900	174	13	RSFSR,[2] Far East
Nagorno-Karabakh .	1,700	150	88	Azerbaijan SSR,[3] Transcaucasus
South Ossetia	1,500	101	67	Georgian SSR,[3] Transcaucasus
Gorno-Badakhshan .	24,600	96	4	Tadzhik SSR,[3] South-central
Total	108,390	1,861	17[4]	USSR

[1] January 1, 1968.
[2] Russian Soviet Federated Socialist Republic.
[3] Soviet Socialist Republic.
[4] Average population density.

Table 7. National Okrugs of the Soviet Union

Okrug	Area (in square miles)	Population (in thousands)[1]	Density of population (per square mile)[2]	Location (all in RSFSR)[2]
Chukchi	284,750	97	0.34	Northern Magadan Oblast, Far East
Koryak	116,400	39	0.37	Northwest Kamchatka Oblast, Far East
Aga (Aginksy) Buryat	7,950	62	8.0	South-central Chita Oblast, east of Lake Baikal
Ust-Orda Buryat ...	8,250	151	18.0	Irkutsk Oblast, west of Lake Baikal
Yamal-Nenets	190,000	74	0.26	Northern Tyumen Oblast, north-central USSR
Khanty-Mansi	227,000	269	1.2	Central Tyumen Oblast, just east of Ural Mountains
Taymyr	332,000	37	0.1	Northern Krasnoyarsk Kray, north-central USSR
Evenki	287,500	13	0.2	Central Krasnoyarsk Kray
Komi-Permyak	12,650	212	17.0	Northwestern Perm Oblast, west of Ural Mountains
Nenets	68,200	37	0.54	Arkhangel Oblast, south of Novaya Zemlya Island
Total	1,634,700	991	0.6[3]	

[1] January 1, 1968. [2] Russian Soviet Federated Socialist Republic. [3] Average population density.

ever, each national *okrug* sends one deputy to the Soviet of Nationalities in the Supreme Soviet of the USSR. All ten that existed in early 1970 were within the RSFSR.

Although the basis for the formation of *okruga* was to recognize ethnic groups, the national peoples are minorities within more than half of their *okruga* and constitute less than one-quarter of the population in three of them. Where the northern tribes remain in the majority it appears to be only because the land has been considered lowest on the list of priorities for exploitation or colonization. In most of these areas the native populations appear to be decreasing or barely holding their own.

Increases in population do not generally reflect growth in minority nationalities but, rather, an influx of immigrants, usually Russians. The city of Norilsk, for example, grew from 14,000 in 1939 to 127,000 in 1968 as it developed into an important mining center. Norilsk is located in the Taymyr National Okrug, but its increased population was Russian rather than Dolgano-Nenets, the peoples for whom the *okrug* was originally established. In the Soviet scheme of government, Norilsk is not even considered to be part of the area in which it is located; it is more important economically than the remainder of the *okrug* and, consequently, is administered by the next higher level of government (see table 7).

CHAPTER 21

POLITICAL DYNAMICS

At the beginning of 1970 every aspect of Soviet society was dominated by the Communist Party of the Soviet Union (CPSU), and the CPSU was dominated by its Politburo. The eleven members of the Politburo wielded absolute control over the destinies of the country's 241 million citizens. The *Rules of the Communist Party of the Soviet Union* as revised in 1961 and amended in 1966 stated that the Party had become "the part of the Soviet people as a whole" yet, in fact, membership remained relatively small and the elitist principles set forth by Lenin still applied in 1970. The role and influence of the Party were all pervasive, however, and Party members were found in leadership positions throughout the entire structure of the government, of the economy, and of society in general.

The Party controlled the citizenry through the maintenance of social and professional organizations to which most people belonged. These organizations included youth groups, athletic societies, trade unions, and cultural societies. All were permeated by Party activists, who provided the means by which the Party maintained contact with the masses and through which it provided approved political education and leadership.

The most important organizations were the youth groups because of their potential of molding younger generations along desired lines. By 1970 most citizens have belonged, at one time or another, to one of the three youth organizations: the Little Octobrists, ages seven to nine; the Young Pioneers, ages nine to fifteen; and the Komsomol, ages fifteen to twenty-eight. These mass organizations have provided sufficient political socialization for at least passive support of the regime by most of the people. The youth organizations also provided an important source for the recruitment of future Party members and potential political leaders.

The political atmosphere, and consequently the social atmosphere, became relatively liberal after the death of Stalin. Terror and fear were rampant during Stalin's dictatorship. Under Khrushchev the situation was mitigated, and liberalization reached the highest point of the post-Stalin period. The collective leadership that succeeded Khrushchev, however, tightened the reigns on society to a limited extent. They clamped down on the cultural field, but allowed some discussion and experimentation in the fields of economic planning and management.

After Stalin's death it became evident that the Soviet Union was not a monolithic society. The existence of interest groups became apparent, based primarily in institutions, though occasionally some coalesced around issues. How much influence these groups exerted, and the extent to which they were permitted to be active, depended upon both the issue in question and the nature of the leadership at a given point in time. Under Khrushchev, the role of interest groups became increasingly important to decisionmaking. This process has continued under the succeeding leadership.

The collective rule of Brezhnev and Kosygin, and their nine fellow members of the Politburo, appeared to be a genuine balance of power. They have not indicated the formulation of a long-range course of action but have moved cautiously, the only apparent goal being the maintenance of political stability and economic progress. Thus, they have allowed experimentation in the fields of economic planning and administration, while maintaining a more or less dogmatic approach in social and cultural affairs.

THE COMMUNIST PARTY OF THE SOVIET UNION

Structure

The CPSU is a highly centralized, hierarchical organization. The All-Union Party Congress, which consists of representatives elected from each of the union-republic party congresses, is designated as the supreme organ by Party statutes; however, in practice it has very little power, if any at all. Its size is too cumbersome to function as a decisionmaking body; at the Twenty-Third Party Congress, held in 1966, there were nearly 5,000 delegates. According to the statutes, this congress is to meet not less than once every four years; however, it did not meet between 1939 and 1952, during which time Stalin was exercising exclusive, one-man rule. Since 1952 Party congresses have been held on a fairly regular basis.

The Central Committee, elected by the All-Union Congress to take over its functions between sessions, is the body in which the political elite is located. In and of itself, however, the Central Committee shares little of the decisionmaking power. It meets too infrequently and has too many members to do more than ratify decisions made by the Politburo. At the 1966 meeting of the All-Union Congress, 195 full (voting) members and 165 candidate (nonvoting) members were elected to the Central Committee.

The Central Committee unanimously elects the Politburo and Secretariat, in which the real power is vested. This is more ratification than election, however, because the slate of officers is dictated by the top leaders themselves. The Politburo is the actual decisionmaking body and has jurisdiction encompassing virtually every aspect of life in the Soviet Union.

The information that is necessary for the formulation of policy for such divergent areas is provided by the departments into which the Central Committee is divided. Many of these departments correspond to the various functions that would usually be associated with the government; their scope ranges from education to international relations. These departments perform a secondary function of supervising the government ministries that correspond to their functional areas.

The Secretariat wields a tremendous amount of political power by virtue of its control over the selection and appointment of key government and Party personnel, as well as the personnel of all mass organizations, such as the trade unions and the youth organizations. This power includes the selection of candidates for elections for posts in the government or other organizations, even on the local level. The Secretariat is also charged with the responsibility of "the verification of the fulfillment of Party decisions." In essence, this gives the Secretariat supervisory powers over the Party, government, and all other organizations.

At the beginning of 1970 there were three full members and one candidate member of the Politburo who were also members of the ten-man Secretariat, including Brezhnev, the general secretary. The overlapping of the membership of these two bodies primarily serves to coordinate their activities.

Below the all-union level, each union republic has its own Party organization, except the Russian Soviet Federated Socialist Republic, which shares the CPSU organization. At the top of the republic Party structure is the union republic congress, which is composed of representatives elected by the provincial conferences. The congress meets once every four years and elects a central committee to conduct its affairs between sessions. In turn, the central committee elects a bureau and a secretariat. The Party organizations of the province, district, and city levels have structures similar to that of the republic Party, except the term *conference* is used instead of *congress* and the adjective *central* is not used to describe their committees.

At the bottom of the Party hierarchy there are about 460,000 primary Party organizations. These organizations, held to be the "basis of the Party," are formed in factories, on collective farms, in offices, in army units, in schools and universities, and "wherever there are not less than three Party members." The Party meeting, which corresponds to the Party Congress at the highest level, meets at least once a month. A bureau is elected for the purpose of conducting daily business.

If a primary Party organization has less than 15 members, it elects a secretary and a deputy secretary instead of a bureau. If there are over 300 members, a committee may be elected, provided the republic central committee or the provincial committee gives approval. Primary Party organizations on collective farms with at least 50 members are also permitted to elect committees. Full-time, salaried officials do not exist at this level except where the primary Party organization has more than 150 members; otherwise, all work is "voluntary."

Operation

The CPSU operates according to the principles of "democratic-centralism" first articulated by Lenin. The Party statutes specify these principles as: "election of all leading Party bodies, from the lowest to the highest; periodical reports of Party bodies to their Party organizations and to higher bodies; strict Party discipline and subordination of the minority to the majority; the decisions of higher bodies are obligatory for lower bodies." Theoretically, these principles allow a great deal of democracy. They imply discussion at all levels until a decision is taken by the majority, at which point discussion ceases and all members are obliged to abide by it. In practice, only the fourth principle, that is, centralism, is operative. Decisions are made by a small circle of people at the top of the Party hierarchy and handed down as binding rules for all Party members.

There is a facade of democracy in the operation of the Party; the lower levels do elect the higher levels. These elections, however, are actually controlled by the highest bodies of the Party. The Secretariat determines who will be nominated, and only one name appears on the ballot for each office. Rank-and-file members usually only have the choice of voting for the designated candidates; although they may register opposition by not voting, this alternative is rarely used because of fear of negative repercussions by the Party leaders. The higher organizations do issue periodic reports of their activities to lower level organizations. These are in the nature of directives, however, and cannot be criticized or rejected.

The interpretation of democratic-centralism that is practiced by the Party was actually made law by the Resolution on Party Unity, passed by the Tenth Party Congress in 1921. This resolution banned the formation of factions within the Party, that is, groups organized on the basis of a platform. Factionalism became a crime punishable by expulsion and, in practice, any opposition to the policy of the top leaders, regardless of whether or not it was centered around a platform, was considered treasonous. In essence, this interpretation overruled the democratic aspects of democratic-centralism. Throughout Soviet history, however, the degree of adherence to this resolution has varied depending upon the Party leader or leaders.

Role

The Soviet Constitution describes the Party as "the vanguard of the working people in their struggle to build communist society and [it] is the leading core of all organizations of the working people, both government and non-government." According to Party statutes, the CPSU "is the highest form of sociopolitical organization, and is the leading and guiding force of Soviet society. It directs the great creative activity of the Soviet people, and imparts an organized, planned, and scientifically-based character to their struggle to achieve the ultimate goal, the victory of Communism."

These quotations indicate the pervasive role of the CPSU in society. Party leaders set the policy for virtually all activities, from the allocation of resources to what is included in the curricula at the various levels of the educational system. Its members permeate all organizations: government, economic, educational, military, and other institutions. The key positions in these bureaucracies are filled by Party members in order to maintain control and ensure compliance with Party directives.

The Party and government hierarchies are actually parallel structures; the Party supervises the activities of the government at each level. This is facilitated primarily by the interlocking relationship of personnel. In early 1970, at the highest level, the chairman of the Presidium of the Supreme Soviet, Nikolai V. Podgorny, and the chairman of the Council of Ministers, Aleksei Kosygin, were also members of the Politburo. Almost all of the ministers in the USSR Council of Ministers were not only Party members, but also members of the Central Committee. The Party-government relationship follows a similar pattern at each level, from the republic down to the village level.

The appointment of key personnel in the government, industry, the military, and other important institutions is done through a system called nomenclature (*nomenklatura*) which is a listing of positions and personnel. A file of job descriptions is maintained by the Secretariat, along with dossiers on each Party member, as well as dossiers on important non-Party people whose loyalty to the system is unquestioned. The purpose of the *nomenklatura* system is the rational selection of personnel, based on professional and political qualifications. In practice, however, the political considerations often outweigh the professional in making appointments.

The secretariats at each of the lower levels of the Party hierarchy also perform the function of appointing personnel to government and other positions at their respective levels. Although these secretariats are elected by the republic central committees or the provincial committees, in practice they take orders from, and are responsible to, the all-union Secretariat.

Although government organizations are responsible for daily

423

administration, they merely implement decisions made by the Party. At the various levels of the Party hierarchy, only a minimum amount of actual decisionmaking occurs, and this is usually restricted to formulating means of expediting the directives from the Kremlin. This, however, is an extremely important task for republic, regional, provincial, and district Party leaders. They are responsible to Moscow for the functioning of the economy, the educational system, the government, youth organizations, and other institutions within their territorial jurisdiction.

The placing of Party members in key positions in the various bureaucracies does not completely assure control. It is possible, and has frequently been the case, that Party members holding administrative positions in an industrial enterprise, for example, will develop interests that center on their occupations rather than on their Party affiliation. The Party has not been able to prevent this situation from developing but has been able to keep it in check by authorizing local Party officials, and even rank-and-file members, to investigate and expose corruption and inefficiency in the various bureaucracies. The Party statutes specifically state that the primary Party organizations, which are organized in production enterprises and other places of employment, "enjoy the right to control the work of the administration" of the enterprises, institutes, and establishments in which they are organized.

The vital function of integrating the political, economic, and social aspects of the society is performed by the Party at all levels. The primary Party organizations, however, have many additional functions that are specifically designated by the Party statutes. They primarily serve to politicize all activities, especially those related to agricultural and industrial production, and for this reason are organized in places of employment, as opposed, for example, to residential areas. In this connection, Party members agitate among their fellow workers for higher productivity. Indeed, political agitators, in general, are recruited from the primary Party organizations.

The primary Party organization is the point of entrance for new members of the CPSU and, consequently, is charged with the responsibility of political indoctrination. Groups are organized for the study of the tenets of Marxism-Leninism and their official interpretation by the ruling elite. At this level, the ideology is presented in a manner that is relevant to the Party members' occupations. This, in turn, facilitates agitation among their non-Communist fellow workers.

Membership

The Party statutes define the composition of the CPSU as "the more advanced, politically more conscious section of the working class, collective-farm peasantry, and intelligentsia of the USSR."

According to the latest available figures, November 12, 1968, there were 13.5 million Party members and candidate members, or just a little over 8 percent of the adult population. Although this is the largest percentage of the population that has held membership in the history of the CPSU, it is still extremely small and indicative that the elitist principles governing membership are still operative. Not only do Party members have to be more "advanced" and "politically conscious," they must also be politically active and undertake various responsibilities for the Party.

Party statutes stipulate that membership in the CPSU is open to any citizen who accepts the program and the rules of the Party. Members are expected to take an active part in Communist construction, work in Party organizations, carry out all Party decisions, and pay membership dues. The demands made on Party members are great, and only those who are willing to sacrifice may join.

The procedure by which individuals are admitted to the Party is rigorous and allows for careful scrutiny of applicants. Admission is only on an individual basis. A person must have the recommendations of three full members who have been in the Party for at least five years. The people supplying recommendations must have known the applicant for at least one year and are responsible for the objectivity of their appraisals of his qualifications. Applicants who are members of the Komsomol (Young Communist League) are permitted to substitute a recommendation from the Komsomol district or city committee for one from a CPSU member.

The primary Party organization holds a general meeting at which applications are discussed individually. Its decision must be endorsed by the next higher Party level, that is, the district Party committee or the city Party committee. If the decision is positive, the applicant is admitted with the status of candidate member for one year. After having passed through this probationary period, he must go through the same procedure to become a regular member of the CPSU.

The motivations behind individuals joing the CPSU are various. Some are firm believers in the Communist ideology and want to participate actively in the "struggle for communism." A more salient reason for joining is that membership in the Party is, in most cases, requisite to attaining positions of influence and responsibility. Indeed, the only way to become part of the political elite is to rise through the Party hierarchy. Achievement-oriented individuals who lack political motivation, however, can pursue careers in the government administration without necessarily belonging to the Party. Other people, particularly those who have excelled in their fields, such as technicians and industrial managers, become members of the Party because of reluctance to decline an invitation to join.

The pressures that the Party can exert on people whom they are trying to recruit can be greater than the demands that will be made of them once they are members. Many people who do possess the required qualifications for Party membership, however, fail to join simply out of fear of the possibility of expulsion. The stigma attached to individuals who have been expelled from the Party is far worse than not being a member in the first place.

The Party as a whole is not the ruling elite; only a small group of men at the top of its hierarchy have political power. Nevertheless, the rank-and-file members function as important communication links between the decisionmakers and the mass of citizens. This communication flow is in two directions: decisions are transmitted down to the masses, and their moods and activities are transmitted upwards through the rank-and-file members. For this reason, the Party recruits members from all social and occupational groups of the population. In practice, it is not the various segments of society that are represented in the Party, but the Party that is represented among the population.

Although there are Party members from all social strata and occupational fields, their proportions within the Party do not correspond to those within the total population. For example, a breakdown of membership based on "social position" for 1967 indicates that the proportion of peasantry in the Party is much lower than their proportion in Soviet society, whereas the percentage of Party members from the intelligentsia is probably twice as large as if not larger than, the percentage of intelligentsia within the entire population.

The 1967 membership breakdown in percentages is: 45.9 percent intelligentsia, 38.1 percent workers, and 16.0 percent peasants. The categories, furthermore, are not entirely accurate. They refer to the "social position" of members at the time that they entered the Party. Very often as a consequence of becoming Party members, workers are promoted to white-collar positions and peasants are promoted to administrative positions on their collective farms. Such changes in status are not reflected in this membership breakdown.

POLITICAL SOCIALIZATION AND RECRUITMENT

Political socialization is a conscious, systematic effort by the CPSU leaders, designed to mold the values and attitudes of the population to actively support their policies and goals. The changes envisioned by the revolutionary leaders in 1917 were not limited to changing the economic relations within the country, nor merely to restructuring the political system. The general goal intended for the mass of the people was to instill loyalty and devotion to the state and its principles. Traditional values and attitudes had to be liquidated and new ones fostered that would facilitate the development

426

of a Communist society. The function of developing the political skills and attitudes necessary for the maintenance of the system is directed specifically to a minority of the population, that is, members of the Komsomol and the CPSU, from which future leaders will be recruited.

Political Education

Educational policy and curricula are determined by the leaders of the CPSU. Consequently, there are political overtones at all levels, from nursery school through the university. Actual political courses, however, do not become part of the curriculum until the last year of secondary school. Before 1960, only one course, on the USSR Constitution, was offered. A second course, Fundamentals of Political Knowledge, was added, however, in the early 1960's. These courses are supplemented by the use of the Marxist-Leninist approach in the teaching of history and other social sciences (see ch. 17, Intellectual Expression).

Formal political education is intensified at the university level. An estimated 10 percent of the curriculum during the five-year program, regardless of one's major field of study, is devoted to required political courses. For those individuals who do not go on to the university after completing their secondary education, the Komsomol, trade unions, and other such organizations provide further political indoctrination.

Aside from the state educational system, the CPSU maintains several schools and conducts seminars to educate its cadres in the fields of Marxism-Leninism, Soviet history, and other politically relevant fields. In conjunction with the political courses, the Party also provides training specific to the responsibilities of the various members. Thus, students in the Party schools receive training in economic production and management, journalism, photography, public administration, agronomy, and any other practical subjects that a Party member will need in order to fulfill his responsibilities.

There are four schools maintained under the Central Committee of the CPSU. The Higher Party School has a two-year program for the purpose of training individuals who are to be appointed to leading positions at the republic and provincial levels of the Party hierarchy. In order to be admitted to this school, an applicant must be at least 40 years old; have had a higher education; have had several year's experience in responsible positions, and have the recommendation of a republic, province, district, or city committee. The Academy of Social Sciences is administered by Agitprop (Department of Agitation and Propaganda) for the purpose of training personnel for theoretical work. The Institute of Marxism-Leninism and the Institute of Atheism also have primarily theoretical curricula.

Below the all-union level, there are several Party schools at the republic, province, and district or city levels to train lesser officials. These schools have either two-year or four-year courses. The two-year programs are designed for people who already have a higher education, and the four-year programs are for people with only a secondary education. Graduation from a four-year higher Party school is considered to be equivalent to a university education.

Mass Organizations

The Party has devised a network of organizations through which it is able to indoctrinate and control the majority of the population who are outside the ranks of the CPSU. The scope and activities of these organizations are diversified, so as to attract the different segments of the population; they include trade unions and unions for artists and writers; cooperatives; youth, women's, cultural, and sports associations; and scientific societies. Most Soviet citizens belong to one or more of these non-Party organizations.

Lenin conceived of these mass organizations as "transmission belts" through which the Party directed all activities of the proletariat. Although this terminology is no longer applied to these organizations, the conception remains. They still provide an important means of mobilizing the population to fulfill Party goals and instilling positive identification with the regime. Even more valuable is the fact that the existence of such diversified social and professional organizations preempts the spontaneous formation of social groups outside of Party control. The Party has consciously fostered the establishment of organizations that will fulfill all the needs that the masses might have.

Article 126 of the Constitution defines the role of Party members in mass organizations as the leading core in all organizations, both public and state. They influence the activities of these organizations to ensure that they conform to Party policy. All of these organizations, regardless of their avowed purposes, have political overtones. Their officials are almost always Communist Party members, and the activists within these organizations are also usually Communists. The presence of Party members in these non-Party organizations provides the means for continued contact between the Party and the general population.

The trade unions are the most prominent and extensive of all mass organizations; even people employed in the arts are unionized. At no time in the history of the Soviet state have the trade unions been delegated power by the Party. They have never been able to influence labor or wage policies but have consistently functioned as instruments of the Party. The primary concern of the trade unions has always been the welfare of the state and fulfillment of eco-

428

nomic plans, as opposed to the interests of the workers. To this end, the trade unions have played a paramount role in the political indoctrination of the workers, as well as in the enforcement of labor discipline (see ch. 33, Labor Relations and Organization).

Once the technological base of Soviet society had been developed and the standard of living began to rise, the trade unions were delegated the function of administering welfare programs for their members. Trade unions now have their own clinics, resorts, day-care centers, schools, and other social welfare programs (see ch. 33, Labor Relations and Organization).

Another non-Party organization, whose branches and activities are extensive, is the All-Union Knowledge Society. It was founded in 1950 as the All-Union Society for the Dissemination of Political and Scientific Knowledge, but in 1963 its name was shortened to the Knowledge Society. The membership of this organization is less extensive than that of the trade unions, but its activities do, in fact, affect large numbers of people. The purpose of this society is to campaign against religion and, in place of religious beliefs, inculcate Communist ethics and values. To this end, the society publishes and distributes millions of antireligious pamphlets and sponsors lectures, discussion groups, and films, which are reportedly well attended. The activities of this society are under the jurisdiction of Agitprop.

Youth Organizations

The hierarchy of youth organizations is perhaps the single most important instrument of political socialization in the hands of the Party. When the Bolsheviks came to power, in November 1917, they did not have a subordinate youth organization. The utility of such an organization, indeed the necessity of it, was recognized early, however, and the Komsomol was formally established in October 1918. Initially, the Komsomol was to serve as a source of recruitment of future Party members and, consequently, was small and elitist. By 1936, however, it began to take on the character of a mass organization in which a whole generation was to be molded. The nature and purpose of the Komsomol has remained virtually unchanged through the 1960's.

By virtue of the CPSU's monopoly over youth organizations and the extent to which these have been developed, most members of Soviet society at least passively support the ruling regime. By the end of the 1960's, most citizens have been, at one time or another, members of one of the officially sponsored youth groups.

The Komsomol is organized along the same lines as the CPSU and is run according to the same principles, that is, those of demo-cratic-centralism. The All-Union Congress of the Komsomol, the highest body in the Komsomol's hierarchical structure, is directly under, and responsible to, the Central Committee of the CPSU. The officials of the Komsomol are required to be members of the Party, and the Komsomol first secretary is a full member of the Central Committee of the Party. Although the age limit for membership is twenty-eight, provision is made in the Komsomol statutes for officers to remain in the organization beyond that age.

The Central Council of the All-Union Pioneer organization is directly under, and responsible to, the Central Committee of the All-Union Congress of the Komsomol. All organizations and government agencies that in some way are concerned with children are represented on this council, including the Komsomol, the Ministry of Education, and the Children's Publishing House.

Children are recruited into the official youth program as soon as they begin primary school. The Little Octobrist organization is designed for children between the ages of seven and nine, with the purpose of preparing them for entrance into the Young Pioneers. They are organized into groups of five, known as "links," which are led by members of the Young Pioneers. Almost all children of this age group are members, and its activities are centered primarily in the school, though there are also extracurricular programs, such as organized play and community service projects. When the children are old enough to join the Young Pioneers, at age nine, initiation ceremonies are held, usually followed by a party. Essentially, the initiation ritual is symbolic of the child's entrance into Soviet society.

The Young Pioneer organization is run by the Komsomol for children between the ages of nine and fifteen, and virtually all children of this age group belong. The program of the Young Pioneers is formulated largely within the framework of the educational system, and each school has a staff member to direct Pioneer activities. The classes are divided into collectives, which also serve as the primary groupings for the Pioneers. The collective serves as a source of control over individual children by means of the pressure to conform that is intrinsic to the nature of groups, and the experience helps to inculcate the collectivisit values that are considered so important to the functioning of a Communist society. In Young Pioneer terminology these collectives are called troops, and each troop is led by a Komsomol member. If a troop has over twenty members, it may be divided into detachments, which are also led by Komsomol members. The leaders of the Pioneers work closely with classroom teachers to teach the children to be good students and good citizens (see ch. 14, Social Values).

Nearly all recreational activities for children between the ages of nine and fifteen take place under the auspicies of the Young Pioneers. The programs that the organization sponsors range from sports and scouting to folk dancing and ballet lessons. Each city has facilities for these purposes, and there are numerous Pioneer summer camps throughout the country. Overt political indoctrination is at a minimum during this period and usually is limited to instilling patriotism and Soviet values in the children. Intensive political indoctrination is reserved for the Komsomol, which the child enters when he is fifteen.

Membership in the Komsomol is less extensive than in its younger counterparts. Only about one-third of the eligible age group are members, though membership is nearly 100 percent among the student population. Indeed, membership in the Komsomol is usually a prerequisite for admission into institutions of higher education. At this level of the hierarchy of youth organizations, political indoctrination is intensified, and greater demands are made of Komsomol members to participate in all aspects of Soviet society. It is difficult to pinpoint the reasons why so many of the youth fail to join the Komsomol, but it is reasonable to assume that the high standards by which the Komsomolite must live and the great demands that are made of him are important factors operating to prevent a person from joining the Komsomol.

Komsomol members are required to "volunteer" to join the armed forces if the government calls for recuits in an emergency, such as the Nazi invasion. They also must "volunteer" to go to work in a factory or on a collective farm when there is a labor shortage. Members who are employed in the military or who are members of the industrial or agricultural force are responsible for the political education of their co-workers who are of the same age group. They receive training for this task during their meetings, which are largely discussions and lectures on Marxist-Leninist ideology. An integral part of this education is agitation for greater productivity. Afterwork activities are planned for workers by the Komsomolites, and they generally help young workers to adjust to the conditions of factory employment. This is especially important for workers from rural communities.

An invaluable surveillance function is also performed by the Komsomol. They frequently inspect enterprises, usually without prior warning, seeking to expose corruption, waste, and inefficiency in the management and laziness among workers. Even the private lives of the workers are subject to the omnipresence of the Komsomol. Since 1955, Komsomolites have formed voluntary police bands for the purpose of patroling streets and public places, such as restaurants, to prevent unconventional behavior, the interpretation of which ranges from drunkenness to wearing one's hair too long.

The nearly universal membership of students in the Komsomol is the result of the Party's desire to inhibit the crystalization of youth groups that could provide the nucleus for political opposition. The potential for such opposition is greater among the student population than any other segment of society. By requiring that students be members of the Komsomol, not only is a large measure of control assured, but the energy of the youth can be channeled into activity that supports the regime.

Komsomolites are frequently called upon to lecture in various factories and villages, to conduct evening courses for workers, and to lead lower level youth groups. Discussion groups meet regularly to supplement formal courses on Marxism-Leninism and to prepare Komsomol members for the task of agitating for Communist goals among the masses. The surveillance function of the Komsomol is even more extensive in the university than it is in the economy or the military. The activities of students are carefully observed, both in the university and at home during vacations; failure to conform to Komsomol standards of behavior can result in expulsion from the university.

The Komsomol is the most important source for recruitment of Party members. Membership in the Komsomol, however, does not automatically ensure that a person will be admitted to the Party or that he will desire admittance. The CPSU often co-opts people who have excelled in their occupational fields, regardless of whether or not they have a Komsomol background. Furthermore, there is evidence that experience as a Komsomol official is not a prerequisite for becoming a Party official; of the persons elected to the Central Committee of the CPSU in 1966, only 2 percent had held an official post in the Komsomol.

The Military Establishment

Another mass organization that has received constant political pressure ever since the Bolshevik Revolution is the military establishment. In the early days when 50,000 tsarist officers served in the Red Army, Commissar of War Trotsky considered it necessary to have a political commissar in every unit down to company size. At times, the role of political commissar overshadowed that of unit commander but, in 1970, the political officer was a deputy commander, subordinate to the regular military commander.

The power of political officers over other military officers declined only after World War II when the concern of Party leaders over the role of professionalism versus loyalty in the armed forces seemed to decline. By 1970, 90 percent of the officers were Party members, whereas, in the forces as a whole, 80 percent of the personnel belonged either to the Party or to the Komsomol. Political officers still maintained direct communications with the Main Political Directorate of the Ministry of Defense but, with a Party or Komsomol cell in practically every unit, the armed forces had become another transmission belt for the Party, since almost every able-bodied young man is conscripted for a term of service with one of the armed forces (see ch. 28, The Armed Forces).

POLITICAL DEVELOPMENTS

Shortly after Stalin's death in March 1953 it became evident to Western observers that the political monolith associated with the Soviet Union was not a permanent feature but rather one dependent upon the totalitarian rule of the man, Stalin. Once Stalin was removed from the political scene, the various components of this monolith were quick to break away and vie against one another for political power. In 1957 Khrushchev appeared to have emerged as the supreme autocrat of the Soviet Union. During his incumbency, however, there were some Western observers who questioned the fact of his dominance and supreme authority. That Khrushchev found it necessary to argue publicly in favor of his policies and frequently criticized opponents of these policies in the press is taken as evidence that his authority was being challenged (see ch. 3, Historical Setting).

There are two major developments in the political system that can be cited with authority: the mitigation of terror and the increased importance of the role of politics. The abatement of terror had important consequences in the fields of economic and public administration. Under Stalin the fear of arrest and execution paralyzed administrators and planners. Creative decisionmaking was necessary to prevent the economy and government from stagnating; but this would only be possible if industrial managers and planners, for example, were not afraid to take initiative in their fields. Since Stalin's death there has been much discussion and some experimentation in order to find a means of maximizing efficiency in economic production and distribution (see ch. 29, Economic Planning and Control; ch. 3, Historical Setting).

The increasing importance of politics at the highest level of the Party was primarily dependent upon the mitigation of the reign of terror that had produced widespread fear in society. Under Stalin, politicking only occurred below the decisionmaking level, that is, between bureaucracies, such as the police, the military, and the state bureaucracies, which were competing for the favor of the dictator. Since Stalin's death, no individual has been able to wield absolute power comparable to his. Khrushchev, who came closest to doing so, at most only had limited authority and was highly challengeable throughout his tenure as first secretary of the CPSU.

Dictatorship

The three basic forms that Soviet leadership has assumed in its more than fifty years of existence are: dictatorship, limited dictatorship, and collective leadership. The first form is characterized by the rule of Lenin and Stalin. Lenin's dictatorship was less extreme and less harsh than that of Stalin. This was the result primarily of the differences in the personalities of the two men. Although Lenin would not tolerate factionalism, indeed he was the man behind the passage of the Resolution On Party Unity, he never suppressed discussion of policy to the extent that Stalin did.

Lenin commanded the loyalty of the Party by virtue of his charismatic personality and therefore could afford to allow his colleagues to challenge him on certain issues. He did not feel that his power was threatened by such challenges and consequently did not find it necessary to liquidate opposition from within the Party. An outstanding example of Lenin's moderation, as compared to Stalin, was his handling of the Workers' Opposition in 1921. In brief, the platform of this group was trade union control over industry. Once they were overruled in the Central Committee and prohibited from acting as a group by the Resolution On Party Unity, Lenin appealed to them to stay in the Party and cooperate, rather than purging them (see ch. 3, Historical Setting).

The dictatorship under Stalin reached extreme proportions, creating a police state in which people were afraid to express opinions even to their closest friends. Stalin's power was based on terror rather than loyalty. Constant fear of challenge to his position as supreme ruler resulted in the perpetual purging of the Party and other bureaucracies. Stalin preempted the power of decisionmaking of the Politburo and undermined the Party's position of leadership in Soviet society. It became one of several bureaucracies that merely implemented the will of the dictator. Below the dictator, the various organizations were left to compete with one another for his favor (see ch. 3, Historical Setting).

Limited Dictatorship

The second form of leadership is characterized by the rule of Khrushchev. In 1957 he achieved the top leadership position by bringing the issue of his tenure as first secretary of the CPSU before the Central Committee. A majority of his colleagues in the Presidium (as the Politburo was called between the years 1952 and 1966) had decided to remove him from office, but he refused to accept their decision and appealed to the Central Committee to overrule it. This was an unprecedented move in Soviet politics but was technically correct according to the delineation of functions in the Party Statutes. By 1957 Khrushchev had manipulated the composition of the Central Committee by virture of his control over the Secretariat and thereby provided himself with a power-base.

The opposition of the anti-Party group, as Khrushchev referred to his opponents, was primarily the result of the conflict between the orthodox and the reformist policy orientations. This conflict was triggered by Khrushchev's "secret speech" to the Twentieth Party Congress in February 1956, which set into motion the process of de-Stalinization.

Western observers ascribe two motivating factors to Khrushchev's action. First, it was a political move, in that it shifted the scales in his favor in the power struggle. In the course of his disclosure of the atrocities committed by Stalin and the irrational bases upon which the latter made decisions, Khrushchev implicated some of his colleagues while disassociating himself. Related to this, the disclosure served to assure the Congress that Khrushchev was against Stalinist methods and would not use them if he were to become the supreme leader. Such an assurance was an extremely important tactic in rallying support for his aspirations to power. The delegates to the Party Congress were largely incumbents of offices that, under Stalin, were most insecure. In essence, Khrushchev was promising them security in return for their support.

The second factor that motivated Khrushchev to denounce Stalin was his desire to move away from the traditional priorities in the allocation of resources. Briefly, his policy was to decrease investment in heavy industry and invest more in agriculture and consumer goods production. This, in turn, required a cutback in appropriations to the military, especially a cutback in the size of the conventional armed forces. The decrease in the defense budget was dependent upon the establishment of a detente with the West. All these innovations were most unorthodox and, in order to implement them, Khrushchev had to discredit the bases of the traditional orientation, which, of course, was associated with Stalin.

Khrushchev's victory in 1957 proved to be temporary. Throughout his incumbency in the office of first secretary, Khrushchev had to struggle to maintain his position of power. There are several examples that can be cited as indicators that Khrushchev was not entirely in control of the political situation. Indeed, there is evidence that he was often forced to accept positions on policy issues that were diametrically opposed to his position. In other instances, Khrushchev was forced to accept compromise.

At the Twenty-second Party Congress in 1961, Khrushchev ordered the expulsion of the anti-Party group. The Congress, however, would not comply. This incident made two facts of his rule evident. First, by 1961 Khrushchev had lost much of the support that he possessed in 1957. Secondly, that Khrushchev found it necessary to bring up the issue of the anti-Party group four years after the crisis is indicative that his victory had been incomplete.

The struggle to maintain his position of authority revolved around the reforms that Khrushchev wanted to institute in the economy.

Even before his defeat by the Twenty-second Party Congress, Khrushchev's incomplete authority could be discerned on the basis of policy pronouncements. There was opposition in the Presidium to many of Khrushchev's actions and, although some of his plans were implemented, his opponents found many opportunities to either modify his policies or overrule them altogether. Although the source of friction was Khrushchev's desire to change the priorities in the allocation of resources, the consequence reverberated throughout the domestic and foreign political spheres.

Khruschev's plan to establish *agrogoroda* (agricultural cities), originally proposed in 1950—51 and brought up again in 1959, was never implemented. He did, on the other hand, succeed in abolishing the machine tractor stations, which had been an obstacle to efficient agricultural production. This particular reform, though opposed when first implemented, was one of the few Khrushchevian innovations that was not overturned by his successors (see ch. 31, Agriculture).

Khrushchev did succeed, temporarily, in making two radical structural changes in both the government and Party organizations, in connection with his economic policy goals. In 1957 he decentralized the management of the economy by reorganizing the Council of Ministers to make it function according to the principle of territorial-production (see ch. 29, Economic Planning and Control). In 1962 Khrushchev instituted an even more radical structural reform, that of the bifurcation of the Party, from the all-union to the district levels. into two parallel structures: one for the control of agriculture and the other for industry. This innovation was actually the result of Khrushchev's search for a greater role for the Party in society.

The division of the Party and the increasing of its role in the management of the economy, however, actually weakened the Party rather than strengthened it. In order for Party officials—that is, those at the republic, provincial, district, and city levels—to participate actively in the practical aspects of industrial and agricultural production, they had to have training in these fields. This posed a threat to the majority of incumbents and aspirants to these positions, whose backgrounds were primarily in Party affairs to the exclusion of practical experience in economic production.

The latter reform, probably more than any of Khrushchev's other policies, caused him to lose support within the Party and was a major factor behind the conspiracy to oust him from his position of power. In November 1964, just a few weeks after Khrushchev's dismissal, the birfurcation of the Party was repealed. In September 1965 Khrushchev's decentralization of economic management and production was reversed, and the centralized ministerial system was reinstituted (see ch. 29, Economic Planning and Control).

When it came to the question of actual allocations of resources to the production of consumers goods and to agriculture, Khrushchev's successes were few and limited. Steel traditionally had been the center of the economic plans and, consequently, received the highest priority in the investment of capital and natural resources. This was the case not only because steel is the basis for the development of a modern, technological society, but Stalin had held that the development of such a society as rapidly as possible was fundamental to the defense of the Soviet state (see ch. 29, Economic Planning and Control).

Khrushchev held that the country was sufficiently developed along those lines to shift the emphasis of investment away from heavy industry toward light industry and agriculture. In this connection, he proposed cutting down on the manufacturing of conventional weaponry and also cutting back the number of conventional troops to be maintained. He argued that conventional warfare had become obsolete as a result of the development of nuclear weapons. Soviet nuclear capability, according to Khrushchev, was greater than that of any other country, and the rocket systems that they already had were sufficient to deter aggression. Thus, according to Khrushchev, it was uneconomical to maintain large numbers of troops and to continue the large-scale production of conventional weapons (see ch. 28, The Armed Forces).

In order to minimize opposition to military cutbacks, Khrushchev sought a detente with the West. In September 1959 he visited the United States and met with President Eisenhower at Camp David. The result was the playing down of the threat of a military confrontation with the West, which facilitated the reduction of troops. This was a very short-lived success, however because the U—2 incident in the spring of 1960 greatly weakened Khrushchev's position. The incident indicated that the Soviet Union was still vulnerable to the West and therefore could not afford to deemphasize heavy industry. The Cuban Missile Crisis in 1962 strengthened Khrushchev's opponents' position, and the number of conventional troops began to increase. At the beginning of 1970 there were almost the same number of troops as there had been before the introduction of Khrushchev's reduction policy (see ch. 28, The Armed Forces; ch. 24, Foreign Relations).

Khrushchev's attempt to establish a detente with the West was one of the major causes of the open rift between the Soviet Union and Communist China. In turn, this development was another factor in the determination of his colleagues to remove him from the scene (see ch. 24, Foreign Relations).

Shortly before his attempt at detente, Khrushchev tried to implement his consumer goods approach indirectly by arguing that the chemical industry, not steel, was primary to industrial development.

If this approach were accepted, Khrushchev would have been able to use heavy industry to produce consumer goods, for example, plastic products. He succeeded in having the program incorporated into the Seven-Year Plan for 1959—65. By the end of that year, however, it was evident that Khrushchev had actually lost the battle: Kosygin, at that time head of the State Planning Committee, reported that all aspects of heavy industry were progressing according to schedule with the exception of the chemical industry (see ch. 30, Industry).

These are but a few examples which indicate that Khrushchev's rule was not secure and that he had to constantly struggle to maintain his authority. His initial reliance on the Party as a power-base was later to prove insufficient. It became necessary to seek wider support and therefore Khrushchev was unable to promote and protect the Party interests vis-à-vis other institutional interests. The frustrations that resulted from Khrushchev's inability to have his reforms implemented caused him to attempt to establish absolute personal rule. The fear of the reestablishment of the cult of personality, this time with Khrushchev as the personality, is one of the reasons cited by his successors for his dismissal.

Collective Leadership

Collective rule is the third form that the leadership has taken. There have been three occasions of apparent collective rule in the course of the history of the Soviet state. Twice, however, it proved to be a facade, behind which there was a fierce power struggle, specifically after the deaths of Lenin and Stalin. Thus, Western observers were skeptical of the credibility of the collective leadership that emerged following Khrushchev's political demise. Based upon the history of Soviet leadership, it was believed that there was a tendency, inherent in the political system, toward a one-man dictatorship. After more than five years of the seemingly viable, collective rule of Brezhnev and Kosygin, however, it appears that they are maintaining a genuine balance of power and are consciously preventing the emergence of a single dictator (see ch. 3, Historical Setting).

No one, except perhaps the top leaders themselves, can be certain of the actual distribution of political power. On the basis of the history of the leadership, however, it is quite possible that Brezhnev has more power than his colleagues by virtue of his incumbency of the position of general secretary of the CPSU. Furthermore, it is impossible to state authoritatively in which direction Soviet society is moving under their guidance. The problems that Khrushchev attempted to solve still exist, and the current leadership must eventually deal with them. Essentially, these problems are: closing the wide gap between industrial and agricultural production; finding a more efficient means of administering an increasingly complex, modern, technologically based economy; satisfying the demands for more consumer goods and creating a higher standard of living, in general; finding a positive role for the Party in a society that is no longer revolutionary; eliminating the gap between the political leaders and the intelligentsia; and the maintenance of Soviet leadership in the international Communist movement.

The reversal of nearly all of Khrushchev's reforms and the return of the government and Party structures to their pre-Khrushchevian forms is indicative of the Brezhnev-Kosygin regime's dissatisfaction with Khrushchev's approach to economic and political problems. Brezhnev and Kosygin, however, appear to be unwilling to make radical policy innovations and seem to have failed to tackle any of the basic problems. Rather, they are administering affairs with an apparent "don't rock the boat" style of operation, which has only maintained the status quo.

The lack of dynamic leadership might be the result of an actual balance of forces in the Politburo; that is, the interests represented by the members of the decisionmaking body may be neutralizing each other, thereby preventing the establishment of long-range goals. Their primary interest appears to be the maintenance of stability and the prevention of the accumulation of power by one man or institution. Some Western observers see a form of paralysis in the collective leadership policies which, they claim, could result in stagnation of the political and economic systems.

The Brezhnev-Kosygin regime has demonstrated a willingness to take a somewhat liberal approach in some areas, while reverting back to orthodoxy in others. In their search for the most efficient means of planning and managing the economy, for example, they have allowed continuing discussion and some experimentation. In this type situation, the role of interest groups and their influence in the decisionmaking process is maximized. The leaders' permissiveness in this area has led them away from the ideologically correct approach in a search for greater efficiency (see ch. 29, Economic Planning and Control).

The cultural policy, however, is becoming increasingly dogmatic and repressive compared to the relative relaxation under Khrushchev. This seeming inconsistency derives from the fact that bending the ideology for economic or political expediency is acceptable, whereas cultural liberalism is neither necessary nor desirable from the ideological point of view. In the past, the cultural intelligentsia, especially the writers, exposed contradictions between official policies and Marxist-Leninist doctrine. Until Brezhnev and Kosygin are able to find the most rational methods for planning and administration and can then formulate ideologically correct explanations for their policies, they appear to be maintaining a strict internal regime and suppressing criticism of the system (see ch. 17, Intellectual Expression).

In the late 1960's there was a great deal of discussion in the Western press about "re-Stalinization." Some Western observers have found indications that the leaders are rehabilitating the memory of Stalin, though gradually. One indicator cited is the revised history of the CPSU, authorized to be published in August 1968. The criticism of Stalin, initiated by Khrushchev, is mitigated in this revised history, but not eliminated.

On December 21, 1969, Stalin's birthday was commemorated for the first time since 1955. This is cited in some segments of the Western press as further evidence of "re-Stalinization." Official statements made by the leadership, however, both praise and criticize Stalin. He is praised for having fostered industrialization and for having led the Soviet armed forces during World War II. On the other hand, he is criticized for having violated Leninist principles of collective leadership, that is, for having instituted the "cult of personality."

The evidence cited appears to consistent with the Brezhnev-Kosygin regime's "middle of the road" approach. Khrushchev's de-Stalinization drive was too extreme for his relatively conservative successors, and they appear to be modifying it by giving Stalin credit for policies that strengthened the state while criticizing those that tended to weaken it.

CHAPTER 22

THE LEGAL SYSTEM

At the beginning of 1970 justice was administered by a single system of courts on both federal and republican levels. With the exception of the Supreme Court of the USSR and the military tribunals, all courts were republican and had the power, along with the federal courts, to enforce federal and republican laws. The Supreme Court of the USSR was at the apex of this system and was the highest judicial agency of the union, which guided all lower courts in administering justice. In the performance of their functions courts were assisted by the public prosecutors, investigators, the office of state notary, a bar, and the police.

The Procuracy of the USSR has comprehensive functions—supervising the legality of activities by all organs of governmental authority, and the conduct of the legal and court system—and is the most important judicial institution in the Soviet Union. It is headed by the procurator general, who is appointed for a term of seven years by the Supreme Soviet of the USSR. He is the most powerful law officer of the government in charge of the enforcement of its policies.

With the establishment of the Bolshevik regime in 1917, the entire prerevolutionary legal system was repealed. In its place a new Soviet law emerged to meet the needs and exigencies of the new era. Soviet law is a system of rules established by the government under the direction and guidance of the Communist Party of the Soviet Union (CPSU) aimed at safeguarding and strengthening the social and governmental system and its economic foundation, based on planned economy and socialist property.

The main distinguishing features of the legal system are the one party rule and integral planning. The CPSU has enormous influence on the legal system and, if necessary, the power to interfere directly with the judiciary. An exposition of the basic principles of the legal system requires a review of all the branches of Soviet law. The various branches of the law, such as constitutional law, criminal law, civil law, and labor law, like the entire body of law itself, are intimately interrelated with the economic system.

Many provisions of the 1936 Constitution and the various codes are not actually applied. Instead, administrative ordinances and circulars have superseded statutory law. Therefore, an interpretation of the legal system requires an explanation of its political significance and repercussions.

Thus, the Constitution indicates that the Soviet government has adopted the most advanced democratic principles, but the applicability of these principles is subject to the unrestricted powers and operation of the CPSU. Although the Constitution contains a chapter on "Fundamental Rights and Duties of Citizens," the exercise of those rights is governed by the fact that the regime holds both political and economic power in its hands. The government, as the most powerful authority and employer, under the control of the Party, ultimately decides the destiny of its citizens.

The system contains many institutions and principles seemingly similar to those of the Western world. Many features of the Soviet judiciary are to be found in the court systems of the West, and in many instances the legal terminology is the same. Such similarities, however, may be misleading with regard to a specific institute, principle, or subject covered by a code or law. For example, under Soviet law collective farms are considered cooperatives, but the collective farms are, in fact, entirely different from cooperatives as the term is commonly understood in the West; collective farms are, in fact, government agencies.

From 1917 to 1958, Soviet legal institutions went through various stages, in conformity with the major political, economic, and social events of the time, such as the period of war communism, the New Economic Policy (Novaya Ekonomicheskaya Politika—NEP), the Stalin era, and the period following Stalin's death.

In 1958 basic federal legislation on the judiciary of the Soviet Union, the union republics, and autonomous republics was enacted and remained in force at the beginning of 1970. This legislation governed the organizational and functional structure of all courts, along with the laws of the individual republics that implemented it.

BEFORE THE REVOLUTION
Early Developments

The origin and development of the legal system in existence when the Bolsheviks seized power go far back to various periods of Russian history in which major events exerted a predominant influence upon Russian legal institutions. Some of the main elements that had a great impact upon Russian law from the earliest stage to the enactment of the Judicial Reform of 1864 were: principles of canon law and Roman law; the Eastern Orthodox Church, which brought Byzantine law to Russia; the Mongol invasion, which developed absolutism; and Muscovite law, which created new legal institutions.

Roman Law and Canon Law

Russian legal institutions developed in a background similar to that of the West. The Slavs in the ninth and tenth centuries occupied the western territory of the present-day Soviet Union. Their social and legal structure was akin to that of the Germanic people who settled in the West. The Slavs were converted from paganism to Christianity by means of which they were highly influenced by, and finally adopted, the canon law of the church and the Roman law of the Christian emperors (see ch. 3, Historical Setting).

Russia and the West were inspired by the Roman Empire and believed that a state could be organized and governed under law and that legislation was its main source. They both followed the basic rules of Byzantine procedure and adopted from Byzantine law the basic elements of contract and torts (see ch. 3, Historical Setting).

Eastern Orthodox Church

The Eastern Orthodox Church has been an important element in Russian legal history. It imported in the eleventh and succeeding centuries Byzantine art and culture and also Byzantine law, which was an integration of Roman law and canon law.

In the Byzantine Empire toward the end of the tenth century, the Orthodox Church had developed the doctrine of caesaropapism, whereby the emperor was the absolute ruler of the state and the head of the church. Consequently, all powers, ecclesiastical and temporal, were vested in the emperor alone. This doctrine was adopted in Russia in the fifteenth century, when the tsars declared themselves the successors of the Byzantine emperors.

Mongol Rule

The Mongol invasion of Russia in the thirteenth century and the ruthless rule of the Mongols for 240 years (A.D. 1240—1480) led to the deterioration of Russian legal institutions. The imposition of strict criminal law provisions and harsh punishments for their violators were the main characteristics of this period. The Mongols were little interested in civil law, being primarily concerned with exacting tribute from the enslaved populations (see ch. 3, Historical Setting).

Muscovite Law

The Muscovite absolutistic state (1480—1689) was built on the ruins of Mongol despotism. During this period the Muscovite state adopted the Mongol principle of compulsory military service. Ivan the Terrible (1530—84), in the struggle against the *boyars* (hereditary nobility of tsarist Russia—see Glossary) created a new nobility based on military and civil service, in order to counterbalance their excessive powers.

Peasants were bound to the soil of their masters. Nevertheless, they enjoyed many personal rights, including the ownership of personal property; were considered citizens; and were entitled to exercise some electoral rights.

The Muscovite legal system was primitive and extremely formalistic. A national system of courts, patterned on Eastern Roman law, was established. All pleadings and testimony had to be in writing. The witnesses still swore that what the plaintiff or defendant said was true. Corruption was widespread.

The Judiciary Before the Great Reforms

Courts

The system of courts in the period preceding the Great Reforms of 1864 was characterized by the judicial reforms of Peter the Great (1672—1725) and Catherine II (1729—96). There was a great variety of courts, with special courts for every class of society.

Judges were elected. As a rule, they had no legal training, and the majority of them were almost illiterate. Bribery continued to be an accepted aspect of the judiciary.

The distinguishing characteristics of the old administration of justice were: secret and inquisitorial proceedings, with their doctrine of formal evidence; the complexity of court and procedure; the corruption of judges; and the complete dependence of the judiciary upon the executive.

Codes

The first collection of laws, called the Code (Ulozheniye), appeared in 1649. Its purpose was to bring together in one code all existing laws. In 1830 Mikhail M. Speransky (1772—1839) succeeded in codifying the Russian laws then in force in the first code enacted since that of 1649.

It was not until 1832, however, that the first systematic publication in Russian legal history appeared. It was a fifteen-volume Body of Laws (Svod Zakonov). Two-thirds of the collection was devoted to the study of public law. A volume of the collection dealt with private law patterned upon the French Civil Code.

The Judicial Reform of November 20, 1864

Enactment

With the reign of Alexander II (1855—81) a new era of modernization of the Russian social and political life was inaugurated. His first reform in 1861 was the emancipation of the serfs, with the allotment of land to them. The Liberation Act was the keystone for the ensuing modern reforms.

In 1861, under the direction of Alexander II, the preparatory work on judicial reform was initiated. The task was completed in 1864, when the General Assembly of the State Council adopted, and the tsar confirmed, the following codes: Code of Civil Procedure, Code of Criminal Procedure, Statutes on Judicial Institutions, and Code of Laws on Punishments to be Imposed by the Justices of the Peace. The entire judicial reform went into effect on November 20, 1864.

Main Changes

The immediate consequence of the 1864 reform was the abolition of the old court organization. The judiciary, in its entirety, was reorganized, and newly created courts were formed to conform with the trend and needs of a modern judiciary. Some far-reaching innovations were: a court system based on the theory of the separation of judicial from executive and legislative powers; trial by jury in criminal cases—no appeal was admissible from a decision of the court with a jury; in all other instances, right of appeal to the next higher court on both issues, of law and fact; a further appeal, a so-called recourse, to the court of cassation, as court of last resort, was permitted on issues of law only—the introduction of the principle of publicity of legal proceedings; the introduction of oral pleadings and oral testimony; the right to be represented by defense counsel; and the transfer of jurisdiction in pretrial investigation in criminal matters from the police to an examining magistrate.

Other changes were: the removal of illiterate judges; the independence of judges in the performance of their duties and their removal from office for misconduct or physical unfitness only; graduation from the faculty of law of a university as the prerequisite for appointment to a judicial position; creation of a hierarchy of government attorneys, headed by the minister of justice, along with the creation of the hierarchy of the courts; and making government attorneys the custodians of legality in every branch of the administration, in addition to their main function of prosecuting crimes before the court. The establishment of the bar was an innovation of extreme importance, since the legal profession had not existed before.

Later Reforms (1864—1914)

The Great Reforms of 1864 were the foundation of all subsequent legal developments up to the Revolution. In the reign of Alexander III (1881—94), however, there was opposition to the reforms, and some amendments, which threatened to frustrate their main goal, were adopted.

The Revolution of 1905 brought about new reforms. An elected parliament, the Duma, a lower chamber of the legislature, was established, and political parties were allowed for the first time. The tsar, however remained the supreme ruler, since the imperial government continued to be responsible to him alone. Legislative power was divided between the Duma and the Council of State, the upper chamber, half of whose members were appointed by the tsar. The imperial government had the authority to issue decrees between the sessions of the Duma (see ch. 3, Historical Setting).

After the suppression of the 1905 Revolution, important legislation was passed. Under the Reform of Stolypin (1862—1911), peasants were given the right to own their land outright, and payment for the grant of land, in accordance with the 1861 Emancipation Act, was terminated.

Substantive and procedural criminal and civil law were also reformed. In 1903 a part of the new criminal code, inspired by the modern criminology of Western Europe, was adopted. A draft of the new civil code was prepared by 1913.

The law reform trend that started in 1905 was brought to an end by the outbreak of World War I in 1914. After the abdication of Nicholas II (1894—1917), a Provisional Government was formed. Headed by the moderate socialist Alexander Kerensky, the new government attempted to transform Russia into a Western European kind of democracy, but it was shortly thereafter overthrown by the Bolsheviks (see ch. 3, Historical Setting).

UNDER COMMUNIST RULE

The Bolsheviks seized power on November 7, 1917, and the All-Russian Congress of Workers' and Soldiers' Deputies elected the All-Russian Central Executive Committee and the Soviet (Council) of People's Commissars. This was headed by Lenin, who established the first Bolshevik government.

Among the important legislative acts of the revolutionary government in the early development of Soviet law was the adoption of the first constitution on July 10, 1918. The Constitution declared the Soviet of People's Commissars, the All-Russian Congress of Soviets and, in the interim between its sessions, its executive committee to be the supreme governing bodies.

The first development of Soviet law is marked by a series of decrees designed to destroy completely the prerevolutionary social, economic, and legal structure of the country. The years of civil warfare and foreign intervention between 1917 and 1921 were known as the period of war communism.

In their efforts to destroy the old world and to create their own socialist order, the Bolsheviks, in the early stage of their regime, attempted to wipe out everything that had any resemblance to the past. The existing court system was abolished in toto. The class system was also abolished, and all titles and ranks were annulled. Property was confiscated and transferred to local Soviet authorities. Private ownership of land and means of production were abolished. Private industrial and commercial enterprises were confiscated. Private trade was prohibited. Inheritance was abolished. Compulsory labor and appropriation of farm surpluses in the villages were imposed. Churches and religious institutions were deprived of the right to exist as legal entities and to own property. All the property of the churches and religious institutions was confiscated.

The 1918 Constitution broadly defined the powers granted to the Bolshevik regime under the term of "dictatorship of the proletariat." It expressly declared:

> The basic task of the Constitution . . . at the present transitional period is the establishment of the dictatorship of the city and village proletariat and the poorest peasantry in the form of a powerful All-Russian state and authority for the purpose of complete suppression of the bourgeoisie, the destruction of exploitation of man by man, and the installation of socialism, under which there will be neither division into classes nor state authority.

The Soviet doctrine of state and law is based on the dictatorship of the proletariat and the domination of the Communist Party. Lenin defined it as "power with no restriction whatsoever, absolutely unbound by any rules of law, and based upon violence" or "unlimited power based upon force and not law." These definitions constituted the backbone of the Soviet doctrine of state and law, which was still applicable after the adoption of the 1936 Constitution. The Soviet leaders were unanimous in their belief that the Communist Party exercises the dictatorship of the proletariat, or as Lenin stated, "our state means the working class, that is, its advanced detail, that is, us (the Communists)."

A contributing element in strengthening the power of the regime is the principle of democratic centralism, which governs the organizational structure of both the Communist Party and government agencies. The principle of democratic centralism applicable to the government machinery gives unlimited power to the authorities of the larger territorial units to repeal the acts of the authorities of the smaller territorial units within their geographic boundaries. Strict subordination of the lower agencies to the higher ones and the binding effect of the enactments of the latter were the basis of this principle. This principle was incorporated into the 1936 Constitution.

Soviet scholars minimized the significance of law as an essential element of an organized society; instead, they considered it a byproduct of economic conditions. According to Marx and Engels, law, as well as the spiritual civilization in its entirety, is merely a superstructure erected over the material basis. In their opinion, this material basis "is formed by the relationship of men in the process of the production of commodities." Economic relations, they assert, are the only determining factors with regard to the form and content of law that is available to the ruling class to keep itself in power. Communist leaders expected that, with the consolidation of the socialist regime, a classless society would be achieved and would cause the withering away of the state and the disappearance of its law.

Initial Developments (1917—21)

One of the first acts of the Soviet government on coming to power was the complete abolition of the entire prerevolutionary legal system. Decree No. 1 of December 7, 1917, on courts, repealed all legal institutions, such as district courts, courts of appeals, the governing Senate with all its departments, military and naval courts, commercial courts, and all existing institutions of investigating magistrates' and procurators' offices, as well as attorneys at law. A network of people's courts and revolutionary tribunals was set up to replace the former judicial system established in 1864. A uniform judicial system was not established, however, until 1923.

People's Courts

A people's court was composed of a leading citizen, as presiding judge, and two lay assessors, who decided all issues by majority vote. It tried civil and criminal cases. Criminal charges were heard in the presence of the aggrieved parties, the defendant, and the defense, composed of relatives and friends. In establishing the facts in a particular case, the court was at liberty to take all the measures it considered necessary. The decisions of people's courts were subject to review by a congress of the local people's judges, which convened within each county. An appeal from a judgment of the people's court could not be lodged unless the sentence exceeded seven days in jail or the payment in satisfaction of a claim was over R300.

In handing down their decisions, the newly elected judges were given no guidance. Under a general instruction they were authorized to use their social conscience and to apply prerevolutionary laws "only insofar as they have not been annulled by the Revolution."

After the abolishment of the legal profession, anyone who enjoyed civil rights could practice law. Under the pressure of necessity, however, this practice soon was discarded, and a body of legal representatives was appointed by local governments. Their salaries were paid by the government, and the clients' fees were collected by the state treasury. There was little civil litigation; criminal matters were mostly in the hands of the Extraordinary Commission (Chrezvychaynaya Komissiya—Cheka; see Glossary) and of special revolutionary tribunals that enforced what was officially called the Red Terror.

Cheka

The Soviet regime has had a particular feature from the start, a protective agency vested with unlimited dictatorial power. The Cheka was created in December 1917, both on federal and on local levels, although no official decree to this effect was ever made public. According to a Communist leader it was an administrative agency that "does not judge the enemy but strikes." It passed "final decisions over life and death with no appeal therefrom." The name of the agency was later changed several times.

An analysis of its operation reveals that the agency could not be considered equivalent to a court, because it was not governed by any substantive and procedural rules, although it imposed punishments as do the courts. Its main task was to fight counterrevolution and whatever appeared to threaten the regime as well as to crush and suppress any opposition to the Communist Party.

Revolutionary Tribunals

Revolutionary tribunals were created to try cases involving the safety of the regime itself, such as attempts to overthrow it, sabotage, and destruction of government property. As a rule, their hearings were public. The accused was not entitled, as a matter of law, to be represented by a defense counsel. Referring to a statement attributed to Karl Marx that political adversaries may be shot but not tried, Pyotr Stuchka, the commissar for justice at that time, wrote that revolutionary tribunals "were not even intended to be courts."

Under later decrees, revolutionary tribunals were not "bound by anything in the selection of punishments." They were instructed that in rendering their judgments they should be guided "exclusively by the circumstances of the case and the revolutionary conscience."

In the period of war communism there was ruthless destruction of prerevolutionary law and social values, and the transition to a new order of equality without law was the prevailing factor.

The New Economic Policy (1921–28)

The destructive measures employed in the period of war communism had catastrophic results. Lenin realized the necessity of returning to the principle of legality. Soviet scholars construed the term *legality* as strict adherence to established rules and procedure, whereas the term *revolutionary legality* was understood to mean observance of laws that, although departure from them was allowed, nevertheless advanced the cause of the revolutionary buildup of society.

A postponement of the transition to a classless society became imperative. The period of the New Economic Policy was a strategic retreat forced by the disastrous economic conditions and famine. Legislation to meet the exigency of the new policy, in the fields of public and private law, was enacted. In a relatively short time, in 1922 and 1923, a new Judiciary Act, a Civil Code, a Criminal Code, and a Code of Criminal Procedure were enacted to provide a legal structure similar to those of Western Europe and prerevolutionary Russia.

In 1922 the Union of the Soviet Socialist Republics (USSR) was created. Under the Constitution of 1924, the federation retained the power to enact the basic principles on the judiciary, legal procedure, and civil and criminal legislation, which field of law was already covered by the legislation of the individual republics. It appears that the codes already enacted by the republics remained in force, since only federal principles on the judiciary were issued. The Judiciary Act created a system of courts that, in many aspects, was similar to those of the West.

The Civil Code incorporated the old principles and subjects of Roman law, such as contracts and torts, real and personal property, mortgages, inheritance, corporations, legal relations, and personal relations. All these novelties reminiscent of prerevolutionary law, however, contained some limiting provisions that indicated their transitional character and bore the mark of the new socialist system. Thus, government control and interference in private transactions were introduced. Lenin instructed the legislators "to enlarge the interference of the state with the relations pertaining to private law" and, if necessary, "to annul private contracts." Civil registration of marriage and divorce was introduced in the Family Code of 1918. The principle of the equality of the legal status of men and women was proclaimed.

The Criminal Code introduced the principle of crime by analogy. According to this principle, a judge who considered an individual socially dangerous could convict him of a crime even though the accused had violated no specific section of the Criminal Code. It was sufficient for a judge to find that the act of the accused closely resembled a crime specified in the code. The doctrine was also applicable vice versa—the perpetrator of an act that was specifically stated in the code to be a crime was not punished if the judge found him not socially dangerous. This provision opened the door to the abuse of power and arbitrariness by the courts in the administration of criminal justice.

The federal reform of criminal law in 1958 did not expressly abolish crime by analogy. This law, however, contains another provision that abolished the material definition of crime in the sense previously accepted. According to one authority, interpretation of the above provision, the application of analogy, was thereby abolished.

The more liberal New Economic Policy did not terminate or alleviate the imposition of harsh punishments by courts and administrative agencies. It continued to follow Stalin's teaching: "The courts shall not do away with terrorism; to promise such a thing would mean to cheat either ourselves or other people."

Private initiative and private rights during the period of the New Economic Policy were not automatically restored. Within narrowly defined limits established by law, however, the so-called private sector was protected. Domestic trade and small businesses were allowed provided such establishments employed no more than twenty workers.

The New Economic Policy came to an end about 1928 with the inauguration of the First Five-Year Plan. It occurred at the time of Stalin's ascendance to political leadership and power and the establishment of his dictatorial regime.

Period Under Stalin (1928—53)

The reversal of the New Economic Policy in 1928 was followed by the nationalization of all industry and the collectivization of the farmers. The succeeding years were years of terror and suffering for the majority of the population. Through total planning the so-called private sector of the national economy was merged with the sector of state economy. The protection of public property became a major goal; for this purpose penal legislation was strengthened.

Forcible methods of collectivization were decreed in the various regions. Stalin launched attacks against the relatively well-to-do farmers called *kulaki*, who objected to collective farming. The term was never defined by law, and it was left to the discretion of the local authorities to decide who should be classified as such. In actuality, the term included all persons who in any way resisted collectivization. A special law was passed for their liquidation as a class. According to the official Soviet *Agricultural Year Book of 1935*, over 5 million families were dispossessed (see ch. 31, Agriculture).

In 1936 the transition from capitalism to socialism was declared to be accomplished. Under the new constitution the Soviet Union became "a socialist state of workers and peasants." The purpose of the Constitution was proclaimed by Stalin to be the "consolidation of a social order desired by and beneficial to the working people" and "the transformation of the dictatorship of the proletariat into a more flexible and powerful system of guidance of society by the state." The main task was to stabilize the existing order and to prepare the country for the transition to communism, the final goal of a perfect society, according to Marxian theory.

The early Soviet leaders saw, however, that the period of transition required the fulfillment of some prerequisites. In the first place, they considered that the people must be prepared and educated; there must be an abundance of goods to satisfy everybody's needs; and finally the threat of encirclement by the capitalist states must be eliminated. They understood that the attainment of these

451

goals would require long and arduous work and, therefore, the existing legal order, characterizing the period of stability, would be of long duration.

The stability propounded by Stalin required the establishment of a new judicial system to guarantee socialist legality and to protect the new social and political system under the Constitution. The Constitution assigned to federal jurisdiction the determination of the fundamental principles concerning the judicial system and procedure and criminal and civil legislation. Only the Judiciary Act of 1938 was passed during this period. Under the 1938 act, all courts constituted a single system. These courts, like other government agencies, continued to follow the guiding directives issued by the highest government and party bodies.

In view of the stated developments, the doctrine of the withering away of state and law had to be reexamined. This doctrine dominated Soviet jurisprudence until the 1930's. After the First Five-Year Plan it was proclaimed that socialism had won "finally and irrevocably," and it was expected that state and law, the entire legal superstructure, would wither away in the immediate future. Stalin, however, was the first to signal alarm and, as early as 1929, to warn that the withering away of the state was still far ahead. Some years later he was more specific by saying:

> The state will wither away, not through weakening state power, but through the intensification of it to the point necessary to finish off the remnants of the dying classes and to organize defense against capitalist encirclement, which is as yet far from being, and will not soon be, destroyed.

Stalin did not categorically assert the impossibility of the withering away doctrine. He only maintained that it was impossible to do away with law before the complete accomplishment of the Communist program.

The essence of Stalin's theory suggests that the period of the socialist society envisaged by him in his constitution should last as long as capitalism exists in the world and should be able to repel aggression and to defend itself against its own destruction. The stability of the existing social, political, and legal order is reflected in Stalin's constitution, which formulates the main tenets of a socialist state.

The 1936 Constitution

Stalin's constitution was formally adopted by the Congress of Soviets of the USSR on December 5, 1936. With some amendments, it is still in force. The new constitution introduced some basic innovations that were consistent with the newly established socialist order. In the first place, it reflected the influence of Soviet scholars who had consistently repudiated Montesquieu's doctrine of separation of governmental powers. Andrei Vyshinsky, formerly Soviet procurator general, in discussing the new constitution, said that in the new order there is only distribution of functions. He affirmed that:

the Soviet regime is permeated from top to bottom by the general spirit of the unity of the governmental power of the toilers. The Program of the Communist Party repudiates the principle of the separation of government powers.

Other main novelties that created the new legal, political, and socioeconomic structure of the country may be summed up as follows: The All-Russian Congress of Soviets and the Central Executive Committee were replaced by a single bicameral Supreme Soviet, the members of which are nominally elected by universal, equal, direct and secret ballot. The Supreme Soviet is a legislative body of the parliamentary type, which convenes twice a year for sessions of a few days. The Constitution contains a chapter on "Fundamental Rights and Duties of Citizens" and also states the principle of the independence of judges. The whole administrative scheme for the central government is framed in such a way as to resemble that of a democratic state.

The constitution states that "the legislative power of the USSR is exercised exclusively by the Supreme Soviet of the USSR." But as a matter of fact, the bulk of the current legislation is formulated by the Presidium of the Supreme Soviet and the Council of Ministers.

As the highest permanent organ of state power, the Presidium has extensive rights and duties that are enumerated in Article 49 of the Constitution. The Presidium has, in addition to regular powers similar to those of a president of a republic, the power to proceed in lieu of the Supreme Soviet in the intervals between sessions of the latter. This power is strictly defined under the 1936 Constitution: it extends, among other things, to the dismissal and appointment of ministers of the Soviet Union, subject to subsequent confirmation by the Supreme Soviet; to the declaration of a state of war in the event of military attack on the Soviet Union or, when necessary, to fulfill international treaty obligations concerning mutual defense against aggression.

One of the most important powers granted to the Presidium is the right to issue decrees. Since the Supreme Soviet meets in brief sessions, much of the legislation is handled by the Presidium and the Council of Ministers. The decrees of the Presidium are binding and operative as soon as they are issued, even before ratification by the Supreme Soviet. In its judicial capacity, the Presidium interprets the laws of the Soviet Union.

The third governmental body of major importance is the Council of Ministers. This body is the cabinet, known until 1946 as the Council of People's Commissars. The Council of Ministers is designated by the Constitution as "the highest executive and administrative organ of state power." Its decisions and orders are issued "on the basis and in pursuance of the laws in force" and "they are binding throughout the territory of the USSR."

The Soviet legal system, with its particular features, differs from that of a constitutional democracy. In the Soviet Union the powers exercised by government bodies actually go beyond those expressly granted to them by the Constitution. Although full power is declared to be vested in representative bodies, these bodies have a large membership and seldom convene. In the intervals between their sessions, their power is delegated to small permanent committees. As early as 1918 the constitution provided for such delegation of power, a provision not clearly defined in the later 1936 Constitution. Nevertheless, Soviet government bodies continue to follow the practice of delegation of power.

Dependency of the Legal System upon Communist Rule

Lenin was the creator of the CPSU, which was formed of disciplined revolutionaries. Their task was to lead the masses to power and, in due time, to transform the proletarian dictatorship into a classless society. Lenin wrote in 1917 "The Party must be teacher, guide and leader."

The activities of the Communist Party are governed by two documents that describe Party aims for a given historical period. Its rules regulate organizational matters and the right and duties of Party members. The guiding principle of the organizational structure of the Party, according to its rules, is democratic centralism, which means rule form the top with no debate after the leaders have reached a decision (see ch. 21, Political Dynamics).

The characteristics of the Soviet system reveal why the Soviet Union is based on the domination of a single political party. Under the Constitution all land, natural resources, industry, communication, banking, large state-organized agricultural enterprises, dwelling houses in the cities, and industrial localities belong to the state. The state, being the sole owner of all natural resources, is in the position to control the entire economy of the country. This control, however, owing to its privileged status, is in the first place directed and guided by the Communist Party, which through the Soviet government implements the economic policy as outlined and adopted by the Party itself. Because of its organizational structure, the CPSU cannot be considered a political party in the Western sense. It is rather an army of civilians, public officials, and privileged workers created for the purpose of propagating and putting into effect the ideas of Marx, Lenin, and Stalin.

The 1936 Constitution was the first formal act of the Soviet government, which legalized the position of, and guidance of the

454

country by, the Communist Party. Article 126, which deals with associations, states that

> the most active and politically conscious citizens in the ranks of the working class, working peasants and working intelligentsia voluntarily unite in the Communist Party of the Soviet Union which is the vanguard of the working people in their struggle to build communist society and is the leading core of all organizations of the working public, both public and state.

In accordance with the constitution, only one political party exists in the Soviet Union, the Communist Party, which is the core of all public and state institutions. The Party stands behind the entire constitutional and organizational structure of the state.

The political, economic, and social activities of all professional and cultural organizations are subject to the general line and the national economic plan established by the central Party and the highest government bodies. The general line lays down the current policy of the Communist Party, which is made compulsory for all government agencies, including the courts, which are not outside politics. Under the doctrine of the unity of the people's power, courts do not constitute a separate power but are "only parts of a single system of power belonging to the working people." Thus, the instructions of the Supreme Court represent the policy of the Party in the same way as do the resolutions of the Council of Ministers. As a rule, these instructions are considered sources of Soviet law.

The status and the overriding influence of the Communist Party within the government machinery, although not officially recognized, are apparent in many instances. For example, decrees and instructions of particular significance are officially published as joint resolutions of the Council of Ministers and the Central Committee of the Communist Party and bear the signatures of the chairman of the Council of Ministers and the general secretary of the Party. Similarly, joint resolutions are passed on a provincial (regional) level.

The functions of the highest Party authorities, the Central Committee, its Presidium (so-called between 1952 and 1966; called the Political Bureau, or Politburo, before 1952 and since 1966), and the general secretary are not governed by law. In the operation of the government apparatus, however, the role of the Communist Party remains paramount and is the main decisive factor in the making of Soviet laws and in their enforcement (see ch. 21, Political Dynamics).

Fundamental Rights

The Constitution contains a chapter on "Fundamental Rights and Duties of Citizens." It was expected by members of the Party that a more liberal approach and interpretation of the rights guaranteeing individual freedoms would ensue. Soon this hope was destroyed by Stalin himself, who stated that the rights guaranteed in the Constitution were couched in such terms as not to impair the dominant position of the Party.

Among the fundamental rights the Constitution recognizes five economic rights: the right to employment, the right to leisure, the right to support in old age and illness, the right to education, and equal rights for women. The Constitution, however, affords individuals no means of enforcing these rights, as for instance, the filing of a suit in court. These stated rights are in the nature of declarations of policy rather than of vested rights. In each of these cases the guarantee of the particular right is followed by a paragraph explaining the way in which the right is assured. Thus, the right to employment is assured "by the socialist system of economic organization, the growth of productivity and the elimination of crises and the abolition of unemployment."

Civil rights and freedoms are covered by Articles 124 to 128. Separation of church and state and church and school are declared in the interest "of ensuring citizens of freedom of conscience." Article 124 also recognizes freedom of religious worship and of antireligious propaganda (see ch. 13, Religion). Article 125 grants to all citizens freedom of speech, freedom of the press, freedom of associations and meetings, and freedom of street processions and demonstrations.

These freedoms are granted with the express limitation that they be "in conformity with the interests of the working people, and in order to strengthen the socialist system." Any other purpose that might jeopardize the cited goal, such as criticism of the regime, is excluded beforehand. The constitutional guarantee consists of "placing at the disposal of the working people and their organizations printing presses, newsprint, public buildings. . . ." Since the Soviet government and the Communist Party are the only representative bodies of all organizations, both public and private, the feasibility of such freedoms being exercised by individuals or private organizations is entirely dependent upon the government and the Party. Under Soviet law printing offices of any kind may be opened only by government agencies, cooperatives, or public organizations.

Freedom of assembly is restricted exclusively to particular groups that are licensed by the Party and the state, such as trade unions, cooperative societies, youth organizations, and sports groups. This limitation follows from the implied constitutional principle that no political organization other than the CPSU may exist. The CPSU, as the core of all organizations, is authorized to supervise the activities of all non-Party organizations and to determine their future status.

The original interpretation of personal freedom as collective consciousness of political and economic organizations was given by Karl Marx who said, "Personal freedom is possible only in the collectivity."

Property Rights

Recognition of some property rights was granted in 1922 during the period of the New Economic Policy. It was further expounded in the Civil Code, which became effective on January 1, 1923. In the course of time, many provisions of the Civil Code and Land Code became obsolete and ceased to govern the determination of property rights, which from then on was regulated by the Constitution and subsequent legislation.

Stalin's Constitution of 1936 does not list the right of ownership among the "Basic Rights of Citizens" stated in Articles 118 to 128. Private ownership is mentioned in Article 4, which states that "private ownership of the instruments and means of production is abolished in the USSR." The Constitution, however, uses a similar term for private ownership, that is, personal ownership. It specifies that the law protects the personal ownership of citizens and enumerates the objects of such ownership as "income and savings from work, dwelling houses and subsidiary home enterprises, articles of domestic economy and use and articles of personal use and convenience. . . ."

One authority stated that the new term *personal ownership* represents a right recognized in a socialist state to its citizens. According to another authority the constitutional protection of personal property as stated in Article 10 extends only to objects of personal needs that are used for consumption or comfort.

With the adoption of the new constitution some private rights to real property were established. The same constitution, in listing the objects of private property, recognized as legal "the small private economy of individual peasants and craftsmen based on their own labor." Therefore, private industry was admitted only in the form of small-scale crafts and small farms operated without hired labor and producing directly for a customer.

The concept of ownership of private property is expressed in the notion that "there is personal property in the Soviet Union but not private property." The word *private* has been replaced by the word *personal* throughout Soviet legal literature. Lenin gave his interpretation of the concept when he stated: "We do not recognize anything private. In the field of economy everything is public and not private from our point of view." Lenin's view expounds the Marxian legal thought.

In 1936, besides government ownership as the most important and privileged category, two additional categories were recognized in Soviet law: personal ownership and social ownership, that is ownership by collective farms and cooperative organizations. One authority suggests that the economic life was within the sphere of public law but that public interest required more decentralization, more personal initiative, and reward as a stimulus. The developments in the economy of the country from 1937 to 1953 may be classed as a fusion of public and private law.

Legislation Safeguarding the Regime

In 1928 Stalin consolidated his own power position that he had achieved by means of the secret police, which at that time reached its full development as an instrument of repression and terror. Appropriate criminal legislation was passed to implement Stalin's new policy. The progressive increase of punishments for crimes indicated an increase of criminal activity. The death sentence was established for seventy individual crimes in forty-seven sections of the Criminal Code of the Russian Republic. It was also provided for in two special laws bringing to seventy-four the total number of crimes for which capital punishment could be imposed.

The unlimited power of the Unified State Political Administration (Ob'edinyonnoye Gosudarstvennoye Politicheskoye Upravleniye—OGPU—see Glossary) was neither stated nor denied officially. Under an ex post facto authentic interpretation of a previous law of November 15, 1923, this power was sanctioned on March 14, 1933. Accordingly, the OGPU was granted the authority to pass sentences of death. On March 15, 1933, referring to the resolution of November 15, 1923, *Izvestia* printed a resolution of the Central Executive Committee of the CPSU that affirmed the right of the OGPU to apply all measures of repression against criminals.

In 1934 Stalin created special boards attached to the Commissariat of Internal Affairs, in order to increase the power of the security police. The boards were not bound to follow the rules of the Code of Criminal Procedure nor were their determinations subject to review by any supreme court. These secret boards, subordinate to the administration, later abolished, constituted a special federal system, in addition to the existing system of federal and republic courts.

Another illustration of this period of terror was the enactment of a statute on June 8, 1934, which stated that a person could be legally sentenced in court for the crime of another, although he was not responsible for the crime. The law provided that if a man in military service took flight abroad by air or otherwise, in time of peace as well as in time of war, the adult members of his family who had knowledge of his plans were subject to imprisonment for from five to ten years and confiscation of property; and those who had no such knowledge, though living with him or dependent upon him, were subject to exile to remote localities for five years.

Under this statute, an innocent person may be subject to punishment although, under the generally accepted principles of criminal responsibility, he could not be punished for the unlawful act of another. No information is available as to whether this law has been repealed.

In December 1934 Stalin ordered that the codes of the individual republics be amended in order to deny the right of a terrorist to have a defense counsel at his trial, the right to be present at the trial, and the right of appeal. In 1937 the rules with regard to counterrevolutionary diversionists and wreckers were changed. Under the amended law they received their bill of charge twenty-four hours before trial, could not appeal, and were executed immediately if their plea for clemency was denied. Both laws were later repealed.

Stalin called for the strict observance of the law but did not consider himself to be personally bound by any standard. He stated when proposing the adoption of a new constitution, "We need stability of law, now more than ever." Legal concepts known in the Western civil law countries, such as money, property, criminal sanctions, and law and state, instead of withering away were accorded new socialist functions and meanings. The guilt of the accused again became an essential element of crime. Revolutionary legality was redefined as the strict observance of laws that had been adopted for the implementation of the achievements of the Revolution.

Instead of bringing stability, legality, and strict observance of established rules, Stalin made this period the most terror ridden in the history of the Soviet people. His domination is described by Soviet and foreign scholars as an arbitrary departure from, and complete disregard of, the existing order. Through the omnipotent secret police, the severe penal legislation, and excessive punishments, he succeeded in suppressing all opposition to his regime and to the Party and in annihilating his personal enemies.

Since 1958

A decentralization movement after Stalin's death resulted in the enactment of a constitutional amendment that again gave the union republics the right to enact laws on court organization and restricted the power of the federation to the enactment of fundamental principles only.

Accordingly, the Supreme Soviet of the USSR adopted on December 25, 1958, the "Fundamentals of Legislation on the Judicial System of the USSR and the Union and Autonomous Republics," which is still in force. On the basis of these general principles the union republics later enacted their own laws. Thus, the Russian Soviet Federated Soviet Republic (Rossiyskaya

Sovetskaya Federativnaya Sotsialisticheskaya Respublika—RSFSR) passed its own Law on Courts on October 27, 1960, amended by edicts of the Presidium, June 29, 1961; October 13, 1961; October 11, 1962; February 20, 1964; and September 9, 1968. As a rule, the union and the autonomous republics strictly follow the federal text, so that no substantial difference exists among the various republican laws on the judiciary.

The 1958 law included most of the provisions contained in the repealed law of 1938. The changes made in 1958 refer primarily to the organizational structure of the courts, their jurisdiction, and method of work but not to the basic principles, such as the tasks of the courts and their functions within the framework of the government, which remained unchanged.

Under the 1958 act, Soviet courts are not merely agencies of state compulsion created for the protection of the social, political, and economic system established by the Constitution. They also have the task in all of their activities of educating citizens in the spirit of devotion to their socialist motherland and to the cause of communism; in the spirit of strict and unwavering execution of Soviet laws; of an honest relationship to state and public duty; of a careful relationship to socialist property; respect for the rights, honor, and achievements of citizens as well as respect for the rules of socialist community living.

Structure and Functions of the Courts

All courts of the Soviet Union constitute a single judicial system governed basically by federal legislation. Under the present constitution individual republics may legislate on their court organization, but it may be done only within limited authority granted by all-union legislation.

The Supreme Court of the USSR is at the apex of the judicial system. By the reforms of 1958, all inferior federal courts, which treated special criminal matters, with the exception of military tribunals, were abolished, and jurisdiction was returned to the courts of the republics. In 1970 the only federal courts were the Supreme Court of the USSR and military tribunals. All other courts were courts of the union republics with the power, along with the federal courts, to enforce federal and state laws. Republican courts, which are called regular courts, trying both criminal and civil cases, are: the supreme courts of the union and the autonomous republics; below them are the provincial, territorial and city courts, and the courts of autonomous regions and national areas; below them are the county (city) people's courts.

In the Soviet judicial system there is no trial by jury. Cases are tried before a trial bench composed of one professional judge and two lay people's assessors who decide jointly by a majority vote all the questions, both of law and fact. The only distinction between professional judges and people's assessors is that professional judges administer justice as their regular and only duty, for which they are paid; whereas the latter serve in their capacity for not more than two weeks a year, do not receive a special salary, and retain their regular occupations. People's assessors sit in federal courts, including the Supreme Court of the USSR, and in all republican courts whenever the particular court hears a case as a trial court of original jurisdiction.

Appeals from an adverse ruling of a lower court by the defendant and protests by the prosecutor against a sentence that has not become final are reviewed by the next higher court. As a rule, a case may be reviewed only once by a higher court. Appeals and protests in higher courts are heard by a bench consisting of three professional judges.

No special training or particular general education is required for the position of judge or people's assessor in either federal or republican courts. According to law, the candidate must be a citizen of the Soviet Union, enjoy the right to vote, and have attained the age of twenty-five by election day.

The 1936 Constitution adopted the traditional formula of many democratic constitutions that "Judges are independent and subject only to the law." It was difficult to reconcile this principle with the repudiation of the doctrine of separation of powers by Lenin, Stalin, and the Communist Party from the establishment of the Soviet regime. Instead, Soviet scholars accepted the tenet of distribution of functions within the unity of the people's power. Accordingly, Soviet judges are not permitted to separate themselves from the aims of the Communist Party. One scholar asserted that three-quarters of the judges at the lowest level and all of them at the highest are members of the Communist Party and subject to its discipline. Strict adherence to the Party policy by the courts is implied; it is also admitted that a judge has a special task to perform, and for the accomplishment of this task he must have special training and ability.

Socialist legality requires that judges base their decisions on established substantive and procedural rules and standards rather than on mere consideration of economic expediency. According to one authority, citizens may find protection in court from a mistaken application of state policy, particularly with regard to matters of employer-employee relations, family disputes, and housing controversies. When the Party leadership considers it necessary to apply extraordinary measures in the interest of security, however, the independence of the court might be at stake.

Judges and judge-assessors of the Supreme Court of the USSR and members of the military tribunals are named by the Supreme Soviet

461

of the USSR. The judges for the supreme court of each republic are named by the Supreme Soviet of the republic and by the provincial Soviets for provincial courts. The 1936 Constitution made an exception with regard to judges of the people's courts who, instead of being named by the local Soviets, are elected directly by the voters from a single list of candidates as proposed by the Party. People's assessors are elected at general meetings of colleagues at their places of work or residence. Judges in all courts are elected for a period of five years, except people's assessors of the people's courts and the military tribunals are elected for a two-year term. Judges and people's assessors of all courts may be recalled by the Soviet or electorate that named or elected them, even before the expiration of their term of office.

Republican Courts. The lowest regular court is the people's court, established in each county or in a city not divided into districts. It functions exclusively as a court of limited original jursidiction. Courts of this kind examine by far the greatest number of civil and criminal matters out of the total number submitted for adjudication in courts at all levels. The people's court, like all Soviet courts, is collegial. The trial bench is composed of one judge and two people's assessors.

The next higher courts vary with regard to their structure in the various parts of the Soviet Union. They are established to correspond to the administrative subdivision of the union and autonomous republics. For instance, in the RSFSR and other larger union republics, the higher courts are established within each territory, region, autonomous republic, national region, national area, and certain cities. In some smaller union republics, which are not subdivided into territories and provinces, only the supreme court of the union republic is above the people's court (see ch. 20, Component Political Subdivisions).

In the RSFSR and the constituent republics of similar structure, the provincial and regional courts and the courts of the autonomous republics function as courts of original jurisdiction in more serious criminal cases and in all civil cases that are beyond the jurisdiction of the people's courts. Provincial and similar courts function as appellate courts for cases decided in the first instance by people's courts. When they are acting in the capacity as appellate courts, their decisions are final. Any higher court has the right to assume jurisdiction as a court of original jurisdiction over any case within the jurisdiction of a lower court. The plenary sessions of the supreme courts of the union republics are an important innovation of the 1958 law.

Under the RSFSR Law on Court Organization of 1960, as amended, the Plenum of the Supreme Court of the RSFSR has the authority to issue guiding instructions to the courts in the application of republican legislation and to initiate legislation. Like previous legislation, the present law provides for the establishment of presidiums in all courts of the union republics, except in the people's courts, to examine, by way of supervision, protested judgments and decisions that have already become final.

The so-called comrades' courts were a special kind of irregular court, which existed during the period of war communism and in the late 1930's. With the beginning of World War II they ceased to function. In 1959 a campaign was launched by Khrushchev emphasizing the need for comrades' courts in building communism. On October 24, 1959, the Supreme Soviet of the USSR adopted a model statute on comrades' courts. This statute provided the basic pattern for the legislation subsequently adopted by all constituent republics.

Comrades' courts were created at factories, offices, organizations, higher educational establishments, collective farms, housing collectives, street committees, or wherever there was a collective, consisting of not less than fifty people, to elect them. Under the amended law they can be set up at places with a collective of under twenty-five persons. Members are elected for a two-year period by open ballot at a general meeting. Members of the court select their own chairman, vice chairman, and secretary. The court meets irregularly. Meetings, presided over by the chairman and including two members of the court appointed by him, are held after working hours. Cases are heard in public. Procedural guarantees, such as the rights of the defendant to be informed of the charges in advance, to have a defense counsel, and to bring in witnesses, are waived. It is stressed that the socioeducational aspect of the offense must prevail over the judicial one.

The court may impose admonitions, reprimands, fines up to R50 (1 ruble equals US$1.10), and damages up to R50. There is no right of appeal from an adverse decision of the court. The court also has the authority to make a recommendation to the people's court that a tenant be evicted from his apartment; that a worker be dismissed from a job or transferred to another job; or that his wages be reduced for a maximum of fifteen days. One authority states that in 1965 there were 220,000 comrades' courts in the country, and in 1967 more than 153,000 in the RSFSR alone.

Federal Courts. Soviet federal courts—military tribunals and the USSR Supreme Court—in deciding civil and criminal matters, are governed by the same provisions as are the courts of the republics, with regard to the composition of the bench and procedural rules. Civil disputes between individuals usually are initiated and decided in the courts of the republics. Although there may be suits by one republic against another, one authority suggests that there is no public record of such suits between the republics in the USSR Supreme Court.

Military tribunals are the only hierarchy of federal courts in the Soviet Union that are not subordinate to republican supreme courts but operate under the direct supervision of the USSR Supreme Court. The Statute on Military Tribunals of December 25, 1958, as amended on February 21, 1968, defines their tasks, structure, jurisdiction, and functions. Military tribunals have jurisdiction over all crimes committed by military personnel and cases of espionage committed by civilians. Before the enactment of the 1958 statute, military tribunals had a wide jurisdiction not only over cases of espionage, but also over many other types of crimes, especially political crimes, committed by civilians.

Citizens in active military service may be elected as people's assessors at general meetings of the military personnel of a military unit or institution for a term of two years. Cases in military tribunals, as trial courts of first instance, are heard before a trial bench consisting of one member of the military tribunal, trained as a military lawyer, and two people's assessors. Appeals from a sentence of such a military tribunal are decided in the next higher military court by a bench consisting of three members of the military tribunals.

The USSR Supreme Court was originally established in 1923 as a consultative body to the Central Executive Committee of the USSR, then the supreme governing authority. Pursuant to Article 43 of the 1924 Constitution, the Supreme Court was authorized to give "authoritative interpretations to the supreme courts of the union republics on questions relating to federal legislation." It had no power, however, to reverse the decisions of the republican supreme courts. It could review such decisions on the motion of the procurator general and submit its opinions to the Central Executive Committee for determination.

The Supreme Court had no authority to rule on the constitutionality of laws. The legislative was to be its own judge on the constitutionality of its actions. This principle was retained in the constitutions of 1924 and 1936, although the USSR Supreme Court was given authority, pursuant to Article 43 of the 1924 Constitution, to render an opinion to the Central Executive Committee, if requested to do so, with regard to conformity with the Constitution of the legislation of a constituent republic. For the first time, in 1934, the Supreme Court was authorized to reverse the decisions of the republican supreme courts without referring the matter to the Presidium of the Central Executive Committee.

Under the 1936 Constitution and the Judiciary Act of 1938, the USSR Supreme Court was granted the power to "superintend the administration of justice by all the judicial bodies of the USSR and constituent republics by means of the examination of protests filed by the USSR procurator general and the president of the USSR Supreme Court against such judgments and orders in criminal and civil cases as have become final."

The structure and functions of the USSR Supreme Court, in 1970, were governed by the Statute of February 12, 1957, as amended on September 30, 1967. Under this statute, the USSR Supreme Court is the highest judicial agency of the nation, which guides the work of lower courts but handles fewer actual cases. Republican supreme courts were strengthened in 1954 by the creation of presidiums in courts above the level of people's courts and by reducing the size of the USSR Supreme Court and assigning a large number of judges from the highest court to the republican supreme courts. The USSR Supreme Court is composed of a president and a varying number of members who include the presidents of the republican supreme courts ex officio. The USSR Supreme Court functions in Plenary Sessions and three divisions: Division for Criminal Cases, Division for Civil Cases, and the Military Division. The jurisdiction of these divisions is both appellate and of a trial court of first instance, the latter involving only cases of exceptional importance. A case is tried before a trial bench consisting of a judge of the USSR Supreme Court and two people's assessors.

The military division of the USSR Supreme Court has original jurisdiction over criminal cases of exceptional importance and over crimes committed by military personnel holding the rank of general or admiral. The same Military Division considers appeals and protests against decisions rendered by higher military tribunals as trial courts of original jurisdiction and, by way of judicial supervision, decides on protests submitted by certain high judicial officials.

The Plenary Session, in the exercise of its appellate and supervisory functions, reviews protests filed by the president of the USSR Supreme Court and procurator general of the USSR from judgments and rulings rendered by one of its divisions. It reviews judgments of the republican supreme courts upon protests of the president of the USSR Supreme Court and the procurator general in case the judgment or decision of a republican supreme court is in conflict with federal legislation or violates the interests of other union republics. The Plenary Session also issues guiding instructions and explanations to courts with regard to the application of the law, makes recommendations to the Presidium of the Supreme Soviet concerning new legislation and the interpretation of federal laws, and decides on conflicts between the judicial agencies of the union republics.

Under the 1967 amendment, the president of the USSR Supreme

Court is allowed to refer to republican supreme court protests against decisions of those courts as an alternative to bringing the protests before the USSR Supreme Court itself for determination.

Private parties are not allowed to bring their grievances before the USSR Supreme Court. This may be done indirectly by petitioning the procurator general, the president of the USSR Supreme Court, or other authorized officials to lodge a protest, thus bringing the case to the USSR Supreme Court. If their petitions are denied, however, no other remedy is available to them.

Procuracy

The Soviet Procuracy was created in 1922. It was organized on a republican basis; the republican public prosecutors were subordinate to the republican ministers of justice. Their status of subordination remained unchanged after the establishment of the federal Procuracy in 1933, although the procurator general of the USSR (who performs some of the functions of an attorney general) was given broad power to intervene in the work of the republican prosecutors. This condition was brought to an end in 1936, when the republican prosecutors were detached from the republican ministries of justice and placed under the direct and sole supervision of the procurator general of the USSR. In 1970 the organization and functions of the federal Procuracy were governed by the Law of May 24, 1955, as amended February 27, 1959; March 3, 1960; February 14, 1964; and December 14, 1966.

Under the amended 1955 law still in force in 1970, the procurator general of the USSR is the most powerful law officer of the government in charge of the enforcement of its policy. His responsibility is general supervision over the strict observance of the law by all ministries and institutions subordinate to them, as well as by all public officials and citizens. The law does not specify whether he has power to supervise the legality of the acts of the highest government authorities, such as those of the Council of Ministers of the USSR, but scholars indicate that they are not within his supervisory jurisdiction.

The procurator general of the USSR is appointed for a term of seven years by the Supreme Soviet of the USSR. He is responsible for his acts to the Supreme Soviet and, in the interval between sessions, to the Presidium of the Supreme Soviet of the USSR. His relations with the Communist Party have not been spelled out in the law. From the entire governmental structure it appears, however, that he must abide by, and follow the directives and instructions of, Party leadership.

The 1955 law established a hierarchy of government attorneys parallel to the hierarchy of the courts. They constitute a single federal system that, with the procurator general of the USSR at the head, was assigned the task of enforcing the law. The procurator general of the USSR directly appoints the prosecutors of the republics, territories, and regions; whereas area, county, and city prosecutors are appointed by the union republic prosecutor, subject to the approval of the procurator general of the USSR. They are all appointed for a term of five years. Local prosecutors perform their duties independently of local agencies, including the local Soviet and Party organization, being subordinate solely to the procurator general of the USSR. Candidates for the position of government attorneys must have a higher legal education and be at least 25 years of age.

The law established, within the Procuracy, the office of the chief military prosecutor. He is a senior assistant to the procurator general of the USSR. This division handles matters pertaining to the jurisdiction of lower military tribunals.

In addition to the general power of supervision, the Procuracy is called upon to perform various other duties within the legal system. As an organ of the administration of justice, its role in criminal and civil proceedings is multifarious and significant. Thus, the procurator general of the USSR has the authority to submit to the Plenary Session of the USSR Supreme Court recommendations requiring guiding directives and instructions on matters of judicial practice for the lower courts.

In criminal proceedings the court and the public prosecutor have equal authority to order the arrest of a suspect of crime. Other law enforcement agencies must obtain the approval of the public prosecutor before making an arrest. A search of a private person's dwelling and seizure of correspondence at postal and telegraph offices may be made only with the approval of the public prosecutor.

The pretrial investigation, the inquiry and preliminary investigation, is supervised by the public prosecutor. In less important cases involving minor violations, the inquiry is conducted by the police. In all other instances, a preliminary investigation is conducted by the investigators, who are officials of the Procuracy or by investigators of the state security agencies. Although the law provides that, in the event the investigator disagrees with the instructions of the public prosecutor, he may submit the case to a higher government attorney; the investigator's decision to file an indictment is subject to reversal by the public prosecutor, and the investigator's decision not to file the indictment is not final, since the public prosecutor has the authority to transfer the case to another investigator. It is also within his discretionary power to conduct the preliminary investigation himself.

The public prosecutor is dutybound to appeal or to protest to a higher court any sentence that he thinks is illegal or groundless. Likewise, any finally decided case may be protested by the authorized government attorney, who may also stay the execution of a judgment until the protest has been decided.

The Procuracy may also intervene in civil litigations, where rights and duties of private persons are involved, in order either to protect the public interest or because some rights of a person are violated. The broad supervisory power implicitly authorizes the Procuracy to institute civil action even without consent of the parties concerned.

Office of the State Notary

In 1926 the federal legislation laid down the basic principles for the state notary. On the basis of the federal principles, the individual union republics passed their own statutes. The RSFSR, the largest republic and a model for all the others in the union, adopted its Law on the State Notary in 1947, which was superseded by the Law of September 30, 1965. This statute, which contains organizational and jurisdictional provisions on this office, was enacted, with slight modification, in all the other republics of the union.

The state notary has been delegated the authority to perform some functions that, as a rule, are within the jurisdiction of regular courts or executive committees of local soviets. The law enumerates the acts to be done by state notary officers in noncontentious proceedings, such as certification of legal transactions, inheritance cases, and matters with regard to aliens and stateless persons.

A person adversely affected by any act of a state notary may file an appeal in the competent court. State notaries are government officials. They are organized in notary offices where notary acts are performed by a senior state notary, deputy senior state notaries, or state notaries.

Candidates for positions as state notaries must have a higher legal education. A candidate without such education may be appointed as a state notary, provided he has been employed for at least three years as a judge, procurator, state notary, jurisconsult (legal adviser), or advocate.

Attorneys at Law

The legal profession makes a distinction between advocates, practicing attorneys who represent individual clients in criminal and civil matters, and jurisconsults, government employees who consult and represent social enterprises and institutions primarily in civil cases. They both have some features in common, although they are governed by different provisions.

Advocates. After 1953 more power was returned to union republics. With the enactment of the Fundamentals on the Judicial System in 1958, the power to legislate on advocates was returned to the union republics.

Advocates practice law in offices operated by colleges of advocates, which are organized on the republican, territorial, regional, and city levels. Colleges of advocates are defined as voluntary associations of persons engaged in counseling defendants in preliminary investigation and at trials of criminal cases, as well as representing citizens and government institutions in civil controversies.

Administratively, a college of advocates is divided into a general meeting or conference of the members, a presidium, and an auditing commission. The general meeting or conference convenes at least once a year to elect the presidium and the auditing commission, approves the bylaws of the college, and gives general guidance to the presidium. The presidium is elected by secret ballot for a term of two years. It organizes legal consultation offices and supervises their activities, grants admission to the college of new members, and disbars those found guilty of having violated the rules of ethics and internal order of the college. An appeal from a decree refusing admission to, or disbarring a member from, the college may be filed to the judicial committee of the autonomous republic or to local executive committees, which may reverse the decree of the presidium. The auditing commission reviews and supervises the financial and economic activities of the presidium of the college of advocates and the legal consultation offices.

Legal consultation offices are created by the presidium of the college of advocates with the consent of local executive committees. The office is headed by a manager, who receives a salary and supervises all the activities of the advocate.

The requirements for admission to membership in a college of advocates are citizenship of the Soviet Union, graduation from a law school on the university level, and experience in judicial work for not less than two years. Individuals without a higher legal education but with at least five years' experience in judicial work may be admitted by the council of ministers of the autonomous republic or local executive committees. The advocate's fee is paid to him through the legal consultant office only. Acceptance of payment directly from the client subjects the advocate to the penalty of being disbarred from the college of advocates.

An advocate must not disclose confidential information communicated to him in connection with legal aid in the given case, nor may he be interrogated as a witness regarding the circumstances of a case that have become known to him in connection with his fulfillment of the duties of defense counsel. This attorney-client privilege has been interpreted by Soviet authorities to be inadequate, since it applies only to a given case and does not prohibit the disclosure of information obtained by the advocate from legal aid in general.

Jurisconsults. Most of the union republics adopted their own statutes on jurisconsults, which necessarily are not identical. Jurisconsults are employed by government enterprises and institutions as

469

full-time employees. They represent the institution in all legal relations and transactions with other institutions, government agencies, and individuals.

As a rule, jurisconsults are appointed and dismissed by the institution that hired them, in accordance with the labor legislation then in force and in agreement with the superior organization. Graduates from a law school on the university level may be appointed to the position of section chief, legal office, senior jurisconsult, and jurisconsult. Individuals with secondary education may be appointed to these offices, provided they have had at least five years' experience in judicial work.

Abolition of the Ministries of Justice

The abolition of the ministries of justice, both federal and republican; the reorganization of the USSR Supreme Court, which became the highest judicial agency to guide the work of all lower courts; and the reorganization of the republican and regional courts in 1956, 1957, and 1963 were small but significant steps that indicated the trend toward the greater liberation and independence of the judiciary from interference by the administration.

After 1946 the Ministry of Justice of the USSR (before 1946 called the People's Commissariat for Justice) exercised general administrative control over all the courts of the nation. It supervised their activities through the republican ministries of justice, which retained supervisory jurisdiction over all courts in the individual constituent republics. When the Ministry of Justice of the USSR was abolished on June 3, 1956, its function of judicial supervision was transferred to the individual ministries of justice of the constituent republics. Between 1958 and 1963, all the union republican ministries of justice were abolished, and supervision of republican court activities was assigned to the presidiums of the various republican supreme courts.

CHAPTER 23

THE POLICE (MILITIA) AND CORRECTIONAL SYSTEMS

Local police in early 1970 were known as militia. The militia was responsible for enforcing laws, maintaining order, and protecting people and property at the local level. It worked in cooperation with, and was supported by, local governments, but it always was directed and controlled by the national organs of state and internal security. Although much of the militia's work supported the national agencies, those agencies retained responsibility for dealing with crimes that were considered political in nature or threats to the state, Party, or society as a whole. The militia dealt primarily with crimes, usually individual in character, that were not of political or national significance.

A citizen who ran afoul of Soviet law or police agencies and was found guilty could be fined, sentenced to corrective labor without deprivation of freedom, banished from certain areas, exiled to a specific location, or sent to prison or a labor colony. The basic penal and rehabilitation institution in early 1970 was the labor colony.

Soviet legislation directed the labor colonies to carry out criminal punishment in such a way that it not only was a penalty for the crime committed but also served to correct and reeducate convicted persons in an effort to improve their attitudes toward labor, society, and the strict observance of laws. This legislation also stated that a further objective of colony regimes was to prevent the commission of new crimes, both by convicted persons and by others, thereby contributing to the eradication of crime. Adults were sentenced to corrective labor colonies; minors (persons under eighteen years of age), to educational labor colonies.

Since the emphasis in penal confinement has been on corrective labor, prisons built since 1917 have been used primarily as places for pretrial detention and interrogation. Those remaining from prerevolutionary days were more generally used for confinement of convicted persons serving court sentences. Although most prisons throughout the land were much less than sanitary, a few of those in Moscow, and possibly in some other major cities, were kept spotlessly clean. Prison capacity totaled about 300,000 in 1917 and, according to one authority, has not changed a great deal during the half century or so of Soviet rule.

Labor colonies, on the other hand, varied widely in function and in inmate population. Conceived and first used in 1919, they functioned for about the first ten years as corrective or penal camps, extracting something from the work of the prisoners that would apply toward the cost of their upkeep and, if possible, instilling a satisfactory approach to work. With the swelling of camp populations from the millions of persons resettled, purged, or deported by Stalin, the camps of the late 1930's and the 1940's became important elements in the labor economy and in the populating of previously uninhabited areas. After Stalin, prison labor lost its national economic significance, the camps were renamed colonies, penal regimes were made less severe, and colony populations were reduced drastically (see ch. 32, The Labor Force).

Prison and labor colony life has been difficult and unpleasant throughout Soviet history, partially because the political prisoners who comprised the bulk of camp populations, until after 1953, were considered outcasts from society and partially in consistency with the policy of making penal regimes severe enough to act as a deterrent to crime. In large part, however, the most hideous of camp conditions—those that caused annual casualties as high as 30 percent in some camps in the World War II period—resulted from poor administration; shortages of food, clothing, and shelter; and work in climatic extremes that had made some of the camp locations previously uninhabitable. Released prisoners frequently complained of official indifference, of intolerable working conditions, and of inedible food but seldom of sadistic or inhumane treatment at the hands of their guards.

CRIME, CRIMINALS, AND PUNISHMENT

A crime is defined in the Soviet Union as a "socially dangerous act," and punishments as "measures taken in social defense." Soviet authorities have been inordinately concerned with crime and have considered that the commission of crimes in general could be construed as a reflection of protest against the system or as an indication that their society had tarnished spots. In consequence, there has been a continuing effort to explain crime away as externally generated or as a residue from the old society that would require time to eradicate.

Offenders have been broadly separated into criminal and political categories. Those classed as "politicals" were the persons suspected of taking actions or harboring opinions considered dangerous to the state, Party, or system. They were usually convicted of espionage, sabotage, wrecking, or terrorist activities. "Criminals" were more frequently those found guilty of crimes against persons and private property, of disruption of public order, and the like. Between 1936 and about 1950, politicals outnumbered criminals in the labor camps by a ratio of four or five to one. The ratio has probably been more than reversed since 1960 (see ch. 8, The Internal Security System).

Punishment for the bulk of more ordinary crimes is intended to reform, reeducate, and rehabilitate the offender and to prevent further crime by impressing him and the public at large with the idea that antisocial pursuits are unrewarding. In the more serious cases the sentence can be considered the retaliation of society, or its rulers, against the convicted person. Such retaliation has been less frequently exercised in the period since Stalin. The death sentence is carried out far less frequently and the proportion of those convicted of political crimes has decreased.

THE MILITIA

The militia approximates the usual uniformed local police organizations of other countries. During the civil warfare years from 1917 to about 1921, it was maintained as a basically military organization, charged primarily with assisting the Red Army. During the early 1920's it settled gradually into the role of the basic local law enforcement agency and in early 1970 had retained that status with comparatively little change.

The militia was originally subordinated to the People's Commissariat of Internal Affairs (Narodnyy Komisariat Vnutrennikh Del— NKVD). A dual subordination, both to the NKVD and to the republic government or to local Soviets, was established. Except for a short period between 1949 and 1953 when it was subordinate to state security, control has always been within the internal security organization. The degree of control exercised from above has varied, but the basic concept of dual subordination remains unchanged.

At the apex of the administrative pyramid, the militia was responsible to the Ministry of Internal Affairs (Ministerstvo Vnutrennikh Del—MVD) in the government organization and to the Administrative Organs Section of the Central Committee of the Communist Party of the Soviet Union (CPSU) in the Party hierarchy. This section was headed by Nikolay I. Savinkin in mid-1968. Savinkin's earlier career had featured a long period of service in the Political Directorate of the Soviet Army. Whether Savinkin assumed the same broad areas of control that were vested in the previous head of the Administrative Organs Section, Nikolay K. Mironov, is not known. Mironov, whose background included several positions within the state security organizations, was the Party official who also had administrative responsibility over the Committee for State Security (Komitet Gosudarstvennoy Bezopasnosti—KGB), the procuracy, and the courts.

The militia is responsible for the protection of public order and public property and for the personal security of the people and their property. Most of its activities are directed and oriented locally. The internal and state security agencies have extensive operations throughout the entire country, however, and relieve the militia of primary responsibility with regard to political crimes or other criminal activity considered dangerous to the state or its major institutions (see ch. 8, The Internal Security System).

In the performance of its work, the militia can demand that citizens observe government regulations, can take measures to maintain public order, and can pursue, arrest, and detain persons suspected of committing crimes. It can commandeer private vehicles and enter and search dwellings or business premises in pursuit of suspected criminals. It can demand cooperation from hotel, apartment, and dormitory managements and caretakers, night watchmen, and other workers in areas where crimes have been committed or where suspected criminals could be hiding. Although it may conduct preliminary criminal investigations, about 65 percent of these are accomplished by the central security agencies, and those relegated to the militia are probably the least important. Militia personnel are armed, and circumstances in which they can use their weapons are specified.

The militia has wide controls over motor vehicle documents, inspection, and operation. It maintains standards of repair, checks drivers' qualifications, and takes action on traffic violations, including related offenses such as drunken driving. It can arrest, pass judgment, and collect fines in such cases. In this or other types of minor offenses, the local police chief, if he thinks the offense does not merit fine or imprisonment, may transfer the case to a people's court or a comrade's court, either of which can take measures exerting pressure on the accused at his work or in his home environment.

The militia administers the internal passport system, issuing passports and checking to see that individuals stay within designated areas. When a person has reason to visit an area outside the limits specified in his passport, the militia issues a certificate, sometimes referred to as a visa. It authorizes movement to a specified place at a specified time and must be in the possession of the traveler, who is required to register with the militia at his destination and upon his return (see ch. 8, The Internal Security System).

In other miscellaneous functions, the militia maintains contact with persons sentenced to exile and enforces a wide variety of regulations concerning firearms, printing appliances, poisons, radioactive materials, photography, and licenses and permits. It maintains address information and traces missing persons and draft evaders. It maintains contacts with resident aliens and foreigners. It supervises crowds in public places and during demonstrations and parades, assisting the movement of traffic and pedestrians. Militia officials participate in street and road construction plans. Since the militia is subordinate to the MVD and operates under the authority of both its security forces and those of the KGB, it has only a portion of the responsibility for the preservation of order.

Militiamen are volunteers. They agree to serve a minimum tour of duty, probably unchanged from the two years stipulated in regulations effective in 1931, but most regard militia service as career work. The rank-and-file include a high percentage of men released from the armed forces or military units of the security forces. A large portion of the officers and noncommissioned officers are products of militia schools, and are transfers from the MVD and KGB, or are governmental and Party appointees. In the mid-1960's deputy commanders for political education were assigned to militia units having more than fifty members. Salaries are not large, but privileges, such as guaranteed housing at reduced rents, increase the attraction of militia work.

The uniform jacket, trousers, cap, and tie are navy blue; the shirt is blue poplin, and the trousers have red piping; cap insignia and banding are also red. For winter there is a heavy overcoat or cloak and, for extreme weather, a sheepskin coat.

LOCAL VOLUNTEER FORCES

In villages and some rural areas, the entire population over eighteen years of age is required to assist the militia for three months of each year. Other such groups are formed on collective farms and in industrial plants, educational institutions, and the like. They are variously referred to by such titles as People's Voluntary Militia, Public Order Detachments, and People's Squads. Their subordination is usually to the local Party organization, indicating that their purpose is primarily political rather than strictly law enforcement. The organizations are collectively referred to as local volunteer forces, although participation is frequently not on a voluntary basis.

These volunteer or quasi-volunteer groups augment the militia on occasions when unusual numbers of police personnel are required. They assist on holidays to control crowds and to prevent small crimes and disorders by patrolling the streets, visiting bars and restaurants, and so forth. They also act as police informers and represent the transfer of a portion of law enforcement tasks to "social" or popular organizations. Much of their work is intended to be of a persuasive or preventive nature.

Volunteer groups appear to be participated in, and accepted, by the public with varying degrees of enthusiasm. They also appear to operate in highly variable fashion, sometimes existing largely on paper, sometimes conducting themselves overzealously. In the latter situations their excesses have occasionally been met with armed resistance. The government has made efforts to improve their image, as well as the militia's, and has matched these efforts by increasing the punishments that can be imposed on citizens who attack them. Although demands for public participation are not nearly so great in urban areas, estimates of the people who may be occupied in this type of militia support work range from 2.5 million to 5.5 million.

SENTENCES NOT INVOLVING DEPRIVATION OF FREEDOM

Persons found guilty of crimes that call for punishment more severe than fines but do not merit confinement can receive three categories of sentences which do not entail loss of their immediate freedom. Corrective labor sentences that are served at the convicted person's usual place of work or at another place designated by the local authorities in his home district are the least severe. In a second category, individuals are banished from specified areas, possibly only the vicinity of their residence, for a definite period of time. Exile is the most serious of the three. It involves banishment, but to a specific area or place.

Corrective Labor

Corrective labor sentences appear to be handed down most frequently in cases where an individual's work, working habits, or attitudes have been unsatisfactory. The sentence involves mandatory performance of "socially useful work" and "political-upbringing" instruction. Work is accomplished under close supervision, and the individual is rated on his work and work attitudes. Although the labor should not interfere fundamentally with the individual's homelife, measures are taken to make the work regime less pleasant than a normal existence, and deductions beyond those usual for taxes and other payments are made into state funds.

Labor accomplished during the period of the sentence is not recorded on the individual's overall or continuous labor records. The time does not apply toward pay raises, and there is no accumulation toward vacations. There are, however, incentives in the program. Exemplary work can result in parole, milder work, or a review of the case by the courts that might restore some or all of the otherwise lost time to the individual's labor records.

Banishment

A person banished is sent away from his place of residence for a specified time. The court determines the size of the local banishment area and adds other forbidden places. The typical sentence has been to the "USSR minus six," meaning exclusion from his home area and the six largest Soviet cities. He can also be restricted from places where work and housing are scarce. Other than as prohibited, he chooses his new residence. The internal passport system and necessary travel documents make it necessary for him to go directly to the place he has chosen. These and local regulations governing the work of banished persons also prevent him from drifting about the country during the period of his sentence. Local Soviets assist him in finding employment.

According to regulations made public in July 1969, "Labor of individuals sentenced to banishment is regulated according to the usual procedure according to labor legislation." This would appear to mean that banished persons receive pay appropriate to the job and work normal hours and that time and labor are entered in their overall labor records, applying toward vacations, raises, and the like. Parole or commutation of a portion of the sentence can be granted if an individual demonstrates exemplary behavior.

Exile

Exile is banishment to a specified area. This can be as severe a punishment as a sentence involving loss of freedom, because exiling has been a means of achieving forced settlement of unpopulated Siberian areas. When this is the case, the individual may find on his arrival that there is one local Soviet in the district to which he is limited, that it is located at a labor colony, which is the only place of work, and that his residence will, of necessity, consist of whatever shelter is available. This could be satisfactory but has, in the worst cases, consisted of caves dug by hand from slag piles. Where nothing could be grown locally or was available for purchase, camp authorities have either fed exiles at prison messes or have allocated them a food ration, deducting an amount from their wages.

The worst conditions reputedly no longer exist, but some of these exiles, special migrants, or settlers have endured conditions no better than those enjoyed by the hardly less fortunate labor camp inmates. In all exile situations, regulations prescribe socially useful work in the job provided by the local Soviet in the district to which the person is exiled. According to these regulations, conditions of labor, wages, and incentives to good work and behavior are the same as in the banishment situation.

Those banished and exiled generally fall into the category of persons referred to as "parasites"—individuals who evaded or refused work considered socially useful by the authorities. Employers who have quotas to fill and are busy with everyday problems are frequently reluctant to employ parasites who, at the best, require extra supervision. Often they are settled together in a single building and given group work with seasonal workers. This type of unsatisfactory condition and other problems arising from the use and retraining of exiled and banished citizens receive continuing critical official and press comment.

PENAL INSTITUTIONS

A convicted individual receiving a sentence depriving him of freedom goes to prison, a corrective labor colony, or an educational labor colony. Many of these institutions are operated by the MVD. Prisons and corrective labor colonies are generally for adults. In some circumstances minors can be confined in prisons, but most of them go to educational labor colonies. The names are generally indicative of the primary emphasis of the institution. Prison convicts perform labor but not to the degree that is the practice in labor colonies. In the adult labor colonies the emphasis is on the labor and its products. The educational program has second priority. The educational labor colonies are set up with the intent of continuing the young inmate's general education and providing specific vocational instruction. There is a penal or work program in addition.

Prisons

Far more labor camps than prisons have been constructed since 1919. New prison areas were either added to internal affairs administration buildings or built adjacent to them in most large towns during the 1930's, and since World War II the state security agencies have constructed special purpose prisons. Neither of these types was intended primarily to house inmates serving sentences but, rather, to detain arrested persons during interrogation periods before trial (see ch. 8, The Internal Security System).

The older prisons have also been used for pretrial detention, but they are more ordinarily occupied by convicted inmates. Capacity inherited from the tsarist period has been estimated at about 300,000. The prison population exceeded that figure considerably during the major purge periods, when some were filled up to ten times their capacities, but it probably represents approximately the upper limit in more normal circumstances.

Conditions in the prisons vary greatly. A few in Moscow are as clean as first-class hotels and are often shown on the conducted tours for visiting dignitaries and penologists. In the better ones convicts get a bath with soap every ten days. Others, particularly in rural areas, are much less sanitary. As a general rule, however, there is a considerable effort devoted to prisoners' health. Inoculations against infectious diseases are frequent and, although dysentery is endemic, epidemics of communicable diseases are rare. To prevent suicide, stairwells have nets, shaving is done with clippers, and hunger strikers are forced-fed. Food is plain and uninteresting but is ordinarily given out in subsistence quantities. Prisoners emerge emaciated after prison terms, but lack of exercise and insufficient exposure to daylight generally contribute more to their deterioration than does inadequate food.

Ordinarily, those sentenced to prison terms are guilty of grave crimes, are recidivists, or are transferred from labor colonies for disciplinary reasons. There is separate confinement for men and women, for adults and minors, and for first offenders and repeaters. Dangerous criminals, those guilty of debasing personal crimes, and prisoners awaiting death sentences are also isolated from other inmates.

Prison mail is censored, and packages are searched. Cells and persons are inspected and searched at irregular intervals. Prisoners do not keep money or valuables in their cells, but what they had on arrival or earn in prison labor is maintained for them and may be spent in the prison store. According to official regulations, each prisoner is provided sleeping space, bedding, clothing, and the necessities for personal hygiene and sanitation.

Until a prisoner—even on the normal, or standard, regime—has demonstrated good behavior, he can receive no parcels and is limited to two visits of up to four hours each per year. He may receive an unlimited amount of letter mail and may send one per month. No prisoner may correspond with anyone in his or any other place of detention. Complaints to prosecutors and other specified government officials are not included in the limitations on correspondence. Regulations direct that these be passed within twenty-four hours to the appropriate authority. Inmates who hold prison jobs can gain additional correspondence, visiting, and other privileges.

A strict regime is provided for second offenders, those committing crimes while in places of detention and, as a punitive measure short of solitary confinement, for uncooperative inmates. This regime is rigorous enough so that it is limited to from two to six months at a time. In addition to a generally harsher existence, exercise periods are cut from one hour to one-half hour a day, no visitors are allowed, and only one letter may be sent out every two months. Prisoners in disciplinary cells or solitary confinement are deprived of their warmer clothing and have no furniture or beds. Cells have bare concrete floors and walls. Exercise periods are reduced by half, and the food ration is cut to between one-half and two-thirds of the standard.

If a person is suspected of having committed a punishable offense, he may also be confined to eliminate the possibility that he might avoid investigation and trial or might engage in other criminal activities. Persons so confined are considered in preventive detention.

479

Regulations state that they may be held in preventive detention for only seventy-two hours unless investigation-period cell blocks are inaccessible, in which case this period can be extended up to thirty days. According to released prisoners, this regulation is frequently complied with loosely. Since the confined individual has not been tried, he retains his rights as a citizen as well as certain other privileges not shared by convicted criminals. He can, for example, be put to work only with his consent. If he warrants discipline, however, he may be given extra work details, lose the privileges to buy supplemental food and to receive packages or, in extreme situations, be confined in a punitive dungeon cell.

Labor Colonies

Felix Dzerzhinsky, first head of the secret police, observed in early 1919 that little use was being made of the labor of people under arrest. He proposed camps "for those who could not work without a degree of compulsion and as a punishment for a remiss attitude toward work, for negligence, tardiness," as well as for criminals and the politically suspect. Construction of the camps began later that year (see ch. 8, The Internal Security System).

Labor camp population was perhaps 30,000 in the mid-1920's, and a high percentage of the inmates were criminals. That number grew to from 7 to 10 million, or more, from 1939 to about 1946. The inmates of that period were largely alleged political deviationists or the victims of population relocations. Annual or more frequent amnesties of entire groups between 1954 and 1957 and the commitment of far fewer individuals after Stalin's death in 1953 reduced colony populations by the late 1960's to a fraction of earlier levels.

The character of camp populations also changed markedly. Beginning with the displacement of the *kulak* (relatively well-to-do peasant) population in 1928 and continuing through Stalin's various purges and deportations, political or noncriminal inmates outnumbered criminals in the camps by as much as five to one. That ratio had probably been reversed by the early 1960's (see ch. 8, The Internal Security System).

The earliest camps were frequently referred to in official publications and legislation as forced labor, concentration, or corrective labor camps. During the early 1930's it became customary to refer to them only as corrective labor camps and corrective labor colonies. During the next two decades, while both camps and colonies were in existence at the same time, regimes in the colonies were the less severe. After about 1957 the term *camp* was dropped altogether, presumably to indicate an overall moderation in the penal system. The remaining corrective labor colonies, however, are divided into five categories and have regimes of varying severity.

Those with the more severe regimes are sometimes referred to as punitive colonies.

Between about 1930 and 1950 the labor camps were an important element in the national economy. This probably developed naturally from evolving circumstances. Dzerzhinsky almost certainly had had little in mind beyond trying to get something useful from his prisoners to apply against the costs of keeping them alive. By the time that Stalin had imprisoned the *kulak* population and large numbers of his competetent managers and engineers, however, it became obvious that the security agencies had become host to a sizable and effective labor force. From that time until nearly the end of the Stalin era, the camps played an important role in canal, railway, and hydroelectric plant construction; in the mining and forestry industries; and in the settling of areas that had inhospitable climates but were wealthy in natural resources (see ch. 8, The Internal Security System; ch. 32, The Labor Force).

Labor camps did not use manpower effectively, and their economic value had diminished by the time of Stalin's death in 1953. A succession of amnesties between 1954 and 1957 reduced camp populations from the high World War II totals to perhaps one-fourth or less of wartime averages. Colony populations continued to decline after 1957 and, by normal attrition between then and 1970, would have reached a level reflecting the rate at which criminal elements were normally confined. There is no indication of what that figure might be. Also, the ratio of prison as opposed to labor colony sentences is not known. Most of those sentenced on minor charges, for periods too short to make a labor colony sentence worthwhile, receive prison terms. At the other extreme, the very worst criminals, who require constant guard, are sent to maximum security prisons. Those sentenced to medium and to long terms but who are not considered prohibitively dangerous and who might be capable of being rehabilitated are sent to labor colonies.

The basic objective in prisoner treatment is no longer utilization of their labor. Although the writings of those who have been released suggest that it may be pursued inconsistently, the official aim is to return socially useful individuals to society. When all facilities are available and the administration adheres to official guidelines, the correcting and reeducating process involves the penal regime, socially useful labor, general education, technical and vocational instruction, and political indoctrination.

According to 1969 legislation, adults go to corrective labor colonies, and minors under eighteen, to educational labor colonies. Both have educational programs with heavy emphasis on social and political indoctrination, and both have general and trade schools. The corrective colonies attempt to teach a trade to younger adults, but those over forty years of age usually receive only a general curriculum. The educational colonies attempt to continue in both general and vocational areas from the point reached in earlier schooling by their young people.

Corrective Labor Colonies

Colonies for adults fall into five categories. The standard, intensified, strict, and special colonies have regimes that are progressively more severe. Colony settlements, the fifth category, feature a much more free regime and are for prisoners showing progress toward rehabilitation. The court sentence specifies the regime it thinks appropriate for the newly convicted individual, and regulations stipulate that, except for the move to colony settlements, the entire sentence will ordinarily be served in one colony. A regime change can occur while the sentence is being served, either as a reward for good behavior or as a punishment for bad behavior or poor performance. One camp complex usually contains colonies with several different regimes, and transfer of an individual from one colony to another with a different regime involves a physical move usually within the same camp complex. In all regimes except the colony settlements, prisoners are segregated according to the same principles that apply in prisons.

Ordinarily, the standard regime is for first offenders who have not committed overly serious crimes. Prisoners work an eight-hour day, six days a week. Holidays are also free of work, but there are no vacations and the work does not apply in the individual's labor booklet toward later vacations, pay raises, and other accruing privileges. Vocational and general educational training is scheduled in addition to the regular workday. Pay and work conditions are determined on the basis of national norms, but the various deductions for maintenance of the prisoner are considerable.

Regulations state that at least 10 percent of his earned wages must go into the prisoner's account. He cannot carry money or valuables on his person but may spend up to R15 (1 ruble equals US$1.10) per month if he has it in his account. He may have visitors up to five times a year. Three are classed as short visits, limited to four hours. Two can be long visits of up to seventy-two hours. Long visits may be made by close relatives only and include the right of cohabitation with the spouse. The prisoner can have unlimited correspondence but cannot receive parcels until he has served one-half of his sentence. The limit then is three per year. All mail is censored except for the complaints or official requests that a prisoner may send to his court or other authorities.

Good behavior is rewarded by a variety of incentives ranging from the inclusion of the prisoner's name on a bulletin board listing of best workers to permission to have extra visitors, pay bonuses, transfer to a colony with an easier regime, or commutation of a part of the sentence. After a portion of the sentence has been served, varying in different circumstances, a cooperative prisoner can proceed unescorted to a place of work outside the colony and work there unguarded. If a prisoner requires extra punishment, it could consist of as little as a warning or reproach, or it could involve loss of visits, packages, and other privileges. In more serious situations it could mean confinement in punitive cell blocks, transfer to a colony with a more severe regime, or transfer to a prison.

First offenders convicted of grave crimes go to colonies with intensified regimes. Second offenders and those guilty of dangerous state crimes are usually sent to colonies with strict regimes. Special regime colonies are for dangerous recidivists and those serving commuted death sentences. Women are sentenced to colonies with standard and strict regimes only. Effort is made to make living conditions less comfortable and to reduce privileges progressively in the more severe regimes. For example, outgoing letter correspondence is unrestricted in the standard regime, limited to three letters a month in the intensified, two a month in the strict, and one a month in the special. Visiting privileges decrease from the three short and two long visits of the standard regime to one of each in the special.

Colony settlements, on the other hand, appear designed as a transition from the colony to a free existence. Transfer is allowed when the prisoner has demonstrated good behavior, dependability, and a cooperative attitude and has served a required portion of his sentence. Supervision is minimal. Movement within the compound is unrestricted between morning and night. Prisoners leave the compound unescorted if they work outside. They wear civilian clothing and retain money, valuables, and personal possessions. They have unrestricted visiting and correspondence privileges. When facilities are available, their families can join them and live in the colony.

Conditions in the northern and far eastern mining camps of the late 1930's and 1940's were especially severe. Information from former inmates indicates that annual death rates averaged about 10 percent in these camps during the World War II years. In a few camps during part of that time, the toll was probably 30 percent per year. Although conditions since Stalin have shown a vast improvement, the few reports from inmates released in the late 1960's indicate that conditions are still extreme by Western standards. Nonetheless, even during the worst years, treatment of prisoners, although most unpleasant, seldom if ever was sadistic. Poor administration, near impossible working conditions, shortages of food, shelter, and fuel, and lack of official concern caused a terrible toll among the prison population. Former inmates, however, do not usually complain of brutal or inhumane treatment at the hand of local guards.

Colonies for minors under eighteen years of age feature more tolerable regimes, additional privileges and, when facilities are available, considerably greater emphasis on education and rehabilitation. General education is programmed to continue from the level reached by the young inmate in his earlier schooling and is provided in addition to vocational courses intended to give him a usable technical skill upon his release.

According to government directives, correcting and reforming of the young inmates in educational labor colonies is accomplished in a five-part program consisting of a penal regime, socially useful labor, a general educational curriculum, technical or vocational training, and political and social indoctrination. There are only two categories of education labor colony regimes—standard or intensified—and girls are committed to those with standard regimes only.

Separation of prisoners by sex and according to the probable category of the criminal conforms to approximately the same guidelines that apply in the corrective labor colonies. The upper age limit for both regimes is seventeen. A girl or boy who reaches eighteen but is progressing satisfactorily in a reeducation program may stay until he completes it, or until he reaches the age of twenty. All who become twenty before their terms are served, however, must be transferred to adult colonies. Labor is performed under general labor legislation codes, and 45 percent of the youths' wages must go into their personal prisoner accounts.

Conditions in the two regimes generally parallel those of the same names in corrective labor colonies, but each has somewhat more privileges than its adult colony counterpart. In the standard regime, for example, the youths may receive about twice as many parcels and may have more than double the visits that are allowed an adult in the corrective labor colony standard regime. Correspondence is unlimited except that the inmate must have permission to write persons other than his relatives. As in the case in corrective labor colonies, all mail except outgoing correspondence to court and government authorities is censored. After six months of good behavior, the young people may work unguarded outside the colony and may go and come unescorted.

The intensified regime, for boys who have committed grave crimes or who are second offenders, allows fewer privileges and has a more severe penal regime. Correspondence is allowed under the same conditions as in the standard regime, however, and the parcels privilege is more lenient than that of the standard regime in adult colonies.

Good behavior is rewarded with extra privileges. Those requiring extra punishment, on the other hand, can have privileges withdrawn. If they are put into isolation rooms, they are allowed no visitors or parcels, and they receive a reduced food ration that cannot be supplemented with purchases from their prisoner accounts.

CHAPTER 24
FOREIGN RELATIONS

At the beginning of 1970 the Soviet Union was a leading world power. Its foreign policy seemed to be based on the desire to extend its influence wherever possible and to avoid direct military confrontation with the West. The Soviet invasion of Czechoslovakia in August 1968 was an example of its desire to maintain its hegemony in Eastern Europe. Activities in the Middle East and the Mediterranean area demonstrated the policy of expanding influence. The limitation of support to North Vietnam to military and economic aid rather than commitment of troops was indicative of the desire to avoid direct confrontation.

Although Soviet leaders continued to adhere to Communist ideology, it appears, at least temporarily, that ideology has become a less important factor than power politics in determining foreign policy. Nevertheless, ideology as a motivating factor remains a basic element in the long term. The men who run the Soviet Union are practicing Marxists-Leninists who have grown up under the system and have been educated and indoctrinated within it. They owe their positions to the system and never cease to reiterate that eventually, and inevitably, the entire world will be Communist. A complex interrelationship of ideology and power politics or national interests exists, and it accomplishes little to attempt to attribute various actions to one or the other or to attempt to devise a ratio of one to the other.

The leaders continued to view the Soviet Union as the vanguard of the international Communist movement and the supporter of forces throughout the world that they considered progressive. Khrushchev's doctrine concerning the possibility of peaceful transition to socialism, augmenting the traditional reliance on revolutionary tactics, had apparently been adopted by his successors.

There are numerous examples of power-political as well as ideological and domestic considerations in the formulation of Soviet foreign policy. Aid continued to flow in large quantities to the United Arab Republic, for example, despite the fact that the Communist Party of that country had been outlawed. Similar examples are found in the support given to Nigeria, Spain, and Greece in 1969 and early 1970. Extensive military aid was granted to the Nigerian government in its struggle against the insurgent Biafrans.

Nigerian officials claimed that Soviet aid was crucial to their ultimate victory. During a critical coal miners' strike in the Asturian region of Spain, the Soviets supplied the Spanish government with large quantities of coal. Economic assistance was also granted to the military junta in Greece.

The objective of foreign policy in Africa, Asia, and Latin America was the penetration of areas that had not previously experienced Soviet influence. The Soviets sought to establish and maintain friendly relations with established governments regardless of their political orientations. In the effort to increase its influence, the Soviet Union was seeking wherever possible to improve its diplomatic, economic, and cultural relations with the countries on these continents.

The Soviet Union was providing military aid and advisers to North Vietnam and the Arab States, among others, but generally avoided the involvement of its own military personnel in armed conflicts, except in the United Arab Republic where Soviet pilots flew operational missions.

The Soviet Union's relations with the West increased in the 1960's, although in early 1970 there were still major issues to be resolved. Trade and cultural activities developed in the late 1960's, and at the beginning of 1970 there were indications that attempts might be made to resolve some of the political differences.

Soviet relations with Communist China deteriorated in the 1960's. The longstanding party-to-party conflict over ideological differences had become a state-to-state conflict over territorial claims and other practical issues. The situation changed drastically in 1969 when the verbal abuse that the Soviets and Chinese had hurled at one another was replaced by actual combat along the borders of the two countries. At the beginning of 1970, Soviet and Chinese diplomats were attempting to negotiate their differences.

DETERMINANTS AND MECHANISMS

Foreign policy is formulated by the members of the Politburo of the Communist Party of the Soviet Union (CPSU). Once determined, policy is implemented by the USSR Ministry of Foreign Affairs, which was headed by Andrei A. Gromyko in the capacity of minister of foreign affairs. The organization of the ministry resembles that of its counterparts in other countries throughout the world. It is divided into several departments that correspond to the various regions and countries with which the Soviet Union maintains relations. Members of the diplomatic corps, as well as all other employees of the ministry, are Communist Party members (see ch. 21, Political Dynamics).

Diplomacy, backed by the military and industrial power of the nation, has become the most prominent mechanism of foreign relations, especially in the post-Khrushchev period. The reliance of Soviet leaders on the activities of indigenous Communist parties to attain foreign policy objectives had decreased markedly, although the role of those parties as disseminators of Soviet propaganda continued unabated. The use of Communists abroad was particularly prevalent during the existence of the Comintern (Communist International) from 1919 to 1943. During this period two parallel courses of Soviet foreign policy were evident as normal diplomatic relations were carried on by the Commissariat of Foreign Affairs while party-to-party relations were in the hands of the Comintern. Although proclaiming itself to be an international organization, the Comintern was completely controlled by the Soviet Communist Party; and its avowed purposes were to foment revolution, to create an international Soviet republic, and to gain recognition for the Soviet Union.

In the years after World War II as the Soviet Union emerged as a great power with increased political, military, and economic capacities, it increasingly relied on the traditional instruments of foreign policy: diplomacy, economic relations, and the military. The Cominform (Communist Information Bureau) an international organization of Communist parties that was established in 1947, never became a viable political instrument as the Comintern had been, and party-to-party relations increasingly became the province of the top level of the CPSU. The absence of an international organization gave party-to-party relationships more of a parochial hue, and the main thrust of these relations became the effort to gain support for Soviet policies. The Sino-Soviet rift caused reverberations throughout the parties of the world, and the Soviet leaders continually sought support for their leadership of the world Communist movement.

Although the Soviet Union continued to articulate policy in ideological terms, ideology, for tactical reasons, was becoming less prominent in determining actual foreign relations. Soviet activities in the international arena, especially since Leonid Brezhnev and Aleksei Kosygin acceded to power, were primarily motivated by power-political considerations—namely, to maintain or if possible to alter the balance of power and to extend Soviet influence. In the late 1960's it became evident that the Sino-Soviet conflict had also become an important determinant of Soviet foreign policy.

The Soviet leaders became increasingly pragmatic in their dealings with other countries. They learned from the mistakes made by Khrushchev and have shown a capacity for flexibility in response to international developments. Economic considerations and access to Western technology emerged as important determinants of foreign relations; in a businesslike manner, Soviet leaders sought trade relations wherever such would benefit the Soviet economy (see ch. 35, Foreign Economic Relations).

Domestic affairs are also important determinants of Soviet foreign policy. The state of the economy influences the extent of activities abroad, and factional struggles among agencies competing for a greater share of the budget affect the choices of policy alternatives. Power struggles within the Party hierarchy also influence the formulation of foreign policy (see ch. 21, Political Dynamics).

The fact that Soviet leaders have become more pragmatic in the formulation and conduct of foreign policy does not imply that they have cast off Marxist-Leninist ideology. The pursuit of power-political objectives is not inconsistent with ideological tenets or with historical precedent. Lenin and all of his successors have advocated pragmatic approaches to specific problems and, at times, dealt with so-called bourgeois governments even at the expense of indigenous Communist movements. Despite such temporary departures from the straight ideological path, however, ideology still affects decisionmaking and provides the framework in which Soviet leaders analyze and evaluate international events.

Karl Marx, writing a half century or more before the Bolshevik Revolution, stated, "The policy of Russia is changeless. Its methods, its tactics, its maneuvers may change, but the polar star of its policy—world domination—is a fixed star." The Bolsheviks, usurpers of old Russia's land and government and inheritors of its traditions and policies, added the element of world communization. The leadership, from Lenin to Brezhnev and Kosygin, pursued the old policies and, by inference, espoused the idea that the ruling center of a Communist world would naturally and necessarily be Moscow.

Secure in the belief that time is on their side, that world communism is inevitable, the Soviet leaders have relaxed their messianic approach to international relations and, when they deem it advantageous, deal with nations of all political hues. Concurrently, their internal and external propaganda machines grind out the familiar theme about the evils of capitalism and imperialism, which causes apprehension on the part of target nations and difficulties in diplomatic negotiations.

THE UNITED STATES

Relations between the Soviet Union and the United States have contained many elements of conflict since the anti-Nazi alliance fell apart after World War II and the entire spectrum of the foreign policies of each became important to the other. United States-Soviet relations have been characterized by the cold war, beginning about 1947, and by the period of relative détente, from about 1963. In the late 1960's and the beginning of 1970, it appeared that some attempts at accommodation were being made by both countries. The basic ideological differences and causes of the cold war had not been eliminated, however, and the many new conflict areas that emerged in the 1950's and 1960's must be disposed of before a real accommodation can be made.

The cold war period was characterized by mutual suspicion that resulted in a rigid division of Europe. The rapid communization of Eastern Europe, plus the maintenance of powerful armies of occupation in central Europe, were a threat to the entire continent. The initiation of the Marshall Plan in 1947, which established a basis for economic recovery of the war-torn countries of Western Europe, was characterized by Soviet officials as an imperialist move to subjugate those countries by the United States. By the time of the fall of Czechoslovakia to a Communist coup in 1948, the lines of the cold war had hardened, and the former allies openly expressed mutual hostility.

The formation of military alliances and the buildup of military forces deterred hostile actions, but serious confrontations occurred that entailed the threat of war. The blockade of Berlin by Soviet forces in 1948 and the subsequent airlift that supplied the city with the necessities of life for several months was one such confrontation through which the Soviets learned that the United States and its allies were determined to retain a free West Berlin. The blockade was finally lifted in May 1949, ending the confrontation.

Another dangerous confrontation occurred in June 1950, when South Korea was invaded by North Korean troops armed and trained by the Soviet Union. United Nations troops, largely provided by the United States, were sent to defend South Korea. Although the Soviet Union provided military aid to the North Koreans, it was Communist China, also relying on Soviet military aid, that provided troops. Thus, a military confrontation between the United States and the Soviet Union was again avoided. The Korean conflict resulted in a stalemate, and the division of that country remained at about the 38th parallel.

The fear created by the experiences in Europe and Asia led, in 1955, to the inclusion of West Germany in the North Atlantic Treaty Organization (NATO). This move intensified the tension in United States-Soviet relations, and Soviet fear of West German rearmament was an important factor behind their effort to maintain control over Eastern Europe.

Attempts to relax the tension between the Soviet Union and the United States had been made throughout the post-Stalin period but without success. Such incidents as the shooting down of the U—2 reconnaissance plane over Soviet territory on May 1, 1960, and the building of the Berlin wall in August 1961 kept the tension high.

The tension was increased in the Cuban missile crisis of 1962. The crisis was caused by the Soviet attempt to install medium-range ballistic missiles in Cuba, which was detected by the United States government in October 1962. In response, President John F. Kennedy ordered a naval quarantine of Cuba and demanded the removal of the missiles. Nikita Khrushchev withdrew the missiles, and the confrontation ended.

The Cuban missile crisis demonstrated the danger involved in the continuing tension of the cold war. Since that crisis the two governments have been pursuing policies which would avoid confrontation. The establishment of a détente did not mean that the two countries had come to any agreement on the problems that had been a source of conflict during the cold war. It did, however, mean a conscious effort to improve relations and to decrease the possibility of war.

Although the arms race continued into the period of détente, several agreements and proposals for agreements have been made to limit it. On August 5, 1963, the Soviet Union, the United States, and Great Britain signed a limited nuclear Test-Ban Treaty that prohibits the testing of nuclear weapons in the atmosphere, outer space, or under water. The Treaty on the Principles Governing the Activities of States in the Exploration and Use of Outer Space, Including the Moon and Other Celestial Bodies was signed on January 27, 1967, by the same three governments. This treaty prohibits putting nuclear weapons into orbit and conducting nuclear tests on other planets or celestial bodies. In early 1970 Soviet and United States diplomats were discussing the limitation of strategic weapons.

Another important feature of relations during the period of détente was the establishment of what is popularly called the hot line, a direct line of communications between the Kremlin and the White House. This was put into operation in September 1963 in order to provide immediate communication between the leaders in the event of a crisis situation that could accidentally escalate into a war. The hot line was used when the Arab-Israeli war broke out in June 1967, and both the United States and the Soviet Union agreed that they would not intervene. Thus a confrontation was avoided in the Middle East.

Since 1963 several agreements have been signed between the Soviet Union and the United States providing for cultural, scientific, and technical exchanges. These actually provided for the continuation of a program initiated in 1958. In 1966 an agreement was signed providing for air transportation between Moscow and New York by Pan American Airways and the Soviet airline Aeroflot. Also, several scientific cooperation agreements have been signed in such fields as water desalinization and environmental control. Cooperation between the United States and the Soviet Union, in concert with sixty-eight other nations, during the International Geophysical Year brought about scientific collaboration in many areas and resulted in agreements for cooperation in Antarctica. All nations involved agreed to retain Antarctica as a militarily free zone.

Despite the areas of agreement, a vast ideological gulf remains between the two world systems. Many issues requiring resolution are stalemated because of ideological barriers.

COMMUNIST CHINA

The Soviet Union maintained what seemed to be close relations with Communist China after the rise to power of the Chinese Communist Party in October 1949. The relationship was based primarily on common ideology and on China's dependence upon the Soviet Union for economic and military aid. In the late 1950's, however, there were signs that the relationship was not developing smoothly. Friction increased in intensity until the existence of a conflict was admitted publicly by Soviet and Chinese leaders.

Ideological differences caused the initial deterioration of the Sino-Soviet friendship. Although the roots of the other areas of conflict—that is, national interest and border disputes—were always present, their development was checked by the mutual belief in a monolithic ideology. When varying interpretations of the same doctrine emerged, nothing remained to prevent other potential conflicts from erupting. Although disagreements on questions of national interest or borders have the greatest potential for leading to armed conflict, these are more easily disposable, whereas ideological differences present almost insurmountable barriers to reconciliation.

The cause of the Sino-Soviet divergence in interpreting Marxism-Leninism was probably Khrushchev's "secret speech" to the Twentieth Party Congress in 1956. In that speech, which lasted several hours, he denounced Stalin's method of rule and the cult of personality, and he also made some radical ideological pronouncements (see ch. 5, The Political System; ch. 21, Political Dynamics).

The Chinese vehemently opposed de-Stalinization for three main reasons. First, they had barely begun their industrialization and collectivization drives, which were based upon the Stalinist model. Second, there existed a cult of personality in Communist China, centering on Mao Tse-tung, the legitimacy of which, in essence, was being challenged by Khrushchev. The third reason was that the Chinese felt that the denunciation of Stalin, by extension, was a denunciation of the homeland of Marxism-Leninsim and would result in the disintegration of the unity of the Communist movement.

The ideological innovations that were promulgated by Khrushchev in 1956 also planted seeds of discord among the Chinese. The basic changes in ideology were that war was no longer to be expected and that it was possible for socialist and capitalist systems to coexist until the latter inevitably broke down. Violent revolution was no longer the sole means of overthrowing capitalism. In advanced countries, Khrushchev held, Communist victories could be achieved by political warfare, propaganda, and parliamentary means. Communism could spread to the African and Asian countries by drawing them away from the Western orbit and eventually attracting them to the Soviet orbit. The only kind of war condoned by this new ideological stance was war of liberation, Communist style, such as in Vietnam, Thailand, and Cambodia.

The foreign policy implications of these innovations were not lost on the Chinese, who favored a militant, revolutionary foreign policy. The Chinese held that the increased military and economic strength of the Soviet bloc could be used to give capitalism its final push from the stage of history. They were against the formulation that war was no longer inevitable because, among other reasons, it meant that the Soviets would not give them the military assistance necessary to regain control over Taiwan. Their reasoning proved to be correct when, in August 1958, they began a military venture against the Nationalist Chinese with renewed heavy bombardment of Quemoy and Matsu and the massing of armed forces on the coast opposite Taiwan, but the Soviets failed to provide support.

The Chinese kept their criticism to a minimum so long as the Soviet Union was providing them with economic and military aid. The Soviets, however, tried to use the extension of aid as a mechanism to control Communist China. The Chinese resisted, and the Soviets responded by first withdrawing military aid and then withdrawing economic aid in late 1960. Once the aid was withdrawn, there was no reason for the Chinese to contain their hostility toward the Soviet Union.

After the Soviets and Chinese publicly acknowledged that there were several issues upon which they held opposing views, the dispute quickly evolved into an actual split in the Communist movement. Not only did the different national Communist parties take sides, but in many cases individual parties split into pro-Soviet and pro-Chinese factions.

Initially, the causes of the break appeared to be ideological. It later became evident, however, that there were important political issues that also contributed to the rift. Indeed, the ideological issues can, in retrospect, be related to issues of power politics. The conflict has developed from one between two Communist parties to one between two of the largest countries in the world and has threatened to lead to war.

There were many underlying factors that contributed to the development of the dispute. Generally, these included different historical experiences, the different conditions under which the Communist parties came to power, and the difference in the levels of development of the Soviet Union and the People's Republic of China (Communist China). In most instances these factors combined to produce discord and, therefore, it is difficult to delineate which issues were caused by what factors.

Historically, the Chinese have viewed their own civilization as superior to all others. The humiliation that they suffered as a result of being forced to allow Western interests to develop within their borders during the nineteenth and early twentieth centuries served to intensify their feelings of nationalism and superiority.

The Sino-Soviet border disputes, which reached their most violent proportions in 1969, have roots extending back to the late 1680's, when the first armed encounter between Russian and Chinese soldiers in the Amur River valley occurred. More direct antecedents of the current border problems are the treaties that were imposed upon the imperial Chinese government by the tsarist government in the latter half of the nineteenth century. According to these treaties, Russia acquired all the territory north of the Amur River, east of the Ussuri River, and portions of what later became Soviet central Asia. In 1896 China granted Russia the right to build the Chinese Eastern Railroad across Manchuria to Vladivostok, thereby giving Russia a hold on the area. The tsars also coveted Sinkiang and Outer Mongolia and tried to increase their interests in those areas.

When the Bolsheviks came to power, however, they sought to disassociate themselves from the imperialist policies of the government that had been overthrown and, therefore, repudiated all the treaties that had been unequally weighted in favor of the tsars, as well as extralegal Russian privileges in China, including Outer Mongolia and Manchuria. This repudiation was not put into a formal document, however, and in 1921 the Red Army moved into Outer Mongolia, which had been a joint protectorate of China and Imperial Russia.

Shortly after the Communist victory in China, Mao paid his first visit to Moscow for the purpose of obtaining economic and military aid, which was vital to the survival of his regime. A thirty-year Sino-Soviet Treaty of Friendship, Alliance and Mutual Assistance was signed on February 14, 1950, but many of its provisions resembled those of the unequal treaties imposed by the tsars. Joint-stock companies were established, primarily for the benefit of the Soviet Union; major railroads were to be administered jointly; and the Soviet Union was given the privilege of maintaining naval bases at Port Arthur-Dairen.

The Chinese did not appear to object, at least publicly, to these conditions. In 1953, however, the Soviets relinquished their share in the control of the Manchurian railroads, and in 1955 they left Port

Arthur-Dairen. These actions, greatly desired by the Chinese, were probably reluctant concessions on the part of the Soviets. Furthermore, since the border issue entered into the Sino-Soviet conflict, the Soviets have pointed with great indignation to a map published by Communist China in 1954, which claims that significant portions of Soviet territory are rightfully part of China.

Althought it is the border dispute that has led to armed conflict between the Soviets and the Chinese and, consequently, has threatened to develop into a war, this aspect of the Sino-Soviet rift was one of the last to emerge. It was surfaced by Khrushchev's reply to Chinese criticism of Soviet behavior in connection with the Cuban missile crisis. In answer to the accusation of capitulating to the United States by withdrawing the missiles, Khrushchev pointed to Communist China's failure to liberate Hong Kong and Macao. The Chinese reminded the Soviet Union and her allies in early 1963 of the unequal treaties, including three which involved Russia that were still operative.

The Sino-Soviet border conflict had not been resolved by early 1970. Communist China and the Soviet Union share over 4,000 miles of frontier, and the boundary dispute had steadily escalated since 1963. Both sides encouraged their people to settle near the disputed boundaries in an effort to maintain a hold on the land that they claim. Each side also massed troops along the disputed borders, and fighting broke out in 1969.

Ostensibly, the move into Mongolia was an attempt to destroy a White Russian force that had gathered there but, in the process, a revolutionary Mongolian government was formed, and China's interests in the area were ignored. A treaty of friendship between the Bolsheviks and the Mongolian revolutionaries followed, and later the Mongolian People's Republic was established. Chinese influence in the area was effectively terminated as the new Republic assumed the role of a Soviet satellite.

When the Chinese Communist Party came to power in 1949, there were several agreements already in operation between the Soviet Union and China. For example, at the Yalta conference in 1945, Soviet rights to the Chinese Eastern Railroad, which they had sold to Japan in 1933, were restored, and they received a thirty-year lease on Port Arthur-Dairen. Provision was also made at that conference for the joint administration of all Manchurian railroads by the Soviet and Chinese governments for a period of thirty years.

The borders have been relatively quiet since talks were initiated in October 1969 between the two countries. The talks, however, seemed destined to be long and drawn out because it appeared that each side had different expectations and purposes. The Chinese seemed interested in concentrating upon settling the border issue and, apparently, viewed the 1969—70 talks as a continuation of the

496

Sino-Soviet border talks that were broken off in 1964. The Soviets, on the other hand, seemed to be demanding that all the issues of contention between the Soviet Union and Communist China be resolved by these discussions, beginning with political and ideological issues. Settlement of the ideological issues would require longer and more complicated negotiations and would postpone settlement of the most explosive issue.

VIETNAM

In early 1970 the only Communist combat operations, other than small-scale guerrilla activities, being actively supported by the Soviet Union was the conflict in Vietnam. Military and economic aid, reportedly amounting to almost R1 billion (1 ruble equals US$1.10) annually, continued to flow to North Vietnam, from which substantial quantities of military hardware were transferred to Viet Cong units in South Vietnam. Propaganda in support of the Vietnamese Communist cause, both within the Soviet Union and abroad, was plentiful and vociferous; but the actual conduct of foreign affairs appeared to follow the more moderate course of no confrontation, which had been predominant since the ouster of Khrushchev.

Although at various times the Soviet press has reported the desire on the part of Soviet personnel to volunteer for duty in Vietnam, no troops have been committed. Such press reports have been attributed by Western observers as attempts to demonstrate Moscow's leadership of the world Communist movement and to indicate its support of the interests of the peoples of Africa and Asia.

The Soviet objectives in continuing its costly aid program to North Vietnam and the Viet Cong undoubtedly involve the desires for an ultimate Communist victory and to demonstrate to the world's Communists that Moscow remains the leader of the international movement. Other important objectives are the diminution of United States influence in Southeast Asia and the concurrent prevention of the spread of Red Chinese influence. Methods of attaining these objectives without direct involvement pose difficult problems for Soviet decisionmakers; however, they continue to advocate a coalition government for South Vietnam in the apparent confidence that such a solution would eventually lead to communization.

EASTERN EUROPE

Soviet interests in Eastern Europe, like earlier tsarist interests, were based upon the desire to secure the western border against invasion and extend their influence far beyond their national borders. The central European plain had throughout history provided a corridor for invaders from the West and was the route that Hitler took in 1941. Stalin believed that the Soviet Union could not rely upon the Eastern European states to serve as allies in the event of a military threat unless these countries were ruled by Communist governments, controlled by the Soviet Union.

As the Red Army moved across Eastern Europe in pursuit of the retreating Nazis, political vacuums were created into which Soviet-trained, indigenous Communists were placed. Many of these Communists had spent the war years in Moscow receiving indoctrination designed to prepare them for roles as puppet leaders. In nearly all these countries the presence of the Red troops was the deciding factor in the establishment of the new Communist governments.

In both Albania and Yugoslavia, Communist-led partisan groups had fought concurrently against other nationalist resistance groups as well as against the Nazis. The Communists were intent on creating conditions that would prevent the return of the legal government, thus permitting them to establish postwar control by the Communist Party. The Yugoslav Communists proclaimed the existence of a provisional government in 1943, and the Albanians followed their example a few months later. When the conflict ended these governments emerged in dominant power positions.

In Albania the local Communists were able to seize control without aid from Soviet troops. In Yugoslavia the prominence achieved by the Communist-led partisans and their leader Josip Broz (Tito) permitted their takeover when Tito entered Belgrade with the advancing Soviet armies. Soviet occupation armies were not established in Albania or Yugoslavia, but the proximity of these forces in nearby countries bolstered the power of the new Communist regimes.

Communist regimes were not established in the other Eastern European countries immediately after the end of the war. Generally, there were three stages to the Sovietization process, although it was not necessary for all of the states to pass through all of the stages or to progress through each at the same speed. In the first stage a coalition was set up in which non-Communist parties were allowed to participate. Coalitions were also characteristic of the second stage, but in this case the Communists had infiltrated and established control over the nominally non-Communist parties. In the third phase all opposition was liquidated, and the country was pulled behind the Iron Curtain.

The German Democratic Republic (East Germany) was not established until 1949. Soviet troops have been stationed there since 1945, when the Allies first occupied Germany; the power of the Communist regime, headed in 1970 by Walter Ulbricht, has been largely dependent upon the presence of these troops.

After the Eastern European states were unquestionably under

Communist control, the Cominform became a mechanism through which Stalin issued directives concerning economic and political activities of these states. The primary purpose of the Cominform was to bring the so-called satellites closer together and to facilitate the establishment of political and economic conformity to Soviet plans. In essence, it was a channel through which Soviet directives could be transmitted.

Soviet policy toward its Eastern European satellites was primarily exploitative until 1953, and economic exploitation was a major cause for the Stalin-Tito split in 1948. By means of bilateral treaties, joint-stock companies, and the Council for Economic Mutual Assistance (CEMA), which was established in 1949, the Soviet Union dominated the economies of the Eastern European states. Furthermore, the Soviet Union exacted heavy reparations from those of her satellites that had been allied with the Axis powers during World War II. The resources and material goods that were extracted from the Eastern European countries were used to rebuild the war-torn Soviet economy. By the time of Stalin's death, however, the Soviets had drained Eastern Europe to the point where it had become an economic liability, that is, dependent upon subsidies from the Soviet Union (see ch. 35, Foreign Economic Relations).

Soviet-Yugoslav relations deteriorated because of economic exploitation and because Tito, the head of the Yugoslav government and Communist Party, sought to maintain an independent course while fostering the economic development of his country. Stalin, on the other hand, sought a virtual integration of all of the economies of Eastern Europe with that of the Soviet Union. Stalin's principal motives in his Eastern European dealings were the furtherance of international communism wherever possible and the expansion of Soviet power regardless. When Tito rejected Soviet demands, Stalin tried to undermine Tito's position of power but failed. Finally, on Stalin's order, Yugoslavia was expelled from the Cominform in 1948.

From the time of Stalin's death in 1953 until 1956, Moscow's hold over its satellites began to relax. The Eastern European regimes were encouraged to institute economic reforms, so that their economies could be rehabilitated and their dependence upon Soviet subsidies diminished. During this period, however, Soviet political controls remained in effect, and Stalinism was still the method of rule.

The de-Stalinization process, which Khrushchev initiated in 1956, had a profound impact upon the Soviet bloc. It resulted in the decline of the satellite status of the Eastern European countries and the reemergence of nationalism. Once Stalinism was discredited, the national factions of the Communist parties began to assert themselves. Eventually, with the exception of Ulbricht in East Germany, the leaders who had been interned in Moscow during the war were deposed, and the national Communists assumed leadership positions in their countries (see ch. 21, Political Dynamics).

During Khrushchev's speech to the Twentieth Party Congress, in which he denounced Stalin, the idea was articulated that all countries did not have to follow the same path in building communism and that national differences must be considered. He failed to explicate how much divergence would be tolerated, however, and this only became clear in the fall of 1956. At that time Soviet troops were sent into Hungary to put down a popular uprising against the Stalinist regime headed by Ernö Gerö. The alternative desired by the Hungarian people was neutralism in foreign policy and nationalism in domestic policy, but Soviet troops crushed the revolt and installed a Kremlin-approved government.

In the process of partially relaxing its hold on Eastern Europe, the Soviet Union was forced to relinquish the dictatorial, terroristic methods used by Stalin. Riots in Poland, which followed the initiation of de-Stalinization, were terminated by negotiation, but the situation in Hungary threatened Soviet hegemony in the entire area. The Hungarians wanted to withdraw from the Warsaw Pact and allow the formation of non-Communist political parties, measures that the Soviets would not tolerate. Internal reforms by the Czechoslovaks in 1967 and 1968 also provoked a Soviet invasion.

The events in Poland and Hungary in 1956 demonstrated to the Soviet leaders that nationalism in Eastern Europe could be held in check only by the use of military force. Rather than pursue such a policy, the Soviet leaders decided to become more permissive in Eastern European affairs, provided developments remained within the framework of communism. Soviet army divisions remained in East Germany, Hungary, Poland and, after 1968, in Czechoslovakia. When the Sino-Soviet conflict became public, the Soviet leaders seemed to be willing to make greater concessions to the Eastern European states in exchange for their support of the Soviet position of authority in the world Communist movement vis-à-vis the Chinese. The only country that left the Soviet bloc other than Yugoslavia was Albania, which allied itself with Communist China about 1960.

There was also an apparent relationship between the relaxation of control over Eastern Europe and the rapprochement between the Soviet Union and Yugoslavia, which was first initiated by Khrushchev in 1955. The doctrine of "separate paths to socialism," which Khrushchev expounded upon in his speech to the Twentieth Party Congress, was actually part of what the Stalinists pejoratively had referred to as Titoism. Khrushchev also dissolved the Cominform in April 1956, a gesture that only held symbolic significance because it had long before ceased to be a viable organization.

500

After 1956 the role of the Eastern European states in CEMA and the Warsaw Treaty Organization, commonly referred to as the Warsaw Pact, began to increase, and summit meetings of Communist parties were held periodically. The function of these states became more than the mere endorsement of Soviet proposals, although it is difficult to ascertain exactly how much influence they have on policymaking.

The amount of influence that an Eastern European country can exert upon the policy formulation of CEMA or the Warsaw Pact probably depends upon the issue and its relationship to Soviet national interests. Thus, Rumania was able to oppose successfully the Soviet proposal to CEMA that it adopt a policy of "socialist division of labor." Such a policy would have prevented Rumania from industrializing its economy and was not vitally important to the Soviet economy. On the other hand, there is evidence that East Germany played an important role in formulating the decision for the Warsaw Pact nations to invade Czechoslovakia in August 1968. Both East Germany and the Soviet Union apparently feared the possibility of the spillover of Czechoslovak liberalization across their borders.

Throughout the 1960's Rumania had been pursuing an increasingly independent foreign policy. Although at times this was embarrassing to the Soviet Union, relatively little pressure was applied to make Rumanian foreign policy conform to that of the Soviet Union. On the other hand, the direction taken by the Czechoslovak foreign policy—specifically, the increased relations with the Federal Republic of Germany (West Germany)—was one of the reasons given to justify the invasion of Czechoslovakia by the Warsaw Pact nations.

The crucial differences between the Rumanian and the Czechoslovak cases were the domestic political developments of these two countries and their geographic positions. These differences, in turn, gained additional significance when the domestic problems of the Soviet Union were considered.

Rumania and Czechoslovakia share borders with the Soviet Union, but Czechoslovakia also shares one with West Germany, whereas Rumania is surrounded by Communist states. For this reason, the Soviet leaders perceived the increase in Czechoslovak-West German relations as more threatening than Rumanian-West German relations in terms of dismantling the buffer that shields the Soviet Union from the West.

In addition to the geographic threat, the Czechoslovak spirit of liberalization contained the danger of spreading to other East European Communist states as well as to areas within the Soviet Union itself. The Soviet leadership evidently decided that Czechoslovak internal reforms and improved relations with the West constituted a threat to its position throughout Eastern Europe. In addition, Czechoslovakia is contiguous to the Ukrainian Soviet Socialist Republic, and the fear of liberalization spreading to the Ukraine may also have been a factor behind the decision to intervene.

Although the Rumanians asserted their national interests in the sphere of international relations, internally they maintained a strict, authoritarian Communist regime. The political atmosphere in Rumania was conservative. In Czechoslovakia, with a democratic tradition dating back to 1918, broad, liberalizing reforms were instituted concurrent with the increase of relations with the West. The reform program had a resemblance to Western-style democracy, and it appeared that that was where the liberalizing process would lead. The first step was the abolishment of censorship, which resulted in criticism of the Soviet Union and the call by Czechoslovak intellectuals for the establishment of a multiparty system.

There are parallels between the situation in Hungary in 1956 and that in Czechoslovakia in 1968 that suggest the limit to which the states of Eastern Europe may pursue independent policies. Beyond this limit, the Soviet Union has used its military power to maintain its sphere of influence. In both Hungary and Czechoslovakia the monopoly of political power held by the Communist Party was threatened as a result of liberalization. Other Eastern European countries have instituted reforms that relaxed the political and social atmospheres but not to the extent that the Communist leadership might lose control.

From the military security point of view, both Hungary and Czechoslovakia border on the Ukraine and are also contiguous to the non-Communist countries of Austria and West Germany, respectively. Hungary tried to withdraw from the Warsaw Pact in 1956 and, although Czechoslovakia only proposed that the pact be revised, the Soviet military leaders seemed to have perceived the eventuality of a similar threat—that is, the disruption of the military alliance system.

In September 1968 *Pravda* published an article in which the Soviet policy toward Eastern Europe was stated and the invasion of Czechoslovakia justified. The doctrine put forth in this article came to be known in the West as the Brezhnev Doctrine, or the Doctrine of Limited Sovereignty. The essence of the doctrine is that, although the individual socialist states are free to formulate policies in accordance with their cultural and economic differences, they are not free to pursue policies that might hinder the development or security of communism either in their own country or in the other socialist states. When the development of communism is threatened, it is the duty of the other socialist states to intervene on behalf of the international Communist movement. Some Soviet theorists have extended the doctrine to include intervention in the internal affairs of nonruling Communist parties by the CPSU if ideological deviation is suspected.

Although the Soviet Union was able to arrest the liberalization of Czechoslovakia and to maintain its strategic position in Eastern Europe, it paid the price of losing some of its credibility as the vanguard of the international Communist movement. The invasion of Czechoslovakia demonstrated to the Communist parties throughout the world that when Soviet national interests come into conflict with those of world communism, the latter will be subordinated to the former. The military intervention evoked criticism against the Soviet Union not only from Communist China, Albania, Yugoslavia, and Rumania but also from the French and Italian Communist parties, which were the strongest Communist parties in the West.

WESTERN EUROPE

Soviet relations with Western Europe after World War II were dominated by the cold war. The Western European countries were highly dependent upon the United States for economic and political assistance in their recovery from the war. In addition, they were dependent upon American military assistance to protect their security against Communist expansion. Consequently, Soviet-West European relations were overshadowed by those between the Soviet Union and the United States.

In the 1960's, however, Soviet relations with the countries of Western Europe began to increase, facilitated by two developments in the international arena. The first was the establishment of the détente between the Soviet Union and the United States. The second development was the relaxation of Soviet control over Eastern Europe and the relaxed attitudes of some of the Western European partners in NATO.

Soviet interests in Western Europe after World War II centered on the fear of Germany, based on the experience of two world wars, and the desire to prevent the reemergence of Germany as an industrial and military power. With Europe prostrate and the Soviet Union emerging as the only military power on the continent, there was also the possibility of spreading Soviet hegemony across all of Europe. From the Western viewpoint, the rapid communization of Eastern Europe, plus the maintenance by the Soviet Union of powerful armies throughout the area, constituted a threat to all of Western Europe. The fear of Germany, combined with the possibility of a Soviet Europe, clearly delineated Stalin's ultimate objectives as being the elimination of United States influence, the disintegration of NATO, and the prevention of German reunification.

In the mid-1960's the Soviet Union began to intensify its pursuit of trade and cultural relations with the governments of Western

Europe, in an effort to spread its influence through normal channels. Concurrently, United States influence began to decline, and President Charles de Gaulle of France began to weaken NATO by demanding that it withdraw from French territory. In August 1968, while the NATO members were negotiating the revision of the NATO agreement and were reducing its forces, the Soviet Union, along with four other Warsaw Pact members, invaded Czechoslovakia. The consequence of this event was the general agreement among NATO members, including France, that the alliance must be strengthened rather than weakened.

Although the invasion of Czechoslovakia provoked indignation in the West and revitalized NATO, diplomatic, trade, and cultural relations between the Soviet Union and Western Europe continued. In 1969 the Soviet Union increased its overtures toward the Western European nations. A special effort was made to initiate the normalization of relations with West Germany. In October 1969 the West German Social Democratic Party, whose platform included improving East-West relations, won the national elections, and Willy Brandt became chancellor. At the beginning of 1970 talks were being held between Bonn and Moscow to explore the possibilities of an accommodation.

The prospects seemed good for some measure of agreement between the two governments. For example, the Soviet government softened its demand that Bonn formally recognize East Germany. Although Brandt refused to give formal recognition, he indicated a willingness to give East Germany de facto recognition. Bonn also indicated that it might recognize the Oder-Neisse line as the western border of Poland. The settlement of these two points could ease some of the tension between the Soviet Union and the West. The prospects of settling the Berlin issue were much dimmer; such a settlement would require an agreement between the Soviet Union, the United States, France, and Great Britain. Any accommodation between the Soviet Union and West Germany would undoubtedly require the latter to totally renounce any intention to arm itself with nuclear weapons.

It is the opinion of many Western observers that the Soviet effort to reconcile its differences with West Germany, and the West in general, was conditioned by its increasingly tense relations with Communist China. Throughout its history the Soviet Union has been afraid of the prospect of having to fight a two-front war. Therefore, it is reasoned that the possibility of war with Communist China, combined with the fear of West Germany's acquiring nuclear weapons, motivated the Soviet leaders to improve relations with West Germany. If this were accomplished, the Soviet Union would be able to turn more of its attention to the China problem.

Another motivating factor for Soviet overtures to Bonn is economic. The West German economy has been expanding rapidly, and an increase of Soviet-West German trade would be beneficial to the Soviet Union (see ch. 35, Foreign Economic Relations).

The Soviet Union in early 1970 continued to call for a conference on European security, in which the states of both Eastern and Western Europe would participate. Initially, the United States was not to be included in the conference but, in January 1970, an official of the Ministry of Foreign Affairs said that the Soviets favored United States participation. He also stated that the Berlin issue would not be included on the agenda. The implications of such a conference, if one were held, might be the stabilization of the division of Europe and de facto recognition of East Germany.

THE ARAB STATES

At the beginning of 1970 the Soviet Union maintained very close ties with several states of the Arab world, primarily the United Arab Republic (UAR), Syria, Iraq, and Yemen. In addition, it maintained diplomatic relations with Algeria, Lebanon, Tunisia, Sudan, Libya, Morocco, Kuwait, and Jordan, but interaction varied from simple trade relations to the granting of military aid.

Soviet policy has met with considerable success in the Middle East, and Soviet influence has grown steadily since the Soviet Union first became active in the area in the mid-1950's. By extending military and economic aid, the Soviet Union was able to virtually eliminate Western influence in the majority of the Arab States. Even more importantly, the Soviet Union has acquired naval bases on the Mediterranean, an objective that was also sought by the Soviet predecessors, the tsars. Fleet units have also shown the flag, for the first time in Soviet history, in the Red Sea, the Gulf of Aden, the Persian Gulf, and the Indian Ocean.

The development of relations with the Arab States clearly demonstrates the flexibility of the Soviet Union in the tactical application of pragmatic and ideological means in achieving its immediate goals of increased power and influence. Even though, with the exception of Israel, the Communist parties in the Middle East have been outlawed for several years, this fact has not inhibited the increasing support the Soviet Union has provided the Arab States. Occasionally, Communists have been admitted into the cabinets of Iraq and Syria for brief periods, depending upon who was in power at a given time. The political situations in these countries are subject to sudden reversals, however, and the Soviets have found it more profitable to maintain relations on a government-to-government level.

Initially, the Soviet Union was able to get a foothold in the Middle East because in the mid-1950's several Arab states were seeking economic and military support that would not contain the conditional provisions that usually accompanied such support from Western powers. They evidently hoped that the alternative source of aid promised by the Soviet bloc would enable them to pursue a policy of political neutralism or nonalignment.

The extension of large quantities of military and economic aid to the Arab States, however, has actually made those states increasingly dependent upon the Soviet Union. In addition to machinery, plants, and military hardware, the recipient nations also admitted large numbers of Soviet technicians and advisers to assist in the training of indigenous technicians and military personnel. With the influx of military and other Communist-manufactured equipment, the Arab States also became dependent upon the donor nations for spare parts. In the on-going process of receiving aid and assistance from the Soviet Union and the Eastern European Communist states, the Arab countries increasingly isolated themselves from contact with many Western nations.

As of January 1970 Soviet military support of the Arabs included flying operational missions on behalf of the Egyptians against the Israelis and supplying pilots, technicians, and advisers as well as advanced technological and military equipment. When the conflict between Israel and her Arab neighbors escalated into a war in June 1967, the Soviet Union had restricted its support to the political arena because of the desire to avoid the possibility of a military confrontation with the West.

The Soviet Union repeatedly condemned Israel as an aggressor and consistently supported the Arab States' position in the United Nations. In essence, their position is that Israel must be forced to withdraw from all of the territory that it occupied during the June 1967 war, a position adopted by the United Nations on November 22, 1967.

The consequence of the Arab defeat by the Israelis was the ultimate strengthening of the Soviet position in the Middle East. The defeat of its client states, Syria and the UAR, was at first an embarrassment to the Soviet Union; but the concurrent drop in United States influence and prestige in the area, aided by massive doses of Communist propaganda, plus the rapid moves to rebuild the destroyed forces, served to eventually enhance the Soviet position. As a result of the Arab military loss and the self-imposed isolation from the West, those states were dependent upon the Soviet Union for replacement of their military equipment and for incrased subsidies to their economies.

The Soviet pursuit of economic interests concurrent with power-political interests and the French attempts to regain influence, particularly in the Arab states of North Africa, have led to various conflicts of interest and some tension in the area. For example,

Algeria, which the Soviet Union studiously courted for several years, was definitely disturbed by Soviet price cutting to gain a contract for the supply of natural gas to Italy, at the end of 1969, a contract that the Algerians desperately wanted and needed. At about the same time, Algeria and France renewed a treaty of friendship and economic cooperation that could intrude upon Soviet-Algerian relations. These events have not caused a rift between the Soviet Union and Algeria, but there is some evidence of strain in the relationship.

TURKEY, IRAN, AND AFGHANISTAN

Soviet policy toward its southern neighbors—Turkey, Iran, and Afghanistan—is the establishment and maintenance of friendly relations. Afghanistan has a neutralist government, which consistently has maintained good relations with the Soviet Union. Since 1954 the Soviet Union has extended economic aid to Afghanistan, which has been the recipient of the third largest amount of such aid.

Until the mid-1960's Turkey and Iran were suspicious of the Soviet Union because of the long historical tradition of Russian encroachment and designs on their territories. As a result, both had joined the Western alliance systems: Turkey as a member of both NATO and the Central Treaty Organization (CENTO), and Iran as a member of the latter. Since 1965 Soviet leaders have actively sought to neutralize Turkey and Iran, and both countries responded positively without, however, withdrawing from the alliances. Turkey and Iran began adopting nonaligned policies concurrently with the acceptance of Soviet economic aid during the late 1960's, although both remain members of Western alliances. Iran also concluded a multimillion-dollar arms aid agreement with the Soviet Union in 1967 despite the continuing close relationship between Iran and the United States.

In early 1970 the only tie between the Soviet Union and her southern neighbors was economic, with the exception of the one military aid agreement with Iran. Politically, Iran and Turkey were maintaining an informal position of neutrality vis-á-vis the Soviet Union. The formal ties with the Western alliance systems were still in effect. Afghanistan continued to pursue a policy of neutralism.

The invasion of Czechoslovakia in August 1968, as well as the Soviet naval buildup in the Mediterranean, which began immediately before the Arab-Israeli war of 1967, reawakened the suspicion of Soviet intentions and the fear of Soviet aggression. The governments of Iran and Turkey, however, kept their neutralist foreign policies and maintained normal relations with the Soviet Union. In return for their neutrality, Soviet propaganda assured them that the Soviet Union would not violate the principle of nonintervention.

OTHER ASIAN AND AFRICAN COUNTRIES

At the end of World War II, colonial empires began to collapse, and many colonies were granted independence by the Western powers. The Soviet Union, under Stalin, failed to recognize the significance of this phenomenon. Stalin continued to adhere to the view that the world was divided into socialist and capitalist camps, a viewpoint that precluded the possibility of some countries existing outside the spheres of influence of the Soviet Union and the capitalist powers. Thus, he did not believe that the new formed states of Africa and Asia were actually independent of their former colonial masters.

After Stalin's death, however, there was a radical shift in Soviet policy toward African and Asian countries. The minimum objective sought was the decrease and eventual elimination of Western influence and the establishment of Soviet presence in the area. Once this was accomplished, the Soviets hoped to foster pro-Soviet attitudes and, ultimately, the acquisition of power by local Communist parties. The priorities given to these objectives, however, were altered considerably after about fifteen years of economic, political, and cultural relations with these countries.

Although the Soviet leaders continued to speak in ideological terms, the goal of fostering the establishment of Communist regimes in Africa and Asia appeared to be less important than undermining Western influence at the beginning of 1970. Soviet relations with African and Asian states became increasingly pragmatic, stressing more the political and economic considerations than the ideological.

The most important mechanism by which Soviet objectives were pursued was that of granting military and economic aid. By extending aid to the countries of Africa and Asis and also by establishing trade relations with them, the Soviets were able to decrease the economic dependence of these countries upon the West, thereby making the political alternative of neutralism viable.

Since 1954 Soviet activities in Africa and Asia have steadily increased. In their effort to undermine Western influence, the Soviets played upon the anticolonial sentiments of the people who inhabit these areas by discrediting the motivations of Western aid policies. While describing Western policy as neocolonial, Soviet leaders stressed the fact that the Soviet Union did not participate in the scramble for colonies, as the Western powers had done. They also reiterated the constant propaganda line that, contrary to Western policy, they did not attach political strings to their aid (see ch. 35, Foreign Economic Relations).

Once the Soviet Union had succeeded in penetrating the African and Asian continents economically, it began to establish political and ideological influence as well. With respect to the internal developments of the countries of Africa and Asia, under Khrushchev the political objective was to encourage the socialist and communist predisposition of many leaders of these countries—that is, nationalization of industries and resources, land reform, and centralized planning. This goal was pursued by directing economic aid primarily to the government-controlled industrial sectors of the economies of these countries. Technicians and advisers were also sent to train local personnel, and many people from Africa and Asia were invited to study in the Soviet Union.

With respect to the foreign policies toward these countries, the Soviet leaders' objectives were to deny the Western powers the resources and markets to be found in Africa and Asia. Even more important, from the point of view of military security, was the Soviet goal of disrupting the Western alliance systems.

The Sino-Soviet conflict provided an additional dimension to Soviet policy in Africa and Asia during the 1960's. The Soviet Union found itself competing with Communist China as well as the West. In the late 1960's, however, the Chinese support of revolutionary groups in Africa and Asia damaged its relations with the governments of some of these countries, while the Soviets, in many cases, successfully pursued state-to-state relations.

Asia

The Sino-Soviet conflict was a significant determinant of Soviet policy in Asia at the beginning of 1970. When Soviet foreign policy first shifted toward active relations with the Asian countries, its primary objective was to counter Western influence and eventually eliminate it. In the mid-1960's, however, the Chinese dimension was added, and the immediate objective of preventing Communist Chinese expansion appeared to have been given the highest priority.

In early 1970 the Soviet Union was seeking to maintain good diplomatic and trade relations with Asian states, regardless of their governments' attitudes toward indigenous Communist parties. Brezhnev in June 1969 expressed the desire to establish an Asian collective security system, assumed in the West to be a policy to contain Communist Chinese expansion. Concurrent with efforts to improve relations with the Asian states, however, the Soviet Union has been playing upon their traditional fear of Chinese imperialism.

The shift in emphasis of policy toward the Asian states became evident in the mid-1960's when the Soviet Union took a neutral position on the Indo-Pakistani conflict over Kashmir. Previously, under Khrushchev, the Soviet Union had supported the Indian position against Pakistan. In January 1966 Premier Kosygin invited the leaders of Pakistan and India to the Soviet city of Tashkent, where he successfully mediated their immediate conflict. The so-called Tashkent Agreement was a major diplomatic achievement for the Soviet Union.

The Soviets began to make overtures of friendship to Pakistan in the mid-1960's for two reasons. First, they wanted to draw Pakistan away from its military alliance with the West, as a member of CENTO. Second, they wanted to prevent Communist China, which had supported the Pakistani military venture in Kashmir, from becoming influential in Pakistan. Thus, in the late 1960's the Soviet Union began extending military and economic aid to Pakistan.

The close economic, political, and cultural ties between the Soviet Union and India, maintained since the early 1950's, continued despite the Soviet change in policy toward Pakistan. Indian national interests have coincided to some extent with those of the Soviet Union, which makes cooperation between the two countries desirable. From the time that India was granted independence by Great Britain, its government has consistently pursued a policy of neutralism and has been hostile to the regional military pacts created by the Western powers. That India has a system of central economic planning was another point in favor of cooperation with the Soviet Union. From the Soviet perspective, an additional factor favoring close relations was that India was one of the few countries in the world where a Communist Party has come to power by election, if only on the local level. Fear of Chinese expansionist activities was also a compelling force for the maintenance of good relations between the Soviet Union and India.

At the beginning of 1970, Indian neutralism actually had a bias favoring the Soviet Union, although India also maintained good relations with the Western nations. Evidence of this bias was seen by Western observers in Prime Minister Indira Ghandi's failure to condemn the invasion of Czechoslovakia and in her mentioning, at the end of 1969, that India was considering establishing full diplomatic relations with East Germany and North Vietnam. India also supported the Soviet-backed Arab position against Israel. The most significant evidence, however, was India's endorsement of Brezhnev's proposal for the establishment of an Asian collective security system, although Indian policy traditionally had prohibited membership in military pacts.

Japan is another nation from which the Soviets sought active participation in its proposed Asian security system. It is believed that the Soviet Union hopes that eventually India and Japan will be able to carry most of the burden in containing Communist Chinese expansion, thereby minimizing the diversion of Soviet economic and military resources to the Far East and allowing the Soviet Union to concentrate on its interests in Europe and other parts of the world.

510

Soviet-Japanese relations in early 1970, however, contained elements of tension, which stem back to the hostility and fear produced by the Japanese defeat of the Russians in the Russo-Japanese War at the turn of the twentieth century. Throughout the history of Soviet foreign policy, Japan has been a factor to be considered in preserving the security of the Soviet Union. Thus, in April 1941 the Soviets signed a neutrality pact with Japan, providing not only for nonaggression between them but also nonaggression by either party in the event of an attack by a third party. The nonaggression pact secured the Soviet Far East and avoided a two-front conflict during four years of war against the Nazis.

At the end of 1969 Japan was still a source of concern for the Soviet leaders. In the campaign for the national elections of that country, the issue of regaining territory lost at the end of World War II was highlighted. An agreement was reached between the United States and Japan providing for the return of Okinawa in exchange for the right of the United States to continue to maintain military bases on Japanese territory. This agreement evoked criticism from the Soviet leaders, who described it as a "dangerous military alliance."

The Japanese interpretation of the Soviet reaction was that the Kremlin was trying to divert Japanese attention from the issue of the Kurile Islands, the southern portion of which the Soviet Union seized at the end of World War II. In late 1969 the Japanese government presented its claim to the Kurile Islands to Premier Kosygin. His response was that the Soviet Union had to retain possession of the islands in order to maintain the balance of power in the Pacific and the Far East.

Soviet-Japanese relations are also related to the issue of Korea. The Soviet Union has tried to maintain close ties with North Korea because of their common ideology and also to prevent the Chinese from becoming too influential in that country. The Japanese, however, maintain good relations with South Korea. The Soviet criticism of the Japanese-United States agreement, therefore, might have been partly a political gesture to North Korea, which has been maintaining increasingly warm relations with Communist China. Furthermore, in discussing the possibility of Japanese participation in the Asian collective security system, Soviet diplomats left the door open to the possibility of both North Korean and South Korean participation.

Africa

Although Soviet policy in Africa achieved some successes under Khrushchev, it also suffered setbacks. Initially, although objectives were basically power-political, Soviet leaders viewed Africa within an ideological framework. They extended aid without considering economic, social, and climatic factors and, consequently, in some instances met with disastrous results.

Under Brezhnev and Kosygin, Soviet policy toward Africa has been based more upon pragmatic considerations. They avoided earlier mistakes and tailored their programs to existing conditions. Trade and aid relations with the African states at the beginning of 1970 were businesslike and based upon more practical foundations. For example, Soviet exports became more competitive in quality with goods available from other countries (see ch. 35, Foreign Economic Relations).

The Soviet objective in Africa in early 1970 was to maintain good relations with existing governments wherever possible, regardless of political orientations. The Soviet Union did not appear to be supporting movements that were trying to overthrow the established governments. A striking example of this orientation in Soviet foreign relations was military support of the Nigerian federal government against insurgent Biafra. Indeed, a Nigerian government official said that Soviet military aid was decisive in the defeat of Biafra.

The Soviet Union was supporting African liberation movements in areas that were still under colonial rule. Their aid, however, was channeled through the Organization of African United (OAU). Soviet relations with the OAU were partly determined by Chinese competition. By channeling aid to the national liberation movements through the OAU, the Soviets hoped to counter Chinese influence within that organization.

LATIN AMERICA

At the beginning of 1970 the Soviet Union maintained diplomatic relations with all of the Latin American countries except Paraguay and Venezuela. The Soviet policy was to maintain good state-to-state relations and increase trade relations with the countries of Latin America. Its primary objective in pursuing this policy was to foster political neutralism. The Soviet Union did not appear to be supporting the guerrilla movements that were active in Latin America, but they did support the legal parties that were anti-American in orientation, which, in turn, assisted guerrilla movements.

Cuba was the only Latin American country over which the Soviet Union had political influence in early 1970. This situation was primarily the result of the economic dependence of Cuba on the Soviet Union, caused by the economic sanctions initiated against it by the United States and the Organization of American States (OAS).

When Fidel Castro came to power in January 1959, he established a Communist regime without the direct aid of the Soviet Union. Consequently, Soviet influence was not the result of political dependence, as had been the case in Eastern Europe. Cuba temporarily sided with the Chinese on ideological points in the Sino-Soviet conflict when Soviet and Cuban interests clashed over the issue of exporting revolution throughout Latin America. Cuban militancy on that point has been disquieting to the Soviet leaders, who are trying to improve their relations with existing Latin American governments.

The Chinese, however, did not have the economic capability to provide the badly needed subsidies to the Cuban economy. The economic situation has become increasingly serious and, consequently, Cuba's dependence upon the Soviet Union has grown. Cuba actually became an economic liability to the Soviet Union, which at the end of 1969 was reportedly providing more than the equivalent of US$1 million worth of economic aid daily.

Apparently, the Soviet leaders did not feel that the price was too high for their political gains. Such aid was preserving a Communist foothold in the Western Hemisphere which, in power-political terms, means Soviet presence in the area. In July 1969 a naval task force from the Soviet Union visited Cuba—the first official appearance of such a force in this hemisphere.

The extension of large quantities of aid has also enhanced Soviet ideological influence over Cuba. The Cubans seemed to have toned down their militancy concerning the spread of revolution throughout Latin America although Castro periodically reiterates his call for revolution. The Cubans also ceased to support the Chinese in the ideological dimension of the Sino-Soviet conflict.

INTERNATIONAL ORGANIZATIONS

The Soviet Union was one of the original signatories of the United Nations Charter and is a permanent member of the United Nations, its Security Council, and most of its specialized agencies. When the United Nations was first established in 1945, Stalin viewed it as an organization designed to further Western interests but joined in order to prevent it from being used against the Soviet Union. From its inception until Stalin's death, Soviet activity in the United Nations consisted primarily of use of the veto in the Security Council.

In 1953 the United Nations became an instrument of Soviet foreign policy toward Africa and Asia. It was in the framework of the United Nations that the Soviet Union began its courtship of these countries. This was initiated by the announcement of a R 4-million contribution by the Soviet government to the Expanded Program of Technical Assistance, a program respected by the governments of

African and Asian countries. By initially distributing aid through the United Nations, the Soviets gained the credibility of these governments, and the way was opened for bilateral aid agreements.

In early 1970 the United Nations served as an additional instrument of diplomacy to gain support for Soviet views on international questions and in the maintenance of state-to-state relations with most countries of the world. The Soviet Union also used the United Nations as a propaganda forum in which to encourage neutralism, or nonalignment, and to give political support to the African and Asian countries. Participation in the various organizations of the United Nations was also used as a means of expanding Soviet influence (see ch. 35, Foreign Economic Relations).

The Soviet Union was also a founding member of CEMA and the Warsaw Pact. CEMA, the multilateral economic alliance between the countries of Eastern Europe, Mongolia, and the Soviet Union, was established in 1949. The Warsaw Pact, a military alliance of the same nations with the exception of Mongolia, was founded in 1955. Both organizations have headquarters in Moscow (see ch. 28, The Armed Forces; ch. 35, Foreign Economic Relations).

CHAPTER 25

PUBLIC INFORMATION

All aspects of the mass communications media were highly developed in early 1970. Although the press and radio were in the forefront, the television industry was rapidly expanding and had assumed a place of importance among the other media. The overall communication network was spread across the vast territory of the country, linking the most remote outlying regions with the capital.

In early 1970 there were over 8,000 newspapers, with an annual circulation of nearly 24 billion copies, and almost 5,000 periodicals, with more than 1.5 billion copies per year. Approximately 980 radio stations broadcast to an estimated 76.8 million radio receivers. There were also 890 television stations, including relay stations, and an estimated 23 million receivers.

The media of mass communication are an indispensable adjunct to the Party and the government bureaucracies. They play an extremely important role in the implementation of official policies and the achievement of official goals.

All newspapers, periodicals, printing establishments, and paper industries were nationalized by the Bolsheviks after they seized power. The leaders encountered some difficulty with the motion picture industry, however, because cinema is an art form as well as a medium of mass communication. It was not until the 1930's, when all creative arts came under strict Party control, that the cinema finally became another instrument of propaganda. Throughout the Soviet era, private ownership and private operation of the press, radio, television, and the cinema have been prohibited. The Party, government, or subsidiary organizations own and operate all media and carefully supervise administration and content.

The development of the means of mass communication has always been given high priority, because the ruling elite recognized the value of the mass media for political indoctrination. Thus, early in the history of the Soviet state, press and broadcasting facilities were extended to the regions beyond Russia proper. Newspapers soon appeared in many of the minority languages, and multilingual broadcasts were heard.

The information aspect of the mass media is not stressed except to further the aims of the Communist Party and the Soviet state. Rather, the media serve as means to communicate policies, interpretations, and directives to the masses and to maximize support for the regime. The content of the media largely consists of official pronouncements, speeches, commentaries on events, and glorification of the achievements of various enterprises. When current events are covered, it is in such a way as to make the Soviet system appear superior to other economic and political systems. Even when the media present entertainment, there is an undercurrent of pro-Communist propaganda.

GOVERNMENT AND FREEDOM OF THE PRESS

According to Article 125 of the 1936 Constitution, freedom of the press is guaranteed to Soviet citizens, but the definition of freedom of the press and the principles behind it are different from those generally understood in democratic countries of the West. The statement of this freedom is prefaced in Article 125 by the phrase, "in conformity with the interests of the working people, and in order to strengthen the socialist system." This phrase is the key to the Soviet concept of freedom of the press. According to Soviet ideology, freedom of the press means freedom from the control of the press by the rich, as in so-called bourgeois societies, and freedom from the individualism manifested in the press of capitalist countries. According to Marxism-Leninism, the interests of the proletariat are central to everything in a socialist society. Therefore, the press must be related to the furtherance of socialist development and can only be free insofar as it is connected with the working class.

The best indication of the official attitude toward the press is found in the words of the Communist leaders from 1917 to 1969. Lenin in 1917 said, "It is necessary to shut down the bourgeois counterrevolutionary newspapers, to confiscate their printing establishments." Ten years later Stalin issued a definition of freedom of the press that has been clung to doggedly through the years: "If it is a question of freedom of the press for the bourgeoisie then freedom of the press does not and will not exist here as long as the dictatorship of the proletariat is the power." Khrushchev at the height of his power declared, "Just as an army cannot fight without weapons, so the Party cannot successfully carry out its ideological work without such a sharp and militant weapon as the press." Finally, a *Pravda* editorial on Soviet Press Day (May 5, 1969) stated, "The press is called upon to actively educate the working people in the spirit of Communist conviction, Soviet patriotism, proletarian internationalism, and implacability toward hostile ideology."

The view of the press and other media of communications as tools of ideology demands that censorship be a necessary function of both the Party and the government. In 1922 the Main Administration for Literary and Publishing Affairs, subordinated to the People's Commissariat of Education, was established to perform the censorship function. From the Russian words *glavny* (main) and *literaturny* (literary), the acronym *Glavlit* was coined and, despite changes in subordination and function, it has remained the title of the censorship board ever since.

Originally, Glavlit was to ensure that the press printed only ideologically suitable materials and was to prevent publication of information that would jeopardize the state either militarily or economically. This function was carried out by reviewing manuscripts and press reports both before and after publication. All printed materials were given numbers indicating Glavlit approval.

The jurisdiction of Glavlit was greatly limited from the outset, however, rendering it less important than informal means of censorship. Certain publishing houses have always been exempt from prepublication review by Glavlit. For example, the editors of the Unified State Publishing House, in existence from 1930 to 1949, supervised the prepublication censorship in the materials they published. The publishing house for the Communist Party of the Soviet Union (CPSU), is also exempt from control by Glavlit. *Izvestia,* which is the official government newspaper and has one of the largest circulations in the Soviet Union, is also outside Glavlit's jurisdiction.

Effective censorship is implemented through the innate system of control, or supervision, found within the Communist Party, in the relationship between the Party and the government, and in the government itself. Most newspaper editors, journalists, publishing house administrators and editors, and directors of news agencies are members of the Party. Before a person may be appointed to such a position, he must have given evidence of loyalty to the Party and demonstrated a clear understanding of Marxist-Leninist ideology.

Training programs for editors and journalists are more concerned with political and ideological indoctrination than with technical competence. These training courses are either run by the Party directly, or their curricula are set forth in Party directives. Thus journalists and editors are aware of the ideological framework within which they must work. They have been taught what is considered news and how it should be presented and what is proper for publication in periodicals and books. In this manner, censorship is present at the very first stages of the publication process.

The CPSU often issues regulations concerning the amount of coverage to be given to various topics found in the press as well as the number of newspapers to be published. The number of people employed in a publishing enterprise and the organization of the press are also decreed by the Party. The Department of Agitation and Propaganda (Agitprop), which is under the Central Committee of the CPSU, ensures that the directives are fulfilled. The Press

Sector of Agitprop controls all aspects of the press and is organized to correspond to the organization of newspapers throughout the country. Its hierarchical structure extends all the way down to the supervision of the local press. Press control is coordinated through reports from lower to higher levels and through conferences. Agitprop also has sectors covering television, radio, and films that operate in a similar fashion (see ch. 26, Agitation and Propaganda).

The Party, state, or subsidiary organizations own and operate all of the communications facilities. It is through these bodies that the mass media are supplied with the necessary equipment and funds for operation. Furthermore, printing presses and duplicating machines must be registered with the police, and the government is the only source of newsprint in the country. Dependence of the mass media upon the government and the Party is absolute and ensures subservience in matters of content.

Glavlit is the least important of the instruments of censorship. All publications do go through that agency for postpublication examination, after which a Glavlit number is assigned, but this process is merely to ensure that no state secrets are published. Under Stalin, this agency was much more active, but after his death the responsibility for prepublication censorship became increasingly less formal. Although the acronym *Glavlit* is still in common usage, the actual title of the organization was changed to the Main Administration for the Protection of Military and State Secrets from the Press, which designates the function of the agency. Glavlit also exercises a measure of control over the film industry, radio broadcasting, lectures, and exhibits.

Glavlit is most active in the area of importation of foreign materials and the exportation of Soviet materials. Again, the concern with exportation is merely to be sure that state secrets are not getting out of the country. The importation of books and periodicals from abroad is a more serious problem from the Soviet point of view. Very few items that are printed abroad are available for public consumption. Most, including books, periodicals, and films, are simply forbidden entrance into the country. Books that portray the social and economic ills of a Western society—for example, those by Upton Sinclair or Charles Dickens—however, are translated and widely circulated. Some materials published in the West, especially in the areas of the physical sciences, the social sciences, and medicine, are imported and kept in restricted libraries, to which special permission is necessary for admittance.

THE NATURE AND FUNCTIONS OF THE MASS MEDIA

The mass media are considered to be highly valuable political instruments. As early as 1902 Lenin, in his essay "What Is To Be

Done?," expounded upon virtues of the press as a means of indoctrination and organization for the revolution. Through the press, he wrote that the people could be made aware of the injustices of bourgeois society and could be exposed to Communist ideology. The press could also serve as a channel through which the revolutionaries would receive instructions from the leaders. When the Bolsheviks came to power in November 1917, the educational and organizational functions of the press became vital to the success of the Revolution.

In 1917 the Bolsheviks set out to revolutionize every aspect of Russian life, from economics to religion. Everyone had to be reached and subjected to information and arguments supporting the goals of the Revolution. Old attitudes had to be liquidated, and new ones fostered. The number of newspapers multiplied, and the expansion of the radio network was implemented in the First Five-Year Plan of the late 1920's.

In converting the mass media into implements of indoctrination, the Communists made two major distinctions between their approach to content and the Western approach. First, the concept of objectivity was considered bourgeois and, in their view, could lead only to apologies for the status quo. Second, the word *news* was redefined in Marxist terminology to connote only items of political or social significance. In essence, everything printed in newspapers and periodicals, as well as everything broadcast, had to be useful in the building of communism. Editors made decisions based on significance to Party goals rather than on whether or not an item or program was newsworthy or entertaining.

Since the Bolshevik ascension to power, the media of communication have been used predominantly for three purposes: political and social education, organization, and control. By controlling the content of the mass media, the Soviets have been able to shape the world view and the social and political attitudes of the masses.

The communications media, especially the radio, are also designed to help raise the cultural level of the population. Several hours a week of broadcasting are devoted to dramatic readings, reading of prose classics and poetry, and discussions about literature. Symphonic music is also extensively broadcast, often accompanied by discussions and interviews with composers and musicians. With the development of the television industry, the visual dimension was added, and live performances of ballet and drama are frequently televised to provide maximum cultural exposure. Such programming is not considered mere entertainment. Cultural advancement is thought to be socially significant and therefore receives official sanction.

The organizational function is carried out by campaigning for the mobilization of the population to fulfill Party or state goals. For example, as the Soviet Union moved toward industrialization, the mass media were actively employed to agitate and organize the masses to work toward fulfilling, and even surpassing, the production quotas set by the industrial plans (see ch. 29, Economic Planning and Control; ch. 30, Industry). This was done by explaining the nature and importance of the goals set and how they could be achieved. Praise of individuals or groups for superior performance in relation to the goals was frequent as was criticism of laggards. Thus the media served to spur individual and group effort.

The media perform their control function primarily through exposure. Corruption in the administration of a particular enterprise, black-marketeering, or other such crimes are brought to light in the form of letters to the editor or editorials. Particular groups or individuals may be singled out for public reprimand for inefficiency. Often, however, this procedure is merely used to shift the blame away from the Party. Public criticism also serves as a warning against not carrying out one's responsibilities adequately.

THE PRESS

Newspapers

The newspaper network is highly differentiated and precisely organized. Differentiation is based primarily on the content and audience of the press, and the organization is designed to correspond with the hierarchical administrative structure of the country.

The first and most important type of press is the all-union, or central, press, which publishes newspapers in Moscow for distribution throughout the Soviet Union. All-union publications primarily serve as instruments of inner-organization communication. That is, the Party press carries instructions to its lower level officials and members, as do the government newspapers, trade union newspapers, and similar organs. For this reason, all-union newspapers are organized both vertically and horizontally. The horizontal divisions are made on the basis of specialization, such as Party, government, youth organizations, the armed forces, industry, and agriculture. The specialized presses, in turn, are organized on a hierarchical basis to correspond to the structure of the administration of each of these functional areas.

Below the all-union level, there are three other levels of newspapers. In descending order they are: republic, autonomous republic, and region; city; and local. The republican, autonomous republic, and regional newspapers are horizontally divided into categories similar to those of the all-union newspapers except where territorial conditions necessitate deviation. These newspapers serve the same function for territorial areas as the all-union newspapers do for the entire nation. They disseminate information and instructions to such groups as the lower level officials for the republican Party and members of the regional government bureaucracy.

The responsibility of the republican and regional press extends in two directions. First, they must discuss the same kinds of topics as are found in the all-union press, such as shifts in policies and international relations. Second, they must disseminate information concerning policies specific to their areas. In this respect they must give detailed information about various industrial or agricultural processes or discuss problems that are peculiar to their territory, such as underemployment of labor or the scarcity of particular commodity or resource. They must also help the Party in the political education of the masses by discussing ideological questions. They cannot generalize on political and economic issues but must provide in-depth discussions on such questions from the territorial point of view.

The city newspapers are local in focus. They deal only with political and economic questions that are related to the city in which they are circulated. Ideological problems are discussed in these newspapers, but only insofar as they can be related to the concrete facts of everyday life. Anything more complicated or abstract is beyond their scope. Many large cities have evening newspapers that carry mostly local news, feature stories, and extensive coverage of sports and amusements. These publications lack the massive propaganda found in other newspapers.

The local press consists of district, factory, and collective farm newspapers, which carry news specific to the particular area or enterprise in which they are distributed. In this category falls a peculiar form of newspaper that is called a wall-newspaper. They are usually single sheets that are mimeographed, typed, or handwritten and posted on the walls or bulletin boards of factories, collective farms, offices of ministries, army units, and any other small unit. They serve to agitate for the fulfillment of assigned tasks or the improvement of the use of time by employees and praise or criticize individuals and groups. The wall-newspapers also help with the task of political education. In this connection the authors of the wall-newspapers often adapt news items from the central organs in such a way as to facilitate local consumption.

At the top of the newspaper hierarchy, the all-union newspapers have the widest circulations, although only a small number of this kind are published. In 1967 there were 26 all-union newspapers published out of a total of 8,524. The total circulation of the all-union newspapers in 1967 was 54,894,000 per issue, while the total circulation of all newspapers was 120,518,000 per issue (see table 8). At the lowest level (the local press), the largest number of

Table 8. *Newspaper Distribution and Circulation in the Soviet Union, 1967*

Newspapers		Circulation per issue
All-Union	26	54,894,000
Republic and region	532	36,995,000
City	591	8,754,000
Local	7,375	19,875,000
Total	8,524	120,518,000

Source: Adapted from *Europa Year Book, 1969,* London, 1969, p. 1139.

newspapers are published, but they have relatively small circulations. Thus, in 1967 there were 7,375 local newspapers published, with a total circulation of only 19,875,000 per issue.

Circulation figures do not give a complete picture, however, because of the practice of reading newspapers in groups. In factories and small communities and on collective farms local agitators often read newspaper items aloud at meetings or in workers' dining rooms during lunch periods, thereby providing greater exposure to the press without expanding circulation figures. Reading rooms with subscriptions to various newspapers and periodicals are located in factories, on collective farms, in university dormitories, and in other large institutions. Many people, therefore, have access to newspapers through reading rooms rather than by means of individual subscriptions or purchases at a newsstand.

The average size of a newspaper is four to six pages. It carries relatively few photographs and cartoons as compared to papers published in the West, although in the 1960's these were included more frequently. Newspapers throughout the country are uniform in content except where local conditions receive coverage. The primary reason for this uniformity is that TASS and Novosti (News) are the only news agencies in the country. Thus different newspapers often carry identical articles. The basic, recurrent themes that run through the press are: the building of communism, the struggle for the achievement of "freedom and socialism" throughout the world, denunciations of so-called imperialists' activities and, since the open rift between the Soviets and Chinese, denunciations of Communist China.

Foreign news coverage, aside from Soviet foreign relations, is brief and often relegated to the back pages of newspapers. Editorials and statements of the government and the Party are always printed on the first page. The only regular features of a typical newspaper that might be considered entertaining are sports coverage and serialized pieces of fiction in the style of socialist realism (see ch. 16, Artistic Expression).

The tone of the newspapers is serious. The private lives either of government and Party officials or other celebrities are not covered. Crime is not reported except when a campaign is being conducted against it. Items on social events are not included except perhaps brief coverage of receptions given by officials for foreign delegations or the reception of Soviet delegations abroad.

The role of the press is primarily functional, and therefore its tone is serious. Most newspapers are published in order to communicate specific types of information to specific audiences (see table 9). The newspaper *Gudok* (Whistle) is published by the Rail Transport Workers' Union and is primarily concerned with the railroad industry. *Trud* (Labor), published by the Central Council of Trade Unions, is directed to union officials and members. The Defense Ministry publishes *Krasnaya Zvezda* (Red Star), which deals with military affairs. *Stroitelnaya Gazeta* (Builders' Gazette) is published by the State Committee for Construction and contains information relevant to the construction industry. *Ekonomicheskaya Gazeta* (Economic Gazette) is an organ of the department of the Central Committee of the CPSU that deals with economic issues. The Ministry of Culture publishes *Sovietskaya Kultura* (Soviet Culture) jointly with the Union of Cultural Workers. This newspaper is concerned primarily with television and radio, the arts, and morals.

The CPSU also publishes newspapers of the general interest type, an example of which is *Sovietskaya Rossiya* (Soviet Russia). This newspaper was founded in 1956 as part of the drive to make the press more diverse and interesting to the population. *Selskaya Zhizn* (Country Life) is also published by the Party and is directed toward the rural population. *Sovietskiy Sport* (Soviet Sport) is published by the Central Council of Soviet Sports Societies and Organizations. On Sundays it puts out an illustrated supplement entitled "Football." *Literaturnaya Gazeta* (Literary Gazette) is a literary weekly published by the Union of Soviet Writers.

Pravda (Truth) and *Izvestia* (News) are the two most important and widely circulated newspapers in the Soviet Union. Often the lower level newspapers take their leading articles from *Pravda* and *Izvestia* or reprint editorials verbatim. Both of these newspapers have printing centers throughout the country. *Pravda* is the organ of the Central Committee of the CPSU, and *Izvestia* is the government organ, published by the Presidium of the Supreme Soviet. Over half of the items covered by *Pravda* are also covered by *Izvestia*, although items often appear in *Pravda* before appearing in *Izvestia*.

Pravda concentrates mostly on Party affairs and ideological issues; thus, it is primarily concerned with domestic news. Foreign news coverage in *Pravda* tends to deal with domestic developments. *Izvestia*, on the other hand, is oriented toward government news

Table 9. Major Newspapers in the Soviet Union

Title	Frequency of publication (per week)	Publisher	Estimated circulation per issue (in millions)
Ekonomicheskaya Gazeta (Economic Gazette)	1	Central Committee of the CPSU[1]	.3[2]
Gudok	6	Rail Transport Workers' Union	n.a.
Izvestia (News) Supplement "Nedelya" (Week)	..do..	Presidium of the USSR Supreme Soviet	8.0[3]
Komsomolskaya Pravda (Komsomol Truth)	..do..	Central Committee of the Komsomol	6.9[3]
Krasnaya Zvezda (Red Star)	..do..	Ministry of Defense	2.4[3]
Literaturnaya Gazeta (Literary Gazette)	1	Union of Soviet Writers	.62[2]
Pioneerskaya Pravda (Pioneer Truth)	2	Central Committee of the Komsomol	9.3[3]
Pravda (Truth)	7	Central Committee of the CPSU	8.5[4]
Selskaya Zhizn (Country Life)	6	..do..	6.7[3]
Sovietskaya Kultura (Soviet Culture)	3	Ministry of Culture and Union of Cultural Workers	n.a.
Sovietskaya Rossiya (Soviet Russia)	6	Central Committee of the CPSU	2.0[2]
Sovietskiy Sport (Soviet Sport)	..do..	Central Council of Soviet Sports Societies and Organizations	2.5[3]
Supplement "Football"	1	..do..	1.5[3]
Stroitelnaya Gazeta (Builders' Gazette)	3	State Committee for Construction	n.a.
Trud (Labor)	6	Central Council of the Trade Unions	2.4[3]

n.a.—not available.
[1] CPSU—Communist Party of the Soviet Union.
[2] Circulation in 1961.
[3] Circulation in 1967.
[4] Circulation in 1969.

and therefore gives more coverage to state relations in connection with its foreign coverage. For example, in covering the Middle East, *Pravda* tends to stress such things as the Arab socialist movement, whereas *Izvestia* gives more attention to trade or aid agreements with various Arab states or visits by Arab delegations. *Pravda* is the only newspaper published seven days a week. All other newspapers are not published on Mondays. *Izvestia* began putting out a Sunday illustrated supplement in 1960, entitled *Nedelya* (Week), which contains comics, political satire, and feature articles.

Large cities have evening newspapers that do not have the serious tone of the other newspapers. They minimize coverage of national and Party affairs, concentrating on local events. *Vechernaya Moskva* (Evening Moscow), an example of such a newspaper, is similar to those in the West in that it contains human interest type items and discusses current films and other kinds of amusements. *Komsomolskaya Pravda* (Komsomol Truth) and *Pioneerskaya Pravda* (Pioneer Truth), published by the Central Committee of the Young Communist League, are also less serious than most Soviet newspapers (see ch. 21, Political Dynamics). The Society of Cultural Relations with Foreign Countries publishes foreign-language newspapers in Moscow for tourists. *Neues Leben* (New Life) is published three times a week in German, and *Moscow News* is published twice a week in English, as is its French version, *Les Nouvelles de Moscou.*

Because the press is not a business venture, little advertising appears in the newspapers. The few advertisements that do appear are in the form of announcements. For the most part, they are either announcements of marriages, divorces, and deaths, which are required by law, or they are publicity campaigns to get rid of consumer goods that the retail stores find difficult to sell.

The traditional view of advertising by the Soviet leaders goes back to Marxist ideology; that is, advertising is a mechanism of the competitive market phenomenon found in capitalist societies. Therefore, the leadership has viewed it as bourgeois and unnecessary in their socialist society. In the late 1950's, however, when consumer goods production was increased, the government found it necessary to use advertisements in order to inform the population of products that were available. Thus, advertisements are merely announcements of what is available and where and are not a source of revenue; they are printed as a public service or as part of the duty to educate the masses. The increase in the amount of space allocated in newspapers for advertising is a reflection of the increase in the amount and variety of consumer goods.

Each union republic has its own newspapers. Some of these are published in Russian, the rest being published in the languages of their populations (see table 10).

Table 10. *Major Newspapers in the Republics of the Soviet Union*

Title	Union-Republic	Published[1]	Publisher	Language
Leninskoye Znamya (Lenin's Banner)	Russian Soviet Federated Socialist Republic	Daily	Moscow Communist Party	Russian
Uchitelskaya Gazeta (Teachers' Gazette)	Russian republic (circulation 1 million in 1967)	Three times a week	Ministry of Education and Teachers' Trade Union[2]	Do.
Leningradskaya Pravda (Leningrad Truth)	Russian republic	Daily	Leningrad Communist Party and City Council	Do.
Moskouskaya Pravda (Moscow Truth)	do	do	Moscow Communist Party and City Council	Do.
Moskovskiy Komosomolyets (Moscow Komsomol)	do	Five times a week	Moscow Communist Youth League	Do.
Vechernaya Moskva (Evening Moscow)	do	Daily	Moscow City Council and CPSU[3] City Committee	Do.
Kommunist (Communist)	Armenian SSR[4]	do	Armenian Communist Party, Supreme Soviet, and Council of Ministers	Armenian
Sovietakan Aiastan (Soviet Armenia)	do	do	do	Do.
Bakinski Rabochi (Baku Workers)	Azerbaijan SSR[4]	do	Azerbaijan Communist Party	Russian
Kommunist (Communist)	do	do	do	Azerbaijani
Sovietskaya Belorussian (Soviet Belorussian)	Belorussian SSR[4]	do	Belorussian Communist Party	Russian
Zvyezda (Star)	do	do	Belorussian Communist Party, Supreme Soviet, and Council of Ministers	Belorussian

Newspaper		SSR	Organization	Language
Rahva Haal (Voice of the People)	....	Estonian SSR⁴	Estonian Communist Party, Supreme Soviet, and Council of Ministers	Estonian
Sovietskaya Estonia (Soviet Estonia)	....	Estonian SSR⁴	Estonian Communist Party, Supreme Soviet, and Council of Ministers	Russian
Kommunisti (Communist)	....	Georgian SSR⁴	Georgian Communist Party	Georgian
Zarya Vastoka (Eastern Dawn)	....	...do...	Georgian Communist Party, Supreme Soviet, and Council of Ministers	Russian
Kazakhstanskaya Pravda (Kazakhstan Truth)	....	Kazakh SSR⁴	Kazakh Communist Party, Supreme Soviet, and Council of Ministers	Do.
Sotsialistik Kazakhstan (Socialist Kazakhstan)	....	...do...	...do...	Kazakh
Sovietskaya Kirgiz (Socialist Kirgiz)	....	Kirgiz SSR⁴	Kirgiz Communist Party, Supreme Soviet, and Council of Ministers	Russian and Kirgiz
Sovietskaya Latvia (Soviet Latvia)	....	Latvian SSR⁴	Latvian Communist Party, Supreme Soviet, and Council of Ministers	Russian
Tsirya (Struggle)	....	...do...	...do...	Latvian
Sovietskaya Litva (Soviet Lithuania)	....	Lithuanian SSR⁴	Lithuania Communist Party, Supreme Soviet, and Council of Ministers	Russian
Tiesa (Truth)	....	...do...	...do...	Lithuanian
Moldava Sotsialiste (Socialist Moldavia)	....	Moldavian SSR⁴	Moldavian Communist Party, Supreme Soviet, and Council of Ministers	Moldavian
Sovietskaya Moldavia (Soviet Moldavia)	....	...do...	...do...	Russian
Kommunist Tadzhikistan (Communist Tadzhikistan)	....	Tadzhik SSR⁴	Tadzhik Communist Party, Supreme Soviet, and Council of Ministers	Russian
Tockikistoni Sovieti (Soviet Tadzhikistan)	....	...do...	...do...	Tadzhik

Table 10. Major Newspapers in the Republics of the Soviet Union—Continued

Title	Union-Republic	Published[1]	Publisher	Language
Soviet Turkmenistani (Soviet Turkmenistan)	Turkmen SSR[4]	...do....	Turkmen Communist Party, Supreme Soviet, and Council of Ministers	Turkmen
Turkmenskaya Iskra (Turkmen Spark)	...do....	n.a.	...do....	Russian
Pravda Ukrainy (Ukrania Truth)	Ukrainian SSR[4]	Daily	Ukrainian Communist Party, Supreme Soviet, and Council of Ministers	Do.
Rabochaya Gazeta (Workers' Gazette)	...do....	...do....	...do....	Do.
Radionskaya Ukraina (Soviet Ukraine)	...do....	Weekly	...do....	Ukrainian
Ukraina (Ukraine)	...do....	...do....	n.a.	Russian
Pravda Vostoka (Eastern Truth)	Uzbek SSR[4]	Daily	Uzbek Communist Party, Supreme Soviet, and Council of Ministers	Do.
Soviet Uzbekistoni (Soviet Uzbekistan)	...do....	...do....	...do....	Uzbek

n.a.—not available.

[1] All listed as "dailies" publish six days per week—no Monday editions.
[2] RSFSR—Russian Soviet Federated Socialist Republic.
[3] CPSU—Communist Party of the Soviet Union.
[4] SSR—Soviet Socialist Republic.

Although newspaper publishing is a massive enterprise, the staffs of the individual newspapers are small because, in keeping with the philosophy of mass participation, at least half of the articles that appear are written by people who are not journalists by profession. The professional newspaper staffs have been directed by the Party to assist nonprofessional contributors in this activity. Usually the various industries and collective farms have correspondents who provide newspapers with articles on the activities or production progress of these enterprises.

In many instances, it is necessary to have nonjournalists contribute to newspapers. Much space in the press is devoted to technical articles concerning industry and agriculture, so that newspaper editors often must call upon engineers, industrial specialists, and agronomists to contribute to their publications.

Another form of mass participation in the press is that of letters to the editor from ordinary citizens. Such letters are largely criticisms of defects in the administration of production within enterprises, criticism of local government administration, or complaints about the lack of consumer goods. Letters to the editor are written about a wide range of topics, but they never touch on controversial issues. The newspaper staffs not only publish many of these letters but also forward them to relevant agencies. The newspapers follow up on complaints to see whether or not measures have been implemented to alleviate the problems.

Letters to the editor primarily serve two functions. First, within prescribed limits, they provide public control over various bureaucratic administrations. Secondly, they serve to channel tensions and resentment away from the system as a whole by encouraging criticism against those who implement policy rather than those who formulate it. Criticism of the system per se is not allowed.

Periodicals

The periodical press, considered to be as important as the newspaper press, is organized along the same lines and performs the same functions. Periodicals are published in each of the union republics in about fifty languages. Every aspect of life in the country—the Party, culture, industry, and the sciences—has periodicals that cover it. Over two-thirds of the total number of periodicals originate in the Russian Soviet Federated Socialist Republic (RSFSR), many of which are of the all-union type. In 1967 there were 3,312 periodicals published in the Russian republic out of a total of 4,704 for the entire country (see table 11).

The Central Committee of the CPSU publishes several ideological and political journals. The leading journals of this type are *Partiinaya Zhizn* (Party Life), *Kommunist* (Communist), *Politi-*

Table 11. *Periodicals in the Republics of the Soviet Union*

Soviet Socialist Union-Republic	Number
Armenian	92
Azerbaijan	108
Belorussian	54
Estonian	125
Georgian	114
Kazakh	94
Kirgiz	47
Latvian	97
Lithuanian	96
Moldavian	60
Russian SFSR*	3,312
Tadzhik	43
Turkmen	36
Ukrainian	323
Uzbek	103
Total	4,704

*SFSR—Soviet Federated Socialist Republic.

Source: Adapted from *Europa Year Book, 1969*, London, 1969, p. 1139.

cheskoye Samoobrazovanie (Political Self-Education), and *Agitator* (Agitator). *Partiinaya Zhizn* deals primarily with ideological and organizational problems, whereas *Kommunist* is basically ideological in scope. *Politicheskoye Samoobrazovanie* discusses economic questions as well as political and ideological topics. The journal *Agitator* is specifically directed to Party agitators, with the purpose of keeping them up to date on the Party's policies. *Voprosy Istorii* (Questions on History) is an ideologically oriented periodical published by *Pravda*. *Komsomolskaya Zhizn* (Komsomol Life) is a theoretical journal that is published bimonthly by the Central Committee of the Young Communist League.

Krokodil (Crocodile), a magazine of political satire, is published trimonthly by *Pravda*. *Krokodil* is one of the most popular periodicals in the Soviet Union. A journal that deals with international relations, *Mezhdunarodnaya Zhizn* (International Life), is also published in English as *International Affairs*. There is also an edition in French.

There are several journals that deal with art, music, literature, theater, and films. The largest category is that dealing with literary affairs. *Don* (River Don), *Inostrannaya Literatura* (Foreign Literature), *Neva* (River Neva), *Novy Mir* (New World), and *Oktyabr* (October) are but a few of the monthlies put out by the Union of Soviet Writers. *Russkaya Literatura* (Russian Literature) is published quarterly by the Institute of Russian Literature of the

Academy of Sciences. *Voprosy Literatury* (Literary Questions) is published monthly by the Union of Soviet Writers and the Institute of World Literature. *Sovietskaya Literatura* (Soviet Literature) is published for foreign consumption in English, French, Spanish, and German.

Dekorativnoye Iskusstvo (Decorative Art) is published monthly by the Union of Soviet Artists. *Iskusstvo* (Art) is published monthly by the Ministry of Culture in conjunction with the Academy of Arts and the Union of Soviet Artists. The Union of Soviet Artists also publishes the monthly journal *Tvorchestvo* (Creativity). Periodicals that deal with motion pictures are *Iskusstvo Kino* (Art of the Cinema), published by the State Committee on Cinematography, and the Union of Film Workers; *Sovietskoye Kino* (Soviet Cinema), published in Arabic, English, French, German, and Spanish, and *Sovietskiy Ekran* (Soviet Screen) are both published by the State Committee on Cinematography and the Soviet Film Producers' Union.

Teatr (Theater), published by the Ministry of Culture and the Union of Soviet Writers, and *Teatralnaya Zhizn* (Theatrical Life), published by the Ministry of Culture, Soviet Writers' Union, and the All-Russian Theatrical Society, cover theatrical affairs and drama. *Sovietskaya Muzika* (Soviet Music) and *Muzikalnaya Zhizn* (Musical Life) are published by the Soviet Composers' Union and the Ministry of Culture. The Magazine *Kultura i Zhizn* (Culture and Life) deals with Soviet culture in general and is aimed primarily at foreign audiences. It is published in Russian, English, German, French, and Spanish.

There are many popular illustrated periodicals, some of which are designed for foreign, as well as domestic, consumption. *Moscow News* is published weekly in English, French, Spanish, and Arabic. *Sovietskaya Zhenshchina* (Soviet Woman) is a monthly, published in Russian, English, French, Spanish, Chinese, Korean, German, Hindi, Hungarian, and Japanese. *Zhurnal Mod* (Fashion Journal) is a quarterly fashion magazine. *Sovietskiy Soyuz* (Soviet Union) is an illustrated monthly, published in Russian, English, German, French, Spanish, Finnish, Serbo-Croatian, Hungarian, Chinese, Japanese, Korean, Arabic, Hindi, Urdu, and Bengali. *Ogonyok* (Light) is a highly political, popular illustrated magazine.

There are hundreds of specialized journals that deal with all aspects of agriculture, education, industry and technology, natural and applied science, and communications. Examples of periodicals that deal with agriculture are *Ekonomika Selskovo Khozyaistva* (Agricultural Economy), *Krolikovodstva i Zverovodstvo* (Rabbit Breeding and Fur Production), and *Lesnoye Khozyaistvo* (Forestry), which are published by the Ministry of Agriculture. The Ministry of Public Health publishes numerous journals on all aspects of medicine and supporting fields, for example, *Antibiotiki* (Antibiotics) and *Laboratornoye Delo* (Laboratory Work).

The Academy of Sciences publishes several journals on the national sciences, for example, the journals *Mikrobiologia* (Microbiology) and *Priroda* (Nature). The USSR Ministry of Education and the Russian republic Ministry of Education publish journals that cover various levels of the educational system in general as well as specific subjects taught in the schools. *Doshkolnoye Vospitaniye* (Preschool Education) is an example of the former, and *Biologiya v Skole* (Biology in the School) is an example of the latter. *Radiotekhnika* (Radio Technology) is one of many communications journals, and *Mekhanizatsia Stroitelstva* (Mechanization of Building) is one example of several industrial journals.

News Agencies

The Telegraphic Agency of the Soviet Union (Telegrafnoye Agentstvo Sovietskovo Soyuza—TASS) has a monopoly on the distribution of news. Its predecessor, the Russian Telegraph Agency, was established in September 1918 by a decree of the Central Committee of the Bolshevik Party. In 1925 TASS was established to take over all news gathering and distribution. The Russian Telegraph Agency remained in existence until 1935 as the news agency for the Russian republic, but from that time on that republic has not had its own agency and has been served by TASS. Each of the other union republics has its own news agency, which is theoretically under the republic Council of Ministers but in practice is run by TASS.

Although TASS is formally under the USSR Council of Ministers, in actuality it is subordinate to the Central Committee of the CPSU. The directorate of TASS is appointed by the Politburo of the Central Committee, and its editorial staff is appointed by Agitprop. TASS is organized into four sections: the Soviet Information Department, Foreign Information Department, Feature Service, and Picture Service. The Soviet Information Department is subdivided to cover the various territorial units and functional areas. TASS supplies feature articles and pictures throughout the entire press network, as well as news items. Radio and television are also supplied with news items from TASS. TASS has correspondents all over the world, although foreign news coverage is minimal in the Soviet press.

The News Press Agency (Agentstvo Pechati Novosti—APN), commonly referred to as Novosti, was established on February 21, 1961, for the purpose of disseminating information about the Soviet Union abroad. Thus Novosti does not impinge upon the TASS monopoly over the distribution of news within the country.

Novosti operates through agreements made between itself and publishing firms and presses in foreign countries.

Book Publishing and Libraries

In 1966 almost 73,000 books and pamphlets were published, with a total printing of over 1.25 billion copies. The great majority of titles—over 65,000—were first editions, with more than 730 million copies printed. Most of the titles were in the fields of politics and ideology, industry and agriculture, science, literature, education, linguistics, and military science. Included in the total number of books and pamphlets published in 1966 were 2,522 textbooks, with a total printing of about 285 million copies, and 2,574 books and pamphlets for children, with a total of about 213 million copies.

Of the 72,977 titles published, 70,547 were in about sixty languages of the peoples of the Soviet Union. The remaining 2,430 were published in thirty-eight foreign languages: 896 in English, 410 in French, 280 in German, 218 in Spanish, and 626 in other languages. Soviet book publishers classify any publication of over five pages as a book or pamphlet, and they include unrevised printings of previous editions as new titles. Translations of a single book into several languages are also counted as new titles. These practices, which are not common in Western countries, make comparative analysis complex and often midleading.

Books and pamphlets are distributed through numerous bookstores, kiosks, discussion circles, and over 350,000 libraries throughout the country. All publishing houses are owned and operated by the Party, government, or subsidiary organizations. There are about 50 major publishing houses and about 150 subsidiary publishers considered to be all-union, specializing in various aspects of Soviet life. There are also several regional publishing houses.

Pravda Publishing House, in addition to its famous newspaper, publishes many political books, pamphlets, and other newspapers and periodicals. Gospolitizdat (State Political Publishing House) also specializes in political literature. The Komsomol has its own publishing house, as do many trade unions and several government ministries. The Ministry of Defense, for example, has the Krasnaya Zvezda (Red Star) Publishing House, which puts out the daily newspaper of the same name and also publishes a monthly magazine, *Soviet Military Review*, in English. The Academy of Sciences is a major publisher of scientific literature, and the USSR Union of Writers publishes several titles, fiction and nonfiction, each year.

Several publishing houses publish books, pamphlets, and other materials for foreign consumption. Novosti Press Agency Publishing House, in addition to providing publications on Soviet life, economy, politics, and science, publishes the monthly periodical *Sputnik* in Russian, French, German, English, and Japanese. *Mezhduna-*

rodnye Otnosheniya (International Relations) publishes grammar books for foreign languages, scientific materials, and United Nations translations. Mir (Peace) Publishers and Progress Publishers translate foreign books into Russian and Russian books into foreign languages. *Sovietskaya Entsiklopediya* (Soviet Encyclopedia) publishes encyclopedias and technical and foreign dictionaries.

In 1965 there were 368,568 libraries containing a total of over 2.5 billion volumes. Libraries in 800 universities and higher educational institutes contained over 200 million volumes, and almost 190,000 school libraries had well over 300 million volumes. Public libraries, the most famous of which is the Lenin Library in Moscow, numbered 127,000 with over a billion selections on their shelves; and more than 50,000 special libraries, catering to scientists, engineers, teachers, and many other specialists, offered almost a million selections. Many libraries have rooms containing foreign books, newspapers, and periodicals that are restricted to a relatively few scholars and others requiring access to such material.

RADIO

Like the press, radio is considered an important instrument of indoctrination. It is probably even more effective in transmitting information to average citizens, because it takes less effort to listen to the radio than to read a newspaper. Formally, all broadcasting activities are under the control of the State Committee for Broadcasting and Television, which is responsible to the Council of Ministers. There is also a Committee for Broadcasting and Television in each union republic, which is under the republican Council of Ministers.

In actuality, the Party maintains control over radio broadcasting by placing its members in responsible positions on the committees as well as among the lower level workers in the broadcasting field. The Party maintains further control by periodically issuing directives concerning radio broadcasting and the radio industry in general. One of the most important means of Party control, however, is the Radio Sector of Agitprop (see ch. 26, Agitation and Propaganda).

The radio network is highly developed and extends to the most remote regions of the vast Soviet territory. According to the latest available figures (July 1968), there were approximately 980 radio transmitting stations, and in 1966 there was an estimated total of 76.8 million radio receivers, or almost one for every three persons. In 1968, 7 million radio receivers were produced and, by August 1969, 4.8 million more had been produced. Of the total number of stations, approximately 824 had high-frequency transmitters, 127 had medium-frequency transmitters, and 29 had low-frequency transmitters.

According to available data, the power of these transmitters ranges from 10,000 watts to 300,000 watts. The reason for such a large number of high-frequency transmitters is twofold: the distance across which domestic broadcasts must be transmitted and the extensive foreign broadcasts that originate in the Soviet Union (see ch.26, Agitation and Propaganda).

Almost half of the receiving network consists of wired radio receivers. The wired receiving network was extensively developed, because it provided the least expensive means, in terms of the amount of equipment necessary, to reach the maximum audience. This was done because of heavy industry's receiving high priority in the allocation of funds and resources at the expense of light industry, in which radio is included. After World War II, the radio industry was given a relatively high priority in economic plans. About half of the transmitting stations had been destroyed, and it was apparent that radio broadcasting would be a fundamental tool in the reestablishment of political control over areas that had been under Nazi occupation. Since that time the radio network has had phenomenal growth. In 1940 there were only 90 transmitters in operation, in 1958 there were 410, and in 1968, 980. In 1950 there were only 11.5 million radio receivers, and in 1966 there were approximately 76.8 million.

Essentially, a wired receiver is a loudspeaker that receives usually one, though sometimes two, programs. The wired receiving network facilitates a large measure of centralized broadcasting. This network is served by radio diffusion exchanges, or relay centers, which relay over wires, programs that originate in Moscow or republic stations. These exchanges sometimes broadcast programs of a local nature, the number of which depends upon how many languages are spoken in the locality they serve. There are over 100 languages spoken by the peoples of the Soviet Union, but central broadcasts are predominantly in Russian (see ch. 10, Languages and Social Communication).

Wired receivers are conducive to group listening, which facilitates political agitation. Such receivers are set up in homes for family listening and in recreation centers, club rooms, or reading rooms for group listening. Programs are also channeled through public address systems on collective farms and in dining halls, factories, and schools.

The number of regular aerial radio sets has been increasing steadily since the early 1950's and, by early 1970, had approached the number of wired sets. In 1966, out of an estimated total of 76.8 million receivers, only 37 million were wired, as compared to 9.7 million wired sets out of a total of 11.5 million in 1950. All receivers, regardless of the type, must have licenses, for which a nominal fee is charged.

As a result of the increase in number of regular radio sets, the population has greater access to foreign broadcasts. This, plus the fact that the Soviets, to a large extent, have ceased jamming foreign programs, has caused the government to change its newscasting policies. Before Soviet news broadcasting had to compete with those of foreign origin, their material was derived primarily from newspapers. Because of this there was a greater lag between the time an event occurred and the time it was announced over the radio, and many news items were not announced at all.

In the latter part of the 1950's, not only did it become necessary for the radio to broadcast news before it appeared in the press, but newscasts had to present items of the nature that were formerly omitted so that the official analysis could reach the population before information from foreign sources. An integral part of newscasting in the Soviet Union has always been, and still is, political analysis. News items are not presented in a straightforward manner but are, in fact, interpretations.

Radio Moscow, the central broadcasting network, has four programs. The first program is the leader in reporting both foreign and domestic news. It is supplied by TASS and, in turn, it either supplies republic and local stations with news items, or its broadcasts are simply relayed by local stations. The newscasts are dispersed between musical and drama programs. The second program is called "Mayak" (Beacon) and was instituted in 1964 in order to compete with foreign broadcasts. It uses the same frequencies as the foreign stations and broadcasts mostly music with hourly, up-to-date newscasts. The union republics have followed Radio Moscow's lead and have also established beacon stations. There is a minimum of newscasting on the third program; its broadcasts are predominantly musical, literary, and drama programs. The fourth program is directed to Siberia and the Far Eastern Regions of the RSFSR. It uses the same newscasts as the first program.

Besides serving as an instrument of political indoctrination, radio also contributes to the cultural education of the population. For this reason, the majority of the domestic broadcasts are programs of music, literature, or drama. Actually, music alone accounts for at least half of Soviet broadcasts. Frequently concerts and operas are presented live. Soviet radio also regularly broadcasts music appreciation programs, in which various types of music or instruments are discussed and composers and musicians are interviewed. Radio is not meant to be entertaining, and musical and drama programs are serious in tone.

Included in broadcasting time are several programs a day directed to children. In addition, several talk-shows on such subjects as science, medicine, economic issues, and public health are broadcast, though not on a daily basis. There are no commercials of the kind presented in the West. Social and cultural events are announced over the radio, however, as well as lists of what commodities are available at which stores. All of these announcements are grouped into one short program, which is repeated every few hours.

TELEVISION

Television is controlled by the government through the State Committee for Broadcasting and Television, which is under the USSR Council of Ministers. Personnel in the field of television and its supporting fields are largely Communist Party members or at least have demonstrated loyalty to Party and state goals, thereby ensuring control over this medium of communication.

Television broadcasting was initiated in 1931 but not on a regular basis. By 1938 Moscow and Leningrad had stations that were in operation regularly. It was not until 1951 that a third city, Kiev, had telecasting facilities. Since that time, the television network has been growing steadily. In 1967 there were 890 television stations, including relay stations. Most cities in the Soviet Union had one station; large metropolitan areas had two; Leningrad and Tashkent had three; and Moscow had four, one of which transmitted in color. The programs are either relayed from Moscow or produced locally. Microwave linkage systems are the primary means of relaying programs; however, coaxial cables are also used.

The government has made agreements for exchange with several foreign television services. Because of the wide linguistic diversity in the Soviet Union, a means of transmitting programs in several different languages simultaneously has been developed. Many of the television sets have switches for language selection.

Although the television transmitting network is fairly extensive, there is a shortage of television receivers. In 1968 there were 22.9 million sets, or not quite 100 sets per 1,000 persons. Television sets are more widely distributed throughout the cities of European USSR than in Asian or rural areas. The Soviets have planned for the annual production of at least 4 million sets since 1966 in order to alleviate the shortage. In 1968 they produced 5.7 million television sets and, by late 1969, an additional 4.3 million sets. The price of television sets is fairly low, and only a nominal license fee is charged.

As with radio, the purpose of television is not primarily entertainment; like the other media, it is an instrument of political and social indoctrination, as well as cultural growth. In order to prevent the distraction of people from more useful activities, there is a minimum of daytime television programming except on Sundays and holidays, though there are two hours of telecasting in the middle of the day. According to 1964 statistics, the central television station in Moscow, from which programs were relayed throughout the Soviet Union, had about sixty-five hours per week of programming, of which 22 percent were films, 19 percent literary and drama programs, 18 percent music programs, 17 percent newscasts, 14 percent children's shows, and 8 percent sociopolitical programs. Concerts, plays, ballets, operas, and sports events are often telecast live. There are also purely educational programs; for example, language courses and informative programs on such topics as public health, the home and family, and youth.

In 1968 Moscow had four television stations. Two of these had regular programming, primarily films and musical and drama programs. One was an educational station, and one transmitted in color. The color station was only on the air a few hours a week.

Besides being subsidized by the government, television stations receive revenue from commercials, though their rates are quite low. Commercials on Soviet television are brief announcements, grouped together, made once during the evening, usually for a ten-minute period. These announcements, like those made over radio, are of cultural events, products available, and job opportunities.

In 1967 a new, ultramodern television center was opened in Ostankino, a suburb of Moscow. It was designed to be the principal programming center for the central television network and to facilitate the reception of five stations in major cities. Although centralized programming increases the strictness of control over content, it has its drawbacks. It cannot appeal to all the interests of the different segments of the population, and this shortcoming has been criticized by the public. The returns of a government survey of the television audience, which were published in 1967, indicate that newscasts, political programs, and educational programs were the least popular and that the people preferred entertainment programs, such as movies, plays, concerts, and children's shows. The poll also indicated that the appeal of television decreased with the increase of education.

FILMS

The motion picture is a medium of mass communication as well as a mode of artistic expression. Because of the duality of function, it took the Bolsheviks longer to establish control over motion pictures than over any other medium of communication. Indeed, the early history of movie production in the Soviet Union is the history of the Bolsheviks' trying to find a balance between the growth of the film industry and control over it. Initially, in order for motion picture production to increase, the skills and talents of non-Communists had to be utilized. The Bolsheviks were unable to permeate the ranks of this industry in a manner similar to that of the news-paper and radio industry. Each time the balance shifted in favor of control, production fell back. By the beginning of 1920 it was necessary for Lenin to direct Maxim Litvinov, deputy commissar of foreign affairs, to get films from the West (see ch. 16, Artistic Expression).

During the New Economic Policy period, production began to increase gradually. In 1922, however, attempts were made to re-establish Bolshevik control over all aspects of the movie industry. From that time, a series of steps were taken, both administratively and economically to accomplish this, until 1936 when the industry was taken out of private hands completely. In 1960 the motion picture industry was under the Committee on Cinematography, which was responsible to the Council of Ministers.

The Party maintains control over the film industry primarily by two means: through a sector of Agitprop that is concerned with film affairs and by placing Party members in key positions, such as directors of studios. Motion pictures are reviewed by censors before being released, as well as at various intervals during their pro-duction.

During the first few years of the Soviet state, domestically pro-duced films were primarily documentaries, newsreels, and short propaganda films, known as *Agitki* (Bits of Propaganda). Except during the New Economic Policy period and during World War II, all films produced in the Soviet Union had a pro-Communist propa-ganda orientation. Even feature films have themes in the style of socialist realism (see ch. 16, Artistic Expression). Throughout Soviet history the number of short documentary films produced has greatly exceeded the number of feature films. Most studios produce newsreels weekly. According to Soviet statistics, in 1965 there were only 167 feature-length films produced as compared to 920 short films.

Films produced especially for television are included under the heading of feature films. Because films are viewed as an additional instrument of indoctrination, often feature films are televised im-mediately after being released to ensure maximum consumption, rather than waiting until after they have been shown in the cinemas.

In 1963 there were approximately thirty-three studios throughout the country. In order to maximize exposure to motion pictures, those produced in Russian have subtitles in the various languages of the union republics, and those produced in other languages have Russian subtitles. Cinema facilities have been constructed widely in rural areas. According to Soviet statistics, in 1965, out of a total of 145,400 projectors set up, 123,100 were in rural areas. According to United Nations Educational, Scientific and Cultural Organization

(UNESCO) statistics for 1966, the latest available, there were a total of 136,800 commercial cinemas and 12,900 mobile units in the Soviet Union. These figures include both 16-mm and 35-mm projectors. The estimated total attendance for 1966 was 4.2 billion, or eighteen visits to the cinema per person.

CHAPTER 26

AGITATION AND PROPAGANDA

The Communist Party of the Soviet Union (CPSU) has developed one of the most comprehensive and tightly controlled propaganda and agitation organizations in the world. The official policy, in broadest terms, that guides this organization is the effort to maintain popular support for the regime and to counter antiregime views. Using censorship and firm control of all media of mass communications, the indoctrination system exerts kindergarten-to-grave influence on every citizen, and escape from some exposure to this all-pervasive propaganda and agitation would appear to be impossible.

Propaganda is one of the most effective tools used by the CPSU to maintain and extend its power and to weaken, if not eliminate, the appeal of any opposing ideas. Underlying all Soviet propaganda is the basic theme that emphasizes the superiority of the Communist system and its historical guarantee of eventual triumph over rival political and economic systems. By assuming and maintaining a position of doctrinal infallibility, the CPSU attempts to control and influence all attitudes and opinions in society.

The machinery for indoctrination that had evolved by 1970 used all the media of communications plus a vast army of oral agitators who transmitted the Party line to the masses through person-to-person contact. The Soviet Union was the first country to produce such a large class of trained, full-time agitators and to afford them a respected and important place in society.

In addition to the internal mission, Soviet propaganda and agitation reached around the world through shortwave radio and a host of books, pamphlets, periodicals, and newspapers printed in dozens of different languages. The basic message usually pertained to the superiority of Soviet-style socialism and the decadence of other political and economic systems.

In the West, agitation and propaganda are usually both referred to as propaganda. In the Soviet Union a definite distinction is made and, despite some blurring of the distinction in modern usage, the two terms retain Bolshevik connotations fifty years after the Revolution.

Lenin accepted the definitions of his original Marxist mentor,

Georgi Plekhanov, to whom agitation meant transmitting an idea to a multitude, whereas propaganda was the discussion in depth of several ideas or theories in a small group. These definitions were adaptable to Lenin's schemes of creating an elitist party as the vanguard of a revolutionary proletariat. The vanguard required propagandizing, but the proletariat needed only agitation. Both aimed at securing support for the regime; only the methods of indoctrination and the target audiences differed.

In Lenin's time, the differentiation between agitation and propaganda was undoubtedly more important than in the modern Soviet state. Lenin recognized the urgency of teaching Marxist theory and philosophy to the relatively small group among his Bolshevik followers who were capable of understanding such complexities. Propagandists were immediately put to work training others to become propagandists and agitators. Lenin also recognized the futility of attempting to teach such themes to a largely illiterate populace; therefore, agitation was the instrument to be used in imbuing at least the spirit of Marxism in the masses of people.

Lenin himself was both propagandist and agitator—propagandist explaining Marxist thought to his cohorts in meetings and in his prolific writings; agitator in the streets of Petrograd with his slogans demanding "All Power to the Soviets" or "Land, Peace, and Bread." Schools were established to indoctrinate Party members, candidates for membership, non-Party activists, and the sympathetic intelligentsia. The subjects included Marxist-Leninist theories, Party policies, techniques of propaganda and agitation—in short, everything necessary to train good Bolsheviks in the arts and skills necessary for maintaining a revolutionary regime.

The Party schools still exist. The curricula have been refined and modernized, but the goal is essentially the same—that is, the training of good Communists who are intellectually committed to the cause and dedicated to spreading the word. Modern communications technology and the increased educational level of the people have somewhat blurred the old distinctions but, on the one hundredth anniversary of Lenin's birth in 1970, both propagandists and agitators had roles in the extensive preparations for commemoration and celebration.

More than half a century ago, Lenin urged his followers to go out among the people as propagandists and agitators in the cause of world revolution. Lenin considered propaganda and agitation to be crucial elements in the building of communism. None of Lenin's successors has ever downgraded the importance of this mission and, in the early 1970's, the Soviet propaganda system was a smooth-running machine—well financed, professional, and capable of worldwide operations.

THE DEPARTMENT OF PROPAGANDA AND AGITATION

The molding of public opinion by the Party at the beginning of 1970 was accomplished through the Department of Propaganda and Agitation of the Central Committee of the CPSU. This department, which has been in existence since the earliest days of the Bolshevik regime, was usually referred to as Agitprop, a name coined from the first four letters of the words *agitatsiya* and *propaganda*, the latter word being the same in both Russian and English. The guidelines used by Agitprop for its vast programs are derived from policy decisions made by the top level of authority in the country—the Party Politburo.

The guidelines established for Agitprop deal with ideological goals or theoretical matters rather than with day-to-day tactics or themes. Agitprop is charged with interpreting and disseminating policies for lower level agencies, and it also has an investigative function to ensure that lower echelons comply with central directives. Each level of Party organization has its own propaganda and agitation organization that is responsible to the local Party apparatus as well as to the central authority of Agitprop. This dual subordination, so common in Soviet affairs, has drawbacks as well as advantages. In brief, the drawbacks arise from the sheer size of the bureaucracy, which sometimes inhibits operational control, while the advantages stem from the fact that the central authority can, when necessary, dictate policies and ideas to the most remote regions of the huge country.

Agitprop is one of several administrative departments of the CPSU Central Committee, and its existence has often been characterized by intense debates over the department's exact purpose and the limits of its authority in influencing public opinion. The directors of this department have often been members of the CPSU Politburo and, as such, wielded considerable influence within the Party hierarchy, thus enhancing the power of the department. Through 1969 Agitprop continued to maintain the broad authority that enabled it to control every realm of intellectual expression and every form of organized activity that might in any way influence public opinion in the Soviet Union.

Agitprop was first formed as a part of the Central Committee shortly after the Revolution and, at an early date, it was entrusted with the ideological guidance of the new state. The department was given the important responsibility of conditioning the people, through education and indoctrination, to accept the dictates of the new regime and to prepare society for its transition to socialism and, ultimately, communism. These guidelines continue to define the basic responsibilities of Agitprop.

During the 1930's Agitprop directed campaigns against religion and worked to ensure that art, music, and literature conformed to the dictates of "socialist realism." In 1930, to cope with Stalin's demands for greater Party control over the implementation of the First Five-Year Plan, Agitprop was divided into the Department of Agitation and Mass Campaigns and the Department of Culture and Propaganda. In 1934 these two departments again were merged into one central organization. In 1939 the department was given the status of a directorate and placed under the control of Andrei Zhdanov. Under Zhdanov's direction the department became infamous for its brutal repression of cultural, intellectual, and artistic expression. This repression was especially harsh in the period immediately following World War II (see ch. 16, Artistic Expression).

Shortly after Zhdanov's death in 1948 the department underwent a series of reorganizations and, until 1957, it was caught in the frequent Party shuffles that characterized the entire system after Stalin's death. The department's status was still nebulous until 1957 when, as part of Khrushchev's administrative decentralization, Agitprop was divided into several sections and each section was attached to the Party organization of a union republic. Throughout the early 1960's discussions of Agitprop's duties in the Soviet press were rare, and the status of the department was never fully clarified.

In 1965 the department was once more centralized and functioning as a section of the Central Committee, exerting considerable influence on the direction and basic content of propaganda. The department was divided into numerous sectors, each having a particular responsibility in the overall guidance of Party propaganda. A central press sector issues directives for local newspapers, holds regional conferences of editors to check their ideological conformity, and ensures that newspapers are correctly publishing and publicizing the Party line.

Another sector of Agitprop performs a similar function for the Soviet book-publishing industry, perhaps the most extensive in the world. Other sectors in 1969 supervised the film industry as well as art, literature, and music. Any form of public expression or influence that might in any way contradict, challenge, or criticize the official government or Party line is rigidly controlled by Agitprop.

Agitprop is omnipotent in its guiding concept that the Party strives to influence the citizen in virtually every aspect of his life—in his home, at his job, and in his leisure time. The citizen becomes the object of a program that seeks as its goal the direction of his behavior in such a way as to fulfill the Party's ideological expectations for society and to ensure support for itself as a ruling force.

The sectors of Agitprop are not operational entities in the sense of actually running the various media of mass communications. This Party organ is, rather, the watchdog, the interpreter, and the director, leaving actual operations to various government agencies. The USSR Ministry of Culture, for example, is a prime element in the dissemination of information through the arts and literature. Other governmental agencies concerned with the mass media are the Committee for Radio Broadcasting and Television, Press Committee, and the Committee for Cinematography. All are carefully supervised by Agitprop. All the ministers and the chairmen of the state committees are members of the Party, and many are members of the Central Committee, thus providing the interlocking of important Party and government posts that is characteristic of the system.

The organizational structure of the Party and government at the national level is duplicated in the union republics and again at the autonomous republic level. Therefore, each of these lower echelons has its own Party Central Committee and its Agitprop, which supervise the same kind of governmental agencies that have been described for the country as a whole. Each of the republic and autonomous republic Agitprops is subordinate to the national department as well as to its own central committee.

DOMESTIC AGITATION

A significant feature of the Soviet state is the careful attention devoted to the manipulation of mass sentiments for the purpose of enlisting support for the regime and its policies. The CPSU has always taken the mobilization of the masses as a serious part of its work. Through a complex and vast network of agitational activities, manned by Party specialists, and through control of the mass media, the Party leadership pursues its objective of channeling popular attitudes and ideas along desired lines.

Agitation can be distinguished from propaganda largely by its greater immediacy, simplicity, and the vastness of the audience to which it is directed. The instruments of agitation include the press, radio, television, and the cinema; and their use differs little from their application in propaganda except in the level and kind of subject matter. Propaganda material usually is more intellectually sophisticated.

The CPSU leadership believes that the most effective agitation is carried out through personal contact. Oral agitation is divided into three categories: mass oral agitation, which employs the use of public address systems, radio or television, and the press; group agitation, which takes place between an agitator and a group of listeners; and individual confrontation.

Mass meetings are held when the leadership deems it necessary to acquaint the workers or peasants quickly and impressively with an important domestic or international policy or an event of particular significance in the life of the country. These meetings are considered by the CPSU to be of prime importance, because they impart a sense of participation on the part of the citizen that cannot be projected through the mass media.

The most ideal method with which to carry on agitational work is for the agitator to personally confront his listener, whereupon he can bring into play a multitude of psychological weapons to enlist the citizen's sympathy and support. The enormity of this task in a country with a population of 241 million, however, restricts its use to all but the most important occasions.

The agitator conducts sessions in factories or on collective farms, usually in groups, throughout the working day and even into the leisure time of the citizen. Known as chats, these sessions are regarded as a basic tool of the agitator among the citizenry and play an important role in convincing the people of the essential correctness of the leadership of the Party. These chats may take place at anytime; however, the favorite period is the lunch break during a work shift. The chats last from fifteen to twenty minutes, and the main theme is usually improved efficiency or productivity within the factory or cooperative in order to speed the "construction of Communism in the USSR."

The chat is one of the few occasions when the citizen can express his complaints to a Party representative. In these sessions the citizens are permitted to express opinions and exchange ideas with the agitators. No criticism of the Communist system, however, is allowed; with that exception, the citizens are permitted freedom of expression. The chats, therefore, serve as a medium for the Party to transmit its messages on a regular basis to the citizens and as a way for public opinion, albeit modified, to reach the Party leadership on the popularity of its policies and leadership.

The reading of a newspaper aloud to a group is another method used by the agitator, and this reading is usually followed by a guided discussion of what has been read. Agitational discussions of this type are frequently conducted under thematic headings, such as "readings from Lenin" or "people's readings about Communism."

A major function of agitation is to stimulate "socialist production," which comprises the use of awards to workers, farmers, or brigades of workers who have exceeded their quotas. This kind of agitation employs the use of leaflets, banners, posters, and medals. To reach farmers or workers in remote areas (an indication of the value the Party places on agitation), "agit-trains" are often formed, complete with Party literature, film projectors, visual aids, lecturers, and regional Party representatives.

Younger workers living in hostels are under the daily influence of the agitator; however, workers fortunate enough to have private living accommodations are usually immune from the attention of the agitator after working hours. Agitators have often forced workers to attend meetings by the simple expedient of locking the factory gates shortly before the end of a work shift. The value of such extreme moves has been frequently questioned in the Soviet press.

The existence of religion in the country after more than fifty years of Communist rule is an embarrassment to the regime; therefore, it is not surprising that much of the agitational effort is atheistic in nature. A common theme has been that modern science "proves religion to be mere superstition." Newspapers and magazines continually relate stories about the conversion of believers to atheism through the efforts of good Communists who have been able to demonstrate the unscientific bases of religion. Some of the Soviet cosmonauts have appeared on television to inform the people that they found no evidence of God during their space voyages into "the heavens."

Another constant theme of agitators from the earliest days of Bolshevism has been that the Soviet Union is in constant danger of attack by hostile forces. In the post-World War II era of Soviet power, the tone of this agitation has changed to explain that any aggressor would be immediately destroyed; however, the basic theme that the Soviet Union and its Communist allies are in constant danger is incessant.

The "cult of personality" of the Stalin era and a similar phenomenon (but to a lesser degree) during Khrushchev's reign, occupied the agitators much of the time and called upon all their resources to show the leader as infallible in any situation. The post-Khrushchev collective leadership has not used the agitational apparatus to make supermen out of any of the leaders or to create any new cult of personality.

The effects of agitation upon the convictions of the people are reported by outside observers to be less than is generally claimed by the CPSU leadership. The artificiality and the affected nature of such agitation, with often blatant contradiction of obvious facts, apparently give rise to widespread distrust among the people. The repetitive nature of routine agitation, with its exclusion of competing or contradictory points of view, sometimes reduces interest in public affairs to apathy.

While there is ample evidence of irritability among average citizens toward the agitational methods employed by the CPSU, the intense and constant indoctrination and the unceasing repetition of slogans substantiating the regime's viewpoint are calculated to induce acceptance, or at least acquiescence, on the part of the people.

Agitational pressure is usually increased in connection with special issues or to publicize measures adopted by the Party and government. Increased agitation also occurs before and during major holidays, such as May Day, the anniversary of the Revolution, and Lenin anniversaries. Agitation has been criticized by some Party propagandists as having outlived its usefulness in an age of advanced techniques and advanced communications technology; however, other Party members lauded the system, and the regime continued to train thousands of agitators.

In the late 1960's agitation was still a definite factor in the overall indoctrination scheme. Before the elections to the Supreme Soviet in 1966, over 3 million agitators were dispersed across the nation to drum up voter enthusiasm for the one-party ticket through person-to-person persuasion. Again, in the elections to local Soviets in March 1969, press reports from all over the country described the intense activities of throngs of agitators in every electoral district.

DOMESTIC PROPAGANDA

The ideological commitment to communism by the millions of individuals who run the affairs of the political system is of critical importance to the continuation of the CPSU as the ruling force in society. The direction of the Soviet Union, a vast country that has undergone a process of rapid industrialization and modernization, requires a sophisticated degree of technical expertise on the part of its managers. Thus, the CPSU is forced to fill high government posts from among individuals who possess the requisite administrative or technical qualifications but who do not necessarily share the Party's philosophy.

Propaganda is the educating and indoctrinating of those individuals, Party or non-Party, who have active roles in the functioning of the political and economic systems. The propaganda subsection of Agitprop is officially charged with the presentation of complex ideological themes, explanation of Party policies and theories, and the general indoctrination of a limited and educated audience. The leadership seeks to instill a devotion to the tenets of Marxism-Leninism in every Party member and an acceptance of the system in every non-Party activist. The regime not only seeks, but demands, commitment from every member of the system, and in the Soviet Union the system enters into every aspect of life. Therefore, it is not only political and governmental officials who must be indoctrinated and then demonstrate conformity, but also the leaders in every endeavor or enterprise.

Propaganda is most intense among Party members, candidates, and non-Party activists. On a somewhat lesser scale, Party propaganda extends to the intelligentsia where, in spite of that, there has been overt resistance, particularly during the late 1960's. Authors and artists have openly demanded a lifting of censorship and a relaxation of the necessity to always conform to the artistic dictates of the Party. Such noncomformist attitudes have demanded and received the attention of propagandists and agitators, who have sought to counter the effects of such "heresy." Some of the dissenters have felt the coercion of the police system, which is always prepared to support Agitprop when such support is deemed necessary (see ch. 17, Intellectual Expression).

Propaganda centers around courses in the history of the CPSU, dialectical and historical materialism, Marxist-Leninist thought, and the political and economic aims and goals of the CPSU. Party propaganda is defined as the oral and printed explanation of the theory of Marxism-Leninism and the programs of the CPSU, but it also embraces a wide variety of fields, such as atheism, industrial and agricultural production, law, business management, science, and many others in addition to ideology and politics.

The major methods of conducting propaganda are through the press, oral discussions or seminars, independent study, and through various institutions operated by the Party's educational system, mostly under the direction of Agitprop. The aim of every propaganda program is not only to exclude views considered hostile to the regime and to indoctrinate, but also to ensure that every medium for the conveyance of ideas is positively attuned to the objectives of the CPSU. Through the selection, training, and supervision of Party candidates and government employees, the CPSU can avoid much of the obtrusive and irritating criticism resulting from the enforcement of direct censorship, although censorship, like the pervasive presence of the secret police, is always available as a weapon of coercion.

Formal indoctrination of Party members and non-Party government officials is provided by the CPSU through a pyramid of educational institutions, usually controlled and administered by Agitprop. This pyramid system is built upon a basis of evening classes and study groups, leading to more formal courses and seminars and finally culminating in the two- and four-year university-level courses given at the Party schools in Moscow or in the republics. Party propaganda is a continuous process, and refresher courses are constantly in progress at all levels of the pyramid.

There are approximately twenty-five schools with the title "Higher Party School" in the Soviet Union. These are located in Moscow, Leningrad, and other major cities. Moscow also has the Institute of Marxism-Leninism, which has branches in several of the republics, and the Academy of Social Sciences (formerly the Marx-Engels Institute); both offer courses designed primarily for rising young Party luminaries. The curriculum of the average Party school stresses Party history, Marxist-Leninist thought, political economy, the history of the international working class, the history of national independence movements, and Party and state administration. The schools, while heightening or instilling the political values of the CPSU in their students, also provide practical training in public administration and law.

Admittance or appointment to a responsible position in the CPSU or the government by any individual who has not mastered the "minimum knowledge of Marxist-Leninist thought and CPSU history" is forbidden by a Central Committee decree, published in 1956. Even experts of a technical nature called in by the government or the Party for a short-term project are not immune to the indoctrination process, since the Party provides a multitude of short intensive courses and seminars.

The highest level of Party education open to non-Party individuals and lower ranking government officials is the system of evening schools known as the universities of Marxism-Leninism. Attendance is voluntary, although considerable pressure is exercised on government employees to attend and advancement without simultaneous enrollment in these universities is doubtful. Since the end of World War II these universities have undergone considerable expansion, and in 1966 estimated enrollment was 200,000. The length of the course of study is two to three years and, the course syllabus is similar to that found in the higher level schools, although not so intense or comprehensive. No method is available to indicate how many individuals enter the schools either from genuine political or ideological motivations or from realization that advancement within the governmental system without attendance is impossible, regardless of academic background or experience.

For the average Party member and Soviet citizen, the CPSU has urged a program of self-education in Marxist-Leninist thought. A Central Committee directive in 1960 pointed out that self-education was a basic method for mastering the essentials of Marxism, a method "fully proved in practice." The leadership noted that, because of the voluminous publishing in the country, it was possible for anyone to secure all the materials to study independently. Only those individuals who lacked the ability for independent study were urged to work in groups or attend seminars called study circles. Independent study in 1969 included a wide network of theoretical seminars to ensure that the individual who embarked on a program was progressing along the proper course.

Circles for the study of the history of the CPSU and Marxist-Leninist thought date back to 1938 and the announcement of the publication of the *History of the All-Union Communist Party (Bolshevik)*, usually known as the "Short Course." During Stalin's reign emphasis was placed on these study circles along with independent study and self-education. The "Short Course" became the standard textbook. After Stalin's death it became increasingly obvious that independent study based on the tendentious, if not falsified, accounts of Stalin's role in Party history was self-defeating.

At the Twentieth Party Congress in 1956 Khrushchev complained about the way in which propaganda had been "cut off" from the building of communism. A number of innovations were immediately introduced by Agitprop toward increasing and intensifying propaganda activities. A new Party history, a substantial revision of the 1938 issue to conform with the denigration of Stalin, was published in 1960 to serve as the new basis for independent study. The text was further revised in 1962 in accordance with the dictates of the personality cult that was growing up around Khrushchev and then revised again in 1965 to account for the premier's forced retirement.

The decree of the Central Committee of the CPSU issued in January 1960 serves as the basis for all propaganda directives. The decree, entitled "On the Tasks of Party Propaganda Under Present Day Conditions," calls for the orientation of propaganda not only toward Party members and government functionaries but also toward the mobilization of the masses in fulfilling the economic tasks of building communism. The decree recommends study circles and seminars in CPSU history and Marxist-Leninist thought, as well as in the international relations of the Soviet Union, domestic policy, and atheism.

In 1969 there were over 1 million leaders of circles, seminars, and political schools active in the Soviet Union. In 1965 it was estimated that over 35 million people, 70 percent of them non-Party, had participated in some level of Party indoctrination and courses. Editorials, frequently appearing in the Soviet press, however, have pointed out the unpopularity of compulsory political study and the general preoccupation of the population at all levels with housing shortages, food, leisure time activities, and other aspects of day-to-day life rather than with ideology.

EXTERNAL PROPAGANDA AND AGITATION

The earliest Bolshevik propaganda and agitation directed to foreign audiences was concerned almost exclusively with world revolution and was aimed principally at European countries that Lenin thought were particularly susceptible. Efforts to discredit existing governments and to spread discontent among the working classes of various nations received the greatest attention. The Comintern (Communist International) was formed in Moscow in 1919 to serve as a directorate for world revolution and to act as coordinator for the worldwide propaganda and agitation agency. Officials of Agitprop closely supervised the efforts of Comintern personnel until the latter organization was finally abolished during World War II.

After Lenin's death and the power struggle that followed, the Party line sometimes faltered, particularly during the period of modified free enterprise known as the New Economic Policy (Novaya Ekonomicheskaya Politika—NEP). Preaching Soviet socialism abroad while practicing modified capitalism at home proved difficult, and the idea of imminent world revolution was considerably dimmed by the mid-1920's.

With the advent of Stalin to full power and the initiation of the First Five-Year Plan, the propaganda theme became an exposition of the successes of the Soviet brand of socialism. Communist Party members from all over the world dutifully attended meetings of the Comintern in Moscow, and many attended long and short courses at Soviet Party schools. In this manner they were trained as propagandists, prepared to take the Party line back home and to train indigenous agitators for the indoctrination of the working classes in dozens of the world's countries.

In the 1930's the Party continued its efforts to prove the superiority of the Soviet system, but the rise of Stalin at home and the rise of Hitler in Germany brought new propaganda themes. Not only was the Soviet system advertised as the best of all possible systems for the entire world, but also the Soviet leader was pictured as the sole source of all Marxist-Leninist interpretation and the infallible leader of international communism. At the same time, a major effort was made to bring about a united front against Nazi Germany.

This phase ended with the signing of the Nazi-Soviet Nonaggression Pact of 1939. Overnight the propaganda line changed, and Western imperialism replaced Naziism as the world's greatest evil. The Nazi invasion of the Soviet Union in June 1941 ended the short-lived detente between communism and fascism, which required another rapid change for the propagandists. Agitprop turned its attention to vilification of the Nazis and praise of the Allies. Stalin abolished the Comintern in 1943 to reassure the Western Allies that his nation was not maintaining a subversive instrument against them while facing a common enemy.

After World War II, the alliance dissolved, and propagandists became the chief combatants of the cold war. The breakup of colonial empires provided fertile fields for Agitprop agents. Because of reconstruction at home, the Soviets could not afford to send material aid, but they could afford to send quantities of printed materials and to beam endless agitational radio broadcasts into the colonies and former colonies. The Soviet Union, standing powerful amidst the ashes of formerly great European nations, pointed to itself as the perfect example of what could be accomplished in a short time by a revolutionary proletariat. Former colonial powers were vilified, while the newly independent countries were pounded with the insistent message that the Soviet way was the only way. Stalin was presented as some sort of a superman, a latter-day prophet who would lead all of the world's peasants and workers out of oppression and bondage.

Khrushchev, during his term in power, took a giant step toward destroying the Stalin image, "the cult of personality" as Khrushchev called it. In so doing, he shook the foundations of the world Communist movement, but the propaganda machine survived and continued to grind out the basic message of Soviet superiority. Khrushchev himself became a traveling propagandist and, on one visit to the United Nations, a shoe-banging agitator. One of the charges made against Khrushchev after his ouster was that he was fostering a cult of personality of his own through the efforts of Agitprop. The post-Khrushchev era has been less bombastic, but the machine grinds on, calling for world disarmament and peace and vilifying the "imperialists."

The propaganda and agitation sent abroad from the Soviet Union generally have three directions: toward the thirteen other Communist-ruled countries of the world; toward countries in Western, Middle Eastern, and Asian alliances that the Soviets consider inimical to their own international position; and toward countries that are nonaligned. Two of the Communist-ruled nations, China and Albania, have become unfriendly and a third, Yugoslavia, has been making its own policies since 1948—all of which necessitates a different orientation of the propaganda and agitation effort. To other Communist nations and to countries with strong indigenous Communist parties, the policymakers in the Kremlin have tried to buttress their propaganda efforts with mass meetings. The general aim of these meetings, as well as of much of the propaganda, has been to reestablish Soviet hegemony over the world Communist movement.

Toward the uncommitted nations, the propaganda has been principally aimed at showing emerging nations that the Soviet Union is the champion of the downtrodden and exploited peoples of the world wherever they may be found. Support for "wars of national liberation" has been constant, despite the seemingly contradictory line of "peaceful coexistence" that has been in vogue since the Khrushchev era. Since 1954 the Soviets have also supported their word barrage with economic aid, trade, and long-term credits.

Toward the remainder of the world, particularly member nations of alliances that the Communists consider hostile, the propaganda message has been designed to divide and weaken alignments. Once again the Soviet Union puts itself forward as the champion of world peace. Various international organizations, such as the World Peace Council, the World Federation of Trade Unions, and the International Union of Students, seek to disseminate the Party line and, despite appearances of internationalism and autonomy, firm control of these organizations is in the hands of Agitprop.

In 1969 one of the most influential international organs for the transmission of Soviet propaganda was the journal *World Marxist Review.* Organized in 1958 and published in Prague, Czechoslovakia, the journal is considered the leading organ of the world Communist movement for the dissemination of propaganda and the influencing of world opinion in favor of the Soviet Union and its political and economic systems. The *World Marxist Review* is published in all major European languages and is widely circulated abroad.

CHAPTER 27

POLITICAL ATTITUDES AND REACTIONS

The political values and orientations of the people in 1970 reflected an admixture of Marxist-Leninist theory and Russian historical tradition, tempered by the practices of the Communist Party of the Soviet Union (CPSU). Despite more than fifty years of Soviet-style communism, attitudes toward leadership and authority in 1970 were, on the whole, strikingly similar to those held by peoples of the former Russian Empire. Other political attitudes and reactions, however, have been formulated during the Soviet era that bear little or no resemblance to those of the past.

Among the more than 100 ethnic groups, social and political differences were more prevalent than similarities. Certain attitudes toward the CPSU, its achievements, the bureaucracy, and authority in general, however, whether entertained by a Soviet Russian citizen in Moscow or a Soviet Uzbek citizen in Tashkent, were often similar.

Many of the Communist theories that have guided the CPSU are based on Lenin's interpretations of Marxist dogma. More important in the development of the values and attitudes of the citizenry, however, have been the practices of the CPSU, which have been broadly based on the doctrine of the dictatorship of the proletariat, a doctrine chiefly attributable to Lenin and one that he defined as "rule based on force not bound by law." The political instrument of this dictatorship has been the Party, which has arrogated the right to complete domination—that is, the right to control the entire political, economic, and cultural structure of Soviet society (see ch. 5, The Political System; ch. 21, Political Dynamics).

In a country where one party has insistently proclaimed that it is the source of all legitimate political power and wisdom, the development of independent values has been circumscribed. Throughout its history the CPSU has dictated the accepted—and solely acceptable—ideological views. As a result, Soviet citizens have been inhibited in their articulation of political ideas, have accepted the Party line, or have paid lipservice to the official ideology. No public opinion polls are published to show the relative popularity of Soviet leaders, nor do people readily express their political views to Western reporters or correspondents. Since the death of Stalin, however, controls have been sufficiently relaxed for Western observers to make some observations concerning the attitudes of the average citizen.

During the 1960's more foreigners visited the Soviet Union as tourists than ever before. The published and unpublished reports of these visitors plus the reports of diplomats, correspondents, and exchange groups can be pieced together to give some idea of what the Soviet citizen thinks about his government, about his way of life, and about the outside world.

The concentration of all policymaking and executive power in a single, all-embracing Party has effectively blocked the emergence of any legitimate political groupings that can assert the interests and aspirations of the people against the centralized authority. As officially formulated, the basic political goal is to engender whole-hearted support of the Party's ideals of self-discipline, the mastery of Marxist-Leninist dogma, and the development of knowledge and skills needed to implement Party policies and plans. As a result, the political values and attitudes of the people are enmeshed within an overwhelming totalitarian system, in which the Party mobilizes all human and material resources toward the creation of a Communist society.

The official ideals, priorities, and goals differ from those of many of the people who, although they value the concept of creating a great and strong country, both economically and militarily, desire freedom from the ceaseless bombardment of official propaganda and the constant demands from them for more work, more contribution of all kinds, and ever-higher production in all sectors of the economy. The objections of the people are not against the Communist system itself but against the rigid, relentless, bureaucratic apparatus that has negated the system's promises for justice, fraternity, and equality. The police pressure is particularly objectionable as an instrument of political control, because its use is interpreted by most people as a lack of trust and respect for their loyalty to the country.

Justification to the people of the pattern of political control developed by the Party and the relations between the rulers and the ruled has not been deemed necessary, because the state's authority and power do not derive from any popular mandate. This authority is based on the dictates of the Party and backed by the security forces. The ruling elite regards its primary mission as the preservation of the victories of the Revolution and the building of a Communist society. The means employed by the Party, however, to perpetuate its rule and attain its goals have created a wide gap between promises and performance and also produced doubt and skepticism in the minds of some people in the value of the goals and in the veracity and good faith of the rulers.

DETERMINANTS OF VALUES AND ATTITUDES

The Soviet people hold certain traditional concepts regarding the authority of the state that are deeply rooted in Russian history. In the period known as The Time of Troubles at the beginning of the seventeenth century, the country had no tsar; an assembly, even with some elected delegates, held temporary power. This assembly did not develop as a representative kind of government, however, but searched for a tsar who would be a symbol of absolute authority. Having found that symbol in the person of the first Romanov tsar, the assembly deteriorated into obscurity and finally disappeared. The tsar remained as the absolute autocrat, and absolutism became a fact of Russian life that was carried over into the Soviet era 300 years later (see ch. 3, Historical Setting).

Absolutism was not considered inherently evil; it was the abuse of power and oppression that brought hardships to the people and, more often than not, the people thought of the tsar or the dictator as being above, and apart from, the oppressive conditions they lived under. Subordinates and bureaucrats were usually blamed for evil conditions and, throughout history, the plea of the peasant was that if only the tsar knew what was going on, or if only Lenin or Stalin knew, then something would be done to alleviate their adversity.

Because rule, whether imperial or Soviet, has usually been arbitrary and oppressive, the people developed defensive mechanisms and evasive tactics to deal with the underlings they considered to be their oppressors. The people learned to heap praise on the minor bureaucrats, offered bribes, pretended failure to comprehend regulations and procedures, or openly evaded orders. The most common attitude has been one of outward acceptance while inwardly remaining aloof and attempting to make the best of existing conditions.

The people's attitudes toward the system are conditioned by the absolute hegemony of the Party, the arbitrary way in which it arrives at decisions, and the disregard of public opinion. Western correspondents who visited the Soviet Union in 1967 to report on the fiftieth anniversary of the Revolution generally reported a lack of revolutionary zeal on the part of citizens with whom they had contact. The attitudes most often expressed concerned the desires for a quieter and more normal life, for more material benefits, and for a lessening of official pressures in their private lives.

It is in the sphere of internal political and economic pressures on the citizens, occasioned by the pursuit of Party goals, that the chief differences appear between the official goals and the private wishes and aspirations of many people. As far as can be ascertained, the average citizen's wish is to be let alone, not to be morally and physically coerced into ever higher tempo of work, and not to be faced with constant demands for more production. These wishes seem to him to be compatible with the ideas and promises originally made by Lenin.

Stalin's long period of absolute rule is viewed by much of the outside world as a reign of terror but, within the Soviet Union, there appear to be conflicting attitudes in general and, sometimes, ambivalent feelings on the part of individuals. There are millions of Soviet citizens who have good cause to remember the excesses of Stalinism, because they suffered personally or had a close relative or friend who disappeared, either never to be seen again or to spend long years in some labor camp. Guilt or innocence in any legal sense had little or nothing to do with arrests, convictions, and sentences during the years of Stalin's terror.

Half the population of the Soviet Union in 1970 had not reached their teens at the time of Stalin's death in 1953. To this large segment of the population, Stalin is a figure of recent history, World War II is even more remote, and the terror of the 1930's is a historical epoch about which they may read and hear but in which they cannot possibly have emotional involvement as do their elders.

Even with the older generations that remember Stalin, there often appears a traditional dichotomy of thought that separates the leader from the system. After Khrushchev denounced the excesses of Stalinism in 1956 and after publication in the Soviet press of Aleksandr Solzhenitsyn's *One Day in the Life of Ivan Denisovich*, open discussion about the period became prevalent. Discussion, however, usually was in terms of "the cult of personality" rather than directly about Stalinism or Stalinist abuses of power.

Many of the so-called dissident intellectuals of the 1960's proclaimed themselves to be good Soviet citizens whose sole aim was to improve, rather than to destroy, the system. Solzhenitsyn, for example, whose novels *Cancer Ward* and *The First Circle* were published in the West but not in the Soviet Union, has stated emphatically that his works do not condemn but criticize, in order to bring about needed reforms in the areas of police surveillance and censorship. Yevgeny Yevtushenko, the well-known poet whose fortunes have seesawed according to the political tone of his poetry, has always stated that he is a good Soviet citizen who only desires improvement of the system. The general attitude of the people toward the dissident intellectuals is almost impossible to determine, and experienced Western observers have urged caution in viewing such dissidence as a movement rather than merely outspoken statements by individuals.

Attempts by post-Stalin rulers to eliminate or reduce some of the primary sources of popular resentment against the Soviet system seem to have had a relaxing effect on the people. The reduction of the application of terror after Stalin's death and subsequent efforts to improve living standards signified an awareness on the part of the new leaders that Stalin's method of rule had had a debilitating effect on the people's relations with the state. In order to make their rule more palatable, therefore, they began making adjustments in the political and economic structure; but they have done so without sacrificing the basic feature of the system, namely, the monopoly of power in the elite of the one-party system.

In effecting changes to ameliorate some of the worst features of Stalinist rule, both Khrushchev during his decade of rule and the Brezhnev-Kosygin duumvirate that succeeded him lost some of the freedom of maneuver, such as the use of terror; but this was more than compensated for by an apparent increase in popular support for the basic political and economic values to which the Party is committed.

Moreover, the post-Stalin leaders have cultivated the national consciousness of the people and have tried to ingratiate themselves to the people through frequent visits to factories, construction sites, and agricultural collectives. During World War II Stalin appealed to the patriotic sentiments of the people, reiterating in particular the nineteenth-century ideas that Russia had a "special mission" to fulfill in the way of assuring world peace and prosperity and that, through the ages, the Russians had had the strength and capacity to endure any hardship. But unlike Khrushchev, Brezhnev, or Kosygin, Stalin kept himself aloof from the people, much more so than any of the autocratic tsars had done.

The Party leadership has tried to maintain a closed society and, for that reason, it has been difficult to gauge the attitude of the people toward the Party. The official position is that the average citizen is dedicated to, and identifies himself closely with, the Party and that he is proud of the Party's achievements. For various reasons, mostly ideological and political, a segment of the population probably conforms to the image created by the official propaganda, but this segment would probably have vested interests in the system. Individuals have expressed dissatisfaction with the system and with official propaganda, but no statistical evidence is available on which to base an assessment of the attitudes of the masses of Soviet citizens.

Many aspects of the Soviet system, however, seem to have won approval by the majority of the people. Among them are the country's rapid industrial development, including state ownership of industries; the strengthening of the country's military might and the prestige and influence it has gained in the world; and the general accomplishments in the state welfare services and in education, arts, and sciences. The dogma of Marxism-Leninism is now rooted in the way most Soviets think about things, and some of them have even been convinced of the virtues of the system, because through its achievements it has given them more self-esteem and pride in their country than they ever had before.

Even many dissidents in society show no interest in returning to capitalism, for they feel that the many shortcomings in the Communist system can be corrected in time by the people once they have been allowed more freedom to criticize them. From interviews and conversations that Western correspondents and diplomats have had with average Soviet citizens in the late 1960's, however, the consensus is that the latter think more about material well-being than they do about politics. This does not exclude the desire on the part of some people for more freedoms, such as freedom of the press, for example, but they generally state that their desires can be fulfilled within the system if it is made to work for the people.

The attitude of Soviet youth—in 1969 about half of the country's population was under twenty-seven years of age—toward policies in general and communism in particular is considered to be of extreme importance by the regime. At the Twenty-third Party Congress in 1966, Party General Secretary Brezhnev complained that the present generation did not possess the revolutionary spirit of the older generation and that it had become apathetic. Since his criticism the Party, chiefly through the Komsomol (Young Communist League), has striven to stir patriotism among the more indifferent youth.

The Komsomol drive has been directed especially at preventing youth from being overly influenced by publication of the works of dissident young writers who have been accused of depicting Soviet society in a poor light. The dissidents hold that patriotism and nationalism are desirable traits but point out that, in pre-1917 Russia, ultrarevolutionary and anti-Semitic elements emerged under the cloak of patriotism.

According to Western scholars who have visited the Soviet Union during the 1960's, a general indifference toward politics prevails among young people, although there is no question about their loyalty to their country. With regard to communism, Soviet youth are reported to feel that, if properly applied, it could be beneficial to society. Their primary consideration, however, is to make their own place in the world without being constantly dictated to by an ever-present bureaucracy. In essence, the youth want to create a good life for themselves.

Day-do-day political activities do not particularly interest the majority of Soviet young people, nor do they like political slogans and outworn clichés. As far as can be ascertained, most of them agree with the Party's general policies in the economic and educational fields but disagree, at times openly, with the suppression of liberals and dissident intellectuals. Most of them seem to be eager to learn how the peoples of the capitalist world live and what they think.

When asked about their top rulers, those young people who answer usually express admiration for Kosygin, whom they regard as an intelligent and dedicated economist. The attitude toward Brezhnev is one of indifference, and he is somewhat derogatively referred to as an *apparatchik* (a man of the apparatus—see Glossary). In an age in which the technicians or technocrats have practically become a class unto themselves, there appears to be a disdainful attitude toward the *apparatchik*, whose entire career has been solely in Party work. Evidently, the enterprise manager or the collective farm manager whose only qualification for his job is his Party standing no longer commands the respect of his subordinates. The Party hierarchy, aware of changed attitudes, has insisted on continuing education for all echelons of leaders in all areas of the economy.

PEOPLE'S ATTITUDE TOWARD THE GOVERNMENT

There is no tradition in the Soviet Union by which the government derived its sanction from the governed. The idea of a government that takes any of its authority and prerogatives from the people is still outside the conception of the average citizen, despite the explicit provision of the Constitution for popular elections of all governmental bodies, from the lowest to the highest. Such elections are conducted regularly, but the people are aware that all they do is approve the candidates presented to them by the Party.

Aside from sophisticated intellectuals and some students who know how the democratic systems work in the West, the rank and file seem to think of political parties, if they think about them at all, as groups of plotters determined to achieve power irrespective of the means employed. The Bolshevik Party suppressed all other political parties after it seized power in 1917 and has since then never allowed the emergence of any other political party or group.

After the great Stalinist purges of 1936—38, political discussion in the Soviet Union became too dangerous even within the top circles of the regime and, in fact, discussions of policy were forbidden even in 1970 in Party organization meetings, although discussions on the implementation of policy were encouraged. Only a handful of Party leaders play a part in deciding policy, but policy is propagated through officials of all ranks, through the whole spectrum of the information and propaganda apparatus and through public lectures and meetings of numerous Party and mass organizations.

With regard to his feelings and attitudes toward the government, the average citizen is guided by the fact that he cannot engage in free political discussion, even if he is inclined to, and that he must, at least on the surface, accept Party policies without question. But this does not imply that he is politically passive or indifferent toward the government's actions, particularly those actions that affect his family or his personal interests. He has in fact learned through experience which governmental orders he must obey and which he can ignore with impunity.

The average citizen also apparently resents the government's policy of holding responsible groups of people for the errors of particular individuals as well as the constant police control and surveillance over all his activities. He has conditioned himself, however, to conceal resentments and to give the outward impression that he willingly submits to everything.

There are, however, some important advantages and benefits that the regime has provided to the people and for which they seem to be grateful. In the political field, a centralized government has given the nation stability and purpose, has afforded the opportunity for personal improvement, and has made possible the economic features of the welfare state that the people seem to approve of and desire. But despite these acceptable features, the whole political style of the regime has created a chasm that sets apart the rulers from the ruled. This has given rise to a general impression that the Party and everything it stands for is against the vital interests of the individual. The invasion of the privacy of his home, the restrictions of his movements through control of housing and employment, and measures that restrict his association with others are particularly abhorrent. Most people view the Soviet bureaucrats as their ancestors saw the bureaucrats of the tsars: aloof, cold, impersonal, distant from most people's problems and wishes, domineering, coercive and punitive, and generally unyielding.

From the time of Lenin until the present, the rulers have made a clear distinction between the bureaucrats and the people. The workers, peasants, employees, and professional people are mere cogs in the wheels of the state apparatus; they are, as Stalin phrased it in 1945, expected to support the regime as the base supports the summit. Because of this situation, the state apparatus does not inspire a sense of identification among the people in general.

The view of the state as an authoritarian power similar to the one the Revolution had overthrown was strengthened by the nationalization of land and forced collectivization, the regimentation of all public life, and the punitive attitude of the central authority. The fact that the bureaucracy is largely recruited from the common people has made no essential difference. To the people the state bureaucracy is a force that is constantly mobilizing them, lecturing and indoctrinating them, and limiting their choice of occupation and freedom to speak their minds.

As for the attitude of the bureaucrats, the most highly motivated

562

among them seem to be convinced of the essential rightness of the Soviet way of life and the legitimacy of the Party as the dominant and monopolistic political force in society. They seem to think always in terms of the future, in the long-range process of building up the country and making it modern, powerful, industrialized, and great. Although many of them admit that things are not easy, they appear to reason that happiness does not lie in today but in tomorrow.

Western scholars have attributed an opportunistic code of behavior to the average citizen in his relations with the bureaucracy; that is, the worker or farmer tries to get as much as possible from the system while giving as little as possible of himself. The theory is borne out by recurrent articles in the Soviet press dealing with opportunists who are discovered even in the Party ranks. The prevalence of opportunism negates the statement of dogma that the people and the state are one.

The official aim is to propagate the myth that the Soviet system is the political incarnation of a people's state. Conversely, the people's attitude toward the government is characterized by a general belief that Party members receive from the state more than they deserve and that others receive less than is due them. There is also a strong feeling that, contrary of the official propaganda line, the interests of the Communists and those of the people do not coincide.

Despite the changes that have occurred in methods of work since Stalin's death, the Party still remains the purveyor of what it dictates to be the truth, controlling all information outlets and the press. Newspapers confine themselves to expounding the current Party line. The large number of national and local periodicals also follow the Moscow directives, at times adapting their material to local conditions. Radio and television, both owned by the government, fulfill the same function. Though the news in general conforms to the Party line, a desire for change is common among the majority of intellectuals and students. A large number of poems, short stories, and novels are being privately circulated, some even published in the more liberal periodicals—*Novy Mir* (New World) and *Yunost*, (Youth), for example—which criticize Stalinist oppressions, express fear of the revival of Stalinist methods of rule, and voice open and unflattering criticism of society.

A small but well-known and vociferous group of writers, including the late Boris Pasternak, Andrei Voznesensky, and Aleksandr Solzhenitsyn, have even spoken of what they term the psychological gulf between the rulers, or "them," and the people, or "us," expressions that were also reflected in the works of such noted writers of the nineteenth century as Gogol, Tolstoy, and Dostoevsky. It is the contention of the dissident writers that they are in search of an authentic national identity and that their primary purpose is to stir the consciences of the people toward a freer society.

The dissidents claim that there is nothing in Soviet law to prevent them from exercising their rights to publish their works at home or abroad. The repressive measures that the government has taken since two writers, Andrei Sinyavsky and Yuli Daniel, were tried and sentenced to hard labor in February 1966 for writing "anti-Soviet propaganda" are indicative of the Kremlin rulers' fear that new and unorthodox political attitudes and values might develop in the people's minds.

Despite the repressive measures against dissident writers and other elements that are struggling for a more liberal policy for the dissemination of news and ideas, information about life in the capitalist countries is seeping in. There are definite signs that more and more people are interested in the outside world, especially in the United States, West Germany, and Communist China, and want to travel abroad. They do not accept the official line as the complete truth, and few of them take Party slogans very seriously. This is particularly true with regard to foreign affairs. In the immediate postwar period the government tried, with some success, to create in the minds of the people the impression that the West, in general, and the United States, in particular, were dominated by warmongering groups committed to waging a war of destruction against the Soviet Union. In the post-Stalin era, however, stress has been laid on the dangers deriving from an emerging "militant" Germany, a danger that many people still keenly feel because of the suffering and destruction during World War II.

Since 1960, however, the anti-West image has been dulled by the increasing campaign against Communist China which, because of its territorial propinquity and vast population, represents for most people a deadly enemy. In any event, there seems to be substantial pride among the people in Soviet strength and in the image of their country as a leading world power.

The changes that have occurred in the way of relaxation of police controls since Stalin's death have not brought any fundamental change in the government's system of political control. The people are fully aware that there is no guarantee that another Stalin may not arise or that police activities may not be intensified again; for the policy that sent millions of innocent people to the execution block or to forced labor camps, as a result of secret police trials in the 1930's and 1940's, has not been fully repudiated. The regimes of Stalin's successors have not been dreaded or distrusted to the degree that Stalinism was, but neither have they been very popular with the people except insofar as they have brought material benefits. This stems partly from the people's awareness that the Party and its leadership suspect everybody and consider every citizen as potentially disloyal until he has proved otherwise.

564

By and large, the people's attitudes toward the government have been conditioned by the quality and behavior of the elite that run the state, by the policies that the Party has formulated for the government, and by the behavior of the rank-and-file Party activists and the bureaucrats. These attitudes have changed for the better since the days when Stalin ruled the country singlehandedly.

POLITICAL ATTITUDES OF THE NATIONAL MINORITIES

As of 1970 the nationalistic aspirations and feelings of the ethnic minorities—about half of the country's population—were still very strong, if not actively flourishing. The contention of the government that its policy of "ethnic democracy" had created harmonious relations among the numerous ethnic groups in the political process of the country is not borne out by facts. All available information shows that many ethnic minorities have no more succumbed to complete Sovietization under Communist rule than they had yielded to Russification under tsarist autocracy. Their attitude toward assimilation and Sovietization has been one of silent defiance, and their basic aim is still the preservation of their national and cultural identities.

The regime itself, in a sense, has fostered nationalist feelings among the major ethnic groups by its policy of encouraging the development of local languages and cultures and nourishing a pride in ethnic identity. The first Party secretary of each of the fourteen non-Russian republics is of indigenous nationality. These indigenous Party leaders publicly speak as Soviet patriots, but in private they often boast of their native culture and betray feelings of what the Moscow propaganda media condemn as "bourgeois nationalism." *Pravda* has published articles complaining that even Party officials in the non-Russian republics cling to nationalistic views and traditions, underestimate the importance of exchange of cadres (Party activist groups—see Glossary) among the peoples of the Soviet Union, and do not trust cadres of other nationalities. The articles have also alluded to ethnic frictions in everyday life and have accused Party organizations of paying insufficient attention to Marxist-Leninist education and to political work and atheist propaganda, especially in the republics with a predominantly Muslim population.

Other complaints in the Moscow press have included charges that "remnants of a nationalistic nature" are still very much in existence in some republics where people idealize the past and preserve outdated customs. *Pravda* articles have also often assailed those who excessively stress the role of their particular republics in the supply of natural resources and labor and have thus attempted to denigrate the contributions of the other republics.

All available information at the beginning of 1970 indicated that the various nationalities still did not share much in common with other peoples in the Soviet Union beyond their minority status. In fact, the behavior of the government toward the minorities attests to their stubborn opposition against being absorbed into a homogeneous Soviet culture. At various times, thousands of officials, teachers, writers, and other members of the intellectual classes have been purged from the Party and state apparatus on charges of harboring "bourgeois nationalist feelings" (see ch. 9, Ethnic Groups).

There have been different levels of ethnic political feelings and aspirations among the national minorities. In the Baltic republics of Lithuania, Estonia, and Latvia, for instance, which were independent states in the period between the two world wars, there is more of an intellectual movement and a striving for greater national identity. In these areas the Russian presence rankles, and people are reluctant to speak Russian. In the Ukraine, where on many occasions intellectuals branded as "bourgeois nationalists" have been tried and imprisoned, there is an unconcealed pride in the Ukrainian language and culture. There have even been instances at Lvov University in which students have refused to use Russian in the classroom. The nationalistic feelings and ferment in the Baltic and the Ukraine are not aimed so much to throw off Soviet rule as to seek greater national identity and freedom.

In the developing regions of central Asia and the Transcaucasus, ethnic feelings revolve around the people's clinging to old ways and customs. Some prefer a family life to a collective one, and private sheep raising to employment in the collective economy. The local Party press in these areas often reminds the people that the Russians have greatly aided in their economic development, that they must learn to live together peacefully, and that intermarriage must be tolerated.

The persistent nationalist feelings and aspirations of the ethnic minorities continued in 1970 to be of deep concern to the Kremlin rulers, who often admit of the "survivals of bourgeois nationalism." An example of this concern was the statement that Politburo member Nikolai V. Podgorny made in November 1969 to the effect that nationalism, irrespective of the form or degree of manifestation, was a bitter enemy of the friendship of peoples. As many Western analysts have interpreted it, one of the major reasons for the Kremlin's decision to invade Czechoslovakia in 1968 was the fear that Czechoslovak national communism would infest not only the Soviet-bloc countries but ultimately the Soviet republics bordering them as well. Although there is no danger of separation in the non-Russian republics, Western scholars suggest that the nationality question may prove to be a thorny one for the Soviet leadership for many years to come.

NATIONAL SYMBOLS AND HOLIDAYS

The official arms of the Soviet Union are a sickle and hammer against a globe depicted in the rays of the sun and surrounded by ears of grain with the inscription "Workers of All Countries, Unite!" At the top of the arms is a five-pointed red star. The national flag is of red cloth with sickle and hammer depicted in gold, and above them a five-pointed star bordered in gold. Each of the fifteen constituent republics has its own arms and flag. Common in all of them is the hammer and sickle, the red star, and the inscription "Workers of All Countries, Unite!"

Immediately after the seizure of power the Bolsheviks adopted the "Internationale" as the official anthem of the Soviet Union. In 1943, however, Stalin replaced it with a new national hymn called "Hymn of the Soviet Union," or "State Hymn of the USSR." Its musical title (first line) is "The Union of Indissoluble Free Republics." It is not known whether the constituent republics have their own anthems.

The symbolic heartstone of the Soviet Union is the Red Square in Moscow, where the Kremlin (the citadel of both tsarist and Communist rulers), the Lenin Mausoleum, and the famous Saint Basil's Cathedral are located. Equally important to the Soviets is the Winter Palace in Leningrad, whose seizure on November 7, 1917, marked the triumph of the Bolshevik Revolution.

Vladimir Ilyich Lenin is considered the father of the Soviet Union and its national hero. His glass-encased embalmed body lies in the huge Lenin Mausoleum, where during visiting hours long lines of citizens wait patiently to view his body. Lenin is genuinely revered by vast numbers of citizens, even among the minority groups, because he is still considered as the champion of the underprivileged and downtrodden. Dying as he did in the midst of the New Economic Policy (Novaya Ekonomicheskaya Politika—NEP) and before the seizure of the land from the peasants and its collectivization, Lenin is not held responsible for Stalin's excesses.

During his lifetime Joseph Stalin was almost deified and was beloved by many people who were not aware of his widespread persecutions and executions. His reputation, however, was tarnished after Khrushchev made public his crimes. Beginning about 1967, the Kremlin rulers have attempted to reassess his contributions to the Soviet state and give him some credit in particular for his part in winning the war against Hitler's Germany. After his death in 1953 his body was laid by the side of Lenin's, but in 1961 it was removed from the Lenin Mausoleum and was placed in a grave behind Lenin's shrine. Stalin, a Georgian, is still revered in much of his native Georgia, and a huge portrait as he lay in his bier hangs in Gori, Georgia, where he was born.

After World War II a number of pre-Revolutionary Russian rulers were restored to prominence in Russian history and presented to the people as heroes after having been discredited by Lenin and his colleagues after the Revolution. Among these were Ivan the Terrible, Peter the Great, and Catherine the Great. They were lauded by the Soviet propaganda media for their efforts to curb the powers of the feudal landowners; to establish a strong, centralized government; and, in the case of Peter the Great and Empress Catherine, to create a great, strong Russia. The national minorities have their heroes, but the Kremlin rulers discourage any signs indicating that they are being worshiped by the local population.

In recent years, the government has been spending large sums of money to restore its artistic and architectural treasures. Orthodox churches and prominent monasteries, tsarist palaces, former private mansions and residences, and even whole towns are being preserved and renewed. Soviet officials say that they are not restoring tsarist ideas, only tsarist beauty. According to Western observers, these measures are appreciated by the people. An example of this appreciation is the large number of people visiting restored museums and churches. The people's appreciation for the revival of old cultural objects is also shown by the popularity of revived Russian operas from the tsarist period, such as *Boris Godunov*, which had been previously banned.

The following are the official holidays of the Soviet Union: New Year's Day, January 1; Women's Day, March 8; International Workers' Day, May 1; The Great October Socialist Revolution, November 7—8; and Constitution Day, December 5.

CHAPTER 28

THE ARMED FORCES

Soviet military strategy has evolved steadily since 1917, reflecting the increase in the power of the Soviet Union, its international status, and new weapons that have become available. Early weaknesses dictated a strategy of exchanging territory for the time required to bring the Soviet Union to total mobilization, after which the masses of its manpower and the distended lines of the enemy would eventually work to bring about a change in the tide of battle. Emerging from World War II by far the greatest power in Europe and second only to the United States in the world, the Soviet Union set about developing forces that would eliminate the need to fight on Soviet soil and that would be appropriate for the support of a foreign policy with expanding interests in areas remote from the homeland (see ch. 24, Foreign Relations).

In 1969 there were about 3.2 million men in the Soviet military services. The army consisted of about 2 million, organized into 140 divisions. Security and border forces, responsible to the police and security organizations, and not within the Army, numbered about 250,000. The navy with about 500,000 men, 130 first line ships, 2,200 small surface vessels, nearly 400 submarines, and a newly formed marine infantry group, had become the world's second largest. Air forces had approximately 500,000 men and slightly over 10,000 combat aircraft. The Strategic Rocket Force had about 250,000 men and missiles deployed at about 750 medium- and intermediate-range ballistic missile (MRBM and IRBM) launchers and at about 1,000 intercontinental ballistic missile (ICBM) launchers.

The forces acquired by mid-1969 allowed the Soviet Union more flexibility than had been enjoyed at any time in the past. As evidenced by existing forces and rates of growth in strategic weapons, the Soviet government had assembled a formidable missile force, a navy capable of maintaining a presence in any ocean, and ground forces adequate to any foreseeable military task. Creation of an elite marine infantry force provided an apparent capability to employ forces in any area on short notice.

The military establishment has always received top priority for scarce resources of both materials and skilled personnel, despite the heavy burden on the society and the economy. Recent programs have made defense costs rise at an increased rate, faster than the expansion of the overall economy. The extent of the burden over the years and of the recent increases are such that Soviet leadership could have tolerated them only because it has seen the armed forces as essential to internal security, for defense against external attack, or for the support of an agressive foreign policy (see ch. 30, Industry).

Universal conscription draws about one-third of the manpower that reaches draft age each year. The conscript works hard, is subject to stern discipline and intensive programs of political indoctrination, has few comforts and little time to himself, but is kept in excellent physical condition and has generally good morale. He is identified with the people and is loyally supported. The officer corps is a separate caste, apart from the troops and from the people. The Soviet officer is a highly regarded professional, a member of a dedicated group. He is respected and well paid.

The position of the defense establishment in the government and its relation to the Communist Party apparatus is unique. The defense organization is within the governmental structure, but is controlled from top to bottom by the CPSU. The Party determines basic military policy and maintains a political apparatus within the force structure paralleling the military command structure. There are party cells within military units, and secret police or internal security representatives infiltrate the entire establishment. Only since the death of Stalin has the military leadership been allowed to air its doctrinal and strategic discussions publicly. This, plus the fact that purges appear no longer necessary to ensure political reliability, probably indicates a slight relaxation of control.

The Warsaw Pact is the only formal military alliance to which the Soviet Union belongs. Members, in addition to the Soviet Union, are Poland, East Germany, Hungary, Czechoslovakia, Rumania, and Bulgaria. Albania ceased to participate in the organization after siding with Communist China in the Sino-Soviet dispute. The Warsaw Pact nations, including the Soviet Union, commit themselves to support of "wars of national liberation" but, with the exception of an agreement with the Mongolian People's Republic, there is no known bilateral treaty that would involve the overt use of Soviet forces. Military assistance is provided to ideologically sympathetic regimes and also in any direction where it might encourage trade relations, promote ports of call for naval vessels, counter or embarrass the West, or merely maintain a presence in order to exploit an opportunity that might arise at a later date.

HISTORICAL BACKGROUND

Red Forces from 1917 to 1939

The Red Army had its origins in a defeated and exhausted country. Karl Marx, the German father of the Soviet Union's official

570

ideology, had stated that revolutions are "the locomotives of history." Marx's Russian disciple, Lenin, activated such a locomotive and successfully gained power, but soon found that there were no existing guidelines for the operation of the postrevolutionary state. One of the neglected areas was the role of the armed forces but, to support and maintain the revolution, the need for an organized army became immediately apparent.

Lenin ordered the formation of an army in January 1918. Leon Trotsky, Lenin's close collaborator and fellow revolutionary, soon became commissar of war and, through his genius as an organizer and leader, the Red Army was created. The new army spent its first four years supporting Lenin's struggle for survival against the varied anti-Bolshevik forces. Despite the fact that many of its officers had no loyalty to Lenin or to his political system, the Red Army ultimately emerged victorious in the civil war that ravaged Russia (see ch. 3, Historical Setting).

The history of military forces of a national character in tsarist Russia had been relatively brief. Peter the Great was a military strategist at the turn of the nineteenth century, but tsarist armies in later years had few other outstanding leaders. The Suvorov military academies of the Soviet Union are named for tsarist Russia's greatest soldier, an exceptional leader and the author of the largest body of Russian military doctrine. More often leadership was mediocre, tactics uninspired, and the country saved, as from Napoleon in 1812, by the inhospitable Russian climate and the difficulties in supplying invading forces over the vast distances involved.

The dozen years before 1917 were especially inglorious for the Imperial Russian Army. Japan humiliated it in 1905. Its World War I losses were staggering. Casualties and mass desertions were such that, although some 15 million men were mobilized, the active force strength never exceeded more than about 3.5 million men at any one time. Casualties alone amounted to perhaps 7 million men. Leadership was inept, training was inadequate, and supplies were almost never sufficient for individual light weapons, to say nothing of artillery and other usually routine support.

After the collapse of the monarchy in March 1917, disintegration of the tsarist forces was rapid. By the time of the Bolshevik Revolution of November 7, 1917, Lenin knew that, to a very considerable extent by his own efforts, the old Imperial Army had been eroded to worthlessness. Up to this time the closest the Bolsheviks had to an organized armed force was its Red Guards. Some units of these guards had been formed ten or fifteen years earlier, occasionally only to watch for police during clandestine meetings. A few units had acquired effective training, most were formed around a nucleus of fanatically loyal Bolsheviks, but others were little better than groups of armed brigands. By November 1917 they numbered perhaps 20,000 men. During and immediately after the revolution, Red Guard strength approximately doubled.

Lenin sued for immediate peace with Germany, but negotiations and sporadic fighting dragged on from November until a peace treaty was signed on March 3, 1918. His weak negotiating position, plus difficulties in unifying his country, made Lenin realize the need for credible forces. On January 28, 1918, he signed the decree forming the Workers' and Peasants' Red Army; two weeks later, on February 14, he established the Workers' and Peasants' Red Navy. February 23, 1918, is celebrated as Army Day, chosen to commemorate the first Red Army action of any consequence. This actually consisted of indecisive clashes between a Red Guard unit and a German force marching toward Petrograd, and took place at Narva and Pskov. The Germans failed to reach Petrograd, largely because the armistice was signed a week later.

Efforts to attract volunteers were unsuccessful. Able to recruit only enough men to bring his total force to about 100,000 by April 1918, Lenin reinstituted compulsory service. About 3 million men were called up by late 1919, and by 1921 approximately 5 million men were under arms. The early Red Army lived off the land, but the people were weary of supporting marauding armies of any nationality or description. The country was exhausted from war, and it was far from united behind Bolshevism. The "democratic" army, electing its officers and lacking any semblance of control or discipline, frequently behaved like an armed mob. With a few notable exceptions, the first group of officers had little capability to lead troops and no knowledge of organization, tactics, or the equipment and support required by their men. The collapse of Germany and the reluctance of the Allied powers to enter another conflict gave the Red Army some respite, but it had, nonetheless, a full-fledged civil war on its hands.

Trotsky, as first commissar of war, saw the need for military professionalism. He called up about 500,000 officers and 130,000 noncommissioned officers from the old tsarist army and set about remedying the worst of the conditions he had inherited. He inducted as many Communist Party members as possible, and during the early years approximately one-half of the total Party strength was in the forces. The bulk of his men, however, were the tired and disillusioned remnants of a defeated army.

Attractions proffered by the new regime consisted of promises of peace, division of the land, and professions that they would be coequals with all their military comrades, including the leadership. The harsh reality of involvement in bitter civil warfare, of being away from home and unable to participate in any new distribution of land, and of renewed military discipline soon became apparent. Conditions were so miserable that of every seven men who died in the civil war, only one was killed in action. Disease, cold, hunger, exhaustion, and the measures used to enforce discipline accounted for the other six. Casualties probably amounted to about 3 million men. Not only was the morale of the men perilously low, the conservative tsarist officers and noncommissioned officers were politically suspect and often militarily unreliable.

The situation required extreme measures to maintain control. Trotsky paralleled his military general staff with a political general staff. To keep his officers from defecting, he held their families hostage. To control their activities while on duty, he introduced the political commissar. In the early days of equivalent rank and coequal authority with the military commanding officer in any unit, the commissar countersigned all military orders. Even the commissar did not escape political pressure. He paid with his life if his commander defected or dabbled in counterrevolutionary activity. Communist Party or Komsomol (Young Communist League) cells were formed in all units. Secret police infiltrated the entire structure. The political officers, party organization, and secret police each had channels of communication to which the commander had no access.

Organized resistance consisted of the White Army and foreign forces, including British, French, Czech, Japanese, and United States units, which intervened to support the White forces. The Whites represented conservative Russian elements but, aside from anti-Bolshevism, had no common objective or ideology. White armies did not lack good military officers. Men such as Admiral Alexander Kolchak, Baron Peter Wrangel, General Anton Denikin, and a few others provided excellent leadership, but the Red Army enjoyed superiority in manpower and fought from the heartland centered around Moscow. The Whites, fighting on the periphery with inferior numbers, had serious supply problems and shared all the difficulties associated with war weariness of the troops and the population that plagued the Red forces. The controls and extensive political indoctrination undertaken by Trotsky contributed to keeping the Red Army intact. It was able to overcome White forces and organized resistance in almost all areas during 1920, although control in the Far East was not established for another two years (see ch. 3, Historical Setting).

Nineteen twenty-one was a year of famine. It has been estimated that as many as 30 million peasants were forced to leave their homes in search of food. In these cold, miserable, and hungry days transient peasants, deserters, and demobilized forces became roving bands of armed marauders. This was also the year of the Kronstadt naval mutiny. The personnel of the naval base near Petrograd had participated in the overthrow of tsarism and had been staunch supporters of Lenin, but the lack of political freedom and food shortages had caused unrest and disillusionment.

A breaking point was reached in 1921, and the naval garrison forces marched on Petrograd under the banner of "Soviets without Bolsheviks." The Red Army Petrograd Garrison prevented the mutineers from entering the city, but refused to follow through on an attack of the Kronstadt ships and forts. Trotsky himself replaced the commandant of the Petrograd Garrison, lined up the Red Army men who had refused to fight, and had one in five of them shot. The attack on Kronstadt was renewed and the mutineers slaughtered. The navy remained an outlaw service for years, regaining an acceptable reputation only during World War II.

The border established between the Soviet Union and Poland by the Treaty of Versailles disappointed the Poles and, with Russia involved in civil war, Poland took the opportunity to invade the Ukraine. The Poles initially penetrated with little difficulty, but the Red Army's counteroffensive proved almost equally easy. Approaching Warsaw, however, the factors that have historically worked to Russian advantage worked in reverse. The Poles, aided by French General Maxime Weygand and French army advisers and supplies, rallied to a fanatical defense of the capital. The Red Army had overextended its supply capabilities, and the Poles had retracted into a defensive position they were able to support. Although engagements were small and isolated by World War I comparisons, the Red Army had employed a million men in this war. The Treaty of Riga that ended the Russo-Polish war reestablished the boundary, not significantly different from that set at Versailles, where it remained until 1939.

It was late in 1922 before the Red Army reached Vladivostok and had effective control over all of the Far East claimed by Lenin. In 1919 White forces and a Czech legion had controlled the Trans-Siberian Railway and most of Siberia. The Japanese had troops in the easternmost portions. With the end of the action in these areas, the boundaries of the Soviet Union were virtually those that remained until 1939, and there was no further organized resistance.

After the civil war and the war with Poland, stabilization of the nation and its economy demanded first priorities. The Red Army had been effective enough to put down opposition and to unify the country, but it was too large, unmanageable, ill-disciplined, and discontented. The 5 million men in the forces were not only an unproductive burden and unnecessary, but also they were potentially dangerous politically. The smoking, chattering, indolent mob that shambled past Lenin and Trotsky in the first Moscow Red Square May Day parade in 1920 was not an impressive military spectacle.

Three million men were demobilized in 1921, 1 million more in 1922. Target strength for the peacetime force was 562,000 men, although it probably never quite got down to that figure. Unreliable elements were weeded out. The new Communist military academies began to turn out a new breed of young, thoroughly indoctrinated officers. Living conditions for the men improved greatly, becoming better than in any earlier Russian army. Discipline and morale gradually improved.

Lenin died in 1924. Wounded in an assassination attempt in 1918, he was increasingly incapacitated after a stroke in May 1922, and the struggle for succession had been in progress during the year or two before his death. Stalin had seen Trotsky as a potential rival and, attaining power, kept him as commissar of war only until early 1925. By that time the most urgent reforms had been accomplished. Trotsky can be given most of the credit for winning the civil war and for taking the first steps with the peacetime army to make it an improved, politically reliable establishment.

In 1928 the political and party machinery was still functioning in parallel with the military organization, but by then the military commander had become reliable enough to be allowed purely operational decisions without a political countersignature. In some instances, the positions of military commander and political commissar were held by the same individual.

Red Army equipment lagged behind that in other major armies by some ten years. The military became a chief beneficiary of the first Five-Year Plan (1928—32), however, and by the mid-1930's modernization efforts began to bear fruit. Adolf Hitler had also appeared on the horizon and, in view of the new German threat, personnel strength was increased, reaching about 1.3 million by 1935. The military budget was tripled during this period. The army now had considerably more armor, including about 7,000 tanks. Aircraft production reached about 4,000 per year. The navy finally came in for some consideration and acquired over a hundred submarines.

Stalin had an opportunity to test some of his new equipment during the Spanish civil war that began in July 1936, although he sent only enough equipment to test it and only enough people to observe it under battle conditions. The small military contingent included some 500 to 600 men, a few aircraft, but a fairly considerable number of tanks. For its influence on future developments, a tank battle observed simultaneously by the Germans and the Soviets turned out to be the most significant event of the war. Tank operations were not followed up properly, and the Soviet observers concluded that, since only ground forces could occupy land, tanks should be used primarily to support infantry. From the same vantage point, the Germans evolved their highly successful blitzkreig tactics, in which they used tanks and aircraft as offensive spearhead instruments, mopping up with infantry after the initial shock attacks.

Although the exercise in Spain made a negative contribution to

Soviet military strategy, the new equipment and vastly improved training establishment were resulting in far superior forces. The forces were also becoming professional to a degree that was disquieting to Stalin. Whether or not the threat to his power approached the proportions he imagined, the measures he took were extreme. During the 1937—38 purges of the military, some 35,000 officers were dismissed, imprisoned, or shot. This represented about half of the officer corps, and the weight of the strike was on the top ranks. The entire Political Directorate, all of the Military District commanders, and seventy-five of the eighty members of the Supreme Military Council disappeared. Overall, Stalin eliminated three of his five marshals, 90 percent of his generals, and 80 percent of his colonels. These included most of the major unit commanders, down to and including division level.

The purge left a docile officer cadre with few experienced men for the top commands. Those remaining knew they had been spared according to Stalin's whim and feared the controlling apparatus to the point where they were, by conviction or otherwise, politically reliable. This situation was heavily responsible for the poor showing of the army during the Winter War of 1939—40 with Finland and during the first two years of the war with Germany. Destruction of the top ranks, however, allowed promotion of younger men during World War II when they were proven to be capable battlefield commanders.

The 1939 Campaign in Poland and the Winter War with Finland

The Nazi-Soviet Nonaggression Pact of August 1939 set up spheres of influence permitting much of eastern Europe to be divided between Hitler and Stalin. A week after Hitler signed, German forces invaded Poland, subduing it almost completely in about two weeks. On September 17th Stalin moved to occupy his portion of Poland and reached a meeting with the Germans at Brest-Litovsk in two days. Warsaw fell in another week. In the period that followed, the Russians took over the Baltic states that had been independent since World War I, annexed Bessarabia from Rumania, and set about securing a buffer zone around the Baltic access to Leningrad (formerly Petrograd) from Finland. Finland refused to cede the land Stalin demanded and, after a provocation had been engineered, the Red Army attacked.

The winter of 1939 was severe even by the standards of that area. Fortifications were more effective than expected, and the resistance of the Finnish people and their forces was stubborn. Red Army leadership, suffering from the recent purges, was inept. The planned twelve-day campaign bogged down completely. The following spring the Russians assembled an overwhelming force and Finland was overcome.

576

This war showed only too clearly that the Red Army had serious deficiencies. The Soviet infantry manual, for example, was rewritten or received major revision approximately twenty-five times between 1938 and 1941. Tank and armor support doctrines were reanalyzed. Discipline was tightened. Officers were encouraged to demonstrate battlefield initiative. Although the corrective measures were not taken in time to prevent near-disastrous defeats in 1941 and 1942, the weaknesses exposed may well have saved the Soviet Union.

World War II

Called "The Great Patriotic War" by the Russians, the Nazi invasion of the Soviet Union began on June 22, 1941, fifteen months after the end of the Finnish war. The German attack was a tactical surprise. It very nearly succeeded in wiping out the effective Soviet forces and in occupying the heartland of the Soviet Union during the summer and fall as Hitler had planned. The Germans destroyed more than four-fifths of the 20,000 Red Army tanks, nearly 10,000 aircraft, killed 1.5 million men, and took another 2.5 million prisoners during the 1941 advances.

The German timetable was thrown off slightly because they had believed a greater proportion of the Red Army was in the front lines. Initial German offensives penetrated the planned distances and eliminated all opposition encountered, but there were more substantial forces in secondary positions than German intelligence had reported. Slowed enough to be caught by the autumn mud and the bitter Russian winter, the Germans found themselves ill-prepared for a sustained campaign. They were short of such fundamental items as winter clothing for the troops and antifreeze for vehicle engines.

Morale of the Red Army was not good in 1941. The marks of the purge were still apparent in the officer corps. Appeals for Party loyalty did not convince the men. Heavy losses and continual defeat were bitterly depressing. Late in the year, however, the demand to save the Party was dropped, and the men were charged with saving the Fatherland. With their backs to Moscow, the troops stiffened and held.

Campaigns in 1942 started in much the same way as they had in June 1941. This time the Red Army finally held at Stalingrad. Hitler's obsession with taking the city allowed the Soviets to encircle and eliminate the entire German force in the area, a loss in manpower Hitler could ill afford and which proved to be the turning point in the war.

In 1943 the initiative went to the Red Army. It was now able to attack with superior forces and equal armor and to choose the areas for engagement. During the remainder of the war the Red Army generated ten major offensives and was victorious in each. Although they played a major role in the defeat of Germany, Soviet forces saw little action against Japan. After early fears of a Japanese attack had died down, only minimal forces had been maintained in the Far East. Stalin had promised at Yalta to join the Pacific war ninety days after Germany surrendered and kept his promise to the day. The atomic bomb had been dropped on Hiroshima two days earlier, and the war continued for only eleven more days, during which the Red Army met little resistance in overrunning Manchuria.

Between June 1941 and May 1945, according to Soviet sources, 7 million military personnel and 10 million civilians were killed, and 3 million disabled. These figures do not include the approximately 3.5 million prisoners taken by the Germans in 1941 and 1942. Men who surrendered on the battlefield were considered in Red Army annals to have deserted.

In spite of such losses, the Red Army grew steadily stronger and, at the end of the war, was by far the largest armed force that has ever been assembled. It had between 16 and 19 million men. It had received over 100,000 tanks and self-propelled guns, over 150,000 aircraft, and about 500,000 artillery pieces during the war. By the end of hostilities, production in each category was in excess of requirements. Men and officers were tough, experienced, confident, and had good morale. The organization had become efficient enough to keep its communication and supply lines open at all times.

Formidable a force as it was, it had weaknesses. The army had learned not to outdistance its support, but although there was a substantial flow of Lend-Lease trucks after 1942 (over 300,000 total), truck transport was never adequate. Railways were used extensively even in supplying units close to the front lines, and at times horse-drawn vehicles were used for supplying troops. Offensive movements would usually be sustained for only about three weeks before waiting for materiel to be brought forward. Frequently, they became bogged down for long periods. Although there were great numbers of aircraft, most of them were inferior to German types. The Soviet Union had no strategic aircraft. Naval operations were unspectacular and were incapable of providing support for Allied convoys bringing vital supplies into the Soviet Union.

Evolution of the Modern Soviet Forces

Demobilization was rapid after World War II. An estimated 11 million men were released the first year, and by 1948 strength was down to about 3 million. Except for augmentations during the mid-1950 cold war years and other minor fluctuations, this has remained the approximate force level. The Workers' and Peasants' Red Army and Red Navy were renamed in 1946, becoming the Soviet Army and the Soviet Navy. The army contracted into about 175 divisions, about one-third of which were kept at full strength. It retained its best tanks and artillery, and 65 of the 175 divisions were armored.

Organizational changes have accommodated to new equipment and changing missions. Stalin had personally directed his forces in World War II and was inordinately proud of his accomplishments. His five essentials for successful conduct of war, in the order of their priority, were stability of the home front, good morale among the troops, superiority in quantity and quality of divisions, superiority in armament and firepower and, lastly, able commanders. According to Stalin, the Soviet method of conducting war was to "coordinate and subordinate all arms and services to the ground forces, which must close with and destroy the enemy armies before victory can be claimed."

Stalin realized, nonetheless, that in the postwar situation the only nation with a potential to harm the Soviet Union or to inhibit its activities was the United States. Also, whereas he publicly gave them little concern, he knew that the United States had nuclear weapons and the means to deliver them within the Soviet heartland without engaging the forces at its boundaries. He thereupon set about developing defenses and comparable weapons of his own. By the time of his death in 1953, in spite of his stated doctrines, much advanced materiel, far removed from that used during World War II, was being produced and research was in progress that would lead to space and long range missile systems.

Soviet military doctrine received extensive public debate after Stalin's death. His successor, Khrushchev, became convinced that initial nuclear strikes would be devastating and probably decisive. This led him to consider general war as an irrational, if not unthinkable, course of action. Since he also believed that conflict between the major powers would inevitably escalate into general nuclear war, he considered that maintenance of large ground forces was unnecessary. He held the navy in low esteem.

Doctrine was again radically altered after Khrushchev. It soon became apparent that the Soviet Union was at a serious disadvantage in its efforts to support "wars of national liberation," ambitions with respect to third powers, or any other interests in areas not immediately adjacent to the Soviet Union. This could not be otherwise with deemphasized conventional forces, inability to move troops to trouble areas, or a doctrine that espoused inevitability of escalation to general war in an engagement between major powers.

More flexible doctrinal views predominated in 1969, and a more flexible force was being created to support them. The military establishment was authorized to build up its forces in all arms. It was acquiring a naval capability that could maintain a presence anywhere in the world and was rapidly expanding its strength in long-range missiles. The army was restored to the strength it had before Khrushchev's reductions and improved in mobility and firepower. Policy statements most frequently heard during the late 1960's were to the effect that preparations should be made for "combined operations by all types of armed forces, all kinds of weapons, employed in close cooperation."

POSITION IN THE GOVERNMENT

The Ministry of Defense is charged with directing, administering, and supporting the military establishment. In the governmental structure the military is beneath the Council of Ministers, which in turn is responsible to the Supreme Soviet and its Presidium. Analysis of the purely governmental structure, however, shows no group that is likely to have responsibility for major decisions relating to defense policy or that would contain the high-level leadership able to allocate national resources among the various ministries and agencies competing for them (see ch. 19, Formal Structure of the Union Government).

The Supreme Soviet is given constitutional authority to organize and direct the country's defense forces and to declare war or make peace. It is a body with over 1,500 members, however, and when it meets, usually for a few days twice a year, it unanimously approves measures that have been prepared earlier. Its Presidium meets between sessions of the Supreme Soviet and can perform most responsibilities where the military is concerned, including mobilizing the nation for and declaring war. Under the Soviet system, however, important decisions are not made by governmental organs, but by the Political Bureau (Politburo) of the Central Committee of the Communist Part of the Soviet Union (CPSU), which is the supreme party organ and makes all high decisions and formulates high policy. In 1969 three Politburo members (Leonid Brezhnev, Nikolai Podgorny, and Pyotr Shelest) and three alternate members were also members of the Presidium of the Supreme Soviet.

The Council of Ministers, which is the highest executive and administrative body in the governmental establishment, contains the heads of nearly a hundred ministries, state committees, and representatives from the various republics. Although it is empowered to control and direct the operations of its member ministries, the group is too large and cumbersome for the whole of it to be involved in prime policy matters of a major ministry such as the

Ministry of Defense. Overall defense policy is determined by the Party rather than by the Council of Ministers, but here again there are interlocking positions. The chairman of the Council of Ministers (premier of the Soviet Union) in mid-1969, Aleksei Kosygin, and his two first deputies, Dmitri Polyansky and Kiril Mazurov, were all members of the Politburo of the Central Committee of the CPSU.

Exercise of control through concurrent occupation of Party and government positions is not confined to the highest levels but extends down through the whole system and has been a feature of Soviet politics since the revolution. In 1969 the minister of defense, Marshal of the Soviet Union Andrei Grechko, was also a member of the Central Committee of the CPSU and a member of the Supreme Soviet of the Soviet Union. Marshal of the Soviet Union Georgi Zhukov, minister of defense under Khrushchev in the late 1950's, climbed all the way to full membership in the Politburo before being forced into retirement because of "violation of Leninist principles." Neither of Zhukov's successors, Rodion Malinovsky and Andrei Grechko, reached such high party position, although both were members of the Central Committee.

Control over the military is vested in the Party, but the military is strongly represented in the Party that controls it. The minister of defense is the highest ranking military officer in the forces. He and the other key members of the Council of Ministers are invariably influential in uppermost Party committees, if not the Politburo. During the mid-1960's the Communist Party had about 13.5 million members and more than 500,000 candidate members, a total of about 6 percent of the population. About 700,000, or approximately 20 percent, of service personnel were either Communist Party members or candidate members. Also, nearly 10 percent of the Party's Central Committee membership was military, which is heavy representation from a group that constitutes about 1.5 percent of the country's population and has only about 5 percent of the total Party strength. About 12,000 servicemen are deputies to local soviets, union republic supreme soviets, or the Supreme Soviet of the Soviet Union.

The relationship between the Main Political Directorate and the Ministry of Defense also illustrates the interplay of governmental and Party control. The Main Political Directorate is on a direct command line beneath and responsible to the Ministry of Defense. When the Party organization is superimposed upon a governmental structure chart, however, the Main Political Directorate is seen to be also subordinate to the Central Committee of the CPSU. It is, in fact, a subcommittee of the Central Committee. The dual Party-governmental system works as well as it does, largely because the same individuals occupy the positions in both elements of the structure (see ch. 21, Political Dynamics).

THE MILITARY ESTABLISHMENT

Service Organization and Mission

The defense establishment is divided into five major service branches: the Soviet Army, the Soviet Navy, the Long Range Air Force, the Air Defense Command, and the Strategic Rocket Force. They are administratively coequal although the army is predominant in size and influence and has by far the greatest share of high-ranking officers and military spokesmen. The navy is the next senior service, having traditions from tsarist days, although the degree of favor in which it has existed during the Soviet period has varied widely.

Although the Long Range Air Force is one of the five independent services, it contains only strategic aircraft and would be the equivalent of a bomber command or the strategic air forces in other more typical air force organizations. Tactical aviation, which includes most of the military air transport capability and the air defense aircraft required to maintain battlefield air superiority, is considered a ground support element and is incorporated within the army. Naval aviation is likewise a part of the Soviet Navy.

Defensive aircraft, for protection of cities and permanent installations within the country, are incorporated within the Air Defense Command, which is the fourth of the independent service branches. This service also has the missiles, radars, controls, and communications that are associated with its piloted aircraft and missile defense systems.

The newest branch, organized independently in 1960, is the Strategic Rocket Force. It controls the longer range missiles that would be employed in a strategic, as opposed to tactical, role. Strategic targets include permanent military bases and industrial and population concentrations. Tactical targets are troop formations and whatever affects the conflict in progress or the movement of forces. Strategic missiles and some strategic aircraft ordinarily have targets selected prior to hostilities. Tactical systems are pretargeted in the same local manner as an artillery barrage would be planned in advance of an attack, but they are also prepared to move and to select new targets as a battle situation develops.

Although the separate service breakdown is not typical when compared with that in the majority of the world's armed forces, the army and navy have the units and missions ordinarily attributed to them. The Long Range Air Force is the only all-aircraft service, and other functions ordinarily accomplished by an air force are either separate, as in the cases of air defense and strategic missiles, or held within other services. Force organization within lower elements is generally standard. The army, for example, has the usual army, corps, divison, regiment, battalion, company, platoon, and squad organization.

582

The military establishment has been organized and used primarily in its deterrence and defensive roles. Internal security is the responsibility of police or special forces which, on occasions such as during the farm collectivization program of the early 1930's, have numbered as many as 750,000 men.

The Army

Tsarist armies and the early Red Army relied on great masses of men in the front line and in reserve, but effectiveness was often limited by shortages of weapons and supplies and, too frequently, by poor leadership. During World War II, the Red Army began to exploit the shock that could be achieved from superior firepower, and in the period since then the Soviet Army has been reorganized and reequipped to the point where it has also acquired a high capability for mobility and the means to support modern mobile forces. It is well trained, competently led, and has excellent discipline and good morale.

Although a sizable number of army personnel are in Rear Services, ground troops of the air defense and tactical aviation forces, and in various other special units, the basic element of the Soviet Army is the division. In 1969 the army had about 140 divisions and maintained about half of them at full strength and in a combat-ready status. Approximately half of the remainder could be ready for action on very short notice. The rest are maintained only at cadre strength and would require a longer time to mobilize and train.

The old rifle division passed from the scene, became fully transportable and was renamed the motorized rifle division. There were about eighty-five to ninety of these divisions in 1969 that, when fully manned, had about 10,500 men each. The typical division had about 200 medium tanks, about an equal number of artillery pieces, nearly 500 armored personnel carriers, and some 2,000 other motor vehicles. It contained three motorized rifle regiments, a tank regiment, an artillery regiment, and an antiaircraft artillery regiment, plus service and support units.

There also were about forty-five tank divisions. At full strength each had about 9,000 men, 300 to 400 tanks, and artillery approximately equivalent to that in a motorized rifle division. It had three tank regiments, one each of motorized rifle, artillery, and antiaircraft artillery regiments, and the necessary service and support units.

Airborne divisions have about 7,000 to 8,000 men and equipment that is necessarily lighter. There were seven of these divisions, and it is believed that all of them were maintained at nearly full strength. The transport aircraft available in 1968 could have lifted three airborne divisions simultaneously, including support units.

At lower levels army organization adheres to conventional patterns. It can vary considerably, however, and a squad might comprise eight to a dozen men. Four of these might form a platoon, which would be led by a junior lieutenant. Three platoons would make up a company, three companies a battalion, three battalions a regiment, and three regiments a division. These could be commanded by a captain, major, lieutenant colonel, and colonel, respectively, or by a rank higher in each case. Depending on local requirements and special functions, there are separate or independent units, most frequently of battalion or regimental size.

Area organization (conforming to the wartime front) consists of Military Districts in the Soviet Union and Groups of Forces in Eastern Europe. The numbers of Military Districts and Groups of Forces have changed from time to time. In 1969 there were fifteen Military Districts and, including the one newly introduced into Czechoslovakia, four Groups of Forces. The Groups of Forces contained twenty-six divisions, plus those in Czechoslovakia, and were maintained at full strength and at a high state of readiness. Ten of the fifteen Far East divisions have also been held at full strength. It is possible that tension with Communist China during the late 1960's will have caused strengthening of the remainder of the units or possibly the introduction of additional units to that area. In 1968 there were sixty to sixty-five divisions in the European Soviet Union. The remaining few were in southern and central Siberian Military Districts.

The Navy

The recent growth of the Soviet Navy has been one of the major military developments since the death of Stalin. Having been a negligible force at the end of World War II, by mid-1969 it had about twenty cruisers, over 100 destroyers, about 1,200 lesser ships of the escort, patrol, minelaying, and landing craft types, and another thousand auxiliary and support ships. A large portion of these vessels were new. The submarine fleet had decreased in overall numbers since World War II, but those taken out of service were short-range boats with limited open sea capabilities. Nearly sixty of the almost 400 submarines in service were nuclear powered. The newest class of nuclear ballistic missile submarines is said to be comparable to the best ballistic missile submarines now in service. Seven of these were constructed in 1968.

The navy had fleet headquarters for forces operating in the Black Sea, the Baltic Sea, the western Arctic seas, and the Pacific Far East. Numbers of vessels were distributed almost equally among the four fleets, but concentrations of certain types of vessels varied in different fleet areas. A large majority of the submarines, for example, were attached to the Northern and Pacific Fleets, where they had ready access to the open ocean.

The navy has medium bombers, transport aircraft, and helicopters, but no carriers for conventional aircraft. Near shore air defense units would presumably take care of naval air defense requirements. At sea the fleets would rely on surface-to-air missiles and antiaircraft artillery only. The navy also has a few long-range reconnaissance airplanes, including perhaps fifty of the 4-turboprop Bear. Aircraft with a bombing mission were armed with cruise-type air-to-surface missiles, intended primarily for use against surface naval or shipping targets.

A small new marine force, literally translated as naval infantry, was formed in 1964. It was considered an elite force and was frequently referred to as the "black death." The men wore berets and distinctive black uniforms.

Historically, the tsarist and earlier Soviet navies were coastal defense forces, little interested in challenging the world's major fleets on the open seas or even in ranging far from the homeland on a regular basis. Efforts to maintain a worldwide presence have been relatively recent. Extensive oceanographic research activities began in the 1950's. The Mediterranean squadron of the Black Sea Fleet was formed only about 1964, although first movements through the Turkish straits after World War II were accomplished ten years earlier. During the late 1960's Soviet naval vessels in the Mediterranean Sea frequently outnumbered those of the Allied 6th Fleet, although in tonnage and in striking power the 6th Fleet was the more powerful force.

Elsewhere, Soviet naval vessels operate regularly off the United Kingdom's Shetland Islands, in the Persian Gulf, and in the Indian Ocean. Soviet ships and planes shadow all major North Atlantic Treaty Organization (NATO) fleet maneuvers and regularly monitor Western space and missile activities. Of the some forty intelligence trawlers, half a dozen remain on station off the United States Atlantic seaboard at all times. Other areas, such as Guam, are under continual surveillance. Some ships in Soviet fishing fleets were equipped for specific intelligence collection tasks.

Performance of the Soviet Navy during World War II was far from extraordinary, but the new navy has developed almost overnight from insignificance into one that by 1969 was second in strength only to the United States Navy and that could maintain a Soviet presence anywhere in the world. Its ships were new, modern, and clean. It was supported by a merchant marine expanding at a rate that, if continued, would make it first in the world by the mid-1970's. The merchant marine may reflect only an increasing commercial interest, but it had the inherent ability to move forces and equipment and establish relations in ports that could be used by naval vessels. The marine infantry force indicated that wherever the fleet operated it would be able to bring ground forces ashore if it chose to do so.

A strategic air force mission was undertaken shortly after World War II, but the Long Range Air Force did not become an independent service until much later. Its first aircraft were the Tu—4 Bull, a piston-engined copy of the United States World War II B—29 heavy bomber. In its most important years it had over 1,000 jet medium bombers and about 200 heavy bombers. At that time the medium bomber force consisted almost exclusively of the Tu—16 twin jet Badger. Even with refueling, the Badger did not have a satisfactory intercontinental capability and could have been employed against most of the United States only on one-way missions. The medium bombers in the Long Range Air Force declined to about 750 aircraft after 1963, their mission largely taken over by missiles. A newer supersonic aircraft, the Tu—22 Blinder, constituted about one-fourth of the medium bomber force in 1969. Although it had superior speed, its range was not significantly different from that of the Badger.

The 4-jet Bison and the 4-turboprop Bear are heavy bombers. The Long Range Air Force had about 100 of each, but it was necessary to use about one-fourth of the total as inflight refueling tankers. These airplanes have intercontinental range and, before the deployment of ICBM's, had primary responsibility for the strategic mission against the United States.

The mission of the Long Range Air Force changed when the strategic missile came of age. Frequent statements by Soviet military strategists on the role of the missile systems made it clear that Long Range Air Force airplanes have been relegated to a reconnaissance or second strike mission in general war. Its aircraft still had a strategic capability against China and could be employed in a variety of ways in limited war situations.

Air Defense Command

The Air Defense Command maintained all fighter aircraft, surface-to-air missiles, antiballistic missile systems, and the associated warning and aircraft control radars, controls, and communications for defense of the homeland against aircraft and missiles. The force was organized into Air Defense Districts, which were similar to but did not necessarily encompass the same areas as the Military Districts. Tactical Aviation forces within the army had the air defense mission in support of battle fronts, whereas the Air Defense Command was responsible for the defense of cities, industries, and all permanent installations within the boundaries of the Soviet Union. Shortly after its creation in 1955, the Warsaw Pact Organization extended the air defense network and controls into its East European member states. Delineation of responsibilities was not known in detail but, inasmuch as Tactical Aviation units were still present with the Groups of Forces in 1969, it can be deduced that battlefield defense policy remained as it was but that static defenses of the member nations had been integrated with and perhaps augmented by the Soviet Air Defense Command.

This service had just under 4,000 defensive fighter aircraft. The later models were among the best performing of the world's airplanes, and all types since the first-generation jet MiG—15, which is no longer considered to be in active units, have been original Soviet designs. The personnel strength of the Air Defense Command was about 500,000, and its missile defenses were the largest and most extensive ever deployed. Newer elements included a peripheral antiballistic missile network along the missile corridor into the European Russian heartland and point defenses against missiles in the Moscow area. A few other major cities may also be defended.

Strategic Rocket Force

The youngest of the independent service branches, the Strategic Rocket Force, became the fifth of the organizationally coequal forces in 1960. Its missiles include all those that would be used in a strategic role. A large variety of missile systems have been deployed, including some with ranges of less than 1,000 miles and some that can attain orbital velocities.

The earliest operational systems were the medium- and intermediate-range ballistic missiles (MRBM and IRBM), most of which were located in the western part of the Soviet Union at the end of the 1950's. By the early 1960's these 1,000- and 2,000-mile systems were deployed at about 750 launch positions.

The initial ICBM force was small and, until after the mid-1960's, was deployed at less than 250 launch positions. Deployment proceeded at a much accelerated rate during the latter half of the decade, probably exceeding 1,000 by mid-1969. Systems included approximately 200 of the very large SS—9 and larger numbers of small missiles. Personnel strength of the Strategic Rocket Forces was approximately 250,000.

The Strategic Rocket Force mission is nuclear strike. Its systems are too expensive, too inaccurate, and too difficult to replace at launch locations for effective employment in a conventional mode. In 1969 the force possessed the bulk of the Soviet Union's intercontinental nuclear delivery capability, inasmuch as the submarine-launched ballistic missile force was still relatively small. The Strategic Rocket Force had no responsibility other than its missile systems, except as it may have participated in the space program.

Military Use of Space

The portion of the space program that has military applications is not always obvious. Missile components can be used in space boosters that may have purely scientific missions. On the other

587

hand, some purely scientific data are of use to the military. The Soviets have been launching photo reconnaissance and electronic intelligence collection satellites since 1962, and up to half of the Cosmos series launched up to mid-1967 reportedly had a reconnaissance function. Others were for communications relay or for use as navigation aids, and some may have been intended for missile early warning or nuclear detonation detection.

The Fractional Orbital Bombardment System that was being tested during the late 1960's might be considered a space weapon in that it attained orbital velocity and, dependent upon its altitude, could remain in orbit the same as any satellite. The package in orbit could be retrofired to reduce its velocity, whereupon the warhead would fall to its target. It could approach a target from the shortest route, or it could take the longer way around the world and come in from the opposite direction. Until it fired its retro-rockets, its target could not be determined. On its long route to the target it might evade defensive radars. On its short route its high velocity would cut several minutes from the flight time of an ICBM. The fact that its orbital flight path would be much lower than the ballistic trajectory of an ICBM could also delay or inhibit its detection by defensive radars.

Mobilization Potential

The 140-division structure of the 1969 army was probably considered the force necessary for winning a short general war or for employment in the initial campaigns of a prolonged conflict. The approximately sixty combat-ready divisions could fight almost immediately. About twenty more have equipment designated to them and are manned with enough personnel so that they could be brought to full strength shortly and be ready for action in four to six weeks. The remainder of the 140 divisions could be ready in ninety days.

The total manpower pool between the ages of seventeen and fifty is as high as 50 million men, but mobilization of more than one-fourth of them is probably not envisaged. The approximately 750,000 conscripts who return to civilian life each year remain on reserve status until the age of fifty, and the pool of men from this group who are considered to be trained reserves is about 10 to 12 million. In any event the limit on the size of the force that would be mobilized would depend primarily on whether the warfare were nuclear or conventional and, if conventional, on the amount of equipment available. Manpower is not considered a limiting factor.

Personnel

The way the individual serviceman contributes to the military establishment reflects not only the training and discipline that govern his moment-to-moment activities, but also the traditions of the people, their history, which includes centuries before the revolution, and the climate and character of the land.

The Soviet soldier with whom the world is most familiar was a member of the Red Army that held off Hitler's forces at Moscow and Stalingrad and then pushed them slowly but relentlessly back toward Berlin. He was acclaimed by his German adversaries and by Allied observers as well trained and highly disciplined, intensely patriotic, and as a formidable warrior who, able to withstand extreme hardship and make do on the barest essentials, fought like a tiger. He was also derided by others from the same groups of observers as slovenly, cruel, illiterate, and as one who might, under pressure, surrender along with thousands of his comrades. In victory he would wantonly loot, kill, and rape. Western military analysts continued to say that he lacked initiative and technical competence and was abusive of his equipment and reluctant to assume responsibility.

The vast majority of conscripts in World War II army were descended from peasants who until 1861 were still serfs. The best of a bare existence required back-breaking labor, and too little or too much rainfall caused frequently recurring famine. Human life was an uncertain thing, a cheap commodity in low regard. Emancipation of the Russian serf came in 1861, but his conditions improved little between then and the Bolshevik Revolution. Things improved markedly for him during the New Economic Policy of the 1920's, but, with collectivization of the farms, the familiar hunger and misery were again the rule, and those who had shown initiative with their newly acquired land suffered the worst. The tsars before the revolution and the leadership since have exercised totalitarian rule and repressive control. Up to World War II, even in peacetime, it was considered unnecessary to notify the next of kin of casualties below the rank of colonel.

The force in 1969 was a far cry from the armies that went into battle during World Wars I and II. Changes in the general educational level of the population have provided the services with much improved basic manpower. World War I troops were largely illiterate. Stalin found the nearly chaotic and totally unstandardized school systems contributing poorly to his industrialization programs, and during the 1930's he retailored education to provide him with quantities of technically trained people (see ch. 15, The Educational System). World War II troops were slightly better educated than their fathers had been twenty-five years earlier, but schools were neglected during the war years. Forces maintained in occupied Germany and Eastern Europe have always been the best available, but a large proportion of sentries with the early occupation troops could not read passes printed in Russian.

As late as 1964 conscripts from rural areas, who constituted the majority of the lower ranking troops, had ordinarily received only about four years of schooling. This caliber of conscript had little exposure to mechanical or electronic equipment and required additional training. Five years later Russian military leaders claimed that over 90 percent of all young servicemen had received at least some secondary or higher education. This probably included inservice training, which is considered the equivalent of the technical training in some of the secondary school programs.

Premilitary training is as old as the Red Army, having been called for in Lenin's decree of April 22, 1918, which reinstituted compulsory service. It grew to proportions where more than 15 million men or youths received at least a portion of one of the services' preinduction training programs during World War II. The basic pattern has been carried on, and most Soviet citizens are exposed to some form of military or military-type training from early childhood. Unless he has a serious physical defect, probably no boy reaches the age of eighteen without knowing the basics of military drill. There is a parallel emphasis on physical training.

The joint services premilitary training organization, the Voluntary Society for Assistance to the Army, Air Force, and Navy, was formed in 1951, combining earlier individual service programs. Training is accomplished most frequently during the last three years of school, but also at factories, offices, and on collective and state farms. Training can be received in night sessions or in summer camps by those who have full-time daytime work. Preconscription training normally lasts 140 hours and is accomplished during the year prior to induction. Secondary school programs are staffed with military officers assigned to the schools.

Premilitary training includes indoctrination into service life, regulations and the oath of allegiance, small arms firing, individual combat techniques, and specialized training in a military-technical specialty. This could consist of instruction in driving a car or motorcycle, operating radio or radar equipment, motor boating, parachuting, gliding, or flying. Sporting events and rifle or pistol competitions are featured.

In premilitary training the emphasis has always been technical. It was necessarily so during the early postrevolutionary years when the technical educational level of the population was very low and the military establishment, such as it was, was ill-equipped to conduct any training in excess of the barest essentials. More emphasis has also been placed on physical education, political indoctrination, and civil defense instruction.

The 2.5 to 3 million youths who become seventeen during the calendar year register for the draft. They are called to duty in a spring or fall callup the following year. If all has gone according to schedule, premilitary training has been completed.

Students are deferred for specific periods. Those with temporary disabilities are deferred until able to serve. Sole supporters of families are deferred indefinitely, and the unfit are exempted. In normal years before 1968, about 750,000 were called annually into the regular services and an additional number brought into the security forces. The total approximated half of the age group remaining eligible after deferments and exemptions were made. Reductions of a year in the conscript tour of duty, which became effective in 1968, would require calling up a larger annual group in order to maintain force strengths at 1968 levels.

A young man's appearance before the predraft review panel and the ceremonies at his induction are elaborate, calculated to impress him with the importance of his service and his responsibilities. The panel could consist of the head of his school, the manager of his factory, the local police chief, the secretary of the local Communist Party organization, a trade union representative, and the chairman of the local soviet. Ceremonies upon being inducted typically include speeches by a general, an old veteran, an on-duty draftee, a youth organization member, and a draftee's mother. The new conscript does not take the oath of allegiance at this time. He takes this only after a period of intensive training, from which he gains an understanding of what his military life will involve, what his duties are, and after he has been able to demonstrate that he can perform them satisfactorily. The oath is taken individually, in private.

The tour of active duty established in 1968 became two years in most ground, air, coast defense, and security forces. It can be longer in special units and is three years in the navy. Early service includes a period of medical examinations, screening for occupational skills, and about two months of basic training. This is omitted if premilitary training had been received. Later training is on an annual cycle. It consists of small arms and personal combat instruction, small unit operations, maneuvers with larger groups of regimental or battalion size, and usually culminates in the autumn with participation in some major field exercise. Much training is conducted in winter or under severe weather conditions and at night. In summer the men live completely outdoors.

The schedule is kept full in all seasons and involves reveille at an early hour. Typically, it is 5:00 A.M. in the summer, six in the winter, with taps at ten or ten-thirty. Military training and physical conditioning take up to eight hours a day. Political indoctrination is scheduled throughout the year, usually for about an hour and a half per day. The normal day has perhaps two to three hours of rest periods and scheduled free time. Otherwise the soldier wakes up, trains, eats, studies, marches to formations, is inspected, and goes to bed in formation. In addition, his sports, recreation, and social life are largely organized. During his conscript tour he can expect one leave in which he can go home. Other leave might consist of organized and supervised visits to national monuments.

Discipline is strict and there is no personal life, but morale is generally good. Living conditions may be harsh, but no more so than the conscript has anticipated. He is performing a perhaps inconvenient but normal and respected life duty. The educational level and professional competence of the individual conscript has improved, and he can still be expected to be in excellent physical condition, willing to subsist with a minimum of comforts.

Men are drafted from any of the many ethnic groups, although there is a conscious effort to make force units homogeneous, and the chances are that none will have a number of any minority group that is far different from its percentage of the total population. Great Russians and Ukrainians account for at least three-quarters of the service personnel (see ch. 9, Ethnic Groups). The soldier remains basically passive, resigned, and fatalistic. He is not the type to be unduly affected by being forced to retreat and, in fact, may be at his best in a defensive situation. He has never been encouraged to think, to solve problems, or to act on his own initiative. He is careless in the use and maintenance of complex equipment.

All conscripts are encouraged to belong to the Komsomol groups. Almost 85 percent of the total armed forces personnel are either Communist Party or Komsomol members. They are patriotic and their morale is good, although there is evidence that some of them think a good portion of the political indoctrination is a bore. It is taken for granted and accepted because it is given on an absolutely unvarying and routine basis.

Some of the Komsomol members appear aggressively enthusiastic. The percentages who are genuinely so, as opposed to those who find it expedient, cannot be determined. There has been press comment to the effect that the lack of martial spirit among draftees has been a matter for concern. During public discussions prior to a 1966 resolution aimed at stimulating greater effort in premilitary training, it was stated that, although 82 percent of the armed forces personnel were Communist Party or Komsomol members, 18 percent were "politically indifferent" and that even some Party or Komsomol members showed political immaturity, displaying apathy and lack of discipline. It is apparent that in recent years there has been a trend toward "humanizing" service life, a movement Stalin would have feared as much as the increase in professionalism. The background of Soviet life and the educational level of the society have been in steady evolution, however, and changes could not but be reflected in the military establishment.

Although the party has always suspected the loyalty and reliability of the military establishment and particularly of the officer corps, the officers have developed into a distinctly separate and privileged group. From the situation in the 1920's when there were no rank insignia or grade differentiations and each professional military commander had a political commissar who was required to pass on his every decision, the officer corps has not only become a distinct social caste, it has also developed stratifications within itself. Ranks were restored in 1935, rank insignia during World War II. Subordinate ranks, field, and general grade officers have separate messes; living standards and social status are vastly different. There are, for example, fourteen standards of food rations for the forces, although some of them depend on the duty situation.

Officers are well paid. The salary of a doctor in the forces is double that which he could expect in civilian life. A marshal receives about 115 times the salary of the newly conscripted private. A major normally has a full-time personal orderly, and a general has a complete household staff.

The elite nucleus of the officer corps is derived from graduates of the Suvorov and Nakhimov cadet schools. The Nakhimov schools train naval cadets; the Suvorov schools prepare cadets for careers in the other services. Boys eight to thirteen years old are selected for these schools. The curriculum lasts five to eight years, depending upon how much schooling candidates had when admitted. Graduates go to an officers' candidate school for three years, receiving commissions upon graduation. The twenty cadet schools supply approximately 1,500 graduates annually. The remainder of those admitted to officers' candidate schools come directly from secondary schools or from higher educational institutions and, less frequently, up from the ranks. The normal officers' candidate school curriculum is three years, but university credits may be transferred in some circumstances.

Officer strengths are maintained at levels considerably beyond organizational requirements, allowing a liberal percentage to engage in advanced educational programs. Courses in the Frunze and Lenin military academies run from one to five years. Three-year midcareer courses are ordinarily attended. The Frunze academy is the equivalent of typical military command and staff colleges. The Lenin curriculum is weighted more toward the political. The apex of the system is the Higher Military Academy, which is attended only by those earmarked for topmost command positions. Normal career progression consists of a rotation through troop, staff, and educational assignments.

Although officers have status, the life of a junior officer is not one abounding in comforts and luxury. Eight or ten may share a room, and the requirement for on-duty studies frequently makes this overcrowding an even greater hardship. Duty is rigorous, and the existence is one inclining toward total involvement. The rewards appear satisfying, however, and the esprit de corps is high. The group that emerged from World War II was tough, experienced, and competent. They were considered flexible within prescribed limits, but inhibited from assuming responsibility or taking any but routine initiatives. These men are reaching retirement age and are increasingly being replaced. There is no evidence that the younger men are less tough and competent, and they have better technical backgrounds and are undoubtedly more professionally able to use and manage modern equipment than were their predecessors.

Officers stay in reserve status to age sixty, ten years longer than enlisted men. Generals retire at sixty and remain in the reserves until sixty-five. All ranks may be called back to active duty for military exercises. Officers in some reserve categories are recalled on a recurring basis for two- to three-month training increments and may get up to thirty-six months of this type of active duty.

Noncommissioned officer candidates may be selected from secondary school graduates at the time of their induction into the service, or they may be chosen from conscripts on duty who indicate that they have the proper attitude and capability. Noncommissioned rank is little sought after. There is extra training, an extra service commitment of at least a year, and there is little pay or other compensation in proportion to the considerably increased responsibility for lower ranking sergeants. The noncommissioned officer is saluted by privates and is not accepted into officer society, which in many assignments can mean that he leads an isolated existence. This may explain why quotas for noncommissioned training are reputedly filled by involuntary means on frequent occasions.

Political Controls in the Armed Forces

Political controls in the forces date from 1918. The task of building an effective Red Army was beset with formidable obstacles. The revolution had been successful in large degree because its leaders had been able to undermine and nearly totally destroy the tsarist armies. The Bolshevik propagandists had urged the men to quit, desert, and go home. The country had had its fill of warfare, death, dislocation, disease, destruction, and the deprivations that came from advancing and retreating armies endlessly living off the land. Revolutionary slogans had done away with discipline by promising to do away with all inequalities between men.

After Lenin's efforts to attract a volunteer army had failed, he reinstituted the draft and gave Trotsky the responsibility for making an army out of the mass of miserable and reluctant humanity that was gathered in. Trotsky called up nearly 50,000 of the old tsarist officers, realizing the necessity for them, but knowing that their political inclinations would be conservative and that they would be unreliable. Trotsky's elaborate system of political controls, although moderated over the years, has continued to be part of Soviet military life.

Political officers, or commissars, were installed in all units. The commissar had rank and authority equal to that of the commander and his cosignature was necessary on all orders. The political officer still exists but, over the years and with increasing stability and reliability of the forces, he has ordinarily become the deputy commander, with rank one grade below that of the commander. He is no longer required to approve orders that are operational in nature. He has generally become the officer in charge of education, recreation, sports programs, morale, and social functions.

The political officer still has a communications channel through which he makes private reports, however, and is required to comment on all matters relating to morale and political reliability, including an evaluation of his commander. Larger headquarters have political staff sections. At the top is the Main Political Directorate, administratively beneath the Ministry of Defense, but responsible to the Central Committee of the Communist Party. The situation has moderated a great deal from the days when an adverse report by the commissar could mean that the commander would not be present some morning and would never be heard from again, but favorable political reports are essential if an officer is to have satisfactory career progression.

The military establishment receives high-priority Communist Party activity, perhaps more than is normal in most aspects of Soviet life. Wherever there are three or more Party or Komsomol members, a Party cell is organized. Inasmuch as these members include more than 80 percent of all service personnel, there are cells in the smallest units. The Party organization can operate independently, but ordinarily cooperates closely with the unit political officer. Leadership in the Party cells is not necessarily related to military rank.

During the civil war years from 1917 to 1921, approximately half of the Communist Party strength was kept in the Red Army, to keep up its morale and to promote revolutionary fervor. The expansion in Party strength was so fast at that time that it was difficult to keep adherance to a strict Party line, and purging of the membership was accomplished regularly during the 1920's.

In addition to the Political Directorate and the Communist Party organizations, the secret police have continually been infiltrated throughout the entire military establishment. Since the Khrushchev era the secret police have been under the Committee of State Security (Komitet Gosudarstvennoy Bezopasnosti) and internationally known by its initials as the KGB. Under whatever initials or ministry the secret police have operated, they also have maintained their own independent communication channels.

Political indoctrination programs administer large doses of the dogma, aimed at convincing the recruit of the superiority of the socialist system and instilling love of the Fatherland. From a military standpoint the serviceman is taught discipline, obedience, pride in his service and its traditions, and to hate his enemies. He is taught, for example, that he has no right to surrender on a battlefield where his comrades may have died. The Military Penal Code calls surrender "voluntary captivity," punishable by death. World War II captives were written off, and no interest was taken in their treatment by their captors. Repatriated prisoners were treated as deserters, traitors, or spies.

For all its efforts, the controlling Party apparatus has found the military an enigma from the earliest days and has never been completely satisfied with its relations with the armed forces establishment. The Party has seen the military not only as one of its most essential instruments, but also as a potential threat to its authority. It has known that professional military establishment tends to become apolitical and that loyalties are likely to develop within it which may become stronger than its ties to a political ideology or a ruling group. This has been a matter of extreme and continuing sensitivity.

The Party has tolerated military professionalism in varying degrees. A Red Army operating along traditional lines was necessary to win the civil war and to unify the Soviet Union. Stalin built up his forces but demanded a politically subservient officer corps, and his purges in 1937 and 1938 were made without regard for the debilitating effect they had on the forces. In World War II, he had to permit the military to manage along conventional lines again, although he continued to have little regard for the role played by his officer corps.

Since the death of Stalin the men in the forces have had to become competent enough to employ and maintain the most modern and technologically advanced types of equipment, and they have been drawn from an increasingly better educated population, more generally accustomed to mechanical and electronic devices. In such circumstances it has become more difficult to hold down professionalism. Ninety percent of the officers, however, are Communist Party members. Political controls do not now prevent the commander from taking any immediate initiative, but any tendency toward political deviation would effectively terminate his career.

Whether because of political indoctrination, repressive measures, or both, the military has not shown any appreciable disloyalty. The Party is still considered to have absolute control over the military establishment, although there have been no Stalin-type purges since his death, and military spokesmen have for the first time been able to state their views freely and publicly on controversial policy matters. Among the troops, in spite of the fact that all of the men known that political and security police representatives are in their midst, personal relations appear hearty and good natured. Such evidence of good morale is seen as a reflection of increased stability, maturity, and general acceptance of the system and the progress of its programs. If there is less severe exercise of control by the Party, it is considered only because it has confidence that heavy-handed measures are unnecessary and that its final authority will not be challenged (see ch. 27, Political Attitudes and Reactions).

About a third of the Soviet male population reaching draft age each year can expect to serve at least two years in the armed forces. The old principles of extreme discipline and total obedience are carried forward, relaxed relatively little even in view of the major technological changes in the forces' equipment and their requirement for highly trained and skilled men. The Disciplinary Statutes of 1946, as revised in 1960, are based on the tsarist military code of 1869. The military establishment has always been a heavy burden upon the population. In major wars the forces have lived off the land, having first priority to anything they have wanted. The armed forces have been the first beneficiaries of all the Soviet industrialization programs. They continue to require a portion of the gross national product that deprives the civilian population of any substantial gain in consumer products (see ch. 6, The Economic System).

For all this, the military establishment is accepted by the people, and the authority of the officer is respected. The ordinary citizen identifies the army as "his" army, an identification he does not feel toward the Communist Party. Moreover, the military is allowed its links with the past. An example is the Suvorov cadet schools, named for the great soldier who fought Russia's battles during the eighteenth century.

The Soviet citizen is not readily able to view his circumstances in a comparison between what they are and what they might have been under another system. The grandfather of the 1969 recruit may only barely remember the revolution, and Soviet society is largely insulated from the rest of the world. Defectors have stated that servicemen tend to discount heavily what they are told about their own country, but generally accept what they are told about foreign lands. It is reasonable to believe that the people credit their forces with having saved the Bolshevik system during the civil war after 1917 and having played a major role in the defeat of Germany in World War II.

The Soviet people probably are genuinely convinced that the armed forces are intended primarily for a defensive role or for deterrence. Justification for actions such as against Hungary in 1956 and Czechoslovakia in 1968 could be approved as defending the system, and those interventions were not costly in life or property. In any event, the men in the forces would not be held responsible for the policy decisions behind the moves. Continuing popular support for "wars of national liberation" that do not involve manpower losses and excessive expenditures can be expected. Such use of the forces would not be regarded as national aggrandizement.

The attitude of the people toward the individual soldier is one of familiar identification. Nearly half of the adult male population has had some service connection and accepts the fact that this will be true for future generations. The fact that the forces are becoming more professional and employ more technically advanced weapons does not alter the fact that military life is participated in over the period of time by nearly one-quarter of the population. Its men are part of the working public, and its officers are a necessary and respected professional group.

Propaganda media paint the military establishment in favorable terms and promote a picture of the military hero who defends Mother Russia. The regular training schedule keeps servicemen busy to the point where opportunities for friction with the civilian population are fewer than would otherwise be the case. Military discipline is not considered excessive to a people who have always been subject to stern, harsh controls. Nothing other than blind obedience has ever been tolerated in the old Russian or the new Soviet military. The Soviet individual, civilian or soldier, is servant to the state and has always been so. Submission to authority may be disliked but it is not resented.

FOREIGN MILITARY RELATIONS

Communist ideology commits the Soviet Union to the support of international communism but, although they have maintained powerful armed forces, Soviet leaders have been reluctant to enter into formal military agreements. In 1969 the Warsaw Pact Organization was the only major military alliance in which the Soviet Union was actively committed to a coordinated multinational use of its forces (see ch. 24, Foreign Relations). An arrangement with the Mongolian People's Republic was in 1969 the only bilateral defense agreement to which it had subscribed publicly.

The Warsaw Pact Organization was established in 1955, on the initiative of the Soviet Union, to counter the West's NATO. The original members were the Soviet Union, Poland, East Germany, Hungary, Rumania, Bulgaria, Czechoslovakia, and Albania. Albania participated in no pact activities after 1961 and was excluded in 1962. During the first five years the pact made some effort to standardize equipment, tactics, and operations among the members, but it was hardly a military partnership. There were no joint exercises and there was little cooperation in military planning. The organization was used, however, to extend Soviet air defenses outward from the homeland.

After 1960 the pact became a more thoroughly integrated alliance. Eastern European forces were assigned a more active role in theater operations, and joint exercises were undertaken. Warsaw Pact forces in Eastern Europe consist of nearly 1 million men in sixty divisions, half of them held at combat-ready status. The Soviet Union is predominant in the organization. All major meetings are held in Moscow, and the commander in chief has always been a Soviet marshal.

The Soviet Union has urged its allies to contribute to the support of the Mongolian People's Republic or to invite that country into the pact, with little discernable success. The Soviet Union has promised to defend the Mongolian People's Republic's 2,500-mile border with Communist China "as if it were its own." Although they had been allies since 1921, the formal defense treaty was signed in the Mongolian capital, Ulan Bator, in January 1966.

Soviet military assistance to other countries has been contributed where there was an opportunity to foster more favorable relations with the Soviet Union or to weaken ties to the West. Between 1954 and 1968 more than the equivalent of US$5 billion of Soviet aid was pledged to about twenty-five developing countries. About one-third of this amount was delivered. This does not include aid to the North Vietnamese and the Viet Cong, who received about 85 percent of their military support from the Warsaw Pact Organization between 1966 and 1969.

Early military aid usually consisted of obsolescent equipment, surplus to the needs of Soviet forces. Aid to the United Arab Republic after the 1967 Arab-Israeli conflict, however, included nearly 100 of the most modern Su—7 aircraft, about 500 modern tanks, 100 amphibious armored personnel carriers, and other amphibious landing craft. Prior to the Vietnam conflict, total Soviet military aid deliveries had averaged about the equivalent of US$400 million annually over a ten-year period, or about 0.1 percent of the gross national product (GNP). Only 5 percent of this aid was provided on a nonrepayable basis.

Sino-Soviet relations deteriorated seriously during the 1960's. Ostensibly a struggle for control of the international Communist movement, punctuated by border disputes and personality clashes, their difficulties may be more basically nationalistic, caused by the pressures generated when two expanding powers meet and have their ambitions frustrated along a border which, in this case, extends for 4,500 miles. Border clashes occurred with increasing frequency during the 1960's, the most serious in 1969. As greater forces have been massed on both sides of the border, the possibilities for more serious developments have increased (see ch. 24, Foreign Relations).

THE MILITARY ESTABLISHMENT
AND THE NATIONAL ECONOMY

Manpower

The total population of the Soviet Union in 1969 was approximately 235 million, of which 45 to 50 million males were in the eighteen-to-forty-five age group. Service strength was approximately 3.2 million. As such, the military establishment represented about 1.4 percent of the total population and 6 to 7 percent of the manpower from the age group it drew upon (see ch. 32, The Labor Force).

These percentages are not high by comparative statistical standards, but are not an accurate reflection of the relative burden of the Soviet military establishment with respect to the allocation of technical and scientific skills. The armed forces have had first priority on industrial planning and for scientific and technologically trained personnel. They have competed with the remainder of the economy for resources and skilled personnel that, until very recently, have been extremely scarce. The equipment in the hands of the military establishment is highly modernized and complex. Civilian consumer products have been held down in quantity, quality, and variety largely because of military priorities. The general public has not yet begun to derive significant quantities of consumer benefits from the extraordinary national industrial and scientific efforts that have so far been undertaken.

Defense Costs

The defense budget for 1968 was R16.7 billion (R1 equals US$1.10). This included expenditures for military pay and subsistence, operations and maintenance, military construction for the armed forces, and at least a portion of procurement. Defense expenditures not appearing in the regular defense budget include military research and development, stockpiling, civil defense, foreign military aid, and space research. The nuclear energy program, for example, is financed under the Ministry of Medium Machine Building. Expenditures for intelligence gathering are also concealed and do not appear in the defense budget. The internal security expenditures probably run about R1 billion and were not included in the defense budget.

The regular 1968 defense budget amounted to 13 percent of the total national budget and about 5 percent of the GNP. The total of actual estimated defense or defense-related expenditures in 1968 had reportedly reached an equivalent on purchasing power of about US$50 billion and would represent nearly 20 percent of the GNP. Increases during the late 1960's averaged approximately 10 percent annually. In view of the reemphasis on conventional forces that followed the Khrushchev years, rapidly escalating space costs, extensive new strategic missile deployment, and increased production of nuclear submarines, this rate of increase can be accounted for.

Since the start of the first Five-Year Plan of 1928—32, there has been a continuing high demand for military equipment and for military-related research and development. The accent has been on heavy industry, producing largely for defense programs. In the past decade the space and missile effort has absorbed vast quantities of scientific talent and research and development facilities. The industrial product that has not gone directly into military-related materiel has to a very considerable extent been plowed back into the means of expanding heavy industrial production, in much the same way that scientific talent not utilized in military and space programs is being used to expand educational facilities to create more scientists and technicians. Consumer goods for the civilian economy have had lowest priority and, in spite of continuing promises to the contrary, there is little to indicate that any significant change to improve the relative supply of consumer products has occurred. The proportion of industrial production that has gone into consumer goods has actually declined from approximately 60 percent during the mid-1920's to approximately 30 percent at the beginning of the 1970's.

SECTION IV. ECONOMIC

CHAPTER 29

ECONOMIC PLANNING AND CONTROL

In Soviet society, where public ownership of the means of production prevails and the authority of the Communist Party of the Soviet Union (CPSU) is supreme, the basic economic task of allocating scarce resources to competing ends is accomplished primarily through a centrally directed planning apparatus rather than through the interplay of market forces. Based on general CPSU directives concerning major economic goals, the planning authorities formulate long-term and short-range plans for the achievement of specific targets in virtually all spheres of economic activity, with primary emphasis on production and investment in heavy industry.

These production plans are supplemented by comprehensive plans for the supply of materials, equipment, labor, and finances to the producing sector, the procurement of farm products by the state, and for the distribution of food and manufactured products to the population. The economic plans have the force of law. They are worked out in great detail down to the level of the individual economic enterprise, where they are reflected in a set of output goals and performance indicators that management is expected to attain.

Adherence by enterprise management to the major plan directives is generally assured through manifold inspection procedures and through a system of incentives and sanctions. Aside from honors and opportunities for professional advancement, incentives are in the form of financial bonuses for performance equal to or better than that called for by the plan. Poor performance entails penalties ranging from reprimand and a reduction of income to loss of position and criminal prosecution. The rigidity of the system is mitigated to some extent by a provision for plan adjustments and by opportunities for limited maneuver on the part of management within the confines of the plan by sacrificing secondary targets for the sake of attaining the major objective.

The staggering difficulty of the planning task, which calls for a delicate balancing of the supply with requirements, involving many thousands of different raw materials, manufactured products, and enterprises spread over the country's vast area and a myriad interrelationships in a dynamic and increasingly complex economy, has inevitably entailed serious planning errors. This problem has been accentuated by a tendency to set overambitious production goals. As a consequence, the economy has been plagued by an intractable materials supply problem.

On the national level material shortages have usually been resolved by diverting resources from low-priority consumer industries and agriculture to high-priority heavy industry. At the enterprise level shortages of materials have generally resulted in wasteful and quality-deteriorating substitutions, in extralegal procurement practices, and in failures to achieve production goals. Overfulfillment of plan targets by heavy industry and underfulfillment by agriculture and the consumer industries has been a regular feature of the Soviet economic performance. As a consequence, the chairman of the Council of Ministers was able to boast in 1966 about the country's remarkable achievements in space and the military's most powerful modern weapons, while admitting that farm output did not meet the requirements of the economy.

The managerial incentive system that was in effect until the mid-1960's and still partially operative in mid-1969 failed to elicit a maximal production effort. Since it was geared primarily to the attainment of the goal for gross output, it actually induced managers to seek approval of low production targets and to neglect quality. The system also tended to inhibit the development of new products and technological innovation, because both these processes usually entail a temporary reduction in output with an adverse effect on managerial income. The attitude of enterprise managers was often tolerated by superiors interested in a good showing by units under their jurisdiction.

Although the planning machinery has undergone frequent modifications over the years, the fundamental planning process has remained virtually unchanged since the inception of the five-year plans in the late 1920's. This process may have served well enough during the early stage of the country's economic development, when the major effort was concentrated on the production of steel; but it has been found increasingly inadequate by Soviet economists, planners, and business managers in dealing with problems of the modern, vastly expanded, and diversified economy since the late 1950's. It has proved particularly unresponsive to the mounting demand by the population for a better supply of consumer goods and to the needs of agriculture.

A slowing down of the economic growth rate after 1958, a decline in output per unit of investment, and the accumulation of huge unsalable stocks of producer and consumer goods, despite many continuing shortages, were widely cited as evidence of the failure of the planning system to make the most efficient use of available resources. Proposals for improvement ranged from still greater centralization of planning, supported by a nationwide network of computers, to the introduction of a controlled market economy based on the exercise of free choice by consumers.

Official response to these proposals was limited to a minor reform of planning and incentives announced in the fall of 1965. This reform modified the incentive system by shifting the emphasis from gross output to sales and profits and granted enterprise managers slightly greater latitude in making operating decisions by reducing the number of plan indicators assigned by higher authorities. It also introduced charges for interest and rent and provided for a gradual transition from centralized material supply to wholesale distribution.

Transfer of enterprises to the new management system had not been completed by mid-1969. Judging by the evidence in the Soviet press, the reform has not significantly improved fundamental conditions of supply, production, and distribution. Decentralization of planning, with a shift in the direction of a market economy, would necessarily involve some loss of control by the CPSU. In the view of most Western observers, Soviet leadership does not appear ready for such a liberalization, as evidenced by its action in stifling incipient reform in Czechoslovakia in the summer of 1968 and its tendency toward more oppressive rule in domestic affairs.

NATURE OF PLANNING

By mid-1969 Soviet centralized economic planning was in the fourth year of a mild revision instituted after a progressively widespread and intensive debate on the subject following the death of Joseph Stalin. The debate revolved around the question of the effectiveness of the planning system in coping with the complexities of a highly developed economy and the ability of the system to assure continued rapid economic growth. Like many of its predecessors, the latest reform merely changed some of the outer aspects of planning but left the fundamental process intact.

Theory and Reality

Economic planning, according to Marxist dogma, is a form of economic management by the state, indispensible both during the transition from capitalism to socialism and in a socialist society. Marxists maintain that planning is based on a profound knowledge and application of several objective socialist economic laws and that it is independent of the personal will and desires of men. The most general of these laws, commonly referred to as the basic law of socialism, defines the aim of economic production to be the fullest

605

satisfaction of the constantly growing material and cultural requirements of the members of society through continued growth and improvement of production on the basis of advanced technology.

The second economic law generally cited in this context is the law of the planned, proportional development of the national economy. This law requires that the development of all branches of the economy be subordinated to a unified planned direction by society and that proportionality among all parts of the economy be preserved.

Centralized planning is presented by its proponents as a way of consciously applying economic laws in the interest of the people through effective use of all natural resources and productive forces. It is said to be strictly scientific, because it is based on relevant Marxist-Leninist theory. It is also said to be supported by a tremendous creative activity of the masses and to provide a clear program of action that enables every individual to find his place in the work for the common cause. Less ardent Marxists acknowledge that the effectiveness of planning depends upon the degree of correctness in the application of the economic laws by state planning agencies and point out the need to develop a truly scientific basis for planning.

Socialist economic laws cannot be conceived as objective or natural laws in the sense that they could operate independently of the will of men. They constitute no more than statements of desirable economic goals. As such, they provide no practical guidelines or objective criteria for determining the priorities among the various economic sectors, which would assure a balanced growth of the entire economy. Neither do they shed any light on the relative advantages of alternative technological processes or methods of industrial and agricultural organization.

The direction of economic development thus depends upon decisions made by planners on the basis of their own evaluation of the country's needs. This evaluation necessarily takes into account political, military, and other noneconomic considerations. Inevitably it is also colored by the personal preferences of the planners. In the Soviet Union economic planning expresses the policy of the ruling CPSU.

Historical Background

Comprehensive, centralized economic planning in the country evolved since the 1920's as a tool of the CPSU in shaping the course of the country's economic development under conditions of public ownership of the means of production and almost complete proscription of private enterprise. The professed goals of planning have been rapid economic growth, military security, and improvement in the living standard of the population.

The task of planners consists in the formulation of concrete, workable plans for achieving the broad goals set by the CPSU. This involves fundamental decisions and directives by the Party regarding rates of economic growth, the allocation of the national product between consumption and investment, military versus civilian priorities, and the direction of technological progress to be followed. The Party's choice has been in favor of military security and a maximum attainable rate of economic growth through rapid industrialization, based on massive investments and on the Marxist tenet that maximum economic growth requires that the output of producer goods develop faster than the output of consumer goods. A corollary of this party choice has been a relative neglect of agriculture and the consumer.

Historically, this economic policy derived from an awareness by the CPSU of a need to develop virtually from scratch, with very limited resources and without foreign aid, an integrated economy capable of supporting its own growth, and from the Party's evaluation of the country's defense needs. To provide the manpower and food needed to sustain industrial development, agriculture was forcibly collectivized and subjected to harsh produce delivery quotas.

Despite the tremendous increase in the country's economic resources and military strength since the 1920's, the Twenty-third Party Congress held in 1966 reaffirmed the priority of heavy industry. It made only a slight concession to consumers by somewhat narrowing the gap between the projected rates of growth for capital and consumer goods and by allocating greater investment to agriculture in the Plan for 1966—70. At the international Communist Party conference held in Moscow in June 1969, Party General Secretary Leonid Brezhnev reemphasized the basic role of the economy in assuring the country's military power.

Economic planning has reflected this concentration on heavy industry. As expressed by a prominent Soviet planner, industry, and particularly heavy industry, plays a leading role in creating the material and technical basis of socialism and communism. It therefore holds the central place in the national economic plan and is the point of departure for working out all other targets.

PLANNING MECHANISM

Comprehensive and detailed economic planning on a scale as vast as the Soviet Union presents formidable problems in coordinating sectoral, functional, and regional aspects of planning and control. In a continuing search for more effective methods of dealing with these problems, and also in part for political reasons, numerous changes have been made over the years in the structure, scope or responsibilities, and authority of the various planning and administrative organizations.

The most radical of these changes consisted in a temporary shift from a predominantly sectoral to a primarily regional approach during the period of 1957 to 1965. It involved the abolition of most industrial ministries and the transfer of their planning and administrative authority to a large number of newly created regional economic councils called *sovnarkhozy*. The major stated reasons for this reorganization were unsatisfactory coordination among the industrial ministries and a lack of an effective regional planning authority.

The regional system proved to be even less effective than the organization it supplanted, and the weaknesses of the ministerial system soon reappeared in a regional context. After a series of reorganizations, the regional planning councils were abolished in 1965 and the ministerial system was reinstituted, although with greater participation by regional bodies in the planning process, at least in theory.

At the top of the planning pyramid is the State Planning Committee under the Council of Ministers. This agency, comprising a large number of sectoral, functional, regional, technical, and statistical departments, is responsible for formulating nationwide plans, integrating the more detailed sectoral and regional plans prepared by subordinate planning levels, and supervising plan fulfillment. It is also responsible for assuring a correct balance among the different branches of the economy, searching out means to speed the growth of the national income, and raising the level of efficiency in production (see ch. 19, Formal Structure of the Union Government).

Economic ministries draft plans within the sphere of their own jurisdictions, direct the planning by subordinate enterprises and supervise enterprise performance. Within the ministries, the planning task is subdivided among several departments called *glavki*, which deal with functional problems, such as finances and procurement, with regional problems, or with a particular segment of the sector under the ministry's jurisdiction, such as woolens in the Ministry of Textile Industry. Each *glavk* plans for its own area of responsibility.

Individual enterprises at the base of the planning pyramid are called upon to develop the most minutely detailed plans covering all aspects of their operations. Generally, enterprises are directly subordinated to a *glavk*, although in some instances there are intermediate organizations in the form of trusts or associations grouping together several enterprises. These organizations also form a link in the planning chain. In agriculture an enterprise is represented by the individual collective or state farm under the supervision of a local party committee. Its role in planning, however, is much more circumscribed.

608

A parallel organizational system for planning exists in each union and autonomous republic. The republic state planning committees are subject to the jurisdiction of both the Republic Council of Ministers and the union state planning committees. They draft plans for all enterprises under union-republic and republic ministries and make recommendations of draft plans of enterprises subordinated to union ministries and located in their territory. The regional system also includes planning agencies created for several major economic regions, which are responsible either to the union state planning committees or to a republic state planning committee, and extends down to the local district and town level (see Ch. 19, Formal Structure of the Union Government; ch. 20, Component Political Subdivisions).

Among functional organizations participating in the planning process the major role belongs to the State Committee for Material-Technical Supply. This agency shares with the State Planning Committee the controls over the allocation of essential materials and equipment. Under the economic reform program of 1965 it has been charged with the task of developing a wholesale trading chain to replace the existing system of administrative allocations. Other functional agencies include the State Committee for Construction, which plays an important part in industrial investment planning and housing construction; the State Committee on Labor and Wages; and the State Committee for Science and Technology, which participates in preparing proposals for the introduction of new technology. The country's Academy of Sciences assists in the development of a scientific base for a unified system of optimal planning and accounting.

Cooperation and coordination among the multitude of planning agencies has been less than perfect. Central planning agencies have often failed to take into account local conditions, interests, and needs, while local bodies have approached the planning task from a narrow parochial point of view. In many instances a clear-cut demarcation of the respective areas of responsibility has been lacking. Thus, for example, no lists of materials were available as late as 1969 to define the limits of jurisdiction in the planning and supply of materials among the State Planning Committee, the State Committee on Labor and Wages, and the economic ministries.

PLANNING PROCESS

Formulation of Plans

The planning process has never been adequately described, but available information suffices to reveal its general outline. Broad economic goals are formulated by the Council of Ministers in accordance with directives of the CPSU and the Supreme Soviet. These include such matters as the growth of agricultural and industrial production, the level of investment and allocations for military expenditures and private consumption. Based on these, and on data supplied by lower administrative levels regarding the current state of the economy, the State Planning Committee works out, through trial and error, a set of control figures covering the major aspects of economic activity in each economic sector and in each republic or region of the country.

These control figures are sent through the various channels and levels of the planning hierarchy for progressively more detailed elaboration. The flow is then reversed, and the detailed draft plans eventually developed by the lowest level—typically the individual enterprise—are sent back up the ladder for review, adjustment, and integration. This process entails intensive bargaining up and down the line, with top authorities pressing for maximum and, at times, unrealizable targets and enterprises seeking to obtain assignments that they can expect to fulfill without great difficulty. Ultimate review and revision of the draft plans by the State Planning Committee and approval of a final national plan by the Council of Ministers, the CPSU, and the Supreme Soviet are followed by another downward flow, this time for amended and approved plans containing specific targets for each economic entity to the level of the individual enterprise.

In agriculture detailed plans for crop and livestock production and production methods are developed and assigned by the planning apparatus to indivudal farms on the basis of centrally determined cropping patterns, production techniques, and output targets for each farming region. These output targets, in turn, are based on State Planning Committee plans for farm produce procurement, which take into account produce sold freely through farmers' markets (see ch. 31, Agriculture).

Timing

In order to have annual production plans for enterprises completed by the beginning of the operational year, preparation of plans normally begins in March or April of the preceding year. Since planning must take into account output levels already achieved, planners have to rely in their calculations on estimates formed many months before actual results become known. The planning of material and equipment supplies must also be done in advance so that enterprises are forced to make detailed requisitions for these items long before they know what their production program will be. These unavoidable conditions of the planning process under the existing system constitute one of the major factors responsible for the development of many unrealistic plans and for a widespread lack of correspondence between production plans and available material supplies. The problem for enterprises is aggravated by frequent changes of plans in midstream by orders from higher authorities.

Despite the substantial leadtime, plans often reach enterprises well after the beginning of the planning period, which results in further confusion and disorganization. An example of this lag in planning, by no means unique, is provided by the Eighth Plan for 1966—70. Although the period covered by this plan began on January 1, 1966, draft directives for the plan were approved only in April of that year; and the enormous, time-consuming task of developing the full plan on the basis of the approved directives still remained to be done. Such delays inevitably reduce the effectiveness of planning.

Types of Plans

Economic planning involves the formulation of both long-term and short-term plans. These plans are expressed predominantly in physical rather than monetary terms; that is, production targets and material consumption are stated in units and weights, and only aggregates, such as total volume of output or of trade, are given in rubles.

Long-term plans point up the general direction that economic development is intended to follow and set forth a series of specific quantitative and qualitative goals to be attained over a period of years by the various economic sectors, territorial units, and individual enterprises. Generally known as perspective plans, they are supposed to provide guidelines for the preparation of more detailed annual operational plans. The annual plans, in turn, are broken down into quarterly and monthly plans, which serve as commands and blueprints for the day-to-day operation of industrial and other economic enterprises and organizations.

Except for a fifteen-year electrification plan announced in 1920, a vague, discarded twenty-year plan ending in 1980, and one seven-year plan, long-term planning has found expression in a series of five-year plans, the eighth and latest of which covers the period of 1966—70. The Third Five-Year Plan was not completed owing to the outbreak of World War II in 1939. The goals of the Sixth Five-Year Plan for the years 1956—60 proved to be unattainable. It was dropped in its third year and was followed by the Seven-Year Plan for 1959—65. Directives for the Eighth Plan for 1966—70 were ratified by the Twenty-Third Party Congress in April 1966 but, contrary to customary procedure, a subsequent formal approval of the five-year plan by the Supreme Soviet did not take place. This failure has been ascribed to differences within the CPSU leadership regarding national priorities.

Plan Contents

National five-year plans have been published in condensed form since the inception of planning, and summary annual plans have been published in the postwar period. Neither quarterly nor monthly plans have ever appeared in print. Published versions of the five-year plans, and to a lesser extent the annual plans, have presented under appropriate headings the targets for the economy as a whole and for its component branches.

These targets, expressed either in absolute magnitudes or in percentages of growth, include such elements as total and per capita national income, industrial investment and housing construction, agricultural production, gross industrial output for both producer and consumer goods, production of major farm commodities and industrial products, retail trade turnover, wages and labor productivity, and consumer services. The plans also call for such measures as technological advances, improvement in product quality, increased labor productivity, reduction in material inputs, and more efficient organization of production. In connection with the planning reform instituted in the fall of 1965, annual plans beginning with 1968 also contain targets for sales, profits, and profitability.

Short-term plans are intended to allow for current adjustment of long-term plans in the light of changed or unforeseen conditions. In actual practice they are more frequently used in efforts to eliminate bottlenecks and other manifestations of disorganization in production arising from planning errors or breakdowns in the supply system. Failure to achieve adequate coordination between long- and short-term plans has prevented enterprises from planning their operations in advance and establishing lasting ties with suppliers, which has had a deleterious effect on production and efficiency.

METHODOLOGY OF PLANNING

Method of Balances

The method used by planners to achieve internally consistent plans, both in a sectoral and a regional context, has been called a method of balances. No very clear exposition of this method has been published. Essentially it consists of preparing balance sheets in which available material, labor, and financial resources are listed as assets and requirements based on planned output as liabilities. The task of planners is to equate both sides through trial and error and successive approximations or, in other words, to assure that the necessary inputs are provided for the planned output, both overall and for each product. To reduce this task to manageable proportions, the most detailed output goals, investment projects, and supply plans are formulated by central authorities only for key branches of the economy, with the rest of the plan developed to the point needed to assure achievement of the main goals.

According to a textbook for CPSU schools, every effort is made in working out the balances to uncover hidden reserves and find new sources for deficit items. In the event that resources are inadequate to cover all requirements, the latter are reduced in strict accordance with establish priorities, making sure that the requirements of high-priority claimants are fully covered. In this process the military and space industries, as well as their supporting heavy industry branches, have been accorded the highest priorities.

In working out material balances, extensive use is made of input and technical norms, which specify for each type of operation the quantity and quality of materials and labor to be used, the intensity of equipment utilization, the allowable time span, and many other relevant factors. It is a cardinal principle of Marxist economic doctrine that these norms must be progressive; that is, they must be made ever more stringent so as to assure a rapid advance in the quality and economy of production. In practice central planning authorities have applied rather arbitrary rates of growth to existing average norms. The resultant plan targets have consequently been relatively, though not absolutely, low for modern, well-equipped enterprises and put a severe strain on older ones in various stages of obsolescence.

Plans for labor requirements and the wage fund are based on output norms per worker in individual economic sectors and industries, predetermined rates of growth of labor productivity in each of these areas, centrally determined wage rates for each category of workers, and the principle that productivity must rise faster than wages.

Separate balances are drawn up for many thousands of items used in production and construction by some 130 distinct branches of industry, all of which must subsequently be reconciled through mutual adjustment and integrated into coherent sectoral and regional production and investment plans. The method of balances is also used in formulating plans for all other aspects of the economy, including the supply of consumer goods to the population, agricultural production, state procurement of farm products, and trade. The integrated sum total of these plans constitutes the national plan. This planning process, which proceeds from the individual product and enterprise, is known as the microeconomic approach to planning, in contrast to the macroeconomic approach, which centers on the broad categories of the national income, such as production, consumption, saving, and investment. This approach plans only a minor role in Soviet planning.

Shortcomings of Planning

Overall national balances and balances involving a few thousand of the most essential materials subject to central allocation are developed by the State Planning Committee. Others are prepared by subordinate planning agencies. This enormous task, involving countless planning bodies with imprecisely delimited responsibilities and authority and well over a million, and perhaps even several million, individuals, poses a most difficult coordination problem.

Planning for individual industry branches is done by separate groups of experts in different planning departments, with inadequate interindustry coordination and consequent inconsistencies in the overall industry plan. A similar lack of coordination, responsible in large measure for the chronic difficulties in capital construction, occurs frequently among the several parts of the investment plan, that is, plant construction, new technology, production capacity, material supply, and financing. Central planning of agriculture has been fraught with particularly grave consequences for production, because it does not take into account the infinite variety of local conditions and deprives farms of the flexibility needed to cope with the vagaries of weather.

Perhaps the most widespread, persistent, and disruptive effect of advance planning by physical balances has been the lack of correspondence, already alluded to, between the production assignments and the material supplies for individual enterprises. Managers have usually sought to deal with this problem by building up excessive inventories through padded estimates of material requirements, creating subsidiary departments for the manufacture of essential components, and resorting to extralegal procurement methods.

The uncertainty of supply has also been responsible for a general tendency among industrial ministries to become self-sufficient by developing their own internal supply bases and to give priority to the needs of enterprises under their own jurisdiction over the requirements, even thou more urgent, of enterprises in other ministries. During the years from 1957 to 1965 the same policies were pursued by various regional organizations.

Ministerial self-sufficiency and inadequate interministerial coordination have resulted in much avoidable waste through needless, often very long, crosshauls on overtaxed railways, duplication of supply and procurement offices, and nonutilization of byproducts across ministerial lines. Together with the supply policies of individual enterprises, it has hampered rational specialization and integration of industry, thereby contributing to the perpetuation of unnecessarily high production costs (see ch. 30, Industry).

In the course of the planning process, decisions must be made concerning such questions as the types of commodities to be produced and their levels of output, kinds of materials to be used for each product and the technology to be employed, ratios of capital to labor in individual industries and plants, types of fuel and power to be developed and used in different industries and regions, kinds of factories and other facilities to be built and their locations, and types of farm crops and methods of cultivation to emphasize. Soviet prices, which are established by administrative order and generally do not reflect either the relative scarcities or the real cost of the products, preclude an optimum choice of alternatives that would assure the most economical use of resources.

In the case of investment decisions, choice of the most economical solution has been further complicated by a Marxist disregard of capital costs and economic rent. Until the reform of 1965, no charges were made for either interest or rent. Administratively determined charges introduced since 1965 have not, in many instances, adequately reflected the relevant economic considerations.

Recognition of the basic problem of rational economic choice is reflected in the following statement contained in the previously cited CPSU textbook. The major principle governing the formulation of plans is a general increase in the efficiency of production, meaning the production of maximum high-quality, essential output with the least expenditure of capital and labor. Neither a generally accepted method nor agreed-upon indexes for measuring the efficiency of production are available at the present time. A noted Soviet economist has estimated that with more efficient management national output could be increased by anywhere from 30 to 50 percent. Others believe this estimate to be conservative.

Planning Reform

The validity of economic plans naturally hinges upon the degree of accuracy with which they reflect actual conditions and the extent to which they promote an optimal relationship and growth of all branches of the economy. The task of reducing the infinite and intricate relationships of a dynamic, modern industrial society to a series of balance sheets or a single so-called input-output table comprising many thousands of products is immensely complex. It requires not only a host of highly trained personnel with profound insight into the operation of the multifaceted economic mechanism but also a wealth of reliable data and appropriate equipment to handle them.

Available resources of these elements have not been adequate for the task, although an intensive program for training economists has been underway, and the use of computers is being introduced. The sheer physical labor involved in developing several plan variants militates against the adoption of optimal plans. A group of economists have therefore advocated the application of mathematical economic methods to planning as a remedy. Other economists, though acknowledging the necessity of centralized economic planning and control in the early stages of the country's development, have questioned the applicability of this method to the economy of the 1960's, even with the use of the most advanced techniques and tools.

In September 1965 a much-publicized reform of planning and material incentives was announced by the Central Committee of the CPSU. Its provisions included the introduction of administrative charges for interest and rent in an effort to reduce the waste of capital and mineral resources; the substitution of profit for gross output as a criterion of plan fulfillment; and some reduction in the number of centrally determined targets for operating enterprises.

ECONOMIC CONTROL

Purpose and Methods of Control

Control over the implementation of planned assignments is exercised by the same administrative structure that is responsible for planning, with the role of watchdog assigned to CPSU units. The administrative apparatus is assisted in this work by the banking system, special accounting and national control organs created for this purpose, and any workers willing to take the responsibility of bringing to light failings within their organizations.

Aside from checking on the progress of work in relation to established targets, anticipating the emergence of disproportions, and correcting plans in light of new conditions or tasks, it is also a function of control to assure maximal use of reserve capacities; to unmask and eradicate parochial, narrow bureaucratic, and antistate policies; to expose plans set deliberately low; and to root out hoarded reserves of materials, equipment, and other productive resources.

Although coercion is considered a legitimate method of economic control, control of plan fulfillment is formally defined not as a mere policing activity but also as a means for analyzing shortcomings of planning and management with a view to developing measures for improving their performance. It is an axiom of the CPSU that effective economic control requires all findings by the controllers to be widely publicized.

At the enterprise level, the operational plan is embodied in a document known as the *techpromfinplan* (technical-industrial-financial plan). This document specifies in detail all aspects of an enterprise's planned operation. The production target, the key element of the plan, is given in terms of both gross output and value of sales; it also lists, in physical units, the major assortment of

616

goods to be produced. The supply section of the plan contains a list of the principal materials and equipment that the enterprise is authorized to purchase during the life of the plan, together with the sources from which they must be obtained.

The labor and payroll section specifies the total amount of the wage bill. Since the rates of pay for each category of workers are prescribed by central authority, the wage bill, in effect, also establishes a limit on the number of workers that can be employed. The financial section of the enterprise plan translates the entire production and investment program into monetary terms on the basis of centrally established prices for materials, equipment, finished products, and similarly determined wage rates. It contains assignments for sales, profits, and profitability; receipts from and payments into the state budget; and a breakdown of capital expenditures.

The enterprise plan also provides product quality specifications and directions for the introduction of new products and technology. It spells out measures for the improvement of production and management methods calculated to enhance the chances of the enterprise to achieve the planned targets for output and cost reduction.

Achievement of plan targets depends heavily upon the level of performance by enterprise management. As state employees, managers are not only under orders to implement their assigned plans but are also under constant pressure to exceed them. In the absence of a profit motive, the method of reward and punishment has been used to elicit a maximum productive effort. Nevertheless, managers have retained a measure of freedom of choice. Within this limited area many have been able to make decisions calculated to protect their position or favoring their own financial interests at the expense of productive efficiency and quality of output.

Depending upon the degree of noncompliance, failure by an enterprise manager to complete the production program in whole or in part has usually entailed a reprimand or a demotion, with a concomitant reduction in income. This fate also overtakes some of the numerous managers driven to unapproved methods in efforts to fulfill the plan. Before the death of Stalin, sanctions were generally much more severe, including the application of capital punishment. Turnover among managers is reported to be very high.

Heavy stress is laid by the CPSU on moral incentives, which consist of public recognition of outstanding performance through widespread publicity and the award of honors, medals, and personal promotion. It is recognized, however, that sactions and moral suasion alone do not provide sufficient motivation for a sustained high-level effort in the interest of the state, and a judicious admixture of material incentives has therefore been considered essential.

These material incentives have been offered in the form of bonus payments for attaining and surpassing various established targets of the annual, quarterly, and monthly plans.

Material Incentives

In agriculture the system of material incentives consists primarily of the distribution of the residual farm income among collective farm members in proportion to their labor contribution, calculated on the basis of prescribed norms for different tasks. Farm managers are entitled to receive an increase in their share as a bonus for overfulfillment of the production plan but are also liable to penalties in the event of plan failure. Since farm output plans have generally been optimistic, incentive payments have not been a significant factor in raising farm productivity (see ch. 31, Agriculture).

In industry the most important bonus payment until 1966 was linked to the target for the volume of gross output, expressed in units or in weights. Lesser rewards were related to targets for labor productivity, cost reduction, economy of materials and wages, and other aspects of the production process. Although payment of the full production premium was officially contingent upon achievement of the secondary targets, this provision was often disregarded in actual practice. The use of gross output as a measure of performance entailed certain undesirable consequences, which led to the gradual introduction of profit as the major criterion after 1965. By mid-1969, however, the all-important steel industry was still operating under the old system, and measures recommended for the improvement of its performance did not include a shift to the new performance evaluation method (see ch. 30, Industry).

Since bonuses for the attainment of output targets and, even more so, for surpassing them were large in relation to managerial salaries, managers were vitally interested in securing low production assignments and liberal allocations of resources. Having better knowledge than outsiders of the potentialities of the plans under their direction, they were often able to conceal the true capacity of the plans and thus obtain approval of production plans that would assure successful completion of the assigned tasks.

Another important reason for seeking low plan targets was a desire to escape the consequences of a common planning practice, whereby new plan targets have been established by raising the highest previously achieved level of performance. This planning practice also induced managers not to exceed plan targets by too large a margin.

The overriding emphasis on output volume, with its associated stress on speed of production, had a deleterious effect on the assortment of goods produced, product quality, and plant maintenance.

618

It often entailed a misuse of scarce materials and equipment and was responsible for an inordinate amount of spoilage. It also made managers reluctant to introduce new products or technology because of the attendant temporary loss of production. The long-term advantages of innovation did not provide a sufficient inducement for its adoption, since managers could not count on reaping the benefits in view of the prevailing high turnover in managerial positions (see ch. 30, Industry).

In construction, performance has been measured by the amount of funds spent during the plan period, which naturally led to many wasteful practices. By a decree published in June 1969, this criterion will be superseded beginning in 1970 by a standard based on the completion of projects in accordance with specifications.

The new incentives program is intended to provide special benefits to enterprises for attaining and surpassing planned targets for profits and profitability. Profitability has been defined as the ratio of total profit to the sum of the value of fixed assets and the amount of officially authorized working capital. It is based on the assumption that the goal of maximizing profits will stimulate enterprises toward greater efficiency and lead to a reduction of waste. As a means of inducing enterprises to seek larger production assignments, rewards for surpassing plan targets have been set at lower levels than premiums for plan fulfillment. This constitutes a reversal of conditions prevailing under the old system.

The core of the incentives program consists in the creation of three special funds for the benefit of the enterprise and its personnel through deductions from profits. A material incentives fund provides for the payment of bonuses to managers, engineering and technical personnel, and office employees. It also serves to supplement bonuses to production workers payable out of the wage fund. A fund for social and cultural measures and for housing is intended to supplement state funds for workers' housing and medical, cultural, and recreational facilities. A production development fund, formed out of profits, depreciation reserves, and receipts from the sale of surplus equipment is to be used for capital improvements of the enterprise.

Continuing Problems

Many theoretical and practical aspects of the new incentives system have not passed the academic discussion stage, and the effectiveness of the system itself is being questioned. A conference of economists on the subject of profits held in Moscow in 1968 identified twenty-six specific problems that required further intensive study and recommended twenty-eight separate measures for improving the operation of the incentives program.

Among the major unresolved problems are the nature and role of profit in a socialist economy, the effect of different methods of business taxation on incentives, the lack of a valid standard for comparing performance levels of different enterprises, and variations in profit levels unrelated to enterprise performance. These variations may arise either from natural advantages, such as superior mineral deposits; location, size, and technological superiority; government price policies; failure of suppliers and transport agencies to honor their commitments; or delayed payments by customers (a sale is considered completed only when payment is physically received by the enterprise).

The amount of the deductions from profits for the benefit of the incentive funds is supposed to be based on the volume of sales during the period and on the amount and the rate of profit. It must also be related to the total wage bill and reflect the degree of adherence to the assortment plan. Much of the continuing discussion about the program concerns such questions as methods of calculating profits and profitability, whether to base deductions on absolute magnitudes or on rates of increase, and the rates at which the deductions for the different funds should be made. A practical difficulty in the administration of the program is presented by the need to redesign the enterprise accounting system. The task of identifying individuals and groups entitled to bonus payments and measuring their contribution entails significant administrative costs, particularly in enterprises where bonuses are paid on a monthly basis.

In the administration of the reform program based on ad hoc decisions by the economic ministries, the basic purpose of increasing efficiency appears to have been overshadowed by a concern for the adequacy of incentive funds. With the exception of a few basic industries, the wholesale price revision of 1967 deliberately established prices that assured a profit to all normally working enterprises and, consequently, excess profits not only to the more efficient but also to the economically more favored concerns. Rates of profit in a number of enterprises reached from 70 to 100 percent in 1968. Differences in rates of profit among enterprises were reported to be as high as fifty to one.

To equalize the relative size of the incentive funds among enterprises regardless of the rate of profit, individual profitability norms were established for most enterprises in 1967, thus obviating the role or profit as a stimulus to efficiency. Administratively determined interest charges in many instances constitute only a tiny fraction of enterprise profits and do not, therefore, serve their intended function of stimulating more economical use of capital.

The basic objective of the reform, which is to increase industrial efficiency by appealing to the self-interest of enterprise personnel through the medium of profit, has not been generally realized. The major reason for this failure is the lack of a direct relationship between efficiency and profit in the Soviet economy. Another important cause is the apparent inadequacy of the material incentives.

Adequate information is not available on the extent to which incomes, and hence incentives, of managers and other personnel have been affected by the reform. Bonus payments by all enterprises in 1968 averaged about eight to ten days' earnings, and payments to production workers out of profits amounted to only about 1 to 2 percent. Yet the equivalent of one month's or even six weeks' pay is considered necessary by Soviet economists to provide an effective stimulus.

The production development funds, in many instances, have yielded only insignificant sums for plant improvement and, in other instances, their use has been restricted by the inability of enterprises to obtain needed building materials, equipment, and construction crews. At the previously mentioned economists' conference it was categorically stated that the incentive program had not solved the problem of productivity in the food-processing industry. There is ample evidence in the Soviet press that the same holds true for other branches of industry.

CHAPTER 30

INDUSTRY

Industry constitutes the highest priority sector of the country's economy. In terms of Soviet statistical concepts and valuation practices, industry's share in the economy's total gross output in 1967 amounted to 64 percent, excluding construction, which contributed another 10 percent. It ranks second in size among the industries of the world, surpassed only by that of the United States. This high level of industrialization has been reached from modest beginnings after the revolution of 1917 and through a rapid recovery from the setback suffered during World War II, as a result of massive infusions of capital and manpower. By 1960, however, and continuing to the end of the decade, industrial growth had slowed to a pace that caused concern among the government and Party leadership.

Western observers and a number of Soviet economists attributed the slowdown to the inflexibility inherent in the highly centralized state planning and management of industry, which limited the ability of industry to adapt to changing conditions. Soviet leadership in the 1960's was faced with two basic problems regarding industry, solutions to which had not been found by the end of the decade. The first problem was presented by a shortage of readily accessible resources to meet both the demands of the military and space programs and the increasingly urgent need for an expansion of the consumer output. The second was posed by a need to allow industry greater flexibility in responding to changing consumer demands, which necessarily calls for an apparently unacceptable loosening of central controls.

A minor economic reform was instituted in 1965 to regain the lost growth momentum. The reform was meant to provide a somewhat broader scope for the initiative of enterprise management and to stimulate productive efficiency through greater incentives to enterprise personnel. After much fanfare the reform languished and, by the end of the decade, had not brought about the desired result.

Industrial growth during the first eight months of 1969 was lower than the rate for any of the postwar years. By the end of 1969 there were strong indications that some of the important industrial goals of the five-year plan for 1966—70 would not be reached (see ch. 29, Economic Planning and Control). At that time the major observable government measures for coping with the problem of the industrial growth lag were confined to experimental modifications of the incentives system and a massive press campaign for a more responsible work attitude and more efficient performance.

The country's vast land mass contains virtually all the mineral, forest, and water power resources essential to modern industry. The bulk of these resources, however, is remote from major population and established industrial centers and is located in regions subject to harsh climatic conditions. Exploitation, therefore, presents considerable difficulty and necessitates costly transportation of raw materials and finished products over long distances (see ch. 2, Physical Environment). Moreover, the more easily accessible minerals, including coal and iron ore, are of relatively low quality and require expensive upgrading. A growing shift from coal and wood to oil and gas for industrial and household uses has been taking place since the mid-1950's. Soviet economists and planners count upon this shift not only to reduce fuel costs, but also to provide a better raw material base for the developing chemical industry.

Industry is heavily concentrated in the European part of the Soviet Union, particularly in the central region around Moscow, the Donetsk-Dniepr area, the northwest, and the Baltic States. Other important industrial regions include the Urals, which are second only to the central region, the Volga region, Siberia, and the Far Eastern region. The areas east of the Urals are primarily producers of fuels and raw materials and account for probably less than one-tenth of the country's output of manufactures. Efforts to develop industry more rapidly in the Asian USSR are hampered by difficulty in attracting workers for permanent settlement in remote and climatically inhospitable regions.

Industry is organized along predominantly functional lines, with individual branches, such as coal, chemicals, textiles, and food, administered by separate ministries through specialized departments. In the interest of greater efficiency, some progress was made by the end of the 1960's toward a greater degree of specialization among enterprises that have traditionally been largely self-contained. For the same reason, the integration of small enterprises producing similar products into single large firms with subordinate branches has been increasingly promoted. Individual enterprises are directed by state-appointed managers, whose primary function is to carry out plans approved by higher authorities. Although the reform of 1965 granted managers somewhat greater latitude in decisionmaking, their authority remains rather narrowly circumscribed (see ch. 29, Economic Planning and Control).

As a safety measure to meet unanticipated increases in planned production quotas, enterprises have traditionally tended to hoard labor. A tightening of the supply of new labor for industrial expan-

624

sion has led to a growing emphasis on better utilization of the available labor force and on measures for raising labor productivity through improved organization, increased mechanization, and stricter labor discipline. These measures have not proved effective, and the growth rate of productivity has actually declined since 1967. In October 1969 the Central Committee of the Communist Party of the Soviet Union (CPSU) approved for general introduction a plan for raising productivity, derived from experiments conducted by the State Committee on Labor and Wages at one of the country's large chemical enterprises (see ch. 32, The Labor Force).

Rapid technological progress has been achieved in large measure through heavy reliance on foreign research and extensive borrowing of foreign techniques. Available scientific, technical, and investment resources, however, have not been adequate to provide civilian industry with advanced technology comparable to that introduced in the high-priority defense and defense-supporting sectors. Innovation at the enterprise level has been inhibited by institutional factors, including production quotas, pricing, and financing (see ch. 18, Science and Technology).

Information on the structure and various other aspects of industry is beclouded by shortcomings in statistics and by official secrecy regarding strategic industrial sectors. These factors present serious obstacles to Soviet economists as well as to foreign observers in attempting to assess the overall industrial posture. The study of the production of nonferrous metals, for example, is impossible for foreign students because of the complete lack of statistics. Any study of the defense industry, including general aviation and electronics, encounters the same statistical vacuum.

Official reticence in the defense sector is well illustrated by an article that appeared in the Soviet newspaper *Socialist Industry* in September 1969. Headlined "50 Years of Defense Industry," the article detailed the development of this industry between 1919 and 1921 and concluded by stating that the defense industry, created under the personal direction of Lenin, continued to develop successfully.

Soviet leadership has consistently given preference to the development of heavy industry, with strong emphasis on its defense-supporting branches. The degree of emphasis on individual branches has varied over time with a view to achieving a better balance. Since 1961 stress has been placed on a preponderant growth of the chemical industry; machine building and metalworking; and oil, gas, and electric power production. At the same time, the gap between the rates of growth of capital and consumer goods has been narrowed.

Investment in industry, including construction, has been quite steady since 1956 at nearly two-fifths of the total annual investment in productive resources. Well over four-fifths of the industrial investment has consistently been devoted to the production of capital goods, and no significant shift in these allocations was evident through 1967. The bulk of the investment has been financed out of the state budget, free of charge until the reform of 1965, and the balance out of enterprise profits and depreciation reserves. In the late 1960's increasing emphasis was placed on the use of long-term bank credit for investment purposes (see ch. 36, Fiscal and Monetary System).

Industrial production in the post-World War II period has been increasingly weighted in favor of capital goods. By 1968 their volume had reached nearly three-fourths of the total gross output. More than four-fifths of this volume has been destined for the further development of the capital goods industry. A significant reversal of this trend, based on a reorganization of industry, is needed to meet the rising public pressure for more and better consumer goods. A small movement in that direction was discernible at the end of 1969, but a fundamental policy reorientation in favor of the consumer was not in prospect.

INDUSTRIAL RESOURCES

Fuels and Power

The country's fuel and power resources are very large, but their location with regard to major consuming centers is mostly unfavorable. About 90 percent of the coal deposits, from 50 to 60 percent of the natural gas deposits, 60 percent of the forest reserves, and up to 80 percent of the hydroelectric potential are located in Siberia and the Far East. Information on petroleum reserves is a state secret, but some unofficial data have, nevertheless, been published. About 80 percent of the commercially exploitable oil reserves known in 1959 were reported to be located in the Volga-Ural region, most of the balance in the Caucasus.

Among major economic centers, only the Ukraine possesses good energy resources. Local resources in the center, west, and northwest of the European USSR are limited to low-grade coal, peat, and oil shale. These areas have large energy deficits, as has also the industrialized Urals region. In 1960 the energy deficit amounted to about 70 percent of requirements in the center, 55 percent in the west, 45 percent in the northwest and north, and 33 percent in the Urals. The movement of fuels and power from producing to consuming regions has necessitated a huge volume of transport by rail, ship, pipeline, and high-tension electric transmission lines.

Fuel output of almost 1.1 billion metric tons in 1967, in terms of conventional fuel of 7,000 large calories per kilogram, was more than triple the volume produced in 1950, and the output of almost 588 billion kilowatt-hours of electricity was about 6.5 times higher for equivalents. Although the bulk of the fuel resources is concentrated in the Asian USSR, the rise in production has been greater by far in the European USSR, to obviate the high cost of transport. During the decade of 1955—65 fuel production in the European areas rose by 402 million tons of conventional fuel, or 150 percent, as against only 98 million tons, or 80 percent, in the Asian region.

During the period 1950—67 the share of oil and natural gas in the total production of fuels rose steadily from 19.7 percent in 1950 to 55 percent in 1967, of which oil constituted 37.8 percent and gas, 17.2 percent. By 1968 this share had increased to 57.5 percent. It was scheduled to rise to 59.5 percent in 1969 and to continue its upward trend. Concurrently, the share of coal in the total fuel balance declined from about 66 percent in 1950 to less than 39 percent in 1968, and even greater declines were registered by peat and commercial firewood. Hydroelectric power provided only about 3.5 percent of the total energy supply in 1965.

The rise in the importance of oil and gas was brought about by a shift in the government's fuel policy, which was embodied in the Seven-Year Plan for 1959—65. Until the 1950's planners concentrated efforts and investment primarily on the development of underground gasification of coal and oil shale. None of these processes proved economically attractive, and the first two were abandoned. The reasons for the belated recognition by Soviet planners of the economic advantages of oil and natural gas over solid fuels are not entirely clear. Western students of the problem have suggested as the principal cause a lack of awareness of the richness of these resources.

By far the largest consumers of fuels are the Ukraine, the Urals, and the center, which, together, account for more than half of total consumption. Other important consumers, although on a much lower scale, are the European west and northwest, western Siberia, and the Volga region. These areas account for about 20 percent of consumption. A small volume of coal and substantial quantities of oil have been exported.

Coal

Total resources of coal are officially estimated at about 8.7 trillion tons. This estimate includes deposits to a depth of 1,800 meters, seams from 40 cm. thick for hard and soft coal and 50 cm. thick for brown coal, and all coal with an ash content of up to 50 percent. In the Donetsk basin seams of 30-cm. thickness are included, and in the Moscow basin brown coal is included with an ash content of up to 60 percent. The largest deposits, totaling 6.6 trillion tons, are located in eastern Siberia. Deposits workable by methods used in the late 1960's were reported to constitute 3 trillion tons.

The immensity of the deposits does not ensure an abundant supply of high-quality, low-cost coal. The great bulk of the large and easily worked deposits is situated in remote, sparsely populated regions of the country. Deposits in the principal settled areas are either of poor quality, requiring expensive cleaning operations, or else are difficult to mine and, therefore, also costly. Coking coal has a high sulfur and ash content, which poses a problem for metallurgy. The cost of mining deposits in two major European basins is about 50 percent above the national average. Substantial costs are also incurred in coal transport. The average length of haul in 1967 was 671 kilometers, but large quantities were hauled over distances as great as 2,200 kilometers (1 kilometer equals 0.62 miles—see Glossary).

In 1968 the output of coal amounted to 594 million tons, a decline of 1 million tons from 1967. Production during the first half of 1969 totaled 297 million tons. Until 1967 production had been rising slowly, only about 17 percent since 1960, primarily because of the growing use of oil and gas. The economic plan for 1969 called for an output of 595.3 million tons, and the five-year plan goal for 1970 was 665 to 675 million tons. Achievement of the 1970 goal would require a tonnage increase in a single year three times as great as the total increase in production from 1965 to 1969

The major suppliers of coal in the late 1960's have been the Donetsk, Moscow, and Pechora basins in European USSR; the Kuznetsk basin (Kuzbas) in western Siberia; the Urals; and the Karaganda basin in Kazakhstan. The Donetsk basin (Donbas) is the largest single producer of coal and the most important source of coking coal for metallurgy. It accounts for about one-third of the coal output and more than half the coking coal. Its output amounted to 205 million tons in 1967 and 105 million tons during the first six months of 1969. The coal seams in the Donbas, however, are thin and steep, and they lie at relatively great depths, which makes for a high cost of extraction.

The Kuzbas contains what is reputed to be one of the richest deposits of coal in the world, including more than one-third of coking grade. Its output, which reached 100 million tons in 1967, is consumed primarily by the iron and steel mills in the Urals and western Siberia and by nonferrous metallurgy plants in eastern Kazakhstan. Although the cost of mining in the Kuzbas is relatively low, owing to the thickness of the seams and the possibility of open-pit mining, the great distance of this basin from industrial consumers (2,200 kilometers from Magnitogorsk in the Urals—) reduces its importance and limits its potential development.

The Karaganda basin, also rich in coking coal, supplies primarily the southern Urals and Kazakhstan. Its distance from the Urals is only half that of Kuzbas. Pechora provides for the needs of the European north and northwest and supplies coking coal to the Cherepovets steel mill. The Moscow brown-coal basin, exploited for about 100 years, is gradually losing importance because of the high cost of its low-grade output and the growing use of oil and gas in the central industrial region.

The huge deposits in eastern Siberia, over three-fourths of the country's total, are located between rich sources in western Siberia and the Far East. Although the cost of mining in the Kansk-Achinsk basin of the Krasnoyarsk region is only one-sixth of the country's average, economical use of the coal from this deposit for purposes other than local fuel is precluded by its high moisture and low heat content. The output of this basin in 1968 was only 1.7 percent of the country's total. Long-range plans envision the conversion of this coal into electric power for transmission to the Urals and the European USSR.

In 1969 experiments in conditioning low-grade eastern Siberian coal were reported to have demonstrated the feasibility of delivering it as far west as Moscow, a distance of roughly 3,500 kilometers, at a cost below that of Donbas, Kuzbas, and Moscow basin coals. A search for improved methods of enriching this coal were continuing in that year, but experiments to use it for metallurgical purposes were said to be lagging because of a lack of cooperation by the Ministry of Ferrous Metallurgy. At the same time, the Ministry of the Coal Industry was taking measures to organize coal-cleaning operations in the Irsha-Borodinsk deposit, about 400 kilometers east of Krasnoyarsk. It was recognized, however, that the future of the "fabled riches" of the eastern Siberian deposits depended upon the development of new approaches to the processing and use of low-grade coal.

Crude Oil

The country's known reserves of crude oil are very large and are being steadily expanded through further exploration. Their magnitude is not well established, but official Soviet sources refer to them as the largest in the world, and Western specialists believe them to be capable of supporting a high level of output for a long period of time. In contrast to coal deposits, the bulk of the oil reserves thus far explored lie in the European USSR, although for the most part at substantial distances from the major industrial centers.

The most important deposits exploited in 1969 are situated between the Volga River and the Ural Mountains, north of the Caspian Sea. This region, often referred to as the second Baku, has far surpassed the old Baku fields and the northern Caucasus both in reserves and in output, although new reserves are being found in these old areas through exploration of lower horizons and offshore sites. Other exploited deposits in the European USSR include fields in the western Ukraine, Belorussia, and the Komi autonomous republic where rich additional sources of oil along the western slope of the Urals were found in 1968. In the same year commercial oil strikes were reported to have been made in Lithuania and the Kaliningrad province on the Baltic Sea.

In the Asian USSR, producing fields are located at Nebit-Dag and Cheleken in Turkmenistan, Andizhan and Chimion in Uzbekistan, at Emba in Kazakhstan, in the Kirgiz republic, and on the island of Sakhalin. Production also started about 1968 on the Mangyshlak Peninsula in Kazakhstan, on the northeastern shore of the Caspian Sea. Very large, promising deposits have been found near the town of Surgut on the Ob' River in western Siberia and in the far north, along the polar seas on both the European and Siberian sides of the Ural Mountains, well above the Arctic Circle. Development of these deposits is hampered by their remoteness, unfavorable climatic conditions, technical difficulties, and labor problems. Some of the new finds may, therefore, not become commercially viable in the foreseeable future.

The crude-oil production of 309 million tons in 1968 was more than double the output in 1960. An output of 326.5 million tons was planned for 1969, and a little less than half of this amount was produced during the first six months of the year. The five-year plan goal for 1970 calls for an output of 345 million to 355 million tons, which implies an increase of from 5.6 to 8.7 percent over the 1969 target. Except for 1968, annual increases in output since 1960 were well above the upper figure. Informal plans released by the Ministry of the Oil Extraction Industry established a target of 460 million tons for 1975, the final year of the five-year plan for 1971—75.

Most of the crude oil is produced in the Volga-Urals region, which accounted for 70 percent of total output in 1966. Although production in this region is scheduled to rise further, its share is slated to decline with the growth of production in other areas. In order of magnitude, the major producers in the Volga-Urals region are the Tatar and Bashkir autonomous republics and the Kuybyshev *oblast* (region) of the Russian republic. Important producers outside this area include the Caucasus, which produced 8.9 percent of the output in 1966, followed by Azerbaijan, with 8.2 percent, and by central Asia and Kazakhstan, with a total of 6 percent. Smaller quantities are produced in various other European and Asian parts of the country, including the Ukraine and Turkmenia.

A pledge by Tatar oilfield workers to increase production in honor of the 100th anniversary of Lenin's birth in 1970 disclosed that output in these fields averaged 75 million tons in the 1965—68 period and set as a target an annual output rate of 100 million tons by April 1970. The economic plan for 1969 established a goal of more than 19 million tons for western Siberia and indicated that the 1968 output in this area was about 12.3 million tons, or 4 percent of the country's total production. According to the minister of the oil extraction industry, this area is scheduled to quadruple its share in the output by 1975 with a planned production of 75 million tons. The same source also disclosed a 1975 goal of 37 million tons for the Mangyshlak Peninsula and the maintenance of an annual 20-million-ton level of output in the old Baku fields.

Natural Gas

The country's reserves of natural gas are known to be huge, although no very precise estimate of their total magnitude has yet been made. Intensive exploration continues to add rapidly to both potential and commercial reserves. As in the case of other energy sources, however, most gas deposits are located far enough from consuming centers to require costly transportation, and their exploitation is complicated by climatic and terrain difficulties.

The potential reserves, including the least certain categories, are rather widely distributed; forty locations were listed in 1966. These reserves were roughly estimated at 67.3 trillion cubic meters. The largest, amounting to about 72 percent of the total, are in eastern and western Siberia and in central Asia, including Kazakhstan. Some of the most important industrial and population centers, however, have practically no reserves. These areas include the center, the northwest, the Baltic republics, and Belorussia.

Developed and commercially exploitable fields are officially estimated to contain about 2 trillion cubic meters of gas. Seventy-five percent of these reserves are located in the northern Caucasus, the Ukraine, and Uzbekistan. These three regions also account for the bulk of the output.

Production of natural gas, including small amounts of oil well gas, has been expanding rapidly since the late 1950's. It reached a volume of about 169 billion cubic meters in 1968 and 89 billion cubic meters in the first six months of 1969, slightly less than half the year's target. The five-year plan goal for 1970 calls for the production of from 225 million to 240 million cubic meters, including about 1 percent of manufactured gas. Achievement of this goal requires a rise of 21 to 29 percent over the 1969 output. Increases of this magnitude have not been attained since 1963. In the years 1964 to 1968 advances in output ranged downward from 20 percent to 7 percent, and the planned increase for 1969 was only 8 percent.

The bulk of the natural gas has been produced in the European areas, which accounted for 76 percent of output in 1967 and were planned to provide 72 percent in 1970. A more rapid development of deposits in western Siberia and central Asia, however, is scheduled to reduce the share of European fields to about 41 percent by 1975. This will require the construction of additional trunk pipelines up to 3,500 kilometers in length.

Pipelines

A large and rapidly expanding network of trunk pipelines with a total length approaching 100,000 kilometers in 1969 has been built to move oil and gas from the producing fields to the consumers. All but 15,000 kilometers of this network have been built since 1955. In 1968 there were 33,500 kilometers of oil lines and 56,000 kilometers of gas lines. Additional oil and gas lines totaling 8,300 kilometers were to be completed in 1969, as against 4,400 kilometers built in 1968.

Despite this rapid development, pipeline construction has consistently failed to meet plan targets and has not kept pace with growing needs, primarily because of a shortage of large-diameter pipe. The lag in pipeline construction has been a major factor retarding the growth of gas output. It also explains the fact that railroads continue to handle a very substantial part of the traffic in crude oil and oil products, even though movement through pipelines, particularly of large diameter, is known to be more economical. In 1967 railroads carried almost 327 billion ton-kilometers for the pipelines. The average length of haul for the two carriers was 1,255 and 671 kilometers, respectively.

Electric Power

Development of electric power has been given high priority ever since the inception of the Soviet state, based on Lenin's famous formula "Communism equals Soviet power plus the electrification of the entire country." Installed capacity and power output have been rising steadily, reaching a volume of about 142 million kilowatts and 638 billion kilowatt-hours, respectively, in 1968, equivalent to a sevenfold increase since 1950. Roughly three-fourths of the entire power output is consumed by industry.

Hydroelectric stations accounted for about 19 percent of the capacity and 15 percent of the output in 1968. Their share in total capacity and output has been rising slowly. The country's hydroelectric potential has been estimated at 340 million kilowatts. The largest reserves are concentrated in eastern Siberia, central Asia, the Volga region, and the Caucasus. Powerful stations have been built on the Dniepr, the Volga, Kama, Kuban, Angara, Yenisey, and other rivers, with capacities up to 4 million kilowatts. Substantial further expansion was underway in 1969.

In the construction of thermal power stations the trend has also been toward ever larger capacities, as exemplified by a 3.6-million kilowatt station being built in 1969 in the Donetsk basin of the Ukraine. Depending upon location and availability of fuel, thermal stations are fired by shale, peat, coal, oil, or natural gas. An atomic power station under construction at Novovoronezh on the Don River is designed for a capacity of 1.5 million kilowatts. Its first section, having a capacity of 210,000 kilowatts, was reported to have produced more than 6 billion kilowatt-hours of electricity by May 1969.

Electric power output is highly concentrated. Eighteen giant stations, each with a capacity of 1 million or more kilowatts, produce over one-fourth of all electric power. Stations throughout the country are united in a number of regional and interregional systems, with the aim of eventually creating a single system for the entire country. Completion of a unified system for the European USSR was planned to be accomplished before 1970.

Other Resources

Ferrous and Alloying Minerals

Iron ore reserves are officially estimated at 95 to 100 billion tons, including 50 billion tons in the commercial category. About half the reserves are located in the eastern regions. The largest ore deposits are situated in the so-called Kursk magnetic anomaly in the central European region, in the Krivoy Rog basin in the Ukraine, the Kustanay basin in Kazakhstan, and in eastern Siberia. Substantial deposits are also located at Kachkanar in the central Urals, on the Kola Peninsula in the northwest, at Kerch in the Crimea, and at several other sites throughout the country.

The richest and most easily accessible ores of Krivoy Rog and of Magnitogorsk in the Urals, the deposits that provided the bulk of the mined ores through the 1960's, have been largely exhausted, and most of the ores now being mined must be upgraded. A number of high-capacity ore concentration plants have been built for this purpose, and additional plants are under construction. Production of iron ore, by far the largest in the world, reached a volume of 177 million tons in 1968, a more than fourfold increase since 1950. About half this output was derived from the Krivoy Rog mines, and roughly 30 million tons were exported.

Adequate reserves of essential steel-alloying elements, such as manganese, chromite, molybdenum, tungsten, vanadium, and others, are also domestically available, although some of them must be mined in remote areas under difficult conditions. In reserves and production of manganese and chromite, the country occupies first place in the world, with an output substantially in excess of its own needs. Production of manganese ore has fluctuated between about 7 million and nearly 8 million tons per year since 1964, up to 1.3 million tons of which have been exported annually. Information on the production of chromite and other alloying elements has not been published. Exports of chromite reached a little over 1 million tons in 1967, and shipments of ferroalloys, 289,000 tons.

Nonferrous Minerals

Available supplies of nonferrous ores are said by an authoritative Soviet source to allow the production of more than sixty nonferrous and rare metals. The ores are generally complex and of low quality—from 0.5 to 2 percent metal content for copper and somewhat higher for lead and zinc. Ore-separation and -concentration facilities have, therefore, been built at all mining sites. A relative shortage of bauxite, the usual source of aluminum, has led to the development of methods for the utilization of nephelite and alunite, which are inferior to bauxite. These methods also yield cement, soda, and potash as byproducts, which help offset the higher cost of processing the low-grade ores.

Most of the nonferrous ore reserves are located in the eastern regions, however, important deposits, including aluminum, copper, lead, zinc, and nickel, are also found on the Kola Peninsula and in the Leningrad *oblast* of the European USSR, and in the Transcaucasus area. The largest reserves and the most intensive mining and primary processing are concentrated in Kazakhstan and eastern Siberia. Kazakhstan and the Urals lead in the production of metals. Uranium production for peaceful and military atomic uses has been concentrated very largely in the Tien Shan mountains of central Asia. Small amounts are also obtained from the Krivoy Rog iron ore basin and from oil-shale deposits in Estonia.

Except for tin, the country appears to be generally self-sufficient in nonferrous metals at the current low level of civilian goods production and at less than optimum consumption for some essential uses, such as the production of steel for construction and pipelines. A number of nonferrous metals, including tungsten and vanadium, are in short supply, in part because of difficulties and high costs of production. Significant quantities of aluminum, copper, lead, and zinc, however, have been exported, primarily to east European allies.

Nonmetallic Minerals

With minor exceptions, resources of nonmetallic minerals are large. A number of these reserves, including potassium, sodium sulfate, phosphates, magnesite, mica, and asbestos, rank as the largest in the world, and deposits of sodium chloride (common salt) are virtually inexhaustible. Substantial and varied resources are

634

found in the Ukraine, the Urals, central Asia, and eastern Siberia. Their exploitation is facilitated by the relatively favorable geographic location of many deposits. A shortage of industrial diamonds was eliminated in the mid-1950's by the discovery of large deposits in the Yakut autonomous republic.

Nonmetallic minerals are used in a wide range of industrial processes, including chemical and fertilizer production; metallurgy; metal processing; porcelain, glass, and optical manufacture; and in the production of building materials. Supplies of raw materials for the cement industry and of decorative rocks for construction, including granites and marbles, are abundant.

STRUCTURE OF INDUSTRY

Availability of Data

Only fragmentary information is available on the structure of industry. An industrial census has never been published, nor has any information on the number of enterprises and available capacities in major industrial branches. Data on the distribution of enterprises by size are given only in percentage terms, with the total number of enterprises in any branch as 100, and the size groupings are not uniform for all branches. Data on the concentration of industrial output are equally unsatisfactory and are available only for 1960.

Production statistics do not separate extractive from manufacturing industries and, contrary to common practice elsewhere, include the production of forestry and fisheries. A distribution of industrial output by major branches has not been published. Available data on the rates of growth of individual industrial branches are not comparable, because of the distortions introduced through the exclusive use of gross value of output rather than value added in measuring production. This difficulty is further complicated by frequent changes in statistical accounting methods and industrial classification.

A publication of the economic research committee of the State Planning Committee, issued in 1968, reported the share of manufacturing in total industry in 1965 to have included about 92 percent of gross output, 86 percent of the number of workers, and 76 percent of the fixed assets, with the balance attributable to the extractive industries. The study noted that prevailing statistical methodology consistently understated the actual share of the extractive industries in total output, but gave no estimate of the probable magnitude of the distortion.

With only a few minor exceptions, information on regional distribution is limited to a breakdown by republics, rather than by industrial regions. The overwhelming size of the Russian republic and its dominant share in total production effectively obscure the regional pattern. Construction is treated as a separate branch of the economy, although the production of building materials is included in industry. Data on strategically important areas of industry are either lacking altogether or are lumped with other categories so as to become indistinguishable.

Number and Size of Enterprises

According to a footnote in the Soviet statistical yearbook for 1967, there were more than 48,000 industrial enterprises in that year operating on a self-sustaining basis, without state subsidies. About 5,500 of these enterprises had more than 1,000 workers and employees each. Information on the total number of enterprises has not been made public.

Although direct comparisons are not possible, available data indicate that the largest enterprises in terms of the number of employed personnel, excluding metallurgy and papermaking, on which information is lacking, are to be found in machine building and in the cotton textile and chemical industries. Some of the largest enterprises in machine building employ more than 20,000 persons and in the oil and cotton textile industries more than 10,000. In terms of gross output, the largest enterprises are in ferrous metallurgy, machine building, and oil refining, the annual volume of production exceeding R100 million (R1 equals US$1.10) per enterprise. The largest knitwear and clothing enterprises have an annual output of more than R50 million.

Concentration of production is quite pronounced in several industries, as shown by the data for 1960, the latest available. For example, 3.5 percent of the machine-building enterprises produced 35.4 percent of the output, and 2.1 percent of the chemical enterprises produced 24.6 percent of the output. A similar concentration of production also prevails in some of the branches of light industry, such as cotton textiles, knitwear, and clothing. In the clothing industry branch, 3.2 percent of the enterprises accounted for 33.5 percent of the output.

Specialization and Scale of Production

Because of past industrialization policies, which were dictated in part by the size of the country, the initially small domestic market, and considerations of military security, many industrial enterprises are characterized by a relatively high degree of vertical integration; that is, their operation involves two or more productive stages from the processing of the raw materials to the completion of the finished product. This holds true not only for such large, integrated enterprises as metallurgical plants and paper mills, but also for machine-building and many other types of enterprises throughout industry.

This tendency has been reinforced by the unreliability of the supply of materials, associated with the administrative division of industry, which has led many smaller enterprises to manufacture needed components in their own plants. Poor planning of the allocation of production assignments has worked in the same direction, so that most enterprises produce a heterogeneous assortment of products. As a consequence, specialization of production is at a relatively low level. Mass production involves only about one-third of the output of industry (see ch. 29, Economic Planning and Control).

In the case of many products, output is widely scattered throughout several industrial branches under the jurisdiction of different ministries. In the early 1960's, for instance, from 60 to 70 percent of a certain type of plastics was produced outside the chemical industry, and only 31 percent of all plastics was produced in specialized plants of that industry in 1965. Plants in heavy industry manufacture an expanding variety and a growing volume of consumer goods, in part from waste materials of their basic output. Light industry produces only about one-third of the total volume of consumer goods.

In many enterprises the number of manufactured items runs into the hundreds, whereas concentrated production of standard components in specialized plants amounts to only 2 to 3 percent of their total volume. Widely prevalent small-scale production caused by such diversity of output necessitates short production runs with frequent machinery changeovers. This entails unnecessarily high costs, with resultant losses estimated by Soviet economists at several billion rubles per year.

The economic advantages of specialization are widely recognized. A provision calling for a rise in the level of specialization, particularly in machine building, and for the construction of specialized plants for the manufacture of parts and subassemblies was included in the Eighth Five-Year Plan for 1966—70. Although progress has been made, the government considers the rate to be too slow. A major reason for the lack of advance is the continued unreliability of the industrial supply and the associated reluctance of enterprises to increase their dependence upon outside supply sources.

Other important reasons are to be found in the same conditions that tend to inhibit economic development generally. These are primarily a lack of coordination of the activities of a multiplicity of ministries and agencies concerned, divergence of jurisdictional interests, inadequate planning and financing, construction delays, and general apathy. In a newspaper article published in September

1969, the deputy chairman of the State Planning Committee specifically referred to the inadequacy of economic incentives for stimulating enterprises and other organizations toward positive action in this field.

LABOR AND PRODUCTIVITY

In round numbers, total employment in industry amounted to 29 million in 1967 and approached 31 million in 1969. About four-fifths of this total were workers. The balance consisted of office and administrative employees and of engineering and technical personnel. More than one-third of the workers were employed in machine building and metalworking, and more than one-fourth in the light and food industries. The construction industry employed 1.5 million workers in 1967, and the chemical and petrochemical, the ferrous metallurgy, and the coal industries employed over 1 million each. Engineering and technical personnel numbered 3.3 million in 1967.

Employment in industry has been expanding fairly steadily and, in 1968, was double the 1950 level. During this period the proportion of engineering and technical personnel in total employment increased from 8.3 percent in 1950 to 11.4 percent in 1967. At the same time, the proportion of apprentices declined from 2.4 percent to 1.6 percent. The proportion of office and administrative employees declined from 5 percent in 1950 to 4 percent in 1960 and remained stable thereafter.

The supply of new labor for industry is becoming scarce, and shortages have been reported in a number of areas. This is reflected in the declining share of the annual output growth attributable to the increase in the number of workers as against the share of output increase achieved through a rise in productivity. In 1968 and 1969 the additional labor accounted for only 2.5 percent of the increase in output, as compared to a range of 3.3 percent to 4.7 percent in the years 1960 to 1967. The tightening of the labor supply has led to increased emphasis on labor productivity (see ch. 32, The Labor Force).

Low and inadequately rising labor productivity has received much of the blame for the failure of industry to meet production and growth targets. According to comparative data published in the Soviet statistical yearbook for 1967, labor productivity in industry was, at most, half as high as in the United States. The annual rates of increase in productivity declined from an average of 7.6 percent in the years 1951—59 to 5 percent in the years 1960—68. For the first eight months of 1969, the rise in productivity was only 4.3 percent. In 1968 the productivity rise was below that of wages.

Among the major reasons adduced for this unsatisfactory situation are poor labor management, inadequate mechanization, particularly in auxiliary shops, and high labor turnover.

One of the main obstacles to raising labor productivity is the practice of planning the wage fund of an enterprise on the basis of past performance. Under the provisions of the economic reform, targets for labor productivity are determined by the enterprise, rather than by higher authority as in the past. The lower the productivity in the base period and the lower the planned rise in productivity, the larger will be the labor requirement and, therefore, the wage fund. A planned reduction in the number of workers concomitant to a planned rise in productivity entails a reduction in the wage fund, which may also affect adversely the enterprise's incentive funds. Enterprises are, therefore, interested in assuming low rates of increase in productivity in their annual plans. Increases in output norms for workers are outside the competence of enterprise managers and are bound to be politically difficult.

In many industry sectors, including the officially favored machine-building and metalworking branches, employment in auxiliary shops is roughly half the total. Mechanization in these shops is generally at a low level, with a resultant low productivity. In machine building, for instance, about 60 to 70 percent of the direct production work is mechanized, but only about 25 to 30 percent of the auxiliary operations. A higher degree of mechanization of these operations, it has been widely argued, would not only increase productivity, but also release much needed labor for further industrial expansion.

Judging by the volume of discussion devoted to the subject in the press, labor turnover appears to be a major problem in industry, although no figures on its magnitude have been published. The instability of labor is ascribed, in part, to transfers motivated by a desire for higher pay and to job dissatisfaction, particularly among the young workers. Of more basic importance, however, is the lack of adequate amenities not only in the new, but also in some of the older established, industrial areas, including the Urals, which is responsible for a substantial degree of migration. Another basic cause is the relatively low status and lower pay accorded to workers in auxiliary occupations.

Complaints are also rife about a widespread disregard for labor discipline, which manifests itself in absenteeism, late arrival at work, carelessness, disregard of basic production and technological requirements, and poor workmanship. Enterprise managers, superior authorities, and even units of the Party have been accused of closing their eyes to violations. Editorials in official organs of the Party have urged stricter application of Lenin's principle of personal responsibility and greater vigilance, including more effective organization of inspection and control over performance, social pressure through publicity and satire, and the use of authorized administrative measures.

The perennial problem of productivity has given rise to a drive for a scientific organization of labor. The problem has been extensively studied without significant concrete results. More than 200 institutes are working on the problems of labor, but their work is uncoordinated and often ineffective. Experiments are also carried out at various enterprises in cooperation with the State Committee on Labor and Wages. All these experiments involve an increase in material incentives for workers.

One such experiment provides for an increase in the wage fund of an enterprise, related to the magnitude of the rise in productivity. In another experiment, involving piecework, the prevailing system of premium payments for output above the established norm was substantially liberalized and penalties for defective work increased. The most notable of these experiments, which is reported to have produced highly satisfactory results, was carried out at a large chemical combine and twenty-three other plants throughout the country.

In this experiment the size of the enterprise wage fund was frozen in 1967, and the enterprise was authorized to apply all the savings obtained through a reduction in personnel toward raising the pay of those remaining. Over a period of two years the combine was able to release a significant number of workers, employees, and engineers while achieving a substantial increase in output. The method used involved not only increases in individual workloads, but also various measures for a more rational organization of labor. Industry-wide application of this approach was approved in October 1969.

Considerable attention and some experimentation are also being devoted to the problem of more intensive use of machinery, particularly in relation to the five-day workweek. Efforts in this direction are complicated by the reluctance of workers to accept staggered days off and by the problem of manning night shifts in industries employing predominantly women, such as textiles, knitwear, and clothing. Greater use of automation is being advocated as a solution.

TECHNOLOGY AND INNOVATION

To a large extent, Soviet industrial products and technology are based on prototypes and processes obtained from abroad. The need for making the utmost use of foreign scientific and technical achievements was reaffirmed in the Eighth Five-Year Plan for 1966–70. In 1969 the director of the All-Union Scientific Research

Institute for Standardization publicly expressed regret over the inability of many research and design organizations to obtain essential data on the best foreign products and to acquire samples for analysis. The prevailing method of introducing innovation has included widespread adaptation of foreign models and techniques and the importation not only of machinery, but also of entire industrial plants erected under the direction of foreign engineers. A large volume of foreign capital equipment was also obtained in the form of reparations after World War II.

Outside the area of military and space production and a narrow range of supporting industry branches, where advanced technology has been introduced, including automation and some computer-controlled operations, mechanization is still incomplete and, in part, obsolescent or even obsolete. In a large segment of industry, mechanization has been limited primarily to the basic production processes. Assembly and other auxiliary operations such as intra-plant transport, warehousing, and loading and unloading, have continued to be performed largely by manual means. Nearly half of all industrial workers are reported to be employed in these operations.

Official policy attaches great importance to technological progress and innovation as means of achieving rapid economic growth and the material basis for building communism. The ultimate aim is full mechanization and automation of production processes. The more immediate goals are the modernization of installed equipment and the mechanization of auxiliary operations, as a means of raising productivity and releasing workers for more essential tasks.

More than 3.5 million engineers, technicians, and worker-innovators are organized in scientific-technical associations for the purpose of speeding technological progress. A large number of scientific research institutes function within the framework of the USSR Academy of Sciences, the Council of Ministers, and the multiplicity of Union and republic ministries. Thousands of worthwhile innovation proposals are reported to emanate annually from industrial enterprises (see ch. 18, Science and Technology).

The most creative scientific and engineering personnel and the bulk of the supporting financial and material resources are channeled into the high-priority sectors. What is left for the remaining industries is generally inadequate to meet the requirements. The results of this policy are evident in the sharp contrast between the achievements in space, aviation, machine tools, steel, and electric power generation and transmission, and the inferior quality of many consumer and less essential capital goods, including such items as refrigerators.

In civilian industry several factors operate to inhibit innovation of products and technology. All innovation involves risks, because the new product or technique may not work out as intended. Furthermore, the benefits of innovation are normally realized only with the passage of time. In the short run, the necessary reorganization of production, retraining of workers, and other essential measures usually entail a loss of time and output. Existing regulations do not allow for any departures by the enterprise from its approved annual production plan, which may be necessitated by innovation. Enterprise managers and engineering staffs are, therefore, reluctant to take risks that offer little prospect for reward but expose them to penalties for failure to complete their current production assignment.

Financing constitutes another difficult hurdle for innovation. Innovation generally calls for capital investment, the magnitude of which depends upon the nature of the change to be made. Since investment is financed predominantly through the state budget, prolonged administrative procedures are required to obtain the necessary funds, which are not always forthcoming because of existing priorities. Small changes may be financed out of the enterprise's own fund for the development of production, created through deductions from profits and depreciation reserves, but this fund is apt to be inadequate in low-profit enterprises most in need of technological advance (see ch. 36, Fiscal and Monetary System).

Administrative procedures are often frustrating. Innovation may not be introduced without official authorization. This authorization is contingent upon review and approval of the proposed product design or technological change by several scientific and technical organizations, and upon agreement among interested ministries and other government agencies. This procedure normally involves considerable delay. Additional delay results from the requirement to submit all requests for the production of machinery and equipment needed for a changeover by mid-April so that its manufacture may be scheduled the following year. In many instances scheduling may be delayed for a year or more by a shortage of machine-building capacity or of necessary materials. Administrative difficulties and delays of many years in securing the evaluation of inventions and in obtaining an inventor's certificate are reported to stifle technological initiative.

Faulty planning also contributes to delays in the technological progress. On the occasion of the machine builders' day in September 1969, the deputy chairman of the State Planning Committee acknowledged that all was not well in the realm of planning the introduction of new machines. Because of lack of coordination in the planning for the manufacture of test models, pilot production runs, and the final scheduling of serial production, enterprises that eventually receive orders for the manufacture of the equipment and their suppliers often find themselves unprepared for the task. Measures are being taken to eliminate this problem through better coordination of planning.

According to the deputy chairman of the State Committee for Science and Technology, the time needed between the conception of a new machine or piece of equipment and the beginning of serial production is from five to seven years and for the development of new technology, from six to eight years. Because of frequent project revisions and construction delays, however, the actual time span is from eight to twelve years. Many products and techniques, therefore, become obsolete by the time they are first introduced. A speeding up of the process, according to this source, would save the country billions of rubles. Existing incentives are not sufficient to stimulate a large-scale effort in this direction.

PRICES

The products of industry must be sold by the individual enterprise at wholesale prices established by higher authorities and included in the enterprise's annual production plan. Determination of prices for specific products is the function of a multiplicity of union, republic, regional, and local bodies and is based upon more than 100 uncoordinated, in part overlapping, conflicting, and obsolete regulations (see ch. 6, The Economic System).

Apart from their broad implications for the use of economic resources, price policies have had a direct and generally deleterious effect on the performance of industrial enterprises. The shortcomings of the pricing system have become even more apparent since the economic reform of 1965, because of the immediate effect of prices on the primary measures of enterprise performance, namely sales and profits and, through profits, upon the size of the incentive funds (see ch. 6, The Economic System).

The major difficulty with existing prices in this context lies in their inadequate correlation with necessary costs of production, lack of sufficient differentiation with regard to product quality, and inflexibility. These flaws have had a negative effect on the assortment of goods produced, on the quality of products, and on product improvement and innovation.

To maximize sales volume, managers of many enterprises concentrate output on high-priced items at the expense of lower priced ones. Since cost of production constitutes an element in price formation, there is also a strong tendency needlessly to use high-cost materials in order to inflate the value of output and thereby the volume of sales. Because uniform prices are often established for a group of similar products with varying costs, production plans are distorted in favor of lower cost items to maximize profits. In the steel industry this has led to shortages of fine-rolled steel sheets, with unfavorable repercussions on the machine-building industry and a substantial waste of metal.

Problems of this kind, involving the frustration of formal production programs, were among the major reasons for changing the criterion of enterprise performance from physical volume of output to sales and profits in the reform of 1965. The apparent effect of this change has been merely to shift emphasis from weight and numbers to prices in the production decisions by managers within their limited areas of choice (see ch. 29, Economic Planning and Control).

Although some price differentials for quality have been introduced since 1965, these differentials have generally not been large enough to compensate for the extra cost of manufacturing a better product. In the absence of effective penalties, a considerable volume of substandard goods, therefore, continues to be produced. In the field of capital goods this situation is responsible for rapid wear of machinery and equipment. In the field of consumer goods it is reflected in a contrast between long queues for quality products and the doldrums of store departments offering inferior merchandise for sale at reduced prices. Government certification of quality, linked to price incentives, has been introduced as a means of stimulating improvement in this field.

In relation to the cost of production, spare parts are usually priced lower than complete machines. The inevitable result has been widespread shortages of spare parts for industrial machinery and equipment and for durable consumer items. These shortages have led many industrial plants to develop the manufacture of spare parts for their own needs as an auxiliary enterprise at substantially higher cost.

Improper pricing is also an important element among the factors that discourage innovation. In many instances prices set for new products do not compensate for the costs involved in a changeover. At the same time, prices of established products remain stable, even when production costs decline as a result of experience and an increasing scale of output. Many enterprises, therefore, prefer to continue the manufacture of obsolescent and even obsolete items in order to protect their profit position. To eliminate the price obstacle to innovation, a proposal has been advanced by an official of the State Committee for Prices to penalize low-quality and obsolete production through a reduction of prices, which would be reflected in enterprise profits and incentive funds.

PRODUCTION

In 1968 the gross output of industry amounted to roughly R 309 billion, an increase of 95 percent since 1960. The increase over 1967 was 8.1 percent, the lowest annual rate of growth in the postwar period, with the exception of 1963, when the increase was of the same magnitude, and 1964, when it was only 7.3 percent.

For the first eight months of 1969 the rate was still lower—only 6.7 percent. A comparison of the average annual rate of growth attained during the first three years of the current five-year plan with those of the preceeding Seven-Year Plan for 1959—66 and earlier periods also reveals a steady decline—from 12 percent in the years 1951—58 to 9.1 percent in the period 1959—65 and 8.9 percent in the years 1966—68.

A somewhat different result, which suggests a slight improvement in performance during the period 1966—68, emerges when the comparison is made with preceeding five-year periods: 1951—55, 13.1 percent; 1956—60, 10.4 percent; 1961—65, 8.6 percent; and 1966—68, 8.9 percent. This minor improvement is attributable to relatively better performance in 1967, when the output increased by 10 percent.

Several Western economists, using different approaches to estimate the rate of Soviet industrial growth in terms of Western statistical concepts, arrived at somewhat differing results but agreed that the rate of growth was lower than the official figure. The most widely accepted estimate suggests an average annual rate of 9.3 percent for the period of 1951—65, which compares with 10.7 percent reported by the Soviet statistical office; for the years 1961—65, the estimate of total output growth ranges from 40.3 percent to 45.7 percent, as against the official Soviet figure of 50.8 percent.

About R230 billion of the 1968 gross output consisted of capital goods, and the balance of R79 billion was in consumer goods. The reported output of capital goods, however, normally includes some consumption goods, such as textiles and dressed furs destined for the clothing industry rather than sold directly to the ultimate user. The output of capital goods was more than double the 1960 volume, that of consumer goods only about 73 percent greater. The gap between the rates of growth of these two categories of goods, however, has narrowed substantially, in part because of growing public pressure for a greater share in the fruits of labor and also because of a recognition by the leadership of a need to improve the supply of consumer goods as a means of stimulating labor's initiative and willingness to work. During the period 1961—65 the output of capital goods rose about 60 percent faster than the production of consumer goods. In the years 1966—68 the rates were almost equal—about 29.3 percent for the former and 27.9 percent for the latter.

The growth of production during the first four years of the Eighth Five-Year Plan for 1966—70 was not adequate to assure the achievement of the targets for most products on which information is usually published (see table 12). With the possible exception of oil, this holds true for basic industrial commodities, such as coal, steel, natural gas, cement, plastics, paper, and synthetic fibers, and for important manufactured products, including steel pipes, machinery, and motor vehicles. Production of equipment for the oil industry actually declined since 1965 and, in 1969, was at a level of only a little more than half the planned output for 1970.

The indicated shortfall is particularly serious for fertilizers, tractors, and farm machinery, because it is bound to retard the badly needed progress in agriculture. In the consumer field only footwear and television sets have a good chance of reaching, or even surpassing, the planned volume. The production of textiles and, even more so, of knitwear, refrigerators, and furniture lagged substantially through 1969. The shortage of consumer goods resulting from the lag in output was publicly attributed by a Politburo member to the competing need for military production.

CONSTRUCTION

In spite of substantial achievements over a period of years, performance by the construction industry has consistently lagged behind official plans. At the beginning of 1968 the construction industry included 14,606 primary contracting organizations, of which 11,410 were under the jurisdiction of union ministries and departments, and 3,196 subordinated to the councils of ministers of union repubics. It also included an unspecified number of inter-collective farm building organizations. Of the total number of primary contractors, 6,925 were engaged in general construction work, the balance divided among a variety of construction specialities, such as earthwork, railway and highway construction, mine building, and equipment installation. The majority of the building organizations are relatively small. In 1968 nearly two-thirds of their total number performed less than the 2 million rubles average volume of work per unit. Contract builders account for somewhat less than 90 percent of the total building volume. The balance is carried out by enterprises with their own resources.

Employment in construction, including employment in building maintenance and repair shops and in machinery-leasing stations, which service the construction industry, numbered 8 million persons in 1967, including about 6.5 million workers and apprentices, 786,000 engineers and technicians, and 344,000 white-collar employees. Almost 6 million of the total number employed were directly engaged in construction. The balance were employed in research, design, project development, administrative, and other activities. In 1968 there were 1,340 project and research organizations doing work for the construction industry, 943 of which were subordinated to union ministries and departments, the balance to the councils of ministers of the union republics.

Table 12. *Production of Selected Commodities in the Soviet Union, 1965, 1969, and 1970*

Commodity	Unit	1965	1969[1]	1970[2]
Electric power	million kilowatt-hours	507	689	830—850
Crude oil	million metric tons	243	328	345—355
Natural gas	billion cubic meters	129	183	225—240
Coal	million metric tons	578	608	665—675
Steel	do	91	110	124—129
Steel pipes	do	9	12	14—15
Fertilizers	do	31	46	62—65
Plastics	thousand metric tons	821	1,452	2,100—2,300
Synthetic fibers	do	407	583	780—830
Tires	million units	26	33	38—40
Metal-cutting tools	thousand units	185	106	220—230
Forges and presses	do	34	43	50—52
Petroleum equipment	thousand metric tons	140	123	210—240
Chemical equipment	million rubles	384	464	780—830
Motor vehicles	thousand units	616	844	1,360—1,510
Passenger cars	do	201	294	700—800
Tractors	do	355	442	600—625
Farm machinery	million rubles	1,446	1,979	2,500
Cement	million metric tons	72	90	100—105
Paper	thousand metric tons	3,200	4,000	5,000—5,300
Textiles	million square meters	7,500	8,527	9,500—9,800
Knitwear	million units	907	1,183	1,650—1,750
Shoes	million pairs	486	635	610—630
Radios and wired radio sets	thousand units	5,200	7,300	7,500—8,000
Television sets	do	3,700	6,600	7,500—7,700
Household refrigerators	do	1,700	3,700	5,300—5,600
Furniture	million rubles	1,800	2,600	2,600—2,800

[1] The 1969 annual rate based on nine months' production.   [2] As projected in the Five-Year Plan (1966-70).

Source: Adapted from *23d Congress of the Communist Party of the Soviet Union*, Moscow, n.d., pp. 335-336; and *Pravda*, January 25, 1970, p. 1.

The construction industry is being increasingly mechanized, but much of the heavy and labor-consuming work is still being performed manually. This accounts for what the government and economists consider an excessively large labor force in this industry. Construction methods are also being modernized, and the use of prefabricated concrete sections is growing.

According to their specialty, building organizations operating on the national level are subordinated either to one of several construction ministries or to the appropriate industrial ministry. Among others, these ministries include the Ministry of Construction, Ministry of Industrial Construction, Ministry for the Construction of Heavy Industry Enterprises, Ministry of the Gas Industry, and the Ministry for Energy and Electrification. The very names of these ministries point to the administrative difficulty of delineating with any degree of precision their respective areas of responsiblity. Below the union level, building organizations are responsible to a variety of republic, regional, and local authorities. Many small construction organizations are united in building trusts.

Overall direction of the construction industry is the responsibility of the State Committee for Construction of the Council of Ministers. This committee is officially known as Gosstroy, an acronym formed from the first letters of the words *gosudarstvennyy* (state) and *stroytel'stvo* (construction). Similar committees also exist at the republic level, with responsibility both to the USSR Gosstroy and to the councils of ministers of the respective republics. Gosstroy includes a number of functional and operational committees. The former are exemplified by the Committee for Building Materials and the Committee for Housing and Architecture, the latter by the Committee for Transport Construction and the Committee for Central Asian Construction. The operational committees exercise direct control over local agencies and enterprises in their respective fields of activity. Among the main functions of Gosstroy is the development of standards and specifications for construction and installation work, based on the findings of specialized research and project-making organizations, and cooperation with the State Planning Committee, ministries, and other agencies in planning the type, location, and financing of construction projects.

Other organizations intimately involved in the planning and operation of the construction industry are the State Planning Committee, the State Committee for Supply, the Ministry of Finance, the Building Construction Bank, and the State Bank. The necessary agreement on policies, programs, and projects and the close coordination of activities among the multiplicity of central and regional agencies essential for satisfactory performance in the building construction field have not always been forthcoming.

The total annual volume of completed construction in terms of adjusted 1955 construction cost estimates rose steadily from R32.9 billion in 1960 to R52.1 billion in 1967 and more than R55 billion in 1968. From 87 to 88 percent of this volume was built for government and cooperative enterprises and organizations, the balance for collective farms and individuals. Nearly sixty percent of the facilities have been erected in the Russian republic. The Ukraine accounted for about 17 percent, and Kazakhstan, for a little more than 7 percent.

Between 1950 and 1967 the annual volume of completed construction projects, excluding collective farm and private-home building, increased by 5.4 times. The detailed data on project completions reflect the government's emphasis on the development of the country's eastern regions. Whereas in most of the established population and industrial areas, such as the central region, the Ukraine, the Urals, and the Caucasus, the rate of increase was from four to less than five times, it was more than seven times for Siberia, nine times for central Asia, and over eleven times for Kazakhstan. Somewhat higher than average rates of increase were also registered in some of the less intensively developed European areas, including the northwest, the Volga region, the Baltic States, and Belorussia. As a result of this development, the share of the eastern regions beyond the Urals in the annual volume of building increased from 20.5 percent in 1950 to 30.6 percent in 1967.

Information on the distribution of building construction by type—that is by industrial, residential, and public purposes—is fragmentary. About 35 percent of the completed construction from 1960 to 1967 consisted of plants and equipment for ten industries. Changes in the relative positions of these industries with regard to the annual volume of construction reflect the government's industrial development policy during this period. The major and steadily growing share—20 percent in 1967—has been for the benefit of machine building and metalworking. A rising share of the construction has also gone to the chemical and the oil and gas industries, each of which accounted for about 11 percent of the construction volume in that year.

At the same time, the relative position of coal, electric power, iron and steel, forestry, woodworking, and papermaking declined. A rise in the share of light industry was accompanied by a decline in the share of the food industry. Although the annual completion of new facilities for these two industries of most direct importance to consumers increased by more than half during the period, their share in the total volume of construction declined. Construction for the building-materials industry increased by only 10 percent, and its share consequently declined appreciably to less than 6 percent in 1967. This development is particularly noteworthy because of the chronic difficulties of the construction industry and the perennial complaints about the inadequate supply of building materials. The industrial construction program has steadily increased the productive capacities for a large number of essential products (see table 13).

Housing construction, which had doubled its pace in the mid-1950's compared with the earlier postwar period, produced an average of a little more than 100 million square meters of useful living space per year between 1960 and 1967. During this period there was a marked shift from rural to urban housing development; urban housing constituted 54 percent in 1960 and 63 percent in 1967. This shift may be related to a need for the provision of better amenities for workers in developing industrial areas.

About 62 percent of the housing completed during this period was built by government and cooperative enterprises and organizations. Another 20 percent was put up by collective farms and the rural intelligentsia, which includes Party and government officials, doctors, teachers, and other professional persons. The balance of 18 percent was built by workers and employees with the aid of government loans. Such private housing may not take the form of individual homes but, rather, of cooperative apartments. This may explain the fact that no individual home construction is reported in official statistics and that apartments account for all the new living space built. There is a growing trend toward the construction of high-rise apartment buildings.

The number of new apartments build annually between 1961 and 1967 fluctuated within the narrow limits of about 2.2 and 2.4 million units. The average size of an apartment, after a slight decline from 1961 to 1962, increased steadily from 42 square meters in 1962 to 45.2 square meters in 1967. In spite of the intensive construction activity, residential housing remains in short supply.

Sustained severe criticism of the construction industry for unsatisfactory performance has been voiced in the Soviet press. The charges have included poor design and project planning, faulty cost estimates, inadequate coordination of activities of the agencies concerned, poor organization of work, shoddy workmanship, excessive costs, failure to meet deadlines, and systematic underfulfillment of planned assignments. A typical example cited in 1969 involved the expansion of facilities at a northern steel mill operating under severe winter conditions. A rolling mill at that plant was installed in a flimsy building without provision for heat, and a high-capacity oxygen installation for the steel furnaces was left under the open sky.

Another charge repeatedly made is the scattering of resources on too many simultaneous projects, with resultant slow progress and frequent suspensions of work entailing a deterioration of partly completed structures. Losses from this source were estimated by a

Table 13. Annual Additions to Industrial Productive Capacities in the Soviet Union, Selected Years, 1961-65, 1967, and 1968

Item	Units	1961-65 (average)	1967	1968 (preliminary)
Electric power	million kilowatts	9.6	9.6	10.5
Coal mining	million metric tons	16.0	19.6	12.5
Coal cleaning	...do	11.2	3.0	n.a.
Iron ore	...do	26.0	15.8	28.0
Pig iron	...do	2.5	4.1	n.a.
Steel ingots	...do	3.1	1.4	1.4
Rolled steel	...do	1.8	2.7	0.7
Fertilizers	...do	4.7	3.3	5.0
Synthetic fibers	thousand metric tons	44.0	15.0	15.4
Plastics and resins	...do	n.a.	n.a.	210.0
Paints and varnish	...do	47.0	89.0	10.6
Tires	million metric tons	2.0	3.2	n.a.
Turbines	thousand kilowatts	618.0	967.0	710.0
Metal-cutting tools	thousand units	7.0	5.3	n.a.
Automobiles	...do	31.3	57.8	43.0
Tractors	...do	27.0	27.8	n.a.
Cement	million metric tons	5.6	2.3	2.8
Looms installed	thousand units	10.5	9.0	11.0
Boots and shoes	million pairs	11.0	22.0	55.0

Source: Adapted from Tsentralnoye Statisticheskoye Upravleniye pri Sovete Ministrov SSSR, *Narodnoye Khozyaystvo SSSR v 1967 g*, Moscow, 1968, pp. 610-611; and *Pravda*, January 26, 1969, pp. 1-2.

high Soviet official in 1969 at over R5 billion per year. The same official attributed the problems of the construction industry primarily to a shortage of necessary resources to meet the demands placed upon it and recommended reducing the number of investment project authorizations by at least one-half. He also made it clear that the common difficulties of the construction industry did not exist in high-priority areas free from limitations on the use of resources, where the construction of essential structures proceeds quickly.

In an effort to correct the unsatisfactory conditions in the building industry, the government issued three lengthy decrees in 1969 that spelled out in great detail various measures intended to improve the methods of planning and the execution of all phases of the construction work. The most important of these decrees made the provisions of the economic reform, previously introduced in most other sectors of the economy, applicable to the construction industry beginning in 1970. Aside from instructions for closer coordination of the work of all the agencies concerned and various administrative regulations, the major innovation introduced by this decree are a change in the evaluation of performance from the amount of funds spent during the year to the value of the completed physical plant accepted by the customer and a system of incentives for early completion of building projects in accordance with specifications. In the light of the results achieved through the economic reform during the first four years of its application to industry, the adequacy of the decreed measures to bring about the desired results in building construction remains to be proved.

CHAPTER 31

AGRICULTURE

At the beginning of 1970, agriculture occupied an important place in the Soviet economy, although the government continued to give a higher priority to industry. The latest available Soviet statistics indicated that agriculture provided employment for about one-third of the labor force but that farming contributed only about one-fifth of the national income. Despite the emphasis on industrial goals, agricultural development nonetheless was a cause of concern among government and Party leaders, for severe difficulties had plagued the agricultural sector of the economy from the start of Communist rule.

The government has exercised broad control over the development of agriculture. In all respects—notably including distribution of land resources, channeling of manpower, allocation of available machinery, and development of new farming areas—its role has been pervasive. Many plans and programs for agriculture have been undertaken, the collectivization of agriculture being one with especially far-reaching effects. Through this process, begun in 1927 and largely completed by the late 1930's, Communist Party power was firmly and finally entrenched in rural society; and the agricultural sector became socialized, as was the rest of the economy. Also in the process, the government, by forced requisitions of produce at artificially low prices, was able to amass much of the capital necessary to support the foundations of a modern heavy industry.

As a consequence of development policy, Soviet agriculture in the late 1960's was highly organized. In the public sector the two kinds of organizational unit were the collective farm (*kolkhoz*) and the state farm (*sovkhoz*). Each such unit was a legal entity, an economic unit, and a specific area of political jurisdiction. Its task was the production of foodstuffs and fibers in kind and quantity determined by central state planning boards. The state farms, on the one hand, were directly owned and run by the state. Farmers were state employees and received wages. The collective farms, on the other hand, greatly outnumbering the state farms, were administered and worked by participating members, who shared the profits among themselves. In both cases, members were permitted to retain small private plots for their own use.

With its vast size, the Soviet Union leads all other nations in total acreage under cultivation. This cultivated portion, however, represents a relatively small part—some 10 percent—of the country's total area, a reflection of adverse climatic conditions. The climate is generally characterized by long and extremely cold winters, short summers, and marginal rainfall. Almost half the country's area is permanently frozen, and in the South large expanses are arid. Three-fourths of the cultivated area is subject to periodic drought.

The country's main agricultural region forms a roughly triangular area extending from the western border between the Baltic and the Black seas eastward for more than 5,000 kilometers to the Yenisey River, near the city of Krasnoyarsk. The region, commonly known as the fertile triangle, contains most of the large cities and major industrial centers.

Climatic conditions in the fertile triangle allow for the cultivation of a wide range of crops, including wheat, rye, and barley. The region is also the country's main livestock-raising area. Fruits, vegetables, and industrial crops are well suited to the forest-steppe and steppe land west of the Volga. The southwestern portion of the triangle has favorable conditions for raising grapes, rice, and tobacco.

Despite chronic shortages of projected goals, agricultural output is usually adequate to meet domestic requirements, except in years of generalized drought when substantial quantities of grain must be imported. The agricultural sector has nevertheless been beset by production problems since the 1917 Revolution. Under Stalin, when the main effort was focused on the burgeoning industrial sector and the greatest concern was for urban and factory workers, agricultural productivity declined seriously. After Stalin's death, attempts were made to improve the lot of collectivized farmers, and there was a greater willingness to increase the procurement prices of farm produce and to increase capital investment in the agricultural sector. Khrushchev made an increase in agricultural productivity a major objective, determining that by 1970 the country would overtake the leading Western states in per capita output of key agricultural commodities.

With the opening of extensive areas of newly plowed land in western Siberia and northern Kazakhstan and a rise in procurement prices, the production of grain, especially wheat, increased sharply from 1955 to 1958. Subsequently, however, adverse weather conditions, problems of overcentralization in planning, and other difficulties resulted in a decline in wheat output in 1959 and 1960, the rate continuing below that of 1958 until 1966. In 1963, because of a severe drought, over 10 million tons of grain had to be imported from abroad.

With Khrushchev deposed, the March 1965 Party Plenum and the subsequent Twenty-third Party Congress in 1966 set more moderate targets in agriculture. The Party leadership promised an increase in investment in the agricultural sector, improvement in rural incomes and living standards, and emphasis on the increased population.

At the beginning of 1970 the basic problems of agricultural production remained essentially the same as they had been under Khrushchev. A major difficulty clearly lay in the harsh physical environment. Aside from this, Western observers attributed the lack of progress in part to a trend toward vast farming operations without reference to optimal size in terms of efficiency and to the inflexibility inherent in centralized management, which also had a limiting effect on personal initiative and responsibility.

BACKGROUND

Russian society on the eve of the Revolution was predominately agrarian; some 82 percent of the population resided in rural regions and received some or all of their income from the agricultural sector of the economy. Of the 367 million hectares of agricultural land in 1913, about 41 percent was owned by the aristocracy, the Church, and the large landowners; an additional 22 percent belonged to the more prosperous independent farmers; and the remaining 37 percent was held by peasants in communal plots. Approximately 11 million peasants were landless.

Methods of production were simple, but abundant harvests were produced in years of favorable weather. The country's foreign trade surplus depended on the massive export of its foodstuffs. In 1913, for example, some 12 million metric tons of grain were exported abroad, the bulk of it produced on the estates of the large landowners and by prosperous independent farmers.

The traditional pattern of landownership dissolved in the wake of the March Revolution, as landless peasants and small farmers began seizing the holdings of the great estates. Their activities were subsequently given legal sanction by Lenin, who the day after his rise to power in November 1917, decreed the nationalization of all land but, in effect, the peasants had already settled the land question by expropriation before the Bolsheviks came to power.

Between 1918 and 1921, nearly all the arable land in European Russia was farmed by peasant households. Food requisitions and the enforced establishment of state farms and cooperatives in early 1919 angered the peasants, who felt betrayed by the revolutionaries. These circumstances, together with the brutality of civil war, with both armies living off the land, adversely affected production as the peasants turned to subsistence farming and hoarding of surpluses. By 1920 agricultural output had declined to 50 percent of the pre-World War I level.

A solution was sought through the New Economic Policy (Novaya Ekonomicheskaya Politika—NEP) set forth under Lenin's direction by the Tenth Congress of the Communist Party in 1921 (see ch. 3, Historical Setting). This provided new incentive for small independent farmers. The requisitioning of so-called surplus grain ceased, and peasant farmers were permitted to trade produce, over and above procurement quotas, on the open market. As a result of the policy of relatively free enterprise in agriculture, by the mid-1920's agriculture had once again become a highly productive sector of the economy, and the country's farms were producing abundant supplies of food.

The Communist Party was weakly organized in the country, however, and had little influence on rural life. The growing prosperity of a group of independent farmers outside the socialized economy was a cause of concern to Party leaders, as was the need to provide funds to finance industrial development. Therefore, in the autumn of 1929 Stalin, in firm control of the country, decided to vigorously enforce the formation of collectives and state famrs. By July 1930 over 300,000 households of *kulaki* (relatively well-to-do peasants) had had their property confiscated and were resettled.

In the old village community, organizations were formally dissolved in areas subject to collectivization and their functions taken over by the collective farms and by rural Soviets. Henceforth, the bulk of the country's farms came under centralized political direction. Resistance to collectivization was widespread, and vast numbers of *kulaki* destroyed their crops and livestock rather than turn them over to a collective. The havoc wreaked by the conflict between the regime and the *kulaki* over enforced collectivization was enormous. Western studies based on Soviet statistics report that 1 million *kulak* households, amounting to at least 4.5 million persons, disappeared during the 1930's.

The collective farm system functioned inefficiently. Liquidation of the most experienced farmers, bad planning, poor organization of work, and unfavorable weather combined with other factors to cause a sharp decline in agricultural production. Famine struck wide areas of the countryside.

Agricultural machinery for collective farms was concentrated in so-called machine tractor stations, which were established in farming regions under direct government control. The stations provided plowing and harvesting services to the collective farms in their vicinity while providing the Party with an organization through which agricultural affairs could be completely supervised. Each station had a political division or section staffed by Party members whose main tasks entailed control and supervision of the collective farms. Many Communists from the cities were sent to the machine tractor stations for the express purpose of giving political guidance to the collective farmers.

During World War II many of the collective farmers greeted German troops as liberators and hoped for the return of the country's agricultural land to peasant ownership, but Nazi brutality soon ended thoughts of liberation. Western aid in the form of large grants of foodstuffs helped carry the country through the ravages of invasion, partial occupation, and preliminary defeats that did not, despite hopes to the contrary, lead to any structural change in the country's agriculture. After the war, conditions remained unchanged. Small remuneration for the farmers, underinvestment in agriculture, and bad weather assured low levels of productivity.

At the time of Stalin's death, in March 1953, both the quality and quantity of the food supply were inferior to that of the precollectivization period. The agricultural sector suffered from extremely low procurement prices and severe underinvestment. Even within the framework of the collectives, the peasants continued to be regarded as potential enemies of the Soviet system. By 1953, 99.7 percent of their households had been absorbed into socialized agriculture. The system of socialized land tenure devised by Stalin and carried out in the thirties remains the mainstay of the country's agriculture at the beginning of the 1970's.

POLICY AND ADMINISTRATION

The Communist Party leadership is the supreme decision-maker in the determination of agricultural organization and production in the country. It sets priorities for agriculture as it does for other sectors of the economy. As a result of the stress put on industry by the leadership, capital input in agriculture has been barely sufficient to permit the sector to function and to provide the government-set quotas for food deliveries.

Major changes in agricultural policy date from 1953, when Khrushchev initiated a sweeping reappraisal of the agricultural sector. One result was a strong trend toward the amalgamation of socialized farms into much larger units. At the same time, the machine tractor stations, which had served to indirectly control collective-farming operations, were disbanded in 1958, and their machinery sold to collective farms. Also, heavier basic investment in the sector by the state went hand in hand with the order for continuous cropping and the opening of the semiarid virgin lands in Kazakhstan as means of increasing grain output. A series of increases in the prices paid by the government to farmers was initiated, as a result of which procurement prices almost doubled between 1953 and 1958, as did average earnings among collective farm members.

The responsibilities of the USSR Ministry of Agriculture were redefined in 1961, its functions being reduced to that of directing agricultural research and innovation alone. The following year a new administrative system for collective and state farms was established, under the direction of a Territorial Production Administration. Under the system, the country was divided into a number of regional zones, each under the direction of a Communist Party-controlled center.

Despite reforms instituted by Khrushchev, the country's agriculture stagnated in the early sixties. An enormous investment in manpower, machinery, and financial resources, notwithstanding, the wheat harvests of 1963 and 1965 were disastrous. Moreover, cropping practices led to an impoverishment of the soil, and yields in field crops, after an initial increase, diminished.

In the early 1960's the cost production of all basic commodities rose markedly; at the same time, while the productivity of workers on collectives increased by about one-third, that of workers on state farms declined. Moreover, the generalized 1963 drought necessitated the importation of considerable quantities of grain from the Western world, a clear indication of Soviet agricultural failure. This major setback contributed to the forced retirement of Khrushchev.

The Brezhnev reforms announced in March 1965 set the tone for the late 1960's. The priority of heavy industry and maintenance of centralized control over socialized agriculture were continued, and innovations were announced in various other respects. These included fixed grain delivery quotas for a period of six years and the payment of a bonus of 50 percent for above-quota deliveries; increase in farm investment and in purchase prices of livestock and animal products; promise of a guaranteed monthly pay for members of collectives; and the creation of a moderate pension for their retired members.

The Central Committee meeting of May 1966, following the guidelines established by the Twenty-third Party Congress in April of that year, allocated R41 billion (1 ruble equals US$1.10) for the agricultural sector in the 1966—70 period. In October 1968, however, Brezhnev announced that actual expenditure by the state during the first three of the five years would amount to no more than R17.3 billion.

Prices paid to farmers by the government for their produce vary according to region. Regions less favored by soil and climate receive more per unit of output than richer ones. In March 1965 Brezhnev announced increases in procurement prices for wheat and rye averaging 12 percent and up to 53 percent for some poorer regions. Outstanding debts of some financially insolvent collective farms have been canceled by the government. Delivery prices paid to state farms are being increased to approach the level of those paid to collective farms.

Despite shortages in promised material inputs and the inadequate training of many workers, gross agricultural production in 1967 officially reached a level 17 percent above the average annual level achieved in the early 1960's. Even this, however, was short of the planned 25-percent increase. In his November 6, 1969, speech President Podgorny, taking into account the 1969 harvest, announced a 19-percent increase in production over the previous five-year (1961—65) period.

FARM ORGANIZATION

Soviet agriculture, based on the premise that all land is the property of the state, is characterized by three basic types of productive unit: the collective farm, the state farm, and the private plot. The state farm, directed and financed by the government, operates with hired laborers whose status is that of wage-earning employees. The collective farm, by contrast, is self-financed and -directed, under the authority of a chairman; and the income of its members, instead of taking the form of wages, constitutes a share of the income of the collective. The private plots are small areas of cultivable land placed at the disposal of various categories of farmers and workers for their own use. The individual cultivator is permitted to dispose of the produce as he chooses.

State farms, first established in 1918, numbered more than 12,700 by 1967 and employed some 7.9 million persons. Most state farms were extremely large. Collectively, in late 1965, they accounted for 312 million hectares of agricultural land, of which 106 million hectares was plowed land. In the late 1960's the average state farm had slightly more than 600 employees with sown area of 6,900 hectares. It had over 2,000 head of cattle and more than twice that number of smaller livestock.

Collective farms—working land to which the government has granted the right of use but which remains state owned—numbered 36,800 in 1967 and had 18.2 million members. In the late 1960's collective farms accounted for 228 million hectares of agricultural land, of which 116 million hectares was plowed land. In 1967 the average collective farm had somewhat more than 400 member households, with about 2,800 hectares of sown cropland, 1,100 head of cattle, and about twice that of smaller livestock. Like employees of state farms, cooperative members were permitted to maintain small individual or family plots to supplement their diet and their income.

Collective farms theoretically remain outside direct state control but, in fact, the Communist Party directs their activities. The man whom they elect as chairman is a member of, and is selected by, the Party. The chairman must oversee the production of commodities determined by state planning boards as well as to provide political leadership for the collective. State farms, similarly, are under the direction of a Party member, who acts as manager and who provides political leadership for the persons under his authority.

Collective farms function on the basis of their own financial resources, since they are economically independent of the directly controlled government economy. State farms, on the other hand, are operated, as are all other Soviet industries, by allocations and directives of the government. Price and quotas are established by the government for agricultural production both in the collective and state farms. Both are bound by Soviet law to ensure the fulfillment of quotas assigned by the agriculture ministry.

The 1969 model charter for collective farms reasserted the right to an individual plot, permitting each household up to 0.5 hectare and allowing it one cow, one calf, one sow or two pigs, up to 10 sheep and goats, as well as bees, poultry, and rabbits in unspecified numbers. This was in conformity with an official policy followed since the early 1930's and with Article 7 of the 1936 Constitution, which stated in part:

> Every collective-farm household, in addition to its basic income from the collective farm, has for its own use a small plot of land attached to the house, and, as its own property, a dwelling house, livestock, poultry, and minor agricultural implements.

The basic income of a collective farm member is determined by the number of workday credits earned. Work performed rather than hours expended is the basis for awarding credits. A tractor driver, for example, might earn three workday credits for plowing a hectare of land in ten hours, but a less skilled farmhand might receive only one credit for the same number of hours of work. Workday units are computed at the end of the year but, ordinarily, a farmer would have already received much of his share in cash and kind during the course of the year.

Peasants are frequently criticized in the Soviet press for spending an inordinate amount of time on their private plots as opposed to that spent on the collective property. This practice is curbed to some extent by the requirement that each collective farmer earn a specified minimum number of workday credits in order to retain membership in the collective. The actual share of collective earnings disbursed for each workday credit varies from one collective to another depending on physical factors, such as soil fertility and climate, as well as the skill and efficiency of the farm manager and the peasantry.

No distribution of accumulated shares is made at the end of the year until collective debts and obligations have been satisfied. After taxes are paid, allocations must also be made to communal funds or reserves that are designated for investments in machinery, livestock, buildings, insurance, seed and feed, and educational and cultural activities. The bulk of collective farm produce is purchased by the state at fixed prices and, despite improvement in the procurement system during the 1960's, the collective farmer in early 1970 remained among the lowest income groups in the country.

Owing to war losses and the emphasis on industry, which have drawn off much of the male element in the labor force, the agricultural labor force is predominantly female. The trend since the beginning of heavy industrialization in the 1920's has been for men to leave the farms to go to work in better paying industrial centers while women stayed behind. According to the 1959 census, women constituted 61.5 percent of the total agricultural work force, 57 percent of the collective farmers, and 91 percent of the persons working on private plots.

Although women perform most of the physical work in agriculture, they hold relatively few skilled jobs. In 1959 women held only 21 percent of administrative, managerial, and specialized posts in that sector of the economy. Of the women in agriculture in 1959, over three-fourths did not have a secondary education.

In the late 1960's the country had more than half a million persons with special skills in some phase of agriculture or in related fields, such as rural electrification or land reclamation. Its more than 100 higher agricultural schools had an enrollment of over 340,000 students, many of whom were outstanding workers sent for specialized training by their collectives or by the state farms on which they were employed. Tuition was free, and all students were provided with stipends.

Research work in agricultural and veterinary problems engages 80,000 scientific workers including more than 1,000 with doctorates and some 10,000 with master's degrees in science. Agricultural colleges annually graduate more than 30,000 specialists, in addition to which specialized technical schools train some 70,000 farming specialists every year. As a result, the number of people with special education employed in agricultural research, supervision, or farming exceeded 650,000 by 1967. The directing agency is the All-Union Lenin Academy of Agricultural Sciences, founded in 1929 in Moscow. It supervises seventeen research institutes and 142 experimental and selection stations.

LAND USE

The amount of agriculturally productive land is limited by climatic and topographic conditions (see ch. 2, Physical Environment). To the north of the so-called fertile triangle lie the treeless Artic tundra, which covers the far north and widens to the east, and the taiga, an immense coniferous forest region. With fleeting and cool summers and long, severe winters with little snow, the tundra is a permafrost zone, suitable only for reindeer herding. The northern coniferous forests stretch south of the tundra from the western border to the Pacific coast. Summer in this region is longer and warmer than in the tundra; there is more snow in winter and usually adequate precipitation in summer.

Although the forest zone cannot supply its own requirements, it plays some role in the production of grain. The main grain crops here are rye, barley, and oats. Grass is widely sown throughout the region. The most important industrial crop is flax, also known as northern silk.

Vast swampy areas in the forest zone hinder the development of farming. The region accounts for most of the over 200 million hectares of swamp and marsh in the country; these are located in the Baltic republics, Belorussia, the northwest section of the Ukraine, and Central Russia. Such land requires extensive and costly improvement measures.

Within the agricultural heartland lies the Central Black Earth region, with extremely rich soil. The area has one major drawback, however; it is subject to wide-ranging drought on an average of once every three years. This is especially true of the eastern parts of the region—the Volga area and northern Kazakhstan. Sometimes, as in 1963, the drought spreads over a vast territory from the Altai Mountains on the Mongolian border in the east to the Carpathians in the western Ukraine, including the entire forest-steppe zone. In such years the drought becomes a national calamity, necessitating large-scale importation of foodstuffs from abroad.

Bordering directly on the steppe zone to the south is a wide belt of semideserts and deserts occupying a considerable part of the lower Volga area, the eastern outskirts of the Caucasus, the central and southern regions of Kazakhstan, and all of Soviet central Asia. Two-thirds of the irrigated land in the entire country is situated in the zone. Outside these areas the deserts are covered with meager vegetation.

The local soils (brown, gray-brown, and gray in the south) are potentially very fertile. With irrigation they produce, as a rule, bigger crop yields than even the best nonirrigated black earth. The only source of water for extensive areas of central Asia and South and central Kazakhstan are the two large rivers Syr Darya and Amu Darya.

Cotton grows well on the irrigated lands of central Asia, south Kazakhstan, and the Transcaucasus. The best tracts of land are allotted to cotton, which has become the main crop there, determining to a considerable degree the zone's economy. Other southern major industrial crops include flax, jute, southern hemp, tobacco, and essential oil plants. Central Asia and the Transcaucasus also are known for their varieties of fruit and grapes.

The humid subtropical zone extends in a narrow strip along the Black Sea coast fringing the southwestern foothills of the Caucasus Mountains. A small section of the zone is situated on the southwestern coast of the Caspian Sea. The entire zone is characterized by a mild and damp climate. The Caucasian subtropics is the only area in the Soviet Union in which winters are extremely mild. Palms, eucalyptus trees, laurels, and magnolias grow here as do tangerines, lemons, and persimmons. Tea and tobacco plantations alternate with orchards and vineyards along the coast.

Land reclamation has played an important role in the development of agriculture. One of the principal efforts to expand the total cultivated area was that undertaken in the Virgin Lands program, which focused on semiarid peripheral zones, particularly in Kazakhstan. In northern Kazakhstan alone, some 40 million hectares of land were brought under cultivation between 1954 and 1962. By the late 1960's, the reclaimed area there represented about 17 percent of all arable land.

Much land has been brought into cultivation or its level of production increased through swamp drainage or construction of irrigation facilities. Swamps that require drainage are mainly located in the northern half of European Russia and in the Baltic region. Between 1913 and 1967 the area of drained land represented some 12 percent of all arable land.

Ambitious plans were set forth in the 1966—70 Five-Year Plan. Irrigated areas were to be increased over 1965 levels by 2.5 million to 3 million hectares; and drained regions, by up to 6 million hectares. By early 1968, however, drained areas had been increased only by less than 1.5 million hectares; and irrigated areas, by 0.5 million hectares.

The Hungry Steppe—a vast plain located at the junction of Uzbekistan, Kazakhstan, and Tadzhikistan—contains an example of the large-scale irrigation projects sponsored by the government. The building of hydropower stations from 1948 to 1956 and the construction of a canal system deriving from the Syr Darya River have permitted the irrigation of over 200,000 hectares of the over 800,000 to 900,000 hectares of the fertile gray soil of the desert region.

Another of the many government-constructed irrigation projects is the Kara-Kum Canal, which begins at the Amu Darya River and crosses the southern part of the Kara-Kum Desert in the direction of Ashkhabad, capital of the Turkmen Soviet Socialist Republic (SSR). The main canal is 850 kilometers long and, in volume of flow, is equal to the largest rivers of central Asia. It is navigable for small ships. When completed, its water will flow toward the shores of the Caspian Sea, and its total length will exceed 1,200 kilometers.

Vigorous efforts have also been made to combat the problem of soil erosion, which causes heavy losses. In 1963 soil erosion damaged some 1 million hectares of farmland in Pavlodar Oblast of the

663

Kazakh Soviet Socialist Republic (SSR). In 1965 wind erosion damaged some 5 million hectares of the Virgin Lands program. As a consequence, the 1966—70 Five-Year Plan called for the planting of trees and shrubs on more than 830,000 hectares of gullies and sands, and protective forest belts were to be planted on 342,000 hectares of land adjoining farms.

PRODUCTION

The contribution of each of the three types of farm organization to total production varies sharply. In 1967 state farms, which had been rapidly gaining importance since the Khrushchev period, contributed 43 percent of the country's grain output as compared with 55 percent by collective farms. Collective farms continued to provide the bulk of other field crops, including cotton, sugar beets, and sunflowers.

Government and policy leaders responsible for agricultural policy sought to make collective and state farms capable, eventually, of meeting all domestic food requirements. In early 1970, however, the government was still dependent on private plot production for a substantial contribution to total needs. Private plots were particularly important in respect to meats, vegetables, dairy products, and eggs. In the mid-1960's, for example, some 29.3 million head of cattle, or about 30 percent of the nation's total, were being raised on private plots, as well as 16.5 million hogs and 33.3 million sheep and goats, representing 28 and 26 percent, respectively, of the national figures. Persons raising livestock on private plots generally bought grain, hay, straw, and silage from collective or state farms and occasionally made arrangements to use their pasturage.

The investment in industry is reflected in the relatively extensive mechanization of large-scale agricultural activities. Nearly all plowing and harvesting is done with machinery. Equipment in use in 1967 included roughly 1.7 million tractors, 550,000 combines, and over 1 million trucks. Western observers estimated that for optimum efficiency, however, nearly twice this number could be used. New equipment was, in fact, being manufactured, allocated, and delivered to the agricultural sector at a rapid pace. In 1968 alone over half a million tractors, combines, and trucks were supplied to agriculture along with a variety of other implements and pieces of machinery.

Mechanization was not equitably developed in all areas of agriculture, however. Milking of dairy cattle and feeding of livestock, for example, were generally done without machinery. Difficulties caused by lack of, or improper, maintenance were widespread. Knowledgeable observers have reported that as much as 90 percent of agricultural machinery has been idled on occasion for lack of spare parts.

Collective farm requisitions for spare parts were reported to have been only 40- to 60-percent filled, according to the November 6, 1968, issue of *Izvestia*. Of 2 million spare parts in storage awaiting delivery, one-half were found to be defective by peoples' control committees in 1966 and 1967.

The output of mineral fertilizer has tended to fall considerably below the assigned production quota, although production has increased considerably in the past two decades. More than 33 million metric tons were produced in 1967 as compared with 5.3 million in 1950. By 1969 total output had reached 46 million metric tons with a revised production target of 57.5 million metric tons.

Crops

Field Crops

In terms of value, plant products constituted roughly 52 percent of total farm output in 1968; livestock products accounted for 48 percent. Grain crops are the foundation of Soviet agriculture. When grains cannot be grown in sufficient quantities to satisfy domestic needs, the effect may be seen in the slaughter of large numbers of livestock.

Grain crops also provide the staple food for the population as well as feed for livestock. In 1967 they comprised some 59 percent of the sown cropland, amounting to 118.2 million hectares, of which 70 million hectares were sown in wheat.

Of the principal grains grown in the mid-1960's, wheat accounted for 49 percent of the total output; barley, 17 percent; rye, 13 percent; corn, 7 percent; and other grains, 14 percent. The major productive regions include the Volga basin, the North Caucasus, Kazakhstan, the Donetsk-Dniepr basin, the Urals, West Siberia, the Southwest, and the Central Black Earth (*chernozem*) region.

Of the area sown in wheat, three-fourths is sown to spring wheat, which is grown especially in the central and eastern parts of the steppe zone. Winter wheat, by contrast, prevails in the forest-steppe zone and the west of the steppe zone in areas with a moderately cold winter and sufficient snow.

The Twenty-third Congress of the (CPSU) in early 1966 gave a priority to grain production, setting a target of an annual average output of 167 million metric tons. The net output in 1966 was about 147 million metric tons, that of 1967 between 122 million and 125 million metric tons, and that of 1968 somewhat over 140 million metric tons. In 1967 the Soviet Union resumed its traditional role as a net grain exporter. Over 5 million metric tons of wheat were exported, and only about 1.8 million metric tons were imported. Estimates for 1968 are of the same order.

Wheat production has improved since the disastrous harvests of

1963 and 1965, which averaged below 50 million metric tons and necessitated large-scale grain, especially wheat, importations. After the record output of 85 million metric tons in 1966, wheat production dropped to 64 million metric tons in 1967 and an estimated 78.5 million metric tons in 1968.

In the late 1960's rye was grown in only one-quarter of the area sown to wheat. Rye cultivation was centered in the forest and forest-steppe zones, and output in 1967 was 12 million metric tons. Barley, grown on about 20 million hectares, is favored for its adaptability to a variety of climatic conditions and its high yields. From record levels of about 24 million metric tons in 1964 and 1966, it had declined to 20.7 million in 1967 and an estimated 22.4 million in 1968. It is used as feed and in the making of alcoholic beverages.

Under Khrushchev, corn acreage was considerably expanded in the mid-1950's to provide cheap and plentiful feed for livestock, especially hogs. In the southern districts it replaced wheat, whereas in the north it replaced traditional fodder crops. Output reached a peak in 1961 with 12.7 million metric tons, declining to 6.4 million in 1965, then stabilizing in 1967 and 1968 at the level of 7.6 million to 8 million metric tons.

Oats are sown on some 6 million to 7 million hectares. Production has fluctuated from over 13 million metric tons in 1958, 3.7 million metric tons in 1963, and 9.6 million to 9.7 million metric tons in 1967 and 1968.

Other grains include millet, buckwheat, and rice. Production of these grains increased in the late 1960's from about 3.8 million metric tons in 1964, to 3.9 million in 1967, and to an estimated 4.3 million in 1968.

Among the varieties of legumes grown are peas in the north; kidney beans in southern Russia, the Ukraine, and Moldavia; lentils in the forest-steppe zone of the Volga and central and eastern Ukraine; and a variety of kidney beans in central Asia. The yearly production of legumes rose from 1.58 million metric tons in the 1957—59 period to 10 million in 1964, then declined to 5.6 million metric tons in 1968.

Land devoted to feed crops increased slightly in the late 1960's. It rose from some 26 percent of total crop acreage in 1965 to almost 29 percent in 1967, with an area of 59.6 million hectares.

Of the roughly 2.4 million hectares devoted to cotton, 90 percent is sown in central Asia, especially Uzbekistan, which yields two-thirds of the total output. The remaining 10 percent is in Transcaucasia. Average annual yield between 1966 and 1968 was 6 million metric tons.

The short flowering period of flax allows it to be sown in the northern reaches of the forest zone of European Russia. In 1968 it was cultivated on approximately 1.4 million hectares with a production of an estimated 500,000 metric tons. Cultivation of another fiber crop, hemp, used in making rope, string, and rough cloth, is concentrated in areas west of the Urals, in the Caucasus, and in the Ukraine.

Sunflowers are grown in the lower Volga and Don basins, the northern Caucasus, and the Ukraine, and their cultivation is spreading to northern Kazakhstan and western Siberia. The total area devoted to sunflowers in 1967 was about 4.8 million hectares, and production was estimated in 1968 at 6.1 million metric tons.

Sugar beet cultivation, totaling 3.8 million hectares, is centered in the western Ukraine, the northwest Caucasus, and eastern areas of Kazakhstan and central Asia. Output has been rising and has exceeded planned targets. In 1968 production was estimated at 93 million metric tons.

Potatoes and other vegetables are major food crops. Total area devoted to these crops in 1967 was 9.7 million hectares, of which 8.3 million were devoted to potatoes. The main districts are found in the acid soils of the forest and forest-steppe zones. Two-thirds of the acreage in potatoes is in central European Russia, the Ukraine, and Belorussia. Western sources estimated an annual average of 82.5 million metric tons in 1966 and 1967 and 91.4 million metric tons for 1968, which still fell short of the average annual planned output of 100 million metric tons for the late 1960's.

Nine-tenths of all vegetables are grown around urban industrial regions ranging from the south to the far north. Despite attempts to increase production, output fluctuated in the late 1960's from 20.5 million metric tons in 1967 to an estimated 18.5 million metric tons in 1968. Melons are cultivated in the irrigated soils of central asia.

Tobacco is cultivated in the southern regions of the country that have humid climate and fine soil. The best varieties are grown in the western Caucasus, the Crimea, Trans-Carpathia, and Moldavia. *Makhorka*, an inferior form of tobacco, is cultivated in more northern climes. The output of tobacco reached a new high in 1967 with 215,000 metric tons; in 1968 it is estimated to have declined to about 200,000 metric tons.

Tea is cultivated in western Georgia, southeastern Azerbaijan, and the northwestern Caucasus. Its annual output stabilized in the 1966—68 period at between 234,000 to 238,000 metric tons.

Other

Fruit orchards have been developed most extensively in the southern regions of the country but also in the Baltic republics, Belorussia, and around the urban centers of the Russian Soviet Federated Socialist Republic (RSFSR), where apples predominate. From the black earth area of the Ukraine and the west banks of the Volga southward, apricots, plums, and the southern variety of apples and pears are grown in large quantities.

Citriculture is centered in western Transcaucasia. The remainder of the region grows walnuts, peaches, apricots, and figs. Grapes, requiring a dry and sunny climate, prevail in Transcaucasia, central Asia, Moldavia, and the southern reaches of the Ukraine and the North Caucasus. Output of citrus fruits has steadily grown in the late 1960's to an estimated 4.2 million metric tons in 1968. The production of other fruits, after a steady increase since 1963, declined from 5.5 million metric tons in 1967 to an estimated 5.4 million in 1968.

Animal Husbandry

In early 1968 the number of cattle was calculated at 97 million head. Sheep numbers were relatively stable in the mid-1960's; the total for the country in 1968 was reported to be 138 million. In the same year the number of goats was only 5.6 million as compared with 17.1 million in 1952. The number of hogs also showed a decline from 70 million in 1963 to 50.9 million in 1968. Reflecting the increasing use of tractors, the number of horses was only 8 million.

Official production figures for 1967 reported 11.5 million metric tons of meat (slaughterweight) and 79.9 million metric tons of milk. Calculations by Western sources of Soviet livestock and livestock products for the same year were: 9.4 million metric tons of meat (liveweight), 71.9 million metric tons of milk, 2.8 billion dozens of eggs, and 394,000 metric tons of wool. Comparable estimates for 1968 were: 9.4 million metric tons of meat, 73.9 million metric tons of milk, 2.9 billion dozens of eggs, and 413,000 metric tons of wool.

Fishing

Fishing, undertaken in both inland and ocean waters, is an important part of the economy. The total catch of fish and marine products in 1967 exceeded 6.5 million metric tons. Estimated catch in 1968 was 6.7 million metric tons, and the goal for 1970 was 8.5 million to 9 million metric tons. The catch was made up of a great variety of fish, sea mammals, and shellfish; but the bulk of it was composed of herring, cod, salmon, flatfish, and fresh-water species, including sturgeon. The country's oceangoing fishing fleet included 20,000 powered vessels, some of which were equipped with self-contained special facilities for freezing or otherwise preserving their catch.

The fishing industry operates mainly in the seas of the Far East. Up to one-third of the total catch of marine products is taken in these waters. Vladivostok, the Kamchatka Peninsula, and the southern edge of Sakhalin Island offer port facilities and have fish-processing factories. Whaling fleets that operate in North Pacific and Antarctic waters use Vladivostok as home port. Shipbuilding and maintenance and forestry and woodworking industries have developed in this area along with the fishing industry.

Northern European fishing areas, centered on the port of Murmansk and in North Atlantic waters, provide one-fifth of the country's marine catch. The two Baltic ports of Kaliningrad and Klaipeda serve as bases for operations in the Atlantic. Other important fisheries are those in the Azov-Black Sea region and the Caspian basin fisheries. The latter are noted for sturgeon, which is processed in Astrakhan, the principal port of the region.

Forestry

Forestry makes a significant contribution to the economy. With more than one-third of its total area, or about 746.8 million hectares, covered with forests, the country has the world's largest forest reserves and is the world's largest timber producer. Nationalized by the decree on land of November 8, 1917, forests are the property of the state. Responsibility for the forests of the RSFSR, which contains 90 percent of the total reserves, is vested in the Main Forest Economic Agency, to which is attached a special institute for forest inspection. Other republics have comparable agencies.

Forestry provides employment for about half a million persons, whereas wood industries involve an additional 2 million persons. Hunting also provides full- or part-time employment for several million persons.

Forests adjoining croplands are a valuable asset in preventing soil erosion and provide food and shelter for fur-bearing animals. Wood is a source of fuel, but its use is declining. Forestry and fur-bearing animals offer an important source of currency for the export market, the value of the annual exports of forestry products reaching about $500 million.

The principal forested areas are in the Ural, Siberian, and Far East regions and in the Northwest. Coniferous forests constitute more than half the timber reserves. Of the deciduous varieties, oak, birch, and beech predominate. Conifers dominate in the Far East, Eastern and Western Siberia, the Urals, and the Northwest. The deciduous stands are more frequent in the less-forested areas of central and southern European Russia, the Caucasus, and the extreme south of central Asia.

Hunting in forest zones is well organized. About 30 percent of pelts procured in the wilds are exported, accounting for as much as 15 percent of the value of Soviet exports in some years. Fur-farming, a related enterprise, provides the furs of mink, silver-black foxes, and light blue polar foxes.

The state maintains some twenty schools of forestry and forest technical institutes for training in all branches of forest management, forest utilization, and wood technology. Numerous experimental stations and laboratories cooperate with special forest research institutions and professional schools of forestry in conducting research.

Much effort goes into conservation and development of forest reserves. In 1967 alone, according to official statistics, 1.25 million hectares of woodland were sown and planted, and in 1968 the area of protective forests expanded by 325,000 hectares.

Productivity in the forestry sector of the economy has been a matter of concern to responsible officials in recent years. In the late 1960's vigorous efforts were being extended to increase productivity by more efficient use of material resources and manpower.

CHAPTER 32

THE LABOR FORCE

The total Soviet labor force was estimated to be 129.4 million at the beginning of 1970. This number included an estimated 3 million members of the military forces. The total population was estimated to be 241.4 million, an increase of 32.7 million since the most recent official census, that of January 15, 1959.

The numerical preponderance of women and the importance of their role in the labor force have been distinctive features of the economy since World War II. The ratio of males to females was gradually improving, although mounting pressures for labor resources and the desire to improve living standards tended to maintain a high level of participation by women workers. The percentage of workers in nonagricultural branches of the economy increased from 20 percent in 1920 to more than 65 percent in 1969. Urbanization and industrialization continued at a rapid pace. City dwellers constituted 55 percent of the population in early 1970, as compared with 20 percent in 1926.

Although there appeared to be no real shortage of manpower, the dwindling supply of surplus labor in rural areas, the appearance of surplus workers in some areas and shortages in others, and continuing heavy demands for workers produced strains on the labor market. There was much concern about labor shortages in the late 1960's. The problem of labor distribution and the training of adequate numbers and types of skilled workers, particularly at midlevel occupations, were also given increased attention.

The decreased rate of population growth in the late 1960's, the tightening labor market, and the impact of labor turnover as a result of increased freedom of internal migration caused Soviet leaders, particularly after 1965, to give added attention to the demographic aspects of national development. These conditions also resulted in an increase and improvement of data collection on population and labor and the establishment of new organizations for developing and distributing labor resources.

The working age groups, defined as sixteen to fifty-nine years of age for men and sixteen to fifty-four for women, contained 54 percent of the population. The youthful character of the population was indicated by the fact that 31 percent was under sixteen years of age.

POPULATION STRUCTURE

War, civil strife, famine, and repressive governmental actions have had major and long-term effects on the size, age distribution, and sex composition of the population. Demographers have estimated that World War I losses were: 2 million military deaths, 12 million civilian deaths, 2 million refugees, and a birth deficit of nearly 10 million. Between 1926 and 1939, the period that included large-scale collectivization of agriculture and various purges, the human cost may have been as much as 20 million lives, of which 15 million were attributed to birth deficits. The estimates of losses for World War II, like those for the other periods, vary. An absolute population decline of 25 to 30 million was probably experienced.

The distribution of the 241.4 million persons by age groups reflects these events (see fig. 9). The small number of persons aged forty-five and over and the low ratio of men to women in this group are, in part, attributable to losses from World War I, the Civil War, and World War II. Low birth rates during World War II account for the disproportionately small group of those twenty-five to twenty-nine years of age. Moreover, the period of sustained growth during the 1950's and early 1960's accounts for the large group of those between ages five and nineteen. The decline in growth rate in the late 1960's is indicated in the group aged four years and under. The net increase in population was 5 million greater for the decade of the fifties as compared with the decade that followed.

The distribution of age groups when viewed in their entirety reflect a predominantly youthful society. Approximately 31 percent are under sixteen years of age, whereas only 15 percent are in the retirement age group—sixty and over for men and fifty-five and over for women. Nonetheless, there is a trend toward an aging population. If growth rates continue at the level of the 1960's, the ratio of persons above normal working age will accelerate around 1981, when persons now forty-four years old will begin to reach retirement age.

An unusually heavy deficit of men has persisted since World War II. At the beginning of 1970 there were almost 18 million fewer men than women, as compared with an estimated deficit of 26 million in 1946. The 111.8 million males and 129.6 million females were distributed by age as follows: under sixteen, 37.2 million males and 35.4 million females; working age group, 65 million males and 67.6 million females; and retirement group, 9.6 million males and 26.5 million females.

The ratio of men per 100 women gradually improved, from an estimated 74 in 1946, 83 in 1959, to almost 87 in 1970. The imbalance was generally confined to the age group forty years and above. At age sixty and above there were two women for every

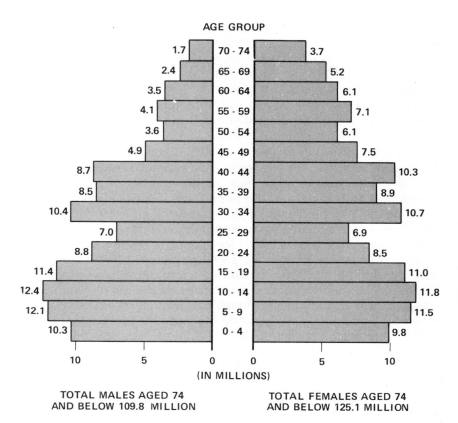

AGE GROUP

	Males	Age Group	Females	
	1.7	70 - 74	3.7	
	2.4	65 - 69	5.2	
	3.5	60 - 64	6.1	
	4.1	55 - 59	7.1	
	3.6	50 - 54	6.1	
	4.9	45 - 49	7.5	
	8.7	40 - 44	10.3	
	8.5	35 - 39	8.9	
	10.4	30 - 34	10.7	
	7.0	25 - 29	6.9	
	8.8	20 - 24	8.5	
	11.4	15 - 19	11.0	
	12.4	10 - 14	11.8	
	12.1	5 - 9	11.5	
	10.3	0 - 4	9.8	

10   5   0   0   5   10
(IN MILLIONS)

TOTAL MALES AGED 74   TOTAL FEMALES AGED 74
AND BELOW 109.8 MILLION   AND BELOW 125.1 MILLION

Source: Adapted from U.S. Congress, 89th, 2d Session, Joint Economic Committee, *New Directions in the Soviet Economy*, Washington, 1966, pp. 667–674.

Figure 9. Population Pyramid, January 1, 1970, Soviet Union.

man. Although the ratio was gradually improving overall, it was estimated that numerical balance will not be reach for another four or five decades if postwar trends prevail.

The severe shortage of males not only required large numbers of women to participate in the labor force, but also left many women without husbands and caused temporary shortages of conscriptees. In 1959, 24 million women aged twenty to fifty-nine years did not have spouses; this was equivalent to half the number of women in the labor force. In 1962 the number of youths who reached conscription age fell to 900,000, which was well below the 2.2 million in 1958 and an equal number in 1969. The decision to register youths for conscription at the age of seventeen instead of eighteen was triggered by the small number who were entering the prime military age group, seventeen to thirty-four years. The number in this group, estimated to be 31.6 million in 1966, was expected to increase to 33.4 million by 1971 and was considered to be near normal after reaching a nadir in 1962.

According to official Soviet sources, the total population of 236.4 million in early 1968 was distributed by union republic as follows: Russian Soviet Federated Socialist Republic, 127.9 million; Ukraine, 46.4 million; Kazakh, 12.7 million; Uzbek, 11.3 million; Belorussia, 8.8 million, Azerbaijan, 4.9 million; Georgia, 4.6 million; Moldavia, 3.4 million; Lithuania, 3 million; Kirgiz, 2.8 million; Tadzhik, 2.7 million; Armenia, 2.3 million; Latvia, 2.3 million; Turkmen, 2 million; and Estonia, 1.3 million. Despite efforts to develop the economy and to increase the number of people in the eastern and northern areas, the population remains heavily concentrated in the European part of the country. Vast expanses of taiga, tundra, and desert remain virtually uninhabited except for scattered locations that have been selected for economic development.

Urban population, numbering 130.9 million in 1968 as compared with 100 million in 1959, constituted approximately 55 percent of the total. The number of city dwellers increased almost four times between 1926 and 1959, and almost half lived in cities with populations over 100,000 in 1959. During the past two decades the annual increase averaged between 3 and 4 million, and city population increased at more than twice the rate of that for the country as a whole. The number of urban areas increased from 4,619 to 5,193 between 1959 and 1965; the number with more than 100,000 inhabitants rose from 148 to 188. The largest cities in order of their size in 1967 were Moscow, Leningrad, Kiev, Tashkent, Kharkov, Gorky, and Novisibirsk.

POPULATION DYNAMICS

The patterns of development in birth rate, mortality rate, life expectancy, and infant mortality closely resemble those of other industrially advanced societies (see table 14). The limited efforts by authorities to control population growth have had little positive effect. Lenin's principle, which stated that the citizen had the basic right to determine whether a child should be born or not, has prevailed. The capability of women to restrict the number of births accounts for the declining birth rate. The major motivations for restricting childbirth include the lack of adequate housing, the widespread employment of women, the desire to improve living standards, and the desire of women to increase their independence (see ch. 11, Family).

Abortions have been the principal influence in the restriction of reproduction. Results of a large-scale survey indicate that the number of abortions exceeds live births and that the abortion rate for women employed in the labor force is 2½ times that of nonworking

Table 14. Birth, Mortality, and Natural Increase Rates per Thousand Population in the Soviet Union, Selected Years, 1913 to 1969

Year	Birth Rate	Mortality rate	Natural increase	Infant mortality (under one year of age)
1913	45.5	29.1	16.4	269
1940	31.2	18.0	13.2	182
1950	26.7	9.7	17.0	81
1960	24.9	7.1	17.8	35
1965	18.4	7.3	11.1	27
1969	18.0	8.0	n.a.	26

n.a.—not available.

women. The influence of other restraints has not been determined. Reports indicate that the quality and distribution of contraceptives are poor.

Comparisons of birth rates for the republics indicated that Slavic people were producing at lower rates than the non-Slavic. Rates in predominately Muslim republics were approximately twice those of the Russian and Ukrainian republics. Birth rates continued to be higher in the country than in the city. Infant mortality has been reduced to a respectably low level; further progress and attainment of the Swedish record of approximately 13 per 1,000 would have only a minor influence on population growth.

Reductions in deaths from natural causes and increases in life expectancy have been significant during the period of Soviet rule. The 6.9 per 1,000 population death rate in 1964, when the age structure was most favorable, is probably a record for the Soviet Union. The rate had increased to 8 in 1969. Life expectancy at birth increased from forty-four years in the 1926—27 period to seventy years in the 1965—66 period. Further progress will be at a slower pace owing to the limitation of total lifespan and despite boasts about the longevity of some Soviet people.

Migration into, and out of, the country has had a negligible influence on the size of the Soviet population during the 1960's. Except for the movement to Poland in the late 1950's of about a quarter of a million persons who claimed Polish citizenship, the policy on migration across Soviet borders has been highly restrictive.

Internal migration, under conditions of increased freedom of movement since 1956, is being given increased attention, because labor turnover and labor distribution problems have appeared. The rate of internal migration for the mid-1960's was estimated at 7 million persons, or 3 percent of the total population, each year.

Data for the period 1961—65, which was computed statistically and not taken from direct reports on migration because the latter are not maintained, indicated the areas of greatest out-migration were the Central Black Earth, Ural, western regions of the Russian republic and the Belorussian republic, and the areas around the Volga and Vyatka rivers. The principal areas of in-migration were central Asia, Kazakhstan, the cities of Moscow and Leningrad, and eastern Siberia. The growth rate of eastern Siberia, a region that has required additional manpower for a number of years, has not been significantly greater than that of the rest of the country since 1956. The movement into this area was greatest from 1939 to 1956; in the succeeding years there has been a strong counterflow westward, to places that offer a more hospitable climate and better living conditions.

The primary organization for recruitment of labor and resettlement under government auspices from the 1930's to the mid-1960's was the Administration for Organized Recruitment of Workers. The organized population movement from country to city before 1956 was controlled by the recruitment administration through contracts between collective farms and industry. Also, this organization recruited workers for the more remote and less favorable areas where labor was required. After 1953 mass appeals and recruitment by the Komsomol (Young Communist League) supplemented the work of the official organ. Between 1956 and 1962 almost 1.4 million volunteers were sent to Siberia and other remote areas on Komsomol travel passes. In 1966 the work of labor recruitment was taken over by state committees for utilization of labor resources at the republic level. Established by a joint Party and government decree in 1966, these committees operate under the central direction of the Labor Resources Department of the USSR State Planning Committee and work through organizations at lower echelons, down to and including the commissions of District Soviets (see ch. 33, Labor Relations and Organization).

It is apparent from the factors of population dynamics which have been examined that probable changes in the mortality rate, life-expectancy rate, and migration will have only a marginal influence on growth rates in the near future. The influence of the birth rate is predominant and, unless the downward trend can be halted, growth rates of the 1960's are not likely to be maintained.

POPULATION POLICY

The government has taken actions that aimed to influence population growth, even though no official policy ever was announced and even though Marxist doctrine denies the need for control of population growth in Communist societies. Both the provision of care centers for some children whose mothers are employed and payments for the support of children are, in part, aimed at increasing the population. Their value as incentives to increase the population has been questioned and, because the amount of payments is small, the program is more properly classed as welfare. The widespread employment of women and liberal abortion laws have tended to reduce population growth (see ch. 11, Family).

The demographic aspects of national development began to receive attention in the mid-1960's after a long period of virtual neglect. Soviet theorists have not abandoned the precept that labor surplus is equivalent to unemployment, and there can be no unemployment in a Communist society. The doctrine states that labor surplus is an inevitable consequence of capitalism. There have been indications, however, of relaxation on the question of population controls. Since 1965 speeches and articles by Soviet demographers have recognized in some instances the need for population controls in developing countries that are confronted with excess population. Soviet votes and participation in United Nations discussions and programs in the mid-1960's indicated willingness to participate in population control measures on at least a limited scale, reflecting a changing attitude on the question.

Although the abortion laws for each of the three periods 1920—35, 1935—55, and 1956—70 have influenced population growth, they do not reflect a consistent policy. The legal abortion law that prevailed from 1920 to 1935 was in accord with Lenin's principle that a citizen has the basic right to determine whether or not a child should be born. The abortion rate reached such proportions, however, that a restrictive policy was adopted in 1936 and continued until 1956. Under this policy the rate of illegal abortions became alarming, and again liberal abortion laws were adopted in 1956. Each of the changes was presented as a measure to protect the health of the people and did not purport to control population growth (see ch. 11, Family).

The increasing interest in population was seen in the creation of the Coordinating Council for Population Problems in the Ministry of Higher and Specialized Secondary Education in 1964 and the establishment in 1965 at Moscow University of the Problem Laboratory of Population, devoted to the study of population problems and the training of graduate-level demographers.

SIZE AND COMPOSITION OF THE LABOR FORCE

The labor force, which has increased over 30 million since 1950, was estimated to number 129.4 million persons in 1970. The flow of persons into the able-bodied age groups, which was at the rate of approximately 2 million per year, was again normal after reaching a nadir in the early 1960's. Nearly 90 percent of the civilian labor force was employed in the socialized sector of the economy—approximately 76 percent in state employment and 14 percent on collective farms. The number of workers in the private sector has remained nearly constant at 11 to 12 million since 1950 and indicated that the growth of nearly 30 million had been entirely in the socialized sector. The continuing trend in industrialization of the labor force was evidenced by the fact that the nonagricultural labor force doubled in size, increasing from 42.5 million to 85.1 million, while the agricultural sector decreased from 49.9 to 41.2 million workers between 1950 and 1970;

Total civilian employment estimated at 119.5 million in 1970 was almost 7 million less than the total civilian labor force. This difference was attributed primarily to the fact that contributions of seasonal workers were computed on the basis of months employed, whereas workers in the labor force who claimed an occupation were counted even if they worked only part of the year. It also indicated considerable losses from low utilization of seasonal workers and other causes. Manpower losses resulting from unemployment were not known. Soviet authorities denied that unemployment existed, despite the admission that labor surpluses had appeared in some areas.

Labor supply that was not reflected in labor and employment official statistics consisted of persons who were on pensions, doing organized extra work, had full-time jobs, or were full-time students. Reports indicated these contributions had been large during the 1960's. In the 1961—62 period approximately 700,000 students of secondary specialized educational institutions took part in volunteer work. Later reports indicated that 70,000 students in higher education worked six to ten months during their fourth and sixth years. During the summer of 1968 over a quarter of a million students were reported to have worked on some 17,000 projects. Also, in 1962 over 2 million volunteers were working at administrative tasks on the district government level. Nearly half of all wage and salary workers in 1965 were reported to be involved in the movement in which voluntary work was contributed on Saturdays and weekends.

The manpower contributions of persons in forced labor status were considered to be insignificant in early 1970, in comparison with the peak level at the outbreak of World War II, when the prison camp population was estimated at approximately 10 to 12 million. A high-level Soviet official stated that there was a 70-percent reduction in prisoners between 1953 and 1957. Individuals continue to be sentenced to terms of labor under conditions of restricted freedom. Prison camps are known to exist, but data on their population and the contributions of persons in forced labor status are not published (see ch. 23, The Police [Militia] and Correctional Systems).

In 1967, when there was a total of 82.2 million in state employment, workers and employers were distributed among the branches of the economy as follows (in millions): industry, 29; construction, 6; agriculture, 9.4; transport and communication, 8.6; trade, 6.4; health services and education, 11.7; science and scientific services, 2.9; household industries, 2.7; and other sectors, 5.5. The number of workers had approximately doubled since 1950 in each of the state sectors of industry, transportation and communication, trade, and health services and education. State farm employment increased about 2½ times during the same period. In the late 1960's, when it was estimated that 300,000 workers left collective farm employment each year, 200,000 were added to state farm employment.

Soviet published data classified workers in state employment in the general category of wage and salary earners. A further breakdown of industrial production personnel for 1967 classified 81 percent as workers; 1.6 percent, apprentices; 11.4 percent, engineer-technical workers; 4 percent, salaried employees; and 2 percent, workers in collective farm and small auxiliary industries.

As a consequence of the heavy deficit of males since World War II, women were added to the labor force in large numbers and were employed in jobs usually reserved for men. Their contribution was significant in science and technology, particularly at the semiprofessional and intermediate professional levels, in comparison with that of women in the industrialized Western nations. In 1970 more than half the labor force were women. The highest rates of employment were in the rural and traditionally Christian areas, which suffered the most during World War II—for example, Belorussia; the lowest rates were found in the more urbanized areas of the republics with heavy Muslim populations—for example, Azerbaijan. The rate of employment of women in their prime childbearing years was extremely high. In 1965, 90 percent of women twenty to thirty-nine years of age were employed. Studies indicated that the total burden of employment, both in the labor force and in the home, fell much more heavily on women than on men.

In 1967, when there was a total of 41 million women in state employment, female workers and employees were represented in the various branches of the economy (in percent) as follows: industry, 47; construction, 28; state farms and subsidiary industries, 44; transport, 24; communications, 66; trade, 74; health, 85; education, 72; science and science services, 45; and credit and insurance institutions, 75. The majority of professional and technical positions were filled by females; however, considering all levels of workers, the bulk of Soviet women were employed in relatively unskilled work and constituted a large proportion of the least-educated element of the population.

In 1959 one-third of all persons sixteen to forty-nine years of age had less than four years of schooling; of these, two-thirds were females. The greatest lag in education of women was found in central Asia. The burden of physical labor fell heavily on women, especially in agriculture where approximately 63 percent of all jobs requiring physical labor were performed by females.

The achievement and productivity of women in the most demanding professions was estimated to be below that of men, despite the fact that more females in the labor force had completed higher education than males. Interrupted careers, loss of worktime, and assignment difficulties tended to offset any advantage in education. In the medical field, where four of five physicians were women, four of five persons holding top-level positions were males. Adverse ratios in the most responsible positions extended into many other fields as well. The trend was toward a progressively smaller role for women in top-echelon positions as the ratio of men to women improved. In the late 1960's the pronounced reduction in the ratio of women admitted to higher educational institutions in the fields of medicine, agriculture, and socioeconomic disciplines showed a preference for men and tended to support the view that economic, rather than idealistic, motivations had advanced women into positions ordinarily dominated by men.

The demands for additional labor supply, plus the desire on the part of women to work in order to improve living standards and to increase their independence, were maintaining high levels of participation by women in the labor force.

LABOR REQUIREMENTS AND SUPPLY

Utilizing the goals for the 1966—70 five-year plan as guidelines, labor analysts estimated the requirements for new workers and employees in the state sector to be 27.7 million for the five-year period. The net increase for new workers coming into the labor force was estimated at 14 to 15 million. Government officials and enterprise managers in the late 1960's increasingly lamented the shortage of workers and indicated increasing pressures on the labor supply. For example, the chairman of the State Committee for Utilization of Labor Resources of the Russian republic stated that in 1968 industry in that republic was short 1 million workers. Reports on employment for the late 1960's indicated that the greatest growth was in sciences and scientific services, trade, and public health; modest growth was in industry; and no significant change had occurred in railroad transportation, construction, and agriculture.

Each year during the 1966—70 plan period, slightly over 4 million persons became sixteen years of age. Many continued their schooling beyond this age, but the primary source for new workers came from the pool of youth who left school or who had completed their education. The abundance of surplus rural labor that had been drawn upon heavily in the early years of industrialization had greatly diminished by the mid-1950's. Since then, urban areas have supplied a large portion of the workers who have been recuited or volunteered for newly developed enterprises and remote areas. The sources for obtaining the additional manpower (the requirements in excess of new workers) were found mainly in better utilization of persons already in the labor force. These included seasonal workers, primarily in agriculture, and workers in excess of needs at some industrial enterprises. Other sources were the employment of additional women of working age, pensioners, the private sector of the economy, and students.

The requirements at various skill levels were reflected in the plans for education and in school enrollments. After a decree in 1963, the government took measures to increase the number of midlevel technicians. The goal for 1970 was to have one specialist with higher education to three or four with specialized secondary education in the agricultural, communications, construction, industrial, and transport sectors. The ratio was 1 to approximately 1½ in the 1962—63 period. Admissions to specialized secondary schools increased almost threefold between 1958 and 1970; the estimated number of graduates for the 1966—70 period was 4.3 million. Total enrollments in vocationally oriented schools in the 1965—66 period were (in millions) as follows: trade and vocational-technical, 1.7; specialized secondary, 3.7; higher educational institutions, 3.9; and training programs for improving skills in factory and other courses, 14.4 (see ch. 15, The Educational System).

SOURCES OF SKILLED MANPOWER

The heavy emphasis on education (which led to substantial increases in the cultural level of the populace) had as a major objective the development of a skilled labor force. In 1970 the median years of school completed by persons sixteen years of age and older was 7.3, an increase from 5 years in 1950. The progress during this period at the top levels was particularly significant. The number who had completed higher education rose from 1.9 to 7.5 million (see table 15).

In 1965 the approximately 400,000 graduates of institutions of higher learning were distributed by field of specialization (in percent) as follows: engineering-industry, 39.5; agriculture, 8.9; socio-economic, 7.9; education-culture, 36.2; and health-medicine, 7.5. In industry the proportion of highly skilled and skilled workers in-

Table 15. Level of Education Attained by Persons Sixteen Years Old and
Over in the Soviet Union, 1950 and 1970

	1950		1970	
	Millions	Percent	Millions	Percent
Population aged sixteen and over	121.3	100.0	168.7	100.0
Higher	1.9	1.6	7.5	4.4
Incomplete higher	0.9	0.7	3.4	2.0
Specialized secondary	5.0	4.1	13.5	8.0
General secondary	6.3	5.2	15.8	9.3
Incomplete secondary (grades 7-9)	19.1	15.8	48.4	28.1
Primary and incomplete seven years (grades 4-6)	41.7	34.3	34.8	20.6
Less than primary	46.4	38.3	45.3	26.9

*Percentages are rounded.

Source: Adapted from U.S. Congress, 90th, 2d Session, Joint Economic
Committee, *Soviet Economic Performance 1966-67*, Washington,
1968, p. 88.

creased from 18.5 percent in 1925 to 64.6 percent in 1961. The number of persons who had specialized secondary or higher educations and were employed in the socialized sector of the economy rose from 8.8 million in late 1960 to 12.9 million in late 1966, and the flow of graduates from these institutions continued throughout the 1966—70 five-year plan at an accelerated rate.

There were special commissions for each of the four basic divisions of the educational system that served as links between employers and the institutions. The Commissions for the Labor Participation of Youths of the Local Soviets of Workers' Deputies worked with the general educational schools in arranging assignments to jobs or to professional-technical schools. The State Committee for Professional and Technical Education assigned professional and technical school graduates who incurred an obligation to work. The Commission for the Personal Distribution of Young Specialists directed the job placement of specialized secondary level and higher education graduates. In February 1966 a joint Party-government resolution directed the republics to take steps to have city and district authorities make allocations of public school graduates to industry, agriculture, construction, and other activities. The proportion of young workers was to range from 0.5 percent to 10 percent.

Extensive on-the-job training was conducted by individual establishments to improve skill levels. Seventy-five or more percent of all wageworkers have undergone such training for periods of up to six months. Special programs, which required two hours' classwork each week for six to eight months, were provided as an additional means to improve job performance and to enhance the worker's potential for advancement.

LABOR TURNOVER

Labor turnover as defined by the Soviets included only those persons who voluntarily quit their jobs or were dismissed for disciplinary reasons. Turnover as a factor in labor distribution became a problem of increasing importance after 1956, because restrictions on movement, imposed by the use of internal passports and permanent labor books, were lifted and job changes became easier. Government control over housing and other benefits and pressures from Party-dominated organizations continued to have restraining influences, but the workers' freedom to move greatly increased.

Despite the fact that in comparison with the early 1950's and the pre-World War II period the amount of turnover decreased after 1956; the volume, direction, and frequency were such that major problems of structural demand for labor resulted. The government's capability to control relocation of workers was greatly decreased. A survey by the Institute of Labor in 1960 revealed that only about 17 percent of shifts were through organized channels. The prevalence of the direct-hire system by enterprise managers facilitated job changes. In Industry, for example, 90 percent of workers were hired by this method.

Studies of industry for the 1961—64 period revealed that the average amount of time lost during job turnover was twenty days. The total loss in industry in 1964 was estimated by Western labor analysts at 320,000 man-years, or 1.5 percent of the total input. The loss of productivity owing to lower efficiency of new workers for all persons who changed employment in 1963 was estimated to be R3 billion (one ruble equals US$1.10).

The problem of labor surpluses in some areas and shortages in others, together with the need for devising means to obtain optimum distribution of labor resources, was of greatest concern and resulted from the uncontrolled labor turnover. Efforts to obtain data on the rate of turnover, reasons for changing jobs, and related information were intensified, beginning about 1960.

The motivations for changing jobs were many and varied. The adventurousness of young adults was evidenced by the involvement of persons thirty-five years of age and under in 85 percent of the turnover. More than half of this group were between eighteen and twenty-five years of age. The departure of youths from farms resulted in an older and heavily female labor force on collective farms. A study by the Soviet Institute of Labor showed that 60 percent of job separations were by the worker's own choice. Dissatisfaction with work and living conditions, rather than with pay, was the primary reason for quitting.

LABOR PLACEMENT

The distribution of labor in terms of the needs of the economy is provided for generally in the central planning mechanism. By virtue of the state's responsibility for its citizens, there is a certain obligation under Article 118 of the 1936 Constitution that, on the surface, guarantees the right to work. The admission of unemployment would indicate the failure to guarantee this right, which has been hailed as a unique innovation. In early 1970 the institutional framework needed to cope adequately with manpower supply and distribution had not been developed.

During the 1920's and until 1933, labor exchanges were utilized to place workers in positions where needed. The Administration for Organized Recruitment of Workers served the same purpose, beginning in the early 1930's, but it was not adequate to cope with the redistribution of workers caused by technological change and conditions of increased freedom of movement. The establishment of regional economic councils (*sovnarkhozy*) in the late 1950's and the efforts after 1965, under the economic reforms, to give enterprise directors greater control over labor resources tended further to reduce the central government's ability to cope with the problem of labor placement. By a joint Party-government decree in late 1966, state committees for utilization of labor reserves were established at the republic level and were given responsibility for recruitment and distribution of labor.

In order to better utilize seasonal workers, the central authority in 1966 issued a decree to permit the organization of industrial and other enterprises not connected with agricultural production on both collective and state farms. The successes of some factory managers to make economies in labor and to find new jobs for displaced workers were publicized, but the problem of placement continued. In the Russian republic some thirty local job-placement bureaus had been established by 1968, and more were planned. Although some policies of Brezhnev and Kosygin emphasized centralism, the trend toward local responsibility for job placement was obvious.

PRODUCTIVITY

The rise in labor productivity during the period of Soviet rule has been acclaimed as a major achievement of the Marxist-Leninist system. Official data using the beginning of the First Five-Year Plan as a basis for comparison indicated that productivity per worker had increased 1,306 percent in industry and 1,015 percent in construction between 1928 and 1967. The generally low level of productivity in comparison with the industrialized Western nations, however, is officially recognized. Statistics published by the Soviet government in 1967 showed that productivity of labor in industry was only 45 to 50 percent as high as that of the United States, while farm labor was only 20 to 25 percent as productive.

The comparatively low productivity is of continuing and increasing concern to the leadership, and economic plans for the 1970's demand substantially greater productivity in all areas of the economy. Labor utilization, which has often been wasteful in the past, has come under increased scrutiny by the economic planners, who now recognize the need for better distribution of labor, greater efficiency, more mechanization, and the upgrading of workers' qualifications. The economic reforms of the 1960's sometimes led to chaotic conditions in some sectors because of the arbitrary establishment of wages, prices, and incentives. In early 1970 the leadership, the managerial elite, and the economists state unanimously and openly that the conflicts must be resolved in order to reach the necessary increases in productivity (see ch. 30, Industry).

The October 1965 Statute on Enterprises, which aimed to improve productivity, accorded managers at individual establishments greater power to hire and fire employees, within limits established in the centrally controlled wage fund. Payment of bonuses from a material incentives fund at enterprise level also was provided. While there were reports of drastic layoffs at some enterprises, the indications were that more personnel had been added overall than had been dismissed during the period following the publication of the statute. Provisions of the statute that based fund allocations on the number of workers tended to prevail over those that aimed to effect manpower economy.

An experiment in the Shchekino Chemical Combine in Tula that began in 1967 provided for the firing of surplus workers and utilization of wage savings as incentive pay for the remaining staff. Fired workers were to be retrained during employment in enterprises where no labor surplus existed. During a two-year period, labor productivity rose by 87 percent, according to the Central Committee of the Communist Party of the Soviet Union (CPSU). Because of the success of the Shchekino experiment, the Central Committee published a decision in October 1969 to apply the methods used there on a general basis.

While there were less technical equipment and less mechanization per worker in comparison with the most advanced Western nations, there were other reasons for the relatively low productivity of Soviet labor. In some cases, work was poorly organized, leading to underutilization of available resources. Another common problem of enterprises was the poor distribution of workers as far as number and type were concerned. The prevalence of excess workers causing underutilization also has been a longstanding problem. Finally, incentives have been lacking, particularly in the agricultural sector (see ch. 30, Industry).

CHAPTER 33

LABOR RELATIONS AND ORGANIZATION

Workers' rights and the activities of organized labor are thoroughly controlled by the centralized authority of the Communist Party and the state. The trade unions, whose membership encompasses 95 percent of workers and employees in state enterprises, play an enormous role in enlisting the support of the masses to achieve the goals established by the Party. The basic interests of workers, such as workhours, wages, and working conditions, are regulated by labor legislation and the planning machinery of the controlled economy and are not subject to collective bargaining. Although unions exercised greater freedom of action in the 1960's than at any time since the 1920's and participated in production conferences, contract negotiations, and settlements of workers' grievances on a broader basis, the worker depended entirely on institutions under state control for improving his welfare.

Substantial improvements were made in wages, working conditions, and protection of workers' rights after the Twentieth Party Congress in 1956 but, as before, the priority of building a large industrial system and strengthening the military posture took precedence over workers' interests whenever there were competing requirements for resources. The advancements of the 1960's were encouraging to the worker, but shortages of consumers' goods and housing continued. Living standards of the worker in early 1970 still lagged well behind those of the industrialized Western European countries.

Trade union activities countrywide were controlled by the All-Union Central Council of Trade Unions, which stands at the apex of the huge were given increased responsibilities, and they continued to serve as the most important transmission belt between the Party and the masses.

THE WORKER AND TRADE UNIONS IN SOVIET SOCIETY

Both before and after the November 1917 Revolution, the Marxist-Leninist party looked to the working class as a primary source of strength to achieve its goals. Although there were variations and changes in labor policies, the domination of the party over matters relating to workers' interests and labor organizations has remained constant in theory and in practice.

Immediately before the Revolution of 1905, when labor unions were first established in Russia, Lenin recognized that the working class, particularly the industrial workers, could serve as an important force in effecting the revolutionary goals of the Russian Social Democratic Workers' Party. The proletariat as viewed by Lenin was an unwieldy mass that required the infusion of class consciousness and class struggle. The working class, he believed, was too much concerned with narrow and immediate objectives which, if pursued, would tend to sacrifice long-term objectives. Only the party serving as the vanguard of the proletariat could determine the long-range interests of the working class. Lenin's insistence on revolutionary means and rejection of evolutionary means was a major difference between the Bolshevik and Menshevik elements of the party before 1917.

From April to October 1917, Lenin and his followers utilized the Soviets of Workers' and Soldiers' Deputies and the factory committees, who were taking over control of enterprises, as the primary organizations to consolidate Bolshevik strength. After the proclamation of Lenin's April Theses, many workers were attracted by the Bolshevik slogan "All power to the Soviets." Seeing the factory committee as a vehicle to gain popular support, the Bolsheviks voiced their support for workers' control of production and distribution.

Once in control, Lenin's party almost immediately took steps to substitute state control for workers' control. A statute of November 27, 1917, subordinated labor to the national economic plan, which was under the control of the Council of People's Commissars. The council was made up entirely of leading party members and included a commissar of labor. Trade unions, which were shortly brought under party control, were substituted for factory committees as the representatives of the workers. In place of shared ownership and control by factory workers of individual enterprises, the Bolsheviks imposed state control, claiming that they were extending workers' control to all industry. Thereafter, the interests of labor were subordinated to those of the Communist Party.

Through the cult of labor the Party attempted to have the worker identify himself with the state and its possessions and perform work out of habit and duty as a contribution to the common good. Obedience to employers, the state, was considered proof of devotion to socialism and of unity with the collective will.

During the early 1920's top Communist Party leaders debated the role of trade unions. Trotsky's proposal for making them state organs for production was formally rejected; however, in practice trade unions did become organs of the state.

The general guidelines for the development of trade unions were contained in Lenin's resolution at the Tenth Party Congress in

1921. After pointing to the need for the strictest subordination of the trade unions to the Party, the resolution called for trade unions to do the following: provide the social base for the proletarian dictatorship exercised by the Party; attain their ends by persuasion (but in exceptional cases they could use coercion); serve as schools of communism for their members; have the broadest voluntary organization of industrial workers; take part in working out economic plans, norms for job performance, wage rates, and regulations for protecting workers; recommend candidates for administrative-economic positions; and serve as schools of discipline empowered to establish courts for trying violators of labor regulations in open session.

In 1929, with Stalin's power consolidated and Mikhail P. Tomsky's removal as chairman of the All-Union Central Council of Trade Unions, as well as a Politburo member, trade unions lost the limited freedom of action that they previously exercised. They became organs for the coercion of the working class and for the fulfillment of production goals of the five-year plans. Trade unions were called upon to cooperate in the promotion of the various campaigns for socialist emulation, first with factories challenging one another, beginning in 1929; then, competitions shifted to individual shockworkers, or *udarniki*, in 1930 and 1931 and, still later, in 1935 emphasis was placed on even more intense individual competitions, called Stakhanovism. As a further means to stimulate production, Stalin substituted piecework for time wages on as broad a basis as possible. By 1938 only 18 percent of workers received ordinary time wages.

In 1933 the Commissariat for Labor was abolished, and many functions of a quasi-governmental nature, including the administration of social insurance, were given to the Trade Union Central Council. The extreme measures of the Stalinist regime completely subjugated the trade unions and the individual workers. As an independent force to further the interests of workers, Soviet trade unions completely atrophied. Workers were tied to their jobs, and drastic penalties were imposed for even minor violations of labor discipline. Millions of workers were sentenced to forced labor in corrective labor camps, and for many there was little or no hope for liberation. Real wages did not reach their 1928 level until 1952. Workers' interests generally were sacrificed to the building of industry and a strong military complex.

A new era that brought improvements to workers and trade unions began in 1956 with the meeting of the Twentieth Party Congress. The improvements during the 1956—69 period included increased freedom for workers to change jobs, increased real wages, increased disability compensation, expanded maternity benefits for employed women, a shorter workweek, improved sanitary and safety conditions, and a more satisfactory system for settling workers' grievances.

The Twenty-second Party Congress promised within ten to twenty years grandiose future benefits, including a thirty-five-hour week, an apartment for every family (eventually rent free), and free transportation. The Twenty-third Party Congress in 1966 reaffirmed the broad, and generally beneficial, policies of the previous three congresses; however, Party leader Brezhnev reported that not all the planned measures for raising living standards could be realized, because agriculture failed to meet production targets, the rate of growth of labor productivity had declined, and additional defense investments were required. No mention was made of the grandiose specific future benefits that had been promised at the previous congress. The Five Year Plan for 1966—70 and actions taken in 1967 and 1968 continued the trend that began in 1956 to improve work hours, wages, and other benefits for workers.

Trade unions expanded their activities and increased their value to the state. Alexander Shelepin, chairman of the Trade Union Central Council, concluded his report to the Fourteenth Congress of USSR Trade Unions in 1968 by stating that trade unions, created and nurtured by the Party, inseparably link all their activities with it and that their source of strength is in guidance by the Party.

GOVERNMENTAL AGENCIES AND REGULATION OF LABOR

The responsibility for administering labor matters rests with a number of government and semiofficial agencies. The State Committee on Questions of Labor and Wages, established in 1955 under the Council of Ministers of the USSR, concerns itself primarily with productivity and wages. Operating directly under this committee is the Scientific Research Institute of Labor, which concentrates on collection of data and analysis of wage and production questions. The state committees on labor resource utilization at republic level, formed after a 1966 decree on this subject, operate under the central direction of the Labor Resources Department of the USSR State Planning Committee. Their main functions involve labor recruitment, placement, and resettlement (see ch. 32, The Labor Force). The work of the Ministry of Higher and Specialized Secondary Education and the State Committee for Vocational and Technical Training, both central government agencies, leans heavily toward manpower planning.

The Ministry of Finance exercises control over personnel staffing matters and administrative expenses of some budget-supported institutions. These agencies and enterprises are required to report personnel staffing schedules and administrative expense estimates annually. Exempted organizations include, among others, those sub-

690

ordinate to the Ministry of Defense and to the Committee for State Security. The number of agencies required to register staffing and administrative schedules with the Ministry of Finance declined steadily during the 1960's, and by 1966 only about 30 percent of some 800,000 institutions and enterprises were still required to register. Personnel staffing schedules and administrative expenses must still be reported, but the procedure is through the hierarchical structure of the enterprises to the responsible ministries rather than solely to the Ministry of Finance, thus relieving the latter of the almost impossible task of auditing the entire economic and administrative structure of the country.

There is no central agency for recruitment of personnel. The various governmental agencies exercise control over recruitment, dismissal, and other personnel actions within their own establishments; however, about 15 to 20 percent of the positions in the government and the economy are considered key positions and are controlled directly by the Party.

The 1936 Constitution enumerates liberal guarantees of personal freedom of Soviet citizens, including the right, as well as the obligation, to work, the right to rest and leisure, and the right to maintenance in old age and in case of sickness or incapacity. The extent to which these guarantees have been fulfilled depended upon the availability of funds and the priorities established by the ruling group. Sometimes the decrees of the central authorities were not consistent with the Constitution. For example, in 1940 a decree established an eight-hour workday even though the Constitution provided for a seven-hour day. After seven years the inconsistency was corrected by amending the Constitution. The legal foundations of Soviet labor are found in the Labor Code and the many decrees, statutes, and regulations relating to labor, rather than in the Consitution.

Labor law is highly uniform despite the fact that decrees may be issued by different agencies of the central government or by the republics. Labor legislation may be promulgated by the Presidium of the Supreme Soviet, the Supreme Soviet, the Council of Ministers, individual ministries concerned with economic matters, and the State Committee on Labor and Wages. The All-Union Central Council of Trade Unions has the right to initiate legislation, issue explanations of existing legislation, and to publish regulations and instructions that have binding force. The most important decrees are issued jointly by the Central Committee of the Party, the Council of Ministers, and the All-Union Central Council of Trade Unions. Others may be issued jointly by the All-Union Central Council of Trade Unions and a government agency.

The Labor Code of the Russian Soviet Federated Socialist Republic, adopted in 1922 and used in the other fourteen republics as well, in 1970 was still one of the principal regulations applying to persons in paid employment. It has been amended and supplemented by hundreds of decrees and regulations. A new code was drafted in 1959 and 1960 but, for reasons that have not been made clear, it was not issued. Labor legislation after 1955 tended to overcome the harsher laws of the 1930's and 1940's. Included in the many measures that generally improved conditions for workers were decrees, resolutions, or statutes on minimum wages; trade union rights and duties; length of workweek and number of workdays; pensions; and labor disputes. Model work rules were issued in 1957 on systematized hiring, dismissal procedures, factory regulations on attendance, safety clothing, sanitation, and penalties for violations of labor discipline.

Violations of rules may result in warning, reproof, reprimand, demotion, or reduced pay for a specified period; absence from work without sufficient reason or persistent breach of rules may result in dismissal. The director of an enterprise may take action, or he may turn a violation over to the Comrades' Court, which is elected from enterprise personnel and is not a part of the regular court system (see ch. 22, The Legal System). In case of dismissal the worker may appeal directly to the civil courts. Top-level managerial personnel involved in violations may appeal directly to the senior administrative agency, and persons under punishment may appeal to the organ that imposed the punishment.

Penalties for avoiding socially useful work or leading an antisocial parasitic way of life tend to be severe. A wide variety of offenses fell under this category. Included were those that involved exploitation of land, housing, or vehicles for personal gain in excess of that permitted by law. A 1961 decree provided that persons found guilty of such practices were to be deported to specifically designated localities where they must work for a period of two to five years. In some cases this sentence has been imposed by the collective of workers at the enterprise, provided it was approved by the executive committee of the local Soviet. Violations of labor regulations by employers, the state, reported by union officials, included arbitrary illegal discharge and transfer of workers, the imposition of excessive overtime work, the introduction of machinery without proper safeguards, and failure to implement safety regulations. Trade union leaders encourage their members to attempt to call individual managers or directors to account, but indictment of the employer is avoided.

Soviet labor law, reflecting the paternalistic character of Party and state, aimed to protect, guide, and train both employer and workers, inculcating a consciousness of mutual rights and obligations. Although bargaining power of workers and unions was narrowly limited, there seemed to be little doubt that civil courts

692

generally made a conscientious effort to protect the rights that were accorded by law.

There was little governmental machinery provided for the settlement of labor disputes, the term used to indicate workers' grievances in the application of labor regulations and the differences between unions and managers. The emphasis after the 1957 decree on labor disputes was to make rapid settlement by the concerned parties as near as possible to the source of difficulty. The aim of grievance procedures was to develop a close and lasting relationship between workers and employer.

The factory labor disputes commissions and the factory committees were the primary means to settle disputes at the enterprise level. If not satisfied with the results at his place of employment, the worker could seek redress by making an appeal to the local People's Court, which was the lowest level of the court system; if further appeal was desired, it could be made to a higher court. Most labor disputes arose out of application of wage rates and production standards, dismissal from a position, penalties for breaches of discipline, and violation by employers of workers' rights. Workers could not challenge labor laws, but they could dispute the fairness with which laws were applied.

The commission on labor disputes to which the worker could appeal was made up of an equal number of representatives from the factory committee and from managers. This commission could resolve grievances by agreement of parties concerned, but it did not have the authority to impose a solution. A worker could appeal to the factory committee if the labor disputes commission did not resolve the problem. The factory committee could impose a binding decision, and further appeal to higher trade union bodies was not permitted unless the decision was made without the required quorum. If a worker appealed to the civil courts, the union could send a representative to assist in protecting his rights, but this was apparently done less than the worker could reasonably expect. There was considerable evidence that the factory committees were more concerned with the interests of production and good relations with the managers than with the interests of the worker, a situation that frequently caused dissatisfaction.

In the negotiation of contracts and other matters in which trade unions dealt with managers, the worker relied upon the union to look after his interests. When differences could not be resolved by local unions and managers, appeal was made to higher trade union and administrative authorities. In the 1960's there were indications that Party and government officials were demanding greater effort on the part of unions in the protection of workers' rights. Strikes were not prohibited, but none had been called by trade unions since the period of the New Economic Policy (Novaya Ekonomicheskaya

Politika—NEP) of the 1920's. Soviet authorities state simply that in a socialist society there is no need for strikes. Western observers, however, attribute their absence to rigid Party control of the economy. Unofficial reports of wildcat strikes included accounts of serious disorders in Temur Tau in 1954 and Novocherkassk in 1962.

WORKING CONDITIONS

Opportunities for employment and the basic terms of employment, such as wages and work hours, are regulated generally by labor legislation and the economic plans. Nevertheless, in the 1960's the increased freedom to change jobs plus increased demands for labor gave the worker greater latitude to choose his place of employment by an enterprise, a prospective employee had to submit his workbook and internal passport. Only in exceptional cases were references or other documents required. The workbook contains biographical data and record of employment. Disciplinary penalties may not be noted in the workbook. The internal passport lists the name, date and place of birth, residence, and nationality. In the state sector of the economy about 90 percent of hiring was by the enterprise managers directly, and terms of employment, in conformity with existing law, were generally by verbal agreement. Written agreements were required for employment in the far north and other remote areas to obtain the privileges and bonuses that were not accorded for ordinary employment. Union membership was not a condition for obtaining employment, but pressure was placed on workers to join.

The standard workweek for most workers and salaried employees, as established by a 1967 decree, was five days, with a total of 41 hours. A shorter workweek was authorized earlier for persons engaged in underground work and in arduous or hazardous occupations, for youths sixteen and seventeen years of age, and other groups such as teachers and doctors. In 1967 the actual hours worked per week in industry averaged 40.4 and in mining (including coal) 38.9 hours. The 1967 decree also stipulated that wherever the character of production and working conditions required, the six-day week would continue. Overtime work was permitted under special conditions but was limited to 120 hours per year. Refusal to work overtime was considered a breach of labor discipline and was punishable. One result of the five-day workweek and two-day weekend was increased demands for consumer and other services that were already in short supply.

During the late 1960's paid annual vacations for most wage and salary earners varied from fifteen to forty-eight workdays. In 1968 approximately 60 percent received from fifteen to eighteen days, 26 percent received from nineteen to twenty-four days, and about

14 percent received from twenty-five to forty-eight days. Increased, or bonus, leave was permitted only to workers in arduous or hazardous jobs. Sick leave was permitted only with a physician's authorization. Full pay was given to persons who were absent because of work injury. Pay during periods of illness unrelated to work ranged from 50 percent to full wages, nonunion members receiving only half the benefits accorded to union members. Maternity leave under normal circumstances was 112 days, and compensation varied from two-thirds to full pay, depending on length of service, union membership, and other factors.

Monthly cash earnings for all wage and salaried employees averaged R112.5 (1 ruble equals US$1.10) in 1968. This was an increase of R33.9 over the 1960 average. If consumer services and other benefits were included, Soviet authorities claimed that the average wage was increased by R35 to R40. In 1967, when the average monthly cash pay for all state employees was R103, the average pay by branch of the economy was: industry, R111.7; construction, R118.1; state and industrial enterprise farms, R84.1; transportation, R115; communications, R78; trade, supplies, and restaurants, R82.5; housing and communal services, R78.6; health services, R82.4; education and culture, R96.5; science and scientific services, R122; finance and insurance, R93; and state and cooperative institutions, R112.5.

Pay differentials have prevailed from the very beginning of Communist rule. In 1965 the use of material incentives to boost production was reemphasized in connection with the new economic reforms. Communist theorists claimed that the principle "the higher the skill of the worker and the greater his production, the more he is paid" is applicable only during the socialist stage of society. Only when the transition is made to a Communist society will the law "from each according to his ability, to each according to his needs" prevail.

The limited data that have become available indicate that the basic pay scales for government officials of minister and deputy minister rank, top-level executives in enterprises, and senior professors are four or more times higher than the average reported for all workers in state employment. In addition, stipends or benefits may be paid for special qualifications or to holders of positions of deference. For example, it was reported that a full member of the Academy of Sciences in 1969 was entitled to a monthly allowance of R500, an addition which almost doubled his basic pay. Extra income could be derived from scholarly work, such as the writing of articles, monographs, or textbooks.

The differential between the highest and lowest reported wage and salary scales was approximately halved during the 1960's; however, the differential in total earnings between the average wage earner and the highest level of employees remained high. Increases in the minimum wage after 1956 contributed greatly to the compression of the extremes in salary scales. In January 1968 the minimum monthly wage was raised to R60. The number of wage earners who were paid according to piecework declined during the 1960's, but a majority were still paid by that system in 1968.

After a period of more than two decades, during which there had been no increase in real wages, a gradual rise began in 1952, and over the next fifteen years real wages increased by 70 percent. Continuing shortages of consumers' goods and housing prevented a corresponding rise in living standards. A Soviet economist estimated that the average per capita real income for the working population in the early 1960's was 55 percent of that of the working population in the United States.

TRADE UNION ORGANIZATION AND FUNCTIONS

The role of trade unions in the post-Stalin era was set forth in a lengthy resolution of the Party Central Committee in December 1957. The organization and regulations for the operations of trade unions were updated in the statute or constitution adopted by the Thirteenth All-Union Congress of Trade Unions in 1963. These basic documents were implemented and supplemented by various decrees, resolutions, instructions, and regulations.

The functions of trade unions are to develop Communist attitudes among working people and to promote cooperation and participation in the building of communism, to put forth an all-out effort in building the technical and material base of communism and to protect the rights and interests of workers that are accorded by law. Trade unions do not have the function of conducting collective bargaining with managers on basic wage rates, work hours, and other matters, because these are fixed by law; however, they negotiate and cooperate with the managers in working out agreements within the framework established by the state.

The basic principles for trade union organization and operation are established by the Party. These principles have not always been observed, but Lenin's proposals adopted in 1921 continued, in early 1970, to provide basic guidance. "That unions must carry on all their activities under the Party leadership" is a fundamental and unchanging principle. Although the influence of the Party in trade unions, purportedly, comes from persuasion by Party members within the unions, the Party issues directives to unions, and Party members dominate the union leadership, particularly at the higher levels.

The principle of "democratic centralism" applies to trade unions as well as to the political system. This provides that union organs

696

from top to bottom are elected by the members; however, all activities must be carried on, and all decisions made, in accordance with the union statutes and the will of the higher trade union organs. Within the limits set by higher authority, the fullest discussion, criticism, and initiative are urged. The "production principle" of organization provides that the national union for an industry has control of all union members in that industry. The principle that unions protect workers' interests has received emphasis only since the mid-1950's, although it was specified in the 1922 Labor Code. The principle that unions are "schools of communism" has been applied fully from the very beginning, when the trade unions came under Bolshevik control in early 1918.

In 1968 Soviet trade unions had a total membership of 86.1 million. About 95 percent of wage and salary earners in state employ, full-time students in higher and secondary specialized educational institutions, and students in technical trade schools were union members. Of the total membership, 14.3 million were in rural unions, including approximately 3 million machine operators and specialists on collective farms. All wage and salary earners were eligible for membership. Most of those who failed to join were young people who had not settled into permanent positions. The privileges of union membership—such as preferential benefits from social insurance and priority in receiving accommodations at sanitoriums, health resorts, children's camps, and nursery facilities—could not be passed up without a significant loss. Union dues were based on pay and ranged from 0.5 to 1 percent of earnings.

Within the trade union organization, the All-Union Congress of Trade Unions is, theoretically, the supreme authority. By statute, it is supposed to meet at least once every four years, but it has not always done so. Between congresses, all-union conferences may be called to consider urgent problems. Delegates to the congresses are elected by the union membership but, instead of acting as labor spokesmen, they act as after-the-fact corroborators of actions and proposals already made by Party and union leaders. The Fourteenth Congress of USSR Trade Unions, which met from February 27 to March 4, 1968, unanimously approved all resolutions and actions, and its proceedings were thoroughly organized and controlled.

The congress elects the All-Union Central Council of Trade Unions, which is charged with directing all activities between congresses. The day-to-day work of the Central Council is carried on by its elected presidium and secretariat. Also, it maintains scientific institutes that conduct research and provide services relating to the safety and health of workers. Two higher schools of the trade union movement train union personnel; one in Moscow specializes in labor economics, and the other in Leningrad prepares personnel for educational and cultural work in trade union clubs. A trade union facility in Moscow, the Hall of Columns, is utilized for assemblies and, when appropriate, as a place for the public to view the remains of Party notables.

The Fourteenth Congress elected a 304-member central council, which in turn elected a twenty-seven-member presidium. The all-union trade union organization, of which the Central Council is the directing force, controls the operations of the Republic Inter-Union Trade Union councils, the Regional Inter-Union Trade Union councils, and the national industrial unions, whose membership extends countrywide by branch of industry. The Central Council and the central committees of the national unions work closely with the various government agencies at the all-union level. The extent to which the union leadership has influenced wages and other benefits for the worker is not clear. Credit for improvements is taken by the Party. Alexander Shelepin, a member of the Politburo, was elected to head the Central Council in 1967, succeeding V.V. Grishin, a candidate member of the Politburo who had held the chairmanship since 1956.

Each of the national industrial unions has a central committee in Moscow, which is subordinated to the Central Council. The number of unions has fluctuated: in 1967 Soviet publications reported twenty-two but, at the Fourteenth Congress of USSR Trade Unions, Shelepin indicated that the shipbuilding union had been added and communications had been separated from road transport, thus making a total of twenty-four. There are indications that at least one other may exist, in the atomic energy industry. According to Soviet sources, the following fields had industrial unions: aviation; geological prospecting; state trade and consumer cooperatives; government employment; railways; cultural work; timber; paper, and woodworking; machine building; health; local industry and municipal services; metallurgy; sea and river transport; oil and chemicals; food; education and scientific institutions; radio and electronics; highway transport; agriculture and state purchasing; construction and building materials; textile and light industry; coal mining; power and electricity; shipbuilding; and communications.

The authority of each of the central committees of the national unions is transmitted through its regional offices to factory, plant, or local committees, which in turn transmit it through the shop committees to the trade union groups. The main fields for which the central committee of each national union sets up departments are labor and wages, safety and protection of labor, and international relations. The principles for organization and operations of unions are laid down in basic statutes and are highly uniform throughout the country. Lines of communication extend from the shops to the top offices of the national unions. Indications are that workers have improved their capability to express dissatisfactions and to move national union bodies to take greater interest in their welfare during the 1960's.

The trade union activists are the functionaries through whom the unions and Party maintain contact with the masses and attempt to achieve labor goals. Meetings, banners, slogans, news media of all types, and clubrooms are utilized to motivate workers. The principal trade union publication is *Trud* (Labor), a newspaper published by the Central Council. Many other periodicals concerning labor interests are published, and widespread use is made of wall newspapers and bulletin boards. At the lowest level the trade union group organizer, assisted by the cultural organizer, has the duty to develop group esprit, instill an understanding of Party policy and aims, and encourage workers to raise their educational and technical qualifications.

Engaged in union work at the beginning of 1968 were 1,985 regional committees, 18,925 city committees, 587,000 locals (with more than fifteen members), and 1,841,200 groups (with fewer than fifteen members). Of the 5.5 million persons serving on committees and councils, 1.5 million were Party members and 3 million were women. From the all-union to district and city levels, committee and council members are elected from lists of candidates that have been approved by the corresponding level Party committee.

At the lower levels committee or council membership frequently consists of almost equal proportions of Party and non-Party members. At the top levels all, or nearly all, committee or council members are Party members. In 1968 the chairman of the Central Council reported that 95 percent of the persons performing union functions were unpaid volunteers. Nevertheless, the trade union bureaucracy is gigantic and provides many of the most secure positions for the Soviet elite.

At the enterprise level the highest authority of the trade union is the general meeting. A two-thirds majority must be present for a meeting to be considered authoritative. The factory or plant committee provides the leadership and carries out union functions on a continuing basis. In large plants there may be as many as 25 members on this committee. One paid union worker is authorized in enterprises with 500 to 2,000 members; greater numbers are permitted for larger enterprises, those with over 35,000 workers being allowed 10 paid union workers. The factory committee sets up permanent commissions for various facets of their work—for housing and welfare, production work, wages, protection of labor, social insurance, cultural work, and others. Representatives of the factory committee participate in the work of the labor disputes commission and make up one-half of its total membership. The commissions of the factory committee are usually headed by a factory committee member, and union members are called upon to contribute.

The trade union group is the basic element of the union. It elects a group organizer and other leaders for the various union activities. In small plants the trade union group may carry on the function usually performed by the factory committee, under the direction of a district or other headquarters of their national union. Under these circumstances the trade union organizer and the plant director constitute the labor disputes commission. Trade union members work jointly with people's control committees in many areas of public control, including housing, transportation, and consumer services (see ch. 5, The Political System).

A primary function of unions is to develop the cooperation and initiative of the masses and bring them into the discussions on production planning and administration in order to achieve the goals set by centralized authority. The various socialist competitions and recreational and cultural programs aim to enhance worker interest and to reduce absenteeism, tardiness, indifference, and failure to respond to instructions and orders. Competitions take many forms and, although claims are made that they are self-generated by individual workers, brigades, and even whole plants, the central trade union, government, and administrative organizations formulate comprehensive plans and issue regulatory directives to ensure wide participation.

Winners of competitions are honored with titles such as "Master of Golden Hands," for an individual within a plant, or "Communist Labor," for a brigade or enterprise. Monetary and other benefits may be awarded as well. During the 1963—67 period a union official reported that 704,000 persons had received orders and medals of the Soviet Union for outstanding performance. The recreational, cultural, and educational programs to improve health, morale, level of education, and understanding of Party objectives are designed to involve as many workers as possible. In 1968 membership in trade union sport societies was 22.4 million, and almost 9 million workers were participating in educational programs from the general through higher education levels.

To further their recreation programs, trade unions in 1968 made use of approximately 20,000 clubs and centers, 36,000 large libraries, 1,700 museums, and 40,000 motion picture projectors and sponsored amateur technical and artistic groups. Health resort and vacation accommodations, supported from social insurance funds, are included in the list of benefits to Soviet workers; however, between 1963 and 1967 less than 10 percent of workers spent their vacations at trade union sanitoriums and rest homes.

Trade unions have a direct and important obligation to spur new technology and innovations in production work. Scientific-technical societies and the societies of inventors and rationalizers within the trade unions are urged to play important roles. Membership in these organizations in 1968 numbered 7.5 million, and it was reported that 11 million of their proposals had been applied during the 1963—67 period.

During the 1960's a greater emphasis was placed on trade union and worker participation in planning and administering production programs than ever before. In 1968 permanent functioning production conferences that enlisted some 5 million workers and employees were operating at 138,000 enterprises to evaluate proposals for improving economic performance. Although providing some know-how for increasing production, these conferences have increased workers' participation in the direction of their enterprises to only a limited extent and have involved workers only in relatively minor matters.

The collective agreements between trade unions and managers were considered as a valuable tool to acquaint workers with their obligations and privileges, rather than instruments for collective bargaining. Some 100,000 collective agreements were made each year in the late 1960's, but only a fraction of enterprises were authorized to make contracts. Subjects included in the contracts were production goals, socialist comptitions, wages, premium payments, job evaluation, and housing. Union participation in checks on plan fulfillment was encouraged as a further means to educate workers and give them an interest in production.

Trade unions have played a major role in the administration of social insurance since 1933, when the Commissariat of Labor was disbanded. In 1968 the chairman of the Central Council reported that unions controlled almost R14 billion of the state social insurance budget. Disability and maternity benefits and programs to provide accommodations at sanitoriums and rest homes are administered by the unions, in cooperation with the Ministry of Public Health and other governmental organizations.

At the enterprise level the commission on social insurance, assisted by insurance delegates, does the bulk of the work, most of which is performed by volunteers. In 1965 about 1.6 million rank-and-file union members were working on social insurance tasks. The commission on social insurance at the factory level determines eligibility for benefits and the amount to be paid in each case. Decisions are subject to the approval of the factory committee. The commission also controls the allocation of privileges at rest homes, sanitoriums, and other facilities. It trains the insurance delegates whose duties include visits to the sick and the provision of medical service and tasks concerned with payments of benefits. The factory committee also has representatives on pension committees of the local governments, which make decisions on pensions.

Supervision, inspection and enforcement of safety measures are primary responsibilities of the trade unions. Research institutes attached to the Central Council study occupational hazards and provide services relating to safety. The council formulates and issues regulations that are binding on all enterprises. The trade union technical inspectors, for all practical purposes, serve in the capacity of government officials. When they find a violation, they submit a written order to the managers and demand that it be corrected. An inspector may request the trade union to exert pressure to force corrective action, and he may impose a small fine on the managers. With approval from higher union authority, he may close the enterprise.

The labor protection commission of the factory committee attempts to improve safety standards and hygiene as well as to protect workers' rights concerning work hours, but it has no enforcement powers. Violations of safety regulations may be reported to the factory committee or the technical inspector. A large part of the safety program is carried on by union volunteers. In 1968 there were 2.5 million volunteer technical inspectors.

PARTICIPATION IN INTERNATIONAL LABOR ACTIVITIES

Soviet trade unions have been particularly active in promoting relations among socialist-oriented labor organizations worldwide. They are a leading force in the World Federation of Trade Unions (WFTU), which has been completely Communist controlled since 1950 and purports to be the most active social force against capitalism and imperialism. Some 200 organizations from 124 countries attended the Seventh Congress of the WFTU, which was held in Budapest in October 1969. Also Soviet trade unions cooperate with those from member countries of the Council for Mutual Economic Assistance and from Yugoslavia on matters concerning labor (see ch. 35, Foreign Economic Relations).

After rejoining the International Labor Organization (ILO) in 1954, the Soviets participated in setting standards and in technical assistance activities. Soviet membership in ILO from 1934 to 1940 had little influence, because participation was limited and sporadic. The election of a representative of the All-Union Central Council of Trade Unions to the Administration Council of ILO for the first time in 1966 was acclaimed an achievement by the Soviet trade union leadership. At the Fourteenth Congress of USSR Trade Unions in 1968, Chairman Shelepin of the Central Council stated that Soviet trade unions were striving to strengthen their ties with the trade unions of capitalist countries and also noted that contact with the trade unions of China and Albania had essentially ceased. Moreover, according to Shelepin, the anti-Communist policy of some leaders of the International Conference of Free Trade Unions, as well as leaders of United States labor organizations, continued to oppose the establishment of trade union contacts with the Soviet Union.

A great effort is made to promote visits and exchanges of labor groups. Between 1963 and 1967 delegations from 110 countries visited the Soviet Union and more than 1,000 Soviet trade union delegations visited foreign countries. Particular attention has been paid to the developing areas of Asia, Africa, and Latin America. In 1968 about 500 trade union activists from these areas had completed courses in Moscow that aimed to strengthen union leadership and promote Communist-oriented activity among the peopel. There is little doubt that a major and primary objective of Soviet efforts in international labor relations is to extend and strengthen Communist influence among working people and promote closer friendship and cooperation with the Soviet Union.

CHAPTER 34

DOMESTIC TRADE

In early 1970 domestic trade was almost exclusively a government monopoly. The only exception was the operation of collective farm markets, which accounted for a small percentage of the overall retail trade. Aside from the collective farm markets, all intra-industry exchange of goods and all retail trade were directed by some agency of the national government or comparable agencies at lower governmental levels. From the beginning of the First Five-Year Plan in 1928, to the death of Stalin in 1953, the main thrust of Soviet economic endeavor was directed toward heavy industrialization and the consumer received scant attention from the country's economic planners. By the late 1950's and more so by the 1960's, however, consumer goods industries received greater allocations from the state budget, and domestic retail trade had grown space. Emphasis was still on heavy industry, but the needs of the consumer were receiving greater attention in the annual economic plans. Because of many years of neglect, however, this sector of the economy lagged behind that of most other industrialized nations.

In early 1970 the consumer had at his disposal a variety of stores in which to satisfy his basic needs. Urban dwellers were able to shop at large and small department stores and centrally located grocery stores as well as many small neighborhood groceries and specialty shops. A large network of government-owned and -operated restaurants, bookstores, and pharmacies was also available. The city dwellers could also shop at the collective farm markets, which often sold assortments of food products not readily available in the state stores.

Various categories of workers had stores and restaurants available at their places of employment but, by 1970, these had declined in importance in the overall retail trade picture. Military personnel and civilian employees of the Ministry of Defense were able to buy from a post exchange system that reportedly continued to do a large volume of retail trade. Rural inhabitants most often shopped in consumer cooperatives, of which a high percentage of the rural population were members. Many peasants continued to shop whenever possible in cities and towns, where quantity and quality of goods usually surpassed those found in their rural cooperatives.

In 1967 over 6.7 million persons, or almost 8 percent of the total working force, were employed in some form of trade. Another 7.5 percent of the labor force was engaged either in transportation or communications. Taxes on the internal exchange of goods and services, which included the turnover (sales) tax, deductions from the profits of state enterprises, taxes on the incomes of employees, and other miscellaneous revenues, netted the government about 63 percent of its annual revenue in the late 1960's.

Price setting for all commodities is a function of the government either at national level or at republic and lower levels. Prices do not always genuinely reflect the costs of production and distribution and have sometimes been maintained at artificially high or low rates in order to attain some political or social goal. Prices have not always been uniform in urban and rural areas, but the trend during the 1960's was toward equalization. Prices in the collective farm markets are free to rise and fall according to supply and demand.

Transportation and communications are also government monopolies and, because of the sheer size of the country and severe climatic conditions, have always presented difficult problems for the economic planners. Moscow is the hub of the transportation and communications networks and, in 1970, most of the better facilities were still concentrated west of the Ural Mountains. All kinds of transportation have received attention insofar as budgetary allocations, new construction, and development are concerned but, in 1970, railroads still carried the major share of the country's traffic and were still considered to be overloaded.

DISTRIBUTION OF PRODUCER GOODS

Intraindustry distribution of producer goods and raw materials is generally directed by the central planners and is referred to as material-technical supply. For example, a ball bearing plant is directed in its annual plan to supply a specific quantity of its product to a machine tool plant or several such users. In fulfilling such allocations, the ball bearing plan accomplishes its function in the socialist economy. There is no cash transaction but, since the economic reforms of the mid-1960's, it is not sufficient merely to fulfill an assigned quota. The enterprise manager has become responsible for the efficiency of his operation and the quality of his product. Subordinate to the USSR Council of Ministers is the State Committee for Material-Technical Supply, whose chairman has ministerial rank. The function of this committee is to supervise the implementation of the plans for distribution of raw materials and producer goods.

Each industrial enterprise submits an annual procurement plan, stating its requirements for the next year to its supervisory organization, which has the authority to change the plan by lowering the requirements. Purchases of essential goods, however, are seldom made directly between the buyer and seller. Definite procedures through established channels must be followed, and these generally depend on the item needed. The purchase of necessary commodities must first go through the purchasing department of the concern to determine whether they are included in the procurement plan. The purchasing department then seeks permission from a higher organization to make the purchase. The higher organization, reviewing the request, issues instructions both to the purchaser to buy the goods and to the seller to sell the goods.

In compliance with such instructions, two firms enter into a contract specifying the amount, quality, price, time, and mode of delivery. Shipments of large quantities of an item are usually made directly from the manufacturer to the purchaser. The shipment of small quantities is not direct, and purchases and shipment are made through a wholesale organization, which is an adjunct of the ministry controlling the production of that product. Usually these wholesale organizations purchase large amounts of goods and store them pending resale to small purchasers.

These procedures, however, may vary according to the kind of product that is the object of the transaction. The government has divided commodities into four categories: funded, planned-centralized, planned-decentralized, and decentralized. Funded commodities are those considered most important by the government, and their distribution is highly regulated and controlled by the State Planning Committee of the USSR Council of Ministers. Purchases of these goods can be made only if the order is accompanied by a special allocation order, which specifies both the purchaser's authorization to make the purchase and the exact amount that he may buy.

The distribution of planned-centralized commodities, being of secondary importance, is governed either by the USSR ministries in respect to goods they control or by the republic councils of ministers. The distribution of planned-decentralized goods is made by local governmental agencies or by local divisions of the wholesale organization of the producing firm. Decentralized goods, those considered the least strategic, are goods that are both manufactured and used in a local area. Sales of these goods require no prior authorization from national or republic organizations.

Failure to comply with the contractual specifications for delivery, kind, and quality of products results in fines and forfeits for the guilty firm or agency as determined by an arbitration board. Material liability is borne by the enterprise that caused the breach of contract. The case may be that the enterprise that appears outwardly liable for failure to meet its contracted obligations is not the enterprise at fault. One of its suppliers may have defaulted on the delivery of a specific item necessary for the contracting firm's production. If this is the case, then liability would be shared and apportioned.

In most cases of arbitration, the primary supplier has been found guilty. Even though an enterprise may have to pay fines, it is also able to collect fines from its producers, and there have been many instances where the fines exacted by an enterprise exceeded the amount of fines it had paid out, thus adding to its overall profits.

WHOLESALE TRADE

Wholesaling activities are carried on completely by organs of the state according to the plans that are formulated and handed down by the planning committees existing at all levels of government, from national to local. The basic wholesale units are depots, storerooms, and warehouses under the jurisdiction of local Soviets; at the provincial level wholesale trade organizations and wholesale offices are supervised by provincial Soviets. The next step in the wholesale hierarchy consists of the autonomous republic and union republic ministries of trade, and at the top of the pyramid is the Ministry of Trade of the USSR Council of Ministers.

Wholesale agencies are usually of two kinds: purchasing and shipping. Although classical Marxism decried the role of middlemen in trade, direct exchange of goods was impossible in a modern society, and the private wholesale organizations that existed during the New Economic Policy (Novaya Ekonomicheskaya Politika— NEP) of the 1920's were converted into a network of government-operated purchasing and shipping agencies to facilitate the flow of goods to the government and cooperative retail networks. From the First Five Year Plan in 1928 to the 1966—70 plan, there have been countless reorganizations of the wholesale trade structure, usually alternating between decentralization and greater centralization. The economic reforms of the post-Khrushchev leadership emphasized greater efficiency and profitability in wholesale trade and also placed much greater emphasis on direct contact between retailer and producer in specific categories where the wholesaler can be effectively bypassed.

RETAIL TRADE

Domestic trade is divided into three categories: state owned and operated, cooperatively owned and operated but state controlled, and collective farm or free markets. State stores, which primarily serve urban areas, handled about 66 percent of the total retail trade in the late 1960's, rural cooperatives accounted for about 30 percent, and the remaining 4 percent fell to the collective farm markets.

State Stores

The entire distributive function of the government-operated sphere of internal trade, according to Soviet sources, was handled in 1969 through about 850,000 retail outlets employing almost 3 million persons. Plans called for the addition of 13,000 new outlets each year but, at the beginning of 1970, officials admitted that the construction of new retail facilities had fallen far behind schedule. The existing retail outlets include tiny street kiosks as well as huge department stores. General policy and planning for all trade are functions of the USSR State Planning Committee of the USSR Council of Ministers; the bulk of the executive function, however, falls on the USSR Ministry of Trade.

A large variety of retail outlets serve the needs of the urban populations throughout the country. Most are state owned and operated, and employees, whether they number in the hundreds in a large department store or just one person operating a street kiosk, are employed by the state. The two kinds of outlets usually found in urban areas are department stores and specialized stores. The latter deal in one product or kind of product, such as shoes or clothing; but in Moscow there is a specialized department store called Children's World, which handles everything needed by children, from babies to teenagers. Another famous Moscow store, the State Department Store (Gosudarstvennyy Universalnyy Magazin—GUM), installed a computer in 1969, according to *Izvestia*, to assist in the handling and ordering of the 330,000 different items sold by GUM. A photograph in another publication about the same time showed a GUM salesgirl using an abacus. *Izvestia* also stated that GUM was serviced by 128 warehouses, which employed 8,000 persons, that 200,000 individuals pass through GUM's doors every day.

Most food purchases in the cities are made in a variety of state stores, all of which are under the jurisdiction of the various ministries of trade. In large cities, stores are usually organized in chains known as trade organizations, such as the Russian Meat and Fish Trade Organization, which has several retail outlets and is subordinate to the Ministry of Trade of the Russian Soviet Federated Socialist Republic. Other examples are the Moscow Cultural Trade Organization, which, among other merchandise, sells television sets, and the Floral Cultivation and Merchandising Trade Organization, which has forty-five outlets in Moscow for the sale of flowers. The manager of the latter complained in 1968 that he did not have the authority to lower prices when his flowers began to wilt and therefore could not compete with the peasants who were allowed to sell homegrown flowers on street corners and could set their own prices.

Complaints were also prevalent in the Soviet press about the shortage of retail outlets of all kinds. Premier Kosygin in an economic message stated that construction of stores was falling far behind the plan for the 1966—70 period. New apartment complexes were supposed to include facilities for retail trade but often, because of redtape or mismanagement, no stores were built, causing residents to travel long distances to purchase basic needs. One trade official also complained in 1969 about the proliferation of specialty grocery stores stating, "The shopper buys fruit and vegetables in one store, goes to another for canned goods, then to another for meat, and to a fourth for dairy products." Committees of the Supreme Soviet of the USSR studied the domestic trade problems in 1969 and urged reorganization and greater efficiency to meet customer demand.

All restaurants in the nation are also considered to be part of the state retail trade network and, like other outlets, are under the ministries of trade. Restaurants include one-room teashops and snackbars as well as large hotel dining facilities. The operation of public dining halls is a huge business in the Soviet Union and is estimated at 10 percent of all retail trade. It also received a share of criticism in the press as workers complained, for example, that they waited in line for inordinate periods simply because dining facilities did not have enough chinaware.

In addition to the USSR Ministry of Trade and similar ministries at lower governmental echelons, various other agencies are also involved in the administration and supervision of domestic trade. The USSR Ministry of Defense, for example, has its own Main Administration for Trade, through which it operates a vast network of stores and restaurants serving the needs of military personnel as well as civilian defense employees. In the late 1960's, estimates of annual turnover in military trade organizations were as high as R2 billion (1 ruble equals US$1.10) to R3 billion.

Another ministry engaged in retail trade was the USSR Ministry of Culture and its namesake ministries at lower levels. Historically, the Ministry of Culture had administered the sale of books throughout the nation but, by 1970, most retail book outlets in rural areas had been absorbed by cooperatives; in the cities many department stores were also in the book business. Many specialized bookshops were still administered by the Ministry of Culture.

The USSR Ministry of Communications has the responsibility for the distribution and sale of newspapers and periodicals throughout the nation and, similar to other national agencies, operates through republic ministries and local agencies. Drugstores are administered by the USSR Ministry of Public Health.

A separate Soviet retail institution that forms a part of the state trade network is known as the Workers Supply Departments. These retail outlets are found in numerous factories and enterprises and cater to the needs only of the employees of the specific enterprise. In a broad sense these stores may be compared to factory cafeterias in Western nations but, in addition to meals, Workers Supply Departments sell groceries and manufactured consumer goods. In previous times of extreme shortages, these stores were important outlets in the overall trade network, and some fortunate employees were able to purchase food and other goods that were often unavailable to the general public. During the 1960's, with the increase in number of retail stores throughout the nation and the increase in the supply of consumer goods, Workers Supply Departments lost much of their previous significance.

Consumer Cooperatives

The consumer cooperative network is the rural counterpart of the urban retail network previously described. Although rural retail trade is concentrated in cooperatives rather than in outlets directly administered by the state, government control equals that of the state retail network. Planning and policymaking are accomplished, ultimately, by the USSR State Planning Committee as is the case with urban domestic trade. Membership in some 18,000 cooperative societies exceeded 55 million in the late 1960's, and over 300,000 retail outlets employing 2 million people served the rural population.

The basic unit of the huge cooperative trade network is the village cooperative, which operates stores and restaurants in thousands of villages throughout the country. Some retail outlets are one-room shops in private homes but, in larger villages and district centers, small department stores form part of the cooperative network. It is not mandatory that a villager be a member of a cooperative to make purchases in a village shop; however, members do receive preferential treatment in the matter of purchasing scarce consumer goods.

Consumer cooperatives are organized on a hierarchical basis; local members send representatives to regional meetings from which delegates are elected to attend meetings of the republic consumer associations. From republic conferences, delegates are elected to attend the Congress of Consumer Cooperatives, which is supposed to meet every four years. Elections to the various meetings, conferences, and congresses have been pro forma affairs, wherein the members usually confirm delegates who have been preselected by local Soviets or Party committees. The entire cooperative structure is supervised by the Central Union of Consumer Cooperatives, located in Moscow. In its functions, the Central Union closely resembles a government ministry.

Prices in cooperative outlets have in the past been higher than those in urban areas. Before 1950, rural prices averaged 13.5 percent higher; during the 1950's the differential had been cut in half;

and during the 1960's price differentials had been virtually eliminated. Despite equalization in prices, by 1970 it was common practice for great numbers of peasants to do much of their shopping in the cities, where goods were more plentiful and where much greater variety could be found. This was particularly true in regard to durable goods such as radios, television sets, refrigerators, and the like.

Membership in consumer cooperatives is not restricted and is open to any villager upon payment of an initial membership fee. This fee usually amounts to R15 to R20, which is payable over a two-year period and which is reported to be refundable if the member decides to withdraw. It has also been reported that cooperative members sometimes receive small annual dividends, but no statistics are available concerning such income. Despite improvements in the overall cooperative retail trade, scarcities and shortages still plagued the rural shopper at the beginning of 1970. Often because of poor facilities and lack of refrigeration, meat and dairy products were still not available in sufficient quantities, and it was estimated that over one-third of the rural population still baked its own bread because of lack of bakeries and poor distribution.

Collective Farm Markets

Private enterprise is incompatible with the Marxist-Leninist brand of socialism practiced in the Soviet Union, but one form that has not been eliminated is the sale of farm produce carried on by peasants in over 8,000 collective farm markets. The Program of the Communist Party of the Soviet Union adopted in 1961 forecasts the withering away of this form of capitalism, but in 1969 collective farm markets still captured about 4 percent of all retail trade and perhaps as much as 9 percent of trade in foodstuffs. In some regions the collective farm markets' share of the food trade is reported to be more than 30 percent. Prices in these markets are not regulated by the government and fluctuate according to supply and demand.

Despite forecasts of Party ideologists, new collective farm markets were still being established. In late 1969 the Soviet press reported the opening of a new market in Tbilisi which, because of its size, will give the peasants a greater share of retail sales in that city. The Tbilisi market contains 1,500 individual stalls and has lodging and transport facilities for the collective farm traders.

Collective farm markets are located in cities, towns, and villages and, in effect, compete witt the state and cooperative retail outlets. Produce sold consists of the surplus from the collective farms after government orders have been filled plus produce grown on individ-

712

ual peasant plots (see ch. 31, Agriculture). Prices in the free markets are often much higher than those in the government controlled outlets depending on the availability and quality of produce in the latter. In some years peasant incomes from sales in the collective farm markets have surpassed regular earnings.

Peasants pay nominal fees for use of facilities in the markets, which are usually controlled by local Soviets or local trade organizations. The free market operators do not escape government control completely, because they are taxed on their market incomes and told by the government what produce may or may not be sold. Sale of grain, for example, is a state monopoly. Nevertheless, collective farm markets continue to thrive and provide an important source of additional income for collective farms as well as an important source of produce for the populace when state stocks are depleted or when shortages occur.

Some collective farmers enter into agreements with consumer cooperatives for the retailing of their surplus and private plot produce. Under such agreements the cooperatives become retailing agents for the peasants, thus eliminating the necessity for the individual farmers to become part-time entrepreneurs. Acting as agents for collective farmers, the cooperatives sell the produce under the free market system and charge the farmers a commission for the services provided.

The Soviet Consumer

The traditional Western view of the Soviet consumer has been that he lives in a perpetual state of shortages of food, housing, clothing, and other various necessities. Although this situation has been true in the past, by 1970 the average Soviet citizen was better fed, better housed, and better clothed than formerly. There is still much room for improvement in the domestic economy but the Soviet citizen, knowing little about the West, does not use Western yardsticks to measure his advances. The average consumer at the end of the 1960's measured his position against conditions that existed five years earlier or at the beginning of the decade and, by such measurement, there could be no question about the betterment in his material life.

A survey of the Soviet press during 1969 showed that many of the reasons for complaints still existed: shortages, poor distribution of consumer goods, and long waits for various items. The survey also showed, however, that the tenor of complaints had changed. At the end of the 1950's, letters to the editors invariable complained about nonavailability of consumer goods; whereas ten years later, letterwriters more often complained about poor quality or about long delays in getting repair services for their refrigerators or television sets.

Disparities remain between the quantity of goods available to the city dweller and that available for rural consumers, and official sources still state that starches constitute too high a percentage of the average person's diet. Nevertheless, changes have taken place, and plans call for greater changes in the near future. By early 1970 the Soviet consumer had at least attained a slight voice in the country's economic plans (see ch. 12, Living Conditions).

Economic planners no longer either ignore the consumer, assign the lower priority to his needs, or attempt to placate him with promises for the distant future. Huge inventories of unsold and unsellable goods accumulating in warehouses in the early 1960's demonstrated that the public would no longer buy any goods simply because they happened to be available. For the first time in Soviet history, planners were forced to determine what the customer did and did not want and to plan accordingly. This does not imply that the Soviet Union has adopted a market economy operating according to supply-and-demand principles. The economic system is still directed from the top but, in a search for efficiency, the planners are concerned not only that requisite quantities of consumer goods be produced but also that they be sold when they reach retail outlets.

One of the worst features of domestic trade from the consumer's point of view, is the inordinate amount of time spent in shopping. The usual procedure for a Soviet shopper is to stand in line at a counter waiting to make a selection. The salesclerk then gives the customer a purchase slip that must be taken to a cashier, a procedure that again requires standing in line. Upon paying for the items purchased, the customer is given a receipt that must be taken back to the salesclerk, again requiring standing in line for actual pickup of the goods. Authorities have taken notice of the great problem of queues, particularly since Soviet economists have estimated that 30 billion man-hours per year are wasted by people standing in lines.

Economic planners are well aware that self-service stores could ease some of the shopping difficulties but, even though such stores began to appear in the 1950's, construction has been slow. An official of the USSR Ministry of Trade estimated in 1969 that only 10 percent of all foodstores were self-service, and the percentage was still lower in other consumer goods outlets. The number of self-service stores in construction plans for 1968 had been 1,100, according to the same official, but only 600 actually were opened. A shortage of modern packaging and packaging machinery is a drawback to more efficient retailing, but officials also state that trade organizations are plagued with obsolete equipment, such as scales and cash registers, which also hampers effective retailing.

The Price System

Under the planned economy, practically all prices are fixed by the government with the objective of meeting the economic goals set by the central planners. Prices paid by consumers depend on whether an article is purchased in a state store, a cooperative, or in a collective farm market. Prices in the collective farm markets are sometimes the same as those in state-regulated outlets, but from time to time, depending on the availability of foodstuffs, they are widely divergent.

Ultimate responsibility for establishing prices lies with the USSR Council of Ministers through its State Planning Committee, Ministry of Trade, and Ministry of Finance. The trend of price setting during the 1960's was toward decentralization because of the tremendous workloads imposed on the central agencies. General pricing policy is dictated from the top but, in practice, only the most important commodities are centrally price. Agencies at republic and lower levels actually have been delegated authority to set prices, but rigid policy control from above has negated moves toward true decentralization or autonomy.

Retail prices set by the government do not actually reflect costs of production and distribution. Prices are used to equalize expected demand with planned supply, and a large portion of the price of most commodities consist of the so-called turnover tax. Prices are manipulated by the state in order to ensure that ideologically important items, such as books and pamphlets, are cheap and readily available. Also, necessities, such as shoes and clothing, are theoretically priced to remain within reach of the lowest income groups but, in practice, these items still require the expenditure of a large portion of the average worker's income.

Prices in the collective farm markets are determined by supply and demand, but the state is also able to influence these prices by regulating the quantities of foodstuffs available in government stores. When supplies in state stores are reasonably plentiful, collective farm market prices drop and vice versa. The official Soviet figure for collective farm market sales for 1968 was R 3.8 billion, which was reported to be about the same as the 1967 figure.

Prices of all retail sales are affected by the amount of the turnover tax, through which the government obtains much of its annual revenue. The turnover tax has varied according to whether the government has wanted to offset demand for scarce items by forcing the prices up or whether the desire was to force prices down to increase demand for plentiful items. Some retail prices on commodities include turnover taxes as high as 50 percent. Inherent in all Soviet price fixing is the ideological constraint of the Marxian Theory of Value, and a continuing controversy ensues among economists as to how best to seek retailing efficiency while remaining on an ideologically correct economic course.

TRANSPORTATION AND COMMUNICATIONS

Transportation and communications, necessary adjuncts to internal commerce, have presented problems to Soviet planners and leaders because of the huge territory to be covered. The task of moving goods and people over the vast country is handled by a complex of railroads, roads, inland and coastal water routes, and airplanes. The development of a transport and communications network able to serve the entire country was visualized by early Soviet leaders as absolutely essential for the growth of the economy and, hence, the stability of the entire socialist system.

Rail Transport

Railroads have been the predominant means of transport in the country since tsarist times. The generally flat topography has been conducive to the construction of railroads, but this benefit has often been offset by extremes of climate and the prevalence of permafrost throughout large portions of the country. Despite natural barriers and enormous destruction of rails and rolling stock in two world wars and during the civil warfare, the government has proceeded with the building of new lines and the reconstruction of old. Railroads remain the most important means of moving freight.

Most railroads are concentrated in the western part of the country, that is, in former European Russia. Rail construction under the tsars was concentrated in this area, because the bulk of the population, the industries, and the known resources were centered there. Seventy-five percent of the population still live west of the Ural Mountains, and the distribution of rail lines remains extremely uneven.

New rail construction under the tsars was usually motivated by military strategy (the need to move troops quickly to the borders) and by the need to supply the centers of population. Construction under the Soviets has been dictated more by industrial considerations. Actually, the construction of new railroads has been relatively limited during the Soviet period. With the notable exceptions of the Turkestan-Siberian, the Southern-Siberian, and the line from Vorkuta to Norilsk, the Soviets have concentrated on making existing lines more efficient, particularly since World War II. Capital investment has gone into double tracking, reconstruction, and electrification rather than into extensive new development. In 1969 it was announced that more than 95 percent of the nation's rail lines had been converted from steam to either diesel or electric.

716

Increased efficiency had also been sought by reducing turnaround time for rolling stock at delivery points, and for years the idle time had shown a downward trend. In his report to the Supreme Soviet on the annual economic plan for 1970, however, the chairman of the State Planning Committee stated, "Because of the increase in the idle time of freight cars at service and freight stations and at spur tracks of industrial enterprises, freight car turnover time has increased." The capital investment in the nation's railroads has been relatively light, and some Soviet critics have complained that more government support is necessary to continue operating while maintaining minimal efficiency. The 1970 economic plan calls for a 15-percent increase in railroad capital investment, which may ease, but cannot cure the overloading of the system that critics have decried. Aware of the heavy demands on the railroads, the government has urged utilization of other means of transport but, at the beginning of 1970, estimates still placed railroad freight traffic as high as 85 percent of the total.

Road Transport

In 1970 the total length of highways was reported to be over 900,000 miles, about 10 percent of which had either macadam or concrete surface. Most of the highway network, particularly that which is hard surfaced, is located west of the Ural Mountains. Moscow, as it is with railroads, is the hub of the road net. Soviet sources imply the existence of a network of superhighways, radiating in all directions from Moscow. Western travelers have reported that these so-called superhighways are most often two-lane hard-surfaced roads. Nevertheless, by 1970 it was possible to travel by automobile from Moscow northwest to Leningrad; west to the Polish border; south to Kiev, the Crimea, and the Caucasus Mountains; east to Kazan; and southeast to Kuybyshev.

The lack of a major national road system in a country as large as the Soviet Union limits the transportation of freight and passengers to trucks and buses and puts an added strain on the railroads. Weather conditions also hamper road traffic during the longer and severe winters but, more particularly, during spring thaws and autumn rains when dirt roads become impassable. The Russian language has the word *rasputitsa*, meaning roadlessness, which aptly describes the conditions prevalent in the countryside during spring and fall.

East of the Ural Mountains only a few of the most important routes are open throughout the year, but the condition of roadlessness is not solely a Siberian phenomenom, since huge areas of the European portion of the country are also affected. Despite all handicaps, freight tonnage carried by truck is increasing, as is interurban bus travel. With announced plans for massive increases in automobile and truck production during the 1970—75 period, greater capital investment in highways can be expected.

Water Transport

Several of the world's greatest rivers are located in the Soviet Union. As transportation routes, however, they are not of major importance because most run north-south, whereas the great need for transportation is in a lateral direction. In addition, the great rivers of Siberia, such as the Ob, the Yenisey and the Lena, flow north into the Arctic Ocean, greatly limiting their usefulness as avenues for freight movement.

Despite limitations, inland waterways are important in the overall transportation scheme and, with many of its great rivers, lakes, and inland seas connecting by seagoing ship canals, the country has over 90,000 miles of navigable waterways. Beginning with the First Five Year Plan, the government constructed canals to connect its inland waterways and, with canal construction continuing into the 1960's, it became possible for large vessels to travel from Murmansk and Arkhangelsk in the north to ports on the Black and Caspian seas in the south. Such transport is limited, however, from six to eight months because most of the waterways are frozen for several months each year.

Passenger service on the country's waterways also increased considerably during the 1960's, although no statistics were available. The Soviets have been particularly proud of their hydrofoil vessels, which travel at relatively high speeds and supplement bus and passenger train service between major cities during the summer months.

Coastal marine transportation has grown in importance during the Soviet period and, with weather permitting, coastal traffic also relieves the strain on the nation's railroads. Since World War II, Soviet coastal shipping has utilized a northern route through the Arctic Ocean carrying heavy cargoes from Pacific ports to ports on the White Sea. This route is usable for only about ninety days each year with the help of icebreakers.

Air Transport

All civilian air transport in the country is under the control of the USSR Ministry of Civil Aviation, which operates the world's largest airline, popularly known as Aeroflot. Aeroflot flight patterns not only crisscross the entire Soviet Union, but the airline also has regularly scheduled international flights to many of the world's capitals.

718

All major cities and towns are served by Aeroflot and, for some towns in remote areas of Siberia, air transport provides the only regular means of travel. Most of Aeroflot's service, however, was for passengers and, as of 1970, the airline as a carrier of freight had made almost no impression on the overall volume of goods moved annually. As a passenger carrier Aeroflot during the 1960's recorded great achievements, and the number of passenger-miles steadily increased. Using modern jet aircraft, passengers are flown from Moscow to Vladivostok in about seven hours, whereas the same trip on the Trans-Siberian Railway requires seven days.

Pipelines

Although construction of a pipeline from Baku to Batumi had been completed ten years before the Bolshevik Revolution, the Soviet government was slow in the further development of this means of transport. During the early Soviet period when Baku on the Caspian Sea was the main source of petroleum products and the Volga River provided an easy transport route, little thought was given to developing pipelines. With the discovery and exploitation of other oilfields, the need for pipelines was more pressing; but in the hectic period of forced industrialization, steel needed for pipelines often went to higher priority projects.

In the 1950's, with many industries changing to oil and natural gas as fuels, pipeline construction received greater priority. By the mid-1960's a number of pipelines were carrying oil and natural gas to Soviet industrial centers, and the "Friendship Pipeline" extended westward into East Germany, Czechoslovakia, and Hungary.

Communication Services

The country is serviced by telephone, telegraph, and postal services, operated solely by the national government under the jurisdiction of the Ministry of Communications. In 1967 there were approximately 8 million telephones in the nation, or 1 for every 31.8 persons, concentrated in the urban parts of European USSR, and only about 1 million in the rural areas of the country. All Soviet towns and most rural settlements have regular phone service, however, even though relatively few telephones are found in individual dwellings.

International telephone service is also available. Service to Europe is provided by means of cables from Leningrad to Denmark, operated by the Great Northern Telegraph Company of Denmark. A cable from Leningrad connects with Vladivostok, and from Vladivostok, service by means of cables that are also operated by the Danish company, connects with Japan, China, and Hong Kong. A special arrangement with India has established direct radio and telephone service between the two countries.

Postal and telegraph services are provided extensively throughout the country. During the late 1960's, close to 70,000 postal and telegraph offices served the nation. Over 4 billion letters, 16 billion newspapers and magazines, 100 million parcels, and 250 million telegrams were carried through this network annually.

CHAPTER 35

FOREIGN ECONOMIC RELATIONS

Foreign economic relations of the Soviet Union played an increasingly important role between the mid-1950's and 1970, both as a means of speeding the growth and modernization of industry and as a tool for expanding economic and political influence among the developing nations of the world. All aspects of foreign economic relations were the exclusive prerogative of the state, including trade, economic assistance to developing countries, and membership in international economic organizations. These activities were conducted through specialized state agencies.

Soviet trade policy distinguished between three different facets of trade—with other Communist states, with the developing countries, and with the economically advanced Western nations. Trade with other Communist states, and particularly with the Eastern European members of the Council for Economic Mutual Assistance (CEMA), was intended to assist in the promotion of a closer economic integration of these countries through specialization in production. Progress toward this goal, motivated by a desire for greater economic and political cohesion of the area, was limited.

Trade with the developing countries, closely linked to economic aid, served to provide essential raw materials and an outlet for manufactured goods not competitive in other markets. Trade with the economically advanced Western nations was relied upon primarily for the procurement of modern industrial machinery and consumer goods. Soviet exports consisted mainly of raw materials and semifinished goods, although exports of machinery and equipment were important in the trade with developing countries.

Between 1960 and 1968 the volume of trade increased by nearly 80 percent. During this period, trade with other Communist states declined from three-fourths to two-thirds of the total volume, primarily as a result of the break in relations with Communist China. Western industrial states accounted for two-thirds of the trade with the non-Communist world. The share of the United States in Soviet commerce, however, was insignificant because of restrictions imposed by the United States on trade with Communist countries. In December 1969 these restrictions were relaxed, but major legal obstacles to the development of trade with the Soviet Union remained in force.

The bulk of Soviet trade was conducted on the basis of bilateral clearing agreements, with mutual balancing of trade in terms of merchandise without the use of foreign exchange. Hard currencies, however, were essential in settling balances with non-Communist trading partners. Although the overall merchandise trade showed a surplus in most years after 1960, the trade balance with the Western industrial states was consistently negative save for 1967. A lack of adequate foreign exchange reserves necessitated partial settlement of these trade deficits through the sale of gold.

Since 1964 the Soviet Union has been able to obtain some long-term loans from Western European sources for the import of industrial machinery. It also made arrangements with several of its CEMA partners to obtain long-term credits in kind for the development of raw material resources. These credits were repayable with products of the investment projects for which the credits were used.

A foreign economic assistance program was developed in the post-World War II period for the primary purpose of spreading Soviet economic and political influence and strengthening the cohesion of Communist states. The major Communist beneficiaries of this program were Communist China before 1960, Bulgaria, and Cuba. Aid to non-Communist nations was concentrated primarily in South Asia and the Middle East; India and the United Arab Republic were the main recipients. As a rule, aid was extended in the form of long-term credits in kind for the development of industry, infrastructure, and agriculture, to be repaid primarily in commodities but also, in some instances, in foreign exchange.

The relatively short duration of the aid loans and ineffective use of the proceeds in some instances created repayment difficulties for a number of countries and thereby increased their dependence on the Soviet Union. This situation was aggravated for countries that had also committed a portion of their limited resources to the payment for military assistance.

The Soviet Union participated in the work of the United Nations economic agencies but was not a member of international trade and financial organizations outside the United Nations. Its major involvement was with the CEMA, where the achievement of the major goals was sought through coordination of national economic plans and various supporting technical programs.

FOREIGN TRADE

Towards the beginning of the 1970's foreign trade was being conducted on a larger scale both quantitatively and geographically than at any time since the inception of the Soviet state. Yet, because of a policy of economic self-sufficiency pursued during most of the post-World War II period, it still occupied a relatively minor position in the economy. Exports absorbed less than 3 percent of the industrial and agricultural production. It is indicative of the low degree of importance attached to foreign trade that, generally, no discussion of it was contained in Soviet texts published before 1968 on the structure of the country's economy and on economic planning.

Beginning in the mid-1950's, however, increasing emphasis was placed on the expansion of foreign trade as an aid in attaining economic and political goals. This trend was raised to the level of official policy in early 1966. Under it, foreign trade was called upon to play an active role in the conduct of foreign policy by promoting three basic objectives. In descending order of importance, these objectives were defined as: increasing the economic power and defense capability of the world Communist movement, assistance to former colonial and dependent countries toward independent economic and political development, and the development of an exchange of goods with the Western industrial states both for mutual economic advantage and as a means of promoting peaceful coexistence.

Foreign trade is subject to a state monopoly. The monopoly is officially justified as being dictated by the nature of the socialist state, which requires a complete integration of import and export plans into the overall economic plan of the country. In the context of trade among socialist states, trade monopoly is considered an essential prerequisite for the planned development of international economic cooperation and for the coordination of national economic plans. Monopoly over foreign trade is said to have been necessary in the past to protect the domestic economy from harmful repercussions of erratic world market fluctuations and from subversive economic actions by capitalist states.

Organization

Government control over foreign trade, exclusive of exports associated with foreign economic assistance, is exercised through the Ministry of Foreign Trade. The ministry is an administrative and regulatory body without direct responsibility for trade transactions. Its major functions include the promotion of foreign trade through the negotiation of trade and payments agreements with foreign countries; the formulation of foreign trade plans jointly with the State Planning Committee and the execution of the approved plans; the direction of the customs service and of transit trade; the issuance of import and export permits; the development of measures for the improvement of all aspects of trade; and supervision over the subordinate agencies that conduct the trade operations at home and abroad. Within the country this supervision is exercised through a network of resident commissioners.

723

The Ministry of Foreign Trade is composed of five trade policy departments organized on a regional basis and seven specialized departments concerned with the import or export of specific groups of commodities. The regional departments are responsible, respectively, for policies regarding European Communist countries, Asian Communist countries, countries of Southeast Asia and the Near East, African and Western countries, and international economic organizations. Of the seven specialized departments, three are for imports and four for exports. Two of the import departments are concerned, respectively, with machinery and equipment from socialist countries and from capitalist countries; the third, with raw materials, foods, and industrial equipment; transport, roadbuilding, and farm machinery; semifinished and consumer goods; and raw materials.

The direct conduct of foreign trade is the province of a number of all-union foreign trade associations and offices. In accordance with the foreign trade plan, these organizations buy export goods from producing enterprises and arrange for their sale in foreign markets. Similarly, they act as import agents for domestic enterprises and also import from abroad products approved by the plan. Each of these noncompeting organizations is authorized to handle a specified list of products or specific services and may engage in either export, import, or both. One of the associations handles the purchase and sale of patents and licenses.

In most instances, products handled by individual associations cut across industry branch lines, and the trade of a single industry branch may be handled by more than one organization. Associations that export machinery and equipment are responsible for servicing them abroad. A national chamber of commerce serves to foster economic relations with foreign countries, arranges international trade and industrial expositions, and has attached to it commissions for maritime and foreign trade arbitrage.

In 1967 there were forty-four foreign trade associations and five offices. Of these, twenty-five were engaged in both import and export operations; seven were limited to exports and six to imports. Five associations provided services, including ship charters, freight forwarding, and advertising. Six others, under the jurisdiction of a separate state committee, specialized in foreign technical assistance. Three of the import-export organizations conducted border trade, and one dealt exclusively with domestic and foreign consumer cooperatives. In that year resident trade missions were maintained in fifty countries, and trade counselors attached to embassies were stationed in thirty-two others.

The advantage of the existing centralized foreign trade organization is reputed to lie in the ability of the trade associations and offices to conduct operations in accordance with national plans and

724

at a minimal overhead cost. At the same time, the trade and the economy are acknowledged by Soviet administrators to suffer as a result of the isolation of industrial producers and import-consuming enterprises from the world market. There is no incentive for producers to raise the quality of products to meet foreign demand and competition, to abide by agreed export delivery schedules, or for the trade associations to negotiate the best possible bargains.

Several measures have been taken in an effort to minimize these adverse effects. Foreign trade associations usually call upon industry specialists to participate in export contract negotiations and often include on their staffs technical experts familiar with the products they import. Production for export is concentrated in a relatively few appropriately equipped and favorably located enterprises. To assure the timely delivery of quality goods, a special premium system has been in effect since 1964. A portion of this premium consists of an allocation of foreign exchange to the enterprise.

In the late 1967 councils on export problems were created by law for the purpose of developing closer business ties between the foreign trade associations and the export producers whose goods they handle. These councils are permanent consultative bodies attached to most export associations. They are composed of association members and high-level representatives of industry and domestic sales organizations, including representatives of ministries, main administrations, and large enterprises producing for export. Participation by officials of the merchant marine and highway ministries was to commence in mid-1968.

The task of the export councils includes the development of detailed recommendations for the improvement of the structure and profitability of foreign trade, for the systematic improvement in the quality of export goods and services, and for the timely and efficient fulfillment of export contract obligations. The councils also serve to inform suppliers of the requirements and potentialities of the export market and to acquaint the foreign trade associations with the capabilities of the domestic industry. Although the initial work of several councils is reported to have produced almost immediate beneficial results, it is recognized that much time and effort will be needed to solve major foreign trade problems.

Trade and Payments Agreements

As a rule, trade with other countries is conducted on the basis of bilateral commercial treaties or agreements covering the exchange of goods and the regulation of payments. Treaties with Communist trading partners and, increasingly, also agreements with European and other non-Communist states are negotiated on a long-term basis, preferably for a period of five years. The effective period of the treaties with most Communist countries is made to coincide with the periods covered by the five-year economic plans. This alignment is intended to provide a more stable base for long-term development planning and to pave the way for closer coordination of the economic plans of the Soviet Union with those of her CEMA partners. One-year trade and payments agreements are negotiated where longer term agreements are not feasible.

Trade Agreements

Trade treaties are in force with all Communist and a number of non-Communist states. These treaties outline the policies and legal conditions that are to govern the mutual trade, customs tariffs, maritime shipping, transport and transit, and the activities of traders. All treaties call for mutual most-favored-nation treatment. They embody lists of commodities to be traded and specify the prices and the quantities of goods to be delivered each year. Less comprehensive trade agreements are entered into with most non-Communist states. These agreements merely contain a list of commodities that the trading partners are prepared to exchange and a mutual commitment to grant export licenses, when required, for the commodities actually traded. The treaties and agreements are supplemented by annual protocols which specify the mutual deliveries that must be made during the year. Provisions concerning payments may either be included in the basic trade documents or else made the subject of separate agreements.

Under trade treaties with Communist countries, mutual delivery of the agreed-upon commodities in the specified quantities and at the stated prices is obligatory. In the case of non-Communist countries receiving Soviet aid, the Soviet Union can exercise leverage to assure deliveries. Agreements with other non-Communist states, particularly with those industrially more advanced, are not binding, and deliveries are contingent upon negotiation of mutually acceptable terms for each individual transaction.

Prices

Prices in the trade with member countries of CEMA are negotiated on a bilateral basis for the duration of the trade treaties, generally for a period of five years. Prices for machinery, which is a less standardized commodity, may be reviewed annually. The last general price renegotiation took place during the 1964—67 period, when many prices were substantially reduced. Because of disparities between the pricing systems used in the several CEMA countries and the tenuous relationship of many domestic prices to costs, prices under trade treaties are negotiated on the basis of world market prices for the individual commodities. For this purpose, average world prices for a period of several years, rather than current or shortrun prices, are used. In calculating these averages, periods of extreme price fluctuations are excluded. The choice of the particular world market and the specific time period to be considered in these calculations are subjects of intensive bargaining between the trading partners.

In the trade with other countries, prices are established through the usual process of negotiation and are apt to reflect the relative bargaining strength of the trading partners. In order to obtain foreign exchange needed to pay for urgent imports and in efforts to gain entry into new markets, however, the Soviet Union, from time to time, sold commodities in the world market or signed a long-term agreement for the delivery of crude oil at less than the prevailing world market prices.

Payments

The predominant form of settling trade balances is through the medium of bilateral clearing accounts or barter, in order to eliminate, or at least to minimize, the need for settlement in foreign exchange, gold, or long-term loans. A number of payments agreements, particularly with the more industrialized non-Communist countries, specify settlement in convertible currency. Agreements generally require settlement of accounts on an annual basis but make provision for limited temporary overdrafts under specified conditions.

Accounts of CEMA partners must be balanced through additional commodity shipments. Multilateral settlement of trade balances among CEMA members through the CEMA International Bank for Economic Cooperation, formally agreed upon in 1963, has not been realized because of the lack of a convertible currency. The transferable ruble, nominally containing 0.987412 grams of pure gold and referred to in Soviet official publications as international exchange, has served only as a unit of account in intra-CEMA trade bookkeeping and has not been used by CEMA members as a means of payment. Deficits with non-Communist trading partners remaining at the end of the agreement period are usually settled in convertible currency and gold or, in some cases, by providing for additional shipments to be made under the protocol for the following year.

Trade Turnover

The total foreign trade turnover in 1968 amounted to a little more than R18 billion (1 ruble equals US$1.10), including almost R9.6 billion of exports and R8.5 billion of imports. This volume represented an increase of 79 percent in total trade since 1960. During this period the trade balance was substantially improved through an increase of 91 percent in exports as against 67 percent in imports. In only two of the nine years was the trade balance negative—in 1960 and in 1964—the latter year because of large grain imports necessitated by the poor harvest in 1963. Surpluses of R1 billion in 1967 and R1.1 billion in 1968 reflected the improvement in the terms of trade achieved since 1964.

During the 1960—68 period foreign trade increased at an average annual rate of 7.5 percent—a rate of expansion comparable to that of world trade as a whole. Although the volume of trade was constantly expanding, the annual growth rates in terms of value fluctuated between an atypical high of 14 percent in 1962 and a low of 3.3 percent in 1966. The major cause of the low rates of increase in 1965 and 1966 was a reduction in the prices of goods traded with the countries of Eastern Europe. In physical terms the volume of trade in 1966 increased by about 6.1 percent. An explanation of the spurt in trade in 1962 is not readily available.

Growth rates in trade volume of 8.6 percent and 10.2 percent attained in 1967 and 1968, respectively, were the highest since 1960, with the exception of 1962. Trade expansion during the nine years was retarded by a decline in the volume of trade with Communist China from R1.5 billion in 1960 to only R86 million in 1968.

Expansion of exports proceeded at a more regular pace than that of imports. Exports have grown steadily since 1960, and annual rates have continued to rise since 1963. Imports, on the other hand, expanded at declining rates from 1961 to 1965, registered an absolute reduction in 1966 following cessation of the emergency wheat imports, and resumed an upward trend at rising rates thereafter.

Direction of Trade

The bulk of the foreign trade has been carried on with other Communist countries. During the nine-year period beginning in 1960, however, a small shift took place in favor of the non-Communist trade partners. Largely because of the decline in trade with Communist China, the share of the Communist countries declined from 73 percent in 1960 to 67 percent in 1968, while the share of other countries rose from 27 to 33 percent. Within the Communist trading group, the share of CEMA members in the annual trade volume was maintained at a stable level of from 84 to 85 percent between 1963 and 1968, but the importance of Cuba and Yugoslavia increased, while that of Communist China declined. During the same period advanced industrial countries accounted for from 63 to 66 percent of the trade with the non-Communist world, and the balance represented trade with developing countries.

Because of restrictions imposed by the United States on trade with Communist countries, the share of the United States in total Soviet trade amounted to only a fraction of 1 percent, with the exception of 1964, when a large, nonrecurrent purchase of wheat by the Soviet Union raised it to 1.2 percent. In December 1969 legislation was passed in the United States that called for a review by the administration of the export-licensing requirements covering more than 1,300 categories of goods. The report of the conference committee of both houses of Congress was introduced on the floor of the House with the statement: "The conferees wish to make clear the intent of Congress that an item which is available from free world nations other than the United States shall be freely exportable from the United States without licensing requirements unless overriding national security considerations still require that the item be controlled." A ban on Export-Import Bank financing of the trade with Communist countries, however, remained in force, as did also the denial of the most-favored-nation treatment to imports from the Soviet Union, which makes them subject to the very high customs rates of the Smoot-Hawley Tariff Act of 1930.

The major CEMA trading partner of the Soviet Union during the 1960's was East Germany, with a turnover of R2.8 billion in 1968. Czechoslovakia and Poland were next in importance, the former leading throughout the period but losing second place to Poland in 1968, when their respective trade turnover amounted to R1.825 billion and R1.874 billion. They were followed by Bulgaria and Hungary, with a respective trade volume of about R1.7 billion and R1.2 billion, and Rumania, which had the lowest volume of only R786 million in 1968. Between 1960 and 1968 trade with Bulgaria nearly tripled, trade with Hungary and Poland grew almost 2½ times, and trade with each of the remaining countries increased by about 60 percent.

Cuba was by far the largest Communist trading partner outside CEMA. Trade turnover with this country amounted to R811 million in 1968, a fivefold increase over 1960. The bulk of this increase took place in 1961. Trade with Yugoslavia increased by roughly the same ratio, from R97 million to R456 million, but the increase was more gradual. Trade with North Vietnam, North Korea, and Mongolia was on a smaller scale.

Among the industrially developed non-Communist countries, the major trading partners in the 1960's were the United Kingdom and Finland, with a turnover for the nine-year period of almost R3.4 billion each. These countries alternated in occupying first place in this group. The Federal Republic of Germany (West Germany), Italy, and France were also important, with a total trade volume for the period ranging from R2.7 billion for West Germany to R2 billion for France. Trade with Italy was growing much more rapidly than with West Germany—so that Italy overtook West Germany in the volume of trade in 1967 and 1968. The annual volume of trade with the United Kingdom and France more than doubled, and it increased by 73 percent with Finland.

India and the United Arab Republic were the two most important trade partners among the developing countries. Much of this trade was the result of massive infusions of economic aid by the Soviet Union. The volume of trade with each of these countries amounted to about R330 million in 1968, a tripling of the volume since 1960 for India and a doubling of that for the United Arab Republic.

Composition of Trade

The basic commodity composition of the foreign trade remained stable during the decade of the 1960's, with only minor or temporary changes in the relative importance of the different commodity groups. This stability is explained primarily by the Soviet practice of fixing quantities for both import and export commodities in long-term agreements for periods of up to five years. Throughout this period, exports were dominated by fuels and raw and semi-processed materials, including food, although machinery and equipment made an important contribution to the export volume. Machinery and equipment, together with consumer goods, accounted for the bulk of the imports.

Exports

The major export commodity categories included machinery and equipment, ores, concentrates, metals and metal products; fuels and power; and food. Together these commodities accounted for two-thirds, or slightly more, of the annual export volume. The balance comprised timber, lumber, and wood products; textile raw materials and semifinished goods; chemicals, fertilizers, and rubber; manufactured goods; and furs.

The first two commodity groups alternated in leading the list of exports and, on the average, accounted for about one-fifth of exports each. Foods declined from 13.1 percent of exports in 1960 to 7.7 percent in 1964, in the wake of the poor 1963 harvest, but recovered to 11.8 percent by 1968. Fuels and power made up about 16 percent of the exports in most years. The shares of the minor groups in the total export volume ranged from less than 1 percent for furs to about 7 percent for timber and wood products.

During the nine-year (1960—69) period, from 35 to 39 percent of the machinery and equipment exports consisted of complete industrial plants. An additional 33 to 36 percent of these exports was composed of tractors and farm machinery, automotive equipment, and aircraft. The balance was accounted for by miscellaneous items for mining enterprises and for a wide range of manufacturing industries. In value terms, machinery and equipment exports of about R2.1 billion in 1968 consisted of R737 million of complete plants, R353 million of automotive equipment, R204 million of tractors and farm machinery, R132 million of aircraft, and R646 million of miscellaneous other items.

A major and growing share of machinery and equipment exports has been directed toward other Communist states, primarily to the CEMA partners. Sales to Communist states in 1968 amounted to R1.6 billion, or 77 percent of the total, of which CEMA members absorbed R1.2 billion, or 57 percent of the total. More than 20 percent was disposed of in developing countries, and barely 2.5 percent in Western industrial states where the quality of Soviet machinery and equipment is not competitive. Machinery constituted nearly half the total exports to the developing countries.

Major export commodities in the fuels and industrial materials groups included crude oil and petroleum products; rolled steel, pig iron, and iron ore; timber and lumber; and raw cotton. Grain, primarily wheat, and vegetable oils were the main food exports. Substantial quantities of sugar obtained in the trade with Cuba were also exported.

Virtually all the products in these commodity groups were shipped to both the Communist and non-Communist areas of the world, but a few products predominated in the trade with non-Communist countries, primarily the industrial states of Western Europe. These items included furs and fur skins; timber, pulpwood, and lumber; petroleum and coal; potassium fertilizers; and sugar, vegetable oils, and fish. Whereas the share of the non-Communist countries in total exports in 1968 was 33 percent, shipments to them of the listed goods ranged from 94 percent for furs to 40 percent for coal. Chromium, timber, pulpwood, and sugar were in the upper half of this range.

Imports

The main categories of imports during the 1960—68 period were machinery and equipment and consumer goods. Machinery imports during this period rose from 30 to 37 percent of total imports. The share of consumer goods in imports, including foods and manufactures, but excluding textiles and fibers, fluctuated between a low of 29 percent in 1960 and a high of 36 percent in 1966; it amounted to 33.5 percent in 1968. Imports of ores and base metals declined in importance—from 17 percent in 1960 to 9 percent in 1968—as did also imports of fuels and of textiles and fibers. Imports of chemicals and wood products remained fairly stable at about 6 percent and 2 percent of total imports, respectively.

About three-fourths of the machinery and equipment was imported from the Communist countries of East Europe, but the industrial states of Western Europe and Japan supplied the major part of the requirements for the automobile, chemical, textile, lumber, paper, and woodworking industries. They were also the source for large imports of merchant vessels, including tankers, refrigerator ships, and icebreakers. Despite their lower volume, these imports from the Western states were of particular importance. They served to introduce into the country the most advanced technology and thus helped modernize industry while obviating the need to divert scientific and technical research and development resources from the higher priority space and defense sectors. A substantial, though undisclosed, portion of the imports of Western machinery was in the form of complete industrial plants.

Non-Communist countries were also the major suppliers of imported foods other than livestock and poultry products. Industrial states supplied virtually all the wheat and three-fourths of the fish and fish products, whereas the less developed countries provided mainly tropical produce, including rice, tea, coffee, cocoa, and fruits. The great bulk of the manufactured consumer goods originated in Eastern Europe, but India and the United Arab Republic supplied a large part of the cotton textile imports.

Among the imports of materials, shipments from non-Communist countries predominated in rolled steel, chemicals, cellulose and paper, textile fibers and yarns, and hides and skins. The bulk of these materials was imported from industrial states, but less developed countries provided substantial quantities of rolled steel, vegetable fibers and wool, and most of the hides and skins. These countries were also the only source of natural rubber imports, while the industrial states supplied all the copper and virtually all the tin.

THE CUSTOMS SYSTEM

All movement of persons, goods, and mail across the country's frontiers is subject to government control. Customs permits are required for all imports or exports by private individuals and by organizations other than the foreign trade associations operating under the jurisdiction of the Ministry of Foreign Trade or of the State Committee of the Council of Ministers for Foreign Economic Relations. The export of art objects and of objects having historical or archaeological significance is prohibited. Individual items of little value may be exported subject to permits issued by the Ministry of Culture.

A new two-column tariff schedule was introduced in 1961, with minimum and maximum and valorem rates. The minimum schedule applies to imports from countries that grant the Soviet Union most-favored-nation treatment; the maximum schedule, to imports from countries that do not grant this privilege. Under the minimum-rate tariff, 155 categories of products out of a total of 244 are exempt from duties; for the remaining categories the rates vary from 1 to 10 percent. The average rate under the maximum tariff schedule is 15 percent.

The reasons for instituting the tariff are not known. The usual functions of a tariff—protection against imports and revenue for the government—are irrelevant in a country committed to state trading, since it is the government that decides what to import and also collects the revenue in the form of the margin that it establishes between the prices it pays and the prices it charges to consumers. The statement concerning customs permits for exports and imports by individuals must have reference to gifts and tourist purchases, because no individual is allowed to engage in foreign trade.

FOREIGN LOANS AND INVESTMENTS

Available evidence indicates that international movement of capital outside the foreign aid program has been on a relatively small scale. Few instances are known of Soviet equity participation in foreign ventures, and none of foreign investments in Soviet enterprise. Long-term hard-currency loans for periods of ten to fifteen years have acquired importance only since 1964. Such loans, extended by major banks in the United Kingdom, France, and Italy, amounted to more than R900 million in the years from 1964 to 1966. They were used to finance imports of a wide range of machinery and equipment, including a complete plant for the manufacture of 600,000 passenger cars per year.

Long-term loans have also played a role in the unpublicized financial assistance provided by Eastern European Communist states for the development of Soviet raw material resources. The extension of these credits has been based in large part on the idea promoted by Soviet economists that such participation by CEMA partners was essential to ensure a continued long-term flow of primary commodities. These development loans, usually bearing a 2-percent annual interest rate, usually take the form of machinery and equipment to be used in the investment project but may also be in the form of other needed commodities. They are repayable in products of the facility to be constructed, repayment beginning when full production is reached.

Projects financed in this manner in the early 1960's included a phosphate mine in the Estonian Soviet Socialist Republic, with participation by five CEMA countries, and a potassium salt-mining and -processing enterprise, with assistance from Poland. Czechoslovakia, which had already extended a credit of some R270 million in 1960, agreed in 1966 to provide R500 million worth of goods between

1967 and 1971, to be repaid with 60 million tons of oil during the 1971—84 period. Similar long-term credit arrangements were agreed upon with the German Democratic Republic (East Germany) in 1967 and 1969. Details of these agreements are not known, except that the 1967 credit is repayable in oil. In 1969 an agreement appears to have been concluded with the Federal Republic of Germany involving the delivery by West Germany on credit of large-diameter pipe in the amount of 1.2 billion or more deutsche marks ($324 million) in return for future deliveries of natural gas.

BALANCE OF PAYMENTS

A balance of payments has not been published; neither are adequate data available on the various elements entering into the Soviet Union's current and capital accounts other than merchandise trade. For the 1960—68 period as a whole and for most years during that period, the balance of the merchandise trade with the different country groupings was positive, except for the trade with the Western industrial states, which was consistently negative except for 1967.

In trade with Communist countries, temporary imbalances are usually eliminated through additional merchandise shipments, while export surpluses arising from shipments of foreign aid goods are financed through long-term credits, largely repayable in kind. No information is available on methods used among Communist countries to balance invisible transactions, such as freight, insurance, interest, and tourism, but it appears likely that these items are also balanced through merchandise trade and credits. It is generally believed that hard currencies are not used for this purpose.

The situation is different with regard to the trade with the non-Communist world. Well over half this trade and more than 80 percent of the trade with the Western industrial nations have been conducted in hard currencies. The inability of the Soviet Union to generate enough convertible foreign exchange through its exports to pay for the hard-currency imports necessitated the sale of substantial quantities of gold to balance the accounts. These sales were estimated to have ranged between US$200 million and US$550 million annually from 1960 to 1965, for an average of almost US$380 million per year. Sales of gold in 1967 and 1968 were much lower, only about US$15 million and US$12 million, respectively. Information for 1966 is not available.

FOREIGN ECONOMIC ASSISTANCE
Role of Economic Aid

With the beginning of the Cold War in the late 1940's, the Soviet Union provided economic aid in various forms to the East European

734

Communist countires, as a means of ensuring the maintenance of their economic and political cohesion. Since 1954 the Soviet Union has also extended aid in the form of long-term loans and grants to developing countries, regardless of their political orientation or form of government. An economic impetus toward this aid activity was initially provided by a need to develop new market outlets for the growing industrial output not salable in economically advanced countries and the associated necessity of granting easy credit terms to prospective buyers as an inducement to abandoning their traditional sources of supply. At the same time, Soviet leaders realized the potential of the aid mechanism as a tool for penetrating areas of the world that had historically been under the influence of Western industrial states. Economic aid and trade have since become instruments in a competitive struggle with these states for political and economic influence in the developing countries (see ch. 24, Foreign Relations).

Foreign aid by Western states has long been denounced in the Soviet Union as an ill-disguised tool of imperialism, and their trade with the developing countries denounced as a means of robbing these countries of their resources. Soviet aid and trade, on the contrary, are proclaimed to be devoid of ulterior motives and directed entirely toward promoting the economic independence of the less developed nations. Yet this aid is counted upon to help concentrate economic power in the hands of recipient governments and to induce social and economic changes in non-Communist states that will ultimately culminate in the establishment of planned economies. Aid has also been used to establish a foothold in strategically important areas of the world. Forty percent of all economic aid has been committed to India and the United Arab Republic, two countries in which the Communist Party has been either under sharp attack or proscribed. Furthermore, in the mid-1960's the idea was espoused that foreign aid should be used to stimulate the inflow of essential raw materials from aid recipients.

Responsibility for foreign economic and technical cooperation, including the associated exports of industrial equipment and technical services, rests with the State Committee of the Council of Ministers for Foreign Economic Relations. One of its major functions is the conclusion and execution of technical assistance agreements with foreign governments for the construction abroad of various industrial enterprises. This assistance includes research and project development, supervision over construction and the installation of equipment, and the training of native technical and key production personnel. Another important, though much less publicized, function of this committee is the provision to foreign countries of military technology and equipment though its Main Engineering Administration. The committee directs the work of six specialized foreign trade associations and participates in the formulation of foreign trade plans. Foreign economic assistance is handled exclusively on a government-to-government basis.

Nature of Economic Aid

Economic assistance has generally been provided for the development of essential economic sectors in aid-recipient countries. The bulk of the aid has been channeled into the construction of publicly owned industrial plants, and most of the balance into agricultural and infrastructure facilities. The Soviet Union does not usually participate directly in the formulation of economic development plans but, rather, selects projects for which it is willing to provide assistance from among those included in the aid-seeking countries' development programs. The nature of the assistance granted is usually conditioned by the stage of the recipient country's development, although deviations from this pattern or miscalculations of a country's absorptive capacity apparently do occur.

In concluding agreements for economic development projects, the Soviet aid organization usually accepts responsibility for the required project research and for the delivery of all equipment, spare parts, and the necessary materials not obtainable locally. The aid organization also provides the technicians needed to direct the construction of the plants or other facilities, the installation of equipment, and the training of indigenous workers and technical personnel. The client countries, as a rule, are responsible for organizing the construction work, the hire and the pay of the local labor force, the provision of local builting materials, the payment of transport costs from port of arrival to construction site for the equipment and materials received from the Soviet Union, and for various other expenditures in local currency.

As a general rule, economic aid has been provided in the form of credits rather than of outright grants. Aside from relatively small gifts to a few countries, the only significant grants known to have been made consist of about R135 million given to Afghanistan for various purposes throughout the early 1960's and a shipment of 200,000 tons of wheat to India in 1967.

The predominant form of economic aid commitment is a long-term development credit, repayable over a period of twelve years or longer and usually carrying a 2.5-percent annual interest charge. About one-third of the commitments made to mid-1969 were in the form of trade credits. These credits, intended primarily to promote the export of machinery and equipment, often require downpayments, allow only five to ten years for the repayment of the principal, and carry a higher interest rate than the development credits. Some aid commitments specify cash payment in freely convertible and local currencies and are thus akin to commercial transactions.

Repayment of aid credits begins either after the completion of deliveries for the particualr project or after the new facility has begun operations. It is usually made through delivery of traditional export commodities and products of local manufacture, including those produced in plants built with the economic aid received. Through loan repayment the Soviet Union has acquired such raw materials as cotton, wool, hides and skins, and nonferrous ore concentrates; foods, including rice, vegetable oils, tea, coffee, cocoa beans, and citrus fruits; as well as a number of manufactured products. Some aid credits, however, require at least partial repayment in convertible currency.

Magnitude and Distribution of Aid

Information on the magnitude of the economic aid program is fragmentary, since relevant data are not officially published. A basic problem in estimating the amounts involved is posed by the lack of a clear-cut distinction between aid and trade. Additional difficulty arises in the valuation of loans provided in kind. The distribution of aid between Communist and non-Communist countries is obscured by changes in the coverage of these categories. Data on aid disbursements are less complete than those on commitments, and information on debt repayment is particularly sketchy.

Commitments

The amount of aid disbursed to Communist countries, including the East European states, Communist China, Cuba, Mongolia, North Korea, and North Vietnam, was estimated by a Western student of foreign economic aid to have been the equivalent of R3.1 billion from 1955 to 1965. This estimate was based on the officially reported annual deliveries of complete industrial plants, the value of which was said by a knowledgeable Soviet official to include also the value of the technical services supplied. Extending this estimate for an additional two years, by using the same method of estimation, yields a total aid disbursement of R3.9 billion through 1967. This sum represents the maximum amount that may have been provided for economic development, because a portion of it may actually reflect sales rather than aid. Trustworthy information on the amount of other forms of aid to Communist countries is not available.

Nearly 40 percent of the aid to Communist countries went to Communist China, most of it before 1961. Thereafter, deliveries to China declined because of the political rift with that country. Deliveries to Bulgaria ranked second in volume and amounted to 20 percent of the total. Beginning in 1957, these deliveries increased steadily to R149 million in 1967. Cuba was estimated by this source to have received the equivalent of about R112 million in economic assistance between 1961 and 1965. Another major Western source, however, estimated disbursements for economic development to Cuba in the 1961—65 period to have been the equivalent of R136 million and placed the total amount of aid provided, including R668 million in balance-of-payments assistance, at around R800 million.

The amount of economic aid provided to the East European member countries of CEMA and Yugoslavia from 1945 to 1968 was estimated at roughly R4.7 billion. The recipients of this aid receiving the largest amounts were Bulgaria, with R1.5 billion, and the German Democratic Republic, with R1.2 billion. Poland and Yugoslavia were estimated to have received about R900 million and R460 million, respectively, while the remainder was divided, in descending order of magnitude, among Hungary, Rumania, and Czechoslovakia. The share of Czechoslovakia was only R55 million, or a little more than 1 percent of the total.

From the inception of the aid program in 1954 to mid-1969, the volume of economic aid pledged in the form of credits to thirty-nine non-Communist less-developed countries amounted to R5.9 billion. About R4.5 billion of this sum, or 77 percent, was extended to countries of South Asia and the Near East, divided almost equally between the two regions. The major portion of this aid went to India and the United Arab Republic, which received about R1.45 billion and R920 million, respectively. African countries received R780 million; Far Eastern countries, R374 million; and countries in Latin America, R188 million. The annual level of new aid commitments increased from an average of almost R365 million in the 1954—64 period to about R500 million in the period from 1965 through June 1969.

Deliveries and Repayments

Economic aid deliveries to less developed countries through the end of 1968 amounted to a little more than R2.5 billion, or about 45 percent of the aid commitments made during the 1954—67 period. These deliveries reached a peak of about R336 million in 1964 but declined to R273 million in 1966 and remained at the same or a slightly lower level in 1967. Because of the aid credit repayments in those years, however, the net outflow of aid amounted to only about R263 million in 1964 and R113 million in 1967. The ratio between the cumulative drawings and aid extensions was quite stable after 1963 and substantially higher than it had been in the earlier years of the aid program.

The highest level of aid implementation was achieved in Afghanistan, India, and the United Arab Republic which, together, received about half the total aid commitments. By the end of 1968 these

738

three countries had drawn 55 percent of the aid extended to them, compared with an average of only about 30 percent for all other aid recipients. In general, the countries of the Near East and South Asia absorbed aid more rapidly than did other areas—about two to three times faster than African countries.

The slow rate of aid utilization by many of the countries that received pledges of assistance was caused primarily by their inability to provide the local currency funds and the qualified manpower needed to carry out their share of the projects. With few exceptions, the Soviet Union refused to assume local project costs and full management responsibility. In the case of a few undeveloped countries, however, including Afghanistan and some of the African states, the needed additional assistance was granted. This supplemental aid included the provision of commodities to be sold for local currency as a means of raising the funds needed for the development projects. Over the years, commodity aid constituted only about 5 percent of the total amount of aid provided to the developing countries.

The extra assistance also entailed the organization of Soviet construction companies in several countries to carry out the building program, the management of local labor engaged in aid-assisted construction of dams and irrigation projects in Algeria, and management assistance in the building of the Aswan High Dam in the United Arab Republic. In several instances specialists were provided to operate newly built facilities for a number of years, although usually the Soviet aid organization provides technicians only for key positions during the initial stages of operation.

In 1968 almost 10,000 nonmilitary Soviet technicians were employed in the less developed countries, and about 1,000 technical students from these countries were being trained in the Soviet Union. By that time more than 130,000 persons had received on-the-job training at Soviet-aided construction projects, and at least 20 technical training institutions had been built in the developing countries.

Information on the magnitude of aid credit repayments is not readily available. Western estimates, however, suggest a rising trend in repayments from about R73 million in 1964 to R160 million in 1967. Repayment of aid credits, usually effected through the shipment of commodities, has caused difficulties to many aid recipients. Less developed countries are generally short of foreign exchange and experience serious balance-of-payments problems. The need to ship export commodities to the Soviet Union instead of selling them on the world market for hard currencies substantially aggravates these problems. In instances where the debt is discharged through the shipment of manufactured products that have a high content of imported materials, repayment is actually made partly in hard currency, to the detriment of the foreign exchange reserves.

Repayment difficulties are compounded for countries in which the aid was used for projects that are either unproductive or slow in yielding returns and, even more so, for countries that mortgaged much of their exports for Soviet military equipment. To enforce repayment, the Soviet Union occasionally insisted on larger exports from debtor countries while reducing its own exports to them. The critical economic and financial situation of some countries, however, including Indonesia and the United Arab Republic, necessitated the granting of various forms of relief from their debt-servicing obligations.

Foreign Aid Policy

Aid policy since the mid-1960's has evidenced a much greater concern than in the past for the application of economic criteria to aid commitments. It has also shown a stronger emphasis on political foreign policy consideration in the allocation of aid (see ch. 24, Foreign Relations).

During the first decade of the aid program, the Soviet Union was willing to advance to almost any less developed country that desired it large lines of economic development credit not earmarked for any specific purpose. These commitments were often made without a study beforehand of the ability of the recipients to use the aid effectively or of the feasibility of the proposed investment projects. Unsatisfactory experience with this liberal aid policy in developing countries that could not effectively absorb the capital aid provided or where unsuitable projects were undertaken led to a more cautious approach. Aid commitments have become increasingly project oriented and contingent upon a satisfactory showing of economic feasibility based on intensive studies.

The growing influence of foreign policy objectives on aid policy is revealed by a shift in the regional distribution of aid commitments since the mid-1960's. Of the total assistance extended to developing nations between 1965 and 1968, about 85 percent was allocated to the Near East and South Asia, as against 67 percent during the 1959—64 period. At the same time, Africa's share declined from 25 to 7 percent, while the Far East and Latin America, together, continued to receive about 8 percent of new commitments. In 1968 two countries in the Near East received more than 99 percent of the new R281 million commitment, with the balance going to Latin America.

These commitments, together with the emergence of Iran, Pakistan, and Turkey as major aid recipients since 1965, indicate that the aid commitment pattern of the second half of the 1960's was directed toward strengthening the country's position in the Near

East and in creating a buffer zone along its frontiers. With the extension of assistance to these three countries, the Soviet Union created an unbroken chain of foreign aid clients with borders contiguous either to its own or to those of Communist China. Six nations along or near the country's southern frontier—Afghanistan, India, Iran, Nepal, Pakistan, and Turkey—received commitments totaling R2.9 billion, about half of which were extended after 1964. Aid extended to these six states constituted half the total economic aid extended to all less developed countries since the inception of the program in 1954 and almost two-thirds the amount provided to the Near East and Asian countries.

To further its foreign policy objectives, the Soviet Union has also engaged in an extensive military aid program for less developed countries. The total volume of military aid extended to some twenty countries from 1955 to 1968 amounted to more than R5 billion. Nearly 60 percent of this amount was advanced to countries in the Near East, including almost 30 percent to the United Arab Republic alone. Indonesia was the second largest military aid recipient, with nearly 25 percent of the total. Other important recipients included Iraq, India, Syria, Afghanistan, and Algeria. Since these arms deliveries must be paid for with commodity shipments and hard currencies, military aid has served to divert scarce resources from economic development and has either caused or aggravated economic dislocation and financial distress in a number of states.

MEMBERSHIP IN INTERNATIONAL ORGANIZATIONS
Council for Economic Mutual Assistance

The Soviet Union is a founding member of the Council for Economic Mutual Assistance (variously abbreviated as CEMA, CMEA, or Comecon), a rather loose regional organization, without executive authority, which joins the Soviet Union with six Communist countries of Eastern Europe—Bulgaria, Czechoslovakia, the German Democratic Republic, Hungary, Poland, and Rumania—and Mongolia. Created in 1949 on Soviet initiative and on political grounds as a counterweight to the Marshall Plan, CEMA was relatively quiescent until 1956 and adopted a formal charter only in 1960.

Organization and Aims

The organization's founding document and charter embody the principle of full national sovereignty of CEMA members, and its statutes require that all organizational and procedural decisions and substantive recommendations be adopted only with the consent of the interested member countries. Attempts by the Soviet Union in 1962 and again in 1968 to transform CEMA into a supranational agency for the purpose of instituting integrated economic planning for the member countries as a whole were successfully challenged by Rumania on the basis of these provisions. Nevertheless, the idea of a socialist economic integration of the CEMA countries has not been abandoned.

The formally stated aim of CEMA is the promotion of economic progress and public welfare in member countries by uniting and coordinating their individual efforts. After the rejection of the Soviet proposal for the economic integration of the member countries, CEMA adopted the more modest goal of an international socialist division of labor. An evaluation of the work of the twenty-third special session of the CEMA Council, which appeared in the official organ of the Ministry of Foreign Trade in July 1969, advanced as the major current imperative the need to strengthen the economic and political unity of CEMA countries in order to achieve victory in the economic competition with capitalism. A similar note was struck by a writer on CEMA matters in a journal devoted to international affairs. This writer hailed the Council activities as serving to strengthen the might and unity of the socialist countries whose community is the mainstay of the international revolutionary movement. These statements indicate the nature of the Soviet Union's interest in promoting CEMA.

In accord with the policies established by the Council and under the direction of an executive committee, CEMA performs its work with the aid of a secretariat, a Bureau for Problems Relating to Economic Plans, an Institute of Standardization, and a series of standing commissions, numbering twenty-one in 1969, on various aspects of the economy and branches of industry. Two specialized international associations were set up in 1964 for cooperation in ferrous metallurgy and the manufacture of bearings, to which all member countries except Rumania belonged in 1969. A third such association was established in July 1969 to deal with a number of minor chemical products, including synthetic paints, pesticides, and chemicals for the textile and shoe industries.

Aside from foreign trade and the associated finance, CEMA activities include the coordination of national economic plans, international specialization and cooperation in production, standardization, and scientific and technological cooperation. Hampered by divergent national interests of the member states, a lack of incentives, and cumbersome procedures, these activities have been largely ineffective.

Plan Coordination

Coordination of long-term national economic plans, instituted in 1954 and established as the basic method of CEMA operations in 1962 and 1963, was still proceeding largely on a bilateral basis with

742

reference to the 1966—70 plan. Multilateral work, limited essentially to compiling raw material balances for fuels, power, certain metals, and some machinery, was not yet completed some time after the plan had come into effect. Although member countries apparently agreed to exchange a wider range of information concerning the 1971—75 plan, coordination remained limited primarily to sectors heavily involved in the production of goods for intra-CEMA commerce and to transport facilities servicing this trade. Persisting differences over the scope of multilateral plan coordination and the admittedly inadequate coordination techniques made for continued primary reliance on bilateral consultation channels.

Product Specialization

Specialization and cooperation in industrial production among CEMA members, intended to bring about greater efficiency and to accelerate technological progress, was conceived in terms of both collaboration between existing industries and the creation of new complexes of interrelated and complementary industries. In practice, most specialization arrangements agreed upon through 1969 consisted of an allocation of production responsibility by type or size of product among countries already producing the items involved, making possible some economies of scale. Although around 2,500 items were covered by CEMA recommendations, primarily in the machine-building, chemical, radio and electronics, and ferrous metals industries, only 68 were adopted. They affected only a small portion of the total output, even within the industries concerned. In machine-building, for instance, the total volume of the products involved constituted no more than 7 percent of CEMA's machinery output.

Standardization

The introduction of common technical standards for industrial products, indispensable for an effective intercountry specialization in production and also essential in view of the extensive trade in machinery and materials among CEMA members, was formally undertaken in 1962. The major problem in this area was posed by the need to reconcile two different, well-developed sets of norms used in the Soviet Union and in the German Democratic Republic. Up to the end of 1967 about 1,500 recommendations on standardization were developed by the various CEMA agencies concerned with this work. The extent to which these standards were adopted by industry is not known.

Scientific and Technical Cooperation

Scientific and technical cooperation has been one of the more successful CEMA activities, although it, too, has not been free of problems. It consists mainly of an exchange of documentation for inventions and technological processes, an exchange of scientists and specialists, and mutual technical assistance. Despite substantial achievements, CEMA spokesmen complained that technological progress through mutual exchanges fell short of needs and possibilities and also lagged behind the progress achieved in advanced industrialized countries.

A major drawback in this field of cooperation has been the requirement for a free exchange of all information and documentation, except for the costs of reproducing the documents. For the most industrially advanced CEMA countries, such as the German Democratic Republic and Czechoslovakia, this meant sharing the fruits of their research with other members who had little to contribute in return. It has also been argued that continued exchange without compensation runs counter to the new principles of management and planning being introduced in member states. The probability of at least a partial commercialization of the scientific and technical information exchange was indicated by the creation in the Soviet Union in mid-1969 of a new foreign trade agency, Vneshtekhnika, for the express purpose of exchanging technology with other socialist countries.

Relations With Other International Organizations

For ideological and political reasons the Soviet Union has declined to join such international economic organizations as the General Agreement on Tariffs and Trade (GATT), the International Bank for Reconstruction and Development (IBRD, known as the World Bank), and the International Monetary Fund (IMF). It has, however, associated itself with the work of the United Nations Food and Agriculture Organization (FAO), the Economic Council of Europe (ECE), and the United Nations Conference on Trade and Development (UNCTAD). In UNCTAD the Soviet Union has supported demands made by the developing countries for freer access to the markets of the developed countries and for various unilateral trade concessions by the latter.

CHAPTER 36

FISCAL AND MONETARY SYSTEM

The financial system of the USSR is an integral part of its planned economy and is subordinate to the national economic plan. After the State Planning Committee prepares preliminary economic plans in largely production terms, it compiles an overall financial plan that translates them into monetary terms. The financial plan reflects the national financial resources available both from the budget and from the accumulations of state enterprises and organizations. The essential function of the financial system is to accumulate and redistribute financial resources to insure the attainment of the regime's economic, social, and political goals. The Ministry of Finance and the banking system are the financial institutions charged with carrying out the economic and financial plans.

The Ministry of Finance is the principal organization concerned with managing financial affairs. The ministry draws up and manages the state budget and supervises the financial system of the country. The banking system for many years was under the supervision of the ministry.

The state budget is the key instrument of the financial system. It distributes a major portion of the national product within investment, consumption, and defense and allocates the investment flows among economic sectors and regions. Receipts from state-owned enterprises in excess of costs are siphoned off into the budget both through taxes and through withdrawal of a portion of profits. Direct taxes on non-state-owned organizations and on the population are a relatively minor source of state income.

The banking system functions primarily as the administrative agent for controlling the flow of payments among enterprises, organizations, and the government in accordance with the financial plans. Payments within the state sector are made almost entirely through transfers on the books of the banking system. These payments are documented so as to conform with the applicable physical and financial plan. The pervasive monitoring of the flow of funds by the state bank makes it easier for financial authorities to detect bottlenecks and various shortcomings of the economic plans. The banking system also attempts to regulate the flow of money in the hands of the population to protect the economy against inflationary pressures resulting from an insufficient quantity of goods and services to satisfy the demands of the population.

THE BUDGET

The state budget is the chief financial plan of the USSR. Through it, the financial resources of the government are collected and redistributed in accordance with the national economic plan. The scope of the budget is considerably greater than that of budgets of Western countries. An estimated 40 to 45 percent of the Soviet gross national product (GNP) is channeled through the state budget. The large scope of the budget is a reflection of the planned economy. Activities covered by the Soviet budget that are undertaken largely by private means in most Western nations include investment in the economy and free health, recreational, and cultural services.

The Budgetary System

The legal foundations for the budget can be found in the Constitution and in the budgetary laws enacted by the Supreme Soviet. The Constitution of July 1918 gave to the Congress of Soviets or its Central Committee the authority to fix revenue and required that expenditures be made strictly for planned purposes. Due to the exigencies of the civil war and economic chaos, the legislation had limited impact. The present system of taxation is based largely on the reforms carried out in 1930 and 1931. At that time separate tax systems were set up for the socialized and private sectors of the economy, and a turnover tax and a profits tax were established as the major sources of revenue. The budgetary system has continued to evolve through legislative action and ministerial decrees, some of which are publicized; others are deemed to be of a sensitive nature and not revealed.

The state budget for the calendar year is prepared under the supervision of the Ministry of Finance. A draft budget is formulated from the financial plan and is submitted to the Council of Ministers where the budget is analyzed for conformity with the State Plan for the National Economy. From the Council of Ministers both the state plan and budget are sent to the Supreme Soviet where they are formally approved, with the customary addition of minor changes usually relating to social and cultural services. With this final approval the budget becomes law.

The state budget is drafted in highly aggregated form at the national level and is disseminated downward to successively lower levels of governmental units, where it is matched against the preliminary draft budgets at each level. After ratification at the top level the legislative organs at descending levels formally ratify their budgets in rapid succession.

After ratification, operational budgets are prepared on the basis of which spending takes place, and budget execution is controlled. Budgetary credits (nonrepayable grants not to be confused with repayable bank credits) are established with branches of the state bank giving the spending unit the right to make expenditures chargeable to the state budget. Credits are opened for each quarter and may be carried over into the next quarter. Unused credits at the end of the year are ordinarily returned to the budget. Central surveillance is maintained over revenues and expenditures on the basis of continual reports from each branch bank to the central office and to the Ministry of Finance.

The state budget comprises a total of about 50,000 various budgets. At the top level, the central, or all-union budget, in recent years has accounted for about half of expenditures of the state budget, including all publicized military expenditures, that part of industry under all-union status, most transportation and communications, foreign trade, formation of state reserves, and certain social services. The republics account for about two-thirds of the remaining expenditures, including much of industry and a major part of specialized and higher education. Local budgets finance small-scale industrial enterprises, trade and services, housing construction, lower levels of education, health, and cultural establishments.

Expenditures

The published version of the state budget is in a highly aggregated and summarized form, making it difficult to appraise the real allocations and activity within the major components. Furthermore, large sums are contained in unidentified residuals.

Budgetary expenditures are broken down into four primary categories: financing the national economy, social and cultural measures, defense, and administration (see table 16). In the 1965 budget plan 45 percent of the total expenditure was allocated to the national economy, 38 percent to social and cultural measures, 13 percent to defense, 1 percent to administration, and 5 percent simply labeled "other." Total expenditures increased by 35 percent during the 1966—69 period, an average of nearly 8 percent annually. Expenditures for 1970 are planned to increase by 5.5 percent over 1969. Usually, actual expenditures exceed the plan by a small amount, but in 1967 and 1968 the actual expenditures exceeded the plan by 4 to 5 percent. The higher expenditure to a large extent was probably due to higher prices, introduced in mid-1967, for many industrial goods.

The budget category "financing the national economy" represents nonreturnable grants to state enterprises and organizations. Unlike other budget categories it deals basically with activity that is largely

747

Table 16. *State Budget Expenditures and Revenues of the Soviet Union, 1965–70*
(in billions of rubles*)

	1965	1966	1967		1968		1969		1970
	Actual	Actual	Planned	Actual	Planned	Actual	Planned	Actual	Plan
Expenditures:									
Financing the National Economy:									
Industry and construction	20.99	21.06	21.87	.....	23.90	.....	22.20	.....	23.90
Agriculture and procurement	6.77	6.30	6.35	.....	9.00	.....	9.20	.....	9.50
Trade (foreign and domestic)	2.27	2.84	3.17	.....	4.00	.....	6.50	.....	6.10
Transportation and communications	2.83	2.61	2.66	.....	2.30	.....	2.60	.....	2.80
Municipal economy and housing	4.23	4.53	4.08	.....	} 11.00	.....	4.90	.....	} 21.20
Other	7.83	7.83	8.78	.....		.....	12.90	.....	
Subtotal	44.92	45.17	46.91	52.80	50.20	58.70	58.30	60.40	63.50
Social and Cultural Measures:									
Education, science, and culture	17.51	18.73	19.67	20.09	21.00	21.90	23.20	23.20	24.50
Health and physical culture	6.67	7.10	7.40	7.45	7.70	8.10	8.40	8.50	9.20
Social welfare measures	13.99	14.93	15.85	15.94	17.10	18.30	19.50	19.60	21.10
Subtotal	38.17	40.76	42.92	43.48	45.80	48.30	51.10	51.30	54.80
Defense	12.78	13.40	14.50	14.50	16.70	16.70	17.70	17.70	17.85
Administration	1.28	1.41	1.44	1.50	1.53	1.60	1.60	1.70	1.71
Other	4.48	4.83	4.24	2.90	9.37	3.60	5.20	6.00	6.80
Total Expenditures	101.63	105.57	110.01	115.18	123.60	128.90	133.90	137.10	144.66

Revenues:

Social Sector:									
Turnover tax receipts	38.66	39.31	40.70	40.10	42.20	40.80	43.00	44.30	46.60
Deductions from profits	30.87	35.67	37.18	41.80	43.80	48.00	48.00	48.20	50.40
Income tax on organizations	1.55	1.15	1.12	1.30	⎱ 26.80	1.10	⎱ 30.60	⎱ 33.50	⎱ 34.30
Social insurance receipts	5.56	6.00	6.29	6.50		7.20			
Other	17.25	14.89	15.08	17.40		22.30			
Subtotal	93.89	97.02	100.37	107.10	112.80	119.40	121.60	126.00	131.30
Private Sector:									
State taxes on population	7.70	8.44	9.04	9.30	10.30	10.50	11.50	11.70	12.70
State loans	0.18	0.22	0.26	0.10	⎱ 0.80	0.30	⎱ 1.00	⎱	0.90
Local taxes and lotteries	0.55	0.61	0.58	0.70		0.60			
Subtotal	8.43	9.27	9.88	10.10	11.10	11.40	12.50	12.50	13.60
Total Revenues	102.32	106.29	110.25	117.20	123.90	130.80	134.10	138.50	144.90
Budget Surplus	0.69	0.72	0.24	2.02	0.31	1.94	0.20	1.40	0.24

*1 ruble equals US$1.10.

self-supporting. Budget expenditures are used for investment in productive facilities, subsidies, formation of state material reserves, and various other purposes. Under the economic reform instituted in 1965, budgetary investment was to be restricted to fina::cing new construction. Enterprises were to finance their own investments from retained profits or bank loans. The share of total centralized capital investments supplied by the budget has dropped from 61 percent in 1965 to 47 percent planned for 1970.

Expenditures under "financing the national economy" are usually divided into five components, of which the largest has been for industry and construction. As recently as the 1968 plan, this component accounted for nearly half of the budget appropriations to the national economy. The share has fallen in the 1970 plan to 38 percent—the decline probably attributable to the shift in investment financing and to the wholesale price revision of 1967, which lowered the number of enterprises operating at a loss.

Financing of state agriculture and the maintenance of procurement organizations form the second largest expenditure under the national economy. Financing of state farms is similar to that of state industrial enterprises; that is, they receive funds for direct investments and some operating expenses, and losses can be made up from the budget. In recent years there has been a movement to make state farms self-sufficient, primarily by paying them the same higher procurement prices received by collective farms. Budgetary funding of agriculture is much larger than is shown under the explicit allocation. Collective farms nominally are not financed from the budget; they are, however, recipients of budgetary expenditures through state procurement of agricultural products.

There is a considerable sum of expenditures remaining under "financing the national economy" after accounting for the allocation to the identified components. The residuals in the two most recent planned budgets are particularly large—R12.9 billion (1 ruble equals US$1.10) in 1969 and approximately R16 billion in 1970. Some observers believe that the residual is a possible location of hidden defense expenditures.

The budget allocation to social and cultural measures covers a broad range of public services: social security and welfare measures, free education, free medical service, the mass media, subsidized recreation and cultural activities, and financing of science. The share of this category in total budget expenditures has leveled off in the late 1960's to 37 or 38 percent, from 34 or 35 percent in the early years of the decade. Budget expenditures for science have increased more rapidly than other components—by 54 percent during the 1966—69 period, compared to 32 percent for the sum of the other expenditures. A large share of the science expenditures may

750

be devoted to military research and development and space activities. In addition to the use of budget funds, enterprises finance about one-third of all expenditures on science development from their own funds.

Budget expenditures identified for defense have formed about 12 or 13 percent of total expenditures since 1965. This relatively low share for defense cannot be taken at face value, however, because no breakdown of the budget category "defense" is ever revealed, and there is uncertainty about what is covered. Rough estimates of defense expenditures by direct means indicate that the explicit defense figure does not encompass all military outlays. Expenditure items under the defense appropriation, according to Soviet financial texts, are vague as to the inclusion of research and development for military and space, stockpiling of military commodities, expenditures for internal security and border forces, civil defense, and military aid to other nations. It may be assumed that some part of these items are not included under the "defense" category in the budget.

After declines in 1964 and 1965, the explicit defense expenditure has grown every year, and in 1968 it increased by 15 percent. The increase planned for 1970 is only 1 percent over 1969 expenditure. Changes in defense expenditures, perhaps even more than other expenditure categories, however, can be strongly influenced by administrative revisions of prices, such as the generally upward revision of industrial prices implemented in 1967 and a planned lowering of some industrial prices in 1970. An unusual feature of the defense budget in recent years is the lack of any divergence between actual and planned expenditures. This stability would not be expected, especially since events such as the intervention in Czechoslovakia must have had an impact on defense spending. This anomaly lends further credence to the possibility that other budget accounts are used for some defense expenditures.

Administrative outlays cover the central administrative institutions and various local governmental organs, the court system, and prosecutors' offices, but not the police. The costs of managing state enterprises and organizations and costs of administering the social and cultural sector are not included under administration.

In addition to the primary expenditure categories there is an unidentified residual, which has ranged from R 5 billion to R 9 billion in the planned budgets since 1966. Some of the miscellaneous expenditure items probably located in this residual include payment of interest on state loans (about R0.2 billion), tax refunds to individuals and enterprises, possibly allocations for long-term credit investment, and various other items. The planned budget probably also includes reserve funds of the councils of ministers of the USSR and the union republics. These are contingency funds and presumably are transferred to the appropriate categories in the report on actual budget expenditures.

Revenues

In the state budget, revenues are planned so that their total will exceed total expenditures. It is a commentary on Soviet fiscal control that there have been no budget deficits since the war year 1943. The budgetary surplus can serve as an anti-inflationary force in withdrawing money from the economy and is a source of funds for the expansion of bank credit.

The Soviet Union relies primarily on indirect taxation for its revenue. Turnover tax receipts and deductions from profits account for about two-thirds of total revenue. Direct taxes on the population—primarily through personal income tax—form only about 8 percent of the total.

The major trend of taxation in recent years has been a shift from turnover taxes to deductions from profits. Both sources of revenue are obtained by setting prices of goods at levels higher than costs of production and appropriating some part of the difference. To some extent there is a trade-off between the two taxes. When wholesale prices of consumption items are raised relative to the retail prices, profits are increased at the expense of turnover tax.

Deductions from Profits

Deductions from profits since 1967 have become the largest single source of revenue. The share of profit deductions in total revenue increased from 30 percent in 1965 to 35 percent in 1969. The growth of profit deductions paralleled a rapid growth in profits resulting primarily from revisions of wholesale prices.

The method of distributing profit between payments to the budget and internal payments to enterprise funds has been revised under the economic reform. Previously, the amount of profit payments to the budget was included as one of the enterprise's plan assignments. The reform divided the profit payment into three parts: a capital charge, a rent charge, and a remainder. The capital charge is a levy based on an enterprise's fixed and working capital—in 1970, 6 percent for most enterprises but 3 percent for some industries or groups of enterprises. The rent payment is mainly for enterprises in the extractive industries that have a particularly favorable location or circumstance. After these payment obligations are met, deductions are made into various enterprise funds—for incentives, social and cultural measures, housing, the development of production, and various other obligations of the enterprise. The remainder of profit, after all the deductions and payments, is transferred to the budget. This profit remainder is the largest of the profit payments, accounting for about one-half of the total planned profit deductions to the budget in 1970.

Turnover Tax

Turnover tax is essentially an excise tax on consumer goods, although the tax is levied on all uses of electricity, natural gas, and oil. The tax rate is established in conjunction with the pricing decision; that is, it is commonly set as the difference between the retail and wholesale price, allowing for a markup for distribution. In Soviet budgetary classification the tax is considered a revenue from the socialized sector because it is assessed on the producer or on a wholesale organization, though ultimately it is paid in full by the consumer. Although actual rates are seldom published they are known to vary widely with highest rates—perhaps more than 100 percent of the price—levied on luxury goods, tobacco, and alcoholic beverages. As a rough indication of the overall tax rate, turnover tax receipts in 1969 amounted to about 30 percent of the volume of retail sales.

Revenue from turnover tax has leveled off in recent years as a result of the reduction or elimination of the tax on many food products. The share of turnover tax receipts in total revenue has fallen from 38 percent in 1967 to 31 percent in 1968. Increased receipts in 1969 and planned for 1970—related possibly to wholesale price reductions—have raised the share slightly. With stable tax rates, the receipts from the turnover tax increase in relation to the increase in retail trade, and perhaps even more as consumers increase purchases of luxury goods carrying higher rates of taxation.

Other Revenues from the Socialized Sector

State social insurance receipts form the third largest revenue source of the socialized sector and account for about 5 percent of total revenue. The state social insurance budget is a separate budget, drawn up and administered by the trade unions, but is consolidated into the overall state budget. Contributions are made by state enterprises and organizations based on wages and salaries and are differentiated by type of work. Rates range from 4.4 percent for agricultural workers to 9 percent for the coal industry workers. The contributions to social insurance have not been sufficient to cover claims, therefore general budget funds are made available.

Organizations not owned and operated by the state—collective farms, consumer cooperatives, and producer cooperatives—pay a tax on their income. Collective farms are taxed at the rate of 12 percent on their net income above a 15-percent profitability rate. Tax rates on cooperatives are generally higher. Income taxes on organizations account for only about 1 percent of all revenues.

Other revenues include income from forestry operations, sale of gold, customs duties, repayment of loans by foreign countries, an entertainment tax, and various other taxes and fees. These revenues are not itemized in the published budget but collectively account for a large share—approximately 17 percent of total revenue in 1968.

Private Sector Revenues

Direct taxes on the population account for about 8 percent of total revenue. The personal income tax, the most important of the direct taxes, was to abolished by 1965 according to a law enacted in 1960. Implementation of this plan was rescinded in 1962, however, and income tax proceeds have grown at a rate faster than total revenue as a result of the rise in personal income. Income tax is paid on a progressive rate schedule, exempting those with incomes of under R60 a month. Payments are also differentiated according to the source of income and size of family. Exemptions are granted, for example, for military personnel (except for officers and career enlisted personnel), for disabilities and pensions, for invention awards up to R1,000 and for wages of medical, veterinary, and livestock workers. Workers and employees with more than three dependents are entitled to a 30-percent deduction. Other taxes on the population include an agricultural tax levied on incomes from private plots, a tax on privately owned horses, and a bachelor and small family tax levied on single men between twenty and fifty years of age and childless couples.

Revenues to the budget from state loans have been insignificant since the abolition of compulsory loans in 1957. A 3-percent state lottery loan yields about R100 million to R200 million annually. Miscellaneous local taxes, lotteries, and fees contribute a total of less than R1 billion annually.

Revenue Division Among the Budgets

In the budgets of the union republics, and lower levels of government as well, the total revenues are planned to be equal to expenditures. This balance is achieved primarily through manipulation of the turnover tax receipts. First, the relatively fixed sources of revenue are calculated, including: deductions from profits of enterprises under their jurisdiction; all revenue from the income tax on collective farms, the agricultural tax, bachelor tax, forestry operations, local taxes and lotteries; and half of the income tax on the population. The gap between these revenues and planned expenditures is filled by retaining a share of turnover tax receipts. These shares are written into the annual budget law. Some republics—the

754

Uzbek, Kazakh, Tadzhik, Armenian, and Turkmen—in addition to retaining 100 percent of their turnover tax collections, have received subsidies from the all-union budget.

THE BANKING AND CURRENCY SYSTEM

Structure and Functions

One of the first acts of the Soviet government upon coming to power was to nationalize the banking system, expropriate the shareholders, and repudiate all foreign debts. A new Soviet State Bank (Gosudarstvennyy Bank—Gosbank) was established as the central bank in 1921. The credit reform of 1930 and 1931 abolished the practice of interenterprise credit, replacing it with bank credit, and the Gosbank was given a monopoly of short-term lending. Since that time the banking and currency system has remained relatively unchanged except for organizational modifications. In 1954 the Gosbank was separated from the Ministry of Finance and given essentially a ministerial status. The banking reform act of 1959 abolished certain specialized banks, transferring their lending functions to the Gosbank. The Investment Bank and the Bank for Foreign Trade have survived as specialized institutions.

The State Bank

The main bank of the USSR, the Gosbank, acts as a combination central bank, commerical bank, and settlement bank. It is the bank of issue, regulates currency and credit, and handles payments between enterprises and organizations. The bank also acts as the fiscal agent for all levels of government, receiving all taxes and payments to the state and paying out budgetary appropriations.

The Gosbank is organized regionally. In addition to the head office in Moscow, which regulates the overall credit system and money circulation, there are main offices in the various republics and district offices in the autonomous republics, *kraya* (territories), and *oblasti* (regions). The district offices supervise the approximately 4,000 branch banks and agencies that are the main point of contact with the clients. In addition, there are several thousand payment and collection points that perform limited banking functions, such as accepting payments for communal services and taxes. The Gosbank serves about 600,000 client organizations and employs over 250,000 persons.

Although most of the activities of the Gosbank are with enterprises and organizations in the socialized sector, it does provide some services for the population. The bank maintains a small amount of personal deposits (R130 million in 1967) and issues long-term loans to individuals, mostly for housing construction. Loans to individuals outstanding at the beginning of 1969 amounted to R725 million. In addition, the bank indirectly has furnished consumer credit through retail stores since 1959, when installment credit was initiated for consumer goods not in short supply.

The Gosbank occupies a position unique to centrally planned economies in that it supervises the financial activities of its clients in support of policies formulated in the planning structure. As a key part of the economic control mechanism, the Gosbank monitors the transactions of enterprises and other organizations to assure fulfillment of production and financial plans, proper use of funds, and the maintenance of financial discipline.

Control over the financial affairs of enterprises and organizations is facilitated by the requirement that nearly all their funds be maintained in non-interest-bearing accounts with a branch of the Gosbank. As interenterprise credit is prohibited, virtually all payments are made through these accounts. The bank receives copies of the financial plan and other information concerning the operation of each enterprise and thus is able to verify its transactions on a day-to-day basis. The bank has the authority to enforce payment for contracts between enterprises and organizations and to assure prompt fulfillment of obligations to the state budget.

One of the most important means of Gosbank control over enterprises is the payment of wages. A time schedule of cash disbursements for wage payments is maintained by the bank, but actual disbursements are made contingent upon the fulfillment of quarterly production goals. Underfulfillment of plans means the enterprise may not receive its planned wage fund in full. A major purpose of the leverage over wage disbursements is to keep labor costs down and prevent wages from exceeding planned limits.

Savings Banks

To service the bulk of the banking needs of the population there is a network of savings banks, numbering 76,500 offices in 1969. Most of these are very small and are operated on a part-time basis by the postal administration. In 1963 control over the network of savings banks was transferred from the Ministry of Finance to the Gosbank. At the beginning of 1970 there were 73 million individual depositors whose total deposits reached over R38 billion.

The services provided by savings banks are much more limited than those provided by institutions in Western countries. They do not engage in lending operations to the population but apparently turn over deposits in excess of a cash reserve to the Gosbank, where they serve as a source of funds for expanding short-term loans in the economy. Wage earners are encouraged to have their pay deposited directly in savings accounts. Interest on savings for deposits repayable on demand is 2 percent and for savings held over 6 months, 3 percent. Depositors may instruct the bank to make payments for rent, utilities, and taxes from their accounts. The savings banks also issue money orders, sell and redeem state bonds, sell tickets for national and regional lotteries, and make certain payments on behalf of the government, such as old-age pensions and various other social security benefits. In addition to the private savings of individuals, savings accounts of nonprofit organizations, collective farms, and low-level municipal entities (such as villages) are carried in the savings banks, as are some current accounts of enterprises and organizations that are not large enough to require concentration in the State Bank.

The Specialized Banks

The Investment Bank—also known as the Construction Bank—is primarily responsible for administering budgetary funds earmarked for capital investment. In addition, the bank issues long-term credit for investment and short-term credit for related construction activities. Before 1959 the bank was called the Industrial Bank. Other specialized investment banks were abolished, and their functions were transferred to the Gosbank. The network of the Investment Bank is similar to that of the Gosbank, with offices in republics, *kraya*, and *oblasti*, and branches in many *rayony* (districts) and cities. In areas not important enough to warrant a separate branch, the Investment Bank uses the facilities of the Gosbank.

The other specialized bank in the Soviet Union is the Foreign Trade Bank, responsible for financial operations connected with foreign trade. It issues credits and makes and accepts payments on behalf of the Soviet foreign trade organizations for the export and import of goods. In addition, the bank carries out noncommercial transactions involving foreign currencies. The Foreign Trade Bank operates in the USSR through accounts with the Gosbank and has correspondent relations with over 1,000 foreign banks. There are Soviet-owned banks in foreign countries, principally London (the Moscow Narodnyy Bank), Paris (Banque Commerciale pour l'Europe du Nord) and Zurich (the Voskhod Handelsbank). These banks, owned by the Foreign Trade Bank and the Gosbank, facilitate trade with the West and provide a point of contact with foreign money markets for dealings in gold and convertible currencies.

In addition to the Foreign Trade Bank and the Soviet-owned foreign banks, the USSR is a member of the International Bank for Economic Cooperation, set up in 1964 to promote multilateral clearances among members of the Council for Economic Mutual Assistance (CEMA). The International Bank for Economic Cooperation has capital contributed to it by the members. Clearing transactions are carried out in "transferable rubles" that are equivalent to

Soviet rubles. These are not convertible and are simply an internal accounting unit. Trade imbalances are covered by short-term credits from the bank at low interest rates (see ch. 35, Foreign Economic Relations).

The Credit System

The Credit Plan, prepared quarterly and annually by the Gosbank, determines the amount of short-term credit to be made available to the economy during the plan period. It is related primarily to the working capital needs of enterprises for meeting their production plans. The Credit Plan specifies the amount of credit by purpose, sector, and territorial distribution and lists the sources of funds. After the plan is approved by the Council of Ministers, it becomes a directive by which the credit operations for each branch bank is governed for the quarter.

The monopoly of control in issuing credit is a means of achieving specific goals, such as increasing the rate of turnover of inventories, and assuring that an enterprise uses its funds in accordance with the production plans. As a rule, funds owned by enterprises for working capital are set and maintained at a low level, adequate to carry only a part of the usual stock of raw and semifinished materials and of goods in process. The remainder of working capital needs are satisfied by credit from the Gosbank, except for construction organizations that receive their credit from the Investment Bank. At the beginning of 1969 short-term bank credit made up nearly half (48.3 percent) of the R181 billion of working capital in the economy.

The bulk of credit for working capital (about three-fourths) is used to carry inventories of materials, unfinished production, and finished goods. The need for this type of credit is greatest in the trade, supply, and procurement networks. Another significant use of short-term credit is settlement credit, by which suppliers are credited for goods shipped before actually receiving payment from the buyer. Settlement credit accounted for about 15 percent of short-term credit outstanding at the start of 1969, down from 19 percent in 1965. Short-term loans for other purposes have been growing rapidly but in 1969 represented only about 10 percent of the total. These include loans for payment of wage obligations to the budget when the enterprise is temporarily short of funds. Loans for introducing new equipment or technology and for expanding secondary consumer goods production are also included in the other category of short-term credit even though terms may be for from one to several years. These medium-term loans have been relatively insignificant in volume, forming 3.7 percent of the total outstanding short-term credit, but have more than doubled in the 1966—69 period.

The interest rate structure for short-term credit was revised by a 1967 decree. Loans for settlement purposes and for seasonal inventories continue to carry a nominal rate of 1 and 2 percent annually. For other types of short-term loans the charges were fixed in a relationship to the charges on existing fixed and usual working capital (6 percent). Loans for usual working capital advances, for example, are charged at the same rate as the capital charge; loans to meet payrolls are 1 percent higher, and overdue loans are charged at 2 percent higher.

Payment of interest, even at the penalty rate for overdue loans, is not much of an inhibiting factor in checking demands for credit. Credit sanctions are frequently imposed when loans are used for other than planned purposes and in order to reduce the volume of overdue loans. The sanctions used vary according to the circumstances and the severity of the case. Usually there is some form of direct administrative action, such as enforcement of a rigid set of priorities over payments, or a higher echelon authority may be required to guarantee future loans. More extreme measures may involved suspension of certain types of credit, taking over collateral and, ultimately, the dissolution of the enterprise.

Long-term credit played a relatively small role in the USSR in 1970. Long-term bank loans outstanding at the beginning of 1969 totalled R12.7 billion, or only 13 percent as much as the outstanding short-term credit; nevertheless, this amount was double the level of 1966. Collective farms are the major recipients of long-term credit, holding 63 percent of the outstanding total at the start of 1969. Another major part goes to finance housing construction both by individuals and by housing cooperatives.

Long-term credit was intended to become a major source of investment financing in the state sector in conjunction with economic reform. It was expected that 35 to 40 percent of all capital investment funds would come from bank credit by the time enterprises and organizations were operating under the new conditions. Budgetary investment is to be restricted largely to financing investment in new enterprises where construction costs could not be recovered in five years; otherwise, investment is to come from the enterprises' own capital and from bank credit. The shift to bank financing apparently has lagged, because by 1969 bank credit reportedly supplied R2 billion or about 3 percent of all capital investment, not including that of collective farms.

Long-term loans are issued at very low interest rates. Collective farms pay an annual charge of 0.75 percent; individuals, 2 percent; housing cooperatives, 0.5 percent, and enterprises 0.5 and 1.5 percent, depending on the planned purpose. The low rates of interest have encouraged enterprises to remain in debt beyond the due date because even the higher interest for delinquent loans—3 percent—is lower than the 6-percent capital charge that takes effect when the debt is retired.

A long-term credit plan is prepared annually but is not part of the main credit plan, which covers only short-term credit. Sources of funds for long-term credit include repayments of loans and from appropriations of the state budget.

The Currency System

The ruble is the basic monetary unit in the USSR, defined by the government to be worth .98741.2 grams of gold, which is the equivalent to the official dollar exchange rate of US$1.10. The gold content has little meaning, however, because the currency is managed; it is not redeemable in gold nor is it freely convertible into another country's currency. In the case of trade with free world countries, transactions are usually carried out at terms that may differ considerably from the official rate of exchange. Trade with other countries is usually balanced bilaterally. It is highly unlikely that the amount of currency is in fact limited by the size of the gold reserve. Gold holdings are never reported.

The major part of currency in circulation consists of bank notes issued by the Gosbank in denominations of R10 and higher. Bank notes are reported to be backed, in part, by gold and other precious metals. Small denomination notes (R1 to R5) and coins are issued by the treasury and are not backed by gold but solely by the credit of the state. The division between bank and treasury notes is arbitrary, as they operate the same way in circulation and both are carried as a liability of the Gosbank. Statistics on currency in circulation have not been published since 1937.

The role of money in the Soviet Union as a medium of exchange is quite different from that of free market economies. It does not give the holder absolute command over resources. In the state sector, money can be used only for purposes specified in the plan. Thus, money is essentially an accounting unit. It is only when the money comes into the hands of the wage earner that it acquires purchasing power. Even then, the value of ownership of money is circumscribed, as the individual can only acquire consumer goods and strictly limited categories of property for personal use.

Monetary payments are of two types: cash and noncash. Payments within the state sector (between enterprises, organizations, and the government) by law are made almost wholly on a noncash basis—simply a bookkeeping matter of transferring funds from deposit accounts. Cash payments are used for virtually all transactions between the government (including state enterprises) and the population and for payments within the private sector (services, sales by collective farmers, artisans, and cooperative producers).

760

The amount of money allocated to the socialized and private sectors is controlled by financial plans. Control over the noncash money supply in the socialized sector is established largely by the credit plan. Control over the currency in the private sector is less direct and more difficult to attain. The "Balance of Money Incomes and Expenditures of the Population," prepared by Gosplan (State Planning Committee) as part of the national economic plan, relates the anticipated money income of different sectors with the projected supply of consumer goods and services. Any imbalance between the two may then be corrected by changes in production, distribution, wages, or prices, but the process is difficult and cumbersome. A cash plan, prepared annually and quarterly by the Gosbank from the balance, estimates the payments and receipts of cash by the bank, the difference representing the emission or withdrawal of money from circulation. A planned currency increase is implemented through a currency issue directive usually by the Council of Ministers. Short-term emissions by branches of the Gosbank are authorized by the center when necessary for a five-day period. When receipts of the branches exceed payments, the money is transferred to a reserve on the same day.

Although the statistics are not published, the amount of currency in circulation reportedly has been growing, both as a result of the growth in money income and through a shift in the collective farm sector from payment in kind to monetary payment. The volume of currency in circulation, however, is very low compared to that of market economies. The circulation of currency for the most part involves only one basic transaction cycle: the currency issued as wages is usually spent in state retail stores and for state services and is immediately redeposited with the Gosbank. The share of currency in this circuit is reported to be 94 percent of total currency flow, the remainder presumably being in the private, cooperative, and collective farm market sphere and in cash hoards.

The building up of cash hoards is regarded as a potentially inflationary situation by monetary authorities. In order to discourage the hoarding of currency, financial authorities push the use of savings accounts, which take currency out of circulation. Savings deposits can also be a source of inflationary pressure, unless restrictions are imposed on their withdrawal. When inflationary pressures threaten stability of the system, the government may increase retail prices or, as in 1947, devalue the currency. The currency reform of 1947 devalued cash holdings by ten to one, while savings deposits and most state bonds were exchanged at rates of two or three to one.

BIBLIOGRAPHY

Section I. General Survey

RECOMMENDED SOURCES

Armstrong, John A. *Ideology, Politics, and Government in the Soviet Union.* (Rev. ed.) New York: Praeger, 1967.

Avtorkhanov, Abdurakhman. *The Communist Party Apparatus.* Chicago: Henry Regnery, 1966.

Barghoorn, Frederick C. *Politics in the USSR.* Boston: Little, Brown, 1966.

Bauer, Raymond A. *Nine Soviet Portraits.* Cambridge: MIT Press, 1955.

Bennigsen, Alexandre, and Lemercier-Quelquejay, Chantal. *Islam in the Soviet Union.* New York: Praeger, 1967.

Berdyaev, Nicholas. *The Origin of Russian Communism.* Ann Arbor: University of Michigan Press, 1948.

Berg, L. S. *Natural Regions of the U.S.S.R.* New York: Macmillan, 1959.

Black, Cyril E. *The Dynamics of Modernization.* New York: Harper and Row, 1966.

Black, Cyril E. (ed.) *The Transformation of Russian Society.* Cambridge: Harvard University Press, 1967.

Bornstein, Morris, and Fusfeld, Daniel R. (eds.) *The Soviet Economy: A Book of Readings.* (Rev. ed.) Homewood: R. D. Irwin, 1966.

Broderson, Arvid. *The Soviet Worker: Labor and Government in Soviet Society.* New York: Random House, 1966.

Brzezinski, Zbigniew K. *Ideology and Power in Soviet Politics.* (Rev. ed.) New York: Praeger, 1967.

Conyngham, William J. "Party, State Relationships in the Soviet Union," *World Affairs,* CXXXII, No. 1, June 1969, 48–63.

Cressey, George B. *Soviet Potentials: A Geographic Appraisal.* Syracuse: Syracuse University Press, 1962.

Dallin, David J. *The Real Soviet Russia.* New Haven: Yale University Press, 1944.

Daniels, Robert V. *The Conscience of the Revolution: Communist Opposition in Soviet Russia.* Cambridge: Harvard University Press, 1960.

763

Dunn, Stephen P., and Dunn, Ethel. *The Peasants of Central Russia*. New York: Holt, Rinehart and Winston, 1967.

Fainsod, Merle. *How Russia is Ruled*. (Rev. ed.) Cambridge: Harvard University Press, 1964.

Geiger, H. Kent. *The Family in Soviet Russia*. (Russian Research Center Studies, LVI.) Cambridge: Harvard University Press, 1968.

Gregory, James S. *Russian Land, Soviet People: A Geographical Approach to the USSR*. New York: Pegasus, 1968.

Grey, Ian. *The First Fifty Years, Soviet Russia 1917–1967*. New York: Coward-McCann, 1967.

Hardt, John P., et al. *Selected Studies in Soviet Economic Trends, Structure, and Institutions*. (Report RAC–R–3Q.) McLean: Research Analysis Corporation, February 1968.

Hazard, John Newbold. *The Soviet System of Government*. Chicago: University of Chicago Press, 1968.

Hulicka, Karel, and Hulicka, Irene M. *Soviet Institutions: The Individual and Society*. Boston: Christopher Publishing House, 1967.

Hunt, R. N. Carew. *The Theory and Practice of Communism*. New York: Macmillan, 1959.

Inkeles, Alex. *Social Change in Soviet Russia*. (Russian Research Center Studies, LVII.) Cambridge: Harvard University Press, 1968.

Inkeles, Alex, and Bauer, Raymond A. *The Soviet Citizen: Daily Life in a Totalitarian Society*. (Russian Research Center Studies, XXXV.) Cambridge: Harvard University Press, 1959.

Juviler, Peter H., and Morton, Henry W. (eds.) *Soviet Policy Making*. New York: Praeger, 1967.

Kirchner, Walther. *A History of Russia*. (4th ed.) New York: Barnes and Noble, 1966.

Lawrence, John. *A History of Russia*. (Rev. ed.) New York: Mentor Books, 1965.

Levin, M. G., and Potapov, L. P. (eds.) *The Peoples of Siberia*. Chicago: University of Chicago Press, 1964.

Lichtheim, George. *The Origins of Socialism*. New York: Praeger, 1969.

Mendel, Arthur P. (ed.) *Essential Works of Marxism*. New York: Bantam Books, 1965.

Riasanovsky, Nicholas V. *A History of Russia*. New York: Oxford University Press, 1963.

Scott, Derek, J. R. *Russian Political Institutions*. (3d ed.) New York: Praeger, 1966.

Swearer, Howard R., and Longaker, Richard P. (eds.) *Contemporary Communism: Theory and Practice*. Belmont: Wadsworth, 1963.

Tatu, Michel. *Power in the Kremlin: From Khrushchev to Kosygin.*
New York: Viking Press, 1969.
Tucker, Robert C. *Philosophy and Myth in Karl Marx.* Cambridge:
Cambridge University Press, 1961.
U.S. Congress. 89th, 2d Session. Joint Economic Committee. *New
Directions in the Soviet Economy,* Part II–A: Economic Per-
formance. Washington: GPO, 1966.
U.S. Congress. 90th, 2d Session. Joint Economic Committee. *Soviet
Economic Performance, 1966–67.* Washington: GPO, 1968.
U.S. Congress. 91st, 1st Session. Joint Economic Committee. *The
Military Budget and National Economic Priorities: Hearings,
Part III, June 23 and 24, 1969.* Washington: GPO, 1969.
U.S. Department of Commerce. Bureau of the Census. *The Soviet
Financial System.* Washington: GPO, 1968.
Vernadsky, George. *A History of Russia.* New York: Bantam
Books, 1967.
Whiting, Kenneth R. *The Soviet Union Today: A Concise Hand-
book.* (Rev. ed.) New York: Praeger, 1966.

OTHER SOURCES USED

Akademiya Nauk SSSR. *Struktura Narodnogo Khozyaystve SSSR.*
Moskva: Nauka, 1967.
Alisov, B. P. *Klimat SSSR.* Moskva: Geograficheskoy Literatury,
1956.
Amalrik, Andrei Alexeivich. "The Fall of the Soviet Empire,"
Atlas, XVIV, No. 2, February 1970, 20–24.
American Association for the Advancement of Slavic Studies.
"Academician Rumyantsev Interprets Communism's 'Basic Eco-
nomic Law'," *Current Abstracts of the Soviet Press,* I, No. 9,
February 1969, 4.
————. "Brezhnev Speech at International Communist Confer-
ence," *Current Digest of the Soviet Press,* XXI, No. 23, July 2,
1969, 3–17.
————. "Ministry for Safeguarding Public Order Becomes Min-
istry of Internal Security," *Current Digest of the Soviet Press,*
XX, No. 48, December 18, 1968, 2–4.
————. "Peoples Control Under New Statute," *Current Abstracts
of the Soviet Press,* II, No. 2, May 1969, 3–4.
Armstrong, John A. *The Politics of Totalitarianism: The Com-
munist Party of the Soviet Union from 1934 to the Present.*
New York: Random House, 1961.
Azrael, Jeremy R. *Managerial Power and Soviet Politics.* Cam-
bridge: Harvard University Press, 1966.
Baranskiy, N. N. *Ekonomicheskaya Geografiya SSSR.* Moskva:
Geograficheskoy Literatury, 1954.

Black, Cyril E. (ed.) *Rewriting Russian History.* New York: Praeger, 1956.

Borisov, Anatolii Aleksandrovich. *Climates of the USSR.* (Ed., Cyril A. Nalstead, and trans., R. A. Ledward.) Chicago: Aldine, 1965.

Brown, Emily Clark. *Soviet Trade Unions and Labor Relations.* Cambridge: Harvard University Press, 1966.

Brumberg, Abraham (ed.). "Myths, Perceptions, Policy: A Symposium," *Problems of Communism,* XIX, No. 1, 1970, 1–27.

Cole, J. P., and German, F. C. *A Geography of the USSR.* London: Butterworth, 1967.

Communist Party of the Soviet Union. 22d Congress. *The Road to Communism.* Moscow: Foreign Languages Publishing House, 1962.

Conquest, Robert (ed.). *The Soviet Police System.* New York: Praeger, 1968.

Cookridge, E. H. *Soviet Spy Net.* London: Frederick Muller, 1954.

Crankshaw, Edward. *Khrushchev: A Career.* New York: Viking Press, 1966.

———. *Russia Without Stalin: The Emerging Pattern.* New York: Viking Press, 1956.

Crowley, Edward L.; Lebed, Andrew I.; and Schulz, Heinrich E. (eds.) *Prominent Personalities in the USSR.* Metuchen: Scarecrow Press, 1968.

Daniels, Robert V. *Red October: The Bolshevik Revolution of 1917.* New York: Scribner, 1967.

De Pauw, John W. "The Private Sector in Soviet Agriculture," *Slavic Review,* XXVIII, No. 1, March 1969, 63–64.

Deutscher, Isaac. *Stalin: A Political Biography.* New York: Vintage Books, 1960.

———. *The Unfinished Revolution: Russia, 1917–1967.* New York: Oxford University Press, 1967.

Dmytryshyn, Basil. *USSR: A Concise History.* New York: Scribner, 1965.

Dunn, Stephen P., and Dunn, Ethel. "Soviet Regime and Native Culture in Central Asia and Kazakhstan: The Major Peoples," *Current Anthropology,* VIII, No. 3, June 1967, 147–208.

East, W. G. *The Soviet Union.* Princeton: Van Nostrand, 1963.

Economist, CCXXXI, No. 6563, June 7, 1969 and; CCXXXIV, No. 6596, January 24, 1970.

Fedenko, Panas V. *Comintern Anniversary Cold-Shouldered by World's Communists.* (No. 554). Munich: Institute for the Study of the USSR, June 24, 1969.

Fisher, George. *Soviet Opposition to Stalin: A Case Study in World War II.* Cambridge: Harvard University Press, 1952.

Fitzsimmons, Thomas, et al. *USSR: Its People Its Society, Its Culture.* New Haven: HRAF Press, 1960.

Florinsky, Michael R. (ed.) *Encyclopedia of Russia and the Soviet Union.* New York: McGraw-Hill, 1961.

Friedrich, Paul. "The Linguistic Reflex of Social Change: From Tsarist to Soviet Russian Kinship," *Sociological Inquiry,* XXXVI, No. 2, Spring 1966, 159–185.

Ginsburgs, George. "The Kremlin Scene: Politics in a Cul-De-Sac," *Current History,* LVII, No. 338, October 1969, 228–231.

Goodall, George. *Soviet Union in Maps.* Chicago: Danoyer-Geppert, 1954.

Gosplan SSSR. *Planovoye Khozyaystvo,* XLVI, No. 12, December 1969.

Gray, G. D. B. *Soviet Land.* London: Black, 1947.

Halm, George N. *Economic Systems.* (3d ed.) New York: Holt, Rinehart and Winston, 1968.

Harcave, Sidney. *Russia: A History.* (3d ed.) New York: Lippincott, 1956.

Hardt, John P., et al. *Recent Soviet Economic Performance: Selected Aspects.* (Paper RAC–P–38.) McLean: Research Analysis Corporation, August 1968.

Hodson, D. J. M. *The Soviet Union.* London: University of London Press, 1967.

Inkeles, Alex, and Geiger, H. Kent. (eds.) *Soviet Society: A Book of Readings.* Boston: Houghton Mifflin, 1961.

Institute of Strategic Studies. *The Military Balance.* London: Institute of Strategic Studies, 1968.

"The International." Pages 405–407 in *Encyclopaedia Britannica,* XII. Chicago: William Benton, 1969.

Kassof, Allen (ed.). *Prospects for Soviet Society.* New York: Praeger, 1968.

Kendrew, Wilfred G. *Climates of the Continents.* (5th ed.) New York: Oxford University Press, 1961.

Kish, George. *Economic Atlas of the Soviet Union.* Ann Arbor: University of Michigan Press, 1969.

Krader, Lawrence. *Peoples of Central Asia.* (Uralic and Altaic Series, XXVI.) Bloomington: Indiana University Press, 1963.

Leonhard, Wolfgang. *The Kremlin Since Stalin.* New York: Praeger, 1962.

Linden, Carl A. *Khrushchev and the Soviet Leadership, 1957–1964.* Baltimore: Johns Hopkins Press, 1966.

Lydolph, Paul E. *Geography of the USSR.* New York: John Wiley, 1964.

McClosky, Herbert, and Turner, John E. *The Soviet Dictatorship.* New York: McGraw-Hill, 1960.

McNeal, Robert H. *The Bolshevik Tradition*. (2d ed.) Englewood Cliffs: Prentice-Hall, 1965.

Mandell, William. *Russia Reexamined: The Land, the People, and How They Live*. New York: Hill and Wang, 1964.

Mehnert, Klaus. *Soviet Man and His World*. New York: Praeger, 1962.

Mellor, Ray E. *Geography of the USSR*. New York: St. Martin's Press, 1964.

Meyer, Alfred G. *The Soviet Political System: An Interpretation*. New York: Random House, 1965.

Mikhailov, Nikolai. *Across the Map of the USSR*. Moscow: Foreign Languages Publishing House, 1969.

————. *Glimpses of the USSR*. Moscow: Foreign Languages Publishing House, 1960.

Milkov, F. N., and Gvozdetsky, N. A. *Fizicheskaya Geografiya S.S.S.R.* Moskva: Geograficheskoy Literatury, 1963.

Miller, Wright. *Russians as People*. New York: Dutton, 1961.

Mirov, N. T. *Geography of Russia*. London: John Wiley, 1951.

Nauchno-Issledovatelsky Ekonomichesky Institut pri Gosplane SSSR. *Sovershenstvovaniye Struktury Promyshlennogo Proizvodstva*. Moskva: Ekonomika, 1968.

Nove, Alec. *The Soviet Economy*. (Rev. ed.) New York: Praeger, 1967.

Pares, Bernard. *A History of Russia*. New York: Knopf, 1953.

Pearson, Ross Norton. *Physical Geography: A Survey of Man's Physical Environment*. New York: Barnes and Noble, 1968.

Pomeroy, William J. *Half a Century of Socialism: Soviet Life in the Sixties*. New York: International Publishers, 1967.

Pye, L. W., and Verba, Sidney (eds.). *Political Culture and Political Development*. Princeton: Princeton University Press, 1965.

Rigby, Thomas H. *Communist Party Membership in the USSR, 1917–1967*. Princeton: Princeton University Press, 1968.

Sachs, Moshe Y. (ed.) *Europe*. New York: Worldmark Press, 1967.

Saikowski, Charlotte. "Lenin's 100th Anniversary: But Where has All the Fervor Gone?," *Christian Science Monitor*, January 23, 1970, 10.

————. "One-Man Rule-Nyet, 'Collective Leadership'-Da," *Christian Science Monitor*, January 16, 1970, 9.

————. "Soviet Industry: Wanted a Management Revolution," *Christian Science Monitor*, January 8, 1970, 13.

————. "What do Russians Really Think About?," *Christian Science Monitor*, January 30, 1970, 9.

Salisbury, Harrison E. (ed.) *The Soviet Union: The Fifty Years*. New York: Harcourt, Brace and World, 1967.

Shabad, Theodore. *Geography of the USSR.* New York: Columbia University Press, 1951.

Sherman, Howard J. *The Soviet Economy.* Boston: Little, Brown, 1969.

Smirnov, I. I. (ed.) *A Short History of the USSR.* 2 vols. Moscow: Progress Publishers, 1965.

Sorlin, Pierre. *The Soviet People and Their Society: From 1917 to the Present.* New York: Praeger, 1968.

Spulber, Nicholas. "The Soviet Economy in the 1970s," *Current History,* LVII, No. 338, October 1969, 214–219.

Thrower, Norman J. W. (ed.) *Man's Domain: A Thematic Atlas of the World.* New York: McGraw-Hill, 1968.

Treml, Vladimir G. (ed.) *The Development of the Soviet Economy: Plan and Performance.* New York: Praeger, 1968.

Tsentralnoye Statisticheskoye Upravleniye pri Sovete Ministrov SSSR. *Narodnoye khozyaystvo SSSR v 1967 g.* Moskva: Statistika, 1968.

――――. *SSSR v tsifrakh v 1967 godu.* Moskva: Statistika, 1968.

23d Congress of the Communist Party of the Soviet Union. Moscow: Novosti Press Agency Publishing House, n.d.

U.S. Congress. 88th, 1st Session. Senate. Subcommittee on National Security Staffing and Operations to the Committee on Government Operations. *Staffing Procedures and Problems in the Soviet Union.* Washington: GPO, 1963.

U.S. Department of State. *Afghanistan-U.S.S.R. Boundary.* (International Boundary Study No. 26.) Washington. Department of State Geographer, 1963.

――――. *China-USSR Boundary.* (International Boundary Study No. 64.) Washington: Department of State Geographer, 1966.

――――. *Czechoslovakia-USSR Boundary.* (International Boundary Study No. 77.) Washington: Department of State Geographer, 1967.

――――. *Finland-USSR Boundary.* (International Boundary Study No. 74.) Washington: Department of State Geographer, 1967.

――――. *Hungary-USSR Boundary.* (International Boundary Study No. 76.) Washington: Department of State Geographer, 1967.

――――. *Iran-USSR Boundary.* (International Boundary Study No. 25.) Washington: Department of State Geographer, 1963.

――――. *Korea-USSR Boundary.* (International Boundary Study No. 59.) Washington: Department of State Geographer, 1965.

――――. *Norway-USSR Boundary.* (International Boundary Study No. 24.) Washington: Department of State Geographer, 1963.

――――. *Rumania-USSR Boundary.* (International Boundary Study No. 43.) Washington: Department of State Geographer, 1964.

――――. *Turkey-USSR Boundary.* (International Boundary Study No. 29.) Washington: Department of State Geographer, 1964.

————. *US-Russia Convention Line of 1867.* (International Boundary Study No. 14.) Washington: Department of State Geographer, 1962.

U.S. Department of the Army. *Strategic Survey.* (DA Pamphlet 550-6 USSR.) Washington: GPO, 1969.

"The USSR and Eastern Europe," *Oxford Regional Economic Atlas.* Oxford: Oxford University Press, 1963.

Washington Post (Special series of articles on the Soviet Union, by Anatole Shub), June 13–22, 1969.

Wolin, Simon, and Slusser, Robert M. (eds.) *The Soviet Secret Police.* New York: Praeger, 1957.

Wren, Melvin C. *The Course of Russian History.* (2d ed.) New York: Macmillan, 1963.

Zagoria, Janet D. (ed.) *Power and the Soviet Elite: The Letter of an Old Bolshevik and Other Essays,* by Boris Nicolaevsky. New York: Praeger, 1965.

(Various issues of the following periodicals were also used in the preparation of this section: *Ekonomicheskaya Gazeta* [Moskva], July 1969–February 1970; *L'Express* [Paris], January 5–February 23, 1970; *New York Times,* May 13, 1969–February 8, 1970; *Pravda* [Moskva], April 1969–February 1970; *Sotsialisticheskaya Industriya* [Moskva], July 1, 1969–February 24, 1970; and *Washington Post,* June 22, 1969–January 15, 1970.)

Section II. Social

RECOMMENDED SOURCES

Abraham, Gerald. *Eight Soviet Composers.* New York: Oxford University Press, 1943.

Allworth, Edward (ed.). *Central Asia: A Century of Russian Rule.* New York: Columbia University Press, 1967.

Amann, R., et al. *Science Policy in the USSR.* Paris: OECD, 1969.

Apel, Willi. *Harvard Dictionary of Music.* Cambridge: Harvard University Press, 1961.

Barry, Donald. "Dissident Intellectuals: Views From Moscow," *Survey*, No. 70, Winter–Spring 1969.

Bauer, Raymond A., and Gleicher, David B. "Word-of-Mouth Communication in the Soviet Union," *Public Opinion Quarterly*, XVII, No. 3, Fall 1953. 197–310.

Bennigsen, Alexandre, and Lemercier-Quelquejay, Chantal. *Islam in the Soviet Union.* New York: Praeger, 1967.

Berdyaev, Nicholas. *The Russian Idea.* New York: Macmillan, 1948.

Bereday, George Z. F. "Education: Organization and Values Since 1917." Pages 353–370 in Cyril E. Black, *The Transformation of Russian Society: Aspects of Social Change Since 1861.* Cambridge: Harvard University Press, 1967.

Bereday, George Z. F.; Brickman, William W.; and Read, Gerald H. (eds.) *The Changing Soviet School.* Boston: Houghton Mifflin, 1960.

Bereday, George Z. F., and Pennar, Jean. *The Politics of Soviet Education.* New York: Praeger, 1960.

Bergaust, Erik. *The Russians in Space.* New York: Putnam, 1969.

Billington, James H. "Beneath the Panoply of Power, the Intelligentsia Hits Out at the Old Order," *Life*, LXIII, No. 19, November 10, 1967, 70–84.

————. *The Icon and the Axe: An Interpretative History of Russian Culture.* New York: Knopf, 1966.

Black, Cyril E. (ed.) *Rewriting Russian History.* New York: Praeger, 1956.

Bowers, Faubion. *Broadway USSR.* New York: Nelson, 1959.

Communist Party of the Soviet Union. 22d Congress. *The Road to Communism.* Moscow: Foreign Languages Publishing House, 1962.

771

Conquest, Robert (ed.). *Religion in the USSR.* New York: Praeger, 1968.

———. *Soviet Nationalities Policy in Practice.* New York: Praeger, 1967.

Cressey, George B. *Soviet Potentials: A Geographic Appraisal.* Syracuse: Syracuse University Press, 1962.

Curtiss, John "Church and State." Pages 405–425 in Cyril E. Black (ed.), *The Transformation of Russian Society: Aspects of Social Change Since 1861.* Cambridge: Harvard University Press, 1967.

———. *The Russian Church and the Soviet State, 1917–1950.* Boston: Little, Brown, 1953.

Davies, R. W., and Amann, R. "Science Policy in the USSR," *Scientific American,* CCXX, No. 6, June 1969, 19–29.

de Custine, Marquis. *Journey for Our Time.* (Trans., Phyllis Peen Kohler.) New York: Pellegrini and Cudahy, 1951.

Dunn, Stephen P. *Cultural Processes in the Baltic Area Under Soviet Rule.* Berkeley: Institute of International Studies, University of California, 1966.

Federov, Yevgeny K. *Science in the USSR.* Moscow: Foreign Languages Publishing House, 1964.

Fedotov, Georg. *Novy Grad.* New York: Chekhov Publishing House, 1952.

Field, Mark G. *Soviet Socialist Medicine.* New York: Free Press, 1967.

Fisher, George (ed.). *Science and Ideology in Soviet Society.* New York: Atherton Press, 1967.

Fitzsimmons, Thomas, et al. *USSR: Its People, Its Society, Its Culture.* New Haven: HRAF Press, 1960.

Florinsky, Michael R. *Russia,* II. New York: Macmillan, 1953.

Gayev, A. "Soviet Censorship Today," *Bulletin of the Institute for the Study of the USSR,* XV, No. 1, January 1968, 14–17.

Geiger, Bernhard, et al. *Peoples and Languages of the Caucasus.* (Janua Linguarum, Studia Memoriae Nicolai Van Wijk Dedicata.) The Hague: Mouton, 1959.

Gibb, H. A. R. *Mohammedanism.* New York: Oxford University Press, 1962.

Gide, Andre. *Retour de l'URSS.* Paris: Gallimard, 1936.

Goldhagen, Erich (ed.). *Ethnic Minorities in the Soviet Union.* New York: Praeger, 1968.

Graham, Loren R. "Science Policy and Planning in the USSR," *Survey,* No. 64, July 1967, 61–79.

———. *The Soviet Academy of Sciences and the Communist Party, 1927–1932.* Princeton: Princeton University Press, 1967.

Herzen, Alexander. *Memoirs.* New York: Knopf, 1922.

Hoffman, Marilyn. "Renaissance Stirs in the USSR," *Christian Science Monitor,* August 8, 1969, 9.

Inkeles, Alex. *Public Opinion in Soviet Russia.* (Rev. ed.) (Russian Research Center Studies, No. 1.) Cambridge: Harvard University Press, 1967.

————. *Social Change in Soviet Russia.* (Russian Research Center Studies, LVII.) Cambridge: Harvard University Press, 1968.

Inkeles, Alex, and Geiger, H. Kent. "Critical Letters to the Editors of the Soviet Press: Areas and Modes of Complaint," *American Sociological Review,* XVII, No. 6, December 1952, 694–703.

Kassof, Allen (ed.). *Prospects for Soviet Society.* New York: Praeger, 1968.

Kohn, Hans. *Pan-Slavism: Its History and Ideology.* South Bend: University of Notre Dame Press, 1953.

Korol, Alexander. *Soviet Research and Development: Its Organization, Personnel and Funds.* Cambridge: MIT Press, 1965.

Koutaissoff, E. "Literacy and the Place of Russian in the Non-Slav Republics of the USSR," *Soviet Studies,* III, No. 2, October 1951, 113–130.

Krader, Lawrence. *Peoples of Central Asia.* (Uralic and Altaic Series, XXVI.) Bloomington: Indiana University Press, 1963.

Kuusinen, Otto V., et al. (eds.) *Fundamentals of Marxism-Leninism.* (2d., rev.) (Trans. from the Russian by Clemens Dutt.) Moscow: Foreign Languages Publishing House, 1963.

Kuznetsov, Anatoly. "Russian Writers and the Secret Police," *New York Times,* August 10, 1969, 1.

Labedz, Leopold. "The Structure of the Soviet Intelligentsia." Pages 63–70 in *The Russian Intelligentsia.* New York: Columbia University Press, 1961.

Leonard, Richard Anthony. *A History of Russian Music.* New York: Macmillan, 1957.

"Letter of A. I. Solzhenitsyn to the Fourth All-Union Congress of Soviet Writers," *Bulletin of the Institute for the Study of the USSR,* XV, No. 8, August 1968, 39–43.

Levin, M. G., and Potapov, L. P. (eds.) *The Peoples of Siberia.* Chicago: University of Chicago Press, 1964.

Leyda, Jan. *KINO: A History of Russian and Soviet Film.* New York: Macmillan, 1960.

Litvinoff, Barnet. *A Peculiar People: Inside World Jewry Today.* London: Weidenfeld and Nicolson, 1969.

McClure, Timothy. "The Politics of Soviet Culture, 1964–1967," *Problems of Communism,* XVI, No. 2, March–April, 1967, 26–43.

Matthews, W. K. *Languages of the U.S.S.R.* Cambridge: Cambridge University Press, 1951.

Medlin, William K. "Education." Pages 241–263 in Allen Kossof (ed.), *Prospects for Soviet Society.* New York: Praeger, 1968.

Meyendorff, John. *The Orthodox Church: Its Past and Its Role in the World Today.* New York: Pantheon Books, 1969.

Mirsky, D. Sviatopolk. *A History of Russian Literature*. New York: Knopf, 1949.

Olgin, C. "The Fourteenth International Congress of Philosophy and Its Impact on Soviet Philosophy," *Bulletin of the Institute for the Study of the USSR*, XVI, No. 7, July 1969, 27–35.

Pei, Mario A. *Languages for War and Peace*. New York: S. F. Vanni, 1943.

Pipes, Richard (ed.). *The Russian Intelligentsia*. New York: Columbia University Press, 1961.

Pirozhkova, Vera. "The Soviet Marxists Under Fire," *Bulletin of the Institute for the Study of the USSR*, XVI, No. 2, February 1969, 3–12.

Raeff, Marc (ed). *Russian Intellectual History: An Anthology*. New York: Harcourt, Brace and World, 1966.

Riasanovsky, Nicholas V. *A History of Russia*. New York: Oxford University Press, 1963.

Rossi, Peter H., and Bauer, Raymond A. "Some Patterns of Soviet Communications Behavior," *Public Opinion Quarterly*, XVI, No. 4, Winter 1952–53, 653–670.

Salisbury, Harrison E. (ed.) *The Soviet Union: The Fifty Years*. New York: Harcourt, Brace and World, 1967.

Scanlan, James P. "Philosophy: A New Openness." Pages 86–100 in Denis Dirscherl (ed.), *The New Russia*. Dayton: Pflaum Press, 1968.

Science News Yearbook, 1969–1970. New York: Scribner, 1969.

Slonim, Marc. *The Epic of Russian Literature*. New York: Oxford University Press, 1964.

————. *From Chekhov to the Revolution*. New York: Oxford University Press, 1962.

————. *Russian Theatre from the Empire to the Soviets*. Cleveland: World Publishing, 1961.

————. *Soviet Russian Literature*. New York: Oxford University Press, 1967.

Spinka, M. *The Church in Soviet Russia*. New York: Oxford University Press, 1956.

Spitsyn, V. I. "The Organization of the Academic Science in the USSR," *Record of Chemical Progress*, XXIX, No. 3, September 1968, 155–160.

Struve, Nikita. *Christians in Contemporary Russia*. New York: Scribner, 1967.

Tsentralnoye Statisticheskoye Upravleniye pri Sovete Ministrov SSSR. *SSSR v tsifrakh v 1962 godu*. Moskva: Statistika, 1963.

Turkevich, John. "Fifty Years of Soviet Science." In Milorad M. Drachkovitch (ed.), *Fifty Years of Communism in Russia*. University Park: Pennsylvania State University Press, 1968.

774

————. "Soviet Science Appraised," *Foreign Affairs*, XLIV, No. 3, April 1966, 489–500.

U.S. Congress. 89th, 2d Session. Joint Economic Committee. *New Directions in the Soviet Economy*, III: The Human Resources. Washington: GPO, 1966.

U.S. Department of Health, Education and Welfare. Office of Education. *Part-Time Education in the U.S.S.R.: Evening and Correspondence Study*, by Seymour M. Rosen. (Bulletin 1965, No. 17.) Washington: GPO, 1965.

————. *Soviet Commitment to Education: Report of the First Official U.S. Education Mission to the U.S.S.R.* (Bulletin 1959 No. 16.) Washington: GPO, 1959.

————. *Structure and Decision-Making in Soviet Education*, by Herbert C. Rudman. (Bulletin 1964, No. 2.) Washington: GPO, 1964.

————. *Textbooks for Soviet Education*, by Nellie Apansewicz. (OE–14123.) Washington: GPO, 1966.

U.S. Department of Health, Education and Welfare. Office of Education. Division of International Education. International Educational Relations Branch. *Education in the U.S.S.R.* (Bulletin 1957, No. 14, OE–14045.) Washington: GPO, 1960.

Voronitsyn, Sergei S. "Intellectual Opposition to the Party Leadership," *Bulletin of the Institute for the Study of the USSR*, XV, No. 12, December 1968, 19–22.

————. "Soviet Intelligentsia Under Greater Pressure to Conform," *Analysis of Current Developments in the Soviet Union*, No. 553, June 17, 1969.

Vucinich, Alexander. "Soviet Ethnographic Studies of Cultural Change," *American Anthropologist*, LXII, 1960, 867–877.

Who's Who in Soviet Science and Technology. (Comp., Ina Telberg.) New York: Telberg, 1960.

OTHER SOURCES USED

Anderson, Paul B. *People, State and Church in Modern Russia.* New York: Macmillan, 1964.

Ashby, Eric. *Scientist in Russia*. New York: Penguin, 1947.

Babitsky, Paul, and Rimberg, John. *The Soviet Film Industry*. New York: Praeger, 1955.

Barghoorn, Frederick C. *The Soviet Cultural Offensive*. Princeton: Princeton University Press, 1960.

Barnier, Lucien. *Secrets of Soviet Science*. London: Allan Wingate, 1957.

Baron, Samuel H. *Plekhanov, the Father of Russian Marxism.* Stanford: Stanford University Press, 1963.

Barry, Donald D. "Housing in the U.S.S.R.," *Problems of Communism*, XVIII, No. 3, May–June 1969, 1–12.

Bellew, Helen. *Ballet in Moscow Today*. London: Burns and MacEachron, 1957.

Benz, Ernst. *The Eastern Orthodox Church: Its Thought and Life*. Garden City: Doubleday, 1963.

Berdyaev, Nicholas. *The Origin of Russian Communism*. Ann Arbor: University of Michigan Press, 1948.

Berlin, Isaiah. "The Silence in Russian Culture." Pages 336–359 in *The Soviet Union, 1922–1962*. New York: Praeger, 1963.

Blumberg, Joe M. "Laboratory Medicine in Russia," *Transactions and Studies of the College of Physicians of Philadelphia*, XXX, No. 1, July 1962, 19–26.

Bowen, James. *Soviet Education: Anton Makarenko and the Years of Experiment*. Madison: University of Wisconsin Press, 1962.

Braden, Charles Samuel. *The World Religions: A Short History*. Nashville: Parthenon Books, 1954.

Burg, David. "Mikhail Dyomin was a Successful Writer in Soviet Russia. Yet He Defected. Why?," *New York Times Magazine*, April 13, 1969, 34–35, 165–170.

Byrnes, Robert F. *Pobedonostsev: His Life and Thought*. Bloomington: Indiana University Press, 1968.

Casey, Robert. *Religion in Russia*. New York: Harper, 1946.

Christian, Ruth C. (ed.) *Soviet Science*. Washington: American Association for the Advancement of Science, 1952.

Cole, Michael, and Maltzman, Irving (eds.), *A Handbook of Contemporary Soviet Psychology*. New York: Basic Books, 1969.

Deineko, M. *Public Education in the U.S.S.R.* Moscow: Progress Publishers, n.d.

Dunn, Stephen P., and Dunn, Ethel. "Directed Culture Change in the Soviet Union: Some Soviet Studies," *American Anthropologist*, LXIV, 1962, 328–339.

————. "The Great Russian Peasant: Culture Change or Culture Development?," *Ethnology*, II, 1963, 320–338.

————. "Soviet Regime and Native Culture in Central Asia and Kazakhstan: The Major Peoples," *Current Anthropology*, VIII, No. 3, June 1967, 147–208.

————. "The Transformation of Economy and Culture in the Soviet North," *Arctic Anthropology*, I, No. 2, 1963, 1–28.

Durham, F. Gayle. *The Use of Free Time by Young People in the Soviet Union*. Cambridge: MIT Press, 1966.

Edie, James, et al. (eds.) *Russian Philosophy*. 3 vols. Chicago: Quadrangle Books, 1965.

Europa Year Book, 1969, I. London: Europa Publications, 1969.

Field, Mark G. "Alcoholism, Crime and Delinquency in Soviet Society," *Social Problems*, III, No. 3, October 1955, 100–109.

————. "Approaches to Mental Illness in Soviet Society," *Social Problems*, VII, No. 4, Spring 1960, 277–297.

————. *Doctor and Patient in Soviet Russia*. Cambridge: Harvard University Press, 1957.

————. "Some Problems of Soviet Medical Practice," *New England Journal of Medicine*. CCXLVIII, No. 22, May 28, 1953, 919–926.

Frank, Semion L. (ed.) *A Solovyov Anthology*. (Trans., Natalie Duffington.) London: William Clowes, 1950.

French, Richard Anthony. "Union of Soviet Socialist Republics." Pages 501–550 in *Encyclopaedia Britannica*, XXII. Chicago: William Benton, 1969.

Friedrich, Paul. "An Evolutionary Sketch of Russian Kinship," *Symposium on Language and Culture*. (Eds., Viola E. Garfield and Wallace L. Chafe.) (Proceedings of the 1962 Annual Spring Meeting of the American Ethnological Society.) Seattle: American Ethnological Society, 1963.

————. "The Linguistic Reflex of Social Change: From Tsarist to Soviet Russian Kinship," *Sociological Inquiry*, XXXVI, No. 2, Spring 1966, 159–185.

Frolov, I. *Genetics and Dialectics*. Moscow: Science Publishing House, 1969.

Fuelop-Miller, Rene. *The Mind and Face of Bolshevism*. New York: Harper, 1965.

Fundamentals of Marxism-Leninism. (2d ed., rev.) Moscow: Foreign Languages Publishing House, 1963.

Galkin, Konstantin. *The Training of Scientists in the Soviet Union*. Moscow: Foreign Languages Publishing House, 1959.

Gargarin, Yury A., and Lebedev, Vladimir. *Survival in Space*. New York: Praeger, 1969.

Glavnoye Upravleniye Geodezii i Kartografii pri Sovete Ministrov SSSR. *Atlas Razvitiya Khozyaystva i Kultury SSSR*. Moskva: 1967.

Gleason, H. A. *An Introduction to Descriptive Linguistics*. (Rev. ed.) New York: Holt, Rinehart and Winston, 1961.

Gorer, Geoffrey, and Rickman, John. *The People of Great Russia: A Psychological Study*. New York: W. W. Norton, 1962.

Gregory, James S. *Russian Land, Soviet People: A Geographical Approach*. New York: Pegasus, 1968.

Gsovski, Vladimir, and Grzybowski, Kazimierz. *Government, Law and Courts in the Soviet Union and Eastern Europe*. New York: Praeger, 1959.

Guillaume, Alfred. *Islam*. Baltimore: Penguin Books, 1968.

Gurvich, I. S. "Current Ethnic Processes Taking Place in Northern Yakutia," *Arctic Anthropology*, I, No. 2, 1963, 86–92.

Hans, Nicholas. *The Russian Tradition in Education*. London: Routledge and Kegan Paul, 1963.

Hetmanek, Allan. "Dissonant Views on Language Questions in Union Republics," *Radio Liberty Dispatch* (New York), May 20, 1961.

Hingley, Ronald. *Russian Writers and Society, 1825–1904*. New York: World University, 1968.

Hollander, Paul. "Leisure as an American and Soviet Value," *Social Problems*, XIV, No. 5, Fall 1966, 179–188.

————. "The Uses of Leisure," *Survey*, July 1966, 40–50.

Inkeles, Alex. "Soviet Reactions to the Voice of America," *Public Opinion Quarterly*, XVI, No. 4, Winter 1952–53, 612–617.

Inkeles, Alex, and Geiger, H. Kent. "Critical Letters to the Editors of the Soviet Press: Social Characteristics and Interrelations of Critics and the Criticized," *American Sociological Review*, XVIII, No. 1, February 1953, 12–22.

Jacoby, Susan. "Better Dressed Russians," *Washington Post*, December 16, 1969, B–1.

Joint Committee on Slavic and East European Studies. *Current Digest of the Soviet Press*, XXI, No. 15, April 30, 1969.

King, Edmund J. (ed.) *Communist Education*. New York: Bobbs-Merrill, 1963.

Kline, George (ed.). *Soviet Education*. New York: Columbia University Press, 1957.

Kline, Nathan S. "The Organization of Psychiatric Care and Psychiatric Research in the Union of Soviet Socialist Republics," *Annals of the New York Academy of Sciences*, LXXXIV, No. 4, April 22, 1960, 147–224.

Kolarz, Walter. *Religion in the Soviet Union*. New York: St. Martin's Press, 1961.

Kolles, Stanley F. "Impressions of the U.S. Mission on Mental Health: Conclusions and Recommendations." Boston: American Psychiatric Association, 1968 (unpublished manuscript).

Korol, Alexander. *Soviet Education for Space and Technology*. New York: John Wiley, 1957.

Krader, Lawrence. "The Cultural and Historical Position of the Mongols," *Asia Major*, III, 1953, 169–183.

————. "A Nativistic Movement in Western Siberia," *American Anthropologist*, LVIII, 1956, 282–292.

Kratkaya Literaturnaya Entsiklopediya, 1962–1969. Moskva: Sovetskaya Entsiklopediya, 1969.

Kurakov, I. G. *Science, Technology and Communism: Some Questions of Development*. Oxford: Pergamon Press, 1966.

Kurganov, Ivan. "The Problem of Nationality in Soviet Russia," *Russian Review*, X, No. 4, October 1951, 253–267.

Laqueur, Walter, and Lichtheim, George. *The Soviet Cultural Scene, 1956–1957*. London: Atlantic Books, 1958.

Harkins, William W. *Dictionary of Russian Literature.* Peterson Littlefield and Adams, 1959.

Lenin, Vladimir. *Selected Works.* 3 vols. New York: International Publishers, 1967.

Lessa, William A., and Vogt, Evon Z. *Reader in Comparative Religion: An Anthropological Approach.* (2d ed.) New York: Harper and Row, 1965.

Levine, Irving R. *Main Street, U.S.S.R.* Garden City: Doubleday, 1959.

London, Ivan D., and London, Miriam B. "Three Flash Studies in Intercultural Communication," *Psychological Reports,* III, No. 2, 1957, 143–148.

Lukashevich, Stephen. *(Konstantin Leontev (1831–1891).* New York: Pageant Press, 1967.

Lunacharsky, Anatol V. *Revolutionary Silhouettes.* (Trans. and ed., Michael Glenny.) New York: Hill and Wang, 1968.

Madison, Bernice. "Welfare Personnel in the Soviet Union," *Social Work,* VII, No. 3, July 1962, 57–69.

―――. "Welfare Services for Children in the Soviet Union," *Child Welfare,* XLII, No. 7, July 1963, 319–331.

Maguire, Robert A. *Red Virgin Soil: Soviet Literature in the Twenties.* Princeton: Princeton University Press, 1968.

Manners, Robert A. (ed.) *Process and Pattern in Culture: Essays in Honor of Julian H. Steward.* Chicago: Aldine, 1964.

Marx, Karl, and Engels, Friedrich. *The Russian Menace to Europe.* (Eds., Paul W. Blackstock and Bert F. Hoselitz.) Glencoe: Free Press, 1952.

Masaryk, Thomas G. *The Spirit of Russia.* New York: Macmillan, 1953.

Massie, Robert K. *Nicholas and Alexandra.* New York: Atheneum, 1967.

Mead, Margaret, and Métraux, Rhoda (eds.). *The Study of Culture at a Distance.* Chicago: University of Chicago Press, 1953.

Medlin, William K. *Moscow and East Rome: A Political Study of the Relations of Church and State in Muscovite Russia.* London: Oxford University Press, 1964.

Medvedev, Zhores A. *The Rise and Fall of T. D. Lysenko.* New York: Columbia University Press, 1969.

Michael, H. N. (ed.) *Studies in Siberian Ethnogenesis.* (Arctic Institute of North America, Anthropology of the North: Translations from Russian Sources, No. 2.) Toronto: University of Toronto Press, 1962.

Miliukov, Paul. *Outlines of Russian Culture.* Philadelphia: University of Pennsylvania Press, 1948.

779

Miller, Hugh. *History of Music.* New York: Barnes and Noble, 1953.

Miller, Margaret. *Rise of the Russian Consumer.* London: Institute of Economic Affairs, 1965.

Mochulsky, K. *Vladimir Soloviev.* Paris: YMCA Press, 1936.

Morton, Henry W. "Law, Social Change and the Housing Shortage in the U.S.S.R." (Speech for delivery at the 1969 Midwest Conference of the Advancement for the American Association of Slavic Studies, Lincoln, April 11, 1969.)

"Nationalities and Nationalism in the USSR." *Problems of Communism* (Special Issue), XVI, September–October 1967.

Nekhamkin, I. *Training of Engineers in the USSR.* Moscow: n.pub., n.d.

Nimitz, Nancy. *Soviet Expenditures on Scientific Research.* (RM–3384–PR.) Santa Monica: Rand, 1963.

Ogloblin, Ivan. *Vocational Training in the USSR.* Moscow: Novosti Press Agency Publishing House, n.d.

Ornstein, Jacob. "Soviet Language Policy: Theory and Practice," *Slavic and East European Journal,* XVII, No. 1, Spring 1959, 1–24.

Planty-Bonjour, Guy. *The Categories of Dialectical Materialism: Contemporary Soviet Ontology.* New York: Praeger, 1967.

Plekhanov, Georg V. *History of Russian Social Thought.* (Trans. from the Russian by Boris M. Bekkar.) New York: Howard Fertig, 1967.

Puzin, Alexei. *Religion in the USSR.* Moscow: Novosti Press Agency Publishing House, 1968.

Rabinovich, Solomon. *Jews in the Soviet Union.* Moscow: Novosti Press Agency Publishing House, 1968.

Rabinowitch, Eugene. "Soviet Science: A Survey," *Problems of Communism,* VII, No. 2, March–April 1958, 1–9.

Raymond, Ellsworth. *The Soviet State.* New York: Macmillan, 1968.

Riasanovsky, Nicholas V. *Russia and the West in the Teaching of the Slavophiles.* Cambridge: Harvard University Press, 1962.

Rudden, Bernard. "Soviet Housing and the New Civil Code," *The International and Comparative Law Quarterly,* XV, January 1966, 231–262.

Schubart, Walter. *Russia and Western Man.* (Trans., Amethe von Zeppelin.) New York: Frederick Ungar, 1950.

Shimkin, D. B., and Sanjuan, Pedro. "Culture and World View: A Method of Analysis Applied to Rural Russia," *American Anthropologist,* LV, 1953, 329–348.

Sigerist, Henry E. *Medicine and Health in the Soviet Union.* New York: Citadel Press, 1946.

Simmons, Ernest J. (ed.) *Continuity and Change in Russian and Soviet Thought.* Cambridge: Harvard University Press, 1955.

Sinor, Denis (ed.). *Aspects of Altaic Civilization.* (Uralic and Altaic Series, XXIII.) Bloomington: Indiana University Press, 1963.

Slobin, Dan I. "The Acquisition of Russian as a Native Language." Pages 129–152 in Frank Smith and George A. Miller (eds.), *The Genesis of Language: A Psycholinguistic Approach.* Cambridge: MIT Press, 1966.

Stalin, Joseph. *Problems of Leninism.* New York: International Publishers, 1934.

―――. *Works.* 13 vols. Moscow: Foreign Languages Publishing House, 1954, 1955.

Starr, Chester G., et al. *A History of the World,* I and II. Chicago: Rand McNally, 1960.

Steinberg, S. H. (ed.) *The Statesman's Yearbook, 1968–1969.* New York: St. Martin's Press, 1968.

Stroehm, Carl Gustav. "Non-Russian Russians: The Stubborn Breeds," *Atlas,* XVII, No. 6, June 1969, 32–36.

Struve, Gleb. "The Second Congress of Soviet Writers," *Problems of Communism,* IV, No. 2, 1955, 3–11.

―――. *Soviet Russian Literature, 1917–1950.* Norman: University of Oklahoma Press, 1951.

―――. "The Writers," *Studies on the Soviet Union,* VII, No. 2, 1967, 158–170.

Teatralnaya Entsiklopediya, 1963–1967. Moskva: Sovetskaya Entsiklopediya, 1967.

Thomas, Lawrence L. *The Linguistic Theories of N. Ya. Marr.* (University of California Publications in Linquistics, XIV.) Berkeley: University of California Press, 1957.

Tomasic, Dinko. *The impact of Russian Culture on Soviet Communism.* Glencoe: Free Press, 1953.

Topchiev, Aleksandr V. *What Soviet Scientists are Working On.* Moscow: Foreign Languages Publishing House, 1960.

Turkevich, John. *Chemistry in the Soviet Union.* New York: Van Nostrand, 1965.

―――. *Soviet Men of Science.* New York: Van Nostrand, 1963.

United Nations. Department of Economic and Social Affairs. *Statistical Yearbook, 1968.* New York: UN Publishing Service, 1969.

United Nations. International Bureau of Education. *International Yearbook of Education, 1967,* XXIX. Paris: UN, 1968.

United Nations. World Health Organization. "Health Services in the USSR," *WHO Chronicle,* XIV, No. 3, March 1960, 97–105.

United Nations Education, Scientific and Cultural Organization.

UNESCO Statistical Yearbook, 1967. Louvain: UNESCO, 1968.

U.S. Congress. 89th, 2d Session. Joint Economic Committee. *New Directions in Soviet Economy,* Part II–B. Washington: GPO, 1966.

U.S. Department of Commerce. Joint Publications Research Services. *The USSR Public Health Program,* 1298–N. Washington: GPO, 1959.

U.S. Department of Health, Education and Welfare. Office of Education. *Final Examinations in the Russian Ten Year School,* by Nellie Apanasewicz. (Revision of Bulletin 1958, No. 6.) Washington: GPO, 1966.

―――. *Higher Education in the U.S.S.R.: Curriculum, Schools, and Statistics,* by Seymour M. Rosen. (Bulletin 1963, No. 16.) Washington: GPO, 1963.

―――. *Medical Education in the Soviet Union.* Washington: GPO, 1963.

Vakar, Nicholas. *The Taproot of Soviet Society.* New York: Harper, 1961.

Varneke, Boris V. *History of the Russian Theater.* (Trans., Boris Braserl.) New York: Macmillan, 1952.

Voyce, Arthur. *Moscow and the Roots of Russian Culture.* Norman: University of Oklahoma Press, 1964.

―――. "Soviet Art and Architecture," *Annals of the American Academy of Political Sciences,* CCCIII, January 1956, 104–115.

Vucinich, Alexander. *The Soviet Academy of Sciences.* Stanford: Stanford University Press, 1956.

Weeks, Albert L. *The First Bolshevik: A Political Biography of Peter Tkachev.* New York: New York University Press, 1968.

Weidle, Vladimir. "Art Under the Soviet Regime," *Studies on the Soviet Union,* VII, No. 2, 1967, 135–151.

Wetter, Gustav A. *Dialectical Materialism.* New York: Praeger, 1959.

―――. *Soviet Ideology Today.* (Trans., Peter Heath.) New York: Praeger, 1966.

Wilson, Edmund. *To the Finland Station.* New York: Doubleday, 1953.

Wolfe, Bertram D. *Three Who Made a Revolution.* Boston: Beacon Press, 1955.

Yelyutin, Vyacheslav. *Higher Education in the U.S.S.R.* Moscow: Novosti Press Agency Publishing House, n.d.

Yermoshkin, Nikolai. *Buddhism and Buddhists in the USSR.* Moscow: Novosti Press Agency Publishing House, 1968.

Zenkovsky, Vasily. *Russian Thinkers and Europe.* (Trans., Galia S. Bodde.) Ann Arbor: J. W. Edwards, 1953.

(Various issues of the following periodical were also used in the preparation of this section: *Current Digest of Soviet Press* [Columbus], July 9–October 1, 1969.)

Section III. Political

RECOMMENDED SOURCES

American Bar Association. *A Contrast Between the Legal Systems in the United States and in the Soviet Union.* Baltimore: Port City Press, 1968.

Anderson, Stephen S. "East Europe: The Politics of Recovery," *Current History,* LVII, No. 338, October 1969, 207–213, 241.

——. "The United States and Soviet Russia," *Current History,* LV, No. 327, November 1968, 281–287.

Anderson, Thornton. *Russian Political Thought.* Ithaca: Cornell University Press, 1967.

Anderson, William. *Local Government in Europe.* New York: Appleton-Century, 1939.

Andrews, William G. *Soviet Institutions and Policies.* Princeton: Van Nostrand, 1966.

Armstrong, John A. *Ideology, Politics, and Government in the Soviet Union.* (Rev. ed.) New York: Praeger, 1967.

Aspaturian, Vernon V. "The Aftermath of the Czech Invasion," *Current History,* LV, No. 327, November 1968, 263–267.

Avtorkhanov, Abdurakhman. *The Communist Party Apparatus.* Chicago: Henry Regnery, 1966.

Babitsky, Paul, and Rimberg, John. *The Soviet Film Industry.* New York: Praeger, 1955.

Bailes, Kendall E. "Soviet Television Comes of Age: A review of Its Accomplishments and a Discussion of the Tasks Facing It," *Radio Liberty Research Paper,* No. 24. New York: Radio Liberty, 1968.

Barghoorn, Frederick C. *Politics in the USSR.* Boston: Little, Brown, 1966.

——. *Soviet Foreign Propaganda.* Princeton: Princeton University Press, 1964.

——. *Soviet Russian Nationalism.* New York: Oxford University Press, 1956.

Becker, A. *Soviet Military Outlays Since 1955.* (Rand Memorandum 3886.) Santa Monica: Rand, 1964.

Beer, Samuel H., and Ulam, Adam B. (eds.) *Patterns of Government.* New York: Random House, 1958.

Berman, Harold J. *Justice in the USSR: An Interpretation of Soviet Law.* (Rev. ed.) New York: Vintage Books, 1963.

783

Berman, Harold J., and Kerner, Miroslav. *Documents on Soviet Military Law and Administration*. Cambridge: Harvard University Press, 1955.

————. *Soviet Military Law and Administration*. Cambridge: Harvard University Press, 1955.

Bialer, Seweryn. "Soviet Leadership: Some Problems of Continuity, Structure and Cohesion." (Paper prepared for delivery at the 1966 American Political Science Association meeting, New York City.)

Billington, James H. "Beneath the Panoply of Power, the Intelligentsia Hits Out at the Old Order," *Life*, LXIII, No. 19, November 10, 1967, 70–84.

Black, Cyril E. (ed.) *The Transformation of Russian Society*. Cambridge: Harvard University Press, 1967.

Black, Cyril E., and Thornton, Thomas P. (eds.) *Communism and Revolution*. Princeton: Princeton University Press, 1964.

Bremberg, A. (ed.) *Russia Under Khrushchev*. New York: Praeger, 1962.

Bryan, Carter. "Communist Advertising: Its Status and Functions," *Journalism Quarterly*, XXXIX, No. 4, Autumn 1962, 500–506.

Brzezinski, Zbigniew K. *Ideology and Power in Soviet Politics*. (Rev. ed.) New York: Praeger, 1967.

————. *The Soviet Block: Unity and Conflict*. Cambridge: Harvard University Press, 1967.

————. "The Soviet Political System: Transformation or Degeneration," *Problems of Communism*, XV, No. 1, January–February 1966, 1–15.

————. (ed.) *Africa and the Communist World*. Stanford: Stanford University Press, 1963.

Cattell, David T. "Politics in Soviet Russia," *Current History*, LV, No. 327, November 968, 257–262.

Clews, Hohn. *Communist Propaganda Techniques*. New York: Praeger, 1966.

Communist Party of The Soviet Union. 22d Congress. *Rules of the Communist Party of the Soviet Union*. Moscow: Foreign Languages Publishing House, 1962.

Conquest, Robert. *The Soviet Political System*. New York: Praeger, 1968.

———— (ed.). *Soviet Nationalities Policy in Practice*. New York: Praeger, 1967.

Cramer, James. *The World's Police*. London: Cassell, 1964.

Crankshaw, Edward. *The New Cold War, Moscow v. Peking*. Baltimore: Penguin Books, 1963.

Dallin, Alexander, et al. *The Soviet Union and Disarmament*. New York: Praeger, 1964.

Daniels, Robert V. *The Conscience of the Revolution: Communist Opposition in Soviet Russia.* Cambridge: Harvard University Press, 1960.

————. *Russia.* Englewood Cliffs: Prentice-Hall, 1964.

Dicks, Henry V. "Observation on Contemporary Russian Behavior," *Human Relations,* V, No. 2, 1952.

Dinerstein, H. S. *War and the Soviet Union.* New York: Praeger, 1962.

Doolin, Dennis J. *Territorial Claims in the Sino-Soviet Conflict.* (Hoover Institution Studies, No. 7), Stanford: Stanford University Press, 1965.

Dragnich, A. N. *Major European Governments.* Homewood: Dorsey Press, 1966.

Ebenstein, William. *Two Ways of Life—The Communist Challenge to Democracy.* New York: Holt, Rinehart and Winston, 1964.

Ely, Louis B. *The Red Army Today.* Harrisburg: Military Service Publishing Company, 1953.

Fainsod, Merle. *How Russia is Ruled.* (Rev. ed.) Cambridge: Harvard University Press, 1964.

Fitzsimmons, Thomas (ed.). *RSFSR: Russian Soviet Federated Socialist Republic,* I. (Country Survey Series.) New Haven: HRAF Press, 1957.

Fraser, Lindley. *Propaganda.* New York: Oxford University Press, 1957.

Friedrich, Carl J., and Brzezinski, Zbigniew K. *Totalitarian Dictatorship and Autocracy.* Cambridge: Harvard University Press, 1961.

Garthoff, Raymond L. *Soviet Strategy in the Nuclear Age.* (Rev. ed.) New York: Praeger, 1962.

Gorer, Geoffrey, and Rickman, John. *The People of Great Russia: A Psychological Study.* New York: W. W. Norton, 1962.

Grzybowski, Kazimierz. *Soviet Legal Institutions, Doctrines and Social Functions.* Ann Arbor: University of Michigan Press, 1962.

Gsovski, Vladimir, and Grzybowski, Kazimierz. *Government, Law and Courts in the Soviet Union and Eastern Europe.* New York: Praeger, 1959.

Guins, George C. *Soviet Law and Soviet Society.* The Hague: Martinus Nijhoff, 1954.

Gupta, Bhabani Sen. "Moscow, Peking, and the Indian Political Scene After Nehru," *Orbis,* XII, No. 2, Summer 1968, 535–562.

Hahn, Walter F., and Cottrell, Alvin J. *Ballistic Missile Defense and Soviet Strategy.* Arlington: Institute for Defense Analysis, 1963.

Hammer, Darrell P. *Towards a Theoretical Model of Non-Competi-*

tive Political Systems: Conflict and Decision Making in the USSR. Chicago: American Political Science Association, 1967.

Hammond, Thomas T. "An American in Moscow," *National Geographic,* CXXIX, No. 3, March 1966, 297–351.

Hazard, John Newbold. *The Soviet System of Government.* (4th ed.) Chicago: University of Chicago Press, 1968.

Hazard, John Newbold, and Shapiro, Isac. *The Soviet Legal System.* New York: Oceana Publications, 1962.

Hazard, John Newbold; Shapiro, Isac; and Maggs, Peter B. *The Soviet Legal System: Contemporary Documentation and Historical Commentary.* (Rev. ed.) New York: Oceana Publications, 1969.

Hollander, Gayle Durham. "Recent Developments in Soviet Radio and Television News Reporting," *Public Opinion Quarterly,* XXXI, No. 3, Fall 1967, 359–365.

Hooson, David. *The Soviet Union: People and Regions.* Belmont: Wadsworth, 1966.

Horowitz, Robert S. *The Ramparts We Watch.* Derby: Monarch Books, 1964.

Humes, Samuel, and Martin, E. M. *The Structure of Local Governments Throughout the World.* The Hague: Martinus Nijhoff, 1961.

Inkeles, Alex. *Public Opinion in Soviet Russia.* (Rev. ed.) (Russian Research Center Studies, No. 1.) Cambridge: Harvard University Press, 1967.

––––––. *Social Change in Soviet Russia.* (Russian Research Center Studies, LVII.) Cambridge: Harvard University Press, 1968.

Inkeles, Alex, and Bauer, Raymond A. *The Soviet Citizen: Daily Life in a Totalitarian Society.* (Russian Research Center Studies, XXXV.) Cambridge: Harvard University Press, 1959.

Inkeles, Alex, and Geiger, H. Kent. "Critical Letters to the Editors of the Soviet Press: Areas and Modes of Complaint," *American Sociological Review,* XVII, No. 6, December 1952, 694–703.

––––––. "Critical Letters to the Editors of the Soviet Press: Social Characteristics and Interrelations of Critics and the Criticized," *American Sociological Review,* XVIII, No. 1, February 1953, 12–22.

Institute for the Study of the USSR. *Soviet Society Today* (Munich), July 1958.

Juviler, Peter H., and Morton, Henry W. (eds.) *Soviet Policy Making.* New York: Praeger, 1967.

Kanet, Roger E. "The Recent Soviet Reassessment of Developments in the Third World," *Russian Review,* XXVII, No. 1, January 1968, 27–41.

Kassof, Allen. *The Soviet Youth Program.* Cambridge: Harvard University Press, 1965.

―――. (ed.) *Prospect for Soviet Society.* New York: Praeger, 1968.

Kolarz, Walter. *Russia and Her Colonies.* London: George, 1952.

Kolkowicz, Roman. *The Soviet Army and the Communist Party: Institutions in Conflict.* (R–446–PR.) Santa Monica: Rand, 1966.

Lapenna, Ivo. *Soviet Penal Policy.* London: Bodley Head, 1968.

Laqueur, Walter. "Russia Enters the Middle East," *Foreign Affairs,* XLVII, No. 2, January 1969, 296–308.

Lenczowski, George. "Soviet Policy in the Middle East," *Current History,* LV, No. 327, November 1968, 268–274.

Leonhard, Wolfgang. "Internal Developments: A Balance Sheet," *Problems of Communism,* XII, No. 2, March–April 1963, 1–9.

―――. *The Kremlin Since Stalin.* New York: Praeger, 1962.

Liddell Hart, B. H. (ed.) *The Red Army.* New York: Harcourt, Bruce and World, 1956.

Linden, Carl A. *Khrushchev and the Soviet Leadership, 1957–1964.* Baltimore: John Hopkins Press, 1966.

Mackintosh, Malcolm. *Juggernaut—A History of the Soviet Armed Forces.* New York: Macmillan, 1967.

Marchenko, Anatoly. *My Testimony.* New York: Dutton, 1969.

Miller, Wright. *Russians as People.* New York: Dutton, 1961.

O'Ballance, Edgar. *The Red Army.* New York: Praeger, 1964.

Rigby, Thomas H. *Communist Party Membership in the USSR, 1917–1967.* Princeton: Princeton University Press, 1968.

Rothermund, Dietmar. "India and the Soviet Union," *Annals of the Academy of Political and Social Science,* No. 386, November 1969, 78–88.

Rubinstein, Alvin Z. *Communist Political Systems.* Englewood Cliffs: Prentice-Hall, 1966.

―――. "Czechoslovakia in Transition," *Current History,* LVI, No. 332, April 1969, 206–211.

―――. *The Soviets in International Organizations: Changing Policy Towards Developing Countries, 1953–1963.* Princeton: Princeton University Press, 1964.

―――. (ed.) *The Foreign Policy of the Soviet Union.* New York: Random House, 1966.

Rudman, Herbert C. *The School and State in the USSR.* New York: Macmillan, 1967.

Salisbury, Harrison E. (ed.) *The Soviet Union: The Fifty Years.* New York: Harcourt, Bruce and World, 1967.

Schapiro, Leonard. *The Communist Party of the Soviet Union.* New York: Random House, 1960.

——————. *The Government and Politics of the Soviet Union.* (Rev. ed.) New York: Random House, 1967.

——————. *The USSR and the Future.* New York: Praeger, 1962.

Schuman, Frederick L. *Government in the Soviet Union.* New York: Crowell, 1967.

Scott, Derek J. R. *Russian Political Institutions.* New York: Praeger, 1961.

Seton-Watson, Hugh. *The East European Revolution.* New York: Prager, 1956.

Shulman, Marshall D. *Beyond the Cold War.* New Haven: Yale University Press, 1966.

Skilling, Gordon. "The Party, Opposition and Interest Groups: Fifty Years of Continuity and Change." (Paper presented at 6th International Conference on World Politics, Berlin, September 1967.)

Sokolovsky, V. D. *Soviet Military Strategy.* (RM–371.) Santa Monica: Rand, 1962.

Sorlin, Pierre. *The Soviet People and Their Society.* New York: Praeger, 1969.

Soviet Criminal Law and Procedure; The RSFSR Codes. (Trans., Harold J. Berman and James W. Spindler.) Cambridge: Harvard University Press, 1966.

Ulam, Adam B. *Expansion and Coexistence: The History of Soviet Foreign Policy, 1917–1967.* New York: Praeger, 1968.

Valkenier, Elizabeth. "The Sino-Soviet Rivalry in the Third World," *Current History,* LVII, No. 338, October 1968, 201–206.

Viator (pseud.). "Cuba Revisited After Ten Years of Castro," *Foreign Affairs,* XLVIII, No. 2, January 1970, 312–321.

Vyshinski, A. Y. *The Law of the Soviet State.* (Trans., Hugh W. Babb.) New York: Macmillan, 1948.

Whetten, Lawrance L. "The Role of East Germany in West German-Soviet Relations," *World Today,* XXV, No. 12, December 1969, 507–520.

Whiting, Kenneth R. *The Soviet Union Today: A Concise Handbook.* (Rev. ed.) New York: Praeger, 1966.

Wolfe, Thomas W. *Soviet Military Policy at the Fifty-Year Mark.* (RM–5443–PR.) Santa Monica: Rand, 1967.

Young, Peter. "Battle of Generations in the Open, *"Life,* LXIII, No. 19, November 10, 1967, 54–59.

Zagoria, Donald. *The Sino-Soviet Conflict, 1956–1961.* Princeton: Princeton University Press, 1962.

OTHER SOURCES USED

Alekseev, A. "Interpreting the Polls," *Radio Liberty Translation.* New York: Radio Liberty, 1969.

Archer, Peter. *Communism and the Law.* Chester Spring: Dufour Editions, 1963.

Armstrong, John A. *The Soviet Bureaucratic Elite.* New York: Praeger, 1959.

Armstrong, Richard. "Soviet Russia," *Saturday Evening Post,* CCXL, No. 22, November 4, 1967, 25–48.

Aspaturian, Vernon V. "Soviet Foreign Policy." Chapter 5 in Roy C. Macridis (ed.), *Foreign Policy in World Politics.* Englewood Cliffs: Prentice-Hall, 1967.

Avtorkhanov, Abdurakhman. "Khrushchev-Brezhnev-Kosygin — The Leadership Debate Continues." (Paper delivered at the 2d Soviet Affairs Symposium, U.S. Army Institute for Advanced Russian and East European Affairs, Garmisch, Germany, June 1968.)

Azrael, Jeremy R. "Soviet Union." Chapter 8 in James S. Coleman (ed.), *Education and Political Development.* Princeton: Princeton University Press, 1965.

Barsukov, M. V., and Kovalev, M. I. "Reorganizing the Militia," *Current Digest of the Soviet Press,* IX, No. 17, June 5, 1957. 10–18.

Bates, Richard W. *Communist Party Control in the Soviet Navy.* Newport: Naval War College, 1967.

Bauer, Raymond A.; Inkeles, Alex; and Kluckholm, Clyde. *How the Soviet System Works.* New York: Random House, 1956.

Berman, Harold J., and Quigley, John B. *Basic Laws on the Structure of the Soviet State.* Cambridge: Harvard University Press, 1969.

Boynton, J. *Aims and Means of Soviet Propaganda.* Chester Springs: Dufour Editions, 1964.

Braham, R. L. (ed.) *Soviet Politics and Government.* New York: Knopf, 1965.

Brzezinski, Zbigniew K. *The Soviet Bloc.* New York: Praeger, 1961.

Brzezinski, Zbigniew K., et al. *Political Controls in the Soviet Army.* Ann Arbor: Lithoprinted by Edwards Brothers for the Russian Research Center of Harvard University, 1954.

Brzezinski, Zbigniew, and Huntington, Samuel P. *Political Power, USA: USSR.* New York: Viking Press, 1964.

Carter, Gwendolen M. *The Government of the Soviet Union.* (2d ed.) New York: Harcourt, Brace and World, 1967.

Chapman, Colin. *August 21st: The Rape of Czechoslovakia.* Philadelphia: Lippincott, 1968.

Churchward, L. G. *Contemporary Soviet Government.* New York: American Elsevier, 1968.

Cleveland, Harlan. "NATO After the Invasion," *Foreign Affairs*, XLVII, No. 2, January 1969, 251–265.

The Civil Code and the Code of Civil Procedure of the RSFSR 1964, No. 11, Law in Eastern Europe. (Trans., A. K. R. Kiralfy.) Leyden: A. W. Sythoff, 1966.

Civil Code of the Russian Soviet Federated Socialist Republic. (Trans., Whitmore Gray and Raymond Stults.) Ann Arbor: University of Michigan Law School, 1965.

Conquest, Robert. "After Khrushchev: A Conservative Restoration?," *Problems of Communism*, XII, No. 5, September-October 1963, 41–46.

——. *The Great Terror.* New York: Macmillan, 1968.

——. *Justice and the Legal System in the USSR.* New York: Praeger, 1968.

——. (ed.) *The Politics of Ideas in the USSR.* New York: Praeger, 1967.

Constitution (Fundamental Law) of the Union of Soviet Socialist Republics. (Soviet Legislation Series.) Moscow: Progress Publishers, 1967.

Conyngham, William J. "Party, State Relationships in the Soviet Union," *World Affairs*, CXXXII, No. 1, June 1969, 48–63.

Dallin, Alexander. *The Soviet Union at the United Nations.* New York: Praeger, 1962.

——. (ed.) *Diversity in International Communism.* New York: Columbia University Press, 1963.

——. (ed.) *Soviet Conduct in World Affairs.* New York: Columbia University Press, 1960.

Dallin, David Y., and Nicolaevesky, Boris I. *Forced Labor in Soviet Russia.* New Haven: Yale University Press, 1947.

Daniels, Robert V. "Khrushchev and the Party Secretaries, 1953–1961." (Paper prepared for presentation at the Midwest Slavic meeting, March 25, 1966.)

Daugherty, William E., and Janowitz, M. *A Psychological Warfare Casebook.* Baltimore: Johns Hopkins Press, 1958.

Denisov, A. I., and Kirichenko, M. *Soviet State Law.* (Trans., S. Belsky and U. Saifulin.) Moscow: Foreign Languages Publishing House, 1960.

Dinerstein, H. S. *Military Force and Soviet Goals.* (RM–2771.) Santa Monica: Rand, 1961.

——. *The Revolution in Soviet Thinking.* (RM–1927.) Santa Monica: Rand, 1957.

——. *The Soviet Military Posture as a Reflection of Soviet Strategy.* (RM–2102.) Santa Monica: Rand, 1958.

Dirscherl, Dennis (ed.). *The New Russia: Communism in Evolution.* Dayton: Pflaum Press, 1968.

Dutt, Clemens (ed.). *Fundamentals of Marxism-Leninism.* (2d ed.) Moscow: Foreign Languages Publishing House, 1963.

Ermarth, Fritz. "The Soviet Union in the Third World: Purpose in Search of Power," *Annals of the Academy of Political and Social Sciences*, No. 386. November 1969, 31–40.

Europa Year Book, 1969, I. London: Europa Publications, 1969.

The Federal Criminal Law of the Soviet Union. The Basic Principles of the Criminal Legislation. The Law Concerning Military Crimes. (The Basic Principles of Criminal Procedure, No. 3, Series Law in Eastern Europe.) London: n.pub., 1959.

Firsov, Boris. "There's No Average Viewer," *Radio Liberty Translation.* New York: Radio Liberty, n.d.

Fisher, Ralph Talcott, Jr. *Pattern for Soviet Youth: A Study of the Congresses of the Komsomol, 1918–1954.* New York: Columbia University Press, 1959.

Fleron, Frederic J. "Toward a Reconceptualization of Political Change in the Soviet Union: The Political Leadership System." *Comparative Politics*, I, No. 2, January 1969, 228–244.

Florinsky, Michael R. (ed.) *Encyclopedia of Russia and the Soviet Union.* New York: McGraw-Hill, 1961.

The Fundamental Law (Constitution) of the USSR Together with the Constitution of the RSFSR. Moscow: Cooperative Publishing Society of Foreign Workers in the USSR, 1932.

Fundamentals of Marxism-Leninism. (2d ed., rev.) Moscow: Foreign Languages Publishing House, 1963.

Fundamentals of Soviet Criminal Legislation, the Judicial System and Criminal Court Procedure. (Trans., George Hanna.) Official Texts and Commentaries.) Moscow: Foreign Languages Publishing House, 1960.

Gehlen, Michael P. "Continuity and Change in the Career Patterns of CPSU Apparatchiki." (Paper delivered at the Conference on Leadership in the USSR and Eastern Europe, Northwestern University, November 1968.)

Gehlen, Michael P., and McBride, Michael. "The Soviet Central Committee: An Elite Analysis," *American Political Science Review*, LXII, No. 4, December 1968, 1232–1241.

Ginsburg, George. "The Kremlin Scene: Politics in a Cul-De-Sac," *Current History*, LVII, No. 338, October 1969, 228–231 .

Goliakov, I. T. *The Role of the Soviet Court.* (Trans., R. Kramer.) Washington: Public Affairs Press, 1948.

Groshev, Ivan Ivanovich. *A Fraternal Family of Nations.* (Trans. from the Russian by Don Domsemanis.) Moscow: Progress Publishers, 1967.

Gross, Leonard. "The Soviet Union After Fifty Years," *Look*, XXXI, No. 20, October 3, 1967, 29–49.

Gsovski, Vladimir. Soviet Civil Law. 2 vols. Ann Arbor: University of Michigan Law School, 1948–49.

Heidenheimer, Arnold J. *The Government of Germany*. New York: Crowell, 1966.

Hekhuis, Dale J. *Comparison of Postwar US and USSR National Security Expenditures*. (TEMPO Report RM 58TMP–1.) Santa Barbara: Technical Military Planning Operation, General Electric Company, 1958.

Hendel, Samuel (ed.). *The Soviet Crucible*. (3d ed.) Princeton: Van Nostrand, 1967.

Holt, Robert T., and Turner, John E. (eds.) *Soviet Union: Paradox and Change*. New York: Holt, Rinehart and Winston, 1962.

Horelick, Arnold L., and Rush, Myron. *Strategic Power and Soviet in the USSR*. (P–3630.) Santa Monica: Rand, September 1967.

Horelick, Arnold L., and Rush, Myron. *Strategic Power and Soviet Foreign Policy*. (R–434–PR.) Santa Monica: Rand, 1965.

"How Russia Really Lives," *Newsweek*, May 26, 1966, 36–52.

"How Russia Survived Marxism: Soviet Life Today," *Time*, XC, No. 19, November 10, 1967, 32–52.

Hulicka, Karel, and Hulicka, Irene M. *Soviet Institutions: The Individual and Society*. Boston: Christopher Publishing House, 1967.

Institute of Strategic Studies. *The Military Balance*. London: Institute of Strategic Studies, 1968.

————. *Strategic Survey*. London: Institute of Strategic Studies, 1968.

Israelyan, V., et al. *Soviet Foreign Policy*. Moscow: Progress Publishers, 1967.

Ivanov, G. *Notes of a People's Judge*. Moscow: Foreign Languages Publishing House, 1950.

Jacobs, Dan N. "Politburo Actors in the First and Fifth Decades of the Soviet Power." (Paper prepared for the 6th International Conference on World Politics, Berlin, September 4–8, 1967.)

Kelsen, Hans. *The Communist Theory of Law*. New York: Praeger, 1955.

Kolkowicz, Roman. *The Dilemma of Superpower: Soviet Policy and Strategy in Transition*. (Research Paper P–383.) Santa Monica: Rand, 1967.

————. *A General and the Apparatchiks*. (P–3298.) Santa Monica: Rand, 1966.

————. *The Impact of Technology on the Soviet Military*. (RM 4198.) Santa Monica: Rand, 1964.

————. *The Red "Hawks" on the Rationality of Nuclear War*. (RM–4899–PR.) Santa Monica: Rand, 1966.

————. *Soviet Party-Military Relations: Contained Conflict*. Santa Monica: Rand, 1966.

Komolov V. (ed.) *USSR: Questions and Answers*. Moscow: Novosti Press Agency, n.d.

Kruglak, T. E. *The Two Faces of Tass*. Minneapolis: University of Minnesota Press, 1962.

Kucherov, Samuel. *Courts, Lawyers and Trials Under the Last Three Tsars*. New York: Praeger, 1953.

Kulski, W. W. *The Soviet Regime: Communism in Practice*. (4th ed.) Syracuse: Syracuse University Press, 1963.

Kuznetsov, Anatoly. "My Diary in the Other World," *New York Times*, August 17, 1969, 17.

—————. "Russian Writers and the Soviet Police," *New York Times*, August 10, 1969, 1.

Lafeber, W. *America, Russia and the Cold War*. New York: John Wiley, 1967.

Lenin and Stalin on Propaganda. London: Lawrence and Wishard, 1942.

Leyda, Jay. *Kino: A History of the Russian and Soviet Film*. New York: Macmillan, 1960.

Linden, Carl. "Khrushchev and the Party Battle," *Problems of Communism*, XII, No. 5, September–October 1963, 27–35.

Lipper, Elinor. *Eleven Years in Soviet Prison Camps*. Chicago: Henry Regnery, 1951.

Lodge, Milton. "Soviet Elite Participatory Attitudes in the Post-Stalin Period," *American Political Science Review*, LXII, No. 3, September 1968, 827–839.

London, Kurt L. "The Soviet Union and the West," *Current History*, LVII, No. 338, October 1969, 193–200, 238–239.

—————. "The USSR, East Europe and the Socialist Commonwealth," *Current History*, LVI, No. 332, April 1969, 193–199.

—————. (ed.) *Eastern Europe in Transition*. Baltimore: John Hopkins Press, 1966.

Lukacs, John. *A New History of the Cold War*. New York: Doubleday, 1966.

McClosky, Herbert, and Turner, John E. *The Soviet Dictatorship*. New York: McGraw-Hill, 1960.

Mackintash, Malcolm. *The Evolution of the Warsaw Pact*. (Adelphi Papers, No. 58.) London: Institute for Strategic Studies, June 1969.

Mead, Margaret. *Soviet Attitudes Toward Authority*. New York: Schocken Books, 1966.

Mehnert, Klaus. *Peking and Moscow*. New York: Mentor, 1963.

Meissner, Boris. "Power Elite and Intelligentsia in Soviet Society." (Paper presented at the International Conference on World Politics in West Berlin, September 1967.)

Merrill, John C.; Bryan, Carter R.; and Alisky, Marvin. *The For-

eign Press. Baton Rouge: Louisiana State University Press, 1964.

Meyer, Alfred G. "The Nature of Communist Political Systems." (Paper presented at the Midwest Political Science Conference, Chicago, April 1966.)

————. *The Soviet Political System: An Interpretation.* New York: Random House, 1965.

Meyer, Frank S. *The Moulding of Communists.* New York: Harcourt, Brace and World, 1961.

Milestones of Soviet Foreign Policy. Moscow: Progress Publishers, 1967.

Miller, D. L. *Strategy for Conquest.* Washington: Public Affairs Press, 1966.

Milosz, Czeslaw. *The Captive Mind.* New York: Vintage Books, 1955.

Moorehead, Alan. *The Russian Revolution.* New York: Bantam Books: 1958.

1969 World Almanac. New York: Newspaper Enterprise Association, 1969.

Oliver, James H. "Citizen Demands and the Soviet Political System," *American Political Science Review,* LXIII, No. 2, June 1969, 465–475.

Olynyk, Stephen D. "Soviet Federalism in Theory and Practice." (Unpublished master's thesis, Georgetown University, 1965.)

The Penal Code of the Russian Soviet Federated Socialist Republic (1926). London: H. M. Stationery Office, 1934.

"The Principles of Corrective-Labor Legislation," *Current Digest of the Soviet Press,* XXI, No. 29, August 13, 1969, 3–10.

Qualter, T. H. *Propaganda and Psychological Warfare.* New York: Random House, 1962.

Raymond, Ellsworth. *The Soviet State.* New York: Macmillan, 1968.

"Report on Results of 1969 Elections to Local Soviets of Union and Autonomous Republics," *Current Digest of the Soviet Press,* XXI, No. 12, April 9, 1969, 17–19.

Rigby, Thomas H. "The Extent and Limits of Authority," *Problems of Communism,* XII, No. 5, September-October, 36–41.

Romashkin, P. S. *Fundamentals of Soviet Law.* (Trans., Yuri Sdobnikov.) Moscow: Foreign Languages Publishing House, n.d.

Rossi, Peter H., and Bauer, Raymond A. "Some Patterns of Soviet Communications Behavior," *Public Opinion Quarterly,* XVI, No. 4, Winter 1952–53, 653–670.

Rostow, W. W. *The Dynamics of Soviet Society.* New York: American Library, 1954.

Rush, Myron. *Political Succession in the USSR.* (2d ed.) New York: Columbia University Press, 1968.

Russia. (Life World Library.) New York: Time, 1965.

"The Russians' Jubilee Year," *Newsweek,* October 23, 1967, 40–63.

Saikowski, Charlotte. "Nationalism in the USSR," *Christian Science Monitor,* January 27, 1970, 9.

Schapiro, Leonard. *CPSU.* New York: Vintage Books, 1964.

Schwartz, Joel J., and Keech, William R. "Group Influence and the Policy Process in the Soviet Union," *American Political Science Review,* LXII, No. 3, September 1968, 840–851.

Seton-Watson, Hugh. *From Lenin to Khrushchev: The History of World Communism.* New York: Praeger, 1960.

Shaffer, H. G. (ed.) *The Soviet System in Theory and Practice.* New York: Appleton-Century-Crofts, 1965.

Sheinin, L. R. *People's Courts in the USSR.* Moscow: Foreign Languages Publishing House, 1957.

Shub, Anatole. "Lessons of Czechoslovakia," *Foreign Affairs,* XLVII, No. 2, January 1969, 266–280.

Smal-Stocki, Roman. *The Nationality Problem in the Soviet Union and Russian Communist Imperialism.* Milwaukee: Bruce Publishing, 1952.

Soviet Criminal Law and Procedure: Fundamental Principles of Legislation. London: Society for Cultural Relations with the USSR, 1958.

The Soviet Parliament. Moscow: Progress Publishers, 1967.

"Statute Governing Labor Colonies for Minors," *Current Digest of the Soviet Press,* XX, No. 24, July 3, 1968, 3–7.

Stewart, Philip D. "Soviet Interest Groups and the Policy Process: The Repeal of Production Education," *World Politics,* XXII, No. 1, October 1969, 29–50.

Suiridov, N. "The Attention of the Party to the Education of the Scientific and Technical Intelligentsia," *Communist,* No. 18, 1968.

Swearer, Howard R. "Bolshevism and the Individual Leader," *Problems of Communism,* XII, No. 2, March–April 1963, 84–94.

Swianiewicz, S. *Forced Labour and Economic Development: An Inquiry into this Experience of Soviet Industrialization.* London: Oxford University Press, 1965.

Taborsky, E. *Conformity Under Communism.* Washington: Public Affairs Press, 1958.

Teifer, George. *Justice in Moscow.* London: Bodley Head, 1964.

Thomas, John R. "Soviet Russia and Southeast Asia," *Current History,* LV, No. 327, November 1968, 275–280.

Thornton, Thomas (ed.). *The Third World in Soviet Perspective.* Princeton: Princeton University Press, 1964.

Towster, Julian. *Political Power in USSR, 1917–47.* New York: Oxford University Press, 1948.

Triska, Jan F. (ed.) *Soviet Communism: Programs and Rules*. San Francisco: Chandler, 1962.

USSR Laws, Statutes, etc. *Constitution of the Union of Soviet Socialist Republics*. Moscow: Progress Publishers, 1967.

"USSR Defense." Pages 534–540 in *Encyclopaedia Britannica*, XXII. Chicago: William Benton, 1969.

United Nations Educational, Scientific and Cultural Organization. *UNESCO Statistical Yearbook, 1967*. Louvain: UNESCO, 1967.

————. *World Communications*. New York: United Nations, 1964.

U.S. Congress. 90th, 2d Session. House of Representatives. Committee on Armed Services. *The Changing Strategic Naval Balance*. Washington: GPO, 1968.

U.S. Congress. 90th, 2d Session. Joint Economic Committee. *Soviet Economic Performance, 1966–67*. Washington: GPO, 1968.

U.S. Department of the Army. Judge Advocate General. International Affairs Division. Foreign Law Study. *The Comrades' Courts of the Soviet Union*. Washington: Foreign Law Branch, International Affairs Division, Office of the Judge Advocate General, Department of the Army, n.d.

U.S. Department of the Army. *Strategic Survey*. (DA Pamphlet 550–6 USSR.) Washington: GPO, 1969.

U.S. Department of State. Bureau of Intelligence and Research. *World Strength of the Communist Party Organizations*. (20th Annual Report, 1968 ed.) Washington, 1968.

Utechin, S. V. *A Concise Encyclopaedia of Russia*. New York: Dutton, 1964.

Washington Post (Special series of articles on the Soviet Union, by Anatole Shub), June 13–22, 1969.

Wheeler, Fenton. "Cuba Takes Own Path," *Washington Post*, December 18, 1969, A–3.

Wilcox, Wayne. "The Protagonist Powers and the Third World," *Annals of the Academy of Political and Social Science*, No. 386, November 1969, 1–9.

Wolfe, Thomas W. *The Evolving Nature of the Warsaw Pact*. (RM 4835.) Santa Monica: Rand, 1965.

————. *A First Reaction to the New Soviet Book, "Military Strategy."* (RM 3495.) Santa Monica: Rand, 1962.

————. *A Postscript on the Significance of the Book, "Soviet Military Strategy."* (RM 3730.) Santa Monica: Rand, 1963.

————. *The Soviet Quest for More Globally Mobile Military Power*. (RM 5554.) Santa Monica: Rand, 1967.

————. *Soviet Strategy at the Crossroads*. (RM 4085.) Santa Monica: Rand, 1964.

Wolin, S., and Slusser, R. M. (eds.) *The Soviet Secret Police*. New York: Praeger, 1957.

World Radio-Television Handbook Company. *World Radio-TV Handbook, 1968*. Hellerup: World Radio-Television Handbook Company, 1967.

Zlatopolsky, D. *The State System of the USSR*. Moscow: Foreign Languages Publishing House, 1961.

(Various issues of the following periodical were also used in the preparation of this section: *The Current Digest of the Soviet Press* [Columbus], October 1963–October 1968.)

Section IV. Economic

RECOMMENDED SOURCES

Akademiya Nauk SSSR. Gosplan SSR. *Ekonomicheskiye Problemy Razmeshcheniya Proizvoditel'nykh Sil SSR*. Moskva: Nauka, 1969.

Akademiya Nauk SSSR. Institut Ekonomiki. *Struktura Narodnogo Khozyaystva SSR*. Moskva: Nauka, 1967.

—————. *Teoreticheskiye Osnovy i Metodika Postroyeniya Raschetnykh Tsen*. Moskva: Nauka, 1969.

Anufrienko, S. V. *Priamiye Khozyaystvenniye Sviazi Predpriyatii i Effektivnost Proizvodstva*. Moskva: Nauka, 1969.

Baibakov, N. K. *O Gosudarstvennom Plane Razvitiya Narodnogo Khozyaystva SSSR na 1969 god*. Moskva: Politicheskoy Literatury, 1968.

Balinsky, Alexander, et al. *Planning and the Market in the USSR: The 1960's*. New Brunswick: Rutgers University Press, 1967.

Bergson, Abram. *The Economics of Soviet Planning*. New Haven: Yale University Press, 1964.

—————. *Planning and Productivity Under Soviet Socialism*. New York: Columbia University Press, 1968.

Bergson, Abram, and Kuznets, Simon (eds.). *Economic Trends in the Soviet Union*. Cambridge: Harvard University Press, 1963.

Berliner, Joseph S. *Factory and Manager in the USSR*. Cambridge: Harvard University Press, 1968.

Bornstein, Morris, and Fusfeld, Daniel R. (eds.) *The Soviet Economy: A Book of Readings*. (Rev. ed.) Homewood: R. D. Irwin, 1966.

Brackett, James W. "Demographic Trends and Population Policy in the Soviet Union." Pages 487–589 in *Dimensions of Soviet Economic Power*. Washington: GPO, 1962.

Brackett, James W., and DePauw, John W. "Population Policy and Demographic Trends in the Soviet Union." Pages 593–702 in *New Directions in the Soviet Economy*. Washington: GPO, 1966.

Broderson, Arvid. *The Soviet Worker: Labor and Government in Soviet Society*. New York: Random House, 1966.

Brown, Emily Clark. *Soviet Trade Unions and Labor Relations*. Cambridge: Harvard University Press, 1966.

Bulletin of the Institute for the Study of the USSR, XV, No. 1, January 1968.

Bush, Keith. "The Reforms: A Balance Sheet," *Problems of Communism*, XVI, No. 4, July–August 1967, 30–41.

Campbell, Robert W. "Economic Reform in Eastern Europe and the USSR.: Economic Reform in the USSR.," *American Economic Review*, LVIII, No. 2, May 1968, 547–558.

――――. *The Economics of Soviet Oil and Gas*. Baltimore: Johns Hopkins Press, 1968.

――――. "Economics: Roads and Inroads," *Problems of Communism*, XIV, No. 6, November–December 1965, 23–33.

――――. *Soviet Economic Power*. (2d ed.) Boston: Houghton Mifflin, 1966.

Chapman, Janet G. *Real Wages in Soviet Russia Since 1928*. Cambridge: Harvard University Press, 1963.

Degras, Jane R., and Nove, Alec. *Soviet Planning*. Oxford: Basil Blackwell, 1964.

Demographic Yearbook. New York: United Nations, 1968.

Deutscher, Isaac. *Soviet Trade Unions: Their Place in Soviet Labour Policy*. London: Oxford University Press, 1950.

Dewar, Margaret. *Labour Policy in the USSR, 1917–1928*. London: Royal Institute of International Affairs, 1956.

Dewitt, Nicholas. "Education and the Development of Human Resources: Soviet and American Effort." Pages 233–268 in *Dimensions of Soviet Economic Power*. Washington: GPO, 1962.

――――. "High Level Manpower in the USSR." Pages 789–816 in *New Directions in the Soviet Economy*. Washington: GPO, 1966.

Dirscherl, Dennis (ed.). *The New Russia: Communism in Evolution*. Dayton: Pflaum Press, 1968.

Dodge, Norton R. *Women in the Soviet Economy: Their Role in Economic, Scientific and Technical Development*. Baltimore: Johns Hopkins Press, 1966.

Drize, I. D., et al. *Fond Materialinogo Pooshchreniya*. Moskva: Ekonomika, 1968.

Ekonomicheskaya Geografiya SSR. Moskva: Prosveshcheniye, 1966.

Ekonomicheskaya Reforma i Uchet na Predpriatii. Moskva: Finansy, 1968.

Felker, Jere Leake. *Soviet Economic Controversies: The Emerging Marketing Concept and Changes in Planning, 1960–1965*. Cambridge: MIT Press, 1966.

Feshbach, Murray. "Manpower in the USSR: A Survey of Recent Trends and Prospects." Pages 703–788 in *New Directions in the Soviet Economy*. Washington: GPO, 1966.

Feshbach, Murray; Weitzman, Murry S.; and Kulchycka, Lydia. "Employment in the USSR: Comparative USSR–US Data." Pages 591–667 in *Dimensions of Soviet Economic Power*. Washington: GPO, 1962.

Florinksy, Michael R. (ed.) *Encyclopedia of Russia and the Soviet Union.* New York: McGraw-Hill, 1961.

Frankel, Theodore. "Economic Reform: A Tentative Appraisal," *Problems of Communism,* XVI, No. 3, May–June 1967, 29–41.

Gamarnikov, Michael. *Economic Reforms in Eastern Europe.* Detroit: Wayne State University Press, 1968.

Goldman, Marshall I. *The Soviet Economy: Myth and Reality.* Englewood Cliffs: Prentice-Hall, 1968.

————. *Soviet Foreign Aid.* New York: Praeger, 1967.

Greensale, Ruth V. "Khrushchev and the Economists," *Problems of Economics,* XII, No. 3, May–June 1963, 27–32.

Grossman, Gregory (ed.). *Value and Plan.* Berkeley: University of California Press, 1960.

Hardt, John P., et al. *Selected Studies in Soviet Economic Trends and Institutions.* (Report RAC–R–30.) McLean: Research Analysis Corporation, February 1968.

————. (eds.) *Mathematics and Computers in Soviet Economic Planning.* New Haven: Yale University Press, 1967.

Holzman, Franklyn D. *Readings on the Soviet Economy.* Chicago: Rand McNally, 1962.

————. *Soviet Taxation.* Cambridge: Harvard University Press, 1955.

Kaplan, Frederick I. *Bolshevik Ideology and the Ethics of Soviet Labor, 1917–1920.* London: P. Owen, 1968.

Kaser, Michael. *Comecon.* (2d ed.) London: Oxford University Press, 1967.

Kassof, Allen (ed.). *Prospects for Soviet Society.* New York: Praeger, 1968.

Kiperman, G. Ya. *Realiztsiya, Pribyl, Rentabelnost.* Moskva: Statistika, 1968.

Komin, A. *Ekonomicheskaya Reforma i Optovye Tseny v Promyshlennosti.* Moskva: Finansy, 1968.

Kortunov, A. K. *Gazovaya Promyshlenmost SSSR.* Moskva: Nedra, 1967.

Ministerstvo Vneshney Torgovli SSR. *Vneshniaya Torgovlia Soyuza SSH za 1967 god.* Moskva: Mezhdunarodnye Otnosheniya, 1968.

Moskovsky Finansovy Institut Ministerstva Vysshego i Srednego Spetsialnogo Obrazovaniya. *Pribyl i Rentabelnost v Usloviyakh Khozyzystvennoi Reformy.* Moskva: Finansy, 1968.

Nash, Edmund. "Recent Changes in Labor Controls in the Soviet Union." Pages 849–871 in *New Directions in the Soviet Economy.* Washington: GPO, 1966.

————. "Recent Trends in Labor Controls in the Soviet Union." Pages 391–407 in *Dimensions of Soviet Economic Power.* Washington: GPO, 1962.

Nauchno-Issledovatelsky Ekonomichesky Institut pri Gosplane SSSR. *Sovershenstvovaniye Struktury Promyshlennogo Proizvodstva.* Moskva: Ekonomika, 1968.

New Methods of Economic Management in the USSR. (Plenary Meeting of the CPSU Central Committee, September 27–29, 1965.) Moscow: Novosti Press Agency Publishing House, n.d.

Notkina, A. I. (ed.) *Struktura Narodnovo Khozyaystvo.* Moskva: Nauka, 1967.

Nove, Alec. *The Soviet Economy.* (Rev. ed.) New York: Praeger, 1966.

Pereslegin, V. *Rezhim Ekonomy v Usloviyakh Reformy.* Moskva: Finansy, 1969.

Popov, V. E. *Ekonomika Ugolnoye Promyshlennosti Sibiri.* Moskva: Gosudarstvennoye Nauchno-Tekhnicheskoye Izdatel'stvo Literatury Po Gornomu Delu, 1960.

Population Bulletin, XXIII, No. 4, October 1967.

Population Reference Bureau. *1969 World Population Data Sheet.* Washington: Population Reference Bureau, 1969.

Pribyl i Rentabelnost v Usloviyakh Khozyaystvennoy Reformy. Moskova: Finansy, 1968.

50 Let Sovetskoi Vneshney Torgovli. Moskva: Mezhdunarodnye Otnosheniya, 1967.

Reed, Richie H. *Estimates and Projections of the Labor Force and Civilian Employment in the USSR: 1950–1975.* Washington: GPO, 1967.

Rosen, Seymour M. "Changing Guideposts in Soviet Education." Pages 817:848 in *Directions in the Soviet Economy.* Washington: GPO, 1966.

————. "Higher Education in the USSR." Pages 269–303 in *Dimensions of Soviet Economic Power.* Washington: GPO, 1962.

Samborsky, G. I. *Avtomatizatsiya i Spetsializatsiya v Promyshlennosti SSSR.* Moskva: Mysl, 1964.

Schroeder, Gertrude. "Soviet Industrial Labor Productivity." Pages 137–162 in *Dimensions of Soviet Economic Power.* Washington: GPO, 1962.

Schwartz, Harry. *Russia's Soviet Economy.* (2d ed.) Englewood Cliffs: Prentice-Hall, 1958.

Schwarz, Solomon M. *Labor in the Soviet Union.* New York: Praeger, 1952.

Shabad, Theodore. "The Resources of a Nation." In Harrison E. Salisbury (ed.), *The Soviet Union: The Fifty Years.* New York: Harcourt, Brace and World, 1967.

Smekhov, B. M. *Perspektivnoye Narodno-Khozyaystvennoye Planirovaniye.* Moskva: Ekonomika, 1968.

Sorokin, G. *Planning in the USSR: Problems of Theory and Organization.* Moscow: Progress Publishers, 1967.

Soviet Economy: Plans, Problems, Prospects. Moscow: Novosti Press Agency Publishing House, n.d.

Spetsializatsiya i Kooperirovaniye Promyshlennosti. Moskva: Gosplanzdat, 1960.

Spulber, Nicholas. *The Soviet Economy.* New York: W. W. Norton, 1962.

————. "The Soviet Economy in the 1970's," *Current History,* LVII, No. 338, October 1969, 214–219.

Swianiewicz, S. *Forced Labour and Economic Development: An Inquiry into this Experience of Soviet Industrialization.* London: Oxford University Press, 1965.

Treml, Vladimir G. (ed.) *The Development of the Soviet Economy: Plan and Performance.* New York: Praeger, 1968.

Tsentralnoye Statisticheskoye Upravleniye pri Sovete Ministrov SSSR. *Narodnoye Khozyaystvo SSSR v 1967 g.* Moskva: Statistika, 1968.

————. *Promyshlennost SSSR.* Moskva: Statistika, 1964.

————. *Strana Sovetov za 50 Let.* Moskva: Statistika, 1967.

23d Congress of the Communist Party of the Soviet Union. Moscow: Novosti Press Agency Publishing House, n.d.

U.S. Congress. 89th, 1st Session. Joint Economic committee. *A Background Study on East-West Trade.* Washington: GPO, 1965.

————. *Current Economic Indicators for the USSR.* Washington: GPO, 1965.

U.S. Congress. 89th, 2d Session. Joint Economic Committee. *New Directions in the Soviet Economy,* Part II–A: Economic Performance. Washington: GPO, 1966.

————. *New Directions in the Soviet Economy,* Part IV. Washington: GPO, 1966.

U.S. Congress. 90th, 2d Session. Joint Economic Committee. *Soviet Economic Performance, 1966–67.* Washington: GPO, 1968.

U.S. Department of Labor. Bureau of Labor Statistics. *Labor in the USSR.* (Bureau of Labor Statistics Report No. 358.) Washington: GPO, 1969.

————. *Labor Law and Practice in the USSR.* (Bureau of Labor Statistics Report 270.) Washington: GPO 1964.

————. *Principal Current Soviet Labor Legislation.* (Bureau of Labor Statistics Report 210.) Washington: GPO, 1962.

USSR Power Industry. Moscow: Energetika, n.d.

Vainshenker, D. I., and Ivanchenko, V. M. *Khozyaystvennaya Reforma i Analiz Raboty Promyshlennykh Predpriyaty.* Moskva: Statistika, 1968.

Vysshaya Partinaya Shkola pri TSK KPSS. *Planirovaniye Norod-*

nogo Khozyaystva. Uchebnoye Posobiye. (Vtoroye, dopolnennoye i pererabotannoye izdaniye pod obschchey redaktsiye professorov Tsapkina, N. V., i Pereslegina, V. I.) Moskva: Mysl, 1967.

Yearbook of Labour Statistics. Geneva: International Labour Office, 1968.

Yevenko, I. *Planning in the USSR.* Moscow: Foreign Languages Publishing House, n.d.

Zagaynov, L. I. *Ekonomicheskiye Funktsii Sovetskogo Gosudarstva.* Moskva: Yuridicheskaya Literatura, 1968.

OTHER SOURCES USED

Akademiya Nauk SSSR. Institut Afriki. *Economicheskoye Sotrudnichestvo SSSR So Stranami Afriki.* Moskva: Nauka, 1968.

Avtorkhanov, Abdurakhman. *The Communist Party Apparatus.* Chicago: Henry Regnery, 1966.

Azrael, Jeremy R. *Managerial Power and Soviet Politics.* Cambridge: Harvard University Press, 1966.

Berman, Harold J. *Justice in the USSR: An Interpretation of Soviet Law.* (Rev. ed.) New York: Vintage Books, 1963.

Conquest, Robert. *Industrial Workers in the USSR.* New York: Praeger, 1967.

————. (ed.) *Agricultural Workers in the USSR.* New York: Praeger, 1969.

Council for Mutual Economic Assistance. *Survey of CMEA Activities in 1967.* Moscow: CMEA Secretariat Printers, 1968.

"The Council for Mutual Economic Assistance-Developments Since the Mid-1960s'." (Unpublished paper prepared for the Joint Economic Committee, U.S. Congress, 1969.)

Current Digest of the Soviet Press, XXI, Nos. 1–35, January–September 1969.

Dewitt, Nicholas. *Education and Professional Employment in the USSR.* Washington: GPO, 1961.

Dobb, Maurice. *Soviet Economic Development Since 1917.* New York: International Publishers, 1966.

Fainsod, Merle. *How Russia is Ruled.* (Rev. ed.) Cambridge: Harvard University Press, 1964.

Gwertzman, Bernard. "Surplus Russian Workers Face Job Loss," *New York Times,* October 10, 1969, C–30.

Hulicka, Karel, and Hulicka, Irene M. *Soviet Institutions: The Individual and Society.* Boston: Christopher Publishing House, 1967.

International Labor Office. *The Trade Union Situation in the USSR.* Geneva: 1960.

Pisarev, I. *The Population of the USSR.* Moscow: Progress Publishers, n.d.

Popov, K. I. *Razvitiye Ekonomicheskikh Sviazei Stran Sotsialisma.* Moskva: Mysl, 1968.

Pryor, Frederic L. *The Communist Foreign Trade System.* Cambridge: MIT Press, 1963.

"Recent Trends in the Foreign Trade of the USSR." (Unpublished paper prepared for the Joint Economic Committee, U.S. Congress, 1969.)

Saikowski, Charlotte. "Manpower Squeeze Besets Soviets," *Christian Science Monitor,* September 20, 1969, 1, 6.

"Shelepin's Report to the Trade Union Congress," *Current Digest of the Soviet Press,* XX, No. 9, March 21, 1968, 3–14.

"Soviet Economic Assistance to Less Developed Countries." (Unpublished paper prepared for the Joint Economic Committee, U.S. Congress, 1969.)

Steinberg, S. H. (ed.) *Statesman's Yearbook, 1968–1969.* New York: Macmillan, 1968.

Tsentralnoye Statisticheskoye Upravleniye. *Trud v SSSR.* Moskva: Statistika, 1968.

"United Nations," *Worldmark Encyclopedia of the Nations.* New York: Harper and Row, 1967.

U.S. Congress. 89th, 1st Session. Joint Economic Committee. *New Directions in Soviet Economy,* Part III: The Human Resources. Washington: GPO, 1966.

U.S. Department of Commerce. Bureau of the Census. Foreign Demographic Analysis Division. *Wages in the USSR, 1950–1967: Education.* (International Population Reports Series, No. 66.) Washington: GPO, 1969.

U.S. Department of State. *Communist Governments and Developing Nations: Aid and Trade in 1967.* (Research Memorandum RSE–120, August 14, 1968.) Washington: Department of State, 1968.

―――――. *Communist Governments and Developing Nations: Aid and Trade in 1968.* (Research Memorandum RSE–65, September 5, 1969.) Washington: Department of State, 1969.

Vneshniya Torgovlya, XLVII–XLIX. Moskva: Izvestiia, 1967–69.

(Various issues of the following periodicals were also used in the preparation of this section: *Economist* [*London*], January–October 1966; *Ekonomicheskaya Gazeta* [Moskva], January–October 1966; *Pravda* [Moskva], January 1–October 31, 1969; and Sotsialisticheskaya Industriya [Moskva], January 1–October 31, 1969.)

GLOSSARY

Agitprop—Department of Propaganda and Agitation of the Central Committee of the Communist Party of the Soviet Union.

apparatchik—Russian colloquial expression referring to a man of the apparatus, that is, an individual whose entire career has been spent in Party work.

ASSR—Avtonomnaya Sovetskaya Sotsialisticheskaya Respublika (Autonomous Soviet Socialist Republic). Regional subdivisions of some union republics, created to grant a degree of autonomy to some of the larger ethnic minority groups.

autonomous *oblast*—A regional subdivision of a *kray* or small union republic, created to grant a degree of autonomy to a national minority.

babushka—Grandmother.

blat—Profitable connections, influence, pull. Often used to describe methods through which industrial managers conceal shortages and surpluses or acquire materials illicitly. May involve anything from black-marketeering to merely overlooking minor production deficiencies.

boyar—Hereditary nobleman in tsarist Russia.

cadre—Organized group of Party activists.

CEMA—Council for Economic Mutual Assistance. A multilateral economic alliance headquartered in Moscow. Members: Bulgaria, Czechoslovakia, East Germany, Hungary, Mongolia, Poland, Rumania, and USSR.

centimeter (cm)—Is equal to 0.39 inch.

Cheka—Chrezvychaynaya Komissiya (Extraordinary Commission). Full title: All-Russian Extraordinary Commission to Fight Counterrevolution, Sabotage, and Speculation. The original Bolshevik security police; 1917—22.

Cominform—Communist Information Bureau. International organization of Communist parties, established in 1947 and dissolved in 1956.

Comintern—Communist International. International organization of Communist parties founded in Moscow in 1919. Dissolved by Stalin in 1943 as a conciliatory measure toward his Western allies.

CPSU—Communist Party of the Soviet Union.

Donbas—Donetsk basin. Major coal mining and industrial area. Located in southeastern Ukraine and adjacent RSFSR.

Duma—Lower chamber of the legislature. Granted by the tsar after the Revolution of 1905.

Glavlit—Glavny literaturny (main literary). Main Administration for Literary and Publishing Affairs, established in 1922 as the formal censorship organ. Later the name was changed to Main Administration for the Protection of Military and State Secrets from the Press, to which the acronym *glavlit* is still applicable.

Gosbank—Gosudarstvennyy Bank (State Bank). Gosbank is the main bank in the USSR and acts as a combination central bank, commercial bank, and settlement bank. It issues and regulates currency and credit and handles payments between enterprises and organizations. It receives all taxes and payments to the state and pays out budgetary appropriations.

Gosplan—Gosudarstvennyy Planovyy Komitet (State Planning Committee). Subordinate to USSR Council of Ministers. Responsible for centralized economic planning.

GPU—Gosudarstvennoye Politicheskoye Upravleniye (State Political Administration). The security police successor to the Cheka, 1922—23.

KGB—Komitet Gosudarstvennoy Bezopasnosti (Committee for State Security), 1954—70. The predominant state and internal security police organization.

kilogram (kg)—1,000 grams. Is equal to 2.2 avoirdupois pounds.

kilometer (km)—1,000 meters. Is equal to 0.62 miles.

kolkhoz—Collective farm.

Komsomol—Young Communist League. Youth group for people between the ages of fifteen and twenty-eight. Administered by the CPSU.

kray—An administrative regional subdivision.

kulak—A relatively well-to-do, independent farmer of the precollectivization period. The term eventually was applied to any peasant who opposed collectivization.

Kuzbas—Kuznetsk basin. Major coal mining and industrial area. Located in southern Siberia, east and southeast of Novosibirsk.

meter (m)—100 centimeters. Is equal to 3.28 feet or 1.09 yards.

metric ton (mt)—1,000 kilograms. Is equal to 1.1 short tons or 0.98 long tons.

MGB—Ministerstvo Gosudarstvennoy Bezopasnosti (Ministry of State Security), 1946—53. From 1949 to 1953 the MGB was the paramount security police organization.

mir—Peasant commune at village level during tsarist period. *Mir* controlled redistribution of land and was held responsible for tax collection and levying of recruits for military service.

MOOP—Ministerstvo Okhrany Obshchestvennogo Poryadka (Ministry for the Preservation of Public Order). Replaced MVD between 1961 and 1968.

MVD—Ministerstvo Vnutrennikh Del (Ministry of Internal Affairs), 1946 to 1962 and 1968 to 1970.

NEP—Novaya Ekonomicheskaya Politika (New Economic Policy). Instituted in 1921, the NEP allowed the peasants to trade produce on an open market and permitted small enterprises to be privately owned and operated. During this period, which ended about 1928, the cultural atmosphere also relaxed.

NKGB—Narodny Komissariat Gosudarstvennoy Bezopasnosti (Peoples' Commissariat for State Security), 1941 and 1943—46.

NKVD—Narodnyy Konissariat Vnutrennikh Del (People's Commissariat of Internal Affairs). Commissariat administering security police organizations from 1917 to 1934. When the OGPU was abolished in 1934, the NKVD became the security police organizations, remaining so until 1946.

nomenklatura—Nomenclature. System of appointing key personnel in the government and other important institutions, based upon lists of personnel and positions.

Novosti—News. Short for Agentstvo Pechati Novosti (News Press Agency). News agency for dissemination of information abroad.

oblast—The primary regional administrative subdivision of the larger union republics.

OGPU—Ob'edinyonnoye Gosudarstvennoye Politicheskoye Upravleniye (Unified State Political Administration). Security police successor to the GPU, 1923—34.

okrug—A national area subordinate to a *kray* or *oblast*, created to recognize a small national minority.

Politburo—Political Bureau of the Central Committee of the CPSU. Foremost policymaking body of the Soviet Union.

Presidium of the Central Committee of the CPSU— The Politburo was called Presidium between 1952 and 1966.

Presidium of the Supreme Soviet— Executive committee of the national legislature.

rayon—Rural *rayony* are country-equivalent district subdivisions of *kraya*, *oblasti*, ASSRs, national *okruga*, and the small union republics. City *rayony* are the boroughs of the larger cities.

RSFSR—Rossiyskaya Sovetskaya Federativnaya Sotsialisticheskaya Respublika (Russian Soviet Federated Socialist Republic). The Russian union republic. It comprises approximately 75 percent of the area of the USSR and has more than one-half its total population.

ruble (R)—The monetary unit, divided into 100 kopeks. The official par value is R1 equals US$1.10.

Soviet—Council. Basic governmental structure at all levels.

sovkhoz—State farm.

SSR—Sovetskaya Sotsialisticheskaya Respublika (Soviet Socialist Republic). A union republic.

TASS—Telegrafnoye Agentstvo Sovietskovo Soyuza (Telegraphic

Agency of the Soviet Union). News agency that has a monopoly
of distribution of news within the Soviet Union.

turnover tax—A sales tax levied primarily on consumer goods.

union republic—The primary administrative subdivision of the
USSR.

USSR—Union of Soviet Socialist Republics. The Soviet Union.

INDEX

abacus: 709
Abastumani Astrophysical Observatory: 358
Abkhaz: 192
Abkhaz ASSR: 412
abortion: 204, 205, 207, 216, 674, 677
Academy of Fine Arts: 342
Academy of Sciences: 277, 336, 350, 351, 353, 354, 373; publications, 531, 532, 533, 695
acronyms: 185
Adegey: 166
Adegey autonomous oblast: 415
advertising: 525, 536, 538
advocates: 468
Adzhar ASSR: 412
Aeroflot: 492, 718
Afghanistan: 24, 125, 188, 507; aid to, 738, 739
Afinogenov, Alexander: 325
Aga (Aginsky) Buryat national okrug: 416
Agitation and Propaganda Department: *See* Agitprop; propaganda
Agitprop: 131, 283, 427, 429, 517, 534, 539, 543, 548, 550
agriculture (*see also* chapter 31, and collective farms; crops; grain; land; mechanization of agriculture; private plots to farm; state farms): 28, 75, 179, 531, 618; economics, 106, 107, 108, 112, 115; labor force, 220, 661, 679; vocational training, 294, 296
agrogoroda: 436
Aguls: 166
Ainu people: 171; language, 193
air forces: 569, 578, 582, 586, 591
air transport: 718
aircraft: 369, 582, 585
Akhmadulina, Bella: 315, 343
Akhmatova, Anna: 313, 315, 339
Aksionov, Vasili: 343, 344
Alabyan, Karo: 310
Albania: 68, 69, 498, 500, 703
Aleksandrov, Aleksandr D.: 355

Aleksandrov, Anatoli: 356
Aleuts: 172; language, 183, 193
Alexander I: 47, 258, 278
Alexander II: 49, 278, 444
Alexander III: 50, 51, 445
Alexandra, Empress: 53
Alexius, Patriarch: 244
Algeria: 507
All-Union Central Council of Trade Unions: 282, 283, 303, 689, 691, 697, 702
All-Union Congress of Trade Unions: 696, 697
All-Union Knowledge Society: 429
All-Union Lenin Academy of Agricultural Sciences: 661
All-Union Party Congresses (CPSU): 378, 420, 688, 689; Twentieth, 95, 435, 493, 500; Twenty-second, 435, 690; Twenty-third, 611, 654–55, 665, 690
All-Union Scientific Research Institute for Standardization: 640–41
Alma Ata: 35
alphabets (*see also* Cyrillic alphabet; Hebrew alphabet; Latin alphabet): 167, 189, 195
Altai mountains: 13, 32
Altaic languages: 183, 189, 191
Altay kray: 406, 407
Ambartsumyan, Viktor A.: 358
Amu Darya River: 15, 24, 34
Amur River: 15, 24, 32
Andropov, Yuri V.: 124
Angara River: 14, 15
Antarctica: 360, 493
Antonov uprising: 151
apparatchik: 69
apprentices: 679
Arab countries: 505, 506
Arab-Israeli war: 492, 506
Arabic language: 188, 193, 531
Aral Sea: 12, 15
Aramaic language: 167, 194
Aras River: 23
architecture: 248, 307–10

Arctic: 12, 360
Argun River: 24
armed forces (*see also* chapter 28, and political commissars): 225, 277, 288, 293
Armenia: 165, 174; languages, 183, 188, 189
Armenian Gregorian Church: 241, 250
Armenian SSR: 26, 29, 60, 165, 402, 403, 404
army: 47, 569, 582–84, 591; Red Army, 570
art and artists: 269, 292, 297, 310–12, 315, 531
Artsimovich, Lev A.: 356, 373
Ashby, Eric: 340
Asiatic languages: 183
Askaryan, G. A.: 357
Assafiev, Boris: 323
assimilation of cultural groups: 7, 84, 158, 164, 172
ASSR (Autonomous Soviet Socialist Republic): *See* autonomous republics
Assyrians: 167; language, 194
Aswan High Dam: 739
atheism (*see also* League of the Militant Godless): 239, 245, 271, 547
autonomous republics (*see also* names of individual republics): 399, 401, 411, 412, 609
Avars: 166, 175
Avicenna: 168
Avvacum: 316
awards and decorations: 129, 700
Azerbaijan SSR: 29, 60, 402, 403
Azerbaijani people: 165, 191
Azers: 329
Azov, Sea of: 12

Baikal, Lake: 12, 15
Baikonur cosmodrome: 366
Baku: 13, 15
Balakirev, M.: 321
Balkars: 145, 166, 177
Balkhash, Lake: 12, 15, 17
ballet: 305, 322–24, 329, 519
Baltic languages: 183
Baltic Sea: 14
Baluchi language: 188
banishment: 476
banking system: 755–60
baptism: 241, 248
Baptists: 241, 252
Bashkir ASSR: 412, 630

Bashkir peoples: 163, 176, 329, 413; language, 191
Basov, Nikolai G.: 332, 356
Belinsky, Vissarion: 326, 339
Belorussia SSR: 25, 26, 402, 403
Belorussians: 18, 160, 161; language, 182, 186, 187
Beltir people: 171
Benois, Alexander: 311
Berdiaev, Nicholas: 336, 337
Beregovoi, Georgi: 365
Beria, Lavrenti: 63, 67, 68, 70, 124, 154
Berlin blockade: 66
Bessarabia: *See* Moldavia SSR
bilingualism: 181, 198
biology: 271, 331, 344, 351, 361
birth rate (*see also* abortion): 174, 216, 222, 674, 676; birth certificates, 206
Black Sea: 14, 15
blat: 270
Blok, Alexander: 313, 319, 337
Blokhintsev, Dmitriy: 368
Bogolyubov, Nikolay N.: 355, 356
Bolshevik Revolution: 8, 58, 349
Bolsheviks: 54, 55, 57, 76, 93, 144, 145, 289, 387, 446, 490, 688
Bolshoi ballet company: 323
Bondarchuk, Sergei: 328
border troops: 125–29
Borodin, Alexander: 321
boundaries: 15, 17, 22–25; disputes, 495, 496
boyars: 42
Brandt, Willy: 504
Braunshteyn, Aleksandr Y.: 362
Brest-Litovsk, Treaty of: 26, 57
Brezhnev, Leonid: 2, 8, 72, 560, 561, 580; agriculture, 658, 690; foreign relations, 509, 512; leadership, 379, 391, 420, 421, 438, 440; military affairs, 607
Brezhnev Doctrine: 502
Briusov, Valery: 313
Buddhism: 171, 256–58
Budker, Gersh I.: 357
Budyenny, S. M.: 58
Bug River: 23, 26
Bukhara: 169
Bukharin, Nikolai: 383
Bukovina: 402
Bulgakov, Mikhail: 325
Bulgakov, Sergei: 336
Bulganin, Nikolai: 68, 69

Bulgaria: 729, 737, 738, 741; language, 182, 187, 191; people, 161
Bunin, Ivan: 313
Buryat ASSR: 412
Buryat Mongols: 171, 191, 256
Byzantine art: 308, 311
Byzantine law: 443
Byzantine Orthodox Christianity: 165, 173

calendar: 45
Cancer Ward: 315
capital investment: 112, 615, 625, 642
capital punishment: *See* death sentence
Carpathian dialect: 186
Caspian Sea: 12, 15, 24
Castro, Fidel: 512
Catherine the Great: 46-47, 277, 568; Jews and, 258
Caucasian languages: 183, 188, 191, 192-93
Caucasoid peoples: 157, 164-67, 177
Caucasus region: 50
Cechetti, Enrico: 323
CEMA partners: 499, 501, 514, 702, 741-44; banking, 757; trade, 727, 729, 731, 738
censorship: 278, 307, 336, 345, 380, 386, 456, 516, 517, 519, 548, 549, 560; letters to the editor, 529
census (*see also* population): 7
Central Treaty Organization: 507
Chagall, Marc: 311, 312
Chagatai language: 179, 191, 196
chamber of commerce, national: 724
Chechen-Ingush ASSR: 412
Chechens: 145, 166, 177; language, 192
Cheka: 120, 121, 123, 141, 448
Chekhov, Anton: 318, 326
chemistry: 288, 360, 369
Cheremis: *See* Mari peoples
Cherenkov, Pavel A.: 332, 356
chernozem: 28
Chernyshevsky, Nikolai: 339
Cherski mountains: 32
children: 59, 205, 217, 223, 234, 236, 268; family system, 204, 206, 209, 211, 218; handicapped, 291-92
Children's Technical Station: 302
Children's World: 709
China, Communist: 8, 24, 71, 703; relations with, 273, 488, 493-97, 504, 509, 522; trade with, 728, 737
China, Nationalist: 494

Chinese Eastern Railroad: 495, 496
Chou En Lai: 71
Christianity (*see also* Protestants, Roman Catholics): 159, 167, 194, 241-53, 316
Chukchi national okrug: 416
Chukchi people: 172; language, 193
Chukchi Sea: 11
Chukhrai, Grigori: 328
Chukotian languages: 183
Church-Slavonic dialect: *See* Old Church Slavonic language
Churchill, Winston: 64, 66
Chuvash ASSR: 412
Chuvash peoples: 163, 176, 329; language, 191
Circassian language: 166, 192
Civil Code: 444, 449, 450
clergy: 75, 160, 231, 243, 245; married, 246, 247
climate: 14, 17, 26, 28, 30, 32, 34, 176, 654, 661
clothing: 229
coal: 31, 35, 116, 626, 627, 647, 651
collective farms (*kolkhoz*): 185, 635, 659, 665, 677-78, 679, 697, 712, 750, 759; forced collectivization, 62, 143
collegiums: 397
Comecon: *See* CEMA partners
Cominform: 489, 500
Comintern: 61, 65, 489, 551
Commander Island: 11
Commissariat of Education: 279-80, 350, 517
commissars: *See* political commissars
Committee for State Security: *See* KGB
committees or commissions (*see also* State Planning Committee): 354, 388, 648, 682, 690
communications (*see also* radio and television, telephone and telegraph systems): 197, 274, 519, 706; budget, 748; services, 182, 198; wages, 695
communist ideology (*see also* Agitprop): 3, 87, 91, 331-41; indoctrination, 275, 279, 297, 302, 517; Marxism-Leninism, 74, 179, 203, 262, 353, 487, 488, 493, 516, 525, 548, 559, 605-6
communist lexicon: bourgeois chauvinism, 329; cold war, 66, 490, 491; cult of personality, 438, 547, 553, 558; democratic centralism, 447,

454; dialectical materialism, 334, 340; dictatorship of the proletariat, 90, 447; hot line, 492; iron curtain, 66; learning through labor, 281; new Soviet man, 262, 275, 281, 301, 312; peaceful coexistence, 70; Socialist Realism, 37, 197, 313; socially useful work, 148, 477, 692

Communist Party of the Soviet Union (see also Agitprop, All-Union Party Congresses, Politburo, purges, security police): 1-4, 60, 70, 181, 420-33; Central Committee, 102, 282, 283, 420, 543; educational policy, 281, 283; labor organizations and, 687, 688, 696; leadership and control, 88, 91, 96, 225, 273-74, 331, 343, 351, 376, 377, 402, 534; legal system, 454; membership, 82, 83, 94, 572, 595; publishing, 517, 523, 529; religion and, 240, 250; security agencies and, 140, 148, 155

computers: 356, 370

Comrades' Courts: 463, 692

conscription: 127, 387, 433, 570, 572, 588, 592, 673

Constitution: 36, 63, 245, 281, 377-87, 423, 446, 447, 452, 461, 516, 691

construction industry (see also housing): 613, 619, 648, 649-50, 652, 748; GNP, 106, 107, 113; labor, 638, 646, 679, 695; materials, 635, 636

consumer goods and services: 228, 437, 438, 525, 623, 637, 641, 644, 645, 646, 647, 651, 694, 696, 713-15, 753; imports, 731; shortages, 104, 109, 597, 600, 601

Cossacks: 75

cotton textile industry: 636, 647

Council for Economic Mutual Assistance: See CEMA partners

Council of Ministers: 102, 124, 139, 283, 377, 378, 390-93, 453, 581, 746

courts: 156, 382, 385, 444, 445, 450, 460-66; civil, 692-93

CPSU: See Communist Party of the Soviet Union

Credit Plan: 758-60

crime: 140, 156, 467; by analogy, 450; political, 472-73, 480

Crimea: 191

Crimean Tatars: 145, 156, 176, 177, 191

Crimean War: 49

Criminal Code: 444, 449, 458

crops: 33, 169, 654, 658, 664, 665-68

Cuba: 491, 512-13, 729, 737

Cui, Caesar: 321

cult of personality: See under communist lexicon

culture change (see also assimilation of cultural groups): 78, 158, 178, 197, 214, 328

currency system: 760, 761

cybernetics: 353, 356

Cyril, Saint: 186, 187, 242

Cyrillic alphabet: 186, 188, 192, 193, 196, 198, 316, 328

Czechoslovakia: 23, 66, 69, 161; invasion, 500, 501, 502, 503, 566; language, 182, 187; trade, 729, 738, 741

Dagestan ASSR: 412, 413

Dagestan peoples: 166, 192

Daniel, Yuli: 306, 344, 373, 564

Dargins: 166

Dargomijski, Alexander: 321

death sentence: 141, 144, 458, 473

Deborin, Abram: 337

Decembrist uprising: 48

defense industry: 600, 625, 747, 748, 751

de Gaulle, Charles A.: 504

Denikin, Anton: 58, 573

deportation of ethnic groups: 145, 166, 168, 177, 273

Derjaguin, Boris V.: 361

Diaghilev, Sergei: 311, 324

diet and food: 107, 109, 115, 117, 170, 228, 229, 709, 714

diseases: 222

divorce: 204, 205, 206, 207, 209, 210, 215, 236

Dnepr River: 15, 26, 27, 29, 31, 310

Dnepropetrovsk: 29

Dniester River: 27

Dobrolyubov, Nikolai: 339

Doctor Zhivago: 306, 315

Doctors' Plot: 67, 146

Doctrine of Limited Sovereignty: See Brezhnev Doctrine

Dolgano-Nenets peoples: 417

Dolgans: 172, 191

Don: 530

Don River: 15, 28, 31

Donets River: 28

Donetsk basin (Donbas): 29, 185, 628

Donskoi, Mark: 327, 328

Dostoevsky, Feodor: 318, 344

Dovzhenko, Alexander: 327

Dubinin, Nikolay P.: 362
Dudinskaya, Natalia: 323
Duma: 51, 52
Dungans: 194
Dushanbe: 35
Dvina River: 26
Dzerzhinsky, Felix: 124, 480, 481
Dzhugashvili, Joseph Vissarionovich: See Stalin, Joseph

Eastern Orthodox Church: 241, 443
Echmiadzin Monastery: 250
economic aid to foreign countries: 9, 508, 512, 513, 733, 735, 736, 740
Economic Council of Europe (ECE): 744
Economic Gazette: 523, 524
education (see also chapter 15, and higher education, schools): 225, 332, 536, 681-82, 695; budget, 748; labor colonies, 484; military, 589-90, 591
Egypt: See United Arab Republic
Eisenhower, Dwight D.: 68, 71
Eisenstein, Sergei: 305, 327
electoral system: 4, 380, 393-95
electric power: See power
Emba oilfields: 35
employment: See labor force
Engelgardt, Vladimir A.: 362
Engels, Friedrich: 3, 203
engineering: 296, 299
English language: 195; publications, 530, 531
Ents: 172
Ermler, Friedrich: 328
Eskimo-Aleut languages: 183, 193
Eskimos: 172
Essenin, Sergei: 313, 314
Estonia: 64, 162, 177, 187, 566
Estonian SSR: 25, 26, 402, 403, 404, 733
Euler, Leonhart: 348
Evangelical Christian Church: 241, 252
Even people: 172, 191
Evenk people: 172, 191
Evenki national okrug: 416
Evtushenko, Evgeny: 315
exile as punishment: 168, 474, 476, 477
Export-Import Bank: 729
exports: 655, 665, 723, 728, 730

Fadeyev, Alexander: 315
Family Code: 450

family life (see also chapter 11): 170, 271-74
Farabi, al: 168
Federal Republic of Germany (West Germany): See under Germany
Fedoseev, Pyotr: 332, 340
feldshers: 226
Fergana Valley: 35
fertilizers: 116, 647, 665
Feuerbach, Ludwig: 334
films: 297, 326-28, 515, 531, 538, 544
Finland: 22, 730; invasion, 64, 576
Finnic languages: 183, 187, 189
Finns: 163, 175, 413
fishing: 668
Five-Year Plan for 1966-70: agriculture, 663; industry, 115, 116, 623-24, 637; labor, 680, 690
flag: 397
flowers: 709
Fokine, Michael: 323
folklore: 165, 170; proverbs, 185
folksongs: 321
Fonvizin, Denis: 326
forced labor: 62, 65, 156, 480, 483, 678
foreign affairs (see also chapter 24, and treaties and agreements, names of individual countries): 91, 384, 564, 698
foreigners and aliens: 121, 133, 136, 137, 474
forestry: 19, 21, 33, 669
France: 504, 729
Frank, Ilya M.: 332, 356
Frank, Semion L.: 336, 337
freedoms (see also censorship, rights of citizens): 37, 77, 307, 373-75, 456
French language: 185, 195, 530, 531
Friendship University: 299
Frumkin, Aleksandr N.: 361
Frunze, M. V.: 35, 58
Frunze Military Academy: 129, 593
furs: 179, 669

Gagarin, Yuri: 365
Gagauz peoples: 167, 191
Galanskov, Yuri: 374
gas: natural, 116, 626, 627, 631, 647, 649, 719
genetics: 352, 362
Genghis Khan: 176
geographic study: 288, 359
Georgian Orthodox Church: 241, 250
Georgian SSR: 26, 29, 60, 402, 403

Georgians: 165; language, 192
Gerasimov, Innokentiy P.: 359
German Democratic Republic (East Germany): *See* under Germany
German language: 185, 187, 188, 195, 531
Germans: 64, 145, 164, 177, 576–78
Germany: 64, 348; East Germany, 498, 729, 738, 741; West Germany, 501, 505, 729
Gerö, Ernö: 500
Ghandi, Indira: 510
Gilels, Emile: 320
Gilyak people: 171, 183, 193
Ginzburg, Alexander: 374
Glavlit: 307, 517, 518
Glazunov, Ilia: 319, 342
Gliere, Reinhold: 319
Glinka, Mikhail: 321
Glushkov, Viktor M.: 356
Gogol, Nikolai: 317, 326
gold: 734, 760
Goldi: *See* Nanai peoples
Goncharov, Ivan: 317
Gorky, Maxim: 13, 31, 307, 312, 313
Gorky State University: 341
Gorno-Altay autonomous oblast: 415
Gorno-Badakhshan autonomous oblast: 415
Gorsky, M.: 324
Gosbank: 755, 756, 758, 760
Gospolitizdat: 533
Gosstroy: 648
government: *See* chapter 19, and Communist Party of the Soviet Union; Constitution; Council of Ministers; local government ministries
GPU: 122, 142
grain: crops, 169, 654, 658, 662, 665; state monopoly, 713
grandmother (*babushka*): 212, 268, 274
Great Britain: 42, 492, 730
Great Fatherland War: *See* World War II
Great Russians: 7, 158, 160, 174, 180, 182, 194, 329
Grechko, Andrei: 581
Greek language: 189; alphabet, 192
Gregorian Church: 165
Grishin, V. V.: 698
Gromyko, Andrei A.: 488
Gross National Product: 106, 107
Gruboyedov, Alexander: 326
Gudok: 523, 524

Gulistan, Treaty of: 24
GUM: 709
Gumilev, Nikolai: 313
Gvishiani, Dzerman: 355
gypsies: 189

handicapped persons: 291–92
Hari Rud River: 24
health services: 223–24
Hebrew alphabet: 188, 193
Hegel, Georg: 89, 334
higher education (*see also* universities): 80, 276, 282, 283, 290, 296–99, 431, 534, 661, 670, 697
highways: 27, 36
Hiiumaa Island: 12
historic site restorations: 333, 568
historiography: 37, 288, 340
History of the All-Union Communist Party (Bolshevik): 550
holidays: 228, 397, 547, 568
Hoover, Herbert: 59
hospitals: 223, 224
housing: 113, 115, 172, 230–33, 748
Hungary: 23, 164, 189; trade, 729, 738, 741; uprising, 500, 502
Huns: 175

iconography: 311
icons: 248
Ili River: 34
Ilichev, Leonid: 344
imports: 640, 724, 731, 732; books, 518; grain, 654, 658
income tax: 78, 754
India: 730, 732, 735, 738
Indo-European languages: 182–89
Indonesia: 740
industrialization: 50, 61, 520, 641
industry (*see also* chapter 30, and labor force, productivity, technology, trade unions): 27, 31, 34, 106, 107; budget, 747, 748; enterprise management, 105, 706
Ingush language: 192
inheritance: 204, 207, 209; taxes, 78
Institute of Scientific Atheism: 245
intelligence collection: 132, 135, 600; military, 120, 123, 128, 134; trawlers, 585; space, 588
intelligentsia: 3, 76, 80, 341, 375, 426, 548
Internal Troops: 151, 153
international organizations: 513, 703
Iofan, Boris: 310

Iran: 24, 125, 507, 740
Iranian people: 165, 167, 175; languages, 26, 183, 188
Irkutsk: 15, 34
iron ore: 28, 116, 633, 647, 651
irrigation: 662
Irtysh River: 14, 15, 32
Islam: 7, 253–56, 264
Israel: 505, 506
Italic languages: 183
Italy: 729
Itelmens: 172; language, 193
Ivan I: 41
Ivan III, the Great: 41–42
Ivan IV, the Terrible: 42, 43, 443, 568
Ivan the Terrible: 327
Ivanov, Vsevolod: 324
Ixhors: 163
Izvestia: 517, 523–24

Jacobites: 165, 167
Japan: 511; language, 189
Jewish autonomous oblast: 164, 171, 188, 259, 415
Jews: 75, 146, 165, 166, 169, 179; language, 164, 179, 188, 193; religion, 258
judges: 445, 461
jurisconsults: 469

Kabardians: 166
Kabardino-Balkarian ASSR: 412
Kachin people: 171
Kafka, Franz: 344
Kaganovich, Lazar M.: 69
Kaliningrad: 26
Kalmyk ASSR: 412
Kalmyk Mongols: 191
Kalmyk Tuvins: 256
Kalmyks: 145, 166, 177
Kama River: 31
Kamchatka Peninsula: 11
Kamenev, Lev: 63, 259
Kandinsky, Vassili: 311, 312
Kapitsa, Pyotr L.: 332, 347, 357, 373
Kapustin Yar: 366
Kara Sea: 11
Kara-Kalpak ASSR (*see also* Karakalpaks): 412
Kara-Kum Canal: 663
Karachay-Cherkess autonomous oblast: 415
Karachay people: 145, 166, 177
Karaganda region: 35, 629

Karaginsky Island: 11
Karaimy people: 191
Karaites: *See* Karaimy people
Karakalpaks: 169, 176; language, 191
Karelia ASSR: 412, 413
Karelians: 163
Karelo-Finnish SSR: 402
Kargin, Valentin A.: 361
Kars, Treaty of: 23
Karsavina, Tamara: 323
Kazakh SSR: 26, 34, 403
Kazakhs: 168, 176, 177, 328, 329; language, 179, 191, 196
Kazakhstan SSR: 166, 174, 402, 404
Kazakov, Yuri: 343
Keldysh, Mstislav V.: 332, 344, 355, 376
Kennedy, John F.: 492
Kerch region: 28
Kerensky, Alexander: 55, 446
Kets: 172; language, 183, 193
KGB: 119, 129–35, 142, 150, 155, 345
Khabarovsk kray: 15, 406, 407
Khachaturyan, Aram: 165, 319
Khakas: 171, 191
Khakass autonomous oblast: 415
Khanty-Mansi national okrug: 416
Khanty people: 172
Kharadze, Yevgeniy K.: 358
Kharkov: 13, 29; University, 278
Khazars: 175
Khronika Tekushchikh Sobyty: 5
Khrushchev, Nikita: 4–5, 67, 68, 69–72; Agitprop, 551, 553; agriculture, 654, 657, 658; leadership, 270, 378, 391, 433–38, 496, 579; social theories, 74, 208, 239, 245, 306, 312, 353, 516; speech denouncing Stalin, 95, 435, 493, 500
Kiev: 13, 29, 39, 40, 186, 308
kindergarten: 284
Kipchak language: 191
Kirgiz peoples: 169, 176, 177, 328, 329; language, 179, 191, 196
Kirgiz SSR: 26, 34, 174, 402, 403
Kirilenko, Andrei: 2
Kirillin, Vladimir A.: 354
Kirov, Sergei: 144, 340
Kirov ballet company: 323
Koenigsberg: 26
Kogan, Leonid: 320
Kola Peninsula: 14, 30
Kolchak, Alexander: 58, 573
kolkhoz: *See* collective farms
Kolmogorov, Andrey N.: 356
Kolyma mountains: 32

Kolyma River: 15
Komarov, Vladimir: 365
Komi ASSR: 412
Komi people: 162, 175, 413
Komi-Permyak national okrug: 416
Komsomol: 283, 302, 342, 344, 419, 429-32, 565, 676; ideology, 244, 274, 560; publications, 525, 530, 533
Konstantinov, Boris P.: 356
Koran: 255
Korea: 25, 169, 256, 491, 511; language, 189, 191
Korneychuk, Alexander: 325
Korolev, Sergey P.: 364
Koryak national okrug: 416
Koryaks: 172, 193
Kosygin, Aleksei: 72, 97, 391, 420, 423, 438, 440; foreign relations 511, 561, 581
Kovalevskaya, Sofia V.: 349
Koybal people: 171
Koznetsov, Anatoly: 345
Krasnodar kray: 406, 407
Krasnoyarsk kray: 406, 407, 629
kraya: 399, 400, 405-6, 407
Kremlin: 309
Kremlin Polyclinic: 225
Krivoi Rog region: 28
Krokodil: 530
Kronrod, Aleksandr: 376
Kronstadt naval mutiny: 151, 573
Krylov, N. M.: 356
kulaki: 76, 143, 273, 451, 656
kul'tbaza: 185
Kumyk people: 166
Kuprin, Alexander: 313
Kurchatov, Igor V.: 356, 367
Kurds: 166, 188
Kurile Islands: 11, 511
Kuybyshev oblast: 13, 31, 630
Kuznetsk basin (Kuzbas): 34, 628
Kuznetsov, Anatoly: 306, 375
Kyakta, Treaty of: 25
Kyzyl people: 171

labor colonies (*see also* forced labor): 140, 143-45, 150, 471, 472, 478, 480-85
labor force (*see also* chapter 32, and trade unions, wages and salaries, work book): 105, 107, 110, 111, 395, 613, 624, 679, 706; collective agreements, 692, 693, 701; competitions and awards, 700; legislation, 384, 691; productivity, 638, 648, 684-86; recruitment, 676, 691; safety and

protection, 698, 702; turnover, 639, 683
Ladoga, Lake: 12, 30
Laks: 166
Lamuts: *See* Even people
land: *mir*, 160; tenure, 52, 62, 385, 655, 657; utilization, 661-64
Landau, Lev D.: 332, 356
languages (*see also* chapter 10, and alphabets): 158, 196; written, 165, 189, 287, 525, 526-28, 530, 531, 533
Lapps: 163, 175; language, 189
Laptev Sea: 11
Latin alphabet: 186, 187, 198
Latin America: 512
Latvia SSR: 25, 26, 402, 403
Latvian people: 162, 177, 566; language, 187
Lavrentyev, Mikhail A.: 355, 368
Laz language: 192
Le Corbusier: 310
League of the Militant Godless: 240, 244, 245
Lebedev, S. V.: 361
legal system: *See* chapter 22
Lena River: 14, 15, 32
Lend-Lease: 64, 578
Lenin (Vladimir Ilyich Ulyanov): 1-2, 54, 55, 56, 57, 59, 60, 239, 434, 457, 567, 655; army, 571, 572, 575; freedom of the press, 326, 516, 518; ideology, 89, 92, 338, 542, 674; labor, 688, 696; minorities, 178; technology, 350, 632; use of terror, 120, 141
Lenin Library: 534
Leningrad: 13, 32, 309, 341
Leningrad Finns: *See* Ixhors
Leonov, Aleksey: 365
Leonov, Leonid: 315, 325
Leontovich, Mikhail A.: 356-57
Lepchinskaya, Olga: 323
Lermontov, Mikhail: 317
Levitan, Isaac: 311
Lezgians: 166
libraries: 195, 534
life expectancy: 222, 675
Lisitzin, Aleksandr P.: 360
literacy rate: 276, 277, 279
literature: 312-19, 339; privately printed, 197, 316; translations, 533
Lithuania SSR: 25, 26, 402, 403
Lithuanian people: 64, 162, 177, 566; language, 187, 191
Little Octobrists: 274, 302, 419, 430
Little Russians: *See* Ukranians

Litvinov, Maxim: 539
livestock: 62, 115, 229, 668
Livonian people: 162, 187
Lobachevskiy, Nikolay I.: 349
local government: 399–401, 405, 409–10
Lomonosov, Mikhail V.: 316, 348
Lossky, Nicholas: 337
Lunacharsky, Anatoli: 312, 324
Lutherans: 162, 241, 253
L'vov: 29, 186
Lysenko, Trofim Denisovich: 331, 344, 352, 353, 361

Macedonian language: 187
machine building industry: 636, 637, 638, 639
Magnitogorsk: 34
Makarenko, A. S.: 268
Malenkov, Georgi: 67, 68, 69, 70
Malinovsky, Rodion: 581
Manichaeanism: 167
Manin, Yuri: 376
Mansi people: 172
manufacturing: 635, 647, 651
Mao Tse-tung: 493, 495
Marchenko, Anatoly: 140
Mari ASSR: 412
Mari peoples: 163, 175
Mariinsky theatre: 323
Maritime kray: 406, 407
marriage: 81, 201, 203, 206, 213; civil, 204, 241; religious ceremonies, 214; to non-Soviet citizens, 207, 210
Marshall Plan: 66, 491
Martynov, Alexander: 326
Marx, Karl (see also communist ideology): 334–35, 490, 570
mass media: See communications
mathematics: 287, 355
Mayak broadcasts: 536
Mayakovsky, Vladimir: 307, 313, 314, 324
Mazurov, Kiril: 581
mechanization of agriculture: 664; machine tractor stations, 436, 656, 657
Mechnikov, Ilya I.: 349
medicine: 225, 299, 532; personnel, 680; research, 362, 363
Mendeleyev, Dimitry I.: 349
Mensheviks: 143, 688
merchant marine: 585
Merezhkovsky, Dimitri: 313
Methodius, Saint: 186, 187, 242

Meyerhold, Vsevolod: 324
MGB: 120, 123, 124, 146, 154
Michael Romanov (tsar): 44, 277
Michurin, Ivan V.: 331, 352
middle class: 77
migration, internal (see also passports): 84, 227, 272, 671, 675
Mikhaylov, Aleksandr A.: 358
Mikoyan, Anastas: 165
Mikulak, Maxim: 340
military academies: 129, 571, 574, 593, 597
military aid to foreign countries: 507, 508, 513, 599, 735, 740, 741
military tribunals: 52, 144, 147, 464, 465, 467
militia: 125, 140, 473–76
Millionshchikov, Mikhail D.: 355
mineral reserves: 12, 28, 29, 30, 31, 33, 35, 114, 633–35
Mingrelian language: 192
ministries (USSR): 392, 393, 404, 614; agriculture, 657; civil aviation, 718; communications, 710; construction, 648; culture, 282, 333, 523, 531, 545; defense, 523, 533, 580, 710; electrification, 648; finance, 690, 745, 746; foreign affairs, 488; foreign trade, 723, 724; heavy industry, 648; higher and special secondary education, 677, 690; public health, 223, 531, 710; trade, 708
Ministry for the Preservation of Public Order: See MOOP
Ministry of Internal Affairs: See MVD
Ministry of State Security: See MGB
Minsk: 26
Mints, Aleksandr L.: 357
Mironov, Nikolai K.: 473
Mochalov, Pavel: 326
Moldavia SSR: 26, 27, 164, 402, 403
Moldavian language: 188
Molotov, V. M.: 69, 70
monasticism: 247
Mongolia: 741
Mongolian People's Republic: 24, 496
Mongolic languages: 183, 189, 191
Mongoloids: 157, 175
Mongols: 40, 176, 189
Monin, Andrey S.: 360
MOOP: 124, 142, 147
Mordovia ASSR: 412
Mordovian State University: 341
Mordvins: 162, 175
Morgan, Lewis H.: 203

Moscow: 13, 15, 31, 145, 148, 185, 308, 478; Lomonosov State University, 341; newspapers, 526; radio and TV, 536, 538; Red Square, 309, 567; Treaty of, 23; University, 296, 317

Moskva River: 31

motor vehicles: 6, 116, 156, 369, 474, 717, 718

mountains: 15, 32

Moussorgsky, Modest: 321

Murmansk: 14

Muscovite law: 443

music: 297, 319–22, 329, 519, 531

Muslims: 75, 163, 165, 167, 168, 169, 201, 212, 220, 255, 329

MVD: 120, 123, 130, 142, 146, 151, 154, 155, 473

Nagibin, Yuri: 343

Nagorno-Karabakh autonomous oblast: 415

Nakhichevan ASSR: 412

Nakhimov academy: 593

names, personal: 185, 209

Nanai peoples: 171

Napoleon: 48

narody: 157

national hymns: 567

nationalism: 194, 263, 565

navy: 505, 569, 573, 574, 578, 579, 580, 582, 584–85, 591

Nedelya: 524, 525

Negidal people: 171, 191

Nekrasov, Victor: 315, 343

Nemirovich-Danchenko, Vladimir: 326

Nenets national okrug: 172, 416

Nesmeyanov, Aleksandr N.: 361

Nesterov, Mikhail: 312

Nestorian Christians: 167

Neues Leben: 525

Neva: 530

New Economic Policy (NEP): 59, 204, 337, 340, 449, 552, 655–56, 693

news agencies: 522, 532

newspapers: 5, 515, 520–29, 544, 546, 699, 710

Nganasans: 172

Nicholas I: 49, 278

Nicholas II: 50, 51, 52–54, 243, 279

Nigeria: 512

Nijinsky, Bronislava: 323

Nijinsky, Vaslav: 323, 324

Nikon, Patriarch: 316

Nivkhy people: *See* Gilyak people

NKGB: 122, 142

NKVD: 142–45, 473

Nobel prizes: 306, 332, 349, 352, 356

Nogai peoples: 166

nomadism: 168, 169, 175, 176, 179, 202

nomenklatura: 397, 423

Norilsk: 417

North Atlantic Treaty Organization: 491, 503, 504

Norway: 22

Novaya Zemlya: 11

Novgorod: 308

Novikov, Vladimir: 308

Novocherkassk: 694

Novosibirsk: 13, 34, 354

Novosti: 522, 532

Novovoronezh power station: 633

Novy Mir: 315, 342, 530, 563

nuclear power: 355, 356, 357, 367–69, 384, 633

Ob River: 15, 32

oblasti: 399–401, 405, 406, 408; autonomous *oblasti*, 414, 415

oceanographic research: 359, 585

Odessa: 14, 15, 29

officer corps, military: 154, 570, 592

OGPU: 122, 142, 458

Oguz language: 191

oil: 31, 626, 627, 629–31, 646, 647, 719, 727

Oistrakh, David: 320

Oka River: 31

Okhrana: 121

okruga: 401, 408, 414; national *okruga*: 416, 417

oktyabr: 342, 530

Old Church Slavonic language: 182, 185, 186, 187, 247, 249, 276, 316

Onega, Lake: 12

Oprichnina: 121

Organization for European Economic Cooperation: 66

Organization of African United: 512

Orochi people: 171, 191

Oroks: 171, 191

Osmanli: See Ottoman Turkish language

Ossetia, North, ASSR: 412

Ossetia, South, autonomous oblast: 415

Ossetic language: 188

Ossets: 166, 175, 188

Ostrovsky, Alexander: 326

Ottoman Turkish language: 191

Outer Mongolia (*see also* Mongolian People's Republic): 495
"Overcoat, The": 317

painting: 310-12
Pakistan: 509, 510, 740
painting: 310-12
Pakistan: 509, 510, 740
palaces of culture: 302
Pale of Settlement: 258
Paleo-Asiatic languages: 183, 193-94
Paleo-Siberians: 169
Pali language: 194
Pamir mountains: 13, 24
Pamirs: 166, 188
Pan-Turkic movement: 190
Paris Peace Conference: 23
part-time education: 79, 289
Pascal, Pierre: 339
Pashto language: 188
passports: internal, 124, 148, 474, 477, 694
Pasternak, Boris: 306, 313, 315, 53
Pavlov, Ivan P.: 349, 351, 356
Pavlov, Sergei: 342
Pavlova, Anna: 323
Pavlovich, Dmitry: 243
Pekar, Soloman I.: 357
People's Court: 448, 462, 693
people's universities: 303
People's Voluntary Militia: 475
Peredvizhniki: 311
periodicals: 529-32, 554
permafrost: 12, 21, 33
Permyaks: 162, 175
Persians: 188
Peter the Great: 44-45, 242, 444, 568
Peter the Great Bay: 14
Petersburg, Treaty of: 22
Petipa, Marius: 323
Petrograd: *See* Leningrad
Petrosian, Tigran: 165
Petrosyants, A. M.: 367, 368
Petrov, Boris N.: 355
Petrov, Vladimir: 327
Petrov-Vodkin, Kuzma: 312
Petrovskiy, Ivan G.: 355
physics: 340
Pioneers: 274, 302, 419, 430
planning, central (*see also* Five-Year Plan for 1966-70, State Planning Committee): industry, 384, 603-21; manpower, 684, 690, 701
plastics: 116, 637, 647
Plekhanov, Georgi: 542
Plisetskaya, Maya: 323

Podgorny, Nikolai V.: 423, 566, 580, 659
Pogodin, Nikolai: 325
Pokrovsky, Mikhail: 340
Poland: 22, 47, 64, 500, 504, 574; trade, 729, 738, 741
police: *see* militia; security police
Polish language: 182, 186, 187, 191
Politburo (CPSU): 67, 97, 377, 420, 455, 488, 580
political commissars: 9, 382, 432, 573, 595
Polyansky, Dmitri: 581
polygyny: 201, 209
population: 7, 403, 404, 407, 412, 414, 415, 672-73, 674-76, 677
pornography: 305
postal system: 182, 198, 720
Potsdam conference: 23
power (*see also* nuclear power): 116, 231; hydroelectric, 33, 310, 626, 627, 632, 647, 651; thermal, 633
Pravda: 523-24, 530
Presidium (USSR): 377, 378, 389, 390, 453
preventive detention: 479-80
prices: 706, 715, 726; agriculture, 657, 658, 711, 713; industry, 643-44, 752
primary education: 79, 284-85
Primorskiy: *See* Maritime kray
Pripet Marshes: 26
prisons: 151, 471, 478
private housing: 232, 649, 650
private ownership: *See* private plots to farm; rights of citizens
private plots to farm: 82, 108, 659, 660, 664, 712
Procurator-General: 144, 385, 466
productivity: agriculture, 654, 658, 664; incentives, 618-21; industry, 625, 638, 644-47, 651, 689; planning, 116, 613
Prokhorov, Aleksandr M.: 332, 356, 357
Prokofiev, Sergei: 319
propaganda (*see also* chapter 26): 394, 424, 516, 533
Protestants: 162, 165, 241, 252
Prut River: 27
publishing: 283, 307, 517, 533, 544
Pudovkin, Vsevolod: 327
Pugachev, Yemelyan: 47
Pulkovo Observatory: 349, 358
purges (*see also* trials): 62-63, 123, 144, 478, 576

Pushkin, Alexander: 317
Pyriev, Ivan: 328

Quiet Don, The: 314

Rachmaninoff, Sergei: 322
Radek, Karl: 54, 383
radio and television: 194, 195, 290, 519, 534-37; TV, 515, 537
railroads: 26, 31, 35, 294, 523, 706, 716; railway troops, 152
rainfall: 12, 14, 17, 21, 27, 28, 32
Rasputin, Grigory: 53, 242-43
rayony: 399, 400, 408, 409
recreation: 137, 227, 700
Red Poppy: 319, 320
Red Star: 523, 524
reindeer herding: 163, 171, 172, 179
religion (*see also* chapter 13 and atheism): 83, 165, 308, 320
Remizov, Aleksei: 313, 337
rents: 231
Repin, Ilya: 311
research (*see also* space): 337, 353, 370; agriculture, 661; demography, 677; earth sciences, 358-60, 585; industry, 370, 640-41; labor, 690, 697, 702; military, 579, 601; science, 347, 355, 361, 367-69
restaurants: 710
Richter, Sviatoslav: 320
Riga: 26; Treaty of, 574
rights of citizens (*see also* freedoms, private plots to farm): 385-87, 443, 455; property rights, 232, 240, 243, 446, 457
Rimsky-Korsakov, Nikolai: 321
rivers: 15
Rocket Force: 582, 587
Rodina clubs: 342
Roman Catholics: 160, 162, 173, 241, 250
Romany language: 189
Rostropovich, Mstislav: 320
Rublev, Andrei: 311
Rumania: 23, 69, 164, 501, 502; trade with, 729, 738, 741
Rumanian language: 25-26, 188
Rumyantsev, Aleksei: 343, 344
rural areas: 78, 82, 224, 300, 380, 714
Rus: 39
Russian language: 181, 185, 193, 194, 287, 301
Russian Orthodox Church (*see also* Old Church Slavonic language): 7, 39, 40, 83, 160, 163, 170, 242-50

Russian Soviet Federated Socialist Republic (RSFSR): 25, 29-32, 32-34, 379, 402, 403, 404, 460, 462, 691-92; newspapers, 526, 529
Russians: *See* Great Russians; Ukranians
Ruthenia: 23
Rutkevich, M. N.: 340
Rutuls: 166

Saami: *See* Lapps
Saaremaa Island: 12
Sagay people: 171
Saint Petersburg: *See* Leningrad
Saint Sophia Cathedral: 308
Sakhalin Island: 11, 171, 193
Sakharov, Andrei D.: 332, 341, 356, 373, 374, 376
Saltykov-Schedrin, Mikhail: 318
Samarkand: 169
samizdat: 197
Samoyedic languages: 172, 175, 183, 189
sanitation: 222
savings banks: 756, 761
Savinkin, Nikolai I.: 473
Sayan mountains: 13, 32
sblizheniye: 158, 179
Schepkin, Mikhail: 326
schools (*see also* education): 154, 277, 396, 461, 469; foreign students, 299; Party schools, 427, 549-50; police, 129, 134; seminaries, 246, 247
scientific endeavor (*see ulso* technology): 288, 355-63, 518, 695, 743, 750; personnel, 679; specialized vocabulary, 196
Scythians: 175
secondary education: 79, 285-89, 681
secret police: *See* security police
security police: 43, 46, 56, 63, 67, 68, 94, 96, 121, 122, 142, 149, 153, 278, 337, 458, 549, 556
security systems: *See* chapters 7 and 8; and labor colonies; terror, use of
Sedov, Leonid I.: 364
Selkups: 172
Semichastny, Vladimir Y.: 124
Semitic languages: 193
Semyonov, Nikolai N.: 332, 352, 361
Serbo-Croatian language: 187
serfdom: 44, 45, 46, 48, 49, 75, 201
Sergius, Metropolitan: 244
Serov, Ivan A.: 124
Severnaya island group: 11
Severny, Andrey B.: 358

Shafarevich, Igor: 376
shamanism: 169–70, 171
Shchekino Chemical Combine: 685
Shelepin, Alexander N.: 124, 156, 690, 698, 702
Shelest, Pyotr: 580
Shevchenko State University: 341
shipping: 718
Shipulo, G. O.: 357
Sholokhov, Mikhail: 307, 314
Shors: 171, 191
Shostakovich, Dmitri: 319, 320
Siberia: 169–72, 174, 477, 676; language, 189, 190, 191; resources, 626, 629
Simonov, Konstantin: 314, 325, 343
Sinkiang province: 168, 191
Sino-Soviet Treaty of Friendship, Alliance and Mutual Assistance: 495
Sino-Tibetan languages: 194
Sinyavski, Andrei: 306, 343, 344, 373, 564
Siomin, Vitali: 344
slave labor: See forced labor
Slavic tribes: 38–40, 160, 173–175, 200
Slaviskiy, Y. P.: 367
sliyaniye: 158, 179
Slovaks: 161, 182, 187
Slovene language: 187
Smirnov, Leonid V.: 364
Smogista: 342
Smolny Institute: 277
social class: 73, 74, 79, 80, 90, 98, 281
social insurance: 233, 234, 235, 237, 749, 753; trade unions, 689, 701
social mobility: 76, 77, 79, 81, 83, 84, 219, 265
Socialist Realism: See under communist lexicon
Soghdians: 167
soils: 21, 22, 27, 662, 663
Soloukhin, Vladimir: 342
Solovyov, Gleb: 362
Solzhenitsyn, Alexandr: 306, 315, 332, 341, 343, 558, 563
Soutine, Haim: 311, 312
Soviet of Nationalities: 387, 405, 413
Soviet of Workers' and Soldiers' Deputies: 54, 688
soviets: 97, 381
sovkhoz: See state farms
space (*see also* strategic missiles): 364, 366, 547, 587
Spain: 488, 575; Spanish language, 531

Speransky, Mikhail M.: 444
Sputnik I: 365
SSR (Soviet Socialist Republic): *See* union republics
Stakhanovism: 689
Stalin, Joseph: 447, 451–59, 558, 575, 576, 578, 656; biography, 54, 60–69, 95, 146, 165, 380, 383; ideology, 77, 194, 239, 244, 260, 338, 544; intellectual freedom under, 345, 516, 518; security system, 141, 143, 144, 481; Tito and, 499; type of rule, 178, 269, 270, 402, 434, 440, 459, 656
Stalinabad: 35
Stalingrad: 65
Stanislavsky, Konstantin: 305, 326
Starov, Ivan: 309
state farms (*sovkhoz*): 653, 659, 679, 695, 750
state notary: 468
State Planning Committee (USSR): 103, 282, 608, 609, 610, 709, 745
status and prestige: employment, 78, 80, 699; government officials, 395; scientists, 348, 373
Stavropol kray: 406, 407
Stolypin, Peter: 52, 53, 446
strategic missiles: 367, 582, 586, 587
Stravinsky, Igor: 319, 322
Struchkova, Raissa: 323
Struve, V. J.: 349
Stuchka, Pyotr: 449
students: 286, 298, 678
submarine fleet: 584
sunflowers: 667
Supreme Court: 382
Supreme Soviet: 377, 378, 387, 453
Suslov, Mikhail: 2
Suvorov military academy: 571, 593
Suzdal: 333
Svan language: 192
Sverdlov, Yakov: 380
Sverdlovsk: 13, 15, 34
symbols, national: 397, 567
Syr Darya River: 34, 169

Tabasarans: 166
Tadzhik language: 188
Tadzhik SSR: 26, 34, 402, 403
Tadzikistan: 198
taiga: 21
Taiwan: *See* China, Nationalist
Tajiks: 168
Tallin: 26
Talysh people: 166, 188

Tamanyan, Alexander: 310
Tamm, Igor E.: 332, 356, 373
Tannu Tuva: 25
Tashkent: 13, 15, 34, 35, 168, 177
Tashkent Agreement: 510
TASS: 522, 532, 536
Tatar ASSR: 412, 630
Tatars: 145, 163, 164, 166, 168, 176, 329; language, 188, 189
taxation: 78, 706, 746, 752-54; turnover tax, 715, 753
Taymyr national okrug: 416, 417
Tbilisi: 29, 712
Tbilisi State University: 341
Tchaikovsky, Peter: 322
teachers: 194-95, 278, 295
technology: 114, 296, 299, 356, 363-64, 369-72, 640, 701
techpromfinplan: 616
Tehran Conventions: 24
telephone and telegraph systems: 182, 198, 719, 720
Temur Tau: 694
Tendriakov, Vladimir: 343, 344
Tereshkova, Valentina: 365
terror, use of: 56, 59, 63, 120, 139, 141, 146, 458; Great Terror, 143-44; Red Terror, 448
textbooks: 283, 300, 533
Thaw, The: 306, 315
theatre: 297, 324-26, 531
Tien Shan mountains: 13
Tikhon, Patriarch: 244
Timakov, Vladimir D.: 362
Timofeyev-Ressovskiy, N. V.: 362
Tishchenko, Boris: 320
Tito, Josip Broz: 68, 498, 499
tobacco crops: 667
Tokamak Three: 369
Tolstoy, Aleksei: 307, 313, 314
Tolstoy, Leo: 318, 328
Tomsky, Mikhail P.: 689
Topchiev, Aleksandr V.: 351
tourists: 137, 525
Townes, Charles H.: 356
trade (*see also* chapters 34 and 35): 9, 109, 748, 757
trade associations: 724-25, 736
Trade Union Central Council: *See* All-Union Central Council of Trade Unions
trade unions: 233, 283, 301, 428, 523, 688, 689, 690-701
Trans-Caspian railway: 35
Transcaucasia: 29

Transcaucasus SSR: 60, 402
Trans-Siberian Railway: 33, 34, 51, 574, 719
transportation: 107, 706, 716-18, 748
Trapeznikov, Sergey P.: 353
Trapeznikov, V. A.: 371
travel: *See* migration; tourists
treaties and agreements: boundaries, 22, 23, 24, 25; commercial, 725-26; Constitution, 390; cultural and scientific, 492; military, 570, 574, 598; nuclear test-ban, 71, 492; Sino-Soviet Treaty of Friendship, 495; Soviet-German Nonaggression Pact, 64, 576; Use of Outer Space, 492
trial by jury: 445, 460
trials (*see also* purges): 141, 147, 306, 344
Trotsky, Leon: 54, 55, 56, 58, 60, 63, 688; armed forces and, 572, 573, 574, 575, 594; biography, 131, 259
Trubetskoy, Eugne N.: 336
Trud: 523, 524, 699
Tsakhur peoples: 166
tsarist era: 43-53, 75, 76, 270, 276-79, 296
Tsiolkovskiy, Konstantin E.: 349
Tukachevsky, M. N.: 58, 63
Tumen River: 25
tundra: 17, 19, 21, 30
Tungus: *See* Evenk people
Tungusic languages: 183, 189, 191
Turgenev, Ivan: 318
Turkestan: 175
Turkey: 23, 507, 740
Turkic Altay people: 171
Turkic ethnic groups: 163, 329; languages, 26, 167, 181, 183, 188, 189, 190
Turkmanchai, Treaty of: 24
Turkmen SSR: 26, 34, 402, 403
Turkmens: 169, 176, 191, 329
Turkomans: 167
Turks: 167, 189
Tuva ASSR: 412
Tuvins: 170, 191
Tuvinskaya ASSR: 25
Tvardovsky, Aleksandr: 315, 342

Ubykh language: 192
Udegeys: 171, 191
Udmurt ASSR: 412
Udmurt peoples: 163, 175
Ugric languages: 183, 189
Ukranian SSR: 25, 27, 402, 403, 404

Ukranians (Little Russians): 160, 161, 180, 566; language, 182, 186
Ulanova, Galina: 323
Ulbricht, Walter: 498, 499
Ulchi people: 171, 191
Ulyanov, V. I.: *See* Lenin
Uniate rite: 160, 250, 251
Union of Soviet Artists: 531
Union of Soviet Socialist Republics (*see also* autonomous republics, Russian Soviet Federated Socialist Republic, union republics): 159-64, 381, 390, 524, 746-55
Union of Soviet Writers: 342, 530
union republics (*see also* names of individual republics): xviii, 14, 25, 195, 399, 402-5, 674, 747, 754; Agitprop, 545; education, 282, 301; law, 381-82, 384, 460, 470; ministries, 224, 404; newspapers and periodicals, 520, 525, 526-28, 530, 532; security systems, 149
United Arab Republic: 505, 730, 732, 735, 738, 739, 740, 741; aid to, 599
United Nations: 513, 514, 744
United States: 46, 64, 490-93, 585, 729
universities: 276, 278, 296, 341, 349
Ural mountains: 13, 30
Uralic peoples: 162; languages, 190
Uralic-Altaic peoples: 175-76; languages, 183, 189-92
Ussuri River: 24, 32
Ust-Orda Buryat national okrug: 416
Ustinov, Dmitry F.: 364
Uzbek SSR: 26, 34, 402, 403
Uzbeks: 168, 169, 176, 191, 329

Valdai Hills: 14
Vannikov, Boris: 367
Vavilov, Nikolay I.: 352
Vavilov, Sergei: 338
Vaygach Island: 11
Vechernaya Moskva: 525
Vedenskiy, B.: 357
vegetation: 19-22
Veksler, Vladimir I.: 357
Vepsy peoples: 163, 175
Verkhoyansk mountains: 32
Vesnin, Victor and Alexander: 310
Vietnam: 497
Vilnius: 26
Vinogradov, Aleksandr P.: 359
Virgin Lands settlement program: 174, 663

Vishnevsky, Vsevolod: 324-25
Vladimir-Suzdal: 308
Vladivostok: 14, 15, 34
vocational training: 285-86, 293, 294, 661
Volga-Don (V. I. Lenin) Canal: 31
Volga Germans: 145, 177
Volga River: 14, 15, 31
Volga Tatars: 176, 191
Volgograd: 31
Voroshilov, K. E.: 58
Vosnesensky, Andrei: 315, 343, 344, 563
Votyaks: *See* Udmurt peoples
Vrubel, Mikhail: 311
Vyshinsky, Andrei: 453

wages and salaries: 74, 77, 82, 617, 690, 695, 761; collective farmers, 660; government officials, 396, 695; in labor colonies, 484; military, 475, 593; police, 128, 134; scientists, 372
wall newspapers: 521
Warsaw Pact: 501, 514, 586, 598
water supply: 222
waterways: 12, 26, 31, 34
White Army: 58, 59, 573
White Russia: *See* Belorussia SSR
White Ukranian language: 186
Winter War of *1939-40*: 22
Witte, Serge: 51
women: 265, 266, 674; crime, 483, 484; education, 277, 278, 279, 296; employment, 78, 83, 226, 235, 237, 679, 695; equality, 202, 211, 219, 220; in agriculture, 220, 661; in industry, 640; status of, 160, 205, 207, 216, 348
word coinage: 185
work book: 148, 694
World Federation of Trade Unions: 702
World Marxist Review: 554
World War I: 53, 57, 672
World War II: 22, 23, 64, 94, 576, 577, 589, 596, 656, 657, 672; forced labor, 472, 678; propaganda, 327-28, 552
Wrangel, Peter: 58, 573
Wrangel Island: 11
writers unions: 332, 339, 342, 530

Yagoda, G.: 144, 145
Yakut ASSR: 411, 412

Yakut people: 172, 413; language, 191, 193
Yalta: 578; Conference, 23
Yamal-Nenets national okrug: 416
Yekaterinsky Institute: 277
Yenisey River: 14, 15, 32
Yerevan: 29
Yesenin-Volpin, Aleksandr: 374
Yevtushenko, Yevgeny: 343, 344, 558
Yezhov, Nikolai I.: 63, 144, 145
Yiddish language: 164, 179, 188
Young Communist League: *See* Komsomol
young people: 419, 429, 560–61; crime, 218, 471, 481; youth organizations, 302
Young Pioneers: *See* Pioneers
Yudenich, Nikolai: 58
Yugoslavia: 68, 161, 498–99, 702, 729, 738

Yukagir languages: 183, 193
Yunost: 315, 563
yurts: 172
Yusupov, Felix: 243

Zakharov, Andrei: 309
Zaporozhye: 310
Zavoyskiy, Yevgeniy K.: 357
Zemsky Sobor: 42
Zhdanov, Andrei A.: 67, 146, 315, 320, 325, 339, 340, 544
Zhdanov State University: 341
Zhukov, Georgi: 581
Zinin, N. N.: 349
Zinoviev, Gregory: 54, 63, 259
Znaniye: 241
Zoshchenko, Mikhail: 315, 339
Zverev, Anatoli: 310
Zverev, Sergey A.: 364

PUBLISHED AREA HANDBOOKS

550—65	Afghanistan	550—38	Liberia
550—44	Algeria	550—85	Libya
550—59	Angola	550—45	Malaysia and Singapore
550—73	Argentina	550—76	Mongolia
550—20	Brazil	550—49	Morocco
550—61	Burma	550—64	Mozambique
550—83	Burundi	550—88	Nicaragua
550—50	Cambodia	550—81	North Korea
550—26	Colombia	550—57	North Vietnam
550—60	Communist China	550—48	Pakistan
550—91	Congo (Brazzaville)	550—72	The Philippines
550—67	Congo (Kinshasa)	550—84	Rwanda
550—90	Costa Rica	550—51	Saudi Arabia
550—22	Cyprus	550—70	Senegal
550—54	Dominican Republic	550—86	Somalia
550—52	Ecuador	550—55	South Vietnam
550—29	Germany	550—27	Sudan
550—78	Guatemala	550—47	Syria
550—82	Guyana	550—62	Tanzania
550—21	India	550—53	Thailand
550—39	Indonesia	550—89	Tunisia
550—31	Iraq	550—80	Turkey
550—68	Iran	550—74	Uganda
550—25	Israel	550—43	United Árab Republic
550—30	Japan	550—71	Venezuela
550—34	Jordan	550—75	Zambia
550—56	Kenya	550—92	Peripheral States of the Arabian Peninsula
550—41	Republic of Korea		
550—58	Laos	550—93	South Africa
550—24	Lebanon	550—94	Oceania